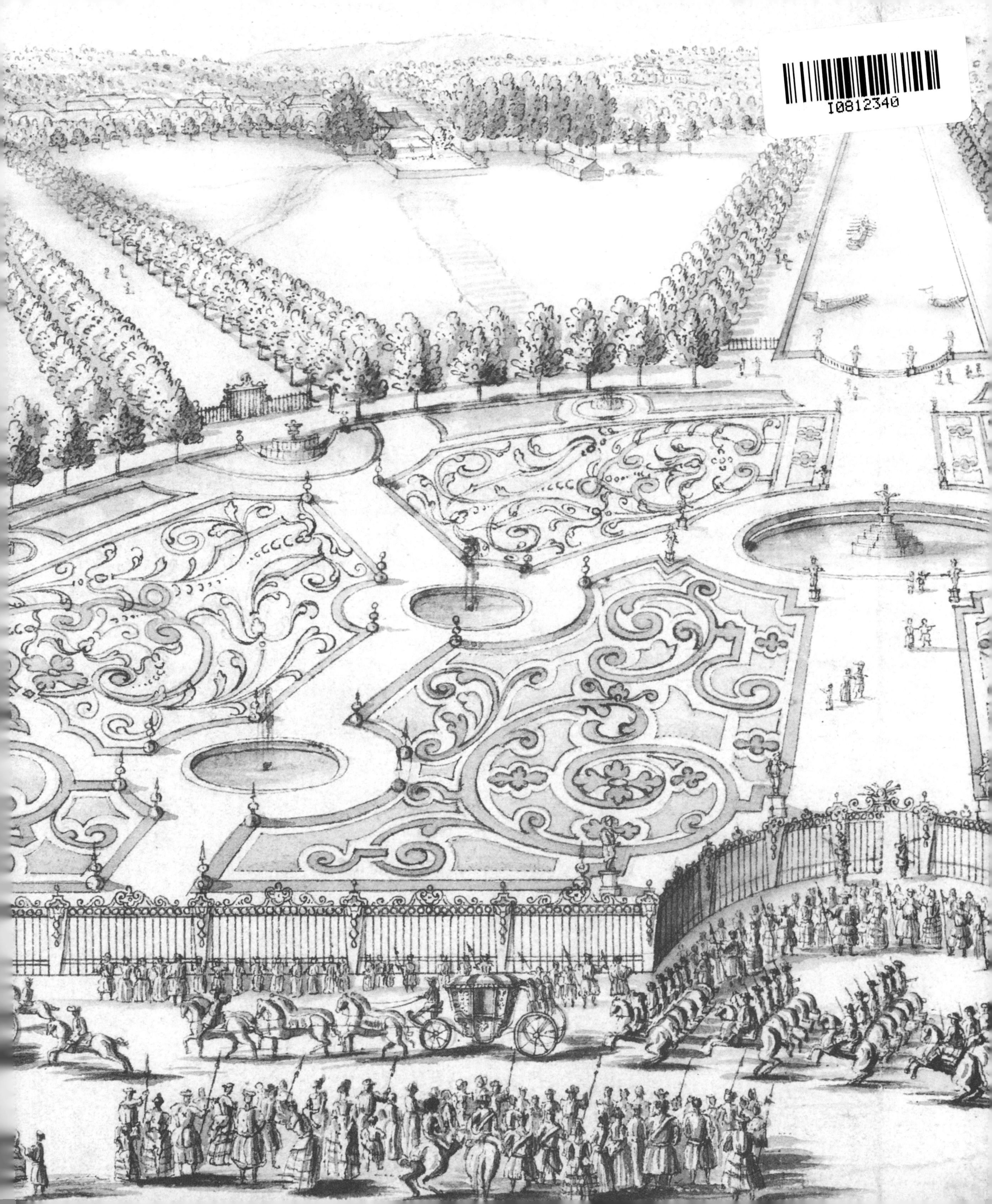

Europe Divided

Huguenot Refugee Art and Culture

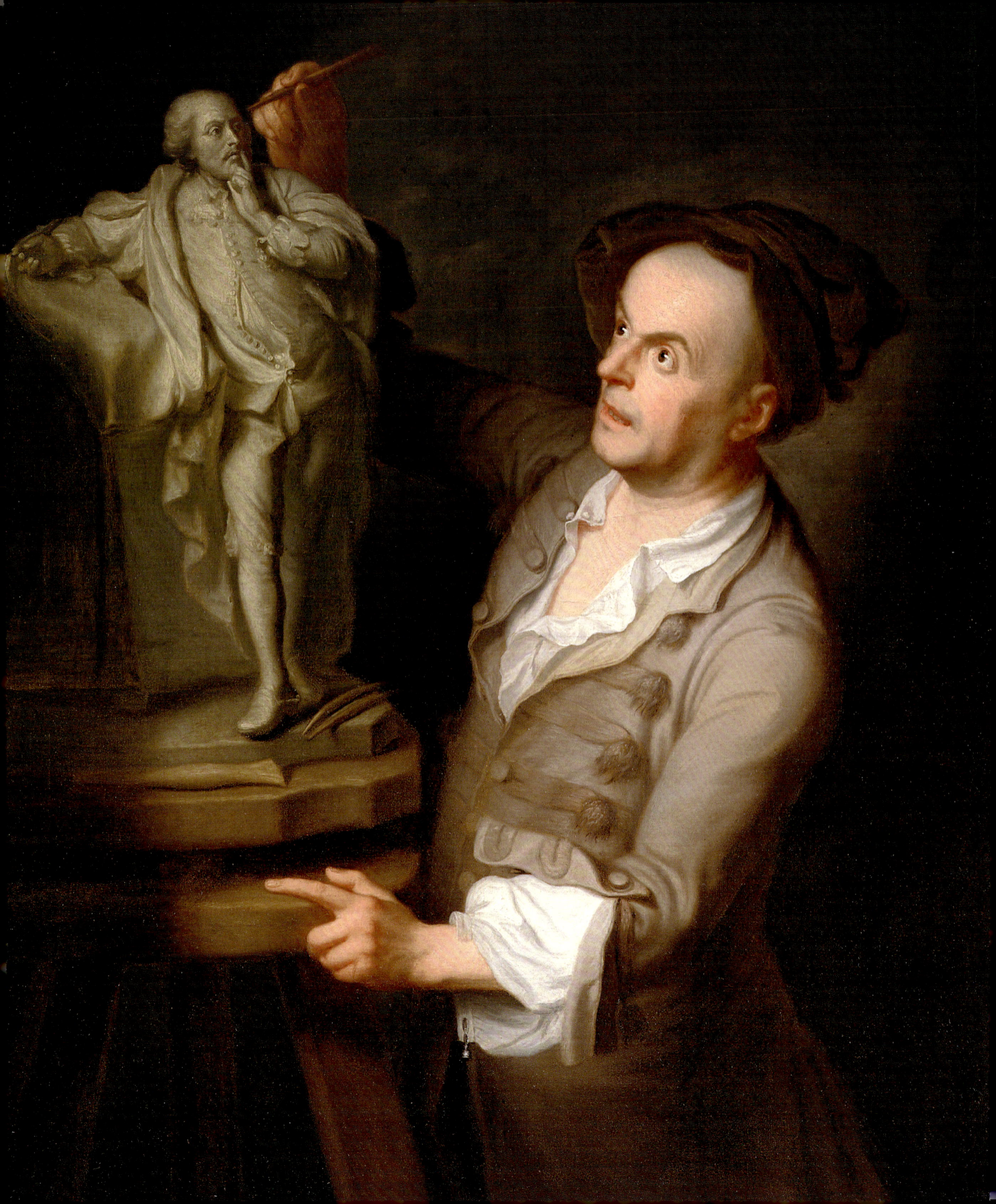

Tessa Murdoch

Europe Divided

Huguenot Refugee Art & Culture

V&A Publishing

First published by V&A Publishing, 2021
V&A Publishing
Victoria and Albert Museum
South Kensington
London SW7 2RL

Vam.ac.uk/publishing

Distributed in North America by Abrams,
an imprint of ABRAMS

ISBN 9781 83851 012 1
10 9 8 7 6 5 4 3 2 1
2024 2023 2022 2021

A catalogue record for this book is available from the British Library.

Designed by Robert Dalrymple
Typeset in MVB Verdigris and MVB Celestia Antiqua
Edited by Johanna Stephenson
Picture researcher: Axelle Russo Heath
Proofreader: Bev Zimmern
Indexer: Nic Nicholas
Maps by ML Design
Colour origination by DL Imaging, London
Printed in China

V&A Publishing

Supporting the world's leading museum of art and design, the Victoria and Albert Museum, London

AUTHOR'S NOTES

In 1752 in the British Isles the Julian Calendar was replaced by the Gregorian Calendar, changing the formula for calculating leap years. The beginning of the legal new year was moved from 25 March to 1 January, so dates occurring between 1 January and 25 March before and including 1752 are indicated as 1751/2.

Chapters 7 and 8 include the term Blackamoor. This has since fallen from general usage. It is repeated here in its original historical context, although it is now deemed discriminatory and offensive.

JACKET ILLUSTRATIONS

Painted looking glass
Antoine Monnoyer, London, 1710–20
See plate 51

Paul Crespin
Unknown artist, London, *c.*1726
See plate 184

Watch case
Augustin Toussaint, London, *c.*1775–80
See plate 205

ENDPAPERS

Design for the Parterre, Hampton Court Palace
Daniel Marot, London, 1689
See plate 60

FRONTISPIECE

Roubiliac modelling David Garrick's statue to Shakespeare
Andrien Carpentiers, London, 1762
Oil on canvas, 125.7 × 100.3 cm
National Portrait Gallery, London (303)
Roubiliac, baptized a Catholic in Lyons, was educated in Frankfurt where the family resumed their Protestant faith from 1710. He trained in Dresden and Paris. From 1730 he became the leading sculptor in London, a friend of the goldsmith Nicholas Sprimont and the actor David Garrick, who posed for the statue of Shakespeare now in the British Library.

MIX
Paper from responsible sources
FSC® C008047

Contents

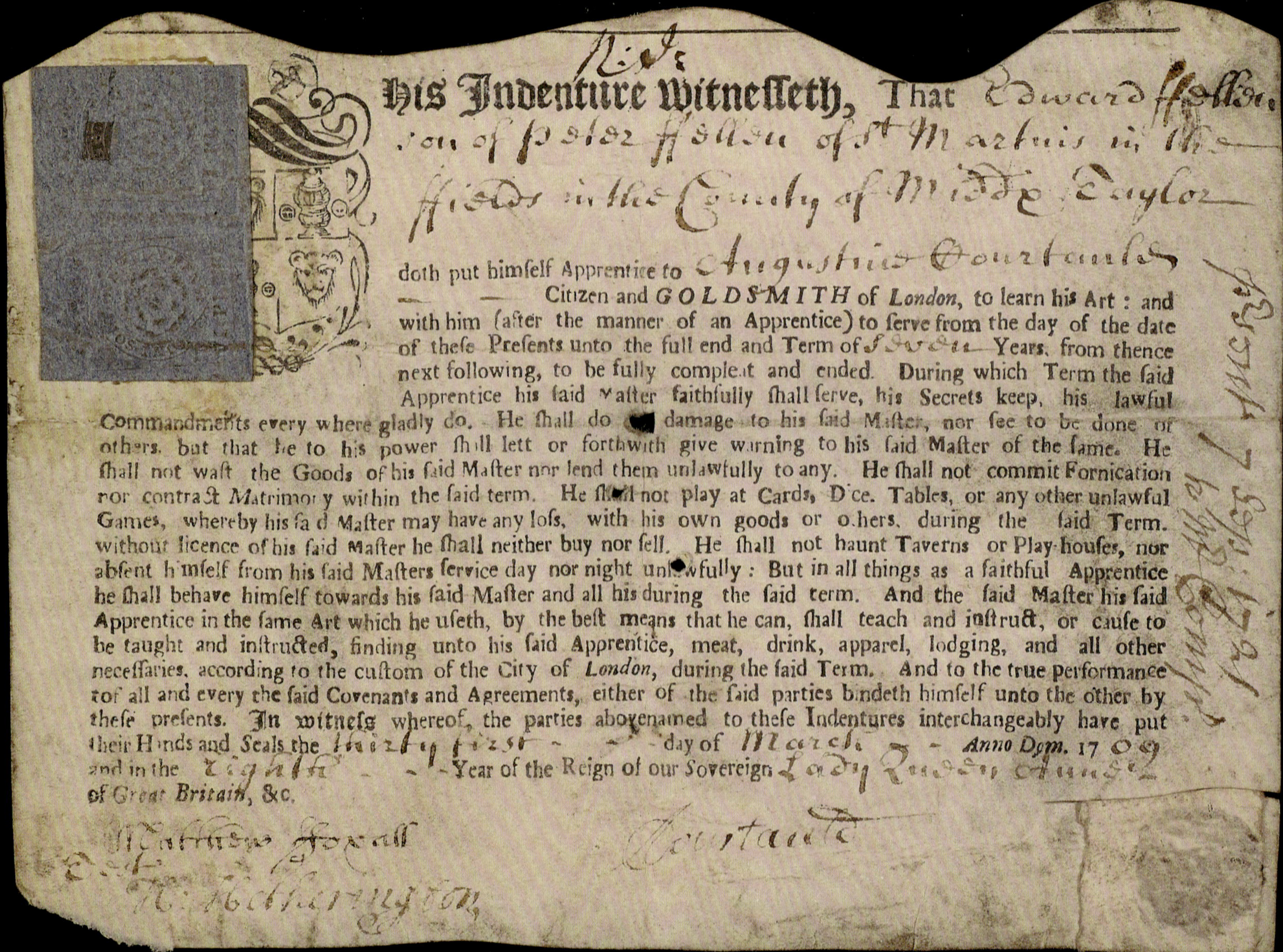

This Indenture Witnesseth, That Edward ffellow son of Peter ffellow of St Martins in the ffields in the County of Midd'x Taylor doth put himself Apprentice to Augustine Courtauld — — Citizen and GOLDSMITH of *London*, to learn his Art: and with him (after the manner of an Apprentice) to serve from the day of the date of these Presents unto the full end and Term of Seven Years, from thence next following, to be fully compleat and ended. During which Term the said Apprentice his said Master faithfully shall serve, his Secrets keep, his lawful Commandments every where gladly do. He shall do no damage to his said Master, nor see to be done of others, but that he to his power shall lett or forthwith give warning to his said Master of the same. He shall not wast the Goods of his said Master nor lend them unlawfully to any. He shall not commit Fornication nor contract *Matrimony* within the said term. He shall not play at Cards, Dice, Tables, or any other unlawful Games, whereby his said Master may have any loss, with his own goods or others, during the said Term, without licence of his said Master he shall neither buy nor sell. He shall not haunt Taverns or Play-houses, nor absent himself from his said Masters service day nor night unlawfully: But in all things as a faithful Apprentice he shall behave himself towards his said Master and all his during the said term. And the said Master his said Apprentice in the same Art which he useth, by the best means that he can, shall teach and instruct, or cause to be taught and instructed, finding unto his said Apprentice, meat, drink, apparel, lodging, and all other necessaries, according to the custom of the City of *London*, during the said Term. And to the true performance of all and every the said Covenants and Agreements, either of the said parties bindeth himself unto the other by these presents. In witness whereof, the parties abovenamed to these Indentures interchangeably have put their Hands and Seals the thirty first — — day of March — *Anno Dom.* 1709 and in the Eighth — — Year of the Reign of our Sovereign Lady Queen Anne of *Great Britain*, &c.

Matthew Foxall

Courtauld

R. Hetherington

Author's Preface

1 Apprenticeship Indenture of Edward Fellen to Augustine Courtauld
London, 31 March 1709
London Metropolitan Archives

Edward, son of the Huguenot tailor Pierre Fellen (Feline), joined his master's household in Church Court, St Martin's Lane. In 1708 Augustin Courtauld registered his mark at Goldsmiths' Hall and married Anne Ribouleau; he was naturalized in 1709. In 1720 Edward Feline married Renée Barbut at the Huguenot West Street chapel and registered his goldsmith's mark from his house in Rose Street, Covent Garden.

I grew up aware that my maternal ancestor was Edward Feline (*c.*1695–1753), a goldsmith apprenticed as Edward Fellen in London in 1709 to Augustin Courtauld (1685–1751), one of the second generation of a family from La Rochelle. The Courtaulds were to become a British household name through their production of silks and man-made fibres as well as silver. Their twentieth-century descendant established the Courtauld Institute of Art to promote internationally the study of art history.

When I was faced with the challenge of choosing a subject for a doctorate in Art History, my decision to document the work of Huguenot artists, designers and craftsmen in Great Britain and Ireland 1680–1760 received encouragement. The resulting thesis, which forms the spring-board for this book, prepared me for my first job at the Museum of London. This brought the opportunity to co-curate *The Quiet Conquest*, a major exhibition on the Huguenots to mark the Tercentenary of the Revocation of the Edict of Nantes in 1985. For that museum I also curated exhibitions of collections of London-made Huguenot silver in 1982 and London-made jewellery in 1990. A British Academy grant in 1989 enabled research into the archives at Boughton House, Northamptonshire, where the patronage of Huguenot artists, craftsmen and designers by Charles II's ambassador to Louis XIV's court, Ralph, later 1st Duke of Montagu (1638–1709), was preserved. The published celebration of Boughton and its collections facilitated my transfer to the Victoria and Albert Museum. There as curator of furniture and then of metalwork collections my research on the Huguenot contribution could continue, admittedly interspersed with increasing administrative responsibilities.

This book could not have been written without the extraordinary opportunities enjoyed as Getty Rothschild Fellow 2019, which coincided with my appointment in January 2019 as Rosalinde and Arthur Gilbert Research Curator at the Victoria and Albert Museum. The Gilbert Collection is rich in Huguenot silver and miniatures and includes Edward Feline's 1731 masterpiece, a royal christening gift. The reader is encouraged to study in person some of the treasures illustrated here. I hope that fresh biographical information about their makers will breathe new vitality into that experience.

In order to distinguish first-generation Huguenot immigrants, I have retained the French version of their given names. The range of spellings of family names and the lack of documentation for many Huguenot craftsmen indicate that this account is limited to the current state of knowledge. New arrivals coincided with the second generation born within established Huguenot communities in their adopted country, an indication of the complexity of the Huguenot diaspora. In London the Huguenots mixed with other French immigrants, including artists, craftsmen and patrons, whose presence enhanced their reputation and opportunities for employment.

This book concentrates on the cultural contribution made by Huguenot families in the British Isles, reflecting research undertaken over forty years, and recent confirmation that Britain welcomed more refugees from Catholic France in the late seventeenth century than the Netherlands. It centres on the British metropolis. London, beyond the rigid French guild systems that dominated Paris and the regional French towns and cities where first-generation refugees were trained, provided the opportunity for Huguenots to network with craftsmen of other skills and other faiths, promoting interdisciplinarity and resulting in regional and international commissions. The global network established by successive waves of Huguenot refugees contributed to their success and eventual assimilation.

TESSA MURDOCH
London, June 2021

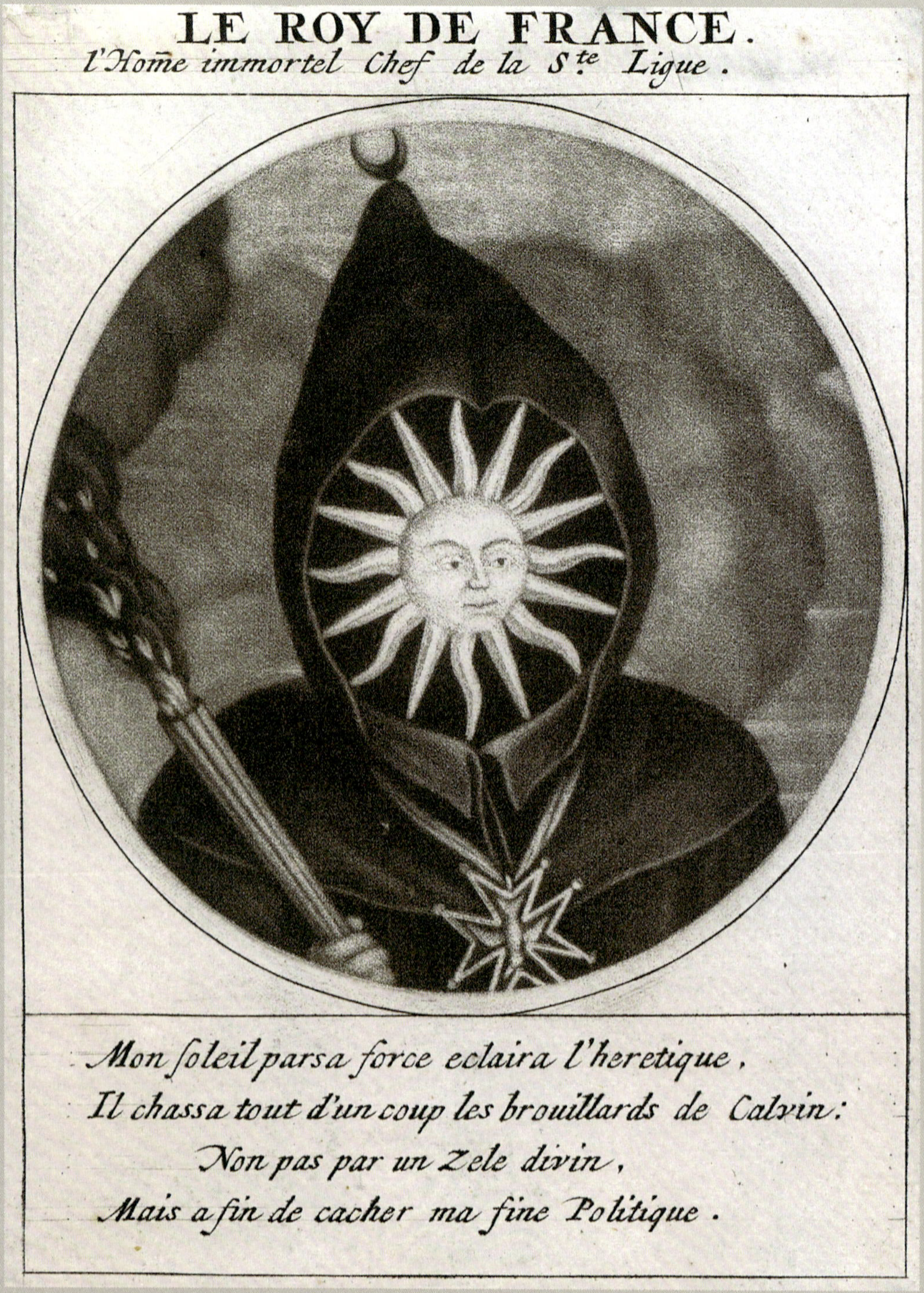

2 *Louis XIV as persecutor of the Huguenots*

Jacob Gole after Cornelis Dusart, Amsterdam, 1691
Satirical mezzotint, 14.4 × 10.6 cm
British Museum, London (S.6693)

This set of prints, with the subtitle *La Procession Monacale conduitte par Louis XIV pour la conversion des Protestans de son Royaume*, consists of satirical portraits of the leading French Catholic persecutors of the Huguenots.

KING OF FRANCE
Immortal Man Leader of the Holy League

My sun in its brightness shall enlighten the heretic,
Scattering all at once the mists of Calvin:
Not out of some zeal divine,
But to conceal my shrewd politics.

Introduction

'Huguenot' is the popular name for the French Protestants, followers of John Calvin (1509–1564). Of disputed origin, the term was previously thought to derive from *Eidgenoss* ('confederate'), a word used in Geneva, where Calvin and many Huguenots settled. However, it was first used in France in the 1550s, where it was linked to the city of Tours and associated with night-time activity.[1] As the influence of French culture pervaded Northern Europe, artists, craftsmen and designers trained in France were welcomed for their skills regardless of their religious persuasion. Some of those who settled in the British Isles in the seventeenth and eighteenth centuries were Catholics or economic migrants who worked alongside immigrant Huguenots and their descendants.

Huguenot artists, designers and craftsmen who left France between 1530 and 1780 and settled and worked in the British Isles were part of an international diaspora spreading across Northern Europe and beyond, to America and South Africa. First-generation immigrants brought skills and discipline that were transferred to the next generation. Their work reflected their training in the French style that was identified as Huguenot in their adopted countries. They met the international demand for French fashion that was dictated by sophisticated European courts and copied by the professional and merchant classes.

How did their Calvinist faith encourage and nurture their creativity? Their tenacity of faith determined their refuge. Their skills were conditioned by their place of origin: for many who came from regional France, this dictated their country of refuge. Most craftsmen who settled in London and Dublin came from regional French cities, including Rouen and La Rochelle, and from other Northern European cities where they had first taken refuge: Amsterdam, Rotterdam, Berlin and Geneva. Many came *en famille*, their strong family identity and network within their communities strengthening their resolve and fostering their identity in exile. Established Huguenot communities of artists and craftsmen in England and the Netherlands in the sixteenth century were a magnet for new arrivals in the late seventeenth century and later. Making the connections between successive generations of Huguenot craftsmen and their families is key to understanding the Huguenot achievement in exile.

In France, domestic silver was melted in 1689 to finance military campaigns so the preservation of Huguenot-made silver beyond the French borders provides evidence for high-style Louis XIV craftsmanship, of which our knowledge is largely limited to contemporary designs, illustrations in still-life painting and tapestries. Small-scale ornament published by Blois-trained Simon Gribelin contrasts with the larger scale of court-trained Jean Tijou and Daniel Marot, contrasting the regional and the metropolitan. Yet they share the same vigorously rendered forms, carefully balanced and proportioned, which in two dimensions anticipate the three-dimensional quality inherent in translation into metal, stone or wood. Gribelin's designs anticipate the subtleties of engraved silver and watch cases. The same substantial quality of ornament is found in architecture, woodwork, ceramics, and decorative painting; ornament which is integrated with the structure of the object or decorative painting. Portraitists channelled their talent into painting or carving portable miniatures, which personalized functional objects, snuffboxes and watches.

The work of British goldsmith George Wickes or gatesmith William Edney reflects the influence of first-generation Huguenot design, although lacking its robustness and plasticity. Gribelin's pattern books were still available after his death as they appealed to the traditional style in 1740s London associated with City merchants. Designs by Tijou and Marot outlived their own lifetimes. Marot's designs brought to British taste the concept that every feature, both inside and out, should reflect the unity of the whole. This was taken up by British designer architects, Marot's contemporary William Kent and, later, Robert Adam. Marot was largely responsible for disseminating the Louis XIV court style in England, associated with émigré craftsmen who had worked for the French monarch before the Revocation. Other Huguenot architects were trained as military engineers. Their contribution to engineering is characteristic of their pragmatic approach to the application of design. Huguenot technical mastery, combined with high standards of execution, attracted and sustained patronage. This vital combination forced native craftsmen to compete.

The role of Huguenot artists as teachers was significant given that the French Royal Academy of Painting and Sculpture was established 120 years earlier than the British Royal Academy of Art. Louis XIV's determination to remove all Protestant artists, both teachers and students, from the Paris Academy was England's gain. The significant increase of figurative decoration on silver and watches reflects the opportunity for life drawing of the female as well as the male model provided at the Chéron Vanderbank Academy in St Martin's Lane. For just four years, from 1720 to 1724, the training set new standards that were adopted by the next generation of artists and craftsmen. Second-generation Huguenots introduced new changes in fashion; the British admiration for the Louis XIV style waned in favour of the lighter, more graceful *régence*, which ceded in turn to the new *rococo* style associated with the court of Louis XV. Again, second-generation Huguenots paved the way for the new style through publication of pattern books. They led native craftsmen in adopting the new designs, attracting commissions and sales. Huguenot technical mastery and understanding of proportion, inherited and learned from the previous generation, empowered their production.

Many refugee designers and craftsmen maintained direct contact with Huguenot relatives settled elsewhere in Europe or family who stayed in France and abjured their faith. They kept abreast of the latest developments in French taste. The work of great second-generation artists Paul Crespin, Paul de Lamerie, L.F. Roubiliac and Nicholas Sprimont runs parallel to the innovative designs published in London by William De La Cour, Vincent la Chapelle, John Rocque (*c*.1704–1762) and François Vivares.

Huguenot mastery and quality of production were promoted by marketing skills, an area in which Huguenot women, trained in the family business, excelled. Huguenot communities established in exile were supported by a core of successful merchants who could underwrite opportunities for craftsmen and promote export of their luxury goods. Some made their name as shopkeepers, effectively marketing the goods made by their fellow émigrés. As French was the fashionable language, their foreign identity attracted the beau monde.

The contribution of the leading artists and craftsmen, some still household names – Marot, De Lamerie, Revere – is set in the context of their lesser-known contemporaries, Chéron, Labelye, Le Marchand, whose work deserves greater recognition. Gideon du Chesne, who received relief from the Threadneedle Street church in 1681, was by the late 1690s working at Boughton and Castle Howard. The family motto 'Persevere' on jeweller Peter Romilly's bookplate sums up the endeavour that contributed to their success. His son Sir Samuel Romilly was Solicitor General.

The charitable support available to new arrivals was crucial. For those whose work is highlighted here, there are many more who worked anonymously. Some, like the architect Samuel Hauduroy, could not rise to the challenge of learning a new language and making themselves understood. Others – the pewterer James Taudin and architects Nicholas Dubois and Charles Labelye – attracted jealousy and rebuke. The opportunity provided to first-generation refugees by leading patrons, Ralph, 1st Duke of Montagu, or William Cavendish, 1st Duke of Devonshire, provides insight into the close working relationship between different specialities that the Huguenots promoted. The support offered by Huguenot merchants in marketing their artistic products developed the international market. This exemplary cross-fertilization between the artistic, business and scientific communities is the most significant aspect of Huguenot refugee art and culture.

The Huguenot refuge over the 250 years encompassed here reached its zenith under Louis XIV. Recent studies of that monarch reinforce the view of Louis XIV's sister-in-law Liselotte, writing to her Aunt Sophie from Marly on 16 May 1696: 'It is difficult to conceive how ignorant the great man is in matters of religion. He never takes the trouble to find out for himself what is right and what is wrong.'[2]

This book presents the current state of knowledge on this wide-ranging subject, which is of lasting human interest. Many readers will be drawn by awareness of their own Huguenot origins. The role of successful Huguenots as collectors and patrons, their assimilation into the British establishment through marriage and business partnerships, the evidence for their books, portraits, silver, jewellery and watches bequeathed as heirlooms, merits separate study. The collection assembled by the merchant George Aufrere was inherited by the Earls of Yarborough and is still largely intact; Sir Peter Delmé, Lord Mayor of London in 1723, 'the greatest merchant of his time', whose collection of paintings was celebrated in his life time, has no official biography. William Fauquier's important collection of contemporary French paintings, sold at auction in 1789, is represented by Chardin's *Boy building a House of Cards* now at Waddesdon Manor; Dr Matthew Maty, trained as a doctor, a profession to which the Huguenots made an extraordinary contribution, was also a scholar curator buying for the new British Museum, which he served as Librarian.

It is hoped that this volume will encourage future generations to engage and uncover further evidence for the network of Huguenot familial contacts which will shed more light on the rich tapestry of their international outreach and exchange. My own interest in Huguenot culture has led me beyond Northern Europe to Australia, Brazil, China, South Africa and the United States. Much remains to be discovered. The Huguenot diaspora extended across the globe and provides an inspiring precedent for accepting and encouraging the potential contribution of refugee communities today.

Huguenot Congregations in the British Isles (excluding London) established before 1700

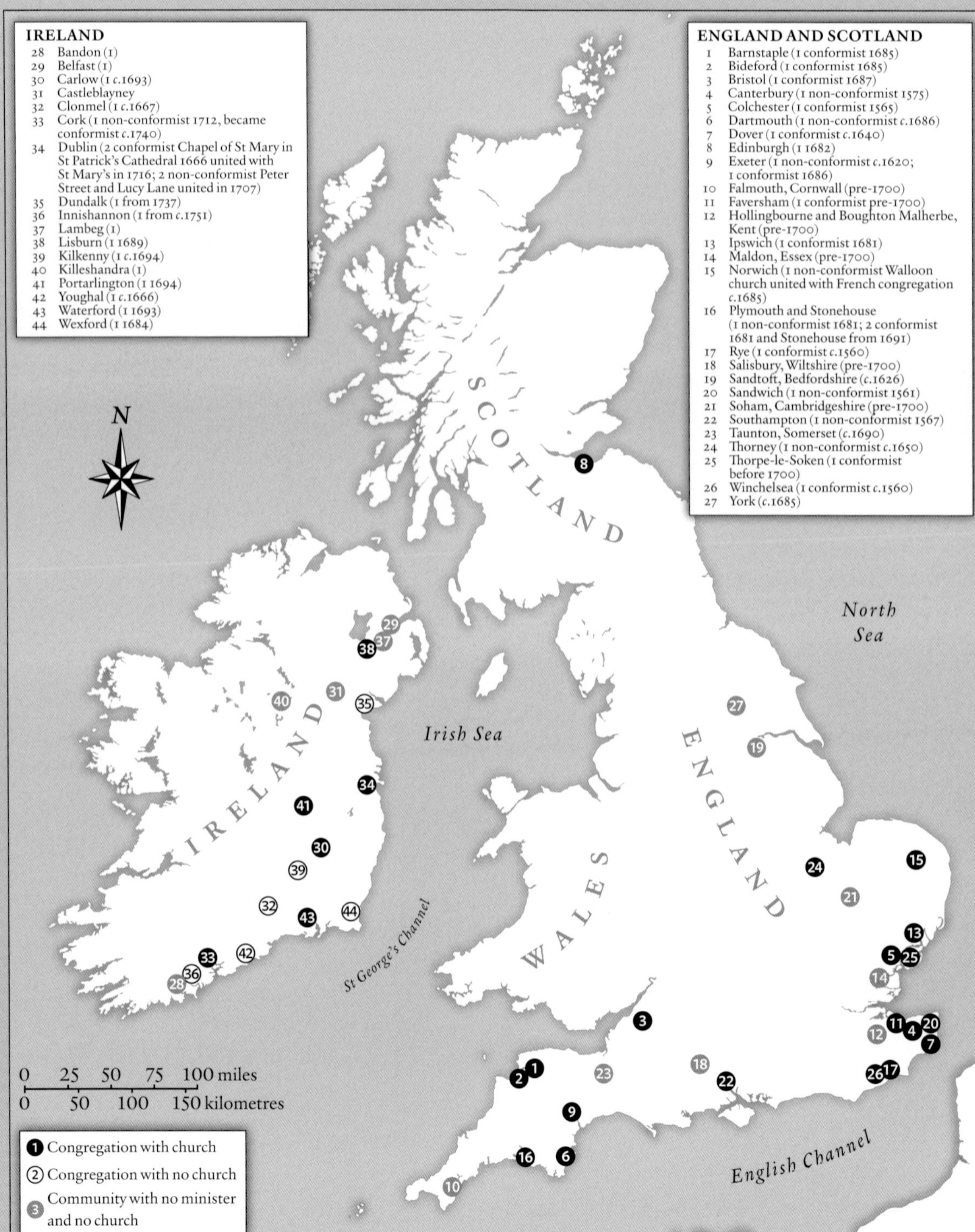

Huguenot Churches in or near London 1550–1750

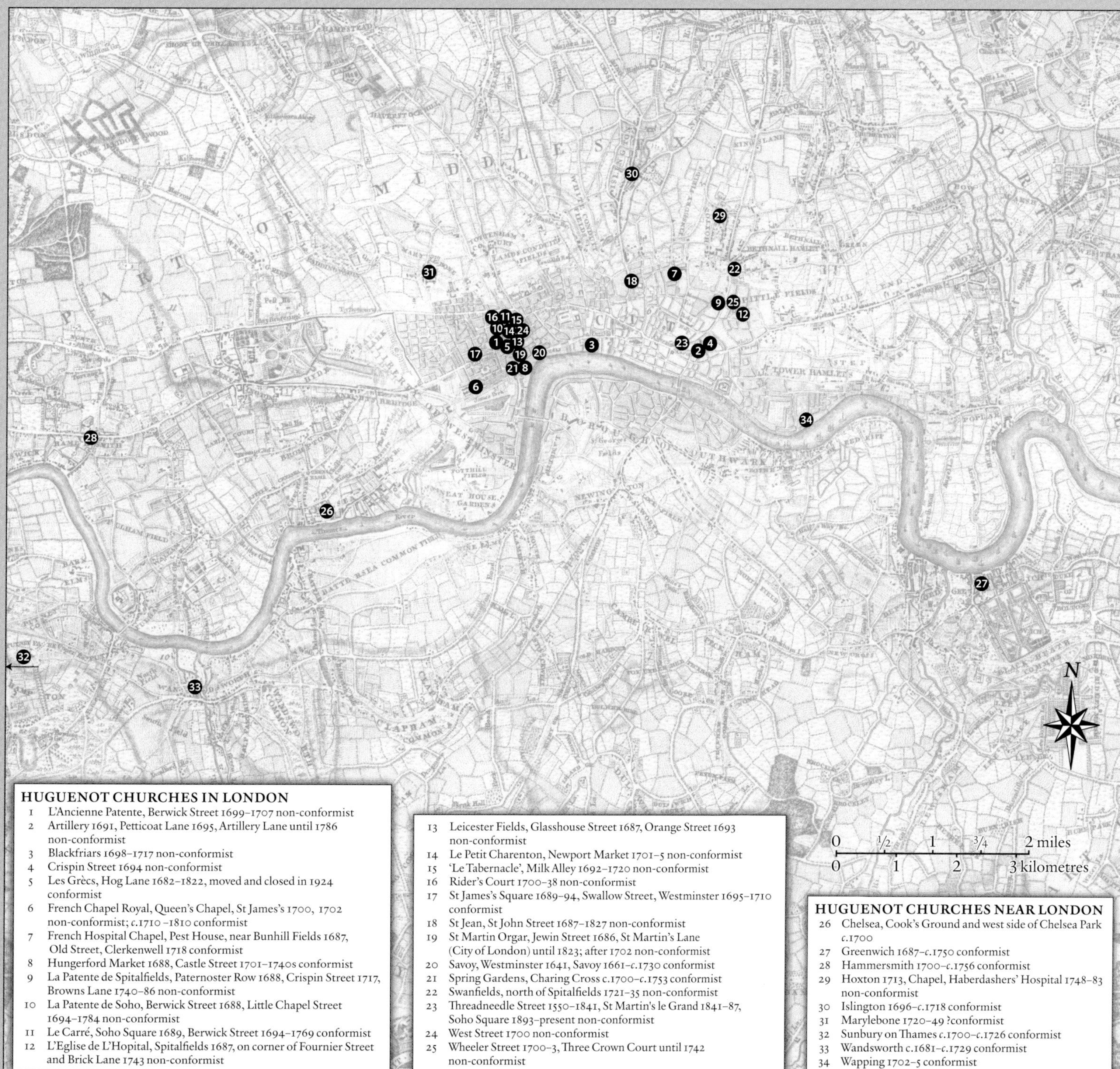

HUGUENOT CHURCHES IN LONDON

1 L'Ancienne Patente, Berwick Street 1699–1707 non-conformist
2 Artillery 1691, Petticoat Lane 1695, Artillery Lane until 1786 non-conformist
3 Blackfriars 1698–1717 non-conformist
4 Crispin Street 1694 non-conformist
5 Les Grècs, Hog Lane 1682–1822, moved and closed in 1924 conformist
6 French Chapel Royal, Queen's Chapel, St James's 1700, 1702 non-conformist; *c.*1710 –1810 conformist
7 French Hospital Chapel, Pest House, near Bunhill Fields 1687, Old Street, Clerkenwell 1718 conformist
8 Hungerford Market 1688, Castle Street 1701–1740s conformist
9 La Patente de Spitalfields, Paternoster Row 1688, Crispin Street 1717, Browns Lane 1740–86 non-conformist
10 La Patente de Soho, Berwick Street 1688, Little Chapel Street 1694–1784 non-conformist
11 Le Carré, Soho Square 1689, Berwick Street 1694–1769 conformist
12 L'Eglise de L'Hopital, Spitalfields 1687, on corner of Fournier Street and Brick Lane 1743 non-conformist
13 Leicester Fields, Glasshouse Street 1687, Orange Street 1693 non-conformist
14 Le Petit Charenton, Newport Market 1701–5 non-conformist
15 'Le Tabernacle', Milk Alley 1692–1720 non-conformist
16 Rider's Court 1700–38 non-conformist
17 St James's Square 1689–94, Swallow Street, Westminster 1695–1710 conformist
18 St Jean, St John Street 1687–1827 non-conformist
19 St Martin Orgar, Jewin Street 1686, St Martin's Lane (City of London) until 1823; after 1702 non-conformist
20 Savoy, Westminster 1641, Savoy 1661–*c.*1730 conformist
21 Spring Gardens, Charing Cross *c.*1700–*c.*1753 conformist
22 Swanfields, north of Spitalfields 1721–35 non-conformist
23 Threadneedle Street 1550–1841, St Martin's le Grand 1841–87, Soho Square 1893–present non-conformist
24 West Street 1700 non-conformist
25 Wheeler Street 1700–3, Three Crown Court until 1742 non-conformist

HUGUENOT CHURCHES NEAR LONDON

26 Chelsea, Cook's Ground and west side of Chelsea Park *c.*1700
27 Greenwich 1687–*c.*1750 conformist
28 Hammersmith 1700–*c.*1756 conformist
29 Hoxton 1713, Chapel, Haberdashers' Hospital 1748–83 non-conformist
30 Islington 1696–*c.*1718 conformist
31 Marylebone 1720–49 ?conformist
32 Sunbury on Thames *c.*1700–*c.*1726 conformist
33 Wandsworth *c.*1681–*c.*1729 conformist
34 Wapping 1702–5 conformist

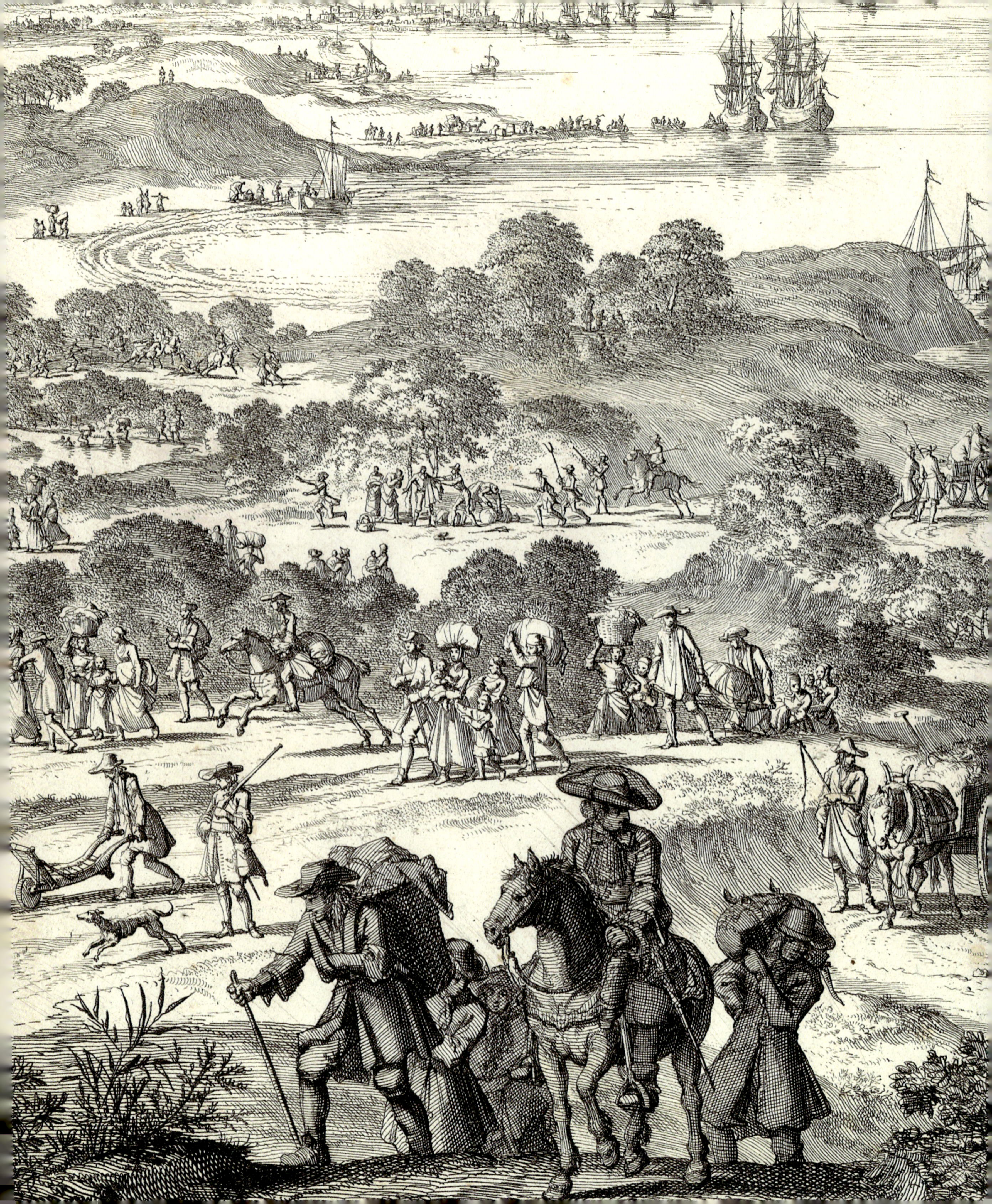

Chapter One
The Huguenot Diaspora

3 *Protestants fleeing France after the Revocation of the Edict of Nantes, 1685–6*
Jan Luyken, The Netherlands, 1696 (detail) see plate 5

In the late seventeenth century the recurring Huguenot exodus created ripples across the known world. Their personal experience as refugees resonates 300 years later, when there are 65 million refugees globally and predictions for the impact of climate change anticipate an additional 125 million refugees forced to leave their homes later this century.

The Huguenot settlers retained their identity through maintaining the French language, already established as the language of Europe through the prestige of the French monarchy and the city and university of Paris. Some Huguenots still spoke French at home in the late eighteenth century, and wrote their wills in French. Their discipline of faith strengthened their ability to ensure that their talent was passed to the next generation, both within their own communities and shared with the indigenous population. Some spread their skills more widely and extended their influence by marrying outside their community. The Huguenots were mainly city dwellers and settled in the capitals and principal towns of Protestant Northern Europe at a time when civic populations were expanding. Their French names endure, so descendants can track their Huguenot ancestors and share inherited stories through Huguenot networks established across North America, Australia and South Africa, and in Europe particularly in the British Isles, France, Germany and the Netherlands.

The interdisciplinary friendships they established are reflected in the records of the Huguenot institutions that fostered their well-being. Thus the sculptor Louis François Roubiliac (1702–1762), first recorded in London in 1730, set up home with Céleste Regnier (fl.1754–71), who ran the family print shop in Great Newport Street, adjacent to Roubiliac's own studio in St Martin's Lane. Roubiliac's daughter by his previous marriage, Sophie, was from 1744 the goldsmith and porcelain manufacturer Nicholas Sprimont's goddaughter, thus demonstrating the close links between sculpture, silver and porcelain and the Huguenots' pragmatic approach to their faith. Roubiliac and Sprimont were both baptized into the Catholic Church, in Lyons and Liège respectively, but this did not prevent their engagement with the Huguenot community in London: they both attended Anglican and Huguenot churches. Leading French craftsmen originally thought to be Huguenot, Joseph Duffour (fl.1730–76), Francis Lapiere (1653–1714), Jean Montigny (1686?–1757) and Jean Tijou (fl.1687–1716), have since emerged from contemporary documents as Catholics, yet the important contributions they made at the hub of immigrant talent justify their inclusion here. The academic 'history painter' Louis Chéron (1655–1725), decorative artist and founder of the St Martin's Lane Academy in 1720, was a friend of René Pelletier (d.1726), carver and gilder, and bequeathed to Pelletier his prints and books. The cartographer John Rocque (*c*.1704–1762) stood godfather to the son of François Vivares (1709–1780), regarded as the father of British landscape engraving.

One skill could morph into another, so Charles Gouyn (1713–1785) and Andrew Planché (1727–1805) used their training as jewellers as a spring-board for developing porcelain manufactories in London's West End and in Derby. A watchmaker, James Vauloué (1702–1742), adapted his skill to invent a new engine for driving the piles for the foundations of the first bridge over the Thames at Westminster, which was designed by the engineer Charles Labelye (1705–1781).

In London and the South East, Huguenots are primarily associated with silks and silver but their most significant contribution, economically and globally, lies in horology, the development of the Swiss watch industry centred on Geneva. The growth of London as the leading centre of clock and watch production in the eighteenth century owes much to the numerical strength of the Huguenot craftsmen, and their ability to attract other immigrant craftsmen and develop the export market.

When Winston Churchill (1874–1965) was researching the life and achievements of his great ancestor John Churchill, 1st Duke of Marlborough (1650–1722) in the 1930s, he became aware of the plight of the Huguenot refugees and the important role they played as soldiers in Marlborough's army. The growing persecution of the Jews in Nazi Germany presented a parallel situation; Churchill was both forewarned and forearmed. But persecution of the Jews, as with the Huguenots, was not a new phenomenon. This parallel empowered composer Giacomo Meyerbeer (1791–1864), from a wealthy Jewish background in Berlin, to empathize with the plight of the Huguenots in his remarkable opera *Les Huguenots*, first performed at the Paris Opera in 1836. I am proud to have both Jewish and Huguenot ancestry and believe that my fascination with both inherited cultures enriches my understanding of their significance.

Huguenot refugees

The 1598 Edict of Nantes, signed by Henri IV, granting the Protestant minority relative freedom of worship in France, was revoked in October 1685 at Fontainebleau by his grandson Louis XIV (plate 4). The Revocation was the climax of 20 years of increased persecution of French Protestants. Tens of thousands fled France (plate 5). The satirical print of Louis XIV dressed as a monk, with a sun instead of a face (plate 2), demonstrates the fear and hatred with which the 'Sun King' was regarded by Huguenots both in France and in exile.[1]

Between 1680 and 1720 over 50,000 French Protestants settled in the British Isles, where many contributed to aspects of British culture, industry and finance and were gradually assimilated. They absorbed British traditions, yet developed French influence in their adopted country. It was they who introduced the word 'refugee' to the English language.[2]

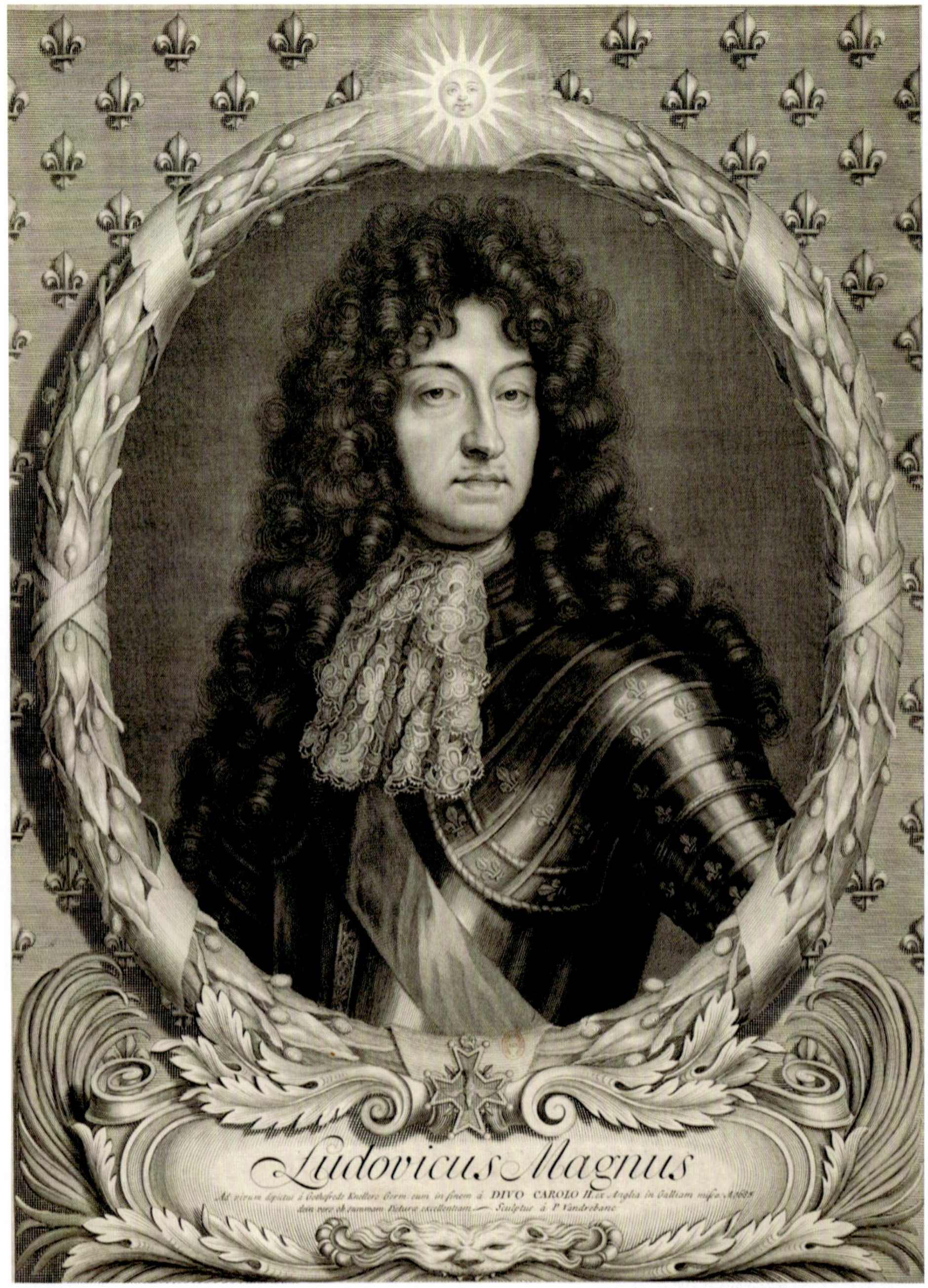

4 *Louis XIV in armour*

Peter Vandrebanc after Godfrey Kneller, London, 1685
Engraving, 58.3 × 42.3 cm
Worcester College, Oxford

In 1652 Louis XIV had declared: 'Inasmuch as our subjects of the so-called Reformed Religion have given us proof of their affection and fidelity, we wish them to understand for this reason they will be maintained and kept in the full enjoyment of the Edict of Nantes.'

5 *Protestants fleeing France after the Revocation of the Edict of Nantes, 1685–6*

From Elie Benoist, *Het weg vlugten de Gereformeerde uyt Vrankryk* (*The Escape of the Reformed Refugees from France*), Amsterdam 1696
Jan Luyken, The Netherlands, 1696
Etching, 29.4 × 36.4 cm
Rijksmuseum, Amsterdam (1896-A-19368-1049,185)

Tens of thousands fled France at the time of the Revocation; if caught, the men were sentenced as galley slaves and the women confined to Catholic convents.

French Protestants were followers of John Calvin (1509–1564; plate 6), the son of a registrar in Noyon, north of Paris. Calvin studied theology in Paris and law in Orleans, but by 1534 had returned to Noyon and converted from the Catholic faith.[3] In October 1534 the authorities reacted violently against reform following the affair of the placards, in which broadsheets printed in Switzerland attacking all aspects of Catholicism were widely displayed in Paris and towns on the Loire. Calvin took refuge outside France, initially in Basle. Here he wrote *The Institutes of the Christian Religion* as a manual to be used alongside scripture. Published in 1536 in Geneva, four further editions appeared during his lifetime.[4]

Huguenots in Geneva

In 1536 Calvin visited Geneva for the first time. Although the Republic was largely Protestant, the leading minister, Guillaume Farel (1489–1565), a Frenchman like Calvin, was struggling against strong Catholic opposition. Calvin accepted Farel's invitation to organize the Reformed Church there and became Reader in Holy Scripture. In 1537 Calvin submitted recommendations on ecclesiastical organization to the city council. Acceptance of the formal confession of faith was compulsory for all citizens who wished to remain in the Republic. Yet Catholic opposition forced Calvin and Farel to leave Geneva in 1538. Calvin went to Strasbourg, one of the most important centres for

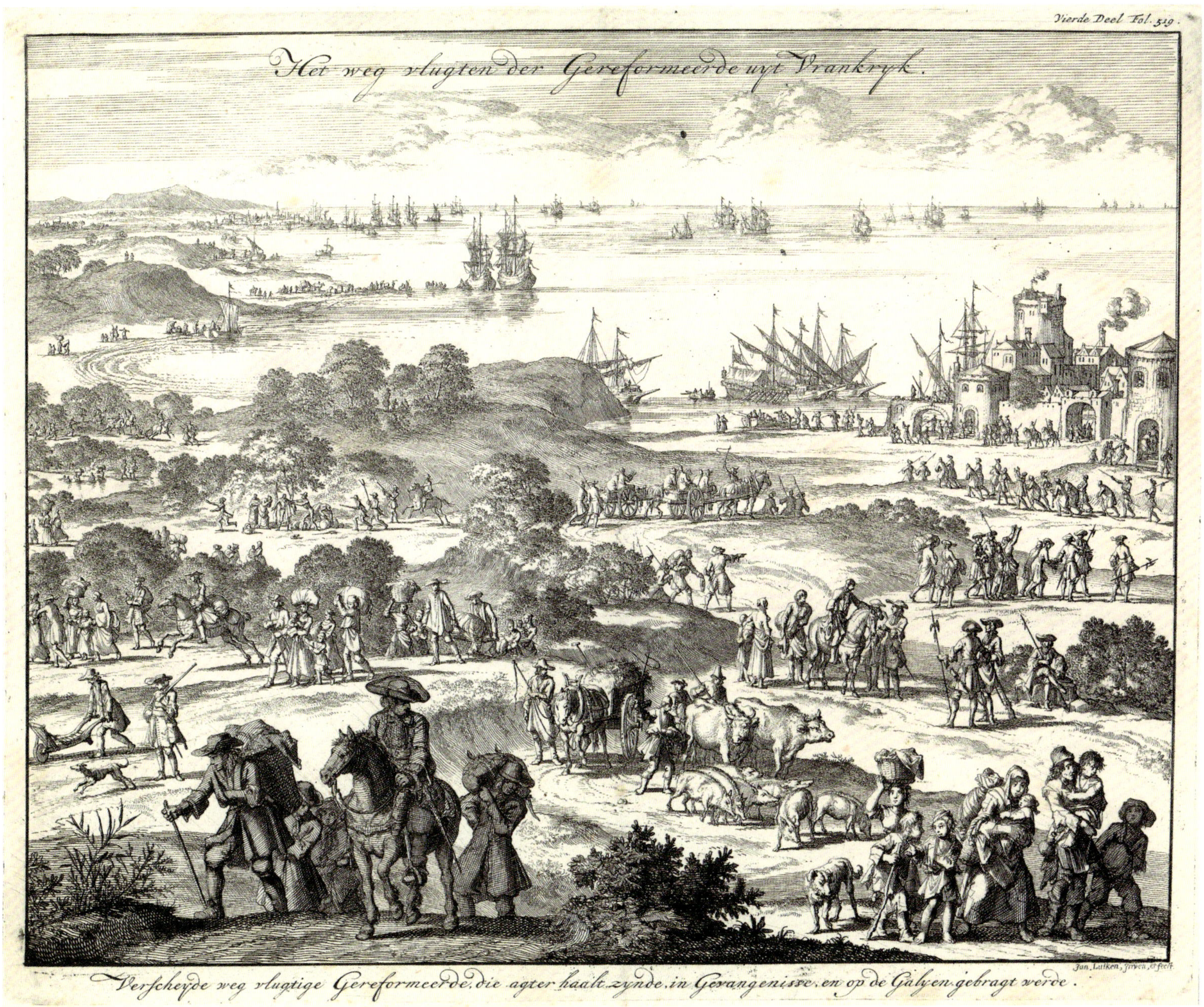

Protestantism in Europe. Here he organized the first French parish as a model for all Protestant parishes in France. He taught theology at the new Strasbourg High School and in 1540 married Idolette de Bure (1506–1549), one of his own converts, the widow of an Anabaptist.

In October 1540 an official Genevan embassy invited Calvin to return. The following year he went back to the city that was to be home for the rest of his life and created a disciplined yet democratic church and government. Geneva welcomed refugees from Italy in 1542, from France from 1547 and from England under Mary Tudor in the 1550s. Between 1549 and 1559 there were over 5,000 new settlers, a large percentage of the then total population of 13,000. Calvin thought that no church could exist unless a fixed rule of life was established in accordance with God's Word. The Genevan church was supervised by the Consistory, six pastors and twelve laymen or elders, in conjunction with the magistracy or temporal government. The Little Council met to decide the city laws and edicts and the General Council of 200 members was elected by the citizens from 800 candidates. The selection of elders was influenced by the church members. Both spiritual and temporal governments were chosen democratically, and united to maintain standards expected of the citizens.

The lives of men and women were regulated: their choice of occupation and their dress, their meals and their songs.[5] In 1544 the Little Council introduced the manufacture of cloth to provide a livelihood for unemployed poor. Abandoned due to competition from Lyons, this was replaced with the manufacture of watches, introduced by refugee French watchmakers. Thomas Bayard (d.1553) from Vézelise, Lorraine, was the first watchmaker to settle in Geneva in 1550.[6] Watchmaking replaced jewellery as Calvin discouraged personal embellishment. Inns were closed and replaced by five 'abbeys', where guests were supervised and given a bible translated into French. Sacred plays were permitted but secular theatre was banned. In 1546 parents who gave their children Christian names that were not biblical were criticized.

The pattern of worship was carefully controlled and citizens were instructed through daily sermons. Discipline was explained in *Ecclesiastical Ordinances* published within a month of Calvin's return to Geneva in 1541. Each church member was encouraged to use their individual talents to benefit the community. The correction of behaviour was undertaken by church elders, although the right to excommunicate was the prerogative of the Consistory. Pastors made annual visits to parishioners' homes to ensure that regulations were observed.

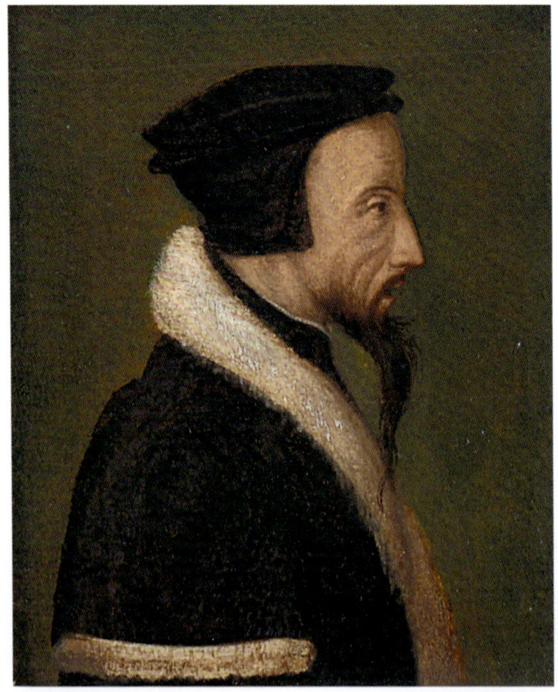

6 *John Calvin (1509–1564)*
Unknown artist, Germany, 1535
Oil on card, 10.2 × 9 cm
Private collection

Born in Noyon, Calvin studied theology in Paris and law in Orleans. He converted from Catholicism in 1535. Calvin took refuge in Basle, where he wrote *The Institutes of the Christian Religion*. He visited Ferrara, and then in 1536 settled in Geneva. 'All those who had some desire for the true doctrine ranged themselves around me to learn, although I was hardly more than a beginner.'

Calvin created an academy modelled on the Strasbourg High School opened by Jean Sturm (1507–1589) in 1538. The inaugural session was held in June 1559. The academy was governed by Théodore de Bèze (1519–1605), Professor of Theology from Lausanne, and nurtured candidates for the ministry. It opened with 162 boys, mostly from France, but within six years its pupils numbered over 1,000 and they came from many European countries. It served as a model for Protestant academies established in France during the seventeenth century.[7]

In 1559 Calvin was given the Freedom of the City of Geneva. His effort to unite Swiss churches had culminated in the 1550 Consensus, yet he did not achieve unification with the Lutheran Church. Reformed Protestantism never lost Calvin's ecumenical impulse. The last five years of his life were dominated by illness; he was succeeded by de Bèze in 1564. Calvin secured the future of Geneva, creating a church, a school and a fortress, and witnessed his influence in France, England and Scotland.

Huguenots in France

In 1536 Calvin dedicated his *Institutes of the Christian Religion* to François I in the hope that his monarch might look favourably on the reformed religion.

However, the Catholic Church was closely integrated with royal authority and any opposition was a political threat to the unity of the French state. From 1547 François I's successor, Henri II, set up a 'Chambre Ardente' in Paris to root out and condemn the reformers as heretics. Within two years more than five hundred people had been condemned for their beliefs. This exercise was repeated at Bordeaux, Toulouse and Aix-en-Provence. Despite this setback, the new faith was nurtured by books and pamphlets printed in Geneva and distributed by travelling preachers. It appealed to most social classes, including Catholic clergy, nobility, scholars, merchants and artisans, but rarely (except in Poitou, the Cévennes and Dauphiné) to the rural peasantry.[8] The Huguenot ethic was largely determined by conditions in Geneva. Their creed dictated the nature of their artistic contribution.[9]

Huguenots contributed art that was functional: well designed, embodying sophisticated technical skills and made to last. Such features are characteristic of Huguenot artistic achievements during the sixteenth and early seventeenth centuries in France and elsewhere in Northern Europe.[10] Bernard Palissy (*c.*1510–*c.*1590), who revolutionized the production of ceramics (plate 7), epitomizes the Huguenot craftsman. Trained as a stained-glass artist in Saintes, he established an academy in Sedan, giving lectures on natural sciences subsequently published as *Discours Admirables* (1580). He created a grotto for Queen Catherine de Medici (1519–1589) at the Tuileries Palace, Paris. His ceramics were curated and displayed on royal buffets by Jean Charpentier, 'Garde-Vaiselle' to the royal household.[11] Palissy's tragic death – he was imprisoned for heresy and died in the Bastille – has contributed to his mythical status as a craftsman hero. During his lifetime Palissy attracted royal patronage; after his biography was published in the mid-nineteenth century in different European languages, his work was avidly collected. His fascination with the natural world appealed to the engagement with natural sciences. He was perceived as a visionary, a wise yet passionate *savant*, poet and mystic.[12]

Palissy's celebrated Huguenot contemporaries include the metalworker François Briot (*c.*1550–1615) from Montbéliard (plate 8); the sculptor Barthélemy Prieur (1536–1611) from the Marne;

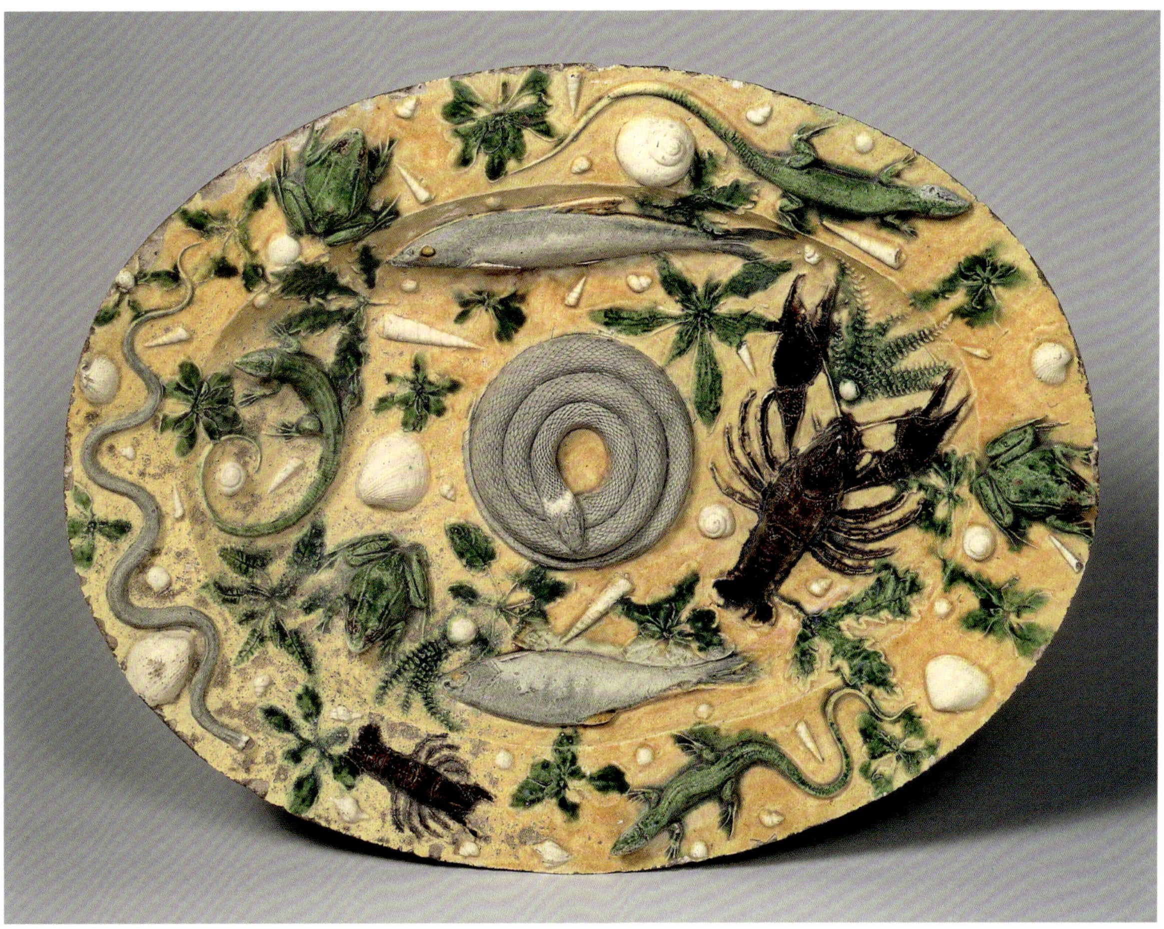

7 Dish

Attributed to Bernard Palissy, Saintes, *c.*1550
Earthenware, 47.9 × 36.8 cm
The Getty Museum, Los Angeles (88.DE.63)

Palissy applied a range of brilliant colours to spectacular ceramic vessels with features cast directly from nature.

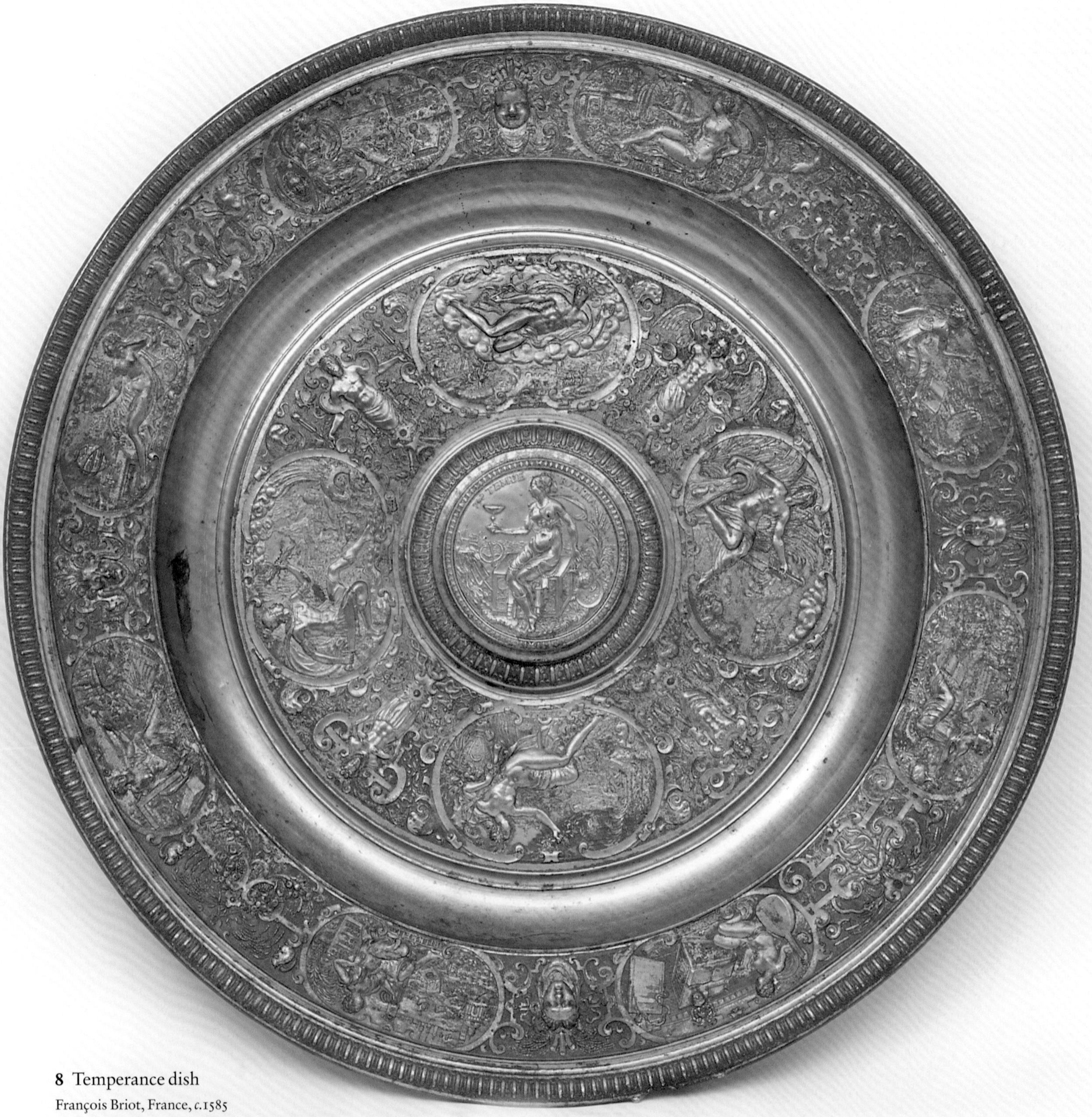

8 Temperance dish

François Briot, France, *c.*1585
Cast pewter, diam. 44.9 cm
Victoria and Albert Museum, London (2063–1855)

The *Temperance* dish is the only signed example of Briot's work, and the model for the Wimbledon Tennis Championships Women's Singles Trophy. The original was intended for display on a princely buffet, probably for Friedrich I, Duke of Würtenburg (1557–1608). Briot was a model carver, medallist and pattern maker based in Montbéliard.

9 Ewer

Susanne de Court, Limoges, 1590–1600
Enamelled copper, ht 29.6 cm
Victoria and Albert Museum, London (553–1883)

Mythological scenes and grotesques echoed the Italianate Fontainebleau court style. This ewer depicts the 'Triumph of Ceres' after Jacques Androuët du Cerceau in the upper section, with two scenes from the life of Moses below, after engravings in Bernard Salomon's Lyons Bible, published by Jean de Tournes in 1554.

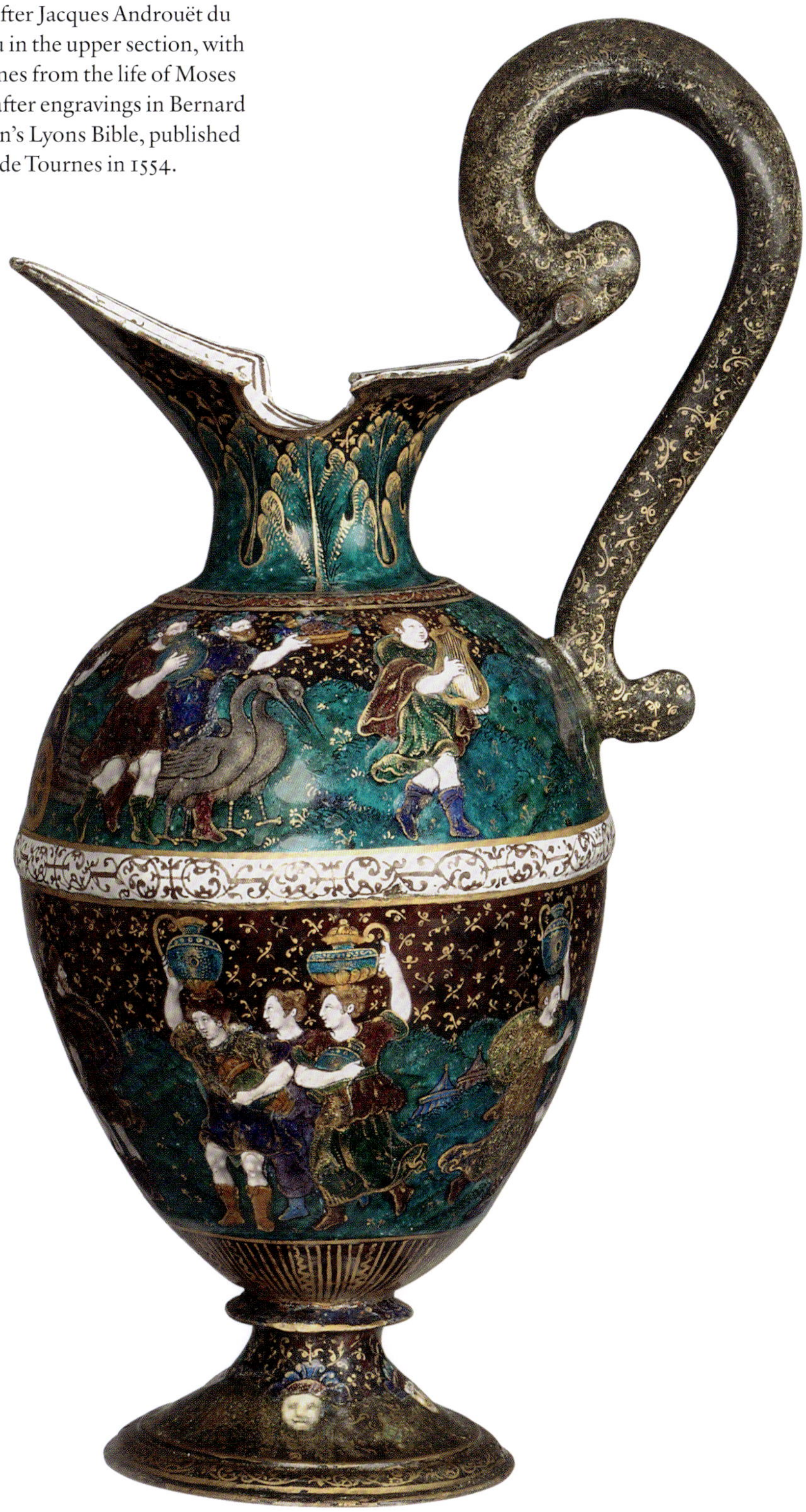

the designer Hugues Sambin (1520–1601) from Dijon;[13] and the designer and engraver Etienne Delaune (*c.*1518–1583) from Orleans. Théodore de Bry (1528–1588), engraver, born in Strasbourg, worked in Frankfurt. Family dynasties of enamellers were established at Limoges by the mid-sixteenth century, when painting *en grisaille* was highly fashionable at the French court; some workshops specialized in Old Testament scenes adapted from Bible illustrations. Secular vessels were intended for display on a table or buffet.[14] Susanne de Court (fl. *c.*1600; plate 9) was the only recorded female enameller (before the nineteenth century) working in Limoges. She worked in the style of Jean Court (fl.1555–85), to whom she was related by either birth or marriage.[15]

At the outset of the French civil wars in the 1560s, about half the French nobility welcomed the opportunity to oppose the Crown under the guise of religion.[16] The Coligny brothers, sincere supporters of the new faith, belonged to a powerful French family; their uncle, Anne de Montmorency (1493–1567), Constable of France, was influential with Henri II. The Queen of Navarre, a strong Calvinist, converted her husband, Antoine de Navarre, duc de Bourbon (1518–1562). His brother, Louis, prince de Condé (1530–1569), became Protector of the Reformed Churches.[17] After Henri II's death in 1559, the Huguenots held the first National Synod in France; 72 French churches were represented and a Confession of Faith and Rules of Discipline were established. The construction of Huguenot places of worship followed, some designed by distinguished Huguenot architects Jacques II Androuët du Cerceau (1550–1614), Philibert de l'Orme (1514–1570) and Salomon de Brosse (1571–1626).

In 1559 regional representatives of Protestant communities professed their allegiance to the young Charles IX and asked permission to meet regularly for worship. They gained royal authority to worship outside towns in the Edict of January 1562. The first Huguenot temple in Lyons (plate 10) was built in 1561. But this disciplined reform movement alarmed Catholic authorities, whose reaction culminated in the Massacre of St Bartholomew on 24 August 1572, when between 2,000 and 3,000 Protestants lost their lives in Paris and a further 7,000 were massacred in the regions. After 1572 the reaffirmation of the Protestant right to restricted worship provoked another Catholic reaction. In 1577 Henri de Condé (1552–1588) laid the foundation stone for the octagonal temple in La Rochelle designed by Philibert de l'Orme. The 12-sided temple at Grand Quevilly, Rouen was designed by Nicholas Genevois in 1599.

Henri, son of the Queen of Navarre, emerged as a new Protestant leader, and in 1584 became heir to the throne; yet the Protestants had to wait 14 years before they achieved religious toleration in the Edict that Henri IV signed at Nantes in 1598.

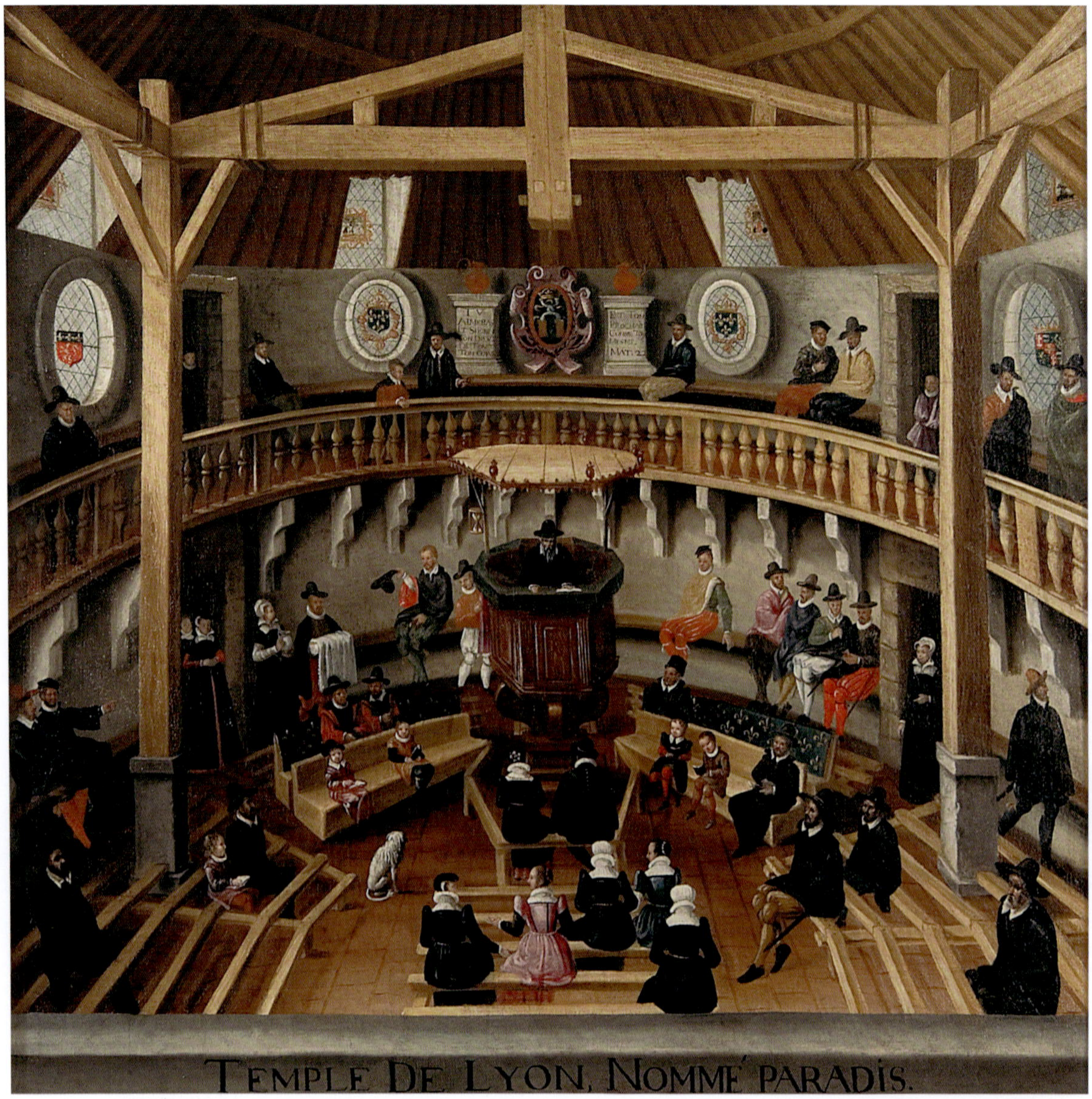

10 *Interior of the Huguenot Temple, Lyons*

Attributed to Jean Perrisin, possibly painted in Geneva, *c.*1569
Oil on canvas, 125 × 123 cm
Bibliothèque Publique et Universitaire, Geneva

The temple shown in this painting remained in use until 1685. There were three ground-floor entrances with access to the gallery via an exterior double staircase. The pulpit is in a central position and the men, seated separately from the women, retain their hats during the service. Jean Perrisin (d.1616) was also responsible for the decoration of Lyons Town Hall (1583) and triumphal arches for Henri IV in 1566, 1595 and 1600.

At Charenton outside Paris, the first temple was designed by Jacques II Androuët du Cerceau in 1606; it was rebuilt from 1623 by Salomon de Brosse (plate 11). At Dieppe the temple in the Faubourg de la Barre was completed with financial support from Henri IV in September 1608; the Caen temple dated from 1612. The Montauban temple was built between 1615 and 1617 to designs by Pierre de Levesville (*c.*1570–1632), an architect from Toulouse.[18]

In 1610 Henri IV was assassinated and the Protestants lost their sympathetic monarch. The Catholic cause was championed by Cardinal Richelieu (1585–1642). Tension developed when the independent province of Bearn appealed to the General Assembly of Huguenots in France for assistance in reacquiring property that Henri IV had restored to the Catholic Church. This incident aroused opposition to the Protestants and culminated in the Siege of La Rochelle in 1628. Although Protestant liberty of worship and civil equality were reaffirmed at the Peace of Alais in 1629, the Huguenots had lost their aristocratic protectors and their four fortress towns, La Rochelle, Montauban, Cognac and La Cité, granted in 1598 through the Edict of Nantes.

The next 30 years saw a lull between two storms of persecution. Many noblemen remained quietly faithful to the Protestant cause, including the de Ruvigny family, Marshal Turenne (1611–1675, who eventually converted to Catholicism) and the Count of Schomberg (1615–1690), who served in the French army from 1651 to 1660.[19] The Protestants found a new protector in Cardinal Mazarin (1602–1661), but on his death persecution was renewed, gathered momentum and culminated

11 *The Temple at Charenton, outside Paris*

Unknown artist, 1623, reprinted for the Society of Parisians in London, 1708
Engraving, 21 × 21.5 cm
The French Hospital, on loan to the Huguenot Museum, Rochester, Kent

The inscription is from Psalm 65 as translated by Clement Marot. The temple was built to the designs of J.A. du Cerceau in 1606 and rebuilt after a fire in 1623 to the designs of Salomon de Brosse; it was destroyed a few days after the Revocation of the Edict of Nantes in October 1685. Members of the Society of Parisians, refugees from Paris who settled within 3 miles of Christ Church, Spitalfields, were aged between 18 and 41. Their number was limited to 61.

in the Revocation of the Edict of Nantes in 1685.

Madame de Sévigné (1626–1696) wrote to her cousin the comte de Bussy-Rabutin (1618–1693) in October 1685: 'You'll no doubt have seen the King's edict revoking the Edict of Nantes. No king has ever done nor ever will do anything more memorable. The dragoons have been very good missionaries up to this point, now its up to the preachers to complete the work.'[20]

For every 7,000 Huguenots who fled renewed persecution, an estimated 70,000 became new converts and enjoyed advantages offered to tempt them back to the Catholic Church.[21] Known as 'new converts', many remained Protestant at heart. There were 750,000 Protestants in France in 1681.[22] Protestants never exceeded 10 per cent of the total population of France. Between 1.5 and 2 million in 1680–5, they were concentrated in South Languedoc, Dauphiné, Montauban, Bearn, Upper and Lower Normandy.

The Revocation gave ministers 14 days to leave France but the Protestant majority were forbidden to leave. Ministers left ahead of their flock and joined already established French churches in countries of refuge. Louis XIV's Minister of War,

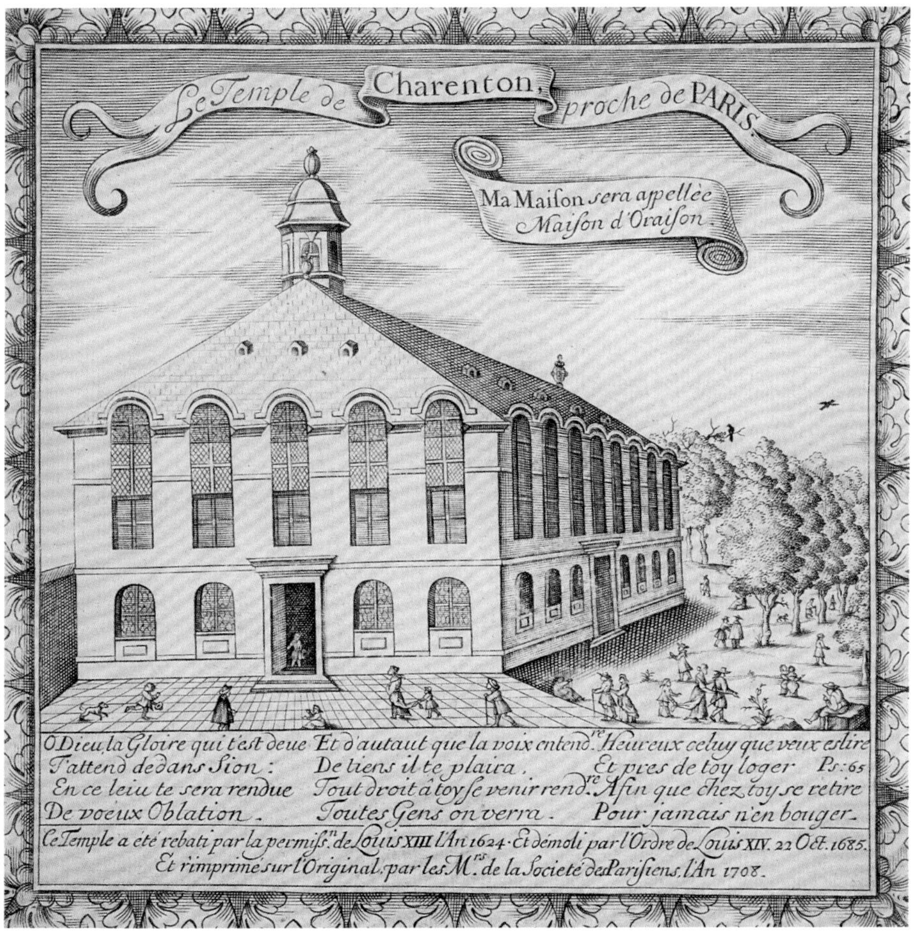

François-Michel le Tellier, marquis de Louvois (1641–1691), wrote that 'The king has always believed that it would be easier to convert his subjects if their Protestant pastors fled abroad',[23] but their presence in exile was an additional enticement for those planning to leave. Most of the Protestants who remained nominally abjured, yet continued to meet clandestinely, particularly in the Cévennes. Here the secret organization of the Protestant Church supported guerrilla warfare under the leadership of Jean Cavalier (1681–1740) in 1702–4. By 1730 the Protestant Church was well organized in South-East France and, after 1750, in Poitou. The Protestants enjoyed relative tranquillity, but years of renewed violence occurred in 1698, 1715, 1724 and 1746.[24]

In Paris it was easier for Protestants to conceal their faith. The French metropolis continued to attract skilled immigrants from Denmark, Germany and Sweden, in particular clock- and watchmakers with close links to London and Geneva, both Lutherans and Calvinists.[25] British, Danish and Swedish embassy chapels provided a relatively safe haven for Protestant baptism and marriage but burial was problematic; Huguenot funerals had to take place at night. After 1750 persecution abated, and with the occasional exception, an informal truce developed between Catholics and Protestants. When in 1762 Jean Calas (1698–1762; plate 12), a respected Protestant mercer in Toulouse, was wrongfully accused of murdering his own son, the resulting enquiry and repeal of the sentence provoked Voltaire's *Treatise on Religious Toleration*. This eventually brought about the Edict of Toleration of 1787, signed by Louis XVI; Huguenots were again able to enjoy freedom of worship and civil equality in France.

THE DISPERSION

Many thousands of Huguenots who left France in the 1680s fled across the Swiss border, which was less guarded than the frontier with Flanders or the French coast. In one day alone, 2,000 refugees entered Lausanne. Many made for Geneva, where over 3,000 refugees settled.[26] These included workers in silk and wool from Nîmes, printers from Dauphiné, goldsmiths from Paris and Dijon and watchmakers from Blois. Although in Geneva refugees were given money to continue their journey as far as Mainz on the Rhine, they could not afford to travel as far as Frankfurt. By the end of 1685 extra funds had been raised by the Protestant princes of German states, empowered through the Augsburg Confession of 1530 to resolve this problem by promoting their faith within their own principalities.

Huguenots in Germany

Less than a month after Louis XIV had signed the Revocation, the Elector of Brandenburg, Frederick William (1620–1688), responded by signing the Edict of Potsdam, which welcomed the refugees. In Frankfurt the Elector's agent was ordered to assist refugees; their goods and stock in trade were welcomed duty free. Huguenot ministers were supported by the state and they were permitted their own system of justice to resolve internal contentions. However, their republican synod was replaced by a High Consistory, a council under the direct control of the minister. At Versailles the Elector's envoy, Ezechiel Spannheim (1629–1710), spread knowledge of the advantages Huguenots might expect in Brandenburg. The Elector's chaplain, Jacques Abbadie (*c.*1654–1727), who later came to Britain with the Duke of Schomberg, visited Holland in 1684, 1686 and 1688 and encouraged refugees to join the community in Brandenburg.

The Elector used the refugees to rebuild the economy following the devastation of the Thirty Years' War. He was successful; the Edict of Potsdam attracted the poorest but most industrious. Their historian, David Ancillon (1617–1692), former Protestant minister in Metz, noted that 'refugees of each province at home are almost all established in one place together'.[27] Centred on Berlin, the French achieved a commercial supremacy and by 1700 numbered about 6,000, representing a third of the total civic population. Berlin citizens, at first jealous of competition, eventually profited from Huguenot example and were trained under their guidance. The French introduced manufactures of tapestry, stockings, silks, hats, gloves, paper and looking glasses, and they worked as tanners, locksmiths, ironmongers, miners and metalworkers. Tapestries woven by Jean Barraband (1650–1709) and his partner and successor Charles Vigne (d.1751) and his son, also Charles (the workshop closed in 1787) are preserved in Berlin's museums. The Barraband family had manufactured carpets in Aubusson: their Berlin chinoiserie tapestries dated *c.*1710 were inspired by French originals.

Huguenots contributed to the Elector's army. Marshal Schomberg was put in command of a regiment of dragoons and his son Meinhardt (1641–1719) a cavalry regiment.[28] Jacques L'Aumonier, marquis de Varennes (1641–1717), and Henri de Briquemault (1620–1692) formed new regiments from refugees who had settled in Brandenburg. Some 20,000 Huguenots settled in cities and villages near Berlin, in particular in the Uckermark region north of the city. By 1690 Berlin had nine ministers and two French churches: the Französischer Dom, built by the Huguenot community in 1705, has accommodated the Huguenot Museum since 1935.[29] A hospital and almshouses were built at the Elector's expense. Etienne Chauvain (1640–1725), Professor of Philosophy, presided over a French college open to all refugees; students were able to use the Elector's private library.[30] A refugee bookseller, Roger, supplied and published French literature and a French periodical, the *Journal des Savants*. Preachers and schoolmasters ensured that the French language was widely used, bringing Brandenburg into closer communication with the rest of Europe.

More prosperous refugees were attracted to Leipzig and Frankfurt, where bankers and merchants established annual markets and provided good business prospects. Frankfurt fair was celebrated for luxury goods in metal, ceramics, glass and jewellery as well as books, wines, spices and draperies. Craftsmen settled in Hanau and Pforzheim, within easy reach of these fairs. Hanau was enlarged in 1597 with a new town to accommodate Protestant refugees from France and the Netherlands; 200 years later descendants

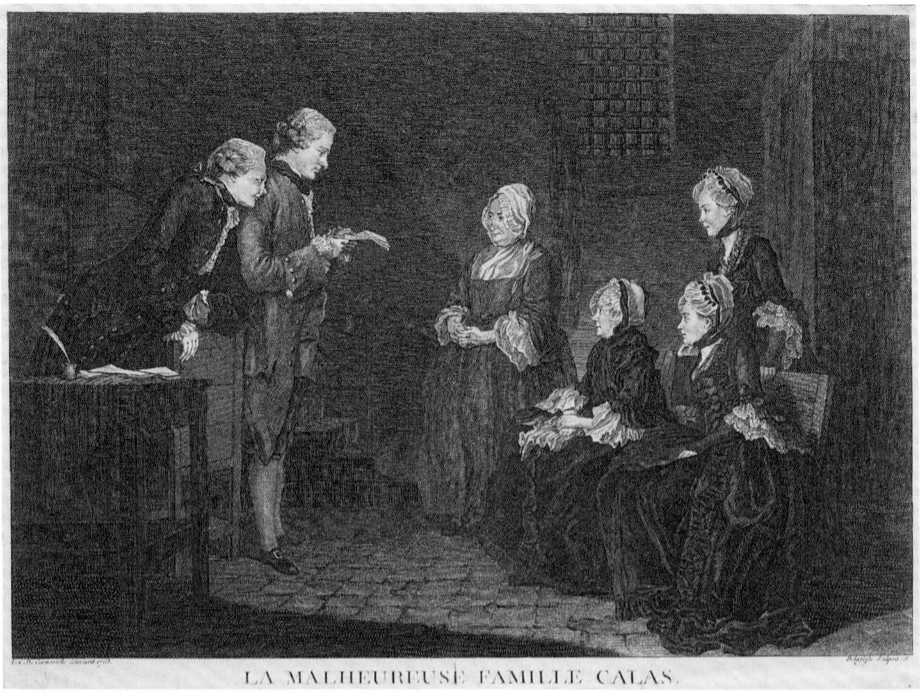

12 *La Malheureuse Famille Calas*

Jean Baptiste Delafosse after Louis Carmontelle, Paris, 1765
Engraving and etching, trimmed to 31.1 × 43.3 cm
British Museum, London (1889,0318.22)

Jean Calas, a linen merchant, was condemned to death following the accusation that he had murdered his son, Jean Antoine, whose Protestant faith prevented him from pursuing his chosen legal career. Voltaire espoused the family's cause and copies of this print were sold in London by Huguenot Paul Vaillant to raise funds. Financial contributions were handled by the Mallets, Protestant bankers. Rose Calas, Jean's wife, was born in Spitalfields in 1710.

of Huguenot jewellers still dominated the production of gold boxes there. Yet in Dresden, Huguenots were forced to worship secretly in a private house that they shared with the Lutherans. There Protestant craftsmen contributed to the market for luxury goods as jewellers and goldsmiths. In the 1720s an exotic bed with hangings woven in feathers (plate 91) was acquired by Augustus the Strong (1670–1733), Elector of Saxony, for his Dresden Japanese palace through Huguenot merchants in Putney, on the outskirts of London.[31] At Erlangen, Christian Ernest, Marquess of Brandenburg-Bayreuth (1655–1712), built a new town for the refugees, despite resentment from citizens in the old town. The Erlangen French congregation, founded in 1686, built its own church in 1693; services continued there in French until 1818, although the town became part of Bavaria in 1810. The original settlers were weavers, dyers and tanners from Vivarais, Dauphiné and Languedoc.[32]

The town of New Isenburg was built by Count Johann Phillip (1655–1718) for the refugees in 1699. He provided for a mayor and four aldermen, a minister, a schoolmaster and an organist. Each settler was given land, fuel and water, and wood to build a homestead and a barn. Their first service was held in 1700 in the open air. Their church building, founded in 1702 and still incomplete in 1706, was finished with financial assistance from Holland. At Hesse-Cassel, Charles I (1654–1730) allowed French immigrants to build churches and appoint ministers and teachers. Here the Huguenot architect Jean Paul du Ry (1640–1714) was summoned from Holland to build two new villages, Karlsdorf and Mariendorf, and a new suburb of the capital, Französische Oberneustadt, where a church was founded in 1698 and completed in 1710. Here the refugees introduced the manufacture of carpets and cloth, hats, gloves, jewellery and ornamental vases. They also settled in Frankenthal and Krefeld. Yet Huguenot settlements in Germany remained distinct from the native population for longer than in the other Northern European countries. They remained a 'self-confident minority, convinced of the superiority of their language and culture'.[33]

Huguenots in the Netherlands

Whereas in Germany the refugees created new towns and founded new churches, the Huguenots were attracted to the Netherlands by well-established Walloon communities.[34] Their churches were founded in Middelburg, Zeeland, in 1574, in Amsterdam in 1578 and in Leiden in 1584.[35] The Dutch were particularly sympathetic to the Huguenot plight, because many Dutchmen living in France had been treated as Huguenots, and funds were raised for their relief by Dutch Anabaptists, Lutherans, Roman Catholics and Jews. When in March 1681 the French Minister of War, the marquis de Louvois, issued instructions to the intendant of Poitou, René de Marillac (1638–1719), to billet troops on the Protestant population, the Dutch province of Friesland responded within eight weeks,[36] guaranteeing refugees the full rights of native citizens. New churches were founded, ministers supported by state pensions and collections made to support poorer refugees. The newcomers chose to settle there because the main occupation in Friesland, as in Poitou, was cattle breeding.

The province of Gelderland attracted silk and velvet weavers. The Utrecht Walloon church was founded in 1580, but through fresh immigration, Utrecht gained such a reputation for textiles that original manufacturers of velvet at Amiens were forced to use the name 'Utrecht' to sell them. Haarlem was also renowned for textile manufacture, its church founded in 1579 with refugees from Valenciennes and St Quentin. Their textiles were 15–20 per cent cheaper than the original manufactures at Lyons, Tours and Paris. The Haarlem new town was built to accommodate the settlers. The poorer refugees were attracted to Rotterdam, where the Walloon church was established in 1605. In 1687 Isaac Dumont de Bostaquet (1632–1709) wrote: 'This beautiful and great city had become almost French because so many inhabitants of Rouen and Dieppe had sought refuge there.'[37] It was here in 1681 that the Ecole Illustre was founded under the authority of Pierre Jurieu (1637–1713), Protestant minister, and Pierre Bayle (1647–1706), Professor of Theology. The two men fled from the Protestant Academy, Sedan, which was suppressed in July 1681. Bayle's *Dictionnaire historique et critique* (1695–7) and the periodical *Nouvelles de la République des Lettres*, which he edited, demonstrate his pioneering separation of Faith from Reason: Bayle is regarded as the 'Father of the Enlightenment'.[38]

Many other French Protestant ministers fled to the Netherlands. By December 1685 there were 180 Huguenot ministers in Holland, and 202 attended a synod held in Rotterdam in April 1686. More than fifty were granted a salary by the Provincial Estates and allocated to places of need. Others included the celebrated Jean Claude (1619–1687), champion of the Huguenot cause, who in 1686 published a vivid account of the injustice of Huguenot suffering in France, *The Complaints of the Protestants cruelly persecuted in the Kingdom of France*. He was Chaplain to William, Prince of Orange. The reception of the refugees in Holland was extremely sensitive. The public press was forbidden to mention their names or their means of escape, in case the information was used by French spies to prevent further Protestants from leaving France; there is little evidence as to how the refugees crossed the Flemish border.

The charity of Amsterdam was proverbial. A welcome was issued to French Protestants in September 1681. The refugees were loaned interest-free sums of money to buy tools and materials for their work. They introduced new textile industries, paper manufacturing and a flourishing book trade. By 1691 the city had acquired over two thousand refugees.[39] Yet the influx was too great for capacity. In 1698 the Estates General begged Charles XII of Sweden 'To take charge of any new immigrants that might come, and to give them lands in his German provinces, for our land shut in by such narrow boundaries is so crowded by French exiles for the faith that it can support no more'.[40] Recent research has confirmed that the numbers of Huguenot refugees who settled in the Netherlands at the time of the Revocation were approximately 35,000 – 50 per cent less than hitherto believed.[41]

Amsterdam was the centre for publishing and attracted authors, printers and engravers. In 1710 the Paris engraver Bernard Picart (1673–1733), former Catholic convert to Calvinism who had moved to Amsterdam, attended a meeting in The Hague of the Knights of Jubilation, an early masonic association. The Knights of Jubilation emerged in Scotland and developed in England from the 1690s. Members included German publishers from Leipzig and fellow French exiles, including Picart's co-publisher, Jean Frederic Bernard (1680–1744).[42] By December 1735 these meetings were banned, being associated with unwelcome British influence: the organization's leaders were linked with British Ambassador Philip Stanhope, 4th Earl of Chesterfield (1694–1773), whose negotiations resulted in the marriage, in 1734, of William IV, Prince of Orange, to Princess Anne, daughter of George II. Bernard and Picart included Freemasonry in their *Religious Ceremonies of the World*, which illustrated masonic symbols.[43] Freemasons welcomed Jews and Huguenots alike, creating an important international network.[44] In London, leading Huguenot designers and craftsmen were members of Solomon's Temple and White Bear masonic lodges, both in the West End. Dr J.T. Desaguliers (1638–1744), the first Grand Master, dedicated *The Constitutions of the Freemasons* (1723) to John, 2nd Duke of Montagu (1690–1749), protector and patron of Huguenots.[45]

Huguenots in South Africa

Overcrowding in the Netherlands encouraged Huguenot families to join the Dutch East India Company settlement founded at the Cape of Good Hope in 1652. In October 1685 the Company Directors passed a resolution: 'to encourage agriculture ... among the said colonists shall be included French refugees of the Reformed Religion, especially those who are cultivators of the vine [and] understand the making of vinegar and the distillation of brandy'. In 1687 this invitation was renewed. Refugees were granted free passage to the Cape; they could take money with them, although only sufficient baggage for the journey. Once there, they would be expected to earn a living. Farmers would be given as much land as they could cultivate, seed for corn, and oxen. The settlers would have to remain for a minimum of five years, after which they could return if they paid their way. Their savings, deposited with the Company, would be repaid on their return.

Between 1687 and 1700, 12 different ships carried Huguenot immigrants to the Cape; by 1726 just under three hundred were recorded as living there. In 1688 the Commander of the Colony, Simon van der Stel (1639–1712), hoped that the French 'would teach the older settlers ... about the cultivation of vine stock and olive trees'. Before their arrival, the settlement numbered under a thousand and consisted of burghers (citizens of the republic), their families and their slaves. The Huguenot refugees were established close to Dutch settlers, mainly in the Drakenstein Valley, along the Berg river, in what became known as Fransche Hoek and Paarl.[46] To this day wine is produced from the original vinestock planted by the Huguenot settler Louis Fourie (1669–1750).[47]

In 1698 a visitor commented that 'the Cape is an extraordinary refuge for the poor French Protestants' and described the home of Isaac Taillefer (1648–1699), a milliner and Drankenstein farmer at Leeuwen Vallei (the Valley of the Lions):

a great yard very well filled, and a large quantity of oxen, sheep and horses, which ... feed all year round without doors. This generous man receives and regales all those that are so happy as to come and see him. He has the best wine in the country.[48]

The Dutch East India Company appointed a French minister, Revd Pierre Simond (b. *c.*1651), who arrived at the Cape in August 1688. He preached in the Dutch church or in the house of a burgher until the French church in Paarl was consecrated in 1720. The Company also appointed a schoolmaster, Paul Roux (1665–1723), in 1693, and he held this position for about thirty years. Roux spoke both French and Dutch and his French pupils were taught to read and understand Dutch. When Pierre Simond returned to Holland in 1701, his successor was forbidden to preach in French, for 'by the use of Dutch in the church and school there, the French tongue will fall into disuse'.

The Company's careful distribution of French refugees and educational provisions were rewarded. In 1724 the Bible was publicly read in French for the last time. When in 1752 the astronomer Nicolas-Louis de la Caille (1713–1762) visited the Cape, he noted: 'I did not meet any person under forty years of age who spoke French unless he had just arrived from France.' In South Africa, the Huguenots were absorbed into the local population more rapidly than in any other country of refuge.

Huguenots in America

From Britain some refugees went on to the American Colonies, where they settled, often with the assistance of funds from Huguenot churches in the British Isles. Earlier attempts to create Huguenot settlements in America in the sixteenth century, most memorably in Florida in 1564–5, as recorded by Huguenot artist Jacques le Moyne de Morgues (*c.*1533–1588), failed.[49] Perhaps as a result, the number of refugees who made the Colonies their permanent home after 1680 was small – about 1,500 by comparison with the 50,000 to 70,000 who settled in Britain.[50]

The Colonies worked hard to attract Huguenots: proprietors circulated pamphlets among refugee settlements on the European continent. The transatlantic journey was difficult, many died on the journey and adapting to the new life was hard. Huguenots were attracted to South Carolina by agricultural opportunities. In 1697 an Act of Naturalization assured the Huguenots all the liberties enjoyed by English residents. They were entitled to own and inherit property and to vote. Although only a minority of the refugees were planters, by 1750 many craftsmen or their descendants had invested in land and the Huguenots were fully assimilated members of a society dependent on slaves for its labour. Huguenot descendants who represented Britain in North America included Francis Fauquier (1703–1768), who served as Acting Governor of Virginia until his death and became known as the 'father of the colonies'.[51] The French church, founded in Charleston in the late seventeenth century, was supported through the eighteenth century by wealthy merchants of Huguenot descent. A Huguenot society, founded there in the 1730s, continues as the Huguenot Society of South Carolina.[52] Destroyed during a major fire in 1796, the Charleston French church was rebuilt as a memorial; its members still gather each October to commemorate the 1685 Revocation of the Edict of Nantes.[53]

The refugees were also attracted to the polyglot society of New York, an old Dutch colony that the English had conquered twice, in 1664 and 1673. In the French church there, founded in 1688, a gallery was constructed in 1692 to accommodate new arrivals. Many refugees lived in rural settlements at New Paltz, New Rochelle and on Staten Island; Historic Huguenot Street, New Paltz, is the oldest continuously inhabited community in North America.[54] As in Carolina, most of the eighteenth-century households had slaves, although the pious Elie Neau (1662–1722), captured by French pirates and imprisoned for two years in Marseilles, returned to New York to establish a school for the city's slaves.

New York City attracted highly skilled craftsmen; the goldsmiths Bartholomew Le Roux (1663–1713) and Simeon Soumaine (1685–*c.*1750) became vestrymen of the conformist Anglican Trinity Church. Merchant families maintained connections with Europe. The Jay family traded with their British relatives, the Peloquins of Bristol, after 1725.[55] In 1776 Oliver De Lancey (1718–1785), son of one of the wealthiest merchants in New York, fled to England as a loyalist.

The French church in New York was used for continuous worship until 1776, when it closed for 20 years. It reopened in 1796, but six years later accepted the authority of the Protestant Episcopal Church and became the French church of Saint Esprit, still the centre of a flourishing ecumenical community.[56]

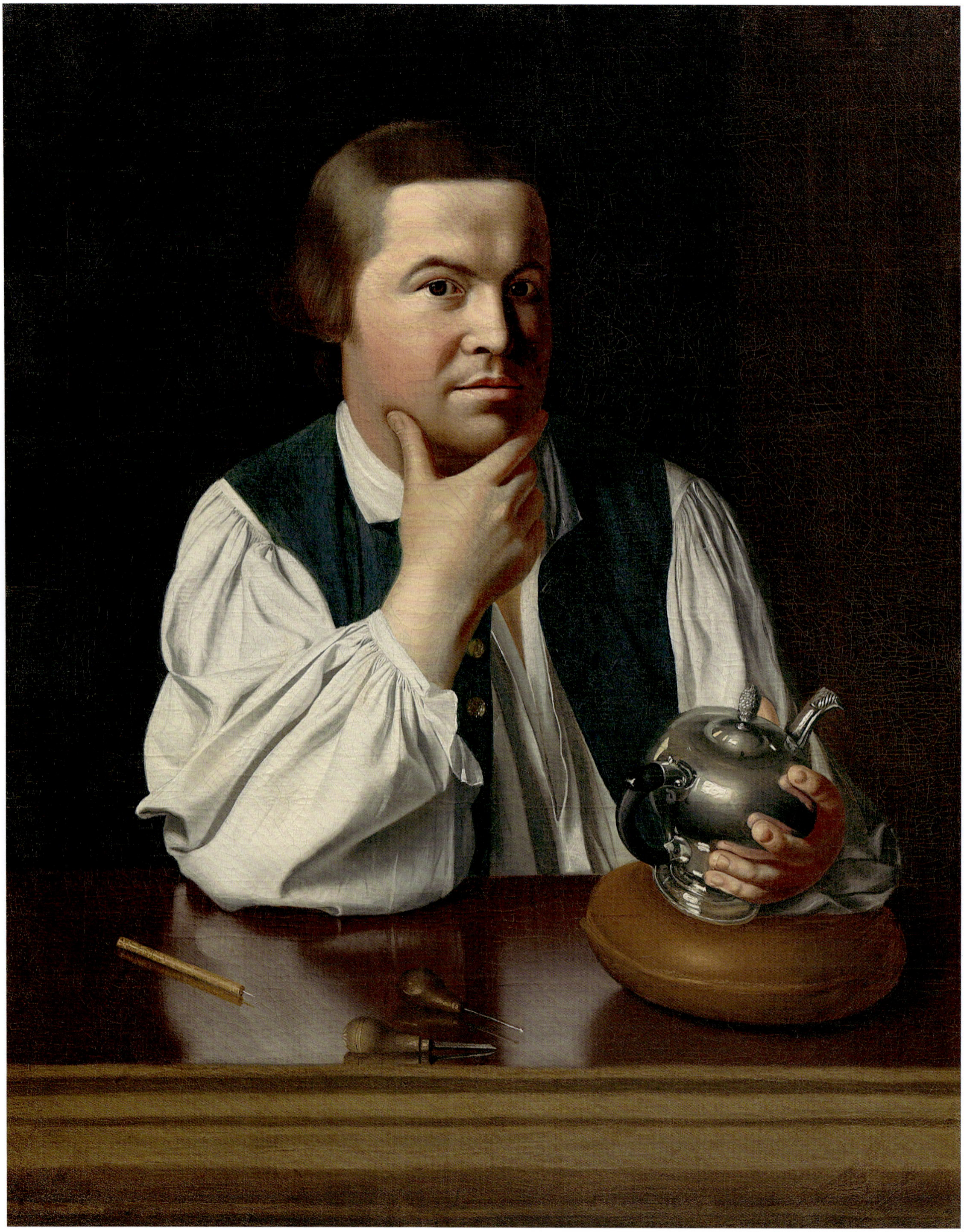

13 *Paul Revere (1735–1818)*
John Singleton Copley, Boston, 1768–70
Oil on canvas, 89 × 72 cm
Museum of Fine Arts, Boston (30.871)

Boston's most famous Huguenot son arrived with his goldsmith father, Apollos Rivoire (1702–1754), in 1715. Revere's role in warning the patriots in Lexington that British troops were coming to seize their munitions was later immortalized in Longfellow's *Paul Revere's Ride*.

By 1696 there were about forty refugee families in Boston, regarded as the capital of New World Protestantism. The city attracted merchant families: André Faneuil (d.1738) and his brother Benjamin (d.1785) built one of Boston's largest businesses between 1695 and 1715, successfully expanding trade ventures developed from La Rochelle earlier in the 1670s. André Faneuil became City Constable and a supporter of the Anglican King's Chapel, founded in 1686. The French church in Boston was constructed in 1716 and enlarged in 1741 through a campaign organized by André Faneuil's nephew Peter (1700–1742/3). In 1742 Peter Faneuil gave a market and meeting hall to the city.[57] Faneuil Hall was designed by John Smibert, London-trained artist and architect who came to Boston via Newport, Rhode Island.[58] Yet by 1748 only seven subscribers remained to pay the expenses of the French church and the congregation disbanded. Boston's most famous Huguenot son is the goldsmith entrepreneur Paul Revere (1735–1818; plate 13).[59]

The Huguenots arrived in America at a time of swift economic growth, which, combined with their creative skills and hard work, resulted in considerable commercial success. As in South Africa, however, the Huguenot migration to America was too small to sustain group cohesion.[60]

Huguenots in Britain

This book places the Huguenot contribution to British art and culture in an international context. Recent research has demonstrated that in the late seventeenth century Britain welcomed more Huguenot settlers than any other nation. Here Huguenots made full use of the opportunities offered by their close contacts abroad. This network was nurtured by Huguenot ministers who often moved across national borders to serve different communities. One such was Jacques Abbadie (*c.*1654–1727), who settled first in Brandenburg and then Holland, and was appointed Dean of Killaloe in Ireland in 1699.[61]

The Fontaines, who initially settled in the West Country, illustrate the extent to which one family could spread its influence – in this case to Ireland and as far afield as the American Colonies.[62] The conditions in which generations of Huguenots lived and worshipped in France explain their reasons for taking refuge. Beyond France they were supported by their churches and charities, and in Britain by Friendly and Charitable Societies, schools and the French Hospital that still serves its founding purpose.[63] Huguenots transferred their loyalty to the British monarchy and became British citizens through naturalization, they served in the British Army and raised volunteer troops when required.

Huguenot refugees practised in London as skilled doctors and apothecaries. They became members of the Royal Society; among their inventions were the planetarium, the self-registering thermometer and the new science of life contingencies, models for pensions and life insurance. Despite their Calvinist background, Huguenot descendants also wrote for the theatre: David Garrick (1717–1779; plate 235), for example, became one of the greatest stars of the British stage. They became librarians (plate 261), antiquaries and men of letters. As craftsmen they introduced new skills to create fashionable styles. Huguenot goldsmiths, jewellers, gunsmiths, sculptors, artists and engravers found a ready market among British collectors who were eager to adopt French taste. London in the mid-eighteenth century offered the latest in sartorial elegance and culinary sophistication. Many refugees and their descendants produced fine clothing, hats, shoes and fans. London's East End, centred on Spitalfields, was renowned for the manufacture of silks; here again,the Huguenots played a central role.[64]

The most significant Huguenot presence occupied London's financial centre, the City. Here the new Huguenot refugees from Louis XIV's France built on foundations laid by earlier Walloon Protestant refugees that had been securely established since Elizabeth's reign. Wealthy Huguenot merchants contributed to the capital of the Bank of England and helped finance William III's wars against Louis XIV, and played an important part in the stock market and insurance companies. They contributed to Huguenot charities, as directors of the French Hospital and members of the French church in Threadneedle Street. Both institutions flourish today and promote an awareness of the wide-ranging contributions Huguenots have made to their adopted nation.

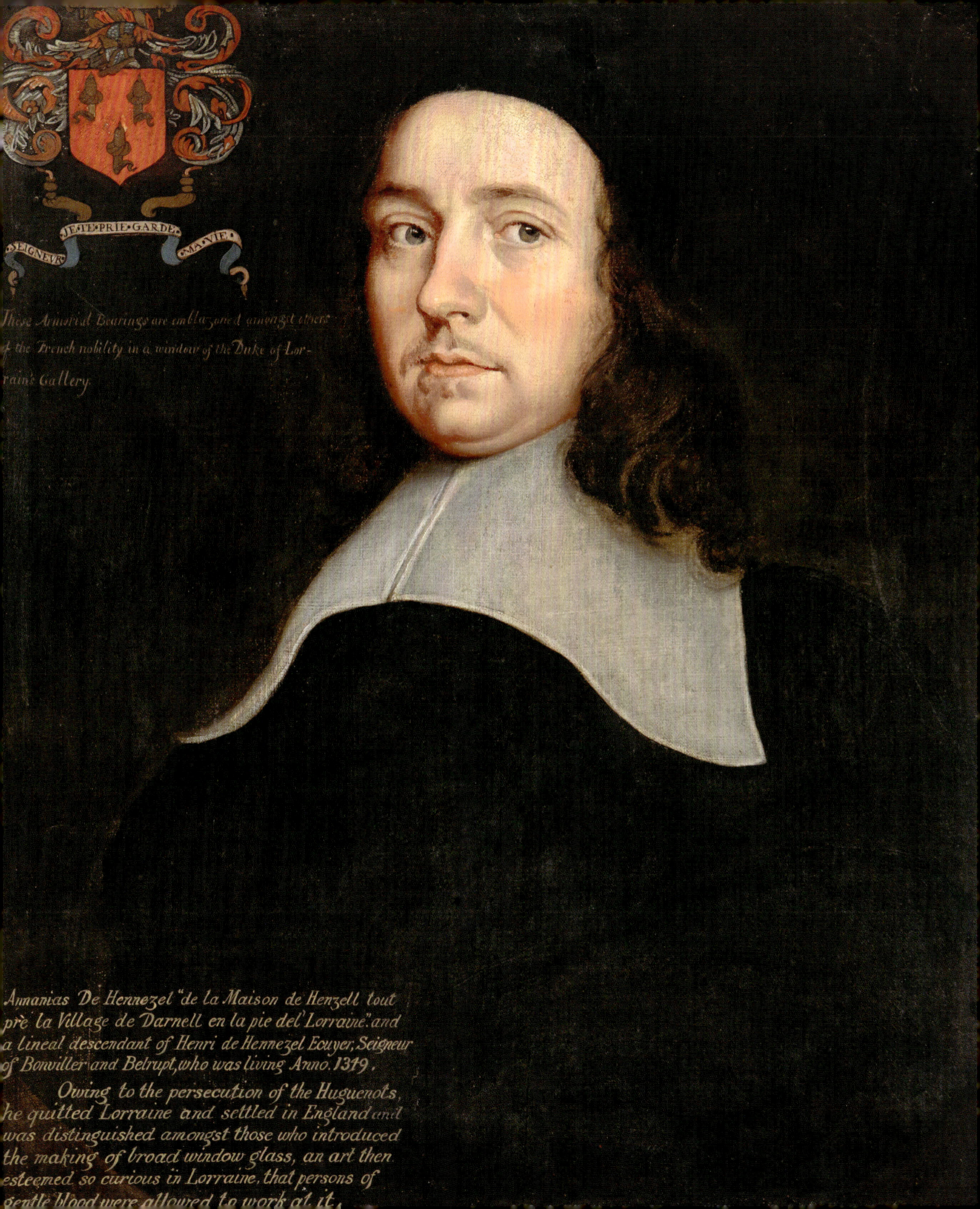
JE TE PRIE GARDE
SEIGNEUR MA VIE
These Armorial Bearings are emblazoned amongst others of the French nobility in a window of the Duke of Lorrain's Gallery.
Annanias De Hennezel "de la Maison de Henzell tout prè la Village de Darnell en la pie del'Lorraine." and a lineal descendant of Henri de Hennezel Ecuyer, Seigneur of Bonviller and Belrupt, who was living Anno. 1319.
Owing to the persecution of the Huguenots, he quitted Lorraine and settled in England and was distinguished amongst those who introduced the making of broad window glass, an art then esteemed so curious in Lorraine, that persons of gentle blood were allowed to work at it.

Chapter Two
The Reception of Huguenot Artists, Craftsmen & Designers in the British Isles

14 *Annanias de Hennezel*
Unknown artist, Lorraine?, 17th century with later inscription (detail)
Oil on canvas, 86 × 80 cm
Private collection

Ananias de Hennezel, from Darnell, Lorraine, manufactured broad-glass (hand-blown sheet glass, ideal for windows), which was considered a respectable occupation for a gentleman. He adopted the name Joshua Henzey and settled in Oldswinford, Stafford, where he became a leader in the local glass manufacturing industry.

Many Huguenot refugees settled in Britain during the sixteenth and early seventeenth centuries. Although 1685 heralded a substantial increase in their number, exiled Huguenots and their descendants were already recognized for their important contribution as artists, glassmakers (plate 14),[1] goldsmiths, jewellers and weavers.

The Huguenots suffered renewed persecution in France from 1661, when the 1598 Edict of Nantes was reinterpreted in proclamations with strong Catholic bias, following the death of Cardinal Mazarin, the Huguenot protector.[2] By 1669 Protestant preaching was confined to a single location in each town. Ten years later Louis XIV's mistress, Madame de Maintenon (1635–1719), wrote: 'the King is thinking seriously of the conversion of the heretics and will soon set to work at it earnestly.'[3] Between 1679 and 1685 some 125 edicts curtailed Huguenot liberties: among other things they were excluded from public office, and marriages between Catholics and Protestants were forbidden. By 1681, in Poitou, Catholic soldiers billeted on the Protestant population tormented their hosts. In July 1681 Charles II responded by granting the Huguenots 'Letters of denization under the great seal without any charge … and free exercise of their trade and handicrafts'. From 1685 the ambivalent attitude of the new Catholic monarch, James II, towards the Huguenots discouraged further settlers until the 1687 Declaration of Indulgence extended toleration to dissenters.

Meanwhile, in France advantages accrued for converts to Catholicism. They were excluded from billeting soldiers, relieved for three years from payment of debt, and children from the age of seven were free to declare themselves Catholic and to demand a reasonable allowance from their parents. It was fear of losing their children if they remained in France that motivated many Huguenots to emigrate.[4] The October 1685 Revocation of the Edict of Nantes was merely the destruction of the document of the 1598 Edict that had tolerated Protestant worship in France. The growing tide of persecution against the Protestants had destroyed their freedom to worship.[5]

Those Huguenots who decided to leave France for the safety of Britain were attracted by the presence of Huguenot and Walloon communities established in the second half of the sixteenth century in London and the South East, including Canterbury (plate 15),[6] Southampton[7] and Norwich. The French Protestant church was founded in London in 1550. By 1700 there were 23 Huguenot churches to the east and west of the City: in Spitalfields, where the community of weavers included many Huguenots, and in Soho, close to the royal court, which attracted craftsmen of luxury goods. In 1718 the French Hospital (plate 16) was established by Royal Charter in Bath Street, Clerkenwell, north of the City and the financial centre.[8]

In 1694 seven of the original 24 founder directors of the Bank of England were of Huguenot or Walloon origin. Sir John Houblon (1632–1712), the first Governor, was the grandson of a Walloon refugee who had settled in Britain. From 1724 banknotes were printed on paper supplied by the Portal family paper mill in Hampshire, founded in 1712. Successive generations of Bosanquets served as directors of Royal Exchange Assurance and several members of the Minet family, originally established at Dover, were Governors of London Assurance.[9]

With the accession of William of Orange in 1688, Huguenot army officers formed regiments and with increased motivation and inside knowledge of the French army, played a vital role in William's campaigns against Louis XIV. By the 1690s Sébastien Le Prestre de Vauban (1633–1707), renowned French military engineer, estimated that the French army had lost between 18,000 and 21,000 fighting men and 500 and 600 officers.[10] In Ireland William's forces were led by Marshal Schomberg, a German who joined the French army in 1650 and had also fought for the Elector of Brandenburg. In 1690, aged 75, Schomberg helped to secure William III's victory at the Battle of the Boyne against James II's combined French and Irish Catholic forces. He rallied the Huguenot troops with the words: 'Allons mes amis! Rappelez votre courage et vos ressentiments; voilà vos persécuteurs!' He was killed in the battle.[11]

William III rewarded the Huguenot soldiers by providing for them in Ireland. Henri de Massue, Marquis de Ruvigny (1648–1720; plate 242), was made Lord Justice of Ireland and granted large estates there; he founded the settlement at Portarlington, to which many Huguenot officers retired.[12] Huguenot soldiers also supported Marlborough's campaigns; one of these officers, Jean Louis Ligonier (1680–1770; plate 266), became Commander in Chief of the British Army in 1757.[13] By 1720 there were some ten thousand Huguenots in Ireland, of which around four thousand had settled in Dublin.[14]

William III's architect, Daniel Marot (1661–1752; plate 59), trained by Jean Bérain the Elder (1640–1711) at the Court of Versailles, designed additions to William's Dutch hunting lodge, Het Loo. He also designed a parterre for Hampton Court Palace outside London (plate 60), furnishings for Queen Mary's Thamesside Water Gallery and Dairy (plate 61)[15] and a royal state coach.[16] At Hampton Court Marot's work was complemented by that of the French gatesmith Jean Tijou (plate 77). High standards of craftsmanship were passed to the next generation: in the 1750s London could boast craftsmen and women of Huguenot descent who were leading exponents of the latest continental style. The work of goldsmith Paul de Lamerie (1688–1751) and sculptor Louis François Roubiliac (see frontispiece) achieved international recognition.

The silk industry centred on Spitalfields catered for a global market: flowered silks exported to the American colonies were designed and manufactured by Huguenots, including the talented James Leman; plate 17). In Ireland the linen industry was fostered by Louis Crommelin (1652–1727), a refugee from Picardy who first settled in Holland and was invited to Ireland by William III.[17] He arrived in 1698 with some twenty followers experienced in manufacturing linen and settled at Lisburn. As a result the export of linen from

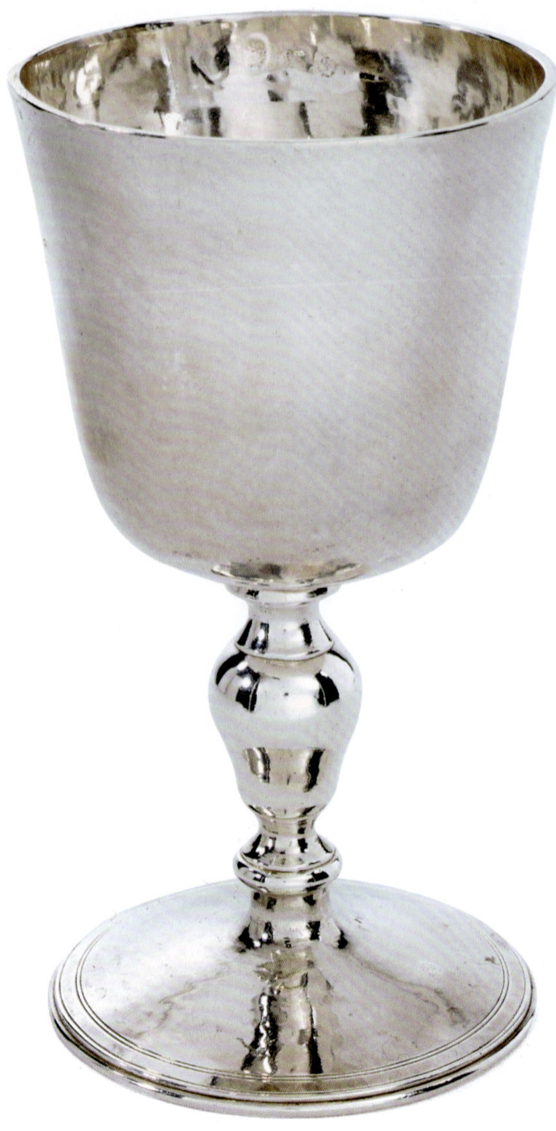

15 Communion cup from the Huguenot chapel, Canterbury Cathedral

From a set of 12, maker's mark 'IT', 1631
Silver, ht 17.15 cm
The French Hospital, Rochester

Made for the use of the Huguenot community that met in the crypt of Canterbury Cathedral from 1576. The base is inscribed 'IBM A l'eglise wallonne de Cantorbery 1632', for Jean Bulteel, pastor, and his wife, Mary. The maker's mark 'IT' has been identified as that of Joseph Taylor, who worked from 1624 until his death in 1646 at Abingdon fighting with the Parliamentarians.

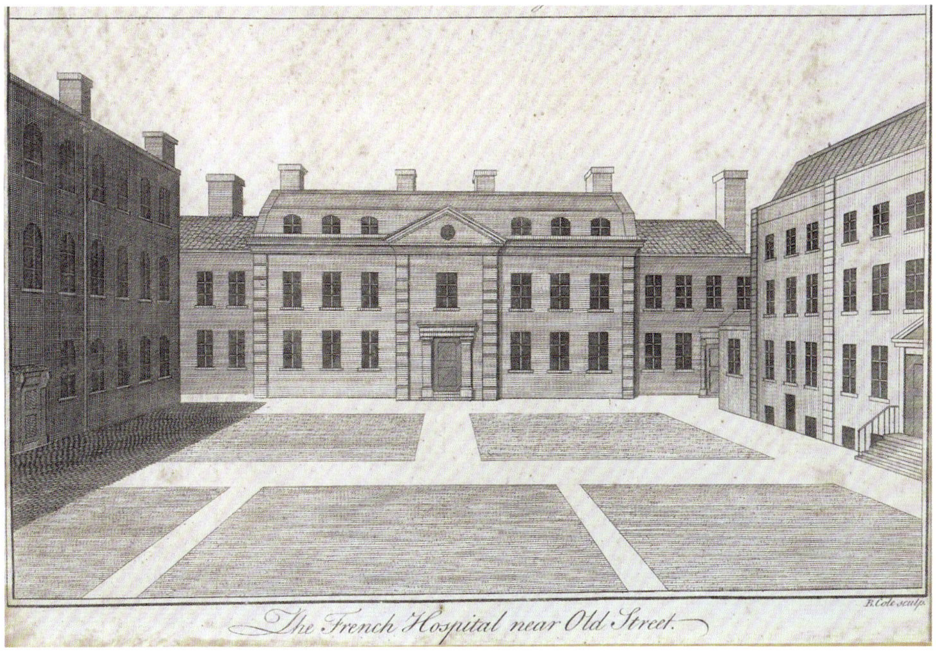

16 *The French Hospital*
From John Maitland's *History of London*, London 1756
Engraving, 16 × 25 cm
The French Hospital, Rochester

Founded in 1708, La Providence, as the French Hospital is still affectionately known by the Huguenot community, provided shelter and medical care for sick and elderly French Protestants and their descendants. The charity was established in its new buildings by Royal Charter in 1718. In 1885 its directors founded the Huguenot Society of London to mark the bicentenary of the Revocation of the Edict of Nantes; the Society led the nationwide commemoration in 1985.

Ireland increased from 300,000 yards in 1683 to 1,819,816 yards in 1713.[18]

In England the size of established communities guaranteed prosperity. Refugees who ventured on to Ireland or the American colonies were often attracted back. James Fontaine (1658–1728), son of a Huguenot pastor from Saintonge, France, fled by sea after the Revocation and landed at Appledore at the mouth of the Bristol Channel. Sheltered at Barnstaple, he opened a cloth manufactory at Taunton. Jealous competitors forced him to sail across to Cork, where he re-established his manufactory and served as minister to a French congregation. Further business rivalry compelled his move to Bearhaven on the south-west coast of Ireland, where he took up fishing. Plagued by French pirate crews, he eventually left for Dublin and founded a school on St Stephen's Green.[19]

James Fontaine's fourth son, John, born at Taunton in 1693, obtained a commission in the army and served in Spain before travelling to America in 1714. He purchased a plantation in King William County, where his brothers Peter and James settled, but John returned to England in 1719. In London he studied watchmaking and worked with another brother, Moses, an engraver. In 1728 he married the daughter of a prosperous Huguenot Spitalfields silk weaver, John Sabatier (d.1780). By 1748 Fontaine had retired to South Wales as a gentleman.[20]

By 1800 the Bosanquet, Courtauld, Garrick, Olivier, Portal and Roget families proclaimed the contribution of this talented minority.[21] In other countries of Huguenot refuge different French names mark a comparable presence. In Britain, Huguenot heritage is remembered by the French Hospital, 'La Providence', providing sheltered housing for elderly people of proven Huguenot descent in Rochester, Kent.[22] In 2015 the French Hospital Deputy Governor Peter Duval, sixth generation to support the charity, established a Huguenot Museum adjacent to La Providence in 2015.[23]

The occupations of over 570 Huguenot artists, craftsmen and women and designers are recorded in the registers of Huguenot churches in the British Isles between 1680 and 1760.[24] London's first Huguenot church was founded by Royal Charter in 1550; 130 years later this well-established community provided an anchor for refugees fleeing persecution from France and a springboard enabling them to travel onwards to Dublin or Cork, or further afield to the American colonies.[25] Huguenots had been forced out of French public life and obliged to find alternative employment. Many from professional backgrounds were attracted to goldsmithing, jewellery or watch-making for opportunities to supply elite patrons, join powerful guilds and engage in banking. They embraced the Reformed faith in its early stages, with its emphasis on individualism, as it gave them a sense of status, self-respect and self-confidence.[26] Despite periods of appalling persecution in France, this enabled them to persevere in their own country – or wherever they settled as refugees.

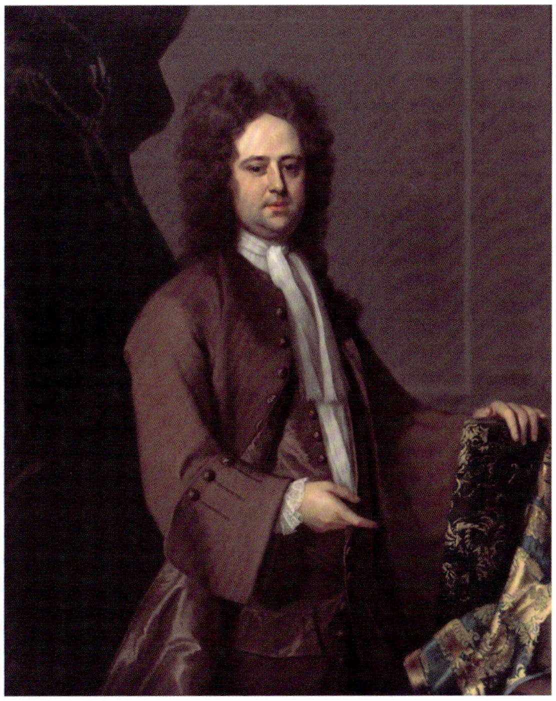

17 *James Leman*
Attributed to Michael Dahl, London, *c.*1720–5
Oil on canvas, 127 × 102 cm
Victoria and Albert Museum, London (E.675–2011)

The sitter has been recently identified as leading silk designer and weaver James Leman, based in Steward Street, Spitalfields, who attended the Threadneedle Street Huguenot Church. Leman's designs for silks (preserved in the V&A) provide a wealth of biographical and technical detail.

Many Huguenots arrived in Britain as experienced metalworkers, sculptors, architects, engineers, carvers, ceramic manufacturers and modellers; as decorative painters they taught art and illustrated books. Approximately one sixth came from Paris and the remainder from regional France. Some Paris craftsmen enjoyed royal patronage in the Louvre 'galleries' or the Gobelins' workshops.[27] In contrast, regional craftsmen belonged to specialist guilds.

Refugee artists, craftsmen and women lived and worked in close proximity; tight communities in London reflected Paris practice but gave craftsmen from the regions the opportunity to develop new skills not possible within the rigid French guild system.[28] A shared vocabulary of ornament across different forms of art and design underlines the influence of European prints, some incorporating the latest style and others relying on time-honoured sources. Thus similar decorative features occur in some Huguenot manufactures dating from the 1680s and the 1750s as Baroque classicism morphed into Classical Revival.

The international prestige of Louis XIV's artistic patronage ensured that French taste was paramount in Europe. After the Restoration, Charles II encouraged a change in English taste greater than any transient turn of fashion; it affected architecture, dress, food and manners, books and daily life. French craftsmen enjoyed more extensive patronage in exile than France, preoccupied with war, could provide.[29] Royal patronage and archives of noble households reveal opportunities met by talented Huguenots. Because French artists and sculptors acquired professional status through the 1648 foundation of the Académie royale de peinture et de sculpture in Paris,[30] the high standards maintained by Huguenots in exile helped to raise British artistic achievement. During the eighteenth century, Britain exported artistic products created by Huguenots to France and other European countries.

When in July 1681 Charles II proclaimed England as a refuge, those bringing stock-in-trade could land this duty-free. Despite this, many fled first to the Netherlands, since Amsterdam was particularly charitable. One contemporary reported that the Amsterdam city authorities loaned money without interest to refugees seeking to buy tools and materials. By contrast, it was rumoured that in England refugees were persecuted, the bank at London was broke, that aliens could not purchase land and that English people were restless and quarrelsome – contriving and plotting against their sovereign and their government.[31] These perceptions were probably the result of the Catholic James II's ambivalent attitude towards French Protestants. With William III's ascendancy to the English throne in 1688, such rumours were dispelled.[32]

The majority of those who fled to England settled initially in London. They had been encouraged in the 1660s to settle in Ireland by James Butler, Duke of Ormonde, who had accompanied Charles II during his exile in France, and later, after William III's successful military campaigns there of 1689–91, in which five Huguenot regiments served. The Huguenot communities in Ireland were dominated by soldiers; any Huguenot artistic achievements were dictated by local demand, which increased with the growth of population and prosperity during the eighteenth century.[33]

Why were Huguenots encouraged to settle in the British Isles? One official source is the motion for naturalizing French Protestants, proposed by Edward Wortley Montagu in the House of Commons on 23 February 1708.[34] Montagu cited the example of the King of Prussia, who used French refugees to regenerate his war-torn country.[35] Huguenots were industrious; work was for them 'the practical exercise of a calling appointed by God'.[36] They had a reputation for honesty and the rapidity with which they settled bills – and expected their own invoices to be paid. The insistence on prompt payment was a form of protection given the general insecurity of their position in France in the 1680s.[37] Work demanded self-discipline, averting temptation.

The distinctive feature of Calvin's creed was belief in predestination: that the future is pre-ordained by God. There was an absolute duty to consider oneself chosen, and to combat all doubts to continue in God's grace. The democratic organization of Huguenot church communities was distinctive: all churches and ministers were considered equal, and preachers were chosen by ballot. Individual responsibility to fulfil daily tasks rationalized the social environment. Ultimately Huguenots were responsible for working out their own salvation. This individual responsibility, shared by large groups of refugees, promoted qualities associated with the Huguenots: reverence, chastity, sobriety, frugality, industry and honesty.

One response to the Act for Naturalizing Foreign Protestants in 1709 was a satirical poem, 'Canary-birds naturaliz'd in Utopia. A Canto' published by the Booksellers of London and Westminster and sold for 2d with the intention of manipulating public opinion. The title referred to the canaries that the Huguenot silk weavers of Spitalfields kept in birdcages beside their looms to entertain them as they worked.[38]

The artistic talent of the Huguenot immigrants is exemplified by Jacques le Moyne de Morgues, painter of flowers and fruit from Dieppe, who accompanied an expedition to America in the 1560s and then settled in London;[39] Salomon de Caus (1576–1626) and his son or nephew Isaac (1590–1648), gardeners and engineers who settled in Germany and Britain respectively; the portrait miniaturists Isaac Oliver (1565–1617)[40] and Jean Petitot the elder (plate 246); and the sculptor Hubert Le Sueur (1595–1650; plates 116–18).[41] All trained in France and worked in England.

Jacques le Moyne de Morgues accompanied René Goulaine de Laudonnière (1529–1574) to Florida in 1564–5 to establish a Huguenot colony there. His account was published in Frankfurt in 1591 by de Bry, with 42 illustrations, as the second volume of a series on voyages to the New World. Possibly the son of Henry le Moyne, embroiderer to Mary, Queen of Scots,[42] Jacques le Moyne was probably trained in Dieppe, a port famous for producing illustrated charts and maps. After settling in London, from 1568 he painted exquisite botanical watercolours. In 1586 in London's Blackfriars he published *La Clef des Champs* (plate 18), with 96 coloured woodcuts of beasts, birds and plants.

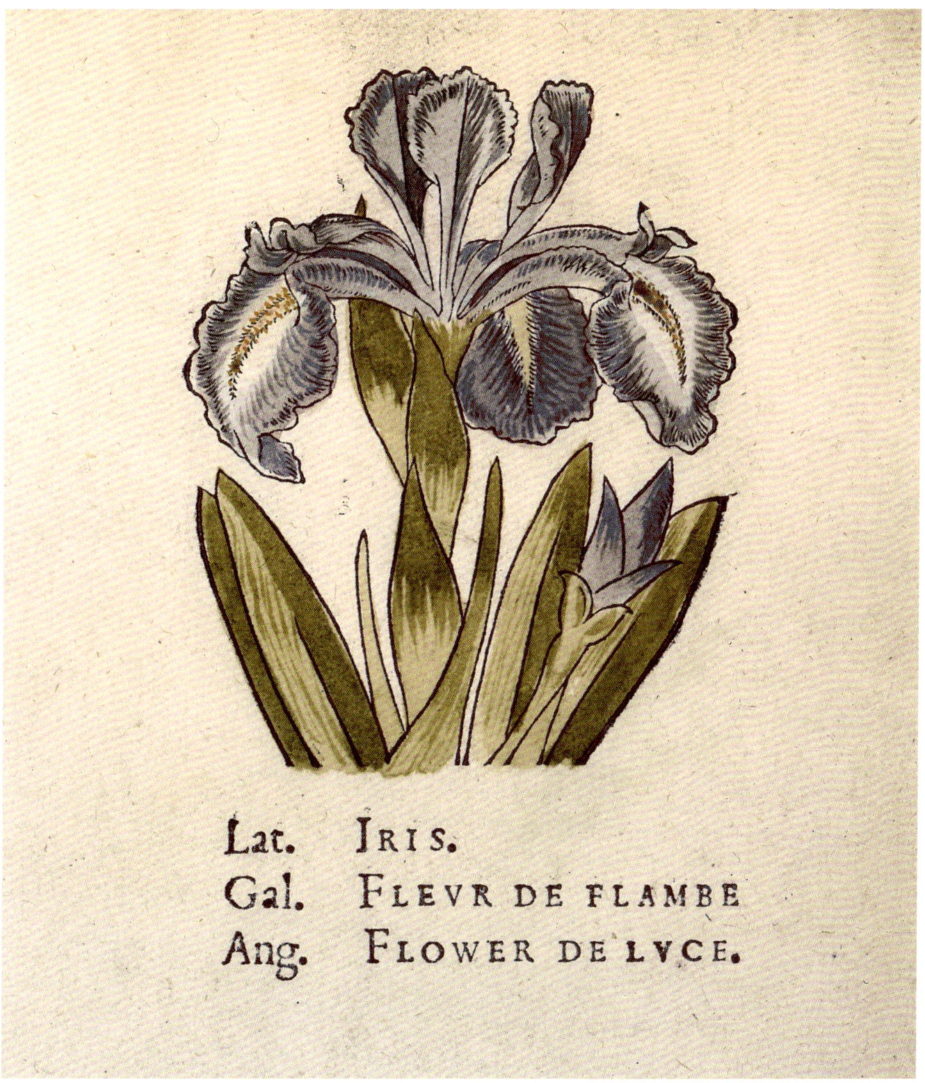

18 *The German Iris*

From *La Clef des Champs pour trouver plusieurs animaux, tant bestes qu'oyseaux, avec plusieurs fleurs et fruitz*
Jacques le Moyne de Morgues, Blackfriars, London, 1586
Coloured woodcut, 22.2 × 28.2 cm
British Library, London (C.70.aa.14)

From a series of 96 coloured woodcuts of the natural world intended as models for the painter, engraver and embroiderer. This is one of only three surviving copies of this book, which was dedicated to Lady Mary, mother of Sir Philip Sidney.

Less well known is the goldsmith Noe Jeopard (fl.1550–d. before 1596; plate 163), who joined the London French church in its foundation year, 1550.[43] In France the designer Jacques I Androuët du Cerceau (1510–1585) established an international reputation, selling his prints through booksellers and publishers across Northern Europe. He dedicated his *Livres des grotesques* (1566) to Renée of France, Duchess of Ferrara (1510–1575), who provided refuge for Calvinist artists and established a Huguenot retreat at Montargis. In 1557 the bookseller Christopher Plantin offered du Cerceau's *Grotesques* at the Frankfurt Fair. Du Cerceau also sold his prints through Protestant publishers in Paris: Benoît Prévost (fl.1550–62) and André Wechel (fl.1554–73), who was based in Frankfurt from 1573. Design books inspired contemporary and later artists and craftsmen. Huguenots attained high standards, creating beautiful objects with a practical use. A talent for portraiture was channelled into enamel miniatures used to decorate watchcases or snuffboxes because the life-size portrait could be interpreted as the product of vanity.

In late seventeenth-century London Huguenot refugees settled initially on the perimeters of the City, in Spitalfields to the east[44] and in Soho to the west; the choice depended initially on the distinction between conformist and nonconformist worship. The Spitalfields churches were all nonconformist, whereas by 1700, of the 14 in Soho seven were conformist.[45] The first West London congregation met at the Savoy Chapel, which was granted to the refugee community in 1661 by Charles II on condition that a French translation of the Anglican liturgy was used. Samuel Pepys (1633–1703) described attending a service there on Sunday 28 September 1662: 'There they have the Common Prayer-Book read in French. And, which I never saw before, the Minister doth preach with [his] hat off, I suppose in further conformity with our church.'[46]

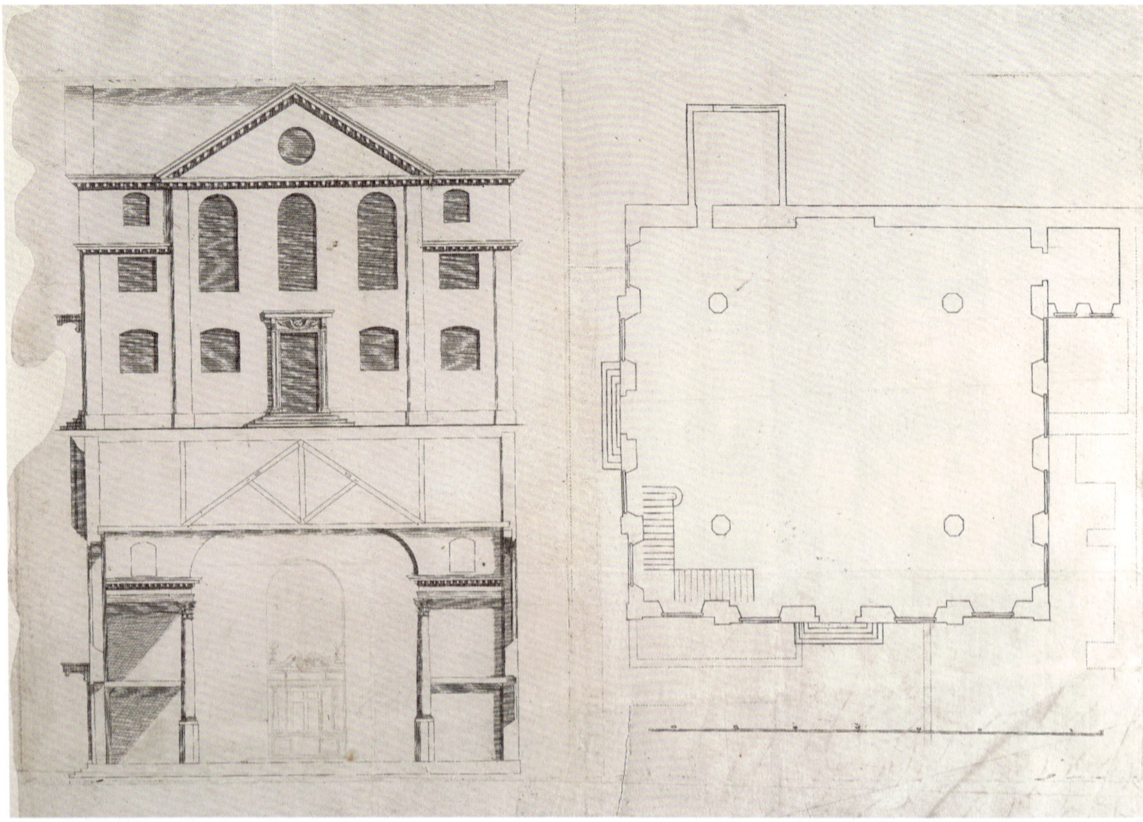

19 Plan and elevation of an extension to the Savoy French chapel, London

Copy after Sir Christopher Wren, London, 1686
Pen and ink on paper, 47.4 × 68.6 cm
The National Archives, Kew (MPA 1/41)

In 1685, to accommodate increased numbers and with the permission of James II, Christopher Wren drew plans to extend the chapel to 'a pious Desine'; the new façade echoed that of the celebrated Charenton temple outside Paris, destroyed by royal order in October 1685. The Savoy extension cost £1,500 and survived until 1771.

In 1685 Sir Christopher Wren (1632–1723) drew up plans to extend the chapel (plate 19).[47]

In 1685 another conformist Huguenot community in West London met in Soho in the Eglise des Grècs, Hog Lane, as shown in Hogarth's painting *Noon*, published as an engraving in 1738 (plate 20). Sixty years after the Revocation, Philip Stanhope, 4th Earl of Chesterfield, advised 'itinerate spirits' in search of 'The French Taste':

> *a much shorter, less expensive and more effectual method of travelling and frenchifying Themselves … if they would but travel to Old Soho and stay two or three months in le quartier des Grecs. – Lodgings & legumes are very cheap there, and the people very civil to strangers. There too, they might possibly get acquainted with some French people which they never do at Paris, and it may be learn a little French which they never do in France neither, and I appeal to anyone who has seen these venerable persons of both sexes, of the refugees, if they are not infinitely more genteel, easier, and better dressed in the French manner, than any of their modern English mimics.*[48]

Some Soho and Spitalfields Huguenot church buildings survive today. In 1732 the ministers, elders and deacons of the Threadneedle Street church petitioned George II for a licence to erect a church and school near the newly consecrated Christ Church, Spitalfields; the purchase money was provided by second-generation Huguenot City merchants, brothers David (d.1741) and Claude (d.1786) Bosanquet.[49] The British-built church compares with de Brosse's second temple at Charenton: rectangular in plan, with galleries on three sides, including the east, and open staircases in the angles. The pulpit was raised above the enclosure containing the communion table. Distinguished only by its pediment and distinctive sundial, dated 1743 and with Latin motto 'UMBRA SUMUS', the church's secular appearance blends with residential housing in Fournier Street. L'Eglise Neuve has catered for changing needs, first as a synagogue, and now as a mosque.[50] The Huguenot church in Artillery Row, Spitalfields, was later converted into the Sandys Row Synagogue for a community of Dutch Jews who settled in London in the 1860s and worked in the tobacco and diamond trades.[51]

Although the Huguenot contribution to British architecture was significant, there are no Huguenot-designed temples here – unlike in France or Germany. They often adapted existing structures, indistinguishable from secular buildings. The interiors contained no religious paintings or sculpture, although Huguenot goldsmiths supplied sacred silver for communion wine and

20 *Noon*

From *The Four Times of Day*
William Hogarth, London, 1736–7
Oil on canvas, 76.8 × 63.2 cm
The Trustees of the Grimsthorpe and Drummond Castle Trust

Huguenots emerging from Sunday morning service in L'Eglise des Grècs, Hog Lane, Soho. Disorderly Londoners on the other side of the gutter contrast with the soberly dressed Huguenots, who demonstrate mutual affection as they emerge from midday worship.

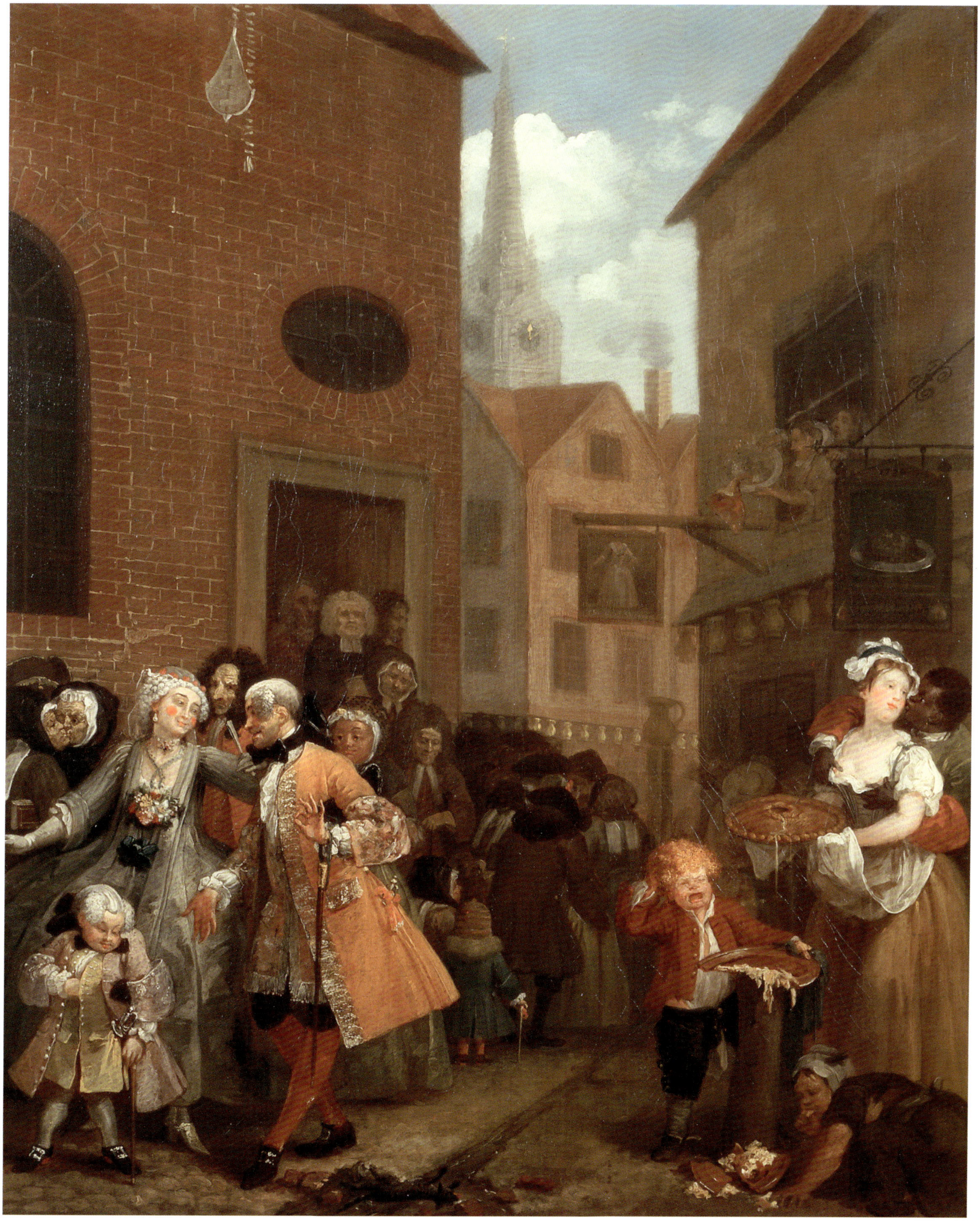

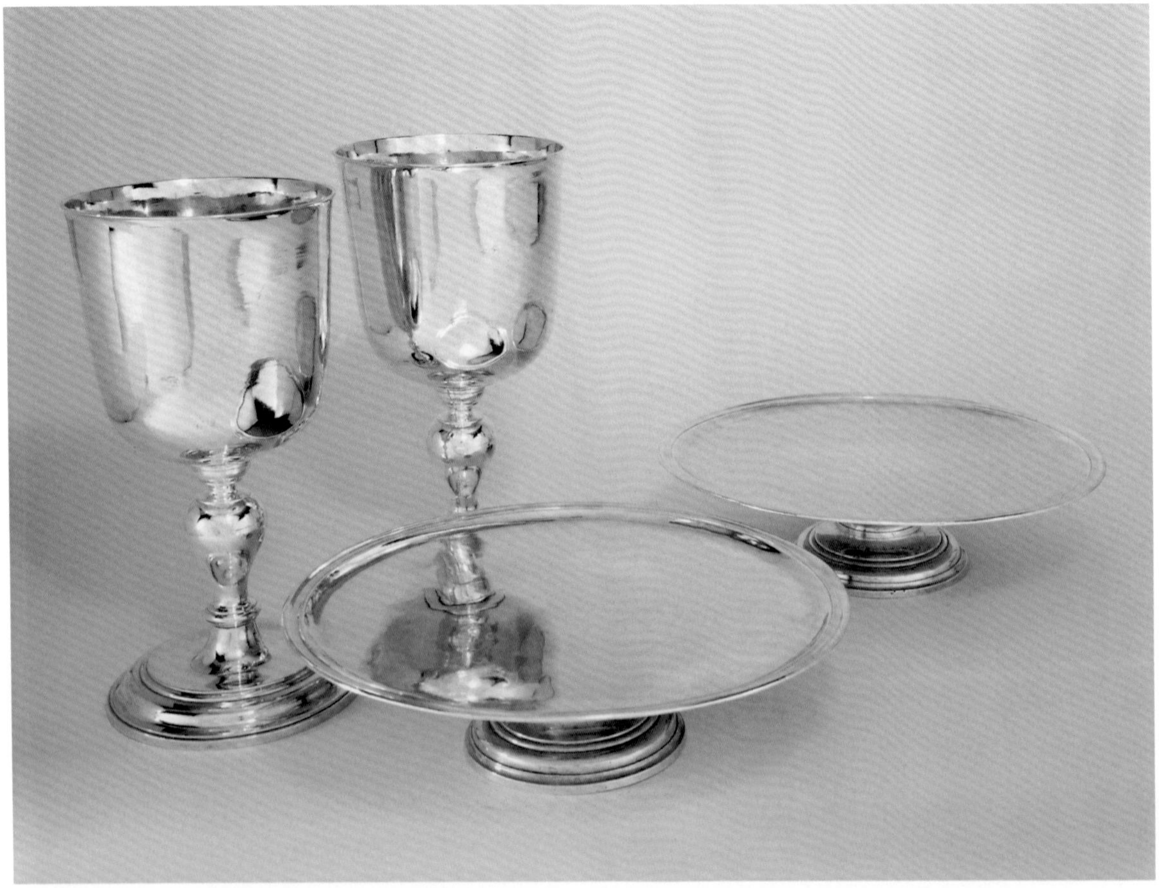

LEFT

21 Pair of communion cups and patens

Louis Cuny, London, 1717
Silver, paten diam. 25.5 cm; cup ht 24.4 cm
The French Hospital, Rochester

Huguenot goldsmiths supplied sacred silver for Communion wine and bread and for collecting alms. Cuny was working at the Three Crowns, Panton Street, when he made this Communion set for the French Church of the Savoy.

bread and for collecting alms. In 1717 Louis Cuny (fl.1697–1733), at the Three Crowns workshop in Panton Street, Soho, supplied communion plate for the Savoy Chapel (plate 21). Jacob Margas (1684–*c.*1730), originally from Rouen, made four communion cups for the Threadneedle Street church; these are still used by the French Protestant church in Soho Square.[52]

The ban on religious imagery in their places of worship did not prevent Huguenots from producing sacred art. The sculptor in ivory David Le Marchand (1674–1726) signed a crucifix (plate 22),[53] while François Asselin (d.1734), a clock-maker from Dieppe, signed a table clock made in about 1695 (plate 23).[54] In 1706 Isaac Liger (1671–1730), originally from Saumur, supplied a silver altar dish for the private chapel at Dunham Massey, Cheshire, the country home of George Booth, 2nd Earl of Warrington; this was engraved by Simon Gribelin (1661–1733), originally from Blois, with a Deposition after a painting by Annibale Carracci (1560–1609; plate 227).[55]

Huguenot artists and craftsmen arrived in large numbers during the late 1680s and 1690s, with encouragement from William III, as persecution in France continued. In 1698 Dr Martin Lister (1639–1712) described 'a certain air of fierceness towards all Protestants and a scorn and contempt for us'; this 'Humour of Bigotry'[56] endured well into the late eighteenth century. It was only with the French Revolution of 1789 that they were again able to enjoy freedom of worship in France. When the engraver Andrew Lawrence, of Huguenot descent, died in Paris in 1747, he was buried at midnight in a timberyard outside the Porte Sainte Antoine, 'the usual burial place of Hereticks' as described his friend and colleague Thomas Major (1720–1799):

> *Lawrence's body was conducted in a Hackney Coach, guarded by order of the Commissaire du Quartier by four soldiers, armed to protect them from the insolence and rage of the Populace, who otherwise might have torn them in pieces, so strong are the prejudices of the common people which are continually fomented by the Romish Clergy against the Protestants.*[57]

The situation in France was not clear cut: by 1700 over five thousand Huguenots were living in Paris, although the extent to which they concealed their true faith is not recorded.[58] Huguenots continued to leave France for Britain during the eighteenth century, among them the sculptor

RIGHT ABOVE

22 Crucifix

David Le Marchand, London, *c.*1700
Ivory, ht 39.37 cm
Victoria and Albert Museum, London (A.42–1983)

In addition to this ivory crucifix, sculptor David Le Marchand also signed a relief of the *Miracle of the Man with a Withered Hand*, a *Madonna and Child* and an *Adoration*.

RIGHT BELOW

23 Table clock

François Asselin, London, *c.*1695
Gilt-brass and ebony, ht 55.3 cm
Formerly in the Time Museum, Illinois (Sotheby's, 19 June 2002, lot 165)

Apparently a Spanish royal commission, the clock is surmounted by a figure of the Risen Christ flanked by four kneeling apostles. The case is decorated with scenes of the Last Supper, the Crucifixion, the Descent from the Cross, the Entombment and the Virgin and Child.

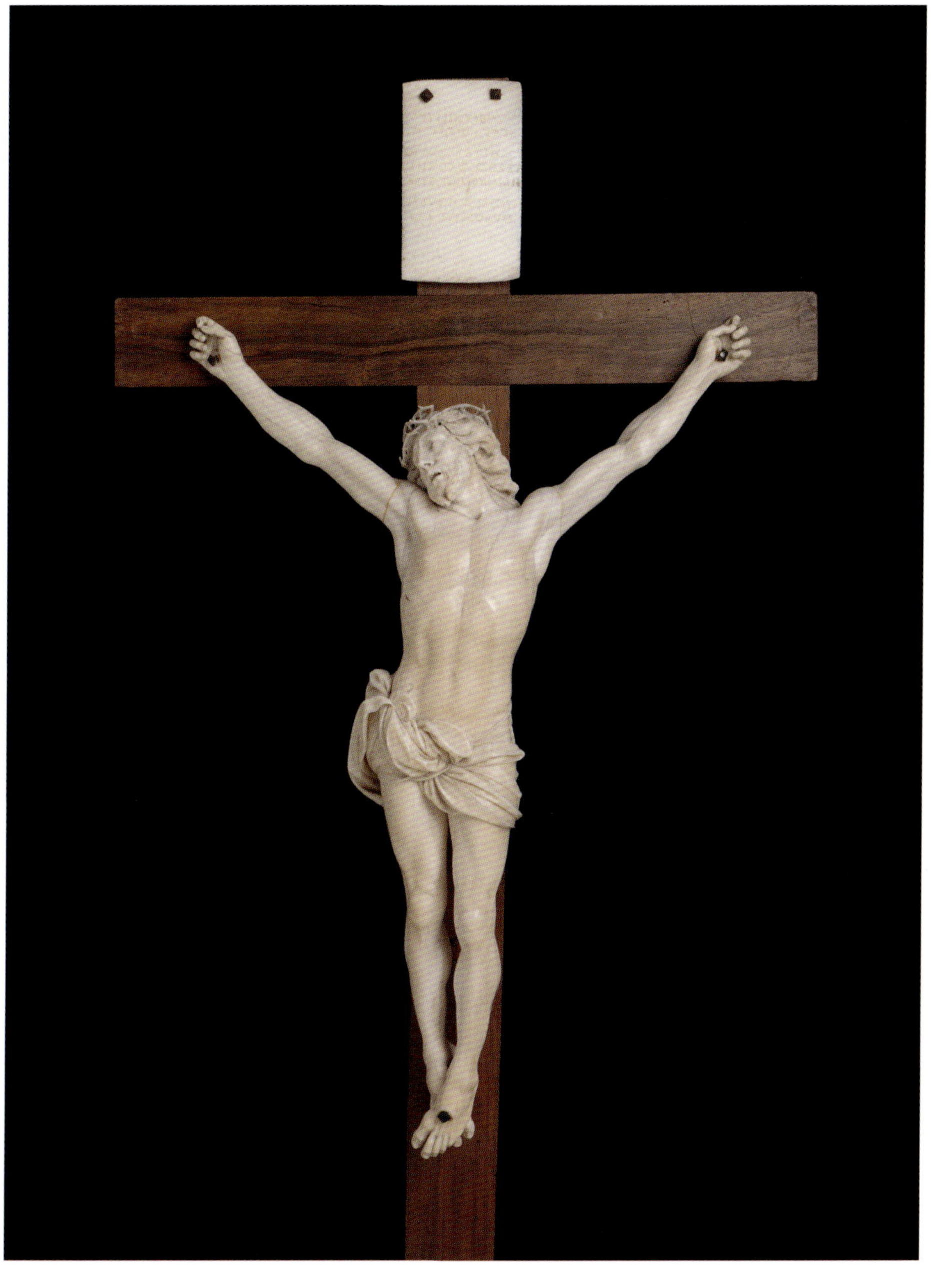

Louis François Roubiliac, who arrived from Paris in 1730.[59] Other artists, whose families settled initially in Geneva, Berlin or the Netherlands, later came to Britain in search of work and joined established Huguenot communities.

Huguenots made reliable tutors for the children of British nobility and gentry. Some former ministers forced to leave France became chaplains to noble families. Monsieur Nicholas Huet, as steward to William Cavendish, 1st Duke of Devonshire (1640–1707), encouraged the Huguenot artists and craftsmen who worked at Chatsworth;[60] his poor English prevented him from taking on an Anglican parish, an opportunity seized by some Huguenot ministers: he was too old to 'learne well enough to be understood by the people' and 'to serve a parish by a proxy I never liked for fear to be saved by proxy too'.[61] Huguenot 'conformist' belief was compatible with Anglican liturgy; the main difference between them lay in church administration. Conversely Huguenot churches attracted English participants keen to improve their French. In 1709 there was a complaint in the recently established City church of St Martin's Orgar that the 'parquet' in front of the pulpit reserved for the elders was entirely filled with young Englishmen who came to learn French.[62]

Prominent members of noble and gentry families who were godparents to children of the next Huguenot generation included the 1st Duke of Devonshire, who attended the baptism of his godson Guillaume de la Plaigne (1709–1764) on 28 May 1709 at Les Grècs.[63] Henry, Earl of Grantham, and the Countess of Arlington, were godparents to Isabelle Ducros, daughter of the minister of the French Savoy Chapel, baptized on 9 November 1710 and named after her godmother. Charles, 5th Earl of Baltimore (1699–1751), attended the baptism of Charles de la Fosse (1636–1716), similarly named after his godfather, on 18 October 1715; and Horatio Walpole (1678–1757),

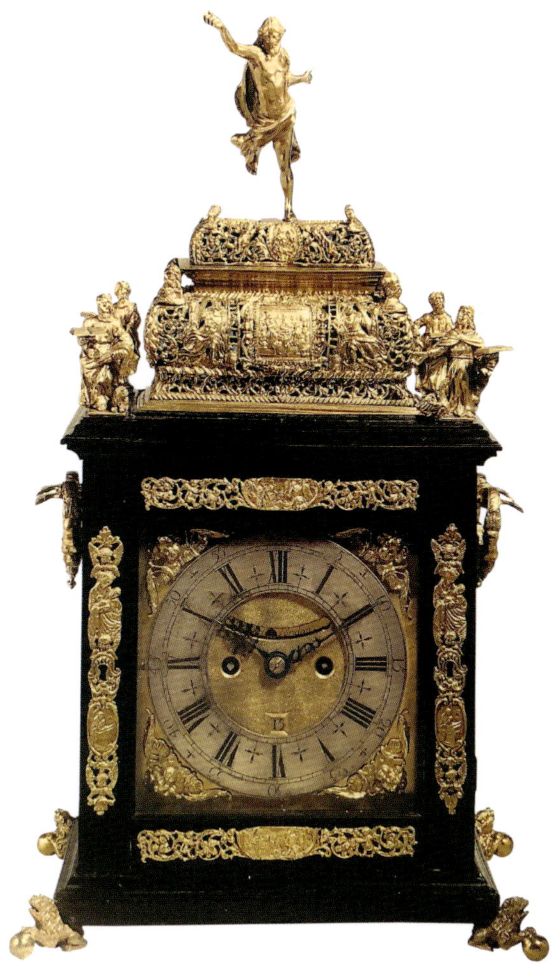

brother of Prime Minister Robert Walpole (1676–1745), was godfather to Antoinette Vatas, daughter of Dr Pierre Vatas, on 28 October 1719.[64] In spring 1740 at the Berwick Street church in Soho, John, 2nd Earl of Ashburnham (1724–1812), and Lady Mary de Grey (1719–1761) stood godparents to Marie Jemima, daughter of the artist Mark Anthony Hauduroy, who was named after her two English godmothers.[65] Hauduroy had married Charlotte Coulon in 1738, in Silsoe church near Wrest Park, the Grey family home, where he decorated the garden pavilion (plate 53).[66] In 1759 the 4th Earl of Chesterfield stood godfather to the son of Jacques Parent, minister of the Hammersmith Huguenot church from 1756.[67] William Blathwayt, the 2nd Duke of Bedford (1680–1711), the 1st Duke of Portland and the 4th Earl of Chesterfield all employed Huguenot household servants and patronized Huguenot artists, designers and craftsmen.

Attending Huguenot services was a good way to improve one's French. In December 1697 Huguenot locksmith Samuel Marc (fl.1689–1718) charged Ralph, then Earl of Montagu, 8d for 'a button to the lock at the Pew in the French church'.[68] This was probably in Les Grècs, the French church closest to Montagu House, Bloomsbury.

Not every exiled Frenchman was Huguenot, and some traded on the Huguenots' good reputation. Daniel Finch, 2nd Earl of Nottingham (1647–1730), Secretary of State to William III, reported in April 1692 that 150 French officers, supporters of James II, had landed on the west coast pretending to be Huguenot refugees; among 20,000 of William's French supporters in London, 'ready to take arms', were several thousands of French 'who passe here for Protestants and goe to the French Protestant Churches who indeed are good Catholicks and would shew themselves to be soe upon James landing'.[69]

In about 1750 Peter Parisot (1697– after 1766), a naturalized Frenchman, trading on the trust that Huguenots had established with their British patrons, set up a carpet manufactory in Westminster with two workmen from the Savonnerie Chaillot factory. Parisot later moved to Fulham, south-west of London, and expanded to include tapestry weaving using the Gobelins' technique. He secured the patronage of William, Duke of Cumberland.[70] Parisot, whose real name was Pierre Nobert, was an anti-Jesuit Capucin priest who had been allowed to visit England by Pope Benedict XIV on condition that he become a missionary. For his new manufactory he attracted a subscription of £10,000 and persuaded his employees to entice members of their families away from French manufactories.[71] The French authorities stemmed Parisot's supply of French-trained workmen by intercepting the correspondence. As a result, his manufactory failed and by 1755 his entire stock was for sale.[72] He disappeared and his tools were bought by 'un certain monsieur Passavant … Suisse de nation et fabricant de serges à Exeter'.[73] Claude Passavant (d.1766) subsequently received a grant from the London Society of the Arts in 1758, which enabled him to salvage Parisot's manufactory. Passavant re-employed the deserters from the Gobelins workshops who had no other skills and did not speak English; they could not return to Paris as they would be hanged for desertion.[74] The Huguenot Passavant turned Parisot's betrayal of trust to good effect (plate 24).

William III's arrival in England in 1688 created ideal conditions for patronage of Huguenot refugee talent: his presence inspired an eager spate of building and collecting. William's Huguenot drawing master, London-born Abraham Raguineau (1623–1681), a citizen of The Hague from 1645, was appointed Keeper of that Prince's picture collection in 1666. He was succeeded by Robert du Val (1633–1732), who purchased and commissioned paintings in London for William's Dutch homes. William's royal possessions were organized by Daniel des Marets (1634–1714) a former Walloon church minister, du Val's father-in-law, who became William's librarian, director of mathematical instruments and 'Comptroller-general of His Majesty's Household in the Netherlands' in 1692.[75]

Queen Mary was also an active patron. Her involvement in rebuilding Hampton Court Palace is recorded in Christopher Wren's *Parentalia*:

> *Upon observing the pleasant Situation of the Palace… [she] proposed a proper Improvement with Building and Gardening, and pleased herself from time to time, in examining and surveying the Drawings, Contrivances, and whole Progress of the Works, and to give thereon her own Judgement, which was exquisite; for there were few Arts, or Sciences, in which her Majesty had not only an elegant Taste, but a Knowledge much superior to any of her Sex.*[76]

After the Queen's untimely death from smallpox in 1694, the patronage of Huguenot artistic talent at court was promoted by Ralph, then Earl of

24 Carpet
Claude Passavant, Exeter, 1757
Wool, 419 × 320 cm
Bute Collection, Mount Stuart

Passavant salvaged the Parisot manufactory in Fulham and re-employed the deserters from the Gobelins manufactory who spoke no English and were unable to return to Paris for fear of being hanged for desertion.

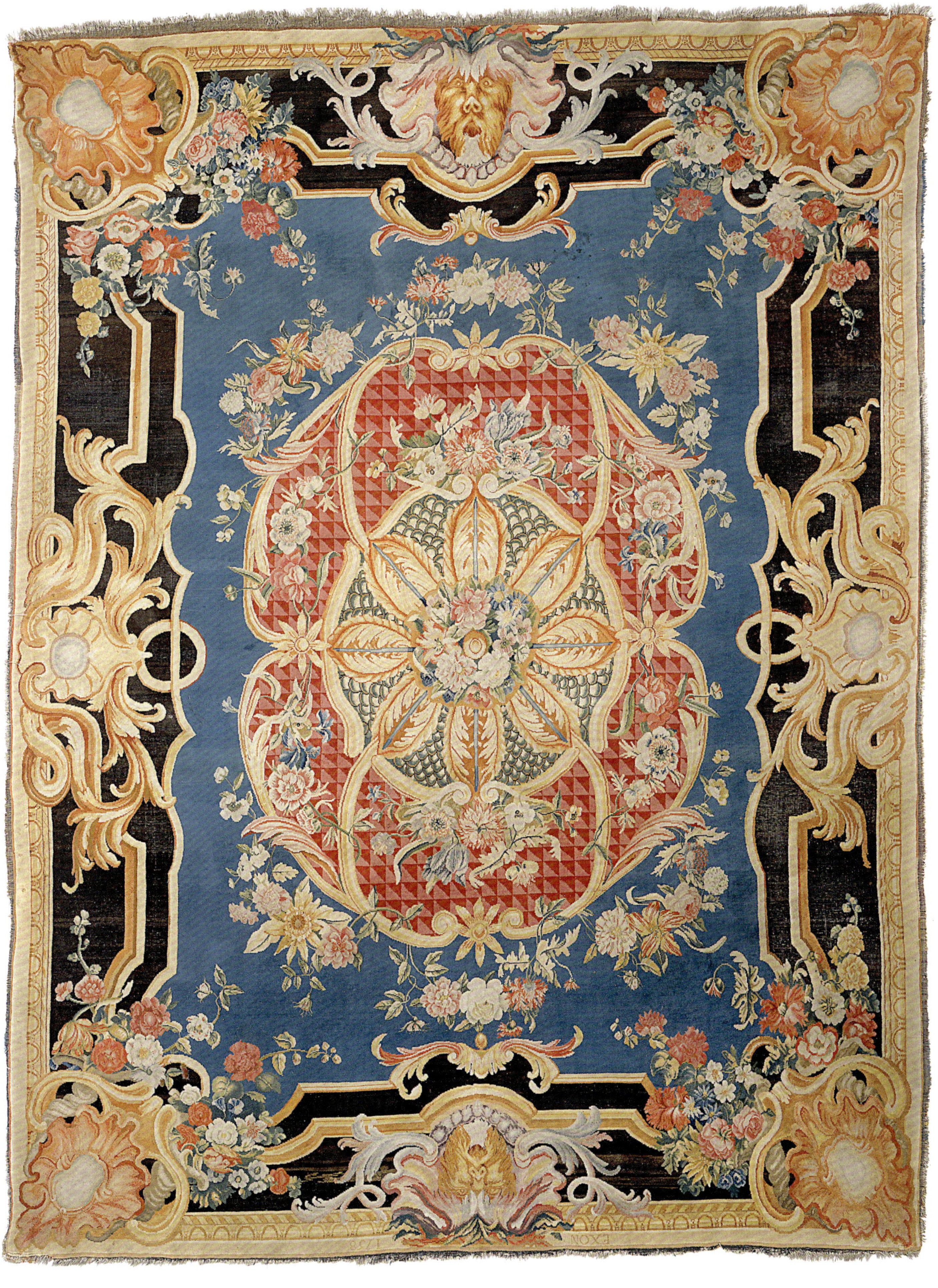

Montagu, who resumed his office as Master of the Wardrobe in 1689. William III maintained personal contact with Daniel Marot, 'Architect to the King', who supervised the decoration at Het Loo, his country palace in the Netherlands, from 1686.

It was almost thirty years before Huguenots again received vigorous royal patronage. When Frederick, Prince of Wales, came to England from Berlin in 1728, he was greeted by a delegation from the French churches.[77] On 6 February 1729 he appointed Philip Mercier (1689–1760), son of Huguenot Berlin tapestry weaver Pierre Mercier (d.1729), as his 'Principal Painter'; in 1730 Mercier became the Prince's Librarian.[78] His duties included the purchase of paintings and literature for the Prince.[79] The Prince and his household, including his Gentleman of the Bedchamber, Charles, 5th Earl of Baltimore,[80] patronized the jewellers Peter Dutens (d.1761; Xref) and Isaac Lacam (d.1757), silversmiths Paul Crespin (1694–1770), Nicholas Sprimont (1716–1771) and Paul de Lamerie, and purchased from 'toyshops', purveyors of adult accessories, owned by Paul Bertrand (1689–1755) in Bath and Mrs Chenevix (1702–1755) in London. Huguenot carvers and gilders Paul Petit (fl.1722–57), Jacob Gosset (1703–1788) and James Riorteau (fl.1718–31) supplied frames for the Prince's collection of paintings.[81]

Some noble families supported Huguenot communities from the 1680s until the 1750s. Between 1727 and 1749 John, 2nd Duke of Montagu, made an annual contribution to La Soupe, the Huguenot charity in Spitalfields.[82] George Booth, 2nd Earl of Warrington (1675–1758), ordered Huguenot silver exclusively, personally compiling the inventory of his purchases.[83] The Russells, Dukes of Bedford (whose ancestor William, Lord Russell, executed in 1683, married Rachel Wriothesley, daughter of Thomas, 4th Earl of Southampton and the Huguenot Rachel de Ruvigny in 1669), patronized Huguenot goldsmiths and tradesmen and gave financial assistance to Huguenots in need.[84] Sir Andrew Fountaine (1676–1753), Master of the Mint 1727–53 and Vice-Chamberlain to Queen Caroline, used his position at court to benefit Huguenot refugees. In 1704 Simon Gribelin inscribed the revised edition of his 1682 book of designs (plate 227) to Sir Andrew.[85]

Huguenot noblemen established in exile also patronized French suppliers and promoted French style. The furnishings for Frederick, Duke (formerly Count) of Schomberg's house in St James's were supplied in 1689 by the French upholsterer Francis Lapiere; the murals were painted by Pierre Berchet (1659–1720).[86] In 1735 the La Touche family, bankers in Dublin, commissioned a plaster ceiling representing *Venus Wounded by Love* after Jean-Antoine Watteau (1684–1721) for the family bank in Castle Street.[87] Paul de Lamerie supplied a tea service (plate 183) as a wedding gift for Suzanne, daughter of Huguenot jeweller Jacques Louis Berchère (1670–1753), who married Jean Daniel Boissier (d.1770) at the church of St Peter le Poor in April 1735. The tea and sugar caddies, cream jug, 12 teaspoons, mote spoon, two knives and pair of sugar flippers were housed in a mahogany box lined with red velvet, embellished with silver mounts engraved with the coat of arms of Boissier impaling Berchère.[88]

Yet indigenous craftsmen reacted strongly against the intrusion. In 1678 the Court of Assistants of the Goldsmiths' Company opposed the bill to enable foreign Protestant craftsmen to exercise their trades in certain places and to take up seven-year apprenticeships. In 1711 a petition was signed by 53 London goldsmiths against foreign craftsmen, 'that by admittance of necessitous strangers whose desperate fortunes obliged them to work at miserable rates, the representing members have been forced to bestow much more time and labour in working up their plate, than hath been the practice of former times'.[89] A similar complaint was taken up in 1733, by Andrew Fullbottom in the *Gentleman's Magazine*: 'Is it not a cruel case that a Tradesman shall not be employed merely because he is an Englishman'.[90] By 1745 the Anti-Gallican Society was formed to 'promote the British Manufactures to extend the Commerce of England, and discourage the introducing of French modes and impose the importation of French commodities'.[91] Many of those involved employed second-generation Huguenot craftsmen. Stephen Theodore Janssen (d.1777) employed the goldsmith Delamain (possibly Thomas; see p.172 below), of Huguenot descent, in the production of Battersea enamels (plate 158). William Hogarth (1697–1764), while deeply committed to campaigning against French taste, willingly associated with Louis François Roubiliac and Hubert François Gravelot (1699–1773) at the St Martin's Lane Academy and employed French engravers to achieve appropriate elegance for the prints of his modern moral subjects such as *Marriage-a-la-Mode*.[92]

In London established Huguenot families also patronized British craftsmen. Thus the Prince of Wales's dancing master, George Denoyer (fl.1721–64); Sir Jacob Bouverie, 1st Viscount Folkestone (1694–1761); and Charles Dartiquenave (1664–1737) were all clients of the royal goldsmith George Wickes (1698–1761).[93] Huguenot merchants in the New World sent their sons back to Europe to be educated. Peter Manigault (1731–1773) from Charleston, South Carolina, came to London to study Law at Inner Temple. He sat to Allan Ramsay (1713–1784) for his portrait, which included a recently purchased clock in the French style; the clock survives in the Manigault House in Charleston.[94]

Native antagonism towards the Huguenots was cooled by advantages gained by taking a Huguenot apprentice, or by placing one's son with a Huguenot master. Leading eighteenth-century London goldsmiths Edward Wakelin (1716–1784) and Thomas Heming (d.1795) served apprenticeships with John Hugh Le Sage (1696–1759) and Peter Archambo (1699–1767) respectively in the 1730s.[95] This practice varied from trade to trade: of 56 Huguenot apprentices recorded in the London Goldsmiths' Company archives between 1680 and 1760, only 12 were apprenticed to English masters. Over two hundred goldsmiths of Huguenot origin were registered with the Dublin Goldsmiths' Company over this period.[96] The apprentice lists of the London Upholders' Company for 1704–60 record that 15 Huguenot apprentices were placed with Huguenot masters and 16 Huguenot apprentices with English masters.[97] Many of these Huguenot names had addresses in Spitalfields, Norwich or Southampton, places with established Huguenot communities.

The French church registers rarely include occupations, so an accurate record of the numbers of Huguenot artists, designers, craftsmen and women who worked in Britain is hard to calculate. Yet by linking family names with artists and craftsmen recorded in guild records, trade cards, rate books and insurance registers, a clearer picture emerges of the presence and influence of Huguenot skills. The fashionable cabinetmaker Pierre Langlois (1718–1767; plates 102–3), working in London from 1759 until his death, was baptized at a West End Huguenot church in 1718. Yet his subsequent training in Paris is not recorded because as a Protestant he could not have been officially apprenticed through the Paris cabinetmakers' guild.[98]

Refugees fled where they could; members of the same family were forced to settle temporarily in different countries. Huguenot church registers record a movement to and from Berlin, Geneva, The Hague, Ireland and America. The Huguenot artistic contribution forms part of the international network established by the refugees, which was itself to boost their progress. A century later, when 12,000 French Catholic priests were forced into exile by the Terror, it is notable that the British government committee set up to provide support for those refugees who settled in ports along the south-east coast where Huguenots had established communities in the late sixteenth century, included descendants of the first wave. Among these were Lewis de Tessier (d.1811), Alexander Champion (d.1793) and John (1773–1847) and Samuel (1768–1843) Bosanquet.[99] One of the exiled priests, Joseph Claude Meffre (1766–1845) from Toulon, converted to the Church of England and served as the last French-speaking chaplain of the French Hospital (1826–45).[100]

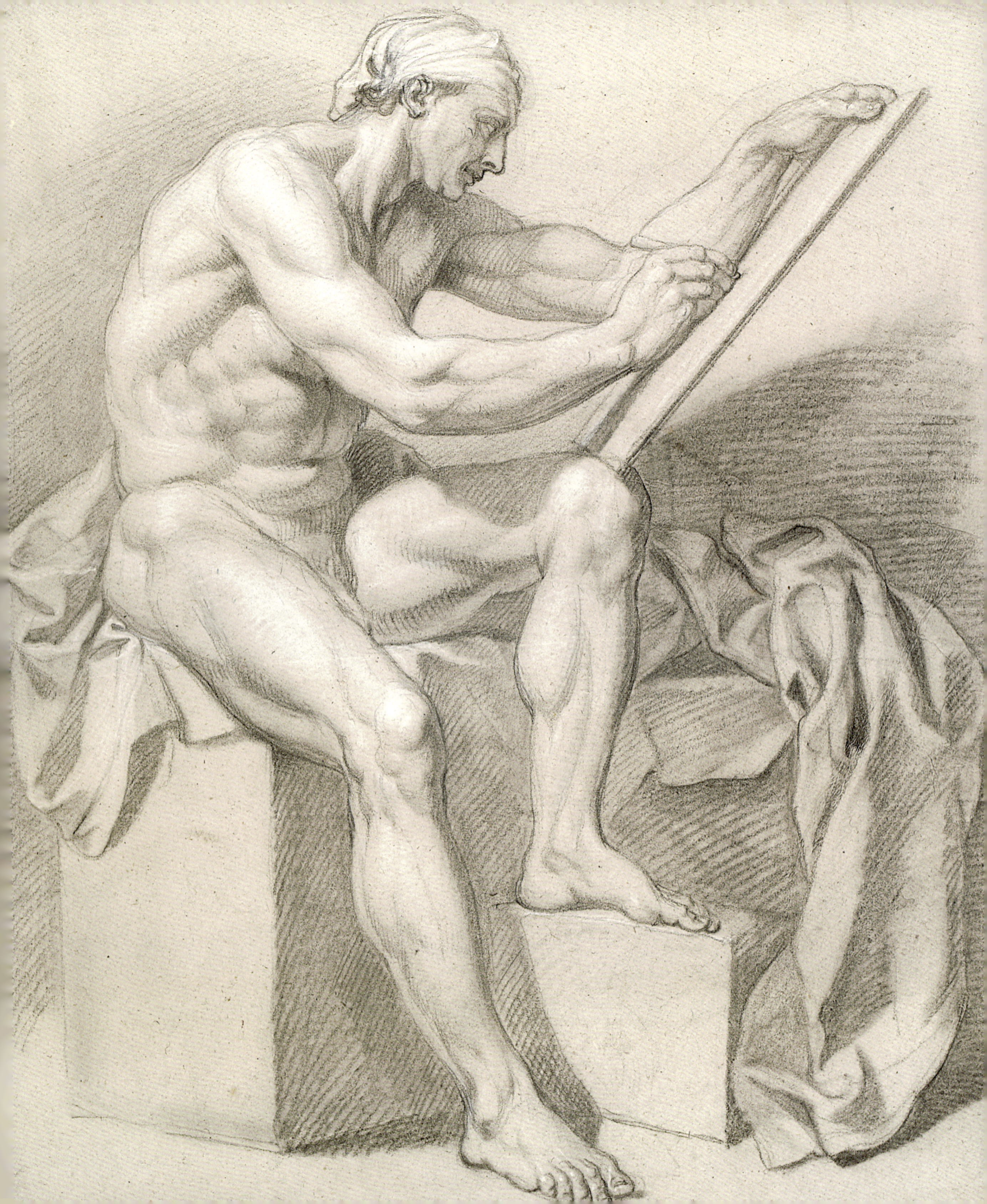

Chapter Three
The Huguenots as Educators

25 *Nude man seated*
Louis Chéron, London, 1711 (detail)
Black chalk heightened with white on grey paper, 65.1 × 56.4 cm
British Museum, London (1953,1021.11.86)

Chéron drew male models of varying ages: a youth, a bald-headed man and a bearded man. The occasional prop, a sword or helmet, made the exercise more interesting. Chéron often used black chalk heightened with white on grey paper for these academic exercises.

At a time of expanding demand for French language teaching among the British nobility, the strong anti-Catholic bias, except during the reigns of Mary I (1553–8) and James II (1685–8), meant that parents ambitious for their children entrusted French Protestants with their education. Art education was part of a wider Huguenot role as educators. Meanwhile, within their own family networks Huguenot artists and craftsmen passed on their skills through apprenticeships, although their children also benefited from schools and academies founded by fellow Huguenots and others.[1]

Private tuition

The British elite turned to Huguenot tutors to educate their children. The first Huguenot refugee to specialize in teaching his mother tongue was London-based Claudius Holyband (d.1593).[2] In 1693 the historian Paul Rapin de Thoyras (1661–1725) was appointed tutor to Henry Bentinck, Viscount Woodstock, later 1st Duke of Portland (1682–1726),[3] and in 1697–8 Sir John Chardin (1643–1712), jeweller to Charles II, accompanied Wriothesley Russell, Marquess of Tavistock, later 2nd Duke of Bedford (1680–1711), to Utrecht, Hamburg, Berlin, Dresden and Nuremberg.[4] William Blathwayt (1650–1717) appointed de Blainville (d. *c.*1733) as tutor to his sons William (1698–1742) and John (1690–1754); between 1703 and 1708 they toured Northern England and the European Continent together.[5] Philip Stanhope, 4th Earl of Chesterfield, was educated by Philippe Jouneau, who served as minister of Le Carré, the Huguenot church in Berwick Street, Soho, from 1690 to 1731. Chesterfield's son was taught Classics by the Huguenot scholar Michael Mattaire (1667–1747) and attended Jean Pierre Coderc's bookshop at Pliny's Head, Little Newport Street, on Tuesdays and Saturdays at 3pm and Thursdays at 5pm between 1726 and 1730,[6] for lessons on 'Modern History, Geography and Chronology, without ... which, the knowledge of History is very imperfect'.[7]

In Ireland, François Maximilian Misson (*c.*1650–1722) served as tutor to Charles Butler, later 1st Earl of Arran (1671–1758), and accompanied him to Europe; Misson was influenced by Pierre Bayle (1647–1706), Professor of History and Philosophy at Rotterdam, regarded as the Father of the Enlightenment. Significantly, Misson bequeathed 11 volumes of Pierre Bayle's *Republic of Letters* to James La Touche (1709–1763) of the distinguished Huguenot banking family, who settled in Ireland.[8] William Petty, 2nd Earl of Shelburne (1737–1805), was educated in Ireland by second-generation Huguenots Revd John Pelissier (d.1781) and Isaac Barré (1726–1802), who accompanied Petty on the Grand Tour.[9]

The Huguenot Germaine Colladon tutored Winwood, Viscount Monthermer, eldest son of

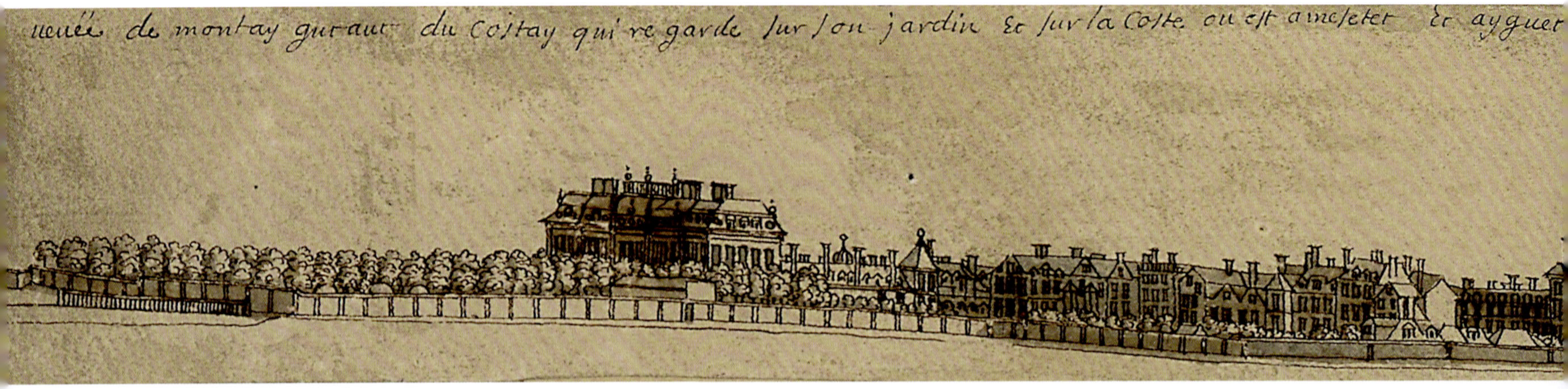

26 *Montagu House, Bloomsbury, from the North West*

François Gasselin, London, *c.*1700
Pen, brown ink and brown wash, 1.5 × 24.4 cm
British Museum, London (1860,0714.4)

Gasselin, a drawing master from Paris, gave lessons to the teenager John, Viscount Monthermer, the Earl of Montagu's eldest surviving son, at Montagu House.

Ralph, Earl of Montagu, who died in May 1702. For this Colladon was paid a wage of £100 in December 1700.[10] Winwood received drawing lessons from François Gasselin (fl.1678–1703) in 1700 and 1702,[11] while his younger brother, John, later 2nd Duke of Montagu, was taught mathematics by Abraham de Moivre (1667–1754), who in 1704 supplied a case of instruments and two geometry books. In 1706 John received three months' teaching from 'Mr. Pelletier, designeing master';[12] this was probably René (see p.121), elder brother of Thomas Pelletier (1680–1739), Cabinetmaker in Ordinary to Queen Anne. Both Gasselin and Pelletier came from Paris. Gasselin, who in 1701 at the Leicester Fields church stood godfather to Corneille François, son of the cabinetmaker Cornelius Gole,[13] was a topographical draughtsman who documented his travels with scenes of villages near Paris in 1678–90 and of Kensington and Whitehall Palaces in the early 1690s. These are preserved today at Chatsworth.[14] Gasselin's London views include: the Old Manor, Marylebone (1700), in which De La Place's French Academy was established;[15] Montagu House, Bloomsbury (plate 26); St James's Palace; and the Royal Hospital, Chelsea.[16] A view of the Binnenhof in The Hague records Gasselin's visit to the Netherlands in June 1692. His drawings of Paris mostly date from before 1685; although his 'riviere de Saine' is dated March 1690.[17] John Montagu travelled to France and Italy with Pierre Silvestre (1662–1718), William III's Huguenot physician, who was otherwise resident in the Montagu family homes, where he supervised building and decoration.

The Huguenots also contributed to music teaching. John Ernest Galliard (d.1747),[18] born in Celle, Germany, son of a French wigmaker, came to London in 1706 as a court musician. In the 1720s he taught Lady Mary, younger daughter of the 2nd Duke of Montagu, to play the harpsichord.[19] Peter Prelleur (1705–1741), a second-generation Huguenot based in Crispin Street, Spitalfields, began his career as a writing master.[20] In 1731 Prelleur published *An Introduction to Singing* as the first part of a much larger work, *The Modern Musick-Master or the Universal Musician*, which included instructions for playing the recorder, German flute, oboe, violin and harpsichord. In 1736 Prelleur was elected first organist of Christ Church, Spitalfields. He died after a short illness in 1741, and the charity children he taught sang at his funeral.[21]

Drawing lessons at school

Abraham Meure's academy (1692–1714) was adjacent to L'Eglise des Grècs, Hog Lane, Soho, where students attended services. Meure (d.1716) also ran the 'Bible d'Or' bookshop in The Strand in 1705.[22] Although the academy was primarily for Huguenot boys, John Monthermer was a pupil in 1704. With a curriculum that included drawing, Meure's Academy was considered one of the best schools in England.[23]

From 1717 the English Academy founded by Martin Clare (d.1751) in Soho Square attracted Huguenot boys who also benefited from regular lessons, including drawing, and conversation in French. They were taught science by Dr J.T. Desaguliers, who had previously helped at his father's school in Islington.[24] In May 1713 Desaguliers offered interested adults a 'Course of Mechanical and Experimental Philosophy; Mechanics, Hydrostatics, Pneumaticks and Optics', at Mrs Hawksbee's in Fleet Street; by 1717 he was instructing the royal family at Hampton Court Palace.[25]

French schools in late seventeenth-century London included D'Agard's, established in about 1680 in the Savoy. Metre's school, next to the White

RIGHT

27 Trade card of William De La Cour

R. White, London, *c.*1740
Engraving on paper, 16.5 × 12.5 cm
British Museum, London (Heal Collection, 89.45)

William De La Cour offered lessons in drawing and painting in watercolours and crayons at home and abroad. He painted stage machinery and designed for 'all Sorts of Trades'. He later moved on to Dublin and then to Scotland, where he taught art at what became the Edinburgh College of Art.

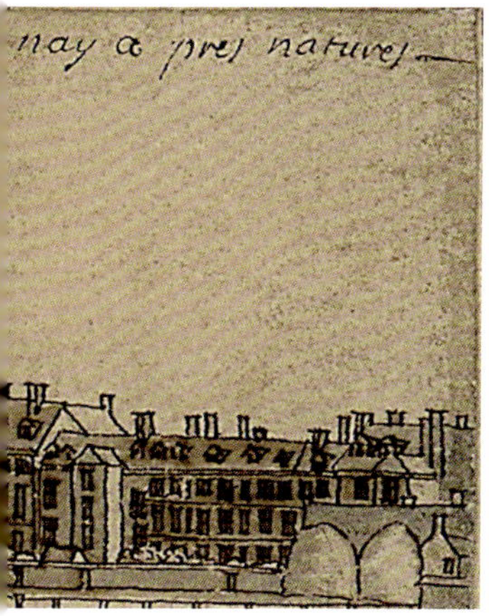

Hart Inn in Long Acre, offered mathematics, geography, classics, dancing, fencing and painting; de Moivre, member of the Savoy Church from 1687, probably taught there. He and Desaguliers often drank coffee at Slaughter's in St Martin's Lane, frequented by the French community, and rubbed shoulders with leading British and Huguenot intellects at the Rainbow Coffee House in nearby Lancaster Court.[26]

Schools in East London advertised 'better Air'. The Widow Sanry's French School, founded in Westminster in 1716, moved to Hackney in 1724. Here Sanry educated young ladies and enjoyed the patronage of Caroline, Princess of Wales.[27] Peter Fargues's Academy, established at 13 Spital Square, moved to Hoxton in January 1744, when *The Daily Advertiser* noted: 'For Twenty-Six Pounds a Year and Five Guineas entrance ... Young Gentlemen are Boarded and Taught French, Latin, Greek, Writing, Arithmetick, Book-keeping and Geography'.[28] Extras included dancing, drawing, music and fencing.[29] Like Meure's in Soho, Fargues's was established adjacent to the local French church.

The Huguenot association with educating the gentry continued into the late eighteenth century, when Mrs Masquerier's Kensington Boarding School for young ladies flourished.[30]

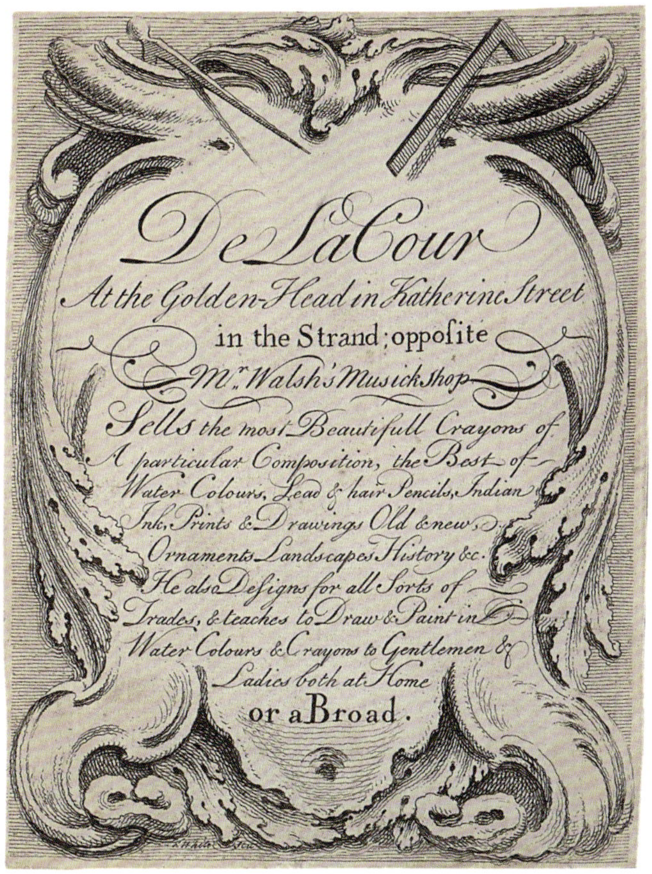

Foubert's Riding Academy

John Monthermer learnt to ride at Foubert's Riding Academy, near Piccadilly.[31] In 1679 Solomon Foubert (d.1696) was forced by royal order to close at short notice his Royal Riding Academy in Faubourg St Germain, Paris, as a Protestant establishment. In 1680 Charles II's £100 donation re-established Foubert's Academy in Sherwood Street, recorded today as Foubert's Place; this relieved 'the expense of sending children to France to be taught military exercises'.[32] After 1696 the Academy was managed by Solomon's son Henry (d.1743), who lived in style in King Street, Covent Garden. On Henry's death, Solomon Durrell, his nephew and executor, took over.

Monthermer, who became 2nd Duke of Montagu in 1709, used his equine training in serving his father-in-law, John Churchill, 1st Duke of Marlborough, in the Wars of Spanish Succession. Montagu retained a lifelong interest in riding and horsemanship and was the dedicatee of *Twenty Five Actions of the Manage Horse ... from Original Drawings of Mr John Vanderbanck*, probably drawn at Foubert's, which was published in 1729 by engraver Joseph Sympson the younger (fl.1727–36).

Artists and drawing masters

Like Gasselin, many Huguenot artists boosted their income by teaching, offering individual lessons; demand for these increased during the eighteenth century. Providing artists' manuals and materials was a good way to attract pupils. The engraver Paul van Somer (fl.1670–94) published a drawing book from his premises in Newport Street, Soho.[33] Nearby, the printseller James Regnier (fl. *c.*1710–52) supplied 'finest Water Colours in Shells, Best Crayons & Straining Frames for Painting, best Lead pencils, Black, White & red chalk, French *and* Dutch Drawing Paper, Portcrayons and Portfolios of all Sizes, Gold and Silver shells, India Ink, All sorts of Coloured prints and varnish for Japanning'.[34] William De La Cour (1700–1767), from 1740 in Katherine Street off The Strand and from 1745 in Coventry Street, Haymarket (plate 27), sold crayons and watercolours 'fit for Gentlemen and Ladies who learn to draw'.[35] De La Cour subsequently moved to Dublin and then to Edinburgh, where he continued to teach as well as practise art. He became first Director of the School of Design founded by the Board of Manufactures at the instigation of Henry Home, Lord Kames (1696–1782).[36]

In Dublin De La Cour's rival was Gabriel Beranger (1725–1817), who joined his cousins there in 1750 and converted the Beranger family coffee house on St Stephen's Green into a print shop.[37] He subsequently moved to 5 South Great George's Street, where he taught drawing. He is best remembered for his topographical views and descriptions of Ireland.

Between 1759 and 1774 printseller and engraver François Vivares produced drawing manuals, including his *Second Book of Principles of Lanskips* (1765)[38] and *A New Book of Principles for Drawing Ornament* 'in the Manner of Chalk fit for Youth to Draw after'.[39] Vivares won the Society of Artists' prize for etching in 1760 and Mary Vivares, possibly his daughter, won a premium for best drawing of beasts by an artist under the age of 20.[40]

Jacob Bonneau (1717–1786), a fashionable drawing master (see p.238), exhibited at the Royal Academy.[41] Daniel Fournier (d.1766), trained as a chaser, became an engraver, draughtsman and wax modeller, and also taught drawing. His 1761 *Treatise of the Theory and Practice of Perspective* was based on the work of mathematician Dr Brook Taylor (1685–1731).[42] François Torond (1742–1812), better known for his silhouettes was a drawing master in Bath and London.[43]

Educating Huguenot artists, designers and craftsmen

Some specialist craftsmen established three-generation dynasties. These include the Courtaulds, goldsmiths (see pp.188–9; plates 194–5), and the Grignions, engravers, clock- and watchmakers (plate 222). Such continuity was achieved through family training: sons and godsons were apprenticed to their fathers and godparents; daughters married their father's apprentices and families were permanently connected. Successive generations carried the same Christian name, an indication of family loyalty but also providing continuity for their patrons. The Willaumes, goldsmiths from Metz (plate 165), and the Tanquerays from Saint-Lô, Normandy (plate 167), became Willaume-Tanquerays; through financial and social success they became landed gentry at Tingrith, Bedfordshire.

Personal accounts of apprenticeship are rare. There are occasional glimpses of life outside the master's house. In 1705 Jacques Bourseau, an apprentice goldsmith, received a grant from the church in Threadneedle Street, 'pour apprendre le Dessein' with the engraver Paul van Somer in Newport Street.[44] Abraham Portal (1726–1809), a talented but reluctant apprentice to Paul de Lamerie, received his primary education in Derbyshire, where his father was vicar. As an apprentice he corresponded with his brother in Switzerland and described the frustration of writing poetry against the din of hammering silver in the workshop from dawn to dusk. The sculptor Henry Cheere (1703–1781) attended Westminster School; his sophisticated administrative skills and business acumen contrasted with those of his assistant Louis François Roubiliac, for whom running the business was a distraction from the sculpture in hand and he failed to make a profit. Born in Lyons, Roubiliac was educated and trained in Frankfurt, Dresden and Paris.[45] A year in Italy in 1752 inspired his mature work.

Specialist schools in London include the 1720s Mayfair establishment led by Vincent La Chapelle (*c.*1690– after 1749; see pp.199–200), the Earl of Chesterfield's sophisticated master chef who subsequently worked at European courts in The Hague, Dresden, Paris and Lisbon. His influential book *The Modern Cook*, published in 1733, was in its fourth edition by 1751 and included new designs for silver vessels.

Robert Campbell's *The London Tradesman*, published in 1747, provided guidance on apprenticeships and suitable qualifications for 367 avocations. This manual of trades informed parents on choice of occupation, transfer of skills and division of labour. Campbell underlines the importance of drawing: lack of skill through inadequate training explained why 'English workmen are so much inferior to Foreigners, especially the French'. At academies in the great French cities, according to Campbell, 'Parents are obliged by the Magistrates' to send their children who 'are taught gratis'.

In 1747 the Huguenot clockmaker David Hubert (fl.1714–48), based in The Strand, founded the Westminster French Protestant Charity School in Great Windmill Street. Its purpose was to educate Huguenot children whose families had fallen on hard times, and to fund apprenticeship premiums.[46] Hubert's portrait and the wooden board recording subscriptions to the Charity School are preserved by the French Hospital (plate 16), the senior charity established by bequest of Jacques de Gastigny (d.1708), which received a Royal Charter in 1718. The subscription receipt, showing a charity boy and girl in school uniform, was engraved by Charles Grignion (1717–1810)

28 *Louis Chéron*
Aubert, after unknown artist, France, 18th century
Engraving, 12.3 × 9.5 cm
National Portrait Gallery, London (D2063)

The son of Henry Chéron, miniature painter, Louis Chéron trained at the French Academy in Paris and Rome. In Paris he decorated his eldest sister's Salon in rue de Grenelle and painted two altarpieces for Notre Dame Cathedral in 1687 and 1690. He arrived in London in 1693.

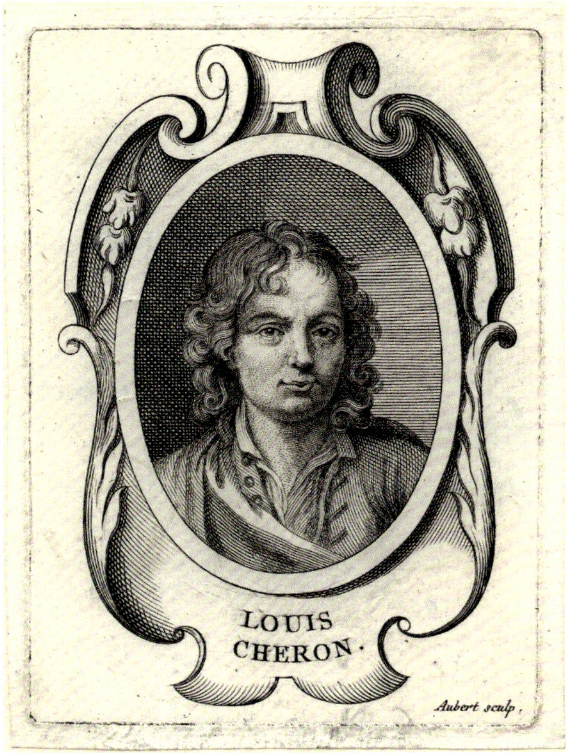

son of Daniel (1684–1753), clockmaker in Russell Street, Covent Garden, who worked with Daniel Quare (1649–1724).[47]

Pupils at the Westminster Charity School included Jean Tijou's great-granddaughters in 1780, and in 1784 the son of William Collett (Caulet; d. before 1787), whose livelihood as a carver and gilder was threatened by the introduction of papier mâché.[48] There was also a French Charity School in Dublin.[49]

Sir Godfrey Kneller's Academy

The painter Louis Chéron (plate 28) and the sculptor Louis François Roubiliac (frontispiece) transformed art teaching in London. Chéron arrived in London in 1693;[50] as a former star pupil at the Paris Academy, he was fined 2,000 *livres* by the authorities for leaving France.[51] When his sister Elisabeth Sophie (1647–1711) died, her will specified that the portion of her inheritance from their mother to which Louis was entitled, some 1,500 *livres*, was dependent on his conversion back to Catholicism.[52] But Louis was firmly established in Protestant London. From 1711 he attended the Academy that met at the house of Sir Godfrey Kneller (1646–1723) in Great Queen Street, near the Soho Tapestry Works, which had been established in 1698. The engraver and antiquary George Vertue (1684–1756) noted that although Chéron's drawing style was heavy (plate 25), 'he was much immitated by the Young people & … by all other lovers of Art much esteem'd & from thence rais'd his reputation'.[53] Yet Kneller relied principally on painter Louis Laguerre (1663–1721), a former director of the Paris Academy and the best draughtsman in Kneller's Academy, for advice on French academic practice. Laguerre was named after his royal godfather Louis XIV; his father was Master of the Royal Menagerie at Versailles. The young Louis Laguerre suffered a speech impediment so he abandoned a vocation in the priesthood for painting; in this he was encouraged by Louis XIV's principal painter, Charles Le Brun (1619–1690).[54] Laguerre came to London in 1683–4 to work for Antonio Verrio (1636–1707), the French-trained Italian who attracted royal and noble commissions for decorative painting.

Chéron's father, Henry (*c.*1609–1677), from Meaux, was a miniature painter and printmaker, skills inherited by two of his four daughters. All four abjured their Protestant faith at Saint-Sulpice, Paris, in March 1668; their mother, Marie Lefevre (1624–*c.*1698), was Catholic.[55] Elisabeth Sophie married Jacques Le Hay (*c.*1645–after 1721), Louis XIV's engineer, and was admitted to the French Royal Academy in 1672 when she presented her self-portrait aged 25. She supported her younger brother Louis financially when he won the Prix de Rome in 1676 and again in 1678, so that he could extend his studies at the French Academy in Rome.[56] Louis Chéron was in Venice from 1683 to 1687, where his huge *Pool of Bethesda*, in the church of San Pantaleone, was commissioned by Antonio Pedrini.[57] On his return to Paris Louis abjured his Protestant faith[58] in order to maintain his connection with the Paris Academy: six years earlier, in October 1681, on the instructions of Jean-Baptise Colbert (1619–1683) to Le Brun, Huguenot office holders and pupils had been dismissed.[59] These included the painter Jacques Rousseau (1630–1693), assistant professor, who fled to London despite Louis XIV's attempts to convert this 'able man' (plate 42).[60] While in Paris, Chéron attended musical evenings and discussions about art with the influential critic Roger de Piles (1635–1709) in Elisabeth Sophie's salon in the rue de Grenelle.[61] He also won commissions from the Paris Goldsmiths' Guild for altarpieces for the Cathedral of Notre Dame on 1 May 1687 and 1 May 1690.[62]

Chéron's student drawings after Raphael's frescoes in the Vatican *Stanze* and *Loggie* and Annibale Carracci's Palazzo Farnese ceiling (plate 29)[63] were purchased by James Stanley, 10th Earl of Derby

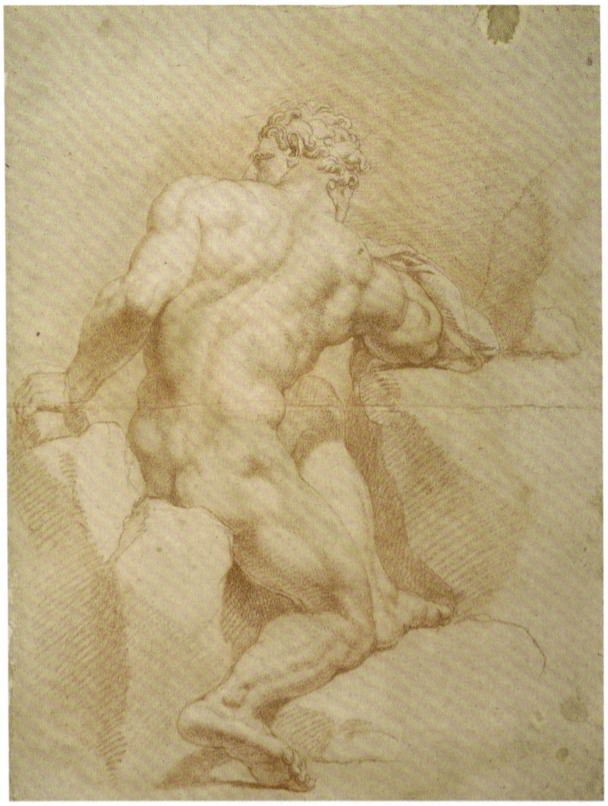

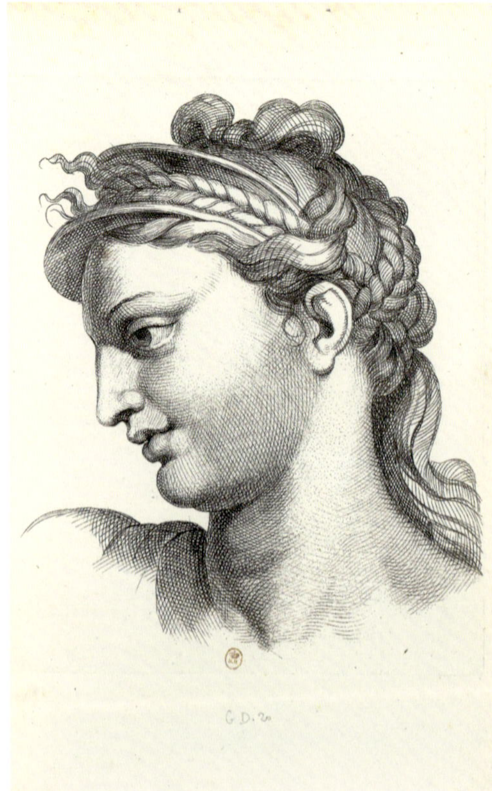

29 Study after Annibale Carracci

Louis Chéron, Rome, 1676–8
Red and white chalk on buff paper, 60.5 × 44.5 cm
British Museum, London (1953,1021.11.1–99)

Most of Chéron's studies after Raphael and Annibale Carracci are bound with later studies, revealing that he used his Roman drawings when teaching at the St Martin's Lane Academy in the early 1720s.

30 *Livre á Dessiner composé de Testes Tirées des plus beaux ouvrages de Raphael*

Plate 8
Elisabeth Sophie Chéron after Louis Chéron, Paris, 1706
Engraving, 44 × 27 cm
Bibliothèque nationale, Paris (FRBNF40353121)

This drawing manual was intended for an international market, bringing Raphael's Roman heads to young British and French artists. Raphael's work was an ideal to which professional painters aspired.

(1664–1736), for £500.[64] They are in red chalk on buff paper with white heightening, the technique then associated with French artists in Rome. Four life drawings dating from Chéron's Roman period all represent the same youth, seated on a rock, dressed as a shepherd or thrusting his spear down the throat of a dragon, imagined in the context of history painting. That these are bound with later studies indicates that Chéron used his Roman life drawings when teaching at the St Martin's Lane Academy in the early 1720s. The prints in his sister's *Livre à Dessiner composé de Testes Tirées des plus beaux ouvrages de Raphael*, published in Paris in 1706, were intended to inform 'le goust des jeunes Estudians en servant de guide' (plate 30);[65] they were probably based on Louis Chéron's drawings after Raphael.

The French artist Nicholas Dorigny (1658–1746) also attended Kneller's Academy, after 24 years in Italy. He abandoned painting for engraving and produced prints after Raphael's *Cupid and Psyche*.[66] Dorigny fostered a closer connection between French and English engravers, and in 1712 invited Claude Dupuis (1685–1742) and Claude Dubosc (*c.*1682–*c.*1745) from Paris to assist with engraving the Raphael Cartoons, then at Hampton Court Palace.[67] Dorigny's engravings were published to great acclaim in 1719, inspiring the Huguenot Simon Gribelin to reissue his smaller 1707 prints of the Cartoons with a new frontispiece in 1720; these were still available from Simon's son, Samuel Gribelin (*c.*1694–1732), in 1735.

The Paris Academy taught sculpture as well as painting but Kneller's Academy only offered life drawing. Yet in 1711–13 it attracted 16 painters, an architect, a sculptor, an ivory carver and seven engravers.[68] They were joined by a surgeon by the name of Mr Geikie, the banker Colonel James Seymour (*c.*1658–1739) and the actor Owen McSwiney (1676–1754). The academy promoted cross-fertilization between disciplines: in 1723 the architect James Gibbs (1682–1754) worked with the sculptor Francis Bird (1667–1731) on the monument to John Holles, Duke of Newcastle, in Westminster Abbey. Owen McSwiney managed the Haymarket and Drury Lane Theatres, so for him attending Kneller's Academy was a good way of spotting talent for painting scenery.[69] George Vertue noted that 'J.Vanderbank, G. VanderGucht, Simpson, Hymore, Kirkall, Baron & severall others as well Painters as Engravers benefitted much by his Cheron drawing'.[70] The Kneller Academy also fostered mutual respect between artists and engravers, many of whom attended the Rose and Crown, an artists' club, between 1704 and 1745. Louis Chéron's wide-ranging book illustrations were engraved by Claude Dubosc, Louis du Guernier (1677–1716)[71] who arrived from Paris in 1708, Claude Dupuis and Elisha Kirkall (1682–1742).

The important link between artists and the medical profession eventually led to the appointment of Scottish surgeon Dr John Hunter (1728–1793) in 1769 as lecturer on anatomy at the newly founded London Royal Academy Schools; his brother William Hunter (1718–1783) taught anatomy at the St Martin's Lane Academy. The mature Colonel James Seymour knew the previous generation of artists – William Faithorne (1616–1691), Peter Lely (1618–1680), Arnold Quellin (1653–1686) and Christopher Wren.[72] Seymour was himself multi-talented: an amateur artist, 'excellent pen man', dealer and collector of 'curious pictures, drawings, prints', 'he well understood jewells' and was 'conversant with practitioners of mechanical works of Arts'.

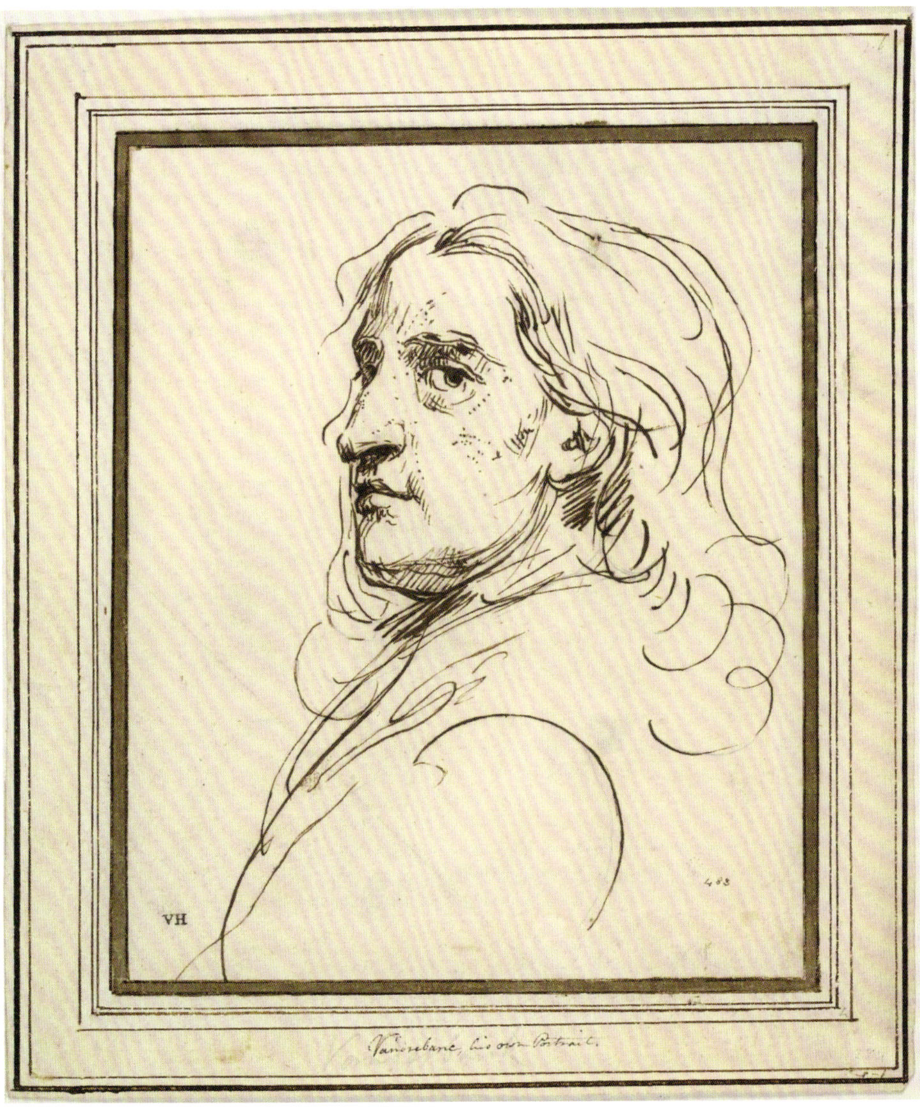

31 *Self-Portrait*
John Vanderbank the younger, London, *c.*1738
Pen and ink, 20.6 × 16.25 cm
Victoria and Albert Museum, London (DYCE 483)

When Vanderbank ran into debt in May 1724 he drew down on the funds of the St Martin's Lane Academy, of which he was Treasurer and Co-Director. In the words of Hogarth, 'the lamp store etc were seized for rent and the whole affair put a stop to' and Vanderbank fled to France for four months in order to avoid imprisonment.

With the exception of a Mr (Gabriel?) Maurer, by whose name Vertue noted 'silver works', and Mr Christian, the seal engraver, Vertue does not mention jewellers, clockmakers or silversmiths in his lists of attendees at Kneller's Academy. However, 'Mr Simpson Senr' worked as a silver engraver and Mr Marlow, who joined the Academy in 1711, may well be Joseph Marlow (fl.1675–1718), engraver and goldsmith jeweller of Lombard Street.[73]

The Academy continued to meet in Kneller's house in Great Queen Street until 1718, although by 1716 James Thornhill (1675–1734) had succeeded Kneller as Governor. He moved the school to Covent Garden after quarrelling with Louis Chéron; Chéron then set up a new academy with John Vanderbank (1694–1739).[74]

The St Martin's Lane Academy 1720–4

Established in 1720, with Louis Chéron as Director and John Vanderbank (plate 31) as Co-Director and Treasurer, the new academy met in an old Presbyterian meeting house in St Peter's Court, off St Martin's Lane with a capital fund of 94 guineas.[75] The initial attendance was 35 – just over half the number at Kneller's Academy in 1711, as the annual subscription at the new academy had doubled to 2 guineas. Chéron directed the programme for artists, engravers, designers and book illustrators. Eight founder members of Kneller's Academy enrolled: Louis Laguerre, Henry(?) Pickering, Stephen Slaughter (1697–1765), Hans Hyssing (b.1678), Bartholomew Dandridge (1691–1754), Louis Goupy (1674–1747), the landscape painter 'Alix Nisbit' and the engraver Joseph Sympson the elder (fl. *c.*1710–50). New members included architect and painter John Harvey (1681–1735), born in Poitou, where Protestants suffered acute persecution in the early 1680s.[76] Harvey specialized in *trompe-l'œil* architecture.[77]

Chéron's academy promoted the link between painting, drawing and the decorative arts. 'Alex Gamble' the enameller may be Ellis Gamble (fl.1712–33), engraver and business partner of Paul de Lamerie, to whom Hogarth was apprenticed in 1712 (plate 32).[78] The anatomist William Cheselden (1688–1752), a distinguished surgeon attached to St Thomas's Hospital, retained his connections with the St Martin's Lane Academy for 20 years (plate 33) and promoted links with the Paris Royal Academy of Science and Academy of Surgery.[79] He also encouraged public interest in anatomy and gave lectures 'chiefly intended for gentlemen' in

Crane Court, off Fleet Sreet, in Spring 1721.[80]

The younger generation of members included William Kent (1685–1748), architect and decorative painter, who had just returned from Italy with Richard Boyle, 3rd Earl of Burlington (1694–1753), and won from James Thornhill the commission for the King's Staircase murals at Kensington Palace. Among the engravers were Joseph Sympson Jr and Nicholas Gabriel Dupuis (1698–1771), younger brother of Claude. Other students included Moses Vanderbank (*c.*1695–*c.*1745), John's younger brother, who managed the Soho Tapestry Works after the death of their father, John Vanderbank Sr; Samuel Barker (d.1727), flower painter, a cousin of the Vanderbanks; John Ellys (1701–1757), the portrait painter; Giuseppi Grisoni (1699–1769), painter and sculptor born in France of Italian parents; and George Schroder (1684–1750), a Swedish portrait painter. Of other names mentioned by Vertue[81] only the painter Jean Charpin (fl.1711–65), who exhibited a *Landscape with Gypsies Merrymaking* at the Free Society of Artists in 1765, may be of Huguenot origin.[82]

The St Martin's Lane Academy complemented the apprenticeship system maintained by the City guilds. Evening sessions were held by lamplight during the winter as an aspiring painter was still expected to pursue an apprenticeship. Drawing the live model was not to be missed, and a master, glad of an opportunity not available in his youth, would probably attend alongside his apprentices. The room was often overcrowded, although the 'Great Room' of Chéron and Vanderbank's establishment was an improvement on Kneller's private house, from where the Huguenot decorative painter Pierre Berchet Senior (1659–1720) had to excuse himself in 1712, 'being not well ... could not bear the smoke of the lamp'.[83] Yet Berchet's widow maintained that he 'drew in the academy very well both in London & at Paris'.[84]

Chéron's life drawings from Kneller's Academy in 1711 and the first St Martin's Lane Academy from 1720 invite comparison. At first he viewed the model through the lens of the Old Masters and his academy drawings reflect his observation of antique sculpture. A comparison of his *Nude man seated* of 1711 (plate 25) with *Study of a female nude* of 1720–4 (plate 34) demonstrates his developing engagement with science through the influence of William Cheselden. The plates for the 1722 edition of Cheselden's *The Anatomy of the Human Body* (first published in 1713) and his *Osteographia, or the Anatomy of the Bones* (1733) were engraved by Chéron's close associate Gerard Vandergucht (1696–1776).

The female model was first studied at a small artists' academy that met in London around 1673; under Chéron and Vanderbank it became a regular opportunity and attracted the attention of the Prince of Wales (later George II). In November 1722, Vertue wrote: 'This Month his Royal Highness with the Lord Herbert Sr And Fountain went to the Accademy of Painting in St. Martin's Lane ... staid there an hour a Woman being then the Moddel to draw after, to whom was given five guineas by order of the Prince.'[85] Yet in drawing the female Chéron was restricted to his perception of antique sculpture and Raphael's Roman paintings;

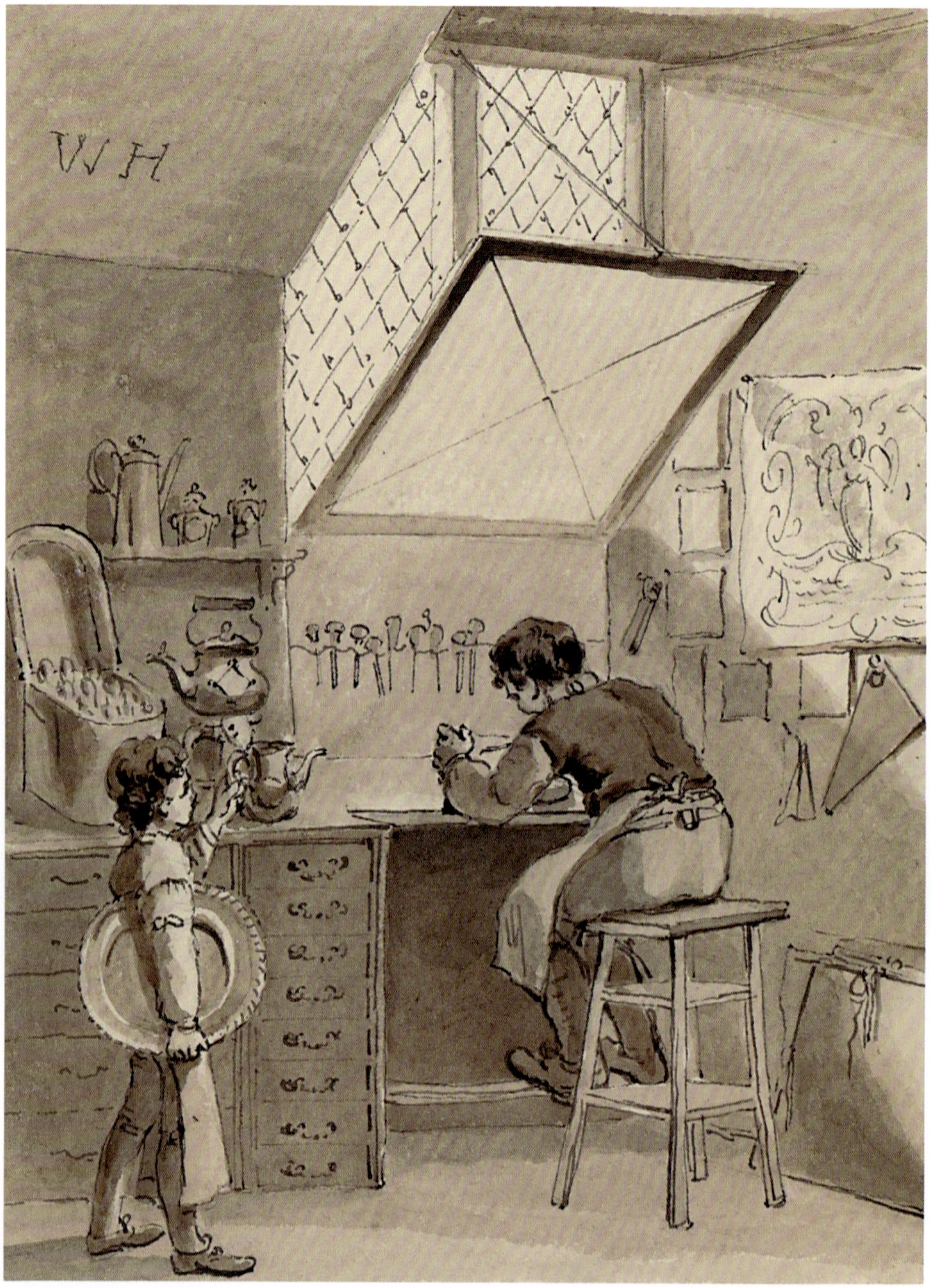

32 *Hogarth engraving his master's shop-bill: the sign of the Angel*

John Thomas Smith, London, 1817
Pen and sepia wash, 18.4 × 14.3 cm
Yale Center for British Art (B1975.3.790)

In 1712 Hogarth was apprenticed to Ellis Gamble, engraver, at the sign of the Angel in Cranbourn Street, Leicester Fields. Gamble later became business partner to goldsmith Paul de Lamerie.

33 *William Cheselden*
Louis François Roubiliac, London, c.1745
Terracotta, ht 61 cm
Royal College of Surgeons, London

Cheselden, surgeon and anatomist attached to St Thomas's Hospital, London, retained his connections with the St Martin's Lane Academy and promoted links with the Royal Academy of Science and Academy of Surgery in Paris. Chéron's later life drawings demonstrate Cheselden's influence.

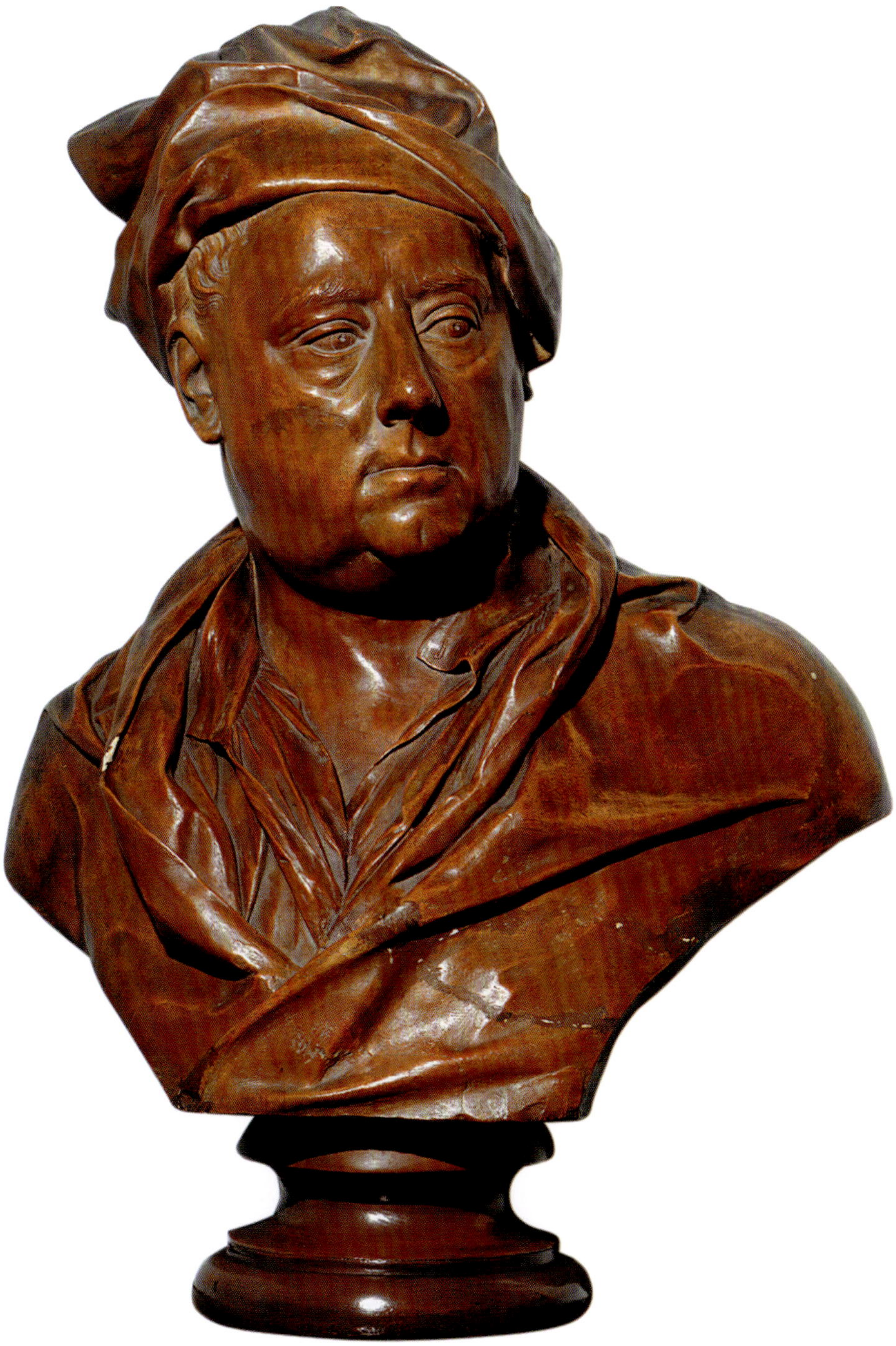

he used a stereotyped face based on his study of Raphael.[86]

It is hard to distinguish life drawings by Chéron and Vanderbank from those by their students. Of the 35 known academy drawings by Chéron dating from the early 1720s, ten are of female models.[87] Five show a woman seated: two from the front, one from behind, one to the left, and one with her left arm raised. Another shows a woman leaning to the right, her left elbow on a ledge (plate 34) and two are studies of a standing woman, in one case holding a scroll. The most daring of these drawings is that representing movement, showing a woman with drapery, fleeing to the left.[88] There are a similar range of positions in Chéron's drawings of male models of varying ages: a youth, a bald man and a bearded man. A standing figure is seen from behind holding a staff; a youth reclines with a staff; a nude man seated in profile to the right draws on a board. The occasional prop, a sword or helmet, makes the exercise more interesting; one study includes a sculptured slab. Louis Chéron used black chalk heightened with white on grey paper for nearly all these drawings.

Hogarth's life drawings reveal his engagement with the French academic tradition introduced by Chéron. Hogarth confessed to 'sometimes, but too seldom' taking 'the life for connecting the parts I had not perfectly remembered and then transfer-r[ing] them to my compositions', in other words drawing from the life in order to connect different parts of the human anatomy.[89]

Chéron's academy figures were published by Gerard Vandergucht in 1713[90] and by Chéron's former student Elisha Kirkall in 1735 (plate 35).[91] Vertue noted that Vandergucht

> *learnt of his Father to engrave and to draw of Mr Cheron & at the Academy, where his constant studies gave good foundation of learning instead of following his Father's stiff manner of Engraving, he practised etching altogether & some means of drawing distinguished himself from amongst many other young men.*[92]

The wider dissemination of Chéron's academy figures through prints demonstrates the crucial role this French artist played in British art education from 1711 to 1735.[93]

There is no record of the use of casts of antique sculpture at the St Martin's Lane Academy, unless the sculpted bas-relief in one of Chéron's drawings can be taken as positive evidence. But drawings and engravings of antique sculpture could be used instead. Copying 'paintings of the most celebrated masters' was another way to improve. Samuel Barker probably used Chéron's connections to study flower paintings by Jean-Baptiste Monnoyer (1636–1699; plate 43) at Montagu House, Bloomsbury. In 1729 Vertue wrote that John Ellys obtained a warrant from their Royal Highnesses 'to coppy any pictures of Vandyke. Kneller. Lilly. with care & study. has made good improvements. in his way of painting'.[94] Likewise Joseph Goupy (1689–1769) 'became eminent in painting in Water Colours, historys in a free masterly manner having Coppyed. multitudes of famous paintings of

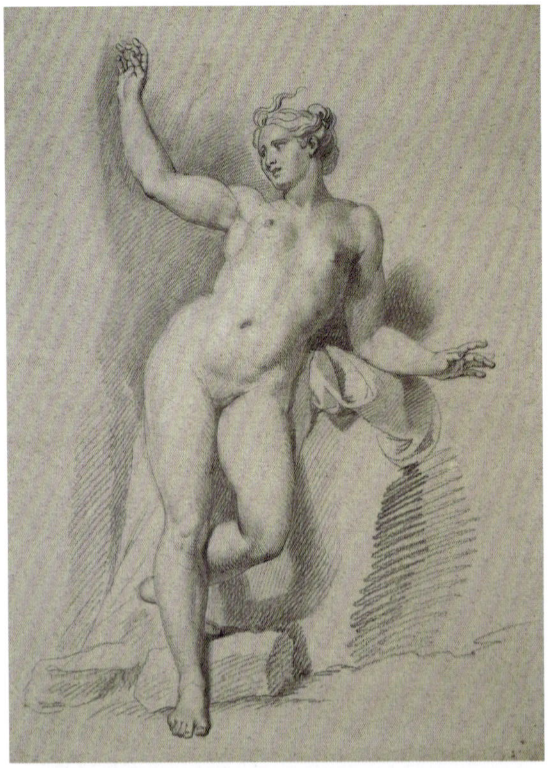

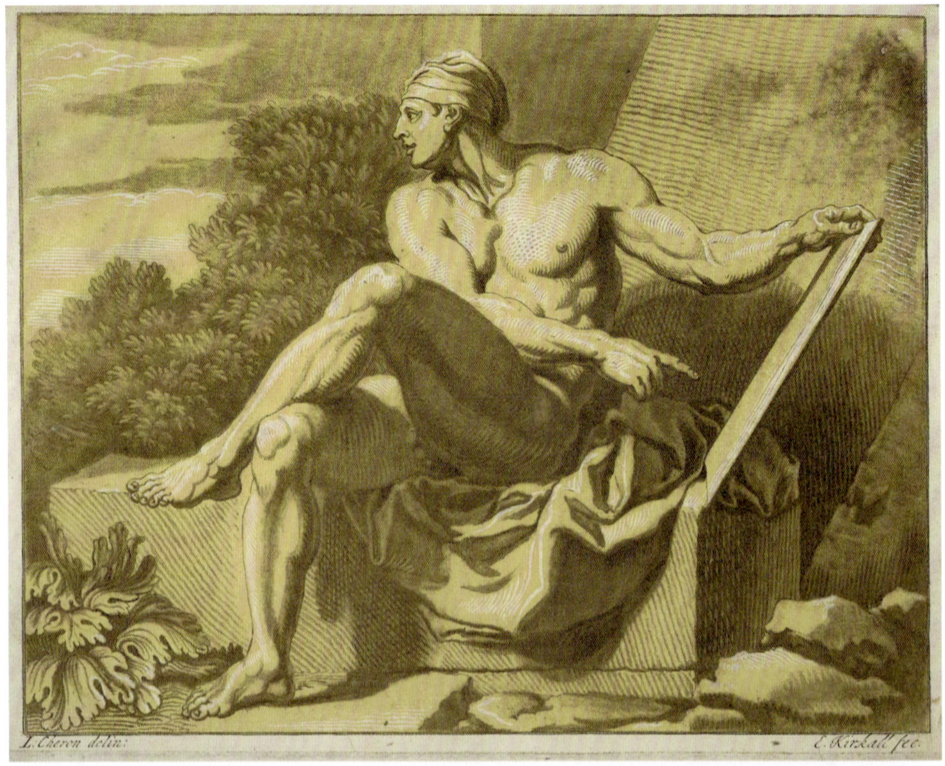

most Eminent Masters'.[95] The success of Joseph Highmore (1692–1780) was due to 'a continual Observation on Nature & the very best of pictures done by celebrated Artists, especially Vandyke'.[96]

The other side of the coin was the painter's ability to act in the capacity of dealer, restorer and advisor, for which the experience of working abroad, above all in Italy, was invaluable. Louis Chéron valued paintings belonging to Ralph, 1st Duke of Montagu, after his death in 1709. These included family portraits, portrait sketches by Anthony Van Dyck (1599–1641), flower paintings by Monnoyer and landscapes by Jacques Rousseau.[97]

In contrast to Chéron, Vanderbank squandered the Academy's finances. In 1724 he drew down on the capital funds in order to avoid imprisonment for non-payment of debts and fled to France for several months. The Academy closed after Chéron's sudden death from apoplexy in May 1725.[98] Thus Chéron deserves most credit for the influence of the St Martin's Lane Academy from 1720 to 1724. The students gained from his willingness to share his experience of the French academy tradition and his 'affable good natur'd temper'; his 'plain open sincerity ... made him agreable & belov'd'.[99]

The St Martin's Lane Academy nurtured artistic ties with France, Italy and Flanders. Vanderbank's artistic allegiance was Flemish; his father is said to have come to London from Belgium. Vertue describes Vanderbank's use of glazes as 'that secrett in oil painting of transparencey'. Through Chéron's French contacts and a network of French cousins a good working relationship with artists in France was maintained while England and France were at peace.

A set of prints entitled *The Most Remarkable Transactions of the Reign of Charles I* (1728) were commissioned by the London printseller Thomas Bowles (*c*.1695–1767). They appealed to Jacobite supporters of the Stuart dynasty, both at home and abroad. The subscription cost £1 11s 6d; and advance payment of 10s 6d guaranteed best paper and early impressions. The prints are of nine paintings that link the St Martin's Lane Academy set – Chéron, Peter Tillemans (1684–1734) and Vanderbank – with contemporary French artists Pierre Angellis (1685–1734), Jean Raoux (1677–1734) and Charles Parrocel (1688–1752). The first and last scenes in the chronological sequence were painted by Chéron and Vanderbank respectively.[100]

As Charles I was married by proxy, in his *Marriage of King Charles I* Chéron avoided having to match up with five other painters' versions of the King's appearance; the painting was probably still on the easel at the time of the artist's death in 1725.[101] Vanderbank's *The Apotheosis or Death of the King* is dated 1727.[102] The nine paintings, with one additional drawing, *The Revolt of the Fleet*,

34 *Study of a female nude*
Louis Chéron, London, 1720–4
Black chalk heightened with white on grey paper, 61.1 × 44.6 cm
British Museum, London (1953,1021.11.71)

The opportunity to draw the female model was a novelty for both native and immigrant artists: naked female models were not allowed in the Paris or Rome academies during the 17th and 18th centuries.

35 *Male nude seated in profile to right with legs crossed, pointing to his board*
Elisha Kirkall after Louis Chéron, London, 1735
Etching, woodcut and mezzotint, 23.6 × 30.1 cm
British Museum, London (X,6.107)

Kirkall's *Six Academy Figures in Chiaro Oscuro, after the Drawings of the late ingenious Painter Louis Cheron, painted in Green and Yellow Tincts, useful for Painters, Carvers and Others*, was priced at 4s. The dissemination of Chéron's academy figures meant that the French artist continued to influence art education in Britain after his death in 1725.

made with Thomas Baston (fl.1721), who drew the shipping within a frame designed by Chéron, were engraved and advertised in 1728. Some of the plates were engraved in France.[103] The London engravers were Nicholas Gabriel Dupuis (*The Marriage of the King 1625*, *The Battle at Naseby* and *The King seized at Holmby*), Gerald Vandergucht (*The Revolt of the Fleet* and *King Charles setting up his Standard*), Bernard Baron (1696–1762, *The King's Escape* and the *Apotheosis*) and Claude Dubosc (*The Trial*). This profit-making venture was aimed at the French and English markets and was a bid to attract royal patronage. It was widely advertised and prompted Vertue to comment: 'Another undertaking by the Printsellers whereby alone may be seen the improvements by encouragement this Art [engraving] has obtaind in London, within the space of Twenty Years.'[104]

The Coronation of George I, engraved by Claude Dubosc after Chéron, was inscribed in French for that market.[105] The enthroned King, flanked by the Prince and Princess of Wales (later George II and Queen Caroline), is surrounded by traditional Virtues. At his feet the lion of England is poised to pounce on the traditional Vices, which Hercules beats down with his club. The design was inspired by Rubens's *Good Government of James I* on the ceiling of the Whitehall Banqueting House. The figure of Hercules, club raised, trampling down the Vices with his right foot, in reverse of the Rubens oval, is taken directly from Gribelin's reproduction print. Chéron was inspired by the baroque exuberance of Rubens's painting, the Vices, falling out of the composition, contrasting with the staid classical figures of the royal family and their accompanying Virtues. Dubosc's print shows Chéron working in the dramatic style of Charles Le Brun as the figures assume a sculptural presence.

Before 1709 Chéron had decorated ceilings with mythological scenes for Ralph, 1st Duke of Montagu, at Montagu House in Bloomsbury, Boughton in Northamptonshire and Ditton in Buckinghamshire. By attending Kneller's Academy, where London's artistic community gathered, Chéron's expanded network resulted in commissions for book illustration and employment for engravers.[106] Some of these came through Huguenot contacts. Chéron designed a frontispiece for *The History of the Life and Reign of Queen Anne* (1722) by Abel Boyer (1667–1729),[107] sold by Abel Rocayrol, from his St Martin's Lane bookshop.[108] The frontispiece shows Queen Anne, flanked by Wisdom and Fortitude, with the Lion of Britain to her right, snarling at the monstrous Hydra of Lerna.

The St Martin's Lane Academy provided an ideal training for book illustration, a source of income for history painters that was less demanding than painting murals.[109] There was real engagement with literary sources: the 'Club of Artists' met at Slaughter's Coffee House and hosted readings from *Paradise Lost* by John Milton (1608–1674).[110] Thornhill and Chéron contributed to an edition of *Paradise Lost* published in 1720 by Jacob Tonson (1655–1736). Illustrating 'classic' authors encouraged discussion and interpretation of the text. Despite their disagreement, Thornhill and Chéron remained neighbours and collaborators, Chéron living at the Green Door in the Little Piazza, Covent Garden.[111]

Vertue stressed the importance of a good literary education for an artist, so Laguerre's Jesuit training with its emphasis on historical sources was useful.[112] Chéron bequeathed 'all his prints, books and figures done in plaister' to René Pelletier, the engraver, carver and gilder and Monthermer's 'designeing master', who was at that time mounting Old Master drawings. Chéron's library included French and Italian books, which were sold at auction in 1740.[113] On his death in 1725, Chéron's sisters in Paris were each to receive £200, if still living, and if not, the money was to be given to 'the poor of the French hospital', the Huguenot charity then in the parish of St Luke's, Clerkenwell.

Chéron and Vanderbank set the pace for the later phase of the St Martin's Lane Academy, 1735–68. Hogarth and Roubiliac taught there in the late 1730s and 1740s. Continuity was provided by seven other members of Chéron's establishment: John Ellys, Bartholomew Dandridge, George Knapton (1698–1778), Joseph Highmore, Arthur Pond (1705–1758), James Seymour and Stephen Slaughter; the last of these was probably connected to the proprietors of the local Slaughter's Coffee House. Studying the female model made attendance 'more inviting to subscribers'. Roubiliac brought the Academy into line with the French prototype by teaching sculpture. An advertisement of 1745 quoted by George Vertue read:

> *For the study of Drawing this winter at the Academy of Painting & Sulpture kept in S^{t}. Martin.'s Lane – Charing X … on Saturday even … will meet at the half moon Tavern in the Strand – to take Subscriptions for the following winter M^{r}. Hayman (History Painter &c.) M^{r}. Gravelot. (designer) M^{r}. Moser (chaser).*

M[r] *Rubilliac (Statuary.) M*[r]*. Yeo. (Seal Graver)*
Mr … (Landskip painter) M[r]*. Wills (portrait painter Treasurer).*[114]

Petrus Camper (1722–1789), a distinguished Dutch physician and anatomist, confirmed in January 1749 that the Academy met for the 'Study of Drawing'. He was introduced by Roubiliac and accepted on payment of his 2-guinea subscription. Camper noted that 'a man and a woman' posed as models, 'The man … three days, the woman two'. The final class of the 1749 season was on the 17 March.[115]

Yet Roubiliac's capacity for drawing has been questioned.[116] His only signed drawing, a design for the monument in Westminster Abbey of John, 2nd Duke of Argyll and 1st Duke of Greenwich (1680–1743), accompanied his contract with the widowed Duchess. The drawing is attributed to 'a more competent artist at Roubiliac's request' for presentation purposes and is signed by Roubiliac as 'designer only'.[117] Yet his assistants, Nicholas Read (*c.*1733–1787) and Mr Siste, were talented draughtsmen. Vertue noted 'a drawing' by Read, 'an accademy figure shows great skill & fire & spirit extraordinary'; and that Siste 'is an Ingenious man draws very well'.[118]

As a former student at the Paris Academy and a director of the St Martin's Lane Academy, Roubiliac assisted with the drawing class. Roubiliac's sketches included an album acquired from his companion, Céleste Regnier, by Josiah Wedgwood.[119] A drawing in gouache for Roubiliac's statue of Shakespeare was recorded in 1916 (present whereabouts unknown).[120] His invoice for the monuments to the 2nd Duke and Duchess of Montagu in St Edmund's church, Warkton, lists three architectural drawings. He encouraged his assistants to draw, probably using his lay figure, which served as a model in the absence of a sitter and provided an opportunity to study the texture and folds of garments.[121] Roubiliac's lay figure (plate 36) is fully jointed, able to adapt to any 'number of attitudes', and its painted head is sufficiently fine to have been carved by Roubiliac himself.[122] The catalogue for the posthumous sale of Roubiliac's effects mentions another, larger lay figure: 'An – exceedingly curious LAYMAN big as the life'.[123] J.T. Smith, whose father, Nathaniel (d.1809), was apprenticed to the sculptor in 1755, remembered: 'Roubiliac seldom modelled his drapery for his monumental figures but carved it from the linen itself which he dipped into warm

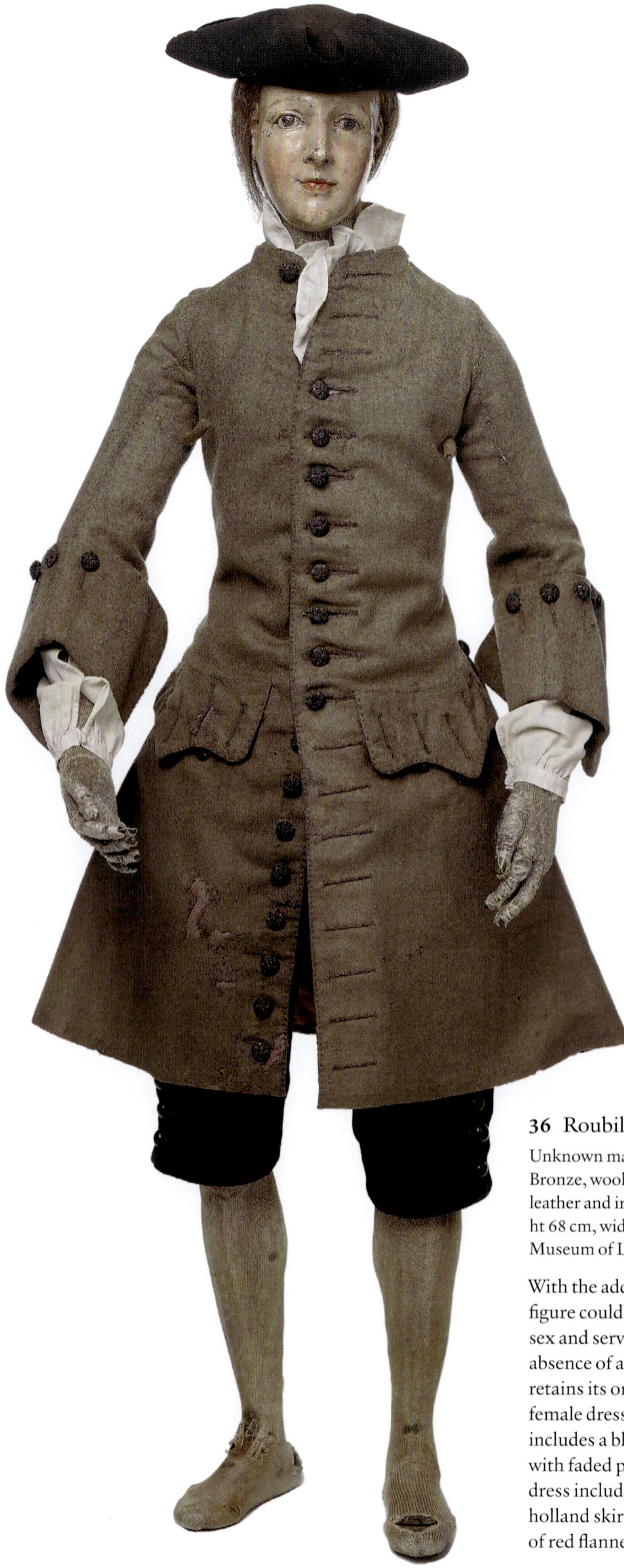

36 Roubiliac's lay figure
Unknown maker, London, *c.*1750–62
Bronze, wool, silk, cork, wood, leather and iron covered with silk, ht 68 cm, width 33 cm
Museum of London (29.130a)

With the addition of a wig, the figure could represent either sex and served as a model in the absence of a sitter. This example retains its original box, male and female dress. The male outfit includes a black silk hat, trimmed with faded pink ribbon; the female dress includes a cambric smock, a holland skirt and a hooded cloak of red flannel.

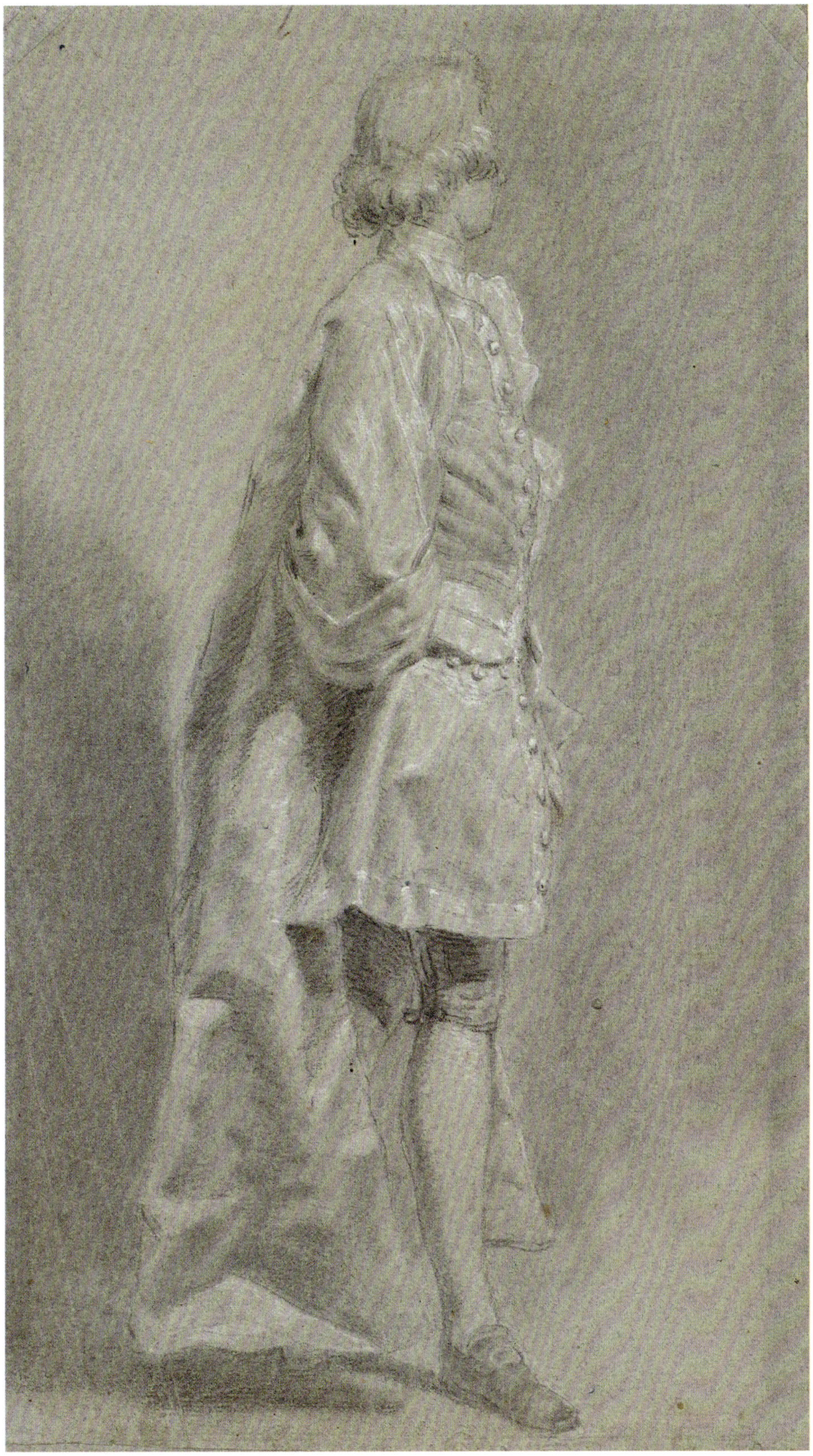

starch-water, so that when he had pleased himself he left it to cool and dry, and then proceeded with the marble.'[124] Roubiliac's contemporary at the Academy, Francis Hayman (1708–1776), paints doll-like features in many of his portraits, betraying his reliance on lay figures.[125]

Whereas students at the St Martin's Lane Academy drew nude models under Chéron and Vanderbank, surviving studies from the 1740s show models now fully dressed. Gravelot's private students included Thomas Gainsborough, Thomas Major and second-generation Huguenot Charles Grignion. Drawings of the same model are known by Gravelot and Grignion (plate 37). Gravelot also taught drawing at the St Martin's Lane Academy in the 1730s alongside Hogarth and Roubiliac, until he returned to France in 1745.

The St Martin's Lane Academy under Hogarth, Hayman, Gravelot and Roubiliac provided ideal opportunities for the interconnection of fine and applied arts and Rococo-style drawing promoted by the latest ornament prints from Europe. These were available at the French book and print shops in The Strand, Charing Cross and Newport Street. John Rocque, later celebrated as a cartographer (plates 229–30), was the first in London to publish this fashionable new style. Rococo-style designs for decorative objects by Gravelot and the talented German chaser Moser survive,[126] while Roubiliac also produced models for porcelain and bronzes.

Although they did not coincide, and they represent successive generations, Chéron and Roubiliac shared the tradition and experience of the French Academy of Painting and Sculpture with their students. Their sense of responsibility and engagement to develop the skills of the next generation was characteristic of the Huguenot ethic.

37 *A gentleman wearing a gown*
Charles Grignion, London, *c.*1737
Black and white chalk on blue paper, 36.9 × 21.1 cm
Ashmolean Museum, Oxford (WA1950.12)

Charles Grignion studied drawing under Hubert Gravelot with Thomas Gainsborough and Thomas Major, and developed a talent for rendering texture.

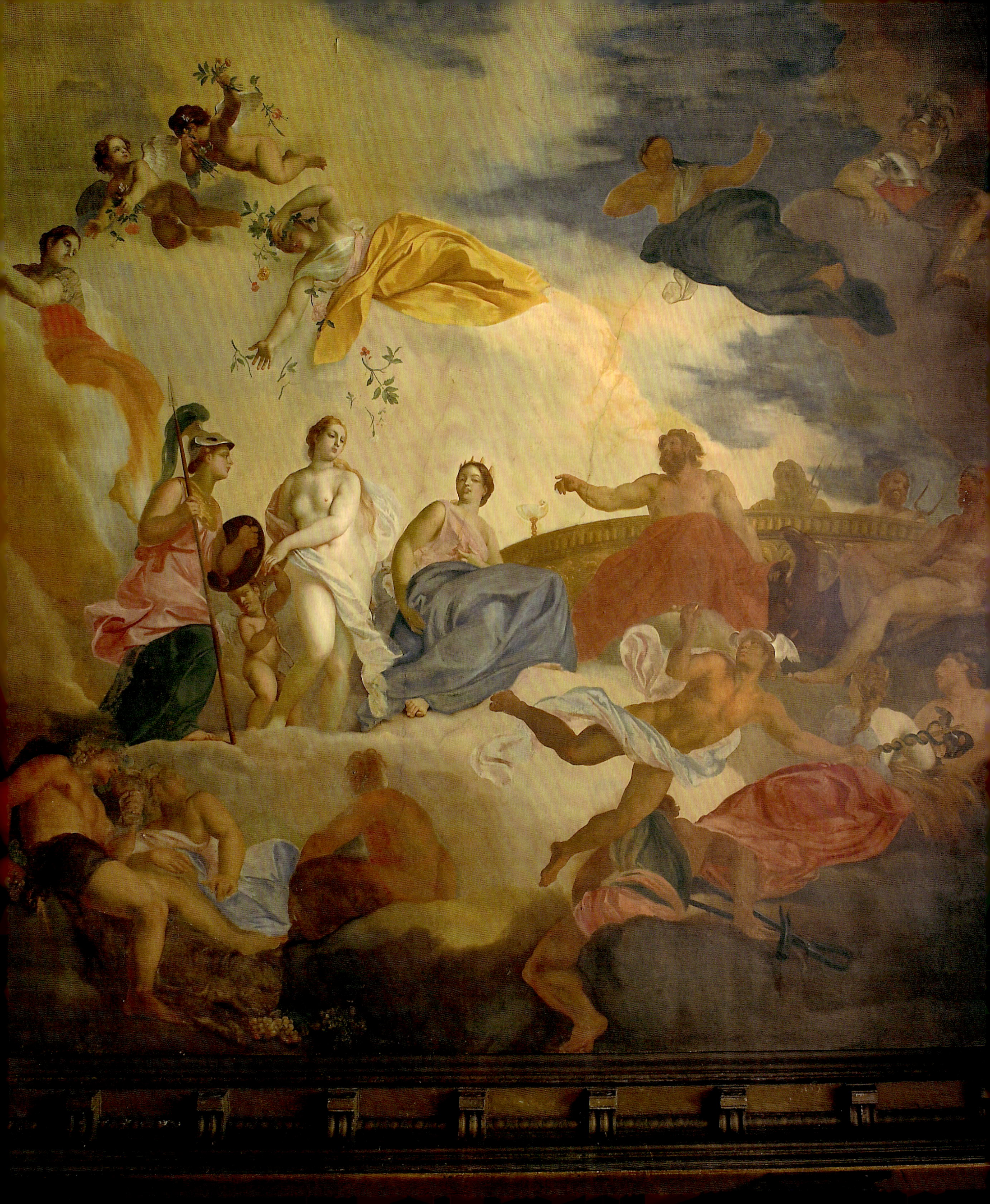

Chapter Four
Decorative Painters

38 *Discord Throwing an Apple at the Banquet of the Gods*
Staircase ceiling, Boughton House
Louis Chéron, *c.*1695
Oil on plaster, 731 × 767 cm
Buccleuch Collections, Boughton House, Northamptonshire

At the Banquet of the Gods, Eris, Goddess of Discord, an unwelcome guest, throws down a golden apple inscribed 'To the fairest', thus initiating the Trojan War. The three claimants for the apple are the helmeted Minerva, standing to the left; Juno, seated; and standing between them, Venus, lightly draped. But Jupiter orders Mercury, below, to delegate the task to Paris. This unusual choice of subject was selected as Mount Olympus was an appropriate celestial setting for the staircase ceiling.

The tradition of secular decorative painting was well established by the seventeenth century but only after the restoration of Charles II in 1660 did it become the preferred means of decorating interior wall surfaces in secular buildings. Hitherto, tapestries had provided a more effective screen from draughts and, although expensive, could be moved from place to place as required. Decorative painting needed less frequent alteration or restoration. Whereas earlier schemes, such as Rubens's ceiling for the Whitehall Banqueting House, were painted on canvas and then positioned, decorative painting was applied directly onto the plasterwork, so the artist had to work *in situ*. The availability of Huguenot artists trained in this technique coincided with increased demand also met by immigrant French and Italian Catholics.

Until 1720 the only significant British decorative painters were Robert Streater (1621–1679) and James Thornhill. The level of competition posed by immigrant artists is revealed by the 1709 commission for scenes from the Acts of the Apostles to decorate the dome of St Paul's Cathedral. Of the five who submitted designs, four were foreigners. Pierre Berchet and Louis Chéron were both Huguenots; Antonio Pellegrini (1675–1741) and Giovanni Battista Catenaro (fl.1692–1727) were Catholics from Venice and Naples respectively. James Thornhill secured the commission largely because of his nationality and the prestige of the newly rebuilt cathedral.[1]

Antonio Verrio, the first foreign decorative painter to settle in England, also a Catholic, was invited in 1672 by Ralph Montagu, Charles II's former ambassador to the French court. Verrio's ceilings for Windsor Castle were later engraved by the Huguenot Peter Vandrebanc (1649–1697; plate 39).[2] From 1676 to 1694 Verrio was assisted by Huguenot gilder René Cousin (d.1701).[3] Verrio was joined in 1677 by the Flemish artist Gerard Lanscroon (1655–1737), and in 1682 by Berchet and his assistant Jacob Rambour the elder (fl.1673–91), an architectural painter who had decorated the royal palaces at Versailles in 1674–82 and Marly in 1679–80.

In 1684 Louis Laguerre arrived with the architectural painter Ricard, possibly from Bruges. Laguerre was Catholic but the religious persuasion of Rambour and Ricard is not recorded. Laguerre married the daughter of the French gatesmith Jean Tijou (plate 77). In 1689 the Catholic Charles de la Fosse, Berchet's former master, and the Huguenot Jacques Rousseau came to London from Paris to decorate the London house of Ralph, 1st Earl of Montagu. They were joined in 1693 by Louis Chéron.[4] Jacques Parmentier (1658–1730), the Huguenot nephew of Sébastien Bourdon (1616–1671), who studied with Charles de la Fosse, worked under Daniel Marot at Het Loo, William III's Dutch country palace, in the 1680s and 1690s. Parmentier resented Marot's authority as Surveyor,

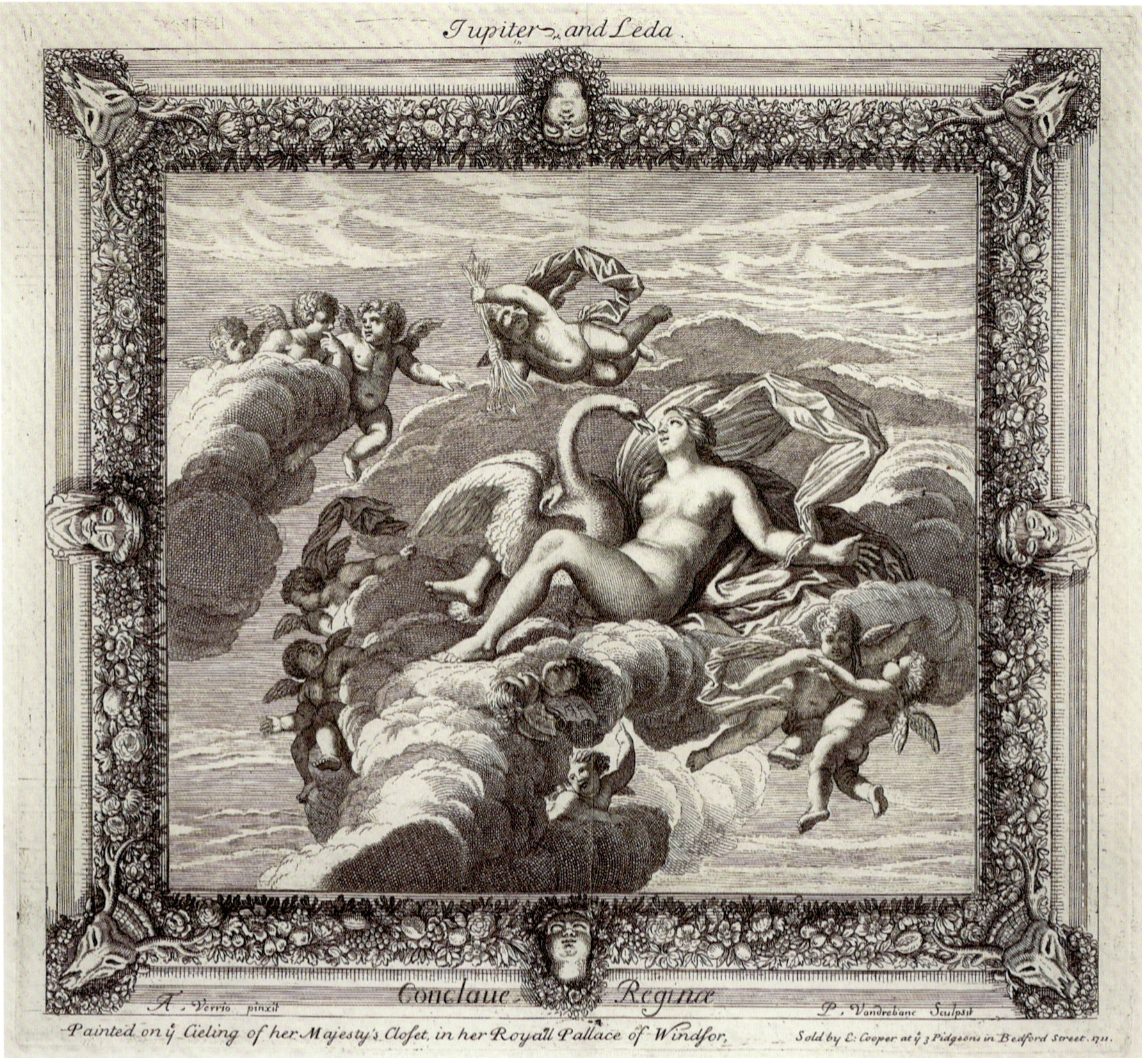

39 *Jupiter and Leda*

Peter Vandrebanc after Antonio Verrio, London, 1711
Etching, 36.9 × 40.8 cm
British Museum, London (1874,0808.1947)

The ceiling of Queen Catherine of Braganza's closet was part of Verrio's scheme of decoration for Windsor Castle, which was remodelled for Charles II's by architect Hugh May (1621–1684). The first foreign decorative painter to settle in England after the Restoration, Verrio was a French-trained Italian who worked in Paris on royal commissions under the court painter Charles Le Brun.

so came to London and painted *trompe-l'œil* sculpture on the main staircase of Montagu House.[5] He was replaced at Het Loo by a Mr Huet, who had worked for Verrio at Hampton Court. Classical or literary subjects were chosen as appropriate context for the patron's status and political circumstances. Religious subjects were selected for ecclesiastical settings.

Decorative painting required a recently plastered surface, which presupposed a new architectural structure. By 1690, 24 years after London's Great Fire, many City churches were rebuilt to Christopher Wren's designs, their ceilings painted by native artists Isaac Fuller (*c.*1606–1672) or Robert Streater. George Vertue noted that Berchet's decoration for a City church was 'done very well' but does not give the location.[6] From 1681 Berchet worked in England as an assistant to Verrio, then returned to France to work at Marly. On his return to England he completed commissions in the West Country and in 1691–4 painted the chapel ceiling of Trinity College, Oxford (plate 40).[7] Berchet then went to the Netherlands for about 15 months to work at Het Loo.[8]

In 1710 Parmentier moved to Yorkshire, where he painted a *Last Supper* altarpiece for the church of Holy Trinity, Hull, and, as a gesture of gratitude for local patronage, another with *Moses and the Law* for St Peter's church, Leeds, described by Vertue thus: 'thunder & lightning rending the Clouds … expressed in fresco upon the roof in Suitable Terror but qualified by the lovely aspects of a choir of Angells & cherubs with Moses & Aaron etc represented & the Decalogue Creed & Lords prayer'.[9] In 1709–10 the 8th Duke of Norfolk (1683–1732) paid Parmentier £40 14s for painting the staircase at Worksop Manor, near Sheffield, which Vertue described as 'his best' work.[10]

Following Chéron's prestigious fellowship at the French Academy in Rome, he decorated his sister's Paris salon at 33 rue de Grenelle: the overmantel with *Moses Striking the Rock*, the walls showing

40 *The Ascension of Christ*

Pierre Berchet, Oxford, 1691–4
Oil on plaster
Trinity College Chapel, University of Oxford

This is Berchet's only known sacred commission in exile, although he later entered the competition for the dome of St Paul's Cathedral, won by the British artist James Thornhill. Berchet's dramatic use of light and foreshortening reflects his French academic training and familiarity with Catholic iconography.

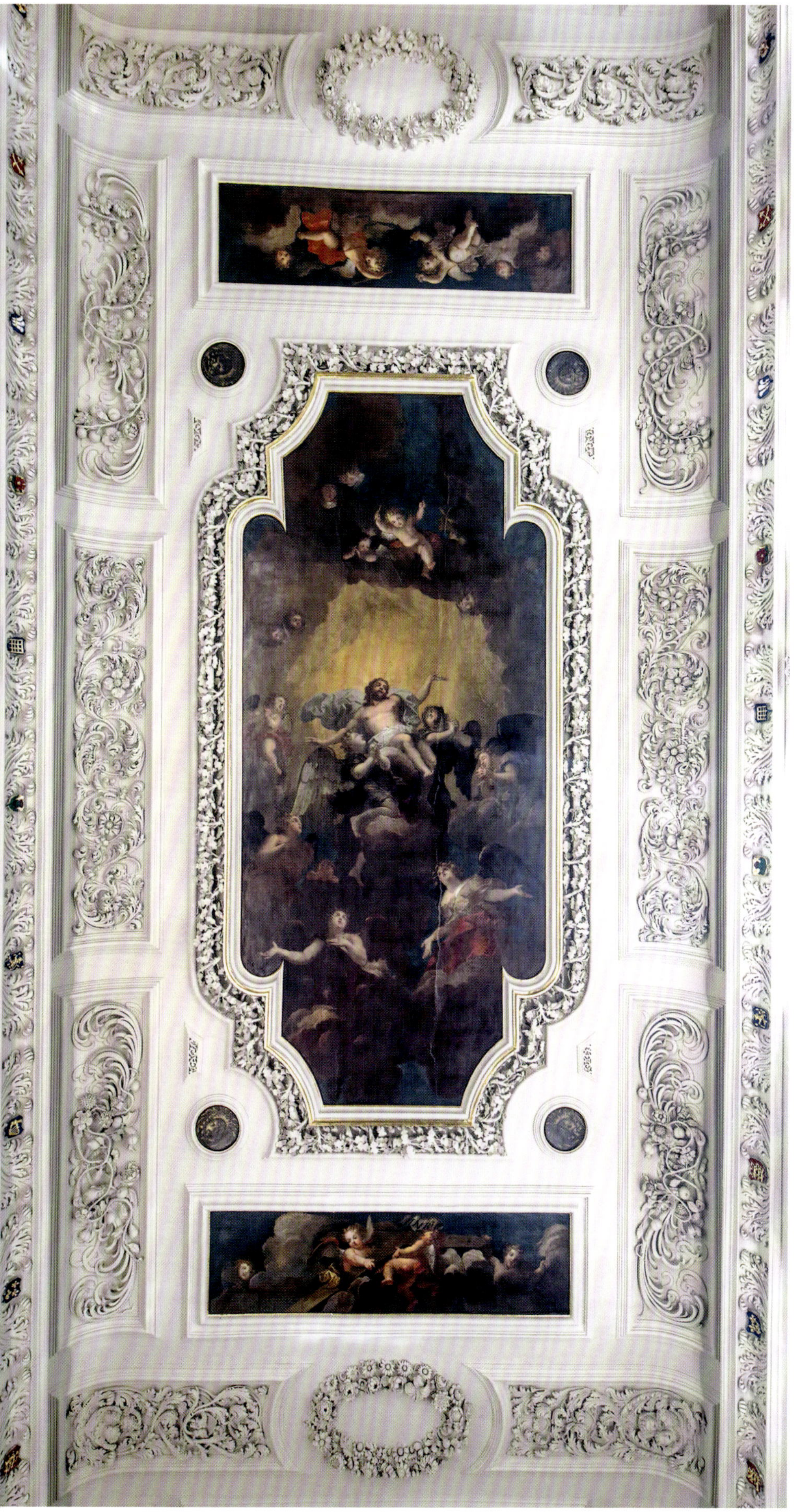

Angelica and Medoro and the ceiling depicting *The Apotheosis of Hercules*.[11] Chéron's reputation was established by the 'two Mays': altarpieces presented in May 1687 and May 1689 to Notre Dame Cathedral by the Paris Goldsmiths' Guild.[12] Before coming to London in 1693, Chéron also painted a *Visitation* for the Cloître des Jacobins, rue Saint-Jacques, Paris. Montagu admired Chéron's paintings in Paris and persuaded him to come to London. At Montagu House Chéron painted ceilings of '2 rooms below' stairs because the ceilings and walls of the principal reception rooms and staircase had been completed two years earlier by Jacques Rousseau and Charles de la Fosse (plate 41).[13] On 9 May 1690 Madame de Rit, the wife of Montagu's steward Elias, wrote to her husband, then in Geneva, that Charles de la Fosse and Jacques Rousseau had raised a glass to his health as they had almost completed painting the salon and were starting on the staircase.[14]

Baptiste (Jean-Baptiste Monnoyer) also worked at Montagu House from 1690 (plate 43), returning to Paris several times before his death in London in 1699. His son, Antoine Monnoyer (1677–1747), also worked as a flower painter in Britain (plate 51).[15] The tradition was continued by Andien de Clermont (d.1783), who was described as 'a disciple of Mr. Baptist' in 1740.[16] The work of these different French artists was described by George Vertue: 'the Staircase painted the Ceiling by Lafosse the Architecture Landskips by Rousseau the bass relievs by Parmentiere … the AntiChamber Ceilg by lafosse – the Salon, a Noble Room the most beautifull & richly adorn'd painted by Lafosse where he has shown all his Art & Skill.'[17]

A French visitor to Montagu House before 1715 praised the combined efforts of this artistic team, singling out De la Fosse's ceilings, *The Apotheosis of Isis* and *The Assembly of the Gods*.[18] When Thornhill complained of not having been paid enough for his murals of *William III Landing at Torbay* and *George I Landing at Greenwich* in the Upper Hall at Greenwich Hospital, he remonstrated that De la Fosse was paid £2,500 for his work for Montagu House. William III tried to persuade De la Fosse to remain in England, but the artist returned to Paris to paint the dome of Les Invalides.[19] Constantijn Huygens (1628–1697) noted the King's admiration for Rousseau (plate 42), who subsequently painted two overdoors for the State Apartments, Hampton Court Palace.[20]

When Montagu House was demolished for the new British Museum by architect Robert Smirke (1780–1867), floral overdoors and overmantels by Baptiste were moved to Boughton House,

Northamptonshire, where Chéron's painted staircase and the ceilings of eight reception rooms are preserved. At Boughton Chéron completed the decoration of the great staircase, five state rooms and the private family dining room in the 1690s. By 1697 the ceiling for 'The littell paynted dining roome bee loe' depicted *The Triumph of Bacchus and Ariadne*. Bacchus, in a gold chariot drawn by leopards, is accompanied by Ariadne in a silver chariot drawn by goats. Ariadne's crown of stars represents the Corona Borealis, the constellation formed when Bacchus rescued her from the island of Naxos and flung her jewelled crown into the heavens. Bacchus is accompanied by the drunken Silenus riding an ass and putti carrying aloft snake-entwined wine jugs. The subject sets the scene for the purpose of the room.

Chéron painted the ceilings of Boughton's Great Hall and adjoining Little Hall in 1705–7. In 1724 a visitor noted that the 'rich Cornishes of the rooms' were also painted.[21] The West Front Colonnade leads to the Staircase Hall, painted in *trompe l'œil* with rusticated stonework echoing the exterior. Here the ceiling represents *Discord Throwing an Apple at the Banquet of the Gods* (plate 38). The upper staircase walls are painted in grisaille with reliefs from the Arch of Constantine, Rome, based on prints by Antoine Desgodetz (1653–1728), who was in Rome when Chéron was studying at the French Academy there in 1676–7.[22] Victorious soldiers with captives at their feet accompany the triumphant Emperor Constantine, who is crowned by Minerva. Within a simulated Doric entablature, pilasters frame four doors, each surmounted by *trompe-l'œil*

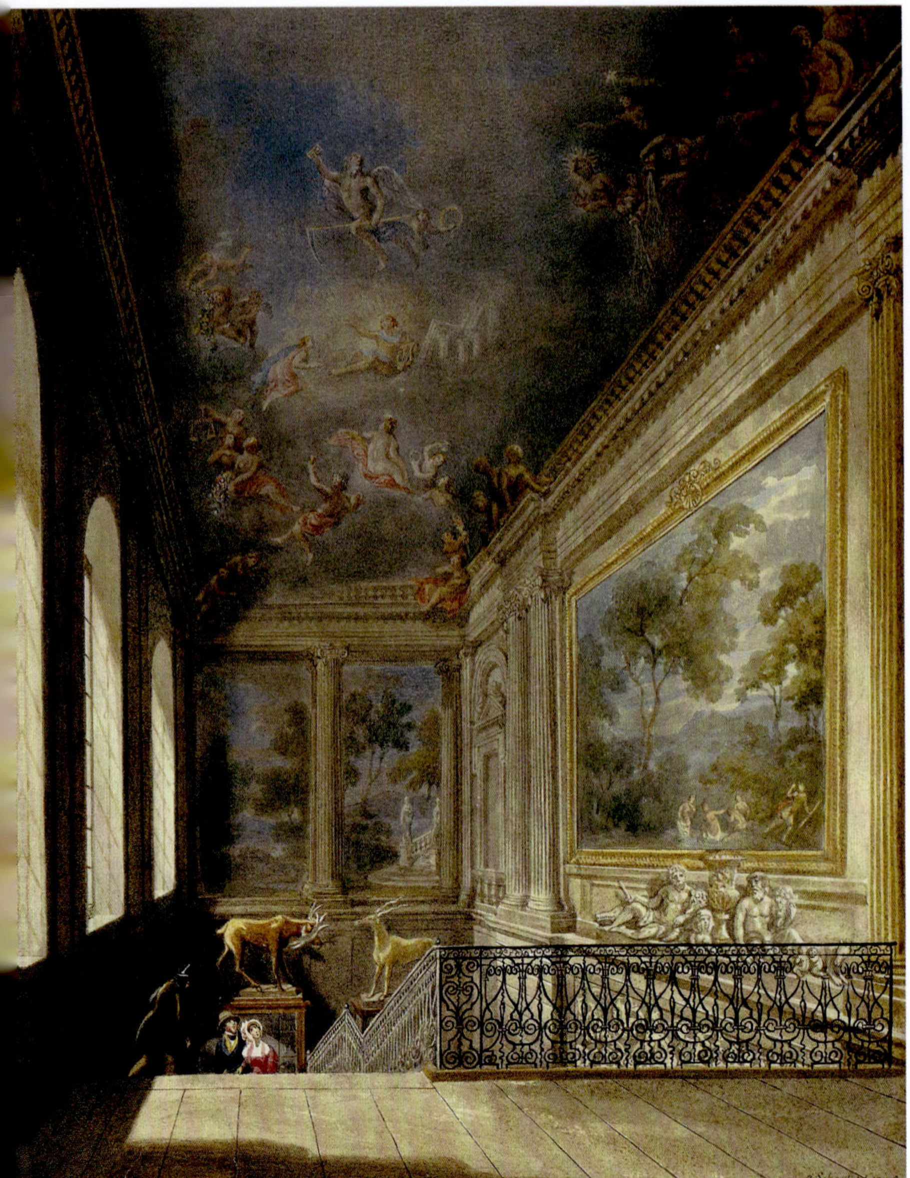

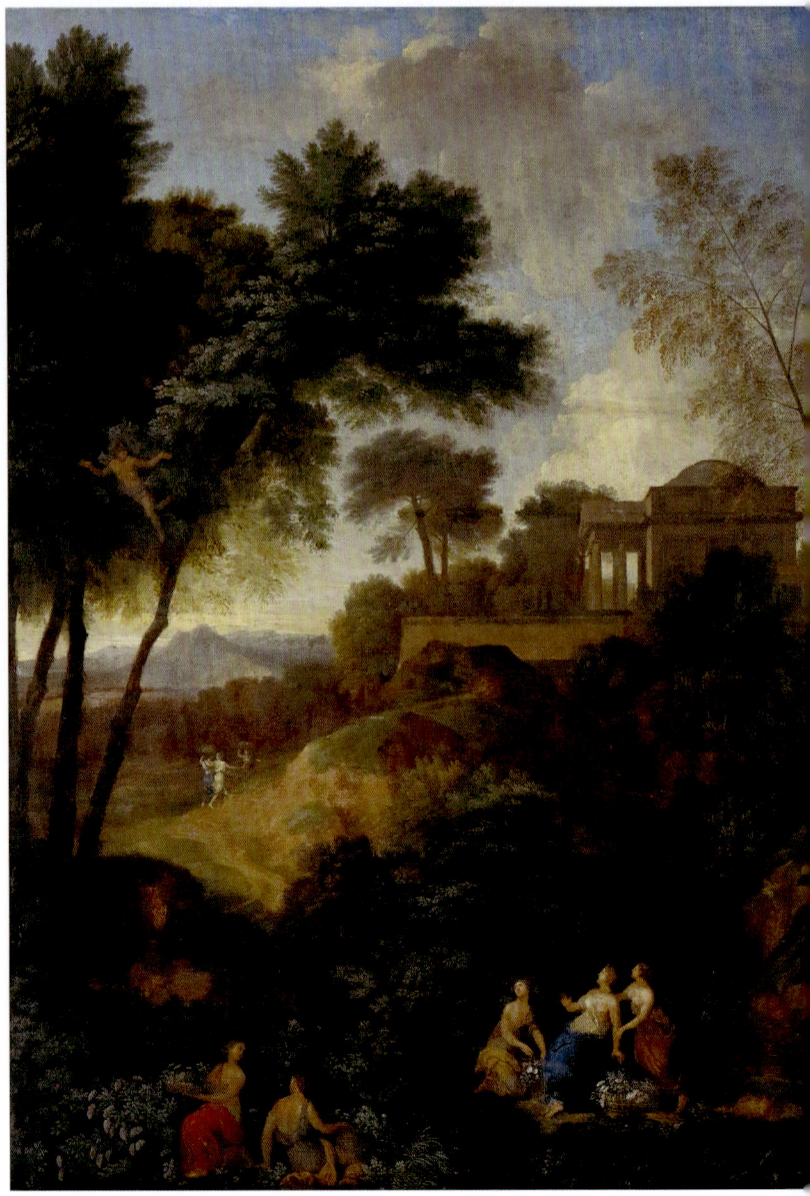

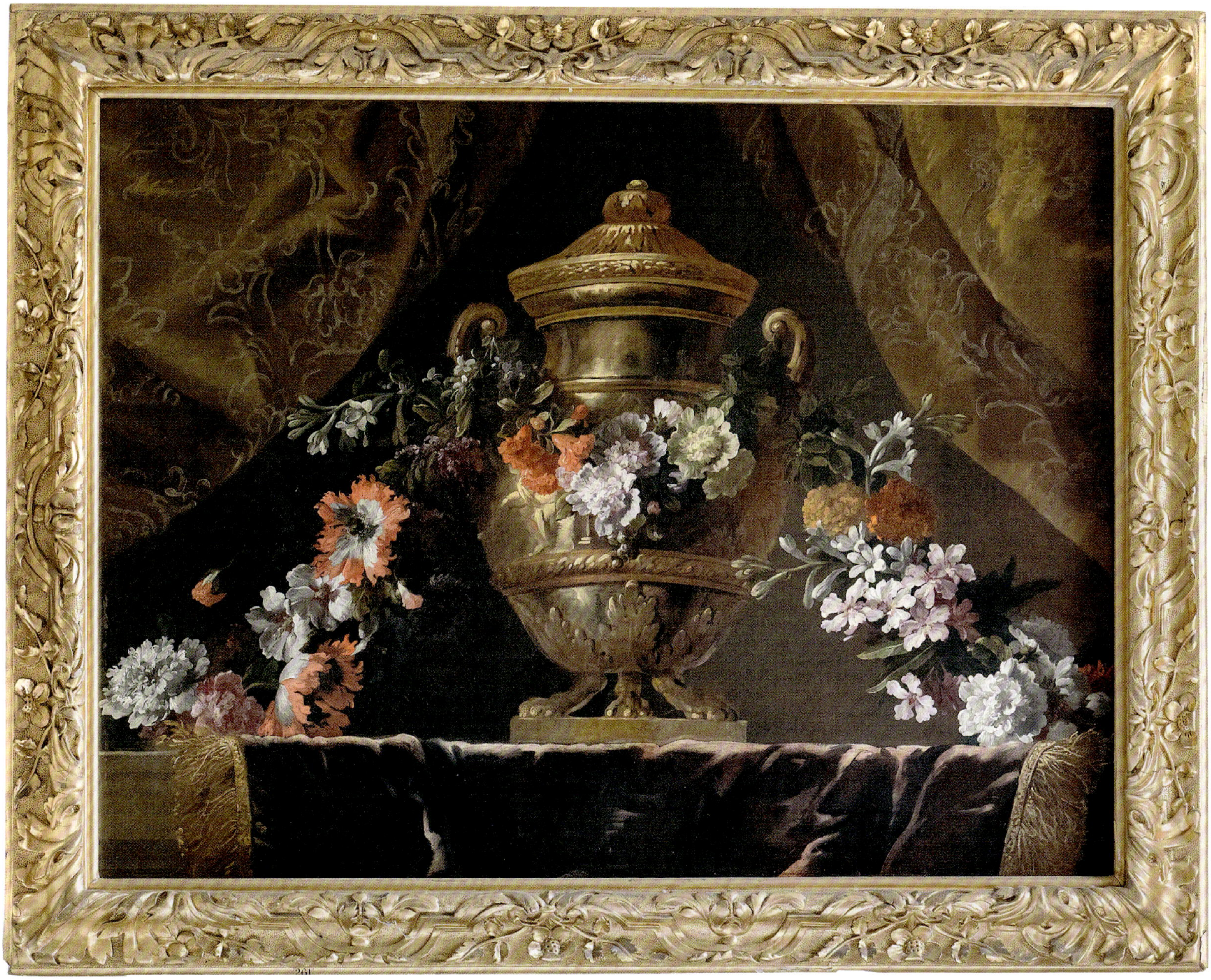

FAR LEFT

41 *The Staircase at Montagu House, Bloomsbury*
George Scharf the elder, London, 1845
Watercolour, 36.2 × 28 cm
British Museum, London (1862,0614.631)

George Scharf painted this view just before Montagu House was demolished for the new British Museum buildings *c.*1845. It shows de la Fosse's staircase ceiling with *Phaëton Asking to Drive the Chariot of Apollo* and, below, *Diana surprised by Actaeon* and landscapes by Jacques Rousseau. The sense of scale and unrestrained movement were much admired by contemporaries.

LEFT

42 *Classical Landscape with Figures*
Jacques Rousseau, London, *c.*1690
Oil on canvas, 193 × 144.8 cm
Buccleuch Collections, Boughton House, Northamptonshire

Rousseau's framed landscape scenes created internal vistas providing virtual space to the sophisticated interiors of Montagu House. The artist's experience of teaching at the French Royal Academy and decorating French royal palaces contributed to the respect with which he was regarded in London.

ABOVE

43 *Still Life*
In contemporary giltwood frame by Pelletier workshop, London, c.1692–1706
After Jean Baptiste Monnoyer, London, *c.*1692
Oil on canvas, 94.5 × 103.5 cm
Buccleuch Collections, Boughton House, Northamptonshire

Like Jacques Rousseau, Baptiste was celebrated as a French court artist. The combination of sumptuous textiles, expensive gilded vessels and flowers representing successive seasons complemented the rich furnishings of the Montagu House interiors, which are described in contemporary inventories.

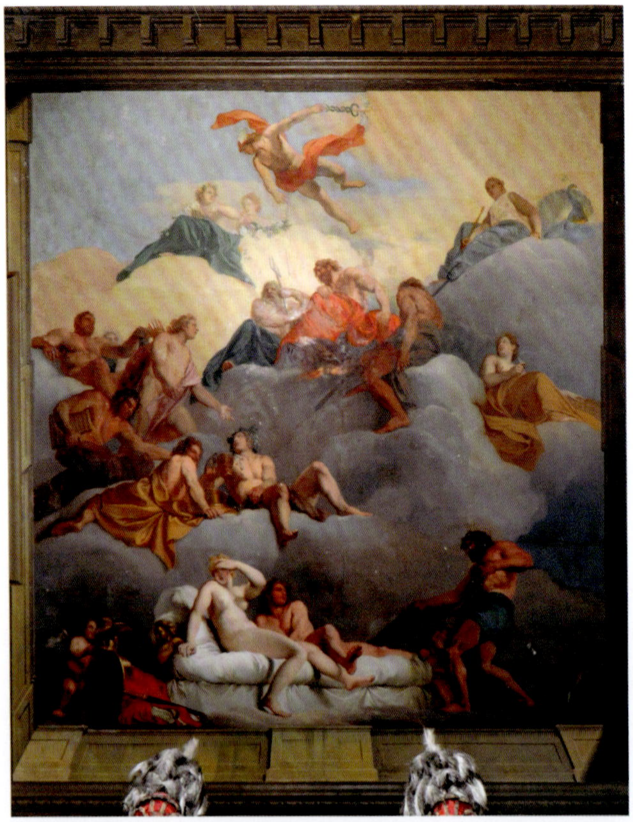

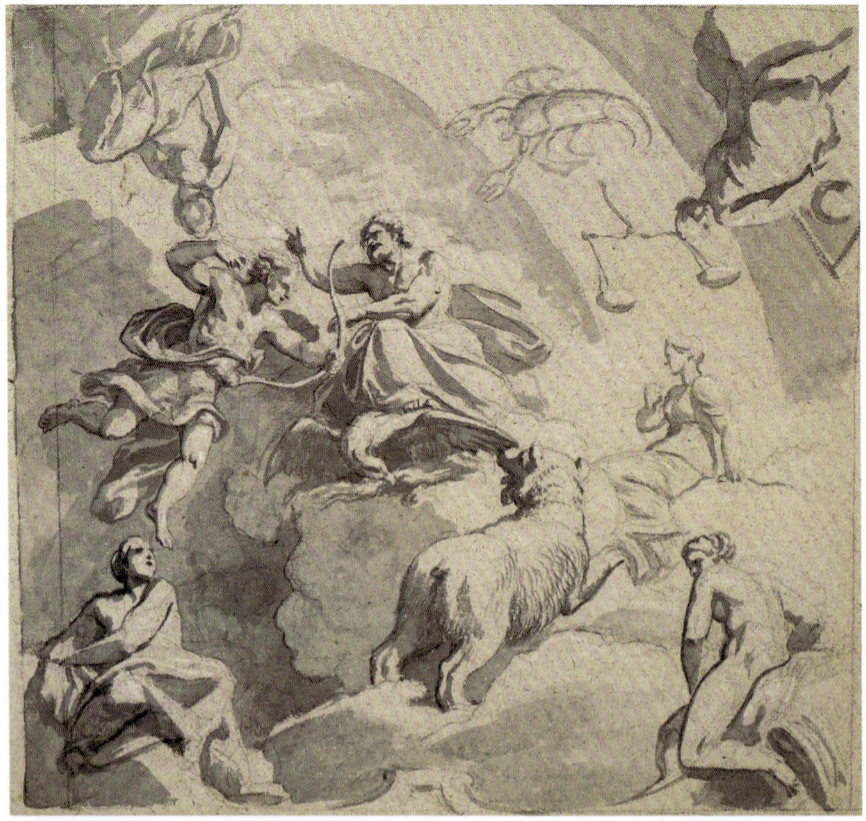

busts of Roman emperors in niches, echoing the plaster busts of the Caesars by Gideon du Chesne (fl.1681–1706) on wooden brackets in the external Colonnade below. A grisaille female figure personifying Abundance presides over the staircase landing (plate 94).

The ceiling of the first state room, at the top of the stairs, represents *Venus Protesting to Jupiter at the Banquet of the Gods*. Venus intercedes with Jupiter for a safe journey for her son Aeneas so he can settle in Italy, where he would later found the Roman Empire, as recounted in the *Aeneid*. Chéron follows Virgil's text closely: Venus is downcast; 'tears stood in her glistening eyes as she spoke ... The creator of the gods and of human kind smiled on her, with the smile which he wears when he calms the storms and clears the sky'.[23] The second state room ceiling shows *The Fall of Pyreneus* from Ovid's *Metamorphoses*.[24] Pyreneus, a Thracian king ruling a territory that he had seized, invites the Muses out of the rain and will not let them go. They take to their wings and he attempts to follow them, flinging himself from a high tower. Melpomene, the Muse of Tragedy, is most prominent, dressed in red and veiled in black; she draws her sword against the figure of Tyranny, who falls into the room, his crown before him.

The status of the third state room at Boughton, the state bedchamber, is indicated by the carved modillion cornice (the projecting bracket under the corona of the cornice). The ceiling here shows *Mars and Venus Caught in their Net by Vulcan* (plate 44) and complements the rich colour of the French 'crimson gold flowered damask bed' in its original setting,[25] echoed by the red of Mars' tunic, Jupiter's robe and Mercury's cloak. Venus appears to sit upright on entering the room but is perceived as supine on leaving. The fourth room was intended as a dressing room. Ralph Montagu's cypher at intervals on the cornice frames *Jupiter Restraining Arcus from Shooting the Bear Callisto* (plate 45). Here Arcas is prevented from shooting his mother, disguised as a bear, but Jupiter sets both in the sky as neighbouring constellations.[26] The subject may refer to the complicated divisions within the house of Stuart that resulted in the accession of William III.

The ceiling of the Little Hall downstairs illustrates *The Return of Proserpine*, abducted by Pluto but heralding the arrival of spring, scattering flowers below her. Her platform of cloud illustrates the account in Ovid's *Metamorphoses*: 'she appears with radiant face, as when the sun breaks through and disperses the watery clouds that have previously concealed him'.[27] The ceiling of the adjacent Great Hall represents *The Marriage of Hercules and Hebe* (plate 46).

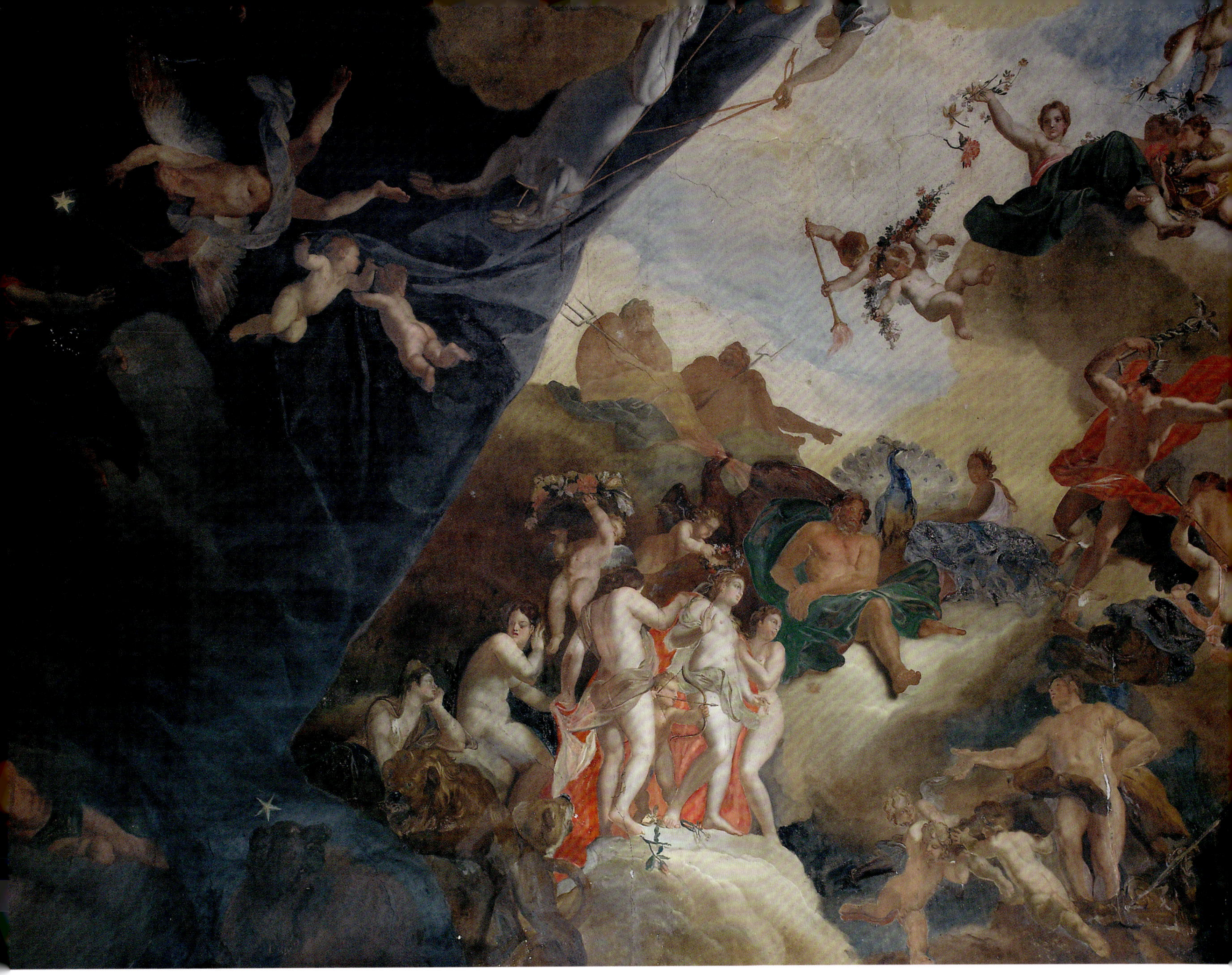

FAR LEFT

44 *Mars and Venus Caught in their Net by Vulcan*

Ceiling of the third state room, Boughton House
Louis Chéron, London, *c.*1695
Oil on plaster, 740 × 680 cm
Buccleuch Collections, Boughton House, Northamptonshire

The subject complements the intended use of the room, the state bedchamber, and the rich colours of the finished ceiling complement the bed hangings. Venus appears to sit upright on entering the room but is perceived as supine on leaving.

LEFT

45 *Jupiter Restraining Arcas from Shooting the Bear Callisto*

Preparatory sketch for ceiling of fourth state room, Boughton House
Louis Chéron, London, *c.*1695
Grey wash over black chalk touched with white on grey paper, 45.5 × 48.5 cm
British Museum, London (1953,1021.11.3)

The ceiling of the fourth state room shows Arcas prevented from shooting his mother, who has been transformed into a bear by the jealous goddess Diana, but Jupiter removes Arcas and Callisto and sets them in the sky as neighbouring constellations. The stars above their heads and Zodiacal belt with the signs for Taurus, Libra, Scorpio and Virgo indicate their ultimate fate.

ABOVE

46 *The Marriage of Hercules and Hebe*

Ceiling of the Great Hall, Boughton House
Louis Chéron, *c.*1706
Oil on plaster, 73 × 1544 cm
Buccleuch Collections, Boughton House, Northamptonshire

Painted after William III's death, the figure of Hercules alludes to Montagu's earlier political allegiance and celebrates his ducal title obtained after the marriage of his son and heir. Brought from earth in Jupiter's four-horse chariot, Hercules was 'set among the glittering stars', rejuvenated and presented with Hebe, the goddess of Youth, as his wife while the gods look on with approval.

The appearance of Hercules on the Great Hall ceiling was intended as an allusion to William III;[28] however, as the scheme was only completed in 1706/7, it reflects Montagu's political activity. During James II's reign (1685–8) Montagu was out of favour at the English court and in political exile in France. The Boughton decorative scheme celebrates the Glorious Revolution: the overthrow of Catholic James II and the triumph of the Protestant William III as King of England. Hercules was often used as a symbol of political strength during William III's reign (1689–1702).[29]

The first triumphal arch erected for William's entry into The Hague on 26 January 1691–2 celebrated the Protestant succession and his strategic marriage. It carried the inscriptions 'Crossing the Seas he delivered Britain where being Honoured with Scepters of large extended power, He is received again into his own country with Publick Joy', and 'He was happily joyned in Wedlock to a Princess descended from an Antient Race of Kings'. A nearby arch was painted with Hercules, Theseus, Phaeton, Perseus and Andromeda, and the coats of arms of England, Scotland, France and Ireland. The entry procession concluded with a festive fireworks display centred on the conjoined letters 'WR' (William Rex), surmounted by a crown and sceptre and flanked by two high pyramids supporting a lion, Hercules and a sun. A contemporary account describes the display:

> *Hercules's Arms were Expanded, firing with Eight several Pauses, to denote his Labours, which were. 1. The Establishment of Religion and Liberty. 2. The securing the Tranquillity of Europe. 3. The Settlement of the Government upon a right Bottom. 4. The Preservation of the Common Interests of the People. 5. The Preservation of Unity amongst the Neighbouring Princes. 6. The clearing of the Sea. 7. The Advancement of the Glory of this State. 8. The concluding of a firm and lasting Peace.*[30]

A comparable political significance informed the scheme at Boughton House. The house was enlarged and decorated to attract a visit from the sovereign. Yet when William III dined there in October 1695 while visiting the Earl of Sunderland at Althorp, the decorative painting was hardly begun. *Discord Throwing an Apple at the Banquet of the Gods* refers to the gradual disintegration of James II's authority and may hint at Montagu's part in the Exclusion Crisis that resulted in his temporary exile in France. *Venus Protesting to Jupiter* and *The Fall of Pyreneus* on the ceilings of the first and second state rooms respectively refer to the downfall of James II; *Mars and Venus Caught in their Net* in the third state room to James's capture; and *Jupiter Restraining Arcus from Shooting the Bear Callisto* in the fourth to his escape to France. William III is thus seen in the roles of Jupiter, Vulcan, Apollo and Hercules, an appropriate tribute to a visiting monarch. In 1698 the Huguenot poet Thomas D'Urfey (1653–1723) exclaimed in his poem *Albion's Blessing*:

> *Thus did Great* WILLIAM *all our ills redress;*
> *Caesar Apollo, Caesar Hercules*[31]

By the next generation the original significance of these paintings had faded. A letter from John, 2nd Duke of Montagu, to William Stukeley (1687–1765), 4 January 1744/5 is written from Ditton Park, where flowery banks inspire an image of Hebe, the Goddess of Youth crowned with flowers:

> *You remember her figure is in the ceiling of my hall at Boughton, which figure some philosophers imagine was formed there by the steams of your toasts daily repeated here, and ascending from the table towards the heavens; which if they had not been stopped by the ceiling, would have formed a better or finer constellation than that of Andromeda; but not being able to make their way through the roof of the Hall they condensed themselves into the figure of Hebe in the ceiling.*[32]

By 1832 the Great Hall ceiling was listed in the Boughton House inventory as 'the fall of Phaeton and Juna commencing her reign' and misattributed to Antonio Verrio. Over the fireplace 'a Basso Relievo … Representing the Infernal Regions, with the figures of Envy Malice and an Infernal Angel bringing down a Mortal' may have represented Alcestis being led to the Underworld by Death, whence she was rescued by Hercules (Euripedes, *Alcestis*).[33] This overmantel was executed in plaster rather than marble, possibly by Gideon du Chesne, who in 1705 replaced the earl's coronet with a ducal one above the Montagu coat of arms on the cornice.[34] The overmantel, destroyed when the panelling in the Great Hall was replaced in 1910, originally formed an appropriate juxtaposition with the scene on the ceiling, *The Apotheosis of Hercules*.[35] William Stukeley believed that Hercules and Hebe were classical prototypes for Adam and Eve. He wrote to the 2nd Duke of Montagu:

RIGHT

47 *Loves of the Gods*

Drawings of two painted panels
Daniel Marot, London, *c.*1690
Pen and ink with traces of pencil, 40 × 12.2 cm
Victoria and Albert Museum, London (8480.6–7)

These drawings, annotated by Marot with the original colours, relate to two from a set of five panels at Boughton, originally from Montagu House. Inscriptions indicate colours used, which, apart from some minor differences, match the Boughton panels.

FAR RIGHT

48 *Apollo and Daphne*

Painted wall panels
Unidentified French artists, *c.*1670
Oil on canvas, 223.7 × 177.5 cm
Buccleuch Collections, Boughton House, Northamptonshire

Painted in oil on canvas, the panels are framed in stone-colour bolection moulding. The central vignettes show two versions of Apollo and Daphne. Other scenes, appropriate decoration for a dressing room or closet, represent Diana and Endymion, Diana bathing, Venus and Adonis, Jupiter and Io and the Triumph of Galatea.

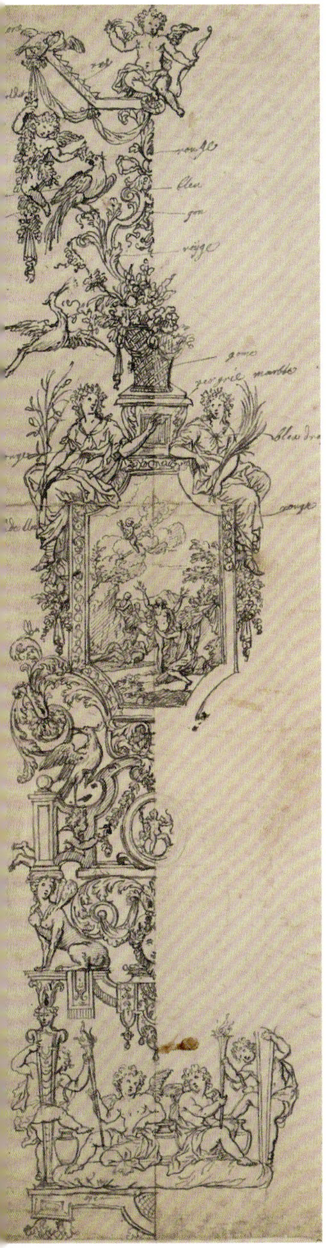

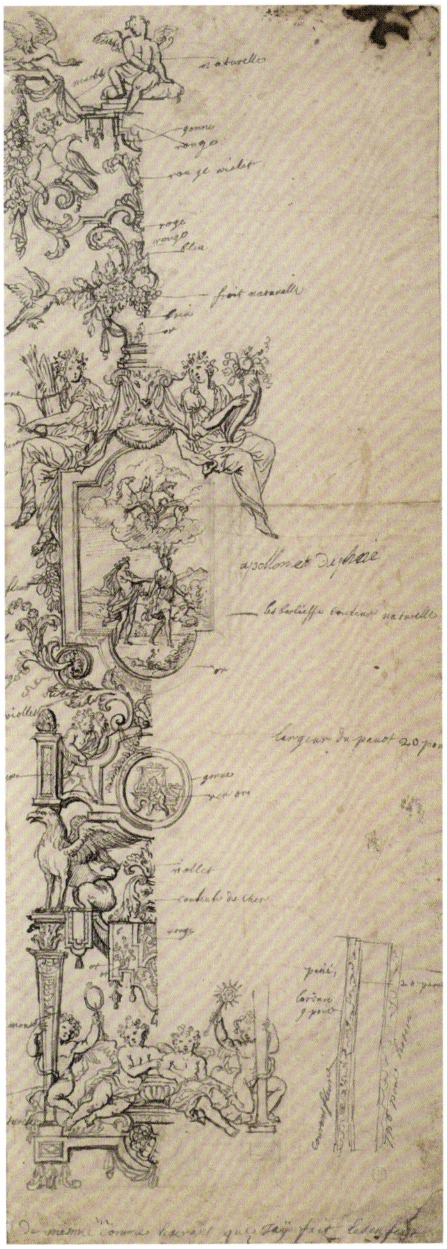

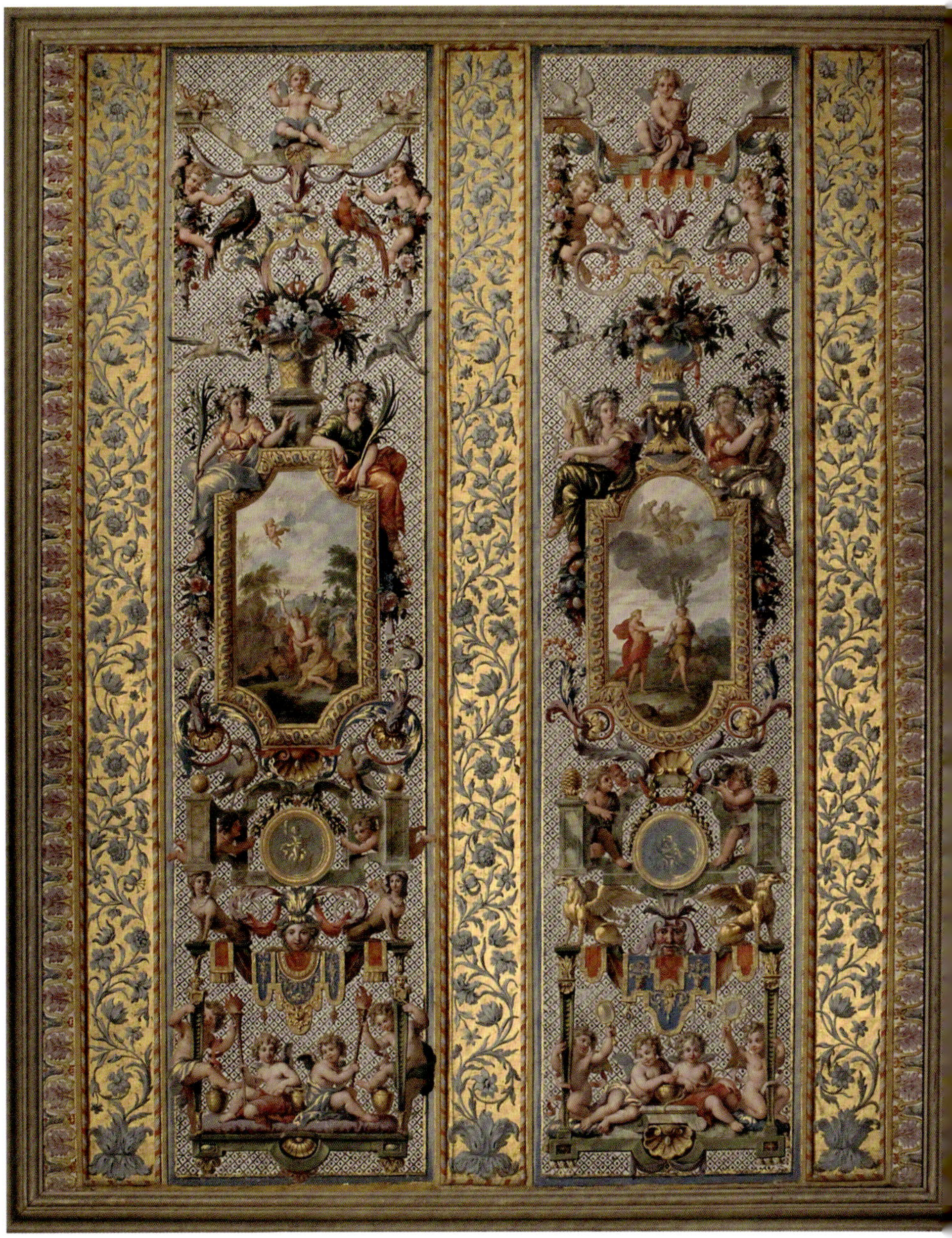

> *The heathen mythology has preserv'd the history of this transaction, in the Story of the Marriage of Hercules and Hebe: which the masterly hand of Cheron has so elegantly painted in your Grace's hall at Boughton, under the name of the most antient Hercules, our father Adam is really understood: Hebe is* EVE.[36]

These compositions were carefully prepared by Louis Chéron. His preliminary studies include *Cupid and Psyche before the Assembled Gods* for the first state room or the Little Hall, *Discord Throwing an Apple at the Banquet of the Gods* for the staircase ceiling (plate 38), *Jupiter Restraining Arcas* (plate 45) for the fourth state room and *Mars and Venus Caught in their Net by Vulcan* (plate 44) for the third state room.[37] In *The Marriage of Hercules and Hebe* on the Great Hall ceiling (plate 46) the dramatic contrast between the curtain of night drawn back to reveal the brilliance of daylight brought by Apollo and his chariot is inspired by Le Brun's ceiling of the Galerie d'Apollon in the Louvre, Paris.

Chéron only achieved limited recognition as a decorative painter. He mastered drawing and composition, but used harsh blues, reds and yellows, inherited from Charles Le Brun, Simon Vouet (1590–1649) and Sébastian Bourdon. Vertue put it kindly: 'his manner of colouring being not so agreable, and as at Rome that is not thought so valuable or estimable as designing (so he had not sufficiently studyed that part).'[38] At Boughton Chéron stands on his own merit; but at Chatsworth, where he spent the summer of 1700 painting panels in the gallery,[39] his work invites comparison with Verrio, Laguerre and Thornhill. Four of the Chatsworth panels represent scenes from *Il Pastor Fido*, a classic Venetian tragicomedy published in 1590, which by 1700 had been translated into French; Chéron was probably familiar with one of the French editions (1676 and 1686). Set in Arcadia, the plot revolves around the loves of descendants of gods and local inhabitants – an ideal country house subject.[40]

The ceiling of the Chatsworth theatre supports 17 panels, some attributed to Chéron.[41] He was paid £40 on 23 August 1700 for painting 'the ceiling of the little dineing roome' and £30 on 14 September for painting the Bowling Green House ceiling. Neither survives. Panels on the theatre ceiling came originally from the library and the billiard room. One of these, which represents the west front of Chatsworth House, has been attributed to Chéron,[42] but the small figure of Venus in a chariot pulled by putti in the foreground lacks his convincing draughtsmanship. In 1688–9, a Mr Bisket, or Birchet, was paid £45 for a 'perspective',[43] so an attribution to Pierre Berchet is possible. The panels representing the story of Andromeda and landscapes are attributed to Thornhill.[44]

Nicholas Heude (fl.1672–1703) paid £20 on 22 March 1689 'for worke to be done at Chatsworth' may be the 'french Painter' for whose diet the housekeeper was given 15s 'when he came to take the Prospect of Chatsworth House'.[45] Heude was excluded from the Paris Academy in 1672 'pour s'etre tabli en Angleterre sans le permission Du Roi',[46] but was later elected a full member and submitted a 'tableau de reception', *The Apotheosis of the Prince de Condé* (now at Versailles). Back in England, Heude worked with Antonio Verrio. He painted the staircase of Viscount Tyrconnel's house in Arlington Street, London, and decorated ceilings at Bulstrode Park, Buckinghamshire, for the Lord Chancellor, George, 1st Baron Jeffreys (1645–1689). Among 'the inhabitants of the four parts of the World, Indians East & West – Asians – Africans Europeans' in the Bulstrode drawing room was Heude's self-portrait, 'the head of the Painter with his Palet in his hand'.[47] Heude later worked for William Douglas, 1st Duke of Queensberry (1637–1695), at Drumlanrig Castle, in 1692 painting overmantels on leather of biblical and secular subjects, some of which still survive *in situ*.[48] Heude died at Queensberry House in College Wynd, Edinburgh, in 1703.

Daniel Marot's chief role was that of designer. Sets of etchings republished in the Netherlands *c.*1712 include designs for decorative panels (plate 48). Annotated drawings by Marot relate to five panels at Boughton House, originally from Montagu House (plate 47). The panels were probably a team effort, the fruit and flowers by Monnoyer, mythological scenes by De la Fosse, and *trompe-l'œil* frames by Rousseau. If this is the case, and the panels were painted in London and not imported from France, they must have been begun before De la Fosse returned to Paris in December 1691. A second series of 15 panels, also at Boughton, attributed to Mark Anthony Hauduroy (fl.1720s) relate to etchings in Marot's first and second *Livre d'Ornemens* (plates 49, 50).

The Hauduroys were architects and painters. Samuel Hauduroy (fl.1691–7), who is recorded at the Threadneedle Street church in 1691,[49] designed the garden front of Dyrham Park, Avon (plate 68), where his relative, another Mr Hauduroy, painted the Balcony Room overlooking the garden and other interiors, in imitation of three different types of marble and exotic hardwoods.[50] This was probably Louis Hauduroy (fl.1689–1713), an elder at the French Savoy church in 1689,[51] who painted the staircase at Culverthorpe Hall, Lincolnshire in 1704–5.[52] At Dyrham the 'Pavillion, Family Parlour, Great Parlour, Great Stayres, Slope Chamber and closet', and the chamber over the servants rooms, were painted 'Walnutt colour' to match the staircase designed by Samuel Hauduroy; the servants' quarters and nursery were painted 'umber'. 'Wainscott colour' was applied to passages, the parlour closet, the hall and pavilion doors; 'Cedar colour' was used in the Great Hall, the slope closet, the church rooms, the stairs and passage leading to the church, the dining room and closet and the lobby. The old parlour lobby was painted cream and the summer house was painted to imitate marble. The walls of one bedroom resembled 'Princes Wood'.[53] Just as walls painted with history subjects were cheaper than tapestry, a skilled house painter could simulate different textures of wood and stone, which was cheaper and much easier to organize and eliminated the cost of buying and transporting wood and marble – as well as the expense of employing joiners to make panelling. Hauduroy also supplied and applied gold leaf.

The Mr Hauduroy employed by Anthony Grey, 11th Earl of Kent (1645–1702), at Wrest Park, Bedfordshire, *c.*1712, 'for painting ye figures in the

RIGHT

49 Design for decorative panels

From the second *Livre d'Ornemens*, republished *c.*1712
Daniel Marot, Amsterdam, *c.*1703
Etching, cut to 27.1 × 18.6 cm
Victoria and Albert Museum, London (E.1672:10–1888)

The painter of the set of panels, *c.*1720, from Montagu House, Bloomsbury now at Boughton House, Northamptonshire, copied Marot's designs for ornamental panels republished earlier that decade.

FAR RIGHT

50 Painted wall panels incorporating the Garter badge of John, 2nd Duke of Montagu

From Montagu House, Bloomsbury
Attributed to Mark Anthony Hauduroy, *c.*1720
Oil on canvas, 300 × 75.3 cm
Buccleuch Collections, Boughton House, Northamptonshire

These panels, from a second set which lined a cabinet room at Montagu House, Bloomsbury are inspired by Daniel Marot's published ornament designs, but personalized with the armorials of the 2nd Duke of Montagu and his wife, Mary Churchill. They are attributed to Mark Anthony Hauduroy, whose family were designers and artists employed at Dyrham, Knole and Wrest Park.

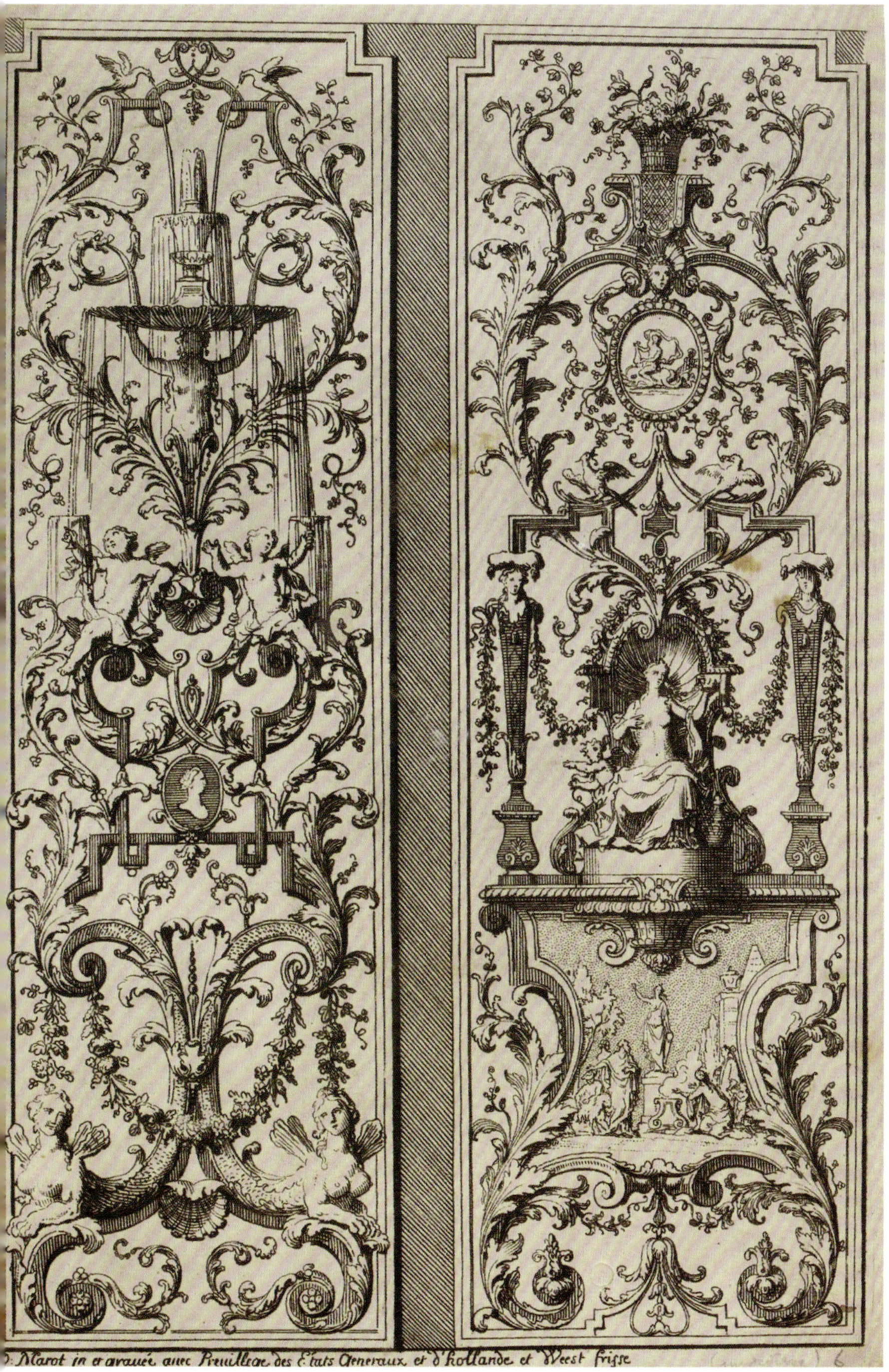

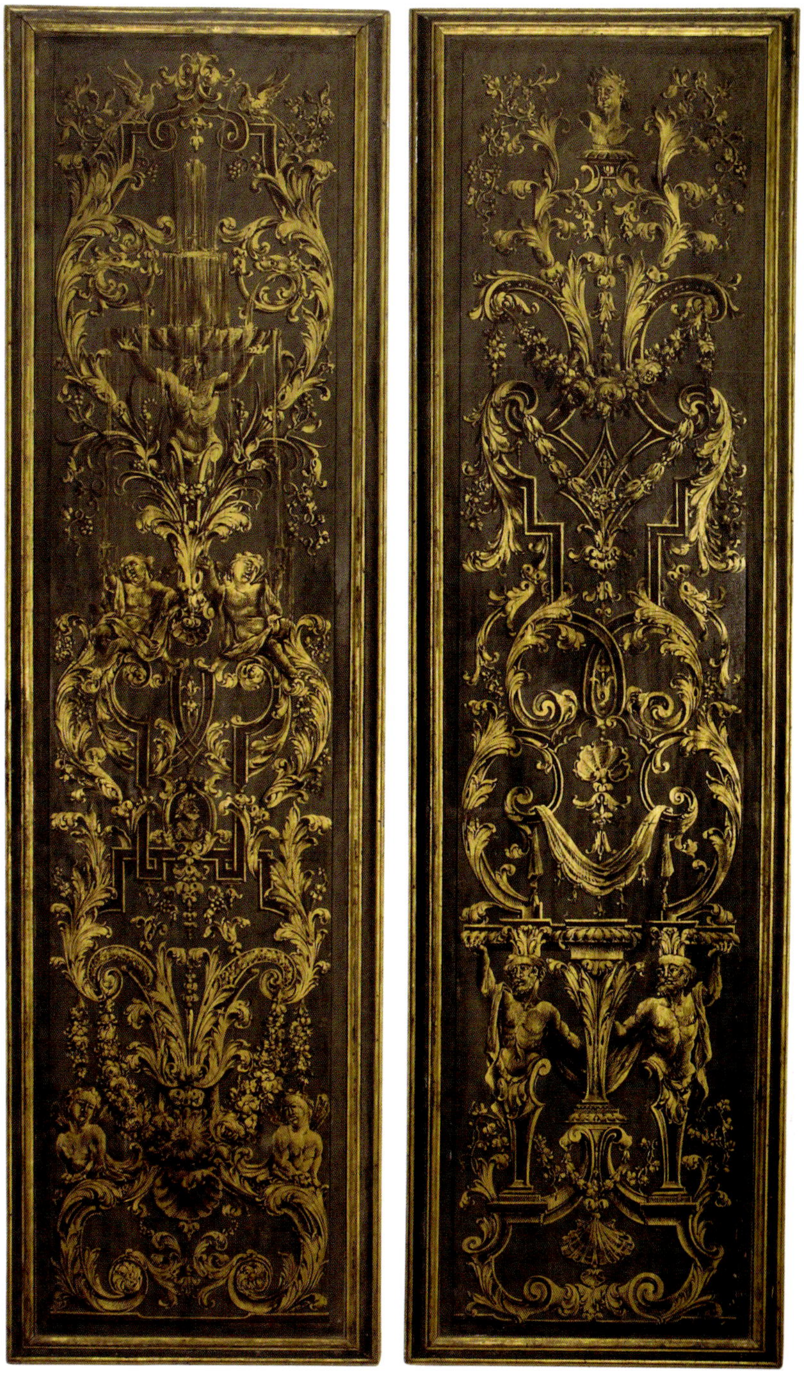

niches at 30s each and for gilding all ye sashes of ye windows' for Cain Hill House,[54] is probably Louis Hauduroy, who witnessed the marriage of Louise Hauduroy in September 1713.[55] The younger artist, Mark Anthony Hauduroy, was working at Knole, Kent, in the 1720s and back at Wrest Park in the 1730s.[56] The painted feature is seen in John Rocque's 1735 'PLAN & VIEW of the BUILDINGS & GARDEN AT REST the seat of his Grace the DUKE of KENT', which includes a plan and the 'West Prospect' of Cain Hill House.[57] Mark Anthony Hauduroy was paid another £110 for painting the 'Great Room' of the Banqueting House designed by Thomas Archer (1668–1743).[58]

Cain Hill House has been demolished but the Banqueting House and the paintings in its Great Room survive, although much restored. The inscription 'HAUDROY PINXIT 1712 [?]' can be seen above the doors inside, and on the door in the third bay to the left on entering the building.[59] The registers of the French church in Berwick Street, Soho, record close connections between the artist and his patron: John, 1st Earl of Ashburnham (1687–1737), was married to the Duke of Kent's

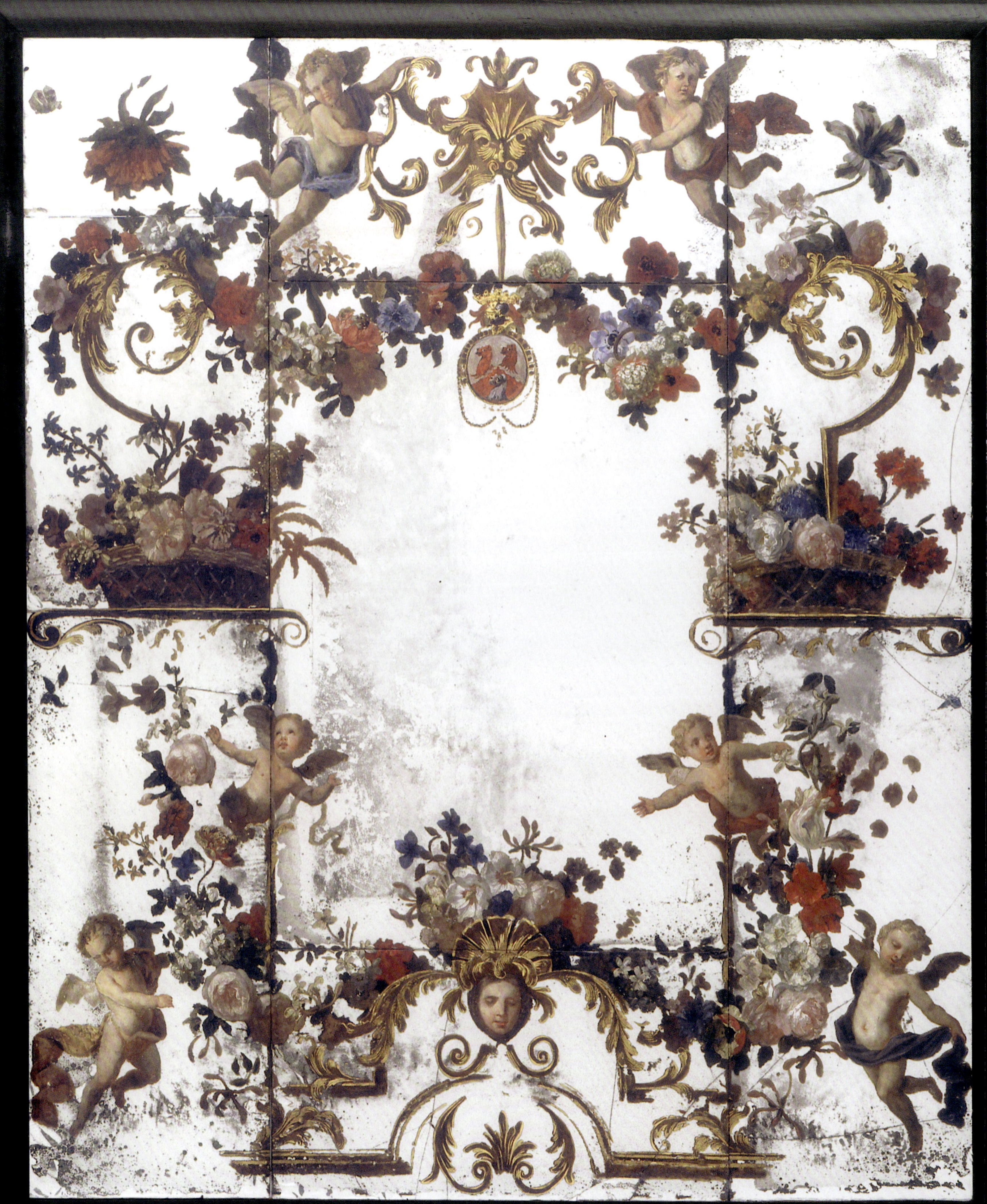

51 Painted looking glass

Antoine Monnoyer, London, 1710–20
Oil on glass, 186 × 158.5 × 6 cm, including frame and mirror plates
Victoria and Albert Museum, London (W.36:1-3-1934)

Elected a full member of the Paris Royal Academy of Painting in 1704, Antoine, son of Jean-Baptiste Monnoyer, shared his father's tradition of flower painting. This genre was continued by the French artist Andien de Clermont, who worked in Britain from 1739 to 1750.

eldest daughter, Lady Jemima Grey; in 1740 she and her younger sister, Lady Mary, stood godparents to Hauduroy's daughter, who was appropriately named Marie Jemima.[60]

An account for work at Knole in Mark Anthony Hauduroy's handwriting dated June 1724 reads:

for ten panells of ornements £12.12.0,
for 3 long panells too by the Chimny an(d) on by ye window £7.10.0.
for mending of a grate panell betwin the windows on under the window
and three little ons £2.5.0.
for gildin mendin and clening of ye ca.rvin and other things £2.10.0.
totall £24.17.0.
for twice coming downe £ 2.2.0.
for mendin ye pictures £ 2.2.0.
£29.1.0.[61]

Hauduroy had evidently been working at Knole for the best part of a year, as another document signed by him, dated 17 June 1723, reads: 'Recd of the Duke of Dorset six Guineas in full for copying his picture'. His work at Knole included painting the back staircase in grisaille with trophies

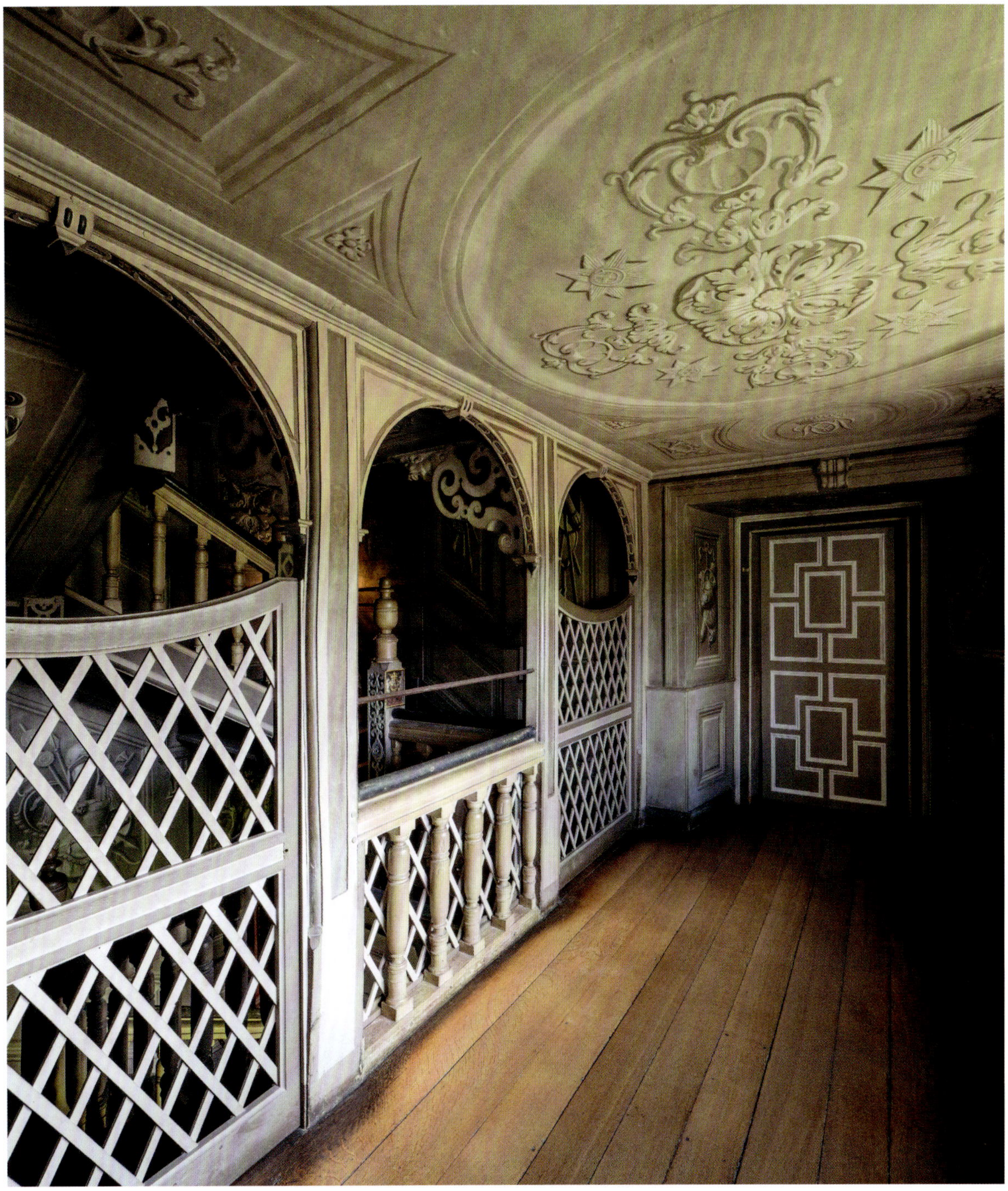

52 The Painted Staircase landing, Knole

Mark Anthony Hauduroy, *c.*1724
Oil on plaster
National Trust

Hauduroy's work at Knole includes the walls and soffits of the back staircase painted in grisaille with trophies, weapons and the coat of arms and cypher of the 1st Duke of Dorset. The staircase provides direct access to the State Rooms from the Colonnade Room.

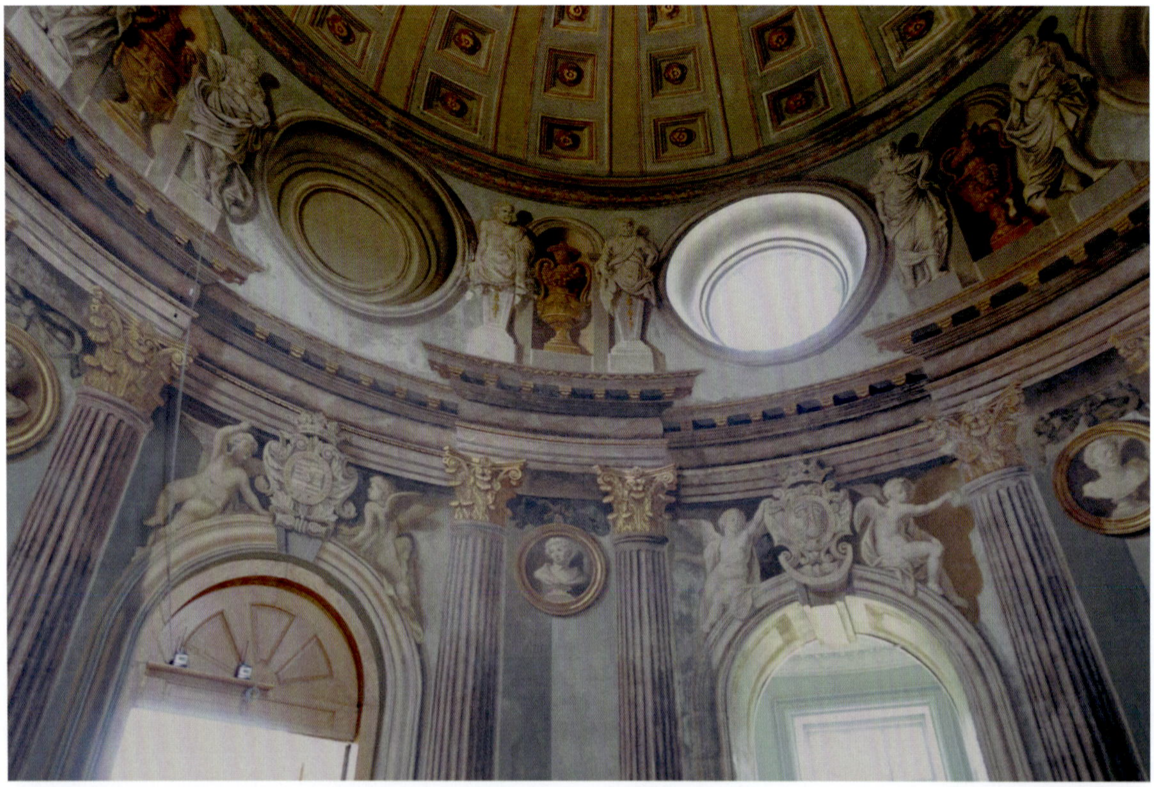

53 Decorative painting in the Banqueting House, Wrest Park, Bedfordshire

Mark Anthony Hauduroy, 1728–38
Oil on plaster
English Heritage

Decorated in brown, white and gold, six *trompe-l'œil* windows alternate with round windows separated by terms and female figures flanking vases in niches. Below cornice level, putti flank the Kent family crest, coat of arms and motto, above round-headed window and door openings, interspersed with six classical busts painted in grisaille within gold frames.

(plate 52), weapons and the coat of arms and cypher of Lionel Sackville, 1st Duke of Dorset (1688–1765). The Colonnade Room at the foot of these stairs is painted with niches containing urns, a variation of the Wrest Park Banqueting House scheme (plate 53). The 1724 account refers to Hauduroy's work in the King's Room at Knole, where the painted dado panelling and window reveals can still be admired. In August 1735 he worked with Gaetano Brunetti (d.1758) colouring and gilding the dressing-room ceiling in the Cavendish Square town house of the 1st Duke of Chandos (1673–1744).[62]

Decorative painting on cloth could be prepared in the studio and then applied as wall covering. Daniel Finch, 2nd Earl of Nottingham, noted that 'The painting upn cloth at my Ld James Russel's in Lincoln's Inn Fields contains between 150 and 160 yards, was painted by Messrs Hoddery for £100 and found cloth was at my Lord's charges';[63] he planned to use this method to decorate the staircase at Burley-on-the-Hill, Rutland, contemporary with Dyrham Park. 'Messrs Hoddery' implies the same team of architect and decorative painter, Samuel and Louis Hauduroy, who worked for William Blathwayt. Yet Mark Anthony was younger than the architect Samuel Hauduroy and he may have worked in England in the 1720s on a temporary basis. Mark Anthony's reconnaissance (in which he produced evidence for his commitment to the Huguenot faith through previous membership to a Huguenot church) is dated 12 April 1739: here he promises 'de demeurer à l'avenir fidellement attaché aux principes de la religion reformée qu'il a succez avec le lait, et a été admis à la participation de la Ste Cene'.[64]

René Feillet (d.1736), a Huguenot history painter based in Clerkenwell,[65] was the brother-in-law of Pierre Champion de Crespigny (1653–1739),[66] founding director of the French Hospital, then also in Clerkenwell. The war with France meant that the 1740s saw little new building in Britain, so there was limited demand for decorative painting. Buildings in Palladian style, with its more rigid classical rules, could only accommodate panel decoration.

The marine artist Peter Monamy (1681–1749), born in London, whose father, Pierre (b. *c.*1650), came from Guernsey,[67] is probably connected to François Monamy (fl.1698), recorded in Stonehouse, Plymouth, in 1698 as from Meschers-sur-Gironde, France.[68] Peter Monamy was apprenticed to a house painter in London from 1696, became free of the Painters Stainers' Company in 1703 and in 1726 advanced to the Livery (the senior category of membership, with its distinguishing fur-edged gown). He was probably based in Cork in the 1710s. Two of his paintings for the supper-boxes at Vauxhall Gardens, representing recent naval engagements (*The Algerine Pirates*) and maritime themes (*Sweet William's Farewell*), were engraved by Paul Fourdrinier (1698–1758; plate 76) and sold by Thomas Bowles in 1743.[69] Monamy was elected a Governor and Guardian of the Foundling Hospital on 31 December 1746.[70]

William De La Cour probably came from Ireland, as a Huguenot family of that name settled in Cork. He was in London by 1740, when he created stage designs for *Busiri*, an opera by Giovanni Battista Pescetti (1704–1766) at the King's Theatre, Haymarket.[71] By 1757 De La Cour was designing stage scenery in Edinburgh. He painted a 'new wood scene' for *Douglas*, a play by John Home (1722–1808), and on 18 January 1759 the *Edinburgh Evening Courant* described the production of *The Orphan of China* by Voltaire (1684–1778): 'The whole appearance of the stage will be entirely new, the scenery, dresses and decorations designed and painted for the occasion by Mons. De La Cour.' In 1758 the architect John Adam (1721–1792) employed De La Cour to decorate a room in Lord Milton's house in Canongate, Edinburgh; in October that year the artist provided an estimate for 'painting a large room for his Lordship's house in Canongate, in arabesques agreable to a sketch'. This entailed 193 yards (176.5 m) of panelling with the 'finest green' and white paint in nut oil, enriching in gold 1,660 ft (506 m) of moulding 'in Cornishes, freezes, Architraves and frets and

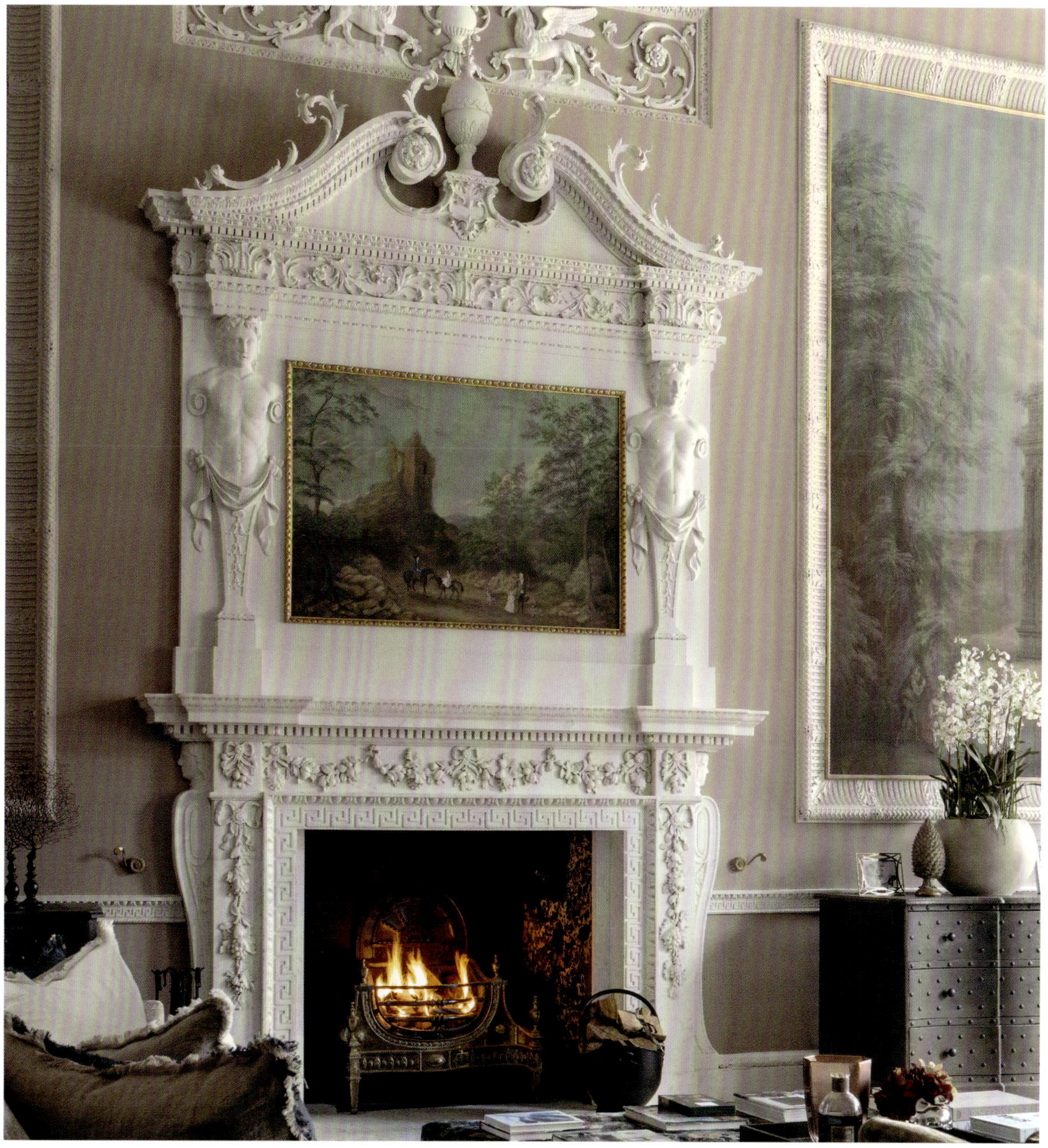

54 Panels painted with arcadian landscapes in imitation of tapestry
William De La Cour, *c.*1760
Oil on canvas
Yester House, East Lothian, Scotland

De La Cour painted scenery for theatres in London, Edinburgh and Newcastle. Robert Adam commissioned this series of arcadian landscapes for the ballroom at Yester House for the Marquess of Tweeddale. The fireplace is framed by scenes of a triumphal arch and pyramids, while the view at the end features Corinthian columns.

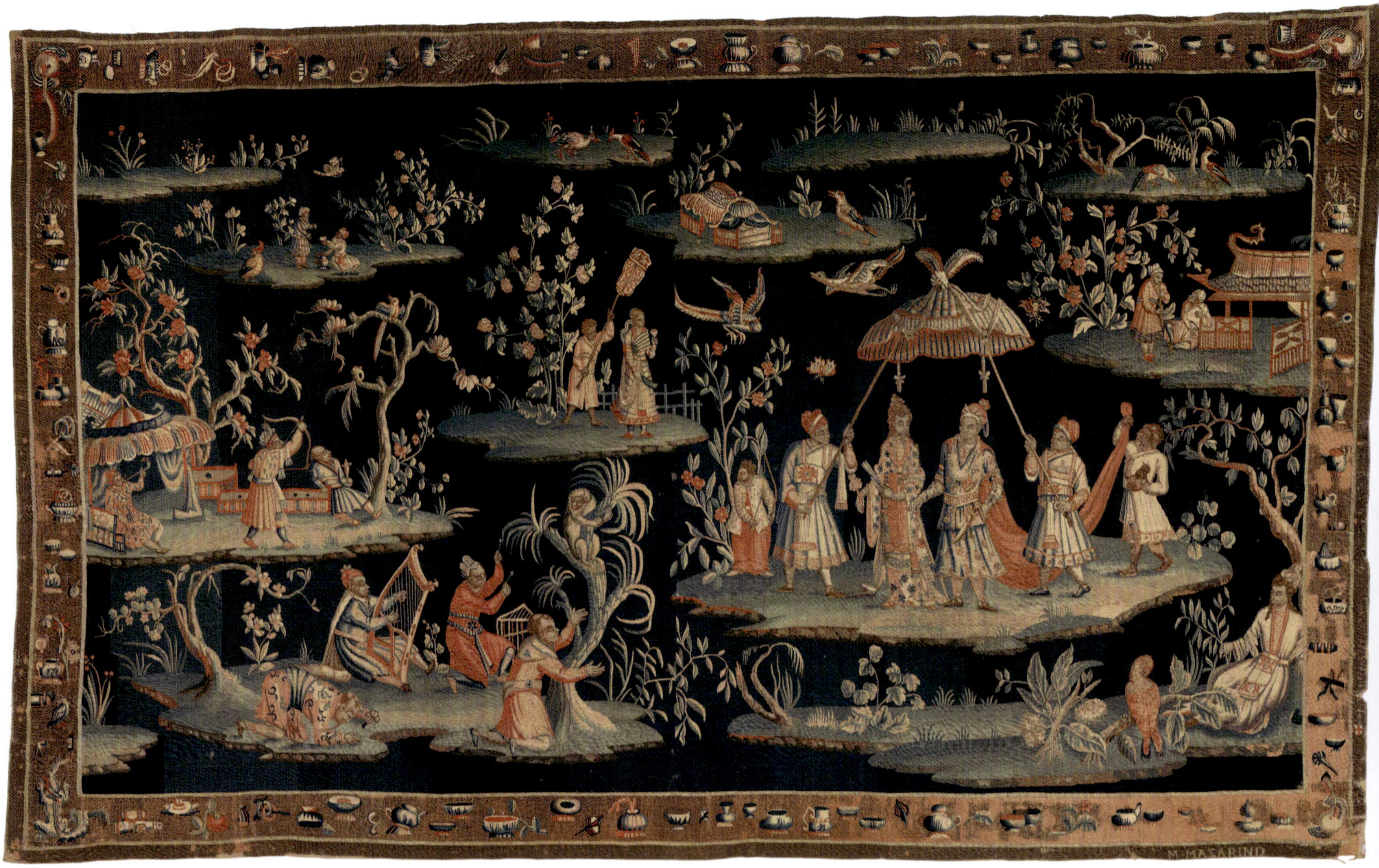

pannels of the doors windows, Bates and Surbates, small and large'. De La Cour asserted that his price of £120 18s 10d was 'moderate': at such low prices he could 'only paint for fame and therefore hopes they wont be established as any precedent'.[72] On completion, this interior was admired by fellow artist Allan Ramsay. John Adam's younger brother, architect Robert Adam (1728–1792), employed De La Cour to decorate the ballroom at Yester House in East Lothian. Here eight panels are filled with oil paintings on canvas of landscapes imitating tapestry; five are signed and dated 'DELACOUR Pinxit 1761' (plate 54).

Tapestry and decorative painting are closely allied. Antonio Verrio originally came to London to design cartoons for the Mortlake Tapestry Factory;[73] 'some small paintings' made by Laguerre 'on Cloath by Order from Queen Anne' were 'designes for Tapestry to be made, wherein was represented. the Queen & ministers of state & several persons of quality concerned in the Union of Scotland'.[74] One of the most prestigious decorative schemes, the Escalier des Ambassadeurs in the Palace of Versailles designed by Charles Le Brun, was painted in 1679–80 by Adam Frans van der Meulen (1632–1690) with scenes of Louis XIV's military campaigns imitating tapestry.[75]

Decorative painting was often accompanied by tapestry. The Boughton House 1718 inventory lists 'three pieces of fine tapestry hangings … history of the Apostles' after Raphael's cartoons woven at the Mortlake factory (owned by Ralph Montagu from 1674 to 91).[76] These lined the walls of the state bedchamber, where Chéron's *Mars and Venus Caught in their Net by Vulcan* decorated the ceiling (plate 44).

Royal Wardrobe accounts include payments to 'arras workers', including a Mr Demay. By 1689 John Vanderbank was chief arras maker and by 1698 the tapestry works moved from dilapidated

55 Tapestry in the Indian manner

Michael Mazarind, London, *c.*1700
Wool and silk, 234 × 392 cm
Victoria and Albert Museum, London (T.1601–2017)

The taste for Indian manner tapestries was established by Queen Mary at Kensington Palace. The small scale of the figures complemented the smaller repeats of luxurious furnishing fabrics and provided more delicate diversion intended to appeal to ladies.

Mortlake buildings, which closed in 1703, to Great Queen Street, Lincoln's Inn Fields.[77] Vanderbank (d.1717), of Flemish descent, came to London from Paris but was not related to Peter Vandrebanc the Huguenot engraver and is often confused with his eldest son, the artist John Vanderbank (co-founder of the St Martin's Lane Academy, plate 31). Vanderbank the elder features in Montagu's private accounts as a supplier and repairer of tapestry between 1695 and 1700, when Louis Chéron was working at Boughton House.[78] On John Vanderbank's death the Soho Tapestry works were managed by his widow, Sarah, and inherited on her death in 1727 by their younger son, Moses Vanderbank, in partnership with the painter John Ellys.[79] Both Moses and John Ellys attended the St Martin's Lane Academy from 1720 to 1724.

By 1700 Stephen Demay, possibly connected with the Demay who worked at the Mortlake works during the 1670s, had established his own manufactory in London. Huguenot church registers describe Demay as 'Tapestry maker at the corner house of Spring Gardens over against ye French Chapel', an annexe of the French Savoy church.[80] A letter from Demay to Lord Nottingham dated 7 September 1701 requests the 'Dimensions of the Months for I have several men that play for wanting of work which is a charge to me'. A later letter refers to the additions to the apostle hangings and requests payment of £142,[81] 'wich I begg ye favour of Your Lordship to be so kind as to send it to mee I being in soe great want of it that I am forced to send mans away for wanting of money therefore I hope your Lordship will have pitty of me'. The total bill 'for ten pieces of the Apostle hangings' came to £758. In 1707–8 Demay received a further £130 for supplying hangings of Hero and Leander. The Mr Demay who supplied '3 peaces of new hangings for the Queen of Scotts Chamber' at Chatsworth was no doubt the same person.[82]

A recent acquisition by the Victoria and Albert Museum is an 'Indian manner' tapestry (plate 55) signed 'M. Mazarind', a tapestry weaver established on the South Side of Portugal Street, Piccadilly, from 1696–1702.[83] The small-figure chinoiserie style is similar to those supplied in 1700 by Leonard Chabaneix (d.1708/9) for Melville House, Fife.[84] The only other known reference to this maker in England[85] is a payment of £118 made to Mazarind by William III's Groom of the Bedchamber Henry Sydney, 1st Earl of Romney (1641–1704), dated 1700–1. The market for tapestry was strong. Other Huguenot tapestry weavers in Soho included Elie Barraband (b. *c.*1656), working in Soho between 1690 and 1705, and Joseph Couloudon (fl.1705–32), who died in the French Hospital in 1734; both had Huguenot tapestry weaving relatives in Berlin.[86]

Painting was a cheaper solution than tapestry for wall decoration. Architectural settings in the Palladian and Neoclassical styles called for panel decoration. British tapestry manufactures competed with prestigious artist-designed tapestries produced at the French Beauvais and Gobelins factories, despite the heavy duty payable, which patrons resented. The Duke of Devonshire petitioned for a reduction of tariff on imported tapestries.[87] In 1723 the Huguenot Jacob Christoph Le Blon (1667–1741), better known for his treatise on coloured printing processes, *Coloritto*, attempted to apply the same principles to tapestry weaving.[88] However, in 1732, when his new company faced bankruptcy, he returned to Paris, concealing his true faith.[89]

Huguenot decorative painters introduced the French style of mural decoration into British interiors. Under the supervision of a designer or architect they worked as a team, which might include a specialist architectural and landscape painter, a flower painter, a figure painter and a gilder. Huguenot artists, exemplified by the Hauduroy family, provided ornamental decoration in the Italian tradition via the school of Fontainebleau, and representational 'History' painting practised by Louis Chéron and other academic artists in the tradition of Charles Le Brun.[90]

The formal artistic training from which Huguenot decorative artists had benefited in France was not available in England until 1711. As decorative painting was the main outlet for history painters during the period 1680–1760, academic training empowered these Huguenot artists to complete such challenging commissions. The enormous scale of decorative painting and its heavy demands on the artist or team of artists involved meant that book illustration and teaching offered them light relief and further employment. The Huguenot contribution to decorative painting should thus be seen in the context of these artists' other achievements.

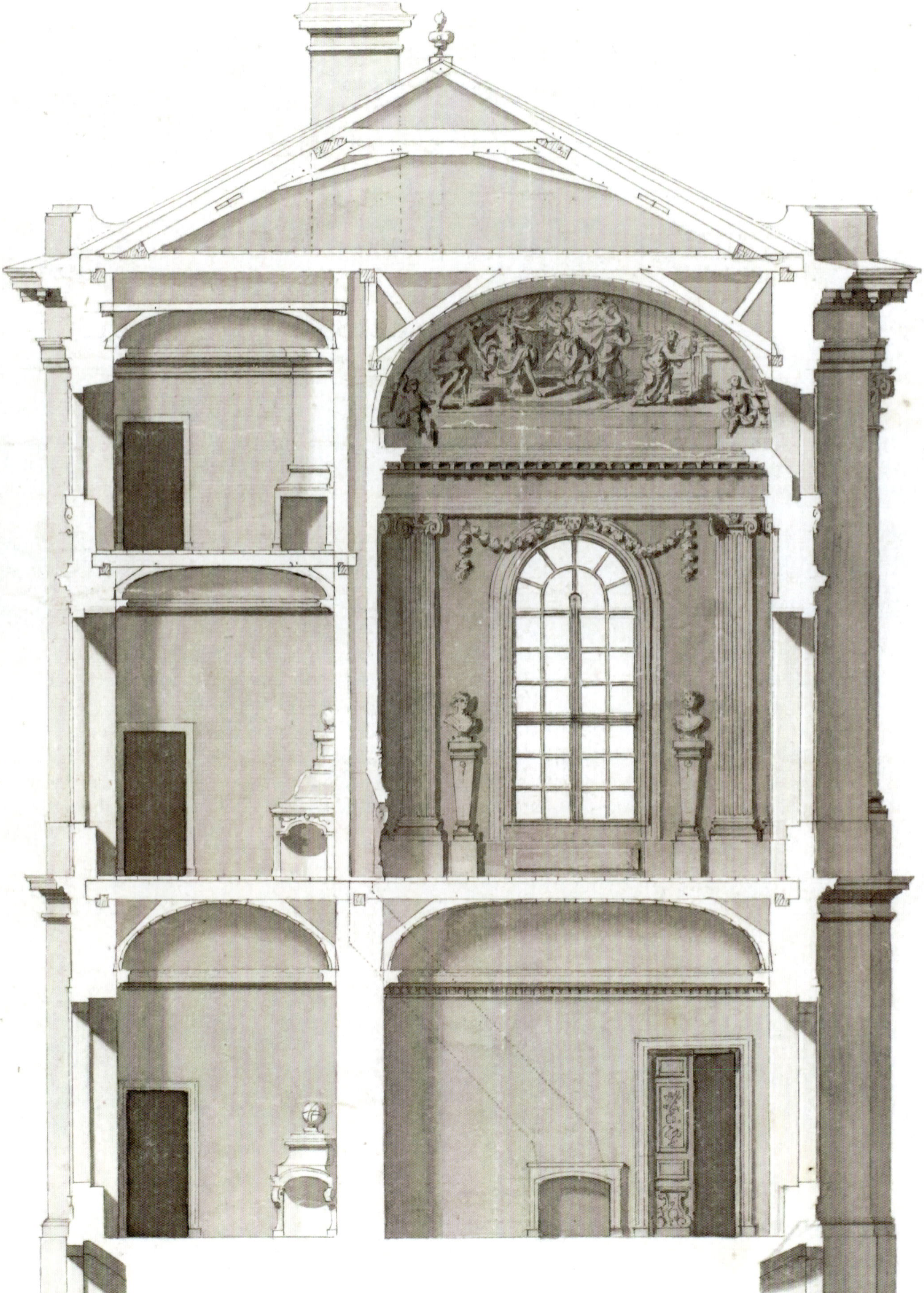

Chapter Five
Huguenot Architects & Engineers

56 Lateral cross-section of the Gallery and adjoining rooms, Wentworth Castle
Jean de Bodt, *c.*1709
Pen, ink and watercolour, 22.8 × 25 cm
Victoria and Albert Museum, London (E.307-1937)

Designed in Berlin for British Ambassador Lord Raby, this design for Raby's castle shows the grand gallery across the North East Front which commanded views of the Yorkshire setting. De Bodt includes corner chimney-pieces in adjacent smaller rooms and indicates ceiling decoration and portrait busts on pedestals flanking the giant pilasters.

The most significant Huguenot contribution to British architecture was in engineering. It was to France that the rest of Europe looked for expertise in engineering and military fortifications: French-trained Huguenot engineers, with experience in the Low Countries creating canals and dykes, and military fortifications, found acclaim in Britain and Ireland. First-generation Huguenot architects working in the French style, Daniel Marot and Jean de Bodt (1670–1745), contributed to English Baroque architecture and interior design, but by 1715, Italian-inspired Neo-Palladianism was dominant. Marot and Bodt settled in Holland and Berlin respectively, where the French Baroque tradition was still in demand. In Britain, second generation Huguenot architects seeking employment adapted their skills to the Palladian style. Huguenot architects and engineers channelled their experience and talent into whatever style or commission was required.

Huguenot architectural carvers and decorators usually followed the dictates of the presiding architect, but absence abroad, as with Bodt, demanded the presence of an experienced surveyor or inspector of buildings, an authoritative role carried out by Jacques Rousseau and Pierre Silvestre for Ralph, 1st Duke of Montagu. Exceptionally, some craftsmen, including Gideon du Chesne and Henri Nadauld, sometimes worked to their own designs. Their efforts added considerable vitality and interest to the architectural context; they deserve more recognition.

Royal patronage

From the sixteenth century the French architectural profession encompassed engineering, that is, the scientific as well as the decorative aspects of building that relied on painters, plasterers, stonemasons and carvers in wood and stone. Leading royal architects Philibert de l'Orme (1514–1570) and Jean Bullant (*c.*1515–1578) were trained as stone cutters. Despite periods of persecution, Protestant architects and engineers sustained roles at the French court. Jean Baptiste Androuët du Cerceau served Henri II and Henri III, and in 1578, six years after the Massacre of St Bartholomew in Paris, was appointed royal architect there. He oversaw the building of foundations for the Pont Neuf, which linked the Ile-de-la-Cité to both banks of the Seine. His father, Jaques I Androuët du Cerceau (1510–1585), and brother Jacques II Androuët du Cerceau (*c.*1550–1614) also enjoyed royal patronage. Jacques I's *Premier Livre d'architecture contenant les plans et dessaigns de cinquante bastiments tous differens* (1559) was the first practical French handbook, providing models for masons and architects and a picture book for patrons;[1] his *Les Plus Excellent Bastiments de France* (1576–9) was dedicated to Queen Catherine de Médicis.[2] The elder Du Cerceau is a key figure in the production of illustrated books on architecture;

his grandson Salomon de Brosse served as engineer to Queen Marie de Médicis from 1601 and became Architecte du Roi to Louis XIII in 1614.[3] De Brosse's design for the Luxembourg Palace was executed between 1615 and 1624. The Temple at Charenton, outside Paris, rebuilt to his designs (plate 11), had a profound influence on later church and synagogue architecture in Northern Europe and beyond, including Christopher Wren's designs for City churches. Inspired by Vitruvius's description of the Roman basilica at Fano, de Brosse's Temple at Charenton was engraved by Jean Marot (1619–1679) in the 1670s.[4]

Salomon de Caus, originally from Dieppe and in Italy from 1595, worked in the Netherlands for Albert, Archduke of Austria, for 12 years, where he met the young Henry, Prince of Wales. In 1610 de Caus joined Henry's household as drawing master and designed the Gallery at Richmond Palace, outside London. His *La Perspective, avec la raison des ombres et miroirs* (1612), the first book on that subject published in England, was dedicated to Prince Henry.[5] De Caus's second book, *Les Raisons des forces mouvantes* (1615) included garden designs for the Prince of Wales. De Caus also designed gardens at Greenwich Palace, Hatfield House and Gorhambury in Hertfordshire.[6]

De Caus's most important work, the gardens at Heidelberg Castle, were created after 1613 for Prince Henry's brother-in-law, Elector Frederick V of the Palatine.[7] A model of Frederick V's electoral territory, this is the most important Mannerist garden north of the Alps. In 1620 Salomon returned to France as Louis XIII's engineer; he designed fountains and supervised the cleaning of Paris streets and squares. His last book, *La Pratique et démonstration des horloges solaires*, appeared in 1624.

Salomon's son or nephew, Isaac, worked in London from 1623, constructing grottos in the Whitehall Banqueting House and the Parnassus for Somerset House, London.[8] As architect to Francis Russell, 4th Earl of Bedford (1587–1641), Isaac de Caus designed houses on the Covent Garden estate in 1633–4 and the grotto at Woburn Abbey, Bedfordshire. A design for a Grotto of Callisto (plate 57) attributed to him may have been intended for one of these projects.[9] From 1632 Isaac was commissioned by Philip Herbert, 4th Earl of Pembroke (1584–1650), to redesign the south front of Wilton House, Wiltshire, and adjacent gardens in latest French style. Subsequent engravings influenced contemporary English garden design. In 1644 Isaac published *Nouvelle invention de lever l'eau plus hault que sa source*.[10]

Balthazar Gerbier (1591/2–1663) came to England in 1616 to work for George Villiers, 1st Duke of Buckingham (1592–1628). Gerbier's social status is reflected in the family group painted by Rubens in 1629, while the artist was staying with them in London (plate 58).[11] Although Gerbier was employed as a diplomat by Charles I from 1629 and served as Master of Ceremonies from 1641, he maintained his interest in military architecture and in 1650 dedicated a lecture on that subject to the parliamentary leader Lord Fairfax. In 1662–3 Gerbier remodelled Hampstead Marshall, Berkshire, the country house of William, 1st Earl of Craven (1608–1697).[12] With English architect Peter Mills (1598–1670), Gerbier designed the triumphal arches that welcomed Charles II back to the City of London.[13] As a young man William of Orange read Gerbier's writings on architecture.[14]

Huguenot architects in exile employed Huguenot craftsmen – carpenters, masons, plasterers and sculptors – and instructed native talent. Often paid little by comparison with the craftsmen they supervised, the architect's identity was frequently later forgotten or confused. Daniel Marot and engineer Charles Labelye gained recognition by publishing their designs for completed projects.

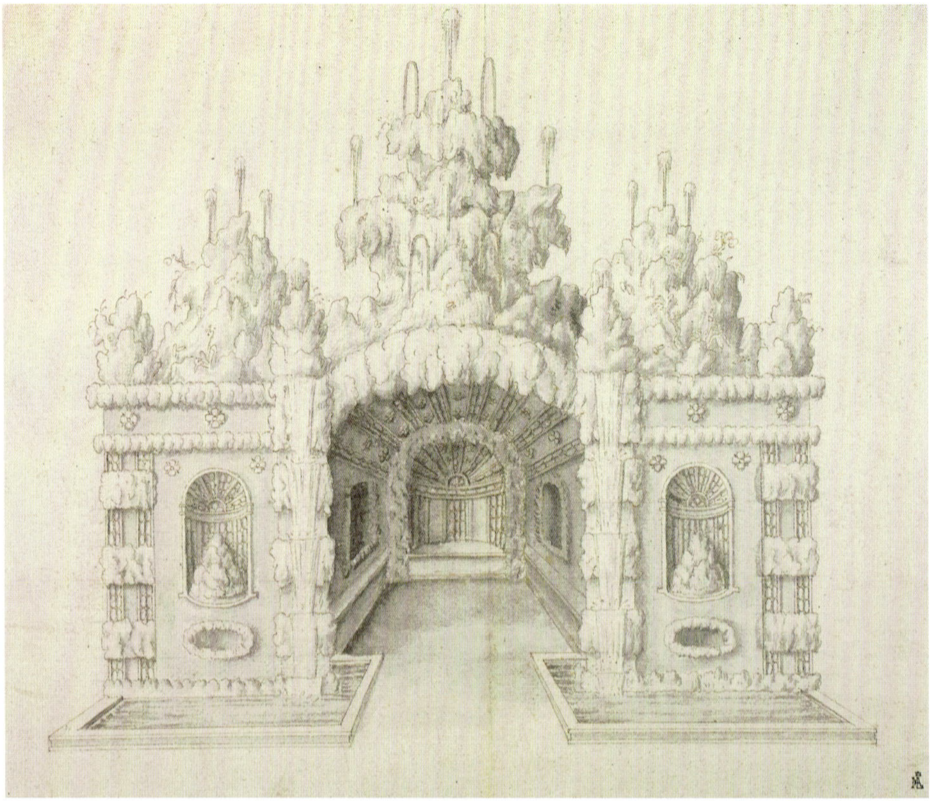

57 Design for Callisto's Grotto

Isaac de Caus, London, *c.*1625
Pen, ink and wash on paper, 29.8 × 24.4 cm
Victoria and Albert Museum, London (3436:403)

Isaac de Caus worked for James I at Whitehall and for the Earls of Bedford and Pembroke at Woburn and Wilton, where he lived with the Herbert family until his death in about 1655.

Daniel Marot was born in Paris in 1661, to Protestant architect Jean Marot and his wife, Charlotte, daughter of Dutch cabinetmaker Abraham Garbrand (d. *c.*1650). Daniel assisted his father with architectural prints, and from 1677 reproduced designs by Jean Le Pautre (1618–1682) and Jean Berain (1637–1711). Berain, with whom Marot trained, was Louis XIV's dessinateur de la chambre et du cabinet du roi. Daniel established his reputation with prints of Lully's opera *Le Triomphe de l'Amour* (1681) and royal propaganda: prints of Queen Marie-Thérèse's funeral and celebrations for the birth of the dauphin.[15]

Yet as a Protestant Marot was forced to leave France. He joined his mother's relatives in the Netherlands, where his brother-in-law, Jacob Gole (1660–1737), engraved his portrait (plate 59). Daniel Marot's prints of royal festivities in The Hague in 1686 – the May Fair, dedicated to William of Orange,[16] and William's December birthday ball at Huis Ten Bosch[17] – secured royal patronage and were sold by Marot in The Hague and Jacob Gole in Amsterdam.[18]

Marot became designer of interiors and gardens for royal palaces and courtier homes, recreating the Louis XIV style for those who admired the palaces of the Louvre and Versailles. From 1686 he worked with the architect Jacob Roman (1614–1716) at William of Orange's hunting lodge, Het Loo near Apeldoorn (a royal palace after 1689) and at Slot Zeist, near Utrecht, for Willem Adriaan (1632–1705), count of Nassau-Odijk, cousin to William of Orange and his ambassador to France. At Het Loo the staircase, inspired by the Escalier des Ambassadeurs at Versailles, was painted from 1692 by Pierre Berchet and Jacques Parmentier, Huguenot artists who previously worked in England and returned there.[19] Marot's 1703 prints show interiors at Het Loo – the Library with mirrored ceiling, intended as Princess Mary's porcelain cabinet, was adapted after her death in 1694. The state bedchamber in Marot's *Second livre d'appartements* (1712) may illustrate the royal bedchamber at Het Loo. Appliqué textiles line the walls and match the bed hangings and upholstered chairs. Overseen by Hans Willem Bentinck, 1st Earl of Portland (1649–1709), Marot also designed the garden and interiors of garden buildings. For the Queen, a three-room grotto furnished with a daybed and decorated with porcelain, was inspired by the 1570s grotto created by Palissy for Catherine de Médicis at the Tuileries, Paris. At Het Loo, the King's garden included a bowling green and a fountain rising to 45 ft with 32 smaller *jets d'eau*.

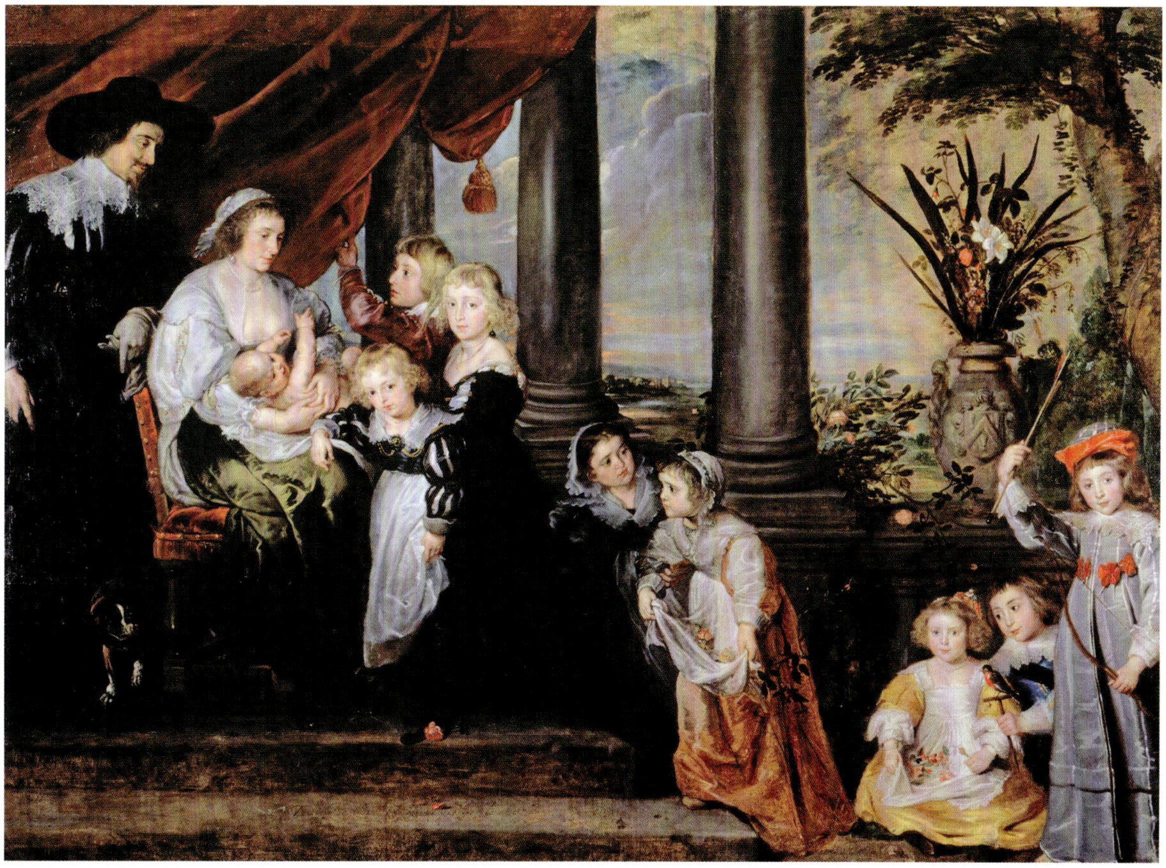

58 *The Family of Sir Balthasar Gerbier*

Attributed to Sir Peter Paul Rubens, London, *c.*1629–41
Oil on canvas, 217.2 × 310 cm
Royal Collection Trust (RCIN 405415)

Gerbier was employed as a diplomat by Charles I and designed the triumphal arches that welcomed Charles II back to London in 1660.

For William III, Marot designed the parterre at Hampton Court Palace (plate 60).[20]

In April 1694 Marot was captured en route to England by the French but fortunately released.[21] In October the same year he married Catherine, daughter of Louis XIV's cabinetmaker Pierre Gole, at the Leicester Fields French church; their eldest children, Daniel and Marianne, were baptized here in 1695 and 1696.[22] In December 1696 Catherine Gole witnessed the baptism of Abraham, son of her cousin Cornelius Gole, furniture maker to the English court.[23]

At Hampton Court Marot designed interiors for the Water Gallery, a Thames-side Tudor building. The upper floor was decorated in blue, white and gold, the gallery furnished with couches upholstered in sky-coloured satin, 25 cane chairs and 12 circular stools painted blue and white. Sets of tables, mirrors and stands, decorated *en suite*, furnished the window piers.[24] The four closets adjoining the Great Room were 'panelled ... with Jappan, another with Looking Glass and two with

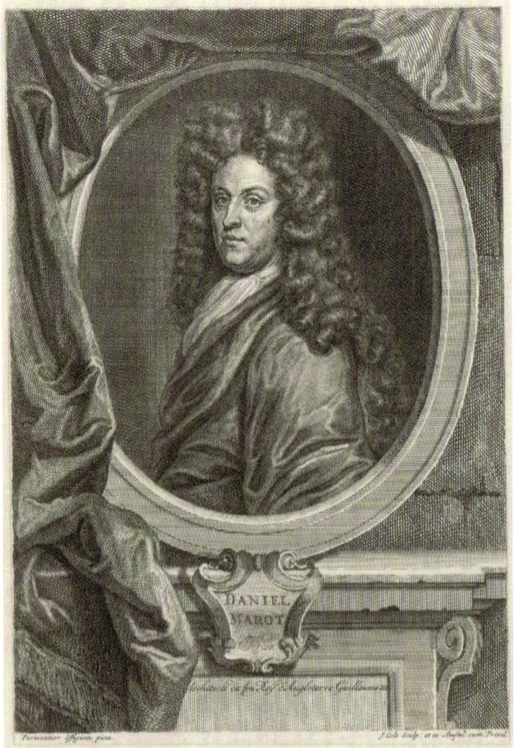

59 *Daniel Marot*

Jacob Gole, Amsterdam, after Jacques Parmentier, *c.*1700
Engraving, 26.8 × 13.8 cm
Rijksmuseum, Amsterdam
(RP-P-1940-327)

Daniel Marot left France for the Netherlands, where this portait was made, as a consequence of the persecution of Protestants that led to the revocation of the edict of Nantes in October 1685.

60 Design for the Parterre, Hampton Court Palace

Daniel Marot, London, 1689
Pen, ink and wash, 19.7 × 51.4 cm
Inscribed 'MAROT FECIT AOUST 1689'
Museum Boymans, Rotterdam

As William III's dessinateur-en-chef, Marot was responsible for Hampton Court Palace interiors and gardens. The parterre design, dated August 1689, was published in The Hague in 1712.

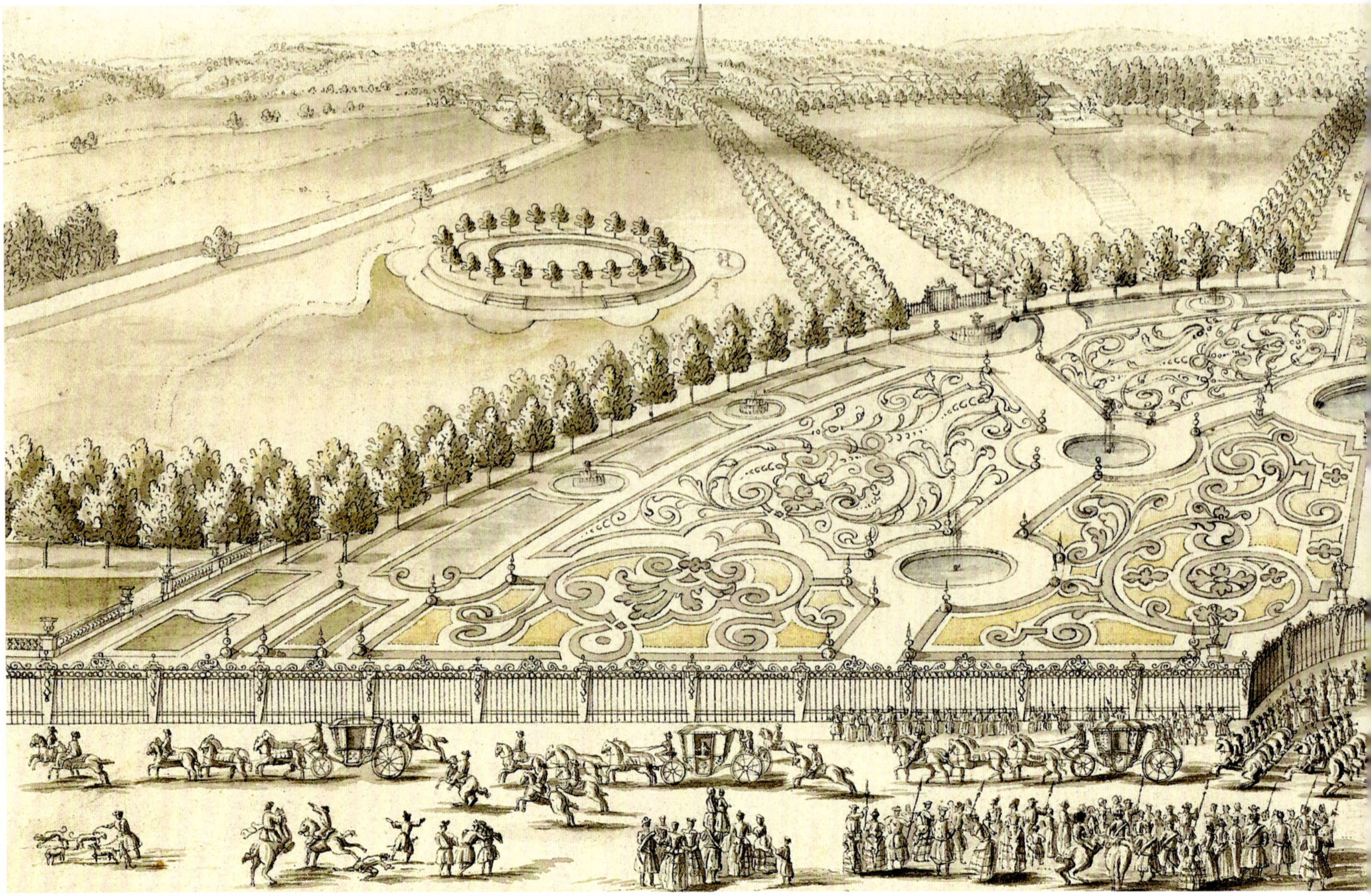

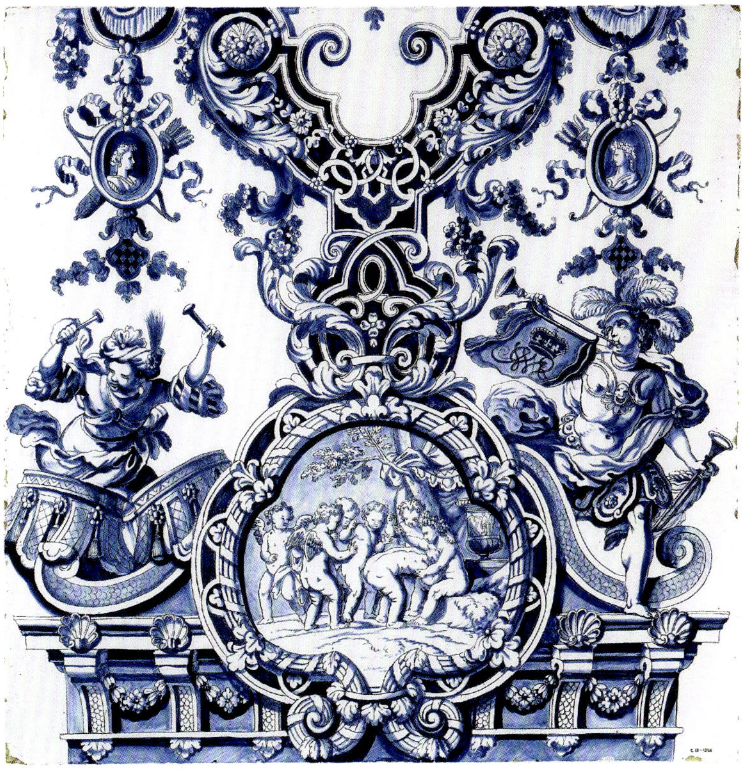

61 Tile

Adrianus Kocx, Delft, designed by Daniel Marot, 1694
Tin-glazed earthenware, painted blue, 62 × 62 cm
Victoria and Albert Museum, London (C.13–1956)

The dairy at Hampton Court was inspired by the Trianon de Porcelaine at Versailles, 'with all conveniences in which [Queen Mary] took great delight'.

work under panels of glass'.[25] The dairy was lined with tiles designed by Marot and manufactured in Delft by Adrian Kocx (d.1701; plate 61).[26] Delftware urns, vases and tall pyramids comprised tiers of box-like units with protruding nozzles, usually referred to as tulip vases, were probably used to grow hyacinths and display a variety of cut flowers.[27]

At Kensington Palace the Queen's bed was of seven-coloured velvet, lined with gold satin and adorned with green and silver *passementerie* (decorative trimmings), with an embroidered gold satin counterpane. Her closet was hung with Indian damask; a blue and gold embroidered

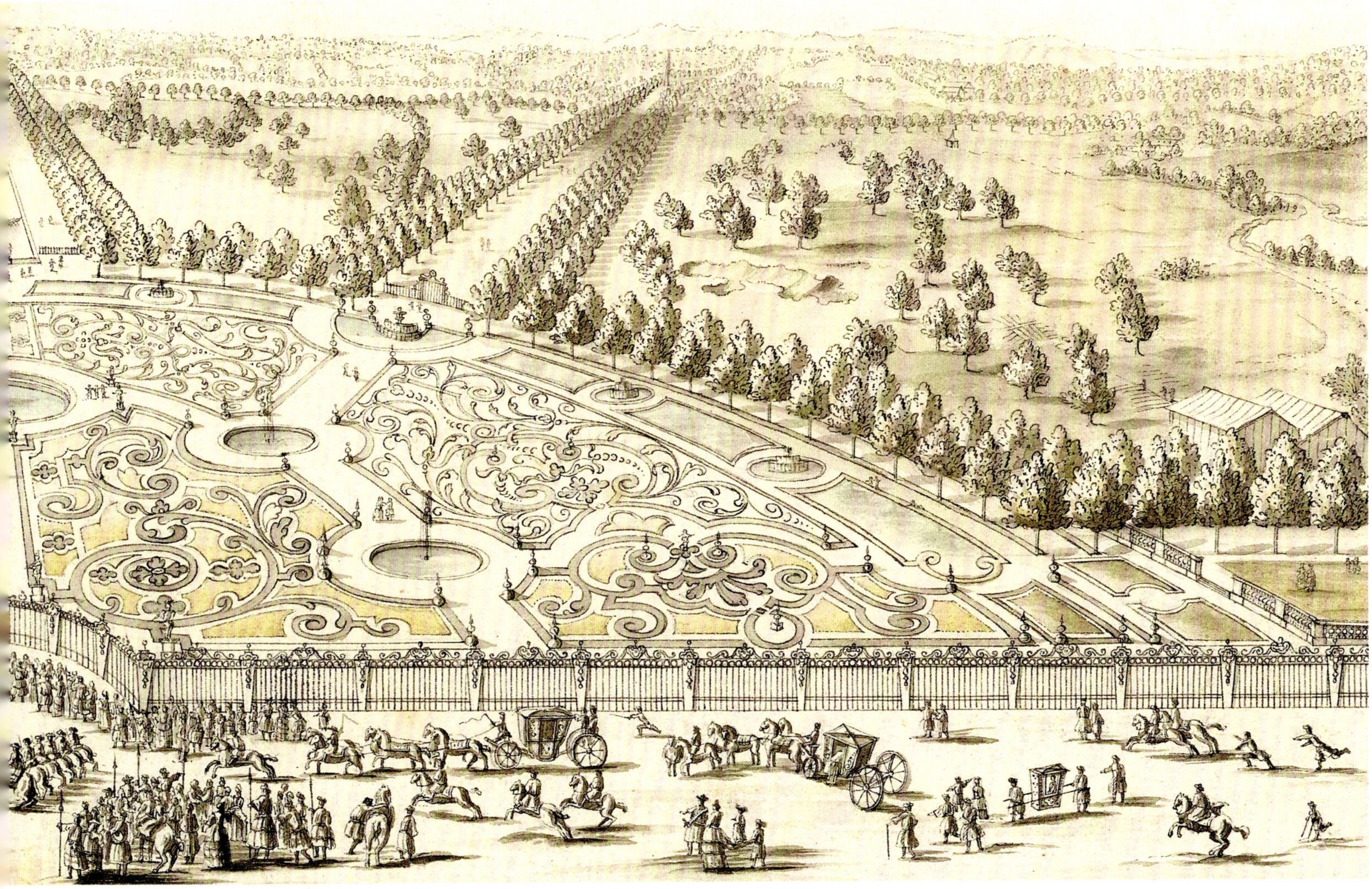

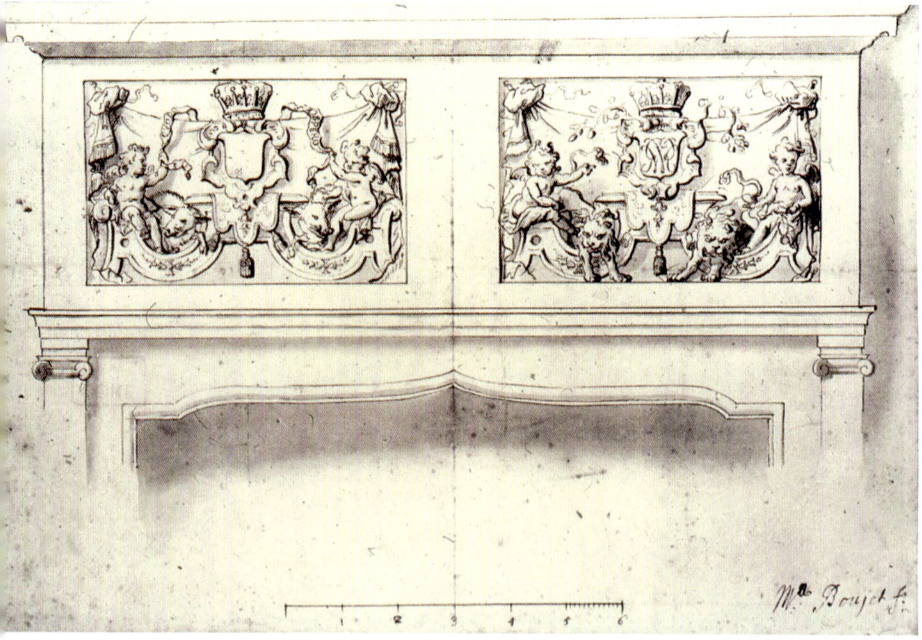

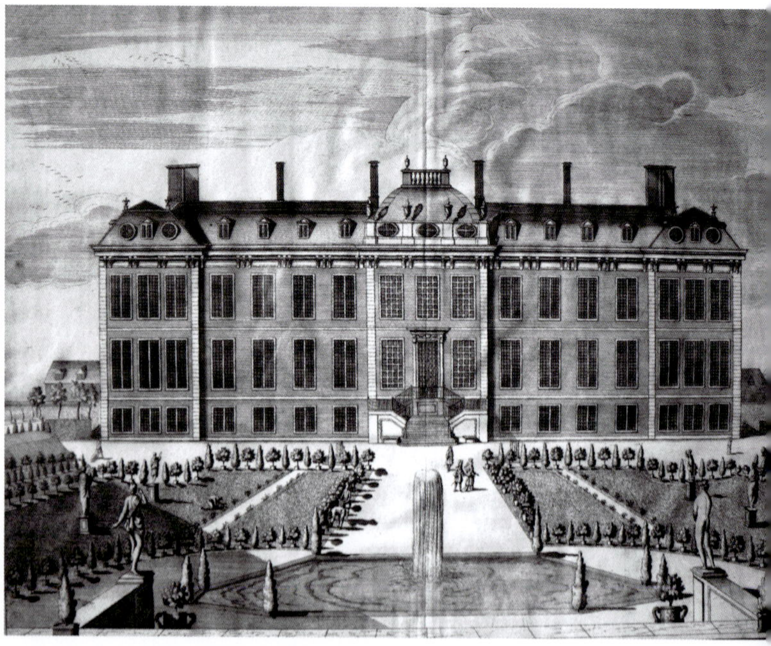

couch, or *sopha*,[28] had a tented canopy of gold and gauze curtains that could be raised and lowered with pulleys, inspired by Turkish prototypes. At Kensington, Queen Mary watched Jean-Baptiste Monnoyer paint her mirrored closet with flowers. Marot designed the 12-acre slope garden with its broad gravel walk flanked by *parterres à l'Angloise*, an English speciality, with *plates bandes* (flower beds) and topiary.[29]

By October 1687 Marot was back in Amsterdam, where his second son was baptized. The Hampton Court Water Gallery and Dairy were destroyed at William III's request after Queen Mary's death in 1694, but the King's interest in the gardens later revived and in 1698 he ordered 'that Mr. Marot should be paid 236 pounds 11 shillings 11-pence sterling' for his garden designs (plate 60).[30] By then, William Talman (1650–1719) was responsible for the palace interiors.[31]

Noble patronage at courtiers' residences

In England Marot contributed to French-style courtier houses completed in the 1690s.[32] These included Montagu House, Bloomsbury; Boughton House, extended from 1688 to include state apartments; and Ditton Park, Buckinghamshire. Building work at Petworth in Sussex was carried out from 1688 for Montagu's son-in-law, Charles Seymour, 6th Duke of Somerset (1662–1748); a payment to a 'Mr. Maro' for £20 in September 1693 may refer to Isaac Marot (b.1672), Daniel's younger brother, described as 'dessignateur' at the French Savoy church in 1707.[33] When Francis Lapiere, London-based upholsterer, supplied to Ralph, 1st Duke of Montagu in 1706, 'a Bed of Striped Tapistry needlework', he paid 'Marot' £1 15s 'for drawing the Cornishes ... drawing the Cupps'.[34] This was probably Isaac Marot, as Daniel had by then returned to Amsterdam.

Daniel Marot introduced the French Baroque style through drawings and prints.[35] The first collected edition of his designs was published at The Hague in about 1703; a second, enlarged edition was sold in Amsterdam in 1712, from Marot's own address. Many of these are signed 'D. Marot Architecte de Guillaume III Roy d'Angleterre'.[36]

Marot's controlling hand designed exteriors and fixtures within and without, including sculpture, clocks, tulip vases and wall coverings. Montagu House, built to Robert Hooke's designs in the 1670s, emulated the Parisian *hôtel* or grand town house, with gatehouse in the street wall opposite a *corps de logis* or main block, with a square-domed centre. As ambassador to Louis XIV in the 1660s and 1670s, Ralph Montagu developed French tastes, deepened in the 1680s during voluntary exile in Montpellier, a Protestant stronghold.[37] Consumed by fire in January 1686, when it was rented to William Cavendish, later 1st Duke of Devonshire (he was still Earl in 1686), Montagu House was rebuilt at Montagu's expense (plate 63). In 1715 Colen Campbell (1676–1729) credited the new design to 'Monsieur Pouget',[38] possibly Pierre Puget (1622–1694) from Marseilles, the nearest large city to Montpellier. The rebuilding was supervised by architectural painter Jacques Rousseau.[39]

LEFT

62 Design for a heraldic overmantel at Dunham Massey

Boujet, London, *c.*1700
Pen and grey wash, 25.1 × 36.2 cm
Royal Institute of British Architects, Smythson Collection, London (RIBA, 1972, vol.B, 98)

Little is known about Boujet, an architectural draughtsman who designed this overmantel for the hall at Dunham Massey, Cheshire, with Lord Warrington's coat of arms, supporters, initials and earl's coronet.

RIGHT

63 *Montagu House, Bloomsbury, The North Front*

John Smith, London, *c.*1714
Engraving, 47 × 58 cm
Buccleuch Collections, Boughton House, Northamptonshire

The north front of Montagu House looked out on a formal garden planted with evergreen shrubs, punctuated by statues and a central fountain, with a view towards Hampstead and Highgate beyond. The garden was maintained by Huguenots François Dursau and Thomas Renard.

Puget's father, François, his elder brothers Jean and Gaspard, and his son, also François, all practised as architects. Pierre Puget was still active as an architect in 1687, producing plans for the Place Royale, Marseilles. Campbell's reference to 'Mr. Pouget' has been linked to an architectural draughtsman named Boujet, who designed an overmantel for the hall at Dunham Massey, Cheshire, for George Booth, 2nd Earl of Warrington, bearing the patron's coat of arms (plate 62).[40]

Montagu House was a status symbol; by employing a French architect, Montagu was asserting triumph over adversity. The Boughton extensions were supervised by Pierre Silvestre, a distinguished Huguenot physician with first-hand experience of architecture – as observer and supervisor in Britain, France and Italy – who was resident at Montagu House and associated with leading scientists and mathematicians at the Rainbow Coffee House, St Martin's Lane.[41] The north front of Boughton (plate 64) is inspired by Jean Marot's 'Profil d'une maison particulier de Paris', published in 1654–60,[42] although the translation of French motifs is hesitant, as if the draughtsman was working from prints.[43] Yet the design incorporates sash windows, a recent introduction from the Netherlands,[44] fitted with large panes of bevelled glass supplied by the Pelletiers;[45] over-mantel mirrors canted forward to maximize artificial light from flanking glass candle sconces (three pairs still *in situ*); and floors of 'parquet de Versailles' created by joiner Pierre Rieusset (fl.1687–1716; plate 94). For Montagu's Buckinghamshire home, Ditton Park (inherited from his mother's family, the Winwoods), the Pelletiers supplied sophisticated *verre églomisé* frames for overmantel mirrors. This technique of applying a design and gilding to the reverse side of glass to produce a mirror finish provided an important source of reflected light.[46]

Silvestre accompanied Winwood, Viscount Monthermer, heir to Ralph, 1st Duke of Montagu, to the Netherlands, Italy, Spain, France and Germany from 1699 to 1702. Charles de Saint-Evremond (1614–1703) wrote to Silvestre: 'From an Inspector of Gardens and Buildings, you will become for some time longer an Inspector of Life and Manners'.[47] Winwood died prematurely and his younger brother, John, became the next Lord Monthermer. He married Mary, youngest daughter of John Churchill, 1st Duke of Marlborough, in 1705, and the following year Silvestre accompanied him to join the allied armies under Churchill's command in Flanders. Back home in September 1707, Silvestre's criticism to Marlborough in September 1707 of the design of the saloon at Blenheim Palace by John Vanbrugh (1664–1726) and Nicholas Hawksmoor (1661–1736) was fuelled by his Italian travels. He sent Marlborough alternative designs for the Saloon[48] and recommended using nine different types of marble

> *having seen at Rome and Genoa chapels and churches entirely encrusted with marbles of amazing beauty. I imagine that the saloon at Blenheim panelled in the same Manner would be one of the most beautiful and most magnificent in Europe. There are plenty of workmen in Rome who work only in these sorts of inlay.*[49]

In 1708 Silvestre supervised the apprentice stonemason at Boughton House, Thomas Drew the younger (1693–1741?), who was taught drawing by Cornelius Gole and mathematics by Abraham de Moivre at the Duke's expense.[50]

64 Boughton House
Extensions supervised by Pierre Silvestre, *c.*1690
The Buccleuch Collections

The north front with its flanking wings and stables beyond to the left were built under the supervision of Pierre Silvestre, Montagu's personal doctor from Bordeaux. The glass in the sash windows was supplied by the Pelletiers, Huguenot craftsmen from Paris.

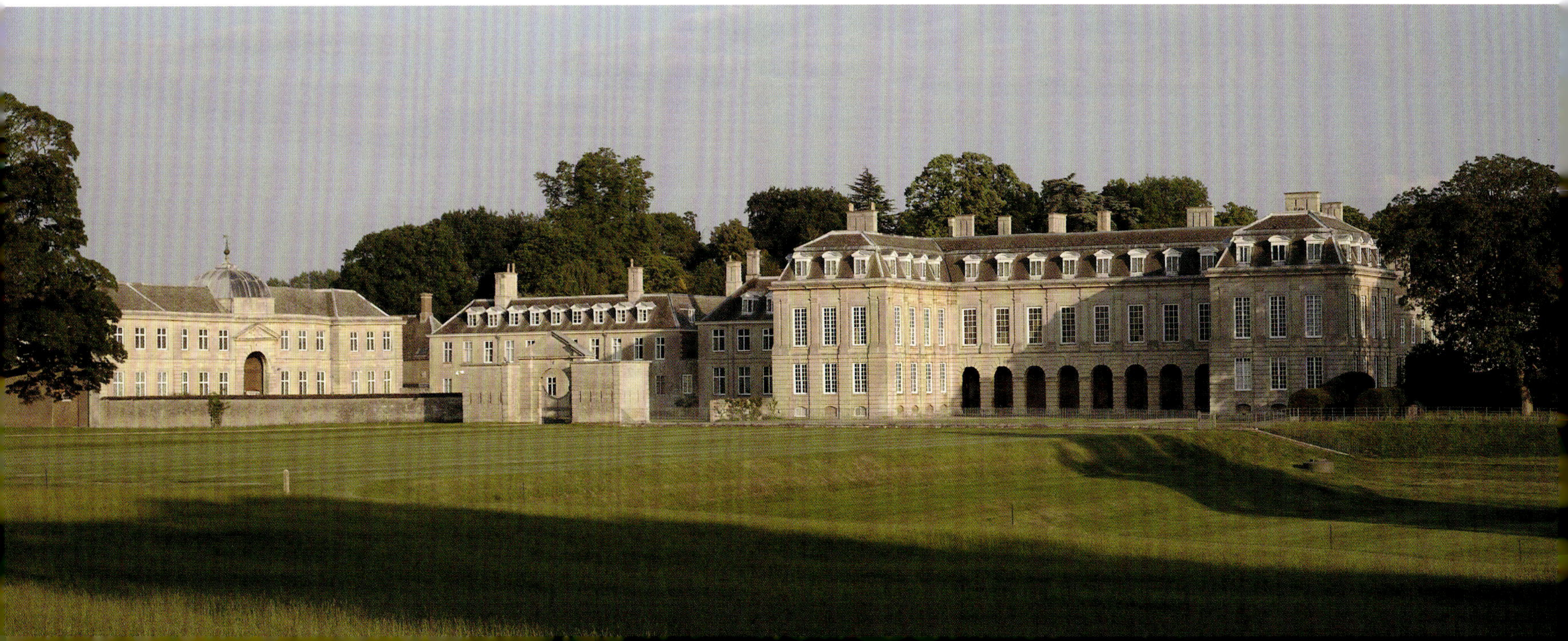

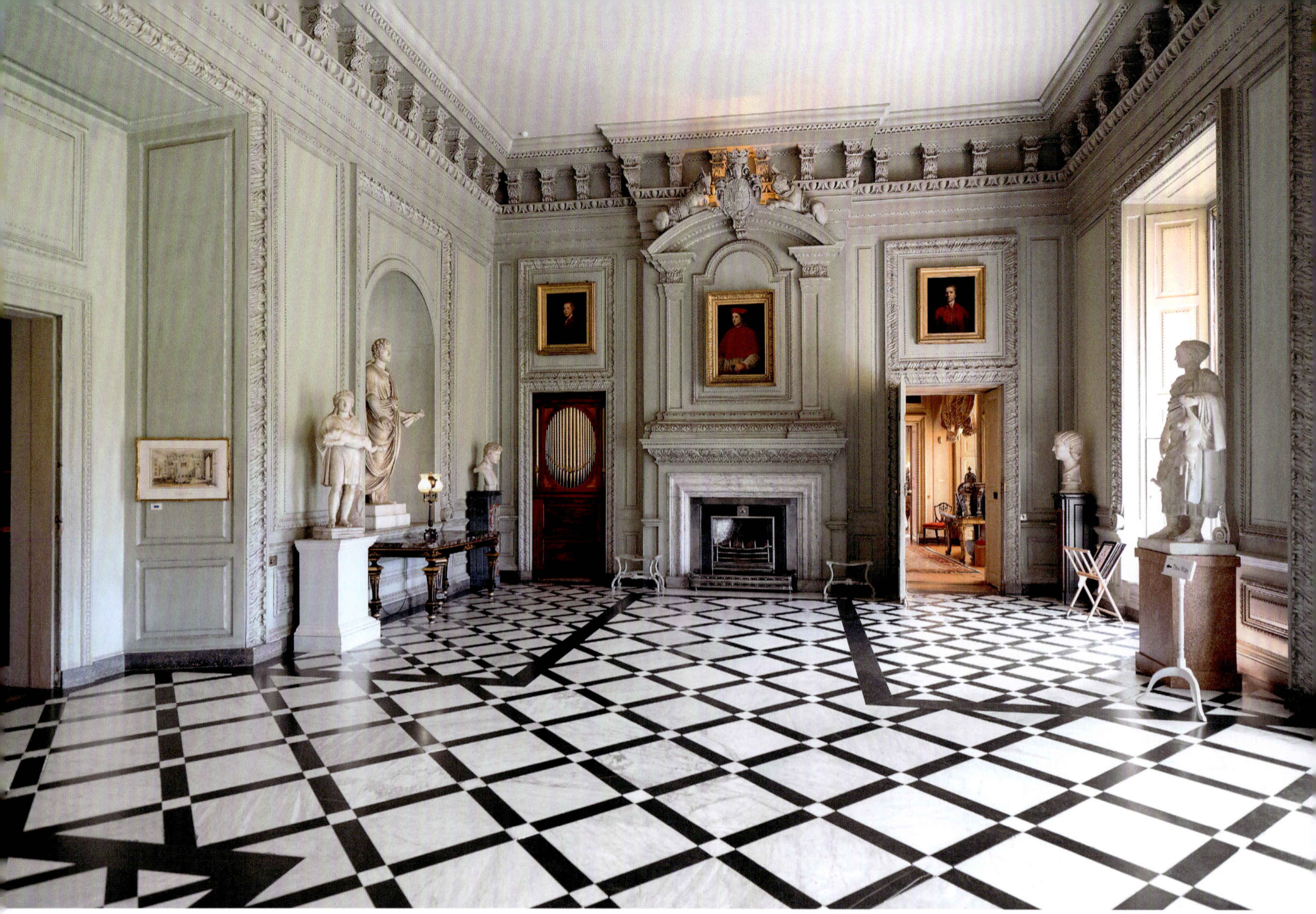

Petworth House was acquired by Charles Seymour, 6th Duke of Somerset through marriage to Lady Elizabeth Percy (1667–1722), Montagu's stepdaughter, in 1682. The French-style square dome,[51] façade and interiors are close to Daniel Marot's published designs. The possible link to Puget is substantiated by a marble bust of William III on the outside of Petworth Town Hall, attributed to Honoré Pellé (1641–1718), Puget's pupil. Marot supplied designs for the interiors of Petworth House. The bracketed frieze, egg-and-dart moulding and semicircular-topped frames cutting into bold segmental pediments in the Marble Hall (plate 65) recur in the Trevesaal, the Binnenhof audience chamber in The Hague, built in 1696–8 to Marot's designs. Begun in 1692, the Petworth dining room (known as the Beauty Room) boasted eight portraits of court beauties by Michael Dahl (1659–1743) separated by mirrored panels so that gentlemen present could enjoy virtual female company.[52]

Jean de Bodt, engineer and architect born in Paris to a German father from Mecklenberg and a Huguenot mother, Rose Louvint de Veral, left France for the Netherlands and service of William III. In 1690–1 Bodt served as an engineer in the artillery train that accompanied William III to Ireland; the following April he moved to Flanders, where in February 1694 he received a warrant 'to perfect himself in the art of engineering'. In October 1697 he returned to England, where he produced designs for rebuilding Whitehall Palace after it was destroyed by fire the following January. Bodt left England in 1699, with his unexecuted designs for Whitehall Palace and Greenwich Hospital, and became chief architect to the Elector of Brandenburg.[53] His only building in England, Wentworth Castle, was designed in Berlin.

As first British ambassador to the Prussian Court in 1703–11, Thomas Wentworth, 3rd Baron Raby (1672–1739), commissioned designs from Bodt for Wentworth Castle in Stainborough,

65 Marble Hall, Petworth House

Design attributed to Daniel Marot with marble floor copied from C.A. d'Aviler's *Cours complet d'architecture*, 1691
National Trust

The deeply carved bolection mouldings of the chimney-piece, door and window frames complement the cornice and unite the interior, reflecting Marot's influence on this great house designed for Ralph Montagu's stepdaughter and her husband, the 6th Duke of Somerset.

South Yorkshire.[54] The seventeenth-century house was acquired in 1708 from Henry Cutler for £14,000; a letter of 15 March 1709 from Lord Raby's brother comments on the cost of rebuilding.[55] Raby had been disinherited in favour of his cousin Watson Wentworth, so his castle was conceived in rivalry to Watson's neighbouring seat, Wentworth Woodhouse.[56] He was inspired by contemporary building in Prussia, including the Berlin Stadtschloss designed by the Swedish architect Johann Eosander (1669–1728); the Berlin Arsenal (Zeughaus), opened in 1706; the Orangery at Charlottenburg Palace, extended in 1709–12; and the Elector's palace at Oranienburg. Raby wanted a long gallery like that in the Berlin Stadtschloss.[57] He was elevated to the title of Earl of Strafford in 1711, and his new castle enhanced his status: 'it is a very fine place to talk of in town, which I have heard say is the right use of a seat in the country'.[58] Among the craftsmen he employed was Daniel Harvey (1683–1733), who worked for Charles Howard, 3rd Earl of Carlisle (1669–1738), at Castle Howard in 1706–24. Bodt's name is not recorded in contemporary correspondence: he is first mentioned in 1756, when Horace Walpole described Wentworth Castle as 'a pompous front screening an old house; it was built by the last Lord on a design of the Prussian architect Bott ... the one pair of stairs is entirely engrossed by a gallery of 180 feet, on the plan of that in the Colonna Palace at Rome.'[59]

Bodt's designs for the façade, cross-section and elevation of the gallery interior (plates 56 and 66), inscribed 'Elevation de la facade du Batiment neuf' and, in a different hand, 'W.T. del et invt', were attributed to William Talman.[60] Talman, with Robert Benson (later Lord Bingley; 1676–1731), at nearby Bramham Park, supervised the execution, assisted by Edward Reeves (*c.*1685–1757), Lord Raby's builder from Twickenham, Surrey.[61] Bodt's design was altered: the rectangular arched-top windows were omitted from the basement; the ground floor windows are supported by twin overlapping Doric pilasters, with distinct *entasis* (slight convex curves in their shafts), their eccentric shape reminiscent of Thomas Archer's work.[62] The façade comprises 15 bays rather than the 13 of Bodt's design, two end pavilions consist of two bays each, and the central bay contains three round-topped windows rather than Bodt's single central window flanked by two storeys of rectangular windows. Decorative sculpture articulates the façade: the coat of arms supported by trumpeting angels, representing Fame, are attributed to Daniel Harvey.[63] Bodt designed the long gallery interior to include a painted ceiling and tapestries but his drawings were modified by James Gibbs. The design is mentioned in an anonymous diary description dated 11 September 1724:

> *My Lord has built a new front of 15 windows to an Old House 190 feet long, which is divided into 7 rooms below all finely carved well hung with Tapestry. the two upper Stories are all thrown into a Gallery 26 feet high 30 broad with two pavilions at each end divided by two noble white pillars & pilasters the Shafts of which are above 14 feet high all in one piece of marble. There hung 8 fine pieces of P[rince]* EUGENES *Victories agt the Turks & French.*[64]

The gallery was complete by September 1724 and in 1725 1st Earl Bathurst (1684–1775) noted 'a very magnificent room now the pillars are up'.[65] The south front was completed in 1762 to the designs of William Wentworth, 2nd Earl of Stratford, concealing the old house. As at Boughton, a French architect created a country residence that reflected European styles absorbed by former ambassadors to France and Germany.[66]

At Dyrham Park, Avon, the elusive Samuel Hauduroy[67] designed the new west front (plate 67), built between 1692 and 1694 to mask a Tudor house. His patron, William Blathwayt, William III's Secretary of State,[68] who served under Sir William Temple in The Hague, inherited the Wiltshire property through marriage in 1686. He decided to rebuild after the deaths of his

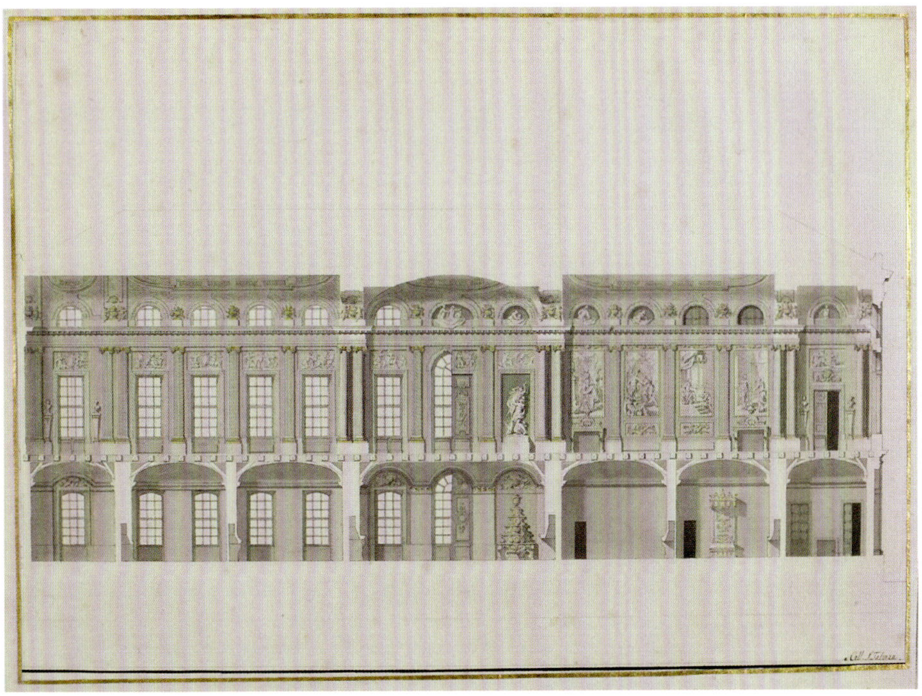

66 Sectional elevation of proposed east wing, Wentworth Castle

Jean de Bodt, Berlin, *c.*1709
Pen, ink and watercolour highlighted in gold, 23.8 × 52.4 cm
Victoria and Albert Museum, London (E.308–1937)

Bodt's only English building, Wentworth Castle was designed in Berlin for Lord Raby, British Ambassador to the Prussian Court. The long gallery was inspired by that in the new Berlin Stadtschloss.

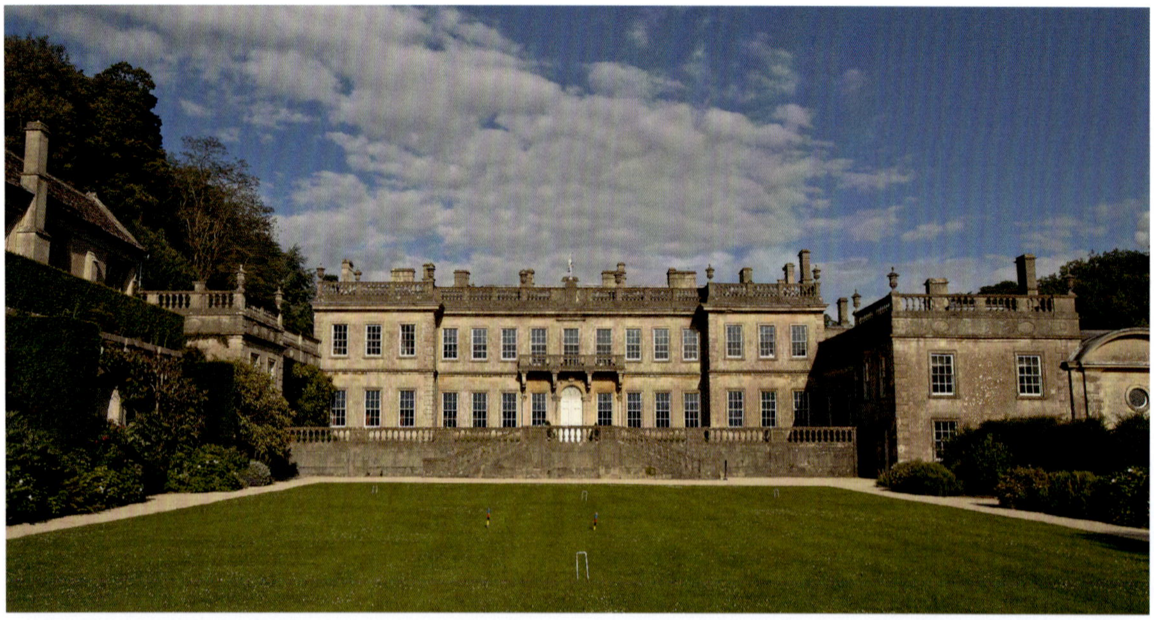

67 West front, Dyrham Park

Designed by Samuel Hauduroy, London, 1691–4
National Trust

Commissioned for William Blathwayt, William III's Secretary of State. Hauduroy's poor grasp of English hampered communication with the builders.

father-in-law in 1689 and of his wife in childbirth in 1691. Samuel Hauduroy only received 10 guineas for his design, whereas his relative, 'Mr Hauduroy', was paid over £185 for painting some of the panelled interiors to resemble marbles and exotic woods.

Samuel Hauduroy's role at Dyrham is recorded in letters, memoranda and designs. His letter to Blathwayt's distinguished uncle, Thomas Povey (*c.*1613–*c.*1705), written from Dyrham while Blathwayt was away in Flanders, suggests that he was employed 'because he was conscientious, penniless, and therefore cheap'.[69] The architect's 10 guinea fee had to cover his subsistence and transport costs from London, which came to 4 guineas. Hauduroy provided detailed drawings for terrace coping, window frames and door panelling.[70] But he was frustrated by the difficulty of making the workmen understand his poor English. Another memorandum listing further designs dates from a later visit.[71] Of these, three plans for the pavilion survive. One of these is for a door with the deleted inscription 'Porte de la Chambre du Conseill' and later annotation 'Form of a Door etc'. This shows panelling and decorative carving in the lintel above, and may be one of 'deux dessins pour le boissage des portes ... pour le bon homme Jacob'.[72] Of four staircase designs, that for the balustrade of the bottom flight (plate 68) is close to a further drawing showing two of three alternative designs for balusters with comments from Blathwayt.[73]

A reference to Lord Nottingham's staircase, perhaps at Burley-on-the-Hill, Rutland, suggests that Samuel Hauduroy worked for Daniel Finch, 2nd Earl of Nottingham, whose Kensington home was sold in June 1689 to William III and became Kensington Palace. In 1694 Nottingham acquired Burley-on-the-Hill, where Hauduroy probably designed the staircase with its twisted balusters.[74] The angular shaping of the handrail at the corner, its moulding and the sides of the treads are similar to the walnut staircase at Dyrham.

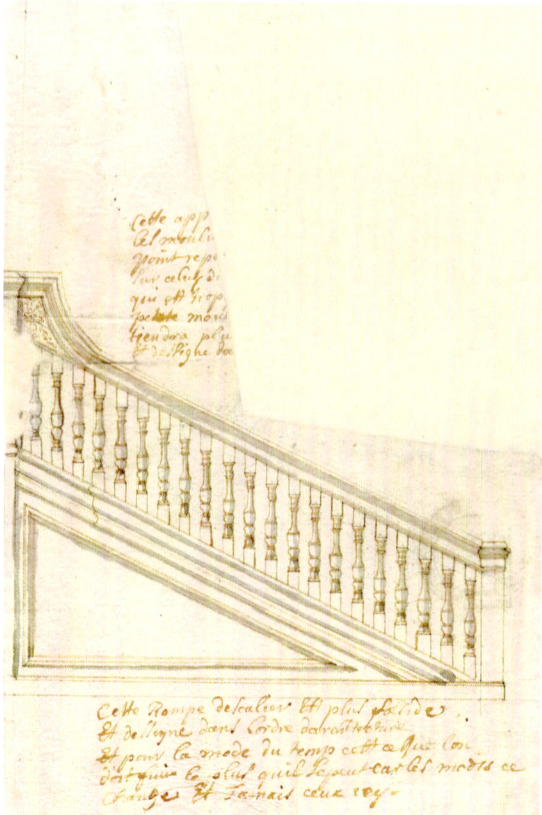

68 Design for the staircase balusters at Dyrham Park

Samuel Hauduroy, London, *c.*1692
Pen, brown ink and grey wash, 24.5 × 15.5 cm
National Trust

Hauduroy supplied four designs for Blathwayt's walnut staircase. The one with a concave moulding is inscribed: 'this will harbor dust very much'; the other, close to the design of the balusters as executed, is inscribed: 'I must confess I think this the best of the three'.

Hauduroy's designs were executed by joiners and masons; Robert Barker was responsible for the staircase. John Povey, Blathwayt's nephew, admired the 'Garden Front ... for the Decoration which are without much carving solid and yet no ways heavy',[75] as in the volutes which support the central balcony. Yet managing Hauduroy was challenging and, like Raby at Wentworth Castle, Blathwayt went elsewhere for the design of the east front: Hauduroy was dismissed and Dyrham was completed to William Talman's designs in 1704. The interiors, dictated by Blathwayt's Dutch taste, particularly the state bedchamber, reflect the influence of Daniel Marot: in summer the hearths held Delft flowerpots with orange trees imported from Italy; pyramidical Delft flower vases displayed exotic tulips or hyacinths.[76]

The Dyrham gardens were celebrated for their water features. A fountain above the great cascade featured a statue of Neptune supplied by the aristocratic Huguenot sculptor 'Chevalier' Claude David (fl.1678–1721), who also worked for Montagu and the royal court. Claude David, originally from Burgundy, was in Rome from 1678 carving ivory crucifixes and succeeded Pierre Puget as sculptor at Santa Maria in Carignano, Genoa.[77] Neptune's role in supporting Aeneas by calming the seas was interpreted as the classical prototype for William III's invasion of Britain, so statues of the sea god were a favourite contemporary garden feature. David also worked for Thomas Thynne, 1st Viscount Weymouth (1640–1714), at Longleat, where, in addition to supplying garden sculpture, he provided two designs for the main entrance doorway. These show a segmental and swan-necked pediment; one of these corresponds to the present front entrance, surmounted by the Thynne family coat of arms and a viscount's coronet. A joiner's bill dated 26 January 1705 refers to 'making a model of the door by Cavalier David's order'. David's presence is recorded in the library at Longleat, whence in 1706 he borrowed 'the life of K Henry the 5th'.[78]

Another gentleman sculptor, Henri Nadauld (1653–1724), designed his own carving, plasterwork and sculpture to complement the architecture of Archer, Talman, Vanbrugh and Hawksmoor.[79] At Chatsworth, where drawings by Nadauld are preserved, he was supervised from 1700 to 1706 by the Duke's Huguenot steward, Mr Huet. Nadauld came from the Ile d'Oléron, near La Rochelle. Like Claude David, his background was lesser nobility: his family's heraldic seal, 'azure, a sun in splendour or', appears on family documents in Derbyshire, where he settled.[80] Nadauld came to England with his wife, Mary, and their eldest son, Pierre, who attended the West Street French

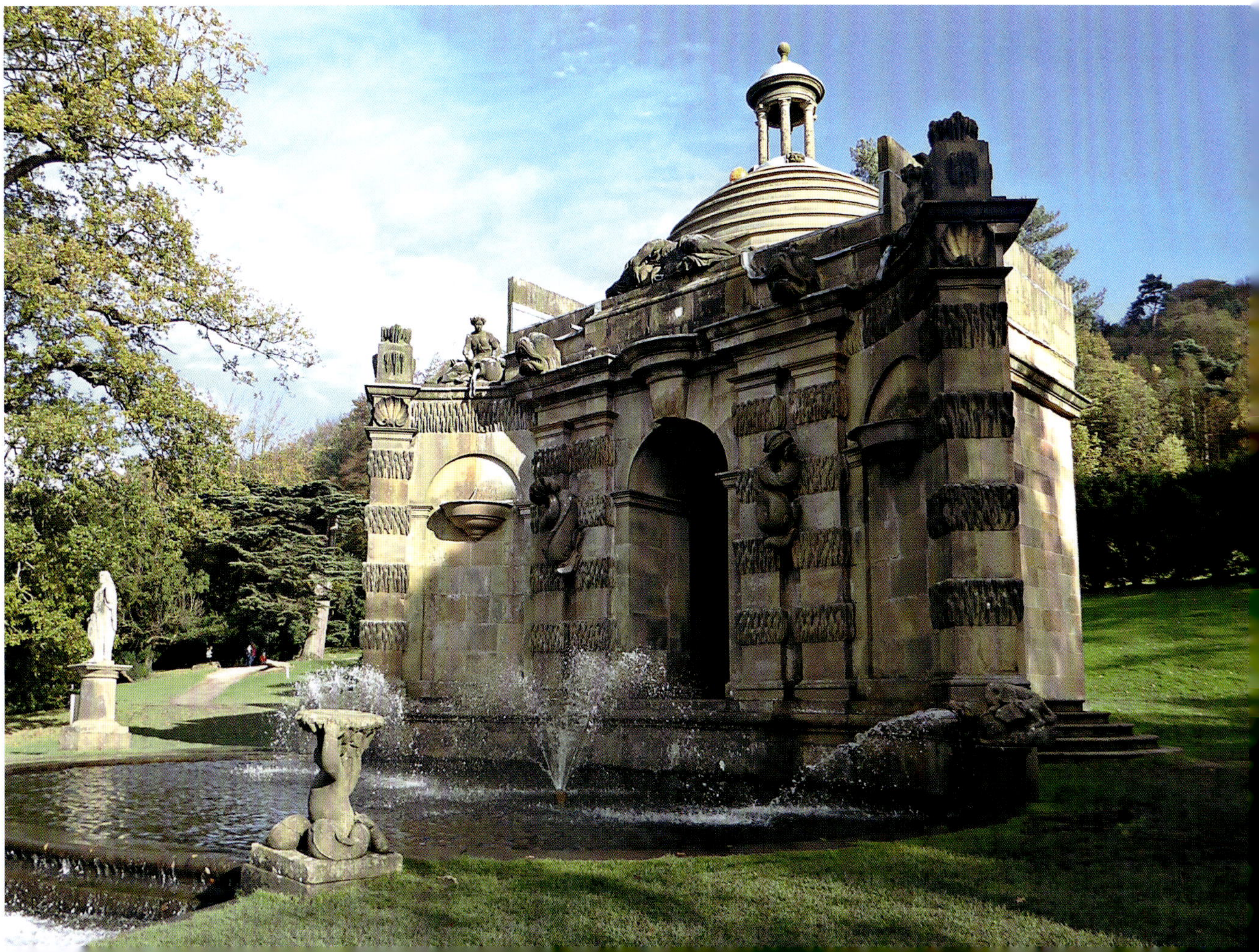

69 Fluvius (river god), frostwork, dolphins and vases

Henri Nadauld, Chatsworth, 1703–4

Nadauld's sculpture embellishes the Cascade House designed by architect Thomas Archer. The sculptor's reclining river god presides over the dramatic fall of water that spills over the stepped dome above and the dolphins which flank the arched opening below. The cascade was inspired by one installed at Marly, the royal French chateau, between 1697 and 1699. It replaced the simpler waterfall devised in 1694 by the hydraulic engineer Grillet, a fellow Huguenot. The dolphins compare with those Nadauld carved to frame a Renaissance French relief of Diana, acquired in 1692 for £16, for the internal grotto beneath the principal staircase.

chapel, Soho. Pierre was naturalized in 1707 and became a surgeon in Ashford, Derbyshire.[81] Henri Nadauld's recreation in France became his English profession. 'Mr. Nadue' worked under Christopher Wren at Hampton Court in 1698. Here he received £50 for plastering the Water Gallery Closet; a nearby shed was provided for 'the Frenchman to burne his Plaister in' and two square stones laid 'to beat his plaster on'.[82] By 1700 he had established a yard in Portugal Row (Piccadilly); he worked at Chatsworth and Castle Howard until 1711.

At Chatsworth Nadauld's sculptural detail enlivened the architectural setting: he provided ornamental carving for the exterior, interiors and garden sculpture.[83] In summer 1700 he supplied 'Figures' for £6 for the west front staircase niches; he was also paid £6 4s 6d for carving (at 2s a foot) '41 foot superficial of Frost worke' around the grotto under the staircase in the west court. Nadauld shared responsibility for the carving on Chatsworth's west front with local Derbyshire sculptor Samuel Watson (1662–1715). He was paid £50 for his 'Ornaments in the Great Frise', £50 for 'the ornaments on each side the 2 Windows over the Entrance' and £7 for '4 Ciphers and Coronetts upon 4 Keystones in the Middle Windows'.[84]

Similar ornaments recur on the south front of Castle Howard. Both juxtapose paired tritons blowing conch shells with paired winged sea horses with entwined tails or tied with ribbons to three-pronged tridents. At Chatsworth, Nadauld's palm-framed cypher, 'wc', for William Cavendish, crowned by an earl's coronet, recurs at intervals on the 'Great Frise'. Nadauld supplied six vases for the west front (still *in situ*) and '22 heads for the two Gallerys in the Inner Court'; these are now on the roof of the glasshouse east of the cascade. In 1704 he provided two figures for the west front staircase niches (still in place) for £24, and was paid 3s per foot for 'carving 94 foot of ffrost worke' for the Cascade (plate 69). For the plaster coving of 'the Vestibule',[85] an exquisite relief of sea horses and acanthus foliage, he was paid £114.

By 1705 'Mr. Nedos' was at Castle Howard carving wooden architraves, cornices and friezes for Lord Carlisle's private apartments. The 'fust closset' and the 'great closit' were destroyed when the new wing was built, designed by Sir Thomas Robinson (1703–1777), but Nadauld's cornices survive in the former saloon, with its lively lion frieze, and former dining room, now the tapestry room and music room respectively.[86] For the north front Nadauld carved metopes and trophies on the returning angles. From October 1706 he carved the frieze in the great curb of the cupola, the four keystones below the curb, the frieze inside the Hall over the composite order and the frieze under the north front main door, with 'Rosses' under the arches, the lintel and 'Three Pine Apples'. The phonetic spelling echoes Nadauld's French pronunciation.[87]

At Castle Howard Nadauld worked alongside fellow Huguenots Gideon du Chesne from London and Daniel Harvey from York, who carved architectural details for the hall interior. Du Chesne, who arrived from Paris with his wife and four children in September 1681, received relief from Threadneedle Street church that October 1681 and again in March 1682.[88] His elder son, John, was paid for 'plastering the painted room' at Boughton in March 1701/2.[89] At Castle Howard, Nadauld supplied 'the freeses over the Cappitels';[90] 'Mr Tushaine' (Gideon du Chesne)[91] was paid for stone cornice mouldings;[92] Daniel Harvey charged for '16 scrowls for the Pelasters of the Cupola att 3s y peece'.[93] Harvey also supplied sculpture for the Temple of the Four Winds and vases for the gardens; some of these were painted green and gilded using leaf gold procured from London by John Harvey, Daniel's elder brother, who painted the ceiling of the grand cabinet.[94]

Developing residential London

From 1680 to 1760 Huguenot architects contributed to the spate of country house building and royal commissions that followed the Glorious Revolution. Public institutions promoted by the expanding merchant class provided new opportunities for architectural patronage from 1720. As Palladianism succeeded the Baroque, there was less scope for originality and reputations were enhanced by the publication of architectural treatises.

Nicholas Dubois (*c.*1665–1735) was appointed by William III as tutor to the Prince of Friesland, father of William IV, Prince of Orange.[95] As 'Architect and one of his Majesty's Engineers', Dubois served in Spain from 1706 and in Flanders under the Duke of Marlborough; he retired on half pay after the Treaty of Utrecht in 1713. In 1715 Dubois translated Giacomo Leoni's *The Architecture of Andrea Palladio*. His introduction throws interesting light on contemporary patronage, the growing professionalism of

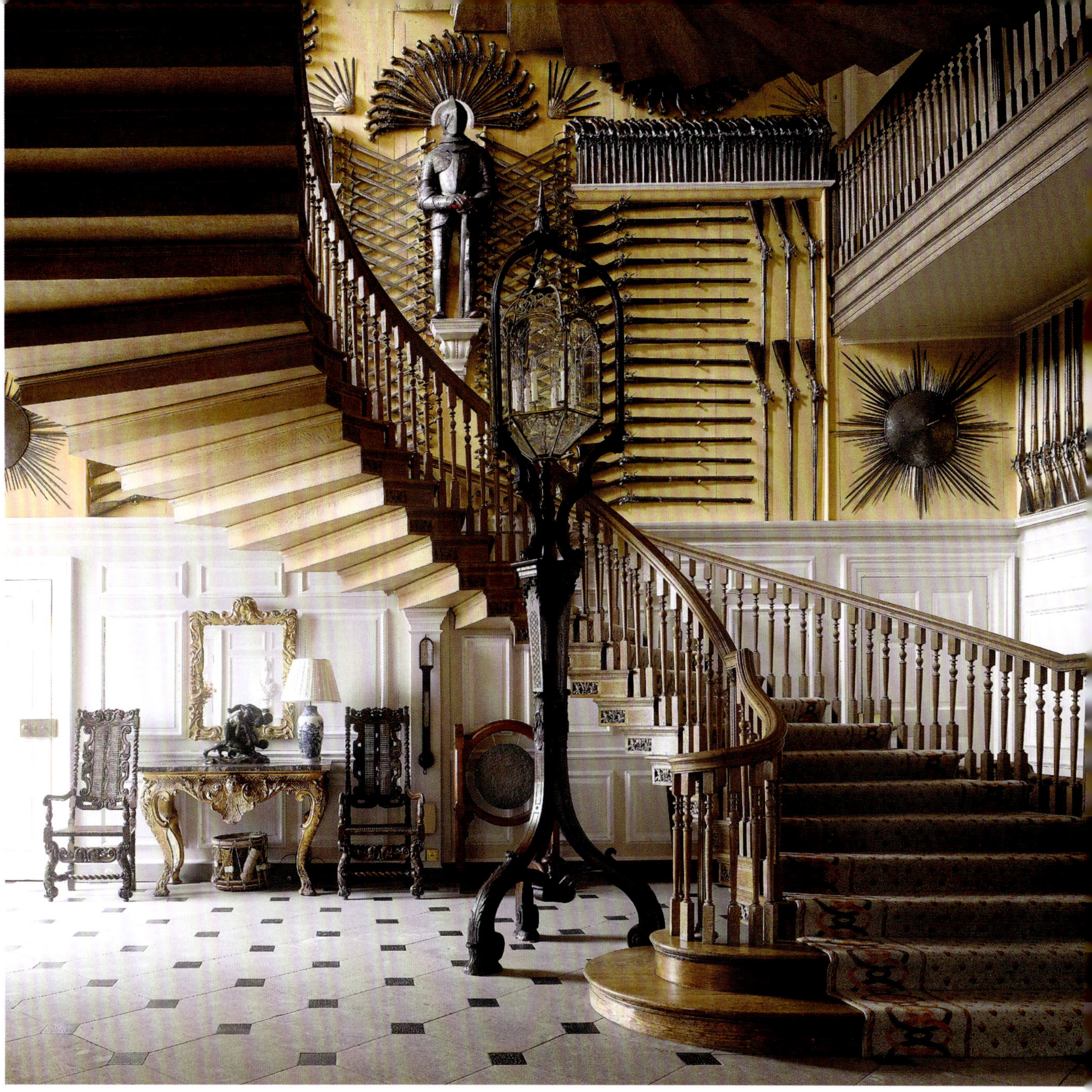

70 Circular staircase at Chevening, Kent

Designed by Nicholas Dubois, London, 1721

Dubois's most successful project was the 'great geometrical staircase' designed in 1721 for the 1st Earl of Stanhope at Chevening, Kent, and completed for his widow. Built in chestnut, the circular cantilevered staircase rises up through two storeys creating a forest of balusters, an astonishing design modelled on that in Dubois's own London home.

architectural practice and the distinction between architect and builder:

> *As most of those who undertake to build, neglect to make any use of any Architect, in order to raise a House ... And because they don't understand the Rules of an Art, they frequently prefer their own fancies to the judgement of the most learned and experience'd Architects; at most they rely upon Workmen, who are often very ignorant, or dare not find fault with any plan, tho' never so bad, for fear of displeasing and so losing their work.*[96]

On 30 May 1718 Dubois formed a partnership with the Italian architect Alexander Galilei (1691–1737), a relative of astronomer Galileo (1564–1642). Galilei studied mathematics and physics at the Florence Academy, which demonstrates Dubois's recognition of the importance of science in architectural practice.[97] Apart from Galilei's work for the Duke of Manchester at Kimbolton Castle, and an association with property belonging to James Brydges, 1st Duke of Chandos, the partnership did not attract major commissions and Galilei returned to Florence in 1719, to serve as court architect.[98] Dubois was also associated with Lewis Dollon, Governor of Guernsey in 1726 and received financial backing from Huguenots James Herault (d.1742) of Twickenham; Charles du Bourgay (d.1732), Governor of Jamaica; Stephen de la Creuze (d. *c.*1744) of Westminster, and John Remy de Montigny (d.1734; not to be confused with the gatesmith Jean Montigny, plate 80).[99]

Between 1717 and 1720 Dubois developed London property on land belonging to Richard Lumley, 1st Earl of Scarborough (1650–1721), in St George's Street, Mayfair, and five properties in neighbouring Hanover Square. Only number 20 still remains, although altered: it was purchased by James Graham, 1st Duke of Montrose (1682–1742), in 1720.[100] Dubois was appointed Master Mason to the Office of Works in 1719[101] and altered Leicester House for the Prince of Wales in 1719–20. In 1720 he set up a builder's company with a monopoly granted by Royal Charter 'to raise a sufficient fund … to buy Old houses in order to build them … to Build good and substantial houses upon neglected and unemployed ground … to provide all sorts of good, proper and fitting materials for Solid Building'.[102]

In April 1720 Dubois shared his plan with his Huguenot backers and James Horne (d.1756), also of St James's, Westminster, later Dubois's personal assistant and Deputy Master Mason to the Board of Works. They agreed 'to have some person of quality' at the helm. Scroop Egerton, 1st Duke of Bridgewater (1681–1744), Lord Chamberlain to the Princess of Wales (who subscribed to Leoni's 1715 *Palladio*), assisted 'in procuring a patent or charter', and his brother Charles Egerton (d.1725) supported the project. Dubois recommended the purchase of 'a considerable piece of Ground … without Bishopsgate called Petty France'. £1,500 was paid for confidential information to secure the property at auction for £4,000, with £300 ground rent. Bridgewater, Egerton and du Bourgay contributed £1,000 each; Lewis Dollon, James Herault, Stephen de la Creuze and Anthony Vezian (fl.1700–39) each contributed £500; and Dubois and Horne agreed to 'contribute their labour and Industry for building upon & Improving the land'.[103]

Dubois carefully surveyed the ground, 'drew a plan … of such houses, shops, stables, Coachhouses and other Buildings' and provided an estimate of the costs for Lord Bridgewater's approval. But the site had belonged to the City of London and the purchase was conditional upon a covenant that the new owner should employ City of London workmen. Dubois 'knew how to choose his own workmen' and was assured that the performance of such covenants was not always strictly required. However, the City authorities complained that they were never paid in full for the property, so Dubois failed to secure planning permission.

By August 1720 Dubois had also 'undertaken to build several large houses for several persons of quality upon new foundations near hide park', where a few years earlier he had designed new barracks for the Foot Guards. Bridgewater felt that Dubois 'would not have leisure to attend to the company's matters as he ought' and therefore recommended that the Petty France property be sold, partly due to the economic climate 'by Reson of the Great fall of stocks, and the Great Decay of public Credit':[104] 1720 was the year in which the South Sea Bubble burst. Bridgewater, Egerton, Dollon and Vezian defended Dubois's Bill of Complaint and all parties were acquitted from performing the agreement. The meetings had taken place in Dubois's house on the south side of Brewer Street, Soho, which he had built between December 1718 and May 1719 with a spectacular circular self-supporting staircase. From the 1730s the large room at the back became John Hickford's concert room, in which the 9-year-old Mozart gave his famous recital on 13 May 1765.[105]

RIGHT

72 *Lewes Bridge*

J.M.W. Turner, London, 1796
Pencil and watercolour, 5.1 × 21.6 cm
Tate Britain, Turner Bequest, 1856 (XXXII B)

Designed by Nicholas Dubois and built by Arthur Morris in 1725, the keystone of the arch inscribed with their names is clearly visible in Turner's watercolour.

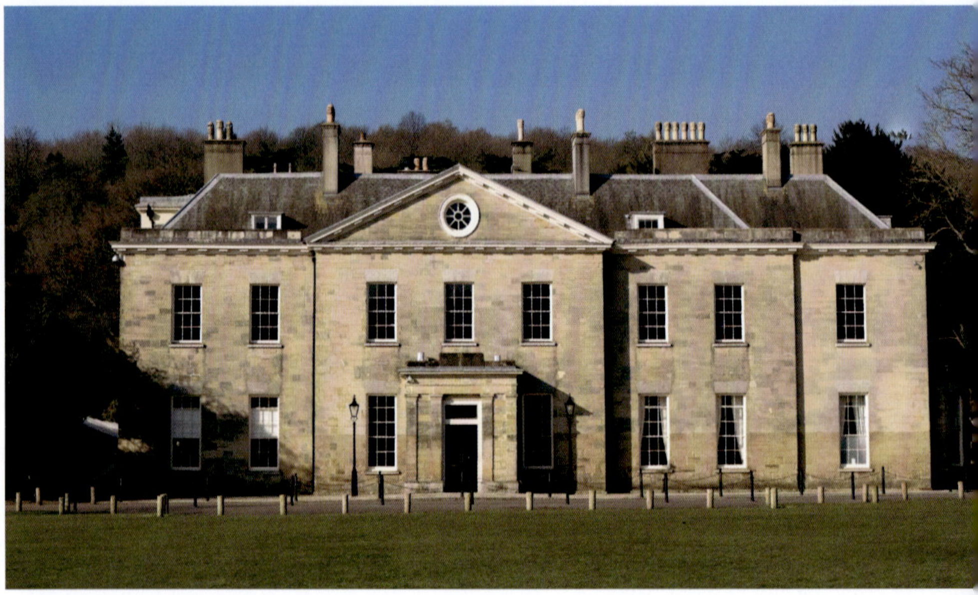

ABOVE

71 Stanmer Park

Designed by Nicholas Dubois, London, 1722–7
East Sussex

Although he was well paid for his role as architect, Dubois was not accepted by the locals when commissioned to design and supervise the rebuilding of Stanmer, near Lewes, West Sussex.

Palladian country houses

Dubois also worked on country houses. His most successful project was the 'great geometrical staircase' designed in 1721 for James, 1st Earl of Stanhope (1673–1721), at Chevening, Kent (plate 70).[106] With French *œil-de-boeuf* attic windows and rusticated entrances, the design of the pavilion wings at Chevening has been attributed to Dubois, although they were in fact built by Thomas Fort (d.1745). For Henry Pelham (1694–1754), brother of Thomas Pelham-Holles, 1st Duke of Newcastle (1693–1768), Dubois rebuilt Stanmer Park, Sussex (plate 71). Acquired in 1721, the total cost of rebuilding came to £14,200. Dubois acted as surveyor and was paid at the high rate of 6 per cent, receiving a fee of £738, a plain brick house

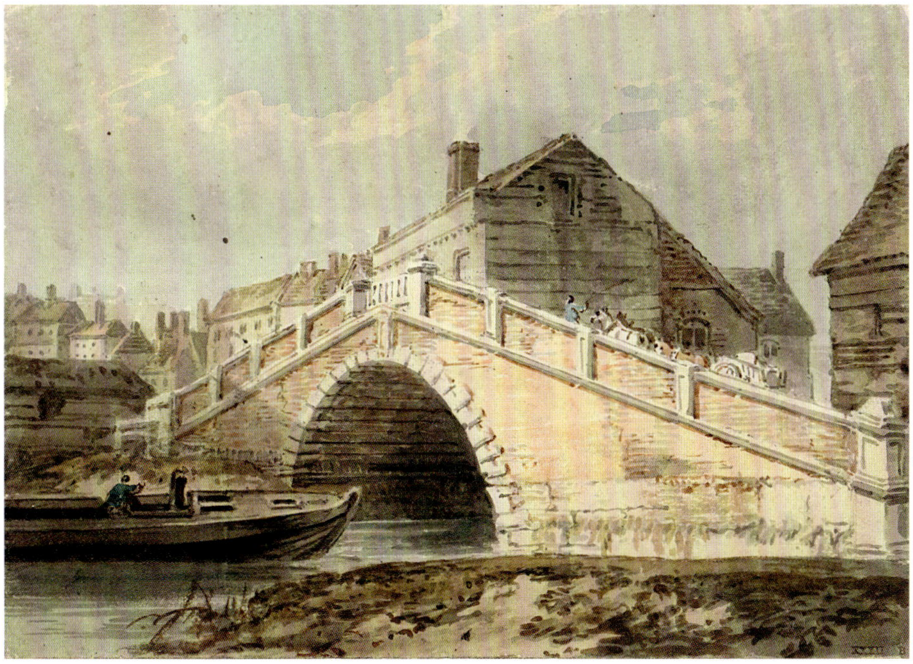

with a low pediment on the main front, its stone facings were taken from a nearby demolished house at Kenwards. (The balustrade was added in the nineteenth century.) A chimney piece carved by Samuel Tufnell, Master Mason at Westminster Abbey, in 'Torbay, White veine & Statuary Marble, with a carved head in the front' followed the design provided by Dubois.[107]

Surviving correspondence between Dubois and his patron between 1722 and 1727 shows that Dubois designed garden features at Stanmer Park, including the Hermitage and pool, and planned to rebuild the churchyard walls, providing a plan for a canal 'that occasioned a dispute'. Dubois fell out with the local vicar and with Lord Newcastle's servants, whose 'behaviour towards me has hitherto been intolerable': they called him 'the french son of a Bitch'. Dubois complained and protested that he never 'acted contrary to the rules of a liberal Education, a man of Honour, an Old Officer to the King and a Gentleman born as I am'.[108]

Civil engineering

It was possibly through the influence of Thomas Pelham (*c.*1705–1737), Henry's younger brother, who inherited Stanmer, that Dubois was commissioned in 1727 to design a bridge at Lewes, Sussex (plate 72), built by the mason Arthur Morris (d.1744). Although the bridge was widened in 1932, the keystone of the arch is still visible on the south side, inscribed:

PEVENSEY RAPES
N. DUBOIS SUVR
A. MORRIS
MASON
1727

Dubois and his wife, Anna, appointed the Earl of Essex to be guardian of his two children in 1734; he died in June 1735, a year before a public commission was set up to build a bridge across the Thames at Westminster.

When the idea was first formed in 1721, James Thornhill, Colen Campbell and John Vanbrugh produced designs.[109] In 1733 a bill was brought before Parliament and in 1734 Nicholas Hawksmoor produced plans, in conjunction with John Price (d.1736) and Batty Langley (1696–1751). Meanwhile, the House of Commons committee appointed in January 1736 consulted Charles Labelye, Dr Desaguliers and Captain Sir Charles Knowles (*c.*1704–1777) as to the most suitable of five possible sites for the bridge. Labelye first came to Britain in about 1720; he was a protégé of Desaguliers, who sponsored his membership

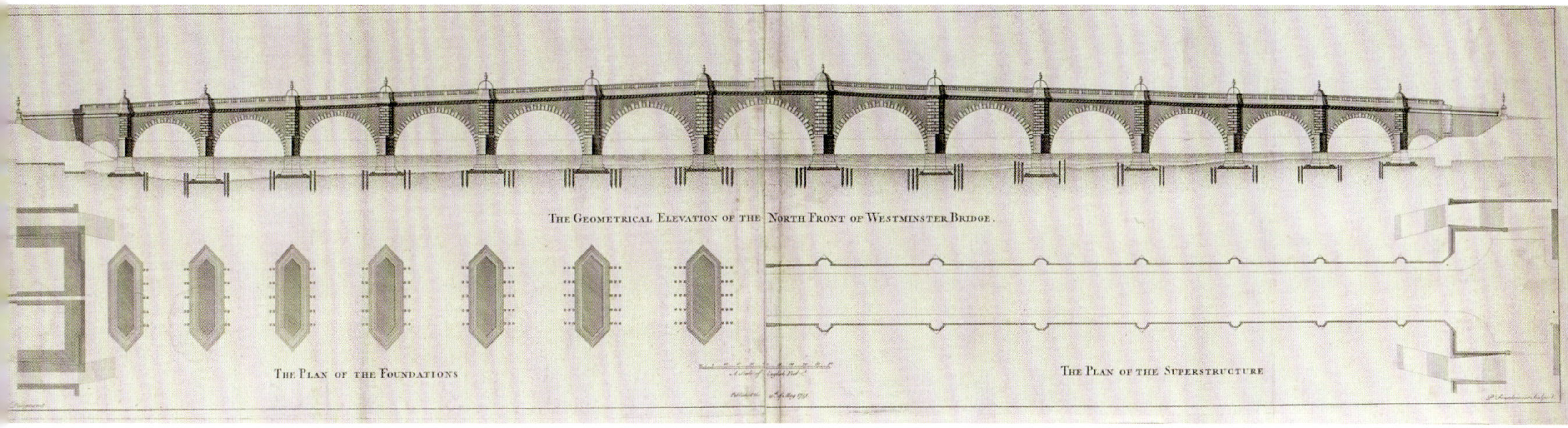

BELOW

73 *Geometrical elevation of the north front of Westminster Bridge with a plan of the foundations and superstructure*

P. Fourdrinier, London, after Charles Labelye, 1751
Engraving, 32.7 × 126 cm
London Metropolitan Archives (p5421031)

On 10 May 1738 the commissioners for the new bridge at Westminster appointed Labelye 'to lay the foundations and conduct the Building of the piers, abutments and superstructure of the said Bridge, and all the works relating thereto'. This is a record of Labelye's final design.

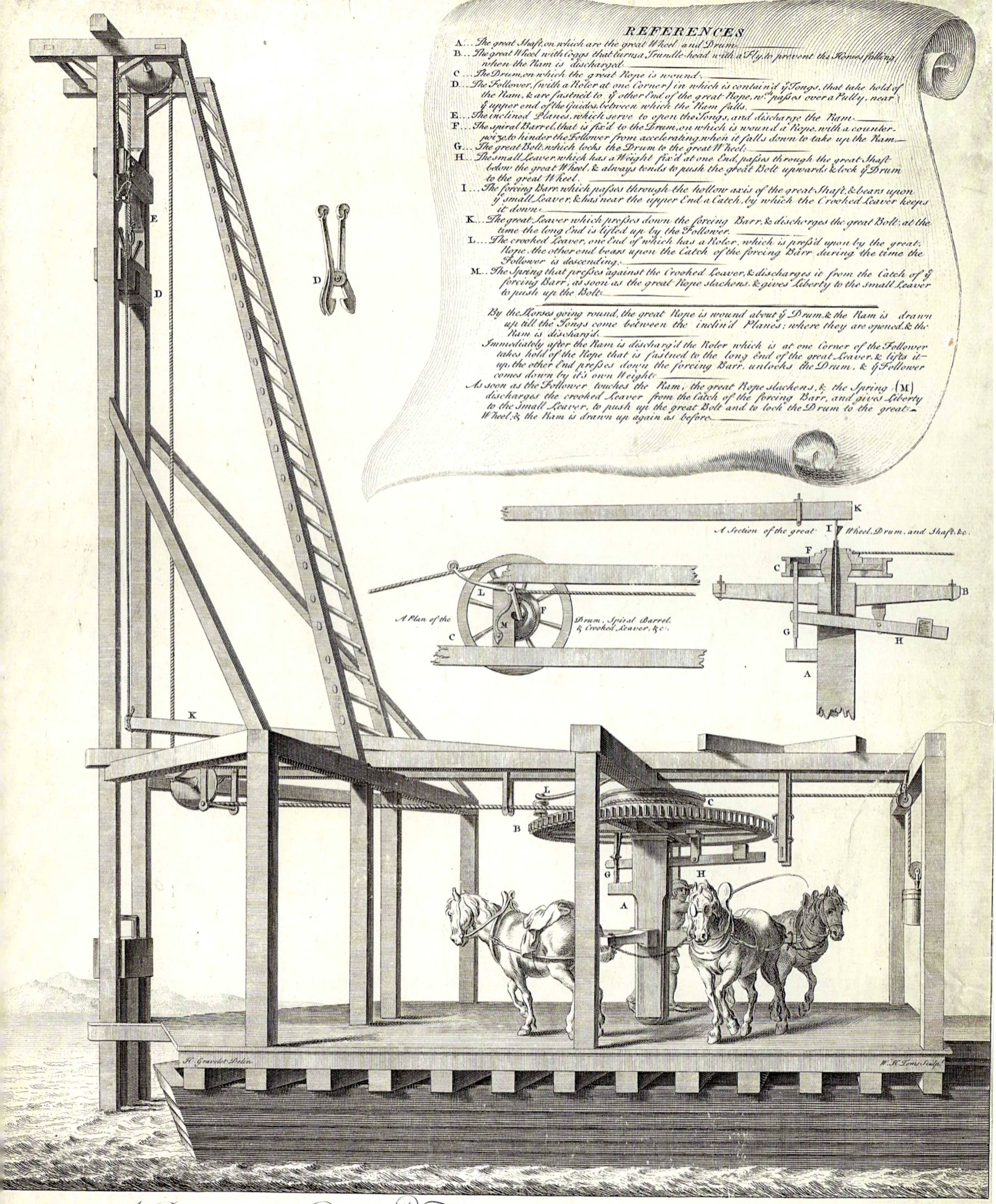

A Perspective View of the Engine, now made use of for Driving the Piles of the New Bridge at WESTMINSTER: most Humbly Inscrib'd to the Hon:ble Commissioners for Building the said Bridge, by the Inventor. — James Vauloue, Watch-Maker. —

Published by James Vauloue Proprietor Novr. 1st 1728.

LEFT

74 *Engine for driving the Piles of the New Bridge at Westminster invented by James Vauloué, 1737*

W.H. Toms, London, after a drawing by H. Gravelot, 1738
Engraving, 43.6 × 34.8 cm
Metropolitan Archives, London (p5424621)

Vauloué's ingenious invention featured a capstan powered by horses that raised a large weight to the top of the shaft. This was released to strike the top of the pile five times in two minutes, driving a firwood pile 14 feet into the river bed in an hour. This device was of great interest and attracted comment in the daily newspapers. The engraving cost 6d and was available at Slaughter's Coffee House, St Martin's Lane, where artists and patrons gathered.

of the French Masonic Lodge in Hemmings Row off St Martin's Lane in 1725 and described him as 'formerly my disciple and my Assistant'.[110] Labelye was in Madrid in 1727–8. Back in London in 1733, he supplied maps and surveys of the Thames at Westminster. In 1734 he assisted the elderly Hawksmoor but only produced his own designs for the bridge in 1736. On 10 May 1738 the commissioners appointed Labelye 'to laying the foundations of the piers' (plate 73).[111]

Although little is known about Labelye, as a marine civil engineer he had experience 'in harbourworks and fen drainage'.[112] His published reports, *The Result of a View of the Great Level of the Fens, taken at the Desire of His Grace the Duke of Bedford, etc. Governor, and the Gentlemen of the Corporation of the Fens* (1745) and *Relating to the Improvement of the* RIVER WEIR *and* PORT *of* SUNDERLAND (1748) appeared during the building of Westminster Bridge. Initial opposition to his appointment was largely a matter of professional jealousy. He was firmly supported by the commissioners, led by Henry Herbert, 9th Earl of Pembroke (1693–1750), with whom he maintained correspondence. David Papillon (1681–1762), great-grandson of the eponymous Huguenot architect and engineer (1581–1655), joined the commissioners and the works committee in 1738.[113] Lord Pembroke laid the first stone in January 1739 and suggested improvements to Labelye's second and final design.[114]

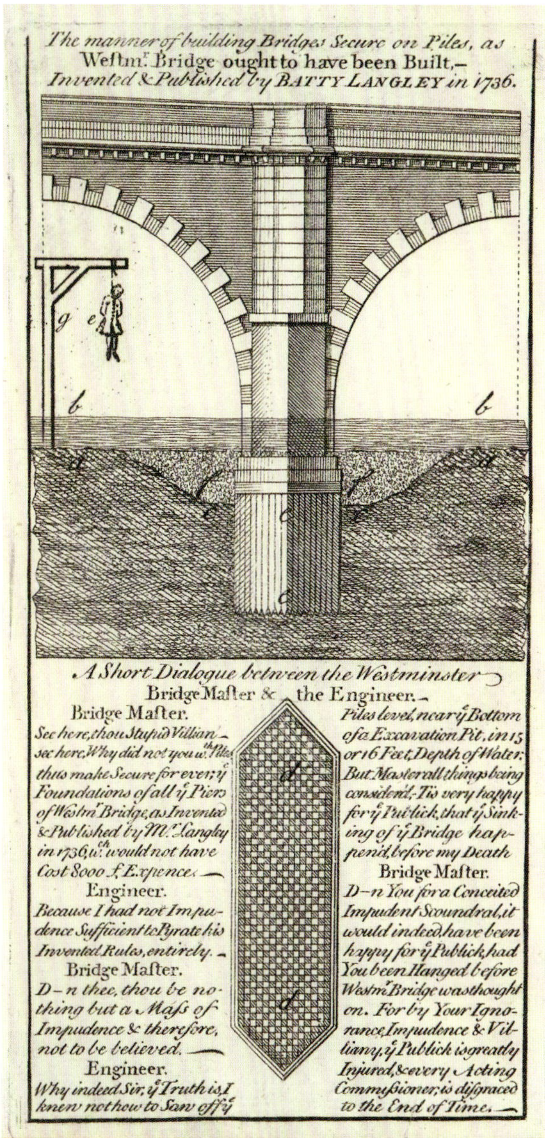

RIGHT

75 *A Survey of Westminster Bridge as 'tis Now Sinking into Ruin*

Frontispiece to Batty Langley's pamphlet, London, 1748
Engraving, 20 × 25 cm
Canadian Centre for Architecture

In September 1747 'one of the great stones, of several hundred weight, in the fifth arch' fell into the water. Langley's pamphlet shows 'Mr. Self-Sufficient' (Labelye) hanging from a gibbet under the left-hand arch.

A pile-driving engine invented by the Huguenot James Vauloué (1702–1742), 'a very ingenious watchmaker',[115] was used for the Westminster Bridge foundations. He was awarded the Royal Society's Copley Medal for his design.[116] A print of the engine, drawn by Gravelot, sold for 6d (plate 74).[117] The model was used by the Huguenot Stephen Demainbray (1710–1782) in his lectures on compound engines. Dr Desaguliers praised Vauloué's engine in a lecture on hydraulic machinery:

> *In works where we are confin'd to Time by Tides, as in making and mending Bridges there must be great care to husband the Power so well as to lose no Time. The late Mr Vauloué Watch-Maker contriv'd the best of that kind that perhaps was ever seen, and about 5 times more expeditious than the best I ever heard of.*[118]

The invention fascinated George III, who owned a wooden model of Vauloué's engine.[119]

Not all Labelye's Huguenot support was effective. Charles Marquand (d.1767), from Guernsey, one of those contracted in 1741 to build Brentford Bridge upstream from Westminster, to Labelye's designs, was given the contract to cut off the Westminster piles for 10s, provide his own tools and retain the longer poles for his own use. However, Marquand was 'seized with a violent fit of the Gout', so for a month nothing happened and then the contract was cancelled. Marquand's excuse was that in his absence his servant had lit a fire with the model of his pile-cutting device.[120] A machine able to cut eight piles under water every tide was invented by carpenter William Etheridge (1708–1776).[121] An engraving of Etheridge's machine, also available for 6d, was sold by Carrington Bowles (1724–1793) in St Paul's Church Yard.

Apart from minor delays, building went smoothly until 17 months before Westminster Bridge was due to open. In November 1747 the last stone was laid by Lord Pembroke, but during

May and June 1747 the first signs of calamity had developed. The balustrade over the West 15-ft pier (the fifth pier from the Westminster abutment) was found to be out of alignment. In September 'one of the great stones, of several hundred weight, in the fifth arch' fell into the water. By June 1748 the mean level of the pier was 2 ft 11 in (89 cm) below the two adjoining piers.[122] For the first time the commissioners disagreed with Labelye: 'I received Order to unload the Pier and to proceed next to take down the two damaged Arches.'[123] The adjoining arches were dismantled and rebuilt, with a reversed arch over the defective pier to relieve some of the pressure, and the bridge was opened to traffic in 1750. The incident produced a flow of bantering criticism and satire. Batty Langley's *A Survey of Westminster Bridge as 'tis Now Sinking into Ruin* had a frontispiece in which 'Mr. Self-Sufficient' (Labelye) is shown hanging from a gibbet under one of his own arches (plate 75). Popular ballads included 'The Downfall of Westminster Bridge My Lord in the Sud', a jibe at Lord Pembroke.[124]

The incident damaged the prestige of this ambitious project. To re-establish credibility and to provide answers for the curious, in 1751 Labelye published *A Description of Westminster Bridge to which are added An Account of the Methods made use of in laying the Foundations of its Piers and An Answer to the chief objections that have been made thereto.* He would not be drawn in to a 'Paper War upon this or any other Account' but was motivated by principles that conform to the Huguenot ethic:

> *It is the Duty of Man to do all the Good in his Power, and to contribute so far as his Abilities will permit to the Welfare of Posterity. I thought it incumbent on me to communicate to others some of the Fruits of my Studies Join'd to above twenty years Practice and Observation.*[125]

Pembroke persuaded the commissioners to present Labelye with an honorarium of £2,000 in recognition of 'his great fidelity and extraordinary labour and attendances, skill and diligence'.[126] In 1751, 'greatly afflicted with Asthma and unfit for Business', Labelye left England for Beziers in the South of France; he died, probably in Paris, some thirty years later.[127]

The lack of an authoritative English treatise on bridges prompted Stephen Riou (1720–1780) to publish *Short Principles for the Architecture of Stone Bridges with practical observations and a new geometrical diagram to determine the thickness of the Piers to the Height and Base of any given arch* (1760). The son of a London Huguenot merchant,[128] Riou refers to Westminster Bridge as

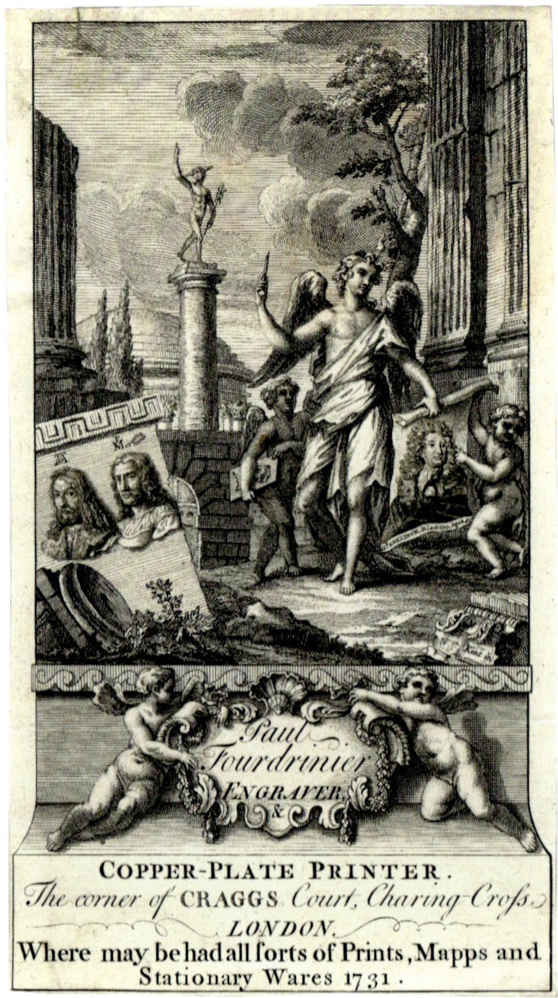

76 Trade card of Paul Fourdrinier

Designed by William Kent, London, 1731
Engraving 23.5 × 14 cm
British Museum, London (Heal Collection, 111.63)

Paul Fourdrinier's trade card was designed by architect William Kent, reflecting Fourdrinier's specialization in engraving architectural plans.

> *a very magnificent stone bridge, which may have afforded much experience … to those who had the opportunities to attend upon this building. It is to be regretted, that the ingenious and honest gentleman, who was appointed over this work did not at the finishing of it publish all the particulars of the mechanism of this grand structure; in a manner he was capable of doing it, to the satisfaction of the curious.*[129]

Riou supplied a design for Blackfriars Bridge, which 'was delivered by a friend of mine to a person of eminence in the city since deceased; but I have reason to believe, that it was by him at once condemned to the obscurity of some dark corner'.[130] The bridge was built to the designs of John Gwynn (1713–1786) in 1759.

The major bridge commission of the first half of the eighteenth century went to the Huguenot Labelye and the leading publications in English on bridge building were written by Labelye and Riou, who was quick to assert that he enjoyed 'the peculiar happiness to be born a subject of Britain'.[131] Yet both men benefited from European training and experience, Labelye claiming 'the first of my studies in architecture was at a foreign protestant academy of note'.[132] In 1736, after the Act for Westminster Bridge was passed, Charles Marquand went to Paris with Captain Sir Charles Knowles to gather information from French engineers about the foundations of piers in deep water.[133] In 1720 the Corps des Ingénieurs des ponts et chaussées was founded; Hubert Gautier (1660–1737) and Bernard Forest de Bélidor (1698–1761) were the French authorities cited throughout the process of its establishment. A bridge over the Loire at Blois, completed in 1720, was also cited as prototype for bridges. Thus the British looked to France for authority in engineering. Samuel Smiles (1812–1904), author of *Lives of the Engineers* as well as *The Huguenots*, commented, 'We depended for our engineering, even more than we did for our pictures and music, upon foreigners'.[134]

As with Nicholas Dubois and Jean de Bodt, Riou's earliest training was with the army; his interest in architecture and engineering was developed through military experience. In 1746 he published *The Elements of Fortification, Containing the Construction, Attack and Defence of Fortified Places, Regular and Irregular* dedicated to Prince William, Duke of Cumberland. The frontispiece, engraved by architectural engraver Paul Fourdrinier (plate 76), shows Minerva, Mars and Fame supporting a portrait medallion of Cumberland.[135] The account was inspired 'by the Scarcity of books in the English language which treat methodically of this art';[136] many of the plates were derived from Vauban and Bélidor. Riou's book made a major contribution to military education.

Huguenot architects in Ireland and Scotland

Abraham Roumieu (1734–1780) was a little-known surveyor of Huguenot descent who was living in St Leonard, Shoreditch, in the 1770s.[137] The son of John Roumieu (1699–1742), a London goldsmith, he was apprenticed to the British architect Isaac Ware (1704–1766) in 1748. In the 1760s he worked for the 4th Duke of Gordon (1743–1827):[138] his unexecuted designs for interior decoration at Gordon Castle are inspired by the Adam brothers.[139] Roumieu's grandson Robert Lewis Roumieu (1814–1877) designed the French Hospital in Victoria Park, Hackney, now the Mossbourne Victoria Park Academy.[140]

In Ireland the leading architect Richard Castle or Cassel (1690–1751) was of Jewish birth but had Huguenot family connections. He settled in Dublin in the early 1730s, where on 27 June 1733 he married Jeanne Truffet (d.1744) of Lisburn,[141] a niece of Louis Poriez (d.1726), who had links to the Lisburn linen industry.[142] The executors of Castle's will included the Huguenot Peter Bernard; and the administration of his wife's effects was granted to Daniel Crommelin (1707–1789), a kinsman of the well-known Lisburn linen weaver Louis Crommelin.[143]

It was through the Huguenot Irish network that Richard Castle met Dr Bartholomew Mosse (1712–1759), who founded the prototype for the Rotunda Lying-in Hospital in St George's Lane, Dublin, in 1745.[144] Dr Mosse then purchased a site for a larger hospital and commissioned Castle to design the building, for which the foundation stone was laid on 24 May 1751. He probably acted pro bono: there is no surviving bill.[145] Castle did not live to see the hospital's completion, as he died in 1751, but he would have approved of the exquisite chapel stuccowork designed and executed by the Flemish sculptor Bartholomew Cramillion (fl.1755–72), further evidence of the patron's sophisticated European taste. Begun in August 1755, the scheme was completed in 13 months for 300 guineas. The ceiling carries allegorical figures of the theological virtues Faith, Hope and Charity and two tablets of the Ten Commandments, supported by angel terms and putti heads. Biblical inscriptions in gold letters on red ribbon extol the challenge and role of children. By August 1758 Cramillion had also completed the altarpiece with a representation of the Lamb with Seven Seals from the Book of Revelation, lavishly decorated with over 20,000 leaves of gold. The work was much admired but the death of Dr Mosse in 1759 resulted in the delay of payment and created considerable anxiety for Cramillion, 'being a stranger' and 'having the most urgent occasion to go to his own country immediately'.[146]

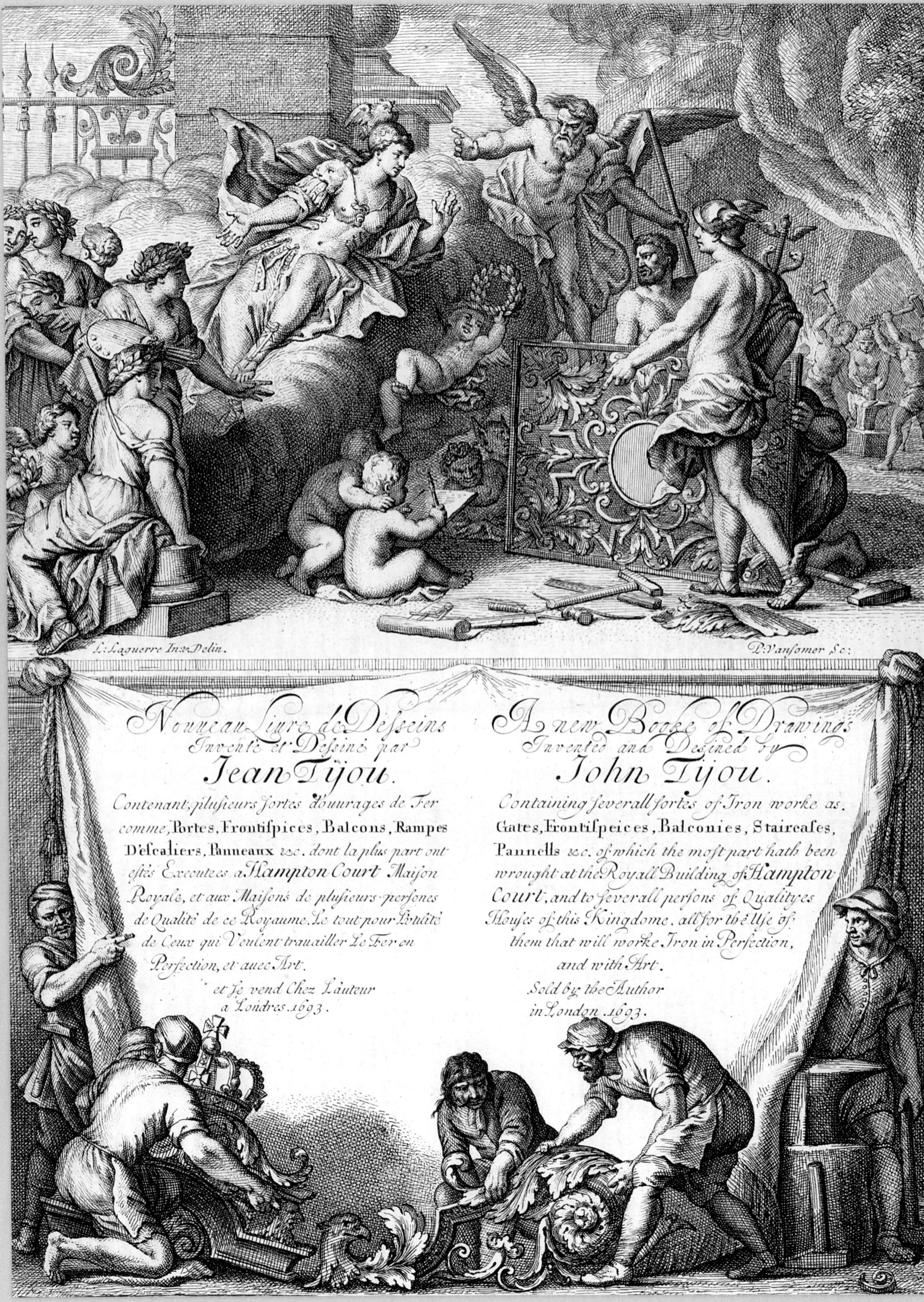
L: Laguerre Inv: Delin.
P: Vanſomer Sc:
Nouueau Liure de Deſſeins
Inventé et Deſsiné par
Jean Tijou.
Contenant plusieurs sortes douurages de Fer comme, Portes, Frontiſpices, Balcons, Rampes D'eſcaliers, Panneaux &c. dont la plus part ont estés Executees a Hampton Court Maiſon Royale, et aux Maiſons de plusieurs perſones de Qualité de ce Royaume. Le tout pour Lutilité de Ceux qui Veulent trauailler Le Fer en Perfection, et auec Art.
et Se vend Chez Lauteur
a Londres. 1693.
A new Booke of Drawings
Invented and Desined by
John Tijou.
Containing ſeverall ſortes of Iron worke as Gates, Frontiſpeices, Balconies, Staircaſes, Pannells &c. of which the most part hath been wrought at the Royall Building of Hampton Court, and to ſeverall perſons of Qualityes Houſes of this Kingdome, all for the Uſe of them that will worke Iron in Perfection, and with Art.
Sold by the Author
in London. 1693.

Chapter Six
Huguenot Metalsmiths

77 *A New Booke of Drawings invented and Designed by John Tijou*
Frontispiece designed by Louis Laguerre and engraved by Paul van Somer, 1693
Engraving, 34.7 × 26.1 cm
Victoria and Albert Museum, London (29394.1)

Jean Tijou worked in England as a gatesmith from 1687 until 1716. In the early 1690s his daughter Eleanor married Louis Laguerre, Louis XIV's godson, who designed the frontispiece for Tijou's 1693 book of designs for ironwork. The workmen assembling ironwork here may represent Tijou and his smithy assistants.

Gatesmiths

He must adorn my Gates with Foliage and Chased Work, and display a bold Fancy in the Disposition of his Scrolls[1]

In 1747 Robert Campbell introduced the art of 'the Black-Smith' as the 'most comprehensive Branch of all the Mechanic Trades'. Variety of employment provided opportunities for 'many different Species of Smiths'. A successful gatesmith required 'Knowledge of Drawing to be able to Design', 'a good English Education' if 'he is to converse with great Men' and 'great Strength of Body'.[2]

French émigré gatesmiths Jean Tijou and Jean Montigny contributed new levels of skill to cast and chased wrought iron still admired at Chatsworth, St Paul's Cathedral, Hampton Court Palace and the gates to Green Park on Piccadilly. They transformed royal palaces, streetscapes, shop signs, town and country houses. Their elegant ironwork defined estate boundaries, interior staircases, perimeters of public and funerary monuments, and church sanctuaries.

Jean Tijou, working in England from 1687 to 1716, is the most celebrated immigrant ironworker, although he is not mentioned in Huguenot church records. Between October and November 1687 Tijou, described as 'serrurier', was paid 2,582.8 *livres* for balcony balustrades on the upper storeys of the chateau of Saint Germain en Laye.[3] In the early 1690s his daughter Eleanor married the Catholic artist Louis Laguerre, Louis XIV's godson, who came to London in 1683 with the architectural painter Ricard.[4] Mrs Ann Tijou, probably Jean's wife, and three Tijou children were buried at St Martin-in-the-Fields between 1700 and 1709.[5] Two generations later (*c.*1780–5), a petition to the Westminster French Charity School on behalf of his grandchildren from Thomas Tijou (*c.*1701–*c.*1780), smallworker in gold, 'near 80 with failing sight', states that his father, John Tijou, was 'a refugee' from 'St Germans [*sic*]' who worked 'at Hampton Court … the whole of the Ironworks', not finished until Queen Anne's reign, when 'only part was paid for'.[6]

Jean Tijou's 1693 *New Booke of Drawings* illustrates private, public and royal commissions. It was advertised in *The London Gazette* on 1–4 October 1694 as available from Tijou's lodgings at the Barber's Pole, at the lower end of the Haymarket.[7] The frontispiece, drawn by Laguerre (plate 77), shows three workmen assembling ironwork – one of whom may represent Tijou himself.[8] The royal crown on the left and the massive stone piers with iron railings evoke the entrance to Hampton Court Palace, where Tijou's smithy was established in 1691. His Fountain Screen at Hampton Court (plate 78) defined the palace boundary on the Thames and proclaimed the prestige of royal estate. Tijou also supplied 773 ft (236 m) of adjacent iron fence to ensure privacy.

Josiah Key (fl.1674–1722), Tijou's neighbour on Hampton Court Green, was paid for supplying the gilded brass locks with chased figurative borders for the State Apartments, as well as 'new stays ... to rivett to Mr. Tijou's Pillars to hinder ye people from pissing on ye Privy Garden'.[9] Tijou's skill is reflected in his higher rates of pay: he was paid £6 a yard for the Greenwich Hospital balustrade, while Key only received 30s a yard for the Hampton Court Chapel balustrade.

Some of Tijou's designs do not relate to known commissions. His vintner's sign (plate 79) reflects the dominance of Huguenot wine merchants in London and in Paris, where even after the Revocation, a network of Protestant-owned wine shops sustained communities of Huguenots.[10] Melchizedeck Girard, who sold wine in West Street alongside the French church in 1701–2, had by 1703 moved to the sign of the Bacchus and Bunch of Grapes (as shown in Tijou's design) in Channel Row on the back side of King Street, Westminster, near the Thames.[11]

Tijou worked outside London at Chatsworth, Derbyshire, for William Cavendish, 1st Duke of Devonshire, under ironworker William Marshall (*c.*1655–1716) in 1697.[12] Here he was joined by French assistants 'Chalet' and 'Raget'.[13] Chalet is possibly John Isaac Chalie (d.1746), whose daughter was baptized at St Martin-in-the-Fields in 1696; Mr Raget is the 'French Smith's Servant' whose travel to London from Derbyshire was refunded in 1689. At Chatsworth the brass-worker Savouret[14] and Mr Grillet advised on the installation of garden water features, including the Cascade; both were French immigrants, probably Huguenots.

At Burghley House, Leicestershire, Tijou was supplied with boards on which to draw; his designs for the great gate are preserved.[15] Tijou also worked at Wimpole Hall, Cambridgeshire; Drayton House, Northamptonshire; and Kiveton Park, Yorkshire. For Cholmondeley Castle, Cheshire, Tijou supplied gates wrought at his Hampton Court smithy.[16] His last recorded

78 Fountain Screen, Hampton Court Palace

Jean Tijou and workshop, *c.*1695
Wrought iron, painted and gilded, ht 3.2 m
Historic Royal Palaces

The celebrated 12-panelled Fountain Screen for the Privy Garden bordering the Thames, incorporating the rose, thistle and harp, representing England, Scotland and Ireland and the Garter Star and cross is Tijou's masterpiece. It defines the palace boundary and proclaims the prestige of royal estate.

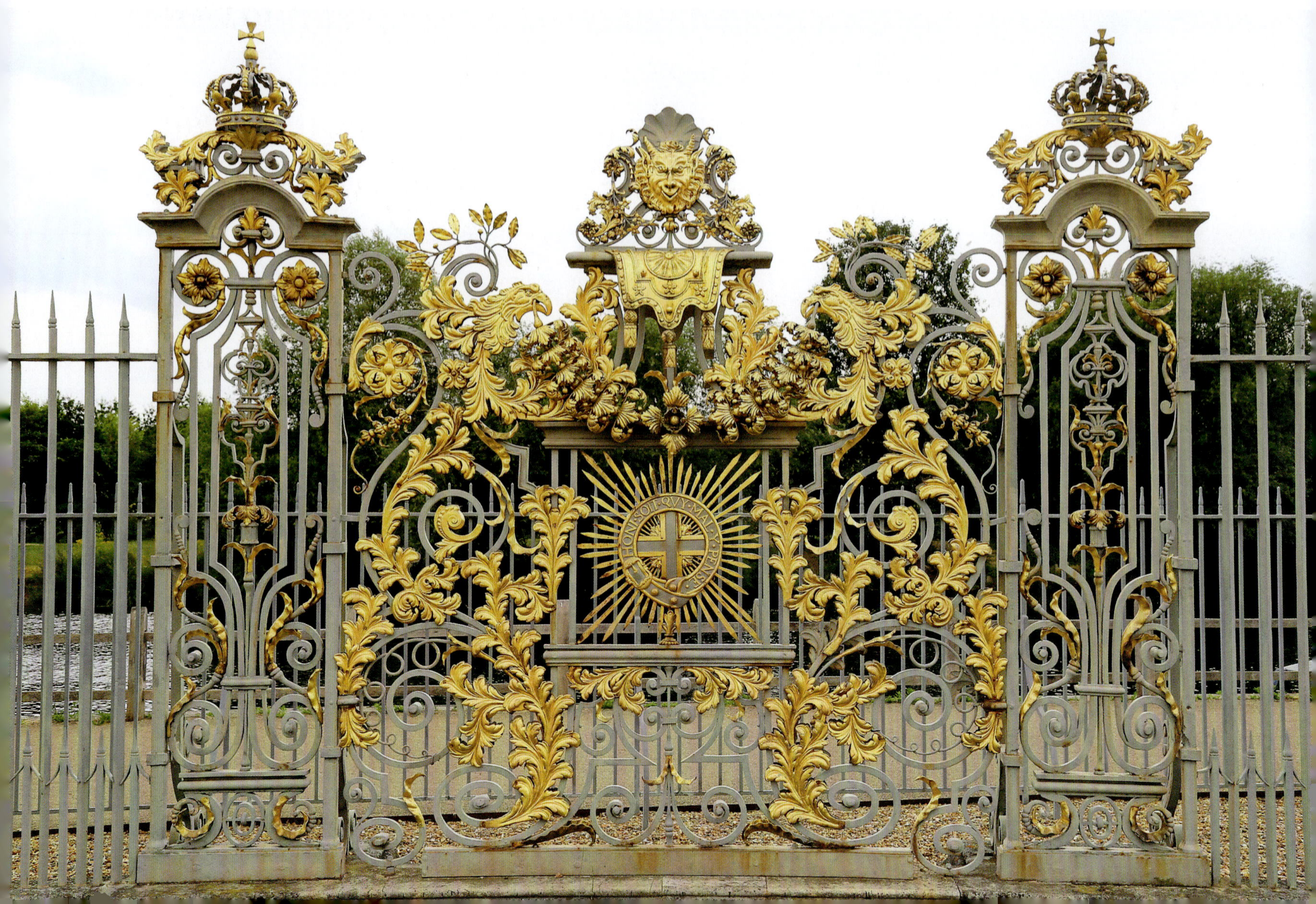

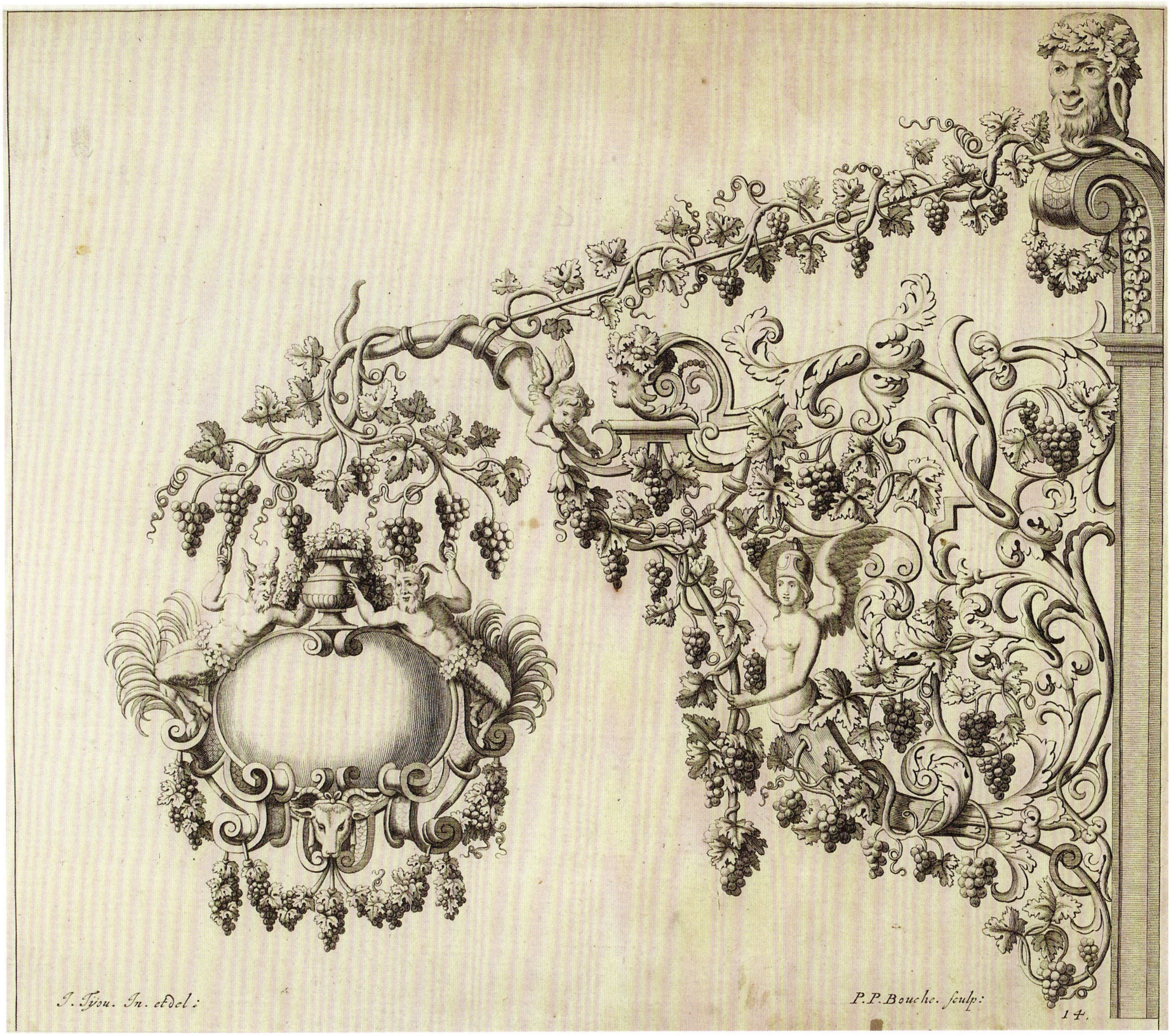

79 Design for a vintner's shop sign

P.P. Bouche after Jean Tijou, 1693
Etching, 26.2 × 34 cm
Victoria and Albert Museum, London (25082.10)

This sophisticated design features Bacchus, Roman god of wine, and his associate, the bearded Silenus. The merchant's name would feature on the pendant label, framed by satyrs and a goat's head.

commission was for Cain Hill House gates, Wrest Park, Bedfordshire for the Earl of Kent, *c.*1716.[17] Tijou made personal recommendations for James Thornhill's visit to Paris in 1716 and probably retired to France; he disappeared without trace, although his 1693 book of designs was published in Paris in 1723 by Louis Fordrin.[18]

Tijou's work for St Paul's Cathedral and royal palaces is documented.[19] Like the Huguenot goldsmiths, his technical skills empowered his designs and embossed repoussé work, creating decorative masks out of beaten metal. Celia Fiennes described Tijou's work at Burghley as carving rather than casting: 'the door on top of the Stepps is of iron carv'd, the finest I ever saw, all sorts of leaves, flowers, figures, birds, beasts, wheat in the Carving.'[20] Tijou probably used a woodcarver to create moulds on which to beat the iron.[21] His assistants at Hampton Court, and from 1700 at Hyde Park Corner (he moved his smithy to Portugal Row, off Piccadilly, in 1705) included English blacksmiths William Bagley (fl.1687–96) and Huntington Shaw (1660–1710). Shaw worked with Tijou at Chatsworth and Hampton Court until his death in 1710; Bagley installed Tijou's ironwork at Cholmondeley between 1687 and 1696.

Meanwhile in London, Tijou's neighbour the gatesmith Jean Montigny married Anne Julian in 1705 at St James's Piccadilly. Montigny may have been related to Tijou: in 1753 Tijou's sons, Thomas and Michael, were named as beneficiaries of Montigny's will and the recipients of 'two family pictures in gilt frames hanging in my little parlour'.[22] By 1710 Montigny had established his own smithy in Bolton Street, off Piccadilly. In 1712 he supplied ironwork for the Temple family at Wootton House, Buckinghamshire.[23] For James Brydges, 1st Duke of Chandos, at Cannons, Edgware, Montigny supplied an elaborate staircase balustrade and exterior railings for over £240 in 1725–6.[24] Following Chandos's bankruptcy and the demolition of Cannons, the railings (plate 80). were adapted in 1737 for the new Mayfair house of Philip Stanhope, 4th Earl of Chesterfield.[25] Among the most lavish ironwork ever made in Britain, they proclaim the patron's status. Intended to impress the visitor on arrival, the railings flanked the main entrance and could be seen by patron and guests from the front ground-floor reception rooms.

Montigny also supplied a weathervane for John, 2nd Earl Fitzwilliam (1685–1728), at Milton, Northamptonshire in 1725 for 3 guineas; and for the menagerie at Goodwood, West Sussex, 'an iron cage for a Tygar, 15 foot two ways with a covering on top' for £77 in June 1726.[26]

Montigny's will reveals his status as a 'gentleman' who owned paintings, silver and watches.[27] He remained in contact with gold chasers Thomas and Michael Tijou in Moorfields, whose name by the 1750s had been anglicized to 'Tissue'. They may have chased the bronze panels for Montigny's railings for Cannons. The codicil to Montigny's will dated April 1754 names 'John Anthony, carver of Warwick Street, St James's' as recipient of a legacy of £10. This is Jean Antoine Cuenot (d.1763), a modeller in wood for iron and bronze work, and carver of interior panelling at Norfolk House, St James's Square.[28] Three substantial gilt-bronze tables made for Norfolk House before 1756 may have been cast and chased from Cuenot's models in Montigny's workshop.

Montigny took over Tijou's workshop and continued to supply sophisticated architectural ironwork from the 1720s to the 1750s. Both may have abjured their Protestant faith before emigrating to London. Montigny's will (1754) states that his parlour had four pictures of 'our Blessed Saviour', which, with 'the Large picture of Our Blessed Lady and the picture of the Samaritan hanging on the staircase', were bequeathed to Catholic priests 'Benjamin Petre, alias White' (1672–1758) and Richard Challoner (1691–1781), a Catholic convert who succeeded Petre as Vicar Apostolic of the London district in 1758. Yet Montigny outwardly conformed to the Church of England, occupying a pew in St George's church, Hanover Square. His friendship with Petre and Challoner may demonstrate the enlightened ecumenical attitude exemplified in Bernard Picart's volumes on comparative religion, *Cérémonies et coutumes religieuses de tous les peuples du monde*, published in London in 1723–43. Montigny's bequest for the relief of poor and deranged persons demonstrates his awareness of the need to support those whose experience of trauma associated with exile was still a strong memory for the next generation.[29]

Locksmiths

Locks provided by Huguenot smiths controlled access to state apartments in palaces and country houses, cabinet furniture and church pews, providing security, promoting privacy and etiquette, and separating royalty and nobility from the public. Huguenot cabinetmakers employed turners and locksmiths from their own community to fit out their work. The *ébéniste* Pierre Pavie is linked with the locksmiths Jacques Marc and Samuel Marc. In 1701 Pavie witnessed Jacques Marc's marriage at the Hungerford Market church and in 1703 Samuel Marc stood godfather to Pavie's son Etienne at La Patente, Soho. In 1696 Pavie received £1 17s from Charles Seymour, 6th Duke of Somerset, 'for making & gilding 4 drawers in his Graces Cabinett to Put bookes in and some other work' for Northumberland House, London.[30] Pavie was still working in Compton Street, Soho, in 1727.[31]

French church registers record locksmiths in London and Bristol.[32] In 1690s Bristol, the leading centre for brass production, Huguenot Isaac Ardouin was working as a *maréchal ferrant* (blacksmith) and his compatriot David Godet as a locksmith. There were three Huguenot smiths in Portarlington, Ireland, in the early eighteenth century.[33] In London, Jacques Nortier and Pierre L'Avenue were in Farthing Street, Stepney, in the 1700s and André Charbonnier was in Nightingale Lane, off Aldgate, in 1701. However, most settled close to the centre of cabinetmaking and coachbuilding in Soho and Covent Garden: in

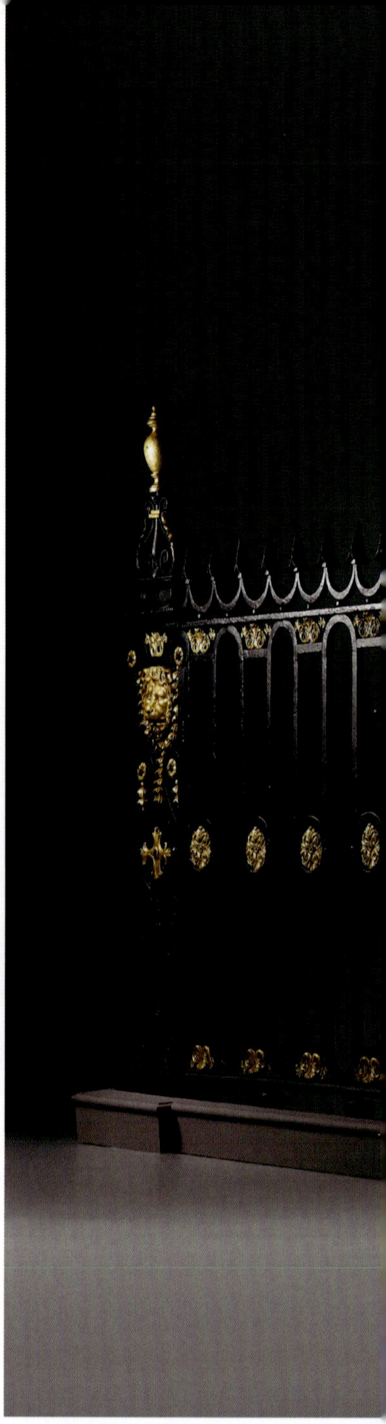

80 Railings from Chesterfield House, Mayfair, originally for Cannons, Edgware

Jean Montigny, *c.*1720; modified *c.*1737
Wrought iron and cast bronze, ht 236 cm
Private collection, Belgium

Made of wrought and cast iron with gilt iron and gilt bronze decoration, the railings have interlaced Cs encircled by the Order of the Garter motto suspended from chased bearded gilt-bronze masks, flanked by acanthus scrolls and floral swags.

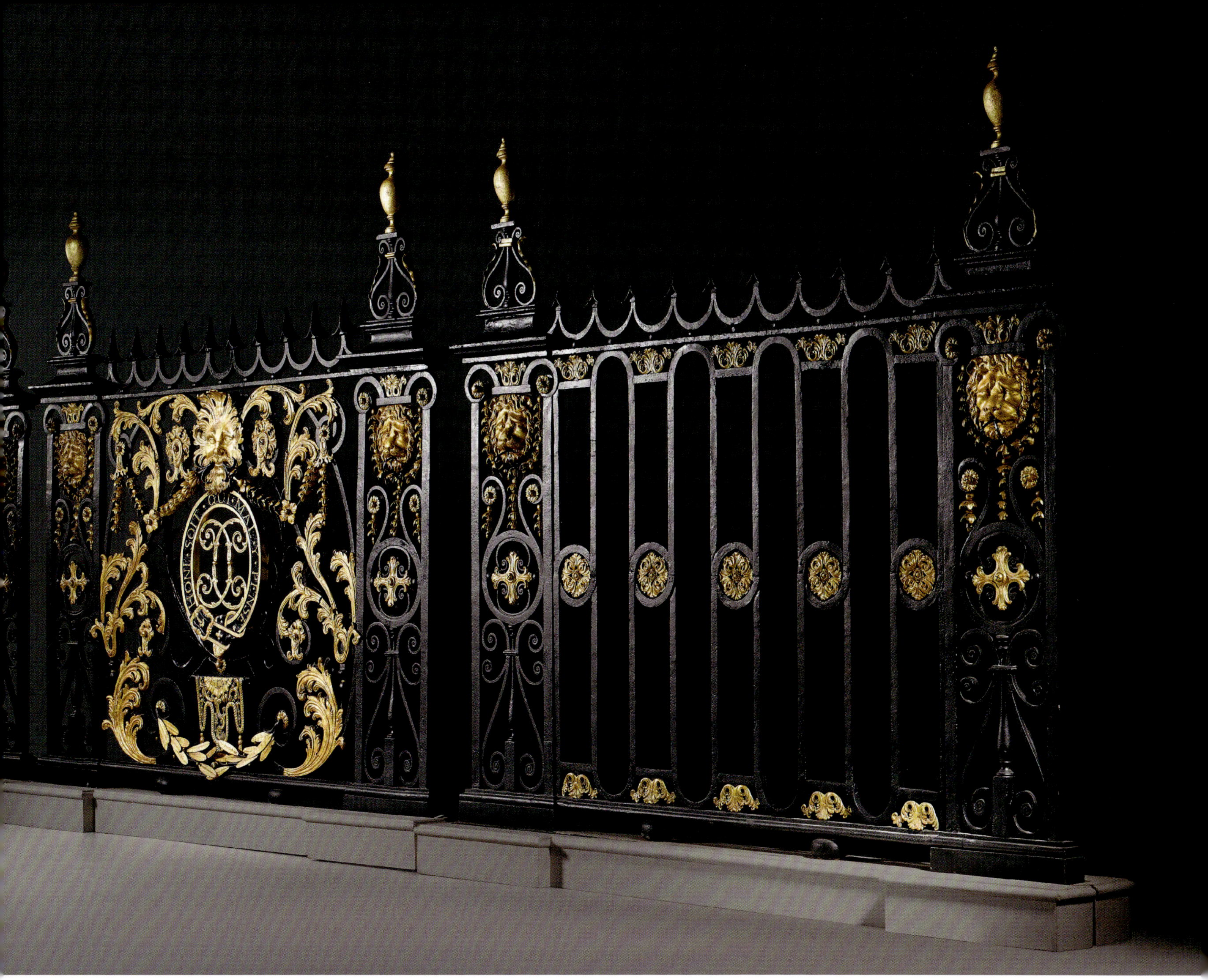

Compton and Wardour Streets, around Seven Dials in Earl Street, Grey Eagle Street and King Street. The church registers demonstrate links between locksmiths and cabinetmakers: in 1713 locksmith Nicholas Gautier (d.1737) stood godfather to Françoise, daughter of the cabinetmaker Lazaire Desbois (fl.1702–23), who worked at the sign of the Clock Case and Cabinet in Compton Street.[34] In 1747 Robert Campbell wrote that the locksmith had to make the keys, wards, springs and plates himself and to employ the founder to cast his cases in brass. 'The nicest Branch of this Art is tempering Springs', which 'requires as large a Share of Ingenuity almost as any Branch of the Trade'. The only education required was 'Writing and Reading'.[35]

Samuel Marc supplied Ralph, Earl of Montagu, in December 1697, with 'a button to the lock at the Pew in the French church'.[36] He worked with Jacques Marc, possibly his brother, at the sign of the Cross Keys, White Lion Street, from 1681 (when they received £5 'to get tools' from the Threadneedle Street church) until 1703.[37] The 'Mr Marke' who was paid the sum of £30 by Charles Seymour, 6th Duke of Somerset, 'in full of all Ironworke', and a further £54 for iron gates and railings in 1689/90,[38] can be identified as Samuel Marc, since he worked on a larger scale than Jacques.[39] Pierre Pavie (fl.1684–1727) stood godfather to his daughter Marguerite in 1696, and Pierre Rieusset (plate 94), carpenter, stood godfather to his son Pierre in

1697. Samuel Marc was godfather to Mathieu, son of Mathieu Andre (fl.1700–6), mason, working at the Blackamoor's Head in Compton Street; he also witnessed the marriage of the cabinetmaker Paul Desmoulins (fl.1698–1719) in 1718.[40] Like the Marc family, Andre came from Caen.

Other ironworkers came from Normandy; Mathieu Fouquelin, based in Earl Street, Seven Dials, from 1695 to 1708, was from Paris. The shortage of locksmiths in the French metropolis around 1700 provided opportunities for English locksmiths to emigrate. A generation later, Pierre François Podevin (1683–1750), originally from Arras, was living with his son at the Golden Lock, Wardour Street, in 1749, when he retired to the French Hospital.[41]

Bronziers

There is surprisingly little information on Huguenot craftsmen who specialized in bronze, although the centrepiece signed by D.R. Gastecloux in 1768 (plate 216) demonstrates that this was another area of speciality. Etienne Baudry, who attended the French church in Leicester Fields and was listed as 'fondeur' in 1688, may have cast in bronze and other metals. In Bristol in September 1720 Francis Billo (d.1754) was admitted a burgess by Vote of Common Council and presented the City with 'a brass Cistern & fountain of his own workmanship'. Brass chandeliers signed by Billo are in St Michael's church, Marblehead, Massachusetts, dated 1732 (the original 1714 church was extended in 1728), and St George's church, Dunster, Somerset, dated 1740 (plate 81).[42]

Billo's daughters were baptized in the Bristol French church in 1719 and 1721. His last apprentice joined him in February 1748/9. He moved from the Bristol parish of St Philip and St Jacob to the parish of St Stephen, where he was buried in June 1754.

Gunsmiths and armourers

During Louis XIV's reign French gunmakers set new standards in design and finish of firearms. Two leading Paris makers, Pierre Monlong (*c*.1635–1701) and Pierre Gruché (fl. Paris *c*.1670–85, m. London 1699), took refuge in London.[43] They settled in Soho, beyond the control of the Gunmakers' Guild,[44] although Monlong's premises were searched in November 1684 and again in February 1686, when he was fined 10s for possession of unproved barrels. Isaac de Seret (fl. *c*.1680–90) and Landreville (fl. *c*.1690–1700) were both from regional France: the de Serets,

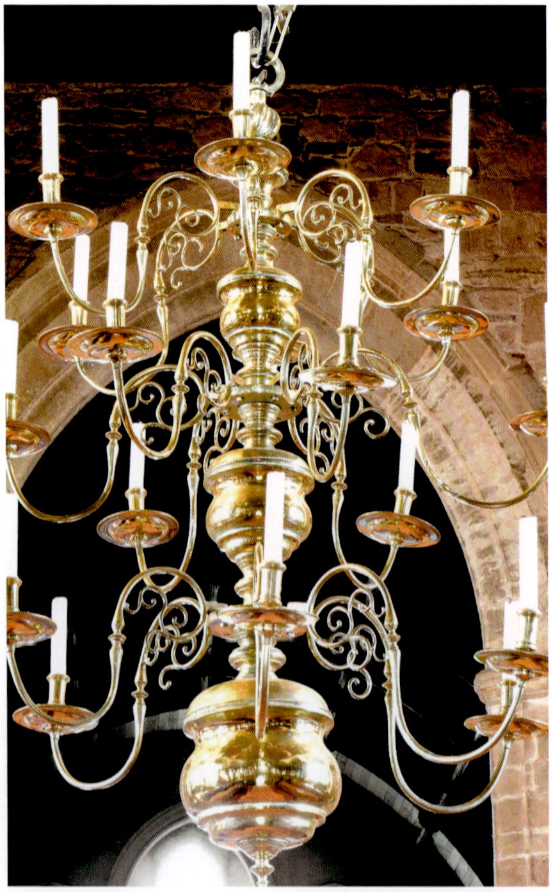

81 Chandelier

Francis Billo, Bristol, 1740
Brass, ht 125.7 cm, diam. 85.7 cm
St George's Church, Dunster, Somerset

Billo, a Huguenot brass founder based in Bristol, contributed to the important local industry centred on Baptist mills started in 1702 by the Quaker Abraham Darby (1678–1717). This drew on local supplies of copper, zinc and coal. Billo's three-tier chandelier provided ample candlelight for this 15th-century priory church.

from Crépy-en-Laonnois, were patronized by William Cavendish, 1st Duke of Devonshire.[45] Their guns combined original mechanisms with high-quality decoration.

Second-generation gunmakers included Henry Delany (fl.1715–46), Pierre Gandon (d. *c*.1743) and Israel Segallas (1715–1774). Segallas, who was from Berne in Switzerland, tested gun barrels for the Armourers' Company; he entered the French Hospital in 1773, no longer able to earn a living due to rheumatism in his hands.[46] In the early nineteenth century Isaac Riviere (1781–1851), a leading gunmaker, was of Huguenot descent: his family originally came from Nérac, Gascony.

Pierre Monlong came from Angers, where his earliest-recorded pair of pistols were made. In 1664 he was appointed Arquebusier de la Maison Roi to Louis XIV. He emigrated to London in 1684 with his wife and two children and was granted denization in 1688. By June 1689 he was Gentleman Armourer in Ordinary to William III.[47] A pair of flintlock holster pistols dating from the mid-1690s inscribed 'MONLONG LONDINI' (plate 82) are considered the finest ever produced as works of art in Britain. The walnut stocks are inlaid with silver filigree work and cut silver sheet representing

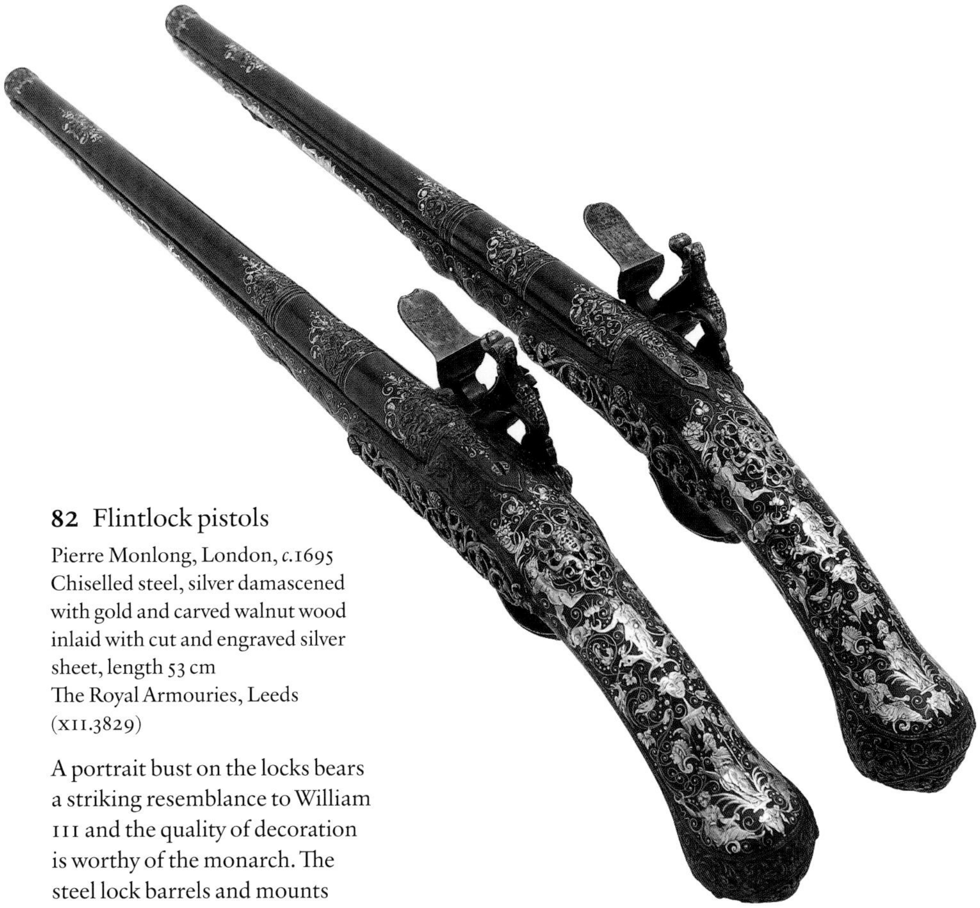

82 Flintlock pistols

Pierre Monlong, London, *c.*1695
Chiselled steel, silver damascened with gold and carved walnut wood inlaid with cut and engraved silver sheet, length 53 cm
The Royal Armouries, Leeds (XII.3829)

A portrait bust on the locks bears a striking resemblance to William III and the quality of decoration is worthy of the monarch. The steel lock barrels and mounts are chiselled and engraved, the barrels enriched with damascened gold set on a blued background. The stamped mark of the maker, 'M' under a heart in a circle, is visible under the breech.

Diana flanked by hounds on the butt, Apollo driving the chariot of the sun in front of the trigger guard, and Fortitude near the fore-end. When Monlong wrote his will on 7 June 1699 he was still 'Gunsmith in Ordinary to the King of Great Brittaine'; probate was granted on 6 August 1701.[48]

Pierre Gruché, from Paris, was established in Compton Street, Soho, when he married Marie des Champs at the French Hungerford Market church in 1699.[49] No London work by Gruché is known but a Paris-made sporting gun signed 'GRUCHE A PARIS' beneath a seated figure of Fame, probably presented to Charles Lennox, 1st Duke of Richmond by Louis XIV, is in the Royal Armouries (plate 83). The stock is inlaid with silver birds, heads of Medusa, lions and *amorini*.[50] Ornamental pattern books published in Paris in the 1670s illustrate the assembly of such sophisticated firearms. The ornament on Monlong's pistols (plate 82) is derived from pattern books published in Paris by Claude (*c.*1635–1693) and Jacques Simonin between 1685 and 1693 and subsequently copied in the Netherlands.

Jacques Gorgo (1689–1727), of Swiss origin, an *armourier* living in Grafton Street in 1702, was married in 1686 at Les Grècs, Hog Lane, Soho. A flintlock breech-loading fowling piece signed 'GORGO LONDINI FECIT' *c.*1690 is innovative (plate 84): this has separate chambers linked to a single barrel by a curved connecting passage, eliminating the usual second barrel, although the gun could still fire two shots in succession before reloading.[51] Another fowling piece, signed 'LANDREVILLE LONDON', is remarkable for its lightness . The maker was probably related to Noel de Landreville (1639–1675), a celebrated gunsmith in Grenoble.[52] The two fowling pieces supplied to the Duke of Devonshire by Isaac de Seret in about 1690[53] are finely inlaid in silver and may have been embellished by Samuel de Seret, the gunsmith's son. Samuel was working in London as a gunsmith from 1690 to 1703; in 1712 he was recorded in London as a goldsmith and by 1715 he had moved to Dublin.[54]

Louis Barbar (*c.*1668–1741) was born in Essendun, Poitou, the son of James Barbar, who had emigrated to France after the Interregnum in England following the Civil War. Louis came to England in 1688 and was made a freeman of the London Gunmakers' Company in 1704. Barbar supplied guns to John Churchill, 1st Duke of Marlborough,[55] was appointed Gentleman Armourer to George I and George II[56] and served as Master of the Gunmakers' Company in 1718.

83 Sporting gun

Pierre Gruché, Paris, 1680–90
Steel barrel, walnut stock inlaid with silver, length 172.2 cm
The Royal Armouries, Leeds (XII.1689)

This incorporates an earlier Italian barrel which has been decorated in Paris to match the French stock and lock. The lockplate bears Pierre Gruché's signature adjacent to a seated figure representing Fame. The stock is inlaid in silver with Medusa-heads, birds, cherubs and lions.

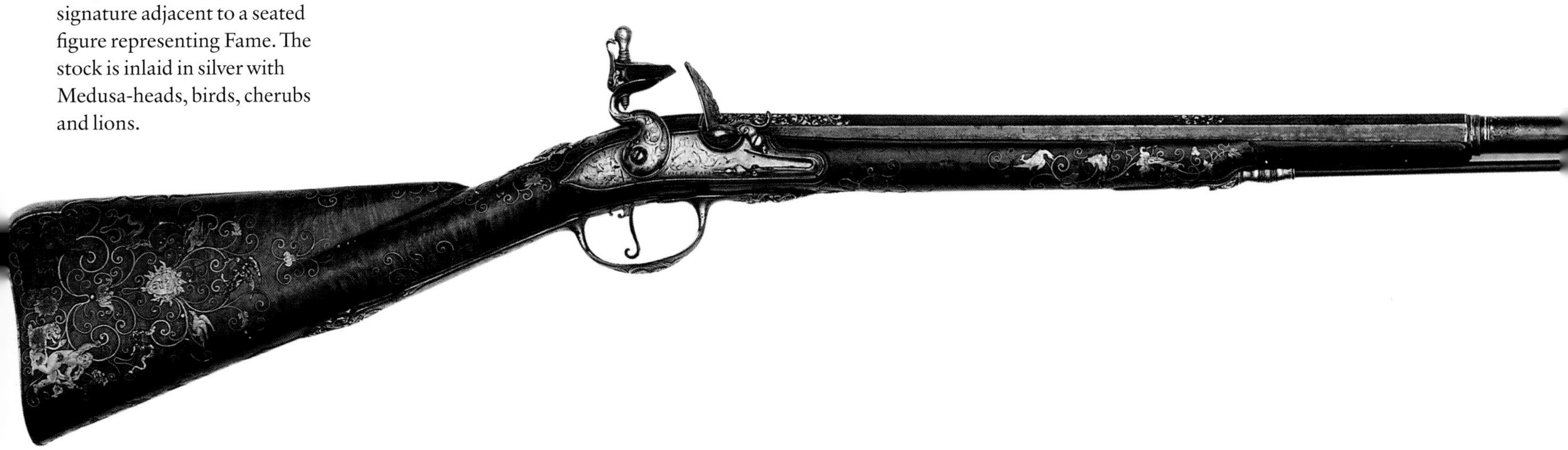

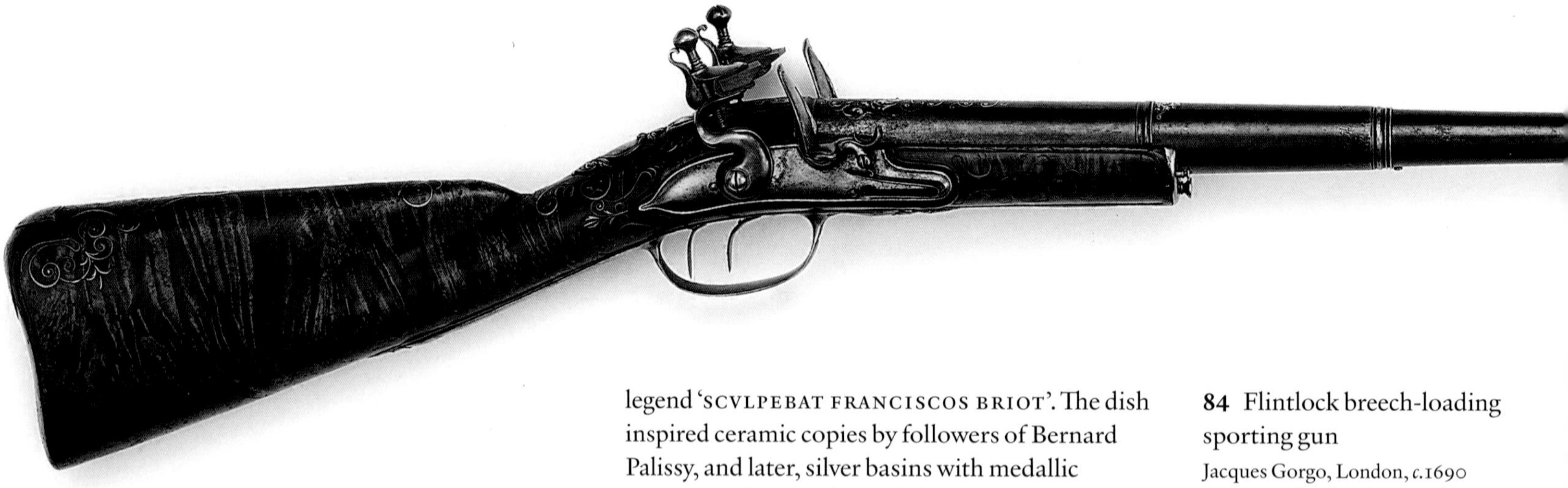

He was working in London's Portugal Street in 1726–39 and in Rupert Street from 1739 until 1741. He supplied guns to John, 2nd Duke of Montagu, between 1711 and 1744 (plate 85) and in June 1718 devised a decorative display at Boughton: 'about 500 musquets, 100 Carbines and 260 pairs of pistols', which, according to the Duke's steward, looked 'wonderfully well'.[57]

Isaiah Fleureau (d.1775), a sword cutler, advertised in 1742 at the King's Arms at the lower end of St James's Street.[58] By 1777 he is mentioned in his uncle's will as sword cutler of Haymarket,[59] and his trade card for that address confirms his location as at 'the lower end of Haymarket fronting Pall Mall'. A small sword with the signature 'Fleureau Hay:Market' on the middle band, dating from 1747–60, was recently sold at auction.[60] Isaiah was succeeded by his son of the same name. His neighbour in St James's was the cutler, razor and surgeons' instrument maker John Savigny (d.1757), at 129 Pall Mall.[61] In 1763 John Savigny the younger advertised cut steel penknives and apologized that demand exceeded the supply.[62] In 1781 the second edition of his treatise on the use and management of a razor was published.[63]

Pewterers

François Briot, model carver, medallist and pattern maker based in Monbeliard, is admired: the 'Temperantia' dish he designed, the only signed example of his work (plate 8), is the model for the annual Wimbledon Tennis Championships Women's Singles trophy. The trophy is an electrotype copy by Elkingtons of Birmingham. Intended for display on a princely buffet, probably for Friedrich I, Duke of Württemberg (1557–1608), the pewter dish has a central medallion featuring the figure of Temperance signed 'FB', with a medallic profile portrait of Briot on the reverse, with the legend 'SCVLPEBAT FRANCISCOS BRIOT'. The dish inspired ceramic copies by followers of Bernard Palissy, and later, silver basins with medallic representations of classical deities interspersed with representations of the Four Elements or the Five Senses, marked by London-based Huguenot goldsmiths Paul Crespin and Paul de Lamerie.

Jacques Taudin (1608–1680), son of Amanieu Taudin (1582–1671), master pewterer in Bordeaux, made an important contribution to pewter production in England before the waves of immigration associated with the Revocation (see pp.15–29).[64] Following his involvement in the republican uprising in Bordeaux known as 'l'Ormée', during which he made contact with Oliver Cromwell, Jacques Taudin, already an established pewterer, arrived in London as a political exile in 1653.[65] He established his business on the west side of St Martin's Lane, Westminster. Here, 'in his own house', representatives of the Pewterers' Company (Guild), driven by jealousy, 'violently assaulted' him, seized his work and threatened to sue him. Oliver Cromwell forwarded Taudin's subsequent petition to the Lord Mayor and Aldermen of the City of London. In 1656 the legal action that the Pewterers' Guild had brought before the Exchequer Court was stopped, and the Guild accepted Taudin as a member two years later.[66] Taudin's petition records the intense reaction of native pewterers, who 'with hammers, or a kind of poleaxe' destroyed his 'ready-wrought' pewter and carried away 'several cart loads' to Pewterers' Hall, amounting to 'one thousand eight hundred three quarters and thirteen pounds' in weight.[67] Led by London pewterer James Jacombe (fl.1639–53), the marauders were accompanied by a constable, who maintained that the Pewterers' Company Charter had overruled Taudin's status as a denizen.

The Lord Mayor's court found that Taudin's pewter had been seized in conformity with the Act of 25 Henry VIII, 'forbidding strangers born out of the realm to exercise or use the craft of pewterer' and a further Act of 32 Henry VIII, which

84 Flintlock breech-loading sporting gun

Jacques Gorgo, London, *c.*1690
Walnut with gold inlay, length 159 cm
The Royal Armouries, Leeds (XII.4094)

The barrel is inlaid with gold floral scrollwork and the burr walnut stock is inlaid with silver wire, decoration probably made by one of the specialist Soho jewellers or goldsmiths.

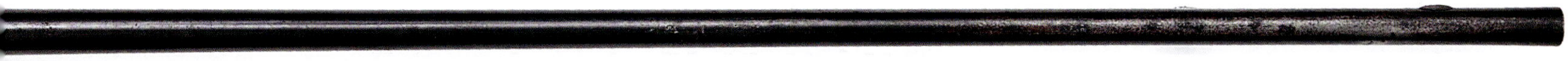

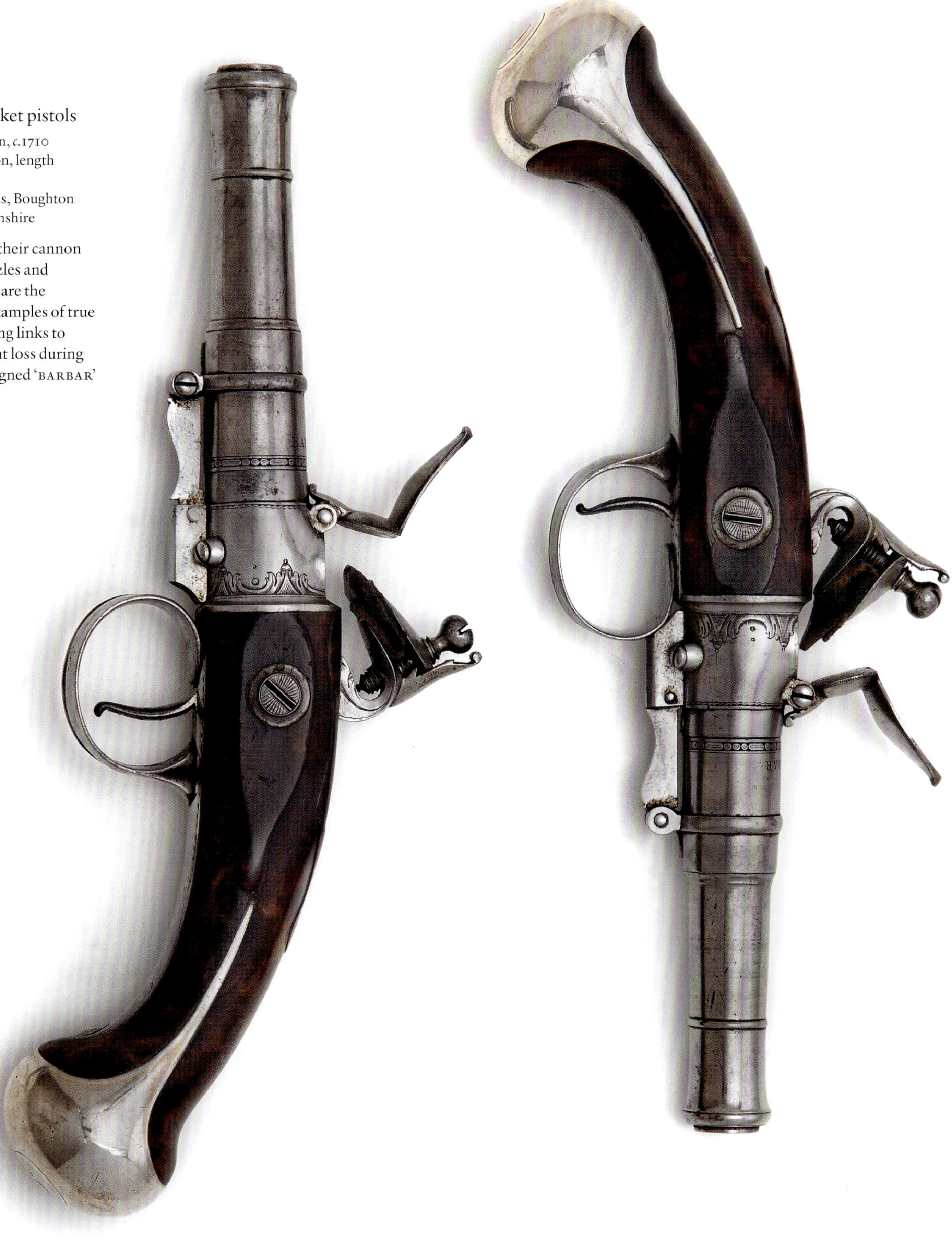

85 Flintlock pocket pistols

Louis Barbar, London, *c.*1710
Walnut, silver and iron, length 21.6 cm
Buccleuch Collections, Boughton House, Northamptonshire

These pistols, with their cannon barrels, flared muzzles and sliding safety links, are the earliest recorded examples of true box locks. The sliding links to the breeches prevent loss during loading. They are signed 'BARBAR' on the barrels.

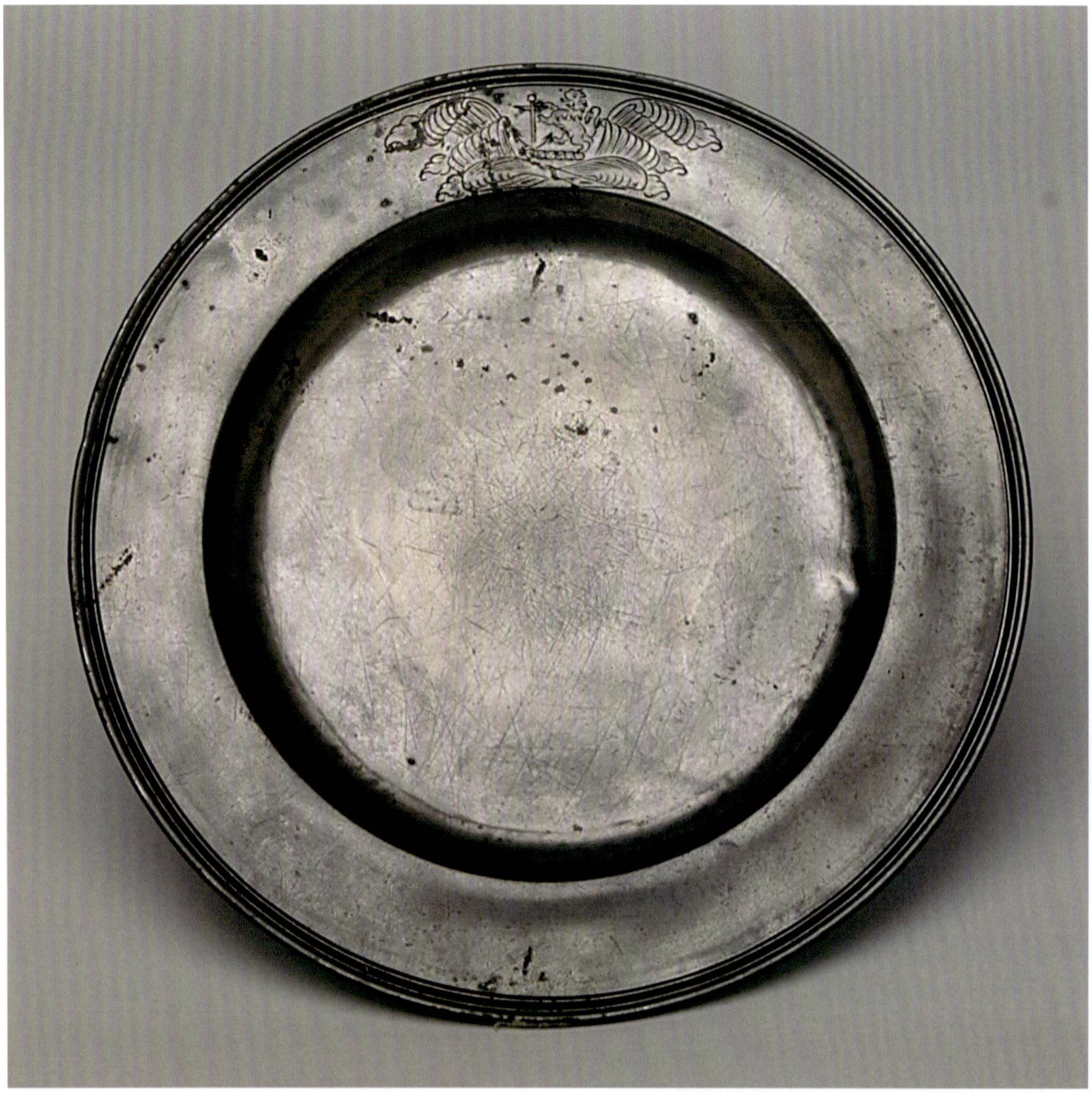

86 Plate, one of a set of five

Jacques Taudin, London, *c.*1675–80
Pewter, diam. 25 cm
Worshipful Company of Pewterers

Bordeaux-born Jacques Taudin, an experienced pewterer, arrived in London in the 1650s. Native resentment continued until Charles II commanded the Pewterers' Company to respect Taudin's right to pursue his craft. He introduced a superior antimony-containing alloy exemplified in this set of plates.

states that 'no alien by any patent of denization shall be privileged against any act of parliament unless such patent contains in it all such privileges particularly expressed by special words'. A writ from the Exchequer Court in 1657 ordered William Hatfield (fl.1632–3; representing the Pewterers' Company) to return the seized pewter to James Taudin, 'which comprised, 32 dozen and 9 dishes, 3 dozen and 7 platters, 15 dozen long plates, 3 dozen trencher plates and one dozen of round plates'. The whole was valued at £114 9s 1d. Six years later, the Pewterers' Company was trying to deny Taudin naturalization:

> *James Taudin afterwards procured his naturalization from the said usurper [Cromwell] who then being naturalised procured orders from the attorney general and other committees to whom the business was referred, to summon the Master and Wardens before them to their great vexation and trouble. Where we were much threatened and commanded speedily to make agreement with him and to admit him a member of the said Company, which we were forced to do.*[68]

Taudin agreed to dismiss between six and ten foreigners who worked for him, but still kept 'eight or ten men constantly at his house beside several that work to him from abroad'. The scale of Taudin's business was impressive. He imported pewter from Bordeaux, where, although his father had died by 1671, his brother Jonas continued as a pewterer. The Company further complained that Taudin

> *allegeth his pewter to be better than ours, which we deny, and are ready to make assay to the contrary … only the name of French pewter is much taken by several of this kingdom and are willing to give him a*

far greater rate than (they give to) natives. Which, if he be naturalised, will unavoidably bring this corporation ... into the condition of the Weavers who are so overspread with strangers that natives are mightily impoverished and their trade much deranged.[69]

Native resentment continued until Charles II commanded the Pewterers' Company to respect Taudin's right to pursue his craft. The Company believed that he had introduced a superior antimony-containing alloy, which may have added to its resentment. The Company never assayed Taudin's pewter, yet one of five of his plates (plate 86) has been found to contain 2.3 per cent antimony, 0.6 per cent copper and 0.2 per cent bismuth.[70]

Charles II's letter dated 7 November 1668 commands the Pewterers' Company:

We expect you will look on the said James Taudin as our servant, and that he shall not have any occasion given him from you or any of you to complain at any time ... against any hard usage he may receive from you. We shall not doubt your compliance with our pleasure hereby signified unto you, and so we bid you farewell.[71]

Taudin was buried in St Martin-in-the-Fields as 'Mr James Touding' on 25 July 1680. He bequeathed 'wrought pewter and moulds' to his nephew James Taudin (d.1692/3), son of his brother Jonas, 'for the long and good service which he hath done unto me ever since he hath lived with me'.[72]

The younger James Taudin, admitted to the Worshipful Company of Pewterers, was required to pay £20 'beside the usual fees'. The will of his uncle, a brief deathbed document, disinherits his grandchildren, 'the children of Henry Lavie [his nephew], merchant of Bordeaux',[73] and charges them not to disturb his nephews James the younger and Pierre Taudin, who came to London from Bordeaux in 1689 and was naturalized in 1698. Pierre Taudin specialized in making chamber pots and worked with Jonas Durand (1694–1730), the younger James Taudin's brother-in law. Thus the Durand–Taudin workshop continued into the eighteenth century.[74] Jonas Durand was succeeded by his son, Jonas Durand the younger (1732–1775).[75]

Only one other name is associated with pewter making in the Huguenot church registers: Mark Henry, of St Anne's church, Westminster, is recorded in 1705; he was probably the Mark Henry Chabrole recorded in the London Pewterers' Company in 1692–3.[76] Some craftsmen worked in both pewter and silver, particularly if they were not guild members who were restricted from engaging in other trades.

The Perchard family from Guernsey illustrate this trend. The brothers Matthew (1703–1777) and John (1704–1758) Perchard and their nephew Peter (*c.*1729–1806) were apprenticed as goldsmiths in London in 1717, 1720 and 1746 respectively, Matthew became Prime Warden of the Goldsmiths' Company.[77] Another member of the family, Hellier Perchard (fl.1709–30), Master of the Pewterers' Company in 1740, supplied the French Hospital in April 1739 when a communion pot used in the hospital chapel was exchanged for '2 Coupes et 2 assietes [sic] d'Etaim'.[78] Members of the French church in Threadneedle Street, by the early nineteenth century the Perchards were working as goldsmiths and jewellers in Charles Street, Hatton Garden.[79]

In 1756 the merchant John Henry Guinand (1686–1755) retained the pewter alms dish in which, as deacon of the Threadneedle Street church in 1727, he collected funds for the church almshouses in Black Eagle Street, Spitalfields. There were apartments for 45 poor men and women, who were allowed 2s 3d and 'a Bushel of coals each Week and Apparel every other Year'. The dish, still in Guinand's possession in 1756, was inscribed 'Le Collecte qui s'est fait a L'eglise Française de Londres & a celle de l'Hopital dans Black-Eagle-Street, pour les Pauvres de la dite Eglize le 10 Mars 1727–8 a produit £1248 7 6'.[80]

Some of the eighteenth- and nineteenth-century pewter vessels used at the French Hospital and the Westminster French Protestant charity school still survive.[81] In addition to the communion pewter, the 1742 hospital inventory lists kitchen equipment, including kegs and sieves, and table pewter: *écuelles* (porringers), plates, beer pots, pint tankards and spoons. For oblations, the wash basins, shaving basins and chamber pots were often replaced due to frequent use.[82]

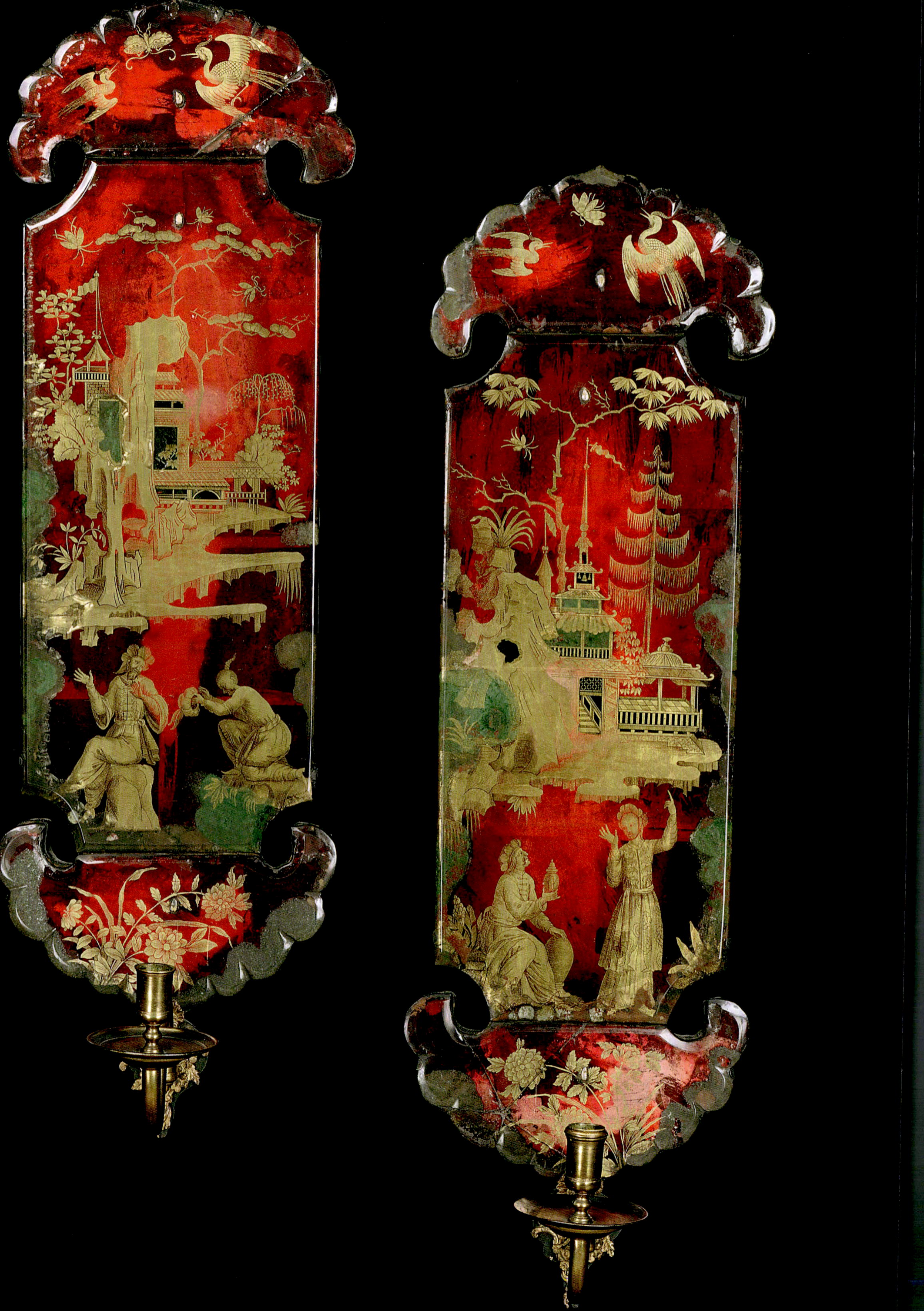

Chapter Seven
Carvers, Gilders, Cabinetmakers & Upholsterers

87 Wall sconces
Attributed to Philip Arbunot, London, *c.*1705
Verre églomisé and brass, 78.5 × 24.5 × 23 cm
Ronald Phillips, London

These unique sconces celebrate the Four Elements: the birds and plants represent Air and Earth, the 'Indian' landscape denotes Water, and candles, when lit, introduce Fire. The chinoiserie decoration appealed to an international market and was selected for contemporary royal diplomatic gifts.

Charles II's court culture demanded French-style quality furnishings and upholstery, which were initially imported from Paris.[1] Louis XIV's diplomatic gifts to British ambassadors inspired emulation. For example, the side table and guéridons representing Summer and Autumn, supplied by Pierre Gole and Mathieu Lespagnandelle (1616–1698; a Protestant sculptor who remained in Paris and abjured his faith in 1686) and presented to Charles Sackville, 6th Earl of Dorset and 1st Earl of Middlesex (1638–1706), ambassador to Paris 1669–70, were displayed at his country home, Knole, Kent.[2] The bureau also by Gole, allegedly presented to Ralph Montagu, Sackville's successor in Paris in 1671–2, was admired at Montagu House, Bloomsbury.[3] These royal gifts are distinguished by sophisticated decorative techniques: marquetry of brass on pewter, their flowers and acanthus scrolls enhanced by surface engraving.

French taste continued to dominate at the English court during the succeeding reigns of James II and William and Mary. Their interior designer Daniel Marot was in London in the mid-1690s guiding production of tables, chairs, coaches, clock cases, picture and mirror frames and upholstery. Marot designed for first-generation Huguenot refugee carvers and cabinetmakers to ensure the unity of all elements of the interior. In London, French upholsterers introduced sophisticated techniques and fabrics to create state beds worthy of a monarch or his representative. Individual craftsmen, John Harvey and the Tabarys produced quality carving in regional Dublin and York and raised local standards. New arrivals from France attracted particular patrons and their skills were recommended by word of mouth.

Second-generation Huguenot carvers and gilders proclaimed the fashionable Rococo style through trade cards and technical mastery which gave them the edge over native craftsmen, although they competed with other European talent. The elaborate carving produced by James Pascall (fl.1733–54) and Paul Petit emulated silver supplied by Paul de Lamerie and marble confections by sculptors Henry Cheere and Roubiliac; picture frames by Pascall and Petit are works of art that enhance and complement the paintings they surround. Pierre Langlois established his London workshop when Britain was at war with France. Langlois supplied sophisticated Paris cabinet furniture to a fashionable British clientele demonstrating the continued advantage of close cultural connections with the French metropolis.

Following Louis XIV's example, Charles II received his most trusted emissaries from his State Bed; more formal receptions took place under a Canopy of State. Such status symbols combined the skills of designer, carpenter, carver and embroiderer, who worked under the upholder (upholsterer), a new profession. Significantly, the London

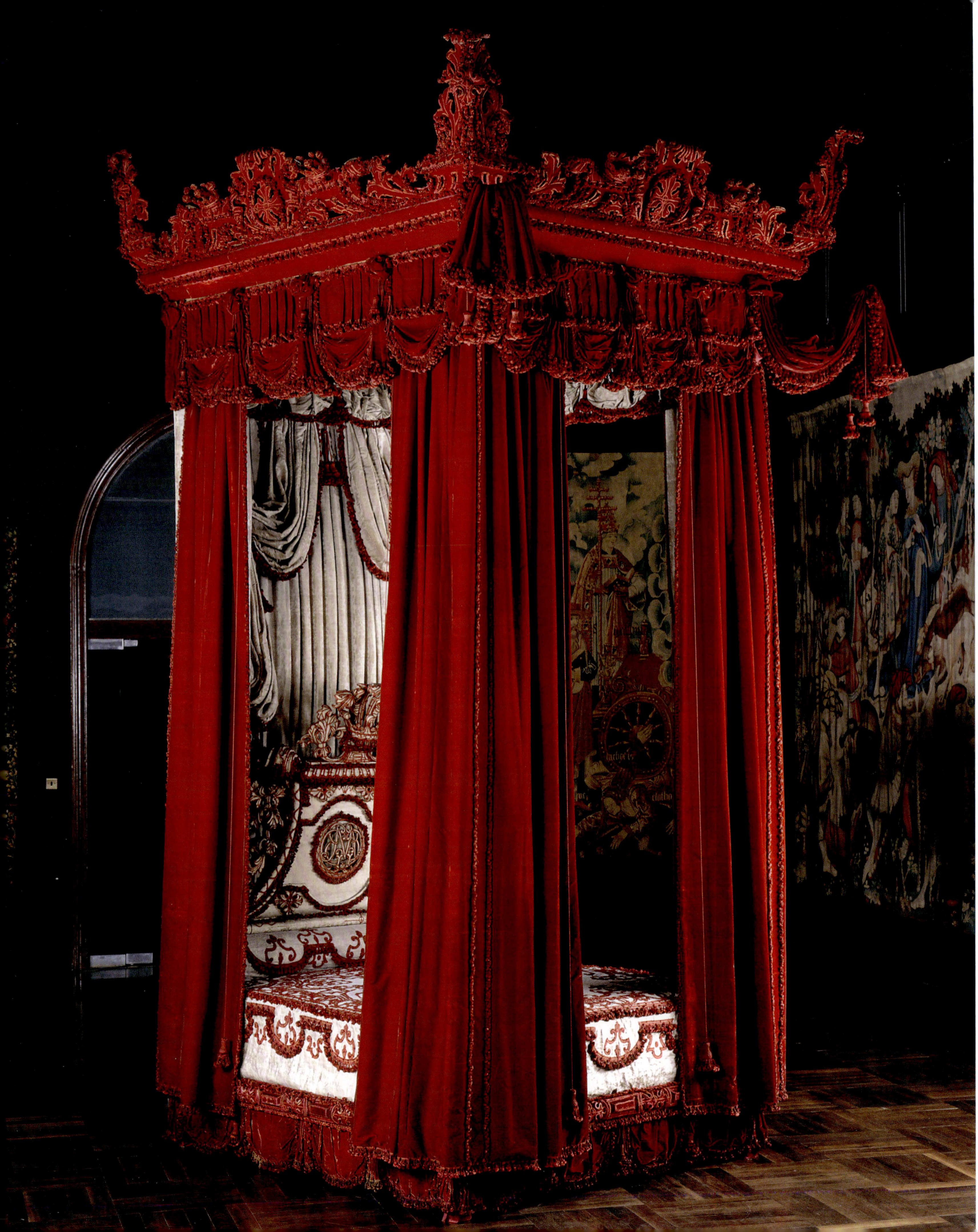

LEFT & BELOW

88 Melville House state bed

Attributed to Francis Lapiere, Pall Mall, London, 1697–1700
White Chinese silk damask and crimson Genoa velvet, 462 × 244 × 274 cm
Victoria and Albert Museum, London (W.35–1949)

Made to the designs of Daniel Marot by a London upholsterer, possibly Francis Lapiere, the bed is lined with Chinese silk woven especially for this commission for George, 1st Earl of Melville. The headboard and counterpane are personalized with the patron's cypher and coronet, to celebrate his status as Secretary of State for Scotland. The bed was installed at Melville House, Fife, *c.*1700, in readiness for a visit from William III.

Upholders' Guild was granted a royal charter in 1668.[4] Within 20 years, sophisticated furnishings produced by first-generation Huguenot craftsmen in London replaced expensive French imports. The Melville House state bed exemplifies new skill levels and demonstrates such collaboration (plate 88).[5] As the Earl of Portland wrote to William III from Paris in spring 1698, French upholsterers in London were producing more sophisticated designs, to higher quality execution, than previously imported from Paris.[6]

Upholders and upholsterers

The cabinetmaker's trade, established in Northern Europe during the seventeenth century, became subservient to that of the upholsterer, who co-ordinated a team of specialist craftsmen.[7] Using luxurious furnishing fabrics imported from France and Italy or woven in Spitalfields, upholstery was expensive.[8] Leading upholsterers with French

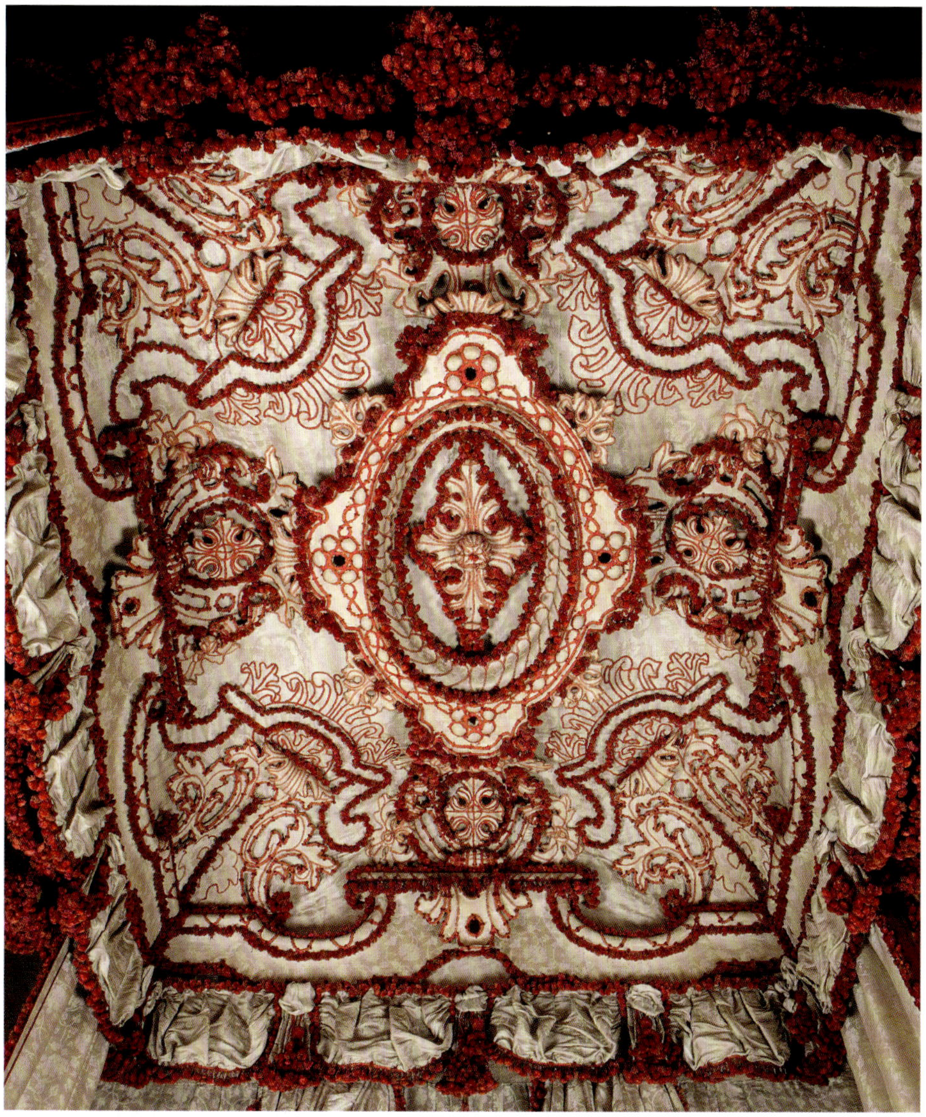

names who worked alongside Richard Bealing (fl.1672–1711), upholsterer at the royal court from 1672 to 1711, and for the Dukes of Devonshire, Dorset and Montagu include John Casbert (fl.1660–77) and his son, also John; Simon Delobel; Philip Guibert (fl.1692–1739); Guillotin (fl.1691–1701); La Grange; Francis Lapiere; Etienne Penson (fl.1701–13); John Peyrard, who came to England in 1672 and 1673 to deliver beds for Charles II; and Jean Poictevin (Paudevin; fl.1677–88). Of these, only Guibert, Guillotin and Poictevin were definitely Huguenots. The work of Isaac de la Haye, upholsterer established in Frying Pan Alley, Stepney, between 1693 and 1705, is not recorded.[9] The full extent to which Huguenot upholstery was subcontracted from established London suppliers, including Gerrit Jensen (fl.1667–1715), cabinet-maker at court from 1675 to 1715, is unknown. James Gronous (fl.1700–39), another Huguenot upholder, at the Black Lion, Wych Street, off the Strand, appraised the entire contents of Montagu House and Ditton Park, Buckinghamshire, after Ralph Montagu's death in 1709,[10] whereas Thomas Pelletier, carver and gilder, only valued Montagu's paintings and furniture.[11] Gronous, Master of the Upholders' Company in 1739, moved in the highest court circles; he was paid £652 for 'equipage, furniture and workmanship' by William Bentinck, 1st Duke of Portland, in 1721.[12]

Philip Guibert worked in London supplying new forms of upholstered furniture. In 1697, for William III, he supplied 'a fine black soffa – of a new fashion' for £14 with a walnut couch with headboard carved with the royal cypher for £8.[13] Courtiers were swift to adopt this comfortable seating. In November 1703 a couch and daybed were supplied for Thomas Osborne, 1st Duke of Leeds (1632–1712) by 'Gilbert ye Joyner by my lady Duches's order'.[14] This furniture was enriched with covers of Genoa velvet, gilded carving, silk fringes and tassels.[15] In 1727 the Great Drawing Room in the Duke's Yorkshire home, Kiveton Hall, was furnished with '14 Chairs & 2 Stools frames Black & Gold. Cover'd wth fflowred Velvt trim'd wth guilt Mouldings & Serge Cases'.[16] The Best Closet had seating with matching covers: '1 Large Couch, 4 Large Sqr. Stools frames Japand, & black Gold Cover'd wth Same Indian Sattin.'[17]

The daybed, accompanying chairs and appliqué hangings in the Queen Elizabeth Room at Penshurst, Kent, *c.*1700, were made to Daniel Marot's designs in the 1690s for William III's Groom of the Stole, Henry Sidney, 1st Earl of

Romney (1641–1704), for his London home, Leicester House.[18] The hangings compare with the description of those provided by Guibert for royal use at Windsor Castle.[19] Marot's published designs (*c.*1703 and 1712) include day beds supported on hoop stretchers accompanied by matching stools, like those from Warwick Castle originally made for William III's Little Bedchamber at Hampton Court Palace (plate 89).[20] Guibert was admitted to the Freedom and Livery of the Upholders' Guild in October 1702 on payment of £4 10s and the prestigious gift of a silver salt cellar formed as the three tents of the Guild's coat of arms (plate 176). Commissioned from Huguenot goldsmith Louis Cuny five years earlier, the gift anticipated Guibert's acceptance.[21]

As masters, Gronous and Guibert took fellow Huguenots as apprentices.[22] Among these was Isaac Deschamps (1666–1714), whose family, based in Compton Street, Soho,[23] was later joined by marriage to that of their neighbour, the goldsmith Nicholas Sprimont (plate 155). London apprentices included Huguenots from regional communities. In 1716 Anthony Guidott (Guidot; 1708–1727), by 1724 at the sign of The Royal Bed in Shug Lane, Marylebone Street,[24] took in his nephew William, son of his brother Richard Guidott from Southampton, without a fee. Paul Columbine (1721–1786), son of Francis Columbine (d.1746), physician, of the Norwich French church, was apprenticed to the City upholder William Braithwaite (fl.1713–24) in London in 1714. Columbine later upholstered furniture for the Earl of Leicester at Holkham Hall, Norfolk.[25]

In 1750 Samuel Phene (fl.1750–75), upholder, established a family business at the sign of the Golden Plow, Little Moorgate. The Phene family came from Canterbury; Samuel's father John Phene, established in Spitalfields, was admitted to the Weavers' Company in 1712. Samuel's brother, also John, a Spitalfields weaver, joined him by 1759. Samuel took Thomas Jones (d.1769) as partner in

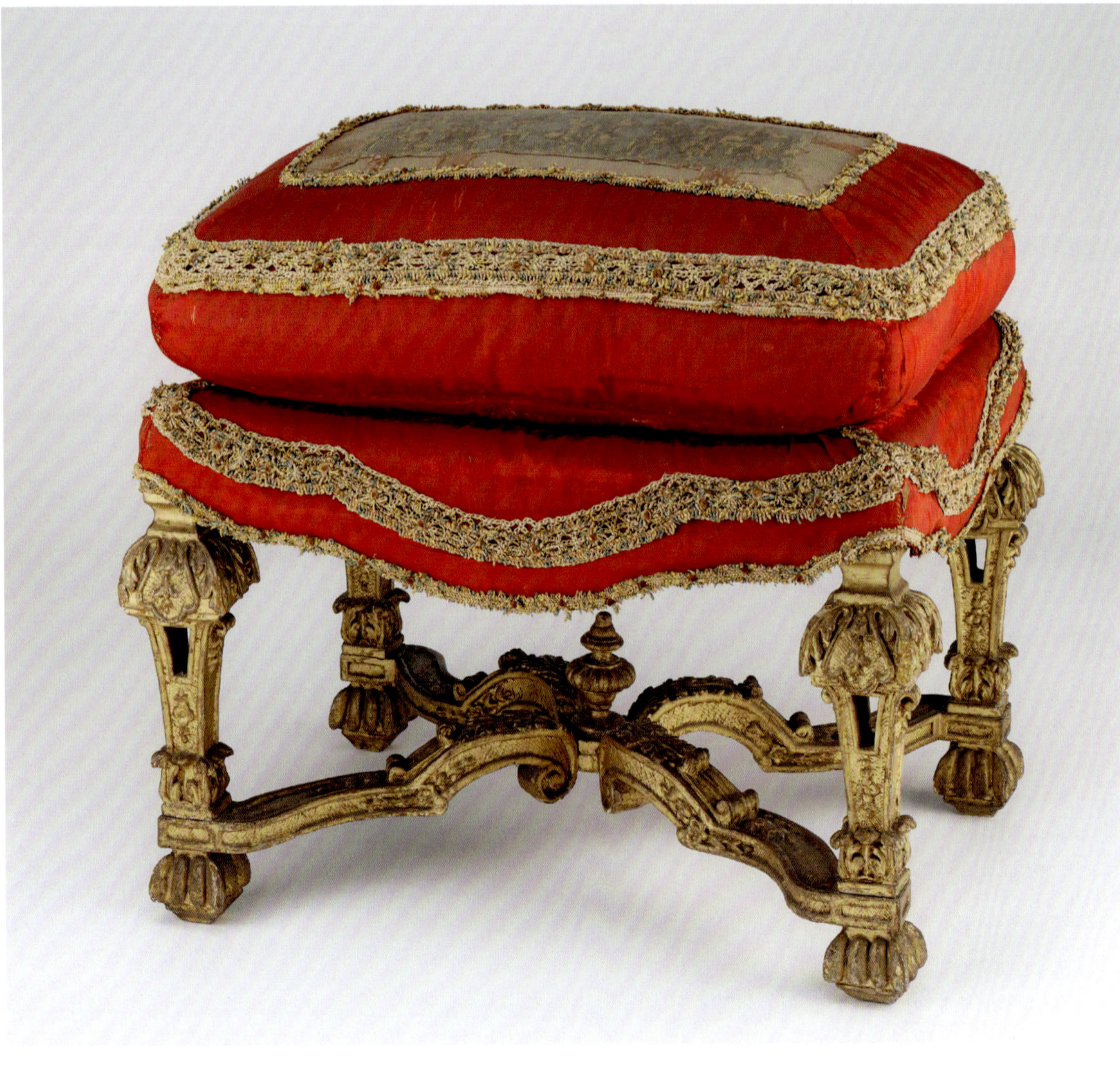

89 The Warwick Castle Stool

Attributed to Philip Guibert, London, 1701–2
Carved and gilt beech, velvet and silk braid, 62.5 × 66.5 × 48.5 cm
Victoria and Albert Museum, London (W.14–2009)

Commissioned for William III at Hampton Court and used by Queen Anne at Kensington Palace, then presented to George Greville, 2nd Earl of Warwick, by George III. One of a pair from a bedroom suite supplied for William III's Little Bedchamber at Hampton Court Palace. The loose valanced cover is tied over an upholstered border by ribbon bows concealed by the cushion. The stool was re-covered between 1790 and 1820, preserving the original trimmings, velvet and upholstery.

1758, but Samuel's son Nicholas (fl.1775–1821) eventually succeeded in 1775. The business continued in the City until 1840.[26]

Huguenot craftsmen worked with the leading Catholic court upholsterer Francis Lapiere. Lapiere is first recorded in London from 1683; being French overruled religious affiliations from the perspective of both patron and supplier. Lapiere furnished Boughton House and Drayton House in Northamptonshire, Chatsworth in Derbyshire and Knole in Kent.[27] His father, Antoine, was a *marchand tapissier* in Paris, so Francis maintained contact with France. In 1689 Lapiere leased colourful furnishings for Huguenot commander Frederick, Count of Schomberg's London apartments in Pall Mall, opposite the upholsterer's own premises. Schomberg died, fighting for William III, at the Battle of the Boyne on 1 July 1690, so the rental was limited to 20 months at £230 and the rented furnishings were returned to Lapiere on Schomberg's death. His bedroom furniture was worthy of royalty: he slept within 'Crimson Genoa Damask' curtains trimmed with crimson, green and white silk fringe; against walls hung with figured 'Flaunders' tapestries, six walnut armchairs were covered with red linen. On the floor was a large Turkey carpet; the blue mohair window curtains and valance were lined with 'Gold coloured Persian'; 'a quilted counterpane' with silk fringes all round ... was of 'musk colour crimson & white'. Between the windows was 'a black table, stands and looking glass'.[28]

For royal use, Lapiere supplied in 1690 'a large very fine Persian Carpet ... For the Gallery at Kensington' for £64, and in 1694–5, two lots of five pieces 'of fine Tapestry Hangings' for the Windsor Castle bedroom of William III's favourite, Mr Keppel, for £236.[29] At Knole, for Charles Sackville, 6th Earl of Dorset, in December 1694, Lapiere made an 'easy Chear freame Japand Black stofed with corled hear & coverd with lynen'; he charged £3 12s for supplying and making 'ye Chear & gilt Neiyle all round & a Coshing' and a blue 'turkey' leather protective cover with an outer serge case.

Lapiere also dealt in paintings, supplying three to Lord Dorset in 1695 for £20.[30] For Chatsworth in 1697 he provided a state bed for £470, which was paid for in instalments (the surviving tester and headboard are in the Long Gallery at Hardwick Hall), and a 'Christall Chandelier' for £27 9s 6d. He may also have procured rock crystal chandeliers for Hampton Court Palace and Penshurst Place.[31] Huguenot carvers and gilders Thomas and René Pelletier supplied Lapiere with furniture frames for upholstery. In April 1706 Lapiere charged £1 5s for stuffing 'two square stools ... finely carved ... with curled hair & covered with linen'; the crimson velvet covers and gold lace embroidery cost twice as much, at £4.[32] The following month the stools were returned to the Pelletier workshop for gilding, which cost £5. The stools were made for the closet at Montagu House, which was being fitted up for John Monthermer's new bride, Mary, youngest daughter of the 1st Duke of Marlborough; they married in 1705.[33]

Attracted by long-term investment opportunities, or by the possibility of returning to France, in 1695 Lapiere had deposited £500 with the then Earl of Montagu 'for a marriage portion' for his elder daughter, Frances;[34] an additional £1,000 followed in 1702. Frances married Joseph Boucher, tailor, also employed by the Montagu household. The £500 was still unpaid on Boucher's death in 1740.[35]

Embroiderers

Some of the specialist Huguenot suppliers of textiles were women.[36] Madame Justell,[37] Marie Pariselle and Esther Regneaux supplied tapestry and needlework chairs for Montagu House between 1703 and 1705.[38] In May 1687 Lapiere supplied the 2nd Earl of Peterborough, who became a Catholic the same year, with 'Vestements for ye prieste' and a bed at Drayton House 'with a dubbel Riseing teaster', which no longer survives.[39] The Drayton state bed dates from 1701; the bedstead, tester, cornices, base mouldings and headboard were probably supplied by Etienne Penson, an upholsterer working at the sign of the Phoenix, Leicester Fields, from 1704 to 1713. Penson was the nephew of Jean Paudevin or Poictevin, upholsterer to Charles II, James II and James II's daughter Princess Anne. Penson was working in St James's, Westminster, in the 1680s, first in King Street and later in Pall Mall and was responsible for the Venetian Ambassador's bed at Knole. He later returned to France, where he died in 1709.[40]

For the state bed at Drayton Penson used a yellow silk taffeta lining woven in Spitalfields supplied by his patron, Lady Mary Mordaunt (1659–1705), former Duchess of Norfolk, who married Sir John Germain (1650–1718) in 1701. This splendid bed, made up by the upholsterer Guillotin,[41] was probably commissioned to celebrate their marriage and allegedly cost £1,500.[42] The original yellow silk counterpane has been recently rediscovered.[43] The outer curtains are of green velvet embroidered with flowers by Rebekah Dufee (fl.1700–1) and Elizabeth Rickson (fl.1700–2), whose contract is dated July 1700; they charged 22s a yard for the needlework.[44] By January 1701 'Two grate curtanes' were complete and a third was in hand. Among the finest surviving early eighteenth-century needlework in England, their embroidery adorns the settee and armchairs in the King's Dining Room at Drayton (plate 90).

Embroidered soft furnishings and dress were a further indication of status. Specialist suppliers included Thomas Benoist, maker of fringes, who received relief through the Threadneedle Street church in 1681,[45] and Abraham David, maker of plumes, who attended the French City church, St Martin Orgar, in 1701. Such specialists may have embroidered dress as well as furnishings. Mrs Mary Gagneron, working for James Brydges, 1st Duke of Chandos between 1722 and 1727, charged £27 6s for embroidering a coat, breeches and a pair of stockings.[46] Meeting the demand for such luxury trimmings was profitable and a trade in which Huguenot merchants prospered. Peter Dufresnoy (d. *c.*1715), like Lapiere, probably Catholic, who supplied spectacular fringes in 1673 for the Duke and Duchess of Lauderdale and from 1686 for the 5th Earl and Countess of Exeter for Burghley House, Lincolnshire, was paid £165 for textiles and lace for Drayton House in 1707.[47] The profitability of trading in trimmings for both furnishings and dress is demonstrated by Joseph Highmore's 1748 portrait of Daniel Sanxay, of Downing Street, Westminster, third-generation Huguenot lace merchant, dressed in blue silk waistcoat trimmed with silver.[48]

For Queen Anne, the Huguenot Stephen Toulouse (d.1728) was paid £110 in 1711

> *For embroidering richly her Majesty's armes and supporters very large according to the Union [of England with Scotland in 1707] all of gold and silver on Crimson figured velvett as also her Majesty's armes and supporters upon the foot Valiance and Cornice … [of a] Crimson figured velvet Canopy of State.*[49]

In 1712 Toulouse was paid £50 for embroidering an altar cloth for Hampton Court Chapel with 'IHS with a Glory about it' in 'gold wyre upon Crimson velvet', and in 1717 he was paid £21 for 'Embroidering richly a Purse with her Majesties arms' for the Privy Seal, for embroidering heralds' tabards '2 Coats at £80 each for Sir John Vanbrugh Knight, Clarenceux and Peter Le Neve Esq, Norroy

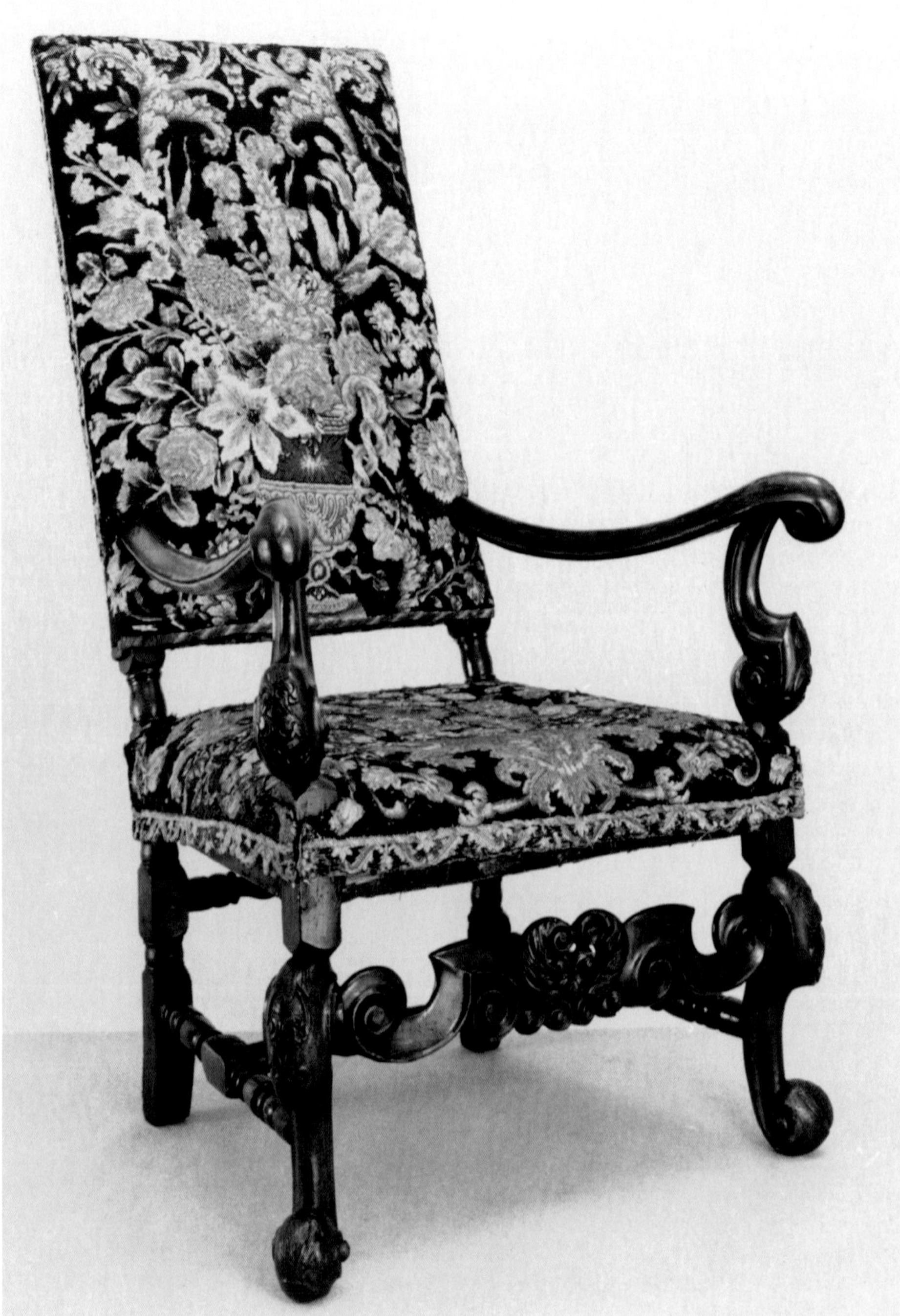

King of arms', and £19 for '4 orders of the garter for John, 2nd Duke of Montagu'.[50] Montagu, who succeeded his father as Master of the Royal Wardrobe, appreciated Toulouse's skills and in 1728 contributed £100 towards the cost of his funeral to the French Savoy Chapel.[51]

Featherworkers

Weaving exotic feathers into sophisticated textiles was the speciality of Monsieur Le Normand-Quesnel, settled in Putney but originally from Rouen. His featherwork hangings were advertised as a 'Lit de Parade' in the *Mercure de France* (1720),

LEFT

90 Armchair from Drayton House, Northamptonshire

Unknown maker, *c.*1685, with embroidery by Rebekah Dufee and Elizabeth Rickson, *c.*1700
Beech frame, needlework, with wool back cover, 122 × 71 cm
Victoria and Albert Museum, London (w.34–1950)

Among the finest surviving early 18th-century needlework, the covers were originally embroidered for the Drayton State Bedroom. The original colours are preserved in a concealed section of matching embroidery still at Drayton. Their impact contributed to the significance of this commission to celebrate the marriage of Lady Mary with Sir John Germain.

when the maker exhibited a featherwork screen in Paris. It had taken Le Normand-Quesnel 20 years to import the exotic bird feathers through the East India Company.[52] When displayed at Somerset House, London, in September the same year, the bed was admired by the Prince of Wales (later George II).[53] Although shown at Exeter Exchange the following January for a further six months, the bed failed to attract a British buyer. Huguenot merchants Nicholas Bosquet (d.1743) of Hackney[54] and Anthony Clerembault (1668–1758) of New Broad Street, London Wall, negotiated the sale of the exotic bed furnishings in 1723 to Augustus the Strong, Elector of Saxony in Dresden, which were intended for the Federzimmer in the Japanese Palace, built from 1727. Installed in Schloss Moritzburg in 1830, the original bed curtains now serve as decorative wall panels and a setting for the featherwork tester; the ensemble is a remarkable survival (plate 91).[55]

Feather pictures and screens by Le Normand, advertised in London in 1720–1 prior to his departure for Europe and sold at Bertrand's Bath toyshop in the 1730s, survive in the collections at Welbeck Abbey. Le Normand returned to Britain and died at Windsor in 1736. In 1753 Mary Clerimbault of Enfield, probably the daughter of Anthoine Clerembault, Le Normand's agent, bequeathed 'a picture of feathers by Mr Le Nordian [*sic*]' in her will.[56]

Cabinetmakers, carvers and gilders

Furniture makers worked with architects, carvers and gilders to complete interior panelling, fireplaces and staircases; they designed and decorated barges, carriages and sedan chairs for prestigious patrons.[57] Unlike Grinling Gibbons (1648–1721), first-generation Huguenot carvers remain under-researched.[58] Daniel Marot's later published designs record carved furniture styles of the 1690s seen in oak benches at Dunham Massey, Cheshire, and walnut chairs at Dyrham, near Bath, although the craftsmen responsible are not recorded.[59] In 1694 Marot married Catherine Gole, niece of Louis XIV's *ébéniste* Pierre Gole in London.[60] Catherine's father, Adrian, and another uncle, Gerrit, were also cabinetmakers in Paris. Despite their Dutch origin (the Gole family originated from Bergen, Holland), the family was not exempt from religious persecution.[61] In 1685, Pierre Gole's son Corneille (Cornelius) left Paris, settling first in The Hague and later in London, where his sister

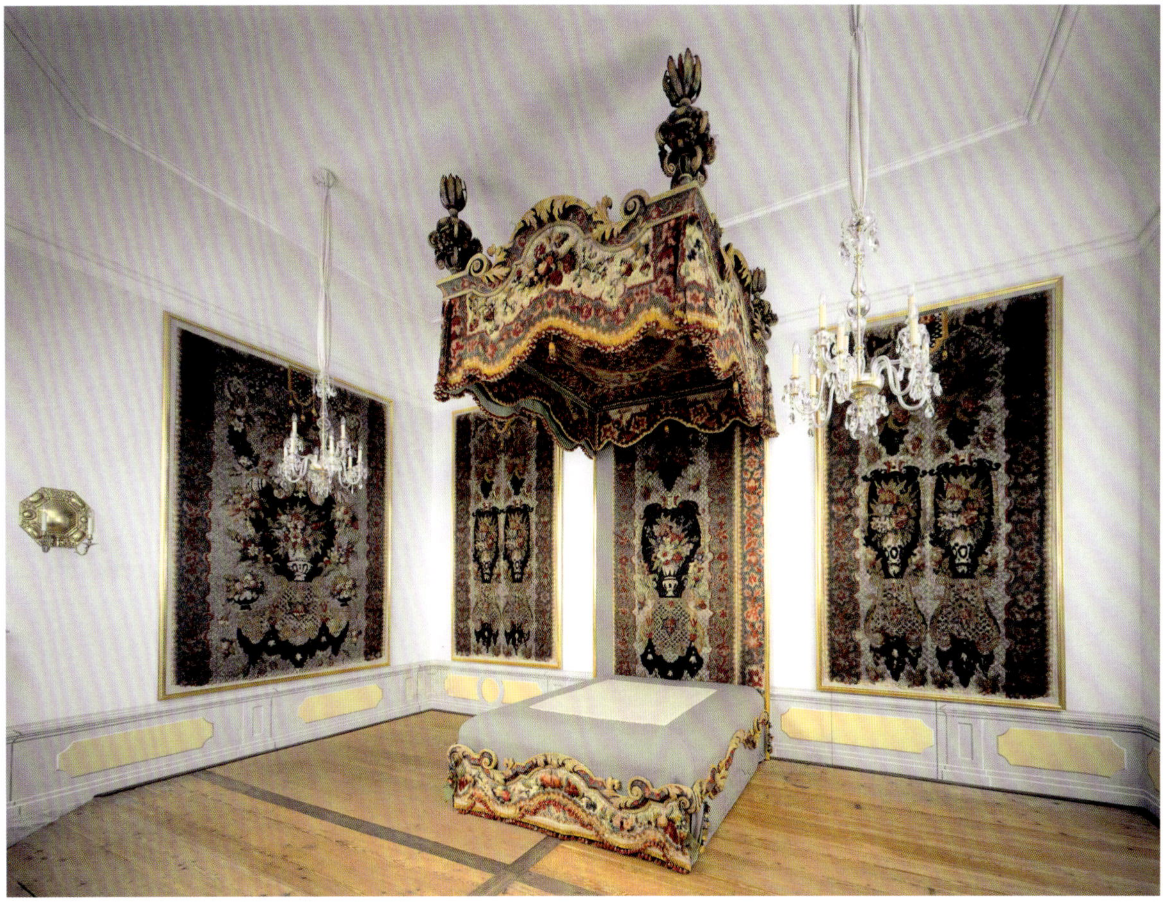

91 Feather Bed in the Federzimmer, Schloss Moritzburg

Nicholas le Normand, Putney, *c.*1708–20
Feathers from exotic birds, some painted, tester 35.4 × 198 × 283 cm
Staatliche Schlösser, Burgen und Gärten, Sachsen

Assembling the feathers from exotic birds took 20 years. They include the dotted black plumes of guinea fowl and scallop-shaped peacock feathers; pink flamingo, ibis and roseate spoonbill feathers; and inky black cassowary plumes. Highlights are provided by the magenta-coloured cotinga and the orange plumes of the male 'cock of the rock' (*Rupicola*), both from the American tropics.

Catherine, Daniel Marot's wife, stood godmother to Cornelius's elder son, Abraham, in 1696.[62]

In London Cornelius Gole worked as a carver, cabinetmaker and designer in Litchfield Street, Soho, specializing in marquetry. In 1712 he published a pattern book of ornament.[63] Gole's link with Salamon Woinsson, carpenter of King Street, Soho in 1704, demonstrates the close network of Huguenot craftsmen working in wood.[64] In August 1691 Cornelius Gole supplied a marquetry table and matching candle stands for £20 for Queen Mary at Whitehall Palace, two looking glass frames 'richly carved with ornaments & flowers and inlaid with wood of all sorts of colours' for £14 and another 'richly carved with cyphers & their majesties arms with an imperial crown'.[65] In 1694 he witnessed the marriage of Isaye Fleureau (fl.1694–1746), clockmaker from Orleans; a long-case clock with a movement by Fleureau of *c.*1700 at Trerice, Cornwall, retains its original walnut case, which was possibly supplied by Gole.[66] He supplied Montagu with a writing desk or 'scrutoire' in 1700–1 for £12 10s; a pair of candle stands and pier table at Boughton, close to designs by Marot, are also attributed to him (plate 92).[67]

Seventeen cabinetmakers and 31 carpenters are listed in the London Huguenot records between 1680 and 1760. Many sought financial relief on arrival in the 1680s, others are recorded in later life no longer able to practise their craft. The only woodcarver named, Pierre Connessant (1681–1748), was born in Holland although his father was originally from Sedan. Pierre was admitted to the French Hospital in 1746, having lost his sight.[68] In 1691–2 Estienne Le Jeune (b. *c.*1620), cabinetmaker, applied for assistance with paying his rent. He was trying to eke out a living producing inlaid borders but his landlord was threatening to seize his tools.[69] Vincent Zeba (b. *c.*1668), *ébéniste* (cabinetmaker), who married at the church of La Patente de Soho on 1 January 1696, had served his apprenticeship in Paris with Jacques Vivares, *menuisier* (carpenter) from 27 April 1682.[70] Other cabinetmakers and carvers with French names have yet to be identified as Huguenots. Christopher Wren's building accounts include payment to Bernard Angier (d. *c.*1718) for £293 in 1685–6 'for Carpenters work in building a Guard House at Windsor Castle';[71] Charles Angeir (*sic*), a carver in Long Acre in 1749, may be a relative, probably his son.

The Tabary brothers, carpenters and carvers in wood and stone, were refugees from Paris. Jacques

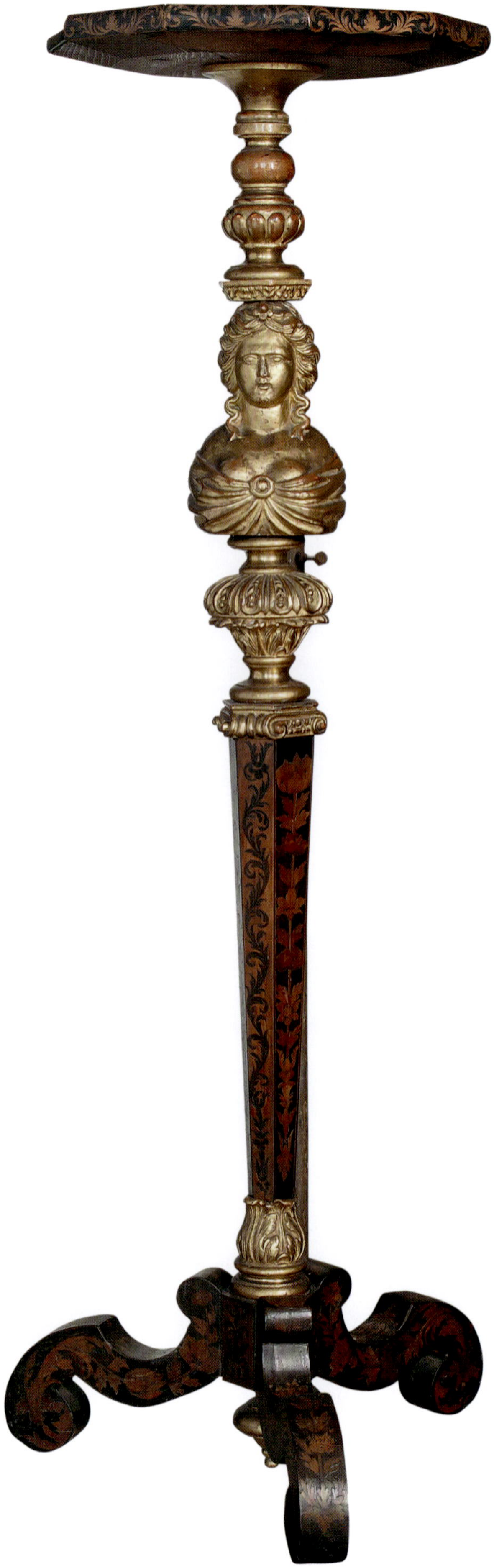

LEFT

92 Candle stand

Attributed to Cornelius Gole, London, *c.*1690
Walnut with marquetry veneer and giltwood, ht 115 cm
Boughton House, Northamptonshire

This candle stand is similar to the pair that Cornelius Gole supplied for Queen Mary's apartments at Whitehall. The marquetry leaves and flowers on the top, fluted base and sides of the tripod feet retain their depth of colour, contrasting with the giltwood bust of Flora and the acanthus knop below. The subtlety of proportion indicates the influence of sophisticated design, probably supplied by Gole's brother-in-law, the architect Daniel Marot.

RIGHT

93 Reredos

Tabary brothers, Dublin, 1683–7
Carved and panelled oak?
Chancel, Royal Hospital Chapel, Kilmainham

Commissioned by the 1st Duke of Ormonde, the chapel, a spectacular addition to Dublin's 17th-century architecture, was described by a contemporary as 'one of the finest the King has in his dominions'. The carving was valued at £250 on completion of the work in 1687. The Tabary brothers also supplied an altar table, now in the National Museum of Ireland.

Tabary (*c.*1635–1687), in Paris from the 1650s, received relief through the London Threadneedle Street church in February 1681/2.[72] In 1682 he was admitted to the Franchise of Dublin as a citizen of the city, where in 1685 his brothers Jean (fl.1685–7) and Louis (*c.*1662–*c.*1731), sculptor and carver respectively, joined him.[73] In France the 'Taborrie' brothers carved choir stalls for the Minimes church, Tours.[74] In Dublin Jacques and Louis Tabary carved decoration for the panelled reredos of the Royal Hospital Chapel, Kilmainham (plate 93), built for retired soldiers from 1684 to the designs

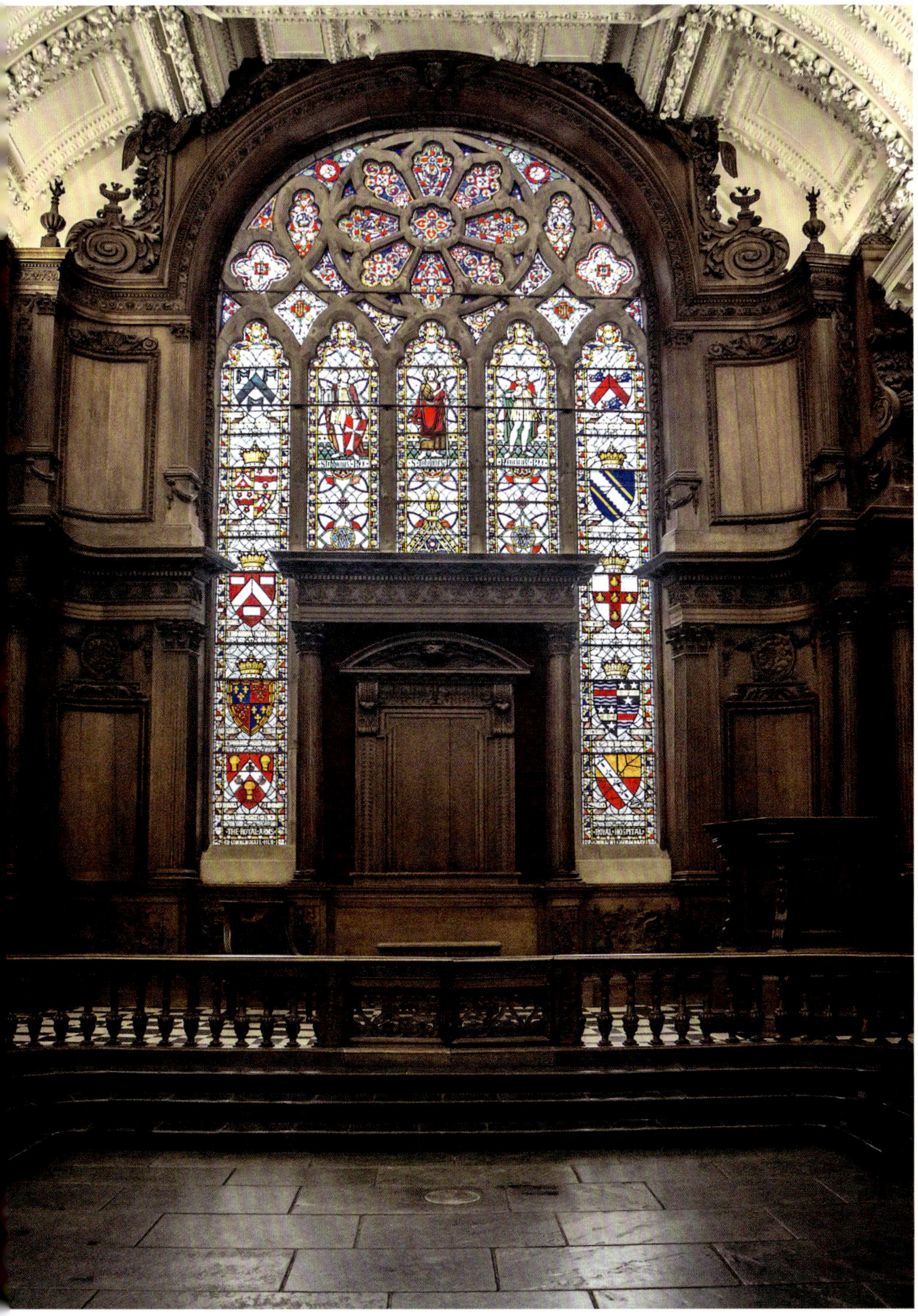

of Sir William Robinson (1645–1712). Consecrated in January 1686 by the Archbishop of Dublin, the chapel is dedicated to the memory of King Charles I Martyr.[75] Giant Corinthian pilasters frame the east window with below, panels representing symbols of hope and purity, the anchor, eucharistic ewer and lily. To the right of the altar a tympanum embellished with putti heads and festoons of flowers was inspired by Pierre Le Muet's 1646 translation of Palladio's *First Book of Architecture*.[76] The Tabary brothers supplied French-style altar rails and the altar table but Jacques complained to the Lord Lieutenant, James Butler, 1st Duke of Ormonde (1610–1688), that £250, paid in January 1686/7, did not cover their costs.[77] Five external trophies of arms above the arcaded courtyard doors, carved in oak but painted to resemble stone, are taken from designs by D. Antoine Pierretz (fl.1647), published in Paris between 1647 and 1666.[78] The royal coat of arms carved by the Tabarys for the Kilmainham Hospital dining room was removed for political reasons in the 1920s and appropriately installed at the entrance to the dining room of its sister institution in London, The Royal Hospital, Chelsea.[79] One of the Tabary brothers was subcontracted by the joiner Pierre Rieusset in London to supply three picture frames for Montagu House. In 1730/1, Louis Tabary, a sculptor from Paris *fort infirme* (very disabled), was admitted to the French Hospital, aged 68 with his wife.[80]

Pierre Rieusset was paid just under £5,000 by Ralph Montagu's executors in 1712 for 'parquet de Versailles' flooring at Montagu House and the State Apartments at Boughton (plate 94), Montagu's family home in Northamptonshire. The technique was invented by Jean Macé (1602–1672), a cabinetmaker from Blois who moved to Paris, where he trained André Charles Boulle (1642–1732). Associated with royal apartments in French palaces, parquet was used on grand staircases at Powys and Nottingham Castles in the 1670s.[81] Laying the parquet on the upper landing of the Boughton great staircase took eight days in June 1706.[82] Rieusset also supplied tables for billiards – a game that gained from its association with Louis XIV's Versailles[83] – as oak parquetry provided a stable surface for the baize-covered tabletop. Rieusset's billiard tables were delivered to Boughton in 1697, to Ditton, Montagu's Buckinghamshire home, in 1702,[84] and to Longford Castle, Wiltshire, home of Jacob Bouverie, 1st Viscount Folkestone, in 1729. Rieusset assembled the Boughton billiard table (plate 95) in the attic, where natural light permitted

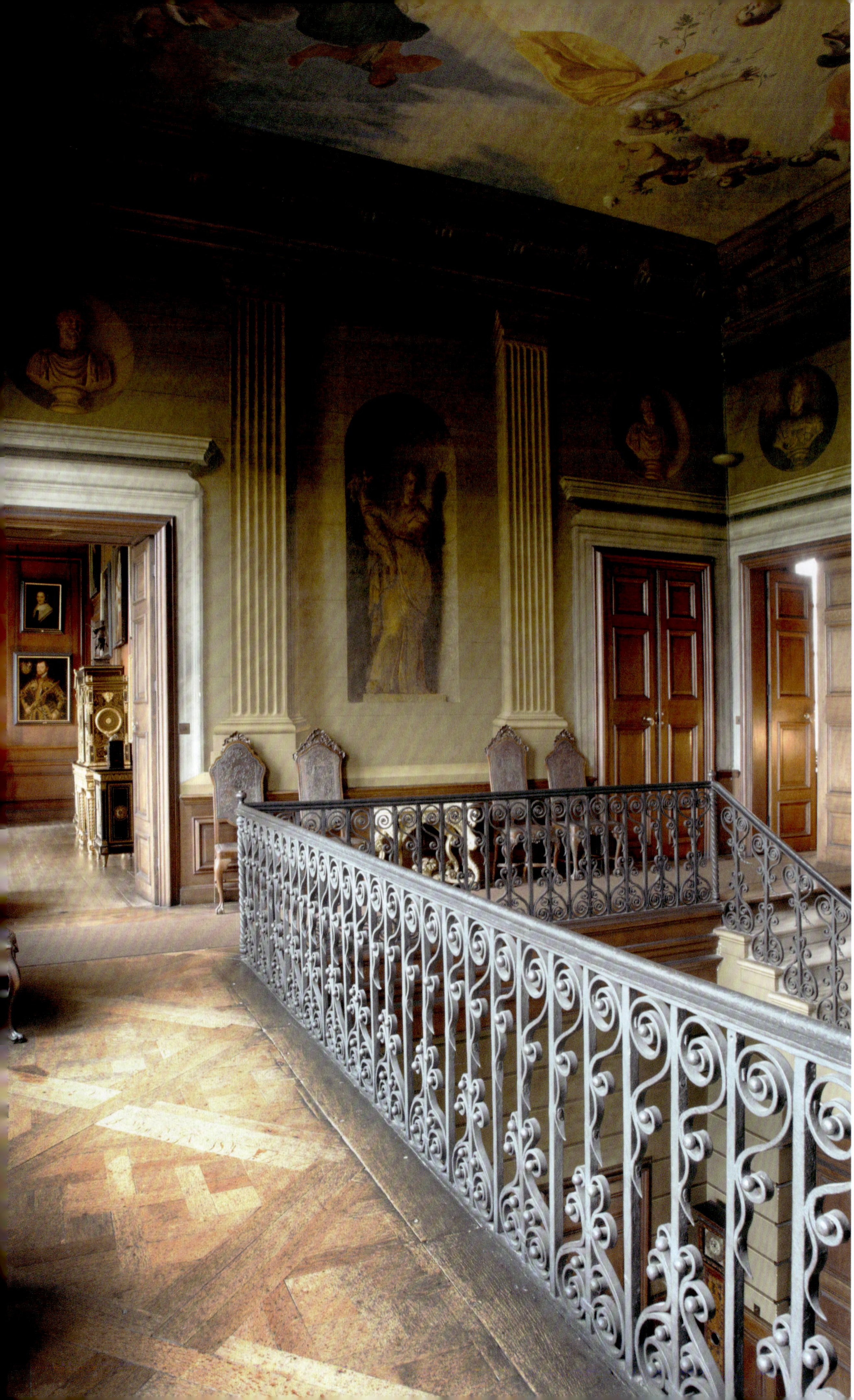

94 Parquet de Versailles

Pierre Rieusset, London, *c.*1697
Oak parquetry, largest lozenge 97 × 10 cm
Boughton House, Northamptonshire

Rieusset was paid just under £5,000 by Ralph Montagu's executors in 1712 for 'parquet de Versailles' floors for Montagu House, London, and for the State Apartments and great staircase at Boughton. The technique was developed in Paris from the 1620s, used for staircases and state bedrooms in England from the 1670s and at Versailles in the 1680s.

95 Billiard table

Pierre Rieusset, London, *c.*1697
Oak, 96.5 × 342.9 × 213.4 cm
Boughton House, Northamptonshire

Rieusset's special skills in oak parquetry were ideally suited to creating the level surface required for playing billiards or for floors with heavy use such as staircase landings. Supported by 12 spiral turned legs linked by stretchers, these reflect the light and contrast with the smooth baize-covered surface of the table.

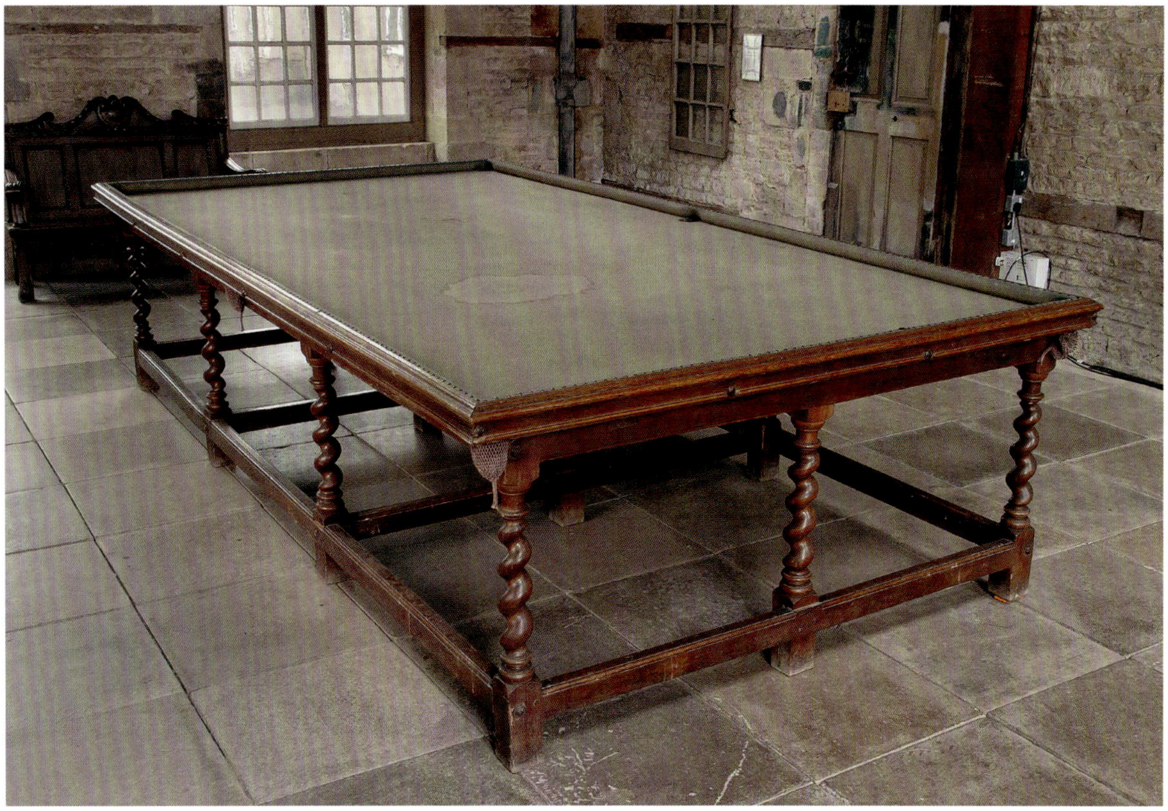

96 Walnut stand for marble table, one of four

Pierre Rieusset, London, *c.*1697
Walnut with original Languedoc marble top, stand
67.3 × 104.2 × 53.6 cm
Boughton House, Northamptonshire

Rieusset supplied turned walnut side tables for royal palaces and for Montagu House, London. Of the two pairs now at Boughton House, one support slabs of red Languedoc marble; a similar pair at Hampton Court Palace, supplied through Jean Pelletier *c.*1699, has white marble tops with black borders.

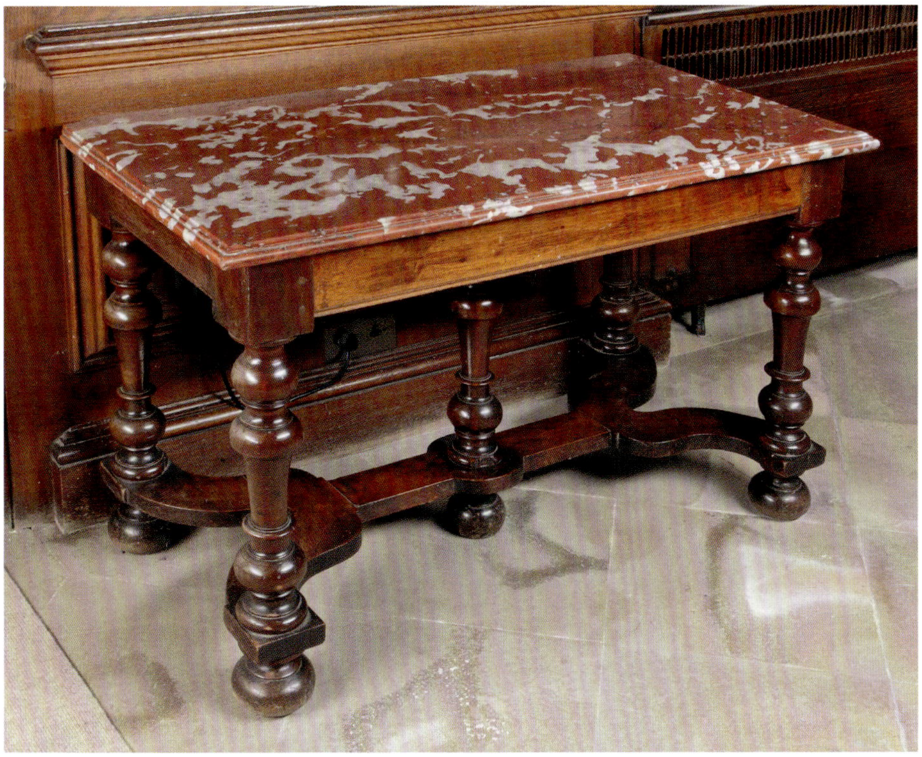

household staff to play on long summer evenings.[85]

Rieusset also worked at Leicester House, London, for Lord Sidney in 1700.[86] His daughter Catherine was baptized in 1702 at La Patente de Soho, when the locksmith Samuel Marc, who also worked for Montagu, stood godfather.[87] The family were then living in Rider Court; by 1716 Rieusset was living in St Anne's, Soho, but also owned property in the City parish of St Lawrence Jewry.[88] He supplied office furniture for Montagu's use as Queen Anne's Master of the Royal Wardrobe;[89] in 1706 he supplied a 'large wainscott Desk 8 foot in length 4 foot 6 inches in breadth & 2 foot 4 inches in height', with several partitions, hinges, locks and keys, covered with green cloth and garnished with galloon and brass nails, for £4 15s. The locks and keys were probably supplied by Samuel Marc. Rieusset also supplied turned walnut side tables for royal palaces and for Montagu's use: one pair at Boughton (plate 96) support slabs of red Languedoc marble, from 1692 reserved for the exclusive use of Louis XIV.[90]

The sophisticated cutting and polishing of marble for buildings and furniture owed much to Huguenot Jacques Besson (1540–1573), inventor and mathematician, who became a citizen of Geneva in 1561 and returned to France where his *Theatricum Instrumentum* (1571) was translated into five different languages and ran into seven editions in 35 years. As a Protestant at the time of the Massacre of St Bartholomew (see p.21), Besson took refuge in England, where he died in 1573.[91]

In June 1688 'Monsr Derigner, a french carver' was recommended to the Master Masons (appointed to the monarch for the 'King's Works') 'to be by some of them employed as soone as possible'.[92] He may have been the sculptor working at the Château de Clagny, near Versailles, in 1678–9 and on the palace stables at Versailles in 1680.[93] Robert Derignée (fl.1691–1701) worked at Kensington Palace for Queen Mary, in 1691 supplying a 'great wainscott frame for a glass 10 feet long and seven feet wide' with gilded figures, for £20, and a chimney glass carved with leaves and jasmine flowers for £52. In 1694 he produced 'three frames for Pictures Richly carved with flowers' and in 1699 charged £30 for 'carving two sconces with festoones, flowers and other ornaments'. It is believed that these handsome sconces were subsequently acquired by Ralph Montagu, as a perquisite of office as Master of the Wardrobe (plate 97).[94]

The fine carved oak reredos in Holy Trinity church, Hull, of about 1753, and panelling in the chapel at Ribston Hall, near Knaresborough, dating from the 1720s, point to skilled French craftsmanship in Yorkshire and may be Huguenot work.[95] Although their church records do not survive, the Huguenot community in York included Daniel Harvey (Harvé), carver in wood and stone, who worked at Castle Howard and Wentworth Castle (pp.85, 88). Jonathan Godier (d.1732), anglicized to Goodyear, probably a member of the Huguenot community, assistant to William Thornton (1670–1721), carver of York, also features in Wentworth Castle accounts for October 1725, when he was paid £33 2s for joinery work.[96]

Carpenter, carver and gilder combined their skills to produce magnificent carriages for royal processions. The 1698 gilded coach made for William III in The Hague to Daniel Marot's designs is exemplary.[97] The body is carved with shells, oak leaves, boars' heads, female masks and lambrequins, and two dogs support a mace decorated with ribbons. Painted panels enclose the lower body and the windows are framed on the outside by caryatid male figures. The coachman's seat is supported at the rear by rampant lions, and four female figures representing the Seasons rest above the main junctions of the wheel and cog. For the prestigious family wedding of Mary Churchill and John Montagu in 1705, the new family vehicles were finished by the Pelletiers, who charged £120 'For gilding the body of a chariot and the carriage and for painting the ground green' and 'for gilding the great coach carriage & with a red ground'. The most sophisticated state barge designed by William Kent for Frederick, Prince of Wales, in 1732, was carved by James Richards (1671–1759) and gilded at a cost of £259 10s by Paul Petit.[98]

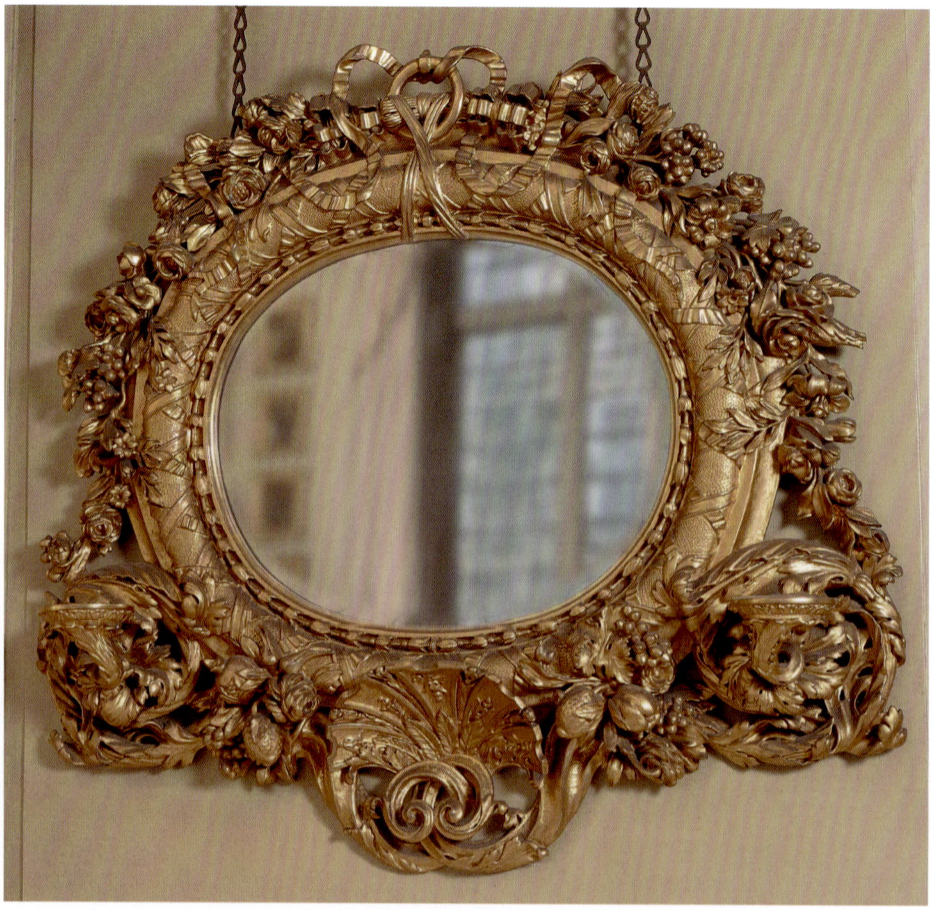

Gold leaf applied to painted murals, picture frames and furniture enhanced and unified the overall effect. Carving and gilding are specialist skills particularly associated with Huguenot émigré craftsmen. In the 1660s René Cousin and his son Peter applied gold leaf to Antonio Verrio's ceilings and murals (plate 39) and Grinling Gibbons's carvings at Whitehall, Hampton Court and Windsor Castle.[99] Under James II, René Cousin repaired 'the Picture frame in front of the Altar' for the Queen's Chapel, Windsor Castle.[100] In 1701 Peter Cousin supplied four large looking-glass frames for Hampton Court, and at Petworth, West Sussex, he was paid in 1690 'for a frame for the head of a man'.[101]

The spectacular gilded frame carved for Edward Russell (1653–1727) celebrated his naval triumphs in 1692 and his appointment as Admiral of the Fleet in November 1693, First Lord of the Admiralty in April 1694 and creation as 1st Earl of Orford in 1697.[102] This limewood frame is flanked by figures of Hercules and Mercury, surmounted by mermen holding the Admiral's coat of arms and with Fame trumpeting his status below. The carver may have been one of the Huguenot sculptors established in Soho.[103]

97 Girandole

Robert Derignée and Jean Pelletier, London, *c.*1691–4
Gilded wood, one of a pair, 94 × 109 cm
Boughton House, Northamptonshire

For Queen Mary II's apartments at Kensington Palace, between 1691 and 1694 Derignée supplied frames for looking glasses and paintings. The naturalistic carving of the flower sprays, held in place by ribbons that also bind the oval border, the acanthus-supported candle stands and the central shell are derived from designs by Jean Le Pautre and exemplify the influence of French ornament prints.

Carver and gilder Jean Pelletier (fl. *c.*1681–1704) left Paris for Amsterdam with his eldest son, René, in 1681. Their business was established in London by 1688, where they were reunited with the younger son, Thomas, his two sisters and their mother, Esther. On the recommendation of Ralph, later 1st Duke of Montagu, Jean Pelletier gilded a suite of two tables, two pairs of stands and two looking-glass frames carved by Robert Derignée for Kensington Palace.[104] A centre table at Boughton House, with an elaborate gesso top carved with Ralph Montagu's monogram beneath an earl's coronet (plate 98), probably dates from 1689. The table top is attributed to René Pelletier, who is listed in 1690 as 'graveur' at La Patente church, Soho.[105] Accounts for 'Jean, René & Thomas Pelletier for … carving and gilding from 16 August 1689', which totalled £1,124, were not settled until 1712, three years after Montagu's death. For the King's Apartments at Hampton Court, in 1699–1700 Jean Pelletier carved four frames for marble pier tables at £28 each and six pairs of large candle stands (plate 99) at £30 a pair. The sum of £417 was still unpaid on the deaths of William III in 1702 and Jean Pelletier in 1704. Thomas Pelletier took over the business in 1702; he became Cabinetmaker to Queen Anne in November 1704 (plate 100).

Jean Pelletier left his 'Wares, Goods, Chattels, ready money, Debts, Plate, Warehouse, hold-stuff, utensills' to his wife, Esther, and 'after her Decease to be equally divided between René and Thomas'. His daughters, Susanne Broquet and Jane Guilbaud, received a shilling each. A writing cabinet supplied by Jane's husband, Jean Guilbaud (fl.1690–1712), cabinetmaker at 'The Crown and Looking Glass' in Long Acre, Covent Garden, retains its label (plate 101).[106] On 31 July 1690 Guilbaud supplied two desks 'inlaid with flowers' for Queen Mary for £30, and in 1691 another 'plain scriptoire' (writing desk) for Whitehall Palace. He may also have made the 'large walnut tree Cabinet with abundance of drawers to it & shelves within the upper body for My Lord's prints',[107] which the Pelletiers supplied to Lord Montagu in November 1704 for £9.

Thomas and René Pelletier were co-partners from 1709;[108] that year Thomas supplied Thomas Thynne with a set of 12 chairs and a large 'sohfe' (*sic*), a table, pair of stands, a looking glass and a fire screen. Lord Montagu's housekeeper at Ditton was paid in January 1710 'for Mr Peltier's 2 mens

98 Centre table with the monogram of Ralph, 1st Earl of Montagu

Attributed to the Pelletier workshop, London, *c.*1689
Carved wood and gilt gesso, 81 × 127 × 68.5 cm
Boughton House, Northamptonshire

The table celebrates Ralph Montagu's enhanced status from 1689 with the cypher 'RM' beneath an earl's coronet framed by palm fronds and flanked by acanthus scrollwork and sprays of jasmine. This raised decoration was cut in the gesso surface and burnished with gold leaf in contrast to the matt gold-tooled background. The sophisticated stand is supported on fluted legs embellished with acanthus leaves and surmounted with Ionic capitals. Such carefully constructed complex gilded profiles reflect light and entertain the eye.

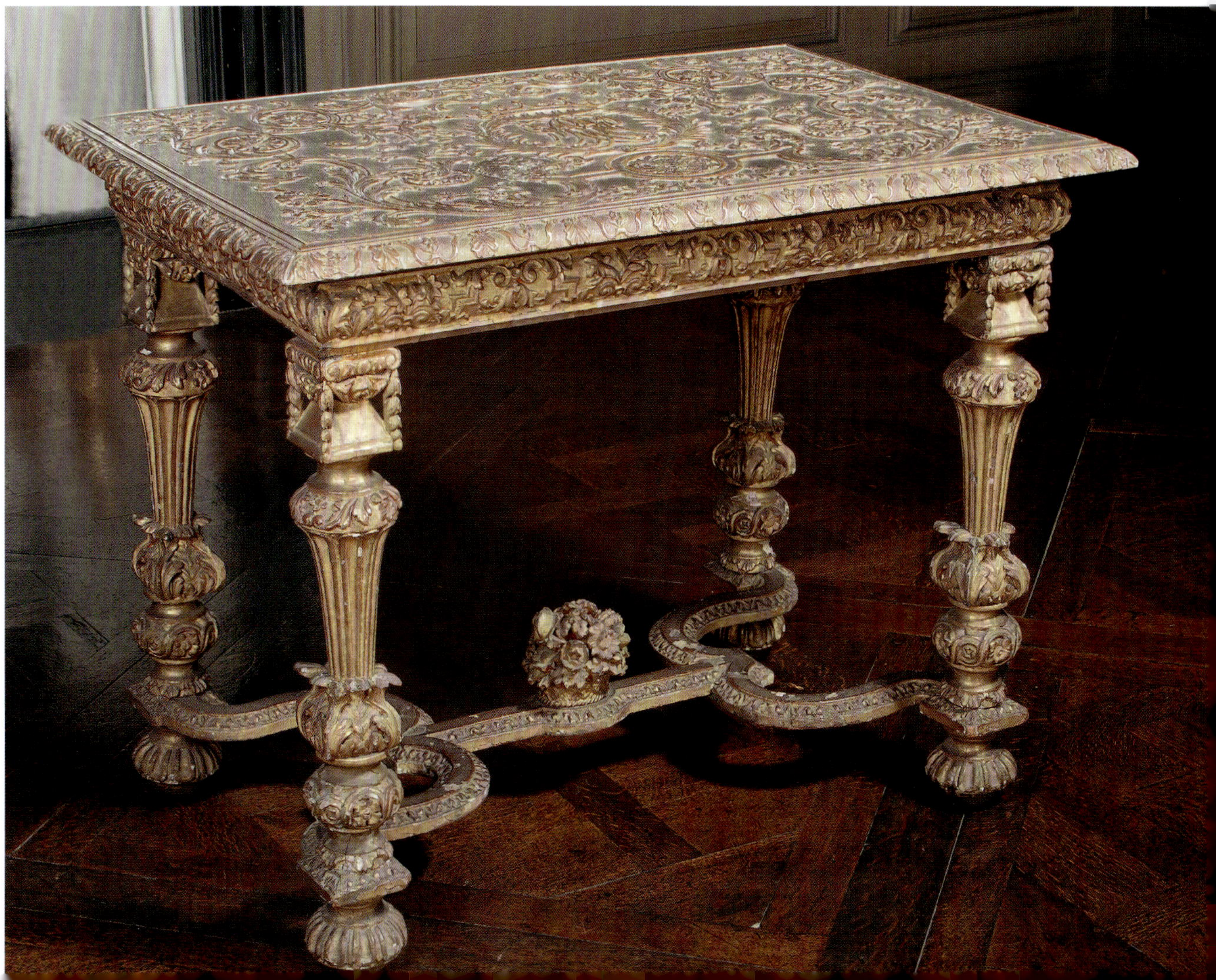

diet'.[109] But in 1711, a month after their mother's death, the brothers quarrelled. Although René was 'best workman', he 'had the misfortune of not understanding English' so he oversaw the work at home, while Thomas minded 'the Business abroad ... Buying up Materialls ... supplying such p[er] sons as they were Employed by' and waiting 'on such persons as had any work to be done'.[110] As the brothers were not on speaking terms, Thomas was their mother's sole executor. René complained that Thomas did not reinvest in the business: he collected customers' debts but used the proceeds for his personal gain, leaving René without financial resources. By 1712 the workshop had closed and the brothers lived apart, René in the parish of St Martin-in-the-Fields and Thomas, as dealer and auctioneer, in the parish of St Paul's, Covent Garden,[111] abutting Bedford House at the east end of Henrietta Street.[112]

René became a mat-mounter[113] and framed more than a hundred Old Master drawings for Thomas Coke (1697–1759) of Holkham, Norfolk.[114] In 1725 René inherited the prints, books and plaster figures belonging to his friend Louis Chéron (plate 28; pp.49–55) and took up residence in Chéron's former house. René's collection of pictures, prints and drawings by Chéron was sold after his death in March 1725/6.[115] René appointed the carver Matthew Gosset (1683–1744) to ensure that his children were brought up in the Church of England.[116] His son Solomon inherited his father's books, drawings and prints; he was apprenticed in 1732 to diamond cutter Peter Saulnier (d.1762) and was working as a goldsmith in Leicester Fields later that decade.[117] The Mrs Pelletier who was paid in May 1727 for mounting a cartoon for James Brydges, Duke of Chandos, at Cannons is probably René's widow.[118] When Thomas Pelletier wrote his will in 1737 he had moved to Kentish Town, where he died in 1739, leaving his estate to his maid, Mary Smith, in gratitude for her long and faithful service.[119]

In London, Huguenot craftsmen with complementary skills clubbed together. Thus James Riorteau (fl.1718–31), listed as *ébéniste* in 1705 at the French Savoy church,[120] kept a shop in Hog Lane opposite L'Eglise des Grècs. The Riorteaus were connected through that church

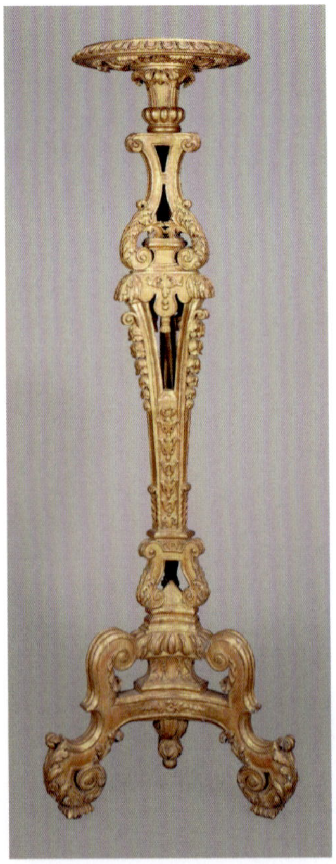

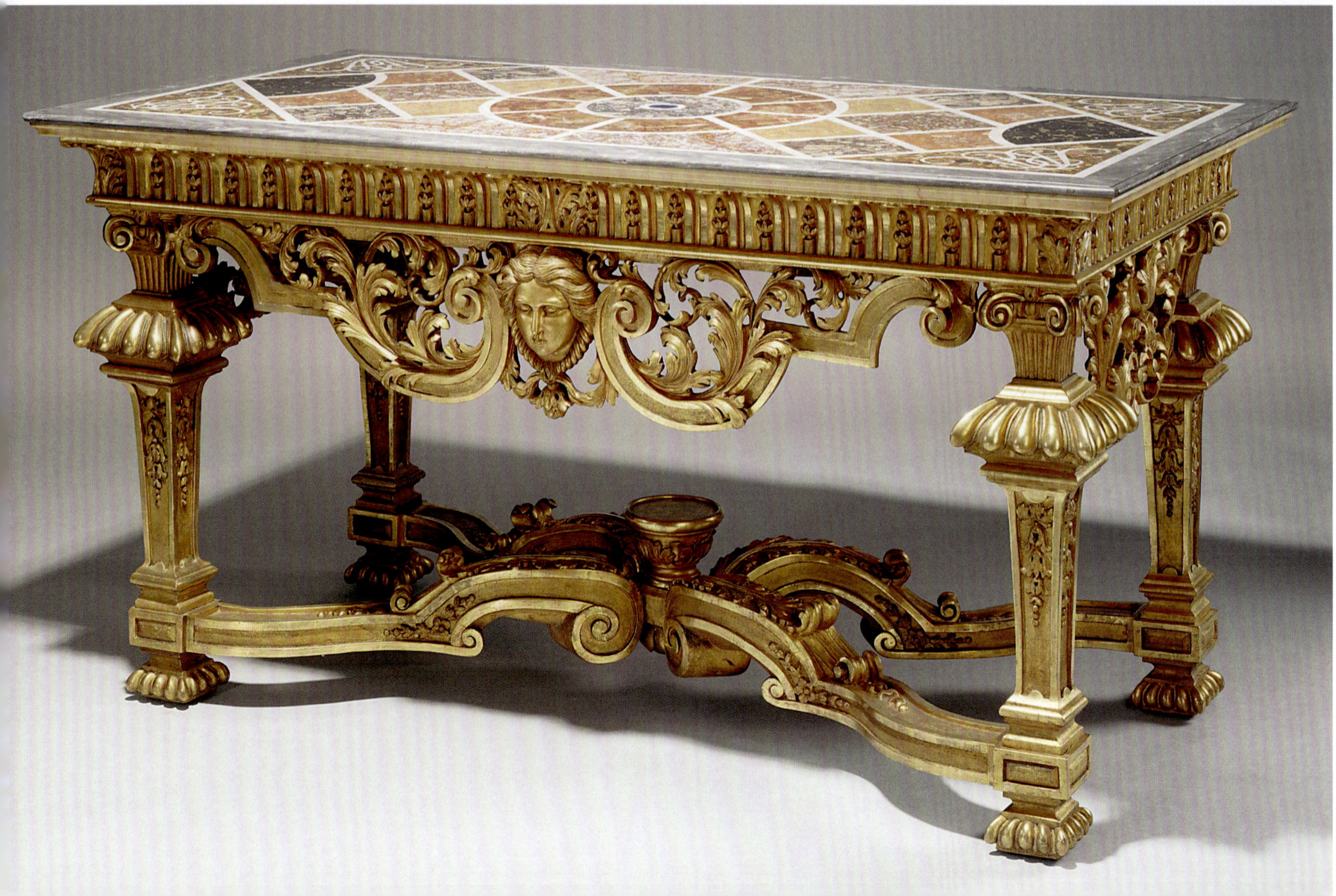

LEFT ABOVE

99 Candle stand

John Pelletier, London, 1701
Carved gilt oak and limewood,
155.5 × 56 × 48.5 cm
Royal Collection Trust (RCIN 1002)

The design is made up of five sections: above the tripod base, chains of bell flowers cascade from a lambrequin fringe, while the source of light at the top played on the sophisticated surface ornament below. This was one of 12 candle stands supplied by Jean Pelletier to illuminate William III's State Apartments at Hampton Court Palace. Matching pairs of stands flanked the giltwood tables that stood between the windows beneath large pier glasses.

LEFT BELOW

100 Pier table

Thomas Pelletier, London, the inlaid marble top attributed to John Nost, *c.*1704
Carved gilt oak, limewood and marble, 82.5 × 154 × 80 cm
Royal Collection Trust (RCIN 600)

This may be the 'Marble inlayd Table upon a Carved guilded frame' supplied for Queen Anne's State Apartments at Kensington Palace by the sculptor John Nost in 1704 and valued at £80. If so, the carved frame was subcontracted to the Pelletier workshop, by then under the management of Thomas Pelletier.

RIGHT

101 Writing cabinet

Jean Guilbaud, London, 1695–1700
Oak, with Guilbaud's trade label,
162 × 110.5 cm
Museum of the Home, London

Jean Guilbaud, cabinetmaker at 'The Crown and Looking Glass' in Long Acre, Covent Garden, was married to Jean Pelletier's younger daughter, Jane. According to his trade label, Guilbaud sold 'all maner of Cabbinet work and Japan Cabbinets, Large Tables, Small suets of all maner of Looking Glasses, Pannells of Glasse, Chimney peaces and all sorts of Glasse Sconces'.

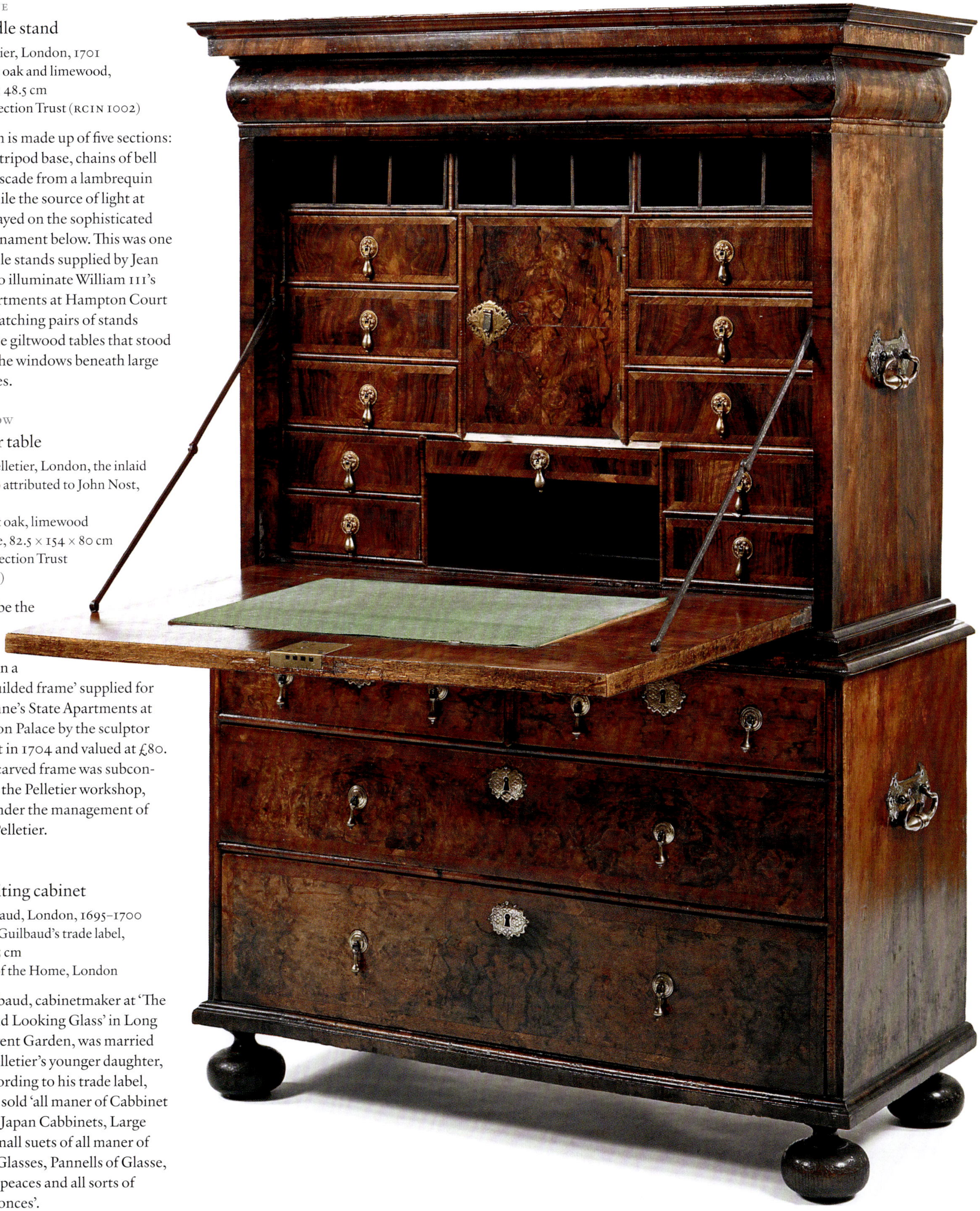

with Abraham Dorselle (fl.1705–15), cabinetmaker at the Angel, Long Acre. In 1718 Riorteau took Abraham Delamere as apprentice. No evidence of Delamere's or Dorselle's work has come to light, but the 'James Riorto' who worked for Frederick, Prince of Wales, in 1731 is either James Riorteau the elder or his son, also James, who was aged 26 in 1731.[121] Paid 6 guineas for preparing a six-leaf screen 'finely carved and gilt', 'Riorto' also decorated the room at Kew Palace in which the screen was installed for a total fee of £139.

Huguenot influence was also achieved through marriage. The celebrated cabinetmaker William Gomm (*c.*1698–1780), established in Newcastle House, Clerkenwell, married in 1737 as his second wife Mary Anne de Moivre,[122] niece of the mathematician Abraham de Moivre.[123]

Pierre Langlois, born in London in September 1718, a son of Daniel and Jeanne L'Anglois, was baptized at Les Grècs.[124] His younger brother was named in 1723 after his godfather Henry, 1st Viscount St John (1652–1742).[125] The family was very well connected.[126] There were Langlois cabinetmakers in Paris in the late seventeenth and eighteenth centuries,[127] and other Langlois craftsmen working in London in the early eighteenth century.[128] Jeanne Langlois, a cabinetmaker's widow, was living in Church Street, St Anne's, Soho, in 1718–20.[129]

Pierre Langlois spent the 1730s in Paris learning to make floral marquetry, but his Protestant faith made official apprenticeship impossible. Perhaps he joined the Huguenot Migeon family, who sustained their faith through five generations.[130] By 1759 he had returned to London, attracted by the opportunity to work beyond the influence of the guilds as a fashionable cabinetmaker until his death in 1767. He made a marquetry writing box for Horace Walpole in 1760, and two marble-topped commodes and matching corner cupboards veneered with Japanese lacquer for Walpole at Strawberry Hill, Twickenham, in 1763.[131] When George Montagu visited Langlois's workshop in March 1763, he was dismayed to find the 'three parts of the Japan' that Walpole 'gave to Langlois to make into commodes … he carried me to see his things, and there it was flaring about the rooms in planks and on the staircase'.[132]

Langlois's first British patron, the 4th Duke of Bedford, lived at Southampton House close to the cabinetmaker's shop in Tottenham Court Road.[133] Langlois's trade card (plate 102) was designed and engraved by François-Antoine Aveline (1718–1780), who until 1743 worked in Paris engraving paintings by François Boucher (1703–1770).[134]

It is possible that Langlois spent some time working in Stockholm. This might explain his connection with the architect Sir William Chambers (1723–1796), who was born in Gothenburg and employed by the Swedish East India Company in the 1740s. In London Langlois made commodes to Chambers's designs: one of four of those made for Princess Amelia (1711–1786), daughter of George II, bears the signature 'F M la Cave' for the engraver François Morellon La Cave (1696–1768; p.216). They were intended for display below tall gilded pier glasses at Gunnersbury Park

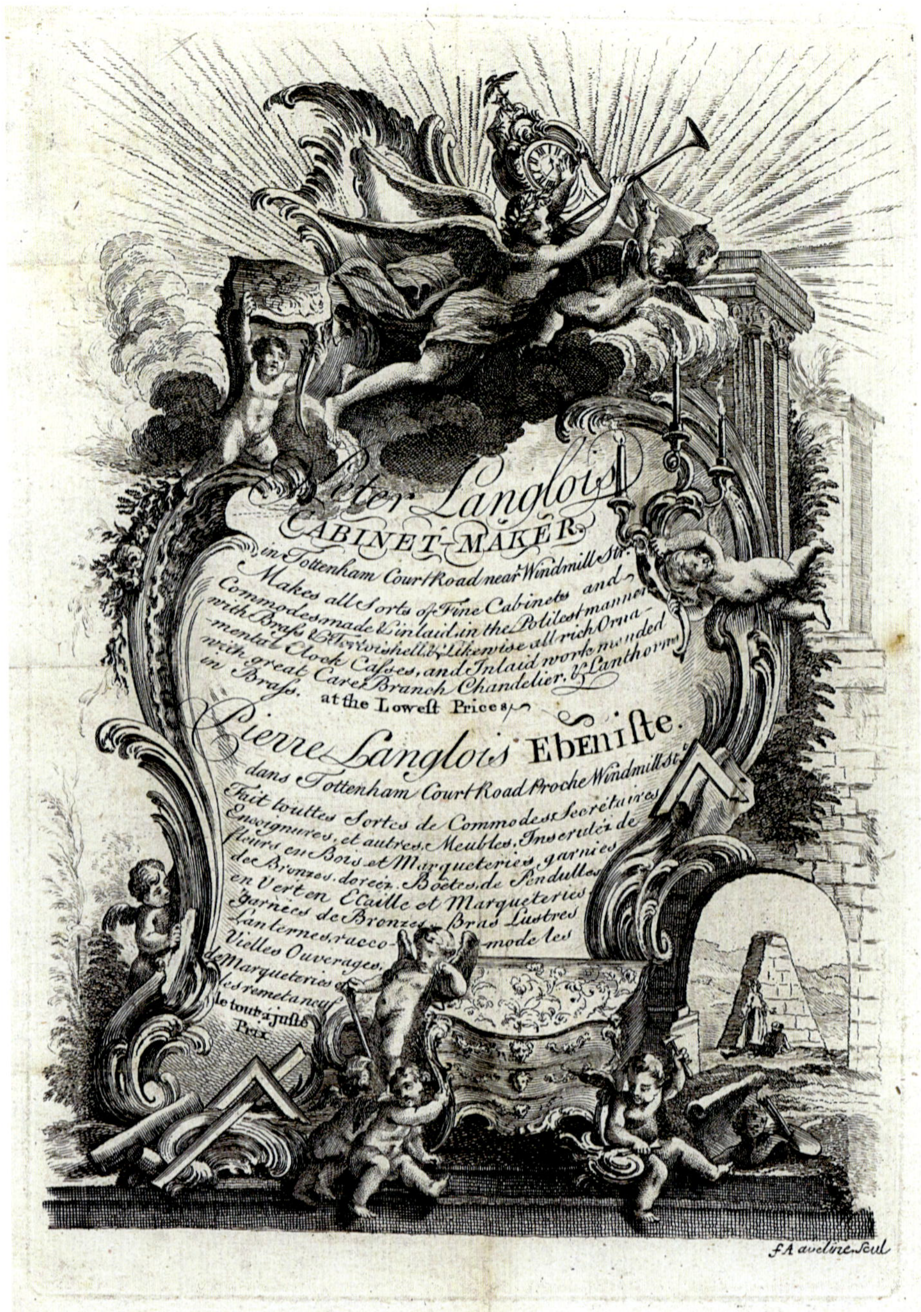

102 Trade card of Pierre Langlois

François-Antoine Aveline, London, *c.*1759
Etching, 23.2 × 16.3 cm
British Museum, London (Heal Collection, 28.121)

Langlois advertised cabinets and commodes, secretaires, corner cabinets and clock cases 'Inscrutez de fleurs en Bois et Marqueteries garnies de Bronzes, doreez' (inlaid with marquetry flowers and mounted with ormolu) from his premises 'in Tottenham Court Road, near Windmill Street'.

(plate 103).[135] In 1764 they were referred to as 'FRENCH COMMODES of exquisite Workmanship, most elegantly decorated with chased and engraved Or Molu'.[136] Langlois's Swedish connections are further corroborated by his friendship with the Anglo-Swedish cabinetmaker Niclas Flodberg (d. *c.*1772) who witnessed the marriage of Langlois's daughter Mary with Dominique Jean (1736–1812) at Old St Pancras.[137]

Dominique Jean worked with his father-in-law, supplied the ormolu mounts on his commodes and managed the business after Langlois's death.[138] In 1769 the industrialist Matthew Boulton noted:

> *mr. Dominique, ou Mns Langlois, Ebenistre, Tottenham Court Road Mr. Dominique married the daughter of Mns Langlois who sells inld wood cabinets on the same side as Piercy Street Tottenham Court you see a sign of commode tables & Mr. Dominique is a french gilder he gets up work himself.*[139]

In 1771 Dominique Jean took Daniel Langlois as apprentice.[140] Daniel's date of birth is not recorded but he was probably born abroad in 1749–50, as he was 66 when he died in 1816. In about 1767 Daniel signed a commode which compares with a pair supplied in that year by Pierre Langlois for the Duke of Bedford preserved at Woburn Abbey.[141] Samuel Servient, goldsmith, living at 'Tottingham Cort Road, ches Mr. Langlois Cabinet Maker' when he entered the French Hospital in 1771,[142] probably assisted with gilding Dominique Jean's mounts.

Pierre Langlois led the taste for marquetry furniture in 1760s London. Correspondence between the celebrated Lennox sisters – Louisa, Emily, Caroline and Sarah, daughters of Charles, 2nd Duke of Richmond (1701–1740) – reveals that Langlois was so fashionable by the early 1760s that he had a waiting list. Louisa wrote from Castletown, Co. Kildare, to Sarah on 22 March 1762: 'I have a commode coming over from Mr Langlois that Lady Anne [her mother-in-law] has bespoke for me. It is one of the cheap ones but I shall like it mightily and wish it was to come soon'. The following February Lady Anne Wentworth wrote to her son, Thomas Conolly (Louisa's husband): 'I hope Lady Louisa will get the commode soon and that she and you will like it. I paid Mr Langlois.' A commode from Langlois's workshops took almost a year to produce. A month later Caroline, Lady Holland wrote to Emily, Duchess of Leinster of Louisa's taste in furniture:

> *I hear she likes L'Anglay's inlaid things. very much, and I would wish to send her something that might suit some of her rooms, whether commode table, bureau*

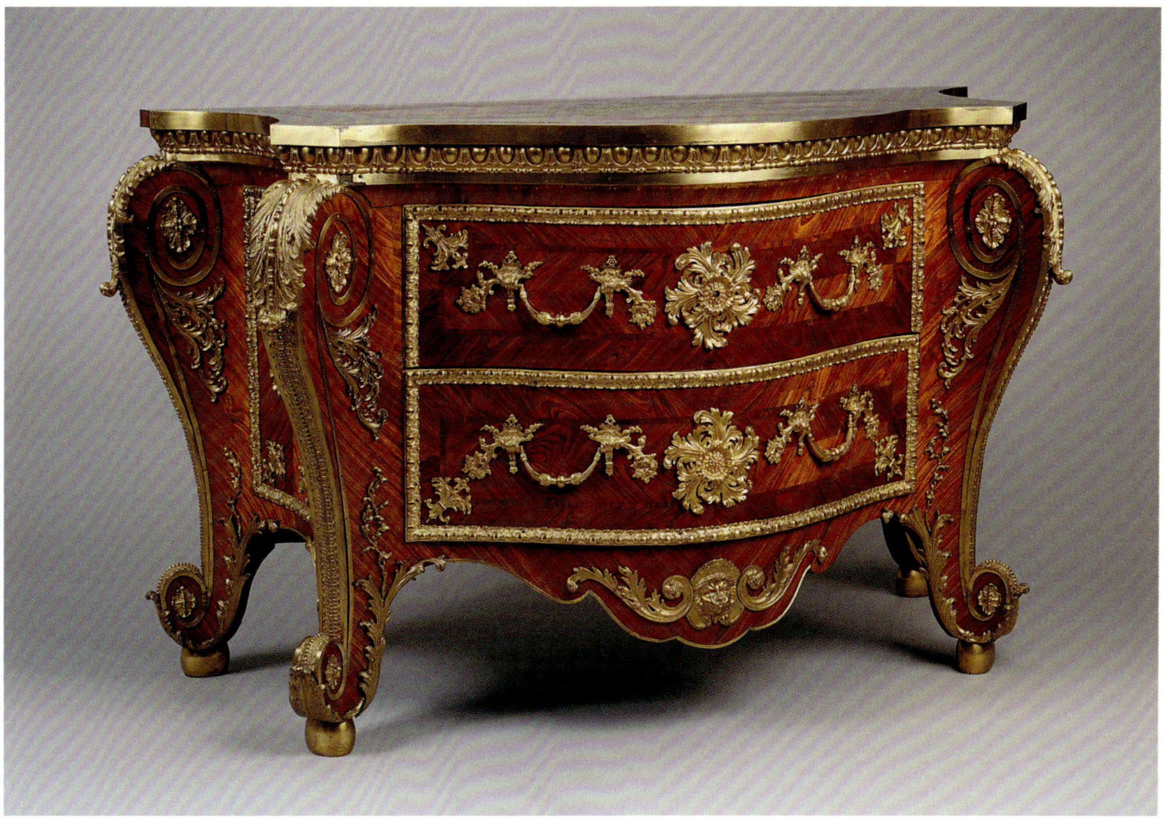

103 Commode

Pierre Langlois, London, possibly designed by William Chambers, with gilt bronze mounts attributed to Dominique Jean, 1763
Rosewood, pine, oak and gilt bronze, 84.5 × 154 × 67.4 cm
Royal Collection Trust (RCIN 21235)

Made for Princess Amelia, daughter of George III, this commode bears the signature 'F M la Cave' for the engraver François Morellon La Cave. The lavish engraved brass inlay includes sprays of narcissi and other intricate floral decoration.

or coins, which to be sure one might vulgarly call corner cupboards, but really they are lovely and finish a room so well. I have two beauties in the Salon at Holland House.[143]

Clocks and clock-case makers

Cornelius Gole may have supplied long cases for clocks, but two specialist Huguenot clock case makers are known by name: Pierre Pavie (fl.1684–1727), listed as a cabinetmaker in 1705–6, was paid £10 for a clock case for William Cavendish, 1st Duke of Devonshire, in 1695.[144] In 1698 Pavie stood godfather to Pierre, son of Pierre Mallet (recorded 1697–1704), clockmaker based in Crispin Street off Petticoat Lane, Spitalfields.[145] Cabinetmaker Lazaire Desbois, at the sign of the Clock Case and Cabinet in Compton Street, Soho, from 1703 to 1723, probably specialized in clock cases.[146] Marquetry long cases framed movements by Henry Poisson (fl.1695–1720) and Daniel Le Count (1676–1714) from Rouen; the latter served the Threadneedle Street church as deacon in 1683–6 and elder in 1689–92.[147] Awarded the freedom of the Clockmakers' Company in 1676, Le Count was still working in 1714, when he had premises on the north side of the Royal Exchange, in Capel Court off Bartholomew Lane.[148]

The arabesque marquetry in contrasting woods on a long-case clock by Henry Poisson was fashionable in England from *c.*1690 to *c.*1715.[149] His son Henry, who anglicized his name to Fish, had premises in the Royal Exchange from 1736 until his death in 1775.[150] Abraham Perinot (1689–1782) worked from Long Acre, Covent Garden. Son of Jean Perinot (fl.1689–1707), master cabinetmaker from La Capelle, Picardy, Abraham signed a tavern clock *c.*1735. By the 1750s he was living in Marylebone. He died in the French Hospital, London, in February 1782.[151]

Makers of looking glass, lacquer, japanning, mosaic work and *verre églomisé*

In 1703 Jean Guilbaud supplied overmantel mirrors and sconces for Hopetoun House, Scotland:[152] the house still contains matching table, pier glass and candle stands, all japanned black, painted with flowers and gilded and also attributed to Guilbaud (plate 105). This attribution is supported by evidence from a 1703 Chancery Court case that lists similarly decorated furniture that Guilbaud supplied to a Mrs Fraigneau, wife of a Huguenot confectioner in Pall Mall.[153] It included 'Japan' cabinets, a black-framed looking glass, a walnut chest of drawers, a Dutch table drawn in gold, four pairs of glass sconces and two flowered pictures.[154] Guilbaud's neighbour in Long Acre, Jean Perinot, supplied Mrs Fraigneau with Japan frames, toilet glasses, a desk, a tea table and glass sconces.[155]

Jacob and Philip Arbunot, like the Pelletiers, came from Paris; the families were closely connected; when René Pelletier stood godfather in 1691, his co-godparent was Marie Arbunot.[156] The Arbunots made furniture using Asian lacquer and its 'japanned' imitation, supplied looking glasses in sophisticated frames and 'China' (porcelain imported through the East India Company). For Lady Mary Germain at Drayton House, in June 1702 Philip Arbunot charged £34 for gilding 'the hinges of 2 cabinets with right gold' and for '2 carv'd frames of right gold'.[157] In July 1703 Philip Arbunot charged Lady Mary £8 10s for 'making up an Indian Chest of yr owne boards finding locks and Hindges and painting the 2 ends', a description that corresponds to a chest preserved at Drayton (plate 104); Arbunot also repaired marquetry furniture.[158] In 1703–4 he provided two double-branched gilded sconces 'scalloped diamond cutt and Engraved Embellished with Crimson and gold Mosaic works with Flowers on the Bodyes of the glass' for £12 7s for Queen Anne's gift to the Emperor of Morocco.[159] This technique of gilding glass

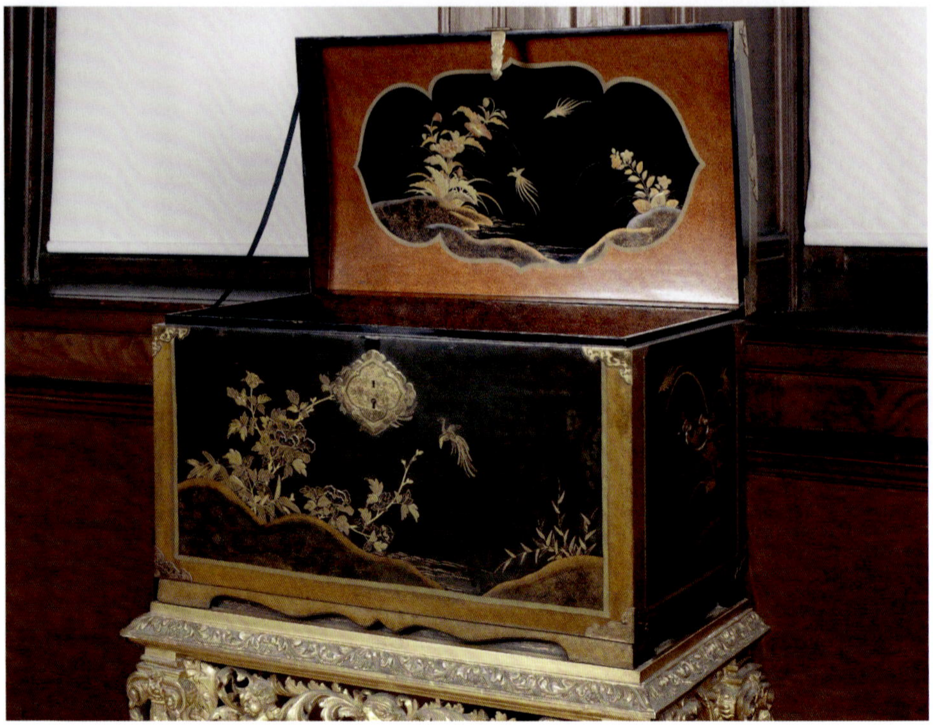

104 Chest veneered with Japanese lacquer

Philip Arbunot, London, 1702, the stand attributed to the Pelletier workshop
Lacquer veneer on oak, japanned borders, brass locks and giltwood stand, 110.5 × 91.5 cm
Drayton House, Northamptonshire

The lacquer panels are decorated with plants and exotic birds; these 'Indian' elements are complemented by the carved giltwood stand, which provides a European frame. The stand was probably subcontracted by Philip Arbunot to the Pelletier workshop.

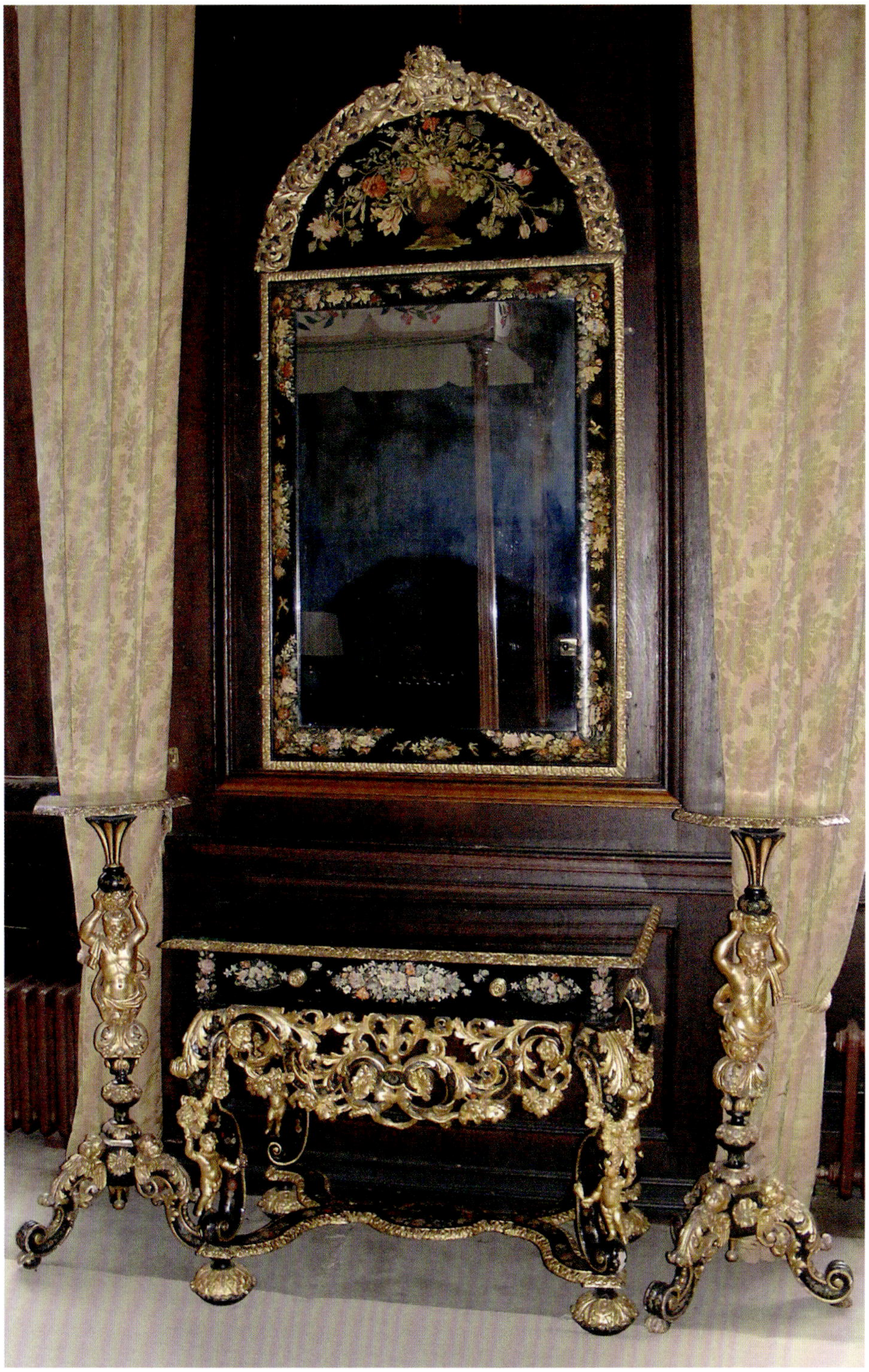

105 Pier glass, table and stands

Attributed to Jean Guilbaud, London, *c.*1703
Japanned black and painted with flowers, mirror 175 × 93 × 13 cm; table 84 × 106.5 × 66 cm, candle stands 110 × 53 cm
Hopetoun House, Linlithgow

Jean Guilbaud worked with specialist gilders, probably the Pelletiers (his wife's family) and japanners, the Arbunots. The identity of the flower painter is not recorded.

from behind, engraving and then applying background colour, in which the Pelletier workshop also excelled, was later known as *verre églomisé* (plate 87).[160] An exceptional looking glass with a *verre églomisé* frame, made for General Charles Churchill (d.1714), bears the Churchill lion crest. Intended for a pier between windows, the associated table was probably accompanied by matching candle stands.[161] Figures of Flora and Zephyr engraved on the looking glass frame support the attribution to the Pelletier workshop; they provided similarly decorated overmantel glasses for Ditton, Buckinghamshire in 1706.

When Jacob (d.1722) and Philip (1702–1727) Arbunot received denization in 1709, they were described as japanners.[162] Jacob worked as a sculptor in the rue de Faubourg St Antoine, Paris, in 1682.[163] He was in London from 1689, when he witnessed the marriage of fellow Parisian Nicholas Doyenne (fl.1689–1703), sculptor.[164] Recorded from 1709 as working on the south side of Long Acre, by 1715 he was at the sign of the Royal Cabinet, at the junction of Church Court and The Strand, where he worked with Philip. In October 1715 a fire at their premises damaged 'a great many of his Glasses'.[165] The shop was burnt out and a notice in the *Daily Courant* indicated the Arbunots' intention 'to leave off trade', describing their wide-ranging stock, including cabinet furniture in walnut, china, tea tables, screens, pictures and strong boxes. In 1719 the Arbunots supplied the Marquis of Annandale with over £300 worth of furniture, including 'a fine pair of Sconces in glass & gold frames & carved as gold heads' at £24. Jacob had died by 1722 but Philip carried on the business until his death in March 1727; in April *The Daily Post* announced the sale of their stock.[166] Successive notices published that spring described the 'Cabinets, Scrutores, Glasses and Glass Sconces, India Tea Tables, China, Ruff Plates and naked glass of all sizes', 'fine large glass and gold Peer glasses Dressing glasses of all sorts Chimney glass & fine large Sconces, and small and Naked glasses'.[167]

The Arbunots, Guilbaud and the Pelletiers probably used a local glasshouse specializing in cast glass as developed in France by Bernard Perrot (fl.1649–1709) in the 1660s and 1670s, but by 1727 Philip Arbunot had a profitable share in the Bear Gardens Glass House in Southwark.[168] Glasshouse Street, Piccadilly, built in 1679, with its French church, was named after a glassworks sited there.[169]

Framemakers

Second-generation Huguenots born or trained in London included skilled carvers and gilders working in the Rococo style. James Pascall; the Gosset family (fl.1716–85) and Gideon Saint (1729–1799) led the production of new-style frames for paintings, looking glasses and marble tables. Pascall at the Golden Head, at the junction of Hanover Street and Long Acre, from 1733, enjoyed close links with engravers and publishers. In 1738 he sold Simon Gribelin's prints of Raphael's cartoons, Rubens's ceiling of the Whitehall Banqueting House and Gribelin's *A Book of Ornaments*; in 1744 he took subscriptions for topographical views of Chatsworth and Haddon Hall by François Vivares.[170] Pascall's workshop and yard in Long Acre was on the Duke of Bedford's estate.[171] His gilded pine and walnut set commissioned for the Picture Gallery at Temple Newsam, Leeds, seat of Henry Ingram, 7th Viscount Irwin (1691–1761), was delivered in August 1746 for a total £364 16s. The set consisted of 20 chairs, four settees, a couch, a pair of console tables, a pair of marble-topped side tables, eight candle stands, a fire-screen and two girandoles, all carved in the latest style (plate 106). Pascall explained to Lady Irwin: 'I am as carefull in charging as possible. there is Upholsters and Cabinett Makers in town would have charged 100 pound more than what I have, but as I am ye Maker my Self and does Everything at ye first hand I can doe what they Cannot.'[172]

Richard Hoare (1709–1754) bought frames from the Pascall workshop between 1733 and 1754, but from 1746 the business was managed by Pascall's widow, Ann, 'with the same hands, and usual Manner, as in her late Husband's time', employing their eldest son, also named James.[173] Charles Wellbeloved (d.1782?), framemaker, who witnessed the elder James Pascall's will, may have worked for the master. Ann Pascall took Ramsay Lawson as business partner until July 1751.[174] Was James Pascall trained by a first-generation Huguenot carver? Is he the Jacques Pascall who, with Augustin Courtauld, goldsmith, witnessed the marriage of Judith Marie Pascall in the Soho annexe of the Leicester Fields church in 1718?[175] The close familial links between craftsmen with different skills created a dynamic melting pot of talent which fuelled artistic inspiration.

The Gosset family of carvers and gilders were established in Berwick Street, Soho, for three generations from 1716.[176] Three brothers were brought up and trained by their uncle Matthew Gosset.[177] Giltwood frames supplied by Matthew (plate 255) for wax portraits of George II and Queen Caroline may have been made by his nephew, Jacob.[178] Isaac (1713–1799) and Gedeon inherited their uncle's house on the east side of Berwick Street in 1744 and worked with Abraham Dallain (*c.*1727–1803), carver and gilder;[179] Jacob Gosset worked at the Golden Table, Oxenden Street, in 1726–9 and then in Warwick Street until at least 1767.[180] He subscribed to Giacomo Leoni's translation of *The Architecture of L.B. Alberti* in 1726. For Frederick, Prince of Wales, Jacob Gosset supplied in 1736 'a carv'd & gilded frame for a whole length portrait for the Duke of Dorset' for £25; he charged a further £35 10s for a frame 'for another version of the same picture' for the Prince's mistress, Mrs Vane (now at Raby Castle) and £21 for a frame with two putti holding a lyre and a symbol of eternity for a 'Child' picture by Jacopo Amigoni of Frederick, Prince of Wales.[181] In the 1730s and 1740s Jacob Gosset supplied the artist Arthur Pond with gilt frames and glasses for pastels;[182] these 'architrave gold frames' complement several of Pond's portraits,[183] as well as some pastels by the artists William Hoare (1707–1792) and Francis Cotes (1726–1770).

Gedeon Gosset supplied picture frames for the Wyndhams, the Earls of Egremont, at Petworth House, Sussex, in 1744 and the Grimston family in 1747.[184] By the late 1750s he had moved to Marylebone. But the Gossets were still linked with

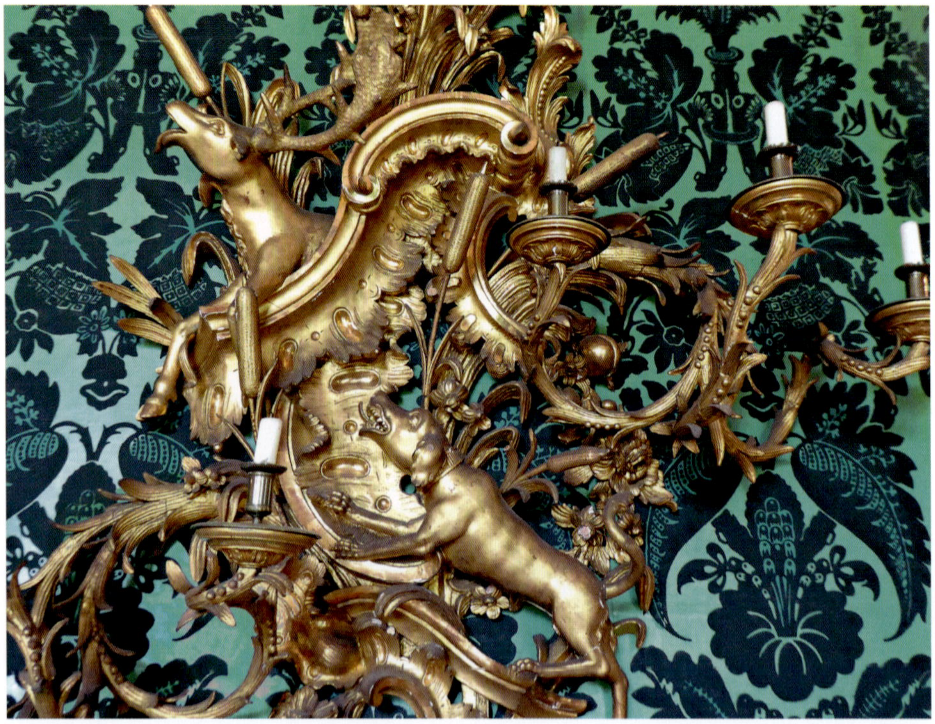

106 Girandole (detail)

James Pascall, London, 1746/7
Giltwood, one of a pair, 211 × 152 cm
Temple Newsam House, Leeds

This is one of a pair, part of a suite of furniture for the Gallery, Temple Newsam House, Leeds. The light from six candles enlivened the carving of hound chasing the stag through bullrushes. The design captures French stylistic influence and may be associated with William De La Cour, who published eight books of ornament in the 1740s.

the Wyndhams in 1748, when William Hogarth sent a sketch for the frame for Lord Wyndham's commission *Paul before Felix* for the Hall, Lincoln's Inn:

> *I have enquired of Mr. Gosset, a Frame maker in Berwick Street about the price of one somewhat in the manner of the sketch below, he believes it may come to about 30 pound Guilt to about half as much unguilt and about five pounds less if my Lord Windham's arms are omitted. Frames may be carried up to a great expense, but he thinks one cannot be made in proportion to the picture for less*

Hogarth adds: 'I have removed the picture home again in hopes of making some improvements whilst the Frame is making.' The sketch at the base of Hogarth's letter is annotated: 'a Moulding of 11 or 12 inches broad with carving at the corners and in the middles' and 'my Lord Windham's armes if Judg'd proper'.[185]

Isaac Gosset supplied frames for portraits by Thomas Gainsborough, William Hoare and Allan Ramsay.[186] In 1751, when praising Isaac's skills as a modeller of wax profiles, George Vertue referred to frame carving as Isaac's original business: 'he still undertakes carving for persons that are willing to pay him well for his labours'.[187] Gainsborough mentions Gosset in letters dated 1762, 1766 and 1768, and Gosset is named in Gainsborough's bank account in 1762 and 1763. It was an enduring friendship: Gainsborough's portrait of Isaac was shown at the Royal Academy in 1780 and Gosset attended Gainsborough's funeral in 1788.[188]

Lady Egremont paid Isaac Gosset as William Hoare's framemaker in 1763.[189] The artist's relative Henry Hoare (1750–1828) of Mitcham Grove was married to Huguenot Lydia Mallortie (1754–1816).[190] His cousin, also Henry Hoare (1705–1785), paid Isaac Gosset for profile wax portraits in 1753,[191] for supplying plate glass for Italian coloured prints in 1758–63, for gold leaf in 1769 and for framing prints, including one in a 'Carlo' frame[192] in 1763 and another in 1774.[193] William Hoare used Gosset as his agent with Charles Yorke (1722–1770) in 1762, Charles Wyndham, 2nd Earl of Egremont (1710–1763) in 1763 and Richard Hurd (1720–1808) in 1765.[194]

Allan Ramsay wrote to Richard Davenport (d.1771) of Calveley on 8 July 1767, enclosing a bill for the frame for his portrait of Jean-Jacques Rousseau (1712–1778): 'Mr. Davenport to Isaac Gosset of Daillain, For a three-quarter frame oiled gold £12.2.0.; and a case for ditto £0.6.0.'. Rousseau stayed in Davenport's house, Wootton, Staffordshire, and Ramsay's portrait remains in the Davenport family.

From 1774 Isaac Gosset was Joiner of the Privy or Great Chamber,[195] and although the position was abolished in 1782, Gosset continued as framemaker to George III until his retirement aged 72 in 1785. Gosset supplied frames at £32 each for Allan Ramsay's full-length state portraits of George III and Queen Charlotte, as many as two dozen pairs between 1772 and 1784.[196] His association with Ramsay is confirmed by payments from the artist in 1770 and 1779 and other payments linking Ramsay or his clients in 1759 and 1767.[197]

Fifty years earlier the patron had taken responsibility for ordering picture frames to ensure that their design blended with the interior in which they would hang. By the mid-eighteenth century the selection of frames and framemakers was usually made by the artist, although an exception is the employment of Paul Petit by Frederick, Prince of Wales. While Ramsay, Gainsborough and William Hoare habitually went to Gosset for frames, Joseph Goupy, John Wootton (1686–1764) and George Knapton patronized Paul Petit, and Thomas Hudson (1701–1779) had his frames made by Joseph Duffour, a Catholic; the exuberant work of Petit and Duffour epitomizes the short-lived Rococo style.[198]

Paul Petit worked in Silver Street, in the parish of St Giles-in-the-Fields, from 1722 until at least 1757; his first apprentice joined him in 1724 and his last in 1757. Yet despite royal patronage, Petit was declared bankrupt in 1738.[199] He is first recorded as working for James Brydges, 1st Duke of Chandos, in September 1723,[200] then for Frederick, Prince of Wales, from 1732 until 1749, gilding seat furniture, a table frame in 'oyl Gold' for William Kent's interiors at Kew Palace and a chimney piece with Apollo's head, festoons of fruit and flowers and male caryatids for Carlton House, St James's.[201] His 'Rich picture frame carved with birds Richly ornamented neatly repair'd and gilt in burnished Gold' for John Wootton's portrait of the Prince with John Spencer (1708–1746) and Charles Douglas, 3rd Duke of Queensberry (1698–1778), cost £21 in 1742 (plate 107).[202] This enhances the painting for which it was made, surmounted by the Prince of Wales's feathers, with C-scrolls, lambrequins and oak leaves, with birds dead and alive indicating a good day's shooting, and hounds' heads, hunting weapons, bows, arrows, a dagger and drinking flask to set the scene. Petit also framed Wootton's *Siege of Lille* and *Siege of Tournay* (both 1742) for the Prince

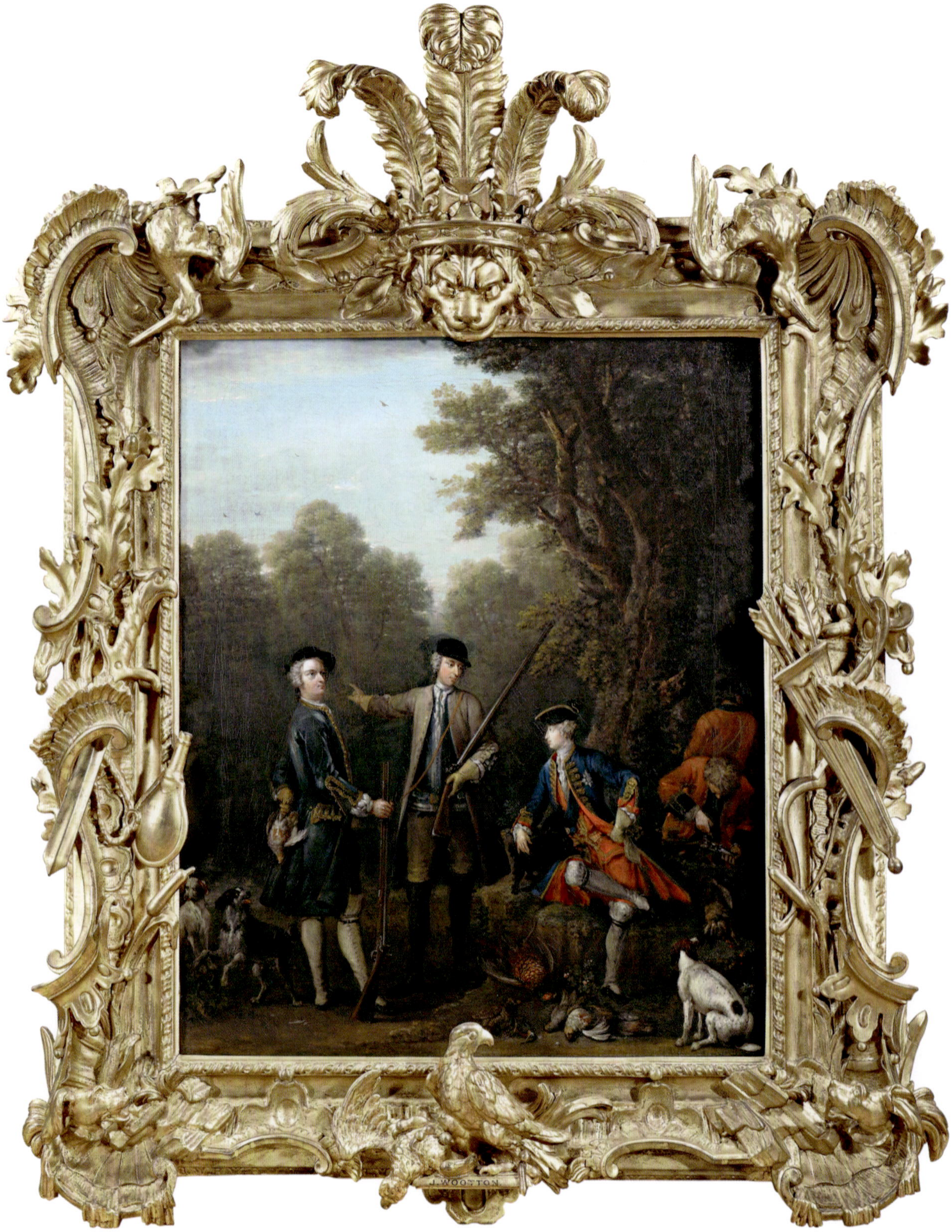

107 Picture frame

Paul Petit, London, 1742
Giltwood, 142.5 × 119.6 × 28 cm
Royal Collection Trust
(RCIN 7402421)

Petit's 'Richly ornamented' frame, surmounted by the Prince of Wales's three plumes, surrounds the portrait of Frederick, Prince of Wales with his hunting companions John Spencer and Charles Douglas, 3rd Duke of Queensberry. Other decorative elements complement the scene: dead and live game birds, hounds' heads, hunting weapons and a drinking flask.

of Wales.[203] Eight years earlier Wootton's *Frederick, Prince of Wales in the Hunting Field*, with figures by Hogarth, was framed by Petit's rival, Joseph Duffour.[204]

Petit's frame for the Prince of Wales's portrait 'with the Prince's Crest at top' with cornucopias 'pouring out Orders and several Medals with several emblems of arts and sciences' costing £197 was sent to Trinity College, Dublin, in 1747. In 1749 the Prince paid Petit over £736.[205] Another richly carved frame by Petit with eagle and sceptre at the top, with two 'Savages supporters Standards in their hand and Trophies of war', surrounds a version of George Knapton's portrait of George III as Prince of Wales; the frame alone cost £150 10s in 1748.[206] In 1739 Petit's bill names Henry Joris as his assistant.[207] He may be identified as Henry Jouret (fl.1755–75), an independent framemaker at the Architrave Frame, Grafton Street, Soho, from 1755, and at the Gold Frame, Maiden Lane, Covent Garden from 1765 to 1775. Jouret's trade card was designed by leading British carver Matthias Lock (c.1710–c.1765).[208] Drawing master Jacob Bonneau designed a trade card for Daniel Bernardeau (fl.1750–3), a turner of hardwood and oval frame-maker at the Golden Coffee Mill, St Martin's Court, near Leicester Fields, c.1750.[209]

Carved gilt picture frames were probably as prestigious as table or cabinet supports, which often included heraldic ornament, indicating the status and identity of the patron. Joseph Duffour's trade card, decorated with scrolls, birds and flowers, claimed that he was the 'original Maker of Papier Maché',[210] although his compatriot Peter Babel (d.1771) was practising as a maker of papier mâché frames and ornaments in St James's Street, Long Acre, by 1763.[211] The competition presented by the 'new invented works in papier-maché' put more traditional carvers out of work. In 1784 William Collett, carver, found work 'grown so scarce as not to find sufficient for a constant employ' and, being 'burthened with a large family', was forced to apply for his son's admission to the French Protestant Charity School, Westminster.[212] Collett's case is echoed by Jean Le Maitre (1737–1816), a woodcarver from Caen, who was admitted to the French Hospital in 1800 as he was unable to find employment because of his inability to work in the fashionable style required.[213]

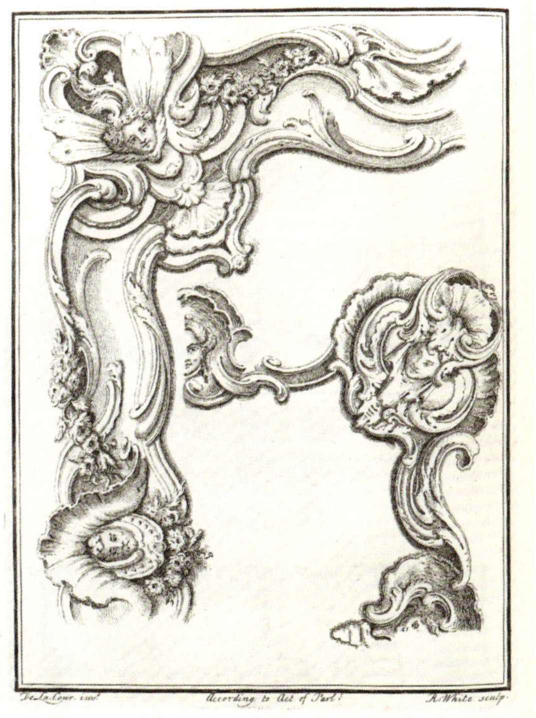

108 Design for a picture frame

From *The fifth book of ornaments: useful for all manner of furniture and all other things*
Designed by William De La Cour, etched by Robert White, London, 1743
Etching, 27.5 × 20.8 cm
Cooper Hewitt, Smithsonian Design Museum, New York (1962-126)

A unique impression of a plate from De La Cour's designs for furniture – another from the same suite in the Victoria and Albert Museum is for six chairs and a table. De La Cour advertised designs 'for all Sorts of Trades'. His *First book of ornament* was etched by Vivares in 1741 and dedicated to Lord Middlesex. De La Cour's designs for jewellery and gold boxes were etched by Jacob Bonneau for *The eighth book of ornament* (1747).

William De La Cour's *Fifth book of ornaments* included designs for picture frames (plate 108) and demonstrates the extent of his influence on 'all sorts of trades'; De La Cour's earlier pattern books were dedicated to Charles Sackville, 1st Earl of Middlesex (1711–1769), Robert Darcy, 4th Earl of Holderness (1718–1778), and John Manners, 3rd Duke of Rutland (1696–1779), all three patrons of the Italian opera, for which De La Cour provided stage scenery. Huguenot craftsmen contributed to the wealth of pattern books available for both patron and craftsman in the mid-eighteenth century. When Daniel Fare (fl.1734–52), frame-maker of Queen Street, appeared before the Committee of the Goldsmiths' Company in 1734, he produced 'several patterns of picture Frames'. Fare can be identified with the Daniel Faure listed in La Patente de Soho as living in the parish of St Giles, Westminster, between 1746 and 1752. Four of his frames still surround portraits in the Goldsmiths' Company Court Room.[214]

The 1760s album compiled by Gideon Saint provides further insight into the business of the carver and gilder.[215] Here cuttings from French and English prints are indexed for ease of reference. Saint's trade card, pasted into the album, advertises his business at the Golden Head, Princes Street, Leicester Fields.[216] He worked for leading architect Robert Adam.[217] The son of Jacques Saint from Saint-Lô, Normandy, Gideon was apprenticed to Jacob Touzey (1685–1749) for a premium of £30 in September 1743.[218] He married within the Huguenot community at St James's church, Piccadilly, in 1762; his bride was Marie Catherine Paisant.[219] From 1775 Saint served the church of Le Carré, Berwick Street, as an elder alongside Gedeon and Isaac Gosset.[220] In 1791 he was elected a director of the French Hospital, joining the three Gosset brothers.[221] Sixty years later the dealer John Smith's reference to the ornament 'Touzets bubble', associated with Saint's master Jacob Touzey, demonstrates the enduring influence that an individual craftsman could have.

Gideon Saint's apprentices included Richard Giles, who paid a premium of 10 guineas in 1765, and George Swain, who paid £20 the following year. By 1790 Saint was living at 13 Charles Square, Hoxton;[222] he retired as a country landowner to Groombridge Place, Kent. His will, dated 21 February and proved 4 May 1799, lists numerous charitable and personal bequests and demonstrates his status and his philanthropy.[223]

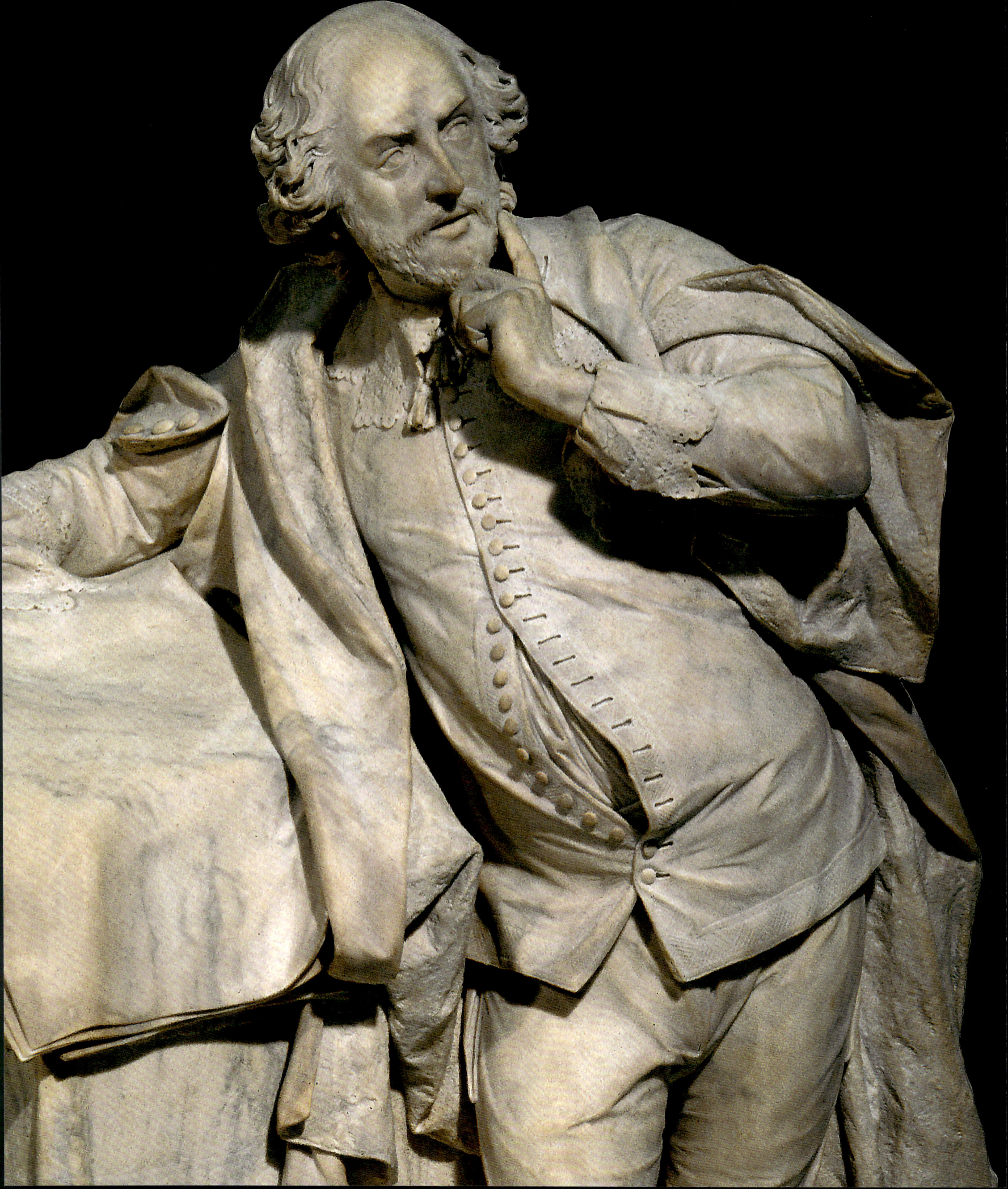

Chapter Eight
Huguenot Sculptors in France & in Exile

109 *Shakespeare*
Louis François Roubiliac, London, 1758 (detail) see plate 134

In the sixteenth century many French artists who promoted the image of monarchy became followers of John Calvin. The style adopted by Protestant architect and engraver Jacques I Androuët Du Cerceau and goldsmith and engraver Etienne Delaune was associated with François I's palace at Fontainebleau and influenced all artistic production, from buildings to jewellery. In the succeeding reign, the sculptor Jean Goujon (*c.*1510–*c.*1567) embellished the Fontaine des Innocents in Paris, designed by Pierre Lescot (*c.*1515–1578).[1] During the 1550s Goujon worked with Lescot on both exterior and interior decoration for the Louvre Pavillon du Roi (plate 110).

In Lorraine, Ligier Richier (*c.*1500–1567) carved astonishingly realistic scenes of the Life of Christ and startling memorial sculpture. Richier's most striking work, the memorial to the *Heart of René de Chalon* in Saint-Etienne, Bar-le-Duc (plate 112), represents the deceased clutching his heart in his hand, his emaciated body still covered by a few shreds of skin.[2] Richier's *Lamentation of Christ* in the church of Saint-Etienne de Saint-Mihiel (plate 111) consists of 13 full-size sculptures, richly clothed, their faces showing deep emotion. It is his most celebrated achievement.[3] In 1560 Richier signed a petition to the duc de Lorraine seeking permission to practise the Reformed religion. After the Council of Trent of 1564, instructions against heresy forced Richier to leave Lorraine and join his daughter Bernardine and her husband, Pierre Godart, who were already established in Geneva. Richier died there four years later, a very rich man.

Barthélemy Prieur embellished the buildings of the Palais du Louvre and created funerary monuments for Anne, Constable of Montmorency, Henri IV and Marie de Médicis (1575–1642). He also produced small bronze statuettes of figures and animals: horses, bulls, cows, dogs, goats and lions, secular imagery that fitted with Calvin's iconoclastic precepts.[4] Prieur's figurative bronzes include groups such as a knight and his lady and individual figures preoccupied with their daily tasks: a maid milking a cow; a woman combing her hair; a woman in regional French dress with a basket (plate 114); a woman seated bathing; a woman braiding her hair; and a seated woman pulling a thorn from her foot.[5] The last three are naked women rather than goddesses and reflect the sculptor's close observation of nature, anticipating by nearly three centuries the sculpture of Edgar Degas (1834–1917). Prieur's work was highly regarded by his contemporaries: his bronze *Woman Cutting her Toe Nails* was in the collection of his friend the architect Jacques II Androuët du Cerceau and listed in his 1602 inventory.[6] It was also praised in an inventory a century later:[7] his *Henri IV Vanquishing his Enemies* was in the French royal collection in 1684 and may be the bronze now in the Victoria and Albert Museum (plate 113).[8]

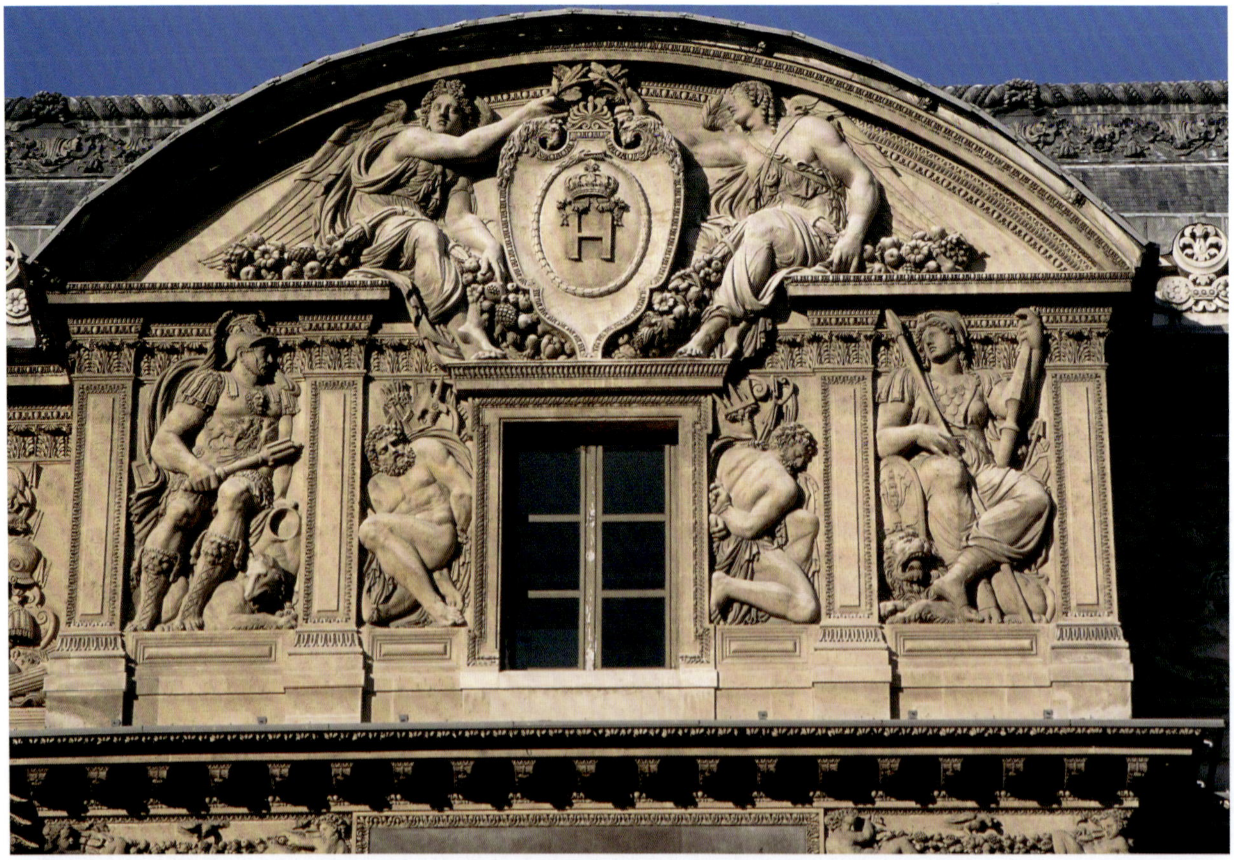

110 Pavillon du Roi, Palais du Louvre

Designed by Pierre Lescot, architectural sculpture by Jean Goujon, Paris, 1550s
Palais du Louvre, Paris

Jean Goujon's winged victories celebrate the reign of Henri II (1547–59), placing a laurel wreath above the crowned 'H' on the central shield and cradling cornucopiae of fruit and flowers symbolizing plenty. Below, Mars and Minerva preside over chained captives.

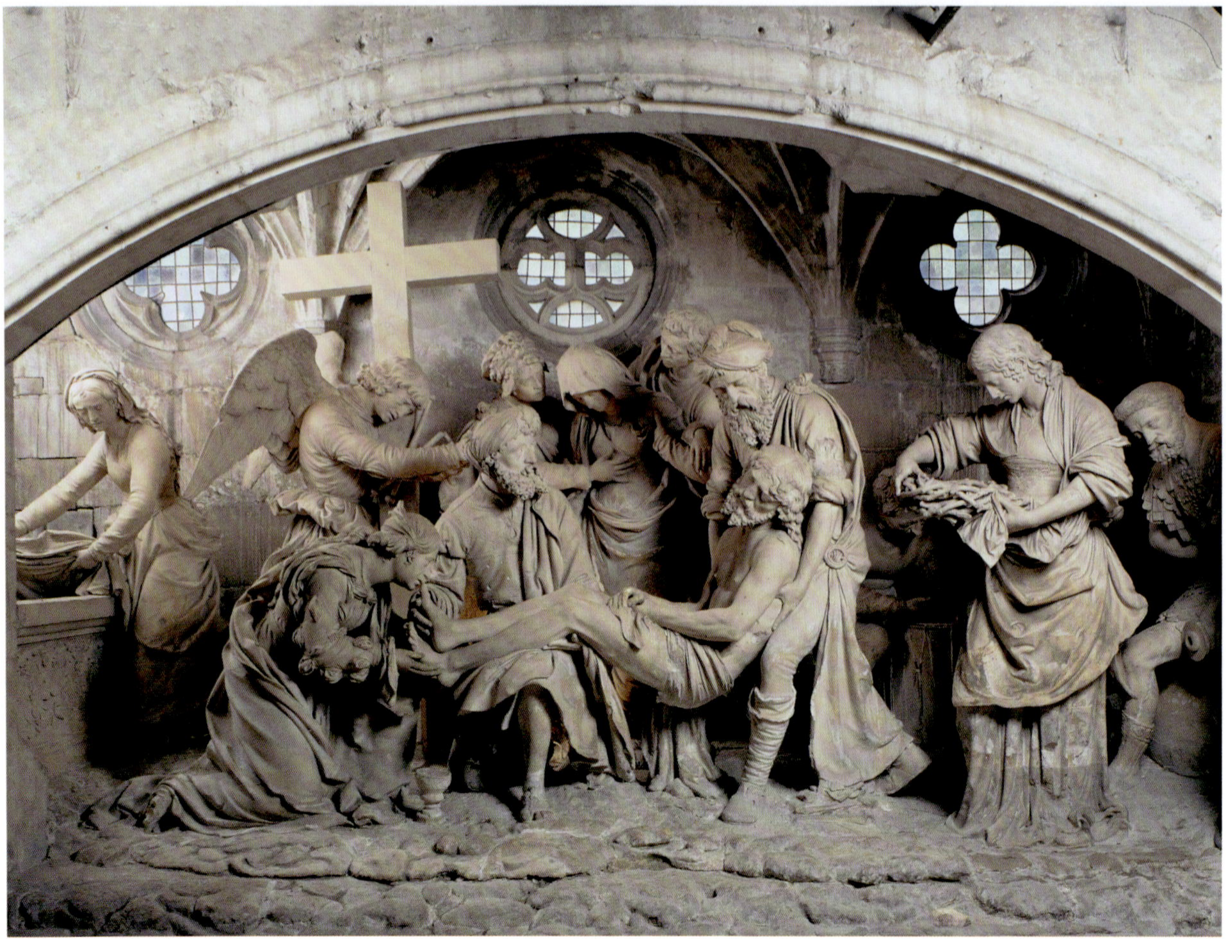

111 *The Lamentation of Christ*

Ligier Richier, Lorraine, 1554–64
Limestone
Saint-Etienne de Saint-Mihiel, Lorraine

The *Lamentation* consists of full-size sculptures whose rich clothes contrast with the emaciated figure of Christ, their faces showing deep emotional response. It is Richier's most celebrated work.

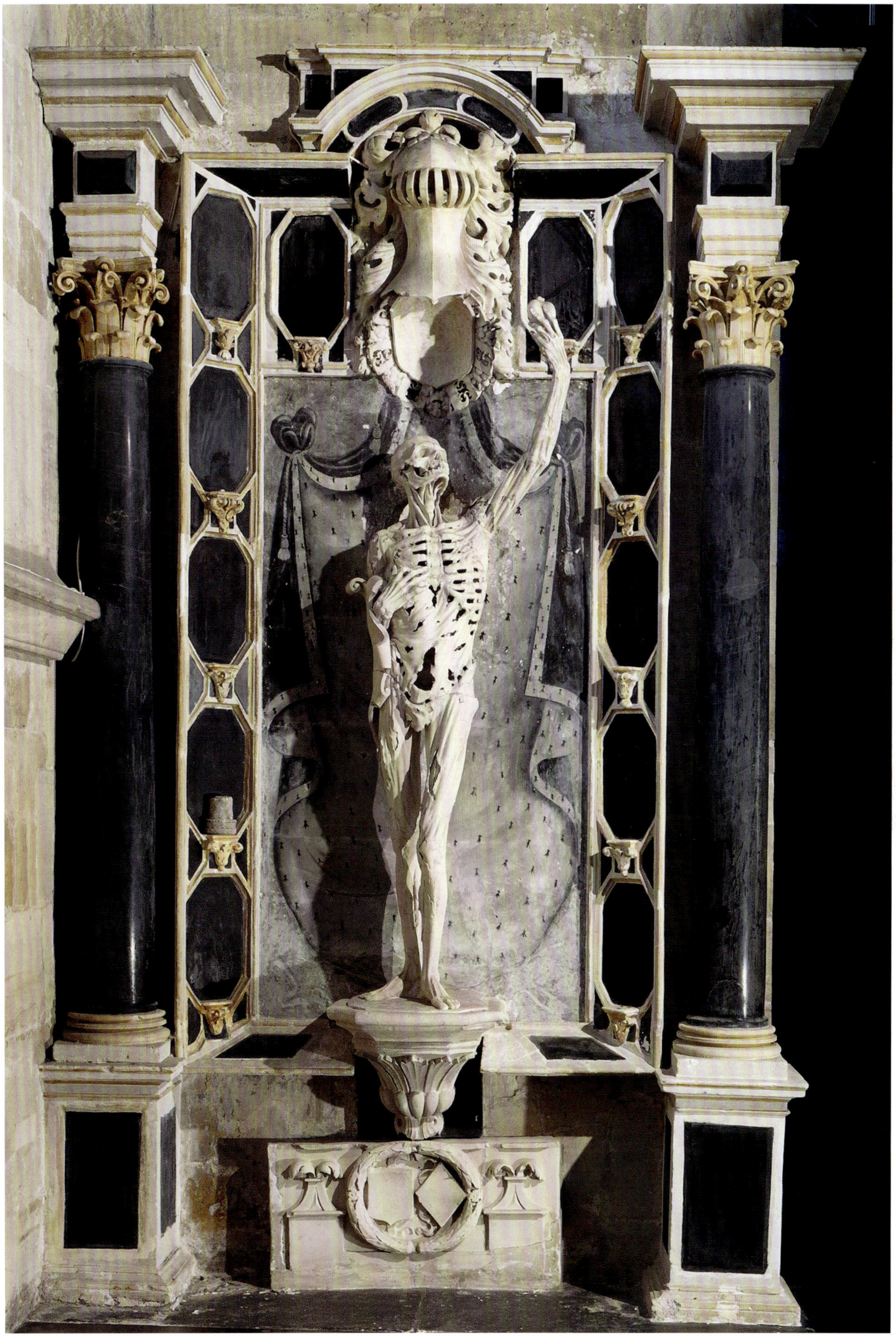

112 *The Heart of René de Chalon*

Ligier Richier, Lorraine, 1544–57
Painted marble and limestone
Saint-Etienne, Bar-le-Duc, Lorraine

Richier's striking sculpture took 13 years to complete. René de Chalon (1519–1544) is shown standing, clutching his heart in his hand, his emaciated body still covered by a few shreds of skin.

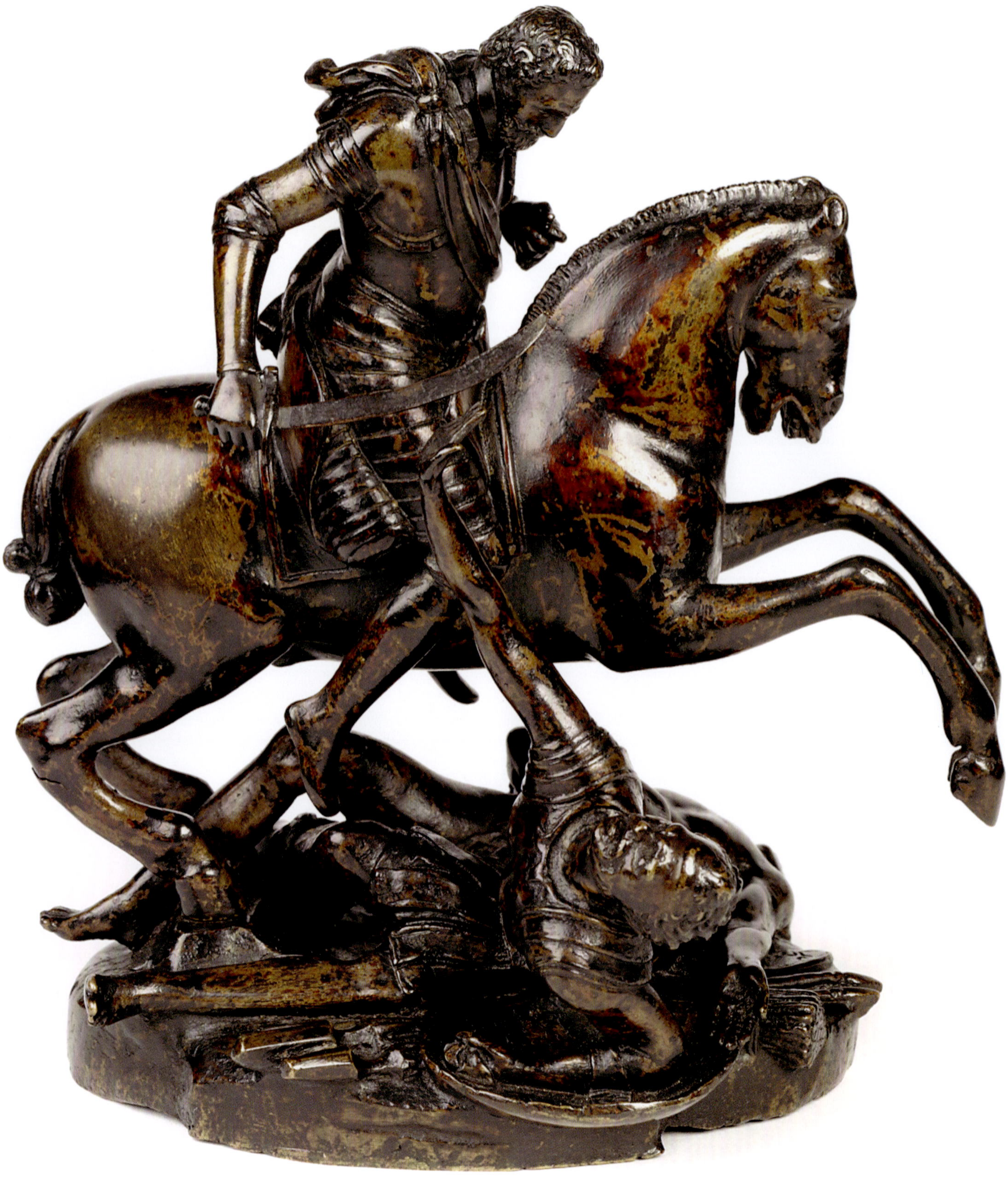

113 *Henri* IV *Vanquishing his Enemies*

Barthélemy Prieur, Paris, *c.*1603
Bronze, 19 × 17 cm
Victoria and Albert Museum, London (A.42–1956)

Prieur's animals have long, slender legs, small heads, short necks and well-arched backs with rounded, powerful hindquarters; their tails are usually dressed. His work continued to be appreciated a century later: Louis XIV's landscape gardener André Le Nôtre (1613–1700) owned a bronze by Prieur of the same subject.

114 A woman in regional French dress with a basket

Barthélemy Prieur, Paris, *c.*1600
Bronze, ht 19.9 cm
Victoria and Albert Museum, London (A.11–1964)

Prieur's bronzes are carefully chased, highly polished and patinated with dark red lacquer.

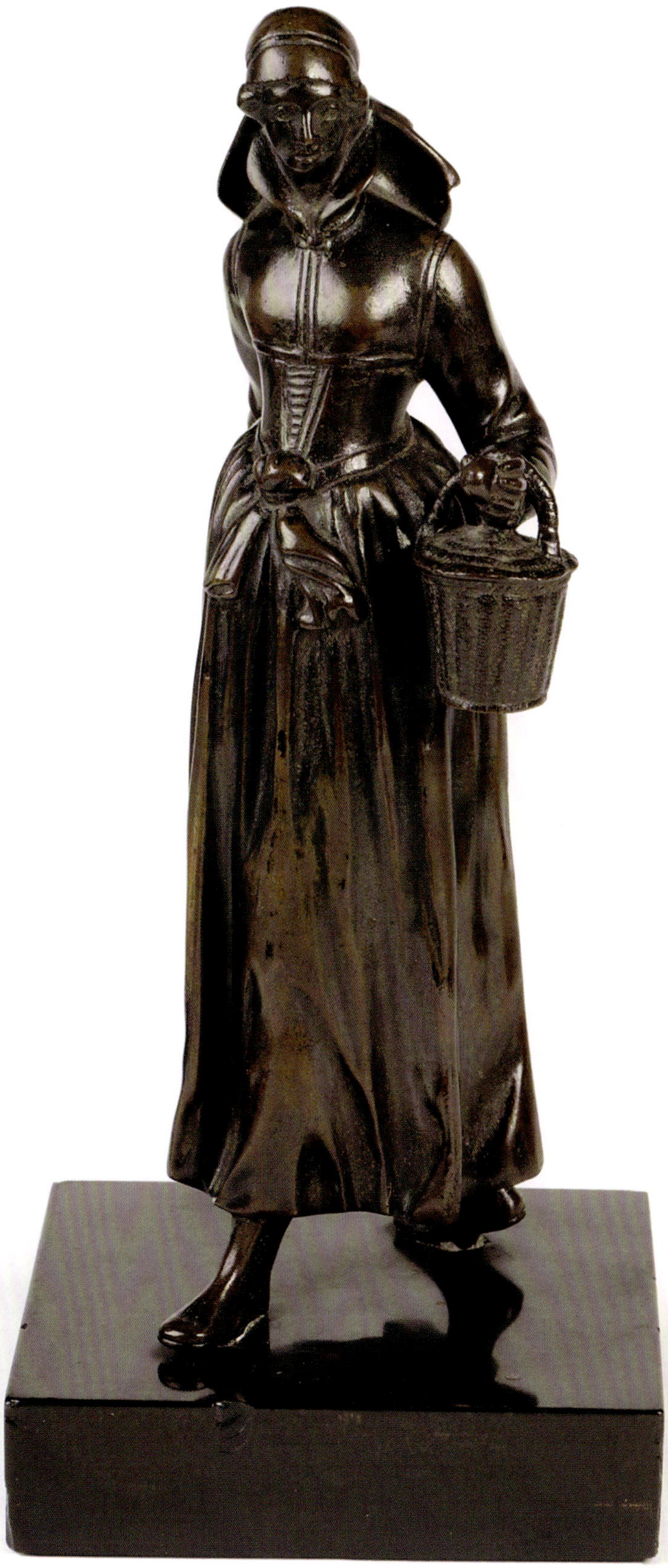

Henri IV commissioned many images of himself for propaganda purposes.

Prieur trained his son-in-law Guillaume Dupré (1574–1642), who in 1600 succeeded him as Sculpteur Ordinaire du Roi and was appointed Premier Sculpteur du Roi in 1611.[9]

Dupré's most important medal, showing Henri IV with Marie de Médicis (plate 115), was cast in bronze and also in gold and silver in 1603. The following year he was appointed joint Contrôleur Général des Poinçons et Effigies des Monnaies with his rival, Jean Pilon (1578–1617). From 1608 Dupré was also responsible for producing cannon for French artillery.

In the sixteenth and early seventeenth centuries the production of bronze sculpture and arms and armour were closely allied. Hubert Le Sueur, son of armourer Pierre Le Sueur (d.1616), was trained in Paris, where he was appointed Sculpteur Ordinaire du Roi to Henri IV. His representation of armour reflects his intimate knowledge from family experience. He specialized in royal subjects. Le Sueur made equestrian statuettes of Henri IV and Louis XIII in Paris around 1615–20: that of Henri IV celebrates the conclusion of the French Wars of Religion of 1562–98.[10] Henri IV and his horse were cast separately. The horse's back has a large hole, concealed by the rider, through which the core material from casting was removed. The head was also cast separately, so that horse and body could be replicated for other commissions. The bronze is attributed to Le Sueur by comparison with a small signed statuette of Louis XIII of *c.*1620 (plate 116), with 'LE SVEVER' struck into the cold metal under the girth of the horse.[11] These statuettes were all made before Le Sueur came to England in 1625, probably at the invitation of George Villiers, 1st Duke of Buckingham, to work for Charles I and Henrietta Maria. Here he created the 1633 life-size equestrian statue of Charles I in Trafalgar Square, originally made for Roehampton House, Surrey (plate 117).

In 1636 Le Sueur created the Diana Fountain at Somerset House for Queen Henrietta Maria.[12] Between 1631 and 1634 he made monumental bronze effigies and seated mourners for the tomb in Westminster Abbey of George Villiers, 1st Duke of Buckingham, the royal favourite who was assassinated in 1628, and his duchess, Katherine Manners (d.1634; plate 118). The small marble statues of their four children were carved by Huguenot Isaac Besnier (fl. *c.*1631–42) for a fee of £56.[13] Besnier may also have worked with other sculptors: in a

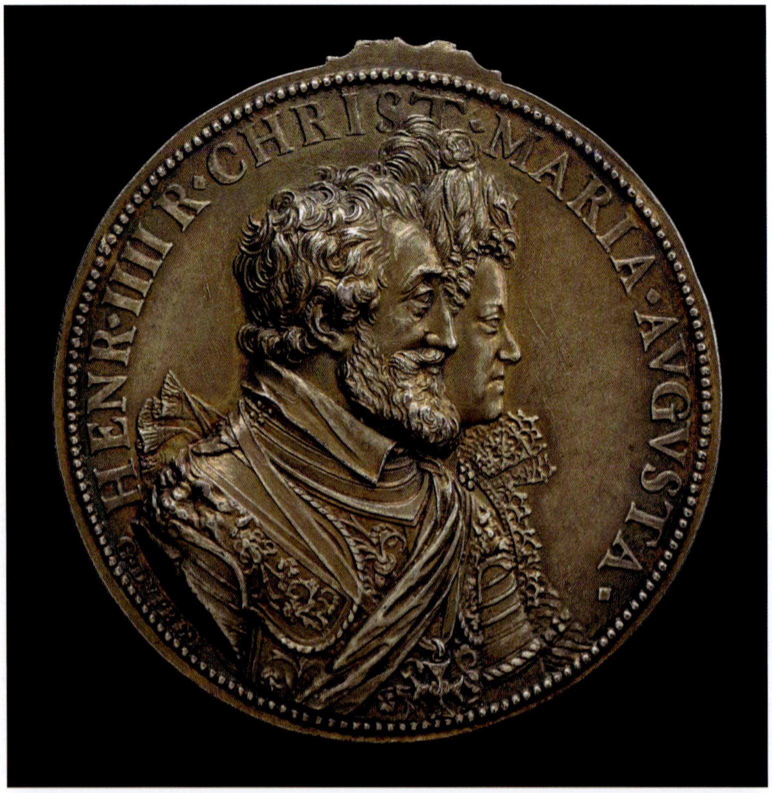

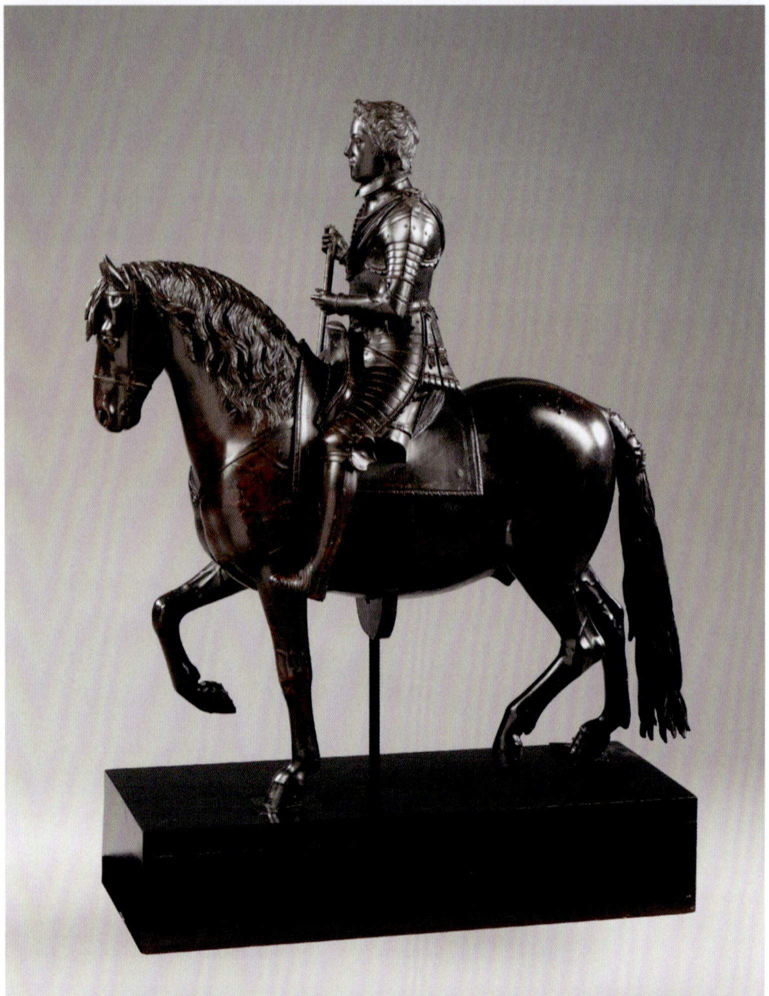

LEFT ABOVE

115 Henri IV with Marie de Médicis

Guillaume Dupré, Paris, 1603
Silver-gilt, diam. 6.75 cm
British Museum, London (G3,FrM.21)

The medal shows conjoined busts of Marie de Médicis and Henri IV in armour, wearing the ribbon and cross of the Order of Saint Esprit.

LEFT BELOW

116 Equestrian statue of Louis XIII

Hubert Le Sueur, Paris, *c.*1615–20
Bronze, ht 94.5 cm, w. 78.5 cm, depth 32 cm
Victoria and Albert Museum, London (A.47–1951)

Louis XIII is shown here as a young adult in contemporary armour. The walking horse was inspired by Pietro Tacca's monument to Henri IV on the Pont Neuf, which was destroyed during the French Revolution.

RIGHT

117 Equestrian statue of Charles I

Hubert Le Sueur, London, 1633
Bronze
Trafalgar Square, London

This Renaissance-style equestrian statue of Charles I in contemporary armour was commissioned by Richard Weston, Lord High Treasurer. After the Civil War the statue was sold to a metalsmith for melting; however, following the Restoration it was installed in its present prominent location in central London.

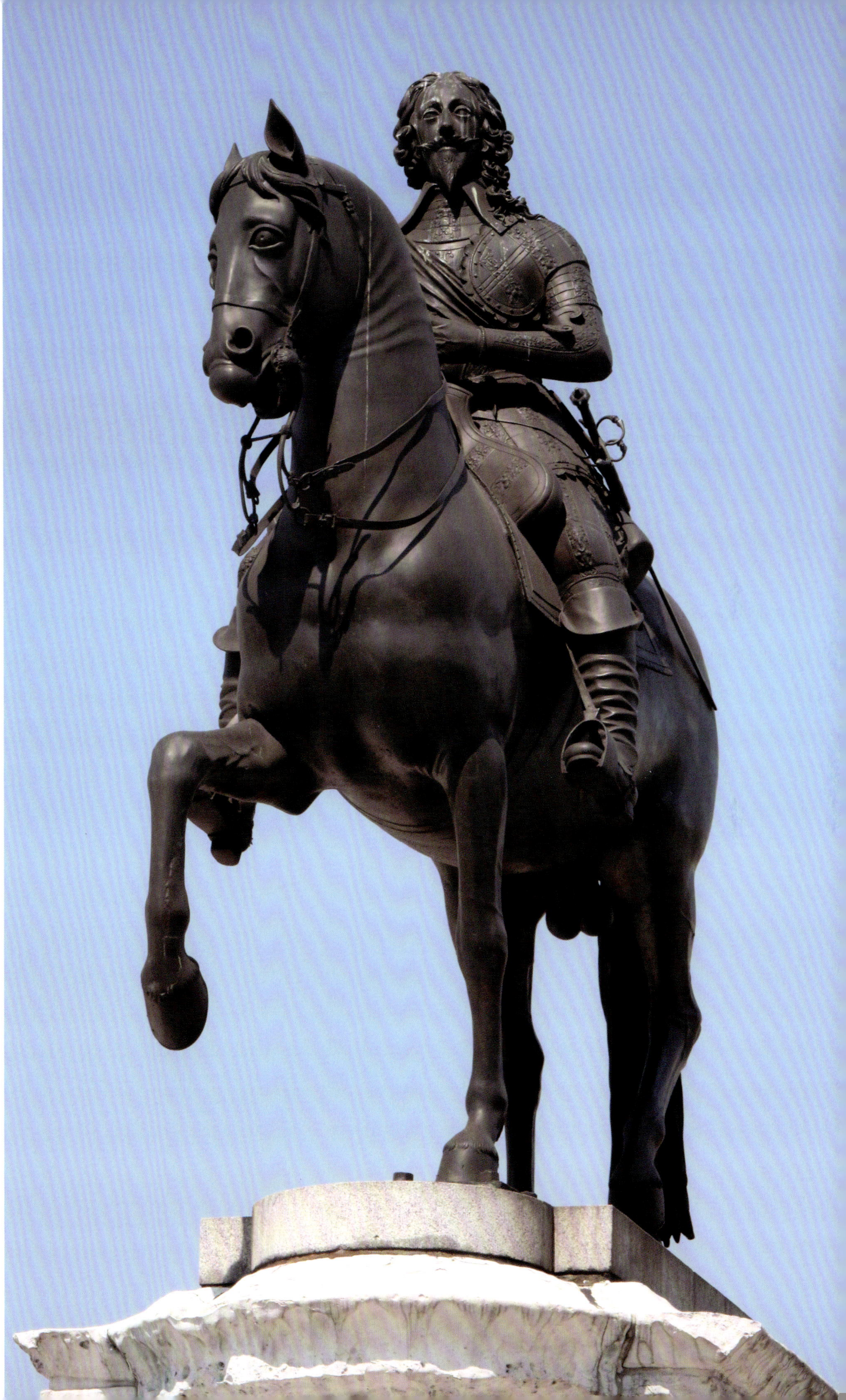

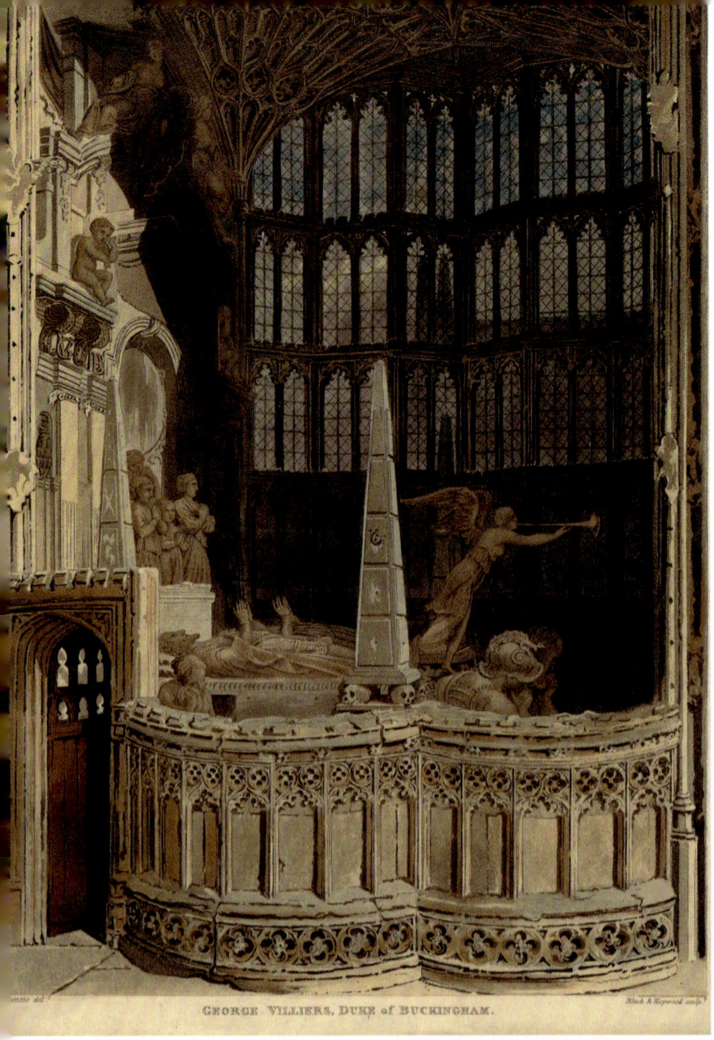

letter written to Balthazar Gerbier (plate 58) in Brussels in February 1632 he refers to the design and carving of marble components for the monument to Richard Weston, 1st Earl of Portland (1577–1635), in Winchester Cathedral. Besnier became Sculptor in Ordinary to Charles I. Inspired by the sculpture of Giambologna (1529–1608), Le Sueur introduced new portrait types, with expressive modelling of the heads and animated features. His heroic equestrian statues emulated those by Giambologna's assistant Pietro Tacca (1577–1640), sculptor to the Medici, Grand Dukes of Tuscany, whose work he had seen in Paris. Besnier and Le Sueur returned to Paris in 1643. Here Le Sueur subsequently made four casts of Jean Warin's bust of Cardinal Richelieu and died after 1658.

Isaac Besnier's brother Peter (d.1693) remained in London and took over Isaac's post as sculptor to Charles I, with responsibility for the 'Moulds, Statues and Modells' in the royal collection and an annual salary of £50.[14] In 1645–9 Peter Besnier was paid for 'covering the naked places of diverse statues' reflecting puritan taste. Having been reduced to poverty, on the Restoration he was reinstated as Sculptor in Ordinary to Charles II 'through faithfulness and constancy'. Peter

118 *Monument to George Villiers, 1st Duke of Buckingham*
R. Ackermann, London, 1812
Aquatint, 24 × 30 cm
National Portrait Gallery, London (D5190)

This marble and bronze monument by Isaac Besnier and Hubert Le Sueur was installed in Westminster Abbey in 1634. In that year 'M. Le Zure' was paid £420 by the widowed Duchess for 'the Brasse works of the late L. Duke's monument'. Their four children were carved in marble by Isaac Besnier, another Huguenot sculptor.

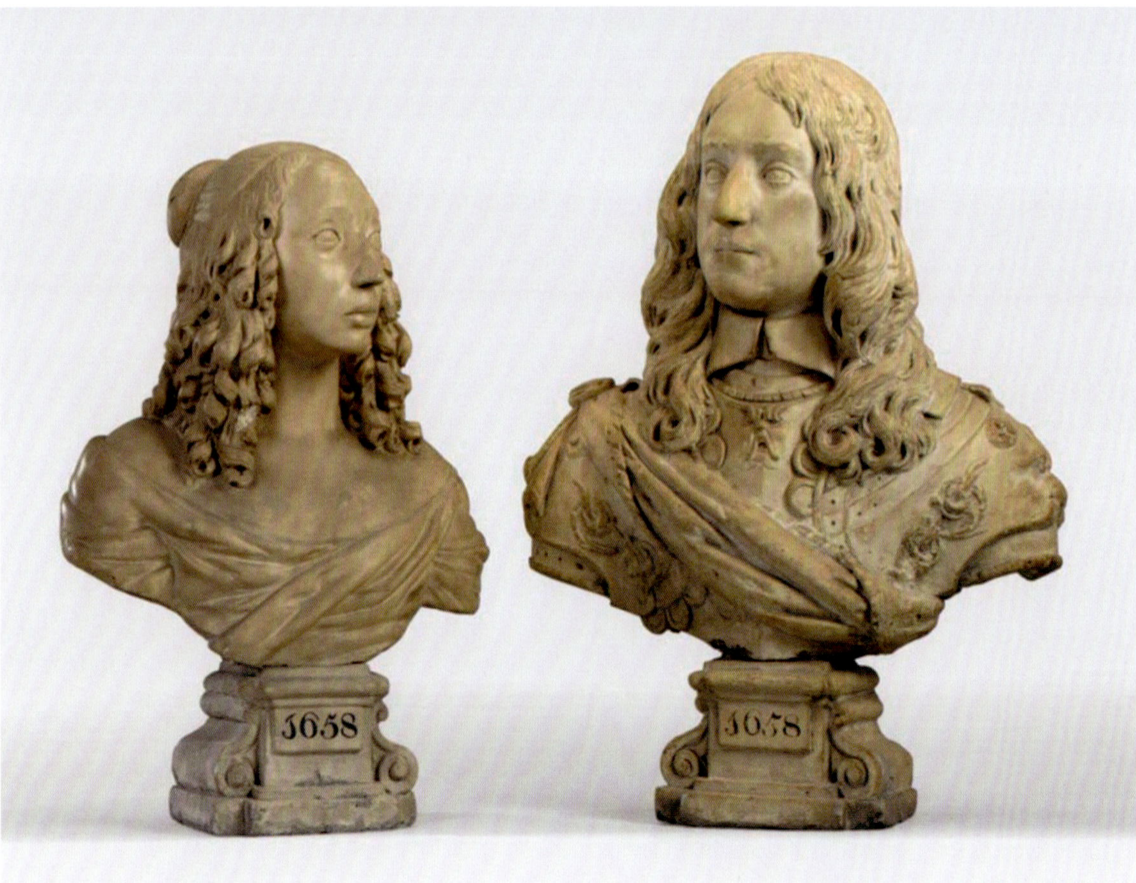

LEFT

119 Busts of Sir William Fermor and his wife, Mary
Attributed to Peter Besnier, London, 1658
Plaster, Sir William ht 72 cm; Lady Mary ht 65.5 cm
Northampton Museum and Art Gallery

Originally from Easton Neston House, Northamptonshire, the busts were acquired at auction by Northampton Museum and Art Gallery on 17 May 2005.

RIGHT

120 *Neptune*
Claude David, London, 1700
Marble, ht 177 cm
Victoria and Albert Museum, London (A.3–1985)

Claude David provided '2 marble figures' for Queen Anne for St James's Palace gardens 'of a curious performance, and mightily commended by such who have any gust of things of this nature'. The Neptune was probably transferred from St James's to Brompton by gardener Henry Wise, who redesigned the palace gardens.

RIGHT BELOW

121 *Vulcan Enchained*

Claude David, London, *c.*1710
Marble, l. 86.5 cm
Victoria and Albert Museum, London (A.3–1981)

Sir Andrew Fountaine commissioned this figure as a companion to a statue of William III for his Norfolk home, Narford. The pair celebrated the Glorious Revolution and anticipated a peaceful succession. They were seen against full-length painted portraits of previous British monarchs.

Besnier's only documented monument is to Sir Richard Shuckburgh (d.1656) in the church of St John the Baptist, Shuckburgh, Warwickshire.[15] In 1673 he received a modest payment for sculpture at Ham House.[16] Also at Ham House, the bronze bust of Catherine Bruce, Mrs William Murray (*c.*1637–9) is attributed to Peter Besnier by comparison with plaster busts of Sir William Fermor (1621–1661) and Lady Mary Fermor (d.1670) previously at Easton Neston (plate 119).[17] The statues of Mars and Minerva on the Great Hall chimneypiece bearing the armorial devices of the Bruce and Murray families, carved before Mrs Murray's death in 1649, are attributed to Isaac Besnier by comparison with allegorical figures supporting the coat of arms on the Buckingham monument in Westminster Abbey (plate 118).[18]

John Besnier, who was paid in 1686 for 'making and casting four large and 16 small statues' for James Butler, 1st Duke of Ormonde, and Thomas Besnier, sculptor in marble and wax, buried in St Anne's, Blackfriars, in 1693, were probably from the same family as Isaac and Peter. Blackfriars, outside the authority of the City of London guilds, had long been associated with immigrant artists and craftsmen.

Like their predecessors in France, Huguenot sculptors who settled in Britain in the late seventeenth century provided architectural and garden sculpture for palaces and noble houses in London and in the country.[19] Engagement with Catholic devotional sculpture did not preclude Huguenot identity: David Le Marchand signed a Virgin and Child and a crucifix (plate 22) in about 1700, although these may have been carved in France or made for a Catholic patron in Britain.[20] Claude David, originally from Burgundy, trained in Rome, where he carved ivory crucifixes. He succeeded the celebrated French sculptor Pierre Puget at Santa Maria in Carignano, Genoa, providing a statue of St Bartholomew. In England by 1700, David's garden sculpture included a figure of Neptune for St James's Palace gardens (plate 120).[21] For William Blathwayt's gardens at Dyrham, celebrated for their water features, Claude David supplied another statue of Neptune for the fountain above the great cascade. He also worked for Ralph Montagu in 1702/3,[22] and in 1708 he was paid £600 for garden figures for the 1st Viscount Weymouth at Longleat.[23] David also carved the monument to James Thynne (d.1709) at Buckland, Gloucestershire, commissioned by Thomas

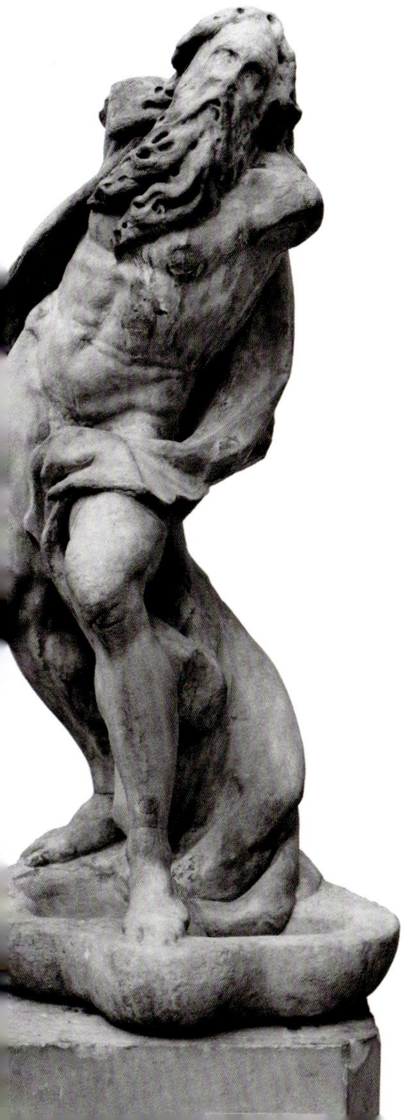

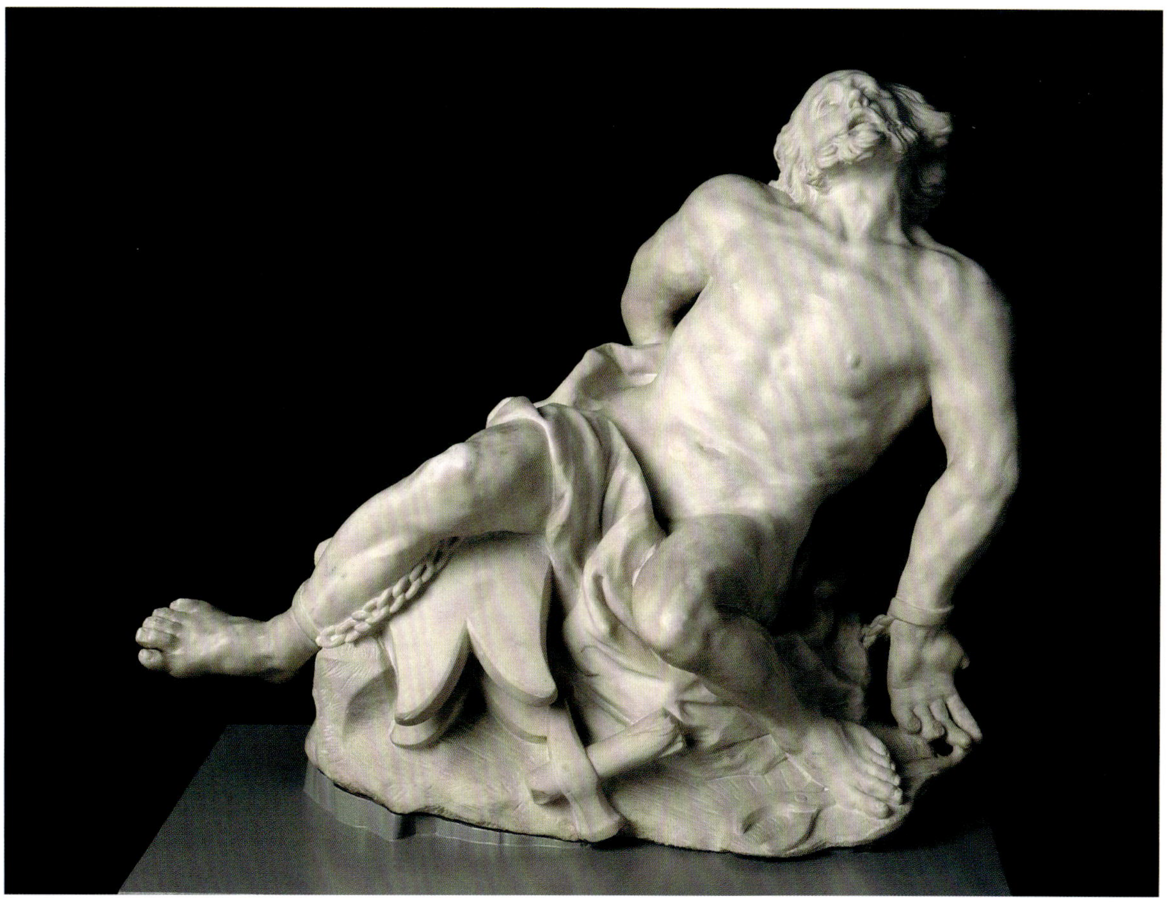

Thynne, Lord Weymouth's father, in about 1718. David's monument to Philip Carteret (d.1710) in Westminster Abbey features a portrait bust in contemporary dress accompanied by a contorted figure of Time characteristic of David's Italian Baroque style.

Claude David planned an ambitious fountain near Cheapside conduit to celebrate the victories of John Churchill, 1st Duke of Marlborough, with the equestrian statue of the commander accompanied by the figure of Queen Anne. A print after his model seen by George Vertue inscribed 'opus equitus Claudii David Comitatis Burgundiae' confirms David's aristocratic French origins.[24] David also tried to raise £2,500 by subscription for an equestrian statue of George I for St James's Square. Neither this nor the Cheapside fountain were realized.

Claude David's *Vulcan Enchained* (plate 121) was commissioned by Sir Andrew Fountaine for Narford Hall, Norfolk, in about 1710; it was seen there in 1728 by Sir Matthew Decker (1679–1749), on the staircase with a statue of William III. Rather than 'fashioning the instruments of war', Vulcan is chained to a rock, his tools, hammer, pincers and anvil resting beside him, celebrating the peace that followed William's accession to the English throne. This is a rare example of mythological sculpture in the round for an interior setting.[25]

In the early eighteenth century the London centre for the production and purchase of garden sculpture and ironwork was Portugal Row, Piccadilly. Adjacent to the smithies occupied by the gatesmiths Jean Tijou and John Montigny were

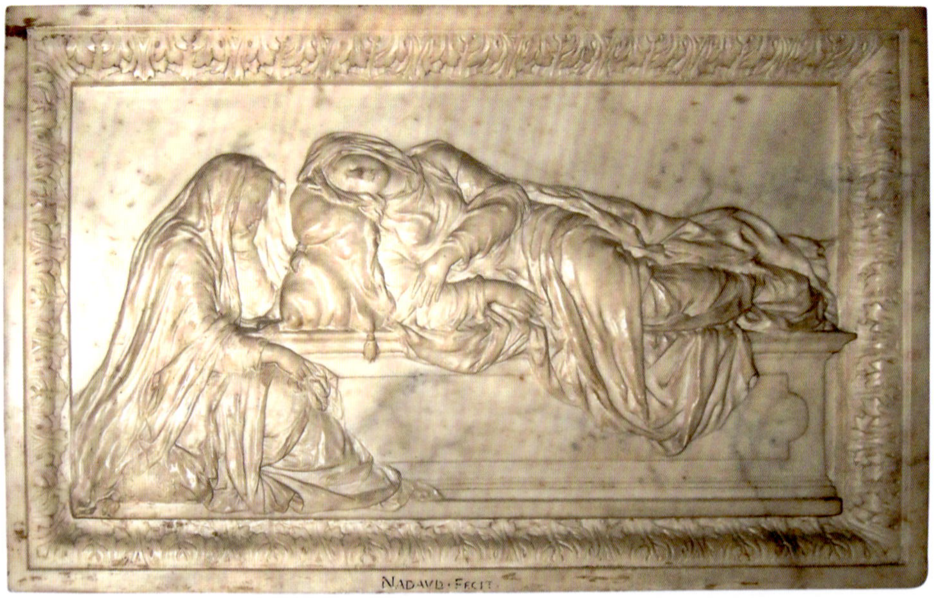

122 *Lady Eland on her Deathbed*

Henri Nadauld, London, 1704
Marble
Westminster Abbey, London

In 1723 John Dart described Nadauld's monument as representing Lady Eland 'on her Deathbed with mourners weeping'.

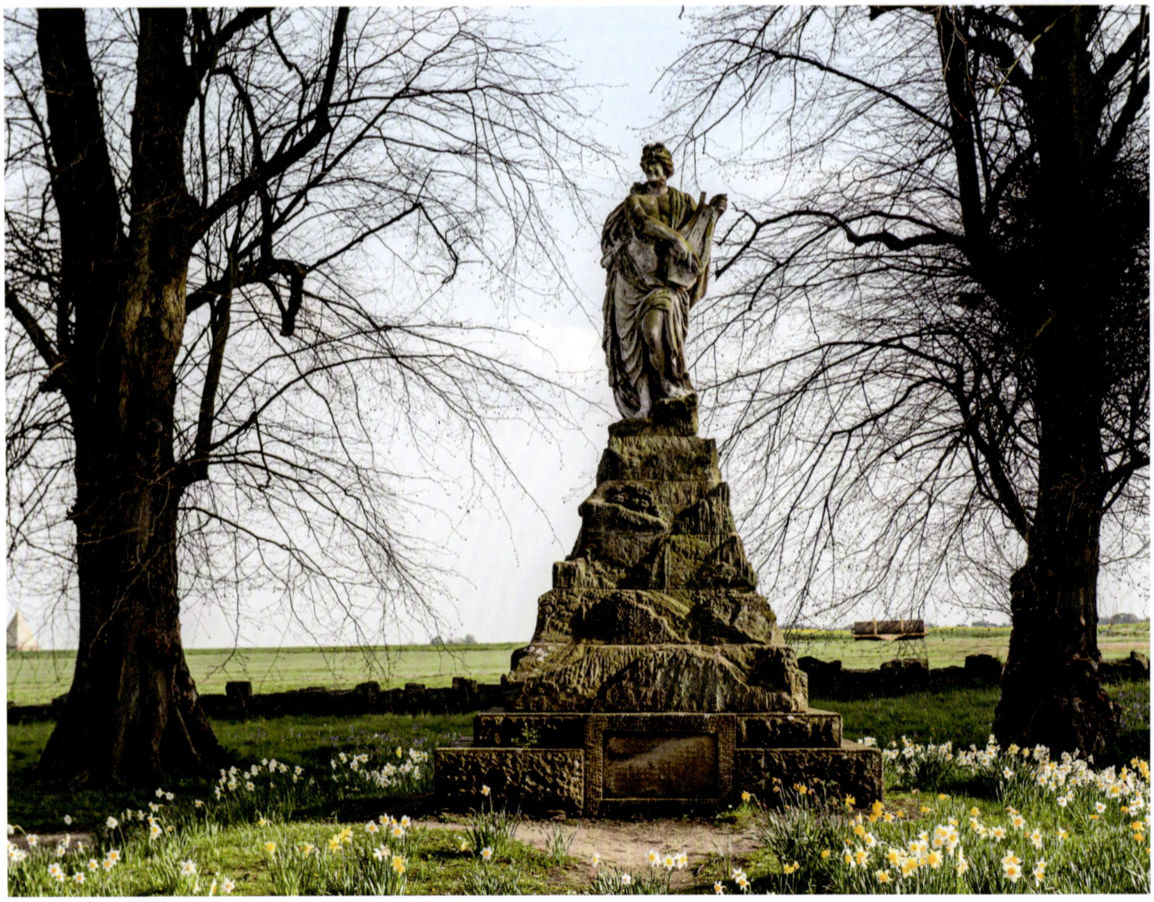

123 *Apollo*

Henri Nadauld, Yorkshire, 1705–9
Roche Abbey Stone
The Castle Howard Collection, Yorkshire

Nadauld was paid £16 for this statue of Apollo, which stands on a pyramidical structure carved in relief with a procession to the Delphi shrine. Nadauld's compatriot, the York-based sculptor Daniel Harvey, was later paid £8 for 'Renewing apollo's Pedistall'.

the sculptors' yards of Henri Nadauld and Andries Carpentière (*c.*1677–1737). Carpentière, a native of the French-speaking Netherlands, complemented Nadauld, who worked principally in stone, by specializing in lead sculpture and supplying the van Nost family of sculptors. Carpentière and the van Nosts were succeeded by John Cheere (1709–1787; brother of Henry Cheere, see pp.147–52), also of Huguenot origin,[26] who was established by 1739 as 'the Statuary at Hide Park Corner'. The Huguenot identity of the Cheere brothers rests on contemporary references to Henry Cheere as 'Chair' and 'De Chair', an established Huguenot name. When competing for the commission to sculpt the bas-relief for the pediment of the Mansion House, Henry Cheere is referred to as Chair; and in the *London Evening Post* of 13 July 1738 the description of the monument to the architect Thomas Archer at St Mary's Hale, Hampshire names the sculptor as De Chair.[27]

Garden sculpture at this time was inspired by figures designed by Le Brun and executed by a team of sculptors for the gardens at Versailles. David Le Marchand carved a miniature ivory version of *Time Revealing Truth* (*Saturn Abducting Cybele*; plate 141), one of four mythological groups created by Thomas Regnaudin (1622–1706) for the Parterre d'Eau at Versailles between 1675 and 1687.[28] Small-scale versions of the groups at Versailles may have been inspired by the illustrations in *Recueil des Figures, Groupes, Thermes, Fontaines, Vases, Statues, et Autres Ornemens de Versailles* (1694) by French engraver Simon Thomassin (1655–1733), in which this statue is named as *Le Temps et L'Occasion* (*Time and Opportunity*).[29]

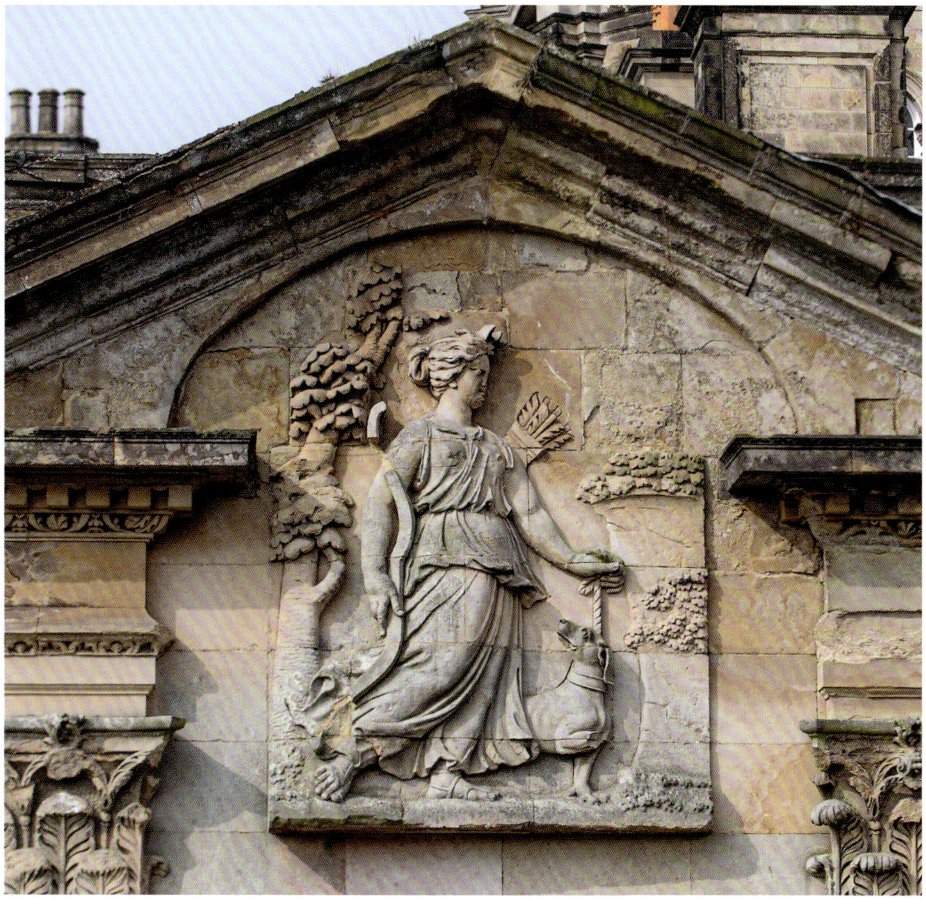

124 *Diana with her Dachshund*
Henri Nadauld, Yorkshire, 1705–9
Roche Abbey Stone
The Castle Howard Collection, Yorkshire

The Dachshund was bred in 16th-century Germany for badger hunting, but its juxtaposition here with the goddess of hunting is original, perhaps inspired by local practice or Nadauld's experience in France.

Henri Nadauld provided ornamental carving for façades, interiors and gardens (plate 69). At Chatsworth in 1700 he supplied a figure of Cleopatra for £22; and in 1701 received £10 for Amphitrite. In 1703 his 'Account of Worke done' includes the payment £36 for figures of Mars, Fortitude and Prudence for the inner court in 'Roach Abby Stone', a white magnesium limestone named after the Cistercian Abbey south of Maltby.[30] Nadauld was paid 12 shillings for travelling to that quarry where he selected the stone. For Chatsworth gardens he supplied sculptures of Antonius for £22 and two river gods for £44, which are still in the canal; and figures of 'Pharsis', Pallas and the Muses. The statue of Pallas is in the walk by the Sea-horse Fountain. Nadauld's *Fluvius*, two dolphins and two vases adorn Thomas Archer's Cascade House (plate 69).[31]

Meanwhile, Nadauld maintained his London yard and in 1704 won a commission for a wall-mounted monument to Esther de la Tour de Gouvernet, Lady Eland (1666–1694), in the Chapel of St John at Westminster Abbey. Now dismantled, only the bas-relief survives, representing the deceased reclining on a plinth, supported by a cushion, with a mourning female figure clutching a handkerchief to the left. It is signed (plate 122). Lady Eland was the daughter of the Huguenot marquise de la Tour de Gouvernet, who lived in St James's Square and who, in 1718, pledged a bequest of £600 to the French Hospital when the new building was under construction.[32]

Nadauld worked at Chatsworth and Castle Howard simultaneously: 'Nadauld hal the carved work that I have done for the Rait honourable the Earle of Carlile at Henderskelfe from 21 June 1705 until 15 December 1709', including 'foure little figures called the foure Sezons made at Chattworths'.[33] For the gardens at Castle Howard he supplied 'a figure called faune', 'an hurne in the Raywood' and the Apollo (plate 123) at the end of the Lime Avenue.[34] The carving on the base is attributed to Nadauld by comparison with that of Diana with her dachshund (plate 124), which was

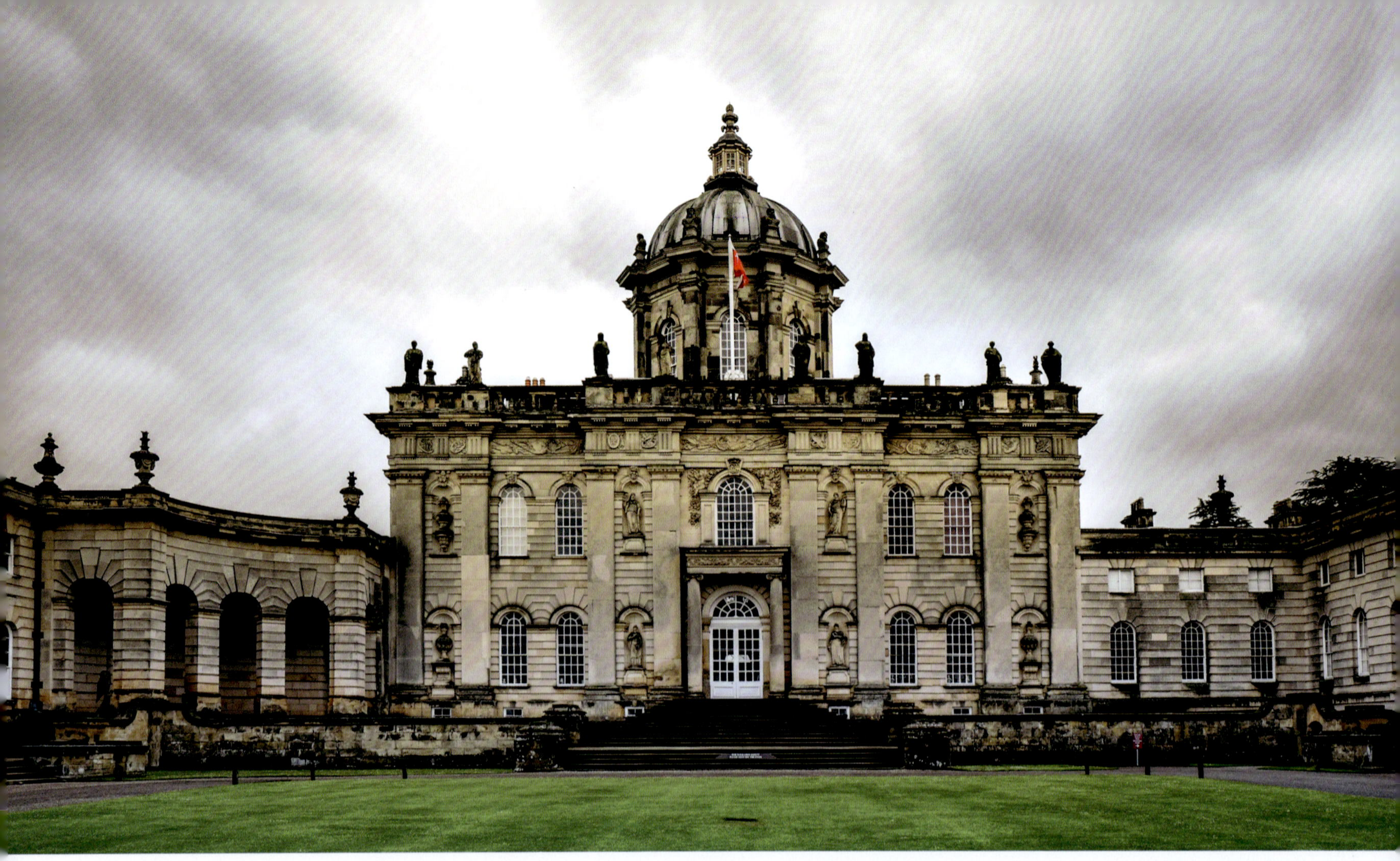

125 North front of Castle Howard

Henri Nadauld's four Vestals (1705–9) are visible in niches flanking the entrance.

moved to the east front when Thomas Robinson designed the new west wing. Castle Howard's south front features Nadauld's statues of Ceres, Flora and Pallas, which stand proud of the pediment, while four Vestal Virgins occupy niches flanking the entrance on the north front (plate 125). Nadauld charged £28 for figures of Seneca and Socrates now in the Entrance Hall.[35]

Andries Carpentière studied 'rudiments of drawing' with a French academician named by George Vertue as Peter Eude (fl.1691),[36] who was subsequently established in Scotland. In 1713 Carpentière completed a statue of Queen Anne for Moot Hall, Leeds, commissioned by Alderman William Milner (*c.*1696–1745). In November 1722 he assisted Gerard van Nost (d.1729) in supplying James Brydges, 1st Duke of Chandos, with an equestrian statue of George I for the gardens at Cannons, his palatial mansion at Edgware; for this van Nost received a fee of £170 and Carpentière £60.[37] In October 1722 van Nost was summoned to Cannons 'to view the Vases upon the House and if there is danger of their falling to propose what he thinks proper to be prevented'.[38] Vertue noted that Carpentière evoked the wrath of the Duke when he built 'some houses and an Inn and in the Middle of the road way put up a Statue for a Sign – not far from the Dukes gate of his avenue'.[39] Later payments to van Nost between 1723 and 1726 totalling over £300 may have been for statues and vases supplied by Carpentière, including the statue of George II now in Golden Square, Soho.[40] Ironwork supplied by Montigny for Cannons between 1721 and 1726 included railings to protect these important sculptures; both van Nost and Montigny had their bills disputed by the Duke of Chandos's audit committee in October 1724.[41] The equestrian statues of George I at the Barber Institute, Birmingham, and at Stowe, Buckinghamshire (plate 126),[42] the latter supplied for £150 for the Whig politician Richard Temple, 1st Viscount Cobham (1675–1749), have been reattributed to Carpentière. The attribution is based on a model provided in about 1716 by the unidentified sculptor C. Burchard, also possibly of Huguenot origin, for James Brydges, 1st Duke of Chandos. By 1718 Carpentière had expanded his workshop to a second site in Portugal Row.

In 1723 Carpentière sent Lord Carlisle a list of lead figures available, with dimensions and cost.

126 Equestrian statue of George I

Andrew Carpentière and C. Burchard, London, cast in 1723–4 after a model made in 1716–20
Lead
Stowe, Buckinghamshire

George I is shown in a classical pose inspired by the celebrated equestrian statue of Marcus Aurelius in Rome. Even the horse has the characteristic raised forehoof found in Roman prototypes.

127 Temple of the Winds, Castle Howard

Andrew Carpentière's lead figures of Sybils (1723) stand on either side of the steps.

He eventually supplied a selection of these for £84, including four statues of Sybils – Sabine, Faustina, Crespine and Giulia Mammea – for the exterior of the Temple of the Winds at Castle Howard (plate 127).[43] The packing cases for these alone cost £9 7s. The statues took nine and a half days to pack using a thousand 'double tenn's nails' at a cost of £21. In 1734 George Booth, 2nd Earl of Warrington, maintained his loyalties to the Huguenot community of craftsmen (plates 62, 180) and commissioned from Carpentière a monument to his father, Henry, 1st Earl of Warrington (d.1694), at St Mary's church, Bowden, Cheshire, near the family home at Dunham Massey. Based on a design by James Gibbs, the deceased is flanked by figures representing Learning and Truth.

In 1744 the sale by Carpentière's widow of 'Metal Statues or Figures in Hard Metal together with his Moulds, Models and Casts in Plaster' provided a further opportunity for the sculptor John Cheere, the younger of two sculptor brothers, to develop his range as principal supplier of lead garden sculpture. At Carpentière's sale Cheere purchased three pieces: *Blackamoor with a Sundial*, *Borghese Gladiator* and *Diana with her Stag*. Similar models in the posthumous sale of John van Nost the elder (1660–*c*.1711) in 1712 had included 'Diana with a buck large life £24'and 'a Gladiator an excellent cast £10'; such traditional subjects were evidently still in demand.[44] John Cheere supplied Castle Howard with a Borghese gladiator and a dancing faun 'cast from a moddle made on purpose' in about 1740, Stourhead with a river god in 1749 and Hampton Court Palace with a figure of Mars in 1752.

John Cheere's Scottish clients included James Murray, 2nd Duke of Atholl (1690–1764), who acquired 'Time with a dial' adapted from van Nost's *Blackamoor*, for Blair Atholl.[45] A wide range of everyday figures included male and female haymakers, a sailor and his girl, Dutch skaters, a gardener, a girl with a bird's nest, a fiddler and bagpiper, and a Highland girl. The *commedia dell'arte* troupe – Harlequin, Columbine, Pierrot, Pantaloon and Harlequin's woman – contributed to the *fête champêtre*, while Bacchus, Pomona and Mercury ensured that the classical tradition was respected. Cheere advised that a gamekeeper 'painted in proper couleurs' should be 'washed carefully every two years and oiled with linseed'.[46] The figure of Bacchus from Kinmount, Dumfries (plate 129),

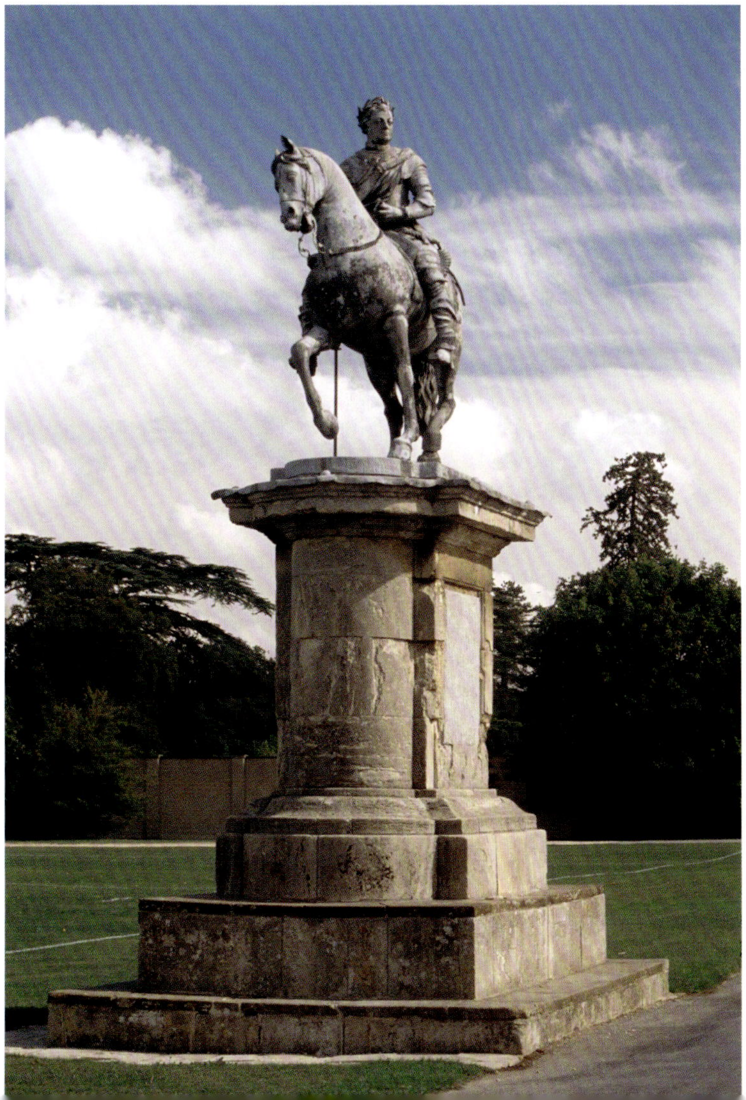

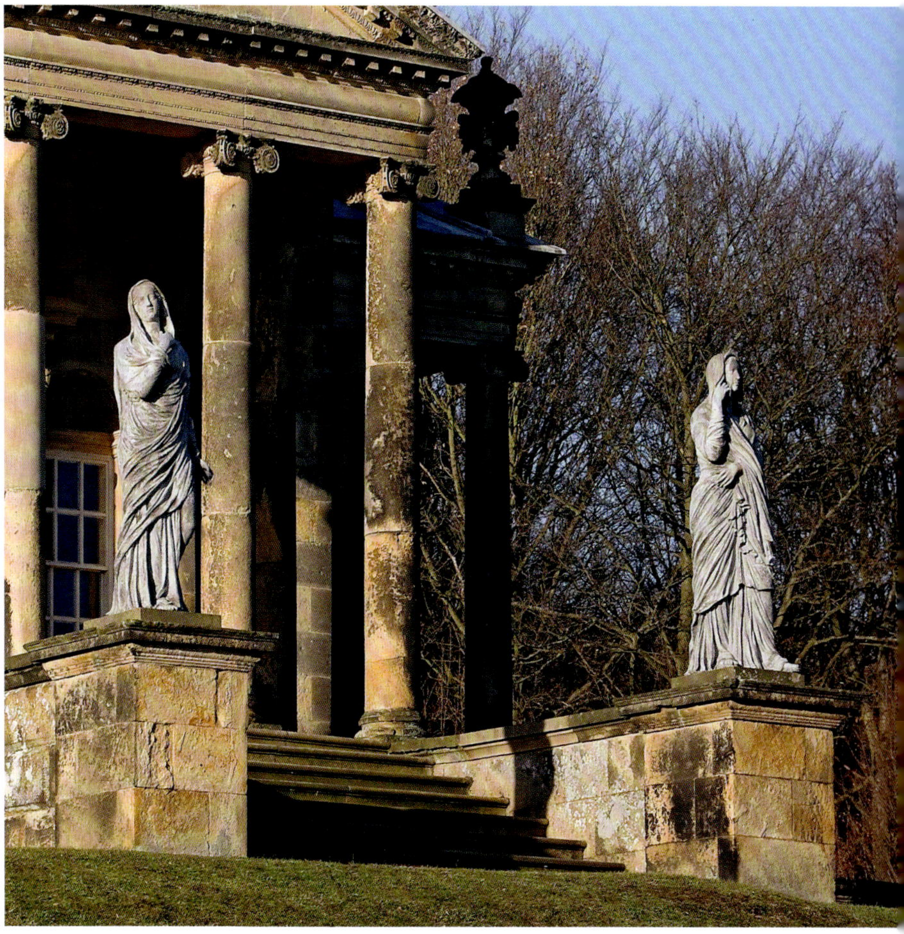

retains its original painted surface. Crowned with a wreath of grapes and vine leaves, the god is clothed in a wolf's pelt and holds a goblet in his outstretched right arm.[47] Prototypes include three lead copies of 'a young Bacchus, Standing Figure' in Nost's sale, which relate to the figure that he supplied for Hampton Court gardens in 1701.[48] John Cheere also provided plaster statues for the interiors at Blair Atholl with the instruction that 'They should be painted over carefully Flake White and Turpentine Oil when they are set up ... and a little drying oile'.[49]

The production of royal equestrian statues gained from opportunity to study horse and rider at Major Foubert's Riding Academy (p.47).[50] Foubert's Academy provided technical instruction for cavalry officers and was attended by Prince William Augustus, Duke of Cumberland (1721–1765) in the 1730s and 1740s. In September 1735, daily papers announced that at 8 o'clock one Tuesday morning, 'her Majesty, his Royal Highness the Duke and the Princesses Amelia, Caroline, Mary, Louisa' travelled in their open chaises 'to Major Foubert's in King Street and did him the Honour to breakfast at his House after which they went to the Riding House, where his Royal Highness went through his Exercise, and about half an hour after nine, they returned to Kensington.' *Read's Weekly Journal* confirmed that 'her Majesty was extremely delighted' at the young Duke's performance.[51] After Major Foubert's death in February 1743 the Academy was carried on by his nephew Solomon Durrell, who received an annual treasury warrant of £500 and continued to attract Royal patronage. In January 1744 *The Daily Advertiser* reported: 'Yesterday their Royal Highnesses the Prince of Wales and Duke of Cumberland were at Major Foubert's Riding House in King-Street, Golden Square, to see some fine Horses that are breaking there for them, and his Royal Highness the Duke of Cumberland rode the Great Horse for some Time.'[52] This provided an ideal opportunity for artist and sculptor to observe and sketch the royal horse and rider.

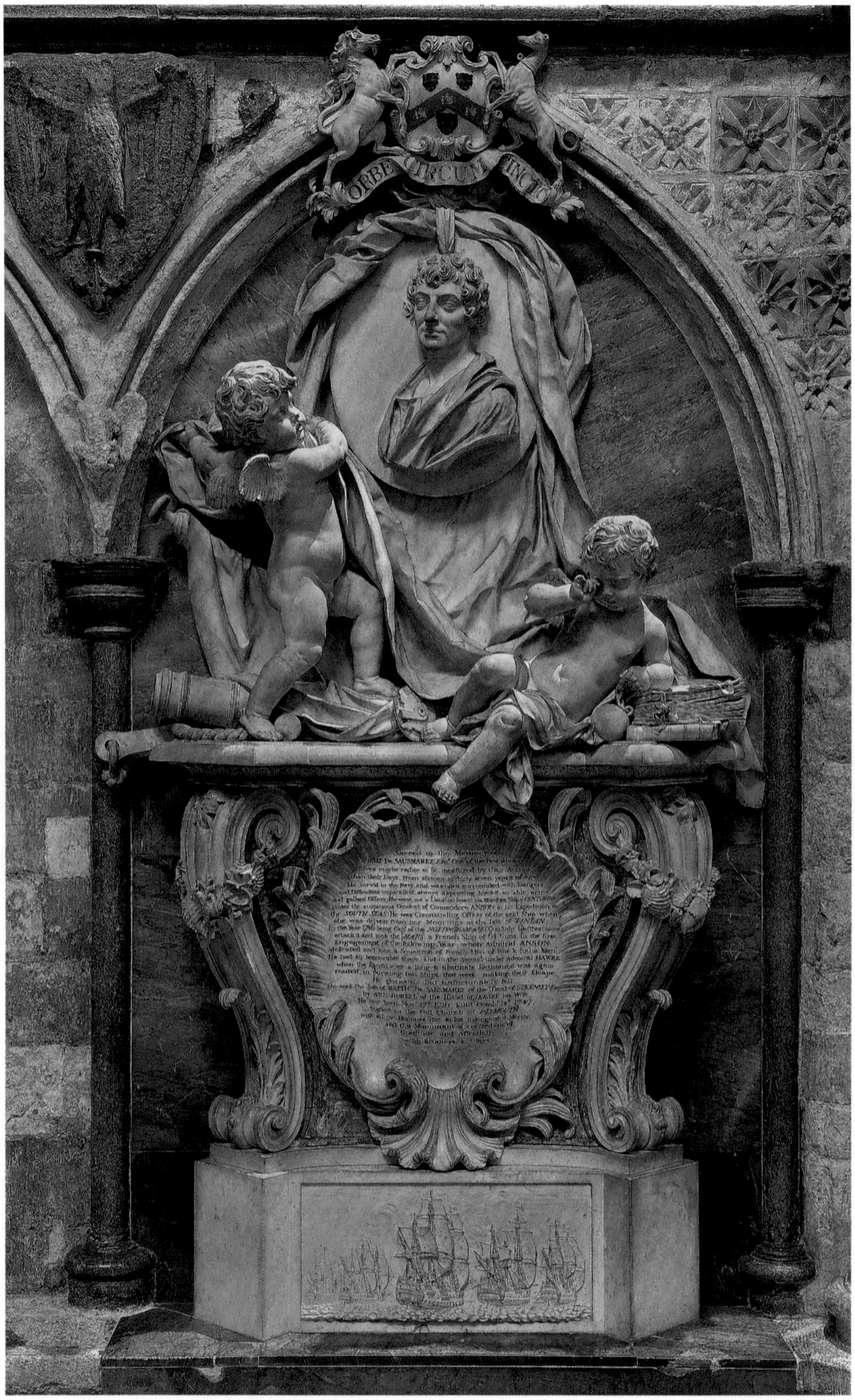

John Cheere's equestrian statue of Frederick, Prince of Wales, dressed in Roman armour, was cast in 1757 for Hartwell House, for Sir Thomas Lee, the Prince's supporter.[53] Cheere's royal statues were commissioned as expressions of loyalty in Ireland and the Channel Islands. In 1746 his lead statue of William Augustus, Duke of Cumberland, originally intended for St Stephen's Green, Dublin, was erected at Parsonstown, King's County,[54] in celebration of the Duke's victory at the Battle of Culloden. Commissioned by Sir Lawrence Parsons, 3rd Baronet (d.1749) at Birr Castle nearby, Cumberland's statue was placed on a marble pillar 50 ft high in the centre of Cumberland Square,[55] where members of the Birr Freemason's Lodge paraded to mark the statue's unveiling. The column, designed by Samuel

LEFT

128 Monument to Captain Philip de Sausmarez

Henry Cheere, London, 1747
Marble
Westminster Abbey, London

The portrait relief of de Sausmarez is draped in mourning by a winged putto whose companion, seated on the ledge below, wipes a tear from his eye. The inscribed shell cartouche, relief of naval battle below and festoons of shells are appropriate attributes for this Huguenot naval hero.

RIGHT

129 *Bacchus*

Attributed to John Cheere, London, *c.*1740
Lead with traces of original paint, ht 183 cm
The Rothschild Foundation at Waddesdon Manor

The *Bacchus* from Kinmount, Dumfries, now welcomes visitors to the wine cellars at Waddesdon Manor, its original paint surface preserved following John Cheere's instructions. Crowned with a wreath of grapes and vine leaves, Bacchus stands in *contrapposto*, bearing most of his weight on his left foot.

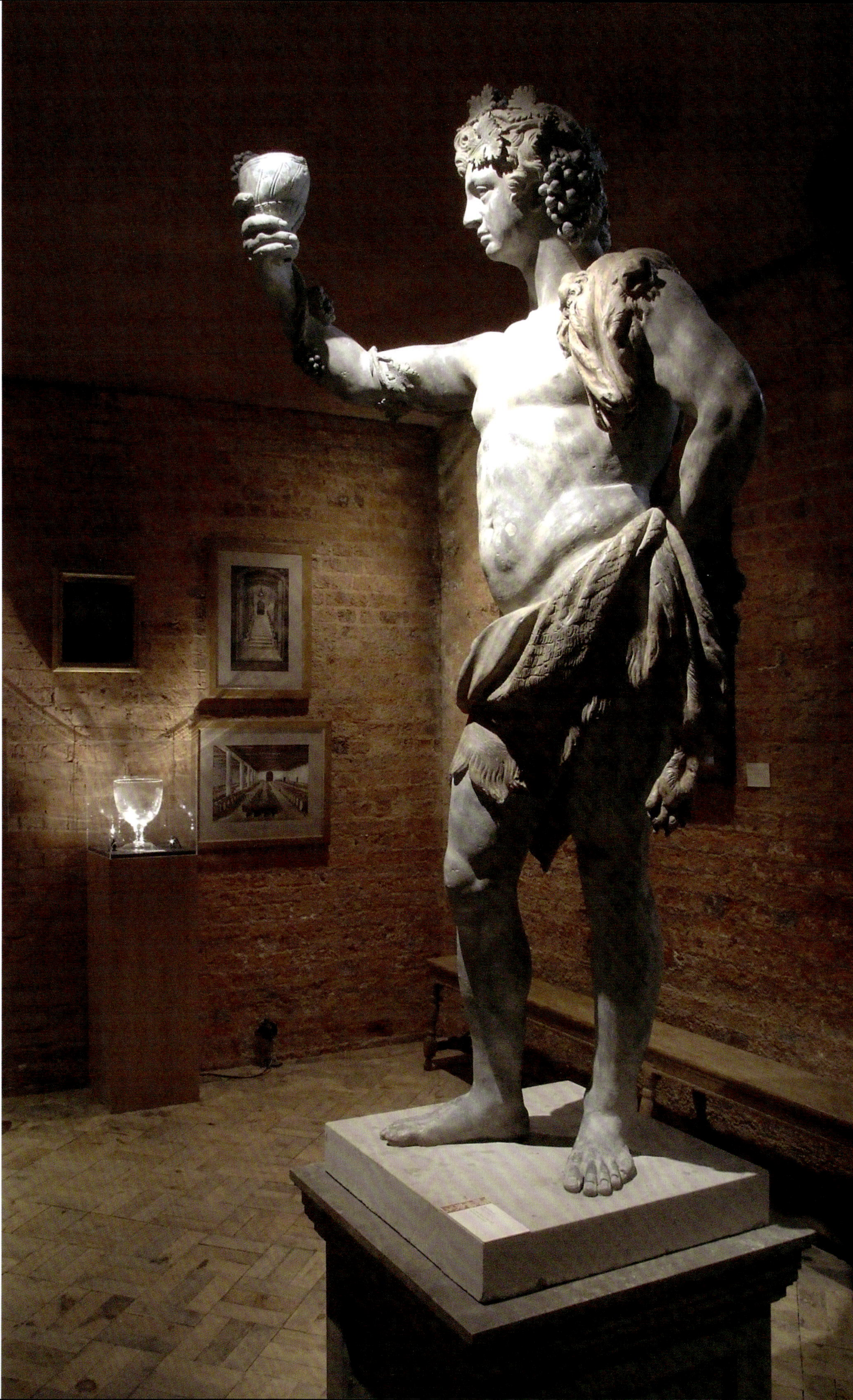

Chearnley (1717–1746), was based on the English 1708 translation of the *Ordonnance des cinq espèces de colonnes*... by Claude Perrault (1613–1688). When the lead figure developed a crack in one leg, Cheere recommended repair by a local plumber and sent Sir Lawrence a complimentary plaster bust of Cumberland polished to imitate marble, 'exceedingly like and very handsome to stand in a room upon a table or a chimney'.[56]

In St Helier, Jersey, the initiative to erect an appropriate feature to replace the cross in Market Square, first considered in 1698, was led by Abraham Gosset (1701–1785), the eldest son of Jean Gosset, a Huguenot refugee from Normandy. Abraham's brothers Jacob, Gedeon and Isaac were established as carvers and wax modellers in London (see pp.128–9, 258). It was Abraham's idea to commission a gilded lead statue of George II from John Cheere. John Cheere's brother Henry later produced a monument to Jersey-born Captain Philip de Sausmarez (1710–1747) for Westminster Abbey, its inscription set within a giant scallop shell attended by delightfully playful putti (plate 128). A second memorial to Sausmarez is in the church of St Andrew, Plymouth, where he is buried. Both memorials were commissioned by Cheere's Westminster neighbour, Captain Philip Durrell (1707–1766).[57] Henry Cheere also signed a monument to Captain Nicholas Le Mesurier (1731–1759) at St Peter Port, Guernsey, in 1759.[58]

On 9 July 1751 John Cheere's statue of George II was erected in Royal Square, St Helier, Jersey. Crowds watched as civil and military authorities paraded through the city accompanied by the Lieutenant-Bailiff, Charles Lemprière (1714–1806). As the statue was unveiled, seven cannon were fired from Elizabeth Castle. The day concluded with fireworks and a volley from five companies of fusiliers who, with the squadron of horse and 30 troopers, made up the procession. A toast to His Majesty's Health followed, and that night bonfires were lit on the hills above town.[59]

From his premises at Hyde Park Corner John Cheere was well placed to arrange transport for heavy lead sculptures to country destinations. His customers included the Huguenot Bouverie family at Longford Castle near Salisbury, who ordered statues of Augusta and Flora.[60] He is best remembered for the series of portrait busts he supplied for private and institutional libraries: in 1749 he provided a series of 'Fellows of this Society', including busts of Sir Christopher Wren and Archbishop Sheldon, for the Codrington Library at All Souls' College, Oxford, where his brother Henry's marble statue of Christopher Codrington was installed in 1734.[61] These plasters could be 'finished' to resemble bronze. John Cheere's small 'bronzed' statuettes were intended for side tables and chimney pieces, while his larger plaster statues for interiors copied from famous antiques furnished Robert Adam's Neoclassical interiors. His most spectacular commission was for 233 statues for the gardens at Queluz, Portugal, between 1755 and 1757. These were ordered through the Portuguese Legation in London at a cost of more than £800.[62] An array of classical and rural subjects created a virtual *fête champêtre*: an Irish clergyman visiting Cheere's yard describes seeing this 'Assembly of Gods and Goddesses, Juno, Minerva, Venus de Medici, Jupiter, Mars, Neptune, Rural Deities, Pan, Frisking Satyrs, Infinite multitude of Dancers, Haymakers, Gladiators, Wrestlers, Huntsman & Fowlers' and accompanying menageries of 'Eagles, Vultures, Hawks, Kites, Ostrich, peacocks, Lions, Leopards, tygers'.[63]

When John Cheere died in 1787 his remaining stock was sold off and his yard in fashionable West London, was closed for residential development. His nephew Charles Cheere offered the Royal Academy one of his uncle's figures; they chose Susannah.[64]

John Cheere's elder brother, Henry, was established in Old Palace Yard, Westminster, with easy access to the River Thames for receiving imported Italian marbles: his pieces feature highly coloured Siena marble and Sicilian jaspers that contrast with the Carrara 'statuary' and grey 'dove' marbles more commonly used at this time. Henry Cheere obtained special marbles from stonemason Edward Chapman Bird (1715–1792), whose yard was nearby at Millbank.[65] Such variety appealed to the pluralist taste for French Rococo, Chinese, Persian and Neo-Gothic styles. In addition to memorial sculpture, Henry Cheere worked closely with architects and surveyors to supply chimney pieces.

In 1734–6 Henry Cheere supplied a new chimney piece for the Parlour at Goldsmiths' Hall (plate 130). This well documented commission throws light on the detailed negotiations that eventually led to a satisfactory outcome. The chimney piece has been attributed to Louis François Roubiliac, who initially worked for Henry Cheere.[66] The Goldsmiths' Company Ledger Books confirm that in July 1735 Cheere was paid £105 for a 'Marble Chimney Piece & Slab' and the following April, £7 10s for a 'pair of marble Covings & a firestone

130 Chimney piece with leopard's head and male terms

Henry Cheere and Louis François Roubiliac, London, 1734–6
Carrara and 'Statuary' white veined marble, 174 × 305 cm
The Court Room, Goldsmiths' Hall, City of London

The leopard's head (the Company's badge) and the male term figures are carved in statuary marble, mounted on slabs of white and veined marble.

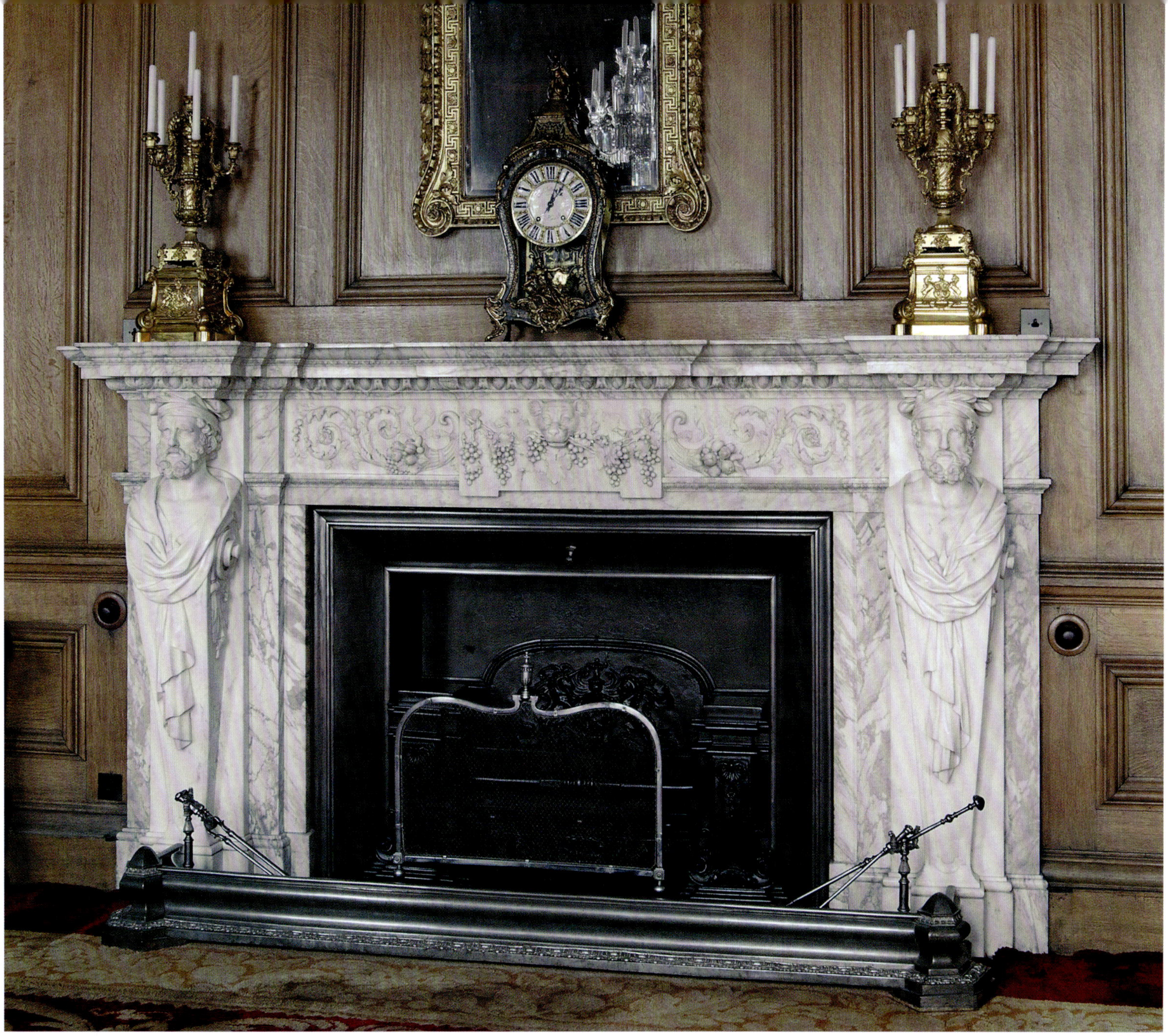

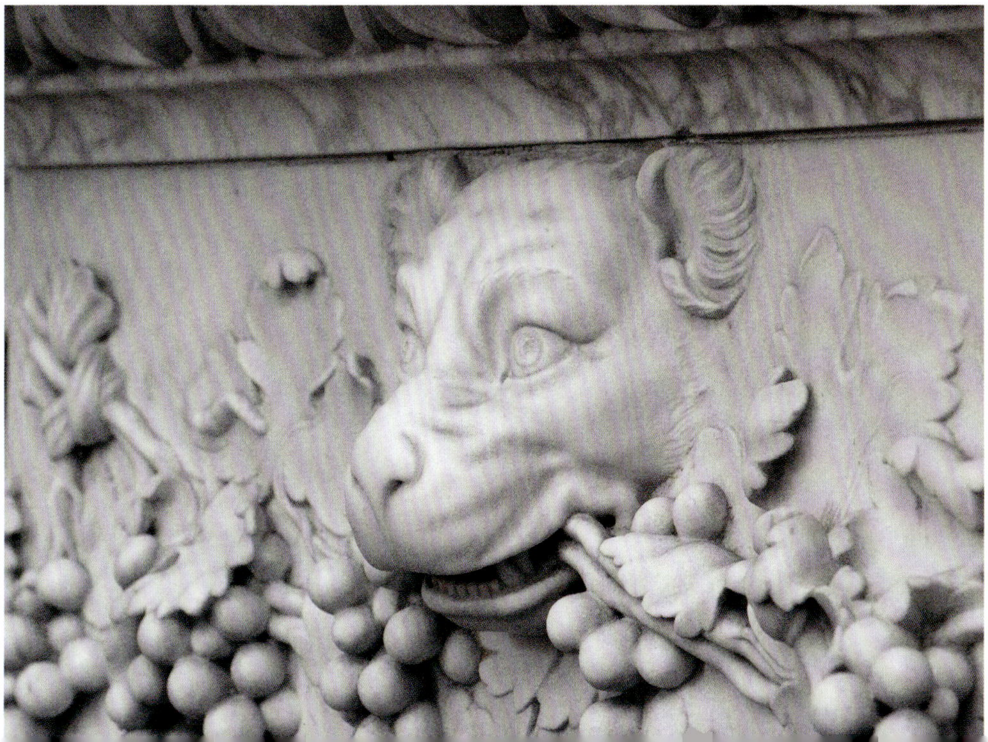

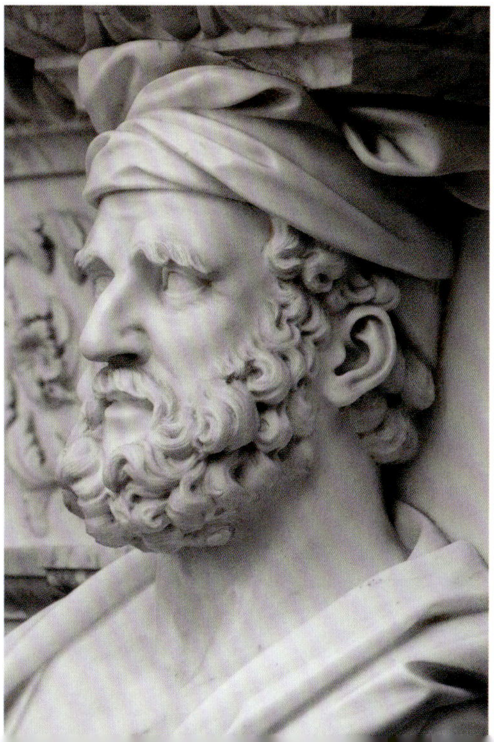

Hearth'.[67] The commission to refurbish the Parlour was initiated in September 1734, when 'three very handsome carved & gilt Frames' for the portraits of Sir Hugh Middleton, Sir Martin Bowes and Sir Thomas Vyner were ordered from Daniel Fare of Queen Street.[68] 'Mr. Cooper the Surveyor' was instructed to 'Design ... a new Marble Chimney Piece and picture frame'. As the previous structure had been removed in attempt to cure the chimney of smoking, a new chimney piece was required. In November 1734 'Henry Cheere agreed to use Statuary Marble and to perform the same in an exquisitely beautifull and perfect manner ... extreamly well polished'. Cheere signed his proposal 'promising to perform the same to the Company's satisfaction and to his own Reputation'. Over the next eight weeks the surveyor and sculptor debated over the quality of marble required. In May 1735 Cheere explained that this discussion had delayed production and requested a further month to complete. The fireplace was fitted with 'handsome coloured new Dutch Tyles' and the royal arms over the door were repainted and gilded. Mr Warden Carter was instructed to provide 'a good new Stove Grate with fire shovel, poker, Tongs & fender'. In order to ensure that this prestigious institutional client was satisfied, Henry Cheere perhaps entrusted the carving to his best assistant, Roubiliac.

Henry Cheere's production of chimney pieces later relied on stock designs and patterns using cast models and employing many different hands. He was his own designer, as correspondence with his Huguenot cousin Sir John Chardin demonstrates. In 1744 he created the monument in Westminster Abbey to Chardin's celebrated father, merchant jeweller to Charles II (plate 131),[69] which bears the inscription 'SR JOHN CHARDIN / SOLI DEO GLORIA / RESURGAM'.[70] Henry Cheere demonstrated the importance of design when recommending William Deards (fl.1740–61), celebrated London toyshop manager, for membership of the Society for the Encouragement of Arts, Manufactures and Commerce in 1755:

> *From architecture and all its ornaments, external & internal, from painting to sculpture, graving and chasing, planting and gardening, and all various performances, in which art and genius, elegance of fancy and accuracy of workmanship are confessedly united, curiosity will descend to the subordinate branches of design, in utensils of all sorts, plate and cabinet work, patterns of silks, jewelling, garniture, porcelain, carriage building and equipage, down even to toys and trinkets; it will expect to find the same manifestations of propriety and elegancy and will reject whatsoever is apparently irreconcilable with the true standards of use and beauty.*[71]

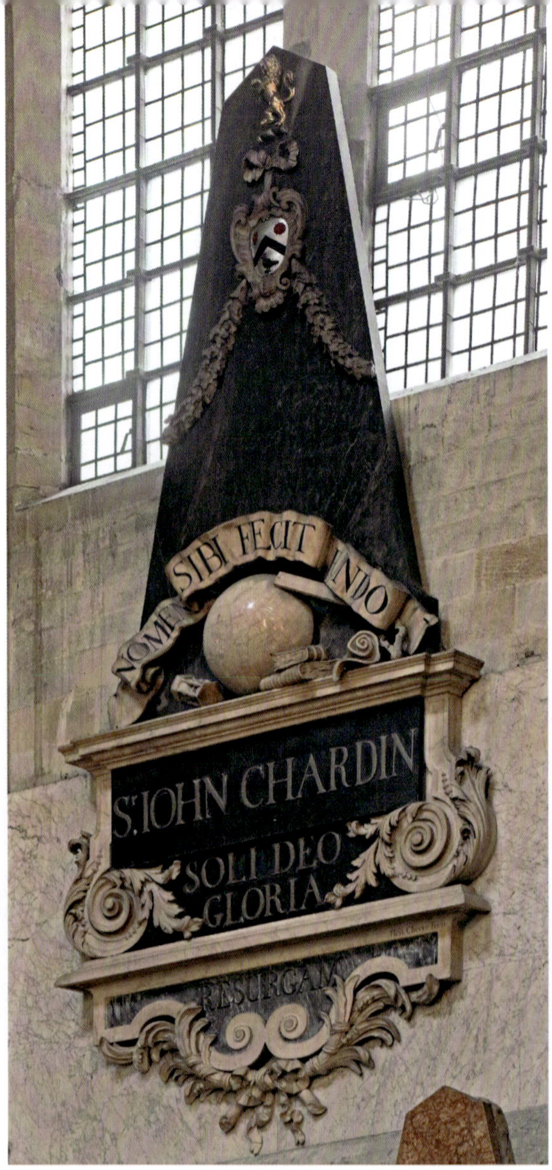

131 Monument to Sir John Chardin

Henry Cheere, London, 1744–6
Black and statuary marble
Westminster Abbey, London

Above the globe are Chardin's motto, and armorial crest, *argent, a chevron sable between two roses in chief and a heathcock in base*.

Henry Cheere was the first sculptor to be elected a fellow of the Society of Antiquaries in 1750, reflecting his social standing and elite education at Westminster School. Like his father, John, a prosperous merchant and churchwarden of the church of St Paul's, Clapham, Surrey, Henry played a responsible civic role, serving as Director of the Westminster Fire Office in 1745–6, Controller of Duties for Westminster Fish Market in 1749 and Principal Vestryman at St Margaret's church, Westminster, from 1742. The commission for a Triton boy for the temporary refreshment stand fountain celebrating George III's accession in St Margaret's parish was awarded to Henry's brother, John.[72]

The successful business career of Henry Cheere contrasts with that of his former assistant

132 *George Frideric Handel*

Louis François Roubiliac, London, 1738
Marble, ht 135.3 cm
Victoria and Albert Museum, London (A.3–1965)

By 1738 Roubiliac established his reputation with this statue made for Jonathan Tyers, proprietor of Vauxhall Gardens, at Henry Cheere's suggestion. Placed under an arch with lead figures of 'Harmony, with bass viol and Genii', the setting was inspired by the Bosquet de la Colonnade at Versailles. The curtain that protected the marble from weather was drawn up when visitors arrived. This, the earliest British sculpture of a contemporary other than monarch, represents the composer dictating music to the putto at his feet.

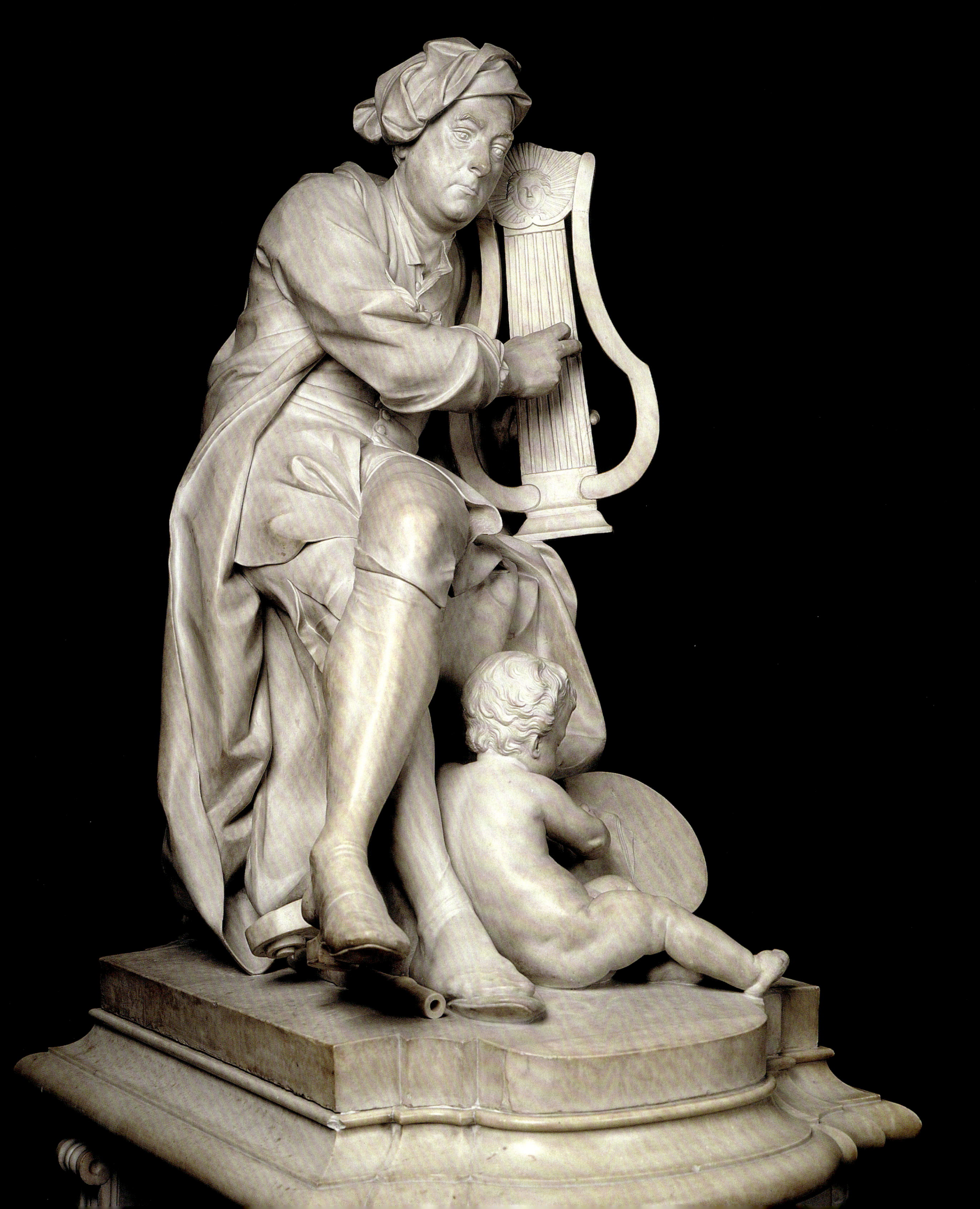

Roubiliac, first recorded in London in 1730 at the White Bear Masonic Lodge in King Street, Golden Square, Soho.[73] One of the Lodge wardens was Charles Labelye, the Swiss engineer who later designed the first Westminster Bridge (see pp.91–4). In 1731 Roubiliac was back in Paris collecting his second prize for sculpture at the French Royal Academy. He returned to London and in April 1735 he applied to St Martin Orgar, the Anglican church near London Bridge, which hosted a Huguenot congregation, for a licence to marry Caroline Magdalen Helot.[74] Roubiliac established his reputation with his 1738 statue of George Frideric Handel (1685–1759; plate 132).[75] Crowds attending the 1748 rehearsal of Handel's *Music for the Royal Fireworks* in Vauxhall Gardens thus enjoyed the composer's virtual presence, on which Dr Matthew Maty (1718–1776), Roubiliac's Huguenot friend, published a celebratory poem in the *Mercure de France*.[76]

Roubiliac's statue of Handel also inspired Sir Andrew Fountaine to commission 'a curious figure of a Lady' for his Norfolk garden in November 1738. Roubiliac employed a female model for nine hours at 7s 6d an hour; the novelty attracted an audience of 'eight of the most celebrated painters', resulting in a 'fine Venus for a Person of Quality'.[77] First introduced in 1722 at the St Martin's Lane Academy in London, opportunities to work from the female model were not available at the Paris Royal Academy until after the French Revolution.

Artists and men of letters gathered at Slaughter's Coffee House, St Martin's Lane, where Roubiliac encountered many of his sitters. In 1741 Vertue noted Roubiliac's 'moddels in Clay … from the Life several Busts or portraits extreamly like … Mr Pope more like than any other Sculptor … Mr Hogarth very like'.[78] Roubiliac created a new vernacular for each: Alexander Pope is captured in loose classical drapery with closely cropped hair, while Hogarth is shown *en négligé*, in the French tradition for artists or writers.[79] The sitter's alertness and energy makes Hogarth the most immediate and penetrating of Roubiliac's early portraits and demonstrates their friendship. Roubiliac also modelled Hogarth's pug, Trump (plate 151), later used as the source for versions in white glazed Chelsea porcelain.[80] Through Hogarth, Roubiliac was appointed to teach sculpture at the St Martin's Lane Academy from 1745. In 1743 he supplied five small-scale bronzes for the *Temple of the Four Grand Monarchies of the World*, a musical clock by Charles Clay with silver reliefs designed by Antwerp sculptor John Michael Rysbrack (1694–1770) and tunes adapted by Handel.[81]

After 1752, Roubiliac's regular payments to Huguenot goldsmith-jewellers suggest probable collaboration in casting figurative bronzes. Robert Campbell noted in 1747 that 'Workers in Metal, especially of the finer Metals, form sensible Figurs, either by casting them in Moulds or forming them with the Hammer … of some kindred to Sculpture & Statuary'.[82] Roubiliac's friend Thomas Harrache (1717–1785), son of the silversmith Abraham

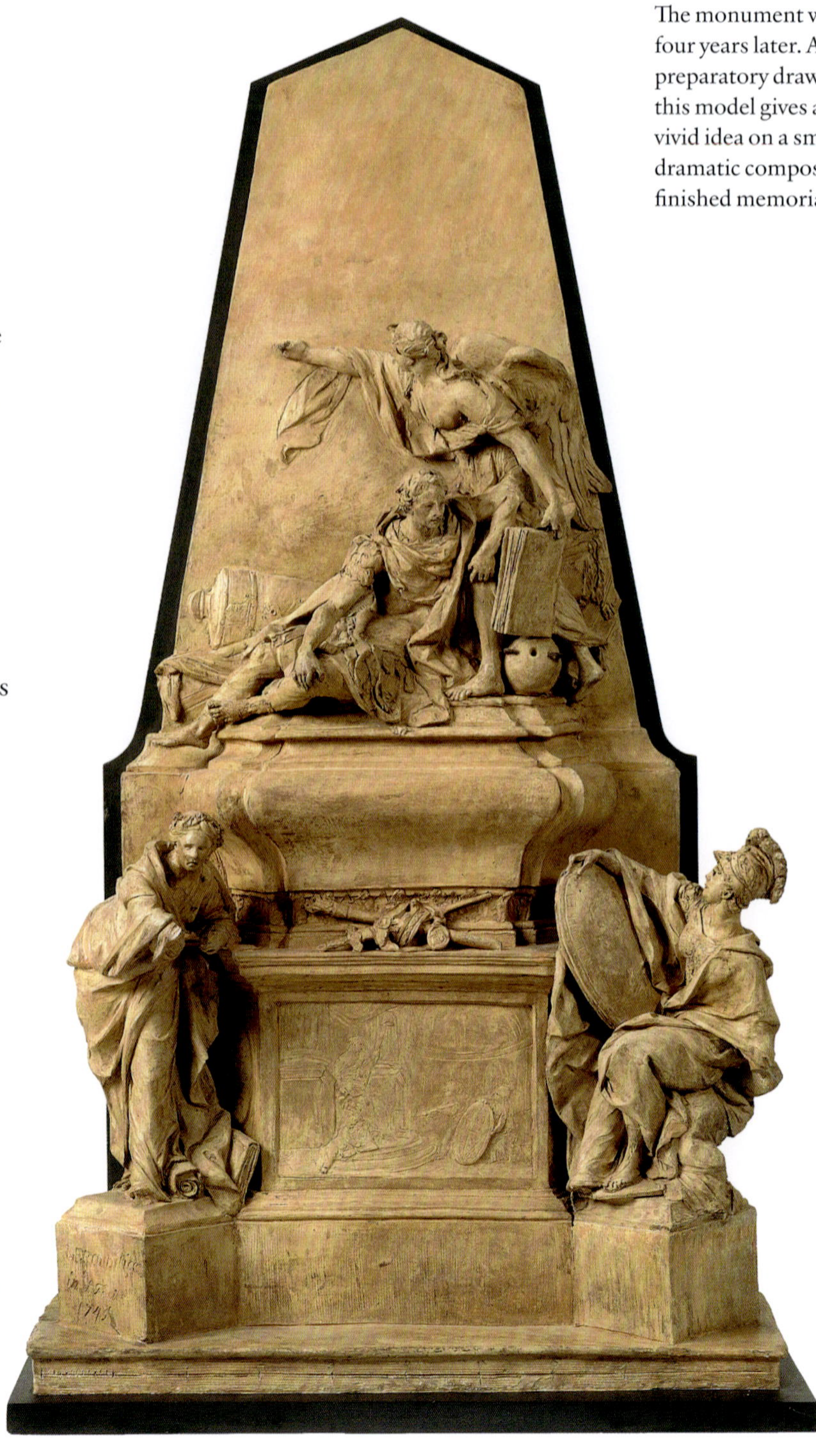

133 Model for the monument to the Duke of Argyll and Greenwich

Louis François Roubiliac, London, 1745
Terracotta, ht 92 cm
Victoria and Albert Museum, London (21:1–1888)

The scale at the bottom indicates that this was the model associated with the contract for the monument, awarded to Roubiliac by the Duke's widow in 1745. The monument was completed four years later. Although several preparatory drawings survive, this model gives a particularly vivid idea on a small scale of the dramatic composition of the finished memorial.

(1661–1722), at the Blackamoor, Compton Street, was apprenticed to his elder brother, Francis (1710–1757), a snuffbox maker, in 1732. From 1743 Thomas was Roubiliac's neighbour in St Martin's Lane.[83] By 1751 Harrache sold bronzes and Dresden china from his new shop in Pall Mall, where in 1774 Paul Methuen (1723–1795) of Corsham Court, Bath, purchased 'A pair of Statuary Marble Vauses mounted in Ormolu' for 18 guineas and 'A fine Antique Bronze of a Laocoon' for 14 guineas.[84] Roubiliac's payment in December 1760 to Charles Gouyn for £50 indicates collaboration with the jeweller-proprietor of St James's porcelain factory (pp.167–9).[85]

In January 1741/2 Roubiliac's second marriage, to Catharine Smart (*c*.1720–1747), took place at St Martin's church, Dorking, near Jonathan Tyers's country retreat, Denbies, Surrey. Here the sculptor created the monument to Robert, 8th Baron Petre (1713–1742), for the garden Temple of Death.[86] The two Roubiliac daughters were baptized at St Martin-in-the-Fields in 1743 and by the minister of the Huguenot Spring Gardens chapel in 1744. Nicholas Sprimont, goldsmith from Liège and founder of the Chelsea porcelain manufactory, stood godfather to the younger, daughter, Sophie (plate 152). Catherine Smart died in 1747 and Sophie, the only surviving daughter, was sent to Paris to join her paternal uncle, Thomas, an engraver.[87]

Roubiliac's earliest large-scale marble monuments are to Dr John Hough, Bishop of Worcester (1651–1743), in Worcester Cathedral (1744) and John Campbell, 2nd Duke of Argyll and Greenwich (1680–1743), in Westminster Abbey (1745–9). In Worcester, Bishop Hough reclines on his monument while the figure of Religion lifts his robes to reveal the relief below. The design compares with the Slodtz brothers' monuments to archbishops Armand de Montmorin and Henri Oswald de la Tour d'Auvergne of 1747 in Vienne, France. Although carved in marble, the Worcester relief was initially intended to be cast in Chelsea porcelain, providing further evidence for links between Roubiliac and Sprimont.[88]

The commission for the Argyll monument in Westminster Abbey (plate 133), won in competition against his main rival John Michael Rysbrack, further enhanced Roubiliac's reputation. The monument celebrates the Duke's role in suppressing the 1715 Jacobite Rebellion and is inscribed with the words of poet William Whitehead: 'Briton behold, if patriot worth be dear, a shrine that claims thy tributary tear…'. Unveiled in 1749, the monument was 'much admired by the Publick … being of a grand composition strikes the spectators with admiration … the attitude of the Statues each well disposed and contrasted … and the Draperys and foldings truely natural … really more like silk than marble'.[89] A signed contract drawing shows that many changes occurred in developing the final composition from Roubiliac's original design.[90] The Duke reclines on a sarcophagus flanked by the figures of Eloquence, leaning on Caesar's *Commentaries* and the *Rhetorical Works* of Demosthenes, and Minerva, martial goddess of wisdom. Above, Fame, writing a memorial inscription, stops at 'GR' for Greenwich: with the Duke's death that title became extinct. Inspired by earlier European sculpture, the design has a dramatic unity of action characteristic of Roubiliac. The prototype for Minerva is the 1715–23 monument to Pope Gregory XIII in St Peter's, Rome, by Camillo Rusconi (1658–1728), and Fame is taken from the 1714–16 monument to Wenzel, Count Wratislaw von Mitrovicz, in St James's Prague, by Johann Bernhard Fischer von Erlach (1656–1723).

In 1749 Roubiliac won the commission for John, 2nd Duke of Montagu's monument in St Edmund's church, Warkton, Northamptonshire; the commission was extended in 1751 to include a memorial to Montagu's widow, Mary. This most important double project cost about £3,000. The Duchess's monument features the Three Fates spinning, weaving and cutting the thread of life in a design inspired by contemporary funeral invitations and an earlier clock case by A-C. Boulle in the Montagu collection.[91]

In 1751 Roubiliac produced the lead figure of Sir John Cass (1661–1718) for his charity school, the Sir John Cass Foundation, in Aldgate. The likeness was taken from Sir John's portrait, enhanced by descriptions provided by trustees of the Foundation.

After his marriage, in January 1752, to Elizabeth Crosby (1727–1755), a Deptford heiress with a fortune of £10,000, Roubiliac reorganized his workshop. He opened an account with Drummond's Bank, where fellow sculptors Henry Cheere, Thomas Carter (d.1795) and Joseph Wilton (1722–1803) were clients.[92] Crosby's dowry never materialized and she died three years later in France. On 20 November 1756 Roubiliac's fourth marriage was announced, to Céleste Regnier, 'a most agreeable and accomplished young lady' whose family owned a print shop at that time in Great Windmill Street.[93] Céleste was the niece of

James Regnier (d.1750), seal engraver, established in Long Acre by 1710 when he was visited by the German scholar and traveller Zacharias Conrad von Uffenbach (1683–1734).[94]

For his marble statue of Shakespeare (plate 134), commissioned by the actor David Garrick, Roubiliac produced his own painted copy of the earliest authentic likeness of the playwright, the Chandos portrait. 'Garrick put himself into countenance and then into posture & desired the astonished sculptor to model away "for behold" said he "the poet of Avon".'[95] The resulting statue epitomizes 'an ideal of passionate genius in ecstasy shared by patron and sculptor' and the vision of Shakespeare as 'genius, savant and master of the passions'.[96] Roubiliac's figure of Shakespeare represents the creative power of the mind to imitate nature: through creativity the artist, whether Shakespeare, Garrick or Roubiliac, expressed divine power.[97] In 1779 David Garrick bequeathed the statue to the British Museum, along with his collection of 'old English plays'.[98]

The 1758–61 monument to Joseph (1695–1752) and Lady Elizabeth Nightingale (1704–1731) in Westminster Abbey was commissioned by their only surviving daughter (plate 135). The affectionate gestures of husband and wife are paralleled by Hogarth's portrait of David Garrick with his wife, Eva.[99] This coherent design reflects Roubiliac's enthusiastic response to 'the captivating and luxuriant splendour of Bernini', for the swooning Lady Nightingale is probably inspired by Bernini's *St Theresa* (1647–52) and the figure of Death, carved by Roubiliac's assistant Nicholas Read, is derived from Bernini's tomb of Alexander VII (1671–8).[100] The monument was intended to generate fear of death: the skeleton was inspired by the memorial to Jean-Baptist Languet de Gergy (1674–1750) in the church of St Sulpice, Paris, carved by René-Michel Slodtz (1705–1764) in 1757. Fifty years later James Peller Malcolm (1767–1815) noted that Joseph Nightingale's 'horror and eager motion can only be described by such actors as Garrick was and Kemble is'.[101]

Roubiliac's bank ledgers also provide information about the sculptor's activity during his last decade. They confirm the names of his studio assistants, subcontractors and suppliers, and the dates they worked with him. Matching credit payments with commissions for which full contract costs survive reveals that Roubiliac was not always paid in full for his work. His will, drawn up just six days before his death, mentions 'all my book debts

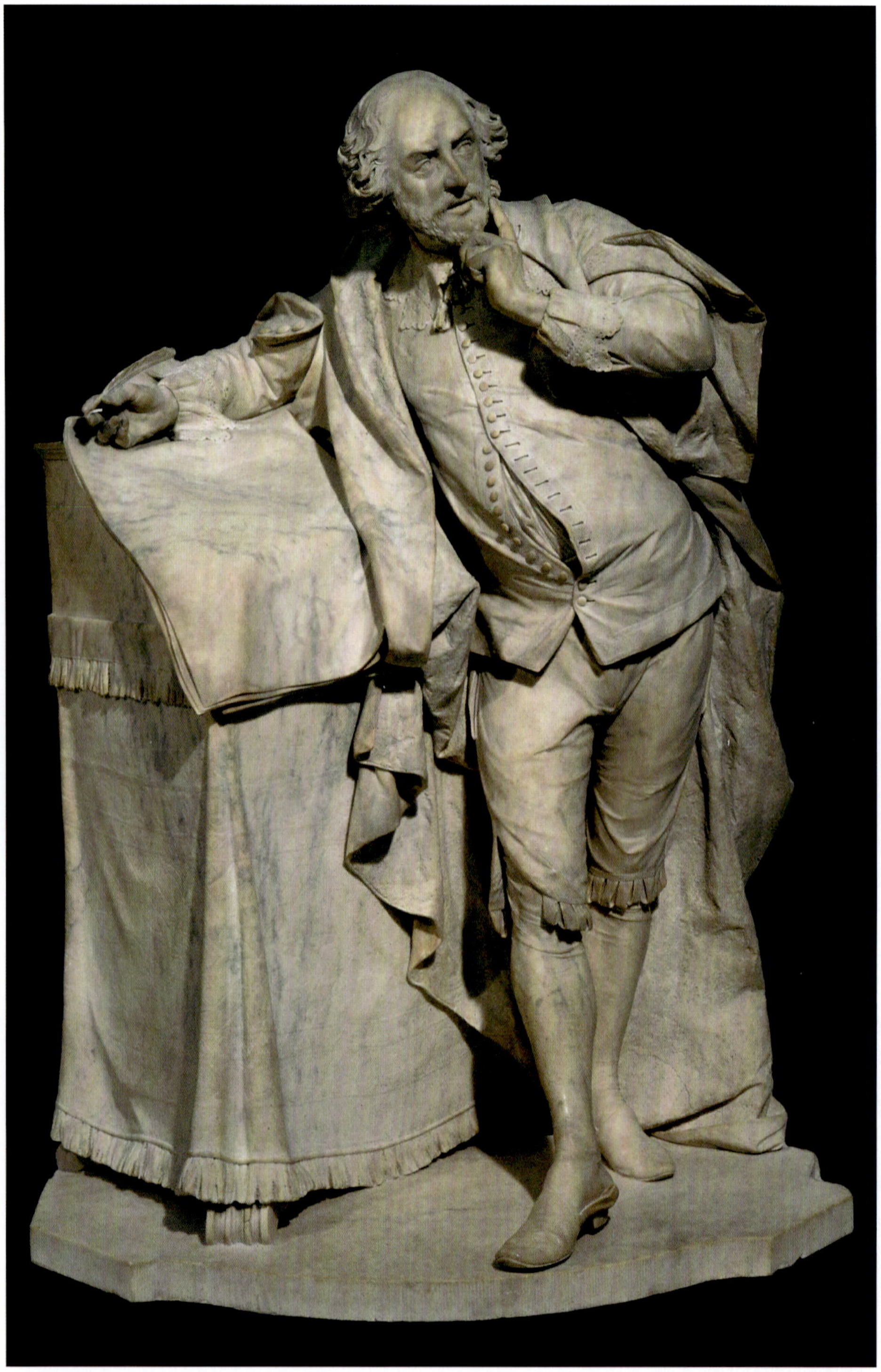

which is due to me to be equally divided into four parts'. Unlike Henry and John Cheere, Roubiliac did not make the time or have the business skills to develop an effective commercial relationship with his patrons.

In Britain French sculptors won leading commissions for monumental sculpture because of their professional standing through Continental training and experience. Yet the conventional equestrian statue or hierarchical funerary

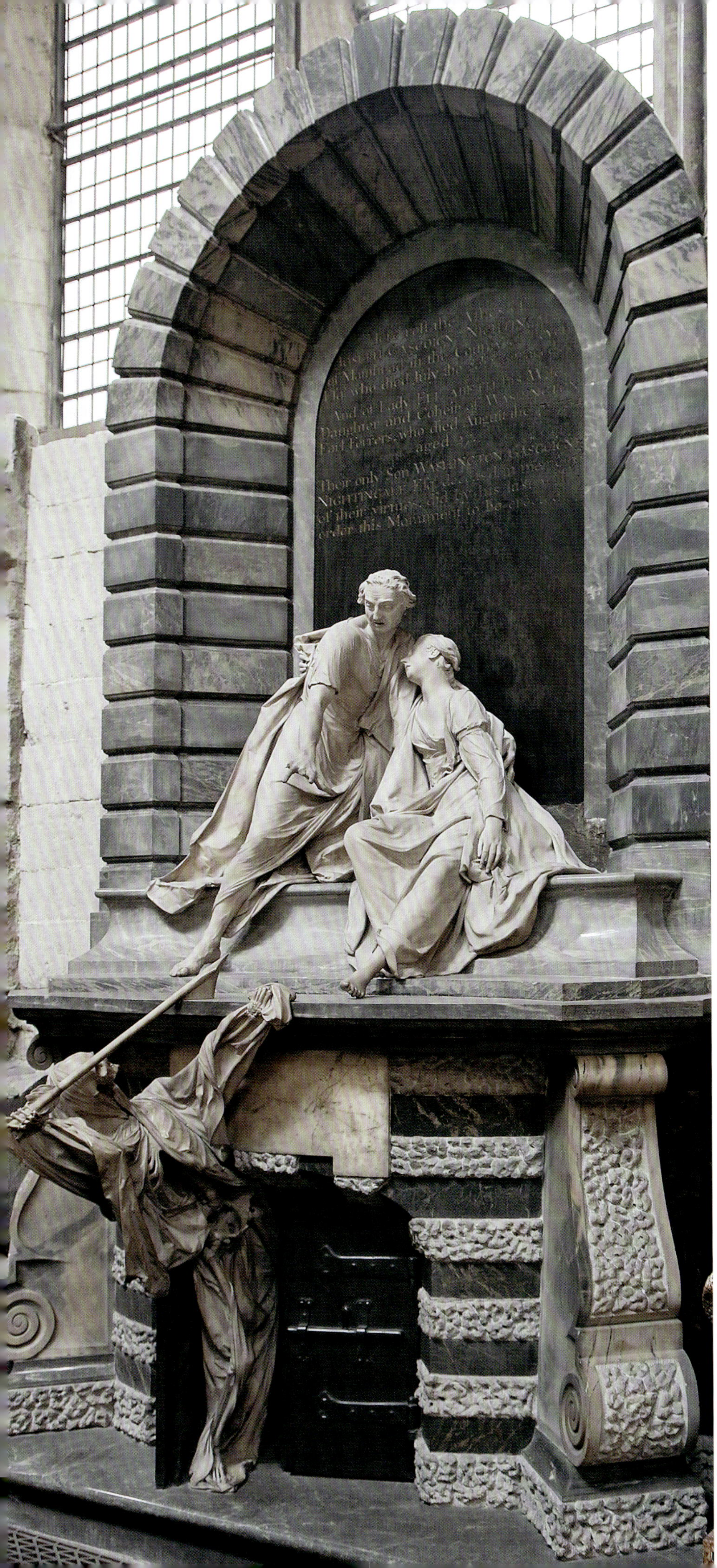

monument left little scope for originality. Although Barthélemy Prieur did not work in England, his fascination with domestic subjects paved the way for the humanizing of secular and memorial sculpture in eighteenth-century Britain. Garden sculpture supplied by Nadauld, Carpentière, the Cheeres and Roubiliac peopled the landscape, adding an element of surprise to the formal garden. Memorial sculpture provided another platform for injecting vitality into the traditional formula of the deceased reclining on a funerary chest within an architectural framework. Nadauld's relief for Lady Eland's monument, although separated from its original context, captures the bereavement of a mother for her deceased daughter, while Roubiliac's Nightingale monument demonstrates the bond between husband and wife. Capturing familial ties in sculptured form reflects the Huguenots' determination to make a significant contribution, informed by their strong domestic and social network that centred on their Calvinist faith.

FAR LEFT

134 *Shakespeare*

Louis François Roubiliac, London, 1758
Marble, ht (without pedestal) 172 cm
British Museum, London (MME.1823,0101.1), transferred to the British Library

Garrick posed for this statue, which was intended for the garden temple at his Thamesside Hampton villa. The figure reflects Garrick's reform of acting styles, his body language and facial expressions successfully expressing conflicting emotions: 'Pity, Anger, Grief, Joy & all the soft tumult of love have in their turn so fired my soul.'

LEFT

135 Monument to Joseph and Lady Elizabeth Nightingale

Louis François Roubiliac, London, 1758–61
Marble
Westminster Abbey, London

Lady Elizabeth died in childbirth in 1731, and the monument re-creates that tragedy, with a pathos seen in Roubiliac's later works. Against a proscenium arch, Joseph Nightingale holds his stricken wife while trying to fend off the dart aimed at her by Death as skeleton emerging from the vault below.

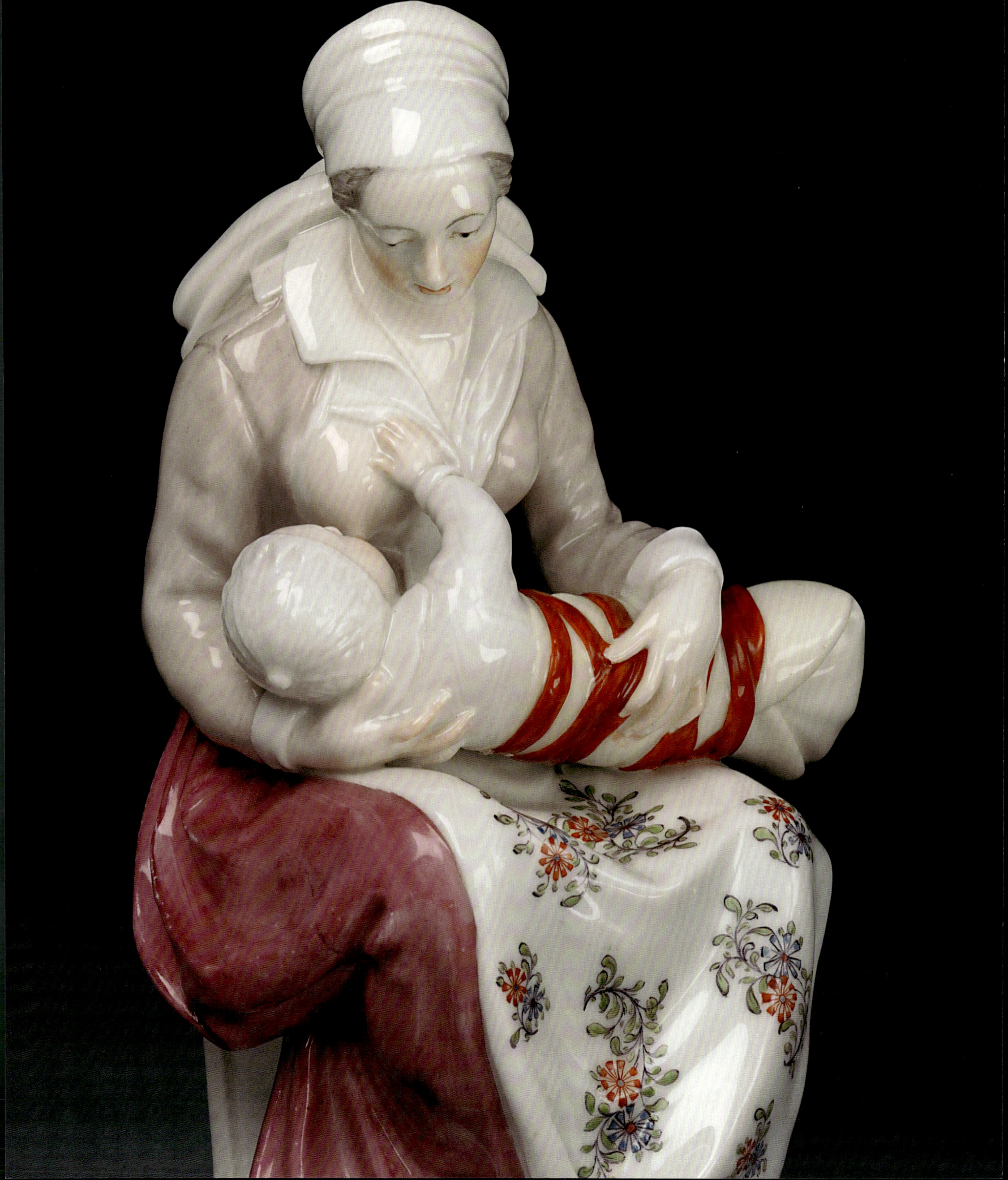

Chapter Nine
The Taste for Porcelain & Ceramic Manufacture in Britain & Ireland

136 A wet nurse
Chelsea manufactory, London, *c.*1753–5 (detail) see plate 148

The taste for collecting Oriental porcelain gathered momentum in England during the 1690s. Queen Mary displayed Chinese and Japanese porcelain in her Kensington Palace apartments (plate 137), while similar collections were shown in small rooms with lacquer panelling at Chatsworth, Derbyshire, seat of the Duke of Devonhire, and at Drayton, the Northamptonshire estate from 1705 of Lady Betty Germain (1680–1769). Porcelain conventionally stood above lacquer cabinets and below on giltwood stands.[1] Some retailers, such as Philip Arbunot in The Strand, supplied furniture and porcelain. In 1703 he sold 'china bottles and cream basons' to Lady Betty Germain, whose china closet survives at Knole, Kent.[2]

Huguenot Peter Anthony Motteux (1660–1718), East India Company merchant, sold 'China and Japan wares, tea and fans' from the Two Fans near old East India House, London, during Queen Anne's reign.[3] A translator and playwright, Motteux was born in Rouen and came to England in 1685. He edited the *Gentleman's Journal* in 1692–4, translated Rabelais and Cervantes, and wrote plays, masques and poems; he described himself as an 'author turned dealer' (plate 138).[4] Motteux promoted the variety of his goods to a mainly female audience and published *A Poem in Praise of Tea* in 1712. In 1711 John, 2nd Duke of Montagu, paid Charles Motteux, another member of the family, £10 for an Indian screen still preserved at Boughton House, Northamptonshire.[5]

The taste for Oriental porcelain inspired European emulation. The earliest-known reference to 'China' manufactured in Britain is a letter from Earl Cowper, written from Derby in September 1728, telling his sister that he had ordered 'a set of china from the Man who makes it here in England'.[6] In 1744 and 1745 the Bow and Chelsea manufactories were established. Their products differed from East India Company imports, although some forms and decoration were inspired by East Asian porcelain.

Talented Huguenot refugee craftsmen working in precious metals also produced luxury goods in ivory and horn. Snuffboxes, toys and fans, made in any combination of these materials, were sold by jewellers or from fashionable 'toy shops' in London's West End supplied by ivory turners, goldsmiths and watchmakers working across the metropolis and beyond. These shops led the taste for luxury goods and nurtured the market for sophisticated domestic vessels and porcelain ornaments made at Bow, Chelsea and Derby in the 1740s and 1750s. The new manufactories were managed by craftsmen trained as silversmiths and jewellers. The obvious prototypes for porcelain tableware were silver vessels. A silver sauceboat with strong contours, chased classical masks and a scroll handle supplied by second-generation Huguenot goldsmith Paul de Lamerie in 1726–7 compares with an elaborate Chelsea porcelain sauceboat and stand of *c.*1760–5, with Rococo scrolled feet, a 'flying' handle and slightly fluted body (plates 139, 140).

Small-scale bronzes and terracotta models copied by wax modellers or ivory carvers similarly provided prototypes for new porcelain figures. A fascination with domestic subjects stems from prints such as those published in 1619 by early seventeenth-century enameller Jean Toutin (1578–1644) from Blois and small-scale sculpture by his contemporary, Barthélemy Prieur (pp.133–7). In early eighteenth-century Dieppe, sacred and secular ivory statues were made as permanent replacements for ephemeral sugar sculpture for table display.[7] In London from 1700, David Le Marchand also made small-scale sculptures in ivory and probably supplied shops run by fellow Huguenot jewellers.[8] Indeed, a 'D. Marchand' – possibly the sculptor – witnessed the marriage of jeweller Antoine Planck to Marie du Barri at the Swallow Street French church, Soho, in 1705/6.[9] Le Marchand's ivory *Venus and Cupid* made after 1718 (plate 142) compares with a mid-1760s Chelsea soft-paste enamel decorated porcelain group (plate 143) in which a more animated and respectably clothed Venus reaches for a dove with her upheld right hand. His *Time, Opportunity and Penitence* of *c.*1700–20 (plate 141) is based on the marble group *The Abduction of Cybele by Saturn* carved by Thomas Regnaudin for Louis XIV's gardens at Versailles.[10]

Apart from early experiments in porcelain manufacture in late sixteenth-century Medici-ruled Florence, the earliest Continental porcelain manufactories were in France: at Rouen in 1673, while experiments at Saint-Cloud in the 1670s led to production in the 1690s. After the Meissen factory opened in Saxony, Germany, in 1710 the second generation of French porcelain manufactories included those at Mennecy in 1734, Villeroy-Mennecy from *c.*1737, Chantilly in 1735 and Vincennes from 1745.[11]

If porcelain was made in Derby as early as 1728, it was linked with European manufactories. In 1722 Thomas Billin took out a patent for what seems to have been porcelain production.[12] Various attempts to manufacture porcelain occurred in London in the early 1740s: in February 1742/3, for example, a Mr Bryand showed the Royal Society several specimens of

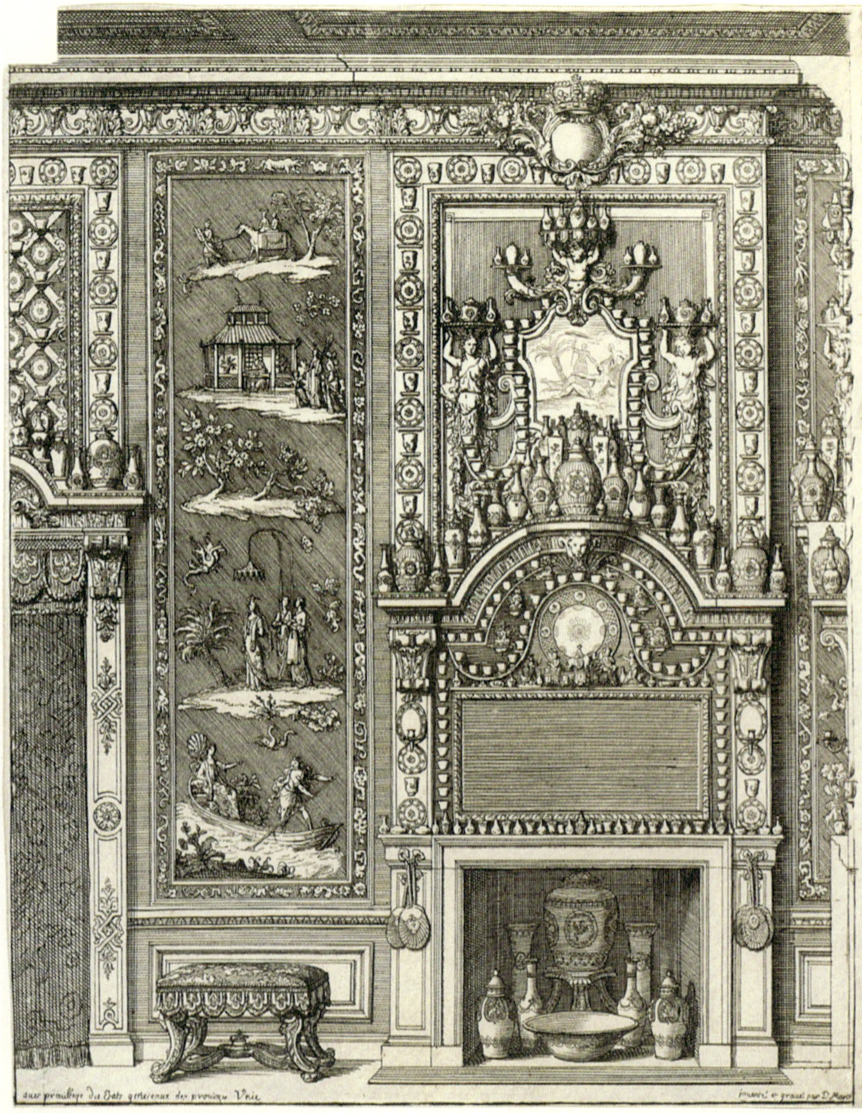

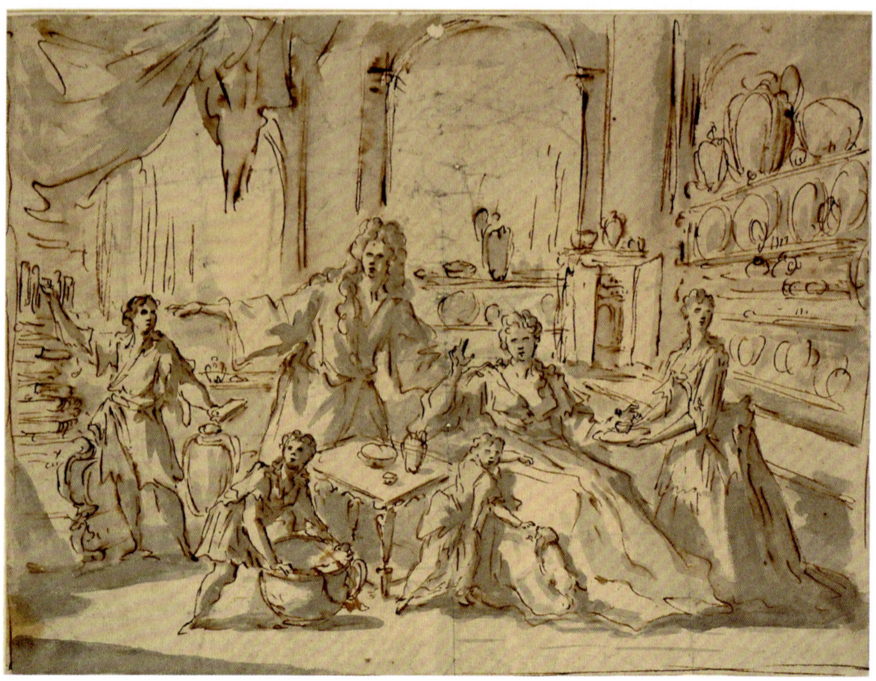

LEFT ABOVE

137 *Nouvelles Cheminée faitte en plusier en droits de la Hollande et autres Prouinces*

Daniel Marot, The Hague, *c.*1703
Etching, 32.2 × 23.3 cm
Victoria and Albert Museum, London
(E.1672:20-1888)

Queen Mary's infectious interest and enthusiasm inspired the fashion for East Asian ceramics in domestic interiors.

LEFT BELOW

138 *Peter Anthony Motteux and his Family*

Giovanni Antonio Pellegrini, London, 1708–13
Pen and brown ink, with grey wash, over graphite, 26.1 × 35.3 cm
British Museum, London (1874,8-8.43)

Richard Steele described Motteux's 'spacious warehouses, filled with tea, China and Indian wares'. Pellegrini's drawing shows the merchant with his family in an interior with porcelain displayed on shelves and books piled high. Pellegrini and Motteux may have met through their mutual interest in the theatre, or through Pellegrini's patron, the 4th Earl (later 1st Duke) of Manchester, to whom Motteux dedicated several books.

RIGHT ABOVE

139 Sauceboat

Paul de Lamerie, London, 1726–7
Silver, 13.1 × 19.2 × 10.4 cm

The Rosalinde and Arthur Gilbert Collection on loan to the Victoria and Albert Museum, London
(LOAN:GILBERT.667–2008)

RIGHT BELOW

140 Sauceboat and stand

Chelsea manufactory, London, 1765
Sauceboat ht 16.5 cm, l. 22.5 cm, w. 11 cm; stand ht 3 cm, l. 28.5 cm, w. 22.5 cm
Victoria and Albert Museum, London
(C.101&A-1932)

The fashionable French *Régence*-style silver sauceboat was part of a dinner service; the Chelsea porcelain sauceboat with Rococo scrolled feet, 'flying' handle and slightly fluted body is painted with exotic birds and flower sprays; the stand protects the table surface from spillage.

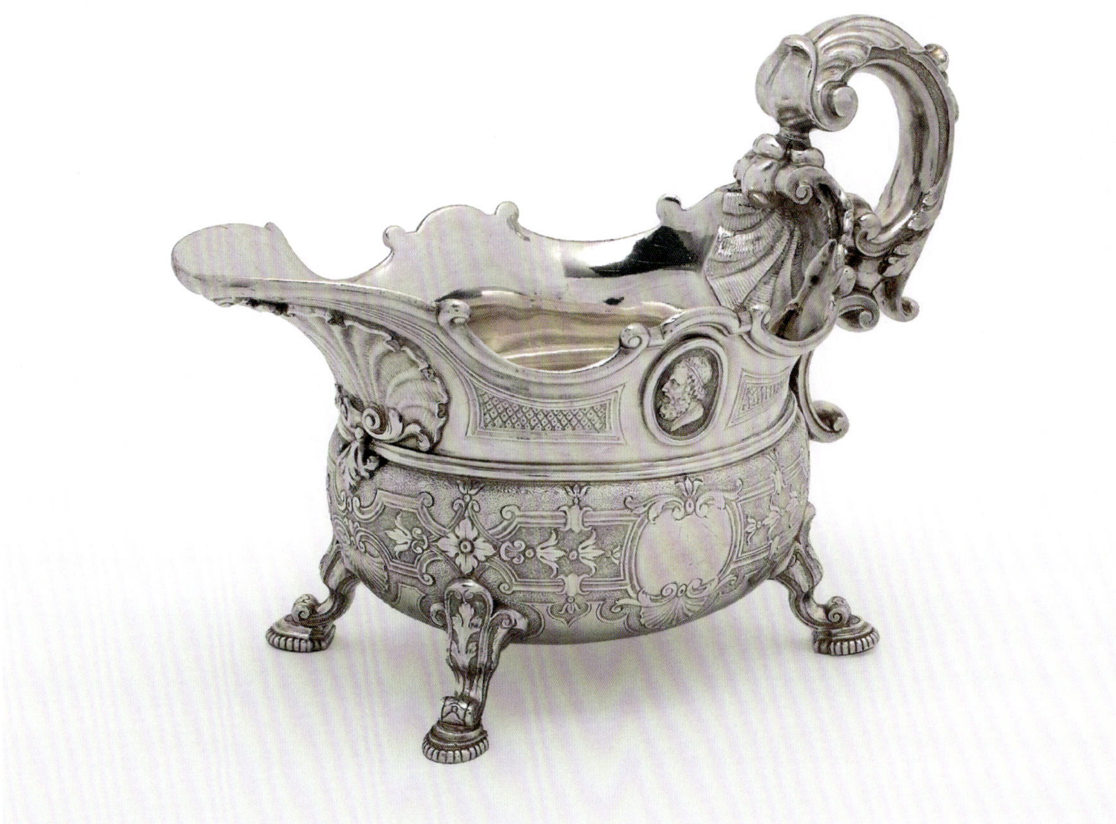

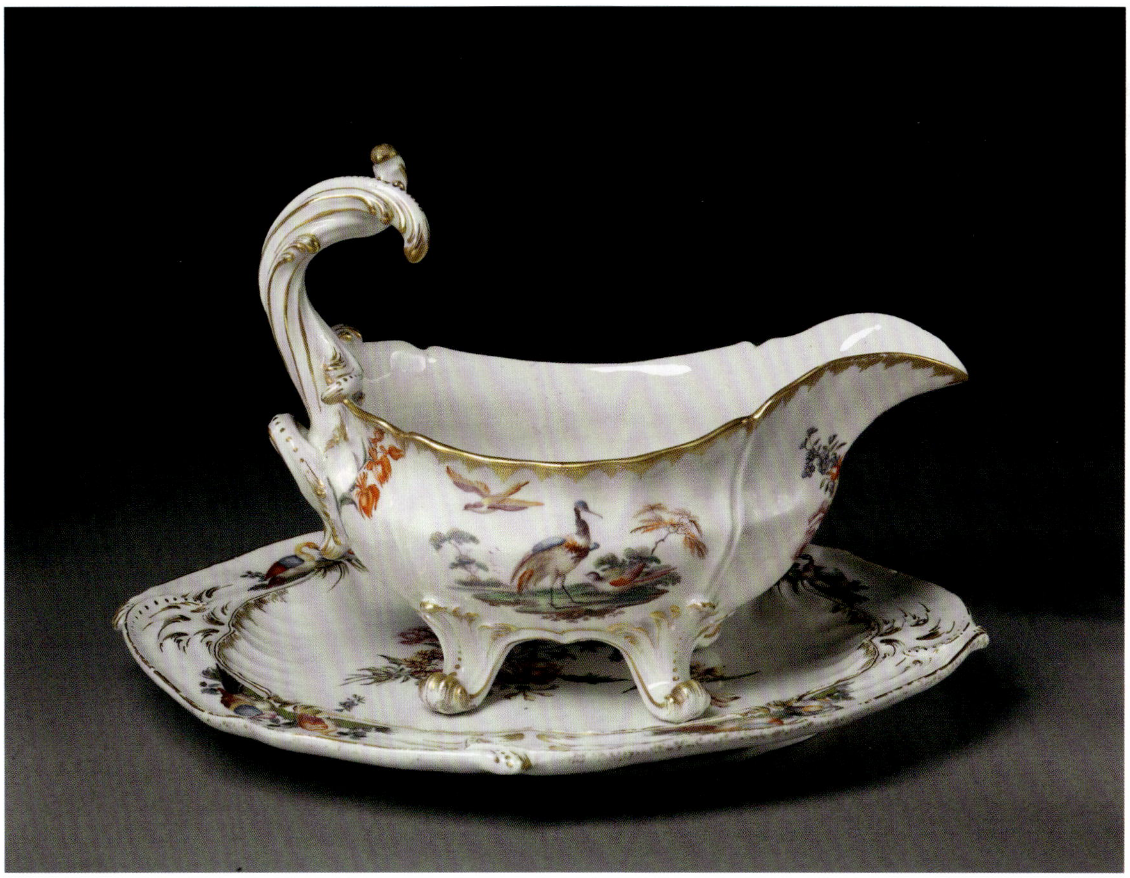

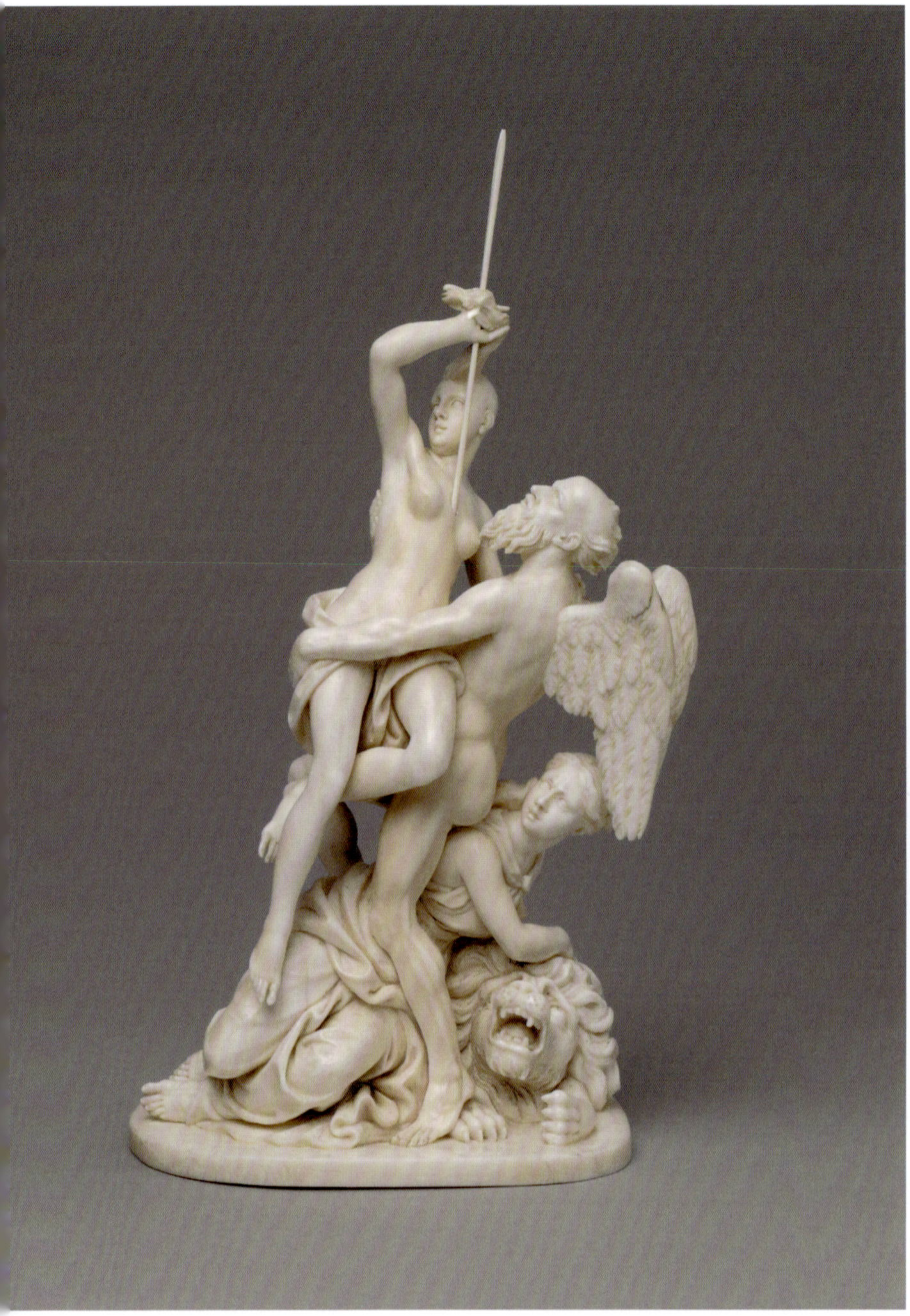

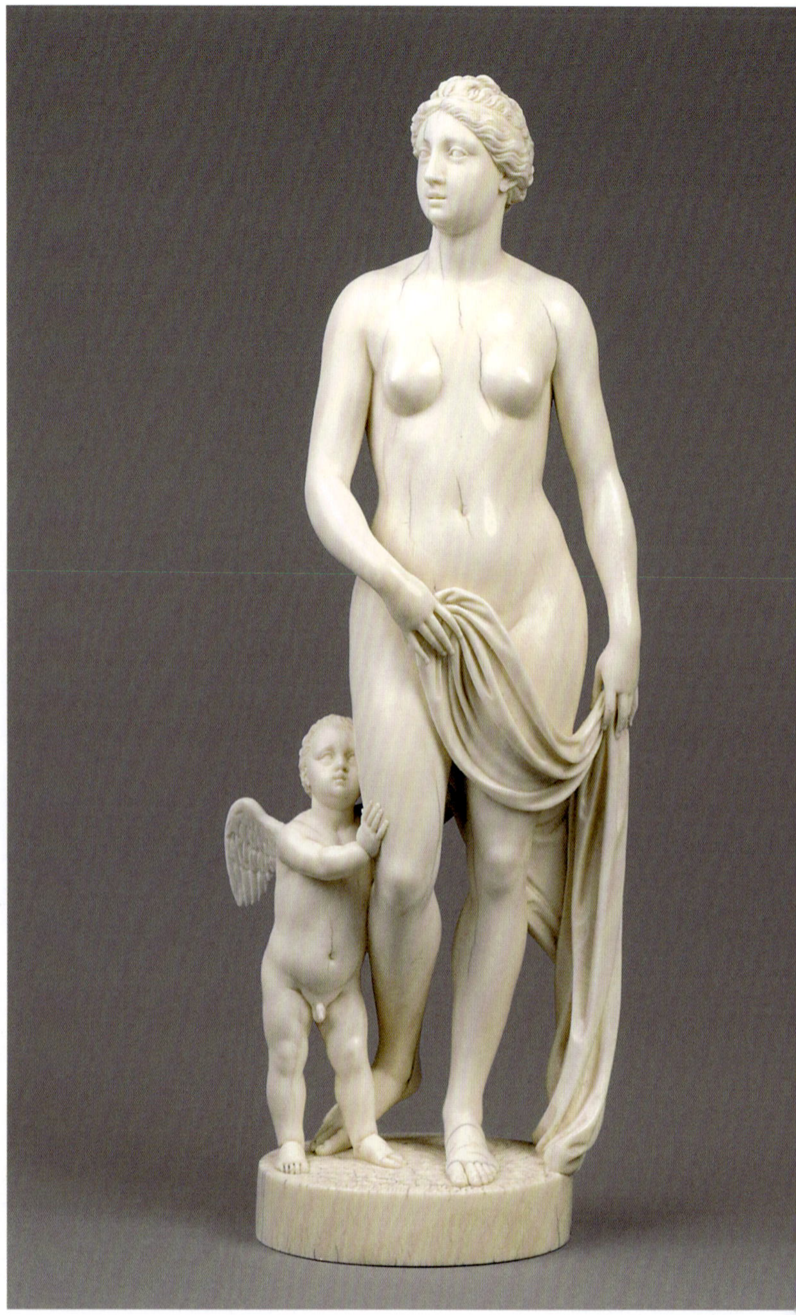

ABOVE LEFT

141 *Time, Opportunity and Penitence*

David Le Marchand, London, *c.*1700–20
Ivory, ht 23.7 cm
Victoria and Albert Museum, London (A.1–1935)

The winged, bearded figure of Time seizes the nymph Opportunity but she takes her own life: tearing her hair, she kills herself with a long spear. Beneath, a female Penitence crouches with a lion. Le Marchand probably used as his source the print after Thomas Regnaudin's marble sculpture *Abduction of Cybele by Saturn* created for Louis XIV's gardens at Versailles. Statuettes based on full-sized sculpture were also produced in bronze.

ABOVE RIGHT AND RIGHT

142 *Venus and Cupid*

David Le Marchand, London, after 1718
Ivory, ht 33.5 cm
Victoria and Albert Museum, London (A.69–1926)

143 *Venus and Cupid*

Chelsea manufactory, London, 1758–69
Porcelain, ht 19.1 cm
Victoria and Albert Museum, London (C.677–1925)

An early 18th-century Dieppe retailer advertised both sacred and secular ivory statues for the mantelpiece. Dieppe-trained David Le Marchand, in London from 1700, carved small-scale figures in ivory. Forty years later the Chelsea porcelain version was clothed and coloured.

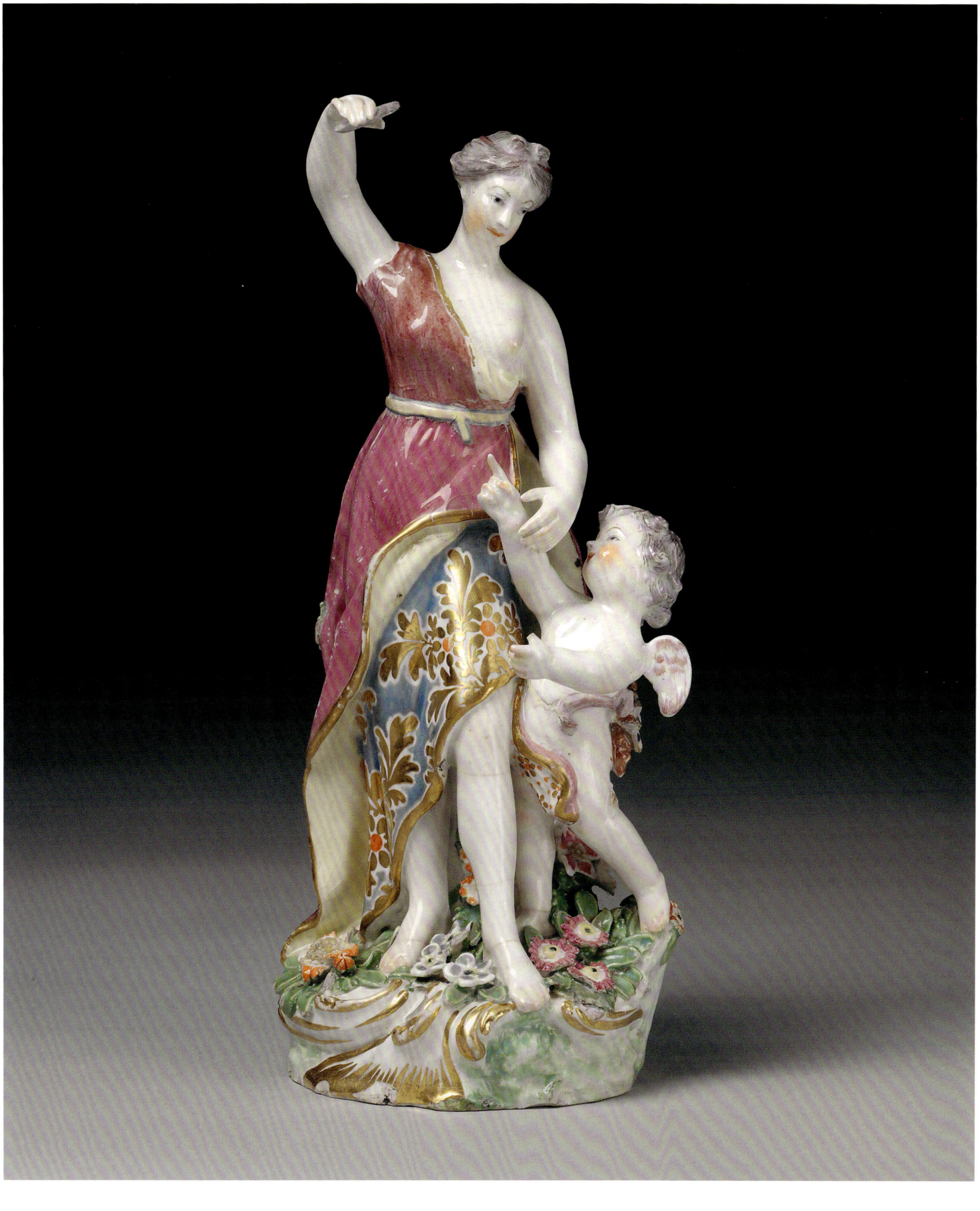

> *a sort of fine white ware made here by himself from native materials of our own country, which appeared as good as any of the finest Porcelaine or China Ware; and ... preferable for its fineness to the Ware of Dresden and seem'd to answer to the character of the true Japan.*[13]

The name Bryand appears in French church registers in London and Dublin later in the century. He may be Thomas Bryand, named in February 1746 as partner of the potter Joseph Farmer of Lane Delph, Staffordshire. The name 'Bryan' occurs in Staffordshire parish registers – the additional 'd' may be explained by local dialect. The partnership only lasted 12 months, as by February 1747 Thomas Briand had died a pauper.[14]

There were links between British potters and Huguenots who had settled in the American colonies. In May 1743, Andrew Duché (1710–1778) from Savannah, Georgia, who claimed to have made porcelain in America and to have discovered supplies of kaolin clay there in 1739, came to London to join Huguenot relatives.[15] His grandfather was from La Rochelle and his father had settled in Pennsylvania. Duché had heard about a London porcelain manufactory, possibly that at Bow, where initial efforts by Bristol merchant Edward Heylyn (1695–1765) and Irish artist Thomas Frye (1710–1762) were under way (although the first Bow patent was for blue-and-white wares). Duché planned to export kaolin clay from Virginia to meet the new demand, yet he returned to Charleston, South Carolina, in 1744, after a fruitless journey, and the export of kaolin clay was undertaken by Cornelius Doherty instead. The Port of London archives confirm that 20 tons of clay to the value of £5 were imported from Carolina in 1743/4. The first patent for the Bow manufactory, dated 6 December 1744, claims that they used 'an earth, the produce of the Chirokee nation in America, called by the natives unaker'.[16]

Some of the figures produced at the Bow porcelain manufactory from 1750 to 1765 are marked with an impressed 'T' or 'To' indicating the name of the 'repairer', the craftsman responsible for assembling the separate sections which make up the model. The mark recurs on porcelain figures manufactured at Worcester, Bristol and Plymouth in the early 1770s. It has been identified as representing Toulouse, the name of a family of modellers from France, possibly including Charles Toullous (fl.1750–d.1807), who occurs in the Bow parish registers in October 1750, and John Toullouse, who died in 1807–9.[17] The name Toullouse is associated with figures representing the Muses, of which only seven of the original nine are known today. Two of these, Euterpe and Erato, are in the Victoria and Albert Museum and dated 1747–50.[18] They are inscribed 'Eraton for the love' and 'Euterpe for the musical instruments' and Clio, another from the set, now in the collections at Castle Howard, as Clion (suggesting that English was not the inscriber's first language and that he may have been of French origin).[19]

The 1745 petition of the Vincennes factory provides the first reference to the manufacture of porcelain in Britain as 'un nouvel établissement qui vent de se former en Angleterre d'une manufacture de porcelaine qui parait plus belle que ce de Saxe'.[20] This probably refers to the Chelsea manufactory established by Soho goldsmith Nicholas Sprimont in 1744. Yet the earliest advertisement for Chelsea porcelain in *The Daily Advertiser* only appeared on 21 and 24 February 1749:

> *The undertaker of the Manufactory of China Ware hereby acquaints the Publick that he has prepared a large Parcel of that Ware, consisting of Tea and Coffee Pots, Cups and Saucers of various Forms besides several other Things as well as for Use as Ornament which he proposes to offer for Sale on Tuesday next, the 28th instant, at the Manufactory at Chelsea, from which time the Warehouse will be open constantly and Attendance given.*

Limited supplies were promptly exhausted, as revealed by the next advertisement, published on 3 March 1749:

> *Mr. Sprimont takes the Liberty to acquaint the Publick that the favourable Reception and general Approbation his China Ware has met with, makes it necessary for him to suspend all further sale thereof at his Warehouse after Tomorrow, that he may have Time to make a sufficient Quantity of such Things he has observed to be most agreeable to the Taste of those who have done him the Honour to look at his Performance. He will nevertheless, till he shall be in a Condition to sell again, receive such orders for Plates Dishes and all Table Utensils, as well as for Tea, Coffee or Chocolate Services, as any Persons may think fit to give him.*[21]

Contemporary newspapers advertised new stock at Chelsea; in 1749 this included luxury tea, coffee and chocolate services, plates, dishes and table utensils. Many were based on Meissen prototypes. Fashionable table wares were designed to appeal to rich, aristocratic clients and to replace expensive

144 Teapot

Chelsea manufactory, 1747
Porcelain, ht 9.84 cm, l. including spout 15.24 cm
Victoria and Albert Museum, London (2877&A-1901)

The flower-decorated teapot is small, a reflection of the high cost of tea in mid-18th-century Britain. In 1747 the tax on tea imported from China was increased and official figures for imports fell. However, smuggling of tea continued.

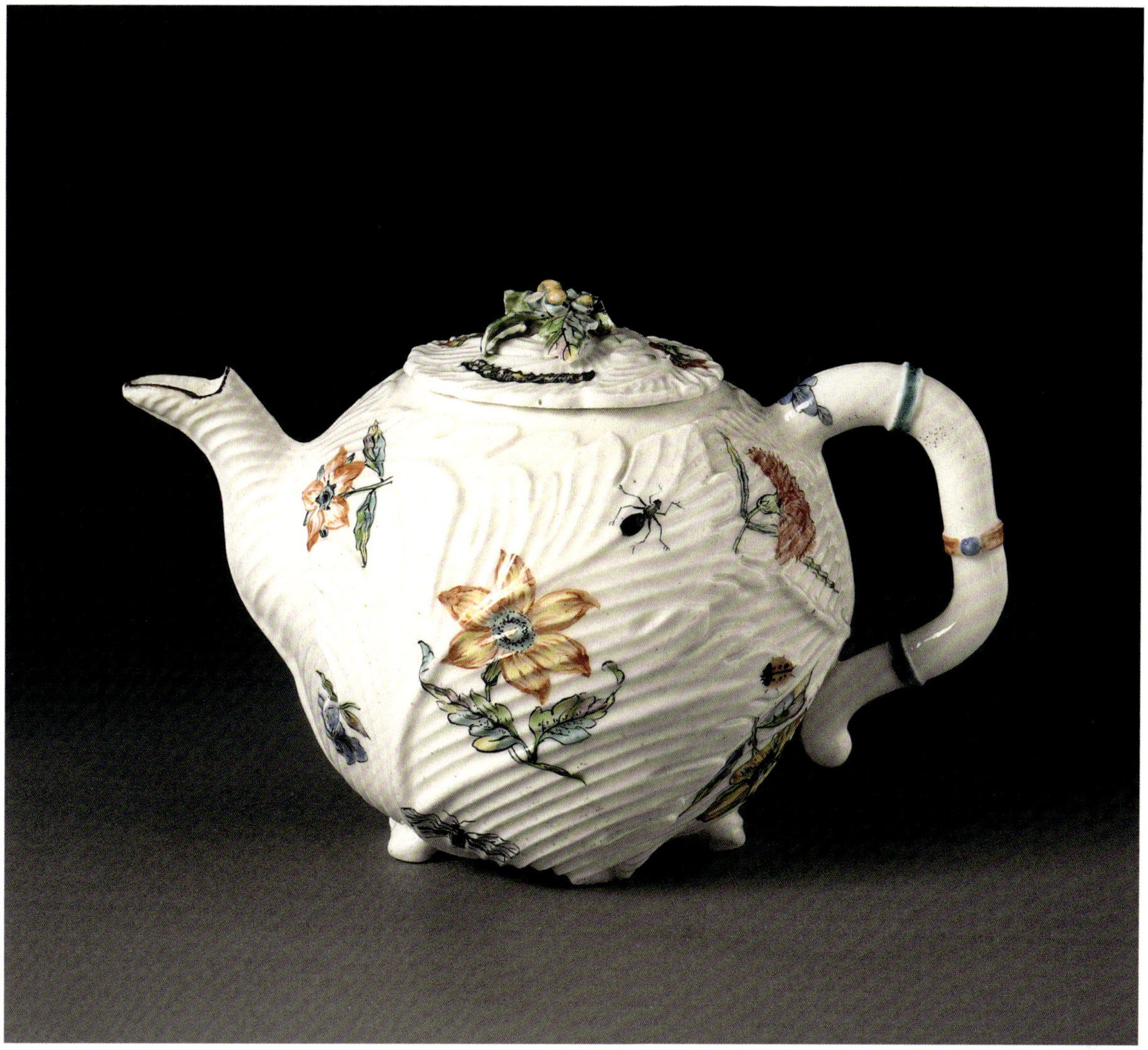

foreign imports. Chelsea porcelain of this date has a glassy composition that could not withstand the thermal shock of contact with boiling water, so the teapot (plate 144) had to be slowly warmed up before use. Partly because of the limitations of the material, and partly out of preference, the Chelsea manufactory concentrated on ornamental pieces and dessert wares.

Sprimont was born in Liège, a Catholic Prince-Bishopric, the son of Peter Sprimont and Gertrude Goffin. He was probably apprenticed to his uncle, goldsmith-jeweller Nicholas Joseph Sprimont (*c.*1678–1744), and in 1736 may also have trained in Paris with the pre-eminent silversmith Thomas Germain (1673–1748) as he travelled through France from Geneva.[22] In February 1742/3 Sprimont took on his first apprentice in London, James Lamistre, of Huguenot origin. In the previous November he married Ann Protin at the Knightsbridge Chapel. Sprimont entered his first sponsor's mark at Goldsmiths' Hall in January 1742/3 from Compton Street, Soho. He had strong links with the London Huguenot community and his marriage in an Anglican church demonstrates his Protestant faith.[23] In September 1744 Sprimont leased and insured a house in Church Lane East, Chelsea.

Nicholas Sprimont's porcelain venture was inspired by a 'casual acquaintance with a chemist', the German F.J. d'Ostermann.[24] His earliest Chelsea products (plate 145) are marked by an incised triangle. Sprimont was more familiar with the latest French Rococo designs than his British competitors (plate 146), while the small novelty teapots made at the Chelsea manufactory, including a squatting 'Chinaman' clutching a parrot (plate 147), were inspired by *grotesque* teapots made at Saint-Cloud. Whereas Saint-Cloud porcelains are smooth, glassy and very white, early Chelsea porcelain paste is much less refined: finer details of modelling are obscured by thick opaque-white glaze containing tin oxide. These early white

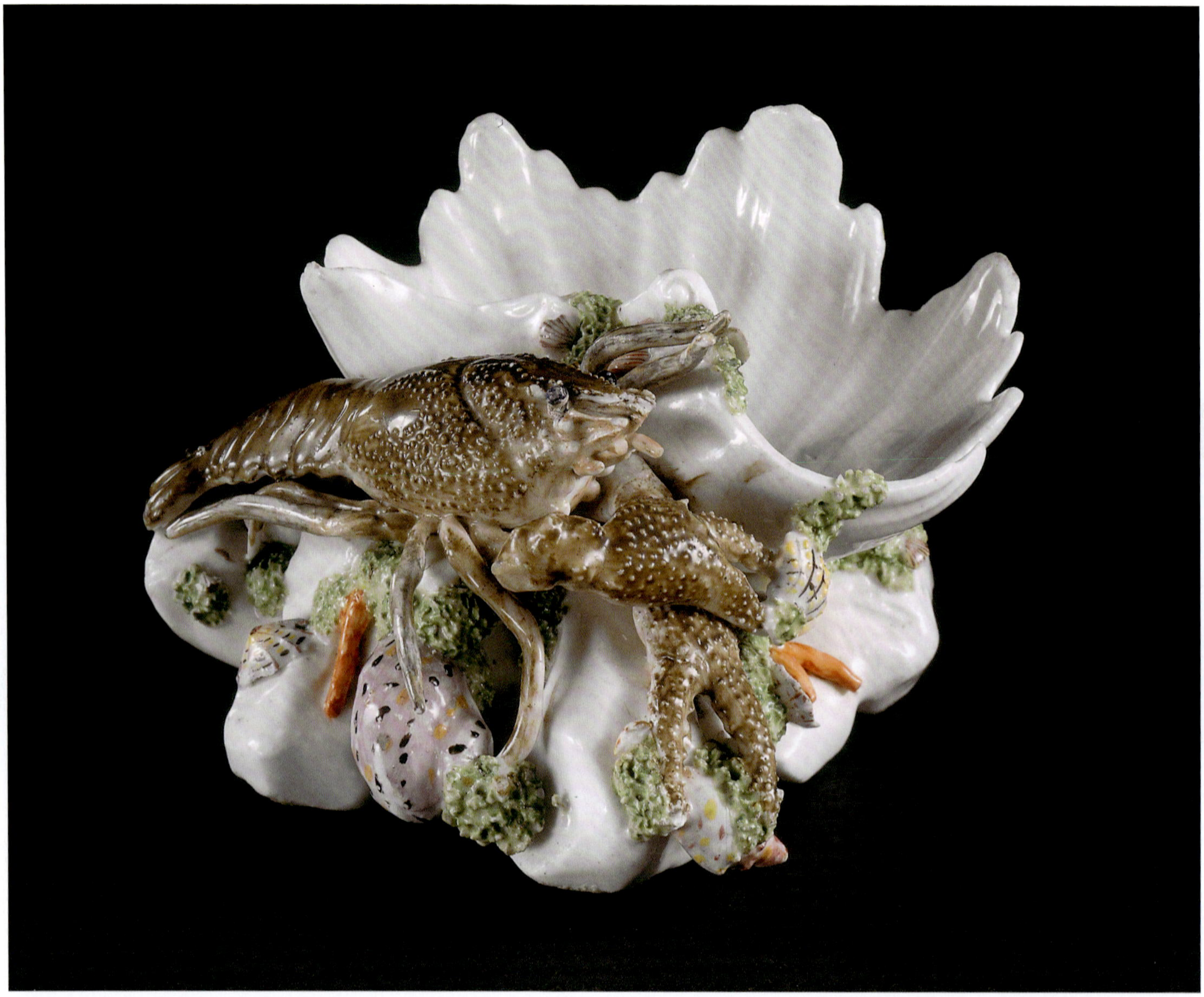

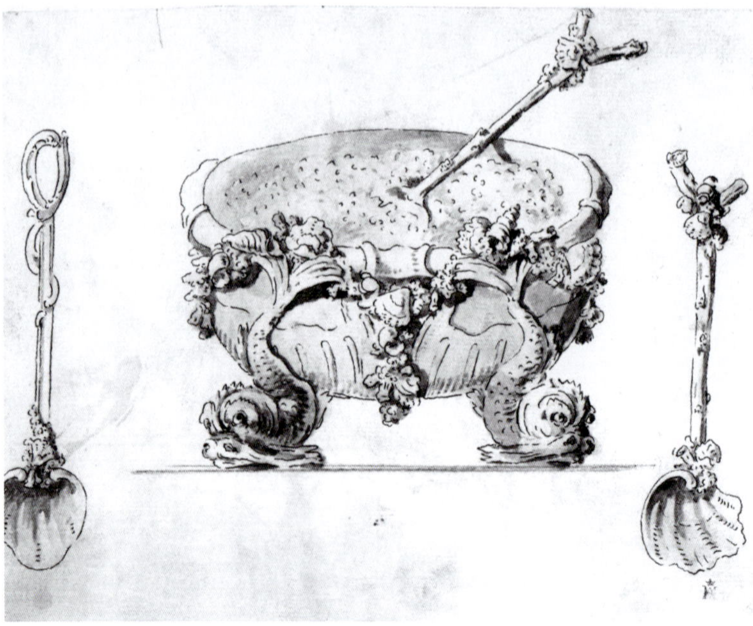

145 Crayfish salt cellar

Attributed to Nicholas Sprimont, London, 1752–6
Chelsea porcelain marked with an incised triangle, 5 × 12.1 cm
Victoria and Albert Museum, London (C.73–1938)

Earliest Chelsea products are marked with an incised triangle and include salt cellars with crayfish based on a silver prototype.

146 Design for a silver salt cellar and spoons

Nicholas Sprimont, London, 1742
Pencil, pen and black ink, brown wash on laid paper, 15.1 × 19.3 cm
Victoria and Albert Museum, London (2592)

This design relates to the marine service supplied to Frederick Prince of Wales by Sprimont and the Huguenot goldsmith Paul Crespin. Dolphins embellish the salt cellar and the spoons have shell bowls, one having a stem imitating coral.

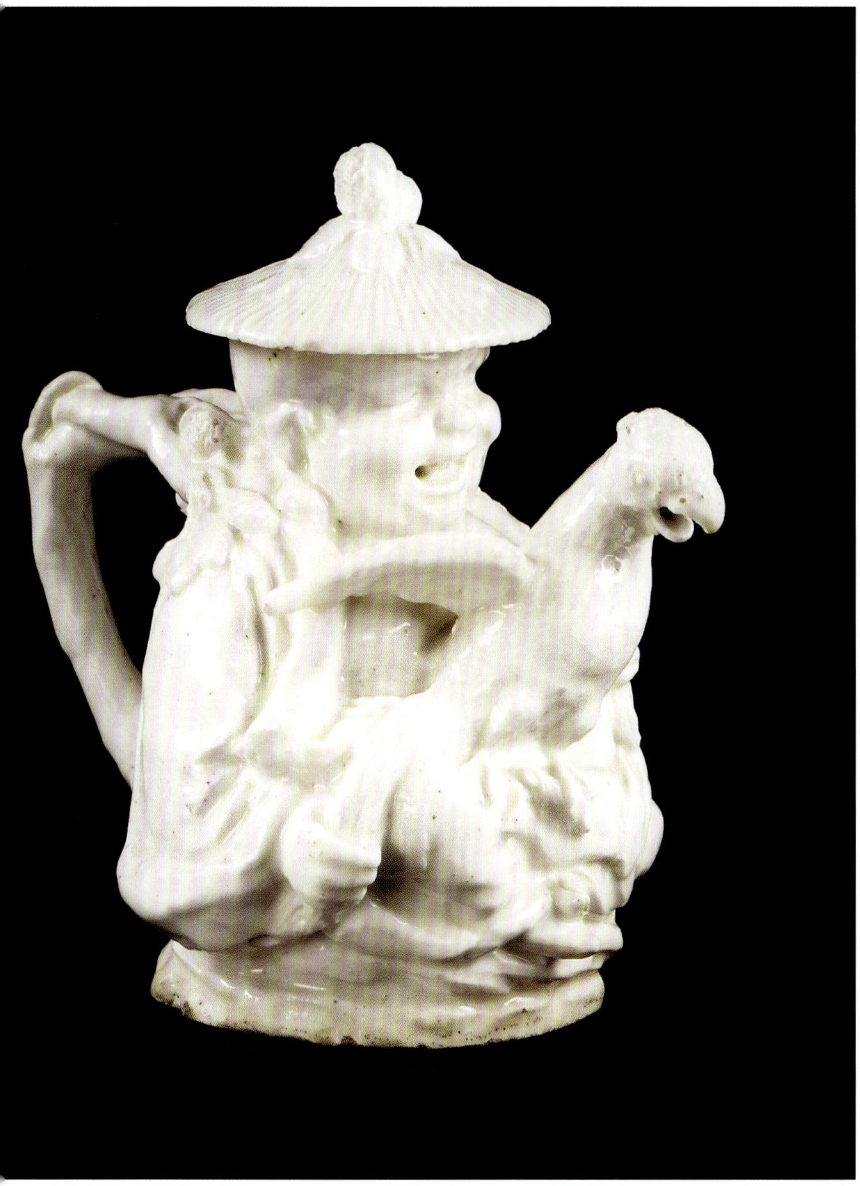

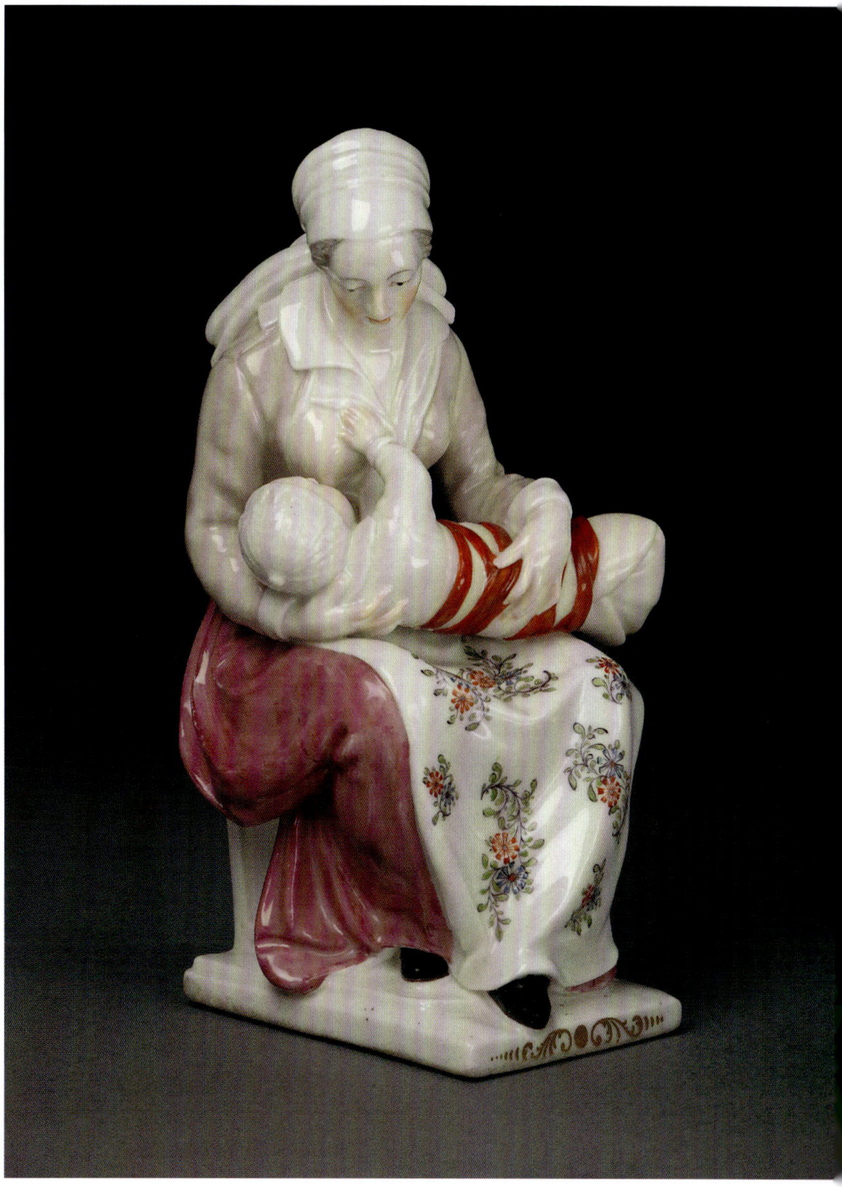

147 Novelty teapot

Nicholas Sprimont and Charles Gouyn, London, 1745–9
Chelsea porcelain marked with an incised triangle, 17.1 × 17 cm
Victoria and Albert Museum, London (C.46&A 1938)

Desperate for new models, the Chelsea proprietors made fashionable versions of cheap, slip-cast teapots mass-produced in Staffordshire. Small novelty Chelsea teapots include this squatting 'Chinaman' clutching a parrot inspired by *grotesque* teapots made at Saint-Cloud, with which Sprimont was familiar.

148 A wet nurse

Chelsea manufactory, London, *c.*1755
Porcelain, 17.8 cm
Victoria and Albert Museum, London (C.29-1938)

The nursing mother with the child at her right breast is inspired by a French 16th-century prototype in earthenware or bronze. She wears a kerchief tied on her head, a tight bodice and a full skirt, over which were painted small sprays of 'Indian flowers'. The child, wrapped in a blanket, wears a close-fitting cap and a coat. Details of faces, hair and hands are delicate.

products were soon succeeded by enamelled wares of great refinement.

By 1747 Sprimont's business was also occupying Monmouth House, Lawrence Street, Chelsea – then the factory showroom – which backed onto his Church Lane property. Although production was in Chelsea, sales were later conducted from a warehouse in Pall Mall, and in 1749 the Lawrence Street site became a manufactory. The business was closed for a year in 1749–50 for reorganization and expansion. Surviving Chelsea figures created during the following decade include a wet nurse sitting with the child at her breast, inspired by a French sixteenth-century prototype in earthenware or bronze (plate 148) and the rare but damaged Chelsea figure of Pulcinella (plate 149).

Competition from Meissen porcelain was considerable. In 1752–3 Sprimont published *The Case of the Undertaker of the Chelsea Manufacture of Porcelain Ware* as an anonymous plea to the government to curb British patrons from importing Meissen to be sold on at auction and by specialist London retailers: 'Considerable parcels are now allowed to pass at the Custom House, as for private use, by which means the shops abound with new stock and public sales are advertised at the very beginning of the winter and in large quantities.' He deliberately imitated Meissen and through his patron Sir Everard Fawkener (1694–1758), a wealthy merchant trading with the Levant and secretary to William, Duke of Cumberland, lobbied the British envoy in Dresden, Sir Charles Hanbury Williams (1708–1759), to send 'over fifty or three-score pounds' worth of models for copying' at Chelsea.[25] From 1756, during the Seven Years' War, supplies of Meissen ceased and French competition was virtually eliminated. Sprimont developed a new line in French-style vases. Over the next two years Fawkener retained an investment in the Chelsea manufactory, to the tune of £1,495, until it closed for a further year due to Sprimont's poor health. When it reopened the gold anchor introduced in 1756 was still used as the mark.

Sprimont was a skilled designer who 'supplies or directs the models of everything'.[26] His design for a tureen for his Chelsea landlord, Thomas Coke, Earl of Leicester, bears an earl's coronet and ostrich supporters (plate 150). Another signed design by Sprimont shows glasses on a silver dish decorated with vine leaves and grapes.[27] As Sprimont had less time to design or model for Chelsea, since being a proprietor was a considerable commitment, he delegated this to others, including Brussels-born Joseph Willems (1716–1766), who modelled for Chelsea for over 15 years. Sprimont also trained 30 parish and charity schoolboys, among them William Brown, who described his experience to the Earl of Charlemont in 1772:

> *I served an apprenticeship to Mr Sprimont of Chelsea who was the first person who brought English china to the perfection it now has arrived at. Under him, I was made master of the various branches of the art, and though painting was my particular department in his manufactory, yet with attention I have obtained a thorough practical knowledge of the whole process.*[28]

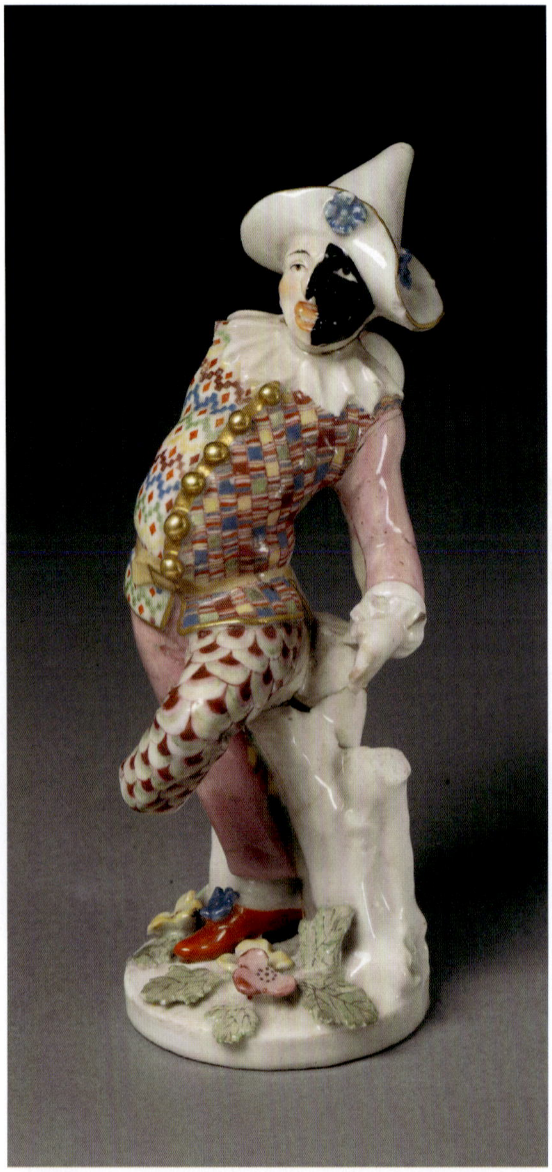

149 *Pulcinella*

Joseph Willems, London, *c.*1755
Chelsea porcelain, ht 16.6 cm
Victoria and Albert Museum, London (C.52–2005)

Copied at Chelsea from Meissen, this figure was found in the grounds of Holland House, Kensington. The figure may have been given in gratitude for the loan of Meissen originals.

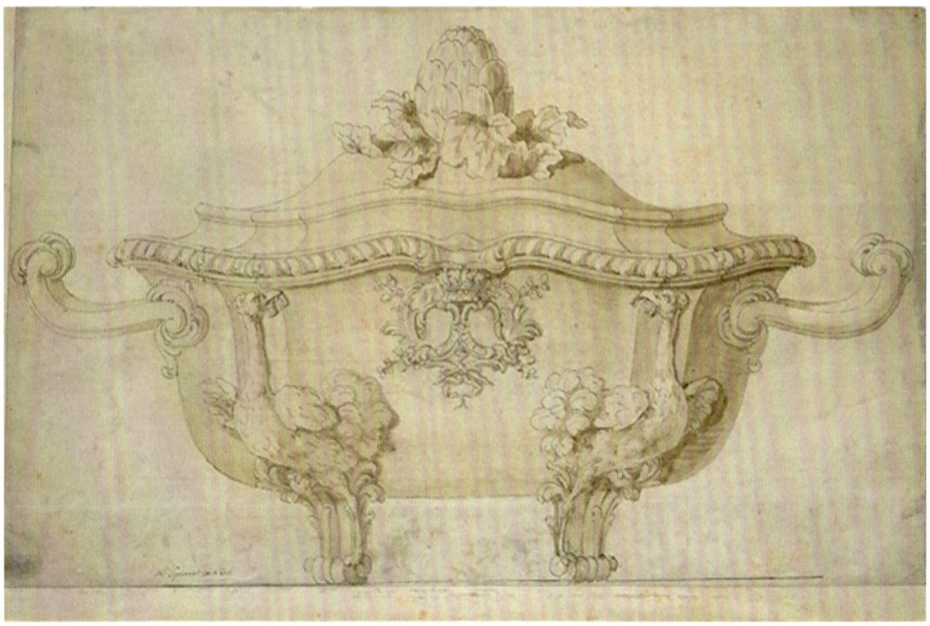

150 Design for a soup tureen for Thomas Coke, 1st Earl of Leicester

Nicholas Sprimont, London, *c.*1742
Pen and black ink with brown ink wash on laid paper, 26 × 43.2 cm
Victoria and Albert Museum, London (E.2606–1917)

Sprimont was a skilled designer who 'supplies or directs the models of everything'. His tureen design bears an earl's coronet and ostrich heraldic supporters for his Chelsea landlord and dates from 1742 to 1744 (when Leicester was ennobled) and the Earl's death in 1759.

151 *Trump, William Hogarth's Pug*
Louis François Roubiliac, London, 1747–50
Chelsea porcelain, 13.2 × 26.5 cm
Victoria and Albert Museum, London (C.101–1966)

Sprimont drew on the London-based Huguenot community for some aspects of his success. Hogarth's pug, Trump, was modelled by Roubiliac, a close friend of both Hogarth and Sprimont.

Sprimont drew on the London-based Huguenot community for some aspects of his success. In 1745 the proposal to insert a relief panel of Chelsea porcelain into the base of Roubiliac's monument to Bishop Hough demonstrates the links between Roubiliac and Sprimont.[29] Hogarth's pug dog, Trump, modelled by Roubiliac (plate 151), dates from 1747–50. An exquisite model of a child's head, also attributed to Roubiliac (plate 152), may represent his daughter Sophie, Sprimont's goddaughter. Roubiliac may have modelled his young daughter before she left for France to live with her paternal uncle, an engraver in Paris, after her mother died in 1747.[30]

Charles Gouyn, a jeweller from Dieppe, was senior partner in the Chelsea manufactory until about 1748. His father, Richard, had owned at least two shops in Dieppe, where the family traded in ivory; as demand declined, they became jewellers. Charles Gouyn lived in the parish of St George's, Hanover Square, from 1737, although he was a rate-payer in the parish of St James's, Piccadilly, for almost fifty years (1735–83). Around 1748 Gouyn left Chelsea to set up his own manufactory in London's West End. Originally attributed to Sprimont's Chelsea factory, Gouyn's products were first identified as distinctive in the 1920s (although their maker was not named until 1993) and associated with one of his earliest ornamental figures, the *Girl-in-a-Swing* (plate 153).[31] Among the products of the 'Girl-in-a-Swing' manufactory, now known as the St James's Factory, were small scent bottles mounted in gold, often with enamelled French inscriptions, appealing to contemporary taste for the pastoral, animals, dance, flowers and music. In 1750 Gouyn was described as 'Late Proprietor and Chief Manager of the Chelsea House'.[32] Ann Gouyn, probably his wife, who in 1763 exhibited 'Two pieces of flowers cut in card' at London's Free Society of Artists and gave her address as 'At Mrs. Carnsu's, Hosier, Piccadilly', may have modelled for the Gouyn factory.[33]

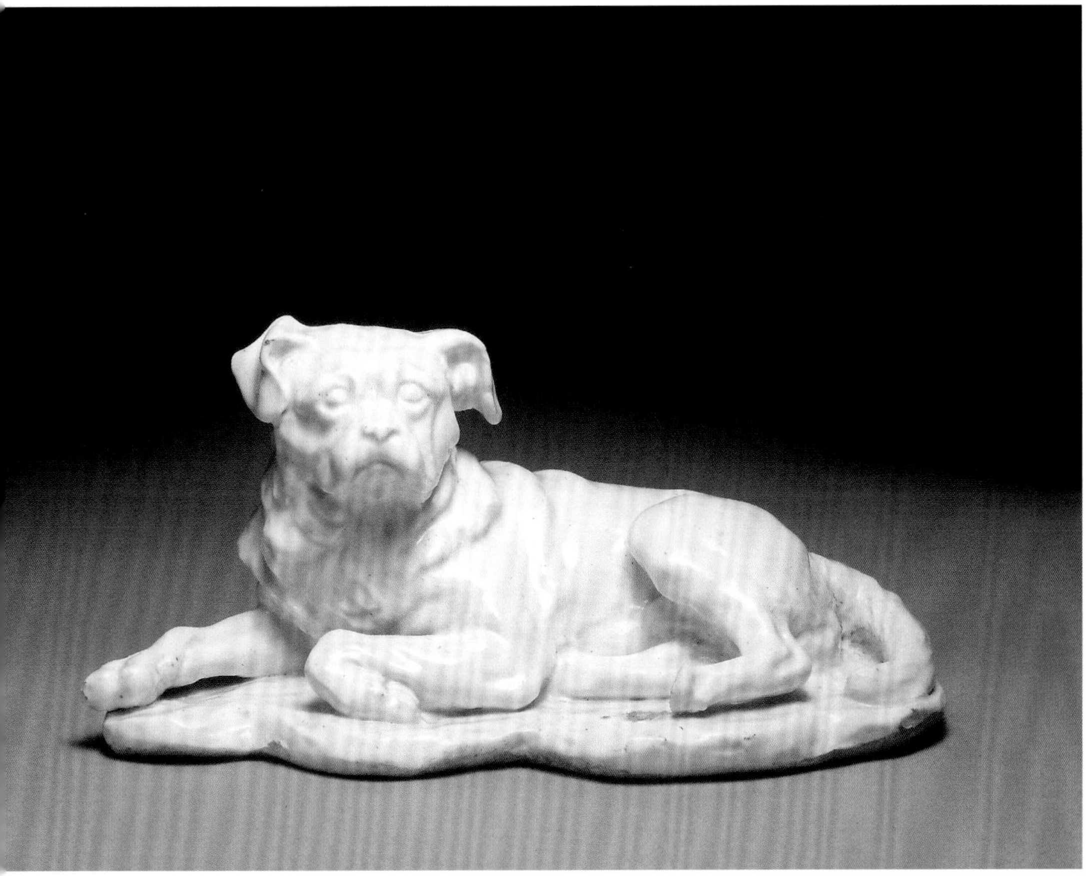

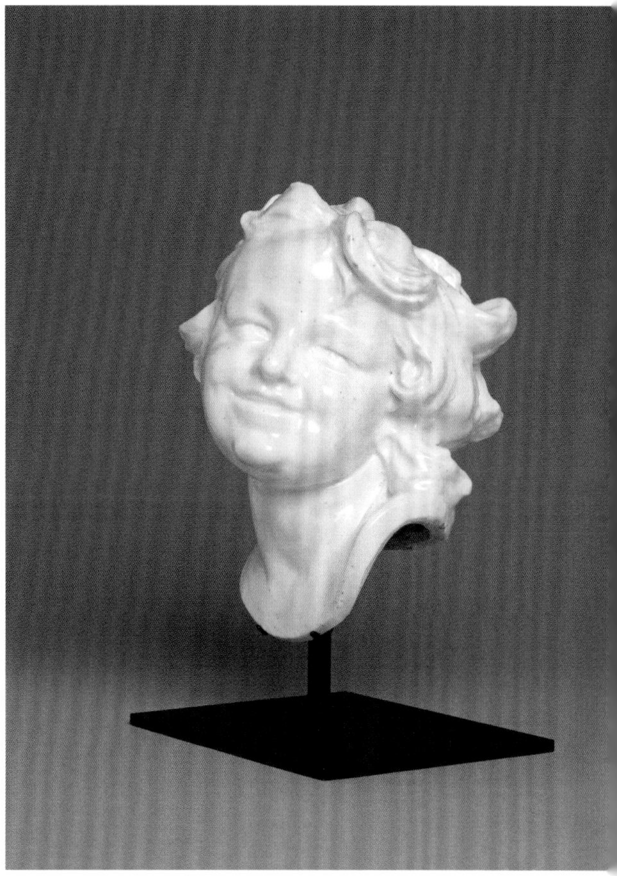

152 *Head of a Laughing Child*
Attributed to Louis François Roubiliac, London, 1748–50
Chelsea porcelain, 19.7 × 16.7 cm
Victoria and Albert Museum, London (C.37–2019)

It has been suggested that this exquisite model may represent Roubiliac's daughter Sophie, Sprimont's goddaughter. The subject was associated with the Flemish sculptor François Duquesnoy (1597–1643), whose work was much admired.

The *Dancing Girl* from Gouyn's factory (plate 154) was influenced by the Chelsea *Columbine* of *c.*1751, itself based on a Meissen model from the *Commedia dell'Arte* series. After Gouyn parted company with Sprimont, he set up the St James's factory near Piccadilly, where he manufactured porcelain until about 1761. Figures and larger models were only made here in the early years: small seals, scent bottles and teawares were the largest output.[34] Gouyn's son Peter was apprenticed to Peter

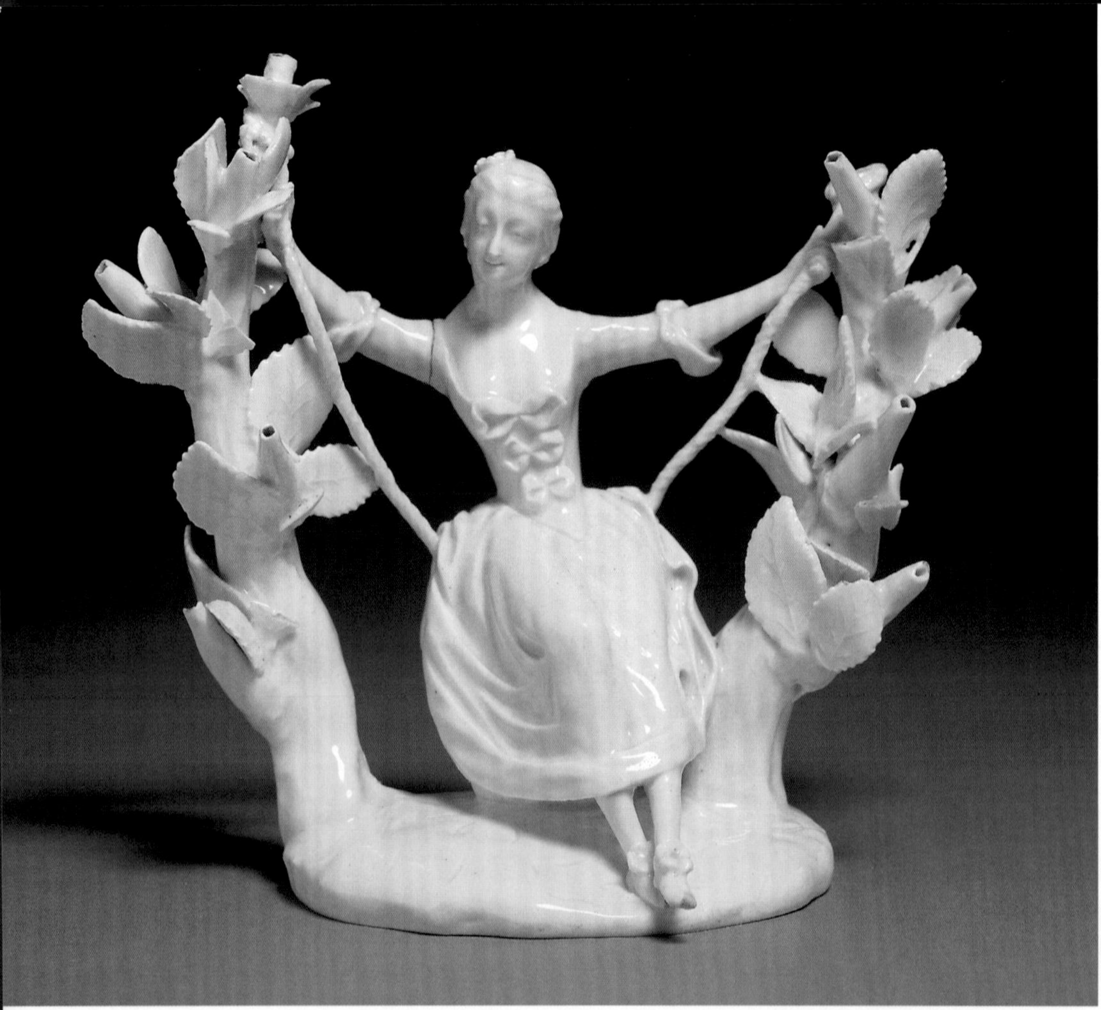

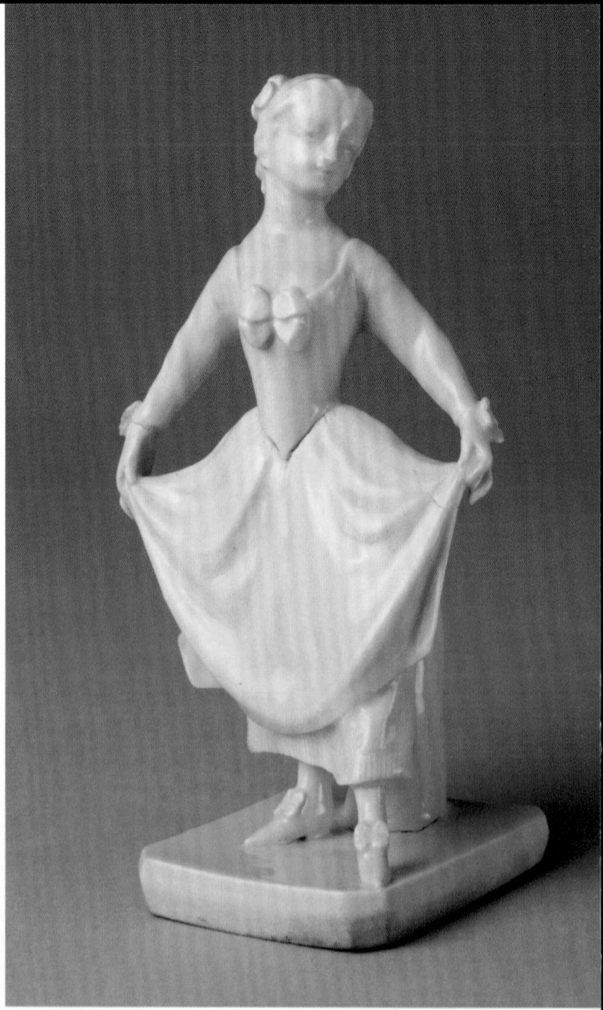

Nicholas Frisquet (d. before 1803), a jeweller of Huguenot descent in Lothbury, City of London, in 1757. In 1763 Charles Gouyn is listed as jeweller in *Mortimer's Universal Directory* but in 1769 he was declared bankrupt. His will was proved on 12 January 1785.[35] Jean Hellot (1685–1766), chief scientist at the Sèvres Porcelain manufactory (who was also a Fellow of the Royal Society in London) describes Gouyn's operation thus:

> *This is how is built the kiln of Chelsea of which the porcelain factory is near the church. It was first established by Mr Gouin, brother of a Paris jeweller of that name, born at Dieppe in the so-called Reformed Faith … Mr. Gouin left, with the loss of part of his Funds, and makes at his house in St. James' St, very beautiful small porcelain figures. The present [1759] undertaker of the Chilsea [sic] factory is one named Spremont [sic] from Liege. The turner was a Frenchman named Martin [not previously recorded]. He left Chelsea and went to Lambeth to work for Jacson [sic] a faience maker. The modeller is one named Flanchet, a pupil of M. Duplessis. The draughtsman is named Duvivier [who managed the decorating studio at Chelsea]: he is Flemish.*[36]

By March 1749 Nicholas Sprimont was keen to declare that he and Gouyn had separated. *The Daily Advertiser* announced that Sprimont 'gives Notice, that he has no sort of Connexion with, nor for a considerable time past has put any of his Ware into that Shop in St. James' Street which was the Chelsea China Warehouse'.[37] The 'Warehouse in Pall Mall on the North side towards the West End' bore the inscription 'Chelsea Porcelaine, made by N. Sprimont is sold here only': as Sprimont wanted to avoid association with inferior products produced by Gouyn's rival manufactory.[38]

By 1754, the production of such 'toys' was well established. The *Public Advertiser* announced sale by auction from 23 November to 21 December that year 'by order of the Proprietors of the Chelsea Porcelain Manufactory' of 'All the entire Stock of Porcelain Toys, brought from their warehouse in Pall Mall; consisting of Snuff-boxes; Smelling Bottles, Etwees, and Trinkets for Watches (mounted in Gold and unmounted) in various beautiful shapes of an elegant Design and curiously painted in Enamel'. The sale included 'A large Parcel of Porcelain Hafts for Table and Dessert Knives and Forks'. In January the previous year Nathaniel Jefferys (1758–1810), Cutler to the King, had advertised 'China Knives and Forks of the Chelsea Manufactory

153 *Girl-in-a-Swing*
Charles Gouyn factory St James's, London, 1749–59
Porcelain, 15.9 × 16.8 cm
Victoria and Albert Museum, London (C.587–1922)

Facing forward, the figurine is less well-finished at the back, evidence that it was intended for display against a wall, on a chimneypiece or in a glazed cabinet.

154 *Dancing Girl*
Charles Gouyn factory, St James's, London, 1750–55
Porcelain, ht 14.6 cm
Victoria and Albert Museum, London (C.328–1919)

This figure was inspired by the Chelsea porcelain figure of Columbine, which was itself based on a Meissen model. There was a great interest in dance which formed part of theatrical entertainment in mid-18th-century Europe.

155 *Nicholas Sprimont with his wife Anne and his sister-in-law Susannah Protin*
Unknown artist, London, 1759–62
Oil on canvas
Victoria and Albert Museum, London, acquired 2021

The undecorated vases depicted here date from 1759 to 1762, the gold anchor period, when the addition of bone ash made the paste retain its shape during the firing process. One vase is based on a Vincennes model by French court goldsmith Jean Claude Duplessis, probably copied from a *potpourri à jour* in the 2nd Viscount Bolingbroke's collection.

in the greatest variety of most beautiful Dresden patterns'.[39] The 1754 Chelsea advertisement explained that 'the things are in lots suitable for Jewellers, Goldsmiths, Toyshops, Cutlers and Workmen in these Branches of Business ... Nothing of the above kind was in their former Sale, nor will anything of the same sort as this be sold from the Manufactory till after next year'.[40] All the items in the sale were marked with an anchor in overglaze red. They competed with silver toys supplied for export by Sprimont's former goldsmith associate Paul Crespin (plates 184–5). Traditionally sold by jewellers, such stock may have been inspired by Sprimont's brother Jean Pierre (1709–1786), a manufacturing jeweller in Liège. Chelsea toys were intended for wholesale to jewellers, goldsmiths, toyshops and cutlers. A scent bottle and candle nozzle found on the Chelsea Church Lane East site suggests that the 'red anchor' toys were made there.

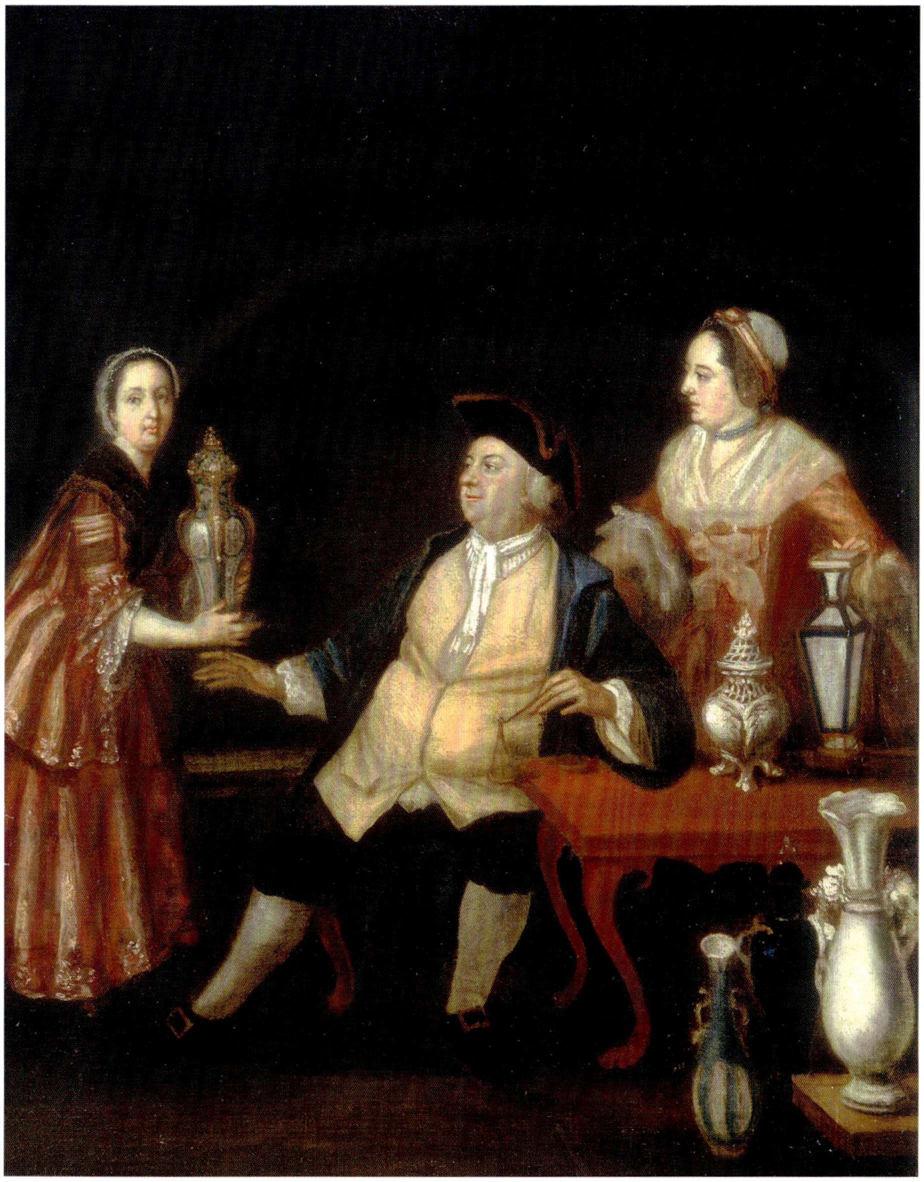

London toyshops included 'the toy woman à la mode',[41] Mrs Chenevix, daughter of Mr Deards, the toyshop owner at the Star at the Haymarket end of Pall Mall. His other daughter, Mrs Bertrand, widow of Huguenot goldsmith Paul Bertrand, ran a 'toy shop' in fashionable Bath that supplied Frederick, Prince of Wales with silver, jewellery, watches and porcelain, including 'A Groupe of China figures' for £5 5s and 'a pair of Old China Candlesticks' for £4 4s.[42] Mrs Chenevix ran the London shop established in Suffolk Street by her goldsmith husband, Paul Daniel Chenevix (fl.1731–42), just off Haymarket (plate 213).[43] In 1749 she sold their Thames-side villa in Twickenham to Horace Walpole (1717–1797), which he rebuilt as Strawberry Hill. Further afield in Norwich, toyshop owner Abraham Pigney (fl.1730–62), a trained ivory turner, was a member of the French church there. His retail business sold glass, china and cutlery between 1730 and 1762.[44]

A group portrait of Nicholas Sprimont, his wife Anne and her sister Susannah Protin (plate 155)[45] shows undecorated vases.[46] A Chelsea example with birds on a *Mazarin* blue ground corresponds exactly to the description of Bolingbroke's Vincennes vase.[47] A decorated vase fits those advertised in 1759 as 'some matchless blue and gold vases ... and other pieces of the Pea Green and Gold, never before exhibited'. Sprimont was diagnosed with thrombosis in 1756. His medical condition is visible in the group portrait and the impact on production was mentioned in a press notice in January 1763. Susannah Protin, standing to the left of Sprimont in the portrait, was then living with the Sprimonts; contributing to the management of the manufactory, she also decorated Chelsea porcelain.[48] In 1751 Susannah signed the apprenticeship indenture of Richard Dyer (b. *c.*1737) and the transferral of the factory lease to the new owner, the jeweller James Cox (*c.*1723–1800). In August 1769 Sprimont specified a bequest of £1,500 to Susannah.

Sprimont's collection of Dutch, Italian, Flemish and French paintings, including works by Poussin and Watteau, furnished his Chelsea home and from 1762 his terraced house overlooking the bridge at Richmond. In December 1758 he announced the sale of 'all his Pictures ... to enable him to carry on his great Undertaking in the Chelsea Porcelain Manufactory till March next'. Eventually sold at Christie's in March 1771, Sprimont's paintings realized £1,239. After his death, Susannah Protin married Sprimont's friend and Soho neighbour, the upholsterer Francis Deschamps. Sprimont was buried in the Deschamps family vault at St Peter's church, Petersham, near Richmond. His widow, Anne, described him as 'a man of the most unsuspecting and benevolent disposition';[49] they had no children. Anne remarried in 1773.

Early products of the Derby manufactory relied on sculptural prototypes; these figures are of high quality and French style and as good as the best contemporary European porcelain. From 1750 to 1756 the manager at Derby was Andrew Planché, son of Paul Blanchet, a Soho coffee merchant, and Marie Ann Fournier; he was the 'Mr. Flanchet' of Jean Hellot's report in the Sèvres archives. Planché's mother may be connected to Louis-Antoine Fournier (fl.1747–74), who worked with Jean-Claude Chambellin Duplessis (1699–1774) at Vincennes in 1747–9 and then at Chantilly in 1752–6 before going on to found the Copenhagen porcelain factory in 1774. Born on 11 March 1727/8, Planché was baptized at the Ryder Court French church.[50] On completing his apprenticeship to Edward Mountenay, jeweller and goldsmith, in Foster Lane, near Goldsmiths' Hall in 1747,[51] he married Sarah Stone at St Pancras church. Hellot notes that 'Flanchet' worked under the great Duplessis in Paris;[52] Planché may have worked for Sprimont at Chelsea before joining Derby. Although Planché played a key role as Derby factory manager, the best dry-edge figures made there have recently been attributed to the Italian sculptor Agostino Carlini (*c.*1718–1790).[53]

The Derby factory was founded before 1750 with assistance from James Marchand, a Westminster potter who married Mary Oldfield at St Alkmund's church, Derby, in 1752. Planché's two eldest sons, Paul Edmund and James, were baptized at St Alkmund's in 1751.[54] An agreement between William Duesbury, John Heath and Planché is dated 1 January 1756, but Planché left Derby by December that year[55] to join the Westminster jewellery business of his uncle, Anthony Planché; he was still there ten years later.[56] The uncle was probably the son of Antoine Plank, the London jeweller listed in 1704/5.

The earliest figurative products of the Derby manufactory include mythological deities taken from sixteenth- and seventeenth-century sculpture. The figure of Neptune was inspired by a 1652 version by French sculptor Michel Anguier (*c.*1613–1686), one of six miniature deities made for jeweller Tessier de Montarsis (fl.1676–1714) later carved in stone for Versailles and engraved by Louis Desplaces (1682–1739). The Derby Pluto and Cerberus have affinities with *Neptune Calming the Waves* of 1737 by Lambert-Sigisbert Adam (1700–1759). A statue of Jupiter by Italian sculptor Alessandro Algardi (1598–1654), commissioned as one of a set of four by the painter Diego Velázquez (1599–1660) in 1650, was used as a source for the model produced at Derby in the 1750s.[57] The Derby figure of Ceres is based on the marble by Renoit Lassau (1629–1714) at Versailles.[58] The goddess, with castellated crown, stands with right hand outstretched (hand broken on one surviving example), and holds in her left hand the tail of a reversed cornucopia, from which flowers and fruit cascade.

Groups representing the Senses (plate 156), dated 1750–3, demonstrate the taste for chinoiserie. Sources include M. de Ferriol's *Recueil de cent Estampes representant differentes Nations du Levant…* engraved by G. Scotin, published in Paris in 1714,

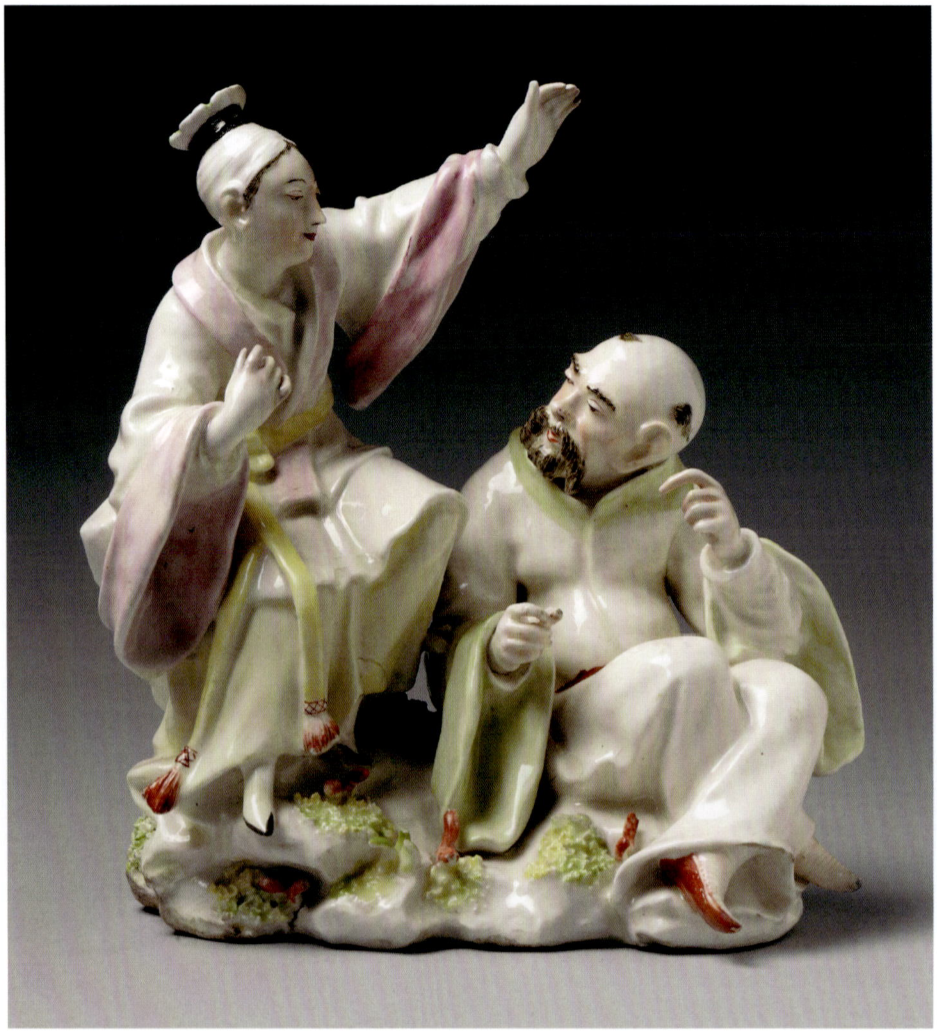

156 *Hearing*
Derby porcelain manufactory, attributed to Agostino Carlini, *c.*1752–5
Porcelain, ht 21 cm
Victoria and Albert Museum, London (C.109–1977)

The Italian sculptor Agostino Carlini has recently been identified as the modeller of the earlier figures produced at the Derby Porcelain Manufactory, with their lively gestures and delicate colouring. The taste for chinoiserie was inspired by contemporary French prints.

157 Barometer with a figure of Urania

Benjamin Vulliamy, London, 1787
Satinwood stand, Derby porcelain, figures, ht 173 cm
Victoria and Albert Museum, London (W.16:1–2-1958)

This barometer by royal clockmaker Benjamin Vulliamy incorporates a figure of Urania modelled by John Deare and produced at the Derby manufactory.

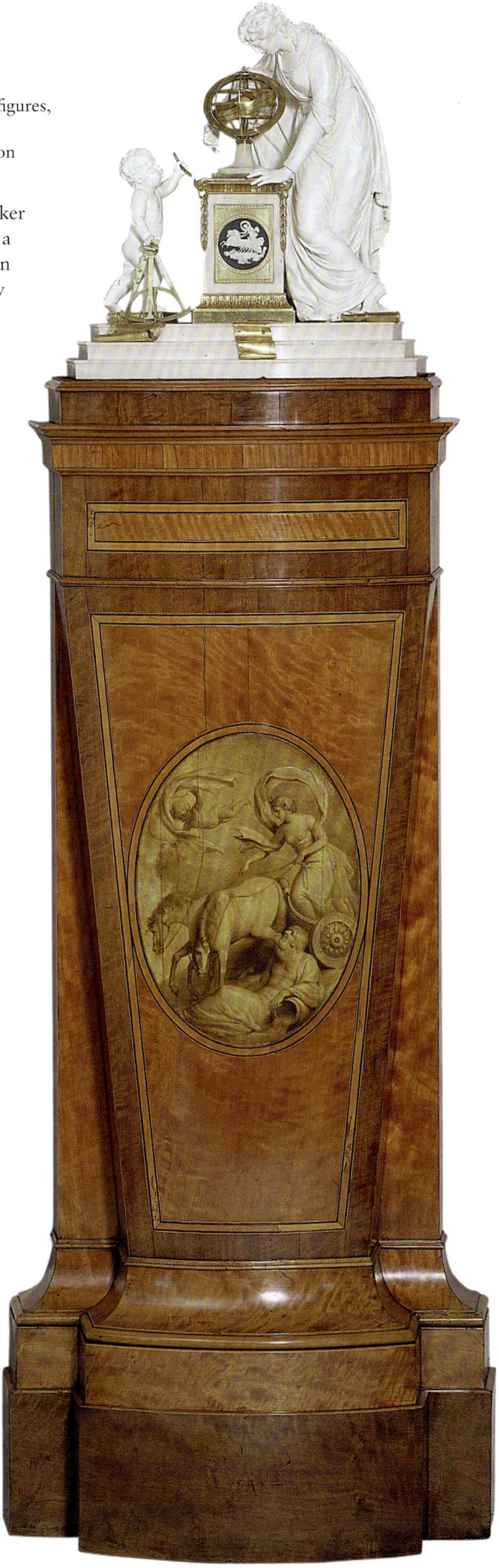

and engravings after François Boucher by Simon François Ravenet (1706–1774). By 1764 Andrew Planché anglicized his name to 'Floor' and toured the North of England with Baker's York Company of theatrical comedy players. In 1768 he joined the Orchard Street Theatre, Bath. He retired in 1799, died in Bath in 1805 and was buried in St James's church there. His nephew J.R. Planché, responsible for developing the pantomime, became Somerset Herald at the College of Arms. Andrew Planché's younger brother, Jacques, a watchmaker trained in Geneva, became assistant to Benjamin Vulliamy (1747–1811), the royal clockmaker who collaborated with the Derby manufactory. Vulliamy's 1787 barometer incorporates a Derby figure of Urania modelled by the sculptor John Deare (1759–1798; plate 157).[59]

Another modeller of Huguenot descent was Jean Voyez (*c*.1740– after 1791), who, like Sprimont and Planché before him, was trained as a silversmith. Working initially as a woodcarver for Robert and James Adam, he was employed by Josiah Wedgwood (1730–1795) from 1768. Voyez upset Wedgwood by modelling a naked figure of his coachman's daughter and was imprisoned for three months. Voyez joined Humphrey Palmer (fl.1760–78) in Hanley, Staffordshire, where he copied Wedgwood's basalt ware.[60]

The London manufacture of enamel boxes at York House, Battersea, from 1753 to 1756 met a growing demand for 'toys and trinkets'. Entries in the Battersea rate books show that the venture first traded under the names of Janssen, Delamain and Brooks. Stephen Theodore Janssen was a prominent merchant stationer and financier; John Brooks (fl.1730–56), the factory manager, probably invented the process of transfer printing using glue bats;[61] and Delamain has been identified as the Dublin-based potter Henry Delamain (d.1757).[62] An enamel plaque, an early example of transferring a printed design, commemorates the foundation by Royal Charter of the 'Free British Fishery Society' or British Herring Fishery Company, on 25 October 1750 (plate 158). The development of this technique was rapid, as this was a swift and effective form of decoration perfected on enamels, porcelain and tiles in London, Liverpool and the Midlands.

Stylistically similar overpainted transfer prints also occur on 1750s Birmingham enamels, inspired by the work of French painters including Jean-Antoine Watteau. Louis-Philippe Boitard (fl.1733–63), a book illustrator and engraver from Paris, moved to London in 1735 and was living in Lambeth Marsh in 1751. He gained notoriety for

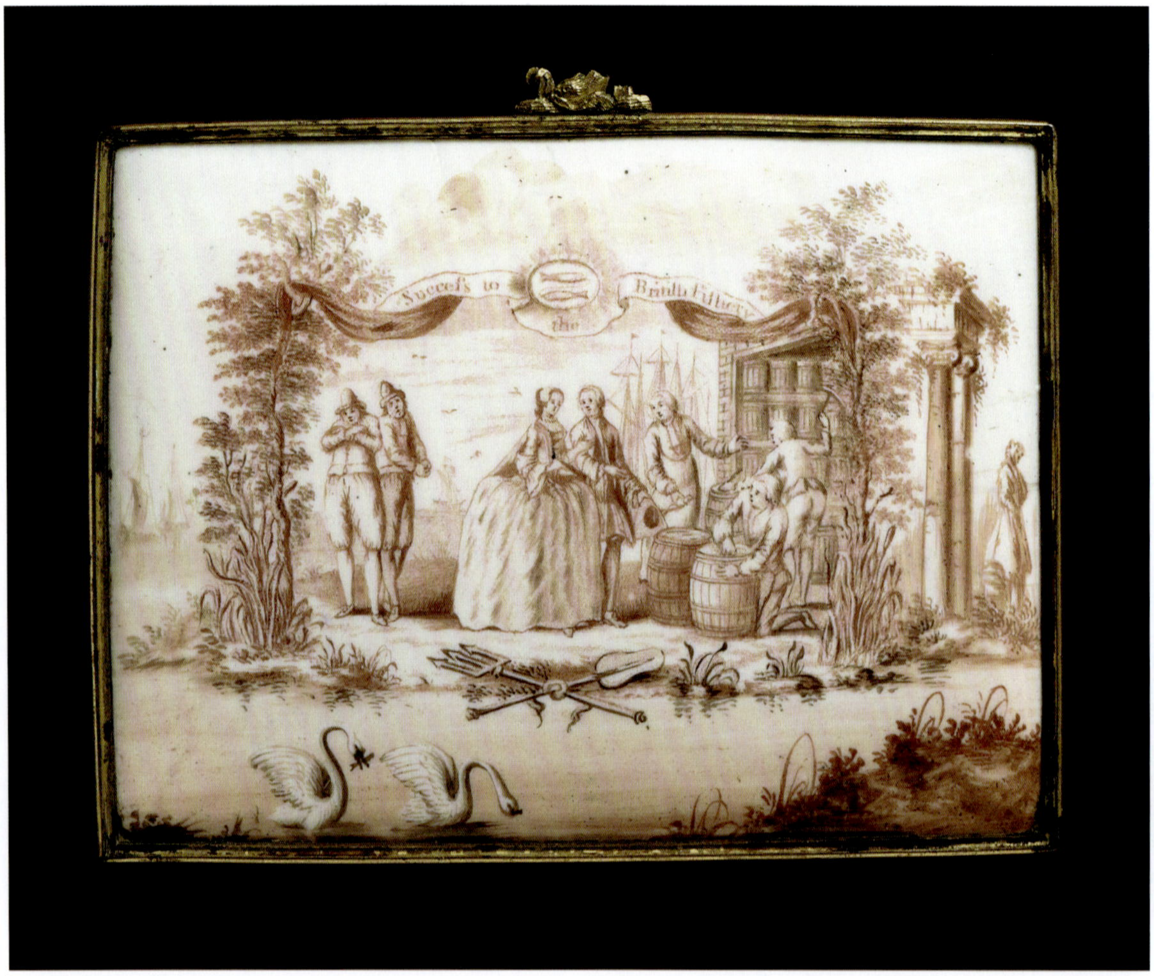

158 *Success to the British Fishery*

Battersea or Birmingham manufactory, 1752
Enamel with engraving after Boitard, 12.4 × 9.8 cm
Victoria and Albert Museum, London (414: 1443–1885)

The powdery appearance of the outlines and overpainting are still experimental. Frederick, Prince of Wales (who died in 1751), the British Fishery Society's first governor, was succeeded by George III. A gentleman, perhaps the Prince of Wales, and a lady watch three Englishmen pack herring into barrels. Two Dutchmen look on, dejected at their loss of trade. Above the banner proclaiming 'Success to the British Fishery' is the zodiac sign Pisces; below are a crossed paddle and trident.

pirating and reducing Hogarth's *The Rake's Progress* to a single print. His prints were used as sources for Bow and Worcester porcelain as well as for Birmingham enamels.

The Delamain connection with Battersea was short lived. A Huguenot goldsmith named Thomas Delamain was recorded in Bath in 1701 and Soho in 1742. Perhaps he was involved with the Battersea project for as a goldsmith, he was well placed to produce mounts for Battersea products in gold, silver or gilded copper. In 1753 his relation Henry Delamain announced that he had purchased the art of printing earthenware. That year John Brooks borrowed money from Peter Gandon, gunsmith of Westminster, probably son of Pierre Gandon, *arquebusier*, baptized at La Patente de Soho, in August 1713.[63] By May 1754 Gandon was declared bankrupt, and by 1756 Janssen had suffered the same fate.

In 1752 Henry Delamain took over from David Davis the Dublin Delftware manufactory, which had been founded by John Chambers (fl.1730s–1747): this is commemorated by a bowl in the British Museum inscribed 'Clay got over the Primate's Coals, Dublin 1753' (plate 159). Delamain produced wine fountains inspired by French faience examples and a pair of wine cisterns with moulded masks probably copied from contemporary Irish furniture. The remains of punchbowls found on the site of an eighteenth-century tavern in Chesterfield County, Virginia, USA, demonstrates that the pottery was exporting to the colonies, probably via Cork, where three of the pottery's agents had retail outlets.[64] Delamain presented pieces for inspection to the Dublin Society.[65] He died in Dublin in 1757 leaving £1,000 to his wife.

The closure of the Battersea factory was followed by the production of white enamelled boxes printed with the words and music of French songs and calendars for 1758 and 1759, with the inscription 'made by Anthony Tregent [fl.1758–9] in Denmark Street'.[66] Born in 1721 at Lunel near Arles in the south of France, he came to England with his parents Antoine and Marguerite Tregent in about 1740. Anthony married Anne Bruce at the Oxford Chapel, Vere Street, in 1750 and eight of their children were baptized at the Leicester Fields French church. In 1752 their second child

159 Punchbowl: 'Clay got over the Primate's Coals'

Dublin Delftware Potter, 1753
Earthenware, ht 21 cm, diam. 42.1 cm
British Museum, London (1960,0702.1)

The inscription refers to Delamain's redesign of the kiln to take coal (cheaper than wood) without discolouring the glaze. Delamain invested over £6,000 transforming the modest pottery into one of the most ambitious Delftware manufactories in the British Isles. It created a vast range of decorative tableware and ornamental items, copying patterns from Chinese export porcelain and forms from Bow porcelain.

was buried at St Mary's church, Battersea, so they may still have been living there when Janssen opened his factory. Tregent worked at the Dial in Denmark Street and claimed to be the 'Inventor of the Enamel New Year's Gift, so much admir'd and in request last year'. Another 1759 calendar box in a gold frame with scrolling border enamelled in translucent green painted with the signs of the Zodiac in *grisaille*, signed 'by Anth Tregent in Denmark Street', is thought to have been presented to the Earl of Bute by George III when he was Prince of Wales.[67] In 1760 Tregent moved to Bristol, where another child was baptized. In 1761 *Farley's Bristol Journal* announced that

> *Mr. Anthony Tregent Two Doors from the Painter's Arms in Milk Street, has just received from London a very extensive variety of the most fashionable and current Articles of Toy and Jewellers goods. To be sold only the wholesale way to Merchants and Dealers and at the very same Price as by the Makers in London.*[68]

According to Pierre Gautier (d.1791), minister of the Bristol Huguenot church, Tregent was well known in Paris, suggesting that his 'toys' were exported to the French capital. His brother James was watchmaker to the Prince of Wales, later George IV, with premises in The Strand, then in Cranbourn Street (plate 160).[69]

The English preferred to choose their own decoration for their dinner plates, buying English-made porcelain in the white and choosing patterns painted by individual decorators' workshops. A contemporary French source on the export of Vincennes porcelain commented that 'The English only want white porcelain, but as they use that for painted decoration, it is sold to them at the same price it would fetch if decorated'.[70] Independent decorators included the Huguenots James Giles, father and son.[71]

James Giles the younger (1718–1780), was the grandson of a Nîmes silkworker who had settled in London in the late seventeenth century and was

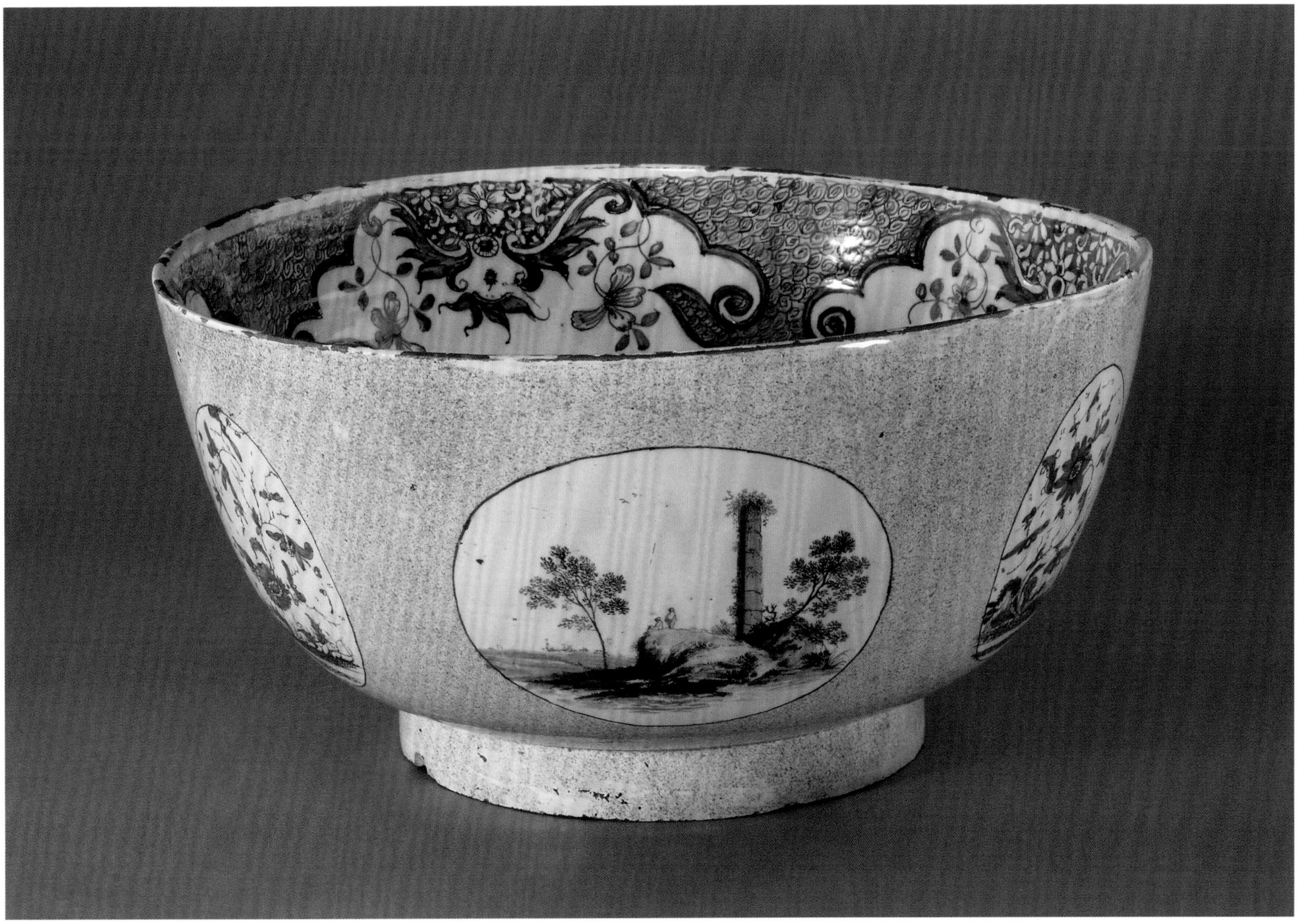

naturalized in 1699. At that time the surname was spelt Gilles.[72] James Giles's elder brother, Abraham, was apprenticed to glass seller Philip Margas (d.1767) on 26 June 1729, when their father, James Giles senior, was described as 'China painter'. The younger James Giles was apprenticed to John Arthur, jeweller of St Martin-in-the-Fields, in 1733. His kiln was used by Thomas Craft (fl. *c.*1760) of the Bow Manufactory, who took a bowl with two penny weight of gold and 'had it burnt in Mr Gyle's kiln, cost me 3s: it was cracked first time of using it'. The bowl is now in the British Museum with its description and history still attached to the underside.

From 1743 to 1748 James Giles the younger worked in Berwick Street, Soho, decorating cordial glasses and scent bottles as well as Worcester porcelain (plate 161).[73] In 1771 he took as partner the Huguenot John Higgons, whose family also came from Nîmes; however, when Higgons died shortly afterwards Giles was unable to buy out his business share. He took additional retail premises in Cockspur Street, near Pall Mall, the site of the Gun Tavern, and continued decorating porcelain until 1776, when William Duesbury (1725–1788) bought the workshop contents.[74] Giles died in August 1780 and was buried in the family vault at Paddington Old Church.

The identification of early work by James Giles is difficult. From 1765 to 1770 he specialized in naturalistic patterns. Four plates given to the Victoria and Albert Museum by Mrs Dora Grubbe, wife of his great-great-great-grandson, who presented Giles's only surviving account book to the English Ceramic Circle, help to document his style.[75] One of these plates shows an Arcadian landscape with figures, ruins and trees painted in green *camieu*.

The London-based Chelsea and St James's porcelain manufactories owed their existence to outstanding skill and enterprise, exemplified by the London community of Huguenot craftsmen and women, trained as goldsmiths, jewellers and enamellers. Andrew Planché played an important role in the early history of the Derby manufactory. James Giles, the most celebrated eighteenth-century London decorator of porcelain, was of Huguenot origin. The production of London-based enamels in the 1750s owed its existence, at least in part, to Huguenot input. Technical mastery, a flexibility of application and discerning taste, absorbed by second-generation Huguenot craftsmen, contributed to the quality of products marketed by three of the earliest British porcelain manufactories in Great Britain.[76]

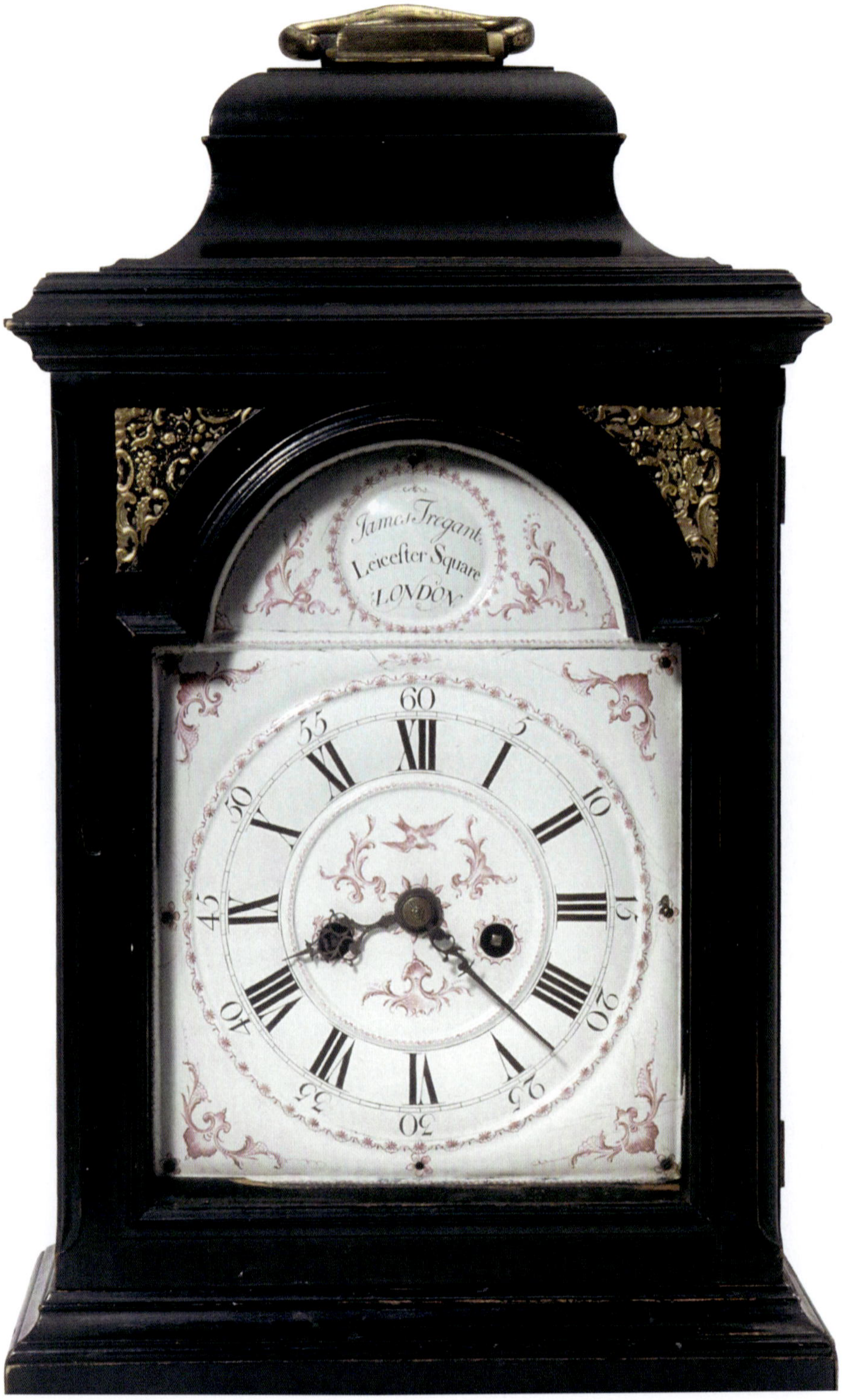

160 Table clock with enamel dial

James Tregent, London, *c.*1770
Ebonized wood case with brass mounts, 46 × 28 × 19 cm
Victoria and Albert Museum, London (414:1508–1885)

A London watch- and clockmaker from 1757, James Tregent joined the Clockmakers' Company in 1781. His name is mis-spelled on the dial.

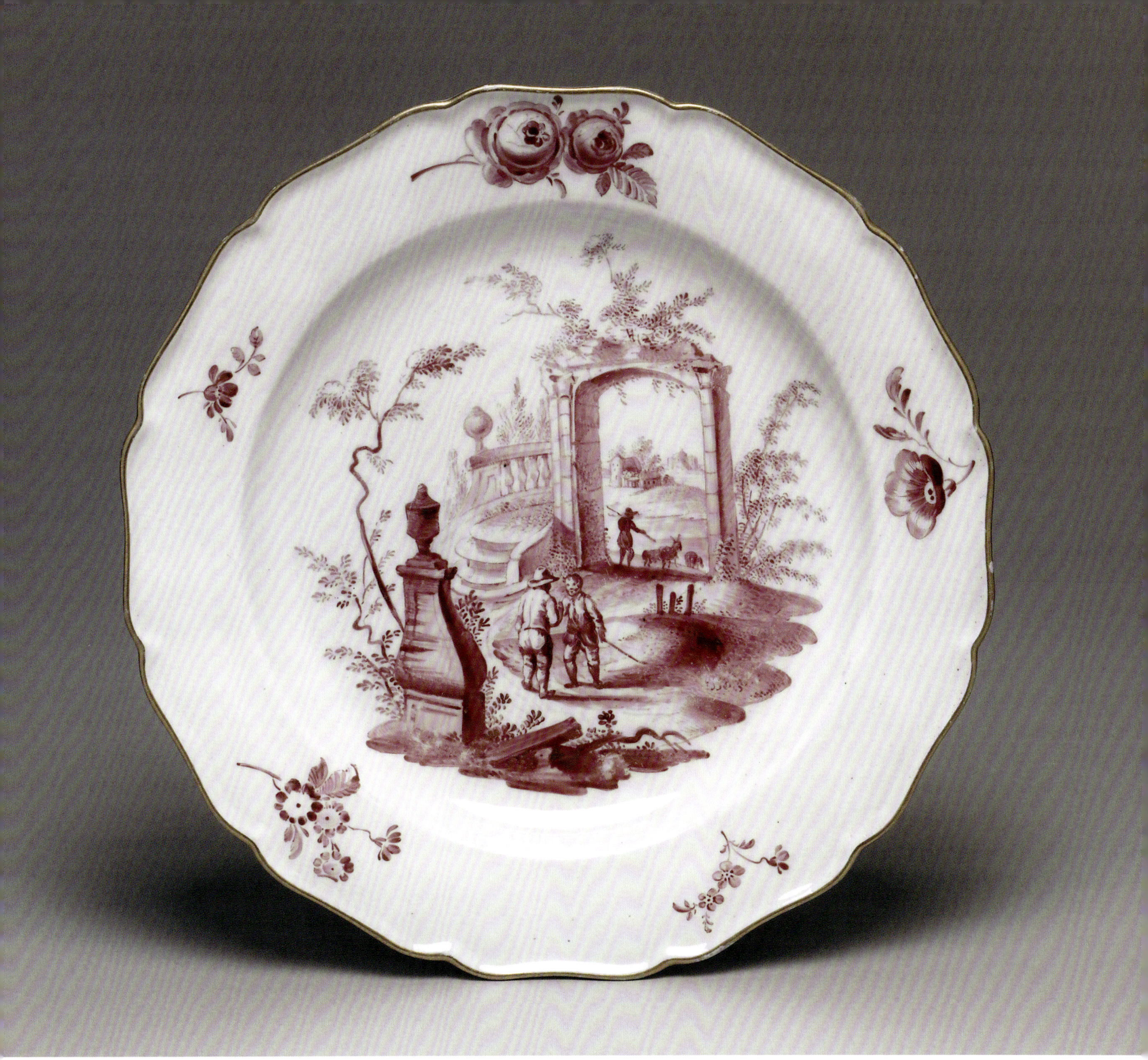

161 Plate

James Giles workshop, London, 1765–70
Worcester porcelain, diam. 22.4 cm
British Museum, London (1940,0401.12)

This is one of 12 surviving plates painted in puce with landscapes and flower sprays with gilded edges. One belonged to a Mrs Grubbe, a descendant of the decorator, James Giles. The combination of architecture and figures is attractive and possibly inspired by the decoration of contemporary porcelain from Tournai.

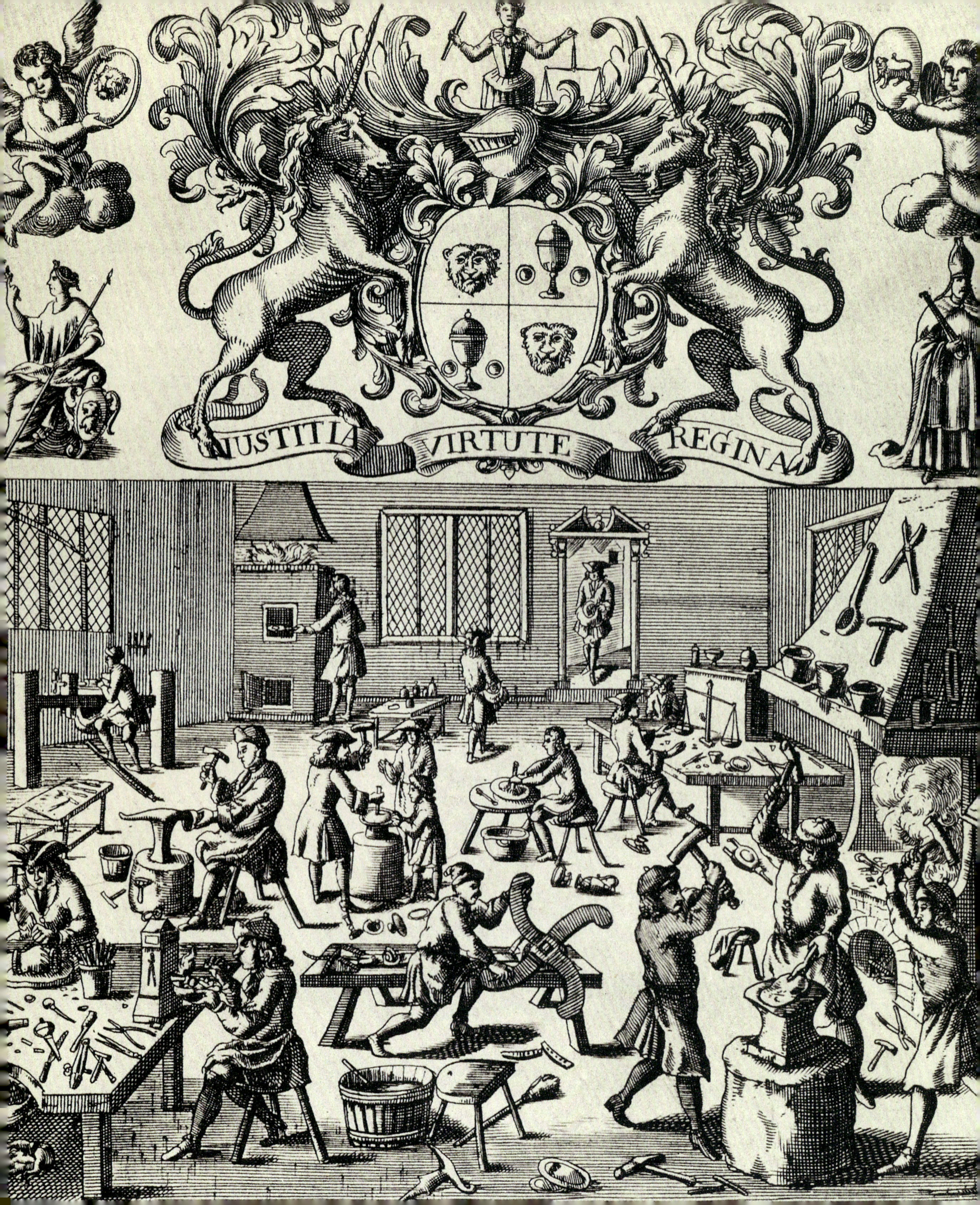
IUSTITIA VIRTUTE REGINA

Chapter Ten
Huguenot Goldsmiths & Silversmiths in the British Isles 1550–1780

162 Invitation to the sermon and dinner
Issued by Louis Mettayer, Steward, The Goldsmiths' Company, London 1701 (detail) see plate 173

From the late sixteenth century Huguenot refugee craftsmen established in London specialized in the luxury goldsmith and jewellers' trades. A century later they also worked as armourers, brasiers, gatesmiths, gunsmiths, locksmiths and pewterers. In seventeenth-century France, Huguenots regularly published ornament prints for enamels and jewellery.[1] In exile they embellished firearms, silver, lock plates, watch cases and clock dials with fashionable ornament, adding coats of arms, crests and family mottos, often with the place and date of manufacture and maker's name. Despite native opposition, Huguenot metalworkers were gradually accepted by long-established London guilds of armourers and brasiers, blacksmiths, clockmakers, gunsmiths, goldsmiths, ironmongers, pewterers and tin-plate workers. Only the goldsmiths' craft had regional assay offices, for which the London guild set the standards.

From the late seventeenth century, over two hundred Huguenot goldsmiths settled in Ireland; those based in Cork were registered with the Dublin Goldsmiths' Company.[2] In regional England, Huguenots who settled in West Country towns, Barnstable, Bath and Bristol registered at the Exeter Assay Office. Thomas Mangy, Huguenot goldsmith established in Hull in the 1660s, was admitted to the Freedom of York in the early years of Charles II's reign.[3]

Huguenot goldsmiths in London

Sixty-three French goldsmiths working in London between 1558 and 1625 catered for the English demand for French silver.[4] The French and Dutch Protestant communities were interconnected. Goldsmith Noe Jeopard was working in the City from 1550 to 1600 (plate 163),[5] and the specialist engraver Nicaise Roussel (1573–1646), from Bruges, was living in Blackfriars in 1573 (it is thought that his family came originally from Rheims).[6] Roussel sought royal patronage: his designs for ornament engraved in 1623 by John Bar, an immigrant from Lorraine, were dedicated to George Heriot (1563–1624), James I's jeweller. By 1617 Roussel, who attended the Austin Friars Dutch church and was described as 'amongst the Goldsmiths, Diamond cutters and Jewelers within ye City',[7] also worked for English goldsmiths. The communion flagons from the City church of St Mary Woolnoth, made in 1587–8, are engraved in Roussel's style with vibrant plant forms, monsters and grotesques; they compare with a later pair of flagons of 1594–5, similarly decorated, which were gifted to the Russia court.[8] In the 1620s Queen Henrietta Maria may have invited French goldsmiths to London: evidence of their presence among the hoard discovered in Cheapside, London, in 1912 includes a perfume bottle decorated with the peapod ornament that encapsulates the latest French fashion.[9]

Mid-seventeenth-century perfume flasks or *ferrières* link one exiled Huguenot goldsmith with Paris craftsmen as they bear marks of Paris and London makers recorded between 1655 and the 1670s.[10] The London-based Jean Le Roy (fl.1655–63), whose marks appear on a flask now in the Victoria and Albert Museum (plate 164), was a member of the Threadneedle Street French church; he moved to the Savoy church, which he later served as an elder.[11] Used for scented water, such flasks graced ladies' toilet services alongside a silver-framed mirror, comb boxes, ointment pots, candlesticks and *écuelles* (two-handled covered bowls). Several *parfumeurs* attended the City French church of St Martin Orgar, where Marchand Parfumeur Jean Merles was married in 1700. Jaques Reynes resided in King Street, Covent Garden, from 1700 and Antoine Nicolas in 1702 was in Newport Street, Soho.[12]

As the number of Huguenot refugees increased, the Goldsmiths' Company admitted goldsmiths by redemption (that is, paying the necessary fine) – a total of 11 between 1682 and 1699. Each of these took several Huguenot apprentices, so by 1714 more than thirty Huguenot goldsmiths were free of the Company.[13] This represented an estimated tenth of first-generation French goldsmiths, jewellers and watchmakers who established workshops in London after 1680. Numerically they flooded the craft, threatening the liveliood of native goldsmiths and creating a network of immigrant craftsmen in adjacent streets in the West End, which imitated the tight-knit community of the French regional guilds. Some joined established dynasties of goldsmiths, jewellers and watchmakers connected with the Threadneedle Street church from earlier in the century, others moved further afield. They nurtured family connections in Geneva, Amsterdam, Rotterdam, The Hague, Berlin, Cassel, Dresden, Erlangen, Frankfurt, Copenhagen, Stockholm and St Petersburg. Others passed through London and travelled on to New York, Boston, Philadelphia, Charleston (South Carolina) and the West Indies.[14]

The international network of goldsmiths is reflected in London apprentices bound in 1715 and 1739 who were sons of Huguenot merchants established in Boston and St Domingo.[15] Later in the eighteenth century the Huguenot network still fostered pan-European connections. For example, Gideon Ernest Charpentier (1733–1797) was born in Emden, Germany, to Huguenot parents; by 1758, when he married, he was living

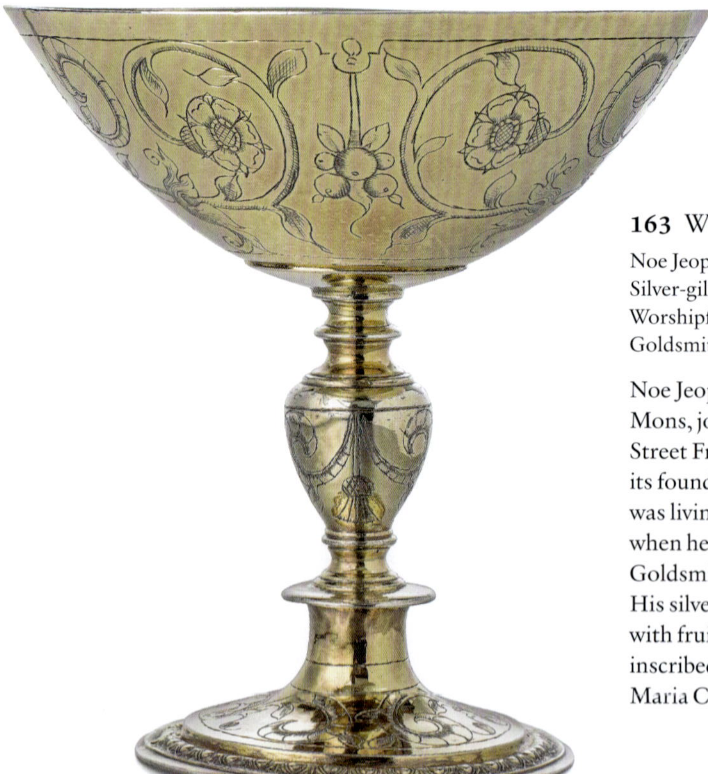

163 Wine cup

Noe Jeopard, London, 1577–8
Silver-gilt, ht 13.3 cm
Worshipful Company of Goldsmiths, London

Noe Jeopard, originally from Mons, joined the Threadneedle Street French church in 1550, its foundation year. Jeopard was living in St Vedast's parish when he was accepted by the Goldsmiths' Company in 1566. His silver-gilt cup, engraved with fruit and Tudor roses, was inscribed as a christening gift for Maria Corbett, 1587.

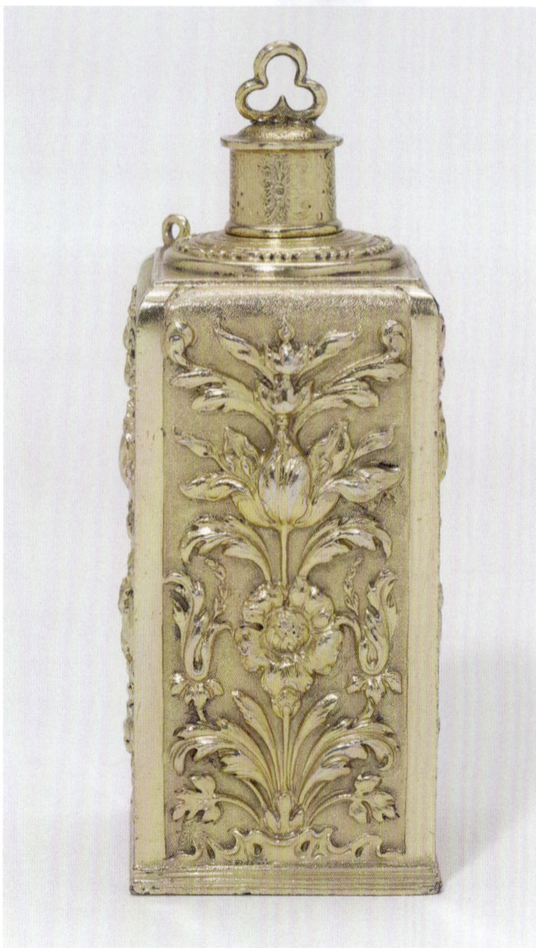

164 Perfume flask

Geneviève Cabarin, Paris, and Jean Le Roy, London, 1671–2
Silver, 17.5 × 6.5 × 6.5 cm
Victoria and Albert Museum, London (806A-C-1892)

Marked in Paris and London, the sides were subsequently soldered to bases recycled from earlier pieces. Did Le Roy incorporate silver marked by Cabarin in Paris to pieces made in his London workshop? Or were the flasks assembled in Cabarin's Paris workshop using substandard silver for the sides and retaining the worn assay marks on the recycled silver bases to make this appear legitimate?

165 Ewer

David Willaume, London, 1701–2
Silver-gilt, 22 × 15.5 cm
Victoria and Albert Museum, London (822–1890)

This small-scale helmet-shaped ewer was supplied as part of a toilet service, for Richard Hill (1655–1727), Lord of the Treasury. The mermaid form of the cast handle reflects the purpose of this vessel, which was used as a water jug. The cut card work (applied cut sheet silver) is typical of Huguenot work.

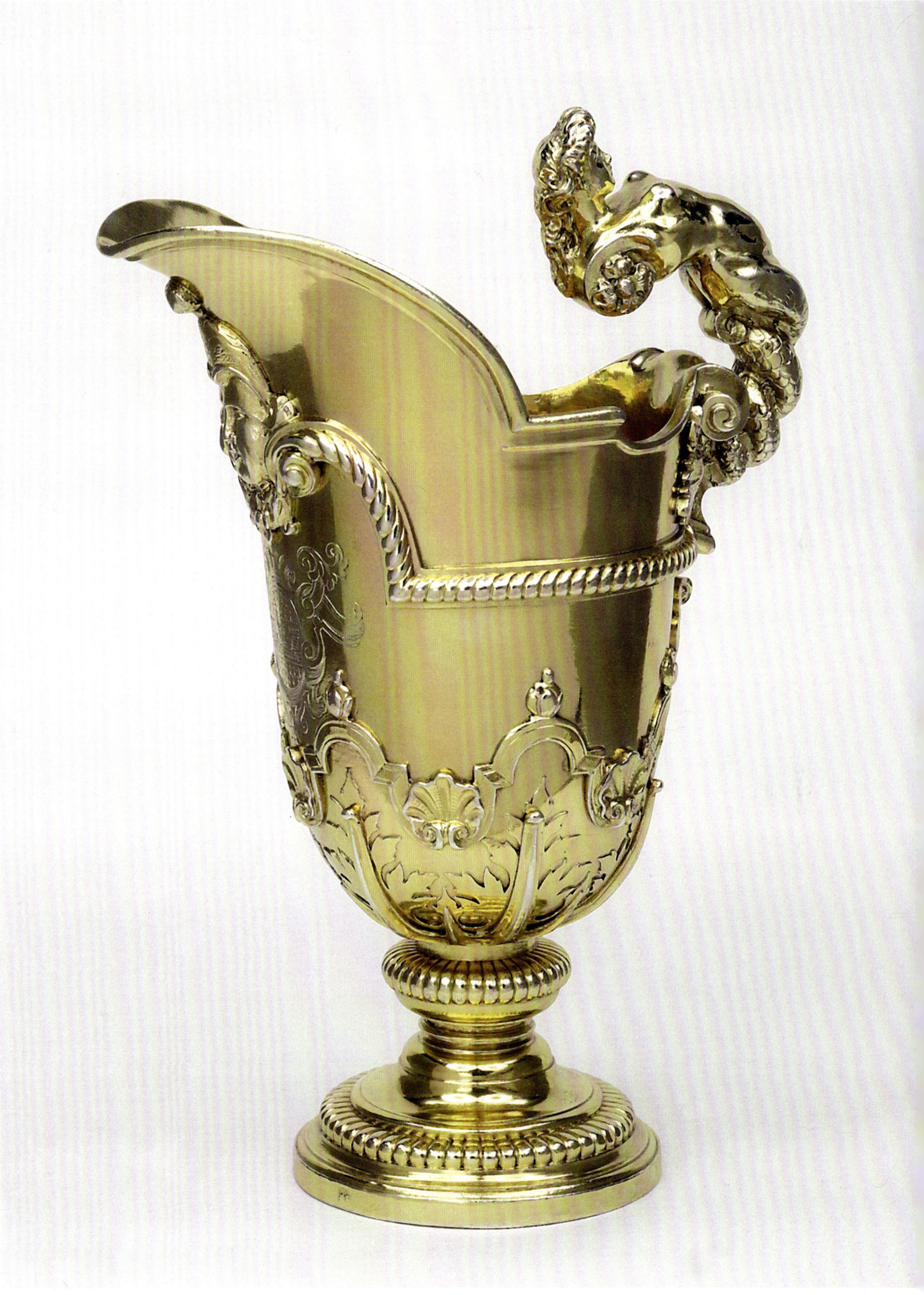

in Great St Andrew Street, Covent Garden. His son William Peter Charpentier (1763–1829) was apprenticed in 1778 to second-generation Huguenot goldsmith Abraham Portal, Paul de Lamerie's former apprentice.[16]

In 1679, 1689 and 1709, in order to finance his war effort, Louis XIV ordered the melt of domestic silver and forbade further employment of goldsmiths in France.[17] Thus Huguenot goldsmiths were attracted to London for economic reasons. Church records in exile reveal their French home towns: Paris, Blois, Dieppe, La Rochelle, Le Mans, Lille, Metz, Rheims and Rouen. Churches in the place of origin provided a *témoignage* (certificate of previous religious observance)[18] and some exiles maintained contact with family members in France who abjured or concealed their faith.[19] Their technical brilliance coincided with a court-led demand for fashionable French styles, so they set new standards and promoted ornament by the Paris designers and fellow Huguenot Daniel Marot.

Huguenot goldsmiths are credited with the introduction of new forms from France: the 'helmet-shaped' ewer (plate 165) derived from Rouen faience, with its matching basin (plate 172), and the pilgrim bottle (also a ceramic form; plate 166); their distinct profiles enhanced social status and lent dignity to display and use. The soup tureen (plate 168) and *saucière* later known as a sauceboat (plate 167),[20] catered for new French recipes, as did the *écuelle*. The latter, a traditional form of two-handled bowl for broth given to a mother after childbirth, in Ireland known as a pottinger, was given a practical cover.[21] The 'machine' (centrepiece) first introduced by French royal chef François Massiolot (1660–1733) cradled fruit, sweetmeats and confectionery throughout the meal.[22] The single-bottle wine cooler provided convenient self-service for gentlemen engaging in confidential discussion at table after dinner.[23]

The steep-sided two-handled cup and cover, a traditional christening gift, was raised on a small foot and acquired a finial, thus becoming more graceful. Subsequently used for commemorative gifts including sporting trophies (plate 192), the form changed with fashion, morphing through the Baroque, Régence, Rococo and Neoclassical styles adopted by successive generations of craftsmen.[24] Huguenots promoted a purity of form, proportion and dignity of ornament, providing vessels for the new hot drinks: chocolate, coffee and tea. The chocolate pot was transformed into an elegant pear-shaped vessel;[25] silver tea bowls proved too hot to handle, although silver *trembleuses* or holders for ceramic cups provided a fashionable alternative.[26] Anne Houblon, Viscountess Palmerston (d.1735), drank chocolate every day

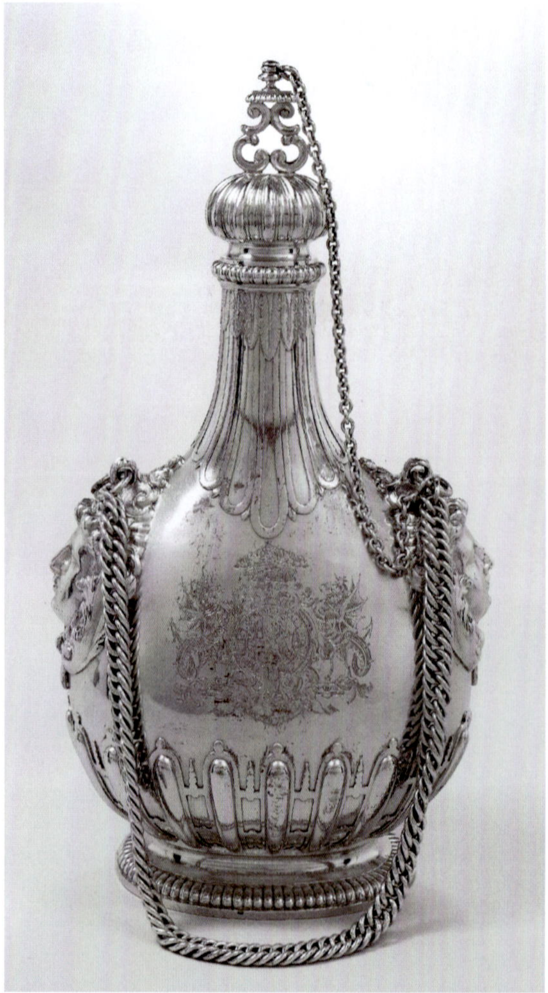

LEFT ABOVE

166 Pilgrim bottle

Peter Platel, London, *c.*1710
Silver, ht 22.5 cm
Victoria and Albert Museum, London
(M.854 & 2–1927)

Peter Platel (*c.*1664–1719) worked on the north side of Pall Mall, 'over against the Duke of Schomberg's'. This pilgrim bottle was made for General Charles Churchill, brother of John, Duke of Marlborough. Named after leather water bottles carried by pilgrims, their form provided ample space for engraved armorials and a vehicle for the cast ornament and cut card work associated with the best Huguenot silver. Displayed on a dining room buffet, the pilgrim bottle proclaimed the status of the patron.

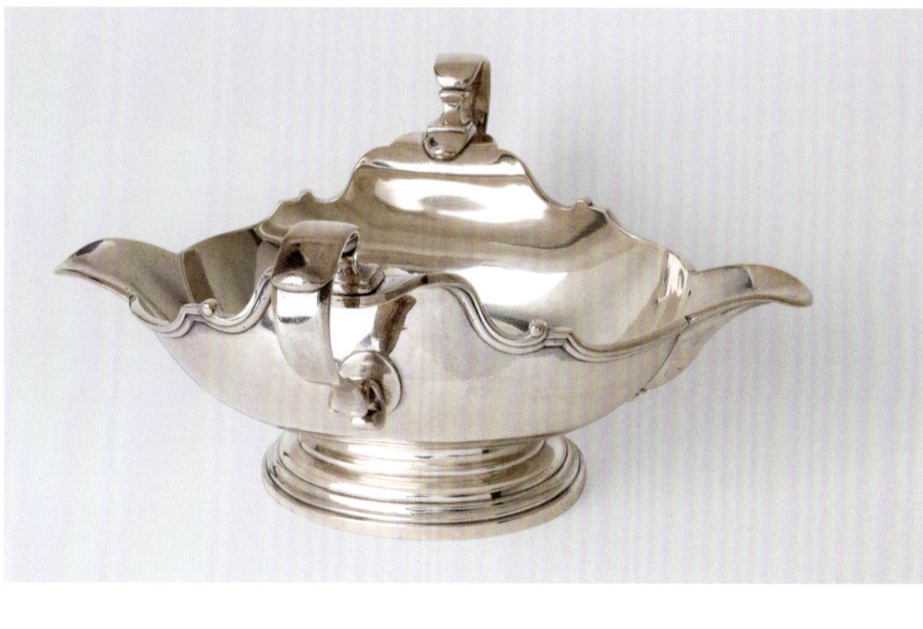

LEFT BELOW

167 Sauceboat

Anne Tanqueray, London, 1727–8
Silver, width 8.25 cm
Huguenot Museum, Rochester

The double-lipped sauceboat was introduced by Huguenot goldsmiths and used to serve new sauces introduced by fashionable French cooks: Vincent La Chapelle provided 30 different sauce recipes in 1733. Anne Tanqueray is the earliest recorded Huguenot woman goldsmith to register her mark at London's Goldsmiths' Hall.

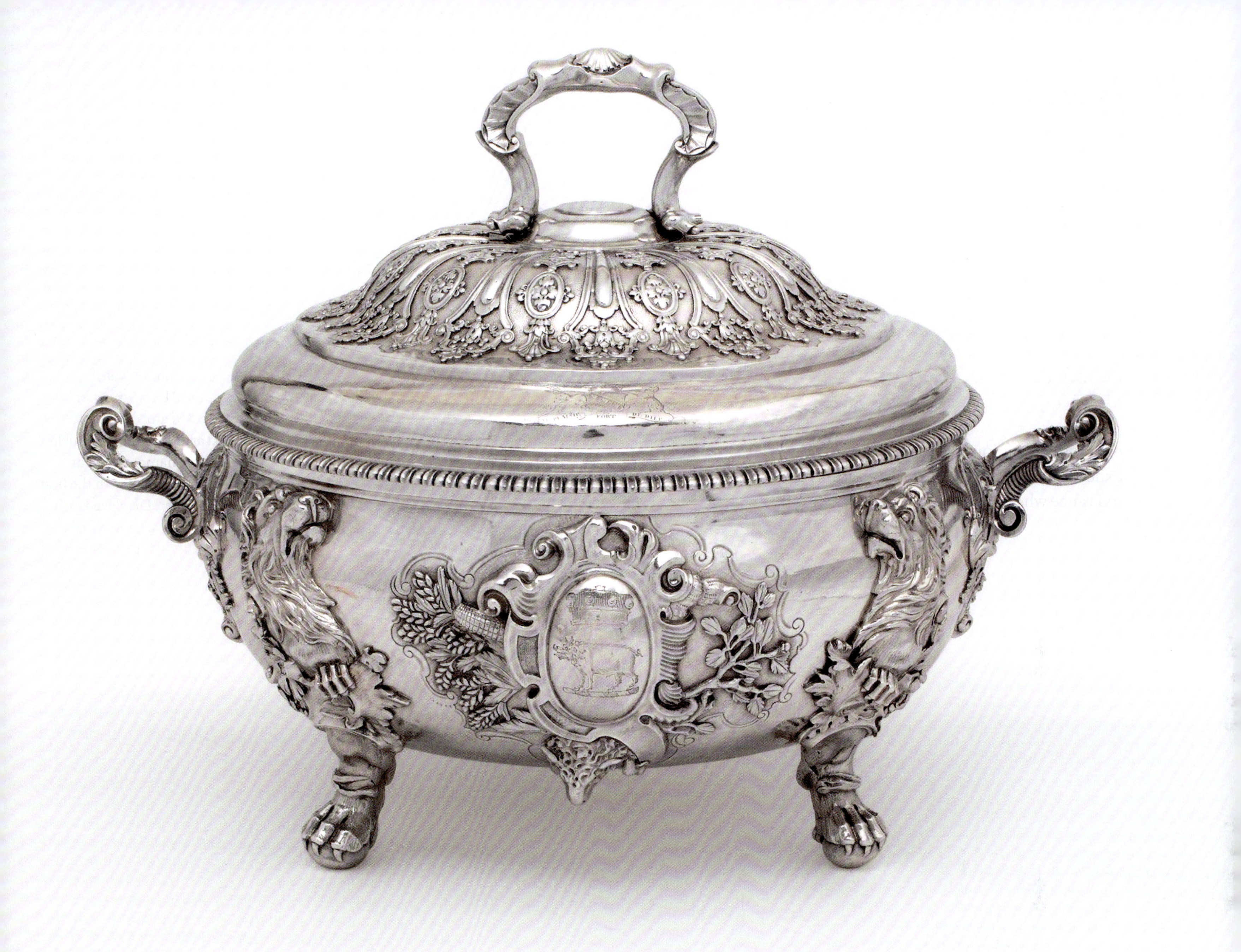

ABOVE

168 Soup tureen

Paul de Lamerie, London, 1722–3
Silver, 27.8 × 38.8 × 30.9 cm
The Rosalinde and Arthur Gilbert Collection on loan to the Victoria and Albert Museum, London (LOAN:GILBERT.723:1 to 3–2008)

Soup tureens supplied by de Lamerie from 1722 were intended for ragout, *olio* or other first-course dishes. This is one of a pair originally supplied for the Edgcumbe family of Plymouth in the French Régence style, sent back to de Lamerie in the 1740s for the addition of Rococo armorial cartouches, replacement feet and handles.

from gold cups made from recycled memorial rings (plate 169) in memory of her distinguished Huguenot ancestors.[27]

As well as new forms, it is believed that the Huguenots introduced new terms that are still used by goldsmiths today. These include 'bouge' (a hollow running round any article or, as in the bouge hammer, used for polishing) and 'paillons' (a term for small pieces of metal used in enamel work or for solder).[28]

The most sophisticated Huguenot goldsmiths used sculptural ornament to personalize silver for display, forming finials and handles into three-dimensional armorial crests.[29] Figurative casting moulds were made from carvers' models. In Soho, Huguenot sculptors, easily located by shop signs, supplied models in wood, clay or lead. By 1700 Matthew André (fl.1700–6) was at the Blackamoor's Head and his neighbour Pierre Bertheux (fl.1702–5) worked at the sign of the Cow in Compton Street; Jean de la Bourde (fl.1698–1701) was at the Dolphin in Princes Street; Abraham le Large (fl.1704–7) worked at Queen Anne's sign in St Andrew's Street; and Nicholas Doyenne (fl.1689–1703), originally from Paris, was at the Two Black Boys in Litchfield Street, where in 1700 his lodger was the goldsmith John Louis Marc,[30] juxtaposing complementary skills.[31] Advertisements in the contemporary press evidence the multicultural talent available.[32] In 1730s London, Huguenots still dominated the international community in Soho and Covent Garden, where Swiss and Germans mingled with Danish, Dutch and Flemish craftsmen.[33]

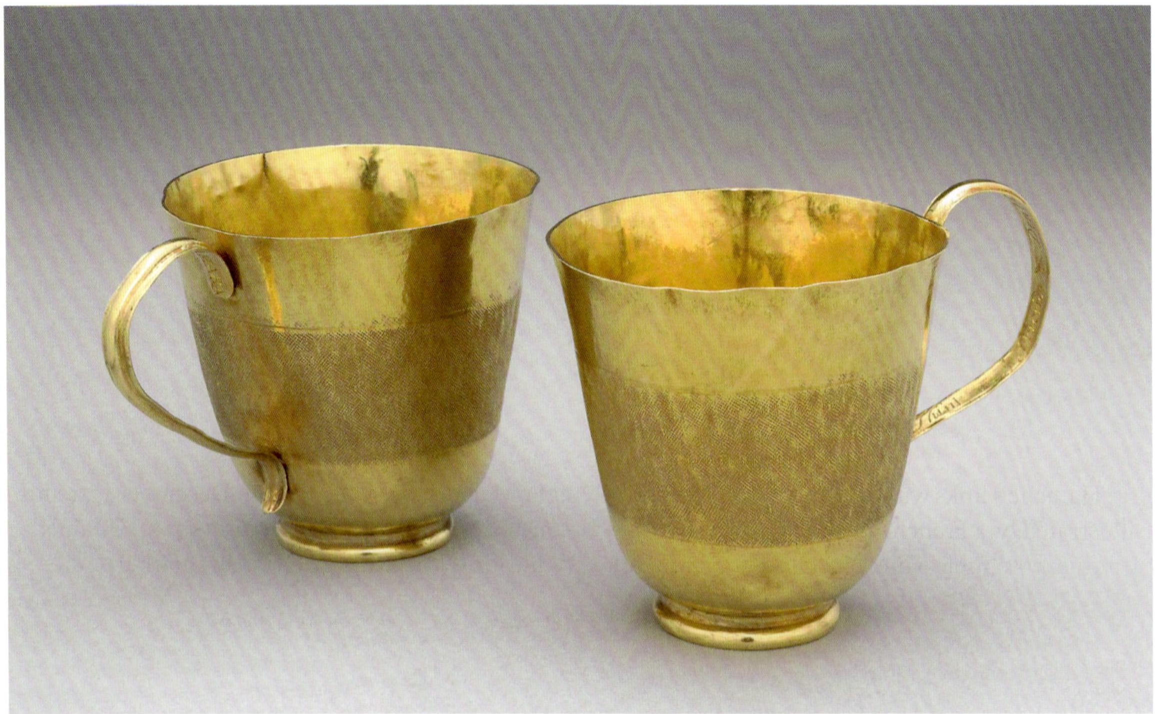

169 Chocolate cups

John Chartier, London, *c.*1700
Gold, diam. 5.9 cm, ht 6.5 cm
British Museum, London
(2005,0604.1,2)

Anne Houblon, Lady Palmerston, bequeathed these '2 lesser Chocolate Cups ... as a Remembrance of Death, and also of the fondest and Faithfullest Friend' to her husband, Henry Temple, 1st Viscount Palmerston (*c.*1673–1757), in 1735. Made by John Chartier out of recycled memorial rings commemorating Houblon family members, their purpose is emphasized by the mottos transcribed onto the handles: 'Let us drink to the dead' and 'Think on yr friends & Death as the Chief'.

THE GOLDSMITHS' COMPANY

In the summer of 1682 the first immigrant goldsmiths of the decade, Louis Berchère (1681–1738), goldsmith and jeweller from Paris, and Pierre Harache (1639–1712) master goldsmith from Rouen, who briefly worked in Paris in 1668,[34] were admitted to the Goldsmiths' Company.[35] Yet Louis Berchère's son Jacques Louis Berchère and his brother-in-law, Jean Louis, had to wait 18 months. Only then could they submit silver for marking and assay to meet the current sterling standard and, from 1697, the Britannia standard, which required a higher silver content. Prior to admission, a certificate confirming Harache's identity was signed by ministers and elders from the Threadneedle Street church, near Goldsmiths' Hall, and the Savoy church, near Harache's workshop at Charing Cross:

> *These are to certify all whome it may concerne yt Peter Harache lately come from France for to avoid persecution & live quietly is not only a Protestant but by his Mats bounty is made a Free Denizen yt hee may settle here freely wth his family ... 28th June 1682.*[36]

Louis Berchère presented his *témoignage* from Charenton, the Huguenot Temple outside Paris.[37] The merchant jeweller Nicholas Maubert (fl. 1663–87), who vouched for Berchère, was son-in-law of the London-based clockmaker David Bouquet (*c.*1607–1665); they both belonged to the Threadneedle Street church. Maubert was a large-scale importer of diamonds through the East India Company supplying the Paris jewellery trade. He was one of three brothers, another of whom imported linen from Rouen.[38] Louis Berchère marked his admission by giving the Goldsmiths' Company a silver scroll salt which the Company sold in 1711. In November 1683 Henry Compton, Bishop of London, lobbied the Goldsmiths' Company to admit John Louis, Berchère's brother-in-law.[39]

In 1682, 1694, 1711 and 1716 the Goldsmiths' Company received successive petitions against admitting aliens to the Freedom (membership).[40] The signatories included Francis Garthorne (1641–1729) and his brother George (fl.1680–97), whose marked work imitated Huguenot style;

170 Makers' marks for Daniel Garnier and George Garthorne

Goldsmiths' Company Register for 1697
Library, Worshipful Company of Goldsmiths, London

Huguenots retained the French form of maker's mark, surmounted by fleur-de-lis or crown, as in Daniel Garnier's mark shown here. The native goldsmith George Garthorne imitated Huguenot style and adopted the French form maker's mark in 1697.

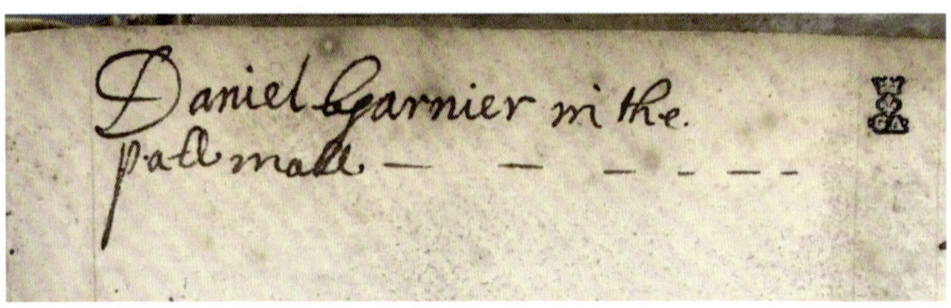

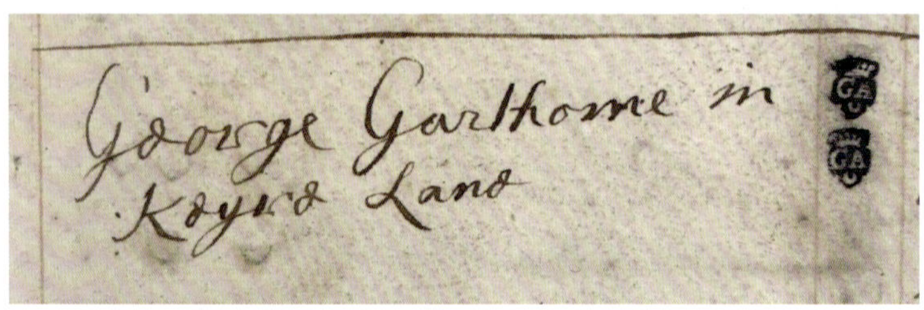

in 1697 George Garthorne used the French form of maker's mark (plate 170) that the Huguenot goldsmiths retained in London.[41] Among the other signatories were Anthony Nelme (d.1722) and his son Francis (fl.1722–59) and Benjamin Pyne (*c.*1653–1732), whose marked silver is comparable to that by leading Huguenot goldsmiths – who may have employed Huguenot journeymen or even marked Huguenot-made silver to maintain their client base and competitive edge.[42] Huguenots had to lobby for admission to the Freedom of the Company, and many failed to achieve membership.

THE HARACHE FAMILY

Pierre Harache's links with the London wine trade are illustrated by a French-form silver taster (used by a vintner to sample wine) made in 1684 that bears his mark (plate 171).[43] London-based French wine merchants included Anthony Reilhan, who supplied Ralph, 1st Duke of Montagu, with a silver 'crane' or corkscrew in 1704. Other merchants specialized in local wines: Degrave supplied burgundy and John Gachon bordeaux.[44] In 1703 Harache sold claret and bordeaux from the basement of his Suffolk Street workshop.[45] It was Pierre Harache who established the family presence in London,[46] although another relative, Nicolas Harache, had attended the Threadneedle Street church in 1668.[47] In 1687 Pierre Harache advertised in the *London Gazette* gold plate with French royal insignia and domestic silver stolen from the London home of Hortense Mancini, Duchess of Mazarin (1646–1699).[48] His patrons included William Cavendish, 1st Duke of Devonshire (plate 172),[49] and John Churchill, 1st Duke of Marlborough.[50] He served the French church in Leicester Fields as an elder from 1693 to 1700.[51] In 1691 he offered the French church in Swallow Street, St James's, a new communion cup of Calambourg wood,[52] with a silver-gilt lining, worth 30s, to replace a silver communion cup stolen from his room where it was being stored for safekeeping.[53] Pierre Harache the elder was buried at St Martin-in-the-Fields on 9 December 1712; his cousin, also Pierre Harache (1652–1718), obtained denization in 1698, registering his mark from Compton Street, Soho. The younger Pierre Harache eventually returned to France and was buried in the Rouen parish of St Maclou in September 1718.

The next generation included Francis Harrache (1710–1757), maker of gold boxes from 1732, who took his younger brother, Thomas (1717–1785), as an apprentice. Thomas who had shop premises first in St Martin's Lane and then in Pall Mall, supplied bronzes, ceramics and jewellery (plate 192). In 1762 he served as executor to sculptor Louis François Roubiliac.[54]

171 Wine taster

Pierre Harache, London, 1684
Silver, ht 2.9 cm
Huntington Library, Art Museum, and Botanical Gardens, San Marino (69.69.1)

In 1703 Harache sold claret and bordeaux from his Suffolk Street basement. French wine was difficult to obtain during the War of Spanish Succession and this helped to finance the goldsmith's business: 'under the House of Mr Harache Goldsmith, there is a cellar, where you may have good claret at 4s per Gallon, some other better at 5s White wine 5s 6d, Canary Bordeaux and French Claret at 8s per Gallon and right excellent wine at 9s per Gallon' (*The Post Man*, 17 April 1703).

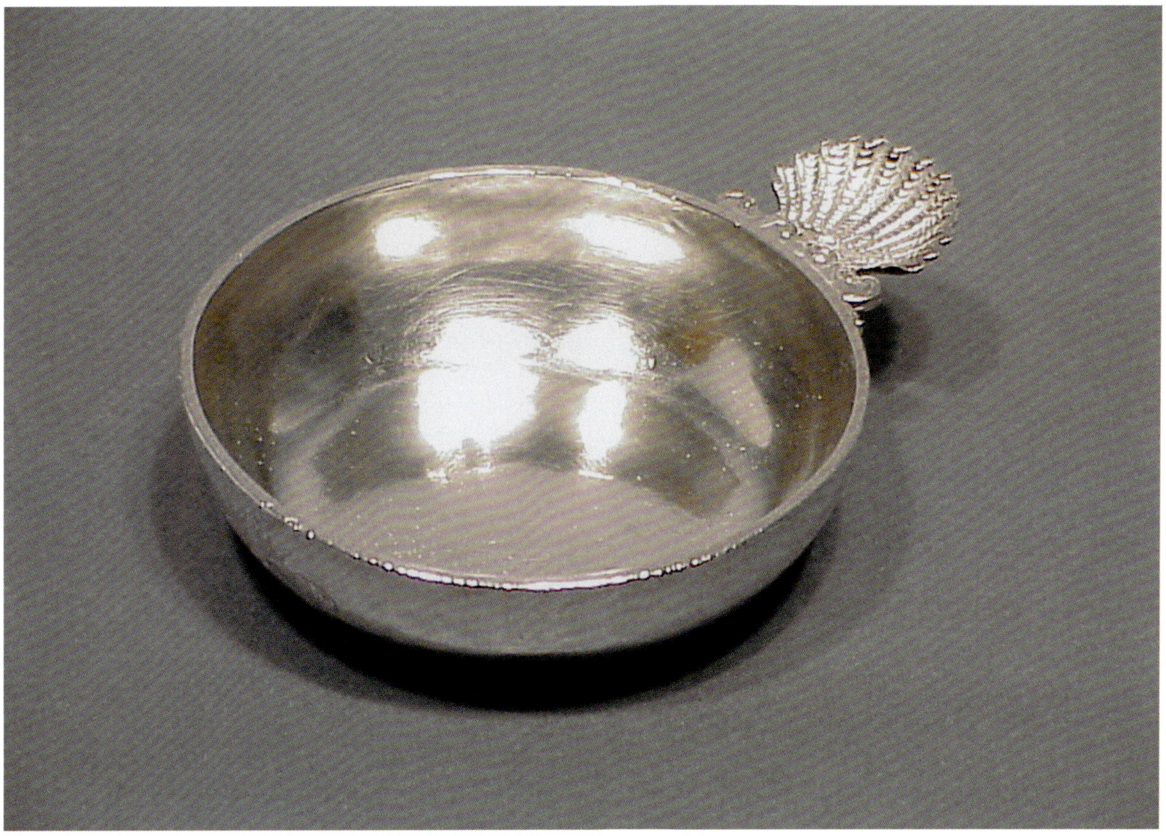

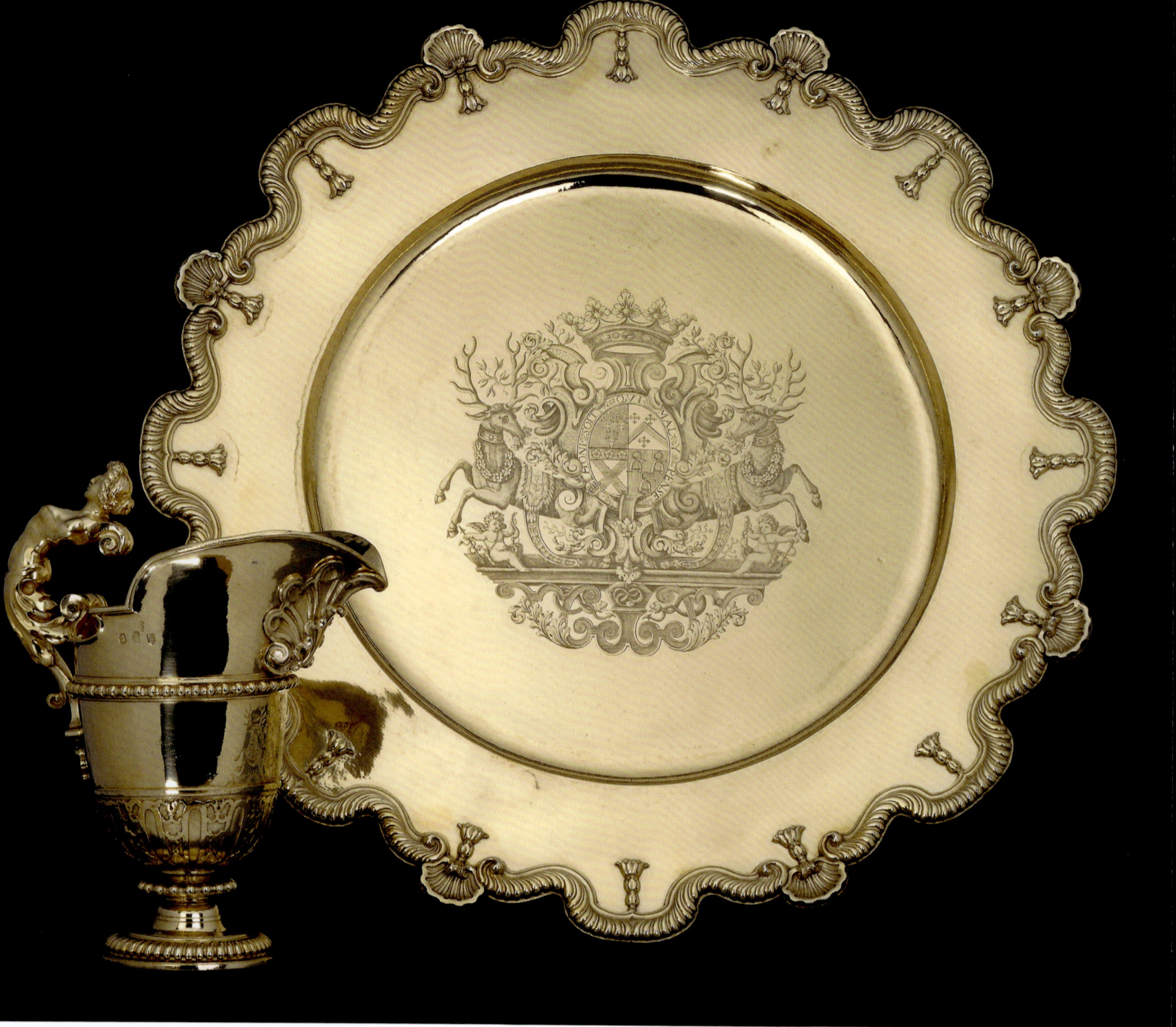

EDUCATION, EXPERIENCE AND SKILLS

In 1747 Robert Campbell advised that a goldsmith needs to be a good designer, have an interest in sculpture and an unerstanding of metallurgy. Goldsmiths needed good judgement, dexterity and a solid education, having learned to draw before being apprenticed at 14. The craft attracted sons of gentry and army officers, as goldsmiths were 'the most genteel of any in the Mechanic Way' and required 'a large Stock to set up'. A superficial understanding of Latin and a working knowledge of French, 'the polite Court language of Europe and a Trading Tongue', were recommended. Bilingual second-generation Huguenot goldsmiths had a head start.

The range of skills practised by goldsmiths are demonstrated in an invitation issued in 1701 by six Goldsmiths' Company Stewards (plate 173), including the Huguenot Louis Mettayer (d.1740), whose brothers-in-law were goldsmith David Willaume the elder (1658–1741) and engraver Simon Gribelin; Mettayer's wife, Anne, was the widow of one of Pierre Harache's associates.[55]

172 Ewer and basin

Pierre Harache, London, 1697
Silver-gilt, dish diam. 65.5 cm; ewer 30.5 × 24.9 cm
British Museum, London (Wilding Bequest 1969,0705.28a & b)

This splendid set combines sophisticated cast ornament with fine engraving of the Cavendish heraldic arms, ducal crest and stag supporters. It was intended for display on the dining-room buffet to emphasize the status of the patron.

173 Invitation to the sermon and dinner

Issued by Louis Mettayer, Steward, The Goldsmiths' Company, London
1701
Engraving, 22.7 × 14.2 cm
Library, Worshipful Company of Goldsmiths

Apprenticed to David Willaume in 1693, Mettayer obtained his freedom in 1700 when he was working in Lichfield Street. He later had premises in Pall Mall, near his former master. In 1747 Campbell noted that the goldsmith 'employs almost as many as there are different articles in his shop'. Fifteen specialists are shown here. The mid-century introduction of flatting mills for reducing the ingot to sheet metal saved effort and time in raising silver with the hammer for hollow wares, as shown in the right foreground.

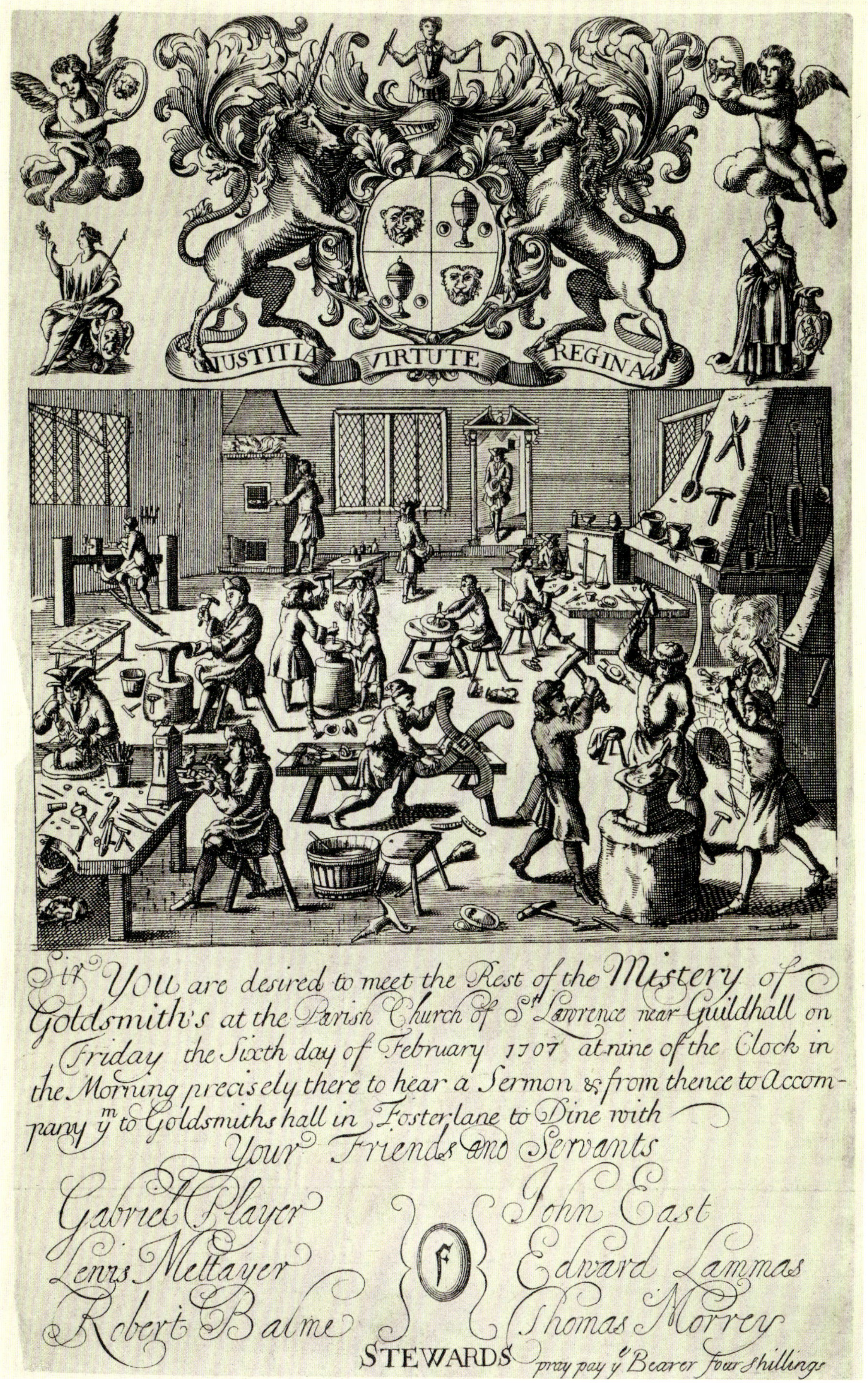

Sir You are desired to meet the Rest of the Mistery of Goldsmith's at the Parish Church of St Lawrence near Guildhall on Friday the Sixth day of February 1707 at nine of the Clock in the Morning precisely there to hear a Sermon & from thence to Accompany ym to Goldsmiths hall in Fosterlane to Dine with

Your Friends and Servants

Gabriel Player
Lewis Mettayer
Robert Balme
John East
Edward Lammas
Thomas Morrey

STEWARDS

pray pay ye Bearer Four shillings

Two apprentices joined the Mettayer workshop in 1709.[56] Mettayer's skills were handed on to his daughter Susanna, free of the Goldsmiths' Company in 1738; his son Samuel followed in 1741, a year after their father's death.[57]

THE PANTIN, BUTEUX AND GODFREY FAMILIES

Simon Pantin the elder (1680–1728), like his master, Pierre Harache the elder, came from Rouen; his family was recorded in London by the mid-seventeenth century.[58] Four successive generations of Pantins were goldsmiths working in related trades.[59] In 1701 Simon the elder registered his first mark incorporating his shop sign, the Peacock, in St Martin's Lane. He moved to the Golden Ball, Castle Street near Leicester Fields, in 1717 (plate 174) and took his son Simon (b. *c.*1702) as apprentice; Simon Pantin the younger registered his own 'Peacock' mark after his father's death in 1728.[60]

In 1720 Eliza Pantin (fl.*c.*1720–66), daughter of Simon Pantin the elder, married her father's godson, Abraham Buteux (1698–1731),[61] son of a Stepney weaver, in St Paul's Cathedral. Buteux was working from 1721 to 1731 in Green Street, near Leicester Fields, but died before November 1731, when Eliza registered her own mark from Norris Street, St James's. She remarried at the City church, St Benet's, Paul's Wharf, in February 1731/2. Her new husband was Benjamin Godfrey, probably her journeyman, who entered his own mark in the year of their marriage and further marks in 1739. Eliza's new mark appears on a silver basket (plate 175).[62]

The dynasties established by the Rouen goldsmiths Harache and Pantin, energetically supported by their wives and including successive generations and cousins, contrast with individual Huguenot goldsmiths such as Louis Cuny (d.1733), whose place of origin is as yet unrecorded.[63] Yet Cuny was closely embedded in the Huguenot community, making a presentation gift for his compatriot, the upholsterer Philip Guibert (plate 176),[64] and sacred silver for the Savoy French church. Free of the Goldsmiths' Company by redemption (that is, paying the necessary fine) in December 1703, Cuny was working at the Three Crowns in Panton Street, Leicester Fields, until 1727. He was elected to the Livery of the Goldsmiths Company in 1708, when he took John Hugh Le Sage, from Alençon, as apprentice. His communion set for the Savoy church (plate 21) included the secular form of wine cup like those made for the Huguenot chapel, Canterbury Cathedral, in 1631–2 (plate 15). Communion bread and wine were distributed around a long table where ministers sat amongst their community.[65] Cuny's apprentices included (from 1717) Isaac Basire (1704–1768), son of James Basire of Wardour Street.[66] Isaac was later established as an engraver in St John's Court, Clerkenwell (p.234); he probably specialized in signatures on dials, meeting demand from local clock- and watchmakers. Huguenot goldsmiths often worked with engravers, jewellers and watchmakers from their own communities.

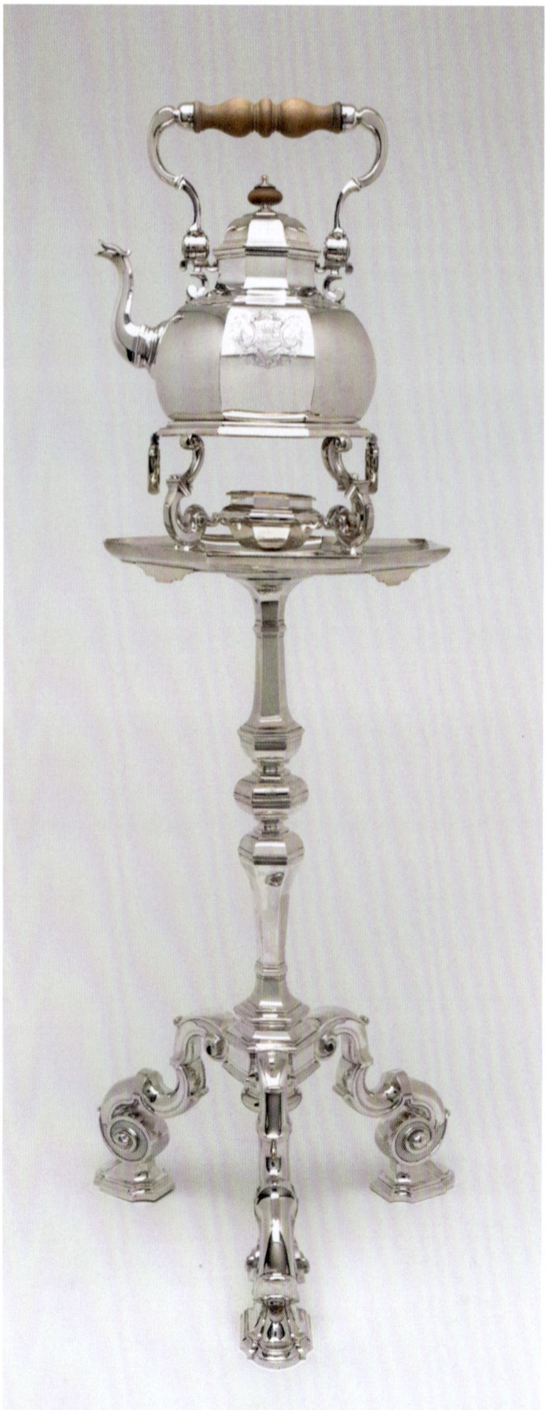

LEFT

174 Tea kettle and tripod stand

Simon Pantin, London, 1723–4
Silver, stand 64.1 × 37.8 × 37.8 cm; kettle 38.7 × 25.4 × 19.1 cm
Metropolitan Museum of Art, New York (68.141.181 a-f)

Simon Pantin welcomed seven Huguenot apprentices between 1705 and 1730: two sets of brothers, Peter and Augustin Courtauld, in 1705 and 1709 respectively, and John and Jacob de Joncourt in 1726 and 1731. Pantin's 1724–5 silver tea kettle and stand were made for the Bowes family, County Durham.

RIGHT ABOVE

175 Basket

Eliza Godfrey, London, *c.*1750
Silver, ht 28 cm
The Fowler Collection, UCLA

On 29 June 1741 Eliza Godfrey registered a new mark. Her trade cards illustrate fashionable Rococo-style tureens, baskets, ewers, coffee pots, candlesticks, two-handled cups and tea kettles and stands, and describe her as 'Goldsmith, Silversmith and Jeweller to His Royal Highness the Duke of Cumberland'. This basket combines sophisticated pierced work with cast border and feet.

RIGHT BELOW

176 Ceremonial salt

Louis Cuny, London, 1697
Silver-gilt, ht 12 cm
The Worshipful Company of Upholders on loan to the Salters' Company, London

This salt, taking the form of the Upholders' coat of arms, *sable three pavilions ermine*, was presented to the Huguenot upholsterer Philip Guibert in 1702 on admission to the Upholders' Livery.

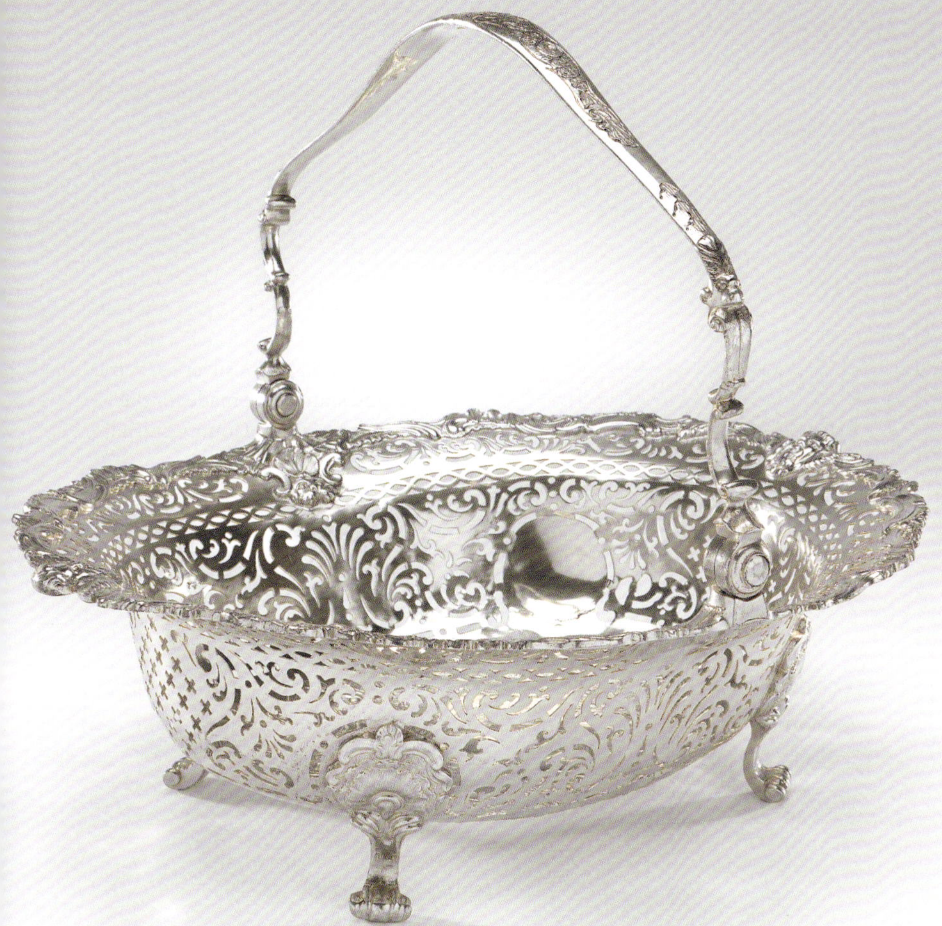

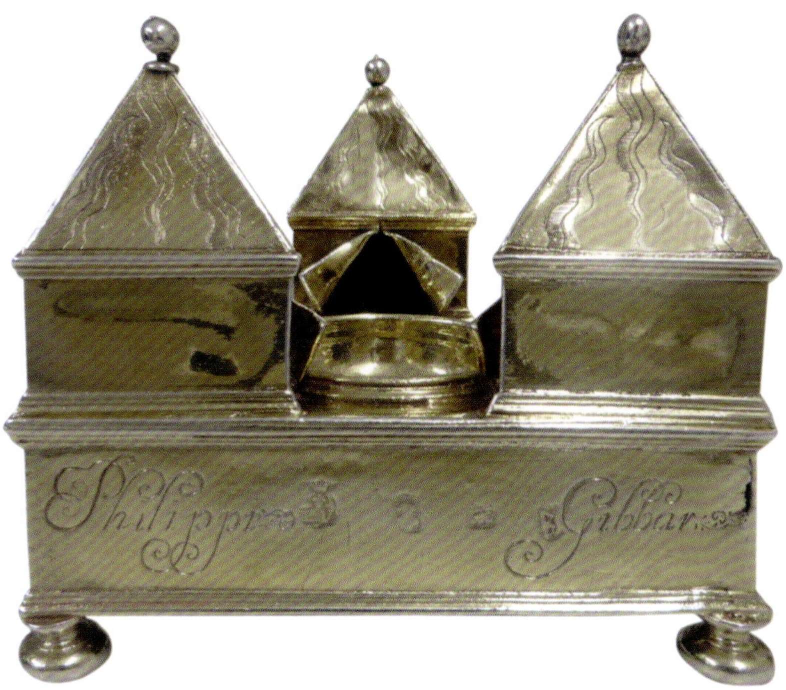

GOLDSMITHS FROM REGIONAL FRANCE AND THEIR DESCENDANTS

First-generation refugee goldsmiths from regional French towns Blois, Le Mans, La Rochelle, Lille, Metz, Saumur and Sedan formed networks concentrated on London's West End. They developed close ties with the Huguenot community in Spitalfields, combining skills and experience to enhance the quality of their work. Jean Chartier (fl.1688–*c.*1731) from Blois, listed in the Savoy French church 'Reconnaissances' on May 1688 and free of the Goldsmiths Company in 1698, married Suzanne Garnier; their son Jean was baptized at Leicester Fields church in December 1697. Their family network exemplifies the characteristic tight-knit Huguenot community. Chartier took his younger son, Daniel, as apprentice in 1720; his daughter Henriette married his former apprentice the goldsmith Pezé Pilleau (fl.1720–76) on Christmas Day 1724.[67] Henriette and Pezé's sons Jean Pezé (b.1729) and Alexis (b.1731) were mentored by their goldsmith grandfather, who was also their godfather.

Daniel Garnier (d.1699), recorded in London until his early death, entered his mark as a large-worker (maker of large-scale silver vessels) in April 1697.[68] The silver toilet service with scenes from Ovid's *Metamorphoses* given by Mrs Strangways Horner to her daughter Elizabeth in 1740, is Garnier's most spectacular commission.[69] In 1697 he completed a silver ten-armed chandelier for William III (plate 177).

In France, Huguenot goldsmiths often catered for specialist markets.[70] One Huguenot speciality in exile was the production of ivory piqué heads for walking canes, traditionally associated with Spitalfields; silver pins were used to personalize these masculine accessories with initials or dates.[71] Another speciality was the production of false teeth. The goldsmith Pezé Pilleau, father-in-law of Henriette Chartier, worked as a dentist in Le Mans before moving to London. In February 1696 *The Post Man* announced that 'Mr Pilleau a French goldsmith ... by an Experience of 18 Years ... has found out a way to make and set Artificial Teeth in so firm a manner that one may chew with them'. Established in St Martin's Lane, he was succeeded by his son, Pezé the younger, who was trained by John Chartier from 1710. By 1720 the younger Pilleau 'continueth to make and set Artificial Teeth and whole Jaws or Rows with the utmost nicety' at the Golden Cup, Chandos Street.[72]

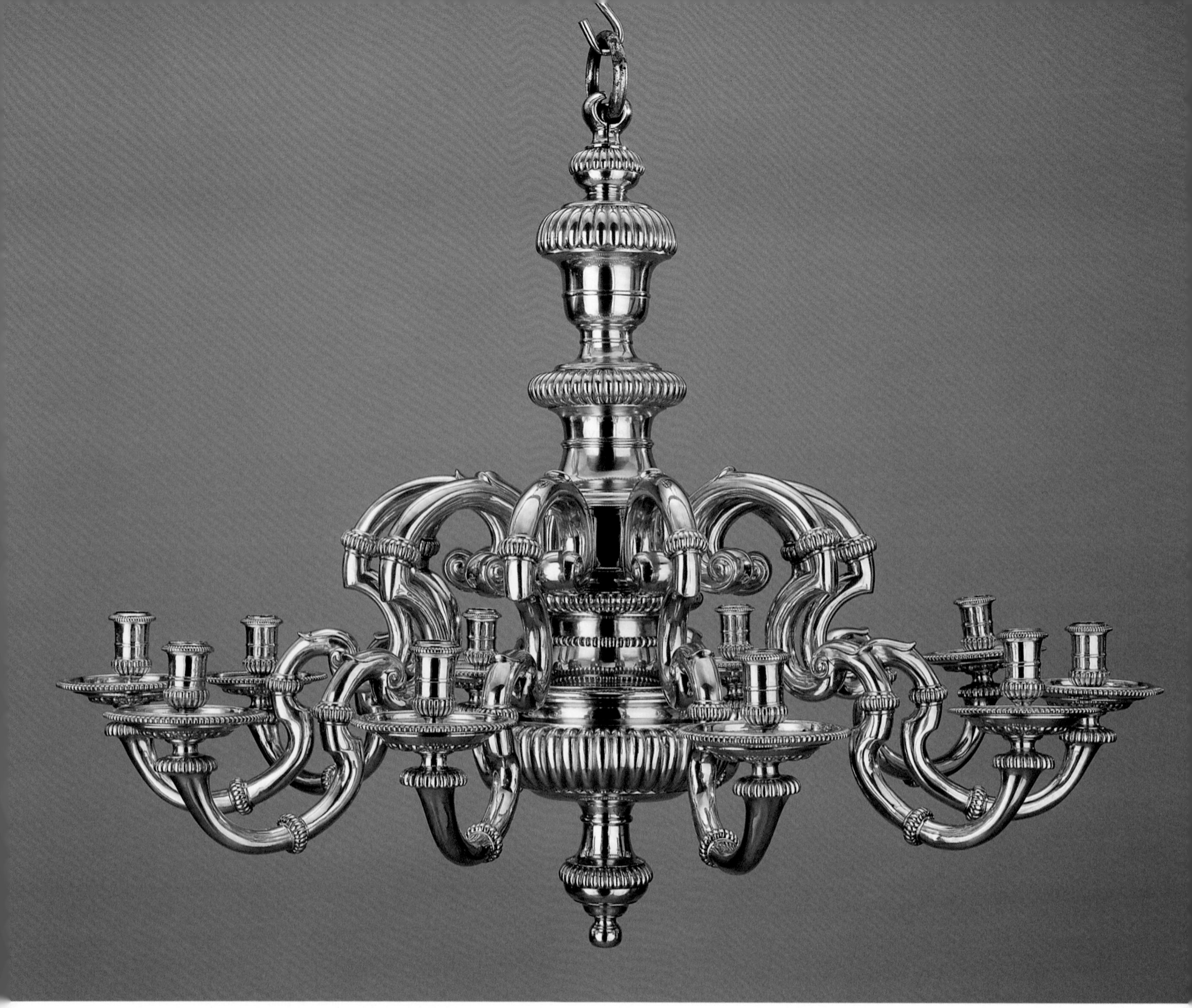

French dentists had the best reputation in eighteenth-century Europe. Peter Hemet (d.1747), another Huguenot 'Operator for the Teeth', lodged with John Fraigneau (d.1756) at the Orange Tree, Pall Mall. Fraigneau was appointed Confectioner to George II in July 1722[73] and his son James (b. *c.*1700) was apprenticed to a goldsmith in 1714.[74] Was John Fraigneau able to recommend his dentist lodger to those who needed treatment following a surfeit of his sugared preparations? In March 1739 Lionel Tollemache, 4th Earl of Dysart (1708–1770), purchased 'a pot of Tooth Powder 'from Paul Daniel Chenevix's Toy Shop in Suffolk Street'.[75] The Hemets continued to specialize in dental care: in 1793 Mary Hemet of St George's Fields, Surrey, bequeathed 'my 5th part in the essence of pearl & pearl dentifrice'.[76]

The Courtauld family demonstrate the links between merchants, retailers and manufacturers in silks and silver.[77] Originally from St Pierre d'Oléron, La Rochelle, Augustin Courtauld joined his father, a wine cooper, in London in 1696 and was apprenticed in 1701 to the goldsmith Simon Pantin. He obtained his freedom in 1708 and married Anne Ribouleau (1709–1751) the following year;[78] their eight children were baptized at Orange

177 Chandelier with ten arms

Daniel Garnier, London, 1691–7
Silver, 86.6 × 83.8 cm
The Colonial Williamsburg Foundation, Virginia

Daniel Garnier, goldsmith neighbour to Platel and Willaume in Pall Mall, was son of Isaac, apothecary at the Royal Hospital, Chelsea. The Garniers came from Vitry-le-François, Champagne, and arrived in London 1694. Daniel registered his first mark in 1697 but died two years later.

Street chapel, near Leicester Fields. Augustin moved from St Martin's Lane in 1729 to the corner house in Chandos Street featured in Hogarth's print *The Enraged Musician*. In 1734 he took on his son Samuel as apprentice. His earlier apprentices, including the author's ancestor Edward Feline (plate 1), were all Huguenots.[79]

Samuel Courtauld (1720–1765) was well placed to attend drawing classes at the St Martin's Lane Academy. His chasing skills are apparent from his shop sign, 'The Rising Sun', which compares with an unmarked basin (plate 178) made for Stephen Fox (1704–1776), later 1st Earl of Ilminster, husband to young Elizabeth Strangways Horner (b.1722). The matching ewer is encircled by bullrushes encrusted with shells, appropriate for a vessel associated with the *toilette*. The Courtauld workshop was adjacent to retailer Peter Dutens, a goldsmith jeweller from Blois, who supplied Frederick, Prince of Wales. As a successful diamond merchant, Dutens was well placed to lend capital to his royal patrons: this was a far cry from his relative John (b.1669), a silversmith in London who, aged 17, received charity from the Royal Bounty.[80]

Another leading first-generation Huguenot goldsmith, Pierre Platel (*c*.1664–1719), originally from Lille, received denization in London on 8 May 1697 and became free of the Goldsmiths' Company by redemption (see p.186) by order of the Court of Aldermen on 14 June 1699, joining the Livery in 1708. Platel took the celebrated Paul de Lamerie as apprentice on 16 August 1703, his £6 premium payable for being apprenticed to a master funded by a grant from the Royal Bounty.[81] Platel made the silver wine fountain (plate 179) for Queen Anne to present to Sir John Walter (1673–1722), her Clerk of the Green Cloth (wine butler), in 1713.[82]

David Willaume came to London from Metz and achieved denization in December 1687. He married the daughter of the Huguenot minister of La Patente, Spitalfields, in October 1690. Three years later he took his brother-in-law, Louis Mettayer, as apprentice, when he was also joined by François Vaillant (d.1721) from Saumur. Further

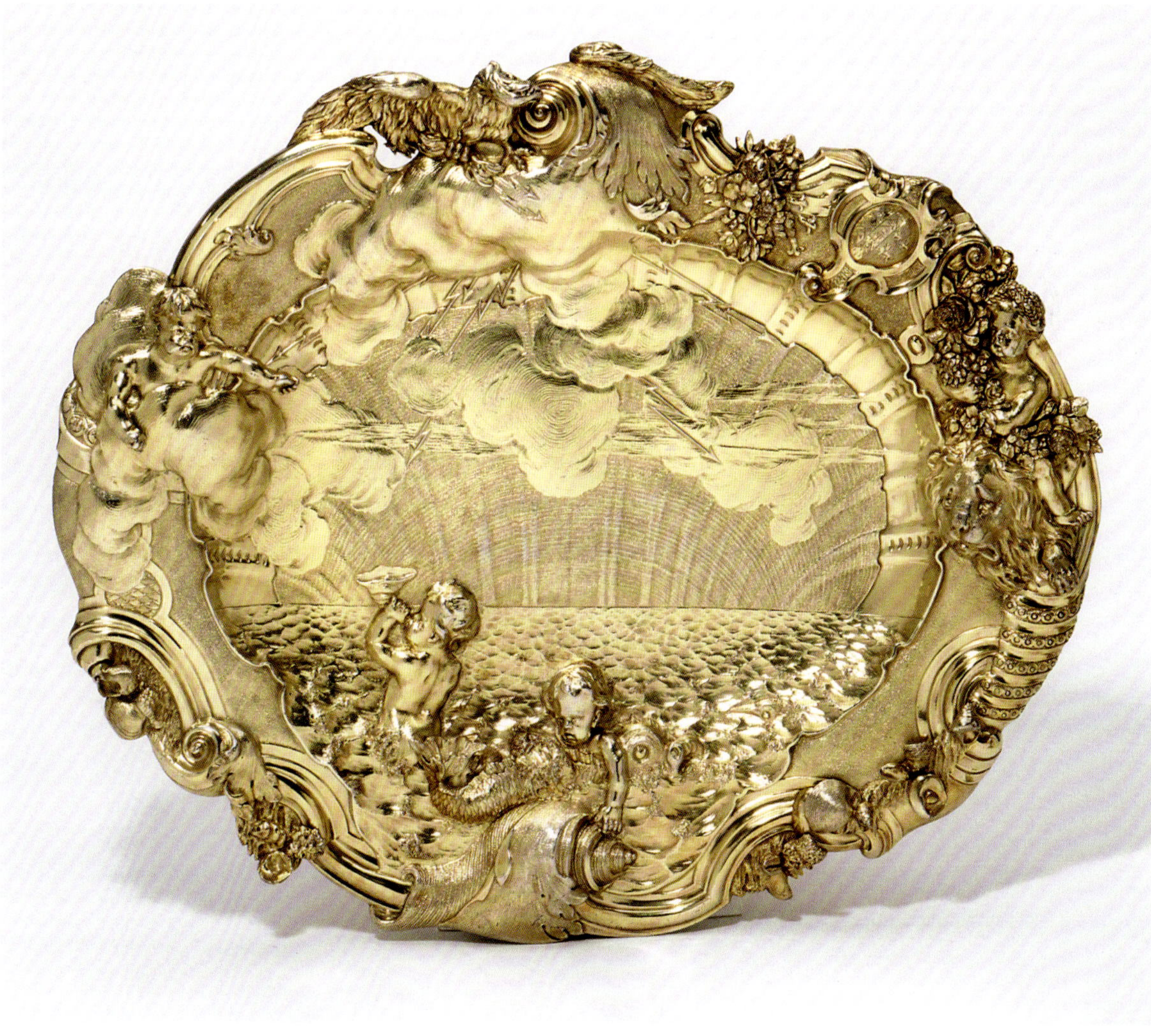

178 Basin

Unknown maker, London, *c*.1740
Silver-gilt, width 42.5 cm
Private collection on loan to the Victoria and Albert Museum
(LOAN:MET.ANON.2:2–1996)

The sophisticated chasing on this unmarked basin made for Stephen Fox, later 1st Earl of Ilminster, is similar to the scene on Samuel Courtauld's trade card, which illustrates the sign of his shop, The Rising Sun. The basin's elaborate frame symbolizes the Four Elements surrounding a seascape; an alighting eagle represents Jupiter and Fire, his thunderbolts piercing the clouds.

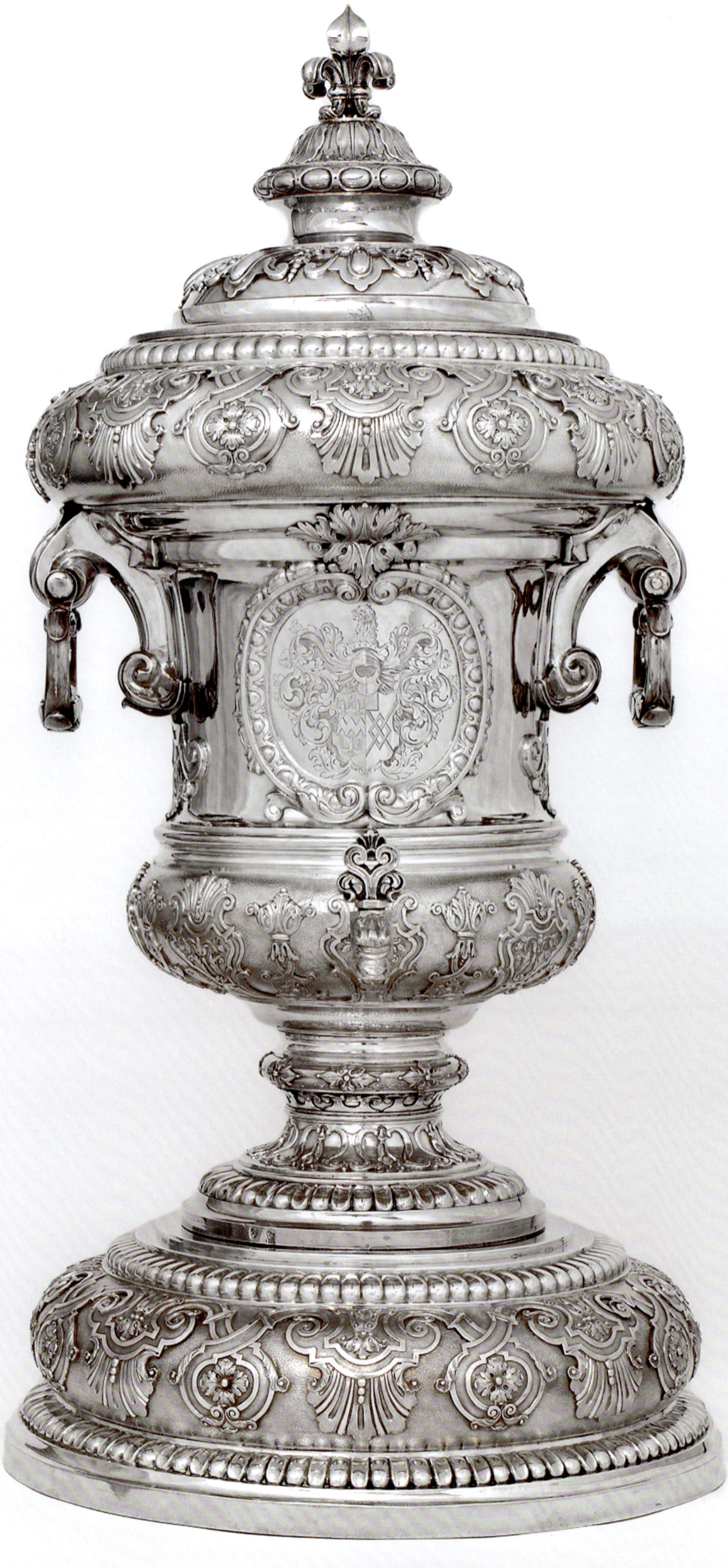

179 Wine fountain

Pierre Platel, London, 1712
Silver, 64 × 35 × 41.4 cm

The Rosalinde and Arthur Gilbert Collection on loan to the Victoria and Albert Museum, London (LOAN:GILBERT.660:1 to 3–2008)

As Clerk of the Green Cloth, Sir John Walter was responsible for the wine served at the court of Queen Anne. This wine fountain was presented to him by the Queen as an heirloom for the Walter family home, Sarsden House, Oxfordshire. After the Peace of Utrecht, 1713, Sir John campaigned to repeal the prohibition on importing French wine. The Latin inscription on this piece records Sir John's wish that this royal gift celebrating restored relations with France should demonstrate to posterity his loyalty to his Queen.

apprentices included John, son of Bartholomew Retry, 'late of Hanno [Hanau] in Germany', and Pierre Le Cheaube, also from Metz. Le Cheaube, who changed his name to Le Chouabe in 1726 when he entered his first independent mark, supplied John Hervey, 1st Earl of Bristol with a tea kettle.[83] Willaume joined the Livery of the Goldsmiths' Company in October 1698 and their Court of Assistants in February 1724/5.[84] In 1714 he attracted the patronage of Caroline, Princess of Wales, who ordered Communion silver for the Huguenot Portarlington church, an Irish settlement of veteran Huguenot soldiers who fought for William III at the Battle of the Boyne in 1690.[85]

From 1719 Willaume combined goldsmithing with banking in his new St James's Street premises. In 1730 he purchased the manor of Tingrith, Bedfordshire, near the Woburn estate of the 2nd Duke of Bedford, his patron from 1702. Invoices in French from Willaume in the ducal archives record purchases of a coronet, a teapot, a bed-warming pan and a set of table forks.[86] He also supplied Ralph, Earl of Montagu with wine fountains and cisterns in 1701–2.[87] Willaume's helmet-shaped ewer (plate 165) was part of a toilet service supplied to the Hill family.[88]

Apprenticed to his father in March 1707, David Willaume the younger (1693–1761) was sent back to France in 1716 to claim his family inheritance in Metz, but the outcome is not known. Free of the Goldsmiths' Company in May 1723, he married Elizabeth, daughter of Charles Dymock of Ampthill, Bedfordshire, and became High Sheriff of Bedfordshire in 1737. In 1717 his sister Anne

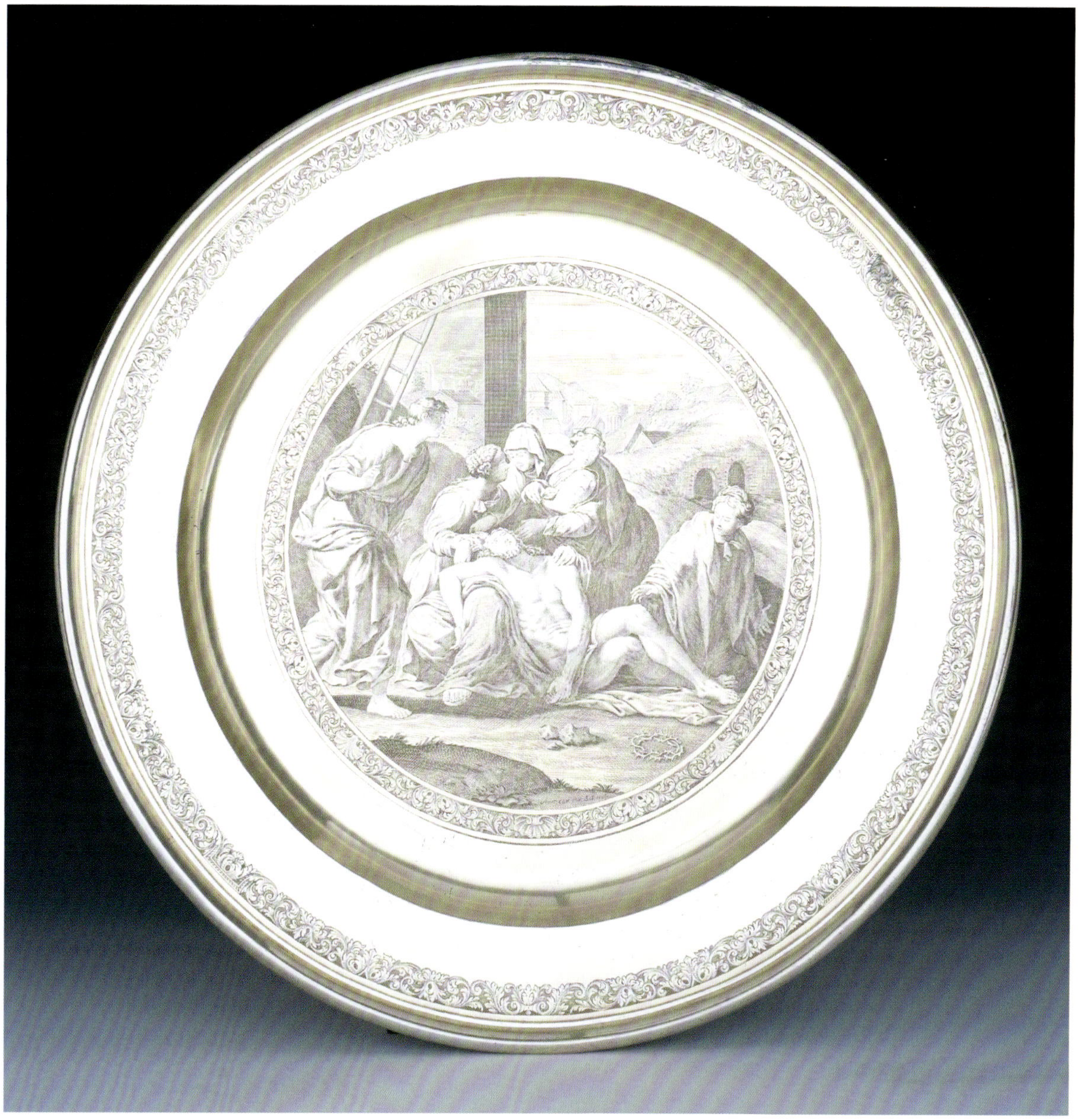

180 Altar dish

Isaac Liger, the engraving signed by Simon Gribelin, London, 1706–7
Silver, diam. 43.2 cm
Dunham Massey, Cheshire, National Trust

Liger supplied this dish, showing the Deposition of Christ, with a Communion cup, paten and tripod candlesticks for the altar of Lord Warrington's private chapel, which was hung with blue Spitalfields silk embroidered in silver with the sacred monogram. The embroidery was perhaps arranged by Liger, who was free of the Broderers' Company from September 1704 'by Redemption by Order of the Court of Aldermen'.

(1691–1733) married their father's apprentice David Tanqueray (fl.1708–30), whose family came from St Lô, Normandy. Anne registered her own mark on her husband's death in 1724 and continued to maintain the family workshop (plate 167) and apprentices. Anne Tanqueray was the first of several outstanding Huguenot women goldsmiths, who included Magdalen Feline (1704–1796),[89] Eliza Godfrey and Louisa Courtauld (1729–1807). Anne Tanqueray specialized in spice boxes, salts and sauceboats, and worked with her brother on elaborate centrepieces and condiment sets.[90] Her great-grandson created Tanqueray gin.

From Saumur, celebrated for its Protestant Academy, came Isaac Liger, who received denization in March 1700. For George Booth, 2nd Earl of Warrington, Liger supplied sacred and domestic silver, toilet services in 1717 and 1728, and chamber pots in 1722;[91] his son, John, entered his mark in 1730 and worked with his father at the Pearl, Hemmings Row, off St Martin's Lane. Liger's altar dish (plate 180) was engraved by Simon Gribelin (plate 228).[92] In 1691 Gribelin married Marie, daughter of Samuel Mettayer, minister of La Patente, Spitalfields, and acquired Louis Mettayer and David Willaume as brothers-in-law; his son Samuel, apprenticed to Mettayer in 1710, became an engraver.

Second-generation Huguenot goldsmiths

Descendants of first-generation refugees, trained by their forebears, maintained high standards. Through international networks they kept abreast of the latest Continental stylistic changes and supplied an increasingly international market.

PAUL DE LAMERIE

Paul de Lamerie was born in the then Dutch city of 's-Hertogenbosch (Bois-le-Duc), in April 1688; his father, Paul Souchay de la Merie (d.1735), was an officer in William of Orange's army. Paul's godparents Jacques Bourse and Marguerite Vignon (d.1699) came from The Hague and Amsterdam respectively. His mother's family were from Normandy: her ancestor Jean Le Roux (1596–1634) settled in Amsterdam in 1619 but there were still relatives in Rouen in 1685. De Lamerie's godmother, Marguerite Vignon, may be connected to The Hague goldsmith Jean du Vignon (1683–1746), who contributed in 1711 to the Communion set for The Hague English church.[93] The de Lameries followed William of Orange to England; Paul Souchay, Paul de Lamerie's father, was pensioned and listed in the Poor Rate records of 1691 as living in Berwick Street, Soho. De Lamerie's uncle, Jean Souchay, also pensioned, had joined the Dublin French church by 1702 and was awarded a further pension in 1715.

De Lamerie grew up in the Soho French community.[94] When he joined Platel as an apprentice in 1703, his master had two small children. Established at the Golden Ball, Windmill Street, near Haymarket, de Lamerie continued his master's association with the Royal Jewel House and served from 1716 as Goldsmith to King George I. Wall sconces with later coat of arms and gilding for Baron Foley are among de Lameries earliest marked silver[95] and incorporate ornament associated with Jean Berain, Louis XIV's court designer. The wine fountain that de Lamerie supplied for the Harpur Crewe family at Calke Abbey, Derbyshire, in 1719 demonstrates his familiarity with Daniel Marot's published designs.[96] His international network extended from Italy and Russia – there was a captive market for Huguenot silver at the Russian court[97] – to the New World, where direct links were maintained with London goldsmiths. For example, Francis Garden (1709–*c*.1768), the brother of London goldsmith retailer Phillips Garden (fl.1739–62), is credited with the design of his brother's elegant London trade card; by 1741 Francis Garden was in Charleston and advertised in *The South Carolina Gazette* as engraving 'in the best Manner … any kind of Metal, Coats of Arms etc'.[98] By the mid-1740s he was working as silver engraver in Boston, Massachusetts.[99]

In Italy, Handel's leading castrato, Senesino (1686–1758), retired to his native Siena and entertained in style, displaying his portrait bust by Roubiliac and using a dinner service supplied by Paul de Lamerie.[100] This may have included as many as 95 pieces: a similar service created by de Lamerie for Sackville Tufton, 7th Earl of Thanet, in 1742–6, comprised two soup tureens, six salts, six meat dishes, two mazarines, two serving platters, 72 dinner plates, four second course dishes and a covered supper dish.[101]

In 1723 de Lamerie formed a business partnership with Ellis Gamble (fl.1712–33), silver engraver, at the Golden Angel, Cranbourn Street, off Leicester Fields,[102] who took William Hogarth as apprentice in 1714 (plate 32). Hogarth engraved de Lamerie's Exchequer Seal Salver for Prime Minister Robert Walpole (plate 181); he may also have supplied de Lamerie's personal bookplate, with figures inspired by Girardon's sculptures

181 Walpole Exchequer Seal Salver

Paul de Lamerie, engraved by William Hogarth, London, 1728–9
Silver, 48 × 48.5 cm
Victoria and Albert Museum, London (M.9–1956)

The central engraving reproduces the obverse and reverse of Walpole's previous seal of office as First Lord of the Treasury under George I. This is supported by the figure of Hercules, symbolizing strength, with Fortitude above. In the background is old London Bridge with the spires of the City of London churches. The border, with Walpole's armorial crest and initials, was probably cut by a specialist silver engraver.

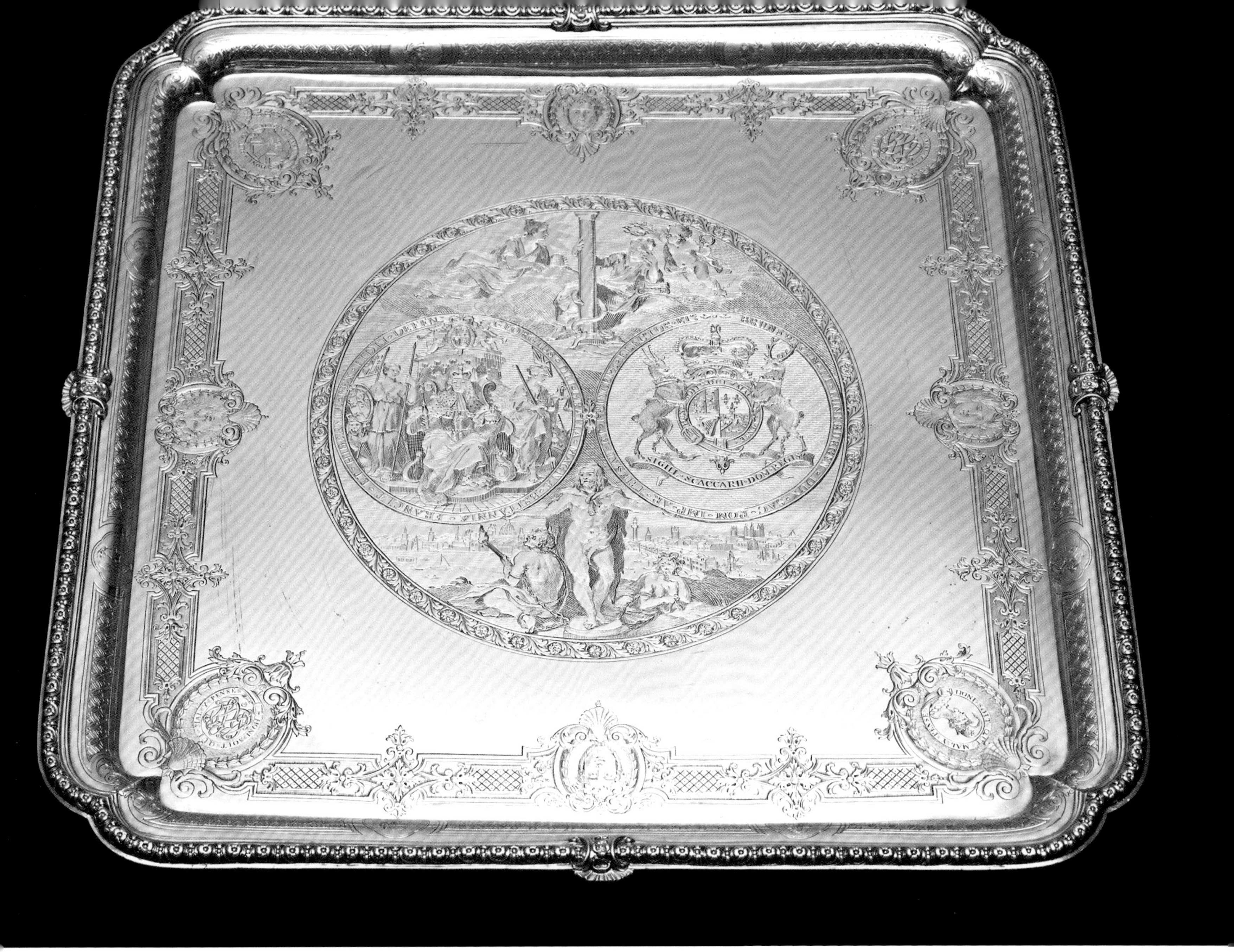

of Autumn and Winter (1675–83) in the gardens at Versailles.[103] Gamble's 'angel' trade card, the engraving of Hercules on the Exchequer Seal Salver and de Lamerie's bookplate all feature the human figure.[104] As an apprentice, de Lamerie could attend life drawing at Kneller's Academy in Great Queen Street, Covent Garden. By 1722 Chéron and Vanderbank's Academy in St Martin's Lane provided opportunities to draw the female model; de Lamerie may have encouraged his apprentices to attend.[105] Figurative ornament chased in relief, cast to form handles of helmet-shaped ewers and wine coolers and engraved on silver by Simon Gribelin and the younger Joseph Sympson, benefited from such training. At these classes, seal engravers, sculptors and surgeons rubbed shoulders with painters (p.51): the drawing skills they acquired raised the quality of production and ornament on applied art.

Published designs were readily available from print shops in Great Newport Street (p.233) and bookshops in The Strand, including Erasmus's Head, run by David Mortier (1673–1728) from 1700 and the Ship, established in 1686 by the Vaillant family[106] and later carried on by Nicholas Prevost (d.1748), who married Suzanne Vaillant

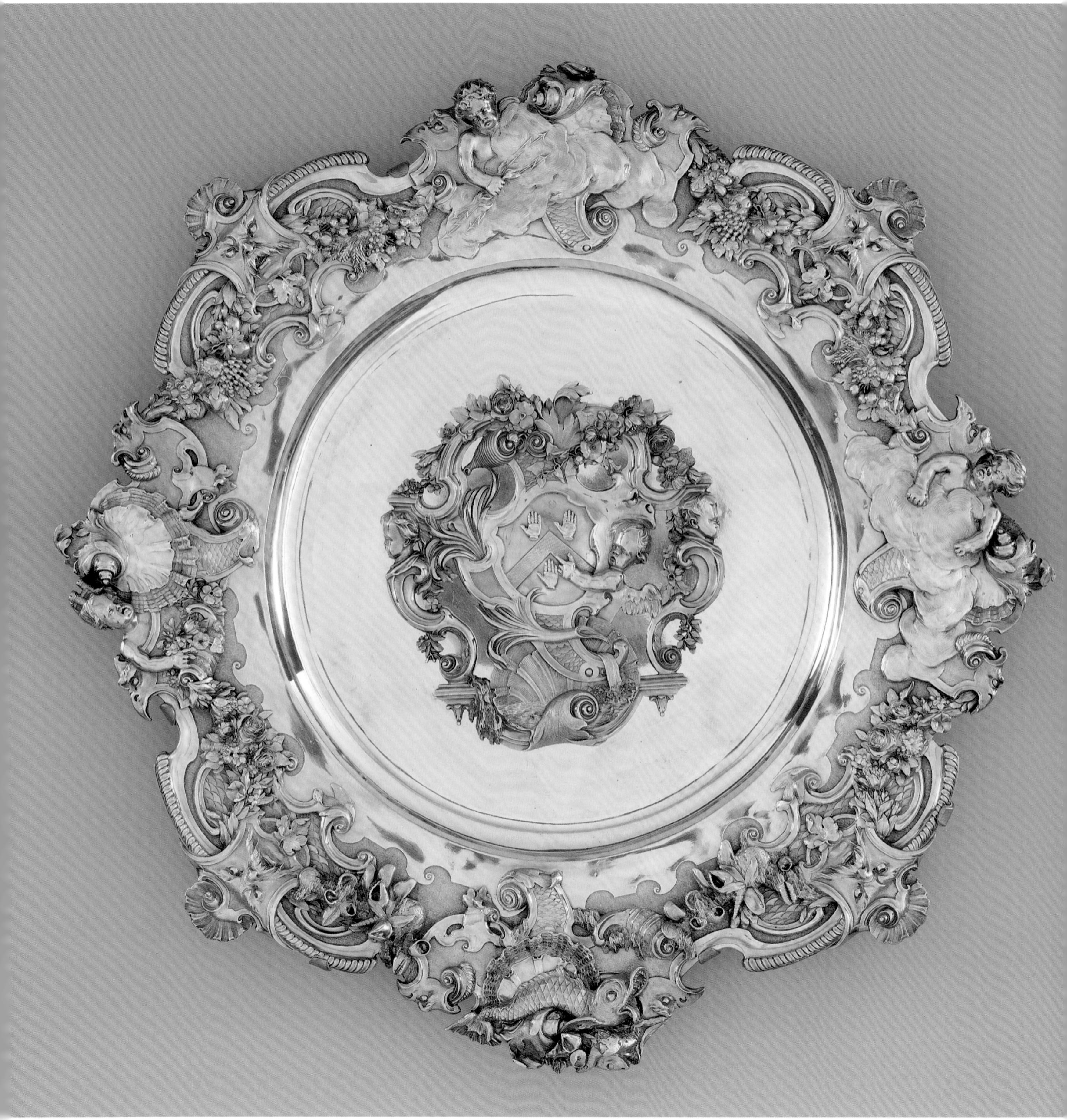

LEFT

182 The Maynard Dish

Maynard Master for Paul de Lamerie, London, 1736–7
Silver, diam. 66.6 cm
Cahn Collection on loan to the St Louis Art Museum, USA

The border displays the skill of the anonymous chaser who worked for de Lamerie, known as the Maynard Master; this dish is the earliest example of his inventive Rococo style. The Four Elements – Air, Earth, Fire and Water – are represented by abstract and organic forms.

(1669–1749). Matthew Varenne (d.1726) was at Seneca's Head near Somerset House from 1712.[107] These shops had links with Amsterdam and sold the latest European publications. Some of them were managed by women, including Céleste Regnier (plate 226) in Newport Street.[108] William De La Cour (plate 27) drew 'for all Sorts of Trades' and may have designed silver with de Lamerie's mark, which has been attributed to the chaser named after the spectacular dish made for Charles, 1st Viscount Maynard (1690–1775; plate 182). Another artist who also designed for goldsmiths was Gravelot – his full name Hubert-Francois Bourguignon (p.57). Trained in François Boucher's Paris studio, Gravelot was invited to London in 1732 or 1733 by the engraver Claude Du Bosc, to work on the English translation of Bernard Picart's *Ceremonies et coutumes religieuses de tous les peuples et de tous les temps* (1733–9).[109] George Vertue noted in 1741 that Gravelot 'practises etching ... in which he has done many curious plates from his own desseins [*sic*] masterly and free and *de bon gout*'. A drawing for an *etui* demonstrates that Gravelot was designing for smaller-scale goldsmiths' work.[110]

In 1735 de Lamerie supplied a tea equipage (plate 183), a marriage gift for Jean Daniel Boissier and Suzanne Judith Berchère. Suzanne was Louis Berchère's granddaughter, baptized at the Threadneedle Street church in July 1702.[111] The gift was commissioned by Suzanne's father, Jacques Louis Berchère, City merchant jeweller and banker in Broad Street, and founder director of the French Hospital in 1718.[112] The silver-mounted mahogany case is personalized with the Boissier and Berchère armorials.[113]

The London General Evening Post noted de Lamerie's death in 1751 as the passing of a 'Tender Father, a kind Master and an upright Dealer'. His kindness is demonstrated by his support for fellow Huguenot goldsmith Jaques Ray, whose mental illness was likely caused by mercury poisoning from gilding silver.[114] Ray's wife, Honor, reported that he had been 'greatly deprived of his senses' for between six and seven years (they had been married since 1718): 'He has left several times his habitation and family running about the streets for several days like a madman forsaking his business of a Goldsmith and crying Oranges and Lemons'. In 1737, with goldsmiths Henry Hebert (fl.1734–6; originally from Le Mans) and John Le Sage (fl.1742–61), de Lamerie signed an indemnity charge for £1,000 worth of damage to support Ray's admission to the French Hospital.[115] 'La Veuve Cuny', Louis Cuny's widow, also contributed. Ray was admitted in October 1737 but escaped in August 1738.[116]

The de Lamerie family had connections to the French Threadneedle Street church: Abraham Maillet (recorded 1739–54), who illustrated the 1739 edition of *Police et Discipline* for that church, witnessed the marriage of de Lamerie's daughter in 1754.[117]

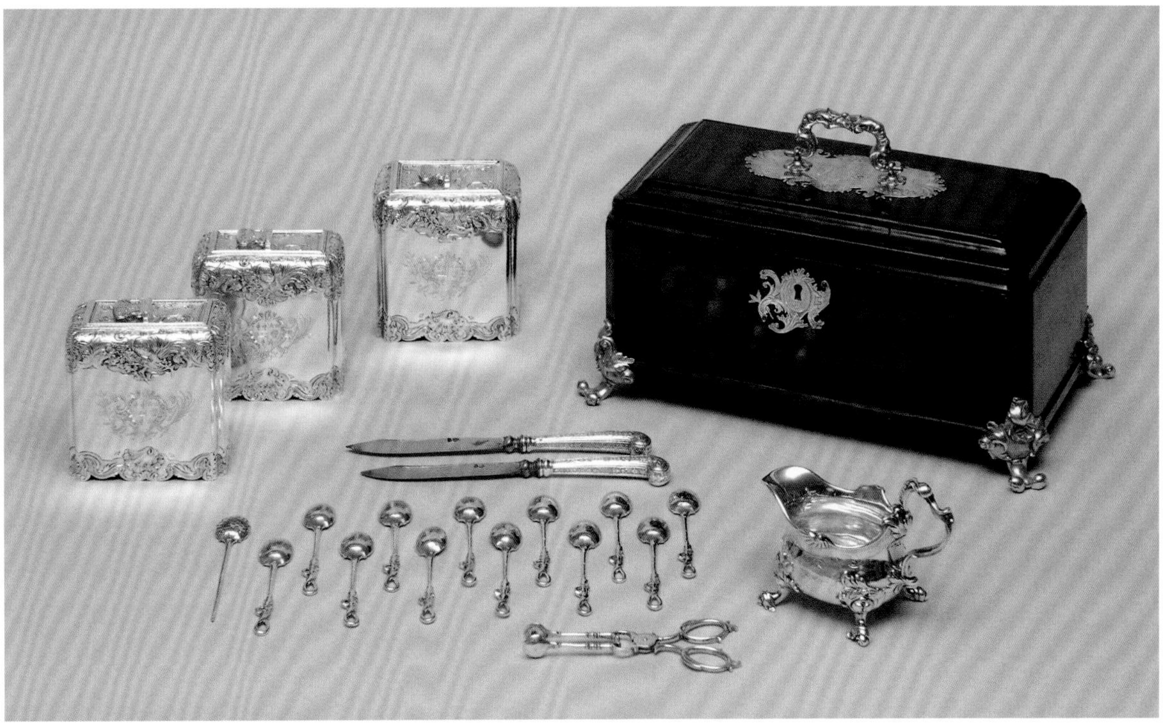

RIGHT

183 Tea equipage

Paul de Lamerie and others, 1735
Silver in mahogany case, caddies ht 11.8 cm high; teaspoons l. 12.2 cm
Temple Newsam House, Leeds

The silver-mounted mahogany case is personalized with armorials to celebrate the marriage of Jean Daniel Boissier and Suzanne Judith Berchère. The tea canisters and sugar box are chased and engraved, masking their rectilinear form in contrast to the cream jug's cast scroll handle and rim punctuated by shells.

De Lamerie had time for external commitments. In 1738 he served as Captain and then Major in the Westminster volunteer regiment. He also served as Warden for the Goldsmiths' Company Court of Assistants. But it was as dealer and retailer that he excelled. By drawing on an international network of designs, supervising the wide-ranging continental and native talent available in London at the time, and manufacturing for export, de Lamerie enjoyed a successful career and a lasting international reputation as 'very instrumental in bringing that Branch of Trade into the Perfection it is now in'.[118]

De Lamerie's silver is closer in style to German than French prototypes. His will was witnessed in 1751 by James Shruder (fl.1733–49), a chaser, recorded in London by 1733 when he took Julian Crispin as apprentice.[119] In his will de Lamerie requests that his journeymen Frederick Knopfell (fl.1752–70) and Samuel Collins (b. *c.*1718) finish the silver in hand at the time of his death. Knopfell, who entered his own mark in 1752, has been identified with Frederick Klupfel, a jeweller with Dresden connections. By 1763 Shruder was described as a 'Modeller and Papier Maché Manufacturer' so he may well have supplied models for silver during his 30-year career in London.

PAUL CRESPIN

From 1727 Paul de Lamerie traded with Paul Crespin at the Golden Ball in Compton Street. Crespin was apprenticed to Jean Pons from 1713. The portrait of Crespin as a working craftsman (plate 184), holding a vase after designs by the Italian engraver Enea Vico (1523–1567), shows that he dealt in antique silver as well as making to commission.[120] The portrait compares with those of David Le Marchand with his ivory bust of Newton and Roubiliac with his terracotta model for David Garrick's statue of Shakespeare (see frontispiece).

For Lord Chesterfield's 1727 embassy to The Hague, Crespin supplied wine coolers by de Lamerie, overstriking that goldsmith's mark with his own. These are copies of the 1723 pair by de Lamerie supplied for Thomas Howard, 8th Duke of Norfolk (1683–1732). Crespin also supplied copies of candlesticks by Lille goldsmith Elie Pacot (1657–1721) originally made for John Churchill, 1st Duke of Marlborough.[121] In July 1724 Crespin's 'Silver Vessel for bathing ... weigh'd about 6030 ounces' when assayed at Goldsmiths' Hall; this was shown to George I at Kensington Palace, who 'was well pleased with so curious a Piece of Workmanship, which can scarcely be match'd in all Europe'.[122] This silver bath was 'Supported on three dolphins, their tails curling up around the outside surface', three mermaids' bodies followed the curve of the double-gilt interior. The sides were decorated with figures of Diana bathing and Perseus and Andromeda; the head of the bath supported Neptune with his trident. Ordered for the King of Portugal by the Portuguese envoy in London, the commission was probably obtained through Crespin's younger brother, a goldsmith to the Lisbon court.[123] The silver bath was destroyed in the Lisbon earthquake of 1755, but Crespin had raised the status of London-produced goldsmiths' work to that of sculpture, demonstrating an ability to model elaborate mythologies in silver relief.[124]

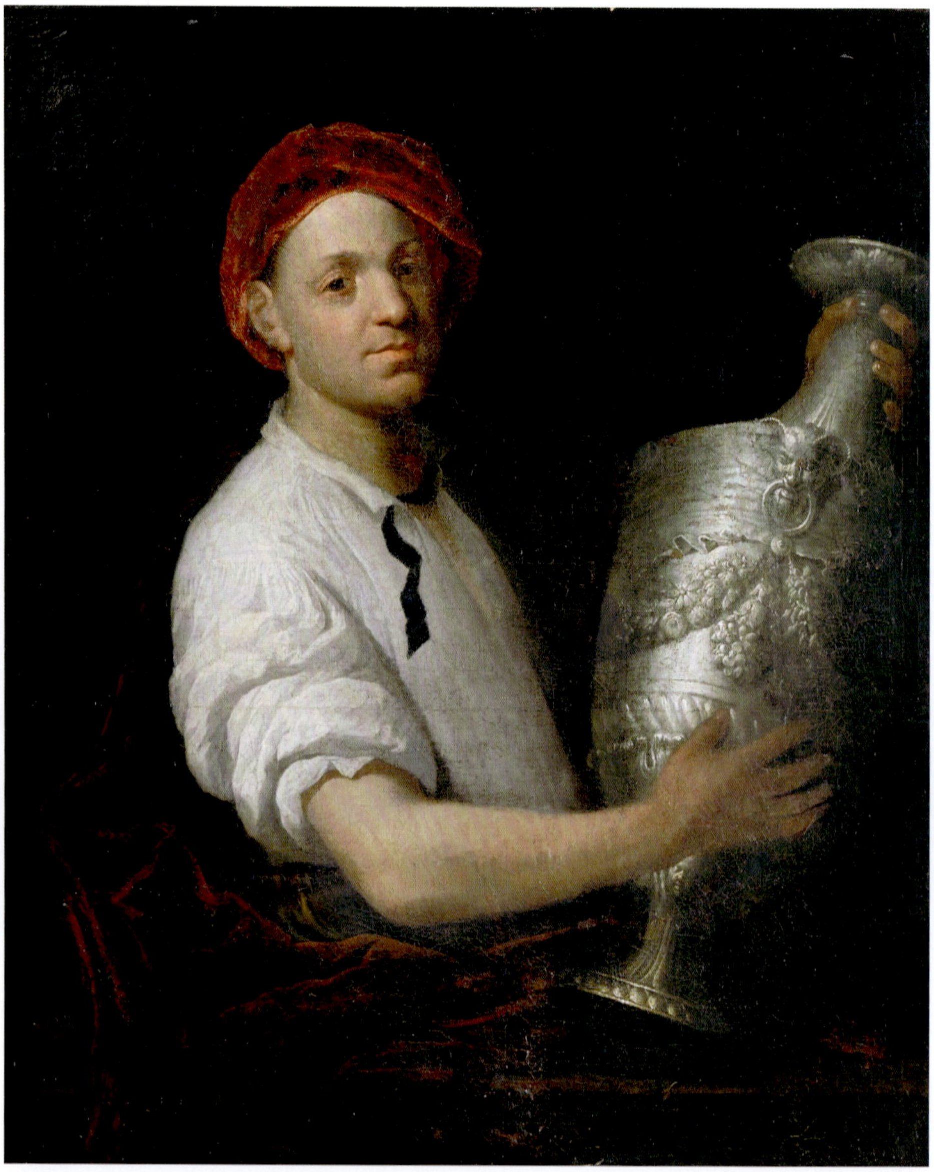

184 *Paul Crespin*
Unknown artist, London, *c.*1726
Oil on canvas, 114 × 90 cm
Victoria and Albert Museum, London (P.29–1985)

Little is known about Crespin's training except that he was apprenticed to Jean Pons in 1713 (presumably the Jean Pens listed as goldsmith in 1705 at the French Savoy church). Crespin established a reputation in the early 1720s for meticulous craftsmanship and for large-scale production for export. He is portrayed here as working craftsman and dealer, holding a vase in an earlier Italian style.

Silver supplied by Crespin to James Brydges, 1st Duke of Chandos, between 1726 and 1728 included candlesticks costing £135. Crespin's sophisticated charger of 1727–8 embellished with named medallion portraits of classical philosophers (plate 185) was probably made for Chandos and passed through marriage to the 2nd Marquess of Buckingham, whose later coat of arms it bears.[125]

Rococo dining silver

In France the earliest manifestations of Rococo appeared in silver. Meissonnier's set of designs for *Chandeliers de Sculpture en Argent* published in 1728, available from the print shops in Great Newport Street, show ornamental details, putti, shells and scrolls from three different angles, intended for the dinner table. Charles Carter's *Complete Practical Cook* of 1730 includes a table setting for an *ambigu* evening refreshment (a buffet with a wide selection of dishes) for a masquerade, with 'a branched light' on either side of the *surtout* (tall centrepiece). The pioneering French cookbook by François Massiolot, *Le Nouveau Cuisinier Royal et Bourgeois* first published in Paris in 1691, had recipes illustrated with woodcuts of silver vessels for serving them. The 1729 edition reproduced Massiolot's 1691 'Machine' frontispiece with attached candles providing a solution to lighting the centre of the dining table. In 1731–2 de Lamerie supplied the first surviving four-branched silver candelabrum made in London for the dining table of Prime Minister Sir Robert Walpole (plate 186). While his candlesticks made in 1744–5 for Mayfair banker Peter Le

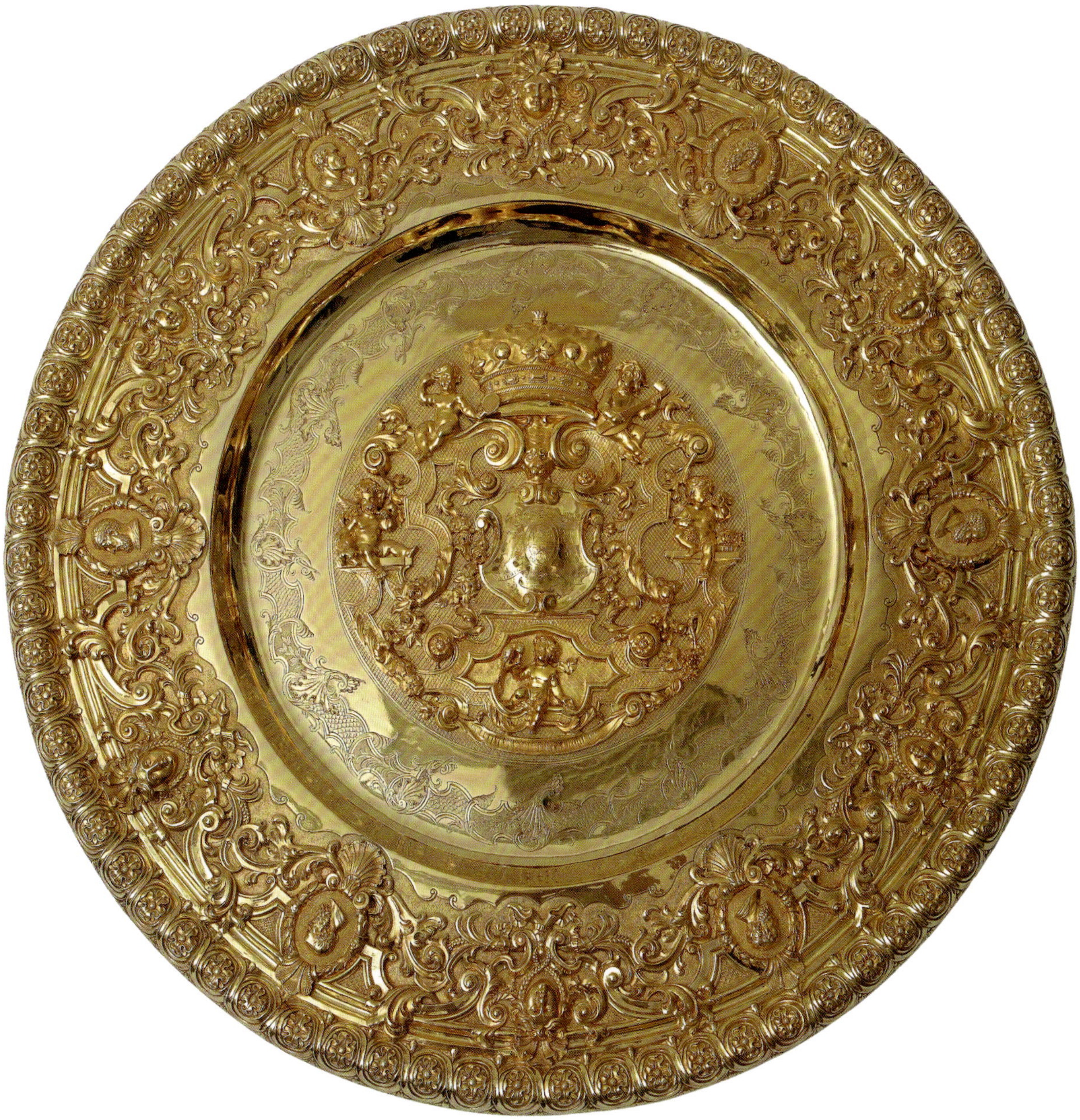

185 Charger

Paul Crespin, London, 1727–8
Silver-gilt, diam. 71.7 cm
The Rosalinde and Arthur Gilbert Collection on loan to the Victoria and Albert Museum, London (LOAN:GILBERT.717–2008)

Medallion portraits of Heraclitus, Democritus, Diogenes, Antisthenes, Zaleucus and Socrates framed by laurel wreaths are identified on the reverse. The basin descended to Richard, 2nd Marquess of Buckingham and Earl Temple of Stowe (1776–1839), whose later coat of arms it bears. The charger was proudly displayed at Stowe to underline Lord Buckingham's sophisticated classical education.

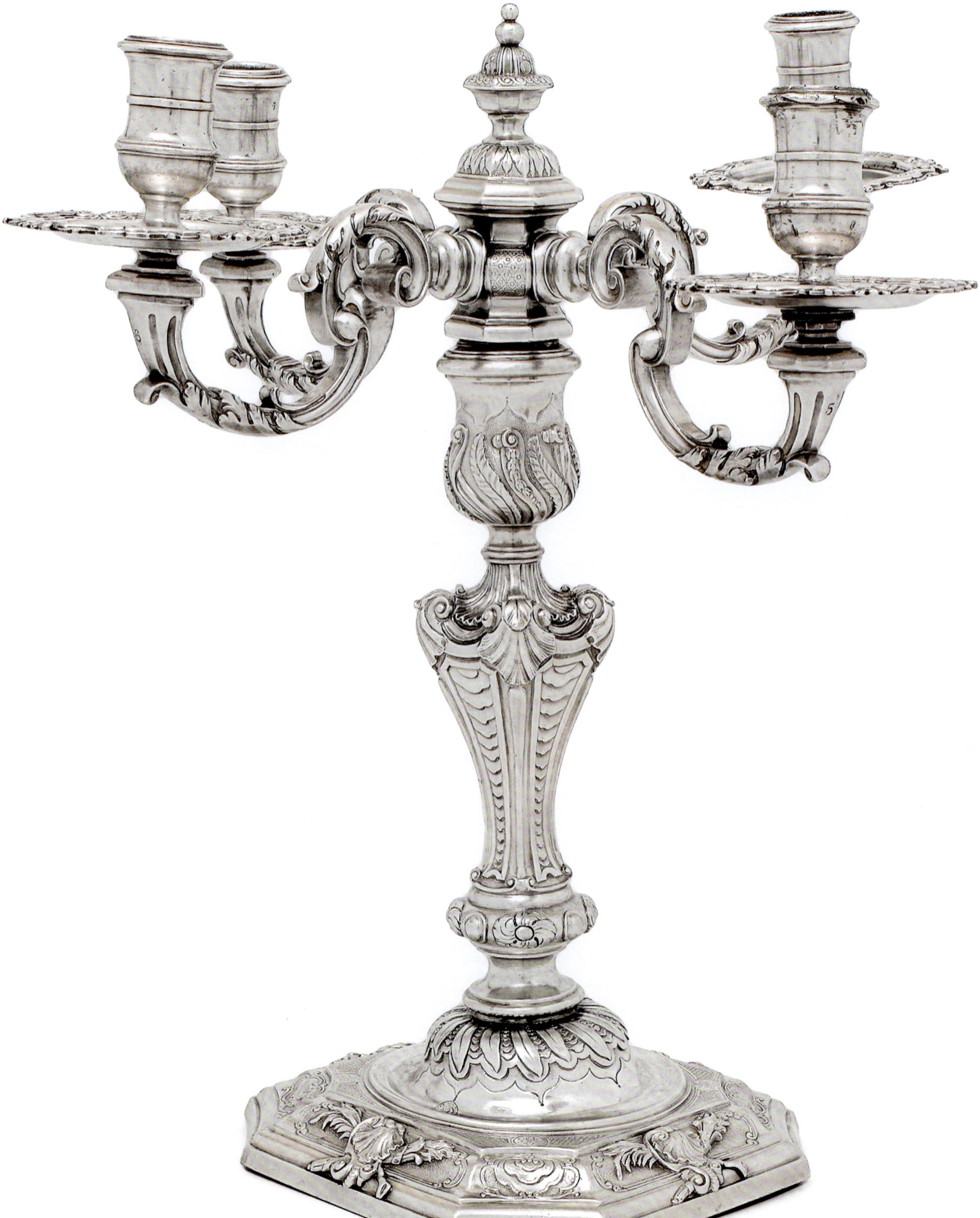

LEFT

186 The Walpole Candelabrum

Paul de Lamerie, London, 1731–2
Silver, ht 32.3 cm
The Rosalinde and Arthur Gilbert Collection on loan to the Victoria and Albert Museum, London (LOAN:GILBERT.690:1-10-2008)

The earliest-recorded four-branch candelabrum made in London provided an effective source of candlelight for Prime Minister Sir Robert Walpole's dining table at 10 Downing Street and later in the Marble Parlour at Houghton Hall, Norfolk.

RIGHT

187 Candlesticks

Paul de Lamerie, London, 1744–5
Silver, ht 23.5 cm
Victoria and Albert Museum, London (M.4&5-2010)

De Lamerie's candlesticks for Mayfair banker Peter Le Heup incorporate beehives and bees from the family coat of arms. Their sophisticated asymmetrical profile suggests familiarity with J.A. Meissonnier's designs for candlesticks published in Paris in 1728.

Heup incorporate bees and hives from the family coat of arms,[126] their sophisticated asymmetrical profile suggests familiarity with Meissonnier's 1728 designs (plate 187).

The drive to provide fashionable silver for the dinner table was encouraged by French cuisine practised by Vincent La Chapelle, Lord Chesterfield's master chef, at his school in Mayfair; he later joined Chesterfield's embassy in The Hague. La Chapelle's three-volume *The Modern Cook*, published by subscription in London in 1733 by Nicholas Prevost, ran into four editions by 1751. The first edition included designs for a *surtout* 'to be left upon the Table until Dessert is Serv'd' (plate 188) and for a terrine or *olio* (plate 189). The engraver was Andrew Motte (1696–1734), brother of the bookseller Benjamin Motte (1693–1738) of Middle Temple Gate, Fleet Street, who took subscriptions for La Chapelle's publication in 1732.[127] La Chapelle's second volume includes a table plan for 15 or 16 covers, with two pairs of tureens: lower, oval vessels with squat feet and boar's head handles and taller tureens at opposite ends of the table. La Chapelle's second edition (1736) was translated into French, dedicated to George II's son-in-law, the Prince of Orange, and was on sale in The Hague in 1742. According to La Chapelle, whose new recipes influenced the form of vessels in which they were served,

> *A cook of genius will invent new Delicacies to please the Palates ... his Art, like all others, being Subject to Change: For should ... a great Man be serv'd in the Taste that prevailed twenty Years ago, it would not please the Guests.*[128]

During the 1730s native goldsmith George Wickes was competing with Crespin and de Lamerie to produce London-made silver in the French style. By the 1740s silver marked by London goldsmiths Thomas Heming and Edward Wakelin, trained by Peter Archambo and John Le Sage respectively, was of comparable quality to silver marked by second-generation Huguenot craftsmen.

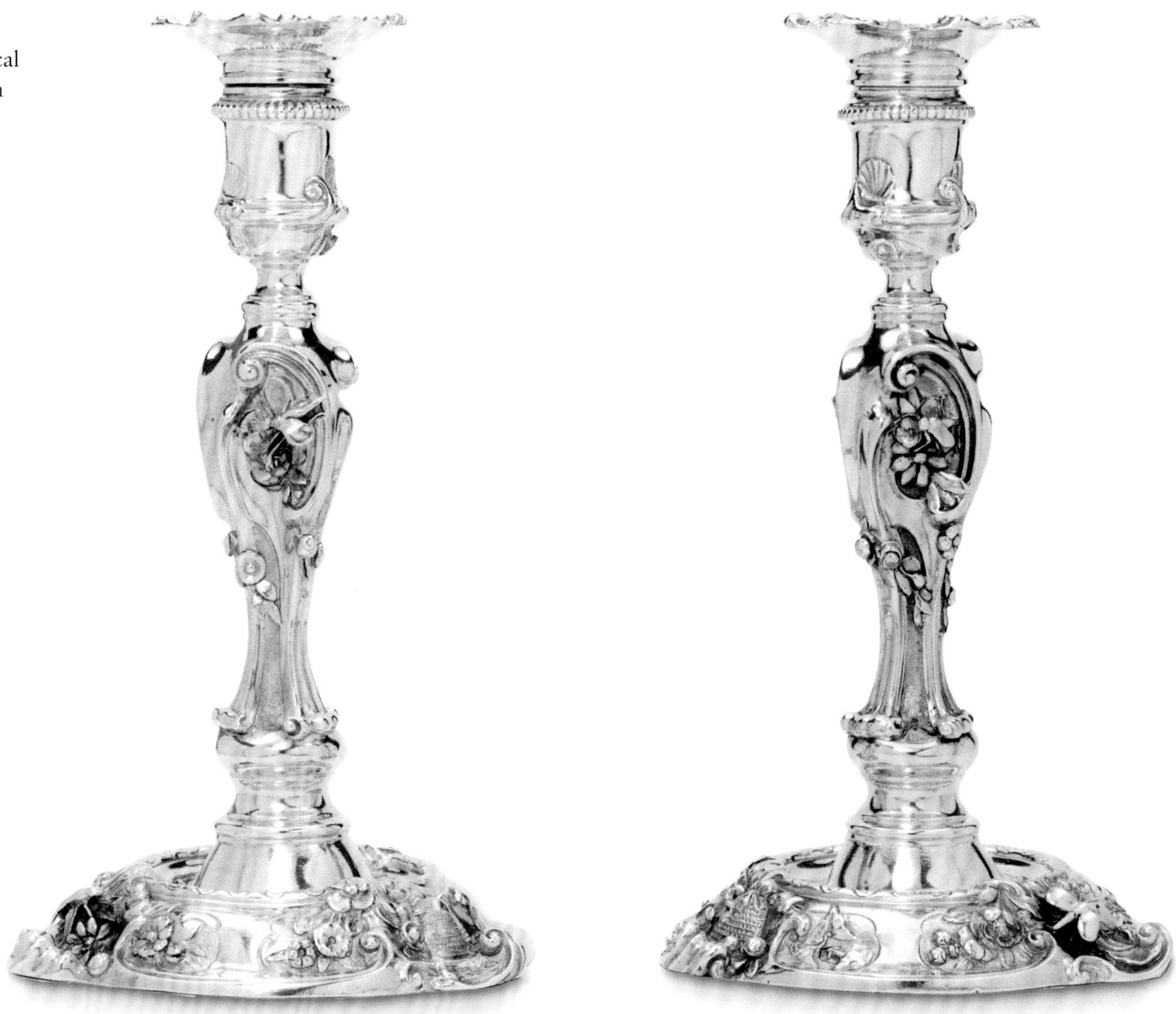

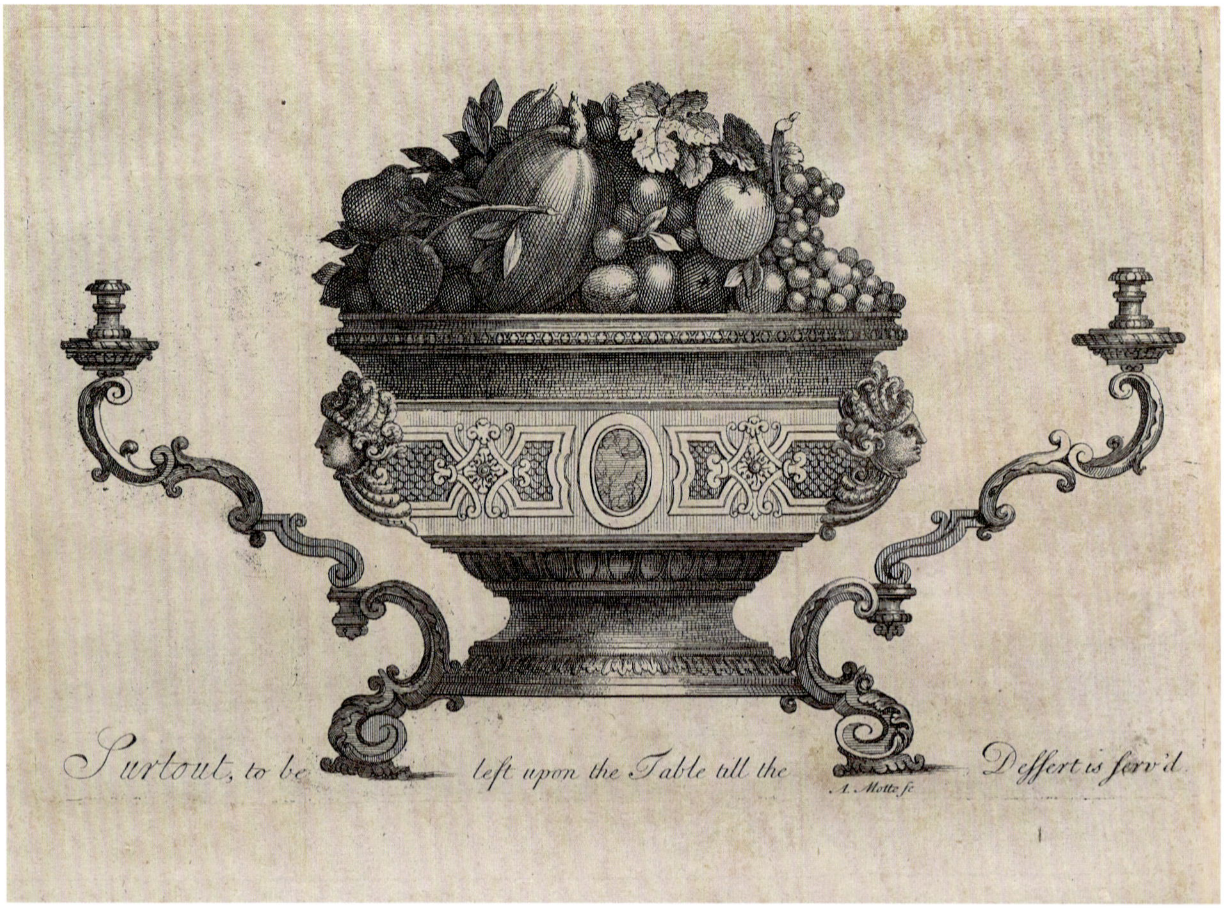

188 *Surtout*

Andrew Motte, from Vincent La Chapelle's *The Modern Cook*, London 1733
Engraving, 12 × 20 cm
Willan Cherniavsky Gastronomy Collection, Getty Research Institute (2019-B592)

The engraver Andrew Motte, one-time lecturer in geometry at Gresham College, London, was the brother of Benjamin Motte who published books by Isaac Newton and Jonathan Swift.

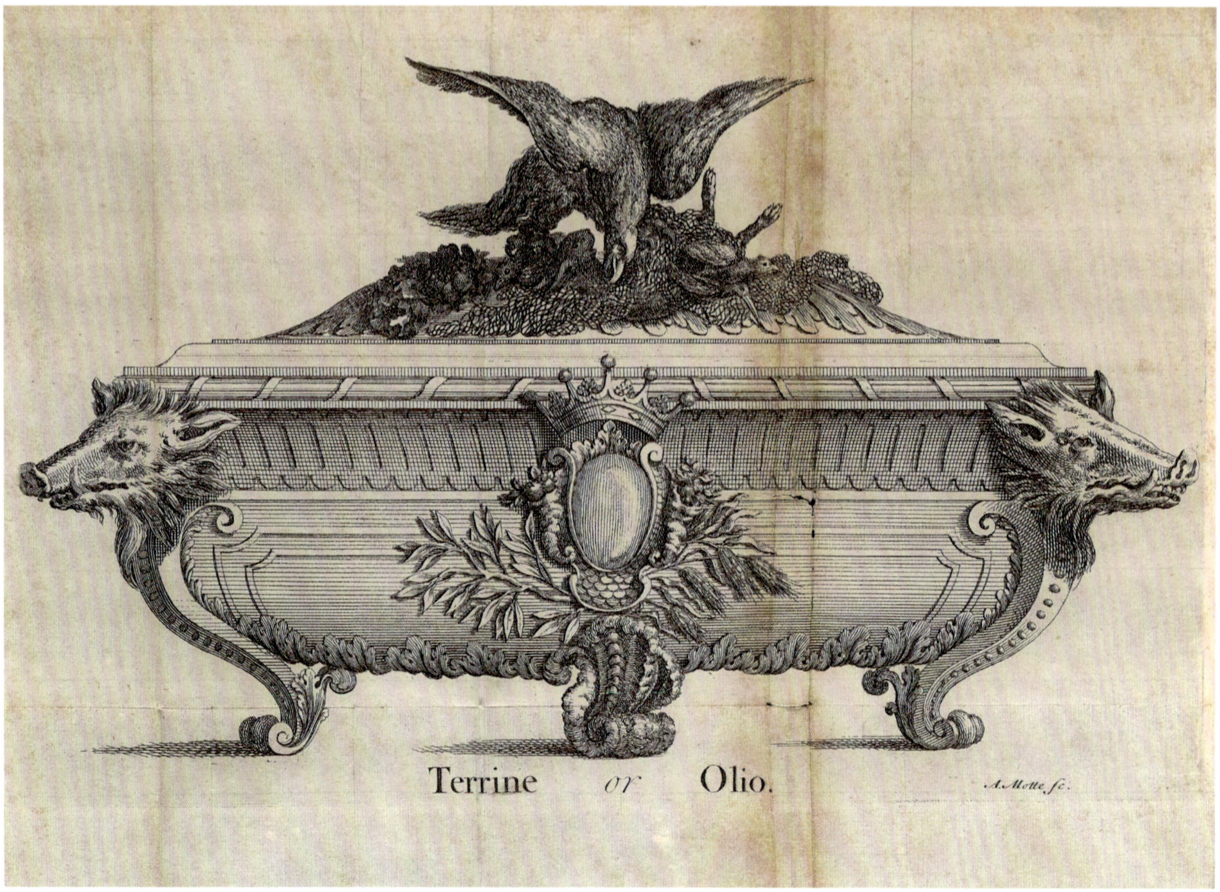

189 Terrine or *olio*

Andrew Motte, from Vincent La Chapelle's *The Modern Cook*, London 1733
Engraving, 12 × 20 cm
Willan Cherniavsky Gastronomy Collection, Getty Research Institute (2019-B592)

The sophisticated illustration of table silver, life-like rendering of the fruit on the *surtout* and the boars' head handles and the eagle and game bird on the cover of this tureen, achieved a new standard for cook books and promoted contemporary goldsmiths. The fourth edition of La Chapelle's *The Modern Cook* was published in London in 1751.

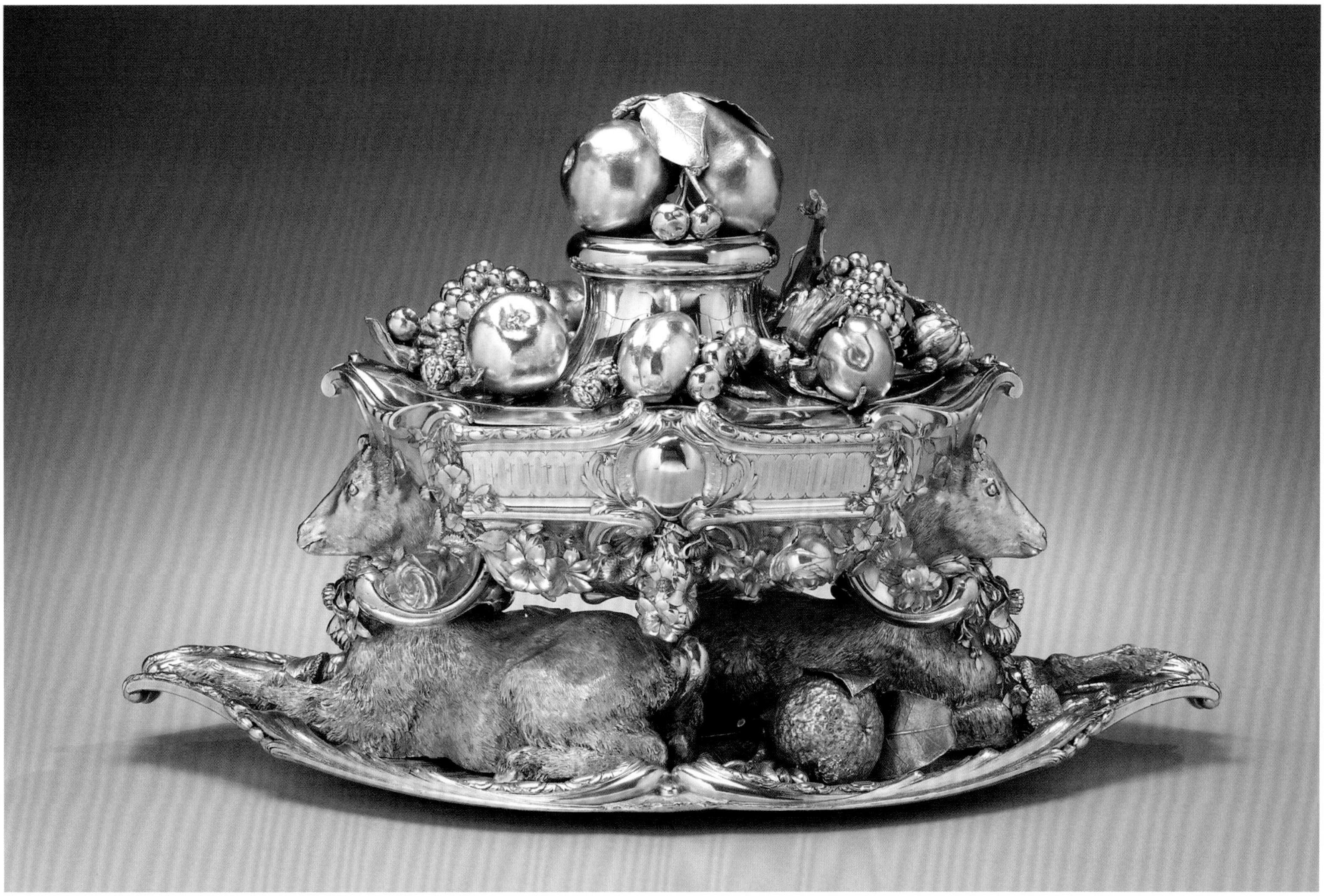

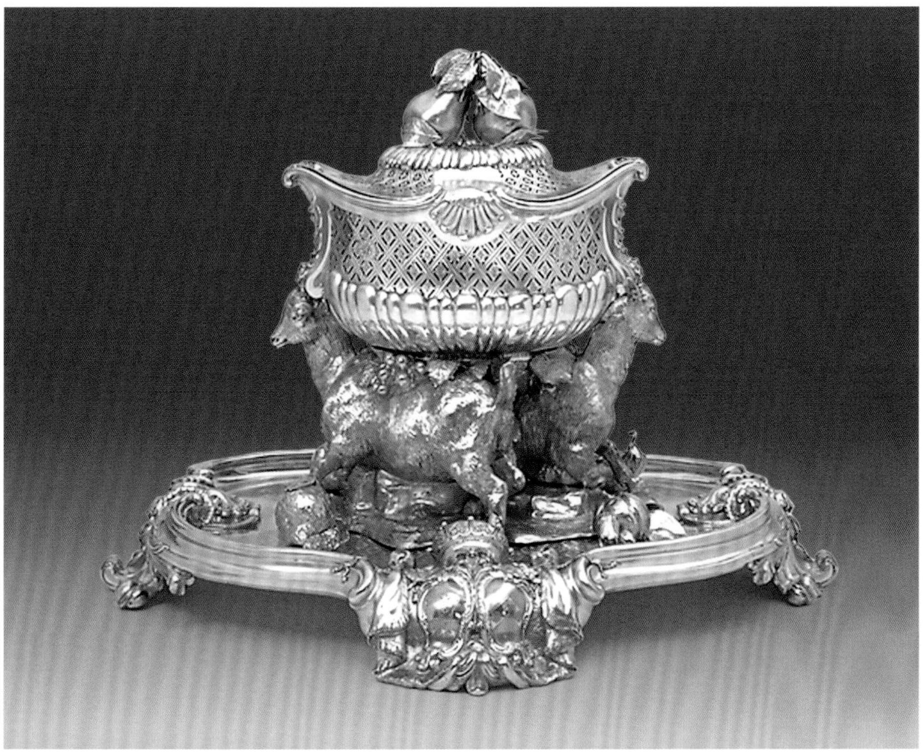

190 Centrepiece

Marked by Paul Crespin but possibly made in association with Nicholas Sprimont, London, 1740
Silver, 36 × 54.5 cm
Toledo Museum of Art, Ohio (1964.51)

Crespin and Sprimont's centrepieces are of sculptural quality and possibly inspired by the *surtout* and terrine illustrated in the first edition of Vincent La Chapelle's *The Modern Cook*.

191 Centrepiece

Nicholas Sprimont, London, 1747
Silver, ht 46.5 cm
Victoria and Albert Museum, London (M.46:1, 2–1971)

The sculptural modelling of the goats and the naturalistic fruit contrast with the central tureen. Sprimont, who was in Paris in the mid-1730s, was familiar with the work of leading French goldsmiths, including Thomas Germain. The coat of arms engraved on the foot of the base are for John, 2nd Earl of Ashburnham, and his wife, Elizabeth, who acquired the centrepiece after their marriage in 1756. It is not known for whom the piece was made in 1747–8, as traces of the earlier armorials cannot be identified.

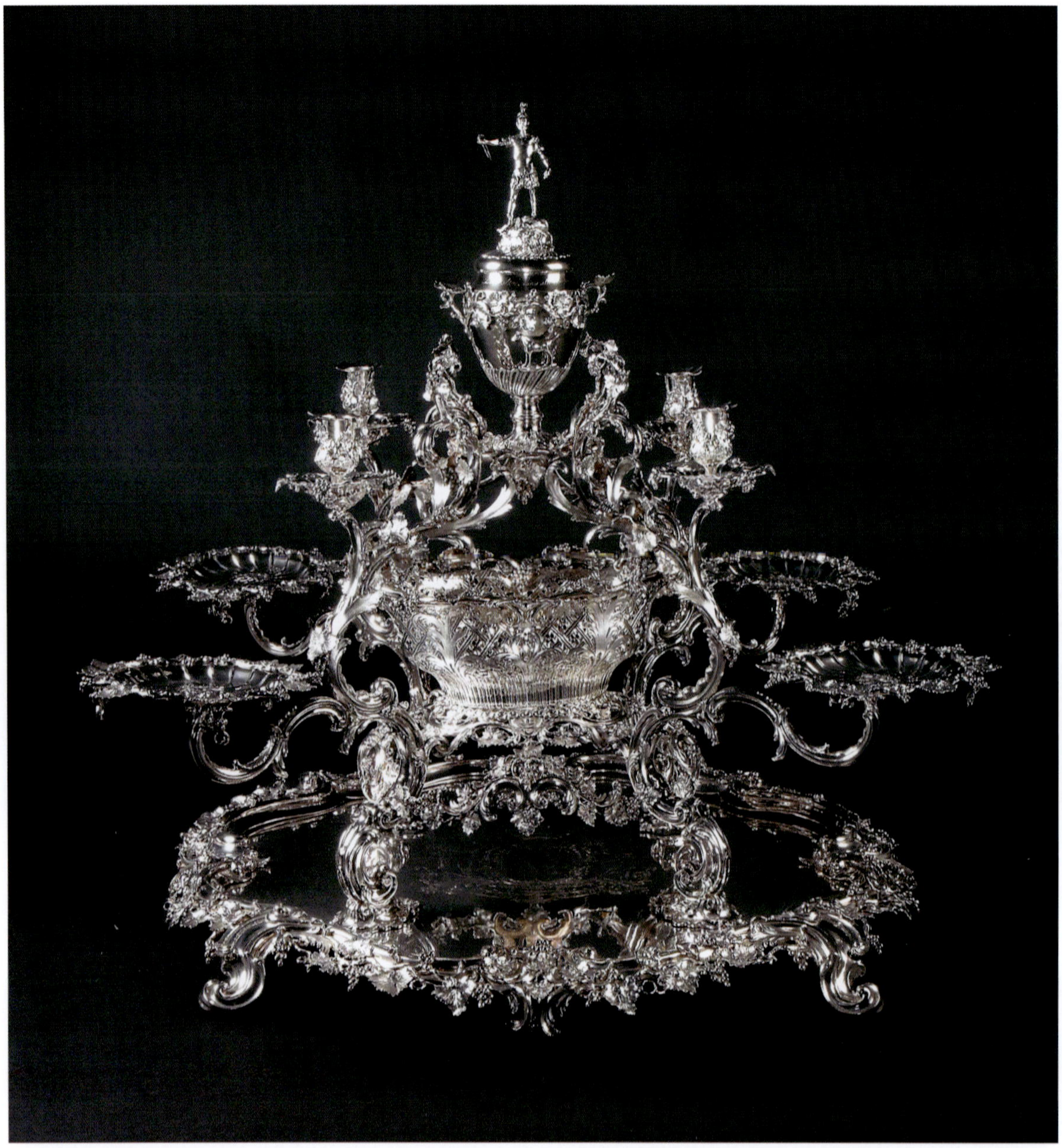

192 Epergne and stand

Thomas Harrache and James Peltro, London, 1755
Silver, 70 × 66 × 55 cm
Kedleston, National Trust

Curzon purchased this 'large table' from Thomas Harrache, retailer in Pall Mall, for £525 15s in 1757. It was adapted as a trophy, surmounted by the figure of Jason, winner of the Golden Fleece to celebrate the race won by Curzon's horse of that name in 1755.

NICHOLAS SPRIMONT

Paul Crespin was associated with the Liège-born goldsmith Nicholas Sprimont, who was established in London by 1742; together they produced the celebrated marine service for Frederick, Prince of Wales. The Neptune centrepiece, marked by Crespin, incorporates an earlier tureen (dated 1720–42) with Turin maker's marks.[129] Sprimont marked accompanying crab and crayfish salts (1742–3) and sauceboats (1743–5).[130]

Sprimont also collaborated with de Lamerie before abandoning the goldsmiths' craft for the manufacture of Chelsea porcelain in partnership with the Huguenot jeweller Charles Gouyn (pp.167–8). Sprimont's tureen design for Thomas Coke, 1st Earl of Leicester (plate 150),[131] may have been made up for de Lamerie, who was responsible for the dinner service at Holkham, Coke's Norfolk home. This included three tureens for use *à la française*; one larger 'terreen' weighed 169 oz (4,791 g) and two smaller ones 95 and 98 oz (2,693 and 2,778 g) respectively. The service was melted down and refashioned in the early nineteenth century.[132]

Silver marked by Sprimont shows a stronger French influence than that marked by de Lamerie. Sprimont was in Geneva in the mid-1730s and may have worked with Thomas Germain before coming to London; he was certainly in Paris in 1736, when, to his surprise, he was imprisoned for whistling during a performance.[133]

Crespin and Sprimont's centrepieces (plates 190, 191) are of sculptural quality and possibly inspired by illustrations of the *surtout* and terrine in La Chapelle's 1733 publication (plates 188, 189), which were in turn inspired by silver made in Paris by Thomas Germain. But by 1747 Sprimont's Chelsea Porcelain manufactory was well established.

Into the third generation

By 1750 Thomas Harrache, established in Pall Mall, continued to attract aristocratic clients. For Nathaniel Curzon, 1st Baron Scarsdale (1726–1804), Harrache customized a silver epergne and stand marked by James Peltro (Paltro; fl.1739–*c*.1759). This was surmounted by Jason, winner of the Golden Fleece, to celebrate the race won by Scarsdale's horse of that name in 1755 (plate 192). Curzon paid £525 15s for this 'large table' in 1757.[134] John Peltro, specialist maker,[135] also marked two of 12 figurative candlesticks supplied by retailer Simon Le Sage[136] in 1758/9 for the

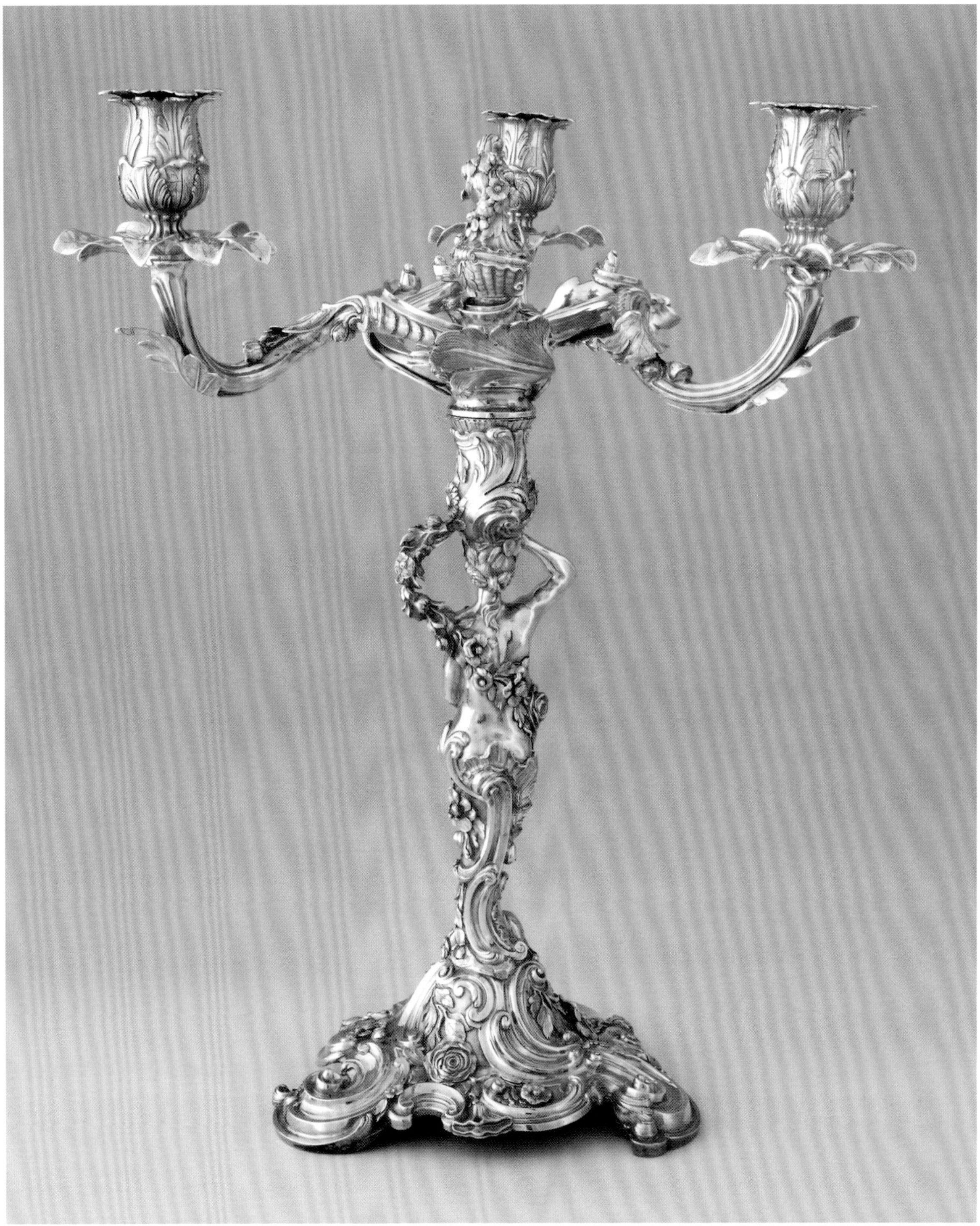

193 Figurative candlestick

James Peltro, London, 1758/9
Silver, ht 57.8 cm
Ickworth, National Trust (852077)

James Peltro, a chaser and engraver, made these sophisticated candlesticks for the dining table of the British embassy in Madrid. The contrasting surface of the supporting figure was enhanced by the shimmering light of four wax candles.

embassy to Madrid of George William Hervey, 2nd Earl of Bristol (1721–1775; plate 193).[137] Le Sage worked at the Golden Cup, Suffolk Street, Charing Cross, with his father, John Hugh Le Sage (fl.1708–39), subordinate goldsmith to George II. The form of this sophisticated figurative candlestick was inspired by the 1740 design by George Michael Moser (1706–1783) made up in London in 1738–9 by German immigrant goldsmith Frederick Kandler (fl.1735–78).[138]

From 1741 Samuel Courtauld (1720–1765) worked for his father, Augustin, as journeyman and registered his first mark in 1746. Three years later he married Louisa Perina, daughter of silk weaver Peter Ogier (d.1740), at St Luke's church, Finsbury. Ogier had come from Poitou in 1729 and was established in Spital Square. On Augustin's death in 1751 Samuel inherited £400 and his father's tools and patterns; he moved to the Crown, Cornhill, facing the Royal Exchange. In 1763 he became liveryman of the Goldsmiths' Company and in 1764 was elected elder of the Threadneedle Street French church. The following year he died and Louisa, aged 37, continued to manage the business: her portrait attributed to Nathaniel Dance (1748–1827) shows her holding business ledgers (plate 194). Louisa registered her own mark and in 1768 a joint mark with former apprentice George Cowles (1737–1811). Cowles married Louisa's niece Judith Jacob, daughter of Samuel's sister Anne and John Jacob, whose portrait has recently come to light (plate 195). John Jacob (fl. *c.*1735–1787) was a talented goldsmith, working at the Acorn, Hemmings Row. Samuel's other sister, Esther, was married to Stephen Goujon (fl.1695–1778), free of the Clockmakers' Company in 1720 and eventually Master in 1760–1.[139]

George Cowles registered his independent mark in 1777, when Louisa registered a new joint mark with her younger son, Samuel II (1752–1821), then aged 25. Louisa Courtauld, John and Anne Jacob continued to speak French at home[140] and John Jacob's will was written in French.[141]

Abraham Portal, Paul de Lamerie's reluctant apprentice from 1740, described his master's workshop in verse sent to his brother Andrew in Switzerland. Although a competent goldsmith, Abraham Portal had literary aspirations.

What sacred muse will now my thoughts inspire
Or deign to touch with poetic fire?
Should I sweet Calliope invoke thy Aid,
Our noisy tools would fright the tender Maid
Do thou great Clio then our toil rehearse
Soften our noisy art in Gentle Verse
Six in the morning from the bed we rise
And rub the sleepy humour from our eyes

The preface to Abraham Portal's play *Olinda and Sophronia*, based on Torquato Tasso's *Jerusalem Liberata*, which was performed in London in 1758, explains that he was 'educated … not in the learned and peaceful retreats of the Muses but in the rude and noisy shop of Vulcan'.[142]

The tenacity of dynasties of Huguenot craftsmen and women reflects their commitment to nurturing skills passed from generation to generation. Their faith excluded them from certain professions in France; their goldsmithing skills lent social status and could be combined with banking. Many apprentices were sons of gentlemen. Subsequent generations, sons of Pierre Platel and Paul Crespin,

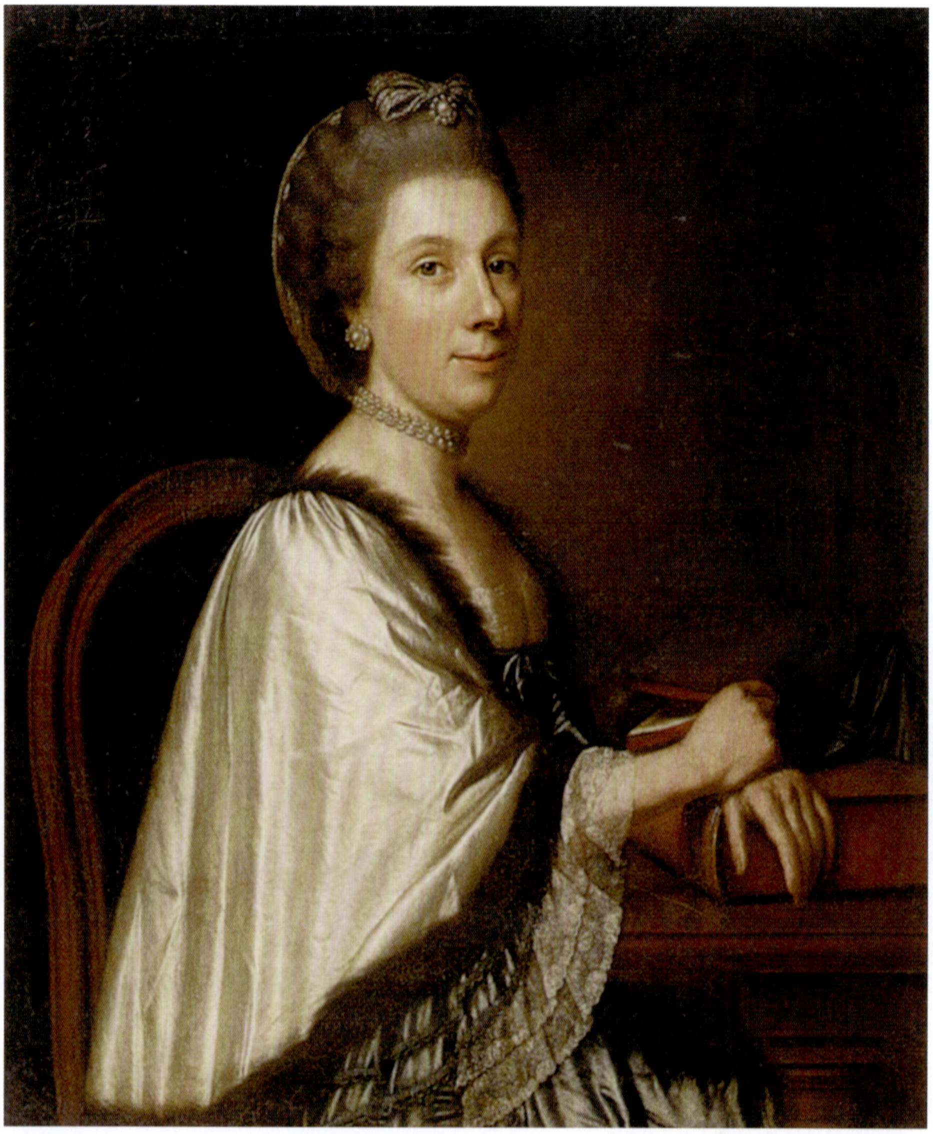

194 *Louisa Perina Courtauld*
Attributed to Nathaniel Dance, London, *c.*1770
Oil on canvas, 76.5 × 63 cm
Private collection, UK

This portrait demonstrates Louisa's status as Samuel Courtauld's widow. Dressed in a fur-edged satin cloak over a silk dress with lace trimmings, with pearls at her throat, she is shown as the manager of her late husband's business, resting her hands on the ledgers.

studied theology and were ordained as Anglican clergy. Engagement with education and the desire to share knowledge were fuelled by intellectual curiosity: as craftsmen they developed scientific interests that informed their awareness of the natural world and boosted their design skills. Several built collections or private libraries: de Lamerie's armorial bookplate is preserved in the Royal Library,[143] while that of Peter Romilly (1712–1782), a jeweller of Frith Street, Soho, and father of the law reformer Sir Samuel Romilly (1757–1818), includes the appropriate English motto 'Perservere'.[144]

International links, fostered through commissions from the colonies, were promoted via a network of family and colleagues who settled there. In 1744 de Lamerie supplied a tea service to the Jewish Franks family of Philadelphia:[145] such fashionable goods promoted the latest styles from France and London.

Apollos Rivoire (1702–1754) was born in Riaucaud, not far from Bordeaux, and sent as a child to Guernsey to escape persecution. He travelled to Boston in 1716 and was apprenticed to John Coney (1655–1722), the leading goldsmith there. Apollos married Deborah Hitchborn, of an established New England family, and their eldest son, Paul, was born on 31 December 1735. Young Paul Revere followed his father's profession: business ledgers for 1761–97 provide insight into the range of Revere's work, supplying domestic silver (plate 13), engraving copper plates and managing a copper mill and a foundry for casting bells and cannon.

The key to Huguenot dominance in the luxury metal trades, as in the other skills they mastered, lay in their tight-knit family networks and careful succession planning, through apprenticeship, training, and fostering a high level of literacy. They specialized and sub-contracted through their social network, using the apprenticeship system to promote links with specialist skills such as chasing and engraving. The Huguenots in London cared for the young and the elderly through their church communities, the Westminster French Protestant School and La Providence, the French Hospital. The family and workshop were physically and psychologically integrated, yet they engaged with wider society marrying in Anglican churches and supporting British organizations. Their combined French and Protestant identity was ideally suited to attract patronage from the British establishment. Thus, as demonstrated in the remarkable history of the Courtauld family, they continued to lead the goldsmiths' trade for as long as they maintained their identity as Huguenots.

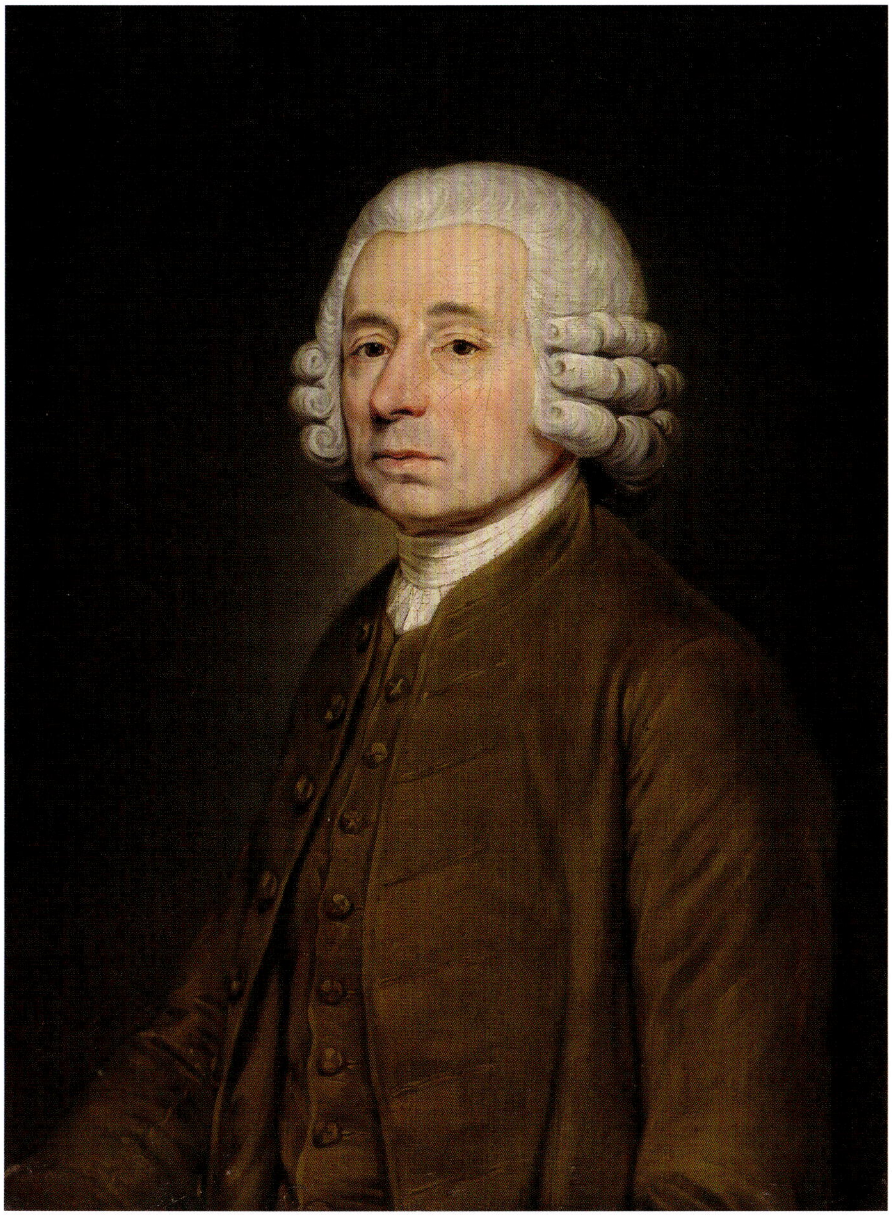

195 *John Jacob*
Unknown artist, London, *c.*1770
Oil on canvas, 69 × 52 cm
Huguenot Museum, Rochester, Kent

John Jacob worked at the Acorn in Hemmings Row off St Martin's Lane from 1734. His wife, Anne, was Samuel Courtauld's sister. They moved to Spur Street, Leicester Fields, in 1760 and by 1784 he was in Panton Street. He supplied jewellery and silver and dealt in second-hand plate and silver lace. His will, dated 1787, was written in French. His grandson George Cowles was apprenticed to Louisa Courtauld and became her business partner.

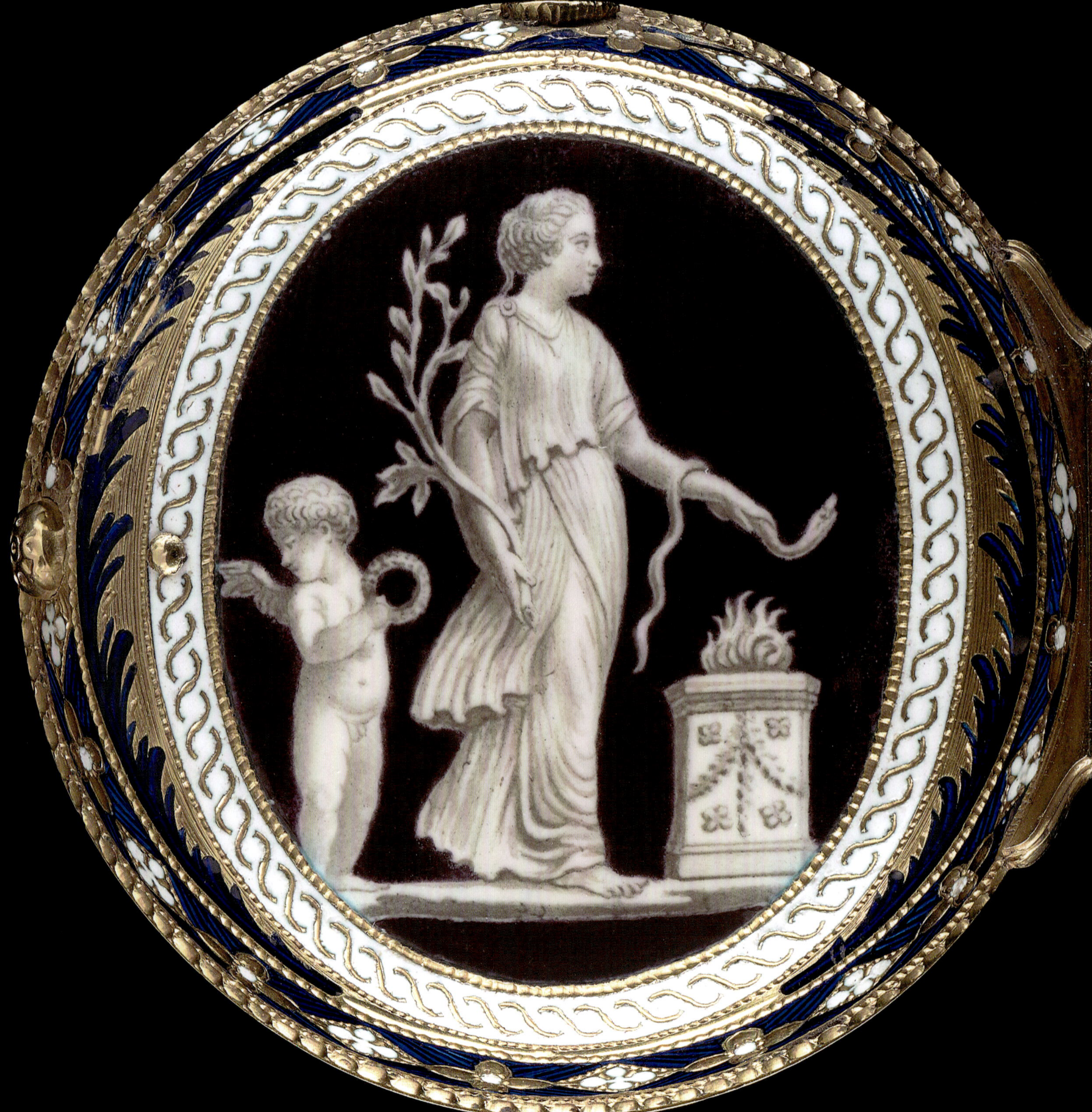

Chapter Eleven

Huguenot Watchmakers & Jewellers: The Manufacture & International Market for Luxury Goods

196 Watch case
Augustin Toussaint, London, *c.*1775–80, see plate 205

Huguenots and horology in London

By 1747 London 'beat all *Europe* in Clocks and Watches of all sorts, and export those useful Engines to all Parts of the known World ... All the Branches require a Mechanic Head, a light nice Hand, to touch those delicate Instruments ... and a strong Sight, there being scarce any Trade which requires a quicker Eye or steadier Hand.'[1] The contribution made by Huguenot refugees to clock- and watchmaking in Northern Europe is probably their most significant legacy to art and technology. Their skills promoted invention and virtuosity, and because they worked closely with jewellers and casemakers, the results were both beautiful and useful.

In 1540 the Huguenot Nicholas Ourseau (d.1590) created the astronomical clock for Hampton Court Palace (plate 197).[2] In 1622 James I's Scottish clockmaker, David Ramsay (*c.*1575–1660), trained in Blois, was joined in Tuttel Street, Westminster, by a Huguenot assistant, Guillaume Petit. French-style clock and watch cases set the standard for London production. The Clockmakers' Company, first proposed in 1622, was established with financial support in 1630 from the Huguenot 'strangers' (foreigners) Petit, James Vautrollier (fl.1622–41), Volant, Josias Cuper (d.1660) and 'Mr Bucket' (David Bouquet).[3] In 1631 the newly incorporated Company endorsed their presence by registering their names.[4] Josias Cuper was joined by his brother Louis by 1622; both were from Blois.[5] Yet these immigrants were all still living and working outside the jurisdiction of the Clockmakers' Company.[6] In 1622 'David Bowkett', originally from Dieppe, was at 'Mr Sampsons house in Blackfriers'; he was still living in that area in 1635. In 1700 Huguenot clockmakers working in Blackfriars included Thomas Chauvain.[7]

In the late seventeenth century Protestant clock- and watchmakers left regional French cities: Blois,[8] Caen, Dieppe, Lyons, La Rochelle,[9] Meaux, Orleans, Rouen and Saumur, as well as Paris. Many went to Neuchâtel and Geneva, where watch-making had been established in the 1570s. Some travelled via Amsterdam and The Hague to Berlin, others settled in Copenhagen. They established a network across Northern Europe.

By 1700, many of those who settled in London's Soho and Covent Garden had links to retailers near the royal court in St James's. The Barrauds, Cabriers, Debaufres, Grignions and Perigals established dynasties with regional and international networks. Although some ninety clock- and watchmakers are named in French church records in Britain between 1680 and 1760, 36 additional Huguenot makers had joined the London Clockmakers' Company before 1732.[10] Many more are named on clock and watch dials, trade cards, in newspaper advertisements and bills. They joined craftsmen established in London and Norwich in the sixteenth and earlier seventeenth centuries and created shops and workshops in Barnstaple, Bristol, Newcastle, Plymouth, Southampton, Winchester and York. Their descendants maintained workshops in nineteenth-century Canterbury and Lancaster. A watch by Henry Lepine (fl.1818–52), working in St Peter's Street, Canterbury between 1826 andd 1830, is preserved in the City of Canterbury Museum.[11]

The Huguenot clock- and watchmaker David Bouquet (Bucket or Bowkett) was admitted to the London Blacksmiths' Company in 1628. Four years later he joined the new Clockmakers' Company, which represented an expanding craft with increased international demand and needed foreign clock- and watchmakers for their skill as casemakers. Bouquet served as elder of the Threadneedle Street French church four times between 1637 and 1662. Bouquet's clocks and watches have exceptionally fine cases (plate 198); a wealthy patron commissioned a silver-cased bracket clock around 1650.[12] He also made watches for merchants: a silver case verge watch made around 1640–50 includes a date indicator with the months and days of the week in French and the time of high tide at London Bridge.[13] Two of his sons, David and Solomon, became watchmakers and joined the Clockmakers' Company in 1640 and 1650 respectively; a third, Hector, was apprenticed to Isaac Mebert or Maubert, a diamond cutter, who married their sister Marie Bouquet. Isaac's brother Nicolas Maubert married David Bouquet's other daughter Suzanne; a third sister Marthe, married Isaac Romieu, who succeeded his father as a jeweller.[14] The watchmakers Adam Roumieu, probably father (b.1667) and son (b.1703), who joined the Clockmakers' Company in 1695 and 1726 respectively, were likely Isaac's descendants rather than new arrivals from France.[15]

During the late sixteenth and earlier seventeenth centuries Huguenot jewellers in London specialized in procuring and setting gems and cutting diamonds.[16] They brought knowledge of the latest design fashion and, from the 1620s, the skill to enamel the settings. Between 1578 and 1635 Guy Hurtu (fl.1568–76) and his brother Jacques (fl.1584–1635), originally from Orleans, worked in both London and Paris, where they responded to demand. Between 1614 and 1619 in Paris Jacques Hurtu published books of jewellery designs for enamelling.[17] Martin Hardret (d.1612), a denizen in London from 1573, and his two sons Abraham and Jacob, supplied the royal family. In 1604 Abraham Hardret was paid £300 for 'a jewell of a table diamond with a picture in it'; Jacob Hardret was jeweller to Princess Elizabeth, charging £520 for 'diamonds, gold and workmanship in enlarging a chain'.[18]

Huguenot goldsmiths and engravers worked closely with other specialists, notably gunsmiths and watchmakers.[19] A pair of pistols made for William III by Pierre Monlong have carved walnut stocks inlaid with cut and engraved silver sheet; barrels decorated with chiselled steel and gold damascening representing wildlife presided over by the goddess Diana (plate 82). In making such

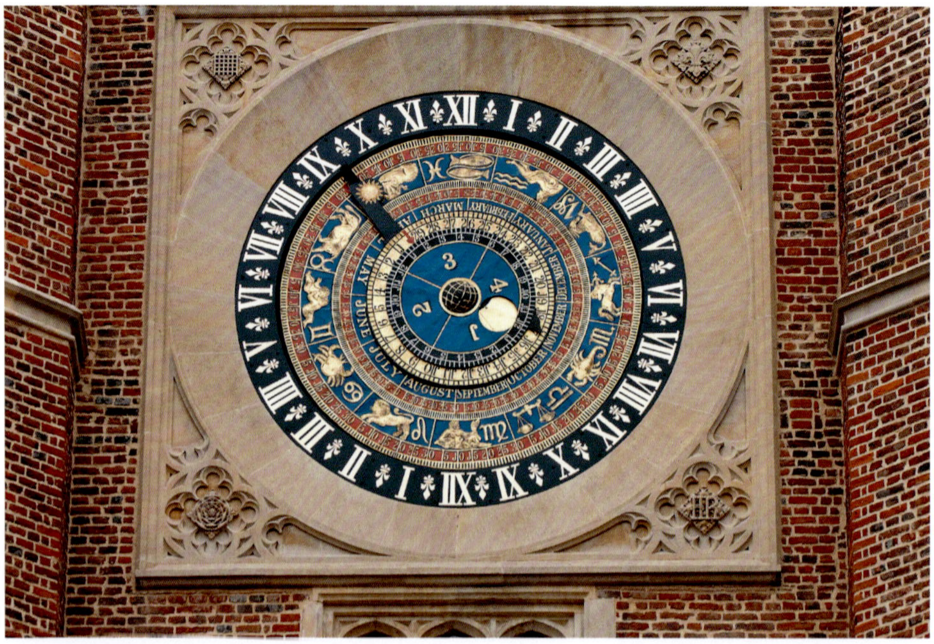

197 Astronomical clock

Nicholas Ourseau, London, 1540
Copper dials, iron and brass mechanism, oil paint and gold leaf; diam. over 3 m
Hampton Court Palace

Before 1550 there were 11 Huguenot watch- and clockmakers in London. They included Nicholas Ourseau, who created this astronomical clock for Hampton Court Palace, devised by German horologist Nicholas Kratzer (1487–1550). Ourseau was still working in Westminster in 1565.

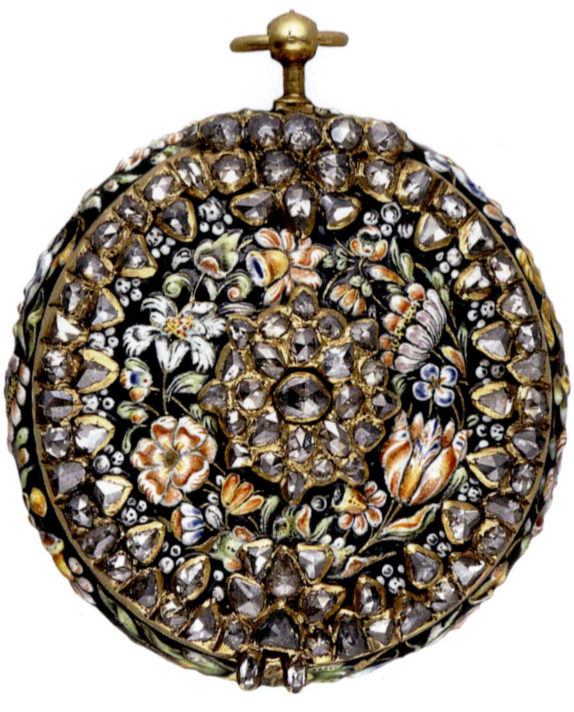

198 Watch case

David Bouquet, London, *c.*1640–60
Enamelled gold, set with diamonds, diam. 4.65 cm
British Museum, London (1888,1201.219)

This exceptionally fine gold-cased watch by Bouquet is enamelled in black and overlaid with floral decoration in realistic colours set with 92 foil-backed diamonds; on the inside the dial is enamelled with a painted landscape.

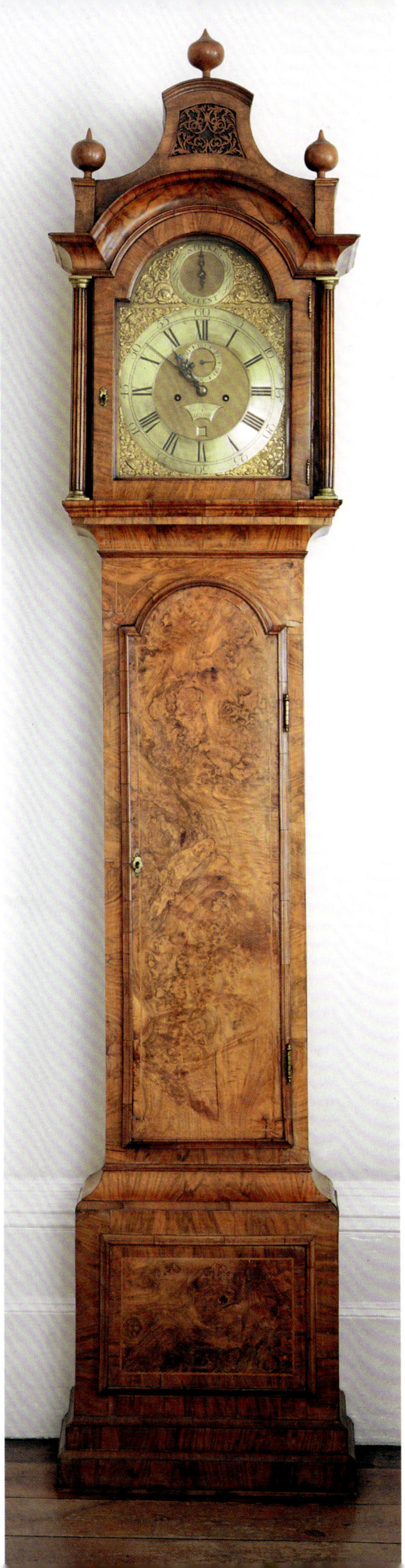

199 Long-case clock
Charles Cabrier, London, *c.*1752
Walnut case, brass dial,
249 × 68.5 × 28 cm
French Hospital, on loan to the Huguenot Museum, Rochester, Kent

This clock was presented to the Corporation of the French Hospital in April 1752 by the maker and furnished the Directors' Meeting Room. It is listed in the 1766 French Hospital inventory.

a commission, Monlong would have engaged a specialist wood carver and engraver. Sporting guns by Isaac de Seret and Landreville, *c.*1690, in the Devonshire Collection, Chatsworth, are engraved with ornament on the stocks and barrels.[20]

Like clock- and watchmakers, jewellers also employed engravers. Isaac Delafons (fl.1780–1815), at Number 12 Corner of Oat Lane, Noble Street, Cheapside, specialized in engraving 'motto rings'.[21] Huguenot church registers reveal that the jewellers' trade was subdivided by specialists *lapidaires* (lapidaries), *diamantaires* (diamond cutters), *graveurs en pierre* (gem cutters) and *metteurs en oeuvre* (gem setters). William De La Cour's eighth *Book of Ornaments*, published in 1747 included designs for jewellery, snuffboxes and watch cases.[22]

Dynasties

Dieppe-born Gideon Perigal (1698–1774), David Lestourgeon's neighbour in Church Street, St Martin-in-the-Fields, was described as silver turner and then as goldsmith when he took the eldest of his three sons, Francis, as apprentice in 1715.[23] Thus Gideon founded a dynasty.[24] Francis Perigal the elder (fl.1741–70), established at the Royal Exchange in 1741, presented a long-case clock to the Threadneedle Street church in 1743.[25] This replaced a clock presented 200 years earlier by Pierre de Dessus La Maire, clockmaker to Queen Elizabeth I, probably destroyed during the Great Fire of London, 1666.[26] Francis Perigal was Master of the Clockmakers' Company in 1756; he was followed by his son, also named Francis (d.1818), who was free in 1756 and Master in 1775. The second-generation clockmaker Charles Cabrier, who was apprenticed to his father in 1719, became Master of the Clockmakers' Company in 1757. Inspired by Perigal's example, Cabrier the younger presented a walnut long-case clock to the French Hospital in 1752 (plate 199).[27]

The Perigal family supplied clocks and watches to the export trade. John (?) Perigal, nephew of Francis Perigal the elder, shared premises with jeweller Lewis Masquerier (d.1757) at The Ring and Pearl in Coventry Street, Charing Cross, from 1770 until 1794 (pp.223–4); the business continued as Perigal & Browne until 1800. The retailers Masquerier & Perigal were instrumental in developing the market for sophisticated automata. Their New Bond Street shop was opened by Gideon Perigal's grandson, another Francis Perigal (1764–1843), Master of the Clockmakers' Company in 1806. This continued as Perigal & Dutereau, 'Watchmakers to

His Majesty', from 1810 to the 1840s. The Perigals were in the Royal Exchange until 1808. An early nineteenth-century mantel clock by Perigal still furnishes the bedroom of Cecil Rhodes's home, Groote Schur, Cape Town, South Africa.

Clock- and watchmakers were at the heart of London's Huguenot community. The Westminster French Protestant Charity School was founded in 1747 by clockmaker David Hubert the elder; the subscription ticket was engraved by Charles Grignion (plate 235) from another Huguenot clockmaking dynasty.[28]

Watchmaking in regional France

Freedom of production in London was in marked contrast to restrictive regional French guilds. In Blois, engraved watch cases and dials signed by the Gribelin family[29] were superseded by *champlevé* and polychrome enamelling using techniques invented by Jean Toutin in the 1620s. An early example is the watch signed by Louis Vautyer (1581–1638) of Blois (plate 200). The temptation to stock jewellery as well as watches had to be resisted if the maker was to retain his good standing with the Blois guild and avoid penalties.

In 1636 the Blois premises of leading Huguenot goldsmith Isaac Gribelin (fl.1616–51) were searched by an officer of the King accompanied by two officials of the Clockmakers' Guild. Gribelin showed them four enamel watch cases, his own silver watch and two others belonging to customers. In the attic the searchers found three pine boxes with 23 gold and four silver watches bearing the names of established Blois and Paris makers, many deceased. There was frequently a delay between making the movement and the case, and it was usual to trade a movement by one maker for another.

Gribelin's response provides an insight into the close links between goldsmiths and watchmakers: 'Goldsmiths have always dealt in clockwork … during the stay of the Queen-Mother [Marie de Médicis] in Blois, one watchmaker and one goldsmith did between them the greater part of the trade in clocks and watches.' Gribelin believed that he could deal in both until litigation between goldsmiths and clock- and watchmakers was settled.[30] In 1632 Pierre Cuper (b.1603), 'merchant watchmaker of Blois', a relative of Josias and Louis Cuper in London, signed a contract with Anthoine Arlaud (*c.*1590– after 1641), 'merchant watchmaker and bourgeois of Geneva', for 'good and faithful merchandize' to be delivered to Marseilles. This was then shipped to Galata near Constantinople, where a colony of Genevois, established in the early seventeenth century, supplied the Turkish market.[31] In seventeenth-century Blois goldsmiths and watchmakers maintained close links with London, Paris and Geneva and supplied the export trade.

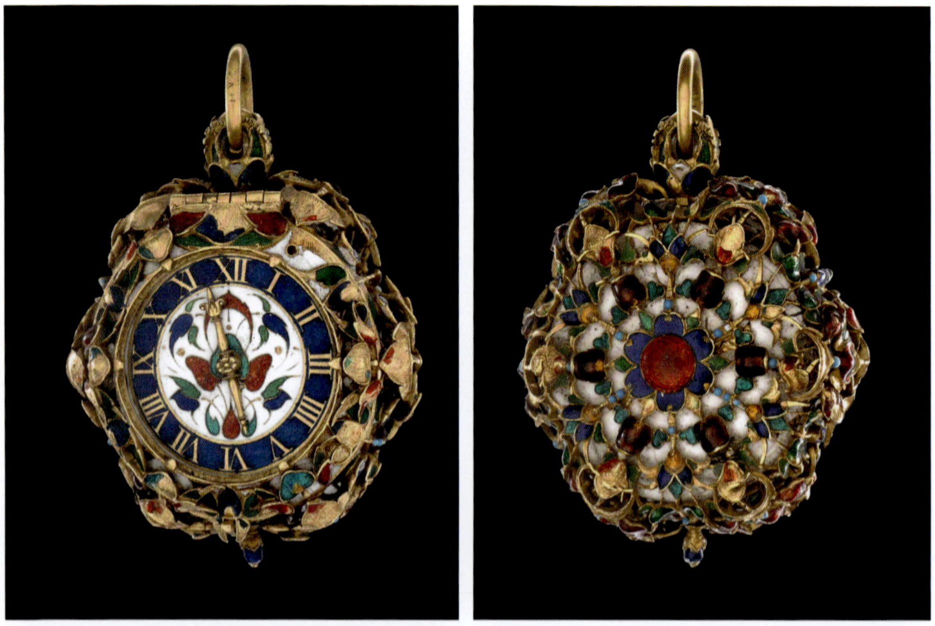

200 Watch

Louis Vautyer, Blois, *c.*1630–8
Enamelled gold, 4.78 × 3.82 cm
Signed 'L Vautyer A Blois'
British Museum, London
(1892,0523.1)

In Blois, finely engraved watch cases and dials were superseded by cases and dials decorated in *champlevé* and polychrome enamelling using techniques invented by Jean Toutin. Such exquisite cases are miracles of production: each had to be fired again and again as new colours were added.

Watchmaking and the jewellers' trades

In pre-Revocation France the clock- and watchmakers' guilds were dominated by Protestant craftsmen. Blois, Dieppe and La Rochelle all boasted thriving communities specializing in such luxury goods,[32] yet most of the clock- and watchmakers who settled in London in the late seventeenth century came from Paris. They included Peter Debaufre (1675–*c.*1730) and his son Jacob (1691–1761), who joined the London Clockmakers' Company in 1689. Living in Leicester Fields in 1695, by 1701 they were working at the Pendulum, Frith Street, Soho.[33] Father and son were naturalized in 1704. The Debaufres's technical innovation, built on close connections between the watchmaking and jewellers' trades, met with resistance from the London Clockmakers' Company.

The Debaufres introduced harder bearings for pivot holes in watch movements with the assistance of Genevan mathematician Nicholas Facio (1664–1753). In his youth Facio had measured the height of Mont Blanc from the terrace of his family's chateau and drafted a map of Lake Geneva. In London he was elected to the Royal Society at the age of 24. The trio tried the hardest stones available, found the diamond too hard to pierce and too easily cleft by use, and settled for agates, rubies and sapphires. They used them as bearings and end stones for the balance staff. Their joint application for the extension to a patent granted in May 1704 for the use of jewelling in watches was presented to the House of Commons.[34] The patent was opposed by the Clockmakers' Company, claiming that other members had used jewelled pivots before 1704 and that the watch that Facio submitted actually had a fake jewel.[35] The Company's justification was that the patent could not be enforced abroad.[36]

In 1704 jewelled watches could be seen at the Debaufres' London shop. Peter Debaufre also invented a dead-beat or 'club-footed' verge escapement with two escape wheels, having between them a truncated cone formed of a diamond, and cut away at the side to form an impulse plane acted on by the wheels alternately. Sir Isaac Newton (1643–1727) had a watch with this feature and spoke favourably of its performance. James Debaufre (1691–1761), Peter's younger son, was born in London and was admitted to the Clockmakers' Company in 1712, when he was living in Church Street, Soho. A gold watch with his signature (plate 201) has an outer case set with panels of coloured glass imitating agate.[37] Contemporary fakes signed 'Debaufre London' demonstrate the selling power of the Debaufre name.[38]

Simon de Charmes (fl.1688–1730), was born in Langres, north-east France, the son of a merchant. He was in London by 1688, free of the Clockmakers' Company in 1691, with another family member, David (possibly his brother), joining the following year. Simon de Charmes served as Company Steward from 1708. He worked at the sign of the Clock in Warwick Street, near Charing Cross.[39] Surviving examples that he supplied include a pair-case watch *c.*1700 with a gold dial plate with steel hands.[40] Another brother and sister lived in Berlin, which may explain his special relationship with Caroline, Princess of Wales, who stood godmother to one of his children.[41] By 1730 Simon retired to his country estate, Charmes (later Grove) Hall, Hammersmith, where he died in 1734, aged 69. The West End shop and workshop were managed in turn by his son Simon (b.1706) and his grandson David, who continued the family business until 1783. In 1736 George Frideric Handel sent his niece's bridegroom 'a gold watch by Delharmes [*sic*] with a gold chain'.[42]

Other watchmakers returned to France from London. Matthew Vaulois (fl.1695–7), who had left France as a child with his parents, was living in St Martin's Court off St Martin's Lane by 1707, when his daughter was baptized at the French church of the Savoy. He was later re-established in Paris, where he worked as a clockmaker's journeyman; in 1736 he was arrested there for attempting to convert a Catholic neighbour.[43]

Joseph Paulet's portable clocks were fitted with a spring balance, an alarm and a calendar. Recorded in London from 1687 to 1726, Paulet worked initially beyond the authority of the Clockmakers' Company – 'Without Temple Bar' – and employed silversmiths, chasers and engravers. One of his clocks (plate 202) bears the royal monogram for Queen Anne, so may have been a royal gift. In 1726 he bequeathed 'one of my best repeating gold watches & all my books except the latin and mathematical' to Michael Garnault, jeweller, and watches to nine other colleagues and friends.[44]

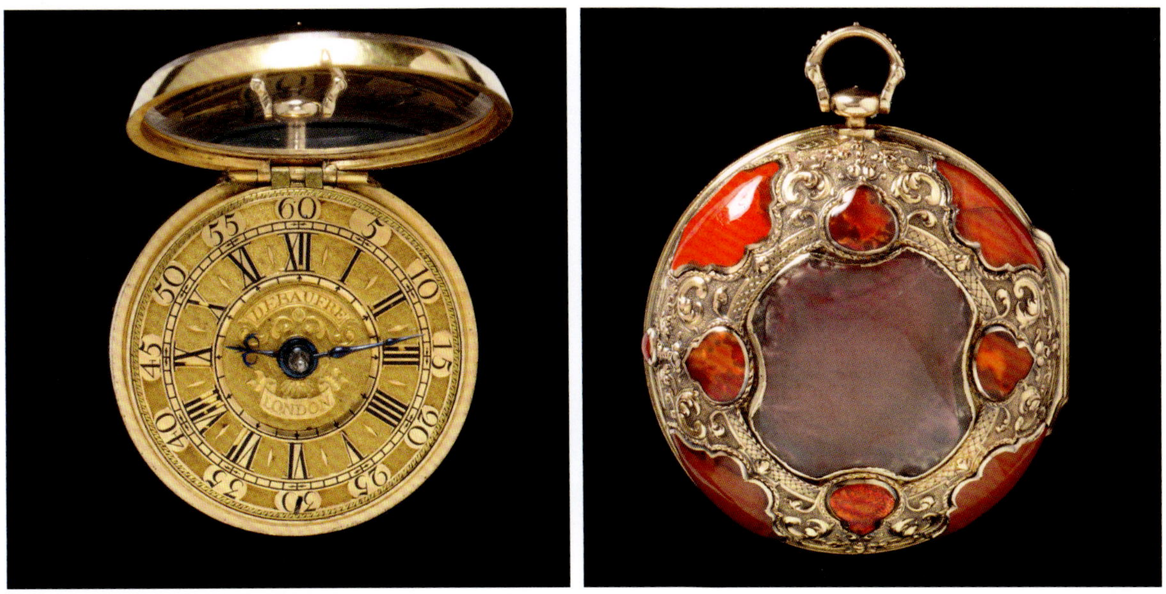

201 Pair-case watch

James Debaufre the Younger, London, 1723–4
Gold set with glass, diam. 4.3 cm
Victoria and Albert Museum, London (2372:1,2–1855)

A second-generation maker, James Debaufre traded on the good reputation established by his father and uncle. This outer gold pair case is set with glass imitating agate and carnelian.

Etienne Asselin (d.1726), a clockmaker in Broad Street, City of London, in 1701,[45] and his relative François came from Dieppe;[46] François was free of the Haberdashers' Company (plate 23).[47] Some sophisticated London clocks were also made to designs by Daniel Marot in the mid-1690s, later published in Amsterdam in 1703 and 1712.[48]

Owning valuable accessories was a mark of status. Monarch, merchant and military officer would reveal their gold snuffbox and watch in good company, sharing a special association.[49] A powerful patron would delegate the purchase of such treasures. The contents of Robert Walpole's pockets were maintained by his valet, Mr Osgood;[50] Prince Carl Anselm of Thurn and Taxis instructed his valet, Adrian Morin, who also dealt in luxury goods, to acquire gold boxes, although he may have commissioned boxes from the Frères Toussaint in Hanau.[51]

The manufacture of such luxuries required high levels of skill: the lid had to fit tightly to contain the milled snuff and the cover was often chased or enamelled with biblical or mythological scenes. Figurative decoration required mastery of human anatomy as well as experience of working precious

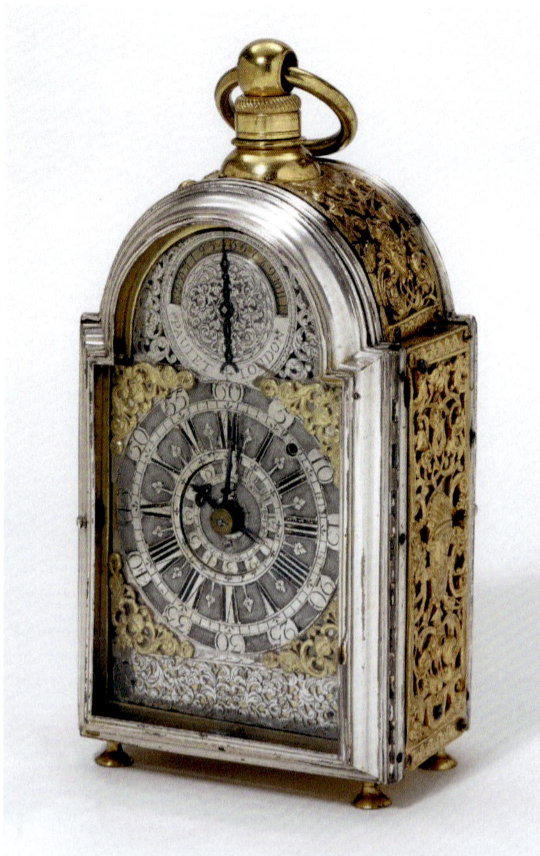

202 Travelling clock

Joseph Paulet, London, c.1710
Chased gilt-brass and parcel-gilt silver, 19.5 × 10 × 7.5 cm
Victoria and Albert Museum, London (420–1869)

This is one of six early carriage clocks signed 'Paulet London'. The universal ball joint from which the case is suspended shields the movement from the jolts of carriage motion. With silver frames, engraved, chased and parcel gilt, these clocks made perfect royal gifts, being both decorative and portable.

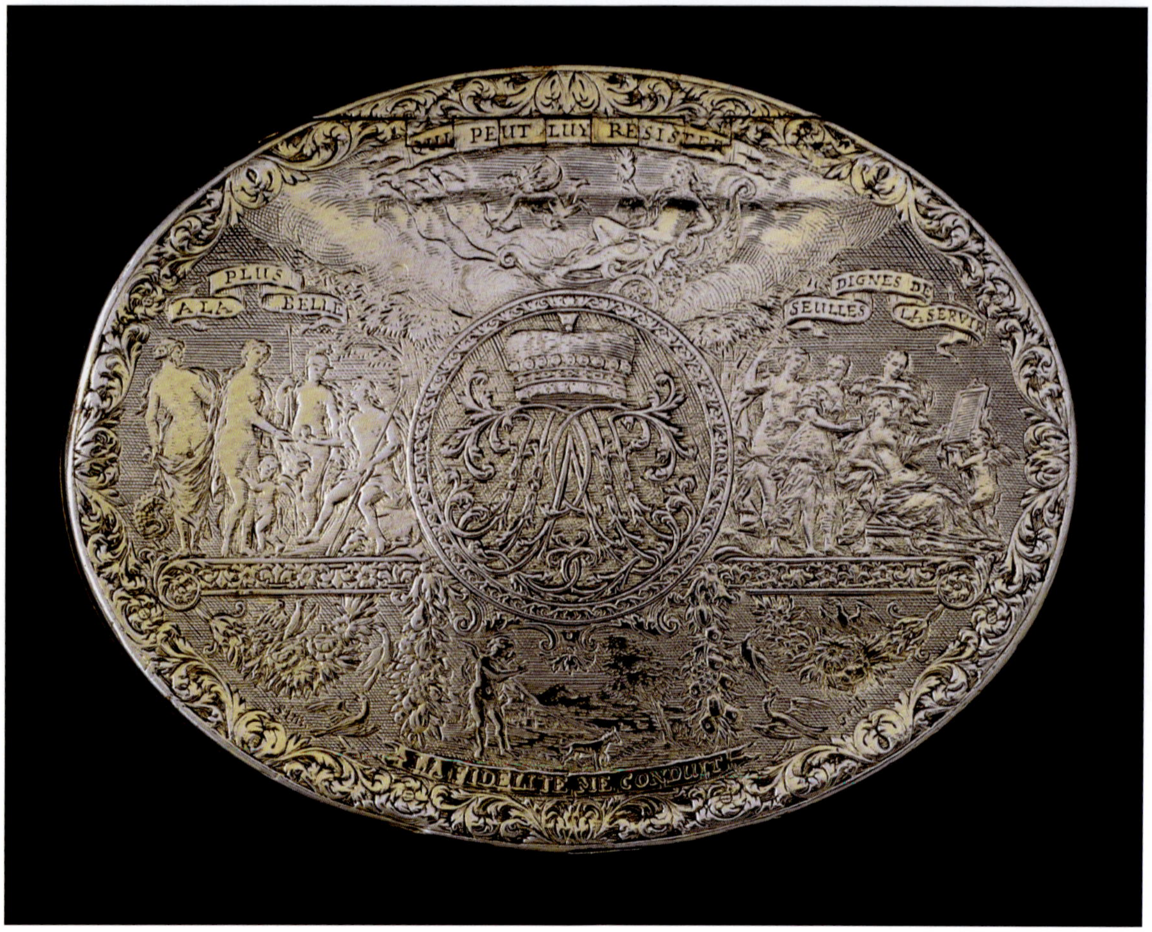

203 Comfit box with the Toilet of Venus

Engraved by Simon Gribelin, London, c.1700
Silver-gilt, 8.5 × 13 cm
Victoria and Albert Museum, London (M.307–1962)

Above the owner's initials and baron's coronet, Venus reclines in her chariot drawn by doves while Cupid shoots arrows from a bow, 'QUI PEUT LUY RESISTER'. To the left is the Judgement of Paris, 'A LA PLUS BELLE' and to the right, Three Graces attend Venus, who admires herself in a mirror, 'SEULLES DIGNES DE LA SERVIR'. Below, Cupid is led by a dog on a lead, 'LA FIDELITE ME CONDUIT'.

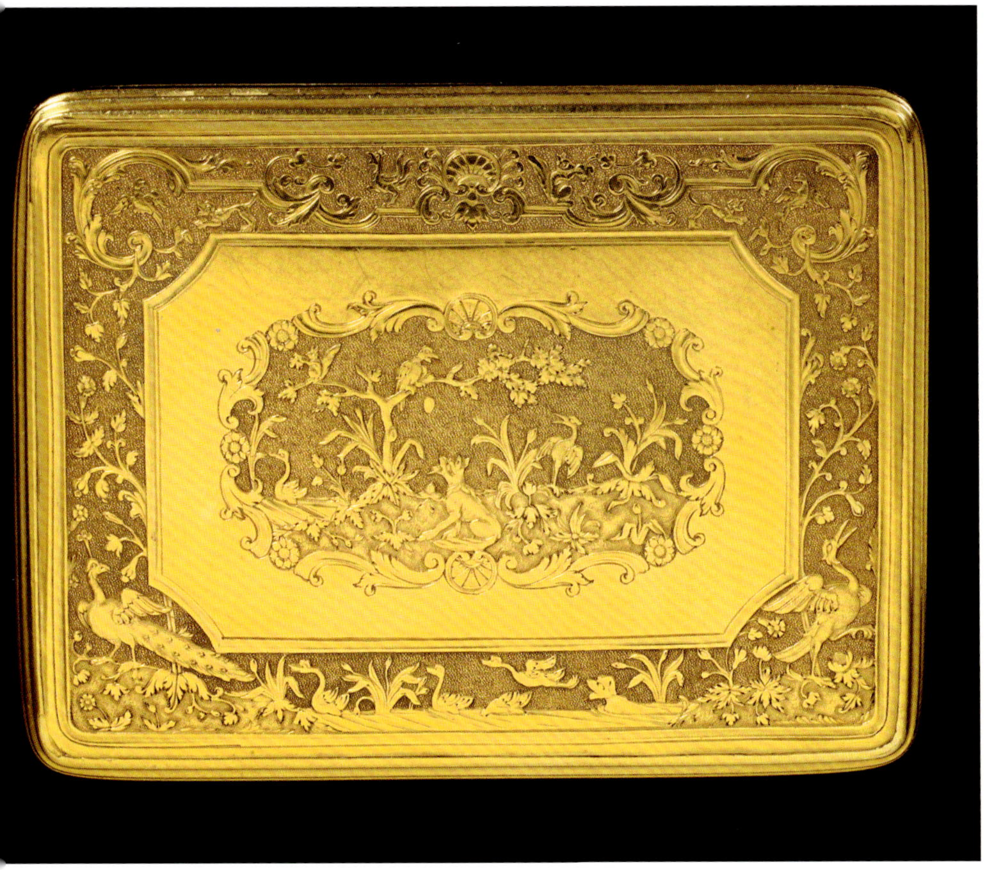

204 Box with the Fox and Crow

Lid chased and signed by Michael Cabaret Lagarene, London, *c.*1710
Gold, 1.5 × 7.9 × 5.5 cm
The Snowman Collection, on loan to the Victoria and Albert Museum, London (LOAN:SNOWMAN.7–1997)

Lagarene sold this gold box featuring a scene from Aesop's *Fables* as retold by the French author La Fontaine in 1668. The crow, flattered into singing, drops the cheese, which falls into the expectant mouth of the fox waiting below.

metal. Paul Daniel Chenevix charged Lionel Tollemache, 4th Earl of Dysart, £55 9s 8d for 'a Fine Carved gold Snuff box' in 1733.[52] Robert Campbell advised in 1747 that 'A Youth' designed for chasing 'ought to have good Eyes, must have a good Genius for Drawing, and … early learned the Principles of that Art'.[53] Chased decoration superseded fine engraving, as seen on the Toilet of Venus comfit box (plate 203), which has illustrations to French mottos signed by Simon Gribelin.[54]

Chasing, particularly of classical figure scenes, was characteristic of London watch case and box decoration from about 1710 to the 1760s. While the most prominent chasers were German or Swiss German in origin, many of the gold chasers who signed their work, or who can be identified from documentary sources, had French names: Barenger, Josias Baril, John Chauveau, Del Grange, Isaac Dubois, David Dupont, Laurence Hamond, James Molière, John Palairet and Villar.[55] Often a Huguenot connection can be established, although it is possible that the lack of signed work means that the Huguenot contribution to gold chasing in London cannot be fully appreciated. Laurence Hamond (fl.1723–59) had a career of over thirty years and took on four apprentices, however only one chasing signed by him is known.

A complication in the written sources is that the term *graveur* could be used to describe both engravers and chasers, two skills that might be practised by one person but were often distinct specialisms. For example, it is impossible to confirm whether Francis Fourestier, witness to a baptism at the French church, Threadneedle Street, in 1714, and described as a *graveur de montre* when he took Pierre Dargent as apprentice in 1718, was chaser or engraver or both.[56]

Silver turners also worked as chasers. Watchmaker David Lestourgeon (1660–1731), originally from Rouen, working adjacent to King Charles Head, Church Lane off St Martin's Lane from 1700 to 1709, captured the market for commemorative watches in coronation year, 1702, by adding chased busts of the outgoing and incoming monarchs on the back of his signed watch movements.[57] Lestourgeon joined the Clockmakers' Company in 1698. He settled first in the City of London, where he worked from 1693 to 1701. One of his former apprentices, Daniel Torin (d.1767), established in Wandsworth, was from 1745 in partnership with his brother-in-law Moses Fontaine (1694–1766), a specialist watch engraver.[58]

Setting up required tools and materials as well as finding appropriate premises. Matthew Gaucheron (fl. *c.*1800), supplier of goldsmiths' and watch-making tools in Tower Street near Seven Dials, Covent Garden, was well placed to cater for the needs of emerging apprentices. His trade card was engraved by John Fougeron (fl.1737–82).[59]

Whereas watches are usually signed on the movement, and sometimes the dial, by the watchmaker or retailer, London-made gold boxes only occasionally bear the name of the retailer or goldsmith. Michael Cabaret Lagarene (fl.1706–25), living in the parish of St Martin-in-the-Fields when he was naturalized in 1709,[60] signed two gold boxes.[61] One of these is chased with Aesop's fable of the Fox and the Crow (plate 204)[62] and the other is mounted with agate, possibly supplied by one of the Huguenot lapidaries based in West London.[63] The witnesses to Lagarene's naturalization were Paul Bertrand and Anthoine Rigal, both described as goldsmiths.[64]

In 1768 enameller Augustin Toussaint (*c.*1754–1802) was apprenticed in London to George Michael Moser. Augustin's father, Louis (d.1785), worked with James Morisset (1738–1815) in Denmark Street, St Giles, from 1767 to 1772; they supplied small enamels to retailing goldsmiths

Parker & Wakelin. Although Moser had made his name as a chaser, he turned increasingly to enamelling, first in the Rococo style and then in the Neoclassical.[65] A watch case signed 'AT' (plate 205) demonstrates Augustin's skill. Morisset continued in Denmark Street until 1800 and specialized in gold and enamelled presentation boxes and dress swords.[66] In 1779 Morisset's competitor William Charron (1736–*c.*1784)[67] supplied the enamel plaques for Admiral Keppel's Freedom Box (plate 206),[68] designed by the sculptor John Bacon (1777–1859) and celebrated in an accompanying publication.[69]

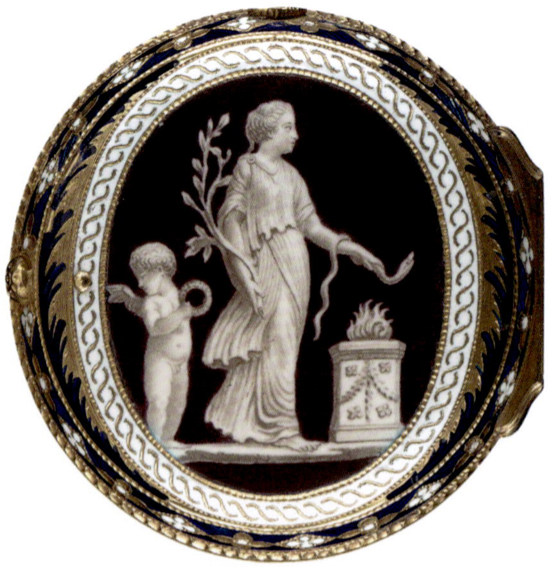

205 Watch case

Augustin Toussaint, London, *c.*1775–80
Gold and enamel, 4.5 × 4.5 × 1.5 cm
Victoria and Albert Museum, London (1065–1855)

Augustin Toussaint was apprenticed to G.M. Moser in 1768 for an enormous fee of 200 guineas, demonstrating the prestige enjoyed by leading London enamellers. This Neoclassical scene *en grisaille* of Hygeia, goddess of health, shows that Augustin had mastered the skills learned during his apprenticeship.

International influences

Specialist foreign and native craftsmen married into the London Huguenot community, combining their skills and international experience, with spectacular results. Watch cases were supplied by specialists. Benjamin Piron (fl.1723–35) of Artillery Ground, Spitalfields, apprenticed in 1723, registered his mark at Goldsmiths' Hall in 1731.[70] This is found on the inner case for a movement signed by J. Rousseau; its outer case is chased with a betrothal scene signed and dated 1735 by J. Haidt (fl.1723–35). A Berlin-trained Moravian who worked in Dresden, Augsburg, Venice and Rome before coming to London via Paris, Haidt married in 1725 Catherine, daughter of Michel Compigné (fl.1698–1703), a Spitalfields watchmaker.[71] The Sacrifice of Iphigenia is chased onto the lid of a gold box signed on the front edge 'BVREL FECIT', *c.*1720. The chaser was probably a relative of Jean Burel, *graveur* from Aix-en-Provence who, in London aged 82 in 1706, received Royal Bounty support (plate 207).[72]

Although London watches had a character of their own, Paris was the dominant influence on the design of gold boxes. The demand for such luxury possessions became a European obsession. In Berlin, Frederick the Great, King of Prussia,

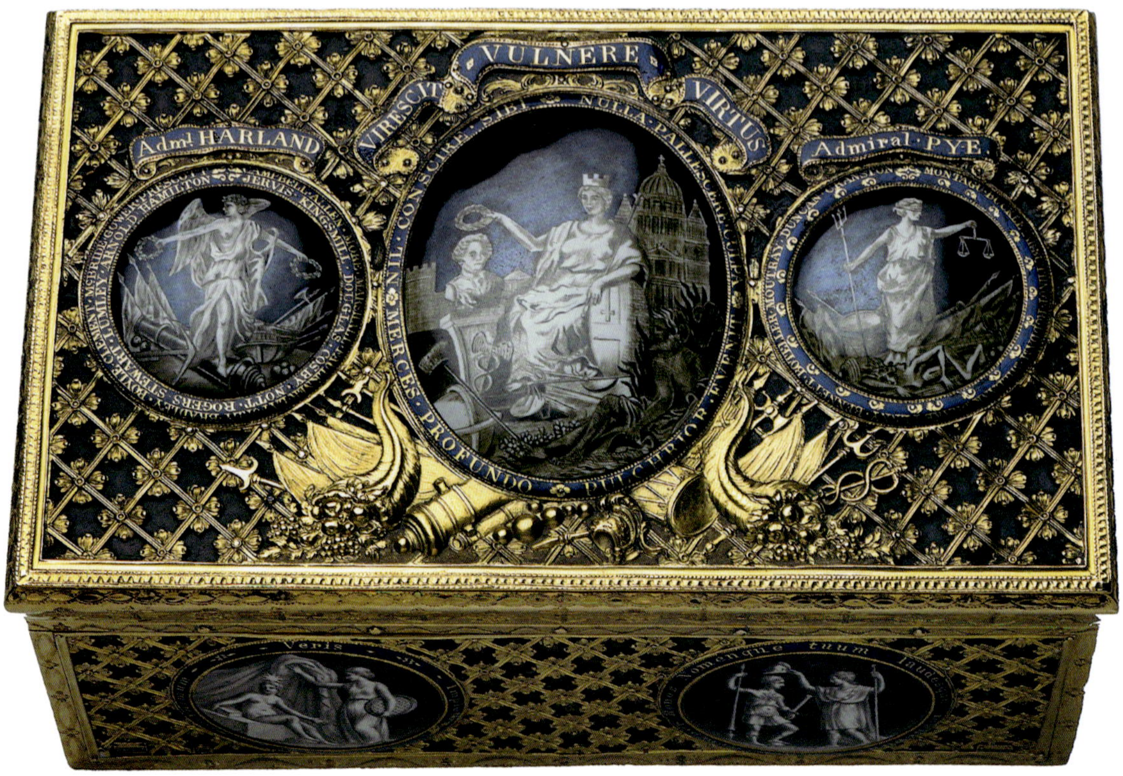

206 Freedom Box

John Bacon, William Charron and Andrew Fogelberg, London, 1779
Wood, gold and enamel, 15.7 × 6.8 × 9.4 cm
Museum of London (25142)

Presented to Admiral Keppel with the Freedom of the City of London in 1779, this box was designed by John Bacon and made by Andrew Fogelberg. William Charron made the enamel plaques and designed the lid, provided a model, 15 drawings, a silver pierced plate and a gold ship for approval. Some costs (the gold alone cost £350) were recouped by publishing an illustrated account of the box available in different versions, black and white, coloured, and embellished with gold leaf.

207 Box with the Sacrifice of Iphigenia

Chased and signed by 'Burel', London, *c.*1720
Gold, 8.7 × 6.6 × 2.6 cm
The Rosalinde and Arthur Gilbert Collection on loan to the Victoria and Albert Museum, London (LOAN:GILBERT.318–2008)

This scene from Ovid's *Metamorphoses* is taken from a 1676 engraving by François Chauveau (1613–1676). Agamemnon, delayed by bad weather on his way to the Trojan War, prepares to sacrifice his daughter Iphigenia to appease the goddess Diana. However, the goddess intervenes and substitutes a stag for Iphigenia, who becomes a priestess.

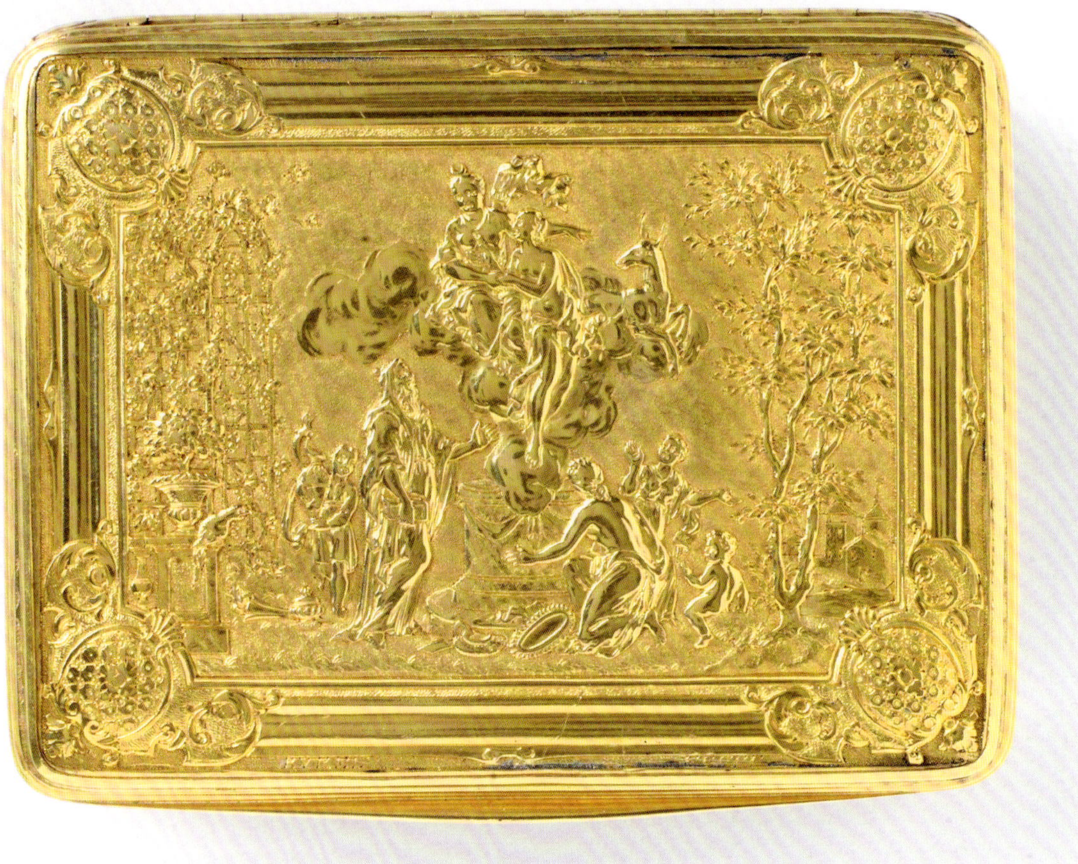

208 Box with Minerva as Patron of the Arts and Sciences

Marked by Daniel Baudesson, painted in enamels by Daniel Niklaus Chodowiecki, Berlin, *c.*1755–80
Gold and enamel, 9.5 × 5 × 4.3 cm
The Rosalinde and Arthur Gilbert Collection on loan to the Victoria and Albert Museum, London (LOAN:GILBERT.333–2008)

Baudesson was born and trained with a Huguenot master in Berlin. This example of his work has enamel decoration by Daniel Niklaus Chodowiecki (1726–1801). The rocaille frame contrasts with the *guilloché* (engine-turned) gold ground, a mechanical technique of engraving with geometric patterns introduced to Berlin in 1754 by the Paris goldsmith P.A. Griot.

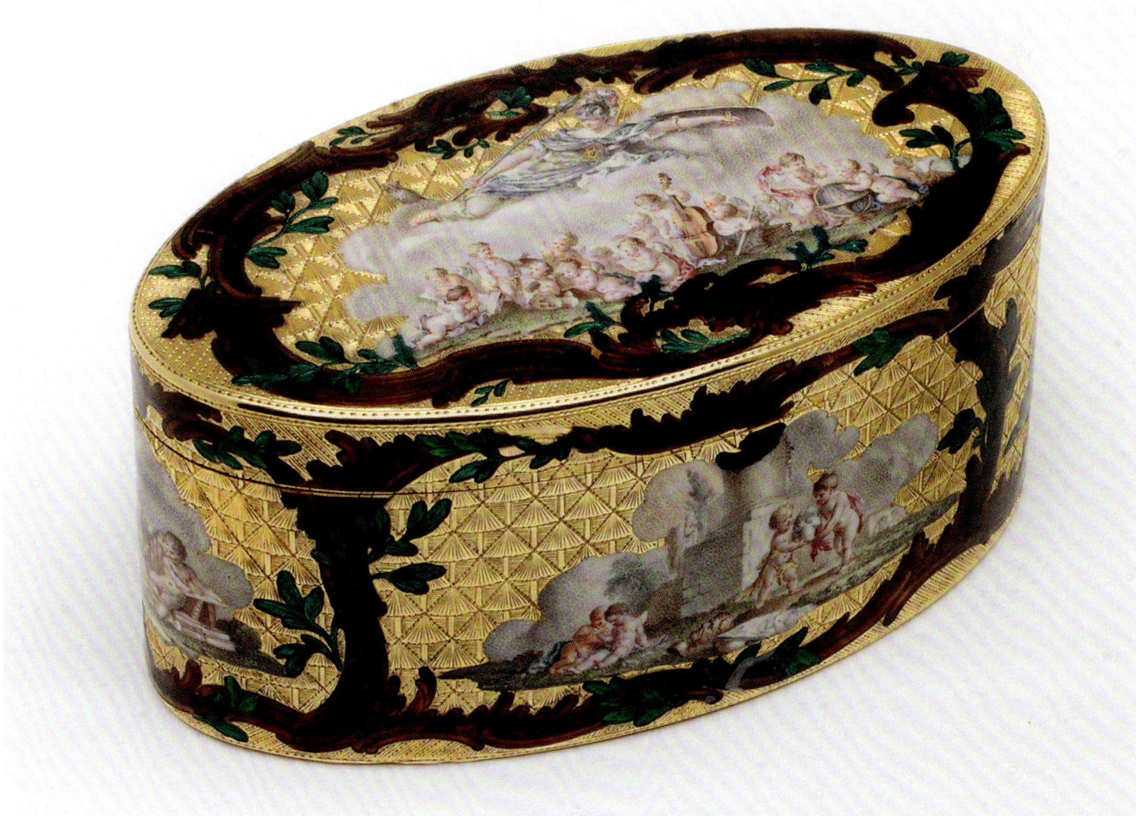

encouraged local goldsmiths to emulate French fashion. Daniel Baudesson (1716–1801) and Philipp and Samuel Colliveaux (fl.1740–60) were of Huguenot descent. Baudesson, born in Berlin, to a refugee from Metz, was trained by Samuel Colliveaux from 1741 and studied in Paris. As Frederick the Great's court goldsmith from 1766, Baudesson supplied 18 boxes.[73] One of these, an oval box (plate 208), is painted in enamel with Minerva as Patron of the Arts and Sciences by Daniel Nikolaus Chodowiecki (1726–1801).[74]

Second-generation Huguenot goldsmiths established in Amsterdam's Kalverstraat, brothers Philippe (1697–1763) and Louis Métayer (1728–1790)[75] and Jean Saint (b.1695; plate 209),[76] attracted prestigious commissions. Jean may have been related to Obadiah Saint,[77] Pezé Pilleau's London apprentice from 1735; to T.D. Saint, who published *A new book of designs for Jewellers work* in London in 1770; or to the carver and gilder Gideon Saint.[78] In Amsterdam in 1744 Jean Saint's daughter married François Thouret, son of a London-based goldsmith. Philippe Métayer, who signed a 1754 cup and cover now in the Rijksmuseum (plate 210), and his brother Louis may be related to the London-based goldsmith Louis Mettayer (p.131). In Amsterdam, the Métayers chased gold watch cases, snuffboxes and cane heads.[79] A cartouche-shaped gold box dated 1739, marked by Louis Métayer,[80] is mounted with a plaque chased by Philippe Métayer with Rebecca at the Well.[81]

Established links between Huguenot craftsmen in London and Amsterdam also include the Amsterdam-based goldsmith Etienne François Morellon de La Cave (p.124), whose father, the London engraver François Morellon de La Cave (1696–1768), worked for William Hogarth from 1739 to 1758.[82]

Laurence Hamond's workshop in the parish of St Giles-in-the-Fields included apprentices Thomas Burges (fl.1731–82), bound in 1731, and Peter Brozett, bound in 1733. By 1744 Hamond was living in Brownlow Street. The lid of a cartouche-shaped box chased with Apollo and Cyparissus is signed 'HA.MOND',[83] yet the box is marked 'F.D.V.' for Frederick de Veer (fl.1731–81), who was working in Angel Court off Throgmorton Street from 1753. Its Rococo scrollwork is close to 1740s designs by William De La Cour and Peter Glazier (1700–1767).[84]

A chatelaine (plate 211) chased for the goldsmith Francis Harrache demonstrates mastery of figurative work. Harrache entered his small maker's mark[85] as a gold box maker in February 1738 from an address in Great St Andrew's Street, Seven Dials; by 1754 he had moved to Little Earl Street.[86] Harrache worked with the chaser Thomas Burges.[87] His father was Abraham Harache, goldsmith (p.153), described as 'marchand graveur' in 1689 and related by marriage to the Gribelin, Mettayer and Willaume families.[88]

New Hanau, Germany, was founded in 1597 for Protestant refugees from the Spanish Netherlands. In the eighteenth century, Huguenot jewellers descended from refugees from France, some of whom had at first settled in Geneva, were living and working there. By the mid-eighteenth century they were making gold boxes that competed with Paris productions; these were acquired by merchants at the annual fair at Frankfurt, close to Hanau. Although there was a town mark for silver made in Hanau, there is no evidence that a gold mark was used until later in the century. Attempts to introduce such a mark by the town authorities in 1752 were rejected by the jewellers: thus their luxury goods could be marketed as Parisian. Etienne Flamant (fl.1762–1770s), a *guillocheur* from Geneva, introduced to Hanau jewellers this sophisticated technique of tooling the gold surface prior to the application of the enamel in 1762; they in turn supplied him with gold boxes for decoration.

Flamant's contract with the Hanau box makers was signed in 1773 by the Toussaint brothers, the

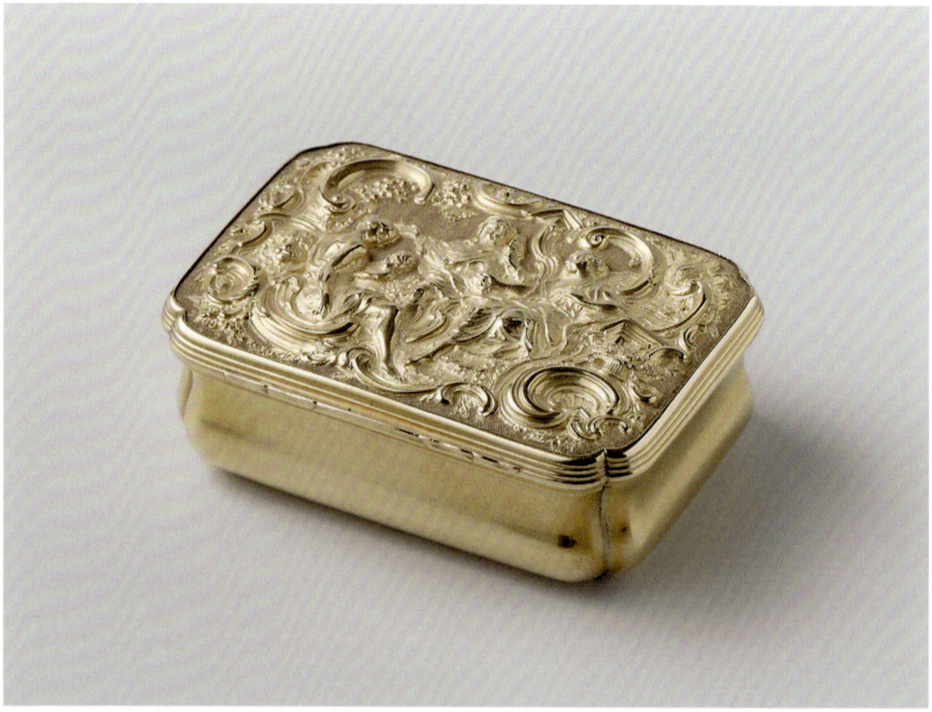

209 Snuffbox with Vertumnus and Pomona

Attributed to Jean Saint, Amsterdam, *c.*1750
Gold, 2.3 × 6.1 × 4.4 cm
Rijksmuseum, Amsterdam (BK.1966-11)

Second-generation Huguenot goldsmiths in Amsterdam's Kalverstraat, Philippe and Louis Métayer and Jean Saint attracted the most prestigious commissions. This snuffbox is inspired by the prints of Juste-Aurèle Meissonnier (1695–1750).

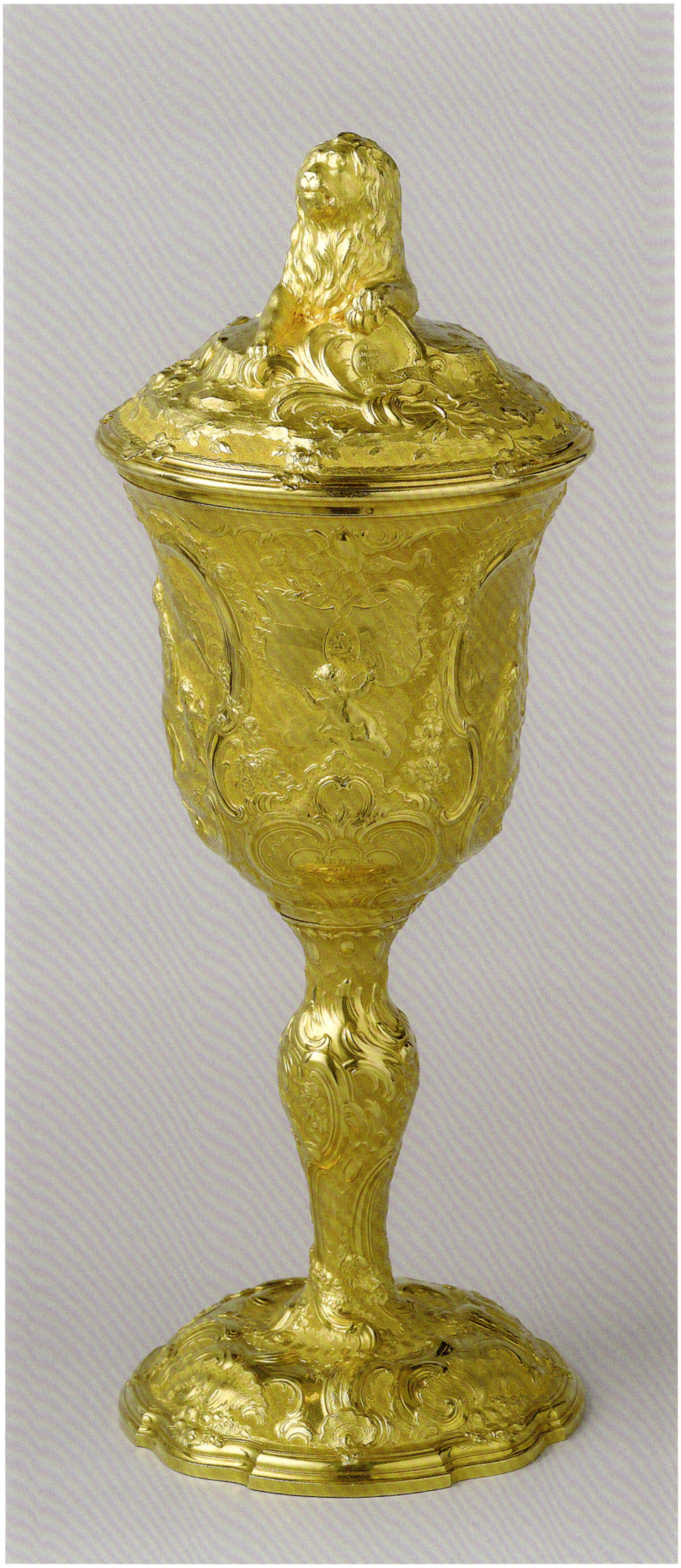

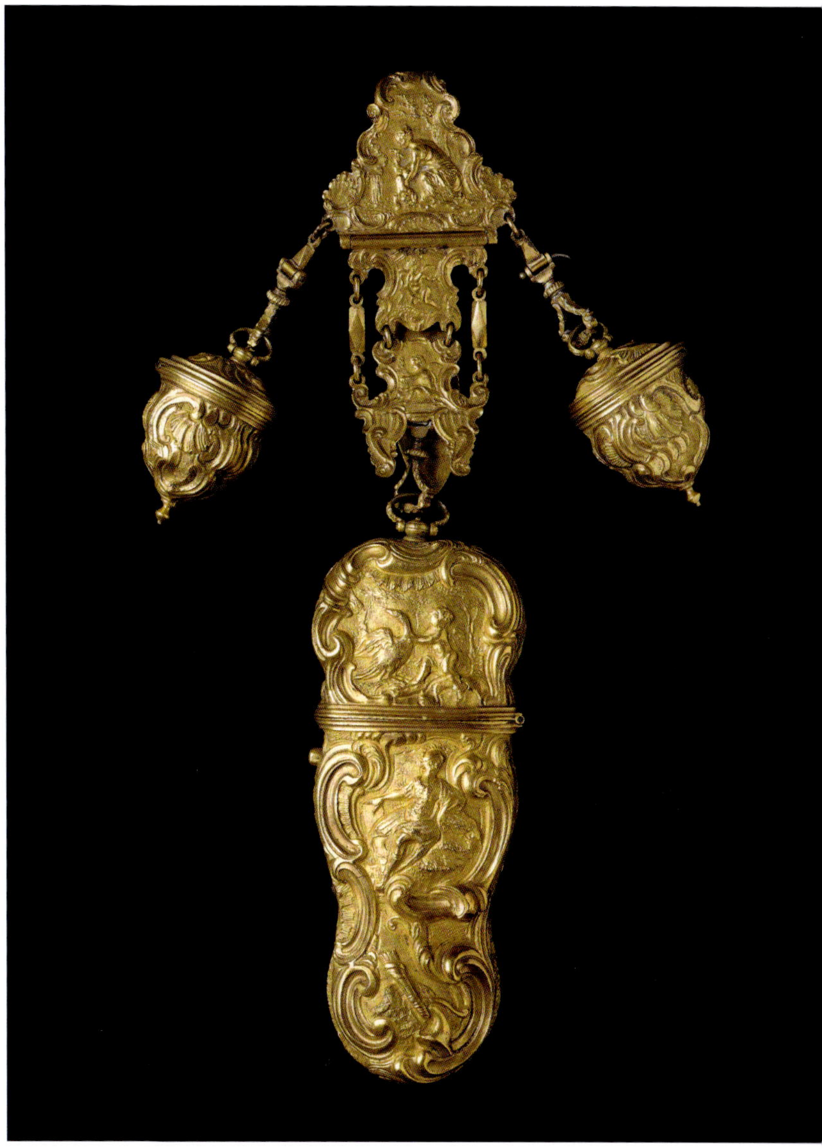

210 Cup and cover

Chased by Philippe and Louis Métayer, Amsterdam, 1754
Gold, 25 × 9.9 cm
Rijksmuseum, Amsterdam
(BK-1981-51)

This gold cup and cover, commissioned to celebrate a marriage, was designed by Louis Fabricius Dubourg (1693–1775) and published in a contemporary print by Jakob van der Schley (1673–1779). The cup bears mythological and Christian imagery and a putto supporting the combined coat of arms of the bride and groom.

211 Chatelaine

Francis Harrache, London, *c.*1740
Gold, l. 19.3 cm; main case w. 4.2 cm
Private collection, on loan to the Huguenot Museum, Rochester

The chatelaine was a practical feminine accessory used to carry personal items such as a pencil, spoon and ear scoop, and vinaigrettes (containing sponges soaked with vinegar) to stimulate the senses when required. The clasp and containers on this example are chased with figures of Venus and putti symbolizing love.

Souchay brothers, Daniel Marchand, Jean Louis Hauchard and Esaias Obicker, all of Huguenot origin. The Toussaints were Huguenots who came to Hanau from Berlin in 1752;[89] by 1762 they had persuaded the talented chaser Jean Jacques Bury (1731–1785) of Strasbourg, who was in Hanau from 1758, to join their workshop.[90] Over a hundred gold boxes bear the maker's mark 'LFT' for 'Les Frères Toussaint', usually with a rosette-shaped mark imitating the Parisian charge mark of 1768–74 (plate 212). They copied the latest Paris productions:[91] their gold *guilloché* ground boxes with enamelled brown 'tree' decoration imitating agate emulated gold boxes produced by the Paris goldsmith Charles Le Bastier (fl.1738–83) around 1775.[92]

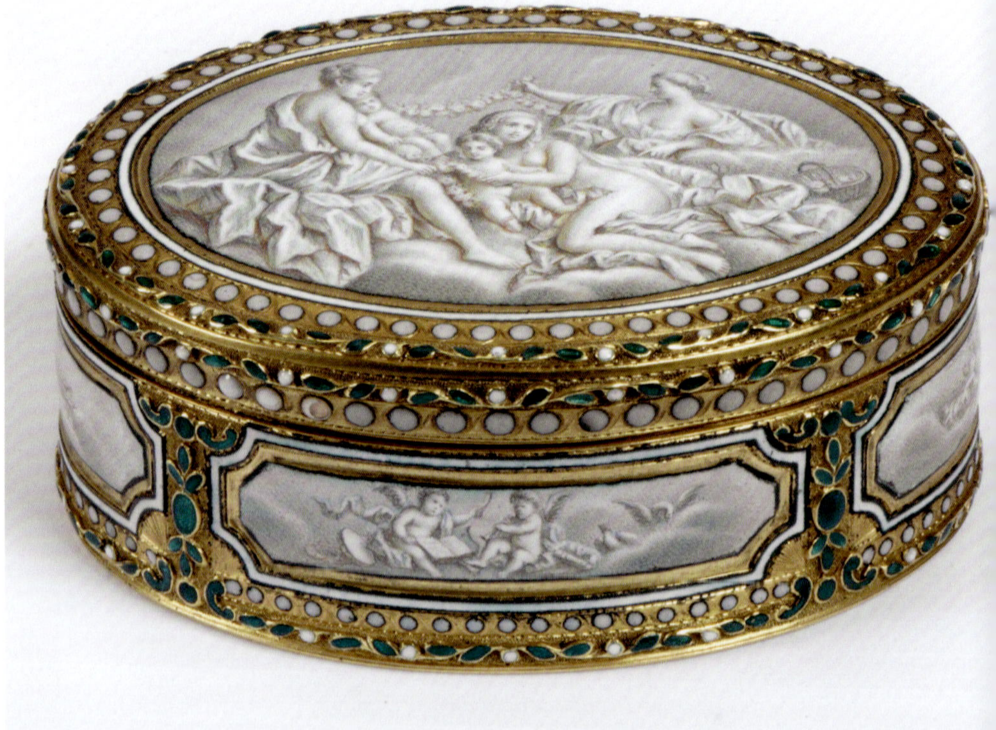

Huguenot 'toy shops' and suppliers in London and beyond

High-quality craftsmanship fed fashionable retailers including, from 1731, Paul Bertrand in Bath.[93] London toyshops were run in Suffolk Street by Paul Daniel Chenevix and, from 1743, his widow, and in Pall Mall from 1751 to 1773 by Thomas Harrache.[94] Robert Campbell noted in 1747 that 'it requires a large Stock to set up as a Master; especially to furnish a Shop'. The Chenevix shop was very profitable: Paul Daniel bequeathed £3,000 in trust to his two brothers (one of them, Richard Chenevix, was Bishop of Waterford), warning that his wife would suffer forfeiture if she 'quits the shop she now lives in or takes a partner'.[95] Several other wives or daughters of Huguenot craftsmen ran successful retail businesses.[96]

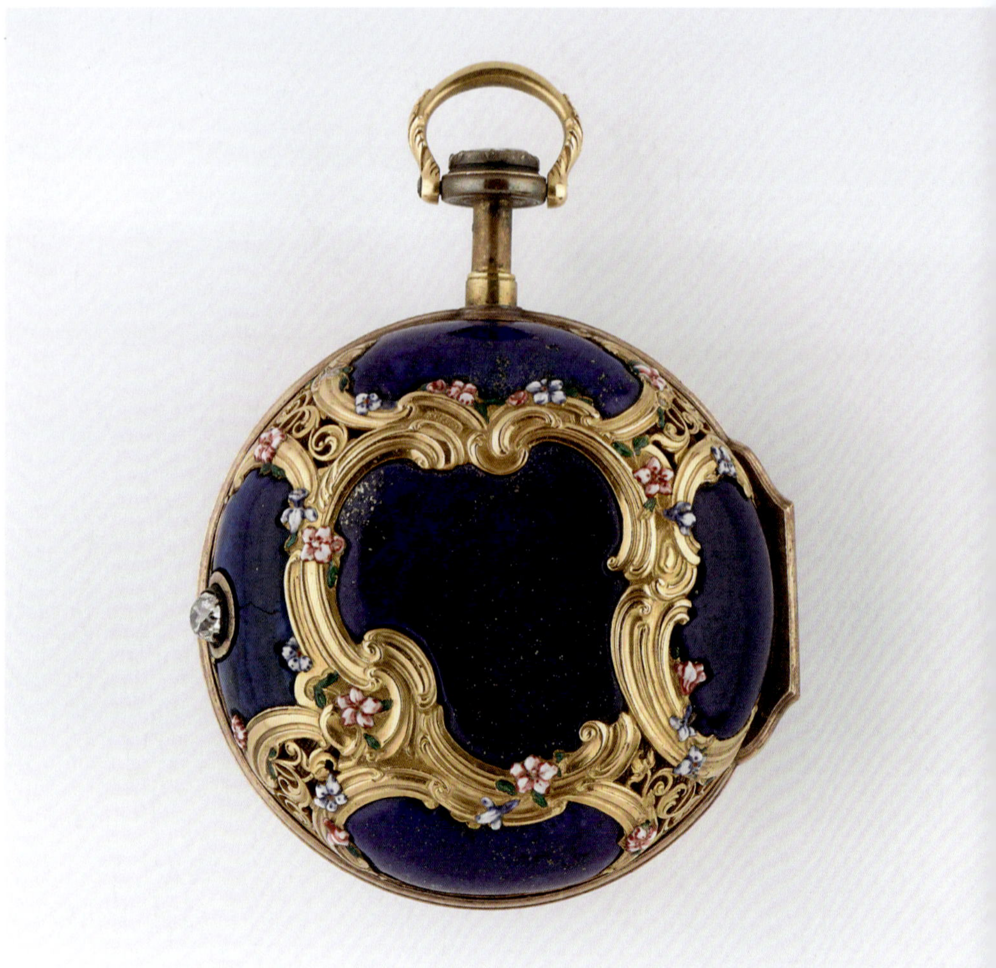

A pair-case watch in a gold lapis lazuli case (plate 213) is signed on the movement 'Paul Daniel Chenevix', although supplied by specialists in the making and decoration of watch cases.[97] From 1700 enamelled watch dials became increasingly colourful and were produced at Battersea in the 1750s. Excavation of the Battersea factory site suggests that some of these dials were hand-decorated, although many were transfer-printed.[98]

James Tregent (fl.1770–1804), watchmaker to the Prince of Wales, later George IV, was based in The Strand and later in Cranbourn Street. The enamelled dial of a bracket clock made in about 1780 signed 'James Tregant, Leicester Square, London' (plate 160) demonstrates the challenge of spelling Huguenot names correctly. James's brother Anthony specialized in retailing enamelled accessories, snuffboxes and calendars.[99]

LEFT ABOVE

212 Oval box

Toussaint brothers, Hanau, Germany, 1775–90
Gold and enamel, 2.6 × 6.6 × 5.1 cm
Victoria and Albert Museum, London (269–1878)

This enamelled box, signed 'LFT' for Les Frères Toussaint, has imitation Paris marks for 1773–4. In Hanau, craftsmen of Huguenot origin succeeded in competing with Paris productions; their goods were sold at the annual Frankfurt fair nearby and marketed through Geneva.

LEFT BELOW

213 Watch case

Paul Daniel Chenevix, London, c.1730
Gold, enamel, lapis lazuli and diamonds, 4.82 × 2.86 cm
Ashmolean Museum, Oxford (WA1947.191.110)

This luxurious timepiece, enamelled and set with lapiz lazuli and diamonds, was supplied by Chenevix to the 1st Duke of Newcastle. The fashionable Chenevix toyshop, advertised in French, was at the Golden Door in Suffolk Street, near Haymarket.

RIGHT

214 Ring

Peter Dutens (?), London, 1736
Gold, diamonds, enamel and hair, 1.5 × 2.5 × 2.3 cm
Royal Collection Trust (RCIN 9020)

The ring displays the Prince's badge and motto, a lock of his hair and an engraved inscription from the *Aeneid*. It was presented by Frederick, Prince of Wales, to Sir John Chardin the younger in 1736.

Manufacturing jewellers

In 1747 Robert Campbell pointed out that working jewellers would gain more profit if they sold direct to the wearer. A jeweller ought to be 'an elegant Designer' but inspiration was readily available from ornament prints: for example, William De La Cour's designs for jewelled pendants were engraved by Jacob Bonneau in 1747.[100] The knowledge and experience to 'judge ... precious Stones, their Beauties, common Blemishes, and ... intrinsic Value' and to 'know real Stones' from 'fictitious Gems' and how to prepare them, distinguished jewellers from goldsmiths. In London their trade was controlled by the Goldsmiths' Company. Huguenot jewellers also settled in regional centres. Henry Servant, from a family of goldsmiths and spoon makers, worked in Bideford before settling in Barnstaple in about 1700 until his death in 1738. A gold posy ring marked by Servant is engraved with the motto 'My Eyes did find my heart made choice of her that makes me now rejoyce'.[101]

Merchant jewellers

Louis and Jacques Louis Berchère[102] and Peter Dutens helped to sustain London's position as centre of the diamond trade during the eighteenth century, catered for by J.H. Desaguliers's *Accounts made Easy: 175 Tables for the use of all Merchant Jewellers* of 1734.[103] They built on the expertise and international network established by their seventeenth-century forbears, which linked the jewellery and watchmaking trades through the production of jewelled watch cases (plate 198).

Sir John Chardin, court jeweller to Charles II from 1681, published his travels to Persia and the East Indies in 1686.[104] Son of Daniel Chardin (1602–1672), a merchant jeweller in the Place Dauphiné, Paris, Chardin and his brother, also Daniel, promoted the diamond trade with India from London.[105] From 1682 the Berchères were at the hub of Huguenot City jewellers, who included Denis Chirac (fl.1712–38), jeweller to Queen Anne, who built Paddington House, on Paddington Green;[106] John Dargent (d.1774) of Lothbury, diamond cutter, working in the 1760s; James Massé of the parish of St Peter le Poer; and Lewis Baril of the church of St Stephen, Coleman Street. When Pierre Deletang, *diamentaire*, originally from Rouen, was admitted to the French Hospital aged 70 in 1760 with rheumatism of the arms, he was recommended by fellow jewellers Messrs Dutens, Raveau, Deschamps and Baril, and by Revd John James Majendie (1709–1782) Minister of the Savoy church.[107] Majendie's son Andrew was based in Madras, where he died in 1782,[108] and Peter Deschamps (d.1770), City merchant, was linked to the Motteux family and to Francis Creuse (d.1758), jeweller.[109] In 1736 Peter Dutens, working in Chandos Street off St Martin's Lane,[110] jeweller to Frederick, Prince of Wales, supplied his royal patron with a mantel clock with a movement by Charles Clay for £61 2s (plate 215). Dutens's bill for that clock[111] reveals that the case was imported from Paris. The dial plate was enamelled blue and white with the days, months and signs of the zodiac, under the supervision of the specialist clockmaker Charles Clay (d.1739), from a detailed design that gained royal approval. A small gold plaque chased with the face of the sun was centred on the dial. Dutens probably also supplied a diamond ring with the Prince's crest and motto (plate 214) as a personal gift to Sir John Chardin's son, also Sir John (d.1755), in the same year.[112] The ring contains a lock of the Prince of Wales's hair and an inscription from the *Aeneid*: 'Semper Honos Nomenque Tuum Laudesque Manebunt' (Your honour, name and praise will endure forever).

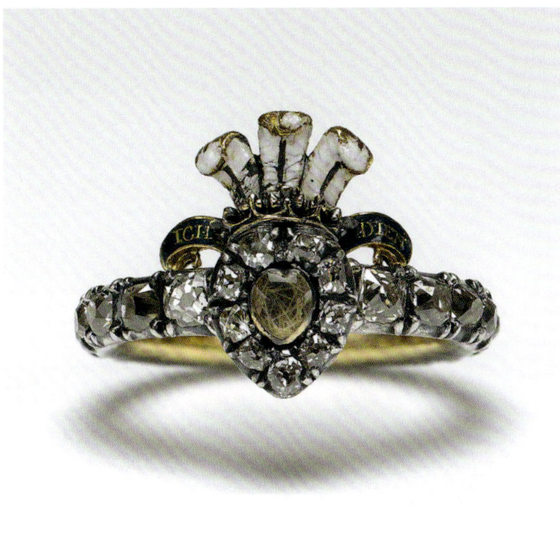

The patent taken out by watchmakers Peter and James Debaufre in 1704 for the introduction of jewels in watchmaking demonstrates the significance of the connections between specialist trades.[113] In 1758 Mrs Delany (1700–1788) was 'dazzled with constellations of diamonds' when visiting Dutens's shop. Her modesty preferred 'one single diamond to all the bouquets, *esclavages*, earrings, and knots; it was so clear, so perfect, so brilliant, and the price but four thousand pounds'.[114] Dutens was supplied by specialist diamond cutters whose skills owed much to John Pantin (1658–1735), of Walbrook in the City of

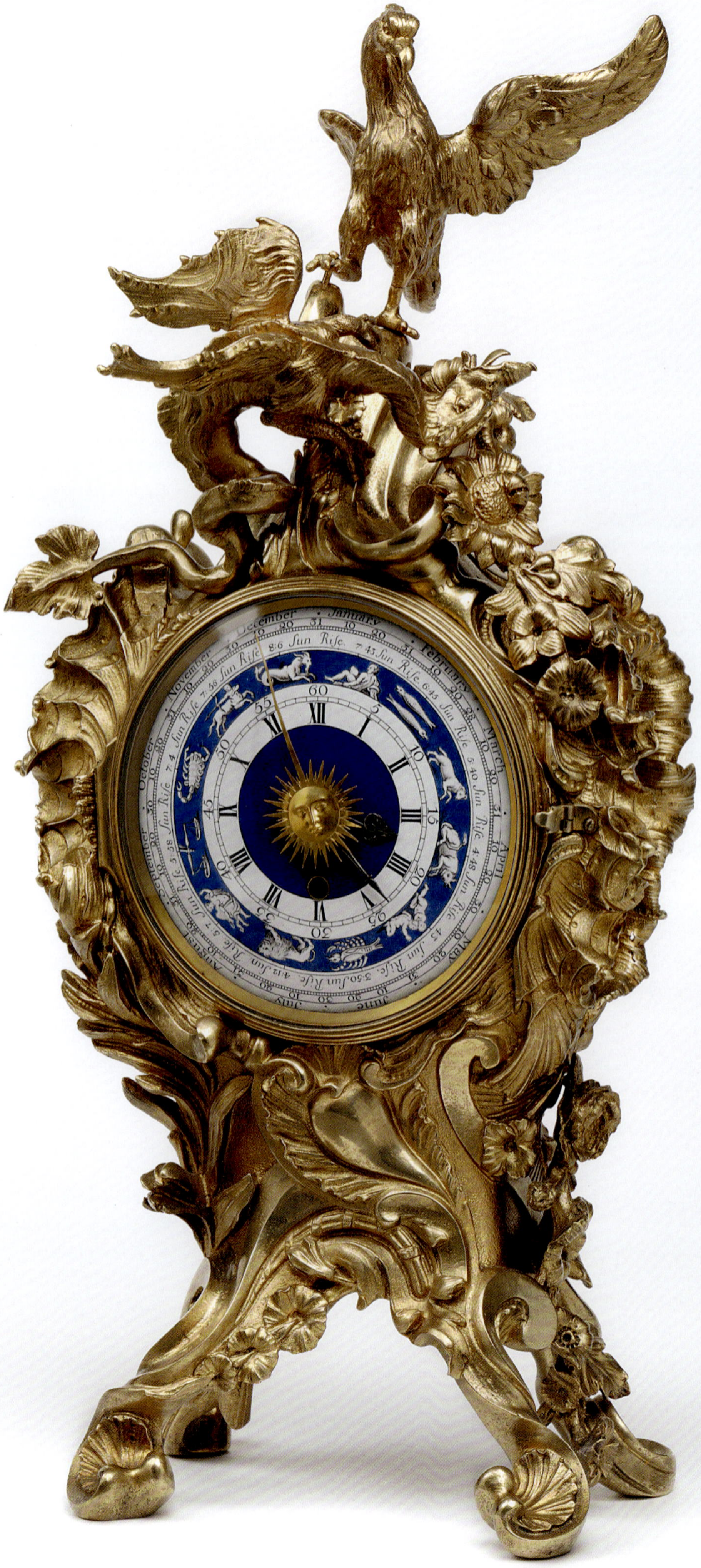

215 Royal mantel clock

Peter Dutens, London, 1736
Gilt brass, cast, pierced, chased and enamelled, max. 40 × 19 × 17 cm
Victoria and Albert Museum, London (M.1–2016)

The dial plate is enamelled blue and white, possibly imitating the dial of the great astronomical clock at Hampton Court Palace (plate 197), which was devised by King Henry VIII. The outer calendar dial and the inner concentric ring indicate the time of sunrise throughout the year and are linked to the central gold mount chased with the face of the sun by a longer, third hand.

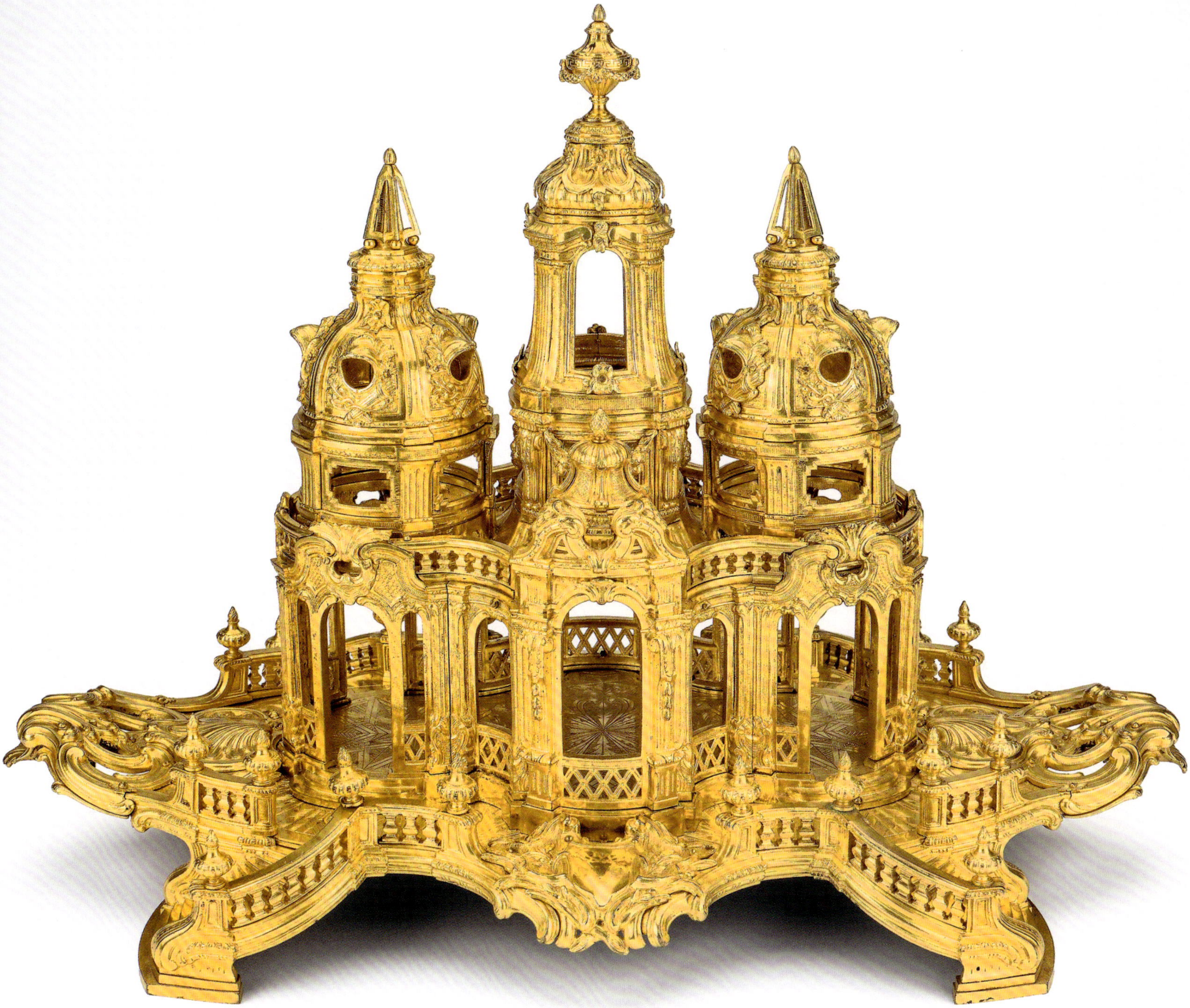

216 Architectural centrepiece

Denis René Gastecloux, London, 1768
Ormolu, 30.5 × 43.5 × 24.5 cm
Art Institute of Chicago (2014.591)

Beautifully cast, chased and finished, this small-scale architectural capriccio reflects European interest in experimental buildings conceived as features in a landscape garden, inspired by temporary structures built to celebrate a national event such as a royal birth or military victory. This centrepiece was inspired by Meissonnier's architectural designs, specifically the temporary Paris pavilion built to celebrate the Dauphin's birth in 1734.

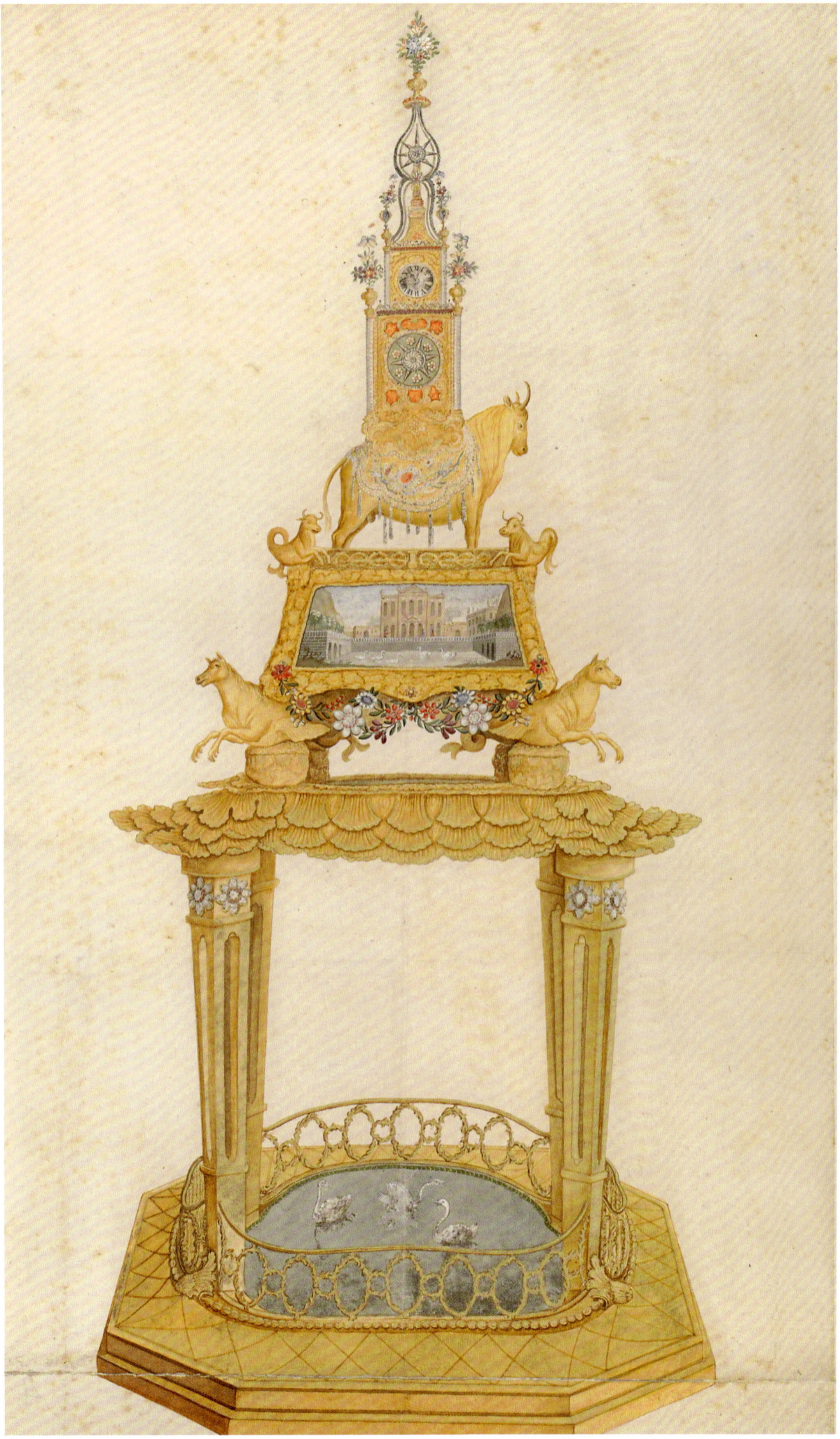

217 Presentation drawing

Attributed to Charles Magniac,
London, *c.*1770
Pencil, bodycolour and gold paint,
44 × 28 cm
Victoria and Albert Museum,
London (E.3985–1906)

This drawing was made for presentation to the patron. It is either a design for or a record of a sophisticated clock that was exported to China. The clock and stand were subsequently separated and only reunited on the evidence of this drawing for an exhibition in Utrecht in 2010.

218 Elephant automaton

Hubert Martinet and others,
London, *c.*1768–72
Chased bronze, with gilt-bronze,
patinated bronze and polychrome
oil paint, white, red, green, blue
and yellow paste, mother of
pearl and glass, carved oak base,
137.1 × 85.1 × 63.8 cm
Waddesdon Manor, National Trust
(2202)

Operated by clockwork, the elephant flaps its ears, moves its tail and raises its trunk as a procession of human figures moves around the base and flowers, embellished with paste, open and close. Moving stars 'display the lustre of the stones' with which they are set, and serpents move 'as if alive'. This sophisticated automaton was intended for export to the East Indies.

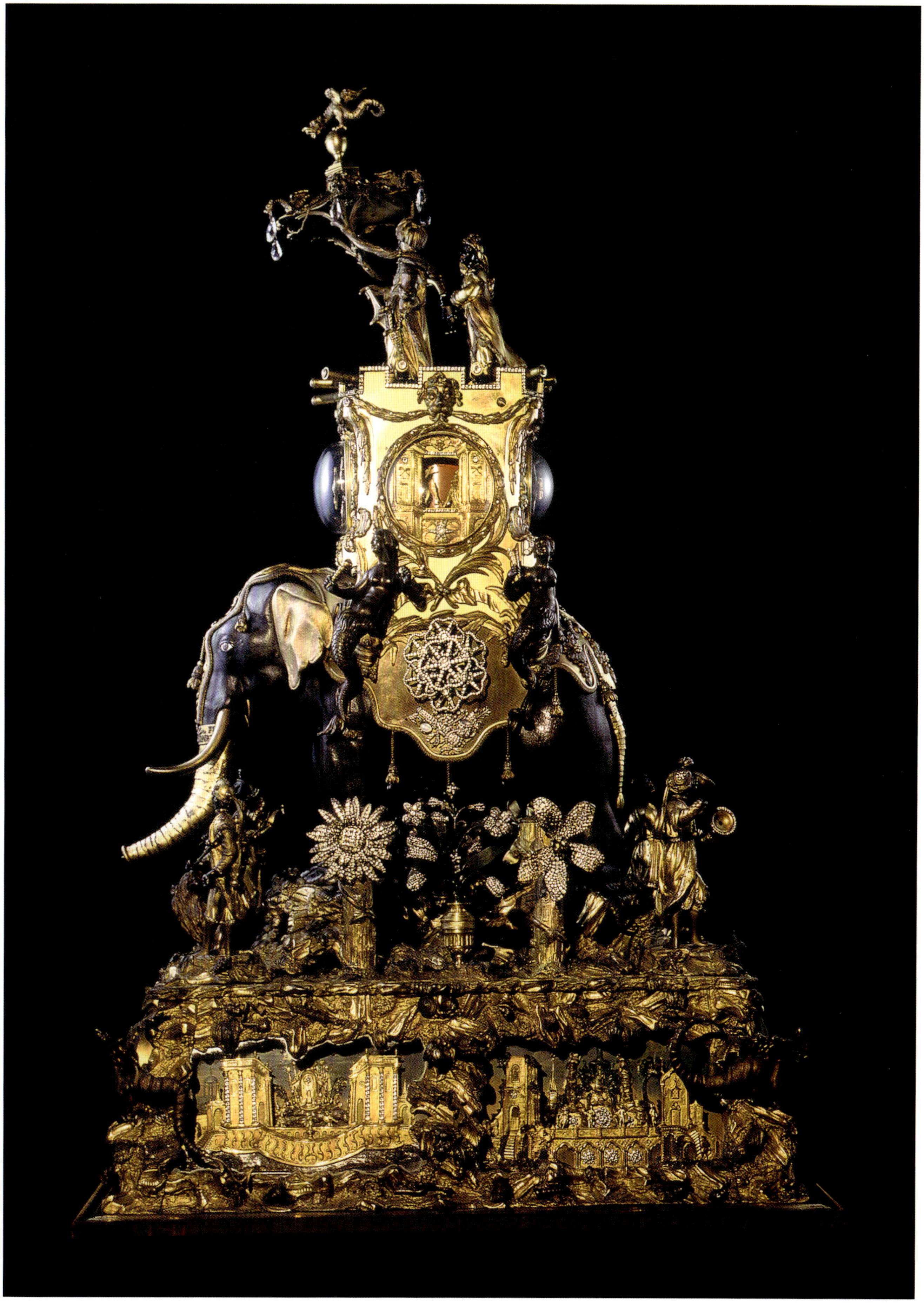

London. Born in Rouen, Pantin left France at the time of the Revocation. On his death he was described as 'the first that brought the Art of Diamond Cutting to that perfection it is now in'.[115] The Berthon family from Chatellerault, Poitou, worked as jewellers and stone setters in the Quartier des Grècs, Soho, but their network stretched from New York and Amsterdam to Lisbon.[116]

Peter Romilly (1712–1782), a jeweller in Frith Street, Soho, was related to the Romilly family of Geneva. In 1762 he charged Charles, 2nd Earl of Egremont, the sum of 15 guineas for 'a Gold carved Watch', a further 5s for 'a Long Gold & silk' watch string and £4 12s for a pair of 'Stone shoe & Knee Buckles'.[117]

The Gastecloux centrepiece

The international network of designers, craftsmen and retailers of Huguenot origin continued to promote exchange across Europe and beyond. A table centrepiece signed 'D.R. Gastecloux' in 1768 (plate 216) demonstrates the skills available. A small-scale architectural capriccio, this is the only recorded ormolu table centrepiece made in London. It was inspired by Meissonnier's temporary Paris pavilion built to celebrate the Dauphin's birth some thirty years earlier, in 1734. Its sophisticated form was intended to remind cultured guests of European travel and stimulate conversation round the dinner table.[118] Formed of over three hundred separate cast elements held in place with rivets, the Gastecloux centrepiece reflects contemporary French practice. Ormolu was a fashionable alternative to silver; the harder metal is well suited to architectural form. Its gilded surface harmonized with silver-gilt plates and cutlery used for dessert; pristine gilding inside the hinged shell compartments suggests receptacles for condiments or snuff. The centrepiece may have held sugared sweetmeats made with saffron, powdered violets, spinach juice and cochineal, providing a colourful and enticing climax for special occasions.

Its maker, Denis René Gastecloux, married Marie, daughter of Isaac Gribelin, goldsmith, and his wife, Marie Vautier, in London in 1743; the bride's family came originally from Blois. René Gastecloux, a bronzier, working in Paris *c.*1740, and Edme Gastecloux, appointed Professor de Fonte et Ciseleur at the Imperial Academy of Fine Arts, St Petersburg, who settled there from Paris in 1770–1, were probably relatives, demonstrating the widespread family links established by the Huguenot diaspora.

As a skilled chaser, Gastecloux is likely to have worked also in gold; an inkstand recently sold at auction bears close stylistic similarities to the centrepiece.[119] Another family member, the clock- and watchmaker Lewis Marie Gastecloux, was working in Parsons Green, Fulham, in 1776.

The bull clock and elephant automaton

The production of sophisticated clocks and automata also catered for the Chinese market. The presentation drawing of a bull clock (plate 217) is attributed to Charles Magniac (fl.1754–70), a 'fine designer and modeller and chaser' who worked for the goldsmith and clockmaker James Cox (fl. London 1749–91).[120] The finished clock was exported to China and is now in the Palace Museum, Beijing, where it had become separated from its original stand with its supporting sea-horses and sea-bulls.[121] Working in Old Change in the City of London in 1767 when he took his son Francis (1753–1827) as apprentice, Charles Magniac founded another dynasty of goldsmiths and watchmakers: by 1790 the Magniacs were established in Clerkenwell.[122] James Cox also employed other Huguenot goldsmiths: Joseph LeJeune, Gedeon Girard, and Albert Ponge from Berlin, whose son John James was born in London in 1737.[123]

The astonishing elephant automaton now at Waddesdon Manor (plate 218) was assembled in rented Clerkenwell lodgings by visiting French clockmaker Hubert Martinet (fl.1770–90), incorporating parts supplied by hundreds of specialists. The retail jewellers Masquerier & Perigal invited viewers to admire this 'machine' in their fashionable premises, for an entry fee of 2s 6d. Although intended for export to the East Indies, that market had slackened by the early 1770s. The proprietors therefore hoped to attract European interest and other customers for their pearl jewellery and watches, including a gold repeater by George Graham (1673–1751).[124]

Musical clocks

From the late sixteenth century, Huguenot clockmakers specialized in musical clocks. Nicholas Vallin (fl. *c.*1575–1603), who came to London from Lille with his father, settled in St Ann's parish, Blackfriars, in the 1580s and was married at the Dutch church at Austin Friars in June 1590. In 1598 he signed a musical weight-driven chamber clock,

219 Musical table clock

Claude Viet, London, *c.*1715
Japanned oak and pine case, brass dial with silver mounts, bronze figurative finials, 101 × 43 × 33 cm
Private collection, on loan to Lyme Park, Cheshire, National Trust

First-generation Huguenot clockmaker, Claude Viet specialized in musical clocks. The sculptural finials include Mercury and four figures carrying Christ's cross. The painted case imitates Asian lacquer, which was fashionable and appealed to the Turkish market. The cast silver spandrels are a further indication of quality.

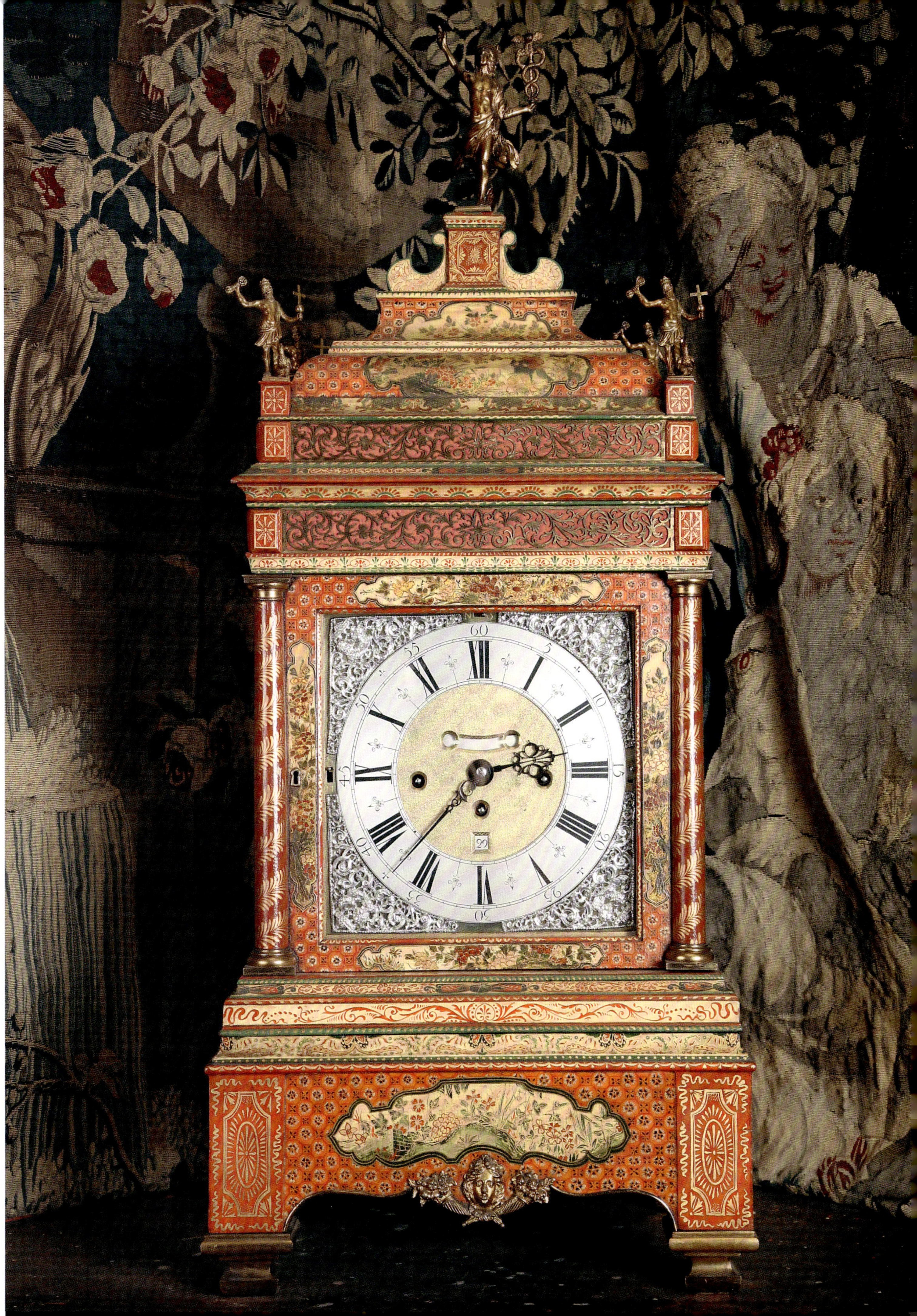

which strikes the hours on the large bell at the top and plays music at each quarter on 13 bells below. Vallin died of plague in 1603, with his father, two of his three daughters and two of his journeyman clockmakers.[125]

A hundred years later Claude Viet (d.1734), originally from Orleans and free of the Clockmakers' Company in 1698, became watchmaker to Queen Anne. A musical clock signed by Viet is at Lyme Park, Cheshire (plate 219). In 1715 he took as apprentice his niece Marie Anne Viet (b.1699), the first woman to be accepted by the Clockmakers' Company. She was named after his wife, Marie Anne (d.1744), whom he married in 1696.[126] When her uncle died in 1734 Marie Anne formed a partnership with his son-in-law Thomas Mitchell (d.1751) and maintained the shop at the Dial and King's Arms, Cornhill; it was still there in 1793. Their sophisticated trade card dated 1742 is signed by engraver James Santor.

Claude du Chesne (fl.1690–1730), who came from Paris, free of the Clockmakers' Company in 1693, worked in Dean Street, Soho and later in Long Acre. He made long-case clocks with fine marquetry cases; one example dated 1705 played six melodies on ten bells with 20 hammers. A 1704 table clock bearing his name has a naively engraved backplate featuring David with the Head of Goliath.[127]

Clockmaker Stephen Rimbault (fl.1744–88), established in Great St Andrew Street, Seven Dials, from 1744, specialized in musical clocks with dials enlivened by mechanical figures. Some dials on Rimbault's clocks were painted by Johann Zoffany (1733–1810): the two had been introduced by Zoffany's landlord, a musical box maker named Bellodi, who pricked the barrels for Rimbault's musical clocks. In gratitude, Zoffany painted Rimbault's portrait (plate 220).[128] Musical clocks by Rimbault and his son Paul (fl.1770–85) are preserved in the Forbidden Palace, Beijing, among examples signed by Huguenots Barbot, Cabrier, Tregent and Lewis Pantin. These include Pantin's balloon-style case for an elaborate gilt-bronze musical clock with a drawer in the base containing a *nécessaire*.[129]

Francis Gabriel Barraud (1727–1795), whose family came from Angoulême, also produced musical clocks. One of these, dating from *c.*1767 and given to the Clockmakers' Company by his descendants, plays four tunes on seven bells. Barraud was Stephen Rimbault's neighbour in Great St Andrew Street, but moved in 1781 to Wine Office Court, Fleet Street.

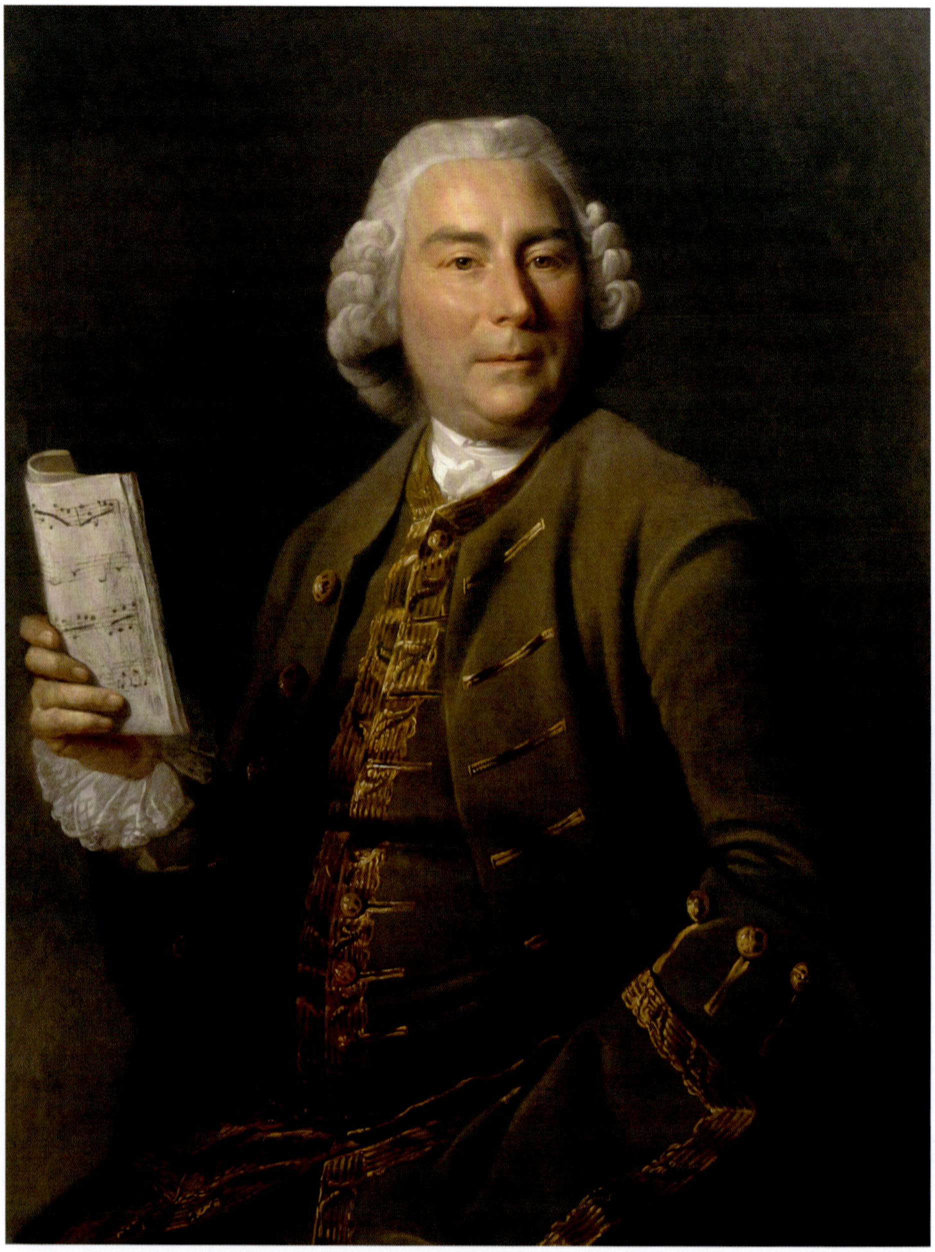

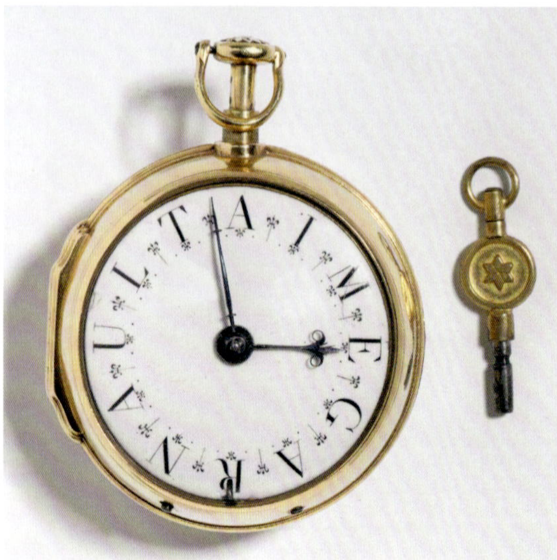

LEFT ABOVE

220 *Stephen Rimbault*

Johann Zoffany, London, 1764
Oil on canvas, 88.9 × 71.1 cm
Tate Gallery, London (N04434)

Stephen Rimbault's musical clocks had dials enlivened by mechanical figures. Johann Zoffany's portrait shows the clockmaker holding sheet music as an indication of his speciality.

LEFT BELOW

221 Pocket watch

Robert Street, case by Samuel Godbehere, London, *c.*1765
Gold and enamel, diam. 5.5 cm
French Hospital at the Huguenot Museum, Rochester, Kent

One Huguenot innovation was to substitute the Roman numerals I to XII for the hours with letters spelling the name of the owner. Aimé Garnault (1717–1782) of Lincoln's Inn Fields, who owned this watch, was the grandson of Ayme Garnault, a merchant jeweller from St Severin, Paris, who settled in Soho.

Retailing jewellers and watchmakers

City merchants were important clients for makers of clocks and watches and well placed to promote the export trade. Clockmaker Paul Chotard at the Dial and Sun, Middle Moorfields supplied watches for export from 1742.[130] One Huguenot patron-led innovation was to substitute the Roman hour numerals I to XII with letters spelling the name of the owner; surviving examples include a watch made for 'AIME GARNAULT' (plate 221) and a long-case clock inscribed 'JACOB HOUBLON'.[131]

In London as in Paris, watchmakers worked closely with goldsmiths and jewellers, both as retailers and manufacturers. Daniel Grignion was established in Russell Street, Covent Garden, by 1720 and worked as finisher to the celebrated London maker, the Quaker Daniel Quare, who died in 1724.[132] Daniel Grignon arrived from Poitou as a child of four in 1688; the family probably escaped via the Netherlands. His name was later anglicized to Grignion. Daniel's son Thomas, born in London in 1713, joined his business in Russell Street. From 1724 Daniel belonged to Solomon's Temple masonic lodge in Hemmings Row, off St Martin's Lane.[133] The lodge was an important source of professional contacts: the Master was the scientist Dr J.T. Desaguliers, from 1719 Grand Master of the London Freemasons; other lodge members were the gunsmith Israel Segalas (d.1735) and engineer Charles Labelye, designer of the first Westminster Bridge, for which watchmaker James Vauloué invented the pile-driving engine (plate 74).

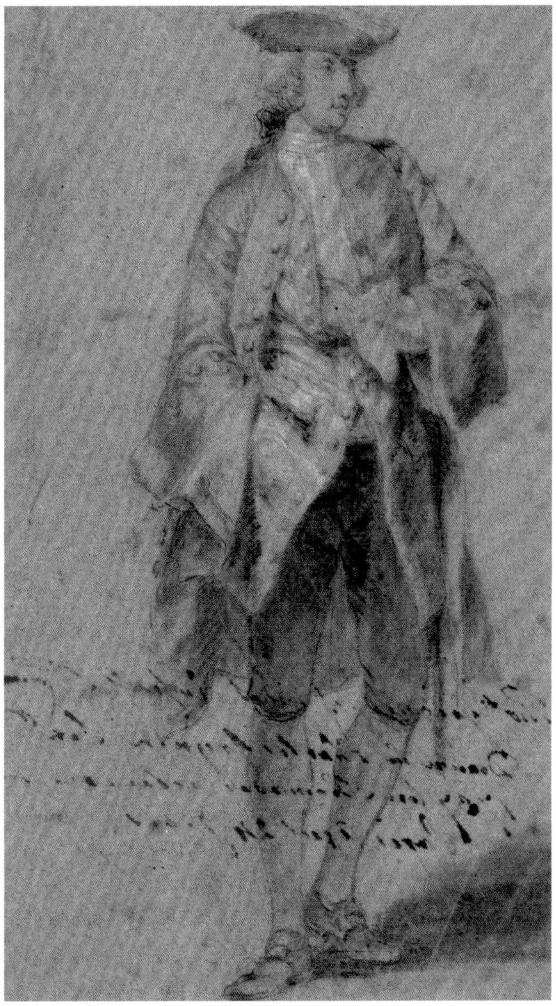

222 *Thomas Grignion*

Charles Grignion, London, 1737
Black chalk and white on blue grey paper, 33.2 × 18.9 cm
British Museum, London (1890,0512.94)

Inscribed on the reverse 'Thos Grignion of Great Russell Street, Covent [Garden] Drawn by Charles Grignion Snr in 1737 on Thomas's return from Paris aged 24 Years'. Thomas is fashionably dressed with tricorn hat, sword and buckled shoes. The artist was his elder brother, who studied drawing with Hubert Gravelot.

Daniel Grignion's elder son, Charles, sketched his brother, Thomas (1713–1784), on his return from Paris in 1737 (plate 222). In 1740 Thomas perfected 'the horizontal principle in watches and the dead beat in clocks' and supplied the turret clock for St Paul's church, Covent Garden. Destroyed by fire in 1795, it was replaced in 1797 by Thomas Grignion the younger (b.1744), who ran the family business from 1763. The Grignions retained their Covent Garden premises for four generations from 1720 to 1825,[134] and mended watches for their landlords, the dukes of Bedford. In 1775 their firm was styled Grignion & Son; a third Thomas Grignion managed the shop from 1800 to 1825.

The Grignions commissioned fine chased watch cases: in December 1750 they charged £31 16s for 'a gold watch going upon jewels No. 1118 chased by George Michael Moser with the *Judgement of Hercules*'. A watch movement dating from 1752, signed by Daniel and Thomas Grignion, is now in the British Museum. This originally boasted a gold case chased by G.M. Moser with the figure of Britannia. Moser chased cases for several other Huguenot watchmakers, including Paul du Pin, John Leroux and Francis Perigal. The watchmaker would supply the plain watch case and commission the chaser to decorate it. Thomas Grignion probably encouraged Moser to decorate watch cases with enamelling: in 1762 Moser showed an enamelled watch case at the Society of Artists annual exhibition in Spring Gardens, adjacent to Charing Cross.

From Soho to Clerkenwell: specialist trades

Although there were Huguenot clock- and watchmakers working in Spitalfields,[135] as the eighteenth century progressed, specialist clock- and watchmakers moved from Soho to Clerkenwell. These included dynasties of Huguenot craftsmen recorded as escapement makers, engine turners, fusee cutters, springers, secretspringers, finishers, and joint finishers. Robert Campbell's seven categories of specialization have apprenticeship fees ranging from £10 to £30 for the main trade, £5 to £10 for the movement maker, spring maker, chain maker, case cap maker and finisher. Campbell explains the division of labour: the 'Watch-maker ... only employs the different Tradesmen amongst whom the Art is divided', adjusts and finishes the movement. New technology improved accuracy: cat-gut, used instead of chains in the seventeenth century, was 'affected by every Change of Weather'; since the 'Invention of the Chain and our Improvement in the Temper of Springs', watches were resistant to the weather.[136]

According to Campbell, the 'Invention of Engines for cutting the Teeth in the several Parts of the Movement ... formerly cut by Hand' reduced the cost of production and promoted precision. Brass wheels were supplied by the cutter and finished by the movement maker; steel pinions were drawn at the mill:

> *[the] Watch-maker has only to file down the Pivots, and fix them to their proper Wheels. The Springs are made by a Tradesman who does nothing else, and the Chains ... frequently made by Women in the Country about London, and sold to the Watch-Maker by the Dozen for a very small Price.*[137]

This is borne out by Huguenot church records. Anne Fenouillet, born in London, was apprenticed to Elizabeth Lignac 'pour apprendre a fair de chaisnettes de montre'; male specialist watch chain makers included Gabriel Veugney, living in Church Street, St Anne's, Soho, in 1700.[138] Other workmen made caps and studs; 'Silver-Smiths ... only make Cases', and 'Workmen ... cut the Dial-Plates, or enamel them, which is ... become much the Fashion'. The watchmaker gave all the parts to the finisher, who had the brass-wheels gilded before assembling all the components and adjusting the time:

> *The Watch-Maker puts his Name upon the Plate, and is esteemed the Maker, though he has not made in his Shop the smallest Wheel belonging to it. It is supposed, however, that he can make all the Movements and Apprentices are learned still to cut them by Hand.*[139]

The watchmaker must be able to judge quality for the price will depend on his reputation.

Campbell confirms that the potential for profit was considerable and even 'a Journeyman has as much as he can earn, for they are generally paid by the Piece; a Finisher may earn Thirty or Forty Shillings a Week, if constantly employed'.

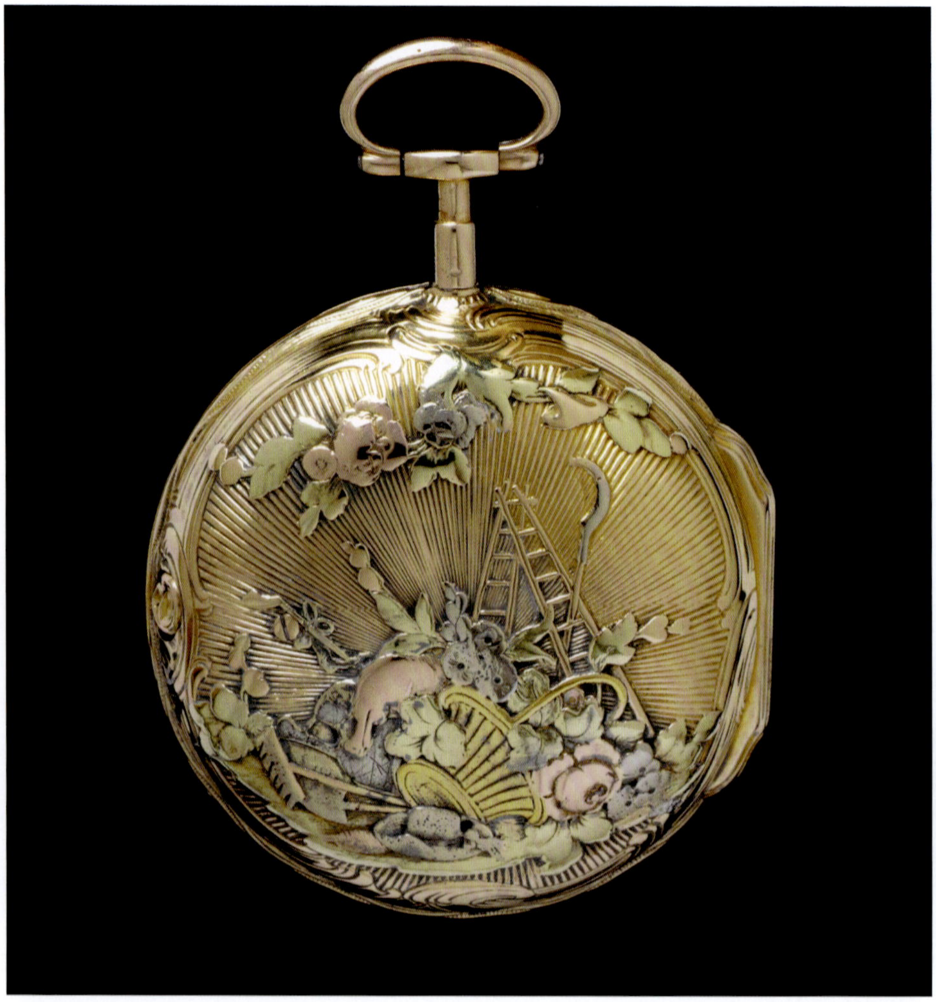

223 Watch
Jean Romilly, Switzerland(?), 1750–60
Four-coloured gold with traces of enamel, 5.2 x 4.3 x 2 cm
Signed 'Jean Romilly, Paris' but probably made in Switzerland; the case inscribed with maker's mark, 'IT' crowned
Victoria and Albert Museum, London (373–1908)

The case is chased with flowers and gardening implements, including a scythe and stepladder. Roses, pansies and leaves in different-coloured gold reflect natural colours. The engine-turned background retains traces of enamel.

A master watchmaker 'ought to have a tolerable Education, and some Smattering of Mechanics and Mathematics'. The watchmaking trade 'is not much over-stocked in Town and no Trade has better Encouragement in our Plantations, or in any other Part of *Europe*. If he understands his Business, he may have Bread almost any where.'[140]

The international market

Genevan watchmakers were the leading migratory workers of early modern Europe. Yet in 1789 'La Fabrique', as the Genevan watch and jewellery trades were known, was still employing 5,000 people out of a population of 26,000.[141] One of the celebrated Genevan dynasties of clock- and watchmakers, the Romilly family, had close links with the Huguenot church there. Jean Romilly (1714–1796), the son of Pierre Romilly (1681–1717), a master clockmaker, was born in Geneva and trained with his father before settling in Paris in 1734. Despite his Protestant faith, he was received as master in Paris 18 years later, on the recommendation of the Conseil d'Etat du Roi. He married

224 Box

John Duval, London, 1769, with ivory turned by George III, 1774
Gold and ivory, 2 × 5.2 cm
Royal Collection Trust (RCIN 65779)

John Duval & Sons, the leading Genevan retailer of such luxury goods, also traded from London and St Petersburg with India, Turkey and China. This gold box is mounted in ivory turned by George III, who subsequently presented the box to John Duval. Duval's grandson recorded its history in an engraved inscription on the inside of the lid.

Elizabeth, the granddaughter of Paris clockmaker Jean Jolly (d.1751).

Jean Romilly (plate 223) was one of the first makers to produce eight-day watches.[142] In 1755, at the Paris Academie des Sciences, he presented a watch that ran for 378 days, although he reduced this to six months. For clocks he used the thermal compensation pendulum invented by Grenier. His few clocks were made to commission, in cases by leading bronziers including C. Cressent (1685–1768) and J.J. de Saint Germain (1719–1791).[143] Romilly's son Edmé-Jean (1739–1779), a pastor in Geneva, moved to London; Romilly's daughter Elizabeth (1742–1814) was the wife of Guillaume Olivier de Corancez (1734–1810). De Corancez was the owner and editor of the *Journal de Paris*, the first French daily literary newspaper, to which Jean Romilly contributed articles, as he did to Diderot's *Encyclopedie*. Jean Romilly and Samuel, the distinguished lawyer son of the London jeweller Peter Romilly, met in Paris in 1780.[144]

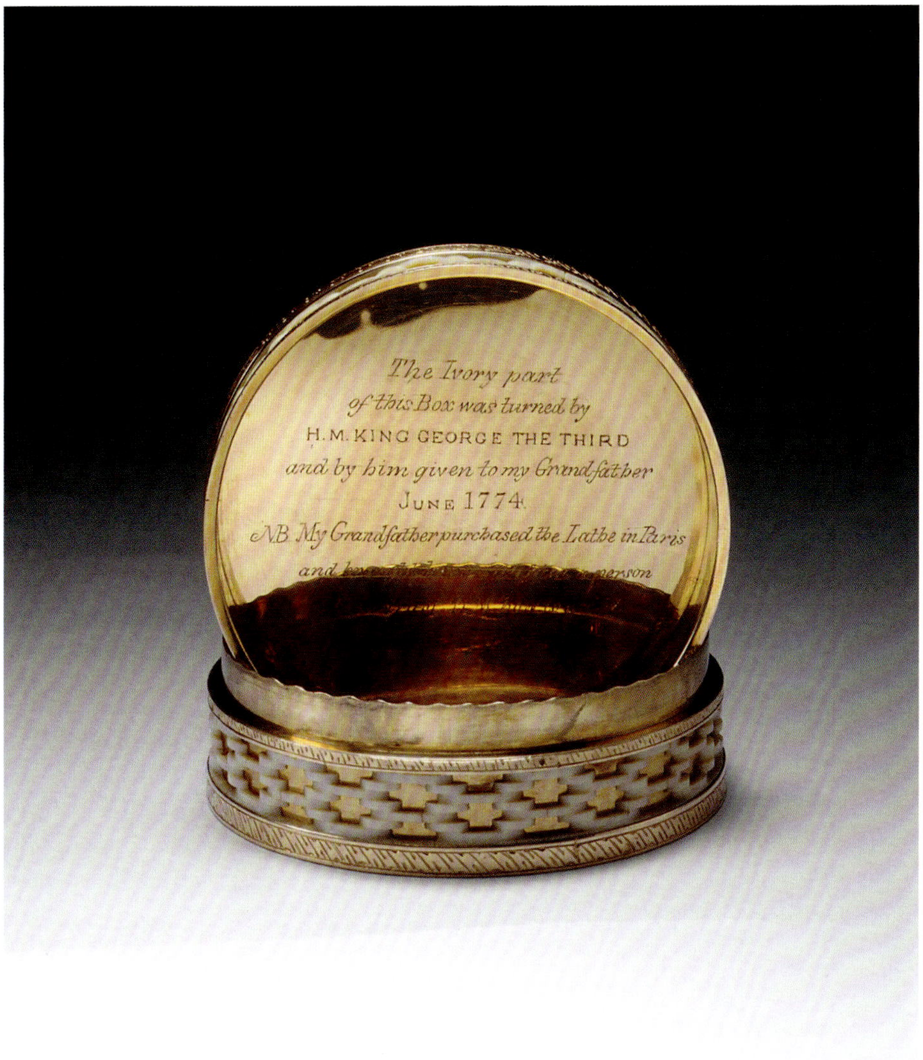

By the 1770s, London's watchmaking fraternity welcomed new arrivals from Switzerland attracted by the established Swiss community, with an independent church (founded in 1762) that met in the former Huguenot Castle Street church and a social network promoted by the United Swiss Society (founded in 1718). A Swiss masonic lodge, 'L'Immortalité de L'Ordre', met at Thirteen Cantons coffee house on the corner of King Street and Litchfield Street, Soho, in 1764 and flourished until 1775; Justin Vulliamy (1712–1797), a clockmaker from Pays de Vaud, Switzerland, established in London from 1739, was a founder member.[145] He also served as President of the London Swiss church from 1762 to 1797.

Watchmaker Josiah Emery (*c.*1731–1794), a founder of the Swiss church in 1762, worked at 33 Cockspur Street, Charing Cross, between 1770 and 1805 and adopted Thomas Mudge's lever escapement; the watch that Emery made for German Count Bruhl proved so effective that he made 33 more at £150 each. In 1781 he was presented with the honorary freedom of the Clockmakers' Company.[146] His business was carried on by Louis Recordon (fl.1778–1817), who from 1780 worked at Greek Street, Soho, and patented a pedometer-winding for watches. After Recordon's death the business continued under Peter Des Granges (fl.1784–1842) until his retirement in 1842.[147]

Benjamin Gray (*c.*1676–1764), clockmaker to George II from 1742, in St James's Street was assisted from 1739 by Justin Vulliamy, who became his son-in-law and succeeded to the business. Vulliamy produced watches of very fine quality: one has an outer case of gold with a crystal and diamond thumb-piece to press back the locking spring, the inner case enamelled in colours with a garden scene. He was another founder of a dynasty: he was succeeded by his son Benjamin, who advised George III on equipment for the Kew Royal Observatory. Benjamin's son, Benjamin Lewis Vulliamy (1780–1854), maintained the family royal appointment and a reputation for excellent finish. Clocks by different generations of Vulliamys are preserved at Windsor Castle: on the mantelpiece in the State Dining Room is a clock by Justin Vulliamy, and in the Presence Chamber another in a marble case forms part of a mantelpiece designed by the sculptor John Bacon. B.L. Vulliamy published an account of the construction of the deadbeat escapement; he was five times Master of the Clockmakers' Company.[148]

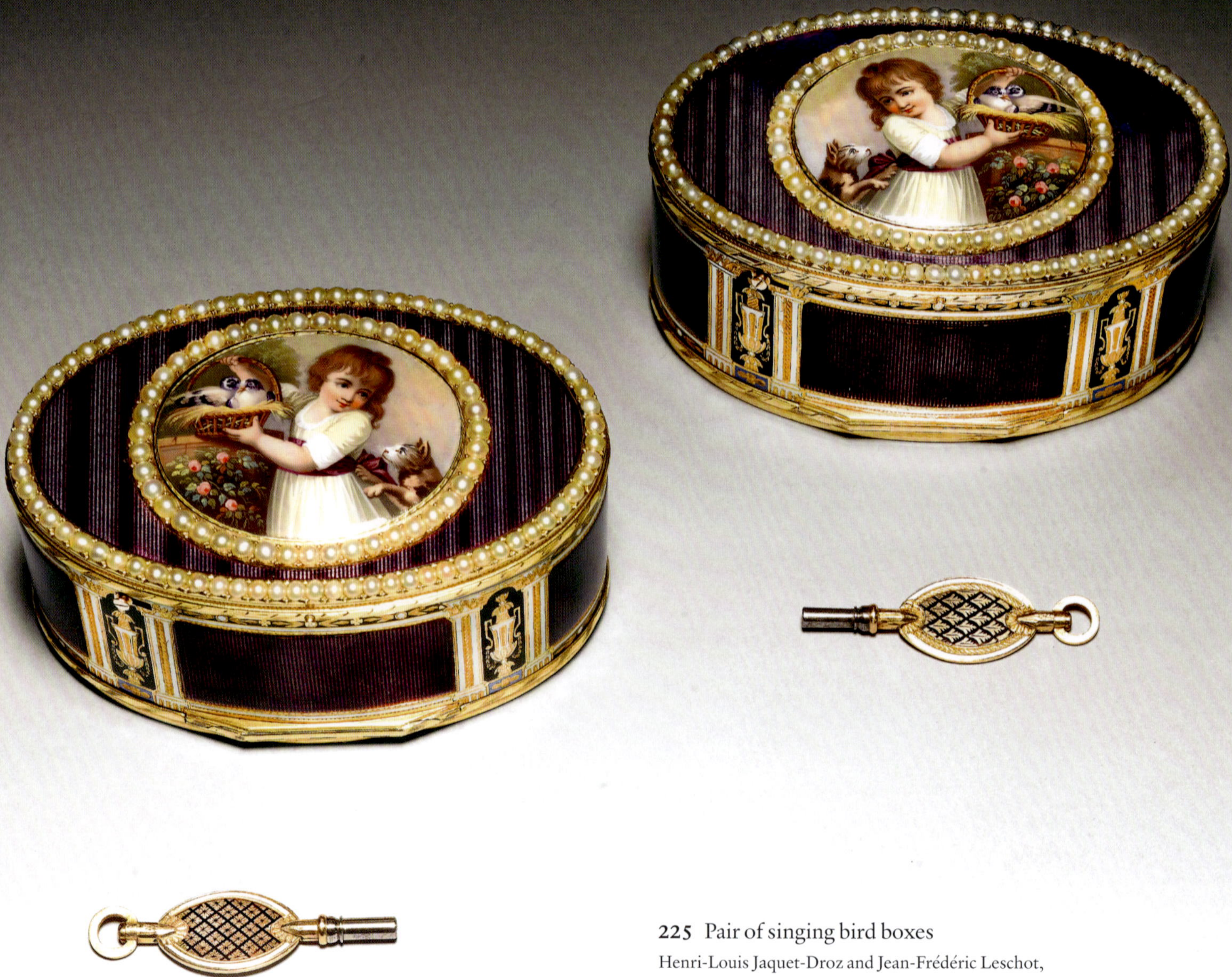

225 Pair of singing bird boxes

Henri-Louis Jaquet-Droz and Jean-Frédéric Leschot, London, 1800–1
Gold and purple translucent enamel, each w. 8.5 cm
Private collection

Swiss maker Henri-Louis Jaquet-Droz and his partner Jean-Frédéric Leschot produced movements for singing birds in gold boxes by Rémond, Gide & Co., which rivalled earlier productions marketed from London by James Cox. This pair was ordered from them by David Duval in 1800–1.

John Duval & Sons, the leading Genevan retailer of luxury goods, established a presence in both London and St Petersburg, where they supplied gold boxes to the court of Catherine the Great. John Duval (fl.1748–1800) was Senior Warden of the Swiss masonic lodge in London, where Louis Duval (fl.1851) was also a member. There is no apparent family connection between him and James Duval (b. *c.*1663–1677), who became free of the Clockmakers' Company in 1677.[149] In 1769 John Duval supplied George III with a French lathe (*machine à guilloché*) and a gold box (plate 224), its ivory decoration turned by George III himself using the lathe.[150] The Duvals developed trade with Brazil: Richard Julius Duval (1802–1864) married and settled there in 1830, after Brazilian Independence from Portugal.[151] The Duvals also traded with Turkey, India and China, where the market for automata was particularly keen.

Another leading supplier of sophisticated automata, Henri-Louis Jaquet-Droz (1752–1791) from La Chaux-de-Fonds, lived in London from 1775 to 1783 and joined the Swiss Society. The business still flourishes today.[152] Jaquet-Droz, with his partner, Jean-Frédéric Leschot (1746–1824), produced movements for singing birds in gold boxes by Rémond, Gide & Co. (plate 225), which rivalled earlier productions marketed in London by James Cox.

No account of the Huguenot contribution to jewellery, plate and horology would be complete without mention of Carl Fabergé (1846–1920), who was of Huguenot descent. His ancestors left France at the Revocation and settled in Eastern Germany. His father, Gustav Petrovitch Fabergé (1814–1872) born in Estonia,[153] served his apprenticeship in St Petersburg from 1830 and set up there as a master in 1841. His son Carl transformed the conventional jewellery business from 1870 by insisting that the value of an object should reside in its craftsmanship rather than its materials.

The close links between the goldsmiths and watchmaking trades provide further evidence for the dynamic integration of Huguenot craft communities in exile and their descendants. This was as characteristic of the Huguenots in the sixteenth and seventeenth centuries as of their descendants in the eighteenth. Thus Joseph Debaufre (1720–1779), only son of James Debaufre the younger, married Susannah, the younger daughter of Paul de Lamerie, in 1750. Paul Crespin's elder daughter, Magdalene, married the Huguenot clockmaker Francis Gabriel Barraud and Crespin's portrait (plate 184) descended in the Barraud family. Like the other Huguenot watchmaking dynasties, the Barrauds contributed to the export trade: a table clock by Barraud is proudly displayed at Middleton Hall, Charleston, South Carolina.

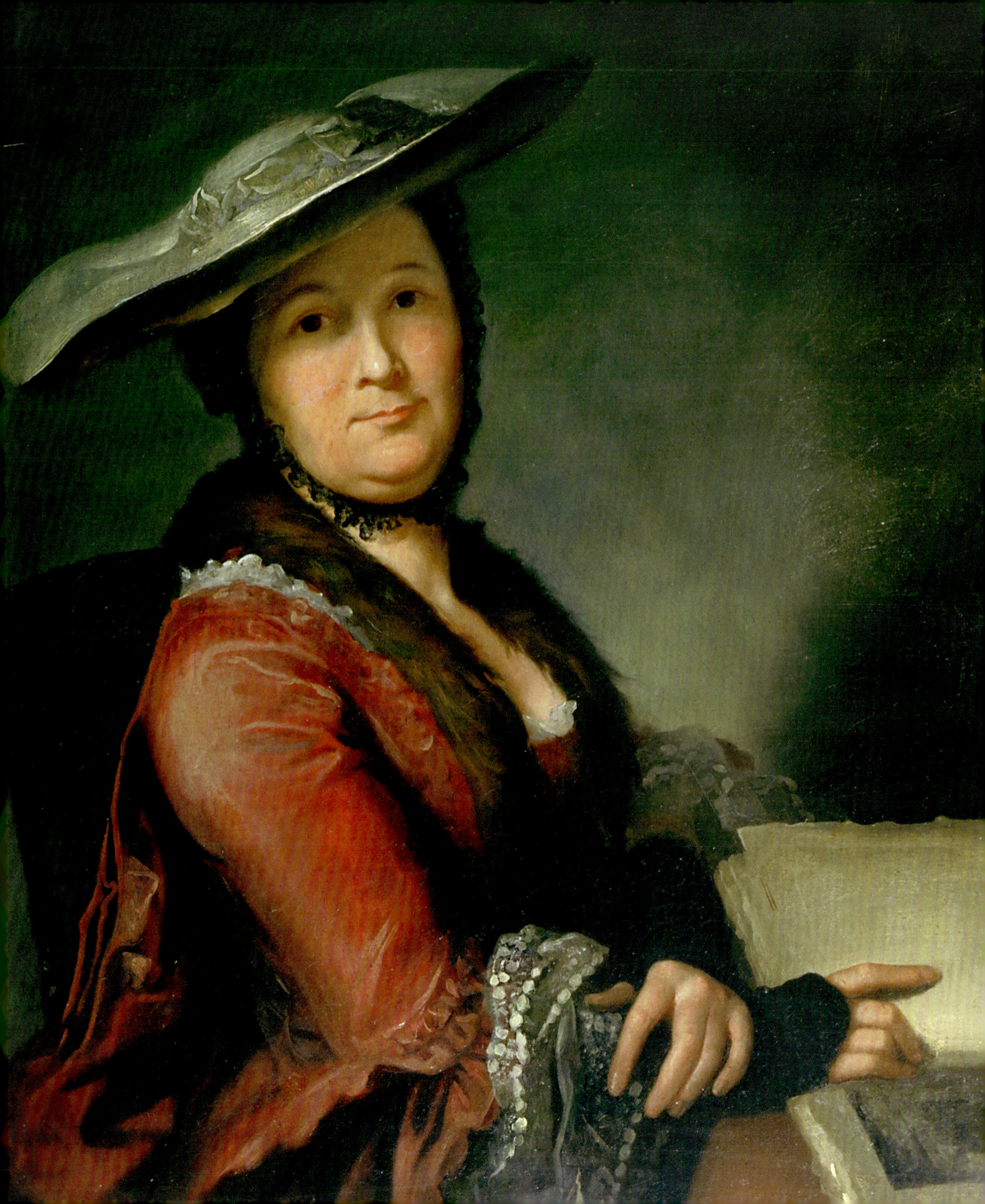

Chapter Twelve
Printmakers & Sellers: Designs, Ornament & Reproductive Prints

226 *Céleste Regnier*
François Xavier Vispré, London, *c.*1760
Oil on canvas, 76.2 × 50.8 cm
Victoria and Albert Museum, London (P.43–1953)

Céleste Regnier managed the family print shop at the Golden Ball, Newport Street, at the heart of London's print market. Portrayed in a red satin dress trimmed with fur and a straw hat, her right hand is placed on an open book of prints. Céleste was the partner of the Huguenot sculptor Louis François Roubiliac, who was also painted by Vispré.

The Huguenots' contribution to printmaking is linked to their engagement with all aspects of applied art and design. During this period French engravers were the finest in Europe, trained in a well-established system. The tradition of decorative engraving of metal went back to medieval times; a specialist *communauté* (a formal community of metalworkers specializing in engraving) existed by 1581 and was incorporated in 1631.[1] As metalsmiths they introduced an ornamental vocabulary derived from designs including those published in Lyons and Paris in 1619 by Orleans-born enameller Jacques Hurtu (p.208); by goldsmith Gédéon Légaré (*c.*1611–1676) around 1630; by Henri Toutin (1614–1683) in Châteaudun in 1628; and from 1670 in Paris by Thomas LeJuge (fl.1648–61), Jean Le Pautre, Paul Ducerceau (*c.*1630–1713) and Jean Berain.[2]

The close community in which Huguenot craftsmen lived and worked promoted exchange of talent. Engravers often designed their own work; they embellished silver, watches and guns, working for specialist craftsmen to produce work of the highest decorative quality. Huguenot engravers, like their fellow craftsmen in silver and wrought iron, brought to their craft a technical mastery. Those who produced pattern books tended to rely, like the first-generation silversmiths and gatesmiths, on earlier design sources. Only through sophisticated patronage, demanding the latest in French taste, were second-generation Huguenot craftsmen, like the celebrated goldsmith, Paul de Lamerie, able to adopt the latest French styles. Huguenot engravers, like craftsmen in other metals, brought a knowledge of the French tradition combined with technical mastery and an alacrity to undertake whatever contemporary patronage demanded from them. In this they were supported by their wives and daughters, Honour Chassereau (d.1803), Dorothy Mercier (1735–1768), Mary Ann Rocque (still working in 1768) and Susan Vivares (d.1792), who managed the business for their husbands and later as widows.

In London, Jean Tijou relied on designs by the Paris master locksmith Hugues Brisville (b.1633), engraved from 1647 by Mathurin Berton (fl. 1647–63) with later prints of around 1662 by Jean Berain.[3] Tijou's *New Booke of Drawings*, published in London in 1693 with a parallel French title (plate 77), influenced British smiths.[4] Bristol gatesmith William Edney (d.1725) used plate 19 of Tijou's book for the design of the gate screen at Elmore Court, Gloucestershire, while Robert Bakewell (1681–1752) in Derbyshire and the Welsh Davies brothers of Wrexham, Robert (1675–1748) and John (1682–1755), harnessed Tijou's vocabulary of cast ornament – the mask, eagle head, acanthus and bay leaf – although their designs lack the unity characteristic of the French master's work.

Huguenot engravers and printsellers

In the London Huguenot church records, five of 18 craftsmen described as *graveur* (literally 'engraver' but also 'carver') are still known by their work. Gideon du Chesne, who received poor relief from the Threadneedle Street church in 1681, was employed 20 years later at Boughton and Castle Howard as a sculptor in wood, stone and plaster. At Boughton he produced plaster busts of the Caesars and the Montagu coat of arms for the stables and the Great Hall.[5] Jean Obrisset (fl.1705–28), originally from Dieppe, worked portraits in pressed horn and turtleshell for lids of tobacco boxes in 1703–28 (plate 257).[6] René Pelletier, from 1691 employed as carver and gilder by Ralph, Earl of Montagu, specialized in *verre églomisé* (plate 87) and cutting ornament in gesso for gilding (plate 98).[7] From Geneva, Abraham Martin (fl.1682–1709), free of the Clockmakers' Company from 1682 and naturalized in about 1709, engraved watches and clocks from his premises in Clerkenwell.[8] Simon Gribelin, who had arrived in London from Blois by 1681, was a 'graveur en taille douce', publishing pattern books for small-scale decoration (plate 227).[9] Sir Christopher Wren wrote from Paris in 1665 that he 'purchased a great deal of *Taille douce* that I might give our countrymen examples of ornaments & grotesks, in which the Italians themselves confess the French to excel'.[10]

Reproductive prints

Among Gribelin's topographical prints is a view of the Royal Naval Hospital, Greenwich, including Wren's additions, completed in 1705. Gribelin was paid £60 for two engravings of St Paul's Cathedral for fund-raising purposes, inscribed 'Ex Autographo Architecti, 1702'. Impressions were given to donors as the cathedral neared completion in 1710.[11] Interest in the building continued and in 1743 Paul Fourdrinier, originally from Caen, Normandy, but established in London,[12] published a 'South East Prospect of the Cathedral Church of St Paul'. Gribelin's plan of Lincoln's Inn Fields illustrated the survey completed by Mr Cavendish Weedon (d.1708) of this seventeenth-century garden square.[13]

Prints of famous paintings might be presented in book form. In 1703 the English edition was published of *The Tent of Darius explained or the Queen of Persia at the feet of Alexander* by André Félibien (1619–1695), translated from French by Colonel William Parsons (1658–1725) and illustrated with Gribelin's print after Charles Le Brun's painting *The Tent of Darius* (1661). In 1707 Gribelin produced the first set of prints of Raphael's cartoons for the tapestries illustrating the Acts of the Apostles, then at Hampton Court. They sold well, although Horace Walpole later wrote that he thought they were too small.[14] The prints inspired Anthony Ashley Cooper, 3rd Earl of Shaftesbury (1671–1713), to employ Gribelin to illustrate the second edition of his *Characteristicks of Men, Manners, Opinions, Times*.[15] Gribelin created a market for prints after Raphael and in 1711, the French Catholic Nicholas Dorigny (p.50) came to England especially to make a set of larger prints of Raphael's Cartoons.[16]

In 1706 Gribelin engraved Annibale Caracci's *Deposition* on a silver altar dish made by Isaac Liger (plate 180) for Lord Warrington's private chapel at Dunham Massey, Cheshire,[17] and in 1712 he produced prints from Royal Collection paintings by Veronese, Tintoretto, Palma Vecchio, Giulio Romano and Andrea Schiavone.[18] Gribelin's prints of Rubens's ceiling in the Whitehall Banqueting House, appeared in 1721.[19] Horace Walpole later complained that none of Gribelin's plates 'gave any idea of the style of the masters they copied',[20] but the engraver's initiative deserves recognition.

Matthew Liart (1742–1781) and Philip Audinet (1766–1837) were cousins, of Huguenot stock.[21] Liart was apprenticed to Simon François Ravenet, French engraver working in London from 1743 to his death in 1774. Liart won a premium at the Society of Arts in 1764 with his engraving of *Jacob and Laban* after Pietro da Cortona; he registered at the Royal Academy schools in 1769. Audinet, whose clockmaker father was apprenticed to Stephen Rimbault (plate 220), engraved a portrait of his elder cousin Matthew Liart shortly before he died.[22] Subsequently Audinet worked for the émigré artist Henri-Pierre Danloux (1753–1809) between 1797 and 1801.[23]

Printmaking dynasties

French church registers include family names of established engravers. Isaac Basire, the son of Jacques Basire (d.1724) of Wardour Street, Soho, was a refugee from Rouen. He established himself in Red Lyon Street, Clerkenwell, the first of four generations of printmakers: his son John, 'copper plate printer' (d.1804), and grandson James (1730–1802) worked in close association with the London-based Society of Antiquaries. John succeeded his father, 'the late Mr Isaac Basire', at 16 St John's Lane near Clerkenwell Gate.[24]

227 *A Book of Severall Ornaments*

Simon Gribelin, London, 1682
Engraved title page, cut to 19.3 × 16.2 cm
Victoria and Albert Museum, London (25905A-2)

Gribelin combines figurative and foliate decoration as a frame for a vignette showing Acteon transformed into a stag after spying on Diana bathing.

228 *Deposition*

From *Livre d'Estampes de Sim Gribelin*
Simon Gribelin after Annibale Caracci on altar dish by Isaac Liger, London, 1706
Pull from engraving on silver, diam. 43.2 cm
British Museum, London (1859,0625.121–542)

The dish was commissioned by George Booth, 2nd Earl of Warrington, for the altar of his private chapel at Dunham Massey. Gribelin produced a series of prints after Old Masters in the Royal Collection but this is the only known sacred subject that he engraved on an altar dish as a substitute for an altarpiece. Gribelin preserved this impression taken from the dish in the album compiled of his work *c.*1722.

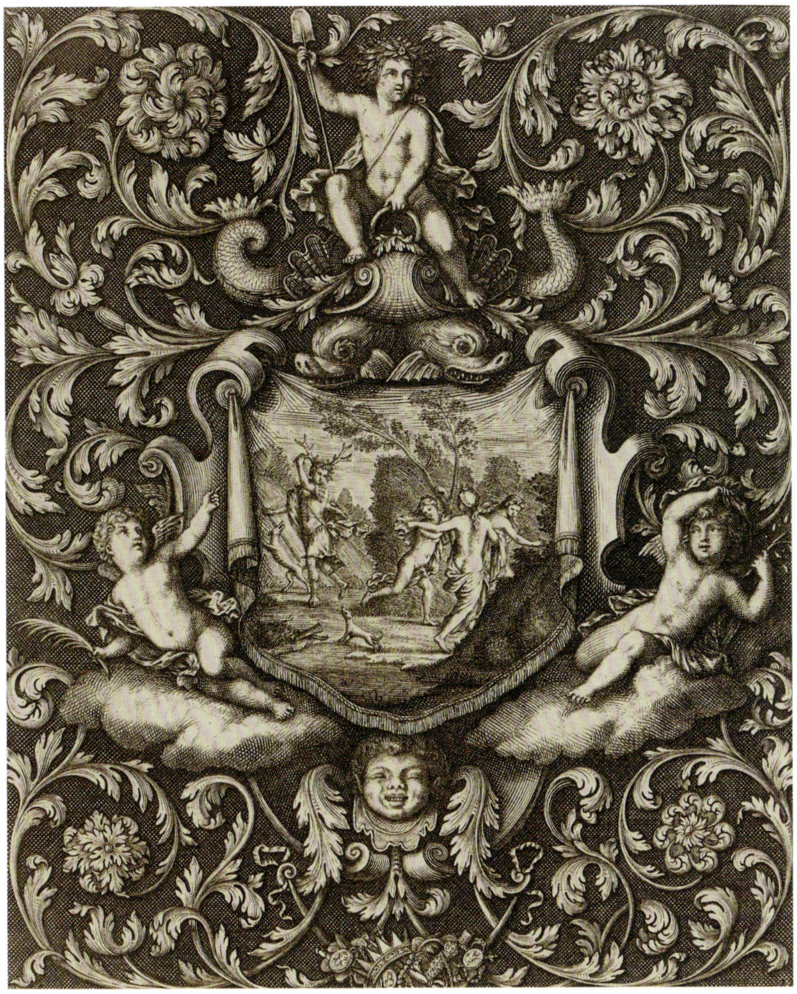

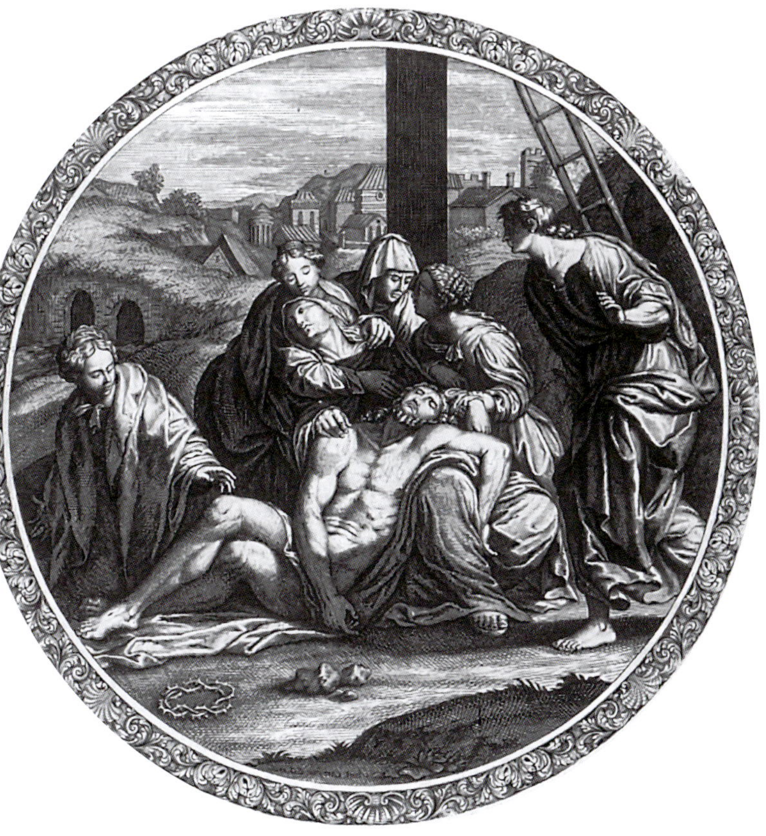

Third-generation James Basire took William Blake (1757–1827) as apprentice in 1772.

Paul Fourdrinier was born in Groningen in the Netherlands and probably studied under Bernard Picart before he came to London in 1720.[25] He established himself as an engraver and copperplate printer, specializing in engraved architectural prints and plans (plate 73) and William Kent's designs for book illustration. His trade card, promoting architecture and engraving, was designed by William Kent (plate 76) and featured Albrecht Dürer (1471–1528), the French architect François Mansart (1598–1666) and the engraver Gérard Edelinck (1640–1707). Fourdrinier's print shop, from 1731 in Craggs Court, Charing Cross, remained in family ownership for 80 years. Paul Fourdrinier died in 1758 and was buried in Wandsworth Huguenot cemetery alongside his wife, Susanna Grolleau (1693–1746), in the Grolleau family plot.[26] Their elder son, Henry (1730–1799), was apprenticed to William Baker, stationer of Lombard Street, with whom he formed a partnership in 1757.[27] A family group, painted in about 1786,[28] shows Henry with his daughter, Jemima (1772–1836) and four sons. His eldest son, also called Henry (1766–1854) and the youngest, Sealy (1773–1847), patented a new method for production of continuous paper in 1807; in 1814 they supplied this specialist machinery to Alexander I, Tsar of Russia. Jemima married John Newman (d.1824); their son, who became a Catholic convert, was canonized in 2019 as St John Henry Newman (1801–1890).

Paul Fourdrinier's business was continued for three further generations by his elder son Henry, Henry's younger son Charles (1767–1841) and Charles's son Charles Kenneth Fourdrinier (b.1766), until 1811.

Cartographers, publishers and surveyors

John Rocque played an important part in the dissemination of the Rococo style in the 1730s by publishing London editions of the latest books of French engraved ornament. His surveys of estates with enticing garden vistas appeared from 1735; in 1736 they included Wrest Park for the Duke of Kent and royal estates at Kensington and Hampton Court, both dedicated to Queen Caroline.[29] The survey of Chiswick House and Gardens, dedicated to Richard Boyle, 3rd Earl of Burlington, was available from Rocque's address, the Canister and Sugar Loaf in Great Windmill Street, St James's, near Paul de Lamerie's premises.[30] The single-page survey of Chiswick Villa includes 13 views of its sophisticated

Neo-Palladian gardens.[31] Rocque travelled to Scotland to survey Drumlanrig, Dumfriesshire, for the Duke of Queensberry,[32] while Wanstead, which he surveyed for Richard Child, 1st Earl Tylney (1680–1750) in 1737, Claremont, surveyed in 1738 for Thomas Pelham-Holles, 1st Duke of Newcastle and Painshill, drawn in 1744 for Hon. Charles Hamilton, were just a day's journey from London. The Watteauesque views included in these plans demonstrate that mastery of perspective was not Rocque's strong point, as his sketch for the view of Richmond Park demonstrates (plate 229). For landscape views Rocque employed the engraver François Vivares (p.48). They were close family friends and Rocque stood godfather to Vivares's son John at the Savoy French church in June 1743.[33]

George Vertue deserves credit for proposing the 'grand design of an ichnographical survey or map of London and all the suburbs' in 1738,[34] perhaps inspired by his own engraving in eight sheets, printed the previous year, of the sixteenth-century map of London by Ralph Agas (*c.*1540–1621).[35] In 1743 Rocque moved to Hyde Park Corner and in 1747 he delivered his *Plan of London and Westminster and Borough of Southwark* in 24 sheets at 26 inches to 1 mile. In 1745–6 Rocque's 16-sheet map showing a larger area on a smaller scale (5¼ inches to 1 mile) was published by John Pine (1690–1756) as the *Survey of London and Environs*, price 3 guineas; and in 1748 Pine published Rocque's *A Map of London and the adjacent Country…* in 16 sheets for 2 guineas. Dedicated to John, 2nd Duke of Montagu (plate 230), this was updated in 1759 to include new roads and buildings.[36] Rocque's *Survey* captures the Soho and Spitalfields streets where Huguenots lived and worked, as well as the location of French churches and charities. Titled in French and English, this accurate plan of expanding London attracted regional and international visitors. Rocque's achievement led to his appointment as 'Chorographer to His Royal Highness the Prince of Wales' (later George III). His knowledge of continental practice facilitated production and inspired comparative studies. In 1762 his *A PLAN of LONDON on the Same Scale as that of PARIS* was dedicated to George Brudenell, 4th Earl of Cardigan and 3rd Duke of Montagu (1712–1790), son-in-law of the 2nd Duke of Montagu. The plan showed 'the beautiful situation of these two Rivals, their Extent, and by how much London exceeds Paris in Acres'.

As 'draughtsman and printseller', Rocque worked next door to the Rummer Tavern, Charing Cross, near Fourdrinier's print shop, from 1749 until November 1750, when his premises were destroyed by fire, as reported in *The General Advertiser*. His brother Bartholomew (fl.*c.*1730–1761), a landscape gardener based at Walham Green (Fulham Broadway), wrote *A practical Treatise of Cultivating Lucerne*; this was printed by John Rocque in November 1761.[37] From 1753 until 1762 John Rocque's stock was available at Old Round Court, on the north side of The Strand,[38] and from 1756 from his brother-in-law Bernard Scalé (1738–1826) in Batchelor's Walk, Dublin. Scalé advertised as a land surveyor in 1758, producing surveys of estates for absentee British landlords 'so that the owner becomes personally acquainted with the circumstances of his estate, the same as if resident thereon'.[39] John Rocque was resident in Dublin between 1753 and 1756, lodging at The Golden Heart opposite Grace Lane, Dame Street, while he produced a four-sheet *Survey of Dublin* in which 'every House' was 'expressed', which sold for 1 guinea; he also produced plans of Cork, Kilkenny and maps of the counties of Armagh and Dublin. Bernard Scalé independently published five plates of the *Dublin Houses of Parliament* in 1767, An *Hibernian Atlas* in 1776, as well as 'A curious map of Ireland for a Watch Case', which cost 6d, in 1762.[40] Scalé married an Essex heiress and was established at Great Warley, near Brentwood, but continued to maintain a commercial presence in Dublin.[41]

John Rocque supplied single-sheet maps of Bristol, York and Bury St Edmunds (advertised as

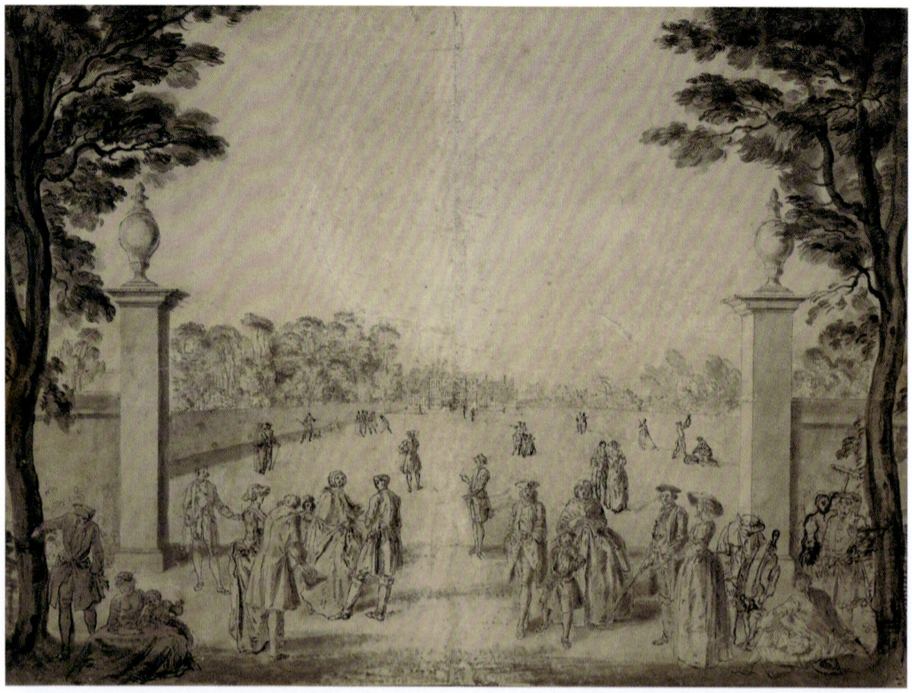

229 *View of Richmond Park*
John Rocque, London, 1734
Pen, grey ink and wash, 40.2 × 54.8 cm
British Museum, London (1880,1113.5556)

Rocque used the diminishing scale of figures and trees to create a sense of perspective but relied on the skill of contemporary engravers to work up his sketches for publication. These vignettes embellished the plans which Rocque published of private estates.

230 *A Map of London and the adjacent Country 10 Miles Round as Survey'd and Publish'd in 16 Sheets by John Rocque Land Surveyor; reduc'd into one Sheet*

John Rocque, London, 1748
Etching and engraving, 50.5 × 67 cm
British Museum, London (1881,0312.85)

The project to map London was suggested by fellow engraver George Vertue in 1738. Rocque sold the maps from his shop in Old Round Court, off The Strand.

'St Edmund's Bury') for 2s 6d; his two-sheet map of Exeter sold for 1 guinea. He sold his one-sheet surveys of Berkshire, Buckinghamshire and Oxfordshire for 3s, Middlesex with parish divisions, in four sheets, for 1 guinea, and Shropshire, also in four sheets for 12s 6d.[42] Rocque introduced the continental method of using different methods of stippling to differentiate heath and arable land, pasture, parks and gardens. He also cultivated Huguenot and naval interest by publishing plans of Brest and Dunkirk with their fortifications; Saint-Malo with a coastal map; Saint-Martin-de Ré, Toulon and Calais; and other European cities, including Montpellier, Nîmes, Dresden and Geneva. Further afield, he provided maps of South America and of 'Lima, Capital of Peru'.

Other French surveyors in London included the mysterious Sieur Bourguignon, who surveyed Thorndon Hall, Essex, for Lord Petre in 1733. He was also employed at Worksop by Lord Petre's Catholic relatives the 9th Duke and Duchess of Norfolk, for whom he produced a planting scheme dated March 1737/8, a nineteenth-century copy of which is signed 'E. Petre invenit, Peter Bourginon delineavit'. He may be connected to Hubert-François Gravelot, born Bourguignon, who produced a map of Santo Domingo in the 1720s but is better known as an artist, designer and engraver (p.57).[43]

Peter Chassereau (1711–1750), architect at the Golden Head, at the upper end of Berwick Street near Soho Square, advertised in the *Gentleman's*

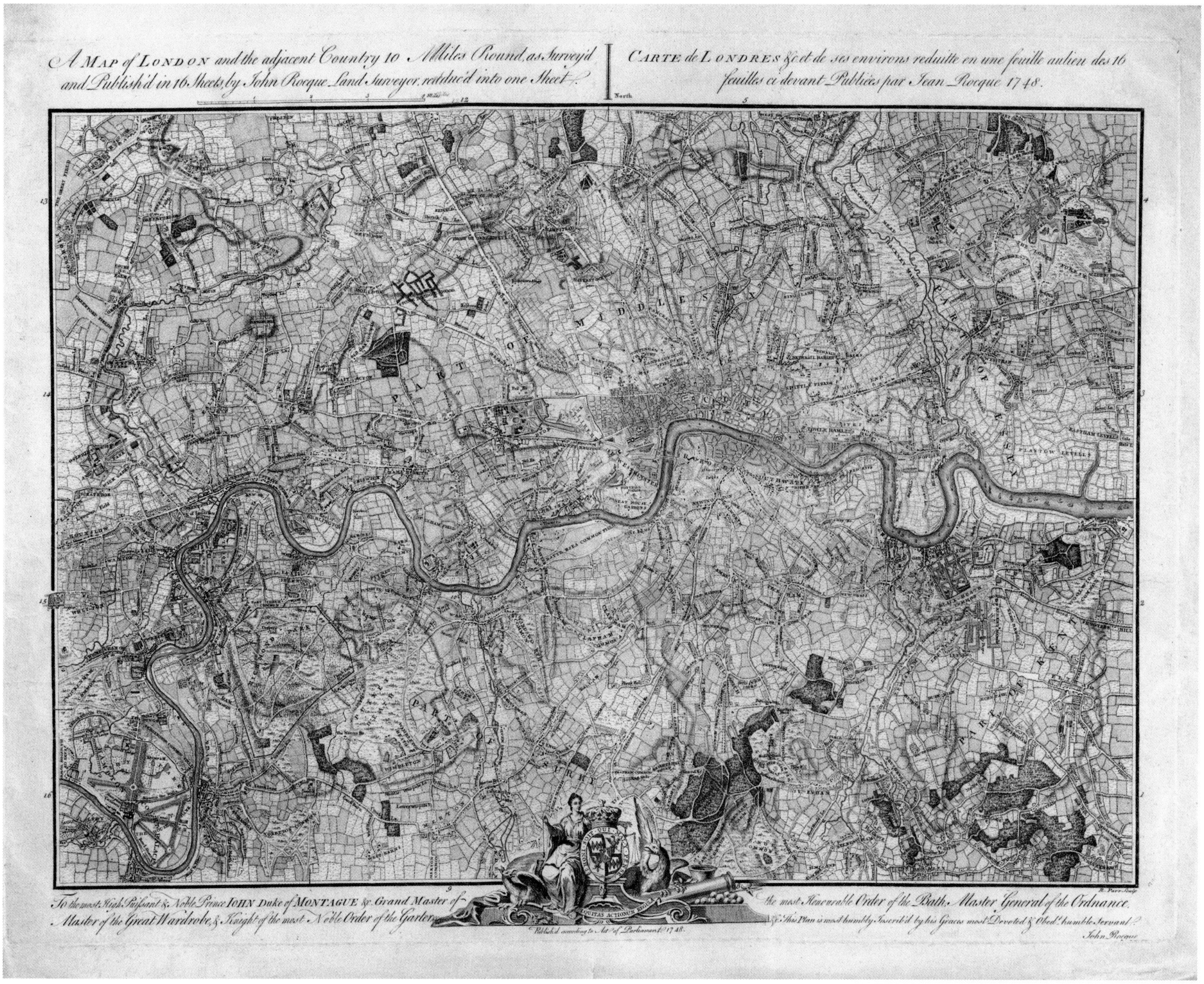

Magazine 1741: 'LAND Survey'd and MAP's … neatly drawn, designs for Building made, and … Prospects of Gentlemen's Seats taken.' His trade card later records his address at The Golden Seal, Hanover Street, Long Acre. Chassereau's 1741 plan of St James's Park records the parish boundaries of St Margaret's Westminster and St Martin-in-the-Fields. He may be Peter Chassereau who advertised in Charleston, South Carolina, in 1735 as a drawing master and surveyor of 'Plans and Elevations of all kind of Buildings both civil and Military … who sets out ground for Gardens and Parks in a grand and rural manner'. Chassereau's map of York was engraved and published by John Rocque in 1750.[44]

The second-generation goldsmith Daniel Pomarede (fl.1742–65) was descended from Pierre Pomarede, a refugee from Bordeaux.[45] Daniel Pomarede also worked as an engraver of silver and maps. In 1746 he illustrated Charles Smith's *The Antient and Present State of County Waterford*, while his map of County Kildare includes a vignette of the horserace 'Run on the Curragh of Kildare' on 5 September 1751 'for a 1000 Guineas won by *Black & all Black* the property of Sr Ralph Gore Bar^t.' against the Earl of March's horse, Bajazet.[46] The scene is engraved on a trophy punch bowl (plate 231) supplied by Dublin silversmith William Williamson (fl.1729–52).[47] In 1753 Pomarede moved to Belfast and was based at John Templeton's in North Street. In 1765 he engraved the bookplate for Belfast Library. He also engraved a frontispiece for a Freemasonry manual for the Royal Arch, Belfast.[48]

Publishing ornament

François Vivares was the son of a 'nouveau converti', Jean Vivares (who abjured so he could remain in France), yet in 1711 the family moved to Geneva to return to their Protestant faith. François came to London in 1727 to study with the Swiss engraver Josef Wagner (1706–1780). In 1749 he opened a print shop at the Golden Head, Porter Street, Leicester Fields, and in 1754 moved to Great Newport Street, where his widow, Susan, continued the business from his death in 1780 until 1792.[49]

Vivares sold artists' materials and Italian, French and Flemish prints, as well as 'Trophies, Flowers, Nosegays and Birds' (flower prints after Jean-Baptiste Monnoyer), which were used by amateur decorators to wallpaper rooms with prints.[50] He traded with France and his prints were also exported to Karlsruhe and Leipzig.[51]

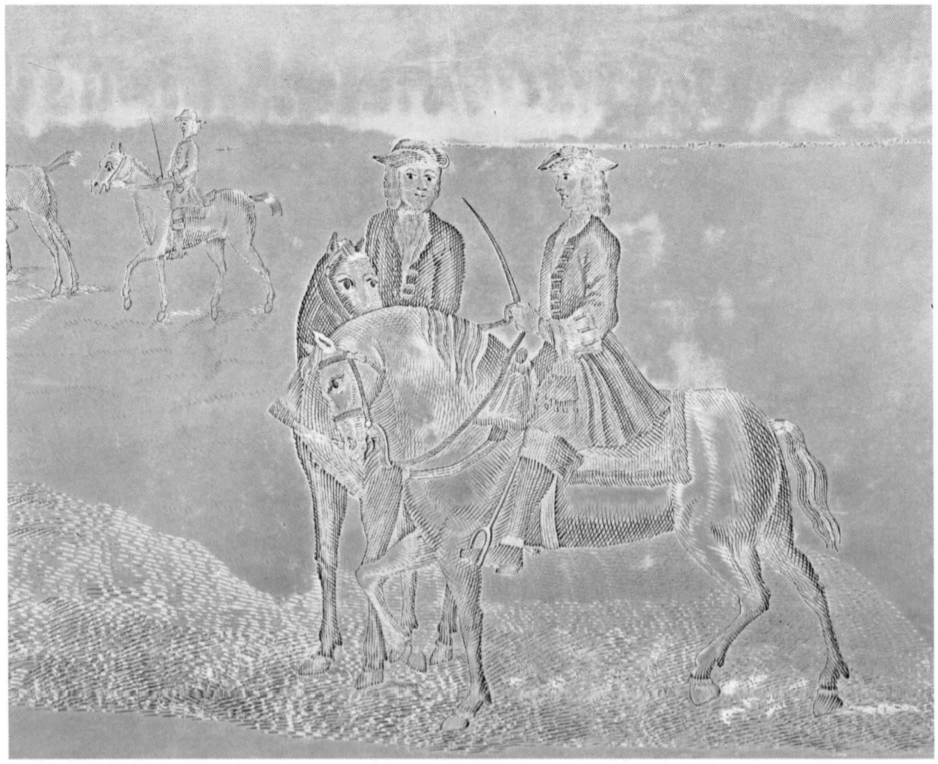

In 1741 Vivares etched plates for designer William De La Cour's *First Book of Ornaments* (plate 232), among the first Rococo pattern books to appear in London, thus establishing De La Cour's reputation.[52] By 1748 De La Cour had published eight ornament books (plate 108) but only plates from the first, fifth and eighth book survive; he etched some plates himself and also employed Jacob Bonneau (p.48).

Engraved ornament circulated widely. The Flemish sculptor John Michael Rysbrack subscribed in 1736 to the London-based Italian Gaetano Brunetti's *Sixty Different Sorts of Ornaments*, which was engraved by Rocque and republished in 1737, an earlier edition having appeared in 1731; it was still available from Rocque's shop in 1759 for 7s 6d. Brunetti's publication was probably also sold through Rocque's agent in Dublin in the 1760s. In 1735 Brunetti had employed the painter Mark Anthony Hauduroy (plates 52–3) on decorations commissioned by James Brydges, 1st Duke of Chandos, for Cannons, his great house in Edgware, and his London house in Cavendish Square.[53]

Landscape prints

François Vivares engraved landscapes by artists Thomas Smith of Derby (*c.*1720–1767) and Arthur Pond in the 1740s; visited Malham, Yorkshire, in 1753 to engrave 'two romantick views;[54] and

ABOVE

231 *The Great Match Run on the Curragh of Kildare Septr 5th, 1751*

Engraving by Daniel Pomarede on punch bowl by William Williamson, Dublin, 1751
Silver, diam. 36.2 cm
Museum of Fine Arts, Boston (1973.482)

The second-generation goldsmith Daniel Pomarede (fl.1742–65) worked as an engraver of silver and maps in Dublin.

OPPOSITE ABOVE LEFT

232 *First Book of Ornaments*

François Vivares after William De La Cour, London, 1741
Etching, 29.3 × 21.4 cm
Victoria and Albert Museum, London (E.731–1907)

The fantastic architectural structure, peopled with chinoiserie and mythological figures creates an exotic context for the title of the publication and the coat of arms of the dedicatee, the Earl of Middlesex.

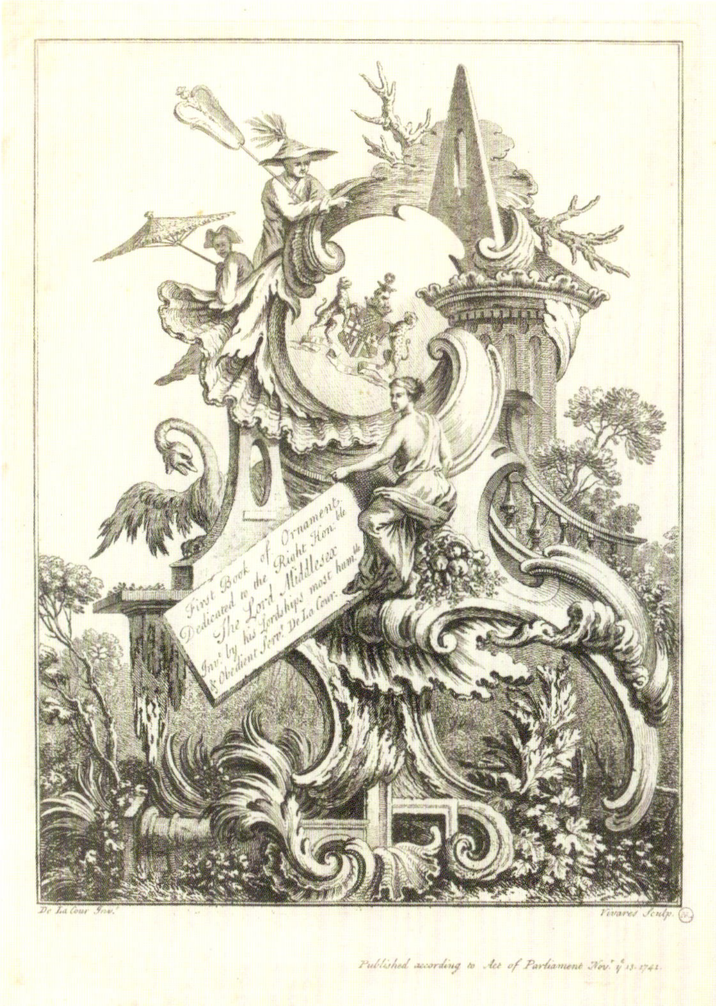

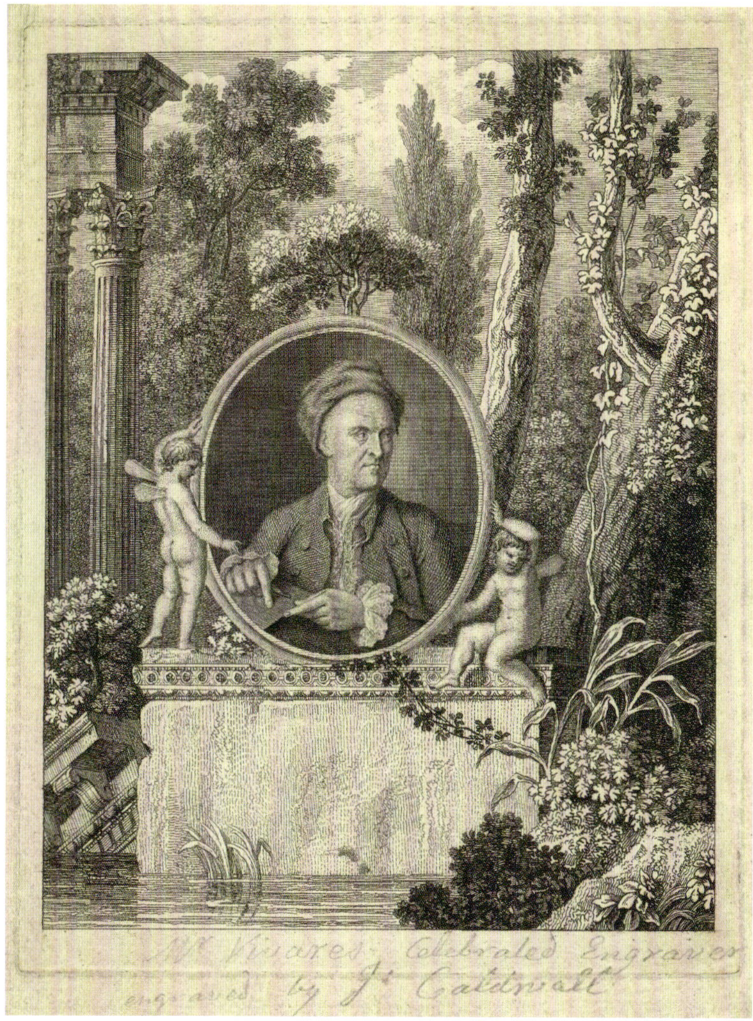

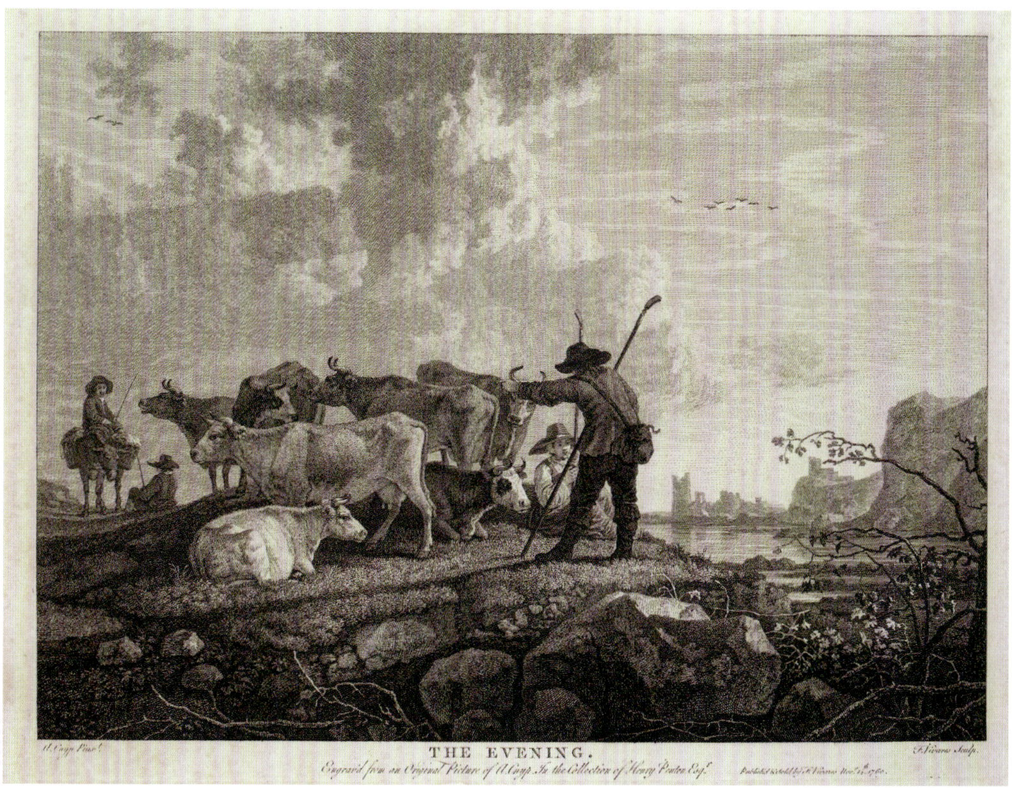

ABOVE RIGHT

234 *François Vivares (1709–1780)*

François Vivares and James Caldwell, London, 1776
Etching and engraving, 20.8 × 16.4 cm
British Museum, London (1849,0512.924)

Vivares came to London from Geneva and maintained a network of European contacts supplying ornament and landscape prints through his London shop, which was managed by his wife Susan.

LEFT

233 *The Evening*

François Vivares after Aelbert Cuyp, London, 1764
Engraving with etching, 28.5 × 37.6 cm
Victoria and Albert Museum, London (E.3152–1990)

Vivares engraved landscapes after Dutch, French and Italian painters and the British artists Arthur Pond, Thomas Smith of Derby and Thomas Gainsborough.

produced prints after Claude Lorrain (1600–1682), the Dutch artists Nicolaes Berghem (1620–1683) and Aelbert Cuyp (1620–1691; plate 233) and Italian Francesco Zuccarelli (1702–1788). His prints were used by James Giles (plate 161) to decorate ceramics: for example, his 1760 print of Gainsborough's *The Rural Lovers* was transferred on to Wedgwood and Worcester wares by Robert Hancock (1731–1817).[55] Two of Vivares's prints were after Gainsborough landscapes belonging to Panton Betew (1724–1799), third-generation Huguenot silversmith and art dealer.[56] Some of his prints include dedicatory inscriptions to owners of the original paintings: a 1752 print after Pierre-Antoine Patel (1648–1707), for example, is dedicated to William Bouverie, 1st Earl of Radnor (1725–1776). Vivares's self-portrait (plate 234) holding burin and copper plate, in an oval frame supported by two cupids and set on a plinth with a pool in front and trees and a classical temple behind, promotes his status as pioneer of British landscape engraving.

Architects, artists and printmakers

Huguenot engravers looked to publishers, painters and architects for patronage. William Hogarth recruited James Basire and Charles Grignion (1717–1810), who from the age of 16 had trained with J.P. Le Bas (1707–1783) in Paris and then studied drawing with Gravelot at his house at the Golden Cup in King Street, Covent Garden, alongside Thomas Gainsborough and Thomas Major (1720–1799).[57] Grignion's print after Francis Hayman's painting of a cricket match was sold during the 1748 cricket season.[58] Grignion and Hogarth worked together on the 1746 print after Hogarth's painting of David Garrick as Richard III (plate 235), an important publicity exercise for actor, engraver and painter alike.[59] At the end of his life, when his sight failed and he was no longer able to work, Grignion was dubbed the 'Father of Engraving' in Britain.[60]

Paul Fourdrinier engraved William Kent's illustrations to John Gay's *Fables* 1727, in addition to Kent's architectural designs, for which Fourdrinier's talent was best suited. These included Kent's designs for Whitehall Treasury in 1734; for Prime Minister Walpole's Houghton Hall in 1736; and for Queen Caroline's Library at St James's in 1737. Fourdrinier's topographical prints include Inigo Jones's rejected design for Temple Bar; the north-west prospect of Westminster Abbey with Wren's design for the spire; the west front and steeple of St George's cathedral, Southwark; the elevation and section of Henry Flitcroft's St Giles-in-the-Fields; and Isaac Ware's design for the Mansion House, the new residence for London's Lord Mayor. Fourdrinier's 1746 print of Matthew Brettingham's triumphal arch in Norwich honouring the Duke of Cumberland (plate 236) is inscribed: 'To the deliverer of his country', a characteristic eulogy for the Protestant victory over the Catholic Young Pretender at Culloden.

Between 1734 and 1749 Fourdrinier was employed by Henry Herbert, 9th Earl of Pembroke.[61] Pembroke encouraged Fourdrinier to record the first Westminster Bridge, designed by Charles Labelye (plate 73). Fourdrinier's prints depict gradual progress: the 1738 timber superstructure designed by carpenter James King (d.1743) was followed in 1740 by 'A Plan of Part of the Ancient city of WESTMINSTER from College Street to Whitehall and from the Thames to St James' Park', with 'the New Streets laid down and intended to be built' by order of the commissioners. In 1743 Fourdrinier engraved King's design for 'One of the five Ribs of the Centre on which the Middle Arch of Westminster Bridge was turned extending 76 feet'. This was followed in 1751 by 'The Geometrical Elevation of the North Front of Westminster Bridge', with a plan of the foundations and the stone superstructure.

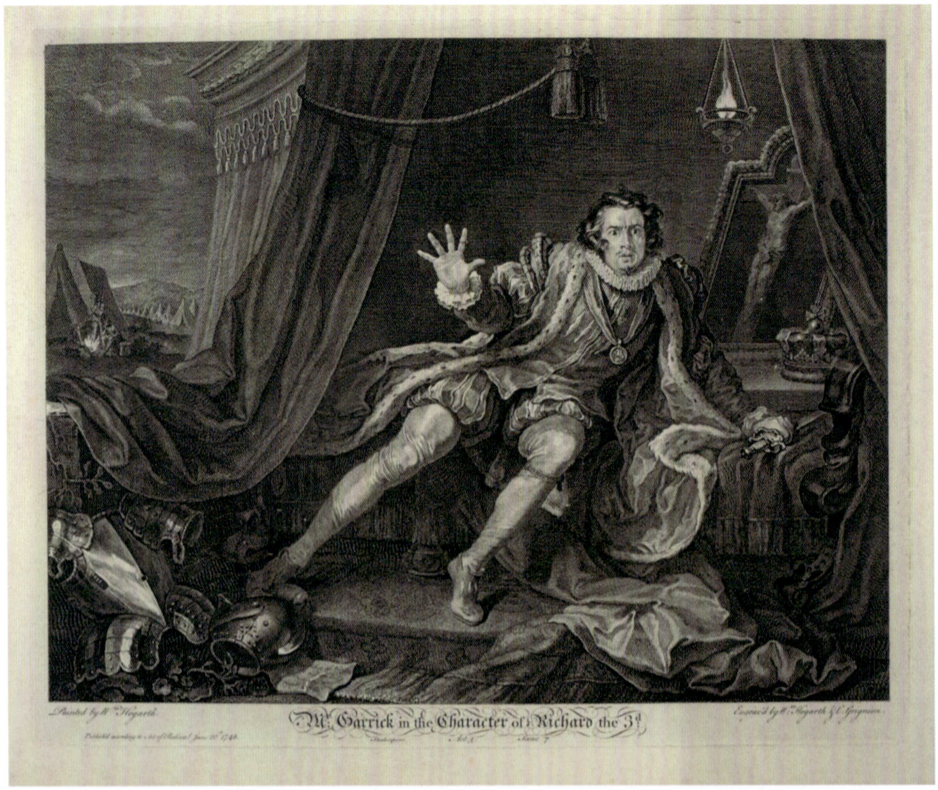

235 *David Garrick in the Character of Richard the Third*

Charles Grignion after William Hogarth, London, 1746
Engraving, 23.4 × 33.4 cm
Victoria and Albert Museum, London (S.119–2007)

The Huguenot actor David Garrick established his reputation through his performance in the title role of Shakespeare's *Richard III*. Grignion's engraving of Hogarth's portrait of Garrick in the role provided an affordable souvenir.

236 *Triumphal Arch erected at Norwich in honour of … the Duke of Cumberland*

Paul Fourdrinier, London, 1746
Etching and engraving, 45.5 × 31.5 cm
British Museum, London (Mm,2.81)

The architectural engraver Paul Fourdrinier was well placed to promote this political tribute to the Duke of Cumberland. Members of the Huguenot community rallied to defend the Protestant British establishment from the threat of Catholic invasion.

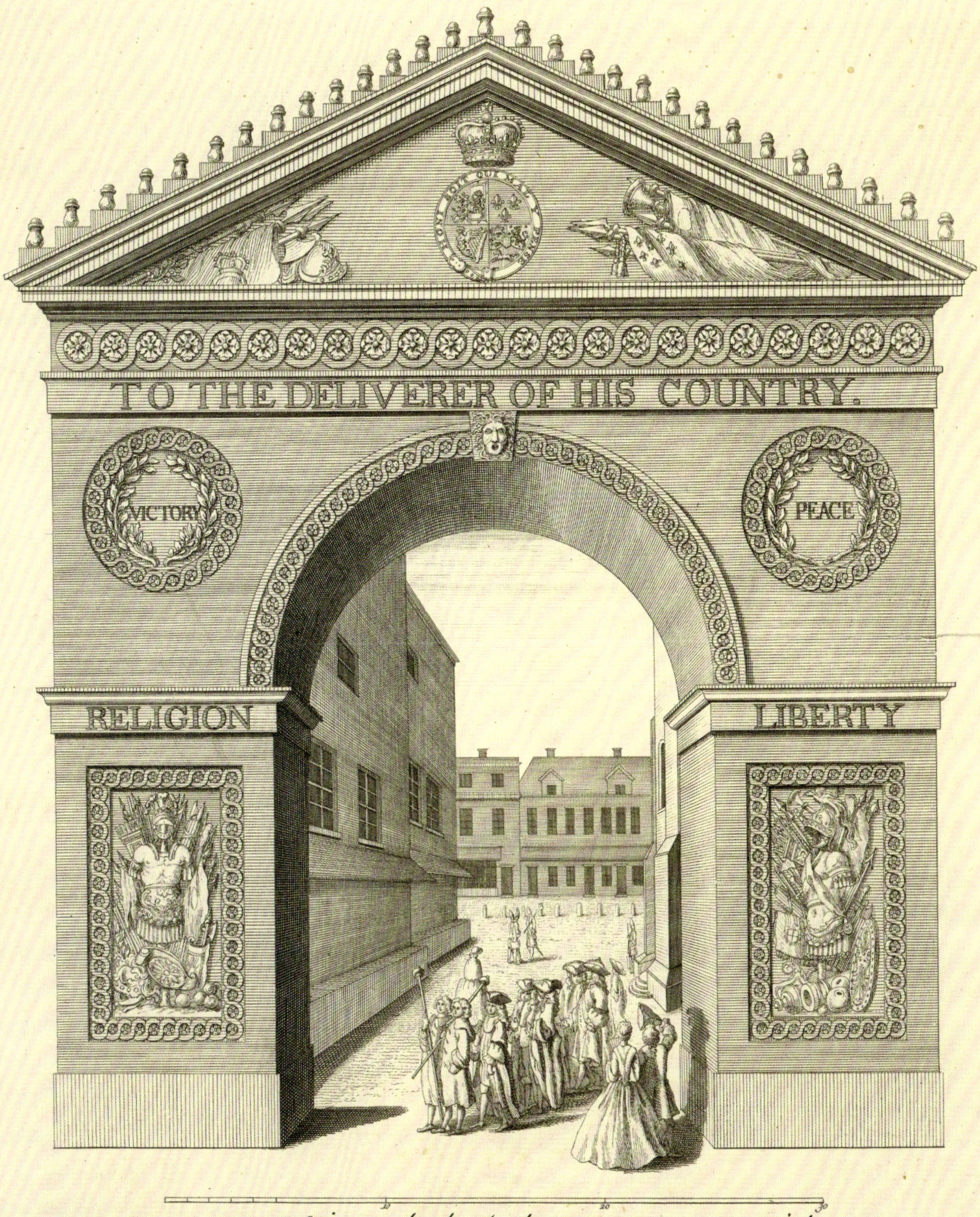

This Triumphal Arch was erected at Norwich
in Honour of His **Royal Highness** *the* **Duke** *of* **Cumberland**
upon the Thanksgiving Day
for the Suppression of the late unnatural Rebellion.
All the Trophies and Ornaments were painted upon Silk which with the Inscriptions
were made Transparent by many hundred Lights placed within.

M. B. delin. 1746. *P. Fourdrinier sculpt.*

Topical and topographical printselling

Gribelin, Fourdrinier and Rocque engraved newsworthy contemporary events. Gribelin's print of Queen Mary's mausoleum in Westminster Abbey, designed by Wren for her funeral in March 1694/5, was copied in Amsterdam by Jacob Gole. For George II's coronation in 1727 Fourdrinier engraved the triumphal arch built to Kent's designs in Westminster Hall, illustrated in *The Ceremonie of the King's Champion attended by the Lord High Constable and Earl Marshall*. In 1730 Fourdrinier was one of three 'loyal' Frenchmen following Prime Minister Walpole's negotiations with France; he rallied to Walpole's defence with his print *Hercules Crushing the Hydra* (plate 237).

Prints of popular London destinations such as Vauxhall Gardens, St James's Park and Ranelagh Gardens were published by Grignion and Vivares. Gravelot, with whom Grignion studied drawing, designed the frontispiece for Rocque's *Views of Middlesex Villages*, engraved by Grignion. In 1752 Henry Overton published Grignion's *View of the Canal, Chinese Building, Rotundo, in Ranelagh Gardens, with the Masquerade*, after a Canaletto drawing. Such attractively decorative prints were often hand coloured later.[62]

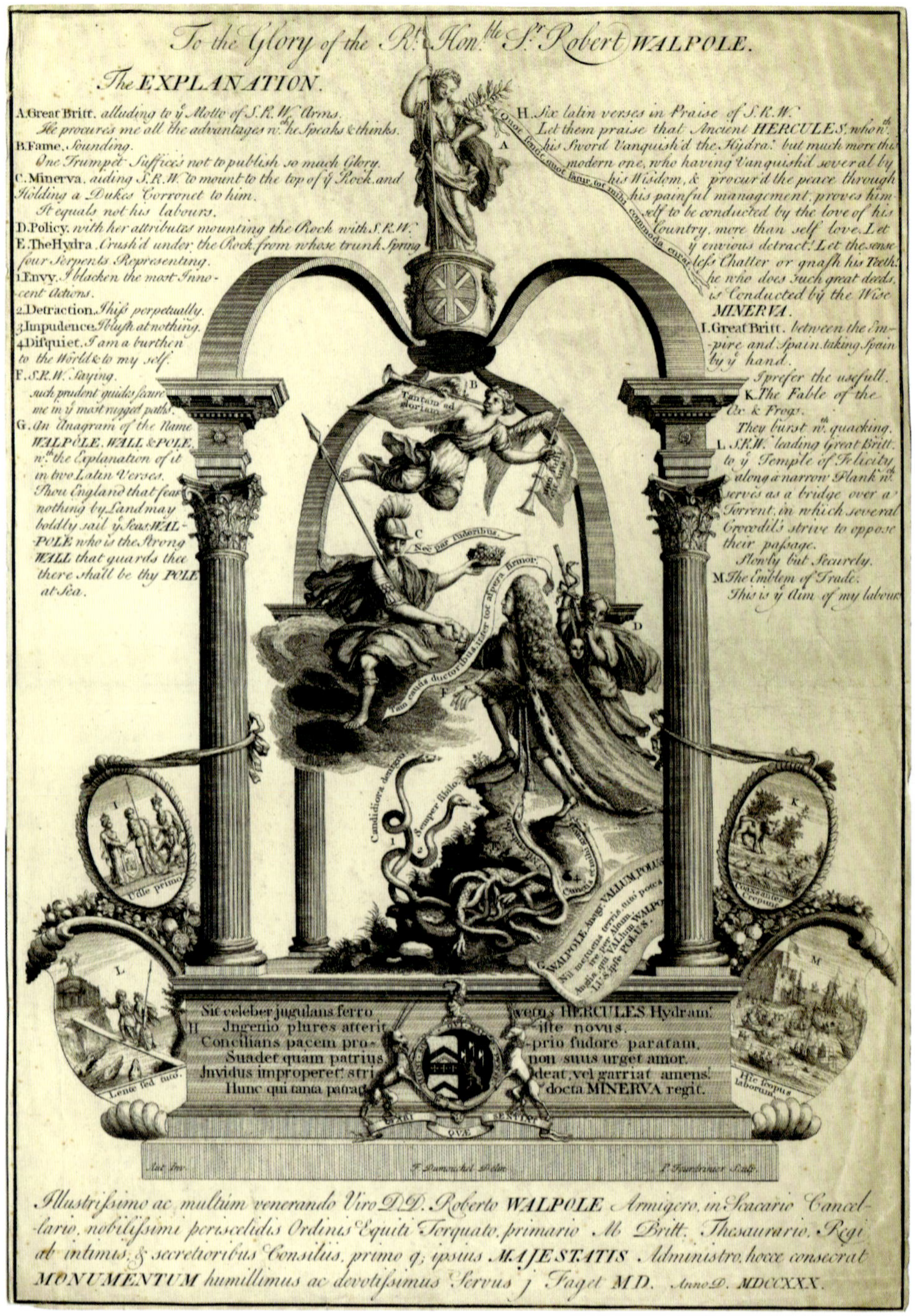

Retailing prints

An engraver often advertised and sold some stock from his studio but supplied publishers who undertook the capital investment in copper, paper and printing equipment. Others were just retailers. From 1681 Paul van Somer supplied prints from his studio at the Eagle and Child in Newport Street, near Leicester Fields,[63] whereas Gribelin sold his own prints direct from his premises, the Corner House, Banbury Court, Long Acre. In 1738, five years after Gribelin's death, his prints of Raphael's Cartoons, Rubens's Banqueting House ceiling and his *Book of Ornament of Twelve Leaves* were sold by his former neighbour James Pascall (plate 106), framemaker at the Golden Head at the junction of Hanover Street and Long Acre. Prints had considerable after-life: Nicaise Roussel's 1623 ornament prints were reissued in London between 1667 and 1672 by John Overton (1639/40–1713).

The Regnier print shop at the Golden Ball (pp.153–4) was at the heart of the market for prints in Newport Street, its range including 'the best Masters, Portraits, Scripture pieces … Hunting Pieces, Battles, Landskips, Shippings, Fishes, Flowers, Gardens, Fountains, Statues, Vases, Antique and Modern Academy Figures, Drawing Books, Birds and Beasts, Ornaments as Compartments, Mask Faces, Trophies, Ceilings, Chimneys, Altars, Organs, Pulpits, Clocks, Looking Glass Frames, Sconces, Tables etc.'[64] John, 2nd Duke of Montagu, bought a print there for his younger daughter, Lady Mary (1715–1775), in December 1727.[65] On 22 April 1730 'Mr Regnier' advertised in *The Daily Courant*,[66] while 'Mr Regnier, seal engraver' who advertised in the same newspaper on 13 March 1712, was probably the James Regnier who was drawing master to Andrew Lawrence.[67] In the 1760s the Golden Ball was managed by James Regnier's niece Nicole, known

237 *Hercules Crushing the Hydra (Glory to Robert Walpole)*

Paul Fourdrinier, London, 1730
Engraving, 43.9 × 33.3 cm
British Museum, London (1868,0808.3537)

In 1730 three 'loyal' Frenchmen, Fourdrinier, Faget and Dumouchel, following the Prime Minister's negotiations with France, rallied to Walpole's defence in publishing *Hercules Crushing the Hydra*. Walpole, on a pedestal framed by four Corinthian columns, climbs a rock. He is accompanied by allegorical figures of Policy (behind him), Minerva offering him a crown (in front), Fame (above) and Britannia (at the top).

as Céleste, Roubiliac's companion (after the death of his third wife), who, like the sculptor, was painted by the French artist François Xavier Vispré in London in about 1760 (plate 226). A 'Bill of Celeste Regnier for Prints' dated 26 October 1763 lists portraits of famous contemporaries, including the Huguenot celebrities Viscount Ligonier (plate 266) and David Garrick (plate 235).[68]

After the artist Philip Mercier's death in 1760, his widow, Dorothy, set up as a printseller and stationer at the Golden Ball, Windmill Street, supplying prints published by others.[69] Her trade card, etched by J.B.C. Chatelain (?1710–1771) after Gravelot, shows the interior of her shop. Customers examine prints and a boy enters carrying a portfolio and a roll of paper. At centre, Dorothy Mercier points to the display of wall-hung prints. She sold 'Italian, French and Flemish Prints ... Flower Pieces in Water Colours, Painted by herself from the life, and Fanns for Ladies, in a New and Elegant manner'.[70]

Six specialist London fanmakers of Huguenot descent listed in the London French church registers between 1681 and 1707 were working in Moorfields, Soho and Spitalfields, making a significant contribution to the production of these fashion accessories.[71] The Chassereau family dominated production for three generations. Jacob Chassereau (1665–1726), a refugee from Niort, Poitou, married in London in 1700. He was joined in London by his younger brother, Jacques (b. *c.*1670), in 1712, whose son François Chassereau the elder (1698–1784) was admitted to the Court of the Fanmakers' Company in 1721, aged only 23. In 1745, designs for fans were published by François Chassereau the younger (d.1767), admitted to the Worshipful Company of Fanmakers in 1755.[72] His wife, Honour, ran the shop at the Fan and Crown, Long Acre after his death. Philip Margas, at the Golden Fan, Bucklersbury, near Stocks Market in the City of London, sold fans to the Countess of Exeter ranging in price from £1 11s 6d to £6 6s for an 'ivory fan' in 1748–9.[73]

Huguenots promoted the taste for chinoiserie, as designers, craftsmen and East India Company merchants. Prints published in London by the engraver P.C. Canot (*c.*1710–1777), of Huguenot descent, from 'the Golden Head Little Chapel Street, Soho', were later sold in Paris.[74] They included *Livre de Chinois Inventé et Dessiné par Jean Pillement* (1758) and *Recueil de different fleurs de fantaisie dans le gout chinois* (1760). From 1770 Canot was, like Ravenet, an associate engraver of the Royal Academy.[75]

Engraved and printed ornament

By the mid-eighteenth century printsellers were selling pattern books for amateur artists. Simon Gribelin, who established his reputation within two years of his arrival in London with the publication of *A Book of Severall Ornaments* (plate 227), must have had financial backing. His book was reissued in 1700 as *A Book of ornaments useful to all Artists* and in 1704 it was incorporated into *A New book of Cyphers, with the coronets of England by Allowance of the Earl Marshall*, by Colonel Parsons.[76] In 1697 Gribelin issued another *Book of ornaments useful to Jewellers, Watchmakers and all other artists*. He had close connections with watch- and clockmaking. His grandfather, Abraham (*c.*1589–1671), was Horloger du Roi to Louis XIII. Simon Gribelin became free of the London Clockmakers' Company in 1686.

Compared to the work of Paris contemporaries Jean Berain and Charles Le Brun, Gribelin's pattern books are traditional, although finely executed. The bold acanthus scrollwork in the 1682 *Book of Severall Ornaments* shows the influence of Jean Le Pautre. Miniature tablets representing paintings are typical of Paul Androuet Ducerceau (1623–1710) and decorative schemes associated with Simon Vouet, particularly his Cabinet des Bains at the Palais Royal, Paris, painted for Anne of Austria.

Gribelin's tiny designs of 1697 do not permit originality as they are so small. Dolphins and rayed Apollo heads were traditional images associated with the French court, but animals and flowers embedded in scrollwork recall designs by the Blois-based Vauquer family. Jacques Vauquer (1621–1686), of the third generation, published his *Livre des Fleurs propres pour Orfèvres et Graveurs* in Blois and Paris around 1680, which was very influential in England in the decoration of watch cases by David Bouquet and others.[77]

Print engravers' skills were extended to other areas of art and manufacturing. In clockmaking, for example, silhouettes were easily interpreted in filigree outer watch cases and the dial and back of the movement were often engraved *en suite*. Ornament on the dials and backplates of long-case and table clocks was usually executed by a specialist engraver such as Abraham Martin. The engraved backplate of another table clock (plate 238) by Jean Constantin (fl.1700–d.1720), member of the Savoy French church, commemorates the 1707 Act of Union of England and Scotland.[78] François Asselin (d.1734), a refugee clockmaker from Dieppe mentioned as an engraver in the Clockmakers' Company Court minutes, probably engraved the backplates of his signed bracket clocks.[79]

For royal or institutional commissions, a specialist engraver was engaged. The frontplate to a bracket clock by Thomas Tompion made for William III between 1695 and 1700 was decorated by a specialist silver engraver, possibly Blaise Gentot (fl.1680–c.1701), as it is close to an engraved table top signed by Gentot at Chatsworth executed before 1710.[80] He may also have engraved the Devonshire armorial cartouches on a gold ewer and basin marked for Pierre Platel in 1701.[81] Gentot signed plate 20 of Tijou's *A new Booke of Drawings* of 1694, which represents the Fountain Screen at Hampton Court Palace. Like Tijou, Gentot was a mysterious yet highly gifted French craftsman, with 'the top reputation of any in Town',[82] who probably returned to France in about 1701; evidence for both men's Protestantism is lacking.[83]

Identification of specialist silver engravers is challenging, although engraving was an established adjunct to the goldsmith's trade. An unusual portrait print of Louis Rouppert (b.1633) of Metz, published in Paris in 1668, shows the goldsmith with a sheet of engraved ornament, standing beside a table with his tools; the engraving served as the title page to a set of ornament prints.[84] The engraving on a set of hexagonal serving dishes or 'waiters' supplied by Benjamin Pyne to William Courtenay (1628–1702) in 1698–9 has been attributed to Gribelin, although it is closer to Gentot's signed work,[85] while the engraved decoration on an oval plate marked for Pierre Harache, attributed by John Hayward to Gribelin, was reattributed by Charles Oman to Gentot as 'the Master of George Vertue'.[86] Yet Abraham Arache, described in 1689 as 'marchand graveur' and as part of the Harache family circle, is a more likely candidate: it is probable that Pierre would have employed an engraver who was a blood relative.[87] Pierre Harache stood godfather to the son of engraver Josias Mauger (fl.1710–13) at the Savoy French church in 1710, demonstrating another significant link between Huguenot goldsmith and engraver.[88]

Much of Gribelin's work as engraver on silver is preserved as inked impressions in an album he compiled in 1722 as a record of his output.[89] He engraved seal salvers for Charles Montagu, Earl of Halifax (1661–1715), who served as Chancellor

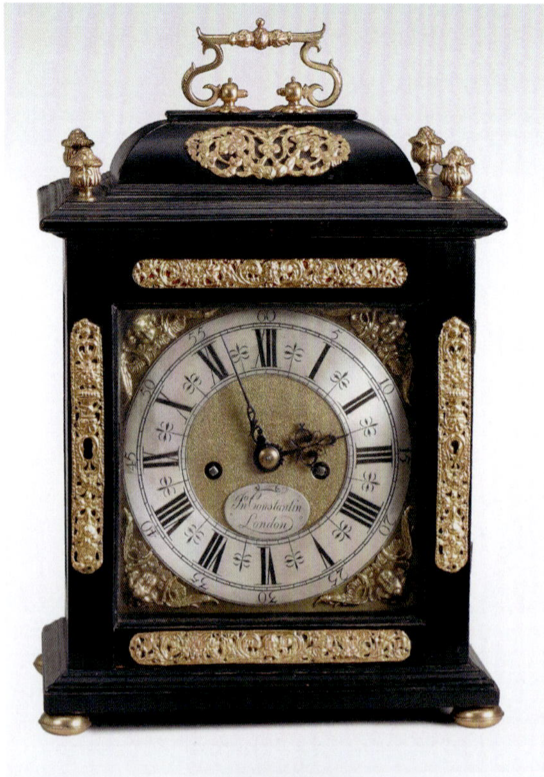

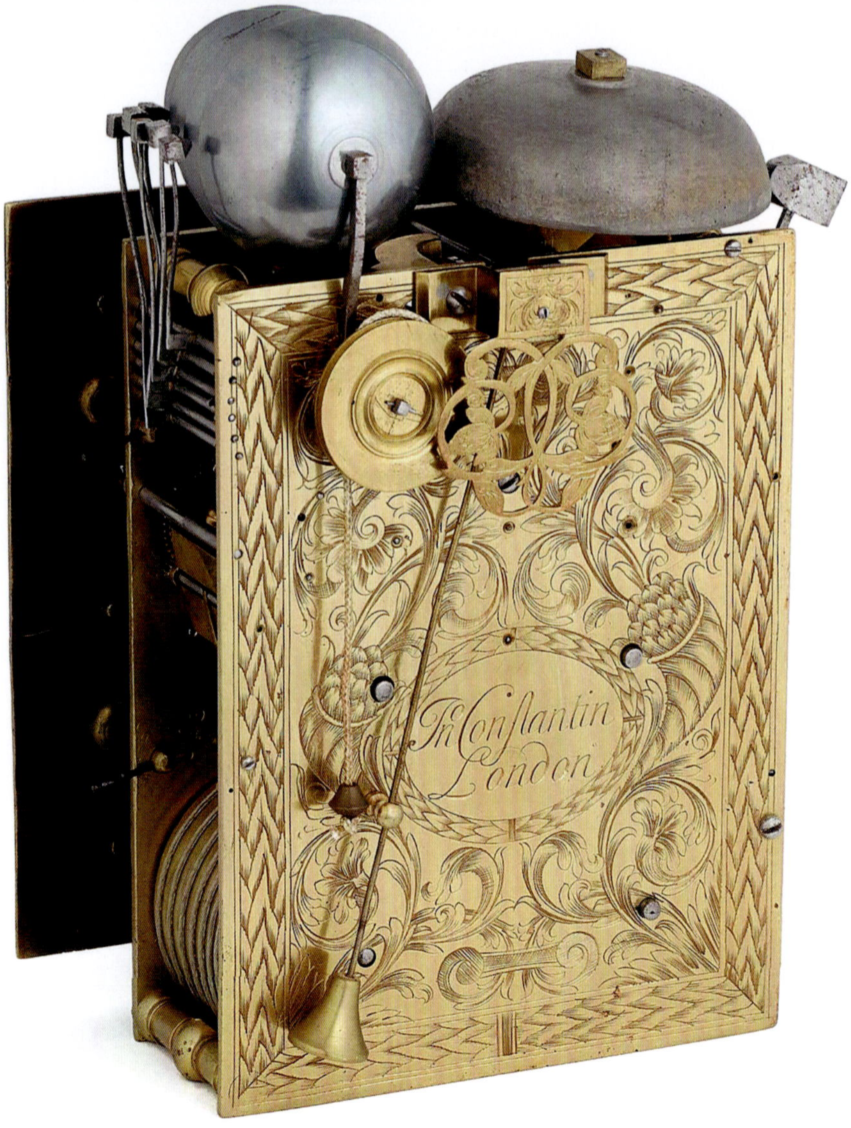

238 Table clock
John Constantin, London, 1700
Ebonized wood, brass
Ht 39 cm
Sunny Dzik and Bonhams

The back plate is engraved with cornucopiae and foliate scrolls.

of the Exchequer 1694–1701, and for Henry Boyle, 1st Earl of Shannon (1682–1764), Montagu's successor in 1701–8. Holders of certain offices of state were permitted to melt down their official seal when this was rendered obsolete by the monarch's death or following political change, as with the Union with Scotland in 1707. Henry Boyle's silver-gilt salvers represent the Great Seal of the Exchequer of William III and that of the Lord Treasurer of Ireland of Queen Anne. They are both signed with Gribelin's initials, 'S.G.', although they do not bear goldsmiths' makers' marks. Halifax's seal salver was supplied by London goldsmith Benjamin Bathurst. As Boyle lived in Pall Mall, the commission for the salvers may have gone to a goldsmith neighbour, Pierre Platel or David Willaume.[90]

Two seal salvers incorporating the arms of Sir Robert Eyre (1666–1735), made in 1728 by Edward Vincent (1698–*c.*1743), are engraved in a similar style and were plausibly attributed by Charles Oman to Samuel Gribelin, who continued to work in the manner of his father, Simon.[91]

The central engraving on Sir Robert Walpole's 1728 seal salver (plate 181) marked for Paul de Lamerie is attributed to William Hogarth. The representation of the obverse and reverse of the Great Seal is supported by Hercules, against a panoramic view of the City of London, with London Bridge in the foreground.[92] An early nineteenth-century drawing (plate 32) shows Hogarth as an apprentice engraving his master's trade card, seated at a window to maximize the light for this concentrated work.[93]

Huguenot engravers also worked closely with other specialists, such as gunsmiths and watchmakers (see pp.103, 208).

Book illustration

Gribelin's designs for book illustrations include plates for *The Gentleman's Recreation*, published in 1686 by Richard Blome (1635–1705). His red chalk drawing for the frontispiece to *De Arte Graphica* by Charles du Fresnoy (1611–1665), translated by John Dryden (1631–1700) and published in 1716 by Bernard Lintot (1675–1736), shows the daughter of Dibutades drawing her lover's outline from his shadow on the wall. The subject, from Pliny, was used to demonstrate the origin of drawing. For the same publisher, in 1716 Gribelin produced illustrations to the poem *Trivia, or the Art of Walking the Streets of London*, by John Gay (1685–1732), and for the first collected edition of the works of Alexander Pope (1688–1744) the following year.

Gribelin's headpieces to Pope's works feature a central cartouche flanked by classical deities framing a vignette with the subject of each poem. The cartouche for *The Rape of the Lock* shows 'unnumber'd Spirits' as winged putti frolicking on the lawn in front of Hampton Court Palace, the poem's setting. *The Wife of Bath's Prologue* is illustrated with a naked lady admiring herself in the mirror, watched by leering satyrs, a parody of the biblical account of Susanna and the Elders. For future reference, Gribelin pasted an impression of each print into a smaller scrapbook later acquired by Horace Walpole.[94]

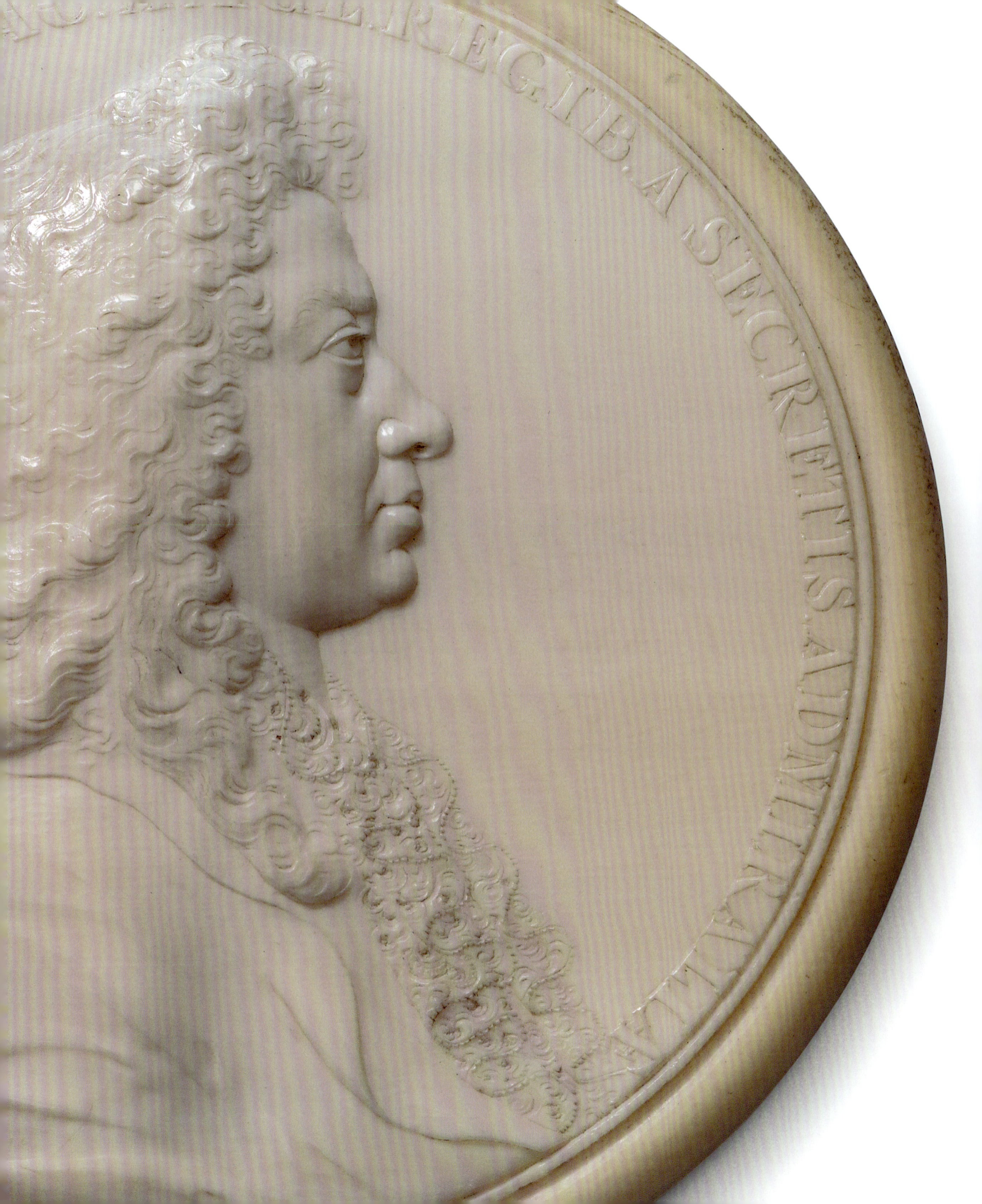

Chapter Thirteen
Huguenots & Portraiture: Allegiance, Identity, Loyalty & Memory

239 *Samuel Pepys as Secretary of the Admiralty*
Jean Cavalier, London, 1688 (detail), see plate 253

The portrait and the Academy

Within six years of its foundation in 1648, the French Academy of Painting and Sculpture recognized portraiture as acceptable for *morceaux de reception*; qualifying art works leading to acceptance as an academician kept for future reference by the institution.[1] Capturing a likeness harnessed different skills and techniques. Life-size portraits were painted in half, three-quarter or full length, sculpted likenesses as busts in the round or in relief, inspired by medals. Miniatures modelled in wax from life were subsequently carved in ivory. Copies, in different techniques and varied in scale, were pressed in horn and turtleshell, chased in silver, painted in watercolour or enamels, cut into silhouettes and engraved. Like coats of arms, portraits identified the owner, their family and friends; miniatures set in snuffboxes and watch cases were more intimate, used to record rites of passage or to cherish memories.

Huguenot Wills demonstrate that portraits in large and in miniature were bequeathed as heirlooms or reproduced for distribution among the friends of the deceased.[2] Royal and political portraits demonstrated loyalty; busts of classical worthies inspired emulation and, cast in relief, provided sophisticated ornament for silver and jewellery. Huguenot artists and craftsmen catered for an expanding market for portraiture that beckoned across Protestant Europe.

Portrait prints

Prints of eminent contemporaries had international appeal. Paris-trained artists established in London from the 1670s included Peter Vandrebanc, pupil of François de Poilly the elder (1622–1693) Louis XIV's engraver from 1664. Vandrebanc's prints of Charles II included a portrait by Henry Gascars (1634/5–1701) of 1675[3] and Grinling Gibbons's 1684 statue of the King in the Royal Exchange.[4] Vandrebanc engraved Kneller's *ad vivum* study of Louis XIV in armour in 1685 (plate 4),[5] and nine plates for gatesmith Jean Tijou's 1693 pattern book. Yet Vertue noted that Vandrebanc died in poverty and his wife had to sell his copper plates. Sir Godfrey Kneller in turn painted portraits of Vandrebanc[6] and Jean-Baptiste Monnoyer.[7]

Paul van Somer, in London from 1674, was born in Amsterdam and trained in Paris. Between 1690 and 1694 he sold the mezzotint of Paul Mignard's portrait of Henrietta and Anne Churchill, daughters of John Churchill, 1st Duke of Marlborough, from his Soho premises at the Eagle and Child, Newport Street. Paul's brother, the painter Jan van Somer (1676–1721),[8] signed the mezzotint portrait of Pierre Mussard (1627–1686), minister at the Threadneedle Street church between 1675 and 1681.[9] As with his brother Paul's print of Israel Antoine Aufrère (1677–1758; plate 240), these portraits of Huguenot ministers were intended for the Huguenot community in London.[10] Paul van Somer engraved the frontispiece to Tijou's 1694

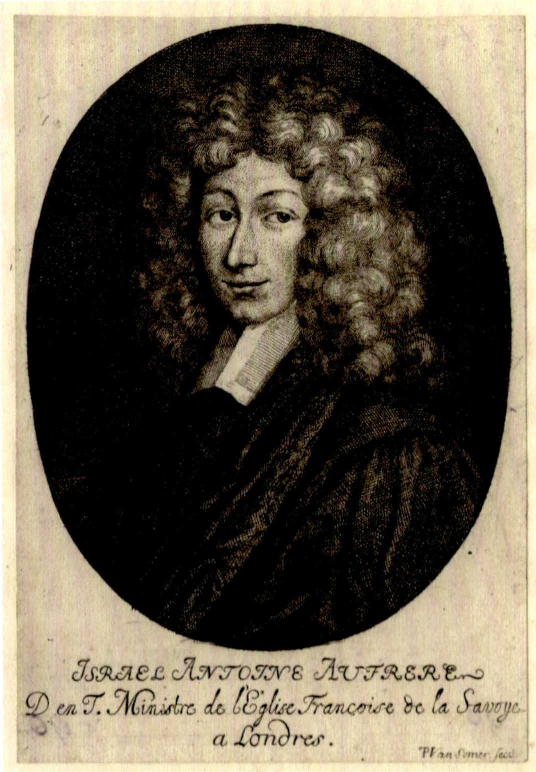

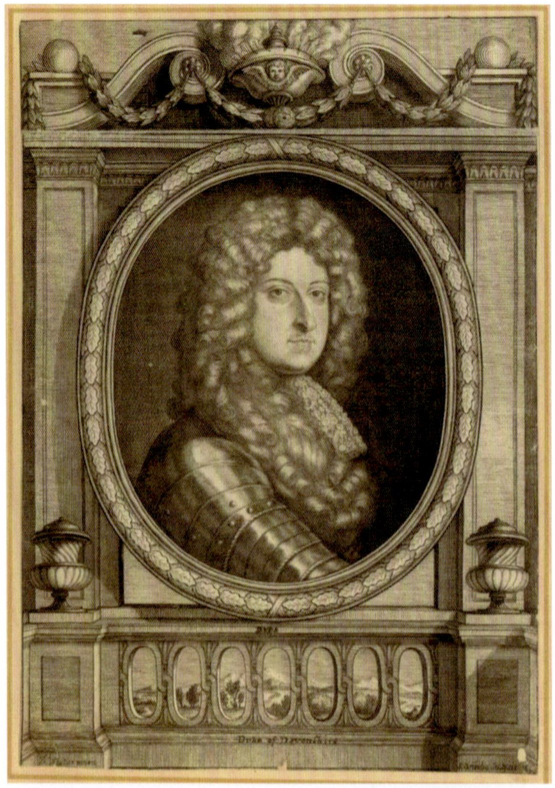

FAR LEFT

240 *Israel Antoine Aufrère, Minister of the Conformist French Church at the Savoy*

Paul van Somer, London, *c.*1700
Etching, 17.1 × 12.1 cm
National Portrait Gallery, London (D1006)

The Aufrère family came from Poitou; Israel Antoine served as William III's chaplain at the Chapel Royal, St James's Palace and as minister of the French Savoy church from 1701 to 1727.

LEFT

241 *William Cavendish, 4th Earl and later 1st Duke of Devonshire*

Simon Gribelin after Daniel Vautier, London, 1689
Engraving, 22.3 × 15.7 cm
British Museum, London (1848,0911.416)

This portrait of William Cavendish, later 1st Duke of Devonshire, champion of the Glorious Revolution and patron of Huguenot craftsmen, was based on a miniature by Daniel Vautier, Gribelin's maternal uncle from Blois, who settled in Marylebone. Gribelin lived in Long Acre, Covent Garden. 'Daniel Vautier … peintre en email', with Gribelin's brother-in-law 'Pierre Berchet, peintre', witnessed Simon Gribelin's marriage in 1691 to Marie, daughter of Samuel Mettayer, minister of the French church, La Patente, Spitalfields.

pattern book (plate 77), which was sold from the gatesmith's lodgings at the 'Barber's Pole … the lower end of the Haymarket'.[11] In July 1694 *The London Gazette* advertised Paul van Somer's 'plate, pictures and other curiosities' for sale by lottery. In 1705, when he was teaching drawing to apprentice goldsmith Jacques Bourseau, he was still living in Newport Street.[12]

Among the portrait prints preserved in Simon Gribelin's collection in 1722 (p.244) are his engraving of the seven bishops committed to the Tower of London, which was sold by Paul van Somer in 1688;[13] a portrait after Daniel Vautier (d.1713)[14] of William Cavendish, later 1st Duke of Devonshire, champion of the Glorious Revolution (plate 241);[15] and a medallic print celebrating William III's victory at Namur in 1695, with a political verse to warm Huguenot hearts:[16]

> *To save the World see* WILLIAM *strike like Jove,*
> *And watchfull Heav'n the Mighty Work approve:*
> *Fame sounds his Praise, Fresh Laurels grace his Brow,*
> NAMUR *submitts and Envy's taught to bow.*
> *Now* LEWIS *from this Moment date thy Fall*
> *The Conqu'rour of* NAMUR *with ease may*
> *Conquer All.*

Engraver Jean Simon (1675–1751) was Gribelin's London neighbour.[17] Simon, who specialized in mezzotint, was born in Normandy and trained in Paris, where his family had connections with the Huguenot temple at Charenton. He lived in Covent Garden at the Seven Stars, King Street, moving to the Golden Eagle, Villiers Street, and then to New Street. He retired in 1742 and his copper plates were sold in November 1761. In 1708 Simon succeeded John Smith (1652–1742) as Godfrey Kneller's engraver and subscribed to Kneller's Academy in 1711.[18] His portraits include Huguenot contemporaries (plate 242) and two champions of their cause, Bishop of London Henry Compton (1632–1713) and, after a miniature by Arlaud, Ezechiel Spannheim, Ambassador to London in 1707 representing the Elector Palatine and Elector of Brandenburg. Spannheim had assisted Huguenot refugees after the Revocation.[19] The beautiful lettering on Simon's mezzotints suggest the specialist services of a writing master. From 1720 Simon published his own prints.

Medallion portraits

Prints of Greek and Roman medals inspired decoration on ceramics, enamels, jewellery and silver.[20] This Renaissance tradition was promoted by sixteenth-century Venetian engraver Aenea Vico[21] and celebrated in ceramics, enamels and pewter as well as precious metal. Classical male heads alternating with female masks were a common device on the borders of silver vessels. The rim of a

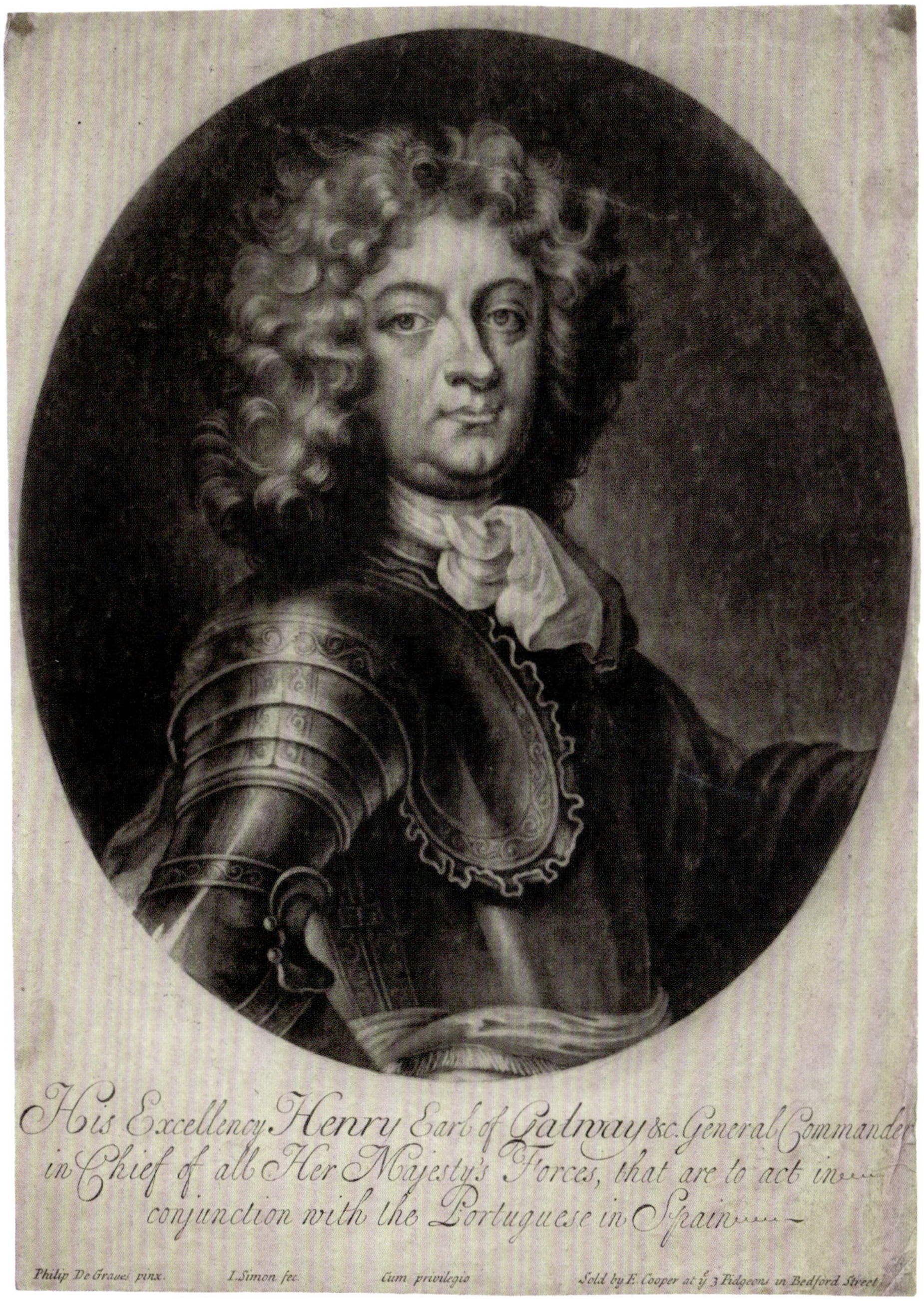

ABOVE

242 *Henri de Massue de Ruvigny, Earl of Galway*

Jean Simon after Philip De Graves, London, *c.*1705
Mezzotint, 34.7 × 25.2 cm
National Portrait Gallery, London (D31117)

Henry de Ruvigny, 1st Earl of Galway (1648–1720) was a distinguished soldier and first Governor of the French Hospital. He fought at the Battle of the Boyne in 1690 and founded the Irish Huguenot veteran community at Portarlington.

charger made by Paul Crespin for James Brydges, 1st Duke of Chandos, carries medallions of classical philosophers, named on the reverse (plate 185).[22] In 1743 the upholsterer 'Mr Deschamps' supplied auction catalogues of the collection of Greek and Roman medallions and medals belonging to the goldsmith and antiquary Peter Birkhead (d.1743).[23] The profile portrait in earthenware of the sixth Emperor of Rome, Galba, attributed to Bernard Palissy, represents widespread engagement with such iconic images.[24]

William III's death and the coronation of Queen Anne in 1702 were commemorated with chased silver busts in relief on the back of watch movements by David Lestourgeon, a silver turner from Dieppe.[25] Paul Beauvais (fl.1696–1730), working at the Crowned Cadran (dial) in Castle Street, Soho, between 1696 and 1703,[26] signed and dated a gold pair-case watch in 1708; the dial bears an unidentified miniature portrait.[27] He may be related to the watchmaker Simon Beauvais. When Simon Gribelin's 1682 *Book of Severall Ornaments* was reissued in 1704 and dedicated to the chronologer Colonel William Parsons, who was probably Gribelin's sponsor, the frontispiece framed a 1696 engraved portrait of Parsons based on a drawing by Pierre Berchet, Gribelin's brother-in-law and a Paris-trained pupil of Charles de la Fosse.[28]

Miniature portraits

The miniature in enamel was a unique Huguenot contribution to the art of portraiture. The technique, developed in Blois, was nurtured in Geneva, and practised by Huguenot artists in exile throughout this period. Blois was an important centre for production of silver, watches and jewellery. In the 1620s the enamelling of watch cases by Jean Toutin was developed by his son Henri in Paris from 1632.[29] Enamelled portraits on watch cases are rare. One example, dating from about 1640, with a movement by Paris watchmaker Jacques Goullons (fl.1626–71), represents Louis XIII and Cardinal Richelieu.[30] The earliest enamel miniature portraits were signed by Henri Toutin, such as that of Charles I, painted in 1636 when the artist was 22 years old, which still retains its original scalloped enamelled frame.[31]

Henri Toutin's 1637 posthumous miniature of Venetia Stanley, Lady Digby (1604–1633), commissioned in Paris, is based on a watercolour by Peter Oliver (plate 243).[32] Extinguished torches and bats' wings embedded in the cartouche complement the memorial inscription on the reverse expressing the widower's grief: 'He tries to snatch a ghost from the funeral pyre and fights a battle with death, exhausting the skills of the artists. Everywhere he searches for thee – O, the bitterness of it'.[33]

Peter Oliver (1589–1647) was trained in London by his father, Isaac, who was a pupil of notable goldsmith and miniature painter Nicholas Hilliard (1547–1619). They worked in watercolour. Isaac's father, Pierre (b. *c.*1525), Rouen goldsmith, met Hilliard in Geneva during the late 1550s. Ten years later Isaac settled in the immigrant community in London's Blackfriars, where he expanded his family network by marrying three times. Sarah, his second wife, was daughter of celebrated portraitist Marcus

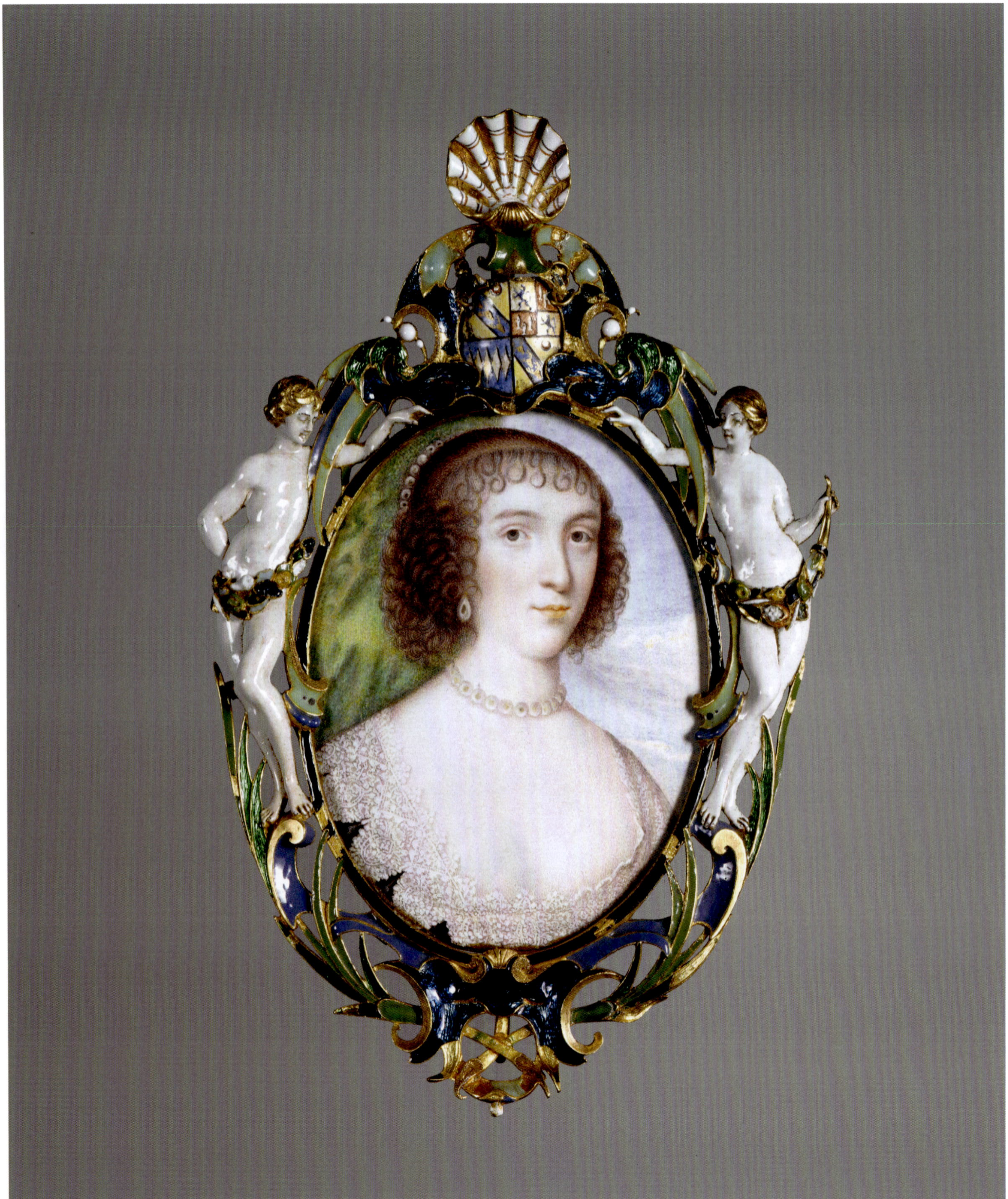

243 *Venetia Stanley, Lady Digby*

Henri Toutin, Paris, after Peter Oliver, 1637, framed by Gilles Légaré
Enamel on gold set in gold and enamelled frame, 12.5 × 8.3 cm
The Walters Art Museum, Baltimore (44.177)

The shell at the top of the frame is symbolic of Venus, flanked by nymphs with cornucopiae symbolizing plenty; the portrait is identified by the Digby coat of arms.

244 *Richard Sackville, 3rd Earl of Dorset*

Isaac Oliver, London, *c.*1616
Watercolour mounted on a Jack of Spades, Rouen-style playing card, 34 × 41 cm
Fitzwilliam Museum, Cambridge (L.D. Cunliffe Bequest 1937, no. 3865)

Cut-down Rouen-style playing cards back some of Isaac Oliver's vellum miniatures.

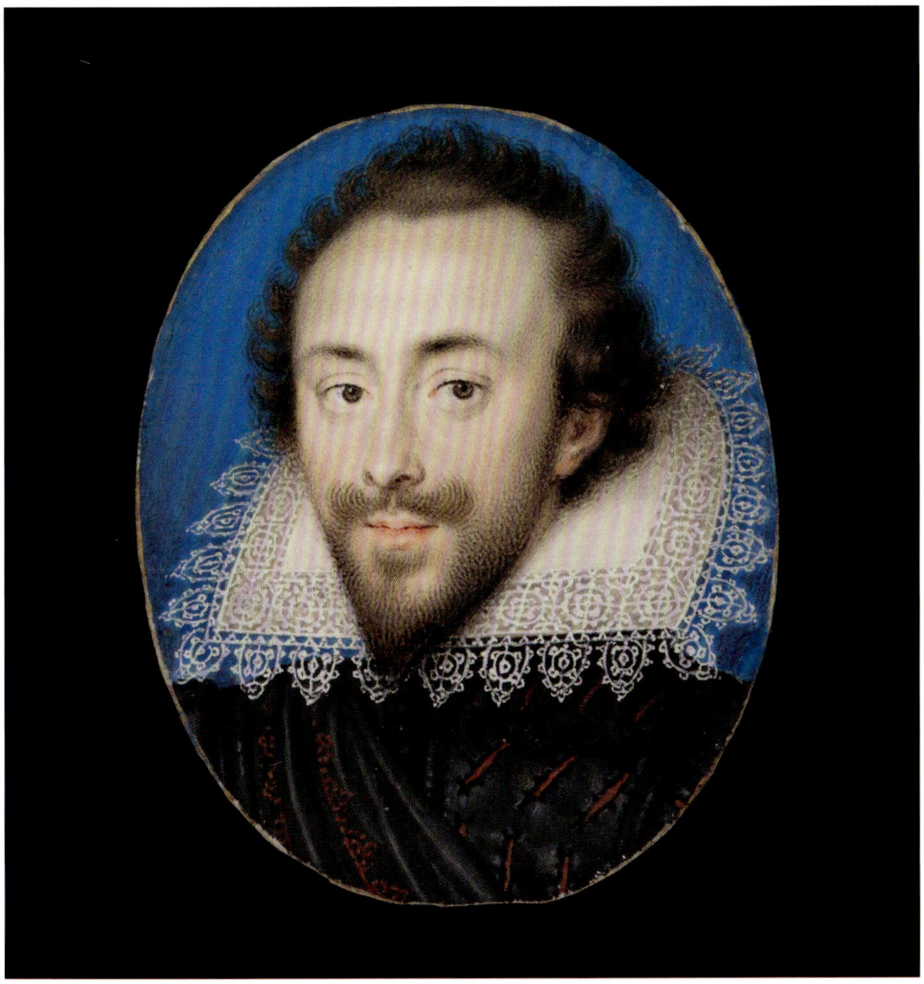

Gheeraerts the elder (1520–1590). Peter, Isaac's eldest son, married Anne, sister of his father's third wife, Elizabeth; the sisters' French father, Jacques Harden (*c.*1550–1626), was a court musician who lived in Isleworth outside London.[34] Isaac's work was experimental and open to continental influence. His portrait of Richard Sackville, 3rd Earl of Dorset (plate 244), is backed by a Rouen-style playing card. His 1598 portrait of Catholic Anthony Browne, 2nd Viscount Montagu, with his brothers John and William, was inspired by a French print of the three Huguenot Coligny brothers.[35]

Isaac Oliver used mercury chloride pigment to achieve white, which blackened with age and was later overpainted. This may be the corrosive face make-up used by ladies, then known as 'sublimate', which Hilliard describes in his *Treatise on the Art of Limning* as 'a white made of quicksilver' that the 'women painters' use. Peter Oliver used a technical innovation, introduced by Balthazar Gerbier, who was in London by 1616. The 'table-book leaf', a sheet of card, was prepared with gesso on each side as backing for vellum for portraits in watercolour and pen and ink. Born in Middelburg to Huguenot refugee parents, Gerbier came to London in 1616 to work for George Villiers, 1st Duke of Buckingham; Gerbier's portrait of his patron is signed and dated 1618.[36]

Horace Walpole closely studied Isaac Oliver's own self-portrait, painted in about 1590, declaring that 'the art and imitation of nature are so great that the largest magnifying glass only calls out new beauties'.[37] However, Isaac Oliver's official portraits did not always attract repeat commissions: his 1589 miniature of Elizabeth I captures her ageing complexion. Yet he became official painter to James I's queen, Anne of Denmark,[38] and his portraits of their children Henry, Prince of Wales, and Princess Elizabeth were treasured by the future Charles I. Peter Oliver worked closely with his father and succeeded as royal miniaturist; his portrait of Elizabeth of Bohemia retains its original gold locket enamelled in dark green and white in the fashionable French *cosse de pois* (peapod) style.[39] Isaac and Peter Oliver were buried at the church of St Ann, Blackfriars.[40]

Huguenot painter David Des Granges (1613–1675), son of Samson de Granges of Guernsey and his wife, Marie Bouvier, was baptized at the Threadneedle Street French church in January 1613.[41] Des Granges trained as an engraver; his earliest miniature is dated 1639. After his marriage in 1636 he moved from Blackfriars to the West End; in 1658 he was lodging with a gunsmith in The Strand,[42] and then lived in Long Acre, Covent Garden, until the 1670s. Des Granges was appointed Limner to Charles II in Scotland in 1651 and later converted to Catholicism. His miniature of Sir Bevil Grenville (1596–1643), the Cornish general killed in 1643, was cherished in its elaborate jewelled case by his widow, who mentioned it in her will in 1647 (plate 245).[43] Des Granges moved to Scotland in 1651.[44]

Royal miniatures set with diamonds presented by Louis XIV to favoured foreign ambassadors[45] were later re-mounted, the diamonds re-set in fashionable new jewels. For example, Henri Toutin's signed portrait of Louis XIV of about 1667–8 is found on a later snuffbox.[46]

Jacques Bordier (1616–1684) remained in England during the Interregnum but by 1668 was operating as a secret agent at Versailles for the Genevese government. His cousin Pierre (1614–1671?), also in England, painted three miniatures celebrating the victory of Thomas Fairfax, 3rd Baron Fairfax (1612–1671), over the royalists at Naseby 1645. The portrait of Fairfax astride his

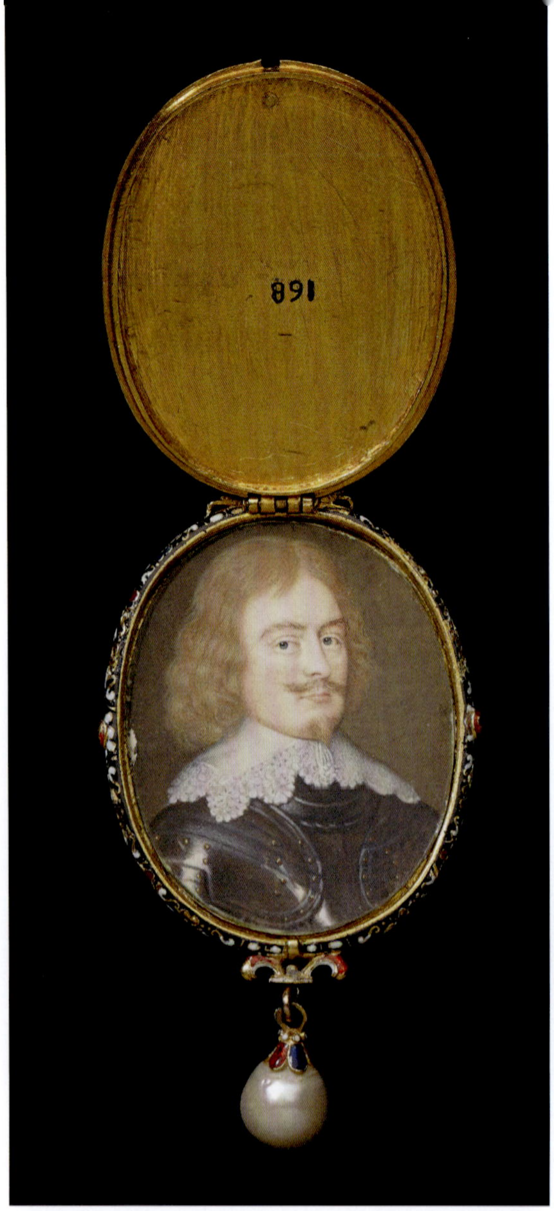

horse, Chessnut, in the battlefield is inspired by Van Dyck's equestrian portrait of Charles I.[47]

At the English court the miniaturist Jean Petitot the elder, who worked in London from 1639 to 1643,[48] was introduced to Charles I's Huguenot physician, Theodore Turquet de Mayerne (1573–1675), who shared his discoveries of 'carnation' flesh-coloured pigment[49] and sat to Petitot. During the English Civil War Petitot left for France and became court enameller to Louis XIV; one of his French royal portraits retains its original frame.[50] In 1687, aged 83, Petitot returned to Geneva, where he encouraged artists to produce enamel cases for the flourishing export trade in watches.[51] He died at Vevey in 1691,[52] recognized as the greatest seventeenth-century miniaturist working in enamels whose career spanned seven decades.[53]

Petitot's eldest son, Jean Louis (1653–1702), trained with miniaturist Samuel Cooper (1609–1672) in London. He married his cousin Madeleine Bordier (1658–1736) and lived in England from 1677 to 1682 and again in 1696. Self-portraits by Petitot father and son proclaimed their skill as they were painted *ad vivum* (plate 246); Jean Louis Petitot's self-portrait is inscribed 'Jean Petitot fait par lui-meme l'an 1676 decembre age 23 ans'. He later settled in Paris, where he maintained his Protestant faith. As there were no legitimate consecrated burial grounds for members of the Reformed Faith in 1702, when Jean Louis died,

LEFT ABOVE & BELOW

245 *Sir Bevil Grenville*

David Des Granges, London, 1643–7
Watercolour on vellum laid on card set in gem-encrusted gold case, 10.9 × 4.2 cm
The Waddesdon Bequest, British Museum, London (WB 168)

This miniature of the Cornish General, shown in armour, is based on an earlier portrait, dated 1636, in family ownership. The miniature is enclosed in an elaborate gem-set enamelled case, decorated with pansies and daisies. It was cherished by Sir Bevil's widow and descendants as an heirloom until it was sold to Ferdinand de Rothschild *c.*1890.

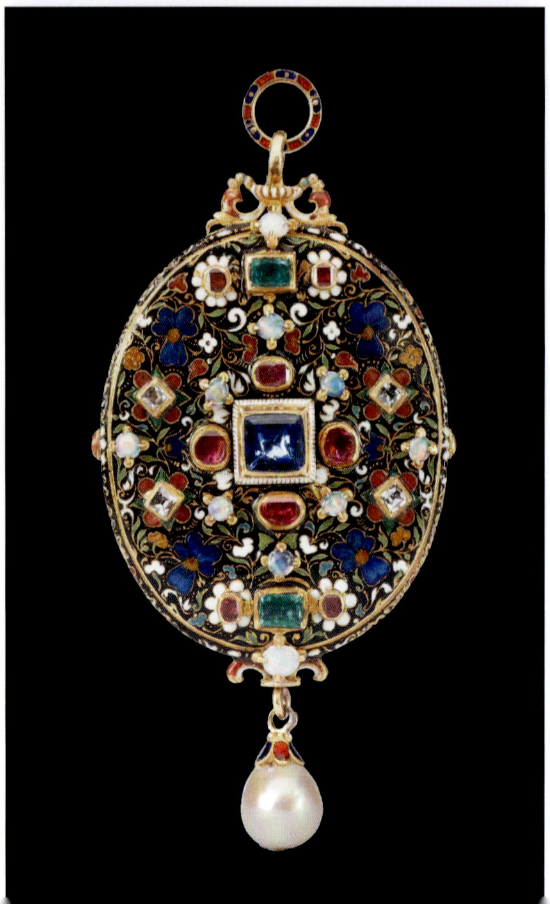

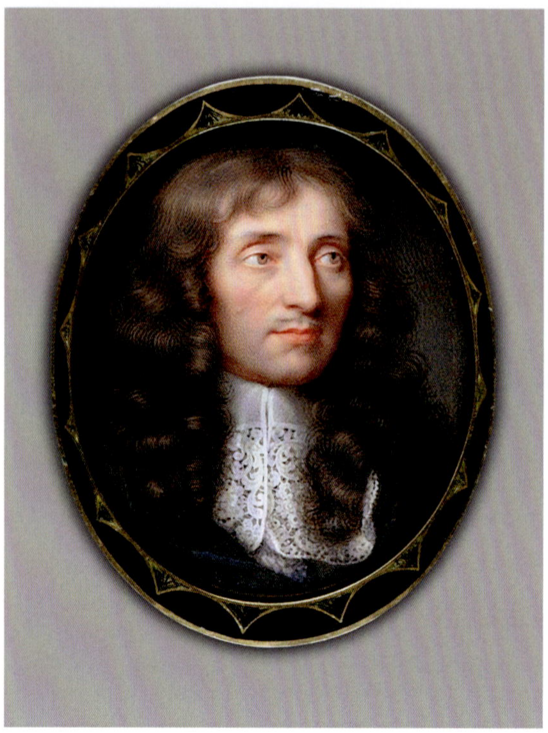

246 *Self-Portrait*

Jean I Petitot, Paris, 1674
Enamel on gold in its original enamelled frame, 2.9 × 2.3 cm
Fondation Custodia, Collection Frits Lugt

This exceptional miniature is among Petitot's finest portraits. He often collaborated with Jacques Bordier, who became his brother-in-law after both artists returned to Paris from London. Bordier is said to have painted the hair, draperies and backgrounds while Petitot concentrated on the more demanding face and hands.

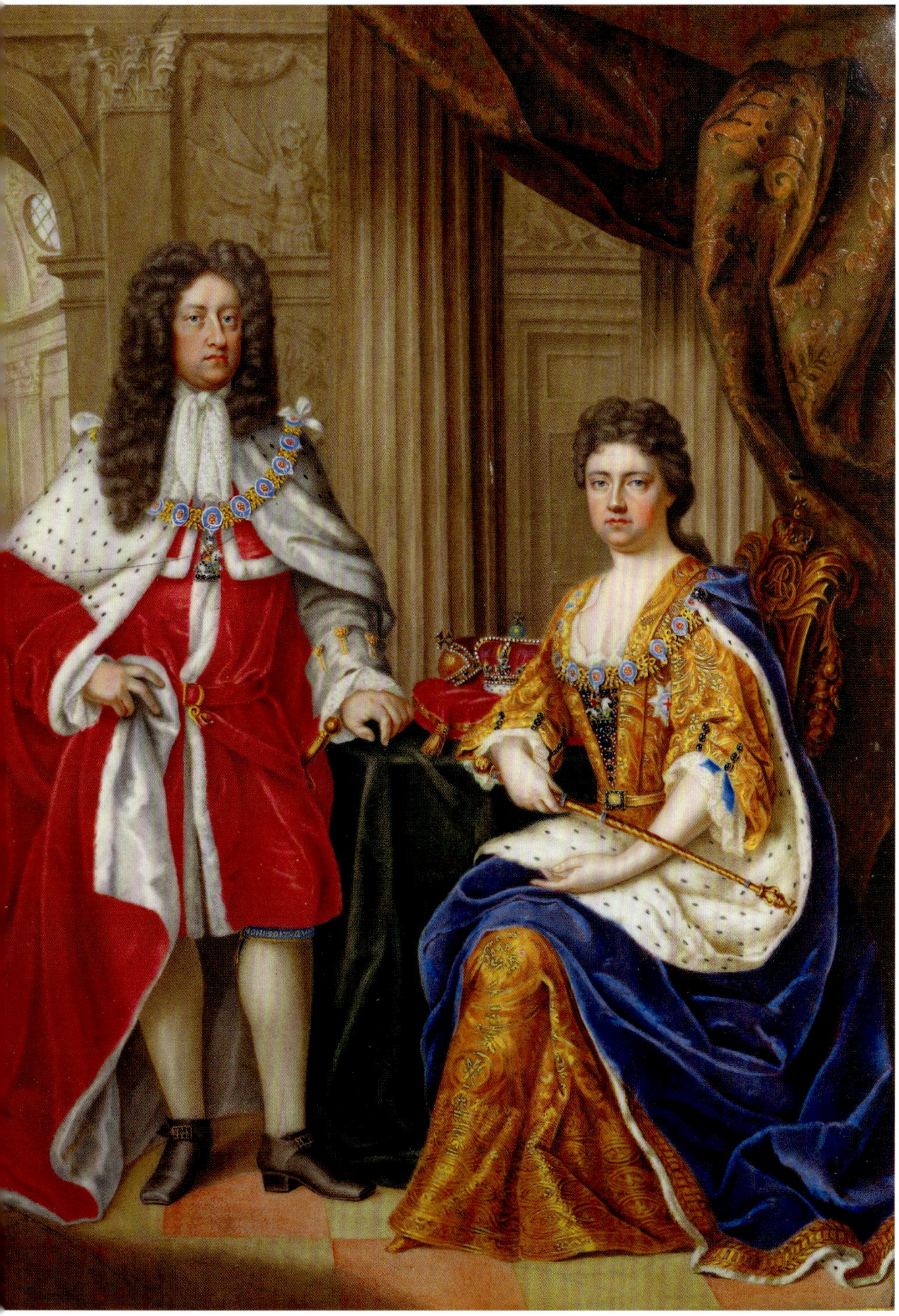

247 *Queen Anne (1665–1714) with Prince George of Denmark (1653–1708)*
Charles Boit, London, 1706
Enamel, 25.4 × 18.4 cm
Royal Collection Trust (RCIN 421497)

Charles Boit, enameller, was the son of a Huguenot silk merchant established in Sweden; his mother was from Calais. Trained as a goldsmith's apprentice, Boit probably learned the art of enamel painting from Pierre Signac (1624–1684), another Huguenot miniaturist in Stockholm, before arriving in London in 1687.

he was buried in his own garden. It is difficult to distinguish his later miniatures from those signed by his father. Their descendants returned to London. François Petitot (1663–1728) bequeathed 'all my pictures in enamel and 'miniatures' to Stephen Petitot (1673–1731), his brother.[54] The taste for miniatures prevailed and Huguenot families bequeathed these small portraits as heirlooms. In 1780 a diamond-set portrait of the merchant silk weaver James Godin (*c.*1697–1762), who worked in partnership with Peter Ogier in Spital Square, was bequeathed by his widow.[55]

Lesser artists, as well as the most celebrated, travelled to find work. David le Clerc (1679–1738), a miniature painter in London in 1715–17 who spent most of his working life in Frankfurt,[56] was son of Rouen medallist Gabriel le Clerc (1648–1690), who had settled in Berne. François Lainé, born in Berlin was in London by 1711; he later became engraver to the East India Company.[57] John L'Admiral (1699–1773), born to Huguenot parents in Amsterdam, was associated with Frankfurt-born Jacob Christoph Le Blon. Both artists practised as miniaturists in Amsterdam and in 1720 came to England, where they attempted but failed to develop a means of printing in several colours.[58]

Swedish-born enameller Charles Boit (1662–1727) assisted James Parmentier from 1691 in copying large paintings. He was appointed court enameller to William III in 1696 and then to Queen Anne, whose larger portrait, of 1706, was framed by Matthew Gosset (p.128). Boit's double portrait of Queen Anne with Prince George of Denmark (plate 247) was probably painted from life. He was paid an advance of £1,000 by Prince George to paint a large-scale enamel in celebration of the victory at Blenheim, with the Duke of Marlborough led to Queen Anne by the figure of Victory, but was unable to complete this technical challenge and forced to leave London. Boit later became a professor at the French Royal Academy of Painting and died in Paris in 1727.[59]

French miniature painters came to Britain in search of patronage. Benjamin Arlaud (b. *c.*1670), from a family of clockmakers, worked in London during the 1710s;[60] his miniature of Johann Christopher Pepusch (1667–1752), son of a Protestant minister in Berlin, was probably painted to mark the award of his doctorate from Oxford University in 1713 (plate 248).[61] Art schools founded in Geneva by David (fl.1684–1704) and Jean André in 1704, and in 1730 by François Picot (1698–*c.*1762)[62] guaranteed a steady flow of talent

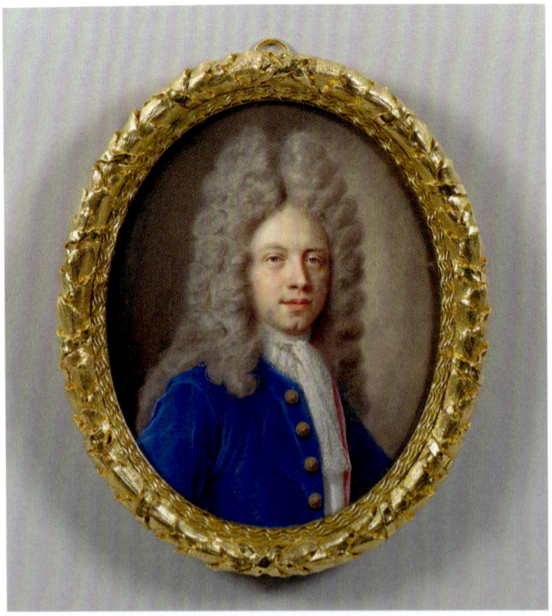

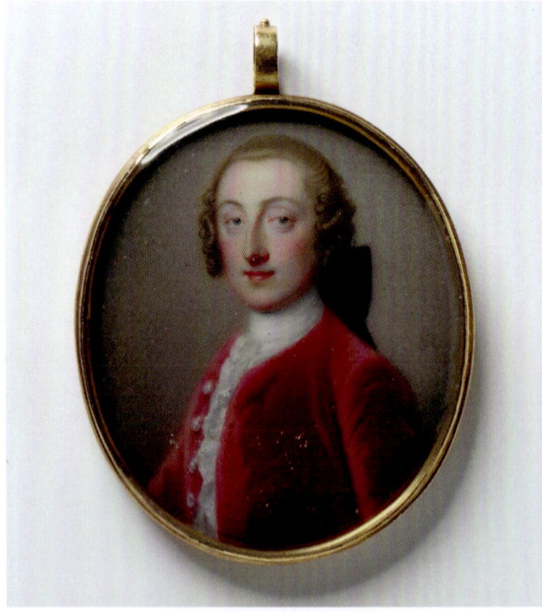

248 *John Christopher Pepusch (1667–1752)*

Benjamin Arlaud, London, *c.*1710–15
Watercolour on vellum, 7.2 × 5.8 cm
Royal Collection Trust (RCIN 420160)

Pepusch conducted the singers in the Duke of Chandos' private chapel from 1717 until 1725. The eyebrows, upper eyelids and corners of the eyes are outlined in red and the face is shaded with greenish grey. Arlaud uses a careful hatching technique to define light and shade.

249 *William Pitt, Earl of Chatham (1708–1788)*

Jean André Rouquet, London, *c.*1745
Enamel, 4.1 × 3.5 cm
Victoria and Albert Museum, London (P.5–1946)

Rouquet, born and trained in Geneva, came to London in 1723 and stayed for 30 years. He then left for France, where, despite his Protestant faith, he joined the Academie Royale in 1753 with a studio in the Louvre. His account, *The Present State of the Arts in England* (1755), singles out Petitot and the Swedish artist C.F. Zincke for praise.

to meet European demand.[63] Jean André Rouquet (1701–1758), for example, trained in Geneva and worked in London's Leicester Square from 1723 until 1753.[64] In the 1740s he painted William Pitt, Earl of Chatham (1708–1788; plate 249), later Minister of War during the Seven Years' War between Britain and France (1757–63).

Itinerant portraitists

Portrait painters also travelled within Britain to gain patrons. In Tunbridge Wells, a Mr Beauvais was 'known for his portraits in watercolour & black lead miniatures'. He gave lessons and dealt in paintings.[65]

The spa city of Bath provided a market of potential sitters with time to spare while taking the waters. Geneva-trained Andrea Mussard (fl.1724–1765), a relative of the French goldsmith Jean Mussard (1644–1703) who published a book of designs in 1673,[66] was working in Bath in 1751.[67] He came to London as a 'Disciple of the famous Rozalba in Venice', celebrated as a 'Limner in enamel & miniature, famous for Likeness and Attitude'.[68] Andrea Mussard charged 10 guineas for enamel, 5 guineas for watercolours and 2 guineas for dry colours and crayons. The higher cost of enamel reflected the risk in the firing. The first colours to be laid on the metal support need the highest temperature. More colour was added and the enamel fired again, the process ending with colours needing the lowest temperature.

John Alexander Gresse (1741–1794) was born in London, the son of a small worker in precious metals from Geneva, Peter Gaspard Gresse (d.1771), who was living in Dean Street, Soho, in 1725. John Alexander trained in Paris with a member of the Scotin family, probably Louis-François (d.1769), and Thomas Major; he occasionally painted miniature portraits and later became drawing master to George III's daughters.[69]

Jean Etienne Liotard (1702–1789), son of Antoine Liotard (1661–1740), a goldsmith from Montelimar who had settled in Geneva, was taught by Daniel Gardelle (1693–1753). Gardelle was a relative of the notorious London-based Genevan miniaturist Theodore Gardelle (1722–1761), who murdered his Leicester Square landlady in 1759, although not before he had painted a portrait of Voltaire.[70] Liotard travelled extensively.[71] In Vienna he painted Empress Maria Theresa, her family and courtiers, and his celebrated *Chocolate Girl* (1743–4; Gemäldegalerie Alte Meister, Dresden), in which a fresh-faced chamber maid carries a lacquer tray with a glass of water and a Meissen porcelain cup filled with dark chocolate to the bedside of her mistress. Venetian pastellist Carriera described this work as 'The most beautiful pastel ever seen'.[72] Liotard was in Paris from 1748 to 1753 as painter to Louis XV, where his British sitters included David Garrick.[73] He visited London between 1753 and 1755 and painted a miniature portrait of John, 1st Earl Spencer (1734–1784; plate 250), which was set in a beautifully carved ivory box,[74] while his own self-portrait (plate 251) promoted his reputation.[75] In 1754 he exhibited from his London premises at the Two Yellow Lamps, Golden Square, Soho; he returned in March 1755 to finish portraits begun the previous

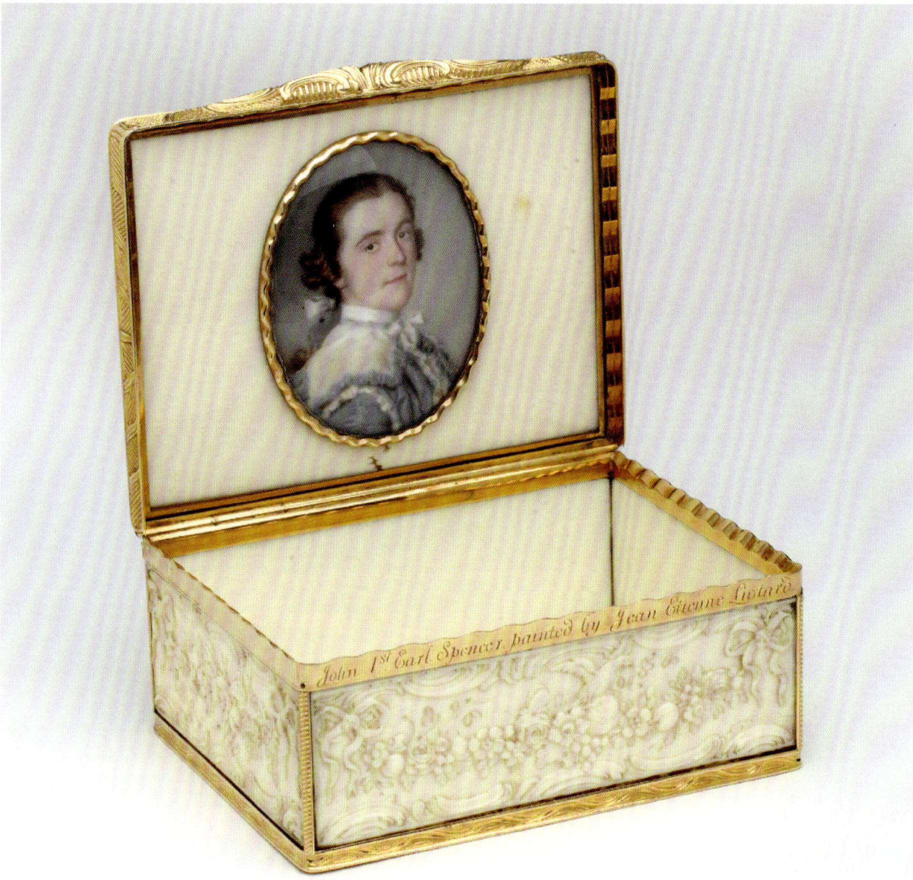

250 *John, 1st Earl Spencer*
John Etienne Liotard, London, *c.*1753
Enamel miniature set in gold and carved ivory box, 8 × 6.5 × 3.7 cm
The Rosalinde and Arthur Gilbert Collection on loan to the Victoria and Albert Museum, London (LOAN:GILBERT.408–2008)

Liotard visited England, 1753–5 when he painted miniatures of John, Earl Spencer and his bride to mark their marriage. The ivory box was possibly imported from Dieppe or made by a second-generation London-based Huguenot ivory carver.

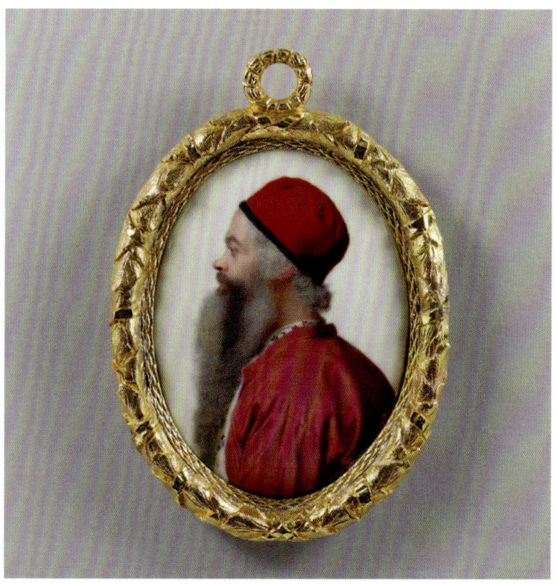

251 *Self-Portrait*
Jean-Etienne Liotard, London, 1753
Enamel with ivory backing in later gilded Hatfield frame, 5.9 × 4.5 cm
Royal Collection Trust (RCIN 421436)

This miniature self-portrait in Moldavian-style dress reflects Liotard's experience in 1742 as court artist in Jassy, Moldavia, and fascinated his British contemporaries.

year.[76] In 1773–4 Liotard travelled to London again to paint members of the royal family. In 1777 he was invited back to Vienna by Emperor Joseph II; he lived in the Hofburg and was considered to be one of the best miniaturists of his time. In his *Treatise on the Principles and Rules of Painting* (1781) he emphasized the importance of draughtsmanship and naturalistic colouring.[77]

William De La Cour, portrait painter in oil and crayons, based from 1745 in Coventry Court, Haymarket, St James's,[78] published pattern books, sold artists' materials and taught amateurs. He moved to the Golden Head, Katherine Street, off The Strand,[79] and in September 1753 left for Dublin, where he had been invited to establish an academy. Here he lived in College Green.[80] By 1757 he had moved to Edinburgh as the first master of the Trustees Academy, where he taught 'the Art of Drawing patterns for the linen and woollen manufacturers'[81] and designed stage scenery for a production of Voltaire's *Orphan of China* in January 1759. His 1765 self-portrait remains in Edinburgh (plate 252).[82]

Ivory medallion portraits

Jean Cavalier (b. *c.*1650–60; d.1698/9), originally from Dieppe, was in London intermittently from 1684 to 1691. He can probably be identified with the John Cavalier whose name is listed among the denizations of Huguenots in London on 16 May 1683.[83] Cavalier's 1684 medallion portrait of Isabella FitzRoy, Duchess of Grafton (1667–1723), was commissioned by her husband.[84] Cavalier's 1684 equestrian relief of Charles II[85] was probably inspired by the equestrian statue in Roman armour cast in bronze by founder Josias Iback (fl.1679–96) from a wooden model 'cut … by a German'.[86] Given by Tobias Rustat (1608–1694), Gentleman of the Bedchamber to Charles II, the statue was installed in the upper court at Windsor Castle in 1680, on a stone pedestal supplied by Grinling Gibbons, where it still stands.[87]

In Holland in 1686, Cavalier carved a medallion portrait of Princess Mary, and two years later an ivory medallion representing Samuel Pepys as Secretary of the Admiralty (plate 253).[88] From 1686 he visited Trier, Stuttgart, Düsseldorf, Hamburg, Hanover and Kassel, and in 1689 Vienna, Munich and Dresden. By 1690 he enjoyed an international reputation, charging £11 for a medallic portrait in ivory.[89] In March that year he and Godfrey Kneller shared sittings for William III's state portrait.[90] The resulting medallion bears the initial 'C' on the arm of the sitter; a second one, of Kneller, is signed lower centre 'I.C.' and shows the Lübeck-born artist in profile to the left, with a Latin legend recording his royal appointment as Principal Painter.[91] In December 1690 a pass and letters of recommendation to travel abroad and return 'pour y travailler aux Choses de son Art' describes Cavalier as 'the King's Medallist'.[92]

Cavalier travelled to Copenhagen with letters of recommendation from Prince George of Denmark in London (5 January 1691) and Electress Anna Sophia of Saxony (13 July 1692), and he worked at the Danish court from 1691 to 1693. On 13 December 1692 he was paid for '10 portraits of the Royal House'. These ivory medallions of the Danish and English royal families were displayed as a group in the Kunstkammer, Rosenberg Castle, from November 1693 to May 1694. They included Princess Anne, Prince George of Denmark (1653–1708) and their son William, Duke of Gloucester, carved in London in 1691.[93] In 1693 Cavalier probably visited Oslo, where he carved two medallions of the Norwegian vice-regent, Ulrik Fredrik Gyldenløve (1638–1704), half-brother to Christian v of Denmark.[94] From 1694 to 1697 Cavalier was back in Stockholm, and from April 1697 in Copenhagen for just a few days, when he sold a toothpick and a box to Christian v. Later that year, with his brother Denis (d.1688/9), he accompanied a Swedish delegation to Russia; they travelled on to Persia but Jean Cavalier died en route, in Azerbijan.[95]

In Britain, David Le Marchand succeeded Cavalier as leading portraitist in ivory and settled first in Edinburgh and then in London; his subjects were distinguished contemporaries and classical worthies. At this period life-size marble and plaster busts were used to punctuate architectural settings: a series by Gideon du Chesne representing the Caesars, dating from around 1700, remains on the North Front Colonnade at Boughton House. Le Marchand's miniature heads of Socrates, Plato, Homer, Cicero and 'two of Medusa, finely copy'd from the antique in ivory' adorned the Great Ormond Street library of Dr Richard Mead (1673–1754). Mead also owned Le Marchand's 'Sir Isaac Newton's head in mezzo relievo'.[96] John Cheere, second-generation Huguenot sculptor, supplied smaller than life-size plaster portraits of contemporary and classical worthies for libraries.[97] As an alternative to plaster busts, in 1754 he offered John Grimston (d.1780), for his library at Kilnwick Hall, Yorkshire, plaster figures of Homer, Virgil, Horace, Demosthenes, Socrates, Shakespeare, Chaucer, Milton, Dryden, Spencer, Locke, Newton, Tillotson and Boyle.

Le Marchand's work was championed by the Raper family, London silk merchants. Matthew Raper I (1653–1713) and his younger son, Moses (1679–1748), served as Directors of the Bank of England; Moses was President of Guy's Hospital

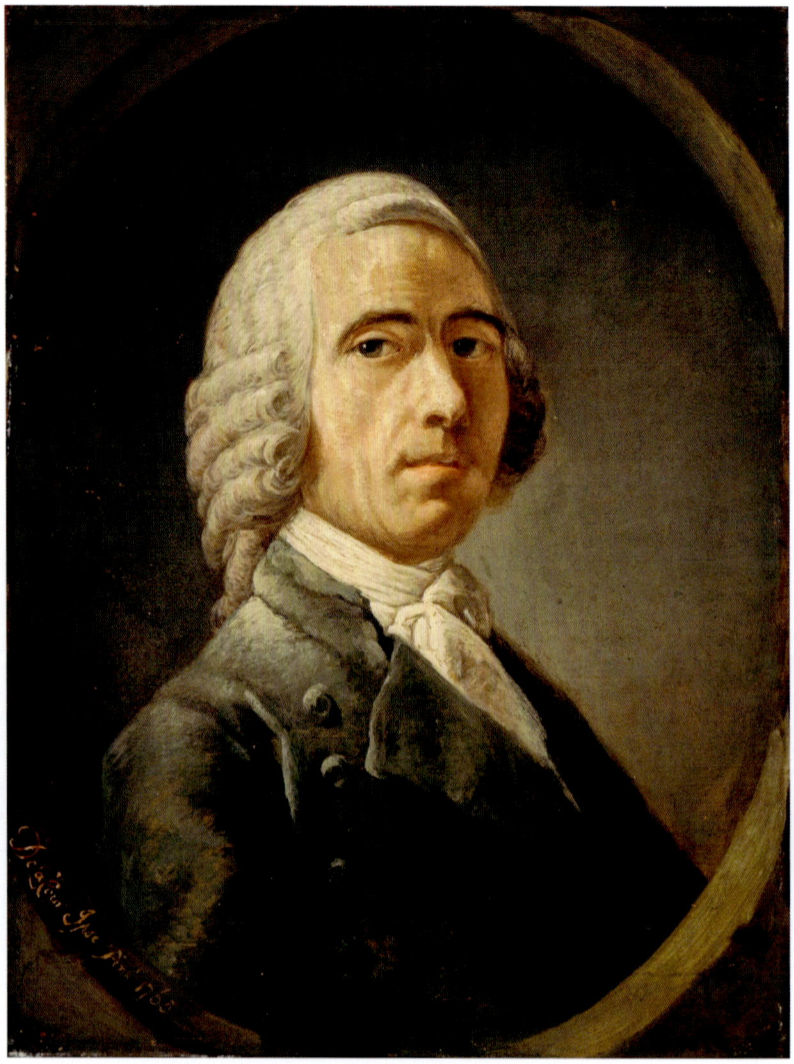

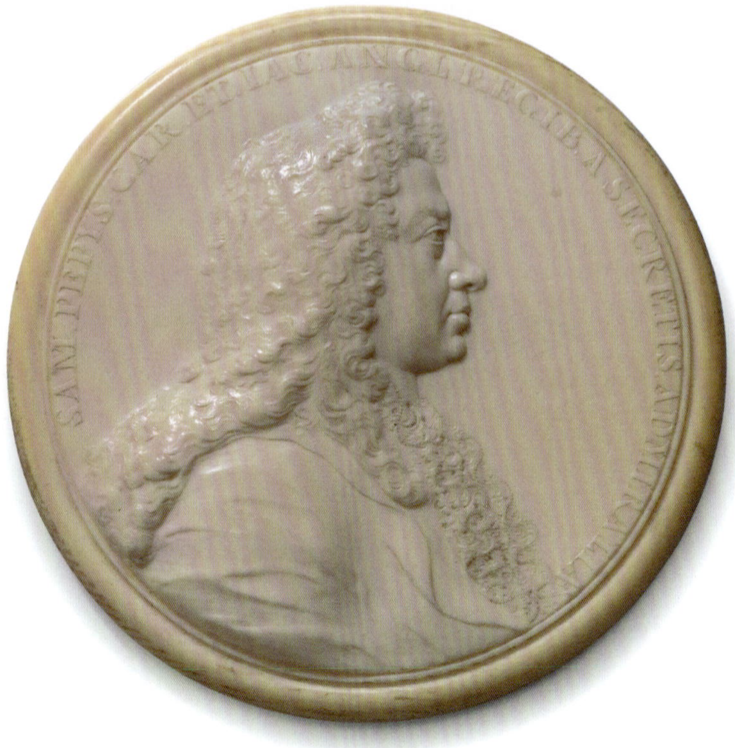

LEFT ABOVE

252 *Self-Portrait*

William De La Cour, Edinburgh, 1765
Oil on canvas, 37.50 × 28.60 cm
Scottish National Portrait Gallery, Edinburgh (PG 1844)

Designer, art teacher and decorative artist De La Cour moved from London to Dublin to Edinburgh. Only a few portraits by him are known although he advertised this skill in London in 1753.

LEFT BELOW

253 *Samuel Pepys as Secretary of the Admiralty*

Jean Cavalier, London, 1688
Ivory, diam. 13.5 cm
Worshipful Company of Clothworkers, London

The pale colour of Cavalier's ivory portraits had novelty value by comparison with bronze, which was more common and, being cast, replicable. The Latin 'medallion' inscription includes the artist's signature. Pepys was persuaded to sit to Cavalier by the artist Sir Godfrey Kneller, who recommended purchase of the preliminary wax as it was considerably cheaper than the finished ivory.

RIGHT

254 *Matthew Raper III (1704–1778) aged 15*

David Le Marchand, London, 1720
Ivory, 20.2 × 15.7 cm
Victoria and Albert Museum, London (A.20–1959)

This full-length portrait relief of the young Matthew Raper III shows this 'sound scholar and able mathematician' standing in a library, demonstrating a proposition in geometry with his left hand and holding a pen in his right. The Chinese-export tripod table, the bookcase with a book aslant, wooden floorboards, and billowing drapery, reflect contemporary French portraiture.

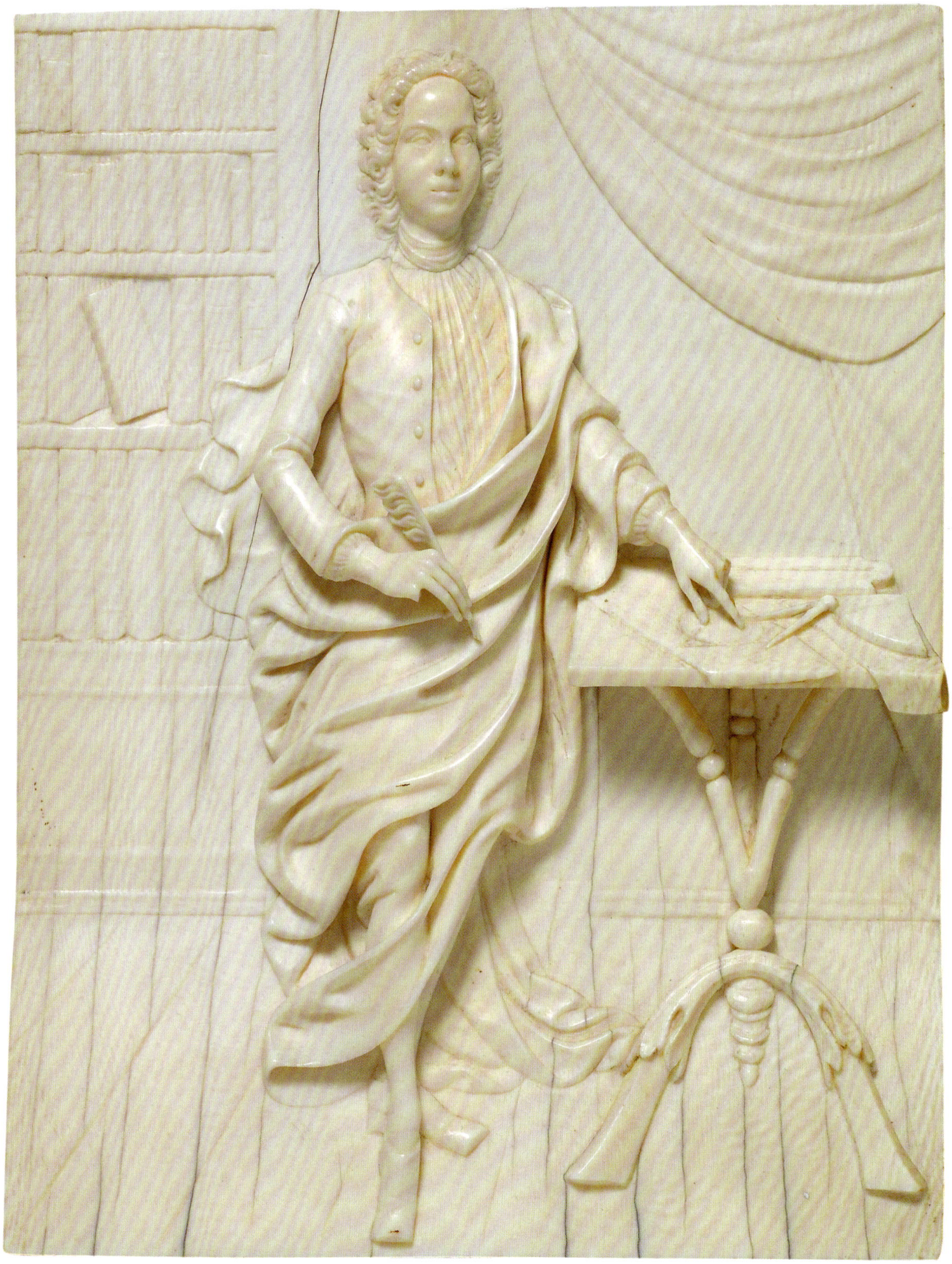

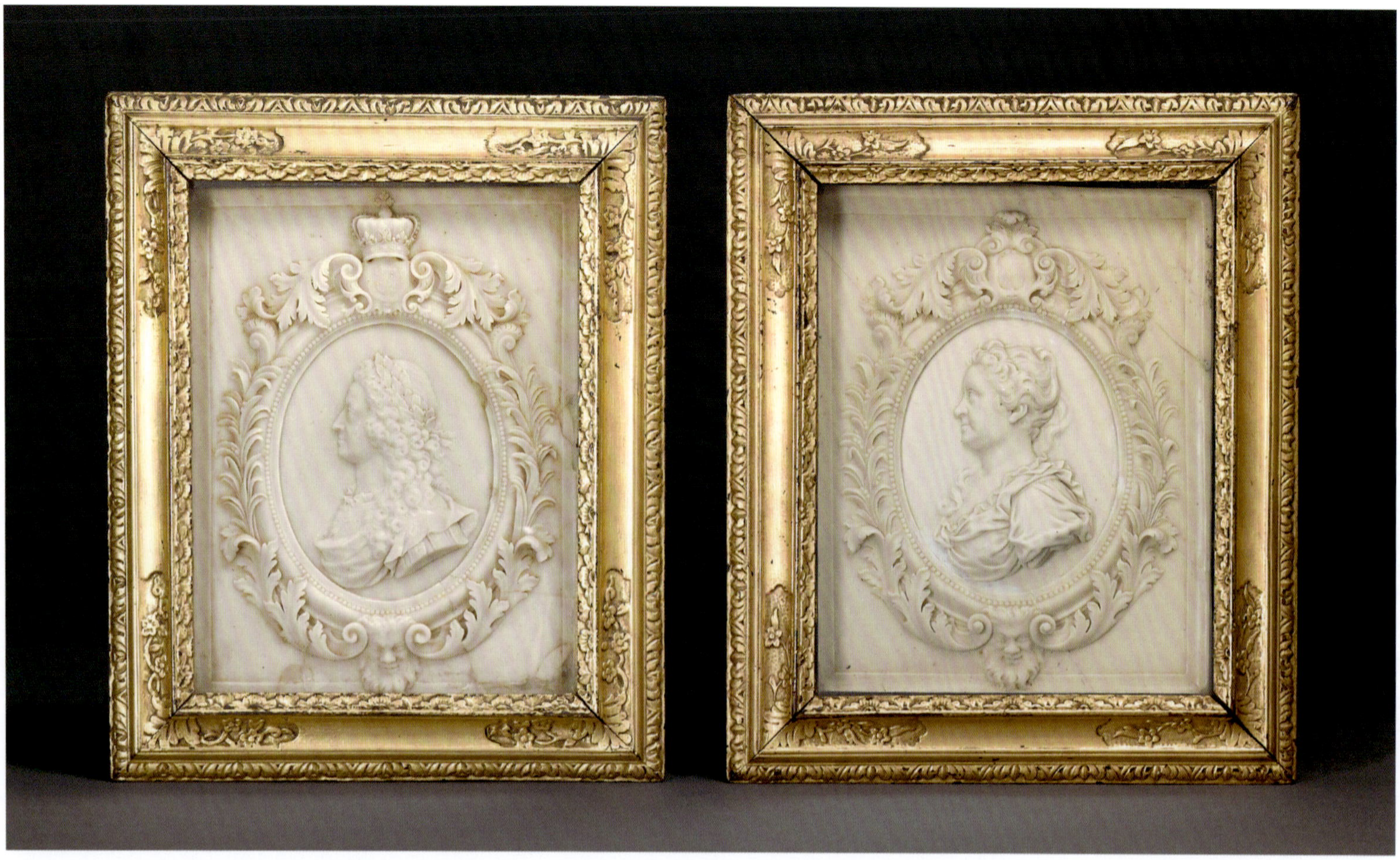

and a Trustee of Thomas Guy's residuary estate. Le Marchand's medallion portrait of Matthew Raper II (1675–1748) and full-length of his son Matthew Raper III (1704–1778; plate 254), a talented mathematician, are dated 1720.[98] The study of mathematics was promoted by Abraham de Moivre, a member of the Savoy church by 1687 and Fellow of the Royal Society from 1697. De Moivre's likeness, 'done from the life ... free and boldly cut' was captured by Jacques Antoine Dassier (1715–1780) in 1741 as one of a set of medals of distinguished contemporaries.[99]

Le Marchand's portraits of the Raper family circle include Thomas Guy (1645–1724), a bookseller who made his fortune by selling South Sea Company stock before the bubble burst in 1720. Encouraged by Dr Mead (both were trustees of St Thomas's Hospital), Guy invested his fortune in founding a hospital in his own name; this was nearing completion at the time of Guy's death and his subsequent endowment bequest of £238,000. Moses Raper, who paid for the operating theatre in 1739, probably commissioned Le Marchand's posthumous ivory of Guy, based on a wax by London-based Flemish artist François Le Pipre (1640–1698).[100] Joseph Highmore's portrait of Le Marchand painted around 1723 features the ivory bust of Isaac Newton created by Le Marchand in 1718; both bust and portrait were inherited by Matthew Raper III, who presented the bust to the British Museum in 1765.[101]

An undated half-length portrait of a woman signed 'g. le Marchand fecit', painted by David Le Marchand's father or brother, Guillaume (1673–1719), is further evidence of this artistic family in Dieppe,[102] a French Protestant stronghold until 1685. Having moved to Edinburgh after the 1694 siege of Dieppe,[103] in 1696 David Le Marchand was authorized to practise as 'designer and cutter in Ivory', provided that 'he take & instruct the children of burgeses of this City and other natives of this Kingdome in his sd. Arte'; there is no evidence that he did this successfully.[104] An ivory portrait of a French aristocrat, and a bust of Louis XIV dated 1700, suggest that Le Marchand was still receiving French commissions.[105] Did he return to France before he moved to London? Or was the portrait of Louis XIV commissioned by a Jacobite with Edinburgh connections who was based at James II's exiled court at St Germain?

255 *George II and Queen Caroline of Ansbach*
Matthew Gosset, London, 1741
Wax in contemporary frames, 27.30 × 22.86 × 4.45 cm
Carnegie Museum of Art, Pittsburgh, Gift of Herbert DuPuy (27.10.355, 27.10.356)

Matthew Gosset's portraits of George II and Queen Caroline set within wax borders of acanthus and palm leaves beneath the royal crown and coat of arms retain their original frames. The Gosset family settled first in St Helier, Jersey, before moving to London. Their recipe for wax imitating ivory was jealously guarded.

Le Marchand's Huguenot sitters in London included Michael Garnault (d.1746), jeweller, son of Pierre Garnault (d.1727), goldsmith from Chatellerault, Poitou. Michael, an associate of Jacques Louis Berchère (p.195), compiled an inventory of jewellery and silver for the 2nd Duke of Bedford in 1711.[106] His brother, Peter (d.1762), merchant jeweller from Saint-Séverin, Paris, was living in the parish of St Anne, Soho, by 1728.[107] Their nephew Aimé Garnault of Lincoln's Inn Fields, Treasurer of the New River Company, commissioned the personalized watch that uses the letters of his name instead of Roman numerals (plate 221).[108]

Like Jean Cavalier, David Le Marchand worked from life, modelling a first likeness in wax, using facial expressions to capture his sitter's vitality; this explains the 'waxy' appearance of hair and drapery in the ivory. Vertue noted 'a vast number of heads from ye life in basso relief'.[109] On 11 July 1722 William Stukeley wrote: 'I sat to Mr Marchand cutting my Profile in basso rilievo in Ivory'.[110] In June 1726 Stukeley recorded the deaths of the 'famous drawer and painter Monsr. Cheron' (Louis Chéron) and 'the famous cutter in ivory, Monsr. Marchand, who cut my profile'. Le Marchand died at 'La Providence', the French Hospital in St Luke's parish, Clerkenwell.

Jacques Constantin (*c.*1655–*c.*1733), a painter and ivory carver also from Dieppe, ended his days at the French Hospital in February 1732–3.[111]

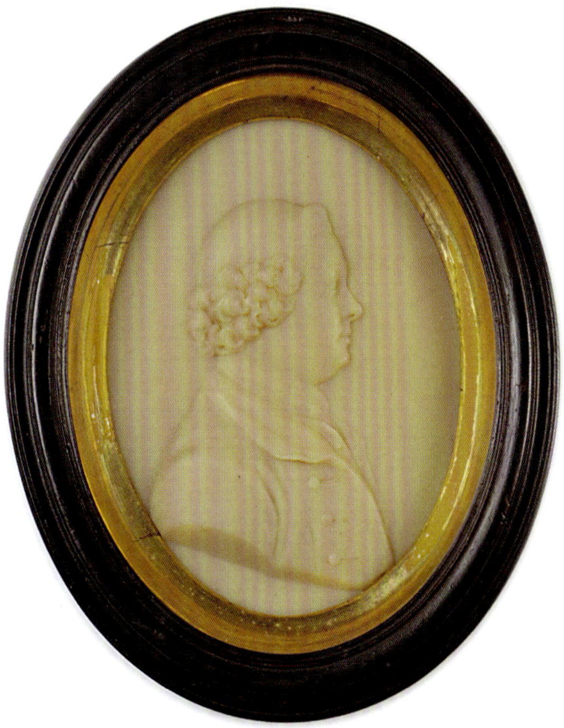

256 *Isaac Gosset, Junior*

Isaac Gosset, London, *c.*1780
Wax in ebonized frame with gold border, 14 × 11.5 cm
Victoria and Albert Museum, London (Schreiber Collection, 414:1369–1885)

Wax portraits by Isaac Gosset the elder in the Royal Library, Windsor include this one of his son, also Isaac (1745–1812). The sitter's son, Revd Isaac Gosset (1782–1855), was vicar of St George's Chapel, Windsor, and chaplain to George III. He was shown his grandfather's waxes whenever he dined at Windsor Castle.

He may be the 'Jacobus Constantin' who carved the allegorical ivory relief of James II, probably to mark the 1685 coronation,[112] and was possibly related to R.A. Constantyn, who signed a portrait of Frederick, Prince of Wales around 1715.[113]

Wax portraits

Preparatory wax models occasionally survive,[114] but wax was also an end product in itself. In 1685, for example, Antoine Benoist (1632–1717) modelled wax portraits of James II and his courtiers,[115] while François Le Pipre discovered wax later in life.[116] Although neither were Huguenots, they developed the market for wax figures, hitherto associated with the royal effigies for state funerals preserved in Westminster Abbey.[117]

Matthew Gosset, carver and wax modeller from Bayeux, Normandy, had settled in Soho by 1709. Perhaps inspired by Benoist's celebrated scenes of the French court shown in Paris, in 1730 Gosset created a wax tableau of the Court of France 'as big as the life, and clothed in habits, the Court … wore last year … given to him for that purpose'. Sir John Percival commented that 'Nothing can be finer done nor more like'.[118] Gosset also produced relief portraits of George II and Queen Caroline (plate 255).[119] He trained his nephew Isaac, whose modelling tools and profile portrait in crayons are still owned by his descendants.[120]

The Gossets modelled sets of wax portraits of classical and contemporary worthies for gentlemen's cabinets,[121] the miniature equivalent of library busts. Portraits of family members (plate 256), including royalty, were displayed together. Isaac Gosset produced a startling likeness in half an hour, and his sitters included George II, 'extreamly like' Queen Caroline, Frederick and Augusta, Prince and Princess of Wales, and George III as Prince of Wales.[122] He made nine wax portraits of relatives to mark the marriage in 1745 of Philip, 2nd Earl Stanhope (1714–1786), and Grizel Hamilton (*c.*1719–1811), including the bride's mother and grandparents, her aunt, brother, sister and husband's cousin, Philip Stanhope, 4th Earl of Chesterfield.[123]

In 1760 *The Daily Advertiser* announced that Mr Gosset's model 'in a composition that imitates ivory' of the late General Wolfe (1727–1759) was available to view in Berwick Street and to purchase by subscription from Mr Deards' toyshop in Dover Street, Piccadilly, and at Mr Russel's, facing Suffolk Street, Charing Cross.[124] The majority of Gosset's models were created as finished works but he also made models for temporary use, including a 'model of ye Queene in a Rich Frame for Mr Hoare the painter' to copy.[125] Gosset's wax model of Henry VIII was acquired by Horace Walpole as a substitute until he could acquire the original hone stone relief.[126]

Miniature portraits in horn, turtleshell and silver, and silhouettes

Jean Obrisset worked miniature portraits in horn, turtleshell and silver (plate 257). In 1676 his father owned an ivory shop in Dieppe before leaving for England.[127] Where there was no medallic prototype, Obrisset used painted sources: his portrait of James I is based on Hilliard's miniatures and his Prince George of Denmark on Kneller's portrait at Kensington Palace.[128] Obrisset catered for those loyal to the Stuart cause with profiles of the martyred Charles I, James II, James III, the Old Pretender and his sister Princess Louise, based on Roettier's medal of 1712. Most of his portrait plaques were set into tobacco box lids but some were intended for display.[129]

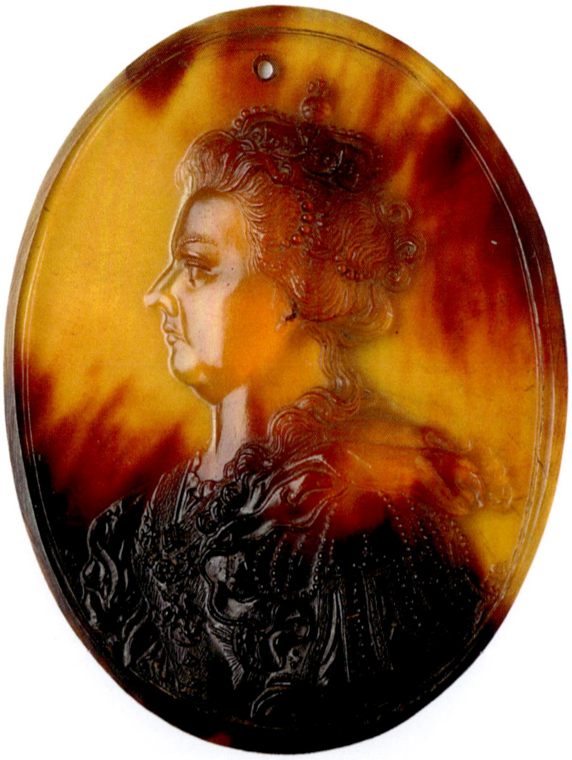

257 *Queen Anne*
Jean Obrisset, London, *c.*1705
Turtleshell pressed relief, ht 6.5 cm, th. 51 mm
Victoria and Albert Museum, London (A.17–1924)

Obrisset may have used Denis Papin's pressure cooker to soften organic materials before making impressions in pressed horn and turtleshell using metal dies. His profiles of monarchs and political leaders were taken from medals.

Francis Torond specialized in profile portraits in silhouette and created conversation pieces of families with servants, pets and furniture. Although Torond's surviving work is later in date, he began his career about 1760 as a drawing master in Bath. By 1776 he had established a London academy in Well Street, off Oxford Street, where he taught drawing, painting, etching and engraving. Later in Berwick Street, Soho, Torond offered drawing lessons to ladies and gentlemen three days a week; he also taught at boarding schools outside London.[130] Torond's silhouettes include *Mr and Mrs Smith of Hailsham and Aunt Everard* (1777; plate 258) and *Jane Parminter, Elizabeth Parminter, Mr*

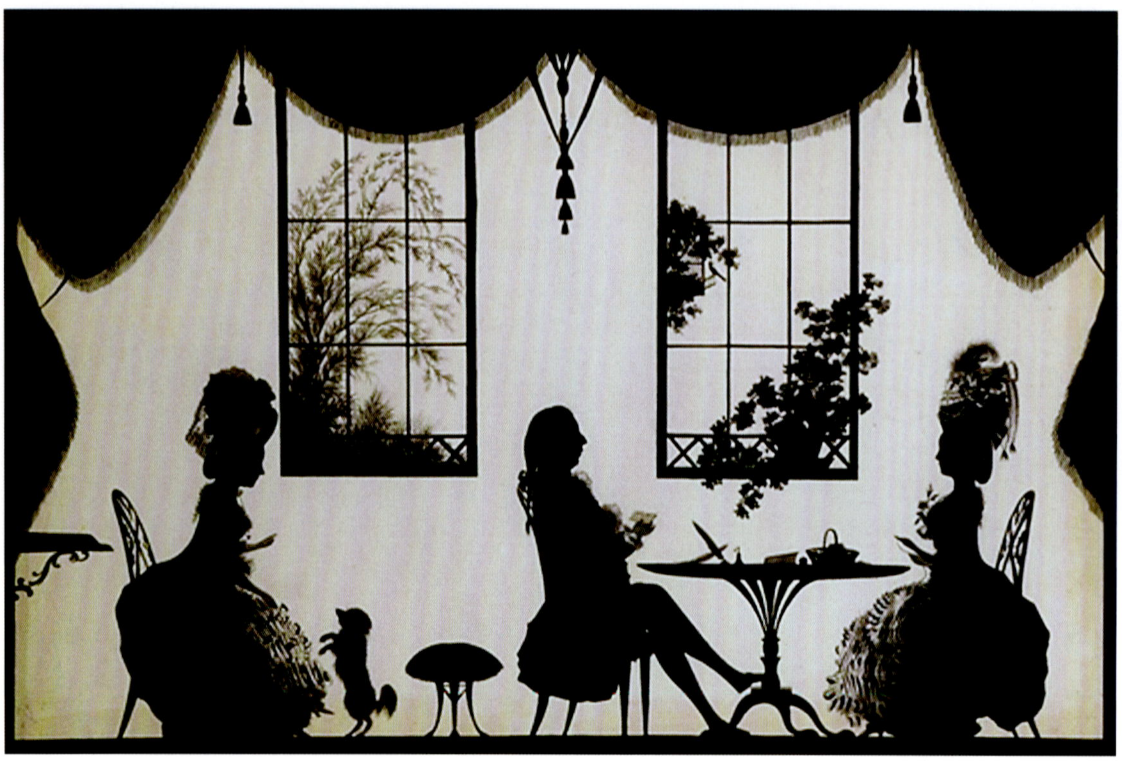

258 *Mr and Mrs Smith of Hailsham and Aunt Everard*
Francis Torond, London, *c.*1777
Silhouette in Indian ink, 40.64 × 61.60 cm
Victoria and Albert Museum, London (P.11–1956)

The silhouette was of French origin, named after Etienne de Silhouette (1709–1767), French Minister of Finance, whose taxation regime led to the phrase 'à la Silhouette' to describe anything that was cheap. This was applied to cut paper profiles, a popular and inexpensive form of portraiture.

Frend, John Parminter and Mrs Frend (1783) preserved at A La Ronde, near Exeter.[131]

Regional presence of Huguenot artists

Born and trained in Berlin under Antoine Pesne (1683–1757), Philip Mercier arrived in London in 1716 having toured France and Italy.[132] As principal painter to Frederick, Prince of Wales from 1729 until 1736, with an annual salary, Mercier produced royal portraits; he received one additional payment, of 10 guineas, in 1735, for a portrait on copper of Princess Mary.[133]

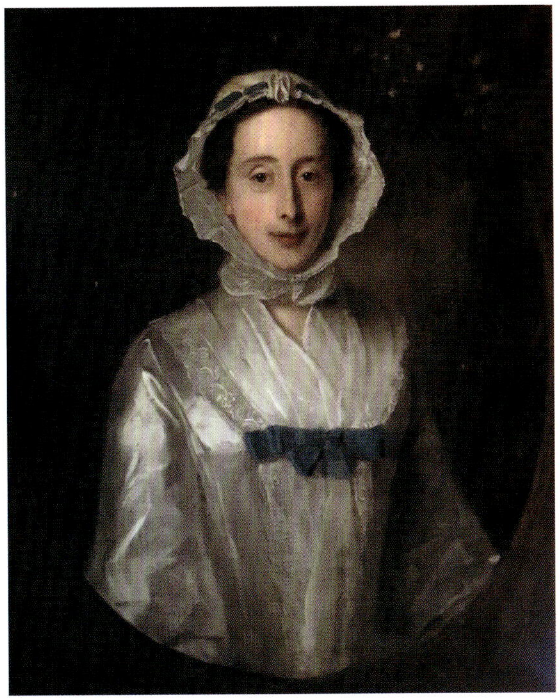

259 *Henriette Raboteau, Wife of William Le Fanu*
Philippe Mercier, Dublin, *c*.1747
Oil on canvas, 76 × 64 cm
Private collection

With the arrival of Amigoni and Van Loo, and increasing competition from British artists, Mercier was forced to seek patronage elsewhere. After some years in York, Mercier travelled to Ireland, where he painted this portrait of Henriette Raboteau. In contrast with Mercier's other female portraits, Mrs Le Fanu wears the dress of a Huguenot married woman. Henriette married in 1734. By 1747 she had produced six children who were baptized at the United French Churches of St Mary and St Patrick, Dublin. HSQS VII (Dublin, 1893).

In 1718 Jean Simon engraved a portrait of the Prince of Wales from a picture brought from Hanover by Philip Mercier (this anticipated the Prince's arrival by 12 years and, as he was absent heir to the throne, it attracted considerable interest).[134] In 1728 another print by Simon announced the Prince of Wales's arrival; later portraits, of 1730 and 1734, demonstrate the Prince's growing maturity. Self-portraits could be used to advertise talent: Simon engraved Mercier's self-portrait and Mercier etched his own family with his first wife.

Prints of military leaders, which were as popular as those of royalty, include one by John Faber the younger (*c*.1684–1756) after Philip Mercier's portrait of General Louis de Jean (d.1764).[135] Other Faber prints after Mercier reflect the demand for images of local personalities in London and Yorkshire, where the painter later settled.[136] These included John Hebden (1712–1765), a celebrated musician, and John Phillips (d.1742), who reached the great age of 116.[137]

In October 1736 Mercier was succeeded at court by John Ellys, who trained at the St Martin's Lane Academy under Louis Chéron and John Vanderbank.[138] With increasing competition in London from other foreign and British artists, Mercier sought patronage in York and Dublin and identified with the Huguenot community. In 1747 he painted Henriette Raboteau (1709–1789; plate 259), wife of William Le Fanu (1708–1797),[139] wearing the dress of a Huguenot married woman.[140] William Hogarth's *Noon* shows mature Huguenot women wearing similar bonnets, lined with black, emerging from Sunday morning service at the Soho French church (plate 20). Mercier's portrait of Marmaduke Fothergill (now destroyed) included Parmentier's portrait of Marmaduke's father in the background.[141] Although in bad condition, the inscription 'Sir Marmaduke Fothergill' his age, 64, and the year 1717 are just visible in Mercier's painting.

Although James Parmentier was mainly a decorative painter,[142] his occasional portraits include Charles II[143] and Charles de Saint Evremond (plate 260), a French political exile associated with London-based Huguenots, who left bequests for French refugees and poor Catholics on his death in 1703.[144] Like Philip Mercier, Parmentier settled in Yorkshire. On 12 March 1703 he painted Ralph Thoresby (1658–1725),[145] who married Anna, daughter and co-heir of Richard Sykes (1654?–1693) of Leeds Manor; Thoresby's collection included Lord Fairfax's coin cabinet and library. A letter from Parmentier to Thoresby dated July 1707 describes Mr Seignior's French school in Leeds, where Parmentier's son was educated.[146]

After Mercier's death in 1760, his widow Dorothy returned to London and set up as a printseller and stationer in Soho.[147] She exhibited four miniatures at the Society of Artists in 1761.[148]

Swiss portraitists: Du Pan and Morier

Barthélemy du Pan (1712–1763) and David Morier (1705–1770) both came to London from Switzerland in 1743. Du Pan was paid £80 'For two pictures of His Royal Highness' Frederick, Prince of Wales, in 1745[149] and his portrait of Dr Matthew Maty, 'drawn by the hand of friendship' (plate 261), was bequeathed by the sitter to the British Museum in 1776.[150] An engraving of William Stanhope, first Earl of Harrington is lettered 'Du Pan Pinxt. Dublin

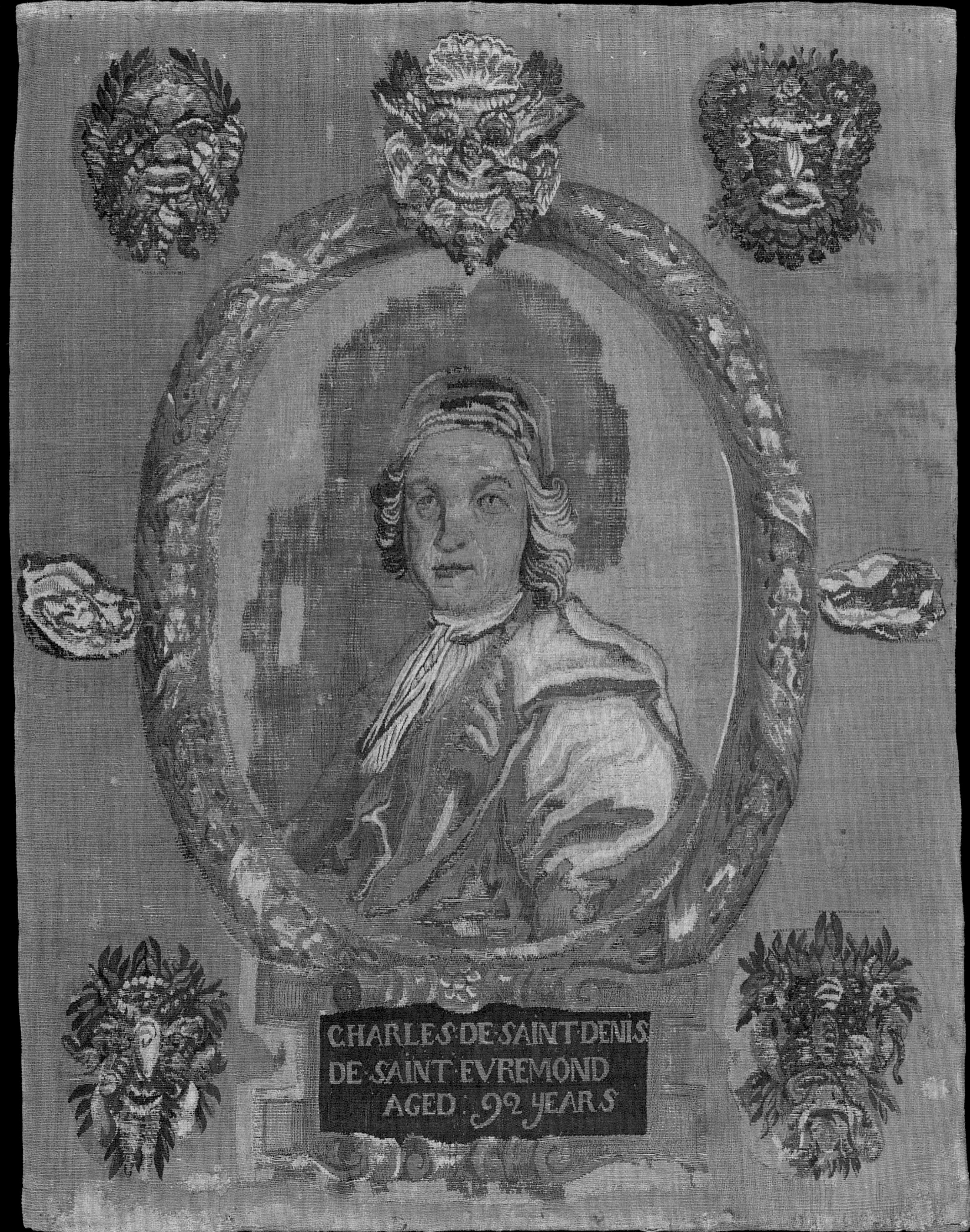
CHARLES·DE·SAINT·DENIS
DE·SAINT·EVREMOND
AGED: 92 YEARS

260 *Charles de Saint Evremond*

John Vanderbank the elder after Jacques Parmentier, London, *c.*1703
Tapestry woven in wool and silk, 76 × 59.5 cm
Victoria and Albert Museum, London (Given by Wendy Hefford, T.36–2008)

A political exile in London from the 1660s, Saint Evremond was closely linked with Huguenot writers and thinkers. Prints after portraits by Kneller and Parmentier painted in his 80s and 90s were circulated, but this unique version in tapestry was woven at Vanderbank's Soho workshop.

261 *Matthew Maty (1718–1776)*

Barthélemy Dupan, London, *c.*1750
Oil on canvas, 77.2 × 63.8 cm
British Museum, London (Painting.37)

Matthew Maty, of Huguenot parents, studied medicine in Leiden. In London from 1740, Maty contributed to the campaign to eradicate smallpox. He also developed a reputation as a journalist – in 1750 he founded the *Journal Britannique*, which publicized British books.

1750'. He returned to Geneva in 1751.

David Morier, whose equestrian portraits are set in the battlefield, secured royal patronage following an introduction to William, Duke of Cumberland, in 1743. In 1764 Morier presented his portrait of George III attended by Lord Ligonier to Queen Charlotte, who rewarded him with 'a Purse of one Hundred Guineas'.[151] Yet Morier died in poverty in Clerkenwell in 1770.

Portrait sculpture

Roubiliac's statue of Shakespeare (plate 109) for David Garrick's garden temple at his Thames-side Hampton villa followed copies of the historic Chandos portrait of Shakespeare made by Joshua Reynolds (1723–1792)[152] and Roubiliac himself.[153] Garrick posed for the terracotta model made in preparation for the full-sized marble.[154] Roubiliac's busts of worthies given to the newly established British Museum by Dr Matthew Maty, its Huguenot Librarian, included the 'ancients' Socrates, Plato, Demosthenes, Tully and Marcus Aurelius'; the 'moderns' Richard Bentley (1662–1742), Isaac Barrow, Charles I, Oliver Cromwell, John Milton, John Ray and Francis Willoughby; and contemporaries Philip

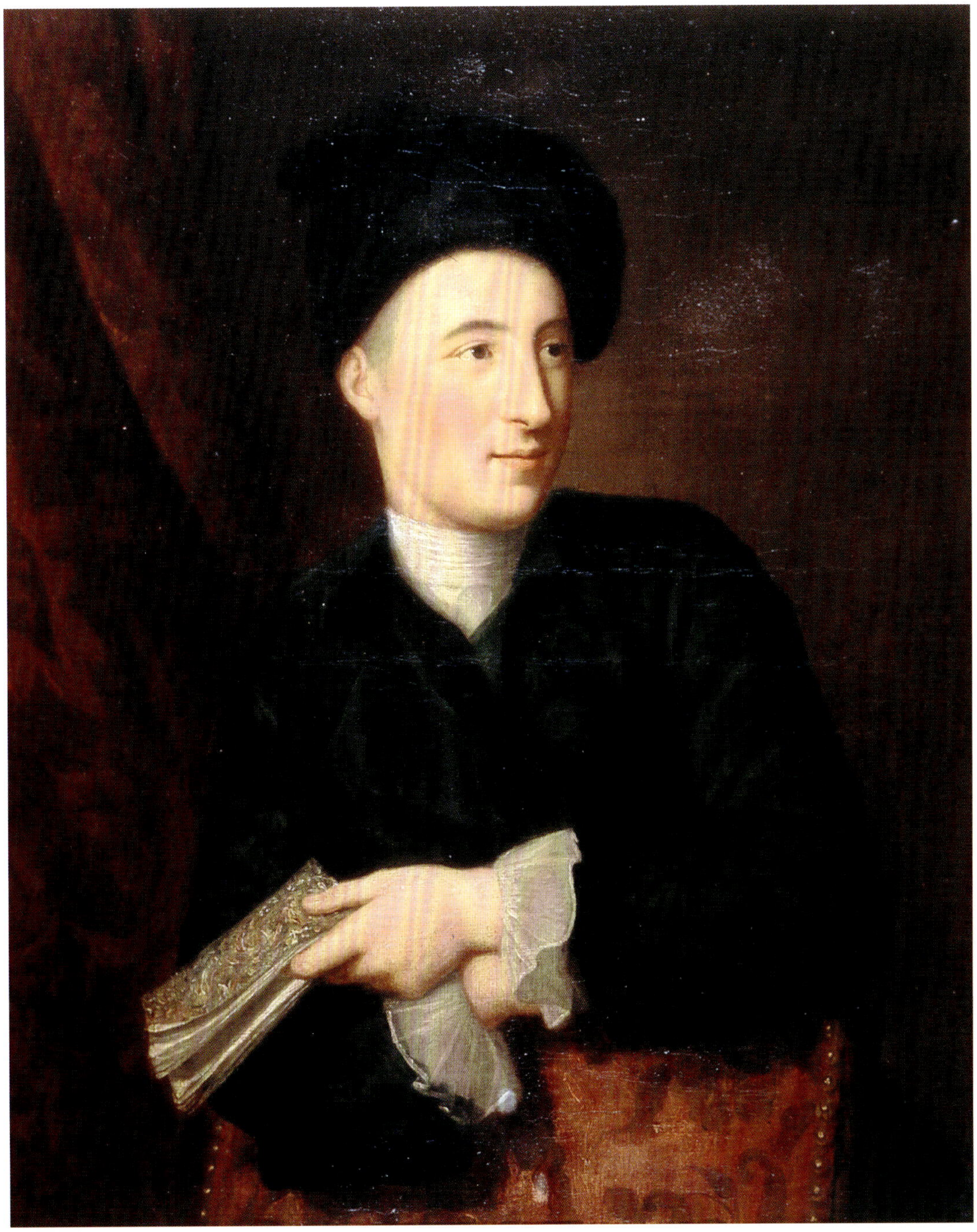

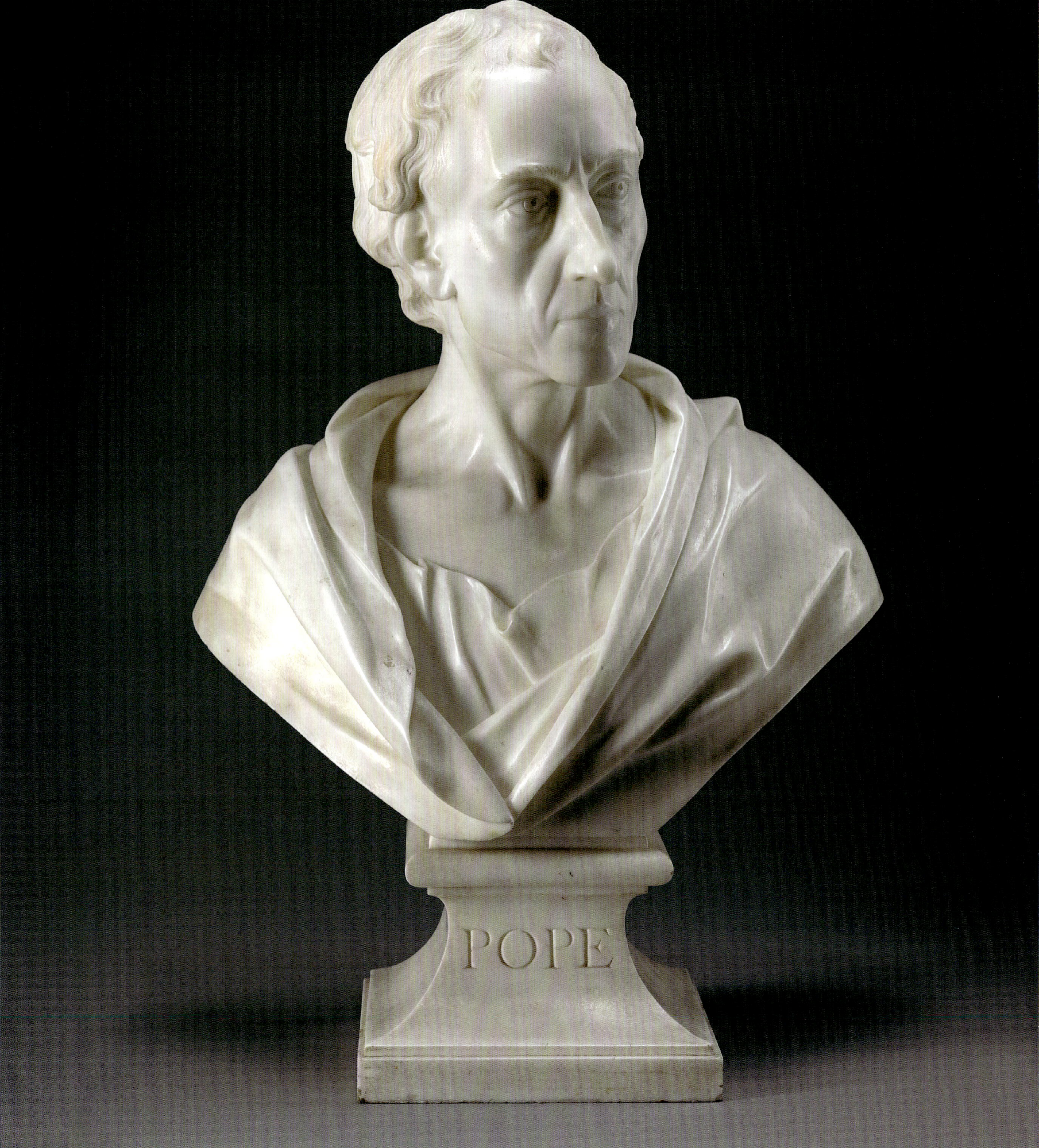
POPE

262 *Alexander Pope (1688–1744)*

Louis François Roubiliac, London, 1741
Marble, 62.9 × 43.2 × 22.9 cm
Yale Center for British Art (B1993.27)

Roubiliac has captured the likeness of the celebrated British Catholic poet, even implying that the sitter was 'much afflicted with headache', as shown by the contracted appearance of the skin between his eyebrows, as Sir Joshua Reynolds later remarked.

Stanhope, 4th Earl of Chesterfield, Martin Folkes, Dr Richard Mead and Alexander Pope.[155] The busts were displayed above the bookcases in the library, following the late sixteenth-century precedent of the private Westminster library of Sir Robert Cotton (1571–1631).[156] Those of Barrow, Bentley and Willoughby relate to marble versions in Trinity College, Cambridge,[157] and a plaster model of the Bentley bust was acquired for the Archbishop of Canterbury's library at Lambeth Palace, probably by Huguenot librarian Andrew Ducarel (1718–1780).[158] Marble and bronze versions of the busts of Alexander Pope (plate 262), Charles I, Chesterfield and Folkes are well known[159] but no marble versions of Socrates, Plato, Demosthenes, Tully, Marcus Aurelius, Cromwell or Milton are documented.[160] Terracotta busts of Thomas, 8th Earl of Pembroke, Sir Francis Bacon, Martin Folkes and Andrew Fountaine at Wilton[161] recur in Trinity College Library, Dublin, where they had been joined by Roubiliac's marble bust of Dean Swift by July 1749.

Roubiliac's medallion portraits of women occur on smaller monuments to Elizabeth Craven in St Mary's church, Scarborough; Elizabeth Smith in St Botolph's church, Aldgate, London; Ann Taylor in St Mary's, Newark; and Mary Clara des Champs de Marcilly, Marchioness of Villette, wife of Henry St John, Viscount Bolingbroke, in St Mary's church, Battersea (plate 263). In St Edmund's church, Warkton, Northamptonshire, at the centre of the 1749 monument to John, 2nd Duke of Montagu, the widowed Duchess stands below, watching a female figure representing Charity hang her husband's medallion portrait, with assistance from a small putto above. This may refer to the memorial medal cast by Jacques Antoine Dassier that was circulated to the Duke's friends after his death.[162]

Dassier's father, Jean (1676–1763), chief engraver to the Genevan Republic, visited England in 1728 and in 1731 produced a medallic series of British sovereigns from William I to George II. A subscription of 4 guineas secured the full set of 13; a single medal cost 7s 6d.[163] Jacques Antoine Dassier made portraits of six of the same sitters as Roubiliac: his medal of John, Duke of Argyll, was struck in 1743, two years before the Duke's Westminster Abbey monument was commissioned from Roubiliac; his medal of Philip Stanhope, 4th Earl of Chesterfield, of 1743 pre-dates Roubiliac's signed marble bust; and his medallic portraits of Martin Folkes (1740) and Sir Andrew Fountaine (1744) anticipate Roubiliac's busts of both sitters carved around 1748 for Lord Pembroke's Library at Wilton House near Salisbury. His medal of Martin Folkes, described by Vertue as 'very like', was 'done from the life, free and boldly cut'.[164] Dassier's medal of Alexander Pope of 1741 is contemporary with Roubiliac's first recorded bust of that poet.[165] Roubiliac is not known to have sculpted Frederick, Prince of Wales, of whom Dassier produced a parcel-gilt medallion portrait (plate 264).

Some marble socles (plinths for busts) were personalized by Roubiliac with the reverse of Dassier's medals of the sitter.[166] His larger medallion portraits in bronze and terracotta of British worthies Cromwell, Newton, Pope, Handel and Inigo Jones superseded Dassier's smaller versions.[167] In 1756 Dassier left England for St Petersburg and visited Copenhagen on the return journey in 1759, which encouraged the international demand for his work.

In 1748 George Aufrère (1715–1801), son of Israel Antoine Aufrère (plate 240), minister of the French Savoy church, commissioned Roubiliac to make a portrait bust of his wife, Arabella, two years after their marriage (plate 265). George was Lord Exeter's steward at Burghley and became Member of Parliament for Stamford, Lincolnshire, in 1765. He began to acquire his collection of paintings and sculpture, 'one of the finest…in this country', for their Chelsea home after 1759.[168]

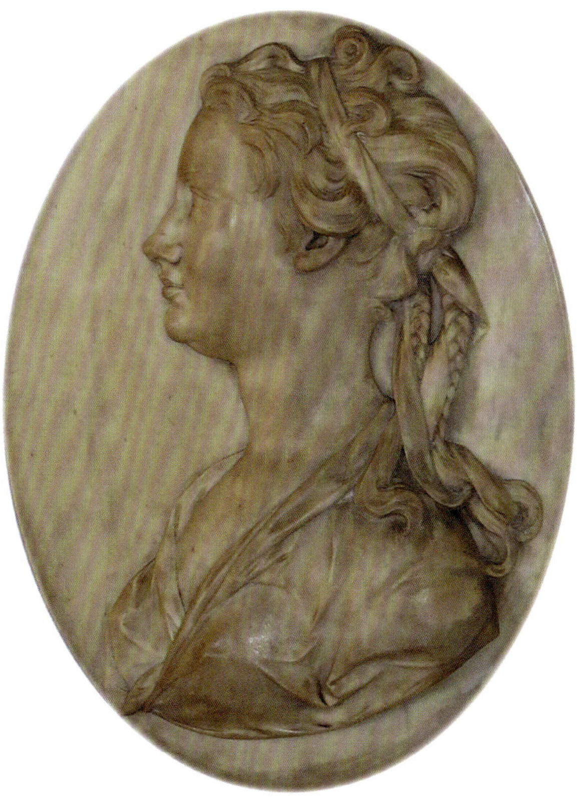

263 *Mary Clara des Champs de Marcilly, Marchioness of Villette*

Louis François Roubiliac, London, 1753
Marble
St Mary's church, Battersea

Medallion portraits are a feature of Roubiliac's smaller monuments to women. This delicate profile portrait of Mary Clara des Champs de Marcilly, Marchioness of Villette, Huguenot wife of Henry St John, Viscount Bolingbroke, graces their joint monument in St Mary's church, Battersea.

Roubiliac captures the authority of a great leader with intensely human character in the portrait bust of his most distinguished Huguenot patron John, Viscount Ligonier (plate 266) who also sat to Mercier. Ligonier fought as a volunteer in the Duke of Marlborough's army in 1702 and rose from Colonel in 1711, Brigadier General in 1735, Major General in 1739, Lieutenant General in 1742/3 and General in 1746, to Field Marshal in 1757.[169]

Reproductions

Huguenot artists and sculptors channelled their technical mastery of different media into portraiture for which there was a constant demand. It is a tribute to the enduring qualities of Huguenot portraiture that originals were used as models for later reproduction. Portraits were copied as miniatures to personalize snuffboxes from the eighteenth century onwards.[170] Casts, taken from medallion portraits or busts by Dassier, Gosset, Le Marchand and Roubiliac were reproduced to meet popular demand. Liotard's portrait of George III as Prince of Wales, engraved by Simon François Ravenet, served as a transfer print to decorate enamel boxes and plaques at the short-lived Battersea manufactory in 1753–6.[171]

During the early 1750s three 'distinguished original' busts of George II, George III as Prince of Wales and William Augustus, Duke of Cumberland, were produced in porcelain.[172] The porcelain bust of George II compares with Roubiliac's bust of the King at Windsor.[173] Did Roubiliac create this model on his own initiative, and was it subsequently used by the Chelsea Porcelain manufactory? George II in armour

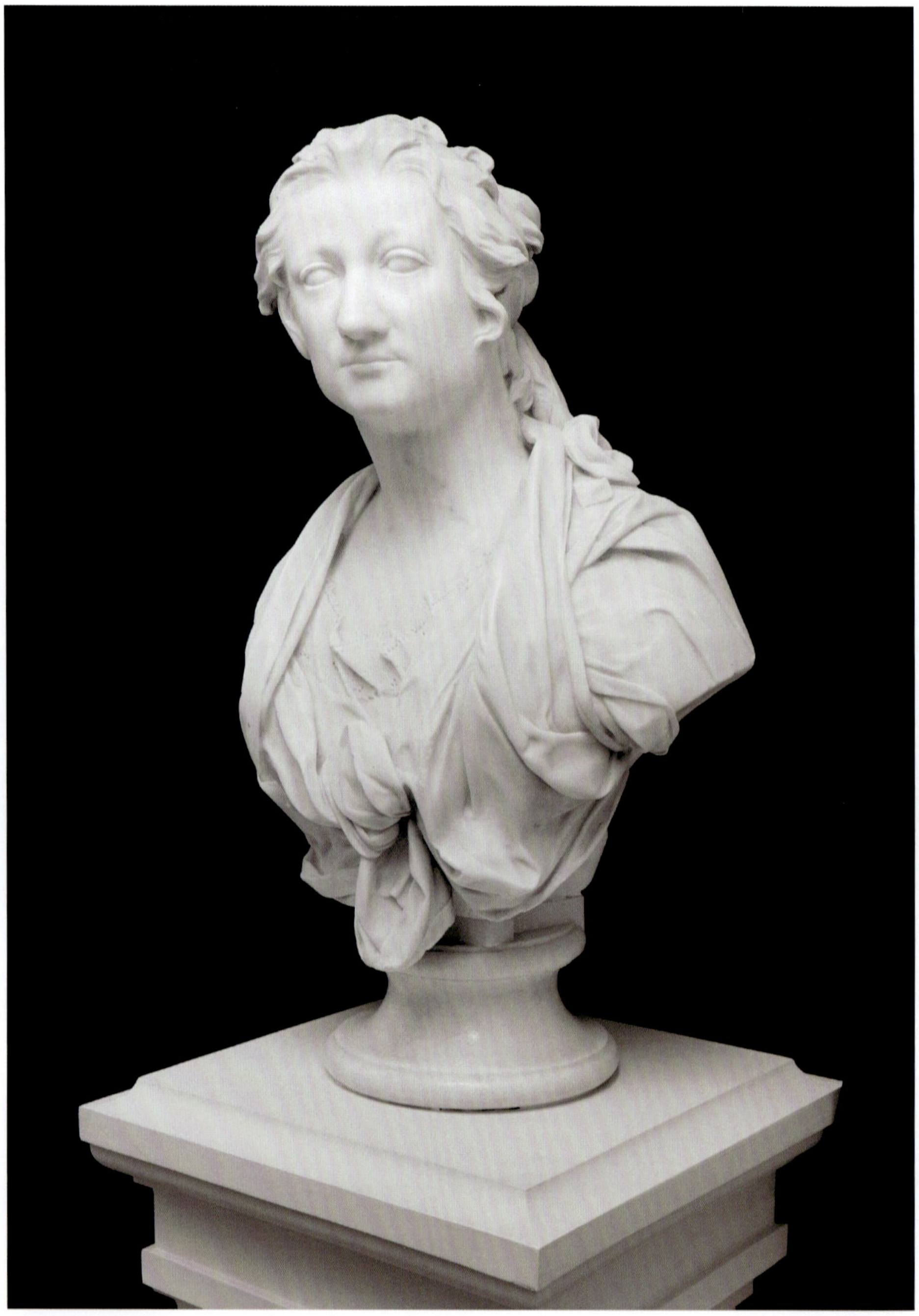

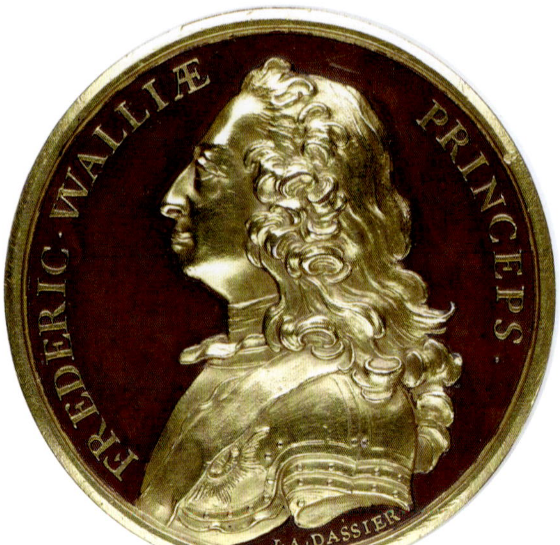

LEFT

264 *Frederick, Prince of Wales*

Jacques Antoine Dassier, London, *c.*1750
Gilt bronze, diam. 5.39 cm
Victoria and Albert Museum, London (310–1880)

Dassier came to London from Geneva in 1740 and published proposals for making a set of medals of distinguished living Englishmen. His contemporary George Vertue commented that the likeness was 'done from the life...free and boldly cut'.

ABOVE

265 *Arabella Aufrère*

Louis François Roubiliac, London, 1748
Marble, ht 69 cm
The Earl of Yarborough

George Aufrère, Lord Exeter's steward at Burghley House, Stamford, was the younger son of Israel Antoine Aufrère. He commissioned this bust of his wife, Arabella, Lady Exeter's niece, two years after their marriage. The Aufrères' important collection of paintings and sculpture, which included Bernini's *Neptune and Trident*, now in the Victoria and Albert Museum, was inherited by their daughter Sophia, who married the 1st Earl of Yarborough.

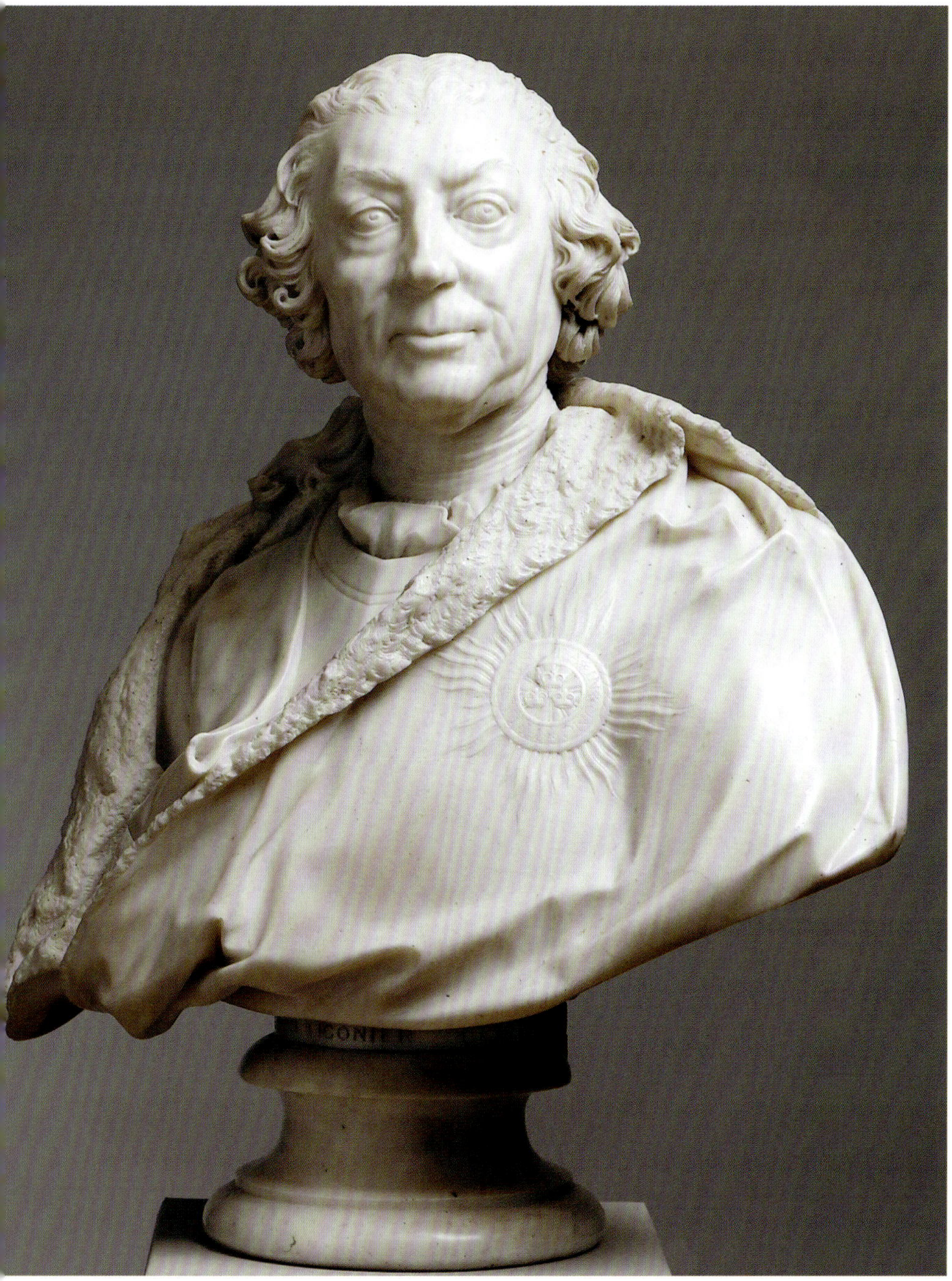

266 *1st Earl Ligonier*

Louis François Roubiliac, London, *c.*1761
Marble, 67 × 71 × 39 cm
Royal Collection Trust (RCIN 35256)

Roubiliac's most distinguished Huguenot sitter, John, Earl Ligonier, fled from Castres to Dublin under an assumed name at the age of 17 and fought as a volunteer in the Duke of Marlborough's army in 1702. He rose through the ranks to become Field Marshal in 1757, the most important military leader in British history between the Duke of Marlborough and the Duke Wellington. Roubiliac's bust captures the authority of a great leader with his intense personality, reflecting the determination with which Ligonier faced the many challenges during his long and distinguished career.

with Garter star and flamboyant drapery was ideal for reproduction as a public image. Roubiliac's main competitor, John Michael Rysbrack, made busts of George II and William Augustus, Duke of Cumberland, but neither sculptor created a bust of George III as Prince of Wales. Casts may have been supplied by one of London's plaster shops or by John Cheere, whose casts of Roubiliac's busts of Newton and Bacon were later reproduced in black basalt at Etruria by Josiah Wedgwood.[174]

Wedgwood wrote to Thomas Bentley (1731–1780) in July 1776: 'People will give more for their own heads or heads in fashion than for any subject and buy abundantly more of them. We should select proper heads for the different European markets and this plan will certainly increase our markets'.[175] Wedgwood's medallion portraits copied originals by Matthew Gosset and his nephew Isaac. Royal subjects included George I (after Matthew Gosset); George II and his children, Frederick, Prince of Wales and his wife, Augusta; his sister Anne, Princess of Orange; and George III and Queen Charlotte after Isaac Gosset. Medallions by Wedgwood with portraits of John Churchill, 1st Duke of Marlborough; John, 2nd Duke of Montagu; Philip, 4th Earl of Chesterfield; Abraham de Moivre; Martin Folkes; and Sir Andrew Fountaine were based on medals by Jacques Antoine Dassier. Wedgwood used an ivory by David Le Marchand for his medallion portrait of Anne Dacier (1654–1720), wife of Huguenot scholar André Dacier (1651–1722), whose ivory medallion portrait by Le Marchand is in the Royal Collection. Anne Dacier abjured her Protestant faith on the Revocation of the Edict of Nantes, remaining in France, where Le Marchand's ivory portrait (now in the British Museum) was probably carved. Wedgwood's medallion portraits of Sir Isaac Newton and Mr and Mrs Matthew Raper were also based on ivories by Le Marchand,[176] while his relief portrait of the Hon. Robert Boyle (1627–1691) was based on a medal cast from the ivory by Jean Cavalier.[177]

Acknowledgements

This book has been over forty years in the making. I am indebted to two generations of twentieth- and twenty-first-century Huguenot descendants, collectors, patrons and scholars; the previous generation are warmly remembered for their encouragement, enthusiasm and generosity in sharing their expertise and providing access to their archives and collections. Huguenot stories of courage and resilience are a source of inspiration in the challenges presented by the global issues we all face.

My first debt of gratitude is to my former supervisor, Professor David Bindman, whose brilliant example and careful coaching nurtured my academic potential. The officers of the Huguenot Society of London, then and now, Irene Scouloudi, Charles Marmoy, Randolph Vigne, Lucy Gwynn and Elizabeth Randall; Dinah Winch, the present and former directors of the Huguenot Museum, and Charlie de Wet, founder of the Huguenots of Spitalfields, have all provided advice and contacts. I am grateful to the officers of the French Church of London, Bénédicte Fougier and Denis Faure, who have recently provided a direct link to the Paris-based Société de l'Histoire du Protestantisme Français. Thanks are due to fellow directors and officers at La Providence, the French Hospital, Emma, Lady Monson, Jane Darwin, Peter Duval, Leslie du Cane, Andrew Gillett, Jonathan Ouvry; the late Stephen de Crespigny, Paul Minet and Peter Minet, the former Governor, Jacob, Earl of Radnor and the present Governor, the Right Reverend The Lord Chartres. Professor Tim Wilson at the Ashmolean Museum, Oxford, with whom I collaborated over the acquisition of Huguenot silver collected by Sir Ernest Cassel in 2004, has been a mentor since the early 1980s.

At the Museum of London from 1981, Rosemary Weinstein entrusted me with the lion's share of the research for the exhibition *The Quiet Conquest: The Huguenots 1685–1985*, which attracted 90,000 visitors. David Challis and Alec Jolly provided the opportunity to publish a full exhibition catalogue, with contributions from expert colleagues, a valuable springboard for the present endeavour. That exhibition led to the published celebration in 1992 of *Boughton House, The English Versailles*, for which Johnny, Duke of Buccleuch, and Duchess Jane generously provided access. Richard and Bizza, the present Duke and Duchess of Buccleuch and their team at Boughton, Paul Boucher, Gareth Fitzpatrick, Charles Lister, Scott Macdonald, Crispin Powell and Kathryn Price have actioned that generosity. Collaborating on the Boughton project with colleagues at the V&A, the National Trust, the Royal Armouries and the Wallace Collection equipped me to serve as V&A curator in Furniture and Woodwork from 1990 to 2002 and subsequently as Deputy Keeper in the newly formed department of Sculpture, Metalwork, Ceramics and Glass. My V&A colleagues over the last 30 years have provided constant encouragement for my special interest in Huguenot artists, designers and craftsmen. I am particularly grateful to Paul Williamson and Richard Edgcumbe for inspiring by example as outstanding scholars and for tolerating my focus and enabling my continued research.

In 2006–7, thanks to Paul and Elissa Cahn and Lewis Smith, the exhibition of silver from the Cahn Family Foundation and the related conference on Huguenot Silver at the V&A provided an opportunity for international exchange. Since 2008 I have worked with the Rosalinde and Arthur Gilbert Collection, rich in Huguenot silver, gold boxes and portrait miniatures. Successive Gilbert Curators Heike Zech, now Deputy Director at the Germanisches Nationalmuseum, Nuremberg, Alice Minter, whose own research on Huguenot goldsmiths from Rouen, and Jessica Eddie have both informed my studies and encouraged exchange of ideas. I am grateful for James Robinson's support and the encouragement of all the Trustees of the Gilbert Trust and the Los Angeles-based Gilbert Public Arts Foundation.

Particular thanks are due to Malcolm Baker, Faya Causey, Judith Crouch, Anthony du Boulay, Richard Edgcumbe, Robin Gwynn, Lydia Hamlett, Kirstin Kennedy, John Mallet, Alice Minter, David Mitchell, Morgan Ng, David Oakey, Sheila O'Connell, Elizabeth Randall, Alicia Robinson, Jacob Simon, Adriana Turpin and Dinah Winch for reading sections of my text and for valuable suggestions; any remaining errors are my own. I would also like to thank past and present colleagues and friends John Adamson, Brian Allen, Charles Avery, Gordon Balderston, Bruce Bailey, Elaine Barr, Geoffrey Beard, David Beasley, Jonathan Betts, Eleni Bide, Howard Blackmore, Vanessa Brett, Clare Browne, Marian Campbell, Frances Carey, Isabelle Cartier Stone, Jeremy and Vivien Cassel, Martin Chapman, Julia Clarke, John Cornforth, Peter de Clercq, Giles de la Mare, Peter Day, Rachel Delphia, Marie Draper, Hazel Forsyth, Celina Fox, Terry Friedman, Richard Garnier, Charlotte Gere, Christopher Gilbert, Mark Girouard, Philippa Glanville, Arthur Grimwade, Susanne Groom, Nicholas Goodison, John Hardy, Susan Hare, Jonathan Harris, Wendy

Hefford, Olivia Horsfall-Turner, Ralph Hyde, Nigel Israel, Gervase Jackson-Stops, Mark Jones, Charlotte Johnson, Catrin Jones, John Kerslake, Alastair Laing, Sarah Lawrence, Lucy Lead, Reino Leifkes, James Lomax, John Mallet, Errol Manners, Philip Mansel, Rosalind Marshall, Christopher Maxwell, James Miller, Lucy Morton, Patrick Noon, Robert Raines, Rosemary Ransome-Wallis, Natalie Rothstein, James Rothwell, Charles Saumarez-Smith, Rosalind Savill, Tim Schroder, Jacques Schuhmacher, Roger Smith, Michael Snodin, Jay Stiefel, Charles Stopford Sackville, Hugh Tait, Christian Theuerkauff, Dora Thornton, Peter Thornton, Sophia Tobin, Charles Truman, Holly Trusted, Will Vaughan, Harry Williams-Bulkeley and Hilary Young. Sandra Robinson assisted me with genealogical advice and research. Dorothy North's compilation of Henry Wagner's notes on Huguenot Wills published in 2007 has transformed the resources offered by the Huguenot Society, as these individual summaries shed new light on the lives of many of the artists discussed in this book.

Further afield, I would like to thank fellow Trustees at Huguenot Heritage and officers of the New York-based Huguenot Society of America; Marie Etta Schneider at Historic Huguenot Street, New Paltz; and the Huguenot Society of South Carolina, in particular Renée Marshall and Dan Ravenel, for their encouragement and hospitality. For the opportunity to teach for the Masters' Program at the Cooper Hewitt Museum, I would like to thank Sarah Lawrence and the students who attended my seminars on the Huguenot artistic contribution. I am grateful to lecture audiences in Australia and Canada; in France, in Paris and Rouen; in Cape Town, South Africa and across the United States who have contributed to my understanding of this fascinatingly wide subject. I would also like to thank Charissa Bremer-David at the Getty Museum, Alexa Sekyra and Marcia Reed at the Getty Research Institute, Matthew Robb at the Fowler Museum, UCLA, Rosie Mills at the Los Angeles County Museum of Art, Catherine Hess at the Huntington Art Gallery, San Marino, Mary Levkoff at Hearst Castle, Mya Chau, my Research Assistant while I was at the Getty, and Lady Marjorie Gilbert for her kind hospitality in Los Angeles. Back in Europe, on the threshold of Brexit, thanks are due to the Reverend Dr Alison Green, Chaplain at the University of Chichester, who suggested the book's title, *Europe Divided*.

The opportunity to work with Rod Kelly and Gareth Harris at their silversmiths' benches in 2019 and 2020 and to register my own mark at Goldsmiths' Hall, inspired by my Huguenot goldsmith ancestors Edward and Magdalen Feline, has helped to develop my understanding of the language and skills required and of the different concept of time when co-ordinating head and hands to work in three dimensions.

I benefited from grants and fellowships as a postgraduate student from the Central Research Fund, University of London and the Sir John Cass Foundation. In 1989 a grant from the British Academy funded my research in the Boughton House Archives. In 2002 a Getty Research Grant covered the costs of further research into seventeenth – and eighteenth-century giltwood furniture, a key area of Huguenot contribution. The Friends of the V&A funded my attendance of the Attingham Summer School in 2001 and Royal Collections Studies in 2006. My V&A scholarship at the Yale Center for British Art in 2014 provided another opportunity to familiarize myself with their relevant holdings. I am grateful to Antonia Böstrom for recommending me and to Tristram Hunt for nominating me for the Getty Rothschild Fellowship in 2019, which provided the resources, collegiate company, advice and space at the Getty Research Institute and Waddesdon Manor to focus on an intensive year of writing, and this volume is the result. At Waddesdon I received a warm welcome and advice from Pippa Shirley, Diane Bellis, Mia Jackson, Rachel Jacobs and Cristina Alfonsin. I would also like to thank the staff of the British Library, Getty Research Library, National Art Library, and above all at the London Library whose gracious provision over the last pandemic year has enabled me to check those vital references and without whose extraordinary service, when all other reference libraries were closed, publication would have been delayed.

Finally my thanks are to my patient editor at the V&A, Coralie Hepburn, as well as to copyeditor Johanna Stephenson, picture researcher Axelle Russo-Heath, designer Robert Dalrymple, proof reader Bev Zimmern, indexer Nic Nicholas and production manager Emma Woodiwiss.

This book is dedicated to my husband, David, who has encouraged me from the outset, and to our daughters, Iona, Frankie and Sienna, our son-in-law Michael and our Kowalski grandsons, Henry, Ollie and Joseph.

Timeline

1536
John Calvin settles in Geneva

1545
First Calvinist community established in France at Meaux

1550
French Church of London is founded in Threadneedle Street

1555
Missionaries leave Geneva for France

1560
The word *Huguenot* first used in France to describe a French Protestant

1562
First French War of Religion

1572
Massacre of St Bartholomew in Paris and beyond

1590
Death of Bernard Palissy in the Bastille, France

1598
Edict of Nantes signed by Henri IV

1606
Protestant temple constructed at Charenton outside Paris

1628
Fall of La Rochelle as Huguenot stronghold

1660
Restoration of the monarchy in England

1681
Dragonnades billeted on French Protestant homes

1681
Charles II welcomes Huguenot refugees

1681
City of Amsterdam welcomes French Protestants

1682
Pierre Harache admitted to the London Goldsmiths' Company

1685
Revocation of the Edict of Nantes

1685
Edict of Potsdam welcomes Huguenots to Brandenburg

1687
Huguenots arrive at Cape Town, South Africa

1687
James II endorses Declaration of Indulgence for Non-Conformists

1688
French Church founded in New York City

1689
William III invades England

1690
Battle of the Boyne: Protestant victory in Ireland

1693
Louis Chéron, artist joins the French Church of the Savoy

1693
Jean Tijou publishes *A New Booke of Drawings*

1694
Foundation of the Bank of England

1694
Daniel Marot marries Catherine Gole in London

1696
David Le Marchant, ivory carver, established in Edinburgh

1696
Pierre Rieusset delivers a billiard table to Boughton House, Northamptonshire

1696
William III grants the Irish estate of Portarlington to the Marquis of Ruvigny

1697
Louis Crommelin establishes the manufacture of linen in Northern Ireland

1698
Renewed persecution of the Protestants in France

1702
War of Spanish Succession, England at war with France

1703
Paul de Lamerie is apprenticed to Pierre Platel, goldsmith, in Pall Mall, London

1709
British Act for Naturalizing Foreign Protestants

1711
London goldsmiths sign a petition against admitting foreign craftsmen to their trade

1713
Peace of Utrecht

1715
Renewed persecution of the Protestants in France

1718
La Providence, French Protestant Hospital, founded in London

1720
Chéron co-founds the St Martin's Lane Art Academy, London

1720
South Sea Bubble bursts

1720
Paul Crespin registers his maker's mark at Goldsmiths' Hall

1724
Renewed persecution of the Protestants in France

1730
Louis François Roubiliac, sculptor, settles in London

1731
James Leman, silk merchant and designer elected Renter Bailiff, Weavers' Company

1738
Roubiliac's statue of Handel unveiled in London's Vauxhall Gardens

1741
David Garrick, actor, makes his London debut as Shakespeare's Richard III

1745
Anti-Gallican Society founded in London

1745
Nicholas Sprimont establishes the Chelsea Porcelain Manufactory in London

1746
Renewed persecution of the Protestants in France

1746
John Rocque publishes a Survey of London and Environs

1747
Westminster French Protestant School founded

1750
Charles de Labelye's Westminster Bridge opens

1752
Charles Cabrier, clockmaker, presents a long-case clock to the French Hospital

1756
Seven Years' War between Britain and France commences

1762
Execution of Jean Calas; the Protestant cause in France is taken up by Voltaire

1762
Foundation of the Swiss church of London

1776
American War of Independence

1778
Paul Revere's Midnight Ride

1787
Edict of Toleration signed by Louis XVI

1845
Death of last French speaking chaplain, the French Hospital

1852
Foundation of French Protestant Historical Society, Paris

1883
Foundation of Huguenot Society of America in New York City

1885
Foundation of Huguenot Society of London

1885
Foundation of the Huguenot Society of South Carolina based in Charleston

1894
Huguenot Patriotic, Historical, and Monumental Society founded in New Paltz, New York State, now Historic Huguenot Street, the oldest inhabited town street in USA

1935
Opening of Huguenot Museum, Berlin

1938
Huguenot Monument, Franschhoek commemorates 250 anniversary of the arrival of Huguenots at the Cape

1967
Huguenot Memorial Museum opened in Franschhoek

1985
Commemoration in Britain and France of Huguenot Heritage

2003
Huguenot Society of Australia founded in Sydney

2015
Opening of Huguenot Museum, Rochester, Kent

2022
450th anniversary of Massacre of St Bartholomew, France

Notes & References

Introduction *pages 9–11*

1 Gray 1983. My thanks to Kathy Chater for this reference.
2 Kroll 1970, p.74.

1 The Huguenot Diaspora *pages 15–29*

1 The prints satirizing leading persecutors of the Huguenots in France were published by Jacob Gole, Amsterdam, in 1691; impressions are in the British Museum and the Rijksmuseum.
2 Gwynn 2018, p.4. The *Oxford English Dictionary* gives the origin of the 'Refugee' as 'Late 17th century: from French *réfugié* 'gone in search of refuge', past participle of *(se) réfugier*, from *refuge*'.
3 Wendel 1980, p.38.
4 Ibid., 'Successive editions of the Institutes', pp.111–49.
5 Wallace 1988, pp.89–90.
6 Landes 1983, p.444 n.4.
7 McNeill 1954, pp.190–6.
8 Treasure 2013, pp.99–101.
9 Harkness 1931, p.164.
10 A. Spicer, 'Huguenots and Art', in Mentzer and van Ruymbeke 2016, pp.170–220.
11 Lestringant 2010.
12 John Winthrop (1606–1676), American scientist elected in London to the newly founded Royal Society in 1663, owned a signed copy of Palissy's *Discours Admirables* (New York Society Historical Society Library), which perhaps inspired the earliest biography in English. C.L. Brightwell's *Palissy the Potter, or the Huguenot, Artist, and Martyr* (New York 1835) was republished in London as *Palissy: The Huguenot Potter: A True Tale* (London 1858). Henry Morley's *Palissy the Potter* (London 1853) fed Samuel Smiles's account of Palissy in *The Huguenots* (London 1867). Berton's 1563 book, translated into English by Thomas Watson in the late sixteenth century, was only published in Brighton in 1876, as *A learned dialogue of Bernard Palissy concerning waters and fountains both natural and artificial*. Despite the revival of Palissy-ware made in France in Tours, Paris and Charente, the earliest full biography in French by Louis Audiat appeared in 1864 under the title *Les oubliés*, II: *Bernard Palissy*. A terracotta bust of the artist was published by Willemin in 1839.
13 Cordellier 2016, pp.223–37, fig.197. The Victoria and Albert Museum has recently acquired a contract design by Sambin for a ceremonial bench in Dijon: www.collections.vam.ac.uk/item/O1330171/contract-drawing-for-a-ceremonial-design-hugh-sambin (accessed 14 January 2020).
14 Wardropper 2004.
15 See www.collections.vam.ac.uk/item/O129038/ewer-court-susanne (accessed 14 January 2020). I am grateful to Judith Crouch, Ceramics Curator at the Victoria and Albert Museum, for sharing her knowledge of Limoges enamels made by Protestant craftsmen using Protestant print sources.
16 Kingdon 1956, p.6.
17 Salmon 1975.
18 H. Guicharnaud, 'An Introduction to the Architecture of Protestant Temples Constructed in France before the Revocation of the Edict of Nantes', in Finney 1999, pp.133–61.
19 R. Dunlop and H. Murtagh, 'Schomberg, Frederick Herman de (formerly Frederick Herman von Schönberg), 1st Duke of Schomberg (1615–1690), army officer', *ODNB* (accessed 23 February 2020).
20 Buckley 2008, p.278. The Marquise de Sévigné, Marie de Rabutin-Chantal, married Henri de Sévigné in 1644 but was widowed in 1651. Well educated, she was a gifted correspondent. Her miniature attributed to Jean Petitot the elder (1607–1691) is in the Metropolitan Museum of Art, New York (inv.622.122.71).
21 Scoville 1960, p.5.
22 Benedict 1991, p.77.
23 Mansel 2019, p.307; Scoville 1960, p.39, citing letter from Louvois to the Marquis de Bouffars.
24 Scoville 1960, p.6.
25 Driancourt-Girod 1992, pp.101, 127.
26 Treasure 2013, pp.369–75.
27 Murdoch 2005a; Murdoch 2006b.
28 Glozier 2005, pp.117, 120.
29 See www.hugenottenmuseum-berlin.de (accessed 14 January 2020).
30 For Huguenot schools in Germany, see Manuel Bohm, 'Sociolinguistics of the Huguenot Communities in German Speaking Territories', Mentzer and van Ruymbeke 2016, pp.291–322.
31 Brett 2014, pp.1–10.
32 Erlangen 1986, pp.61–5, 192–203 (for the New Town); 92–9 (for the Brandenburg-Bayreuth patronage); 134, 150 (for the church); 152–9, 168–91 (for the weavers).
33 Lachenicht 2007.
34 Berg 1845, pp.43, 211, 338.
35 Cerny 1987, p.56.
36 Luria 1993.
37 Ressinger 2005, p.143.
38 A. Garrett, 'Enquiry, Sceptism and Enlightenment', in Fitzpatrick et al. 2004, pp.57–64; and L. Simonutti, 'The Huguenot Debate on Toleration', in ibid., pp.65–77.
39 Scoville 1960, p.124.
40 Lane Poole 1880, p.70.
41 Van der Linden 2015, p.2, cited by Gwynn 2018, p.201.
42 Hunt, Jacob and Mijnhardt 2010, pp.25–7, 279–82.
43 Ibid., p.280, fig.11.4.
44 Clark 2000, p.301.
45 Carpenter 2011, pp.85–6.
46 Nathan 1939, p.58; Coertzen 1988, pp.68–70.
47 Louis Fourie arrived at the Cape in 1685 after fleeing France and surviving a 185-day sea voyage from Texel in the Netherlands. He settled on a piece of land on the slopes of the Groenberg Mountain, today known as Wellington in the Western Cape. Fourie was granted the De Slange Rivier farm in 1699 by the then Governor of the Cape of Good Hope, Willem Adriaan van der Stel (1664–1733). Fourie farmed and made wine here until his death in 1750, pioneering winemaking at the Cape. See www.lintonparkwines.co.za/our-story (accessed 14 January 2020).
48 Nathan 1939, pp.33, 69, 120; Coertzen 1988, p.152.
49 Harvey 2008, pp.111–63.
50 Butler 1983, p.49; Gwynn 1985, pp.29–30, believes that this figure is overstated.
51 See Francis Fauquier's Will, *The William and Mary Quarterly*, 8, no.3 (January 1900), pp.171–7, for a memorial ring commemorating his brother William. See also www.collections.vam.ac.uk/item/O123481/ring-unknown (accessed 14 January 2019).
52 See www.huguenotsociety.org (accessed 14 January 2020).
53 Ibid.; Eastman, Donohoe and Thompson 2018, pp.140–1.
54 See www.huguenotstreet.org (accessed 14 January 2020); Carlo 2014.
55 Whitelock 1887.
56 See www.stesprit.org (accessed 14 January 2020).
57 See www.nps.gov/bost/learn/historyculture/fh.htm (accessed 14 January 2020).
58 Fairbanks 1975, p.28, no.26.

59 Fischer 1994.
60 Van Ruymbeke 2011; The Huguenot Memorial Museum, Franschoek, www.museum.co.za (accessed 16 January 2020).
61 Jacques Abbadie, *The art of knowing ones-self, or, A diligent search into the springs of morality* (London 1695).
62 Maury 1853.
63 See www.frenchhospital.org.uk (accessed 16 January 2020); Murdoch and Vigne 2009, p.86.
64 Rothstein 1990, biographical index.

2 The Reception of Huguenot Artists, Craftsmen and Designers in the British Isles *pages 31–43*

1 The best-known of the Protestant glassmakers was Jean Carré (*c*.1520–1572), born in Arras, who came to London from Antwerp. Ananias de Hennezel (b.1570) from Darnell, Lorraine, manufactured broad-glass, which was considered a respectable occupation for a gentleman. He adopted the anglicized name of Joshua Henzey and settled in Oldswinford, Stafford, where he became a leader in the local glass industry. His portrait is still in the possession of his family and bears a later inscription: 'Annanias De Hennezel "de la Maison de Henzell tout prè la Village de Darnell en la pie del Lorraine" and a lineal descendant of Henri de Hennezel Ecuyer, Seigneur of Bonvillerand Belrupt, who was living Anno 1349. Owing to the persecution of the Huguenots he quitted Lorraine and settled in England and was distinguished amongst those who introduced the making of broad window glass, an art then esteemed so curious in Lorraine, that persons of gentle blood were allowed to work at it'; Grazebrook 1877; Guttery 1956, pp.14, 15, 17, 28 and 58. There were three Henzey glassmakers named Ananias. Among other Lorraine families of glassmakers who settled in England were the Thisac, Thiétry and Houz families (Barrington Haynes 1948, p.110).
2 Treasure 2013, pp.301ff.
3 Grant 1934, pp.160–1.
4 For a declaration relating to the children of the Huguenots in Paris, 12 July 1685, see 'Reglemens concernant les Religionnaires depus l'année 1685 jusques & compris 1734', Musée du Protestantisme, Paris.
5 Agnew 1874, p.5.
6 Oakley 2015; *Huguenot Society Quarto Series*, v.
7 Scouloudi 1958–64; *Huguenot Society Quarto Series*, IV.
8 Murdoch and Vigne 2009, pp.13–18.
9 Gwynn 1985, pp.155–9. A portrait of third-generation Huguenot Daniel Minet (1729–1790) attributed to Thomas Gainsborough (1727–1788), *c*.1779 is in the Library of the Society of Antiquaries, London.
10 Mansel 2019, pp.320, 350.
11 Glozier 2005, p.146; R. Dunlop and H. Murtagh, 'Schomberg, Frederick Herman de (formerly Frederick Herman von Schönberg), 1st Duke of Schomberg (1615–1690), army officer', *ODNB* (accessed 23 Februry 2020).
12 Hylton 1984.
13 Gwynn 1985, pp.80, 88.
14 M. Yardeni, 'Assimilation and Integration', in Mentzer and van Ruymbeke 2016, pp.273–90, at pp.278–9.
15 Ozinga 1938; T. Murdoch, 'Marot, Daniel (1661–1752), architect, designer, and engraver', *ODNB* (accessed 16 January 2020).
16 Murdoch 1985, no.268, pl.12.
17 Lee 1936, esp. chap.7, pp.176–202.
18 A. Gordon and L. Clarkson, 'Crommelin, (Samuel-)Louis [Samuel-Lewis] (1652–1727), linen manufacturer', *ODNB* (accessed 4 April 2020); Gill 1925, pp.7, 341; Scoville 1952, pp.309–10.
19 Maury 1853, pp.229–32.
20 Alexander 1972, pp.25–7.
21 See *ODNB* for 14 Bosanquet entries, 14 Courtauld entries and 5 Portal entries. Entries for David Garrick, Laurence Olivier and P.M. Roget demonstrate the important Huguenot contribution to literature and theatre: P. Thomson, 'Garrick, David (1717–1779), actor and playwright', *ODNB* (accessed 16 January 2020); M. Billington, 'Olivier, Laurence Kerr, Baron Olivier (1907–1989), actor and director', ibid. (accessed 16 January 2020); T. Murray, 'Roget, Peter Mark (1779–1869), physician and philologist', ibid. (accessed 16 January 2020).
22 See www.huguenotsociety.org.uk/ (accessed 16 January 2020).
23 See www.huguenotmuseum.org (accessed 16 January 2020).
24 Murdoch 1982b, appendix, 'The Professions of Émigré Craftsmen as recorded in the Registers of the Huguenot Churches in Great Britain and Ireland', pp.237–56.
25 For information on those who settled in the American colonies, see D.L. Barquist, 'Huguenot goldsmiths in Colonial New York and Philadelphia, 1680–1750', in Murdoch 2008, pp.61–70, and B.C. Wees, 'Huguenot goldsmiths in Colonial Boston and Charleston' in ibid., pp.71–84.
26 Hill 1961.
27 Cornelius Gole (1657– after 1716), son of Louis XIV's cabinetmaker Pierre Gole (*c*.1620–1684) and brother-in-law of Daniel Marot, grew up in an environment of royal French patronage. Lunsingh Scheurleer 2005; Turpin 2014.
28 See, for example, Vial 1945.
29 For the impact of military campaigns on art patronage during Louis XIV's reign, see Mansel 2019, p.318.
30 Spicer 2016.
31 *An accurate Description of the United Netherlands*, 1691, pp.27, 111. While the Bank of England was not founded until 1694, C. Hoare & Co. was established in 1672 and Child & Co. the following year.
32 Gwynn 1980.
33 For a general account of Irish art in the eighteenth century see Laffan and Monkhouse 2015.
34 Halsband 1960, p.9.
35 Boyer 1722, p.369.
36 Troeltsch 1959.
37 Turner 2011.
38 The Guildhall Library, City of London, has an original copy; the canto was reprinted in 2018. See Murdoch 1985, no.134, p.102; www.ourmigrationstory.org.uk/oms/huguenot-silk-weavers-in-spitalfields (accessed 16 January 2020).
39 Hulton 1977, pp.10–12.
40 MacLeod 2019, pp.142–75.
41 Avery 1980.
42 Harvey 2008, pp.256–60.
43 Mitchell 2017, p.387.
44 Cruikshank 2016.
45 Gwynn 1975.
46 Latham and Matthews 1971–83, vol.3 (1971), p.207.
47 The National Archives, MPA 1/41; Somerville 1960, p.229.
48 *Common Sense*, November 1738, reprinted in Maty 1777, vol.1, pp.99–104.
49 Sheppard 1957, p.223.
50 See www.bricklanejammemasjid.org.uk (accessed 16 January 2020).
51 R. Cole, www.sandysrowsynagogue.org/history (accessed 22 October 2019).

52 Jones 1908, pp.5, 10, pls III, VI; see www.egliseprotestantelondres.org.uk (accessed 16 January 2020).
53 Avery 1996, no.93, pl.6, pp.104–6.
54 Formerly in the Time Museum, Rockford, Illinois. Sotheby's, New York, 19 June 2002, lot 165.
55 Lomax and Rothwell 2006, pp.43, 44, 198 n.20.
56 M. Lister, *A Journey to Paris in the Year 1698* (London 1699), p.178.
57 See Whitley Papers, Department of Prints and Drawings, British Museum, vol.VIII, pp.429–551.
58 Garrioch 2014, pp.76–9.
59 Bindman and Baker 1995, pp.62–3.
60 G.C. Gibbs, 'Huguenot Contributions to England's Intellectual Life and England's Intellectual Commerce with Europe, *c.*1680–1720', in Scouloudi 1987, pp.20–41.
61 Monsieur Huet, 'A letter to Mr. James Whildon, dated 8 February 1699/1700' (Chatsworth Archives), quoted in Murdoch 1982b, p.12.
62 *HSQS*, XXXVII, introduction.
63 Guillaume de la Plaigne is an ancestor of the celebrated actor Derek Jacobi, as revealed in the BBC One television programme *Who Do You Think You Are?* first broadcast in 2015.
64 *HSQS*, XXVI, pp.20, 24, 36, 46, 214.
65 *HSQS*, XXV, p.18.
66 I am most grateful to Mr Alan Hunter, former administrator at Wrest Park, Bedfordshire, for providing this information (in 1982).
67 *HSQS*, XXVI, p.106. Charlotte Hauduroy's brother was Charles Coulon, watchmaker of Panton Street, Soho, her executor in 1762. The National Archives, PROB 11/878/422.
68 'The Accounts of the Executors of Ralph, 1st Duke of Montagu, 1712', vol.1, p.499 (Archives, Boughton House, Northamptonshire).
69 *Report on the Manuscripts of the late Allan George Finch, Esq.*, 1957, pp.107–8.
70 Parisot promoted his venture in 1753 by publishing *An Account of the new manufactory of Tapestry after the manner of that of the Gobelins and of Carpets, after the manner of that at Chaillot.*
71 Darcel 1878, p.286.
72 A letter dated August 1752 from M. Grignon, one of Parisot's 100 employees, addressed to his father, tries to persuade his brother Estienne to learn the manufacture of the Savonnerie for two and a half years, and then come to Fulham to work for Parisot, where 'ne sera pas regarde comme un jeune apprentif, mais comme un homme en remplissant son devoir avec les ouvriers avec qui il travaillera' (he will not be regarded as a young apprentice but as a journeyman amongst equals).
73 *Bulletin de la Société de l'Art Français* (January 1877), pp.95–9, at p.97.
74 The letters of Giuseppi Baretti, in England by 1751, note that Monsieur Parisot disappeared and that most of his tools were bought by a certain Monsieur Passavant. 'Quelques malheureux déserteurs des Gobelins, qui etaient venus servir monsieur Parisot après avoir risqué la potence s'ils avaient avaient été pris pendant qu'ils se sauvaient de France … ils ne savoient d'autre métier que le leur, ignoraient entièrement la langue et ne pouvaient retourner en France ou ils auraient été pendus pour leur désertion. M. Passavant ramassa dans les rues de Londres le petit nombre de ceux que le faim et la misère avaient encore epargnés et les fit conduire á Exeter ou il se fait un petit revenu de leurs travaux'. Baretti adds: 'Comme monsieur Passavant et un négociant très-habile, il a trouvé le moyen, sans aide de prince, de duc, ni de seigneur, de gagnier quelque chose avec sea tapisseries.'
75 Van Gelder 1979, pp.30–4. Raguineau painted portraits of William in 1660 and 1661.
76 Wren 1750, p.326.
77 *HSQS*, XXXVII, introduction 'pour aller faire compliment à son Altesse Royale sur sa venue dans ce royaume'.
78 Ingamells and Raines 1976–8, pp.1–70.
79 French books among those purchased by Mercier include *Oeuvres de Crebillon*, Paul Rapin de Thoyras's *History Of England…*, Bernard de Montfaucon's *Monuments de la Monarchie Française*, Morery's *Dictionary* and Du Thou's *Histoire de son Temps*. Frederick Prince of Wales, Household Accounts (Offices of the Duchy of Cornwall), IV (1733–4), p.221; V (1734–5), p.244.
80 Charles, 5th Earl of Baltimore's Receipt Book, 26 March 1729 to 17 July 1750, is preserved in the library of the Maryland Historical Society, Baltimore.
81 Frederick Prince of Wales, Household Accounts (Offices of the Duchy of Cornwall), V, VI, VIII (1734–44), pp.134, 141–5.
82 Accounts of John, 2nd Duke of Montagu 1725–46 (Archives, Boughton House, Northamptonshire).
83 'The Particular of my Plate & its Weight', Lomax and Rothwell 2006, appendix II, pp.167–83.
84 Scott-Thompson 1937, pp.93–102, 184, 186, 224–5, 363.
85 Gribelin 1941, inscribed 'combien vous avez pour Agreable mes Foibles Efforts, par que vous m'y faites donc j'en auray (comme de tous les Autres) une Eternelle Reconnaissance'.
86 Lord Chamberlain's Account for 1689, fol.107 (National Archives); Croft-Murray 1962, pp.243ff.
87 Curran 1967, p.25, pls 15, 16.
88 Wells-Cole 1976.
89 Tait 1972, pp.267–77.
90 From the Auditor, *The Gentleman's Magazine*, 3 April 1733.
91 Mew 1928.
92 Simon 2007, p.24.
93 Barr 1980, pp.62–3, 121, 124.
94 McInnes and Mack 1999.
95 Murdoch 1986, citing Grimwade 1976, pp.543, 691.
96 T. Sinsteden and T. Murdoch, 'Names of known, believed or possible Huguenot goldsmiths of Dublin', in Murdoch 2008, pp.150–5.
97 Register of Apprentices, Upholders' Company, Guildhall Library MS 7142.
98 T. Murdoch, 'Pierre Langlois', in *Masterpiece 2019 Handbook*, p.68; Murdoch 2001b.
99 Beinecke Library, Yale University (Osborn c 42), Collection of papers of Eardsley-Wilmot, 1750–1815, 'Report of the Distressed French Immigrants, Subscription to succour the distress and misery of the French Clergy, who had taken refuge under the British Government'. These Catholic refugees were distributed across the South Coast in Dover, Rye, Shoreham, Brighthelmstone (Brighton), Portsmouth, Southampton, Poole, Hastings and Eastbourne, and established in the King's Barracks at Winchester.
100 Murdoch and Vigne 2009, p.45.

3 The Huguenots as Educators
pages 45–57

1 Hetherington 2019.
2 Howatt and Widdowson 2004, pp.26, 37. Holyband published *The French School Master* in 1573 and *A Dictionarie French and English* in 1593. His family name was an Anglicization of Sainliens. He came from Moulins.
3 Gibbs 1975, p.269.
4 Scott-Thomson 1940, pp.83ff.; Labib-Rahman 1981, pp.309–18.
5 Hardwick 1977; Ford 1976, pp.19–31; De Blainville, M., *Travels through Holland, Germany, Switzerland, and Other Parts of Europe; But especially Italy*, London 1743.
6 Gwynn 1985, p.82. Jouneau came from Barbésieux. For Coderc, see Swift 1983, p.136.
7 Root 1929, pp.97, 100, 118, 139.
8 Agnew 1871–4, vol.2, pp.10, 155, 314–16; vol.3, p.152. C. Spence, 'Misson, Francis Maximilian [formerly François Maximilien] (*c.*1650–1722), traveller and author', *ODNB* (accessed 27 March 2020); *HSQS*, LX (2007), p.283; www.latouchelegacy.com/history-of-the-la-touche-family.php (accessed 27 March 2020).
9 I am grateful to David Oakey for this information.
10 Buccleuch 2016, pp.20–5. Germaine Colladon was a cousin of Sir Theodore Colladon (d.1712), physician to the Royal Hospital, Chelsea, who attended William III on his deathbed. Germaine was named after his great-grandfather Germain, who was John Calvin's assistant in Geneva (v. Larminie, 'Colladon, Sir John [Jean] (1608–1675), physician and political agent', *ODNB* [accessed 7 April 2020]). For the Colladon family, see Agnew 1871–4, vol.1, pp.162, 238–9. The Colladons were later connected to the Montagus by marriage. In 1725 Sir Theodore's daughter Anne married Charles Montagu of Papplewick, Nottinghamshire, a cousin of John, 2nd Duke of Montagu.
11 Gasselin was paid 'on acct for teaching Mr [Winwood Monthermer] to draw £25 on 18 July 1700 and again on 12 February 1702/3: 'Mr Gasselin Drawin[g] Mr [Master] in full to 23 Janry last £13 15'. Mr de Moivre, who taught mathematics to Winwood's younger brother, John, was paid £10 1s 6d on 9 December 1704 for instruments, books and '2 months teaching' and £16 10s 6d on 21 August 1705 for '7 months teaching my Lord Monthermer'.

Boughton, MS Elias de Rit's Accounts 1698–1705. Murdoch and Boucher 2013, pp.57ff.
12 Bedford Record Office, x800/1, fol.6, Accounts of Mark Anthony, Steward to Ralph, 1st Duke of Montagu at Montagu House, Bloomsbury.
13 *HSQS*, XXIX, p.79.
14 Blunt 1975.
15 Gasselin's drawing of Marylebone Manor House was engraved by J.T. Smith in 1807 with the inscription: 'In this house a considerable school was kept many years by Mr De La Place and after by Mr Fountaine, on whose sucession the building was demolished in 1791. Dedicated to the Nobleman and Gentlemen educated at the said school' (British Museum, London, inv.1880,1113.4647).
16 These drawings are in the Marylebone Public Library, the British Museum and the Yale Center for British Art. *A Country House in a Park* (Yale Center for British Art, inv.B1977.14.5534) may represent Boughton House, Northamptonshire, with its newly built French-style wing, adjacent to the Tudor hall.
17 François Gasselin, who attended the Paris Academy in 1708, 1712 and 1713, may have been connected to the artist of the same name recorded in England.
18 *The General Advertiser* announced on 25 March 1749 the auction at Mr Prestage, Saville Row, on 5 April, following 'The Collection of Pictures and Library of John Ernest Galliard Esq., deceas'd, with some fine Prints, Busts and other Curiosities, lately bought abroad'.
19 R. Langley, 'The Music', in Murdoch 1992a, pp.174–7; Boughton House, MS Accounts of the 2nd Duke of Montagu 1725–1766: 'To Jn Ernst Galliard for teaching Lady Mary as per Bill', £16 16s; R. Fiske, and R. King, 'Galliard, John Ernest', *GMO* (accessed 7 April 2020).
20 See R. Platt, 'Prelleur, Peter', *GMO* (accessed 3 February 2020).
21 'Greek Street Area: Portland Estate, Greek Street', in Sheppard 1966, pp.170–90. Prelleur's 15 hymns composed for Charity School Children were published in 1758 with the title *Divine Melody*.
22 *HSQS*, XVI, pp.11, 144. Mr Meure's lodger in 1705 was the goldsmith Jean Batut.
23 In 1704 Robert Pitt wrote to his father, Governor of Madras: 'My two brothers are at Mr Meure's Academy esteemed the best in England. They learn Latin, French and accounts, fencing, dancing and drawing'. Hans 1951, p.115.
24 Gwynn 1985, p.263; Murdoch 1985a, no.152, p.112. The rules of the Soho Academy were published in French and English (M. Clare and C. Barwis, *Rules and Orders for the Government of the Academy in Soho Square, London* [London 1740]).
25 *The Weekly Journal or British Gazeteer*, 14 September 1717: 'His Majesty and the Royal Family continue in perfect health, at Hampton Court where among others the ingenious Mr Desaguliers FRS has the Honour to divert them with several curious Performances upon Globes, and other Philosophical Experiments; for which Purpose he has a Lodging allow'd him in one of the Pavilions of the Garden.'
26 Harvey and Grist 2006, pp.163–4.
27 *The Daily Courant*, 16 December 1724, issue 7229, p.1.
28 *The Daily Advertiser*, 27 August 1743, issue 3934, and 2 January 1744. *Public Ledger*, 30 April 1760, issue 95, announces the annual meeting for 'the Gentlemen Educated at Mr Fargues' Academy at Hoxton'.
29 Dancing cost 15s a quarter and half a guinea entrance; drawing was one guinea a quarter and a guinea entrance; music was two guineas a quarter and a guinea entrance; and fencing cost three guineas a quarter. There was one guinea entrance fee for attending the French Chapel for the first time and half a crown a quarter thereafter.
30 British Museum, Department of Prints and Drawings, Heal Collection, inv.104.54.
31 Boughton House, Mr de Rit's Accounts, 1706–7.
32 Manchee 1937.
33 Phillips 1933. Paul van Somer, *Figurae Variae*, n.d. The British Museum has 11 plates (invs 1937,0802.1.48–1937,0802.1.59); the title page is inv.1937,0802.1.48.
34 He may be the Mr Regnier who taught drawing to the engraver Andrew Lawrence (1706–1747). T. Major, 'A short sketch of the life of Mr Andrew Lawrence, engraver' (1785), MS, British Museum, Department of Prints and Drawings, inv.1870,0514.2357.
35 *The Daily Advertiser*, 13 February 1745.
36 Croft Murray 1962–70, vol.2 (1970), pp.250a, 325a.
37 O'Mullane 1946.
38 Sloan 2000, no.39b.
39 A copy is preserved in the Bodleian Library, Oxford (inv.17023 d 1). Clayton 1997, p.161; *A New Book of Principles for Drawing Ornament* (1774) is in the Getty Research Institute, inv.2961-913 P860001* [bx.2, f.10]).
40 Clayton 1997, p.187.
41 Hammelman 1975, p.19; Jacob Bonneau's father engraved designs and trade cards. His grandfather Pierre Bonneau, engraver from Rennes, left France in 1687 and abjured Catholicism on his arrival in Jersey. He later settled in London. Murdoch 1985a, no.294. His card for George Beacher, copperplate printer of Drury Lane, illustrates the printing process: see Clayton 1997, pl.25. His card for the wood turner Bernardeau advertised bowls, mahogany stands for china dishes and 'all sorts of oval frames'.
42 *Wherein the Principles of that most Useful Art laid down by Dr. Brook Taylor, are fully and clearly Explained by means of Moveable Schemes properly Adapted for the purpose*. See *ODNB* under Fournier, Daniel.
43 Woodwiss 1965.
44 Phillips 1933.
45 I am grateful to Gordon Balderston for sharing his discovery (via www.ancestry.com) that the Roubiliac family left Lyons for Frankfurt in 1710, where they attended the Protestant church until 1718. Pierre Roubiliac, the sculptor's father, died in Berlin in May 1723. Gabrielle, the sculptor's sister, died in Dresden in March 1724 (email 1 November 2017). See forthcoming article by T. Murdoch and S. Robinson in *The Burlington Magazine*, 2022.
46 Premiums paid include that for John Chazaux who was apprenticed to goldsmith Guillaume Devis in 1752; see Evans 1930–3, p.531.
47 School subscribers were directed to David Hubert his son Stephen, an apothecary, and to addresses in Soho and the City; they included Huguenot descendants and members of the British establishment. A receipt to Lady Ravensworth for one guineas' subscription in 1791 is signed by Mr Artaud, the Treasurer (Huguenot Society Library).
48 Murdoch 1985, no.117, p.92 and no.295, p.204.
49 *HSQS*, LX, p.47, under 'Broca, Theophilus', who left the school a bequest of £10. He also mentions Revd Charles Pelissier. For an account of the French School in Myler's Alley, Dublin, see O'Mullane 1946, pp.121–34.
50 Louis Chéron was accepted at the Savoy Church in 1693. *HSQS*, XXII, p.13: 'Le sieur Louis Chéron paintre âgé de 30 ans, de Paris, qui a signé, s'estant présenté au Consistoire et ayant témoigné la repentance de sa faute en a fait aujourd'huy sa reconnoissance et réparation publique et a été admis à la paix de l'Églize sur la promesse d'être désormais fidelle à Dieu jusques à la mort et de se conformer à la discipline de cette Églize, en foy de quoi le d. Sr. Louis Chéron a signé ce présent acte au Consistoire de la Savoye, ce 1er octobre 1693'. 'Le peintre Louis Chéron', *BSHPF*, 63, no.3 (May/June 1914), pp.279–80.
51 He won the Prix de Rome in 1676 and 1678. In 1715 his Paris relatives received a refund for the earlier fine of 2,000 *livres*. Simon 2007, p.64.
52 Greder 1909, p.97; 'Artistes huguenots. – Louis Chéron', *BSHPF*, 55, no.1 (January/February 1906), pp.91–2.
53 Vertue III (*The Walpole Society*, vol.22 [1933–4]), p.22.
54 Vertue II (*The Walpole Society*, vol.20 [1931–2]), p.124.
55 Greder 1909, p.2.
56 Guiffrey and Barthélemy 1908. Chéron's sister Elisabeth Sophie 'l'a entretenu pendant dix-huit ans en Italie ... pour faciliter ses progres dans la peinture & il a repondu ses grands soins'. D'Argenville 1762, vol.2, p.370; D. Cast, 'Chéron, Louis (1660–1725), painter and illustrator', *ODNB* (accessed 13 March 2020).
57 Ivanoff 1962. The painting measures some 20 x 30ft. Simon 2007, p.64. According to François Marandet (pers. comm.), the preparatory oil sketch for the *Pool of Bethesda* is in the Wellcome Library, London.
58 Pannier and Vergnet-Ruiz 1936.
59 'The King having been informed that the Sieurs Testelin, Secretary of the Academy of Painting and Sculpture, Michelin, Assistant Professor, Ferdinand, Besnard, Rousseau [Jacques Rousseau, who also took refuge in England] Conseilleurs of the Academy, and Espagnandelle and Ferdinand, Academicians are all of the so called reformed religion, His Majesty commands me to inform Monsieur Le Brun that

he wishes them to be deprived of these functions and that the Academy should elect others in their place who are Catholics. His Majty also wishes that no pupil be admitted into the Academy who is not a Catholic.' Evans 1972, p.152.

60 Louis XIV's secretary wrote to the Chief of Police, Nicholas Gabriel de la Reynie: 'His Majesty wishes that you should continue your efforts to try to convert Rousseau, painter, and he will be very satisfied should that conversion succeed because he is an able man.' Douen 1894, vol.3, p.271.

61 Simon 2007, pp.58–9, citing d'Argenville: 'One could often hear in this salon the brother Louis, the sister Elizabeth-Sophie; the illustrious Roger de Piles and several savants of the highest order discussing the most interesting points about painting & the fine arts. Music followed these excellent discourses.'

62 Auzas 1949; Laharie 1999: pl.3 is Chéron's *Le Prophete Agabus précisant á saint Paul ce qu'il doit souffrir á Jérusalem May de 1687*. The preparatory sketch is in the Fine Arts Museum, Caen. According to François Marandet (pers. comm.), the sketch for the 1690 May *Salome and the Head of St John the Baptist* is in a private collection. The altarpieces in Notre Dame survived the 2019 fire.

63 Croft-Murray and Hulton 1960, vol.1, p.282, nos 122–4. The two albums were acquired from Knowsley by the British Museum in 1953.

64 Vertue III (*The Walpole Society*, vol.22 [1933–4]), p.22. Lord Derby acquired another group of 72 drawings for 265 guineas at Chéron's posthumous sale in 1726; see Stainton and White 1987, p.218; Vertue III, p.28.

65 There is a copy in the Bibliothèque nationale, Paris. The work is listed in sale catalogues of the artists Louis Goupy, Thomas Major and P.A. Rysbrack, as 'A drawing book of Cheron'; 'the book of Elizabeth Cheron complete' (sale catalogue of Louis Goupy's effects, 14 February 1747 [5th day], lot 81). Thomas Major and P.A. Rysbrack owned Elisabeth Sophie's engravings of gems: sale of Thomas Major's effects, 1747/8, lot 30: 'Thirty seven antique gems by Cheron'; sale catalogue of P.A. Rysbrack's effects, 17 April 1774, lot 20: 'A drawing book of Cheron' and lot 54: 'The book of Elizabeth Cheron complete'.

66 Vertue III (*The Walpole Society*, vol.22 [1933–4]), pp.8, 19–20.

67 A title page engraved by Nicolas-Henry Tardieu (1674–1749) after a design by Louis Chéron may have been intended as a frontispiece, designed for both the French and English markets and lettered: 'A Paris chez F. Poilly, Graveur rue Saint Jacques a l'image Saint Benoist' and 'by John Bowles at the Black horse in Cornhill'.

68 Vertue describes the attendees from 1711 to 1713: the architect James Gibbs (1711); the history painters James Thornhill and Antonio Pellegrini (1711); six portrait painters, Mr Gibson, Mr Dahl, Mr Hysing, Mr Borman, Mr Closterman and Mr Gouge (1711); two limners, Mr B. Lens and Mr Mortiz (1711); three landscape painters, Mr Boul (Bowles?), Mr Tillemans (1711) and Mr Nesbit (1713); one painter 'of huntings' (a sporting artist), Mr Wootton (1711); five artists simply described as 'painters', Mr Pickering, Mr Byng, Mr Vanderbank, Mr Weedman and Mr Swartz (the last two are described as assistants to Kneller); three painters in watercolour, Mr 'Goupee senr' and Mr 'Jo. Goupee Junr' (Goupy), and Mr Bodin (1711); an artist in crayons, Mr Lutterel (1711); a statuary, Mr Bird (1711); an ivory carver, Mr Dubberman (1711); a seal engraver, Mr Christian (1711); seven engravers, Mr N. Dorigny, Mr Vertue, Mr Duguernier (1711), Mr Simpson Sr (1712), Mr G. Vandergucht Jr (1713), Mr Carwitham (1713); a mezzotinter, Mr Simon (1711); a surgeon, Mr Gejkje; and a banker, Colonel Seymour. Mr Swiney, 'a player', was presumably Owen McSwiney, the actor. Of those with French names, the engravers Du Guernier and Simon were of Huguenot origin; Bodin and Chauvin may have had Huguenot connections.

69 In 1724 Vertue notes 'Mr. P. Tillemans & Mr. Jos. Goupee both joyntly imploy'd to paint/make a Sett of Sceenes for the Opera house in the Haymarkett which were much approv'd of'. Vertue III (*The Walpole Society*, vol.22 [1933–4]), p.21.

70 Vertue III (*The Walpole Society*, vol.22 [1933–4]), p.22; Gerard Vandergucht was son of Michael Vandergucht. T. Clayton, 'Vandergucht, Gerard (1696/7–1776), engraver and art dealer' *ODNB* (accessed 13 March 2020).

71 Du Guernier, a pupil of Louis de Chatillon (1639–1734), enameller, may be related to the miniaturist Louis du Guernier (1614–1659), a founding academician of the Royal French Academy of Painting and Sculpture. Du Guernier the elder came to London in 1708 and with Nicholas Dorigny became a director of Kneller's Academy. Vertue described du Guernier as 'rather Low than Middel sise, very obliging, good Temper, gentleman like & well belov'd by all his acquaintance' (Vertue II, *The Walpole Society*, vol.20 [1931–2] p.131). He engraved book illustrations by Louis Chéron and Kneller's portraits of the 2nd Duke and Duchess of Queensberry. Libson-Yarker 2018, no.13.

72 Vertue noted that 'great age gave him an early opportunity and acquaintance with artists long ago dead as Mr. Faithorne, Sir P. Lelly, Mr. Simons modeller, Quellin, Sir Chris. Wren'. Vertue III (*The Walpole Society*, vol.22 [1933–4]), p.86.

73 Vertue II (*The Walpole Society*, vol.20 [1931–2]), pp.90–1; III (*The Walpole Society*, vol.22 [1933–4]), pp.85–6. Mitchell 2017, pp.316, 420.

74 Vertue VI (*The Walpole Society*, vol.30 [1951–2]), pp.169–70: 'there began some fractions encouraged by S^r^. James Thornhill – M^r^. Cheron which at last broke it up and afterwards – Thornhill got it under his management – for some two or three years then partyes rose against him. then he drew them to his own house in Common Garden – in a large room – gratis … growing tired with this and M^r^. Cheron and John Vanderbank – undertook to keep on they began in S^t^. Martin's Lane in a great Room'.

75 John Vanderbank subscribed 15 guineas and James Seymour, the artist son of the banker Colonel Seymour who had attended Kneller's Academy, contributed 10 guineas. Bignamini 1988, p.84.

76 Ibid., p.36. Harvey was also associated with the group of artists known as the St Luke Virtuosi. His portrait was painted by John Smibert (1688–1751).

77 Vertue III (*The Walpole Society*, vol.22 [1933–4]), p.12.

78 Murdoch 2014, fig.1; Yale Center for British Art, inv.V 2571.

79 Simon 2007, p.65.

80 Advertisement in *The Daily Courant*, 21 March 1721, cited by Bignamini 1988, p.90 n.13.

81 Leonard Simson, Hen. Welden, Nash Jeames, Jean Charpin, Norris Jeamison, George Hay Gart, Jacob Smith and Wm. Cooper.

82 Bignamini 1988, p.64.

83 Vertue VI (*The Walpole Society*, vol.30 [1948–50]), p.169.

84 Ibid., p.169.

85 Vertue III (*The Walpole Society*, vol.22 [1933–4]), p.11.

86 Vertue II (*The Walpole Society*, vol.20 [1931–2]), p.128. Bignamini and Postle 1991, p.73, no.56.

87 Croft-Murray and Hulton 1960, vol.1, p.278, nos 66–73, and p.280, nos 91–2. Two further studies of the female model by Chéron were sold at Sotheby's, New York, on 13–14 January 1989 (lots 241, 242); another is in the Fogg Art Museum, Cambridge, MA.

88 Croft-Murray and Hulton 1960, vol.1, nos 92–9, p.260.

89 Benthall *c.*1955; Vertue noted that Hogarth was 'from a perfect natural genius improvd by some study in the Accademy under the direction of Cheron & Vanderbank'. Vertue III (*The Walpole Society*, vol.22 [1933–4]), p.38.

90 Bignamini 1988, p.92 n.3.

91 Advertised in the *Daily Journal* and *Fog's Weekly Journal*, 15 March 1735, as for sale from E. Kirkall, engraver in Dock-Well Court, Whitefriars. A single undated print by George Bickham after Chéron was published from May's Buildings, Covent Garden.

92 Gerard Vandergucht, '6 prints after Monsr Cheron's Accademy figures'. Vertue VI (*The Walpole Society*, vol.30 [1948–50]), p.189.

93 Bignamini and Postle 1991, p.67, no.42.

94 Vertue III (*The Walpole Society*, vol.22 [1933–4]), p.38.

95 Ibid., p.138.

96 Ibid., p.29.

97 Chèron's valuation is quoted in full, as it gives some idea of contemporary values in English pounds sterling.

37 Little pieces of Vandick at 3l [£] each	111
1 peece of Pousin	10
2 peeces of Rieussau litle	10
1 peece of Baptist	10
3 peeces over ye doors 5l [£] each	15
2 peeces of Rieusau bigger	10
2 peeces of Baptist 6 each	12
4 more of Baptist 5l [£] each	20
2 little peeces of Botson	8
1 landskip of Forest	8
2 landskips of Crebidge 7l [£] each*	14

1 landskip of Fouquier**	10
3 peeces of Ldy Montagu & Monthermer & ye present Duke	20
1 Cleopatra after Guido	2

* In the Dks Dressing Room are 2 landscapes on Copper by Apelyn called Crabelje, amongst the Artists at Rome on account of a Contraction in his Fingers probably the two above alluded to.

** In the D's Closet is a landscape by Fouquieres likely the same.

The valuation, which came to a total of £266, is signed 'Valued by us Cheron, M. Antonie'. Antonie was the name of the Duke's Huguenot steward.

98 Vertue III (*The Walpole Society*, vol.22 [1933–4]), p.22; Hogarth, *Apology for Painters* cited by Simon 2007, p.20.

99 Vertue III (*The Walpole Society*, vol.22 [1933–4]), p.22.

100 Between 1722 and 1729 six scenes were painted in England and three in France, all approximately the same size (62 x 75 cm). Angellis painted *The King seized by Cornet Joyce at Holmby House*, *The King's Escape from Hampton Court* and *The Trial of the King* in 1722. Born in Dunkirk, he worked in Flanders and Dusseldorf before coming to England in 1716; he was still living in Covent Garden in 1726 but returned to France and died in Brittany. Parrocel, 'Painter to the French King', was responsible for *The Battle of Naseby* and *King Charles before Hull*; Jean Raoux painted *The King taking leave of his Children* and Peter Tillemans *King Charles setting up his Standard and making his Declaration*.

101 Hymen's breeches are left in outline and the silk stockings fail to cover the knee on the left leg of the King's proxy, Claude de Lorraine, duc de Chevreuse.

102 Raines and Sharpe 1973–4.

103 Tardieu engraved Parocell's *King Charles before Hull*, and Mons. L'Epicier, who was in England in 1722 'but stay'd not long & returnd to Paris', engraved Raoux's *The King taking leave of his Children*.

104 Vertue VI (*The Walpole Society*, vol.30 [1948–50]), p.191.

105 No English-titled print is documented and the only impression known is in the Bibliothèque nationale, Paris.

106 Vertue III (*The Walpole Society*, vol.22 [1933–4]), p.22, noted that Chéron 'got into good business was particularly much imploy'd for designs for Engravers of which there are abundance in most of the best printed books prints done in London for some years before his death'.

107 Boyer came from Castres, Upper Languedoc. Barrell 1992.

108 Abel Rocayrol, bookseller, was recorded in Covent Garden from 1719 and then Green Street, Leicester Fields, from 1722 to 1739. Swift 1983, p.136.

109 Horace Walpole described Chéron as 'master of Vandergucht but not in England'; Michael Vandergucht (1660–1725) frequently engraved Chéron's designs in England.

110 Simon 2007, p.82.

111 Russell 1988.

112 Vertue II (*The Walpole Society*, vol.20 [1931–2]), p.152.

113 *The London Daily Post and General Advertiser* announced the auction on 21 November 1740 of 'the Pictures, Prints, Drawings, Mathematical instruments and books in French and Italian late of Mons Louis Cherone History Painter deceas'd in Mr. Heath's Great Room in Hart Street. Covent Garden'.

114 Vertue III (*The Walpole Society*, vol.22 [1933–4]), p.127.

115 'Petri Camperi Itinera in Angliam 1748–1755', *Opuscula selecta Neerlandicorum de Arte Medica*, XV, 1838 (copy in Library of the Royal College of Physicians, Edinburgh). I am most grateful to Kim Sloan for this reference

116 Whitley Papers, Department of Prints and Drawings, British Museum, under 'Roubiliac', quotation from *The Middlesex Journal*, 18 September 1770: 'When a meeting of Statuaries was held about the Alto Relievo at the Mansion House, the late celebrated Roubiliac, among others attended. The other artists delivered drawings of their designs & when Roubiliac was asked for his, he said "I have brought no plan – I do not draw but if you will give me a lump of clay & let me be shut up in a room I will do something for you".'

117 Physick 1969, p.119.

118 Nicholas Read's obituary explains that he first studied at the St Martin's Lane Academy but that his father 'prevailed with Mr. Roubiliac to take him into his house to instruct him in drawing and modelling' *The Gentleman's Magazine*, 1787, part II, p.614; Vertue III (*The Walpole Society*, vol.22 [1933–4]), p.154.

119 Meteyard 1865, p.406.

120 Andrews 1916.

121 Benthall *c.*1955, p.34.

122 Munro 2014, pp.43, 48, figs 57–8, p.232 n.22; Esdaile 1929. With the addition of a wig, Roubiliac's lay figure could serve to represent either sex. It retains its original box, male and female dress, and a military uniform, made for a smaller figure. It is made of cork, covered with silk stockingette. The male outfit consists of a black silk hat, trimmed with faded pink ribbon; the female dress includes a cambric smock, a holland skirt, a hooded cloak of red flannel, and a large pocket which was tied round the waist and worn in front. This is possibly the same lay figure that John Hamilton Mortimer provided for the Society of Artists in 1770 as a result of a Committee meeting on 30 October 1770, at which it was directed that 'the layman be set with drapery on the Fryday and Saturday in each week from the hours of six till nine'. I am grateful to John Sunderland for this information.

123 Esdaile 1928, p.218.

124 Smith 1920, vol.2, p.28.

125 Allen 1987.

126 See Edgcumbe 2000, pp.85–132, for a full account of Moser's career and influence.

4 Decorative Painters
pages 59–75

1 Croft-Murray 1962–70, vol.I (1962), p.7.

2 Clayton 1997, pp.67–8, fig.7. The print is inscribed: 'Painted on ye cieling [*sic*] of her Majesty's Closet, in her Royall Pallace of Windsor'; 'Sold by E: Cooper at ye 3 Pidgeons in Bedford Street. 1711.' This plate records the lost composition in what was then the King's Closet, painted before 1677. Griffiths 1998, cat.169.

3 Croft-Murray 1962–70, vol.I (1962), pp.246–7.

4 *HSQS*, XXII, p.13.

5 Vertue III (*The Walpole Society*, vol.22 [1933–4]), pp.39–40: 'Monsr Marot was Surveyor to the King & director of the workes of building, painting etc was in great favour & esteem with that Prince but Parmentiere ... thought himself above the direction of Marot and differd with him came to England again so lost an opportunity of being well imployd & perhaps of Making his fortune. haveing had some notice taken of him by the King, but Parmentiers high spirit rather always made him more enemys than Friends to this very day being passionate & sarcastical.'

6 Simon 1974 contains a useful chronology.

7 Vertue I (*The Walpole Society*, vol.18 [1929–30]), p.87. Kemp 2013; Kemp 2019, p.11.

8 Vertue I (*The Walpole Society*, vol.18 [1929–30]), p.187.

9 Vertue III (*The Walpole Society*, vol.22 [1933–4]), p.111. The decorative scheme was destroyed when the church was rebuilt in the nineteenth century. Parmentier also painted 'at Hull an Altar piece the Lords Supper' (Vertue III [*The Walpole Society*, vol.22 (1933–4)], p.29), which has been overpainted but survives in Holy Trinity Church.

10 Binney 1973, p.680; Vertue II (*The Walpole Society*, vol.20 [1931–2]), p.35.

11 Greder 1909, p.96. A sketch for *The Apotheosis of Hercules* was with the Baulme Gallery, Paris.

12 Laharie 1999.

13 Vertue III (*The Walpole Society*, vol.22 [1933–4]), p.21.

14 'Nous avons beu ce matin à votre santé avec M de la fosse et M Rosseau [*sic*]. Ils ont Presque achevé le Salon et commençeront bientot l'escalier'. Murdoch 1992a, p.70 n.14.

15 Edwards 1935; Cornforth 1993; Salvi 2002. Antoine Monnoyer became an associate of the Paris Academy on 28 April 1703 and an Academician on 25 October 1704.

16 *London Daily Post* (19 December 1740) announced the sale of Clermont's collection, which was eventually sold by Mr Ford from Clermont's own apartments at the Lower End of Thrift (Frith) Street, St Anne's, Soho, following a further announcement on 2 April 1750. The collection included Italian, French and Flemish paintings and 'his own Works in Flower Pieces and designs by him for curious Pieces of Needlework and some valuable Miniatures'.

17 Vertue III (*The Walpole Society*, vol.22 [1933–4]), p.22; IV, 1935–6; p.43. Chéron's 'manner of

Colouring being not so agreable … that … many noble workes of Rouseau, Baptist & lafosse whose fine manner of Designing & agreable colouring so much outshone Cheron's works that quite discouraged everyone to imploy him in that way'.
18 'Ces trois peintres François arrachent aux Anglois l'aveu sincère qu'on ne peut aller plus loin en fait de peinture. On y trouve l'effet de grandes ordonnances, soutenues d'un grand colour, d'une belle touche, & accompagnés d'ornamens, d'architecture et de fleurs ravissantes' ('These three French painters captivated the English with a new standard of decorative painting. Their grand designs, sensitively executed in striking colours, were accompanied by ornament, architecture and ravishing flowers'). D'Argenville 1762, p.332.
19 Ibid., pp.339–40.
20 Huygens 1876, p.365.
21 Friedman and Linstrum 1973.
22 Montfaucon 1682, pp.232–3; Lemonnier 1917, p.1.
23 Virgil, *Aeneid*, book I, ll.216–93.
24 Ovid, *Metamorphoses*, book V, ll.270–96.
25 Restored in 1705 by upholsterer Francis Lapiere, who was paid for 'taking a Crimson & gold Damask bed all to pieces & new making it up again to go to Boughton' (Executors' Accounts, fol.581). The bed was given to the Victoria and Albert Museum in 1916 by the 7th Duke of Buccleuch and returned on loan to its original setting in 2006; Cornforth 2006.
26 Ovid, *Metamorphoses*, book II, ll.498–510.
27 Ibid., book V, ll.566–78.
28 Cornforth II, 1970.
29 Chéron's *Hercules slaying the Hydra* is in the Victoria and Albert Museum (inv.99–1870).
30 'An Exact Relation of the Entertainment of His Most Sacred Majesty King William At The Hague: Written by an English Gentleman', from *An Accurate Description of the United Netherlands* 1691, pp.1–40, at p.24.
31 T. D'Urfey, *Albion's Blessing. A Poem Panegyrical on His Sacred Majesty, King William the III…* (London 1698), ll.7–8.
32 Stukeley 1882, p.64.
33 1832 Inventory of Boughton House, MS (Boughton House).
34 Cornforth III, 1970, p.687.
35 Ovid, *Metamorphoses*, book IX, ll.240–73.
36 Murdoch 1992, p.68.
37 An oil sketch for the ceiling of the Great Hall was in the private collection of Mr David Griffiths in 1957, and an oil sketch for the ceiling of the third state room with the Old Master Galleries in 1950, was acquired by the Tate Gallery in 1963.
38 Vertue III (*The Walpole Society*, vol.22 [1933–4]), p.22.
39 On 18 June 1700 Chéron was paid £25 for 'Painting the six Panells in the Gallery'; Chatsworth Building Accounts 1685–9 (Chatsworth Estate Office, Derbyshire), vol.VI, p.1.
40 Five drawings signed by Louis Chéron, in the same circular format as these panels, which vary slightly in style, are evidently closely related to the panels. A careful identification of the subjects of these signed drawings relates them to the surviving panels and proves the attribution to Chéron. The drawings also assist in the identification of the two panels that are no longer to be found at Chatsworth. Two of these drawings were sold at Christie's on 20 July 1976 (lot 7) and at Colnaghi's, also in 1976.
41 Thompson 1949, pp.165, 168–9, cites evidence in a notebook in the 6th Duke's hand to the effect that Chéron also painted panels in the wainscot of the dining room.
42 Croft-Murray 1962–70, vol.1 (1962), p.245.
43 Chatsworth Building Accounts 1685–9 (Chatsworth Estate Office, Derbyshire), fols 148, 159; 1687–94, fols 25, 47.
44 Thompson 1949, pp.145, 178, 185–9.
45 Chatsworth Building Accounts 1685–9 (Chatsworth Estate Office, Derbyshire), fols 44, 46, although it is tempting to relate this entry to the panel in the theatre gallery: a new west front was not planned in 1689 and was only begun in 1700.
46 'for moving to England without the king's permission'. Dussieux 1856, pp.271–2.
47 Vertue IV (*The Walpole Society*, vol.26 [1935–6]), pp.48, 139, 147: painted 'History. ornaments. Ceiling etc by N. Heude', 'said to be done in the reign of K.Will'.
48 Heude was working under contract for £15 per month from March to December 1692; two overmantels of Lot and his family leaving Sodom and Hercules are still *in situ*. Heude painted on green linen provided in July by the architect James Smith (pers. comm., Crispin Powell, Archivist to the Buccleuch Collections, 8 July 2020). Apted and Hannabuss 1978, pp.46–7.
49 Colvin 1995, p.472.
50 Blathwayt Papers, Gloucester County Record Office, E.234: 'An Account of ye measure of Mr. Hauduroy's Painting & ye Prices agreed for ye doing of it'. The only item recognizable today is 'The Balcony Room', which was repainted in the nineteenth century. Hauduroy charged £33 15s for '225 yards & 1 foot marble Colour at 3s per yard', and £19 18s 4d for 'laying 199 Bookes of Gold at 2s ye Booke'.
51 Gwynn 2018, p.199.
52 Croft-Murray 1962–70, vol.1 (1962), p.248; vol.2 (1970), p.218.
53 Bristow 1980.
54 Papers of the Earls of Kent, Bedford County Record Office. Hauduroy was paid £24.
55 *HSQS*, XXXIX, entry for 1713.
56 *HSQS*, XXV, p.42. In his 'Reconnaissance', Mark Anthony Hauduroy explains that he inherited his Protestant faith from his parents.
57 Godber 1963 includes a reproduction of John Rocque's *Survey*.
58 Further payments from the Duke of Kent to Mark Anthony Hauduroy are recorded in that Duke's account with Hoare's Bank, 13 February 1728: 'To Ant: Hauduroy 10 & 15 £25 0s 0d; 25 July 1738 – To Mark Anthony Hauduroy £15'. My thanks to Dr Andrew Hann of English Heritage for this reference (pers. comm., 2 October 2019).
59 The next door to the right is inscribed 'BERTRAND ITHRUM 84 RESTAURAVIT' and the next door is inscribed 'H. WHACEY RESTAURAVIT 91 [?]'.
60 *HSQS*, XXV, pp.18, 42. On 12 April 1739 Mark Anthony Hauduroy made his 'reconnaissance' to the consistory of that chapel, promising to remain faithful to the Protestant religion in which he had been born and took communion – presumably at Easter. Gedeon Gosset the elder (1709–1785) was a witness.
61 Sackville Papers, Kent County Record Office, Maidstone, TJZ 69, A 232.
62 Collins-Baker 1949, p.285. In December 1735 Mark Anthony Hauduroy received three large portraits of William III, Queen Mary and George I valued at £16, in part payment. Hauduroy also charged £3 4s 6d for two frames for portraits of the Duke of Suffolk and Queen of Bohemia for the Dining Parlour.
63 Finch 1901, vol.1, p.69.
64 'to remain faithful to the principles of the Reformed Faith into which he was born and to participate in Holy Communion' (*HSQS*, XXV, p.42).
65 Feillet was paid for restoring a cartoon of Eve obtained from the auctioneer Cock for James Brydges, 1st Duke of Chandos. Collins-Baker 1949, p.88 n.89.
66 *HSQS*, LX, p.166.
67 Deuchar, S., 'Monamy, Peter', *GOA* (accessed 23 March 2020).
68 *HSQS*, XX, p.107.
69 Gowing 1953, pp.19, 22; the sale of the prints was announced in the *London Daily Post and General Advertiser* on 19 April 1744. For *Sweet William's Farewell* see Simpson 2020.
70 Nichols and Wray 1935, p.251. A signed painting in the Victoria and Albert Museum is *Vessels at Sea* (www.collections.vam.ac.uk/item/O131665/vessels-at-sea-oil-painting-monamy-peter, accessed 20 March 2020).
71 Fleming 1962.
72 Saltoun Papers, National Library of Scotland.
73 'English Baroque Sketches', ibid., under Antonio Verrio.
74 Vertue II (*The Walpole Society*, vol.20 [1931–2]), p.126.
75 The scheme was engraved and the prints were evidently well known in England. The sale catalogue of 'The Prints, Drawings & books of Prints of Mr Thomas Major by him lately collected Abroad' (1747) included lot 76, 'le grand escalier de Versailles par le Brun'.
76 A typescript copy of this inventory is in the library of the Victoria and Albert Museum.
77 Thomson 1930, p.361.
78 Boughton House, Accounts of the Executors of Ralph, 1st Duke of Montagu, 1712, vol.1, fol.330, when he received £328. By 1705 Vanderbank received a further £448 5s 0d from Ralph Montagu.
79 Sheppard 1966, 'The Soho Tapestry Manufactory: The Vanderbanks and John Ellys' (website accessed 5 August 2019).
80 *HSQS*, XXVI, p.6.

81 Finch 1901, vol.1, pp.95–6.
82 Chatsworth Household Accounts 1685–99, 1699 (Chatsworth Estate Office, Derbyshire), fol.178.
83 *Export of Objects of Cultural Interest 2016–17*, Case 8: 'English Tapestry in the Japan Indian Manner', pp.31–3 (www.collections.vam.ac.uk/item/01386215/tapestry-mazarind-michael, accessed 28 January 2019).
84 Leslie-Melville Papers, Scottish Record Office, GD 26/6/123/13. Bills from Leonard Chabaneix are dated 19 September, 10 December and 19 December 1700. One of these payments is for the chinoiserie tapestry hangings shown in the 1911 *Country Life* photograph of the Tapestry Room (the room next to the State Bedroom on the principal floor) at Melville – they are described in the bill from Leonard Chabaneix as 'trois piece de Tappisserie Japan Chameaux', for which he charged £8 6s 4 1/2d.
85 By kind permission of Viscount De L'Isle. De L'Isle papers, Kent Archives and Local History Service.
86 Hefford 1983–4.
87 Thomson 1930, p.362.
88 *L'harmonie du coloris*, published around 1725, demonstrates Le Blon's invention of a three-colour printing process that was a predecessor to chromolithography. The book could be acquired from 'W. and J. Innys ... and at the author's lodgings at the Dial and Bible in the Strand', as stated in their 'Monthly Catalogue' of May 1725. See www.collections.vam.ac.uk/item/01438226/lharmonie-du-coloris-dans-la-book-le-blon-jacob (accessed 7 July 2020).
89 Thomson 1930, p.496.
90 The discovery of a previously unpublished oil sketch by Chéron, *A Feast of the Gods with Venus and Bacchus*, *c*.1710, illustrated in Hamlett 2020, p.103, no.92, indicates that the reassessment of Chéron's contribution is overdue. For a reassessment of Chèron at Boughton House see Marandet 2017.

5 Huguenot Architects and Engineers *pages 77–95*

1 Rosenfeld 1989.
2 Knecht 2008, p.363.
3 R. Coope, 'Brosse, Salomon de', *GOA* (accessed 28 June 2019).
4 Known as 'Le Petit Marot', *c*.1654–60, reprinted Farnborough 1969.
5 MacLeod 2012, no.21, p.83.
6 Strong 1979, pp.85–104; Morgan 2007.
7 The designs were published as *Hortus Palatinus*, 1620.
8 This is shown in Robert Smythson's ground plan of Somerset Place and Gardens, *c*.1611, Thurley 2009, pp.97–8.
9 Strong 1979, pp.138–65.
10 The full title in French, *avec quelques machines mouvantes par le moyen de l'eau et un discours de la conduite d'icele*, was published in London. For the De Caus family, see R. Zimmermann, 'Caus, de family', *GOA* (accessed 8 February 2020); Strong 1979, pp.138–65.
11 See www.rct.uk/collection/search#/4/collection/405415/the-family-of-sir-balthasar-gerbier (accessed 22 November 2019).
12 Colvin 1995, pp.396–8.
13 J. Wood, 'Gerbier, Sir Balthazar (1592–1663/1667), art agent, miniature painter, and architect', *OCNB* (accessed 8 February 2020).
14 For Gerbier's *Princely virtuous academical discourse*, see van Gelder 1979, no.44, p.88 (illustrated).
15 See www.collections.vam.ac.uk/item/0675236/print-jean-berain (accessed 8 February 2020). In September 1682 the *Mercure de France* commented on Daniel Marot's print: 'Faite par un jeune homme qui égale deja les plus habile graveurs, et qui se sera autant connaîtres par luy-mesme, qu'il est connu a Paris par le nom de feu son pere. Ils est fils du Sr Marot, architecte et graveur, qui a laisse beaucoup ouvrages au Public.'
16 A copy of this rare print is in the Metropolitan Museum of Art, New York.
17 The print of the birthday ball is inscribed 'J'ai porte donc a Votre Altesse Royalle ce qui'il ya de plus beau et de meilleur au monde, s'il est bien reseu je suis content'.
18 British Museum, inv.1870,0514.2959. A portrait of the Princess, above, is flanked by vignettes of the façade of Huis Ten Bosch and the court banquet.
19 Jackson-Stops 1975.
20 Lane 1949. The design is in the Boymans Museum, Rotterdam. See Murdoch 1985a, no.264, p.184.
21 In a letter to his brother Christian, dated 13 April 1694, Constantijn Huygens wrote: 'Ce pacquetboate qui a este pris est le mesme avec lequel Je suis venu icy. Le capitaine s'appelle Stevens. Le pauvre Marot mandé par la Reine, pour venir ici, y a esté fait prisonnier aussi'. Ozinga 1938, p.89.
22 *HSQS*, XXIX, pp.52,57.
23 Ibid., p.59.
24 Sotheby's, 10 July 1998, lot 87; Turpin 1999. The table is inscribed under the stretcher: 'La Galerie Thames'.
25 Morris 1982, pp.59–60. This 'work under ... glass' may be the hangings embroidered to Marot's designs preserved at Hampton Court Palace.
26 De Jonge 1971, p.91.Ceramic tiles and milk pans are preserved at Boughton House, the Rijksmuseum, the Victoria and Albert Museum and Hampton Court Palace. The delftware bears the 'AK' monogram of Adrianszoon Koex (who ran the Greek A factory at Delft from 1687 to 1701) and the 'PAK' monogram of his son Pieter Adrianszoon, who ran the factory until his death in 1703, when it was managed by his widow until 1722.
27 Pavord 1999, p.182.
28 The early seventeenth-century French word was based on the Arabic *suffa*.
29 The formal garden was cleared away in 1727.
30 Records of the Council of Nassau Demesne include a letter from Secretary Caspar Frederick Henning, paymaster 'of the money set aside for the use and service of his Majesties gardens at Hampton Court and Newmarket'. Henning drew up accounts for the new gardens at Hampton Court from 12 March 1698, so Marot must have supervised the layout of the gardens there after his return to the Netherlands. Lane 1949, p.19.
31 Marot's ceiling design incorporating a royal crown, may be connected. Royal Institute of British Architects 1972, under 'Marot'.
32 Jackson-Stops 1973a.
33 *HSQS*, XXXI, pp.8–9; *HSQS*, XXVI, p.16. There were other well-connected Marots among the London Huguenot community. Henri de Massue, Earl of Galway (1648–1720) and 'Mme Marie Temple', daughter (?) of Sir William Temple (1628–1699), former ambassador in Paris, stood godparents to the daughter of Maixant and Ester Marot in 1697.
34 Jackson-Stops 1981.
35 Ward-Jackson 1958, p.6; impressions are in the collections of the British Museum and the Victoria and Albert Museum.
36 *Oeuvres du Sr. D. Marot contenant plussieurs pensez utille aux architects, sculpteurs, orfevres, & jardiniers, & autres le toutes en faveure de ceux qui s'appliquerent aux beaux arts*, inscribed 'Ce vand Chez l'Auteur'. Rosenberg, Slive and ter Kuile 1972, p.411. For Marot's prints, see Bowett 2007.
37 Boyer 1722, p.46.
38 Campbell 1715, pls 34–6.
39 Reff 1967. A contemporary painting attributed to Mignard, inscribed 'Le Duc et la Duchesse de Montaigu arrètant le plan de Montaigu house qui leur est presenté par un Architecte francais' (Sotheby's, London, 7 July 2011), provides possible visual evidence; the painting was likely executed in Paris, where Mignard painted portraits of Ralph Montagu and his first wife, Elizabeth (d.1690). No portrait of the younger François Puget (1651–1707) survives but his portrait of his father, Pierre, hangs in the Louvre; a self-portrait by Pierre Puget was recently on loan to the Museum of Aix-en-Provence (Colvin 1995, under 'Pouget'; reproduced in Murdoch 1992b). François also acted as his father's agent at the court of Louis XIV from 1683 to 1688, accompanying Pierre's celebrated sculptures *Milon de Crotone* (1683) and *Perseus and Andromeda* (1685) to Paris. François could have delivered his father's design for Montagu House to Ralph Montagu in Montpellier or Paris. This summary benefits from communications with Richard Hewlings and Alastair Laing following the Victoria and Albert Museum/Boughton House 'Louis XIV Style' conference in December 2015.
40 Royal Institute of British Architects 1972, under 'Boujet'; Girouard 1962, pp.64, 181–2. An illustrated pedigree of 1711 for the second Earl of Warrington bears a close resemblance to Boujet's other drawings; Hardy and Jackson-Stops 1978, fig.1. Boujet's design for a pediment sculpture now in the Metropolitan Museum of Art, New York, Minerva flanked by five putti representing the Arts, with Garter ribbon and Minerva's spear, may have been intended for the rebuilding of Whitehall Palace after the 1698 fire, or for one of the new Oxford or Cambridge colleges.

Information supplied by Gervase Jackson-Stops. The drawing was in Sir James Thornhill's collection.

41 I am grateful to Richard Hewlings for sharing his observations on Pierre Silvestre as a connoisseur of architecture. Born in Bordeaux, Silvestre established a medical practice in Paris and in Amsterdam in 1685 became physician to William of Orange, whom he attended at the Battle of the Boyne in 1690. Admitted to the London College of Physicians in June 1693, Silvestre was naturalized in July 1696 and elected Fellow of the Royal Society in March 1699. He died in 1718 in London; his mother was his executor. His elder brother remained in Bordeaux as a Councillor of the Parlement of Guienne. *HSQS*, LX, p.341.

42 *Le Petit Marot*, *c*.1654–60 (see note 4).

43 Cornforth 1970.

44 Louw 1983.

45 G. Jackson-Stops, 'French and Dutch influence on Architecture and Interiors', in Murdoch 1992a, p.63.

46 Murdoch 1992b.

47 Hayward 1930, p.341.

48 Green 1951, pp.85–6, citing Blenheim archives MS A.2–31. Green attributes the letter to Louis Silvestre (1669–1740) but neither of these two Paris-trained artists was in Britain in 1707.

49 Quoted by Richard Hewlings, unpublished paper delivered at the Victoria and Albert Museum 'Louis XIV Style' conference visit to Boughton House, December 2015.

50 Boughton House MSS, vol.2, fol.908, Accounts of the Executors of Ralph Duke of Montagu 1709–1712: 'Laid out by Order of his Grace Ralph Duke of Montagu by Peter Silvester' in 1708, for which Silvester was recompensed on 17 April 1712; 'Paid to M[r]: Cornelius Gole for teaching Thomas Drew to draw ... £4 18s 8d'; 'To M[r]:de Moivre for teaching the said Drew the Elements of Geometry ... £2 3s 0d'; 'To M[r]:Thomas Hews for binding the said Drew his Apprentice and the Charge of his Indenture ... £1 1s 6d'; 'Paid for some Tools for the use of the said Drew ... £1 0s 0d'. Thomas Hughes was a London-based stonemason working at Kensington Palace in 1689–92; at St Alphege, Greenwich, in 1712–14; and St John, Smith Square, in 1714–28. He was appointed Master Bricklayer in the King's Works in 1718, an office that gave him a place on the Board of Works. Richard Hewlings, pers. comm.

51 Jackson-Stops 1973a, p.1873.

52 Marot used reflective glass for interiors for Queen Mary at Kensington and Het Loo. See, for example, her china cabinet at Het Loo, which became William's library after her death.

53 Harris 1961.

54 Jacobsen 2012, pp.209–30.

55 Quoted in full in Cartwright 1883, p.79.

56 My thanks to Dr Terry Friedman for this reference.

57 A. Hagemann, 'Lord Raby and the Cultural Milieu of the Berlin Court of Frederick I', in Eyres and Lomax 2014, pp.9–22, at p.17; M. Charlesworth, 'Lord Raby in Berlin: Architecture, Art and Amour' in ibid., pp.23–42.

58 Letter from Lord Bathurst (1717), Cartwright 1883, p.443.

59 Letter to Richard Bentley, Lewis 1937–83, vol.35, pp.266–7.

60 Formerly in the collection of Francis St John, Thorpe Hall, Peterborough; the volume containing the cross-section is inscribed 'Bt. at M. Talman's Sale Feb. 1725/26 £7.10s'.

61 A plan of the cellars, in the Sheffield Record Office, is inscribed: 'Dessein & lettre de Thomas Thackray Aout 1714', and a plan and elevation for a garden pavilion, Franco-Prussian in style, are probably contemporary copies. Lady Wentworth, writing on 28 April 1709, relates that 'Mr. Benson' was 'to look after your building in Yorkshire'. Two years later, on 22 May 1711, Peter Wentworth advises his brother: 'When I was at the Duke of Shrewsbury's my Lord Scarborough was there and he was talking of his building and they did agree that there was no Building without a Surveyor ... wch agrees with the advise Mr. Benson is always desiring to send you'. Cartwright 1883, pp.84, 200.

62 Archer's work shows the influence of Bernini and Borromini and is closer to the Italian Baroque than any other contemporary British architect. My thanks to Terry Friedman for this observation.

63 Harvey's presence at Stainborough in May 1720 is recorded in the contract for carving Corinthian capitals in Roche Abbey stone.Wilkinson 1883, p.374; Wentworth Papers, Sheffield Record Office, CLD 1121v, p.7. He was still working there in 1724, when three letters were delivered to 'Mr. Harvey the carver at York' for a charge of 2s 4d.

64 I am indebted to Dr Friedman for this reference Yorkshire Archaeological Society, anonymous MS 328.

65 Cartwright 1883, pp.455–6.

66 Kuke 2002, pp.165–9.

67 Elias, son of Elizée Hauduroy was baptized at the Threadneedle Street church on 7 May 1665. *HSQS*, XIII, p.178h.

68 Girouard 1962b.

69 Samuel Hauduroy also designed features for Blathwayt's London home, Little Wallingford House, Whitehall. The papers and designs in the Gloucester County Record Office include the following letter 'Pour Monsieur Povey a Witthall': 'Je ne croy pas Monsieur qui soit besoin de vous faire Un grand discour sur tout ce que Jay fait pour Monsieur Bladthwayt tant pour la Campagne que Jay fait tout seul a durham ou bien lorce que Jy ay ette en Compagnie de Monsieur bladhwayt car pour la fois que Jy ay eté moy seul on peut voir facilement par le pland general que Jy ay fait Sy Jay perdu le temp quay Jy ay este ettant un pland d'une aussy grande fatigue qui Sen peut voir veu que toute les proportions en sont prise avec toute l'exactitude imaginable. Et cett en pland a garder a toujours de plus Jaye escrit toute bel auteurs Et le panchan(t) de la terre Et fait le dessein de la facace avec le pland de ce qui est execute a present Et tout cela pour la valeur de six guinée car del dix que Monsieur Bladhwayt me donna auparavant que de partir il m'en a coute quatre pour les fraix du carrosse Et de ma nourriture pour ce qui est du voyage que Jay fait avec Monsieur blatheways il scait tres bien la fatigue que Jy ay eu a instruire Et corriger les ouvrier a visiter avec luy tout les lieux l'un apres l'autre et ecrire tout ce qu'il faloit faire de plus J'ay fait les desseins de Caping de la terasse, le dessein d'un pavillon le dessein de la Muraille de la terasse Un dessein de chambranle des fenestre quil faut adjouter a la façade Et le pland de toute la maison attaché avec le pland des ecurie Jay fait de plus pour le bon homme Jacob deux desseins pour le boissage des portes un dessein pour les trois grande fenestre du bout de la hall avec un dessein en forme dalcove vous voyez pas tout cecy Monsieur. Sy lorsque Javoir visité de Jour avec Monsieur bladhwait tous les androit ou ii faloit faire des augmentation J'aurois peu faire tant d'ouvrage sy Je ne mettois levé tout les Jours deux heure devant le jour, Et me coucher tous les jours passé minuit sy Javois peu faire tout cecy Je ne dit rien qui ne soit vray et dont Monsieur bladhwayt ne soit le temoins c'est pour quoy Je prie Monsieur bladhwayt de considerer tout ces choses Et de croire que toute peine merite recompance principalement quand on le fait avec autant dassiduité comme Jay fait Je croit Monsieur que cecy et assé pour vous instruire de tout. Je suis Monsieur, Votre tres humble Serviteur, S. hauduroy. Pour les deseins que Jay fait a Londre Monsieur bladhwayt en a la memoire Et Je vous prie Monsieur de vous resouvenir de votre billet et que Monsieur Bladhwayt ne resteroit que dix Jours en campagne.'

70 Gloucester County Record Office, Blathwayt Papers, E 236.

71 'Desseins que Jay fait pour Monsieur Bladthwayt du depuis que je suis revenue de Durham Cest a dire du temp quil a esté en flandre et ceux que J'ay fait du depuis qu'il est revenue Premierement trois plans pour les trois estages du pavillon, du coste des escuries. Plus un dessein de Cheminée pour la Sale neufue. Plus un dessein de l ambrassement de la porte Et du reste qui sert d'Elevation Jusqua La corniche de la ditte Salle. plus Un dessein de la Corniche de la ditte Salle qui regne tout autour. Plus un dessein de cheminee pour le banquetin house. Depuis le retour de Monsieur Blathwayt de flandre Jay dessigné Un dessein de L'escalier de Milord Nottingham

Un autre dessein ou les proportions dudit escalier sont dessigne en grand avec les proportions de lescalier que Jay prise aupres de bichop guates. du depuis le retour de monsieur bladhwayt de durham Jay dessigné un dessein de cheminée pour la Salle du pavillion du cote de l'Eglise. Plus deux plans de la facade de la maison ou sont dessigné toutes les partition que l'on y doit faire.'

72 'two designs for the woodwork of the doors ... for [my] good man Jacob'. Pencil, brown ink and grey wash, 32.5 x 15.5 cm (Gloucestershire Archives). The design includes 'la Corniche de la ditte Salle', so could fit the later description of 'un dessein de lambrassement de la porte'.

73 Goulding 2017, illustrated p.10. This is inscribed: 'Cette Rampe descalier Est plus solide Et dessigne dans lordre d'architecture Et pour le mode du temp c'est ce que l'on doit fuir [?] le plus qu il le peut car les modes ce changes Et jamais ceux ci'.

74 See note 71. Burley-on-the-Hill was bought from the executors of the 2nd Duke of Buckingham, although John Lumley of Northampton (the architect of Ampthill Park) was employed there by 1697.

75 Kenworthy-Browne 1978, p.11; Finch 1901, vol.1, p.69. Lord Nottingham considered employing Messrs. 'Hoddery' to decorate the staircase walls.

76 Archer 1975.

77 Morgan Ng (pers. comm.) has suggested that Claude David may have been introduced to Montagu by Pierre Silvestre, who had visited Genoa and Rome.

78 Roscoe et al. 2009, p.339; Longleat Archives of Thomas Thynne, 1st Viscount Weymouth, 200 01/01/1705.

79 Roscoe et al. 2009, pp.689–701.

80 Craven 1988.

81 A family pedigree is preserved in the Huguenot Society library.

82 Beard 1975, pp.43, 231.

83 Nadauld's first recorded payment for work at Chatsworth is dated 28 April 1700.

84 Chatsworth Building Accounts (Chatsworth Estate Office, Derbyshire), vol.VII, p.63.

85 Nadauld was paid £14 6s: ibid., p.93.

86 'Worck done since 1710' lists 'Carving the Corniche in the Sallon', 'Carveing the corniche in the danain romme': ibid., G2/2/33–4. I am most grateful to Miss Oppenheimer, Archivist at Castle Howard. The entry in the accounts for the 'dainain room' specifies '81 modillions', which remain; the lion frieze in the Tapestry Room is stylistically close to Nadauld's drawings at Chatsworth.

87 Saumarez Smith 1990, pp.63–6.

88 *HSQS*, XLIX, pp.79, 194.

89 'Mr de Rit's Accounts 1698–1705', Boughton House.

90 He was paid £31 14s for 114 ft of carving at 4s 6d per foot.

91 Gideon du Chesne supplied the 'upper sima of the composite cornich, the under sima reverst' and 'the Ovill or Egs in the Beding mold' for a total of £21 4s 4d.

92 Saumarez Smith 1990, p.66; Roscoe et al. 2009, p.378. Gideon du Chesne worked with his son John in wood and plaster at Boughton.

93 Castle Howard Building Accounts, G2/2/32, Nadauld's Account 1705–9.

94 Saumarez Smith 1990, pp.93, 104, 138–9; Castle Howard Building Accounts, G2/2/53. The account is dated 1727–8.

95 Obituary, *Gentleman's Magazine*, 1735.

96 G. Leoni, *The Architecture of Andrea Palladio*, trans. N. Dubois (London 1715). translator's preface, p.2.

97 'Captain Nicholas Dubois of Leicester Fields in the Parish of St. Martin in the Fields ... and Seignior Alexander Galilei of St. James's Parish ... agreed to become co-partners & joint dealers together in all Designs, Buildings, Architecture, Drawings, both Military and Civil, to commence from the Day of these presents and to be continued for the Terme of Five years from thence', Toesca 1952, pp.212–17.

98 E. Kieven, 'Galilei, Alessandro', *GOA* (accessed 8 February 2020).

99 *HSQS*, LX, p.148; Du Bourgay lived until 1732, although his will was written in 1719.

100 Colvin 1995, pp.323–5.

101 Colvin et al. 1976, p.87.

102 According to Dubois's defence at the Court of Chancery in 1721, the company was inspired by 'the great number of new buildings which were daily erecting in and about the city of London, and the necessity of rebuilding a great part of the city in a few years by reason that the houses which were rebuilt after the fire in the year 1666 had been built in hast & with indifferent materials and the great abuse and fraud of Common Builders and Workmen' (Colvin 1976, p.87).

103 The National Archives, Court of Chancery Papers C 11/1998/15. Nicholas Dubois v Mayor of London.

104 The National Archives, Court of Chancery Papers C 11/1999/15. Nicholas Dubois v Lewis Dollon, Anthony Vezian and others.

105 Sheppard 1963, vol.XXXI, part 2, p.121.

106 Bryant 2018, pp.4, 16.

107 Oswald 1932.

108 Tipping 1921, figs 21 and 22; British Library, Add. MS 33085, pp.285–6, 351–2.

109 For a full account of the first Westminster Bridge, see Walker 1979.

110 J.T. Desaguliers, *A Course of Experimental Philosophy* (London 1745), vol.2, p.506.

111 Walker 1979, p.82.

112 Ibid.

113 Ibid., pp.64, 109.

114 Lees-Milne 1962, pp.98–9; Walker 1979, pp.95–6. For the earlier David Papillon, see Airs 2017.

115 The Vauloué family of watchmakers came from Bourges. In 1769 François Vauloué was admitted to the French Hospital aged 64 on the recommendation of the jeweller Louis Masquerier. His business had failed. He had served as an elder at the French church of La Tremblade. His father, Pierre, had been admitted in 1736 and had died there in 1737. *HSQS*, LIII, under 'Vauloué'.

116 *Read's Weekly Journal*, 12 December 1738. C. Labelye, *A description of Westminster Bridge* (London 1751).

117 'A Perspective View of the Engine made use of for driving the Piles of the New Bridge at Westminster, engraved by Mr. Toms after Mr. Gravelot ... sold at Slaughter's Coffee House, and Mr. Harding's both on the Pavement in St. Martin's Lane' (London Metropolitan Archives, inv. p5424621).

118 Walker 1979, p.91.

119 This is with the George III collection in the Science Museum, London, inv.1903–2 (www.sciencemuseum.org.uk/objects-and-stories/george-iii-royal-passion-science, accessed 8 July 2020).

120 Walker 1979, pp.154–5.

121 See Colvin 1995, p.353.

122 Walker 1979, pp.172ff.

123 Labelye 1751, p.81: 'This order was the first and only one that ever I received from the Commissioners, contrary to my judgement or opinion and which I obeyed, but I own not without some concern.'

124 Walker 1979. p.181.

125 Labelye 1751, pp.iii, 103.

126 Lees-Milne 1962, p.99.

127 Walker 1979, p.221.

128 S. Riou, *Short Principles for the Architecture of Stone Bridges with practical observations and a new geometrical diagram to determine the thickness of the Piers to the height and base of any given arch* (London 1760), p.ix.

129 Ibid., p.92.

130 Ibid., pp.iv, 111.

131 Colvin 1995, p.440.

132 S. Riou, *Short Principles* (note 134), cited in Murdoch 1982, p.122.

133 Colvin 1995, p.640, under 'Marquand'.

134 Walker 1979, pp.52, 55.

135 Murdoch 1985a, no.144, p.108.

136 S. Riou, *The Elements of Fortification* (London 1746), Preface.

137 *HSQS*, LX, p.329.

138 An architectural book in the sale rooms in 1972 was inscribed: 'Abraham Roumieu Architect 1756'; Colvin 1995, p.836, under 'Roumieu'.

139 Register House Edinburgh, Gordon Castle Plans 1072–4, dated 1766–7.

140 Murdoch and Vigne 2009, pp.50–1.

141 My thanks to Gordon Balderston for advice on Richard Castle. James Truffet, Louis Poiriez and five members of the Crommelin family are listed in the 'Account of Royal Manufacture of Linnen Cloth' in Lisburn for the half year 25 September 1711 to 25 March 1712. The most accurate account of Richard Castle's complex family background is in the online Dictionary of Irish Architects published by the Irish Architectural Archive, www.dia.ie/architects/view/347/CASTLE%2C+RICHARD (accessed 8 July 2020).

142 A service of blessing in French took place on 18 June 1733, led by Abraham Viridet, minister of the French Protestant community that met in St Mary's Chapel in St Patrick's Cathedral, Dublin. *HSQS*, VII, p.115.

143 For Louis Crommelin and his family in Lisburn, see Scouloudi 1964 (genealogy as inscribed on gravestone); Best 1997, pp.176–83 (Samuel Crommelin's pedigree chart on p.180).

144 Curran 1967, pp.51–6.

145 Cox 2002.

146 Curran 1967, pp.51–2. The original contract is today on display in the hall of the hospital. McDonnell 2007.

6 Huguenot Metalsmiths

pages 97–107

1 R. Campbell, *The London Tradesman, being an historical account of all the trades, professions, arts, both Liberal and Mechanic, now practised in the Cities of London and Westminster* (London 1747), pp.165–6.

2 Ibid.
3 Guiffrey 1887, p.1230. My thanks to Sandra Robinson for this reference.
4 Jackson Stops 1971, p.183. Vertue III (*The Walpole Society*, vol.22 [1933–4]), p.124.
5 Saunders 2005, p.350.
6 *HSQS*, LVI, p.112.
7 Clayton 1997, p.294 n.70; Griffiths 1998, no.190, p.273.
8 Laguerre's original drawing in black chalk for the frontispiece is illustrated by Davis 1982, at that time in a private collection. See Croft-Murray and Hulton 1960–3, vol.1, p.400.
9 Saunders 2005, p.305.
10 Garrioch 2014, pp.130, 141.
11 'Advertisements and Notices', *Post Man and the Historical Account*, 7–9 October 1703. Davis 1982, p.205. Advertisement for Mr Melchizedeck Girard, wine merchant at the sign of the Bacchus and Grapes, who advertised in the same broadsheet in November 1701 and March and April 1702 from West Street 'over against' the French church near Newport Market.
12 Saunders 2005, pp.311–12.
13 Ibid., pp.272, 290, 332, 333, 345.
14 Ibid., p.290.
15 Ibid., p.355.
16 Edwards 1975, p.22.
17 Bedford County Record Office, L 31/309: 'Mr. Tishue Iron gates etc £64'.
18 Lee-Woolfe 2018, pp.204, 218, 238, 242, 243. The original manuscript is in the National Art Library, V&A MS 86 EE 86 pp.9, 75; Davis 1982, p.249.
19 *Wren Society*, vols VII, XV, XVI, XVIII.
20 Morris 1982, p.83.
21 Edwards 1977, p.15. Josiah Key bequeathed 'all my tools and materials and all my patterns of metal or wood to cast by' in 1711; Saunders 2005, p.306.
22 Saunders 1980.
23 Saunders 2005, pp.314–19.
24 Collins-Baker 1949, pp.149, 159n.
25 *Export of Objects of Cultural Interest, 2016–17*, Case 18 'English gilt-bronze painted & cast iron railings', pp.52–3, www.gov.uk/government/news/rare-chesterfield-house-railings-at-risk-of-leaving-the-uk (accessed 15 July 2020).
26 Saunders 2005, pp.316, 317.
27 Jean Montigny was not connected to John Remy de Montigny, who had lived in Duke Street, St James's, and served the Huguenot charity, La Providence, as a director from 1723 until his death in 1734, when he was living in Greenwich. Murdoch and Vigne 2009; *HSQS*, LX, p.113.
28 Murdoch 2006c.
29 Saunders 2005, p.319.
30 I am indebted to Gervase Jackson-Stops for this information.
31 Beard and Gilbert 1986, p.682.
32 Murdoch 1982, vol.2, appendix pp.246–7.
33 They are described as smiths (*maréchal*), so were either locksmiths or possibly blacksmiths in this country town. They were Solomon Courier, Pierre Delessard and Jacques Duclos. *HSQS*, XIX, pp.26, 45, 63; Murdoch 1982, vol.1, p.246, 'Professions of Emigré Craftsmen: Locksmiths'.
34 *HSQS*, XXIX, p.15; Beard and Gilbert 1986, p.241. Desbois was still there in 1723. Nicholas Gautier is recorded between 1703 and 1734.
35 Campbell 1747, pp.166–7.
36 Boughton House, Northamptonshire, Archives: 'The accounts of the executors of Ralph, Duke of Montagu, 1712', vol.1, fol.499, entry for 15 December 1697.
37 *HSQS*, XXVI, p.4. John Lewis Marc, recorded as a silversmith in 1704 at the Savoy Church, was still working in in 1727, when he registered as a smallworker.
38 West Sussex Record Office: Petworth House Accounts 172.
39 G. Jackson-Stops in Murdoch 1992a, p.63 and n.40. In September 1703, when Samuel Marc stood godfather to Etienne Vanier, son of Etienne Vanier, a carpenter, then working in Rose Street, Soho, Marc was described as 'serrurier en grosses oeuvres'; *HSQS*, XXXV, p.22.
40 *HSQS*, XXIX, pp.55, 64, 75; *HSQS*, XXIX, p.114. Paul Desmoulins is recorded as a cabinetmaker from 1698 to 1719: *HSQS*, XXVI, p.5; *HSQS*, XXIX, p.117. See also Beard and Gilbert 1986, p.242.
41 *HSQS*, LIII, under 'Podevin, Pierre François'.
42 Sherlock 2002, fig.6. The Dunster chandelier cost £16 5s and was described in the churchwardens' accounts as 'the Candle Stick'. The Marblehead chandelier was the gift of the Eldridge Family. Mr Eldridge was a Royal Customs Collector for the Port of Marblehead. His grandson Eldridge Gerry signed the Declaration of Independence and was a United States Vice President.
43 Hayward 1963–4, p.655.
44 The Gunmakers' Guild maintained standards of production and proved or tested gun barrels before they were offered for sale. Its authority extended for a 10-mile radius beyond its premises in the City of London.
45 *Treasures from Chatsworth* 1979, nos 171 and 172.
46 *HSQS*, LIII, under 'Segalas'. He was living with the 'Milk Man' in Old Street when admitted. He died ten months later.
47 Hayward 1963–4.
48 He is not the Peter Molan, buried in St Martin-in-the Fields on 23 November 1699 (www.collections.royalarmouries.org/object/rac-object-31799.html, accessed 7 August 2019) as his will was written on 7 June 1699, Royal Armouries, PROB-11-461-247.
49 The Gruché *arquebusier* family were from Corbeil-Essonnes in the Ile de France: Claude Gruché, *arquebusier*, was son of François Gruché, *arquebusier*, who was married in Corbeil-Essonnnes in 1700. There was a gunpowder mill in Essonnes from *c.*1650. My thanks to Sandra Robinson for this information.
50 See www.collections.royalarmouries.org/object/rac-object-35079.html (accessed 7 August 2019).
51 See www.collections.royalarmouries.org/object/rac-object-1059.html and www.collections.royalarmouries.org/object/rac-object-15204.html (accessed 7 August 2019).
52 *Treasures from Chatsworth* 1979, no.172. A gun signed 'Noel de Landreville' is the Glasgow Museum Collections on display at Kelvingrove Museum, inv.E.1939.65.vv.
53 *Treasures from Chatsworth* 1979, no.171.
54 Murdoch 1985, no.325.
55 The Duke of Marlborough's pair of pistols signed 'Barbar' have descended in the Churchill family.
56 S. Bevan, C. Blair and A.V.B. Norman, 'The Armoury', in Murdoch 1992a, pp.159, 165, 167, fig.173. The gunsmith Peter Riou was paid by the Huguenot steward Mark Anthony for cleaning arms between 1709 and 1713; ibid., p.159.
57 Letter from the 2nd Duke of Montagu's Huguenot steward Charles Lamotte, June 1718: 'put up in that room next to your former appartment', Murdoch 1992b. For a photograph of the Old Armoury, Boughton House, as laid out by Louis Barbar, see Murdoch 1992a, p.158.
58 *The Daily Advertiser*, 15 November 1742, issue 3689. Huguenot cutlers and razor makers include James Bernardeau (d.1752/3), based at Russell Court, Drury Lane, from 1726 (see www.academia.edu/7181556/_Sprimont's_Complaint_Buying_and_Selling_Continental_Porcelain_in_London_1730_1753, p.15, accessed 13 October 2020). Bernardeau supplied cutlery with Chantilly porcelain handles in the Kakiemon style
59 *HSQS*, LX, will of Jacob Boursot, 4 February 1777, proved 27 May 1778. Fleureau's shop bill head in the Banks Collection, Department of Prints and Drawings, British Museum, inv.52.27, carried an invoice dated 1766. Jacob Boursot's father, James, a haberdasher in The Strand, died in 1735.
60 Christie's, South Kensington, 18 June 2009, lot 63.
61 John Savigny's trade card is in the Banks Collection, Department of Prints and Drawings, British Museum, inv.D.2.145. P. Savigny was the direct descendant of Nicholas Savigny, cutler, in St James's, who married at St Martin Orgars in 1714. *HSQS*, XXXVII, no.499.
62 *The Daily Gazeteer*, 31 October 1763, issue 3078.
63 See www.catalogue.nla.gov.au/Record/4882782 (accessed 27 March 2020).
64 Homer 1984, pp.118–22.
65 Coyne 1994, pp.545–8.
66 Hatcher and Barker 1968, p.22; Homer 2018.
67 Homer 2018.
68 The petition is dated 31 March 1663. Welch 1902, vol.2, p.122. Taudin was naturalized in 1663. National Archives, HL/PO/30/10/1/316.
69 Welch 1902, vol.2, p.124.
70 Hatcher and Barker 1974, nos 40–4.
71 Welch 1902, vol.2, p.137.
72 Hatcher and Barker 1974, pp.225–7. James Taudin the younger was established in London by 1675, when he married Isabeau Lavie.
73 Welch 1902, vol.2, p.169.
74 Chassin du Gerny 2007, pp.131–7.
75 See www.pewterbank.co.uk/wp-content/uploads/2020/07/Some-interesting-Tickets-on-Old-Pewterware (accessed 25 March 2020) for a

remarkable wavy-edged bread dish marked for Jonas Durand, 1699, with the crest of the Earls of Lonsdale. Jonas Durand also supplied the Montagu household with pewter. Murdoch 1992b, p.349.

76 Welch 1902, vol.2, p.164. Mark Henry Chabroles (fl.1689–93) appeared before the court and was told he must not keep any shop because he was a stranger and alien. In December 1689 his premises were searched. In October 1690, when it was discovered that he was a Protestant refugee, he was given permission to work 'for some time longer'. In June 1693 he was advised to leave the trade 'as the laws of this kingdom are against his excercising it', although he was allowed to continue until 24 August that year. Ricketts 2001, pp.65–6.

77 See www.theislandwiki.org/index.php/Biographies_of_silver_makers (accessed 25 March 2020).

78 Murdoch and Vigne 2009, pp.25, 111–16, fig.20 and appendix pp.111–16: 'Inventory of the contents of the French Hospital, 1742'.

79 In 1808 James Perchard registered his mark as a smallworker in partnership with William Brooks and worked from 14 Clerkenwell Green until 1817.

80 W. Maitland, W., *History of London from Its Foundation to the Present Time* (London 1756), book VI, p.1303.

81 Murdoch 1985, nos 113, 114, pp.92–3.

82 Murdoch and Vigne 2009, pp.111–16.

7 Carvers, Gilders, Cabinetmakers and Upholsterers *pages 109–31*

1 Thornton 1978, pp.48, 225.

2 Drury 1991.

3 Lunsingh Scheurleer 1980.

4 Beard 1997, p.4.

5 Murdoch 2002.

6 Jackson-Stops 1971b; G. Jackson-Stops in Baarsen et al. 1988, pp.200–9.

7 *The London Tradesmen* (1747) confirms that the Upholder co-ordinated 'Journeymen … Cabinet Makers, Glass-Grinders, Looking-Glass Frame-Carvers, Carvers for Chairs, Testers and Posts of Bed, the Woollen-Draper, the Mercer, the Linen-Draper several Species of Smiths, and … many Tradesman of the other mechanic Branches'.

8 Fowler and Cornforth 1974, pp.25–6.

9 Murdoch 1982, p.255.

10 Murdoch 2006c, p.84.

11 Murdoch 1998; 'Pelletier', www.npg.org.uk/research/conservation/directory-of-british-frame-makers/p/ (accessed 16 September 2019).

12 Beard and Gilbert 1986, p.376.

13 Ibid., p.377. The sofa was 'filled up with fine hair, and its cushion filled up with downe, the freize [*sic*] and cheeks all molded and fringed'.

14 Gilbert 1978, vol.2, pp.264–8; Wood 2008, pp.28, 36, nn.49, 83–4.

15 Bowett 2002, p.244.

16 One of these chairs is in the Victoria and Albert Museum (W.11–1964) and illustrated in Bowett and Fraser 2015, fig.10.

17 Murdoch 2006c, pp.248, 250.

18 Bowett 2002, pp.248–9, pl.8:36; Baarsen et al. 1988, p.45, fig.48.

19 Wood 2012, pp.69–70.

20 Ibid., pp.45–104.

21 Beard 1997, p.107, citing Guildhall Library MS 7141/1 fols 4, 311.

22 They were Josiah Casimire (fl.1714–24), Daniel Demée (entered the Upholders' Company in 1735), Isaac Deschamps, Anthony Guidott, Isaac Nourtier (entered the Upholders' Company in 1712) and Edward Noys (entered the Upholders' Company in 1722/3). For a list of admissions to the Upholders' Company, see Walton 1973, pp.51–79.

23 Beard 1997, p.156, citing Guildhall Library MSS 7141/1 and 7142. As Nicholas Sprimont's widow, Ann Protin (*c*.1724–1794) became sister-in-law to Francis Deschamps (1731–1808) in 1772, when he married her sister Susannah.

24 Heal 1953, p.72.

25 Paul Columbine was buried at the Norwich French church in 1784. *HSQS*, LX, p.70; Cornforth and Schmidt 1980, pp.427–31.

26 Beard and Gilbert 1986, p.693. Rothstein, 1990, p.219. Their descendant the architect John Samuel Phené (d.1912) was a director of the French Hospital and Master of the Clothworkers' Company in 1906–7. Murdoch 2009, p.196.

27 Beard and Westman 1993.

28 National Archives, LC9/280/107, fols 71–2.

29 National Archives, LC5/43; LC5/44, fol.28; LC9/280 no.74, fol.75.

30 Sackville Papers, Kent County Record Office, Maidstone, O 269 A 196/1: 'For 8 large turkey skins … to cover ye Chear £3.12.0; For making of ye Caas For ye Blue lethor chear £0.3.0.; For 6 yds 1/2 – of Blue Serge to Make ye Caas at 2s 6d yd £0.16.0.; For sewing silk & hooks & yes £00.02.00.'

31 Chatsworth, Building Accounts, 1697 (Chatsworth Estate Office, Derbyshire); Beard 1997, p.128, pls 92–4.

32 Boughton House MSS, Accounts of the Executors of Ralph, 1st Duke of Montagu, fols 93–6, 820–31.

33 Murdoch 1997.

34 Murdoch and Boucher 2013, pp.52–3.

35 Murdoch 1992b. Boucher provided mourning rings for the 1st Duke's funeral in 1709.

36 For Mary Pariselle, who supplied Ralph, Duke of Montagu, with tapestry seat covers, see Murdoch 1992b, p.349. Pariselle was paid, in December 1703, £10 on account for tapestry chairs and again for the same in August 1704 and July 1705; Esther Regneaux was paid £8 in March 1704 for two tapestry chairs; and in August 1705 Madame Justell was paid £20 for three silk and needlework chairs.

37 Possibly the wife of Henri Justell (1620–1693), William III's librarian, who outlived her husband and died in 1720.

38 Marie Pariselle was paid £6 2s 10d for worsted by the Duchess of Norfolk, Drayton Archives, MM/A/427.

39 Drayton Archives, MS 2475: £52 paid to Dorothy 'de lapere' 'for the use of my husband ffrancis d'lapier'. There was a charge of 15s for 'ye Upholsterer yt went downe with ye Bed to Drayton'. Drayton Archives, MM/A/18.

40 Beard and Gilbert 1986, p.689; for Penson's relationship to Poictevin, see Beard 1997, p.139. Poictevin returned to France, where he died in 1709. The upholsterer Guillotin of Castle Street, near Air Street, also supplied beds for Drayton. Drayton Archives, MS 2530.

41 Drayton Archives, MS 2530.

42 Friedman and Linstrum 1973, p.270.

43 Information from Bruce Bailey, Archivist at Drayton.

44 Beard 1997, pp.135–6. On 24 July 1799 they were paid 22s a yard 'for ye embroadery of ye bed they to find Silks and all other things fitting for ye use', with an advance of £6. They received £7 'for finishing ye embroidered curtain and four pound in hand for ye beginning of ye other curtain'.

45 Possibly the Thomas Benoist of the parish of St Giles-in-the-Fields, who died on January 1695/6 and was living in the parish of St Giles-in-the-Fields. Administration was granted to his widow, Judith (*HSQS*, LX, p.396).

46 Collins-Baker 1949, p.200; Huntington Library, Stowe Papers, ST 24/131 December 1722 ST 30, entry for 30 June 1730.

47 My thanks to David Mitchell and Annabel Westman for discussing their latest findings on Dufresnoy. A. Westman, 'New Light on the Textiles at Ham House', in Rowell 2013, pp. 248–61, at pp.250, 255; Westman 2019, pp.43, 250 n.25, figs 3.18, 3.19, 3.20, 4.6; Drayton Archives, MS 2475.

48 Huntington Library and Art Gallery, inv.2016.15. For the Sanxay family, see Murdoch 1985a, no.127, p.96. The Sanxays came from Tonnay-Boutonne, Aquitaine, and settled first in Exeter before moving to Cheam, Surrey, where Daniel's father, also Daniel Saxnay (d.1739), was headmaster of Cheam School. Sanxay 1907, p.83.

49 National Archives, Lord Chamberlains' Accounts LC9/284, fol.25 no 4. Toulouse charged £16 for embroidery and the canopy. Murdoch, 1992, pp.352–5.

50 National Archives, Lord Chamberlains' Accounts, LC9/283, fol.62; LC9/284, fol.637; LC9/285, fol.27.

51 Boughton House, Household Accounts of John, 2nd Duke of Montagu, 1725–46. The payment was received by 'An. Degulbourg & John. Desmanule, Church-Wardens of ye french Savoye', Murdoch 1992b, p.352.

52 Le Normand's obituary, *The Daily Post*, issue 5374 (2 December 1736), cited by Brett 2014a, p.6.

53 *The Freethinker*, 23 September (1720), no.262 cited by Brett 2014a, p.6.

54 Nicholas Bosquet's will, proved 28 April 1743, mentions his former partnership with Anthony Clerimbault and provides the instruction 'no papist to inherit any part of my estate', *HSQS*, LX, p.42.

55 Cassidy Geiger 1999. See also Brett 2014a.

56 *HSQS*, LX, p.68.

57 In 1681 four coachmakers received relief through the Threadneedle Street church; they were Pierre Marteau, Andrew Martinet, Henri Massiennes and Pierre Menardeau (*HSQS*, XLIX).
58 For Gibbons, see Esterly 1998.
59 Hardy and Jackson-Stops 1978; Kenworthy-Browne 1978, p.8.
60 Lunsingh Scheurleer 1980.
61 Ibid.
62 *HSQS*, XXIX, p.59. A second son, Corneille François, was baptized in the French Leicester Fields church in 1701.
63 *British and Irish Furniture Makers Online*, www.bifmo.history.ac.uk/entry/gole-cornelius-1689-91 (accessed 21 July 2020); Hardy and Turpin 1993. The only known copy is in the Library at Chatsworth.
64 Cornelius Gole stood godfather to Catherine, Salamon Woinsson's infant daughter, in October 1704 at the Huguenot Church of Leicester Fields. *HSQS*, XXIX, p.89.
65 Beard and Gilbert, 1986, p.349.
66 *HSQS*, XXV, p.25, pp.20, 25. Isaye Fleureau is described as 'horloger, bourgeois de la ville d'Orleans', Mr Gaulle, as *ébéniste*. In January 1746 Isaye Fleureau stood godfather to Françoise, daughter of Gedeon Gosset.
67 Turpin 2014.
68 Murdoch 1982, appendix: 'Professions of émigré craftsmen as recorded in the Huguenot registers of Great Britain and Ireland', pp.238–9: cabinetmakers and carpenters; *HSQS*, LII, under 'Connessant, Pierre'.
69 *HSQS*, XXXVII, p.38.
70 Alcouffe 2008 p.303.
71 *Wren Society*, vol.VIII, p.14. John Angier, cabinetmaker in London in 1806, may be another descendant; see Beard and Gilbert 1986, pp.14–15.
72 *HSQS*, XLIX, p.178. *British and Irish Furniture Makers Online*, www.bifmo.history.ac.uk/entry/tabary-james-john-and-louis-1655-1699 (accessed 21 July 2020).
73 James Tabary received his *témoignage* (confirmation of Huguenot status) in Paris in December 1681 and was in Dublin by 1683.
74 Lami 1906, p.5.
75 Glin and Peill 2007, pp.32–5, figs 23–7.
76 *The First Book of Architecture by Andrea Palladio. Translated out of Italian: with an appendix touching doors and windows. By Dr le Muet architect to the French King* (plate 177). Pierre le Muet's English translation was published in London in 1683.
77 'Whereas James Tabarick Carver sett forth in his Petition, that he was not allowed the full value of his worke in carving framing and setting up the altar-piece. Rayle, Pannell and Table in the Chapell of the Hospitall it did appear by the Certificate of Mr. Robinson his Maty Surveyr that the said Altarpiece as it then was fixt was valued at two hundred and fifty pounds, wch he declaring to be the full value thereof, according to the best of his Judgement unlesse the said Tabarict should add other workes thereto which was intended Ordered that the said Two hundred and fifty pounds be allowed the said carver as the present worth of the said worke, and that if any other embellishment should be added hereafter, that the same shall be payd for according to the vallue thereof.' Minutes of the Governors of the Royal Hospital, Kilmainham, Dublin National Archive, RHK, 1/1/1/ under 27 January 1686, fol.36.
78 Glin and Peill 2007, p.36.
79 Ibid.
80 *HSQS*, LIII, under 'Tabary'.
81 C. Rowell, 'Floor', *GAO* (accessed 18 March 2020).
82 G. Jackson Stops, in Murdoch 1992a, pp.63–4. Rieusset was paid £24 18s 'to go to Boughton with my man' for '27 ½ yards of Parkett at 18s per yard for the Gt stairs'. Cornforth 1970, p.627 suggests that this is the earliest use of the technique in England.
83 See, for example, Antoine Trouvain, 'Third Apartment', from *Appartements ou amusements de la famille royal à Versailles* (1694–8) Getty Research Institute, inv.2011.PR.20. *The School of Recreation or the Gentleman's Tutor* (London 1684), pp.184–202, included instructions on the game and the necessary equipment.
84 Boughton House, Executors' Accounts, fol.666: bill of Pierre Rieusset, joiner, who charged for setting up a billiard table between March and May 1697 and supplied a billiard table and the frame with turned feet for Ditton Park in October 1702 for £22.
85 Murdoch 2006c, p.51.
86 By kind permission of Viscount De L'Isle from his private collection held at Kent Archives and Local History Service, Maidstone, U1476 70/3, Charges of Furniture for Leicester House 1698–1700: 'To Mr Mazarin for Tapestry £118' and 'In Repayring of Leicester House from the years 1698 to the year 1700 to Mr Rousset Joyner £25.0'.
87 *HSQS*, XXXV, no.6.
88 Beard and Gilbert 1986, p.747.
89 National Archives, Lord Chamberlain's Accounts LC9/280, no.64.
90 Murdoch 1997, p.737, illustrated fig.8. A reference to a table bought through the French ambassador indicates that Montagu acquired French furniture through diplomatic channels. Boughton MSS Executors Accounts 1712, vol.2, fol.646; www.marcmaison.com/architectural-antiques-resources/red_languedoc_marble (accessed 27 March 2020).
91 Battison 1966.
92 *Wren Society*, vol.VIII, p.14.
93 Versailles, Comptes, vol.I, pp.1076,1289, 1326; vol.II, pp.22, 62, 68, 88, 160, 324.
94 Derignée was employed by Montagu in 1707, when he received £10 for 'Carver's work': Marc Antonie's accounts, Boughton House, cited in Murdoch 1997, p.739 n.47.
95 Hall 1979, figs 78–80, pp.38, 62; Jackson Stops 1973b.
96 Wilkinson 1883, p.421; Beard and Gilbert 1986, p.347, citing BL Add. MS 22141, fols 102, 114, 129; Beard 1981. A note in *Hobson's Journal* for 2 June 1732 records that 'Jonathan Godier the Joyner died about a fortnight ago, at Doncaster; he killed himself with drinking, He did most of the Joyner work at Stainborough hall then servant to Mr. Thornton; as also the best Staircase at the Banks'.
97 Murdoch 1985a, no.268, col. pl.12. First used by the Speaker of the House of Commons, Charles Abbot (1757–1829), in the early nineteenth century, it was purchased from Lord Redesdale for £1,060 and repaired in 1801.
98 Beard 1970.
99 Beard 1989, pp.23, 24, 188. René Cousin, gilder. Peter Cousin, gilder, picture and mirror frame maker: see National Portrait Gallery *British picture framemakers, 1600–1950*, www.npg.org.uk/research/conservation/directory-of-british-framemakers/c (accessed 21 July 2020).
100 Colvin et al. 1976, pp.168–9, 289–91, 283, 320, 322, 323, 325, 326, 327, 330, 334.
101 Beard and Gilbert 1986, p.202; Jackson-Stops 1980, pp.798–800.
102 See www.fitzmuseum.cam.ac.uk/aboutus/support/admiral-russells-frame (accessed 21 July 2020).
103 Nicholas Doyenne, who was working as a sculptor at the Two Black Boys in Litchfield Street from 1689 to 1703 and attended the French churches of the Savoy and Hungerford Market, is a possibility.
104 Pelletier's bill for 'burnished gold worcke done for the Queen … at Kensington' dated 26 October 1690, covers 'guilding a screene' £8, 'a great frame for ye greate Glass' £18 and 'a frame for the glass over ye Chimney of the said closett' £8; Pelletier was gilding carvings supplied by Derignée earlier the same year. National Archives, LC9/280, nos 14,16; LC9/281, fol.66; Beard and Gilbert 1986, p.241.
105 *HSQS*, XLV, p.49.
106 Gilbert 1996, pp.324, 325, 456. https://collections.museumofthehome.org.uk/object26802 (accessed 17 May 2021).
107 Boughton House, MSS Accounts of the Executors of Ralph, 1st Duke of Montagu, vol.II, fol.825.
108 René explained that Thomas was responsible for the clients while René stayed in the workshop. This remained the situation from 1702 until 1712, when the brothers separated.
109 Bedford Record Office, X 800/8, fol.22: accounts of Mark Anthony, Steward to Ralph, Duke of Montagu, cited in Murdoch 1998, p.370; British Library Thynne Papers M.904/45, fol.349. Thomas Pelletier was paid £42 for the larger set of chairs, 10 guineas for the sofa, £142 10s 10d for the set of table, stands, looking glass and fire screen.
110 Boughton House, MSS Legal Depositions Box CIV, Part I, quoted in full in Murdoch 1998, pp.369–70, appendix IV, pp.372–4.
111 Boughton House, MSS Accounts of the Executors of Ralph, 1st Duke of Montagu, I, fols 231–2, 819.
112 *Daily Courant*, 10 December 1711. Thomas's house on the south side of Covent Garden was insured for £450 and another house owned by him in Maiden Lane for £250, with the Hand-in-Hand insurance company: Beard and Gilbert 1986, p.687. Sales held at Pelletier's Covent Garden

house organized by James Graham included one on 6 March 1711/12 (P. Mason 1992, 'The Picture Frames', in Murdoch 1992, pp.90–5, at p.92) and the James Graham sale in the same month: Murdoch 1998, p.370. See Pears 1991, pp.72, 243 n. 92, for the sale of Old Master pictures, 'late Mr Tho Pelletier's', held at his 'late dwelling house' in Henrietta St, Covent Garden, in 1713. See 'The art world in Britain 1660 to 1735' at www.artworld.york.ac.uk (accessed 21 December 2013).

113 Thalmann 2008, pp.66–7.

114 Murdoch 1998, p.374.

115 *Daily Courant*, 5 March 1726, information provided by Richard Stephens.

116 Murdoch 1998, p.371.

117 Ibid., pp.370, 374, with full text of the will. René and his wife, Mary Catherine, were living in the parish of St George's, Hanover Square. Solomon Pelletier lived until 1797.

118 Huntington Library, Stowe Papers 85, fol.220.

119 London Metropolitan Archives, MS 25628/80.

120 *HSQS*, XXVI, p.9.

121 The Frenchified use of English in the bill suggests the father's involvement, given that the younger Riorteau was born and educated in London. Offices of the Duchy of Cornwall, Frederick, Prince of Wales, Household Accounts, vol.11, fol.224, 9 April 1731:

1731 Apr. y 9

For loocking out an India screen too Days in the Citte £1.1.0.

For carrying Do to St. James to Shew it 0.5.0.

For carrying ditto home again to my house £0.5.0.

For making two packing cases for Do. £1.10.0.

For carrying Do to Que by Land and by Water £1.0.0.

For sawing and Prepairing a six leafe screen and finearing the Pannells with Do £20.0.0.

For painting the Old Panells in Coleurs and Speckling the borders £40.0.0. For varnishing the Room in Green and Guilding the Plaine Moldeings £25.0.0.

For foure large Pannells and too Narrow slips Grav'd and Painted to Imitate the other Pannells £25.0.0.

For Guilding the Plaister Cornish and Sealing £30.0.0.

Total £144.01.00.

122 See www.bifmo.history.ac.uk/entry/gomm-william-richard-1698–1794 (accessed 2 April 2020).

123 *HSQS*, LX, p.110.

124 National Archives, RG 4/4644: born 10 September, baptized 28 September 1718.

125 Pierre Langlois's will, proved 17 May 1742, is in the National Archives, PROB 11/718/186.

126 Wood 2014. Henry Langlois's godmother, Marie-Léopoldine zu Löwenstein-Wertheim-Rochefort (1689–1763), was the wife of Konrad Sigmund, Count of Starhemberg (1689–1727), Imperial Envoy to George I's court from 1720.

127 'Les sieurs Langlois, pere et fils', cabinetmakers, were in the Faubourg Saint-Antoine, Paris, in the late seventeenth century; Pierre Eloi Langlois was a master cabinetmaker in Paris in 1774.

128 James Langlois, goldsmith, was working in St Andrew's Street, Seven Dials, in 1738; Grimwade 1982, p.575.

129 From Saint-Lô, Normandy, Jeanne Langlois was 68 when she received £4 5s 4d through the Royal Bounty; Phillips 1933.

130 Garrioch 2014, pp.103, 108, 115.

131 Snodin 2009, pp.271–2 (and fig.301), 338–9, cat.264.

132 Thornton and Rieder 1971, p.285.

133 Fowler and Cornforth 1974, p.26. Langlois worked for the 4th Duke of Bedford from April 1759.

134 British Museum, Department of Prints and Drawings, Heal Collection, 28/120.

135 Two of the commodes are now at Woburn Abbey, one at Blenheim Palace, and one in the Fitzwilliam Museum, Cambridge.

136 From the advertisement for the sale of the contents of Gunnersbury Park following Princess Amelia's death.

137 London Metropolitan Archives: St Pancras Old Church, P90/PAN1/050, Marriages, 20 October 1764: 'Peter Dominique Jean' (signed 'Dominique Jaen [*sic*]') married to 'Mary Françoise Joseph[ine] Langlois' (signed 'Mari Francis Langlois'); witnessed by 'Petter Langlois' and 'Nicolaus Flodberg'.

138 'Dominick Jean' died in St Marylebone on 1 December 1812, aged 76, and was buried on 6 December at St Pancras Old Church (London Metropolitan Archives: St Pancras Old Church, P90/PAN1/175).

139 Goodison 1968, pp.105–6.

140 National Archives, IR 1/27, fol.26v, duty paid 22 June 1771 on the indenture of Daniel Langlois to 'Dominique Jean of Saint Pancras in Middlesex Water Gilder &c'. See also 'Daniel Langlois', shorter notice in *Furniture History*, I (1965), pp.62–3 (and pl.XII).

141 Now in the Fitzwilliam Museum, Cambridge.

142 *HSQS*, LIII, under 'Servient'.

143 Murdoch 2001b; Tillyard 1994.

144 *HSQS*, XLV, p.286; *HSQS*, XXXI, p.42; Chatsworth, Household Accounts, 1685–1699, fol.117, 24 March 1695; *British and Irish Furniture Makers Online*, www.bifmo.history.ac.uk/entry/pavie-peter-1690–1727 (accessed 21 July 2020).

145 *HSQS*, XLII, p.147.

146 *HSQS*, XXXVII, no.457. Desbois came from Autun in Burgundy.

147 Information kindly provided by Robin Gwynn; Daniel Le Count or Le Conte was naturalized in 1675.

148 *London Gazette*, issue 5283 (4–7 December 1714): 'Daniel Le Count was lately in possession of a shop on the North side of the Royal Exchange'. In 1684 Le Count was awarded a 15-year lease for this premises from the Corporation of the Sons of the Clergy; this was renewed in 1699 (London Metropolitan Archives A/CSC/722, 726). A long-case clock by Daniel Le Count *c.*1690 is in the Victoria and Albert Museum (W.23–1929).

149 G. Campbell, 'Seaweed marquetry', *GOA* (accessed 18 March 2020).

150 Baillie 1967.

151 Murdoch 1985a, no.361, pp.248–9. Rose 1978, pl.24; *HSQS*, LIII, under 'Perinot'.

152 Wills 1971, pp.108–9; Beard and Gilbert 1986 p.378; Symonds 1955, p.108. The bill from Jean Guilbaud, 'Cabinett maker att ye Crown and Looking Glass in Long Aker', in the Hopetoun Archives, dated 9 February 1702/3, is for chimney glasses and 'three paire of Sconces' for £36, which included the packing and transport by ship from London to Hopetoun, Scotland. I am grateful to Linda Balfour, Archivist at Hopetoun House, for sharing this information.

153 Information provided by Richard Stephens (personal communication, 2 February 2017). On 28 January 1702 Madame Fraigneau (Fraignan) entered Guilbaud's Long Acre shop and told him that she was commissioned to furnish a house for Aron D'Almanza, where he was to renounce his Jewish faith and be received into the Church of England, in a grand ceremony witnessed by Queen Anne with the Duke of Devonshire as godfather and the Duchess of Marlborough as godmother. Almanza was fresh out of prison, and there was no money to pay for Madame Fraignan's opulent purchases. But the debt set off a chain of claim and counter-claim that echoed through the courts for 35 years, drawing in not only Jean Guilbaud and the Fraigneaus, but fellow cabinetmaker Jean Perinot and framemakers René and Thomas Pelletier. National Archives, Chancery Court Proceedings, C 5/317; C 5/240/19.

154 A pier glass, table and candle stands at Hopetoun were attributed to Guilbaud in Baarsen et al. 1988, no.87, p.145.

155 Susanne and Alexander Broquet were witnesses at Jean Perinot's marriage in 1695, *HSQS*, XXXI, p.36.

156 *HSQS*, XXVI, p.36.

157 Philip Arbunot charged £2 for fetching the goods from Mill Bank, for 'two leather covers for 2 cabinetts lin'd with flanell. He also supplied china bottles, cream basons and blue and white beakers'. Drayton Archives, MM/A/472.

158 Gervase Jackson-Stops kindly drew my attention to this reference. Drayton Archives, MS 2476. Hinton and Impey 1998, fig.26, p.57.

159 National Archives, LC9/282, fol.11.

160 Trench 2000, p.517; Murdoch 2020c.

161 Christie's, London, 23 May 2012, lot 300.

162 Heal 1953, under 'Arbunot'.

163 Alcouffe 2008, p.33.

164 *HSQS*, XXXI, p.33.

165 *The Post Man*, 27 October 1715, cited in Beard and Gilbert 1986, p.16.

166 Beard and Gilbert 1986, p.16.

167 *The Daily Courant*, issues 7972 (4 May 1727), 7984 (18 May 1727), 8037 (19 July 1727) and 8039 (21 July 1727). Jacques Ouvrier, glazier, received relief through the Threadneedle Street church in 1682, *HSQS*, XLIX.

168 Melchior-Bonnet 2002, pp.50–1. National Archives, PROB 11/615/438.

169 Cunningham 1850, p.204; Buckley 1915, pp.7, 26, 31, 37.

170 *The Daily Post*, 21 February 1738.

171 Beard and Gilbert 1986, p.679.
172 Hill 1981; Gilbert 1978–98, vol.1, no.45, pp.61–2; vol.2, pp.716–19.
173 Richard Hoare's private account, Hoare's Bank, Stourhead Papers (Beard and Gilbert 1986, p.679). Further payments follow for £30 12s in 1743, and to his widow, Ann, more than £37 in total for picture frames and gilding in the years 1747–51, with a final payment for gilding frames of £16 in 1754.
174 'James Pascall', www.npg.org.uk/research/conservation/directory-of-british-framemakers/p (accessed 16 September 2019).
175 *HSQS*, XXIX, p.23.
176 Gosset 1892.
177 Isaac Gosset married Françoise Buisset at the French church in Berwick Street in 1737; his brother Gedeon, who served that community as an elder, was a witness. *HSQS*, XXV, p.38.
178 These are in Carnegie Museum of Art, Pittsburgh (gift of Herbert DuPuy, invs 27.10.355 and 356; Pyke 1973, p.59. Matthew Gosset provided Paul Methuen with a frame for £14 0s 0d in 1720. Archives, Corsham Court; Department of Furniture, Victoria and Albert Museum.
179 *HSQS*, LX, p.82.
180 'The Gosset and Dallain Families', www.npg.org.uk/research/conservation/directory-of-british-framemakers/g/ (accessed 16 September 2019).
181 Offices of the Duchy of Cornwall, Frederick, Prince of Wales, Household Accounts, vol.VI, fol.317. The portraits were formerly at Easton Neston and at Raby Castle.
182 Jacob Gosset was executor of Peter Adam Bosquian, engraver, St Martin-in-the-Fields, in 1736. *HSQS*, LX, p.42.
183 Pond's notebooks record payments in 1736 to 'Gosset the Framemaker on account' and in February 1737, £22 to Gossett for frames. Pond continued to use 'Gosset the frame maker' from 1735 until 1749: Simon 1996, p.62; Whitley Papers, Department of Prints and Drawings, British Museum, under 'Arthur Pond'; Lippincott 1991.
184 Gedeon Gosset received £19 for picture frames and glass from the Grimston family, Beard and Gilbert 1986, p.358.
185 Murdoch 1985; the letter was first published in Dobson 1891, p.136. Lincoln's Inn Treasurer's Accounts confirm that the payment of £25 for this frame was made to Isaac Gosset on 26 April 1751. 'Paid Isaac Gossett for the Picture frame in the Hall by Order of Council the 24th Instant £25' (Lincoln's Inn Library, Archives, C2a31; information kindly supplied by the archivist, Josephine Hutchings, August 2012); see www.theframeblog.com/2012/10/19/hogarths-framemaker/ (accessed 16 September 2019).
186 J. Simon, 'Thomas Gainsborough and picture framing', www.npg.org.uk/research/programmes/the-art-of-the-picture-frame/artist-gainsborough (accessed 16 September 2019).
187 Vertue III (*The Walpole Society*, vol.22 [1933–4]), p.160.
188 See note 186; Sloman 2002, p.66.
189 Simon 1996, p.88.
190 *HSQS*, LX, p.80, under 'D'Aussy, Charles of Southampton', died 1781.
191 Wiltshire Record Office, 383/6, Stourhead account book; Henry Hoare private account, information supplied by Evelyn Newby, 1992.
192 A frame with a prominent curved top edge of distinctive profile, named after the Italian painter Carlo Maratta (1625–1713).
193 Dodd 2016, nn.9, 25, 28, 31.
194 British Library, Add. MS 35636, fol.252; Add. MS 35637, fol.50; Kerslake 1977, p.292. William Hoare wrote from Bath to Charles Yorke in London on 9 August 1764: 'Mr. Gosset has the account of the pictures I have had the pleasure to do for you & I will desire him to wait on you'. In October 1764 William Hoare wrote that Gosset has received the amount due and thanked him. In 1763 he wrote to the 2nd Earl of Egremont that he had 'given orders to Mr. Gosset my Framemaker to wait on you, who will give you a Receipt for me'.
195 Bucholz 2006.
196 Millar 1963, p.94; Simon 1996, p.453.
197 Simon 1996, pp.446–7. For example, the Findlater London accounts, 1758–9, include reference to payment, presumably by Lady Findlater, to 'Allan Ramsay for my lord's picture and mine and for frames from Isaac Gossett', National Records of Scotland, GD248/939/5, Seafield Papers.
198 'Joseph Duffour', www.npg.org.uk/research/conservation/directory-of-british-framemakers/d (accessed 16 September 2019); Simon 1994, p.18. His son William Duffour (d.1787) was also a framemaker, initially in partnership with his mother (*Daily Advertiser*, 7 February 1776).
199 *The London Gazette*, 13 May 1738, and *London Daily Post and General Advertiser*, 17 May 1738: 'Bankrupt Paul Petit, now or late of Silver Street in the Parish of St James in the Liberty of Westminster…', cited in www.npg.org.uk/research/conservation/directory-of-british-framemakers/p (accessed 16 September 2019).
200 Huntington Library, Stowe Papers, 24/1 fol.281: £24 paid to 'Petite' the gilder.
201 Petit charged £16 15s 8d for 'A frize carv'd Apolloes head and Raised and festoons of fruite and flowers with other ornamts two Men opening off Chimy 2 to Cornish and 2 to pedestal over Cornish all Enrich'd put up at Carleton House'.
202 Frederick, Prince of Wales, Household Accounts, vol. XV, fol.329; Millar 1963, pl.195.
203 Frederick, Prince of Wales, Household Accounts, vol.XV, fol.375.
204 The Wootton paintings are now in St James's Palace. Frederick, Prince of Wales, Household Accounts, vol.IV, fol.216, Duffour was paid £57 15s for the frame. Millar 1963, p.183.
205 Hobbs and Oakey 2015, pp.87–104.
206 Frederick, Prince of Wales, Household Accounts, vol.XVII, fols 530ff.
207 Ibid., vol.IX, fol.236.
208 This advertises 'Black and Gold Frames for Paintings, Prints and Glasses, and all sorts of Ornaments Carved and Guilded', British Museum, Department of Prints and Drawings, Heal Collection, 95/7; Heal 1953, p.9. 'Jouret', noted as a framemaker by George Vertue *c.*1751 (British Library, Add. MS 23096), was paid by Lord Monson for a peartree looking-glass frame in 1755. Jouret worked for the artist Richard Crosse (1742–1810) in 1775–7. He was paid £5 5s for framing and packing Dr Wright's picture in January 1775, £4 1s for two oval glasses etc. in October 1777, as well as other small amounts for picture framing (V&A National Art Library, MSL/1929/2154, 2188).
209 His business was carried on after his death by his widow, Anne, in Russell's Court, St Martin-in-the-Fields. In 1766 she left her stock in trade to her daughter Anne Holroyd; *HSQS*, LX, p.32.
210 British Museum, Department of Prints and Drawings, Heal Collection, 32/15.
211 See www.npg.org.uk/research/conservation/directory-of-british-framemakers/b (accessed 16 September 2019).
212 Murdoch 1985, no.295.
213 *HSQS*, LIII, under 'Le Maitre, Jean'.
214 Minutes of the Committee of the Goldsmiths' Company, vol.VII, p.7, meeting of 1 October 1734.
215 Simon 1996 fig.145; Heckscher 1969.
216 Saint advertised 'Sconces, Girondoles, Chandeliers, Brackets, Tables, Chimney-Pieces, Picture Frames, &c, in the best and most Reasonable manner'. He took out insurance on these premises in 1764; London Metropolitan Archives, Sun Fire Office policy registers, 157/215557.
217 Gideon Saint is mentioned in Robert Adam's bank account in 1768; Beard 1978.
218 For further details of the Tousey family, see 'John Tousey', www.npg.org.uk/research/conservation/directory-of-british-framemakers/t/ (accessed 16 September 2019). John Tousey was in Princes Street in 1759–79, according to rate books.
219 They had six children between 1763 and 1773.
220 *PHSL*, 9 (1909), pp.123–4.
221 Murdoch and Vigne 2009, pp 91, 98, 101. The Gosset brothers were elected in 1760, 1764 and 1778 respectively.
222 In 1790 Saint witnessed the will of the Revd John Carle.
223 National Archives, PROB 11/1325/11.

8 Huguenot Sculptors in France and Beyond *pages 133–55*

1 Knecht 2008, pp.107–9.
2 The sculpture was moved from the collegiate church of Saint-Maxe, abandoned in 1782.
3 *Ligier Richier* 1985; Bourdieu 1998; Denis 1911.
4 Bresc-Bautier and Scherf 2009, pp.102–3.
5 These small scale domestic bronzes were acquired by Henry Huntington from the collection of J.P. Morgan in 1917. Huntington Library and Art Gallery, invs 17.15, 16, 17, 18 and 20.
6 'une autre figure de cuivre faicte de la main de Mr Barthelemy, laquelle figure est une femme qui

rogneles ongles de ses pieds', Bresc-Bautier and Scherf 2009, p.136; Seelig-Teuwen 1973, p.224.
7 Le Notre inventory no. 346, described as 'une autre figure du feu Roy a cheval avec deux captives dessoubz, prisé', Guiffrey, 1911, p.254
8 This bronze (V&A A.42–1956) was formerly no. 144 in the *Inventaire des collections de la Couronne* and was recorded in the Louvre in 1603. See www.collections.vam.ac.uk/item/o66313/henry-iv-destroying-his-enemies-statuette-prieur-barthelemy/ (accessed 4 July 2019).
9 G. Bresc-Bautier, 'Dupré, Guillaume', *GAO* (accessed 4 July 2019).
10 Evelyn 1995.
11 There are two versions of the Louis XIII statuette in the Victoria and Albert Museum, A.47–1951 and A.1–1994. Only the second of these is signed by Le Sueur.
12 Now in Bushey Park, Middlesex.
13 McEvansoneya 1993. Besnier's wife witnessed a baptism at the Threadneedle Street church in 1642.
14 C. Avery, 'Seventeenth-century sculpture at Ham House', in Rowell 2013, pp.158–77.
15 White 1992, pp.75–9.
16 Lightbown 1993.
17 Avery 2013 (note 14), pp.160–2.
18 Northampton Museums and Art Gallery, www.english18thcenturyportraitsculpture.blogspot.com/2017/11/busts-of-sir-william-fermor-and-his.html (accessed 3 October 2019).
19 Baker 1995a, pp.3–12.
20 Avery 1996, nos 92, 93, p.104.
21 Whinney 1988, p.449 n.15; Malcolm 1807, p. 242.
22 Boughton House MSS, Elias de Rit's accounts 1698–1705, 2 March 1702/3: 'Dr Sylvestre by my Lds note for Signr David £20'; 21 April 1703: 'To Dr Sylvestre for Signr David for mending bustes upon acct £10'; 8 June 1703: 'To Signr David in ful for mending Bustes £20'.
23 Longleat, Thynne family collections, 1718 Thynne pages 185, fol.331, cited by Roscoe 2009.
24 'the work of Chevalier Claude David from the county of Burgundy'. For Claude David, see Bilbey and Trusted 2002, pp.71–2; and Baker 2000, pp.28–31.
25 Baker 1993, p.15; Baker 2000, pp.30–1.
26 Jean Sheare and Judith Hauduroy were fellow godparents at the baptism of Françoise Marie Goodsense in June 1719: *HSQS*, XXXI, p.20; *HSQS*, LX, p.211.
27 Craske 2007, p.130.
28 Avery 1996, pp.52–3, no.3.
29 Thomassin 1694, pl.77.
30 Wright 1982.
31 Chatsworth, Building Accounts (Chatsworth Estate Office, Derbyshire), vol.VI, fols 1, 16, 17, 24, 91; vol.VII, fol.57.
32 Murdoch 1988; Monson 1998. A gravestone in the North Ambulatory beside the tomb of Eleanor of Castile records that Lady Eland was buried in Westminster Abbey with her mother and grandmother. For an illustration see www.westminster-abbey.org/abbey-commemorations/commemorations/esther-de-la-tour-de-gouvernet-lady-eland (accessed 3 October 2019).
33 Castle Howard Building Accounts, G2/2/32.
34 Ibid., Nadauld's account, 1705–9; G2/2/53: Daniel Harvey's account, 1727 and 1728.
35 Castle Howard Building Accounts, G2/2/32.
36 Vertue IV (*The Walpole Society*, vol.24 [1935–6]), p.35. Vertue may be referring to the decorative painter Nicholas Heude (see p.68) as no further references are known to Peter Eude.
37 Jenkins 2007, pp.82, 85.
38 Stowe Papers, Huntington Library, ST 24/1f.255.
39 Vertue III (*The Walpole Society*, vol.22 [1933–4]), p.83.
40 O'Connell 1987.
41 Stowe Papers, Huntington Library, ST 24/2. Collins-Baker 1949, p.149.
42 Morris 2018, illus. p.142.
43 Saumarez Smith 1990, p.146.
44 O'Connell 1987.
45 For the part played by Cheere's sculpture in the Hercules Garden at Blair Atholl, see Dingwall 1992, pp.161–2.
46 Friedman and Clifford 1974.
47 Waddesdon Manor, Collection of Wine Antiquities, Rothschild Foundation.
48 O'Connell 1987.
49 Friedman and Clifford 1974.
50 Ansell 2017.
51 *Daily Gazeteer*, 3–5 September 1735; *Read's Weekly Journal*, 6 September 1735.
52 *Daily Advertiser*, 4 January 1744.
53 Wheeler 2006.
54 *General Advertiser*, 17 October 1746,
55 *Dublin Journal*, 3 June 1746.
56 D. Bridgewater, 'Statue of the Duke of Cumberland, by John Cheere formerly on a Column at Emmet Square Birr Ireland', www.english18thcenturyportraitsculpture.blogspot.com/2016/08/statue-of-duke-of-cumberland-by-john.html (accessed 4 July 2019).
57 See www.westminster-abbey.org/abbey-commemorations/commemorations/philip-de-sausmarez (accessed 3 October 2019). Craske 2000, pp.100–1.
58 Murdoch 1983.
59 For the restoration of the statue of George I, see www.members.societe-jersiaise.org/geraint/statues/gi1999.html (accessed 3 October 2019).
60 Nito and Rilo 2006, p.5.
61 'Journals of visits to England in 1761, 1762', British Library, Add. MS 27951, fol.16.
62 Smith 2017.
63 Friedman and Clifford 1974, appendix B.
64 Bignamini 1988, p.119.
65 Henry Cheere's bank account at Drummonds shows payments to Edward Chapman Bird.
66 There is no evidence to support the statement that this came from Cannons. Pevsner and Cherry 1978, p.242.
67 Goldsmiths' Hall, London, MS: The Goldsmiths' Company Ledger Books 1729–1746: fol.131, Account of Repairs 1734 4 July 1735 'To Heny Cheere for a Marble Chimney Piece & Slab' £105; fol.145, Henry Cheere 1735 Account of Repairs; 1736 April 29 'To Heny Cheere for a pair of marble Covings & a ffirestone Hearth in full' £7 10s.
68 Goldsmiths' Company Committee Minutes, vol.7: 1734 to 1740, 10 October 1734, fol.7: 'At this Comee Daniel Fare of Queen Street, Picture frame maker produced several patterns of picture Frames and they ordered him to make Three'.
69 Drawing V&A 8933.20, 21; 'The Letter Book of Sir John Chardin', vol.II, Cumbria Record Office, Carlisle D/Lons.
70 See www.westminster-abbey.org/abbey-commemorations/commemorations/sir-john-chardin (accessed 31 January 2020); Cheere's preparatory drawings for this monument are in the Victoria and Albert Museum, www.collections.vam.ac.uk/item/o800292/design-cheere-henry-sir/ (accessed 31 January 2020). In 1746 Sir John Chardin, 2nd Baronet, gave a portrait of his father to the Ashmolean Museum, Oxford, in a spectacular frame embellished with telescopes and other scientific instruments referring to travels in Persia, Turkey and India (Ashmolean Museum, inv.72661).
71 Craske 2007, p.165.
72 Friedman 2004, p.269.
73 Bindman and Baker 1995, pp.48, 62–3.
74 The wedding took place at St Martin-in-the-Fields, but Caroline died six years later.
75 Smith 1920, cited in Simon 1985, pp.39–40.
76 Cited in Murdoch 1983, pp.28–9.
77 Ibid.
78 Vertue III (*The Walpole Society*, vol.22 [1933–4]), p.105.
79 The marble bust of Pope is in the City Art Gallery, Leeds, and the terracotta of Hogarth in the National Portrait Gallery, London.
80 Mallet 1967; Ireland 1793, vol.1, pl.1.
81 Murdoch 2013.
82 Campbell 1747, p.141.
83 *Daily Advertiser*, no.3848 (Thursday 19 May 1743). Information shared by Gordon Balderston, 4 May 2016.
84 Methuen Archives, Corsham Court.
85 Roubiliac lent money to and borrowed from Benjamin Maisonneuve, jeweller in Craven Street, off The Strand, who also had an account with Drummonds. Roubiliac paid him £60 on 9 March 1759 and £112 on 29 June 1761; he received a note from Maisonneuve for the same amount a month later, on 31 July 1761. Murdoch forthcoming *Sculpture Journal* 2021.
86 Penny 1975; Allen 1981.
87 My thanks to Sandra Robinson for sharing this new discovery (personal communication, March 2020).
88 Sir Theophilus Biddulph to an unnamed correspondent, presumably John Byrche, 7 May 1745 (William Salt Library, Stafford, Salt MS 478, B); Bindman and Baker 1995, pp.279–85.
89 Vertue III (*The Walpole Society*, vol.22 [1933–4]), pp.143, 146, 148–9.

90 Both are in the Victoria and Albert Museum. The model (89.5 × 50.2 mm) is signed 'L.F. Roubiliac int. et Fecit 1745'. For the contract drawing 72.5 × 43 cm; inv.21–1888, design no.8381. See Physick 1969, pp.119–21.
91 T. Murdoch, 'Spinning the Thread of Life: The Three Fates, Time and Eternity', in Dethloff, Murdoch and Sloan 2015, pp.46–54.
92 Murdoch forthcoming *Sculpture Journal* 2021.
93 *Evening Advertiser*, no.421, Saturday 20 November to Tuesday 23 November 1756; *Gazetteer and London Daily Advertiser*, no.4742 24, November 1756. Information kindly shared by Gordon Balderston, 4 May 2016. There is no evidence that this marriage actually took place (information supplied by Sandra Robinson), although Céleste remained Roubiliac's partner until the sculptor's death.
94 Murdoch 1983.
95 Cunningham 1829–33, vol.3 (1830), p.54.
96 Craske 2007, p.155.
97 Bindman and Baker 1995, pp.77–9.
98 *HSQS*, LX, p.180.
99 Royal Collection, RCIN 405682.
100 John Flaxman noted that Roubiliac was inspired by Bernini's *Ecstasy of St Teresa* (1647–52; Cornaro Chapel, Santa Maria della Vittoria, Rome) and the tomb of Alexander VII (1671–8; St Peter's, Rome).
101 Bindman and Baker 1995, pp.325–30 citing *Londinium Redevivium*.

9 The Taste for Porcelain and Ceramic Manufacture in Britain and Ireland *pages 157–75*

1 Somers Cocks 1989.
2 Sackville West 1998, pp.29–30. Philip Arbunot was paid £4 3s (Drayton Archives MM/A/427); I am indebted to Gervase Jackson-Stops for this reference.
3 For Motteux, D. Hopkins, D. 'Motteux, Peter Anthony [formerly Pierre-Antoine Le Motteux] (1663–1718), journalist and translator', *ODNB* (accessed 6 April 2020); see *Transactions of the English Ceramic Circle*, 1, part 3 (1933), p.48. For Pellegrini's sketch, see Stainton and White 1987, no.183, p.231.
4 *The Spectator*, 30 January 1712.
5 Buccleuch 2016, pp.94–5, citing Boughton House MS.
6 Thorpe 1955, p.151.
7 'Figures saintes montées sur des pedestaux et autres figures pour garnir les cheminées', cited in Bazin 1972, p.9.
8 Avery 1996, pp.52, 53.
9 *HSQS*, XXVIII, p.22. The bride's father was probably Peter de Barry, who attended the French church of Hungerford Market from 1688 to 1695 (*HSQS*, XXXI, pp.3, 7).
10 Wittkower 1937–8. The Regnaudin sculpture is now in the Tuileries, Paris.
11 Lane 1961, p.3.
12 Charleston and Mallet 1969, pp.87–8.
13 Gardener 1930.
14 Mountfort 1969.
15 Hood 1968.
16 Ramsay, Gabszewicz and Ramsay 2001.
17 I am grateful to Tony du Boulay for drawing my attention to the Toulouse family; see Du Boulay 1996, p.448. Adams and Redstone 1981, p.140.
18 First published by Toppin 1929.
19 Erato C.31–1959; Euterpe C.30–1959. Adams and Redstone 1981, p.140.
20 'a new enterprise formed in England to manufacture porcelain which appears to be more beautiful than that made in Saxony [at Meissen]'. Clarke 1958, p.46; Clarke 1955, p.28.
21 Bellamy Gardner 1928, pp.16–17, citing *The Daily Advertiser*, 3 March 1749.
22 Jones and Garibaldi 2006; Funck-Brentano 1903, p.288. Letter from John Mallet (former Head of Ceramics at the Victoria and Albert Museum and leading authority on Chelsea porcelain) to this author, 25 November 2005, notes that there was a 'Spreman', or some similar spelling, recorded as working or training under the great Paris goldsmith Thomas Germain; if so, Sprimont may have known the Italian goldsmiths from Turin Andrea Boucheron and Lorenzo Lavy, who also trained in Germain's workshop. Boucheron's mark appears on the elaborate Neptune centrepiece made for Frederick Prince of Wales, son of George II and heir to the throne, which was also marked by the London-based Huguenot goldsmith Paul Crespin but associated with Sprimont.
23 Young 1998.
24 Mallet, J., 'Agostino Carlini, Modeller of 'Dry-Edge' Derby Figures?', in Walford and Young 2003, pp.42–57.
25 Clarke 1988. Some pieces from the Meissen service made for the Earl and Countess of Northumberland were also copied at Chelsea at this time.
26 Rouquet 1755, p.143.
27 Society of Antiquaries, London, MS 263. The drawing is in a scrapbook of Jacob Schnebbelie, sometime draughtsman of the Society, and was presented on 28 June 1877 by Frederic Ouvry, President of the Society 1876–8. See B. Nurse, 'Ouvry, Frederic (1814–1881), antiquary and lawyer', *ODNB* (accessed 17 March 2020).
28 Tait 1998–9.
29 Bindman and Baker 1995, p.280.
30 I am grateful to Sandra Robinson for sharing this exciting discovery, to be published in full in 2022.
31 An identical model is preserved in the Museum of Fine Arts, Boston, accession number 53.1019.
32 *The General Advertiser*, 29 January 1750, quoted in Lane and Charleston 1962.
33 Young 1999, p.123 n.35.
34 Valpy 1994. The stock of Kensington-based porcelain dealer Errol Manners included a porcelain seal representing the Marquis of Granby after a print of 1760; *Transactions of the English Ceramic Circle*, 18, part 3 (2004), pp.398–407, specifically pp.403–7.
35 Gardener 1930, p.23.
36 Discovered by Tamara Preaud and published in Dragesco 1993.
37 Bellamy Gardner 1928, p.16.
38 Burrell 1962.
39 Gardener 1942, p.136.
40 Lane and Charleston 1962, p.128.
41 Referred to thus by Horace Walpole in a letter to Horace Mann in June 1747: Toynbee 1903–5, p.278.
42 Archives of the Duchy of Cornwall: Accounts of Frederick, Prince of Wales, vol.VIII, fol.369.
43 The trade card advertised 'toute sorte de Bijouterie en Or et en Argent de l'ouvrage des meilleurs ouvriers, comme aussi des Curiosities de toute especes en Or et en Argent, Ambre Ecaille de Tortue Et pareillement Pierreries et Vaiselle d'Argent en tout genre'. 'A L'enseigne de la Porte d'Or' in Suffolk Street is in the Department of Prints and Drawings, British Museum, Heal Collection, inv.119/7.
44 Smith 1974, pp.195–6.
45 The painting is now in an American private collection, although it has been on loan to the Mint Museum, Charlotte, North Carolina.
46 'Deux pots purris affortis, À quatre pieds dont les cartouches peints à oiseaux' bought by the 2nd Viscount Bolingbroke in October 1755 from the marchand mercier Lazare Duvaux.
47 E. Manners, 'Some Continental Influences on English Porcelain', paper read to the English Ceramic Circle at the Courtauld Institute on 15 October 2005.
48 A discovery by Nancy Valpy cited in du Boulay 1996.
49 T. Murdoch, 'Nicholas Sprimont', *ODNB*.
50 *HSQS*, XXX, p.33.
51 Planché was apprenticed on 30 July 1740: Tapp 1936–7, p.157.
52 Barkla and Barkla 1996.
53 The term 'dry-edge' was first used by Bernard Watney, Ceramics Curator at the Victoria and Albert Museum (Watney 1976). For the attribution to Carlini see Mallet 2003 (see note 24).
54 James Planché only lived for three years; he was buried in December 1754. Planché's younger sons, James 'the bastard son of Andrew Planché and Margaret Burroughs', and William, 'the son of Andrew Planché and Sarah his wife', arrived in 1756.
55 Barrett and Thorpe 1971, pp.1–15.
56 Bradshaw 1990.
57 Victoria and Albert Museum. Watney 1975, p.352; John Mallet notes: 'I seem to recall some time ago thinking that the Neptune might be after Michel Anguier, but finding it was if anything closer to Bernini. These comparisons seem so diverse as to be unlikely. If the Gods are by Carlini, he would not have needed a model'. Letter to the author, 25 November 2005.
58 Possibly by way of a reduced bronze copy or engravings in *Receuil des Figures, Groupes, Thermes, Fontaines, Vases, Statues, et autre Ornaments de Versailles*.
59 R. Smith, 'Some Problems in the Design and Manufacture of Vulliamy's Sculptural Clocks', in Walford and Young 2003, pp.124–37; Barkla 1995.
60 Reilly and Savage 1973, p.329; Charleston 1963.
61 For the glue bat method see www.printedbritishpotteryandporcelain.com/how-was-it-made/glue-bat-printing (accessed 4 September 2020).

62 Hughes 1967, p.49.
63 *HSQS*, XLV, p.29.
64 Laffan and Monkhouse 2015, pp.182–5, citing Mary Delamain's petition to the Irish House of Commons on 9 November 1759, and Francis 2000, pp.46–66.
65 Westropp 1935, pp.12–14.
66 Benton 1972, p.149 (www.britishmuseum.org/collection/object/H_1895-0521-11, with advertisement from *London Daily Advertiser*, 23 and 29 December 1758 [accessed 9 September 2020]). A calendar box for 1758 attributed to Anthony Tregent is in the Metropolitan Museum of Art, New York, inv.03.26.3
67 Bute collection; Christie's London, 3 July 1996, lot 57.
68 Cited by Benton 1972, pp.122–3, who also notes that in 1798 Anthony Tregent's second son, Jacques, witnessed the will of Benjamin Brett, a toymaker, in Wolverhampton.
69 Benton 1972, pp.150–1; Anthony Tregent's correspondence with Mr Pierre Gautier is preserved in Dr William's Library; Murdoch 1985a, no.372. I am grateful to Judith Crouch for information about the V&A clock (email correspondence, 26 July 2018).
70 'Les anglois ne demandent que de la porcelaine toute blanche, mais comme ils pourroient en faire usage pour y ajouter des peintures on leur vend cette porcelaine blanche aussi chère qui si elle etait peinte'. Clarke 1958, p.55.
71 Massey 2005, pp.71–2; Smith 1995.
72 Not to be confused with Abraham Gilles, cabinet-maker from Rouen who stood godfather in July 1694 at La Patente de Soho (*HSQS*, XLV, no.156).
73 Coke 1983.
74 This statement from Jewett 1878 has been subsequently disputed.
75 It is now deposited in the Library of the Society of Antiquaries. For Giles, see Marshall 1951, p.2; Mallet 2012.
76 Du Boulay 1993; du Boulay 1996 p.443.

10 Huguenot Goldsmiths and Silversmiths in the British Isles 1550–1780 *pages 177–205*

1 M. Bimbenet-Privat, 'Huguenot goldsmiths in France prior to the Revocation of the Edict of Nantes (1598–1685)', in Murdoch 2008, pp.7–19, at p.9.
2 J. Bowen, 'Huguenot Goldsmiths in Ireland: Cork', in Murdoch 2008, pp.85–99; T. Sinsteden and T. Murdoch, 'Names of known, believed or possible Huguenot goldsmiths of Dublin', in Murdoch 2008, pp.150–5.
3 'Admissions to the Freedom of York: 12–22 Charles II (1660–72)', in Collins 1900, pp.124–38. BHO (www.british-history.ac.uk/york-freemen/vol2/pp124-138, accessed 22 February 2020). Hughes 1952, p.1826. Bennet 1991, vol.1, pp.136–48.
4 Evans 1930–3, p.500.
5 Mitchell 2017, pp.386–7, frontispiece. Acquired by the Worshipful Company of Goldsmiths from the celebrated collection of Lord Swaythling; Christie's, London, 6 May 1924, lot 110.
6 *Revue de Champagne et Brie, biographie, archaeologie*, 13 (1901), pp.653–4 (gallica.bnf.fr/ark:/12148/bpt6k65805893/f660.image.r=Roussel?rk=21459;2, accessed 13 January 2021). David Mitchell suggests that there was more than one craftsman called Nicaise Roussel.
7 *HSQS*, X, part II (1903), p.262.
8 Dmitrieva and Murdoch 2013; Oman 1961, pp.31–2; they were presented by James I's ambassador John Merrick (*c*.1559–1638/9) to Patriarch Filaret (1553–1633), the father of Tsar Mickhail Feodorovich (1596–1645).
9 M. Bimbenet-Privat in Murdoch 2008 (see note 1), p.14, pl.V.
10 V&A 806A & C-1892; V&A 806 & B-1892; www.collections.vam.ac.uk/item/096318/perfume-flask-cabarin-genevieve (accessed 22 February 2020). Email from M. Bimbenet-Privat to K. Kennedy, 23 December 2013 in object file, V&A Metalwork Collection.
11 Gwynn 2018, p.298; Sitwell 1960, p.151, lists John le Roy (Goldsmith Extraordinary to the King) in December 1666 and John le Roy (Goldsmith in Ordinary to the King) on 19 May 1668. He is not to be confused with Pierre Le Roy, master clockmaker from Meaux, Brie, who married at Hungerford Market in July 1692; the marriage was witnessed by Messieurs Massi (Massy) clockmakers. *HSQS*, XXXI, p.35.
12 *HSQS*, XXXVII, p.451.
13 Mitchell 2017, p.65.
14 D. Barquist, 'Huguenot goldsmiths in Colonial New York and Philadelphia 1680–1750', in Murdoch 2008, pp.61–70; B.C. Wees, 'Huguenot goldsmiths in Colonial Boston and Charleston', in ibid., pp.71–84. Louis Dupont (fl.1736–53), who registered a mark in London as a largeworker 20 September 1736 with an address in Wardour Street, Soho, then moved to Compton Street, where he was declared bankrupt in 1747, is recorded in Saint Domingo by 1752. A sugar caster marked by Dupont is in the Barker collection of Jamaican silver NMS (National Museum of Scotland). His son Stephen, born in London in 1739, was bound apprentice to Samuel Courtauld in 1753. When his brother Oliver Dupont (b. *c*.1740) was apprenticed to Isaac Chartier (fl. *c*.1754–77) in 1754, Louis Dupont was described as a London merchant. Grimwade 1982, p.497; Evans 1930–3, p.530.
15 Peter Chardon's father was a merchant in Boston, Massachusetts, when Peter was apprenticed to a London goldsmith in 1715.
16 Evans 1930–3, p.530. For an account of Abraham Portal, see Portal 1993.
17 Tait 1972, p.280.
18 The 1743 *témoignage* of François Richard, wigmaker, signed by the officers of the French church in Berlin, is preserved in the archives of the Westminster French Protestant Charity School (illustrated in Murdoch 1985a, no.156, pp.114–15).
19 M. Bimbenet-Privat in Murdoch 2008 (see note 1), pp.8–19, 118–28; Murdoch 1982, pp.259–62.
20 See www.shrubsole.com/news/?p=621 (accessed 30 March 2020). Before 1740 the word 'saucer' (from the French *saucière*) was the term used for a sauce server; 'sauce-boat' was first used in Hannah Glasse's *The Art of Cookery* (1747).
21 *Ecuelle* is a French term first used in 1856, according to the OED *Online*; cf. the 1682 porringer with one ear illustrated in Mitchell 2017, fig.64, p.126, and marked by Mary King, 1682/3. The more familiar term 'porringer' (Irish 'pottinger') was adapted from the French word *pottinger*, a two-handled vessel used to serve soup or broth, Cunningham 2016, p.117.
22 Micio 2005.
23 Murdoch et al. 1985a, pp.229–42.
24 Hayward 1959, pp.32, 47; Hartop 1996.
25 Hartop 1996, no.68 pp.290–3.
26 A pair of saucers with *trembleuse* stands (frame for porcelain cups to prevent spillage) made by David Tanqueray in 1718/19 is in the Wilding Collection, British Museum.
27 See www.britishmuseum.org/collection/object/H_2005-0604-1(accessed 24 September 2019).
28 I am grateful to Rod Kelly for discussing these terms with me.
29 Heraldic ornament was used on English silver from the late sixteenth century as symbolic of status.
30 Murdoch 1982a, appendix: 'The professions of émigré craftsmen as recorded in the registers of the Huguenot churches in Great Britain and Ireland', p.249.
31 Marc gave this address on his marriage at the French church of the Savoy on 28 November 1700 (*HSQS*, XXVI, p.140).
32 The Banks and Heal collections, Department of Prints and Drawings, British Museum, have trade cards for many Huguenot craftsmen and suppliers.
33 Snodin 1984. George Michael Moser's Academy in Salisbury Court, which moved to Greyhound Court, Arundel Street, in 1726 was an important meeting place for the community of Swiss and German artists in London. Bignamini 1988.
34 M. Bimbenet-Privat in Murdoch 2008 (see note 1), p.17.
35 Cousins 2005, p.72. Information kindly confirmed by David Mitchell. Louis Berchère was admitted on 16 June 1682 and Peter Harache on 21 July 1682. London Metropolitan Archives, Court of Aldermen, Rep.87, fol.186.
36 Hayward 1959, p.17.
37 *HSQS*, XXI, p.18.
38 Mitchell 2017, p.65; British Library, East India Company ledger L/A/G/1/1, fols 295, 405 (reference supplied by Robin Gwynn via Edgar Samuel). I am grateful to David Mitchell for his advice on the Maubert family connections. Isaac Maubert was a diamond cutter.
39 Hayward 1959, p.18.
40 Archives of the Worshipful Company of Goldsmiths 1682, 1694, 1711 and 1716.
41 Hayward 1959, p.27; Grimwade 1976, no.739.
42 Grimwade 1976, p.635.
43 Huntington Library and Art Gallery, inv.69.69.1.

44 Murdoch 1992b.
45 *The Post Man*, 17 April 1703: see www.vam.ac.uk/blog/museum-life/huguenot-goldsmiths-silver-and-wine-in-war-time-britain (accessed 11 October 2019).
46 For Pierre Harache's presence in London, see www.sothebys.com/en/auctions/ecatalogue/2017/treasures-l17303/lot.22.html (accessed 11 October 2019).
47 McKinley 2017, p.650.
48 Bleuzen 2008–9, p.58.
49 See www.britishmuseum.org/collection/object/H_2005-0604-1 (accessed 11 October 2019).
50 Murdoch 2007.
51 Gwynn 2018, p.304.
52 Calambourg was a green scented wood imported from the East Indies; see Pomet, Lémery and Pitton de Tournefort 1748, p.74.
53 *HSQS*, XXXV, p.xxxiii, quoted by Grimwade 1976, p.534.
54 Thomas Harrache served as the sculptor Roubiliac's executor in 1762 (The National Archives, PROB 10/2312). The will was dated 6 January 1762; another version, published in Bindman and Baker 1995, pp.95–7, is PROB/11/872/125. I am grateful to Gordon Balderston for this information, shared on 4 May 2016.
55 Anne was the widow of Stephen Hobbema (1674–1705), who in 1703 signed a receipt for payment of £23 18s for a silver tea kettle supplied by Pierre Harache to St George, a Dublin-based client. See McKinley 2013, reproduced p.100.
56 Alcorn 2006, pp.46–8, no.2.
57 Grimwade 1982, p.596 The Mettayers came from Île de Ré, near La Rochelle.
58 Bleuzen 2008–9, pp.65.
59 Grimwade 1976, pp.612–13. Robinson 2021 forthcoming.
60 Abraham Pantin, goldsmith of St Giles-in-the-Fields whose will was written in 1731, was probably a close relative. An affidavit was signed by Isaac Cornafleau, goldsmith in the same parish. *HSQS*, LX, p.298. When the younger Simon Pantin died in 1733 his widow, Mary, entered her own mark, running the business until their son Lewis registered his mark in 1734. His son Lewis Pantin the younger, at the Crown and Sceptre on the corner of Mitre Court, Fleet Street, from 1770–81 (Heal 1947), made clock cases; two signed by Lewis Pantin are in the Palace Museum, Beijing: Harcourt-Smith 1930, p.22, pl.25.
61 Abraham's mother was Elizabeth Joncourt, so Pantin's apprentices, the Joncourt brothers, were relatives by marriage.
62 Skerry 2018.
63 Grimwade 1982; Cuny appears in the denization list for 8 May 1697 with goldsmiths Peter Platel from Lille and John Chartier from Blois. *The Gentleman's Magazine* reported Louis Cuny's death on 14 December 1733.
64 Exchange of emails with Lucy Wood and Tim Schroder, October 2018; Hayward 1959, pl.68a.
65 Murdoch and Vigne 2009, pp.41, 78.
66 ForJacques Basire, see *HSQS*, LX, p.24, probate granted 1724. Isaac's son John was a copperplate printer in Charterhouse Street when he wrote his will in 1804.
67 *HSQS*, XXXI, p.49.
68 Free of the Goldsmiths' Company in May 1696 'by redemption according to an order of the Lord mayor and Court of Alderman', Garnier paid the customary fine of 46s 6d to the City and £10 to the Goldsmiths' Company. James Beschefer (1683–1753), taken on as an apprentice in 1697 and turned over to Garnier's neighbour Pierre Platel on his master's death in April 1699, left the goldsmiths' trade for the army in 1714. Goodway 2000.
69 This is on loan to Hampton Court Palace. See Fairclough 1996.
70 M. Bimbenet-Privat in Murdoch 2008 (see note 1).
71 Murdoch 2020b.
72 *The Post Man*, 12–15 March 1720.
73 *Daily Journal*, 28 June 1722.
74 'PETER HEMET Junior, OPERATOR for the TEETH ... is removed from the Strand to Mr. Fraigneau's [the Prince's Confectioner] near St. Albans Street in Pall-Mall' (*The Daily Journal*, 28 June 1722); 'Anthony Fert, Dancing Master ... Enquire for him at Mr Fraigneau's at the Orange Tree in the Pall Mall ... or at the French School in Gun street, Spittle-fields' (*The Post Man*, 30 December 1714). A 'Jno Fraignean' paid the poor rates on the north side of Pall Mall in 1729. Evans 1932, p.537.
75 Accounts of 4th Earl of Dysart from Paul Daniel Chenevix, Tollemache Family Archives, Lincolnshire, MS 925.
76 *HSQS*, LX, p.210.
77 Gerstein 2019.
78 Tunnicliffe 2019.
79 Murdoch 2005b.
80 Phillips 1933. John Dutens, a silversmith from Blois, received £1 10s for 'Cloaths & linen' in 1687/8.
81 Phillips 1933.
82 See www.collections.vam.ac.uk/item/O158040/wine-fountain-platel-pierre (accessed 19 January 19).
83 Goodway 1998; Goodway 1999.
84 Liveryman are freemen of the City of London entitled to wear the livery of the guild to which they belong and to vote in the election of Lord Mayor and other officers. The Court of Assistants is the council of senior members managing the affairs of the livery company.
85 Murdoch 1985a, no.82, p.76; Murdoch 2005a; Murdoch 2006b.
86 Murdoch 1985a, no.335.
87 Glanville in Murdoch 1992, p.153, figs 157–8.
88 Kaellgren 1994, p.162.
89 Murdoch 2005b.
90 Anne Tanqueray accommodated her husband's apprentices: Thomas Guesnard (b. *c.*1700) from 1714, Paul Jullion (b. *c.*1703) from 1717 and Peter Buhet (b. *c.*1709) from 1723.
91 Lomax and Rothwell 2006.
92 Isaac Liger goldsmith was linked with other trades through familial ties. He stood godfather to René, son of Abraham Blanchard (1705–1740), clockmaker in Newport Street in 1710; Anne Ribouleau and her husband, the goldsmith Augustin Courtauld, were godparents to René Blanchard's siblings Anne and David in 1709 and 1720. In 1737 the clockmaker Simon de Charmes the younger (b.1706) was godfather to the younger Abraham Blanchard's son William. Abraham Blanchard the younger (d.1775) was a watchmaker. A long-case clock by Abraham Blanchard the elder was with Alan Smith Antique Clocks in 2019. Josias Blanchard (Blanchet; 1680–1715), clockmaker at the Green Ball, Porter Street, married Judith Garnault in 1702. *HSQS*, XXXI, pp.16, 17, 21, 28, 42. A table clock *c.*1690 by Jean Garnault at The Hague was exhibited by Amsterdam dealers Mentinkenroest at The European Fine Art Fair, Maastricht, 2020.
93 See www.collections.vam.ac.uk/item/O107603/the-hague-plate-communion-beaker-and/ (accessed 11 October 2019).
94 T. Murdoch, 'International Influences on Paul de Lamerie', in Murdoch 2008, pp.99–116.
95 See www.collections.vam.ac.uk/item/O156684/sconce-lamerie-paul-de/ (accessed 11 October 2019).
96 Colvin 1985, p.37.
97 The presence of Huguenot chaplains of the Russia Company, Philip Lernoult (1737–1742) and his successor, Daniel Dumaresq (1713–1805), based in St Peterburg, may have promoted the work of Huguenot goldsmiths at the Russian Court. See Cross 1997, pp.97–9.
98 Cohen 1953, p.54. Francis and Phillips Garden were related to Dr Alexander Garden, who advertised in *The South Carolina Gazette* on 1 August 1743: 'one of the Masters to teach the Greek and Latin tongues & in the FREE SCHOOL'. Dr Garden's brother-in-law was the Huguenot Henry Peronneau, who had moved from Charleston to London; *HSQS*, LX, p.304.
99 Murdoch 2008, pp.114, 116 n.33.
100 Roubiliac's bust of Senesino has recently been acquired by the Metropolitan Museum of Art, New York.
101 Sotheby's, London: The Thanet Dinner Service, 22 November 1984.
102 In 1723 De Lamerie and Gamble took out a joint policy with the Sun Insurance Company for £1,000 for 'Goods and Merchandise in their Dwelling house' in Cranbourn Street. This covered de Lamerie's stock while it was engraved on Gamble's premises; by 1726 Lamerie had a separate policy for £500 worth of household goods and stock in his own Windmill Street premises. By 1728 their partnership had ended and they took out separate policies. Hare 1990, p.10.
103 The bookplate is in the Royal Library, Windsor, and is reproduced as frontispiece to Murdoch 2008.
104 Murdoch 2014b.
105 'Alex Gamble', recorded as attending Chéron's Academy, may be Hogarth's master and de Lamerie's partner Ellis Gamble. The students at St Martin's Lane academy included the Huguenots Daniel Manganelle, Michael Olivier from 1724, Charles Bardin from 1736, Peter Archambo, son of goldsmith Peter Archambo the elder, from 1738, and Henry Ainge from 1743.

106 From 1705 the Vaillants published the official accounts of Royal Bounty charitable distribution to Huguenot refugees.
107 Swift 1983, pp.123–40.
108 Pierre Regnier, son of Daniel Regnier of Paris, surgeon, who was apprenticed to the goldsmith Louis Berchère in London in 1696, was probably a relative.
109 A surveyor named Peter Bourginion was employed by 8th Lord Petre at Thorndon, Essex in 1733, but no connection with Gravelot has been found.
110 See www.collections.vam.ac.uk/item/O78189/print-gravelot-hubert-francois (accessed 11 October 2019).
111 *HSQS*, XVI, p.224j.
112 James Louis Berchère was said to be worth £120,000: Henry Wagner, 'Pedigree of the Huguenot Refugee Families of Berchere and Baril', *The Genealogist*, n.s., XXIII (April 1907), pp.248–51 (information from Robin Gwynn). See *HSQS*, LX, p.31 for a summary of the will of James Louis ('Lewis') Berchère, written in 1750; probate granted on 8 May 1753. His sons-in-law Lewis Baril (d.1761) and James Massé (d.1761) were both City jewellers. Each of his four daughters received a legacy of £1,000. By 1738 Lewis Berchère was described as 'a gentleman of Hackney' so had evidently retired from business. Lewis Baril was a business associate of Denis Chirac, jeweller of St Martin-in-the-Fields, and Chirac's brother-in-law Anthony Rigal, jeweller of Duke's Court, St Martin's: *HSQS*, LX, p.67. Denis Chirac's will was dated 15 July 1738.
113 The teaspoons with their intertwined handles were outsourced; the knives and sugar nippers bear the mark of John Allen, a specialist smallworker.
114 I am grateful to Nigel Israel for this suggestion.
115 Murdoch and Vigne 2009, p.20.
116 C. Marmoy in *HSQS*, LIII, entry for 1737, under 'Ray'.
117 Murdoch 1985a, no.70, p.66. For the details of Mary de Lamerie's marriage, see Phillips 1935, p.55.
118 P. Glanville, 'Lamerie, Paul Jacques de (1688–1751), goldsmith', *ODNB* (accessed 23 February 2020).
119 There is no recorded connection between Paul Crespin and Julian Crispin, although the former's name is sometimes misspelled as Crispin.
120 See www.collections.vam.ac.uk/item/O132677/paul-crespin-oil-painting-unknown (accessed 11 October 2019).
121 Cartier and Cartier 1994.
122 Symonds 1940; Delaforce 1997.
123 Delaforce quotes the description of de Saussure, a Huguenot friend of the Crespin family.
124 Murdoch 1985c.
125 V&A LOAN:GILBERT.717–2008. The 1st Duke of Chandos paid Paul Crespin £135 for 'candlesticks and all demands' in April 1726; 'in full of 3 Bills £13 2s' in October 1727; and again £1 7s in November that year. There were further payments to Crespin in 1728 and 1729 for relatively small amounts but the exact nature of all the purchases is not given. Huntington Library and Art Gallery, San Marino, California, Stowe papers ST 82 fol.196. In 1796 the 2nd Marquess of Buckingham (1776–1839) married Lady Anna Eliza Brydges (1779–1836), Chandos's granddaughter and sole heiress.
126 The Le Heup coat of arms are *gules three beehives between eleven bees volant or*.
127 The proposal for printing by subscription *The Modern Cook* by Vincent La Chapelle appeared in *The Daily Journal*, issue 3561 (2 June 1732). Benjamin Motte published books by Isaac Newton and Jonathan Swift.
128 La Chapelle 1733, Preface.
129 Jones and Garibaldi 2006.
130 See www.rct.uk/collection/search#/3/collection/51271/sauceboat-and-stand; www.rct.uk/collection/search#/4/collection/51392/salt-cellar (accessed 11 October 2019).
131 See www.collections.vam.ac.uk/item/O1029812/design-for-a-sprimont-nicholas; www.collections.vam.ac.uk/item/O1008704/a-design-for-sprimont-nicholas (accessed accessed 11 October 2019). Another design by Sprimont is in the Society of Antiquaries, MS 263, see Esdaile 1944a.
132 Mortlock 1997.
133 Funck-Brentano 1903, p.288: the wonderfully named author published a second edition of his prize-winning book about this prison; information from Sandra Robinson.
134 Cornforth 1996, figs 4 and 5, p.129.
135 Grimwade 1976, no.1575. James Peltro, who entered a mark as a largeworker in 1739 at the Golden Head, Heneage Lane, is probably closely associated with John.
136 A set of four candlesticks bearing his mark were sold at Bonhams on 24 March 2005 (lot 69).
137 Rothwell 2017, pp.158–9.
138 See www.collections.vam.ac.uk/item/O688877/design-for-a-moser-george-michael; www.collections.vam.ac.uk/item/O64957/candelabrum-kandler-charles/ (accessed 11 October 2019).
139 Edgcumbe 2000, pp.43–4: *HSQS*, LX, p.46.
140 Gerstein 2019, pp.43–54.
141 The National Archives, PROB 11/1150/52.
142 Portal 1993. The family originally came from Bagnols sur Coze, Languedoc.
143 Murdoch 2007, frontispiece.
144 Murdoch and Vigne 2009, pp.109–10. Illustrated on the endpapers, Romilly's bookplate is in the fashionable wreath and ribbon style. It is in the De Crespigny collection.
145 See www.metmuseum.org/art/collection/search/204882 (accessed 11 October 2019).

11 Huguenot Watchmakers and Jewellers: The Manufacture and International Market for Luxury Goods *pages 207–31*

1 Campbell 1747, pp.250–2.
2 Shears 1959–60, p.164.
3 Memorandum of the Clockmakers' Company 31 March 1630. They were James Voutrolier (Vautrollyer) and his associate, Louis Cuper; Josias Cuper; William Petit, who worked with David Ramsay; and Elie Volant, who had been lodging at a baker's house in Holborn. My thanks to David Mitchell for sharing the 1622 Petition of London Clockmakers with me and highlighting this early presence of Huguenot makers in London.
4 Atkins and Overall 1881.
5 Morgan 1883.
6 Thompson 1996, p.417; Public Record Office State Papers, Domestic Series, 14, vol.127. Members of the Clockmakers' Company were described as 'Brothers'; 'Strangers' indicated that they were foreigners: despite being Brothers and within the jurisdiction of the guild, they were still living outside the City walls. Among the 'Brothers' listed on 16 October 1632 (after incorporation) were the 'Strangers': James Vaultrolier, Josias Cuper, Davyd Backquet, Ely Volant, William Petit and John Droeshout.
7 *HSQS*, XXXI, p.40.
8 An octagonal watch signed 'FONNEREAU LA ROCHELLE' and dated *c.*1640 is in the Museum of London; Murdoch 1985a, no.352.
9 Other leading Huguenot watchmakers from Blois included Henry (fl.1692–1745) and Jacob Massy (fl.1715–33). Henry Massy supplied Lord Monthermer with a silver watch in August 1703 for £9 (Boughton House, Mr de Rit's Accounts 1698–1705). Watches by both makers are in the British Museum and there is a long-case clock by Henry Massy at Stourhead. An alarm watch signed by Nicholas Massy (1641–1698) in a case marked 'ALR' for Adam and Lewis Roumieu, embellished with the cypher of the owner, is in the Metropolitan Museum of Art, New York; Baarsen et al. 1988, no. 84.
10 Morgan 1883. They are Beauvais, Barrachin, Bouchet, De Lande, Delavespere, Dettacher, Delandre, D'Argent, Du Castel, De Mere, Desbois, Gobert, Guignier, Jaques, Le Grand, Le Comte, Le Feburg, Le Roux, Limoniere, Latour, Mussard, Massy, Mesniel, Motteux, Marchant, Marduit, Pasquier, Plavene, Pamphillion, Pomeroy, Regaud, Roumieu, Raimond, Sylvester, Vassiere and Vaslet.
11 City of Canterbury Poll Book 1826.
12 Thompson 1996, pp.420–1, pl.XXXVIb; www.collections.vam.ac.uk/item/O7790/lantern-clock-bouquet-david/ (accessed 30 January 2020).
13 Thompson 2008, pp.40–1.
14 *HSQS*, XIII, pp.35, 42, 44.
15 Morgan 1883.
16 Murdoch 1991, p.96, no.132.
17 See www.collections.vam.ac.uk/item/O562231/blackwork-engraving-hurtu-jacques (accessed 30 January 2020); www.collections.vam.ac.uk/item/O676938/print-hurtu-jacques (accessed 30 January 2020). Fuhring and Bimbenet-Privat 2002, pp.98–105.
18 Mitchell 2012, p.145.
19 *Treasures from Chatsworth* 1980, nos 171 and 172.
20 Hayward 1963–4, p.655.
21 Delafons's trade card is in the British Museum, Heal Collection, 59.52. He was a member of the multi-generational Delafons family of jewellers and clockmakers established in the West End and the City from 1738 to 1815.

22 Six plates of De La Cour's 1747 book are held by the Victoria and Albert Museum, E.1386–1391–1925.
23 The escape from Dieppe in 1688 of their relative Jean Perigal, ivory turner, is one of the most evocative narratives, Perigal 1888, pp.14–22.
24 Shears 1959–60, pp.158–173, 174–5.
25 This is preserved in the French Protestant Church Library, Soho Square.
26 Thompson 1996.
27 Murdoch and Vigne 2009, pp.31–3, fig.29.
28 The British Museum has a watch signed by David Hubert *c.*1750 (1958.1201.695) and an ebony-cased table clock from the Lloyd Collection (2018,8027.4), *c.*1740. David and his relative James were naturalized in 1709, when both were living in the City of London, David in the parish of St Faith under St Paul's and James in St Stephen's, Walbrook. *HSQS*, XXVIII, no.46.
29 For examples see Murdoch 1985a, no.351. There is an astronomical clock by Abraham Gribelin in the Ashmolean and a shell-shaped watch by him in the British Museum.
30 Develle 1913, pp.108–14, cited by Landes 1983, pp.216–17. Isaac Gribelin's nephew Nicolas (1637–1719) was received as Master at the Faubourg Saint-Germain-des-Près around 1660 and appointed Clockmaker to the Dauphin before 1674. Nicolas Gribelin established a workshop in the rue de Bussy and remained in Paris, where he collaborated with André Charles Boulle. He was Master of the Paris guild of clockmakers in 1675.
31 Landes 1983, p.238.
32 Bourriau 1934; Murdoch 1984.
33 *HSQS*, XXV, p.29: on 15 December 1701 Jacob Debaufre married Marie Roux at the Huguenot church of Le Carré and Berwick Street.
34 'An Art of Working Pretious or more Common Stones (whether Naturall or Artificial), Christal, or Glass, and certain other Matters different from Metals, so that they may be employed and made use of in Clockwork and Watchwork and many other Engines nor for Ornament only, but as an Internal and Usefull Part of the Work or Engins itselfe, in such Manners as have not heretofore been used'. Landes 1983, pp.136–7.
35 Bromley 1977, no.3, p.80.
36 'Reasons of the English Clock and Watchmakers against the Bill to Confirm the Pretended New Invention of using Precious and Common Stones about Watches, Clocks and other Engines' (broadside, London 1705?), quoted by Landes 1983, pp.138, 425 n.11.
37 See www.collections.vam.ac.uk/item/O114464/watch-and-pair-debaufre-james/ (accessed 30 January 2020).
38 Murdoch 1985, no.356, p.246, is in the British Museum (1958–1201,822). Another in the Museum of London has an outer case chased with the Judgement of Solomon, signed 'Mauris Fecit'.
39 16 November 1705 *The Daily Courant* announced: 'Lost between Convent Garden and Leicester Fields, on Wednesday Nov 14th a silver watch with a silver chain. Whoever brings the said watch to Mr. S de Charmes, Watchmaker, at his house, the Sign of the Clock, the corner of Warwick Street, Charing Cross shall have 2 Guineas reward.'
40 Murdoch 1985a, no.353, p.244. For Charmes Hall, see www.british-history.ac.uk/vch/middx/vol2/pp158–165 (accessed 3 August 2017).
41 De Charmes had married Elene Dieu in December 1696 at the Huguenot church in Berwick Street; they had six children, two sons (David and Simon Gideon) and four daughters (Anna, Martha, Eleanor and Judith).
42 Murdoch 2020a, p.50.
43 *HSQS*, XXVI, p.15; Garrioch 2014, p.139.
44 The National Archives, PROB 11/610/374. Carriage clocks by Paulet are preserved in the Victoria and Albert Museum (V&A 420–1869; www.collections.vam.ac.uk/item/O126854/watch-and-pair, accessed 30 January 2020) and the Metropolitan Museum of Art, New York (www.metmuseum.org/art/collection/search/203676, accessed 30 January 2020). Baarsen et al. 1988, p.141, no.83.
45 A table clock signed Etienne Asselin is in the Library at Ascott, Buckinghamshire (National Trust). The elaborately mounted bracket clock by François Asselin was in the Time Museum, Rockford, Illinois. See also www.millingtonadams.com/antiques/george-i-ebonised-moon-phase-quarter-striking-musical-bracket-clock-by-stephen-asselin-london/1559 (accessed 30 January 2020).
46 François, possibly the François 'Asselinne' who died in 1734, mentioned in the Court Minutes of the Clockmakers' Company, 7 November 1687, as an engraver. The National Archives, PROB 11/666/2; Murdoch 1982, p.38 and footnote p.199.
47 Baarsen et al. 1988, p.166.
48 Garnier 1994.
49 In 1757 Thomas Grignion, second-generation Huguenot watchmaker, repaired the Countess of Plymouth's gold watch 'broke by a fall'. British Museum, Heal Collection 39.44. See John Russell's 1801 pastel portrait of Mrs Sherlock taking snuff from her gem-set box, Metropolitan Museum of Art, New York, inv.1975.217.2.
50 Murdoch 2015.
51 L. Seelig, 'Gold Box Production in Hanau: The Extended Workbench of Frankfurt and its Trade Fair', in Murdoch and Zech 2014, pp.74–91. For the Frères Toussaint boxes, see ibid., plates 6.6 and 6.7.
52 Hare 1990, payment to William Trumbull, Easthampstead Park, Berkshire, D/ED F22 fol.43; T. Murdoch, 'From the Gate to the Hearth: Metalwork at Ham House', in Rowell 2013, pp.232–47, citing Chenevix's bill (Buckminster Park, Leicestershire, Tollemache MS 925).
53 Campbell 1747, p.145.
54 Above, the reclining figure of Venus in her chariot is drawn by doves with Cupid shooting arrows from a bow, 'QUI PEUT LUY RESISTER'; to the left is the Judgement of Paris, 'A LA PLUS BELLE'; to the right, Three Graces attend Venus, who admires herself in a mirror, 'SEULLES DIGNES DE LA SERVIR'; and below, Cupid is led by a dog on a lead, 'LA FIDELITE ME CONDUIT'. See www.collections.vam.ac.uk/item/O104444/snuff-box-gribelin-simon/ (accessed 30 January 2020). The box is also engraved with the cypher and crest for Frederick Augustus, Duke of Sussex. The engraved top is signed twice 'SIM GRIB'.
55 John Palairet was apprenticed in 1736 to David Dupont. The Palairet family was based in Bloomsbury, Marylebone and Soho, with branches in Southampton and St Petersburg in the 1770s and 1780s. Edgcumbe 2000, p.133; *HSQS*, LX, pp.297–8.
56 Edgcumbe 2000, pp.17, 44. My thanks to Richard Edgcumbe for this information.
57 Murdoch 1985a, no.354, pp.244–5; Thompson 1996, p.427, pl.XXXVIIIa and c for a silver pair-case watch with chased bust of Queen Anne inscribed 'Regn Incip 8 mart 1702'. David Lesturgeon joined the Clockmakers' Company in 1721.
58 Elizabeth Fontaine married Daniel Torin in 1729. A long-case walnut clock, *c.*1745, by Moses Fontaine and Daniel Torin, was with the London dealers Raffety and Walwyn (Bonham's, 24 September 2013, lot 189). See Alexander 1972, who reproduces a portrait of 1735 by Thomas Worlidge of Moses Fontaine with engraving tools, inscribed 'MF AE 40', from a copy then in possession of Mrs William Hirschfield of Delray Beach, Florida.
59 John Fougeron engraved plates for *A New Geographical Dictionary* (London 1759–60), and a view of Lincoln Cathedral (www.collections.vam.ac.uk/item/O514535/a-new-geographical-dictionary-print-fougeron-john (accessed 30 January 2020) and www.collections.vam.ac.uk/item/O589797/the-south-prospect-of-the-topographical-print-fougeron-john (accessed 28 March 2020). He was probably a relative of Ignace Fougeron, who exhibited at the Society of Artists, London.
60 *HSQS*, XXXV, nos 171, 173, where his name is given as Cabaret Michel Lagarene. He was naturalized in 1709. Morisette Lagarene, living in the same parish, whose will was proved on 28 April 1735 was probably his widow. The National Archives, PROB 11/670/439.
61 One of the boxes is signed Michel Cabaret Lagarene, the other is mounted in gold with the signature 'M. Lagarene London'. M.C. Lagarene wrote his will in 1716.
62 The 1703 translation into English of La Fontaine's fables by Bernard Mandeville brought these texts to a wider English readership. M. Goldsmith, 'Mandeville, Bernard (bap.1670, d.1733), physician and political philosopher', *ODNB* (accessed 31 March 2020).
63 Victoria and Albert Museum, LOAN:SNOWMAN.8–1997. Other Huguenot lapidaries recorded in contemporary records include Jean Brison (1689–1705), 'proche la boulle d'or, Lichfield Street; Jacques De La Fond (fl.1713–23); Luc Maurice (fl.1701–7), who attended the Leicester Fields church (*HSQS*, XXIX); and Jean Legaigne, who attended the Savoy church in 1705. Nicholas Cellier, in Fore Street in 1706, attended La Patente in Soho. Murdoch 1982b, appendix: 'Jewellers'; Records of the Sun Insurance Company: London Metropolitan Archives.
64 For Bertrand, see Brett 2014b.

65 Edgcumbe 2000, pp.147–8.
66 Blair 1972; J. Clarke, 'Swiss Gold Boxes: Myth or Reality?', in Murdoch and Zech 2014, pp.61–73.
67 William Charron was the son of John Charron who was apprenticed to François Fourestier in 1717 a 'graveur de montre'. John Charron founded Charon and Son, watch case engravers of Little Chapel Street, Soho, listed in Mortimer's *Universal Director* 1763. His apprentices included Francis Guiot in 1726 and Peter Benazech in 1741. Edgcumbe 2000, pp.39–40.
68 The box was supplied by retailer John Newman but the mahogany frame, veneered with oak, was made in Birmingham and the gold box bears the mark of Swedish goldsmith Andrew Fogelberg, working in Church Street, Soho.
69 Entitled *A Description of the Freedom Box voted by the City of London to the Hon. Augustus Keppel Admiral of the Blue to which is linked a succinct account of his services*. Murdoch and Snodin 1993.
70 Grimwade 1990, p.289.
71 A silver pair-case watch signed 'Compigné Winton' in the British Museum has a later case marked for 1768 (not 1718 as stated in Murdoch 1985a, no.360). The movement was supplied by David Compigné, who was probably Michel's brother.
72 See www.collections.vam.ac.uk/item/O156750/snuffbox-burel (accessed 30 January 2020). Truman 1991, no.95, pp.282–3; Edgcumbe 2000, fig.12, p.36. The goldsmith David Willaume stood godfather to Simon Burel, son of Jean and his wife Elizabeth Bolet, baptized 16 March 1690 at the Hungerford Market Huguenot church, indicating established connections within the goldsmiths' trade.
73 T. Murdoch, 'Biographies of Huguenot goldsmiths in Berlin and Cassel', in Murdoch 2008, pp.133–5.
74 Truman 1991, no.77; Zech 2015, no.29, pp.90–1; W. Baer, 'Gold Boxes in Berlin: Thoughts on their Production for and beyond the Royal Court during the Reign of Frederick the Great', in Murdoch and Zech 2014, pp.97–8, pl.7.6.
75 Philippe Métayer was probably Louis Métayer's father. In 1773 Antoinette Bernard, his widow, declared her son Louis Métayer as her heir. *HSQS*, LX, p.32, under Bernard.
76 Truman 1991.
77 The Saint faimly came from Bayeux and Saint-Lô in Normandy and settled initially in Jersey. See www.theislandwiki.org/index.php/Biographies_of_silver_makers (accessed 25 March 2020). Pierre Saint abjured at St Helier in 1687, having brought with him his wife and their sons Jean, Jean-Pierre and Jean-Jacques.
78 In April 1719 John Bosquet, a refugee living in Paddington, bequeathed £25 for the education and maintenance of his nephew John Saint and £300 when he attained the age of 21. *HSQS*, LX, p.42.
79 For Philippe and Louis Métayer, Jean Saint and the designer Louis Fabrice Dubourg, see Baarsen 2001, pp.98–109; Edgcumbe 2000, pp.17, 59, 103.
80 Baarsen 2001, nos 29, 31, 35.
81 Ibid., no.29, pp.100–1. Another box by Métayer is chased with Odysseus and Achilles, see Snowman 1990, pl.877. www.masterpiecefair.com/en/blog-details/126/object-of-the-month-a-dutch-gold-snuffbox-with-rebecca-at-the-well (accessed 20 May 2021).
82 Edgcumbe 2000, p.17; Citroen 1975, p.140. For Huguenot goldsmiths in the Hague, see J. Pijzel-Dommisse, 'Huguenot goldsmiths and their Influence in The Hague in the late 17th Century' and appendix 2, 'Huguenot Goldsmiths and those that worked in the French style in The Hague, 1680–1730', in Murdoch 2008, pp.20–44 and 129–33 respectively. F.M la Cave's headpiece after Hogarth for the Foundling Hospital broadsheet is in the British Museum (1868,0822.1552). La Cave also engraved Hogarth's Election series in 1758 and the blank invitation to the Vine Tavern, Long Acre (British Museum, Banks Collection, C,2.339).
83 Edgcumbe 2000, fig.54.
84 Snowman 1990, pl.564.
85 Goldsmiths who specialized in small-scale work registered a different category of mark that was also smaller so that it could be accommodated.
86 The National Archives, PROB 11/832/283. Written in May 1754, the will was proved 29 August 1757.
87 Edgcumbe 2000, fig.15, pp.51–2, 56. For gold boxes marked by Harrache with panels signed by Burges, see *A La Vieille Russie* and Sotheby's, London, 10 June 1974, lot 47; Sotheby's, Monaco, 29 November 1975, lot 35.
88 Abraham Harache is described as a silversmith in his 1722 will (*HSQS*, LX, p.206) and an engraver in 1689 (*HSQS*, XXIX, p.32). Le May 2005, pp.364–76.
89 It is not known whether Les Frères Toussaint were connected with Augustin Toussaint of London. For their Huguenot origin, see Willem Wijnaendts van Resandt cited by L. Seelig in Murdoch and Zech 2014 (see note 51), p.88 n.20.
90 Information kindly provided by Lorrenz Seelig via email (7 April 2020).
91 L. Seelig in Murdoch and Zech 2014 (see note 51). Seelig confirms that Esaye Obicker was buried in the Wallonian church in Hanau. He reports that he has identified another 20 gold boxes marked for Les Frères Toussaint since his 2014 publication (email 7 April 2020). For the latest account of Huguenot jewellers in Hanau, see Seelig 2015, pp.49–51, and Seelig 2018, pp.100–3.
92 Zech 2015, illustrated p.51.
93 Brett 2014b.
94 Brett 2004; Brett 2010.
95 *HSQS*, LX, p.66.
96 Surviving trade cards record the businesses of Susanna Passavant and Marianne Viet. Susanna Passavant was apprenticed to George Willdey and maintained a day book from which information was transferred to stock books and customers ledgers. Brett 2010, p.19.
97 Murdoch 1985a, no.362, p.248. It is signed on the dust cover at the back of the movement.
98 Crouch 2005.
99 See www.metmuseum.org/art/collection/search/188870 (accessed 30 January 2020).
100 All six sheets of De La Cour's *Eighth Book of Ornaments* are in the Victoria and Albert Museum (1386, 1387,1388, 1389,1390, 1391–1925).
101 Kent 1992, p.131, no.M.138. Of three finger rings in the British Museum bearing Servant's mark (1961,1202.3, 1961,1202.49 and AF.1287), two were given by Dame Joan Evans, historian of Huguenot goldsmiths and jewellers. Henry Servant was married to Elizabeth de Barry, daughter of the goldsmith Pierre de Barry, at the French church, Castle Street, Soho, in 1699. At that time Servant was described as a jeweller of 'Bethisford', an oral spelling of the French pronunciation of Bideford, Devon (*HSQS*, XXXI p.37). Servant was buried at Barnstaple on 31 October 1738. The mark illustrated is possibly a variant of the 'HS' serrated outline to the punch on this ring.
102 Jacques Louis Berchère was the son of Louis Berchère, who was born in Paris and presented his *témoignage* from Charenton in 1681 (*HSQS*, XXI, p.18). He was endenizened and free of the Goldsmiths' Company in 1682, when Nicolas Maubert stood surety for him (London Metropolitan Archives, Court of Aldermen, Rep.87, fol.186); he was naturalized with his son Jacques Louis in 1685. He visited Holland and Germany in 1692 (French Church of London, MS 7, p.537; Mitchell 2017, p.63). Louis (Lewis) subscribed £100 to the Tontine, 1693 and served as an elder of the Threadneedle Street church in 1697–1700. His son Jacques Louis Berchère served as deacon in the same church from 1701 to 1705 and as an elder in 1709 and 1718. As a merchant jeweller and banker of Broad Street, Jacques Louis Berchère was said to be worth £120,000 (Wagner 1907, p.346). He was a foundation Director of the French Hospital (*Proceedings of the Huguenot Society*, VI, p.71). For further information about the Berchère family see Agnew 1886, vol.2, p.501, and for a summary of Lewis and Jacques Louis Berchères' wills, *HSQS*, LX, p.31.
103 For Peter Dutens, see Murdoch 2017.
104 Chardin 1686; www.collections.vam.ac.uk/item/O1389040/the-travels-of-sir-john-book-none (accessed 30 January 2020).
105 A. Eurich, 'Chardin, Sir John [Jean] (1643–1712), traveller and merchant', *ODNB* (accessed 31 January 2020); Samuel 2000.
106 *HSQS*, LX, p.67. Chirac died in 1738 and appointed Louis Berchère and Lewis Baril as trustees of his daughter Susanna's inheritance.
107 *HSQS*, LII, under 'Deletang, Pierre'. He died in 1763.
108 *HSQS*, LX, p.265.
109 Ibid., p.138.
110 V&A 12859.2.
111 Offices of the Duchy of Cornwall, the Accounts of Frederick, Prince of Wales, vol.VI; Murdoch 2017, pp.51–60.
112 See www.rct.uk/collection/search#/1/collection/9020/ring-0accessed (accessed 30 January 2020).
113 Guildhall Library, MS 3940. The patent was for 'a Certain new Art or Invention or working & Figuring precious or more common stones & certain other matters different from Mettalls so that they may be

Imployed and made use of in Clockwork or watchwork and many other Engines; not for ornament only, but as Internall and useful part of the Work or Engine itself in such manner as have not here to fore been used, and very much conducing to the greater perfection of Watches and clocks.'
114 Llanover 1861, vol.3, pp.413, 478.
115 *General Evening Post*, 15 January 1735, issue no.4370.
116 HSQS, LX, p.33. In 1747 Isaac Berthon (1663–1747) left over £17,000 in bequests to relatives in London and Amsterdam. Named craftsmen include Michael Berthon, engraver, and John Berthon, jeweller or stone setter.
117 Petworth House Archives, 377/C 11 Other minor charges were for mending the top of a silver essence bottle, replacing a lost brilliant (diamond), mending gold patch boxes and providing a silver lining to a mother-of-pearl shuttle. A new pair of gold scissors with a green case cost 8 guineas.
118 See www.artscouncil.org.uk/sites/default/files/download-file/Export_of_Objects_of_Cultural_Interest_2013-14.pdf (accessed 16 January 2019). elephant-musical-toy-waddesdon-manor-buckinghamshire (accessed 14 May 2021).
119 Sotheby's, Paris, 28 November 2016, lot 8.
120 Young 1996; Goodison 1974, p.21, cited by Smith 2000, p.355.
121 Van Wely 2010.
122 Charles Magniac's son Hollingworth Magniac (1786–1867) was a distinguished collector of medieval works of art acquired with a fortune amassed through trading in opium with China. C. Sebag-Montefiore and R. Grace, 'Magniac, Hollingworth (1786–1867), merchant and connoisseur of medieval art', ODNB (accessed 28 March 2020).
123 Smith 2018.
124 *The Gazeteer and New Daily Advertiser*, 13 February 1772. See Betts and Smith (forthcoming 2021). See www.apollo-magazine.com/125.
125 Thompson 2004, pp.36–7.
126 Shears 1959–60, p.168. Marie Anne was the daughter of Etienne Viet baptized at the Huguenot church of Le Carré on 9 April 1699. HSQS, XXV, p.6.
127 Thompson 2004, p.98.
128 See www.tate.org.uk/art/artworks/zoffany-stephen-rimbault-n04434 (accessed 30 January 2020); a bracket clock by Rimbault is in the Victoria and Albert Museum (W.30–1959). Rimbault put Zoffany in contact with the artist Benjamin Wilson (1721–1788), through whom Zoffany met his first major patron, the Huguenot actor David Garrick.
129 Harcourt-Smith 1930, p.25.
130 Chotard was apprenticed in 1720 and free of the Clockmakers' Company by 1742.
131 The watch, in the French Hospital collection, is on view at the Huguenot Museum, Rochester, Kent; Murdoch and Vigne 2009, p.87, fig.109. The JACOB HOUBLON long-case clock is with the direct descendants of the first owner; the dial is signed 'Rob. Lemley' and inscribed 'God Save the Hour – Britains Strike Home, 1742'. Aime Garnault's brother Michael was a City jeweller associated with the Berchère and Baril families. Other relatives include Jean Garnault, a clockmaker in The Hague in the 1690s, and Peter Garnault, a merchant in Amsterdam during the 1720s and 1730s.
132 See E. Radford and J. Evans, 'Quare, Daniel (1648/9–1724), maker of clocks, watches, and barometers', ODNB (accessed 2 March 2020), who state that Thomas Grignion worked as finisher to Quare, but he was only 11 when Quare died.
133 The Grignions never joined the Clockmakers' Company.
134 Their landlords were the Dukes of Bedford, so papers relating to the Grignion family are preserved in the Bedford Estate Papers, deposited in the London Metropolitan Archives.
135 Jean Crucifix witnessed the naturalization of David Tollier, gunsmith of St Mary Whitechapel, in 1709 (HSQS, XXVII, no.118). Robert Crucifix, clockmaker, was working in Spitalfields until his death in 1735 (HSQS, LX, p.78). There is a wall clock signed 'Crucifix' in the Garrick Club, London. See also Edmunds 2013.
136 Campbell 1747, pp.250–1.
137 Ibid., p.251.
138 HSQS, XXIX, pp.12, 66, 76, 98, 108, 114, 137, 139. The clockmaker Joseph Martineau witnessed the marriage of Gabriel's daughter Louise in 1726.
139 Campbell 1747, p.252.
140 Ibid.
141 Landes 1983, pp.254–6.
142 Victoria and Albert Museum, LOAN: GILBERT.310–2008.
143 See a clock by Romilly paired with a barometer, now at the J. Paul Getty Museum, California (invs 71.DP115 and 71.DP116).
144 Wagner 1907, p.346.
145 Smith 2015.
146 An example with ruby cylinder, helical balance spring and compensation curb is in the Clockmakers' Company Collection, on loan to the Science Museum, London.
147 The shop continued under the management of Edward Dent.
148 In recognition of his services, the Clockmakers' Company Company presented Vulliamy with a piece of silver in 1849.
149 Morgan 1883.
150 K. Jones, 'Gold Boxes in the British Royal Collection' in Murdoch and Zech 2014, fig.16.2, p.211. This was part of a group of 200 piqué boxes given to Queen Mary in December 1917 by Lady Mount Stephen. The box is inscribed 'The ivory part / of this Box was turned by / H.M. KING GEORGE THE THIRD / and by him given to my Grandfather / JUNE 1774. / NB My Grandfather purchased the Lathe in Paris / and brought home with him a person / to instruct H.M. how to use it / Henry Duval'.
151 For members of the Swiss Masonic Lodge in London see Smith, 2015, p.341. David Duval, born in Frankfurt 1751, married in London in 1791 and served the French Hospital as a Director from 1786 and as Deputy Governor from 1813 to 1836. His son Richard Julius Duval, born in 1802, married in 1830 Maria Isabel, daughter of Manuel José da Costa Machado of São João del Rey, Brazil. They settled in Minas Gerais and had six sons and five daughters.
152 See www.jaquet-droz.com/en/the-extraordinary-history-jaquet-droz (accessed 31 January 2020).
153 Romadzka 2005.

12 Printmakers and Sellers: Designs, Ornament and Reproductive Prints *pages 233–45*

1 Griffiths 2016, pp.219, 236.
2 Hayward 1959, pp.5, 8.
3 Jackson-Stops 1971, pp.182–3.
4 Ibid., pp.262–6. *A New Booke of Drawings* was advertised in *The London Gazette* on 1–4 October 1694.
5 Murdoch 1992a, pp.62–3, figs 58, 60. The plaster busts are still *in situ*.
6 Phillips 1931. Murdoch 2020.
7 Murdoch 1997; Murdoch 1998, pp.363–74.
8 Listed in HSQS, XXX, p.35. Abraham Martin signed a watch case with a movement by Delander and another by Thomas Tompion, 1683 (Ashmolean Museum, Mallet Collection, no.86). Thompson 2007, p.42.
9 Gribelin published *A Book of Severall Ornaments* (London 1682); *A Book of Ornaments Usefull to Jewellers, Watchmakers, and all Other Artists* (London 1697); *A New Book of Ornaments Usefull to all Artists, Invented and Engraved by S. Gribelin* (London *c.*1704). His *Livre d'Estampes de Sim Gribelin* with 425 prints is in the British Museum, Department of Prints and Drawings (1859,0625.121–542). See O'Connell 1985.
10 Wren 1750, pp.261–2.
11 O'Connell 1985, p.38, no.15, cited by Clayton 1997, p.21. Griffiths 2016, pp.318–19.
12 Simpson 2017. The print is lettered 'Sir Christopher Wren Architectus / Published April the 28. 1743 / Engraved and Sold by P. Fourdrinier the corner of Craigs Court Charing Cross London'; British Museum, inv.1880,1113.3296.1–2.
13 These prints are contained in Gribelin's presentation volume preserved in the Department of Prints and Drawings at the British Museum.
14 *The London Gazette*, 15–19 May 1707, announced: 'The seven cartons [sic] of Raphael d'Urbin, drawn and engraved from the Originals in the Gallery at Hampton Court, by S. Gribelin, are sold by Charles Mather, near Temple Bar in Fleet-street; and by the said Gribelin, in Longacre, the Corner-House of Banbury Court. Price 15s'. The antiquary George Vertue noted that 'vast numbers of them sold': Vertue III (*The Walpole Society*, vol.22 [1933–4]), p.7; Walpole 1769 (1849), p.964.
15 Letter from Lord Shaftesbury to Thomas Mickelthwayte, Naples, 19 April 1712 (The National Archives, 30/24/Box 239). Paknadel 1974; O'Connell 1988.
16 Hsieh 2009.
17 Oman 1978, p.79, pl.9.
18 'Six of her Majesty's Pictures Drawn and Engraved from the originals of Paulo Veronese, Jac. Tintoretto, Old Palma, Jul. Romano, and

Andr. Shiavone in the Royal Palace of Windsor and Kensington' were advertised in the *London Gazette* of 27–29 May 1712 for 16s the set.
19 When the panels were repositioned in 1951 the arrangement was based on Gribelin's engravings, which were taken to be the earliest and most authoritative rendering of the ceiling. However, Gribelin lined up the longitudinal pictures on the same axis, as engravings; unlike a ceiling, they cannot be viewed from four different angles, so his work only served to confuse the issue. Held 1970.
20 Walpole 1769 (1849), p.964.
21 Le May 2003.
22 See www.collections.vam.ac.uk/item/0697123/matthew-liart-c1736-c1782-engraver-print-audinet-philip (accessed 1 March 2020); Murdoch 1985a, no.241, pp.168–9.
23 Portalis 1910, cited by Le May 2003, p.75.
24 British Museum, Department of Prints and Drawings, Heal 99.18; 99.19. Isaac Basire was one of five Huguenot engravers who subscribed in 1726 to Samuel Sympson's *A New Book of Cyphers*, 1726. The others were Peter Bosquian, Paul Fourdrinier, Andrew Motte and James Regnier.
25 Simpson 2020.
26 The inscription on the Grolleau family tomb records the burial of Paul's wife and other family members: 'Mr. Lewis Grolleau died 26th December 1715, aged 53. Also, Mrs. Mary Grolleau, his wife, died February 5th 1729. Also their daughter Mrs. Susannah who died 16th November 1746. Also, Jane Fourdrinier, daughter of the above mentioned Mrs. Susannah died 8th May 1752, aged 15. Also, Mr. Paul Fourdrinier, husband of the above mentioned Mrs. Susanna died in 1757 [*sic*]. Also, Mrs. Mary Lloyd, daughter of the above Lewis Grolleau, died 5th October 1770, aged 57 years', cited by Simpson 2020, p.223.
27 Murdoch 1985a, no.258.
28 Ibid., no.259
29 Ibid., no.19.
30 A copy of the survey is in the Victoria and Albert Museum, V&A E.352–1944. For Rocque, see Snodin 1984, no.B2.
31 See www.collections.vam.ac.uk/item/078204/plan-du-jardin-vue-des-plan-rocque-jean (accessed 1 March 2020).
32 Murdoch 1985a, no.247.
33 *HSQS*, XXVI, p.87.
34 William Oldys records in his diary for 3 March 1738 a meeting between George Vertue and John Rocque about the proposed map of London: 'Went to Lecester Square with Mr. Ames, and saw Mr. Vertue there, but Mr. Rocque and he are not yet come to an agreement.' Phillips 1952, pp.10–11.
35 See www.collections.vam.ac.uk/item/0976859/londinum-antiqua-print-vertue-george (accessed 1 March 2020).
36 R. Hyde, 'Portraying London mid-century: John Rocque and the Brothers Buck', in O'Connell 2003, pp.28–33.
37 *HSQS*, LX, p.325. Bartholomew Rocque's Treatise was announced in *London Chronicle*, 10–12 November 1761.
38 For a 1759 list of Rocque's stock preserved in the Heal Collection, British Museum, see Murdoch 1985a, no.246 (illustrated). British Museum, Heal Collection, 17.132 (www.britishmuseum.org/collection/object/P_Heal-17-132, accessed 23 July 2019). British Museum, Heal Collection, inv.17.133 is the list of stock available from Rocque's widow, Mary Ann, in 1765 (www.britishmuseum.org/collection/object/P_Heal-17-132, accessed 1 March 2020).
39 Strickland 1913, pp.322–3.
40 O'Mullane 1946, pp.129–31; www.libraryireland.com/irishartists/bernard-scale.php (accessed 25 March 2020).
41 Stuart Mason and Bensusan-Butt 1985.
42 Elliot 1987, p.64, no.34; British Library, Maps, K.top.xi.68.
43 Binney 1973, p.681; Clutton and Mackay 1970; K. Rorschach, 'Gravelot, *GAO* (accessed 23 July 2020).
44 Cohen 1953, pp.30, 54, 63, 69. Colvin 1995, p.245. Peter Chassereau's wife, Anne, described as 'very weak' when she wrote her will in 1740, was living in Berwick Street when she died in 1740. *HSQS*, LX, p.64.
45 The family originally came from Clairac, Guienne. A Susanna Pomarede mentioned in the will of Dublin watchmaker Abraham Barbault in 1751 may be a relative: *HSQS*, LX, p.371.
46 A copy of this map in a private collection in the Isle of Man was published by John Noble and James Keenan, Dublin, in 1751: Philips 1973, pp.34–5, sold 27 June 1973, lot 37.
47 Alcorn 2000, no.266, pp.347–9; a copy of the map is in the British Library, Map 12170.
48 See www.libraryireland.com/irishartists/daniel-pomarede.php (accessed 25 March 2020).
49 Clayton 1997, p.211.
50 Archer 1989. Ornament prints by Vivares were used to create print rooms at Blickling, Rokeby, Ston Easton Park, Somerset and Woodhall.
51 Clayton 1997, pp.269, 272.
52 Snodin 1984, no.C11 p.45 E.731–1907.
53 Huntington Library San Marino, Stowe MS ST 30: James Brydges 1st Duke of Chandos Accounts with Walter Ferguson, House Steward 1729–35, fols 169, 172. Collins-Baker 1949, p.285.
54 One is in the Victoria and Albert Museum (www.collections.vam.ac.uk/item/0188624/a-view-of-amazing-rock-print-vivares-francois, accessed 1 March 2020).
55 Belsey 2002, p.11.
56 Clayton 1997, pp.182, 233; Belsey 1997.
57 M. Sullivan, 'Gravelot [formerly Bourguignon], Hubert-François (1699–1773), book illustrator and engraver', *ODNB* (accessed 1 March 2020).
58 *The General Advertiser*, 9 November 1750, cited by Clayton 1997, p.145.
59 Simon 2007, pp.20–1, 33–4, 97; Einberg 2016, p.274.
60 Charles Grignion in *The Monthly Magazine*, 1808.
61 Wilton House, Household Account Books. The earliest payment, of £1 9s 6d on 28 March 1734, is for 'bookbinding'.
62 Clayton 1997, p.165.
63 P. van Somer's address is given in the lettered inscription on the engraving of the seven bishops committed to the Tower by James II in 1688.
64 British Museum, Department of Prints and Drawings, Heal Collection of Trade Cards, 100/60.
65 Boughton House, Northamptonshire, Accounts of John, 2nd Duke of Montagu, reads: 'To Jaqs Regnier, fr. Print deliver to Lady Mary, as pr Bill £1.05'.
66 www.britishmuseum.org/collection/object/P_Heal-100-60, note by Ambrose Heal on mount of trade card.
67 Thomas Major, MS Account of Andrew Lawrence, British Museum, Department of Prints and Drawings, 1870.0514.2357.
68 Archives, Petworth House: 'Celeste Regnier supplied 71 Prints of Giacomo Freij at the prices mark'd £15.17.0. and Single Mezzotinto portraits of Augustus Keppel £ 0.7.0. Admiral Saunders £ 0.7.0. Lord Edgecombe £ 0.7.0. Lord Ligonier £ 0.12.0. Lord Albemarle £ 0.2.0. Lord Hardwicke £ 0.6.0. Mr Legge £ 0.5.0. Mr Pelham £ 0.6.0. Garrick with Tragedy & Comedy £ 0.10.6.'
I am indebted to Gervase Jackson-Stops for this information.
69 My thanks to Sheila O'Connell for clarifying the role of the printseller in eighteenth-century London.
70 British Museum, Department of Prints and Drawings, Heal Collection of Trade Cards, 100/51.
71 Murdoch 1982b, listed on p.240.
72 British Museum, Department of Prints and Drawings, Banks Collection.
73 Philip Margas, of the same address, appears in the accounts of Lord Coventry, Croome Court, as supplying 'a draught & making a frame to a Japan Cabinett according to my lady's Orders'. Margas also supplied a rosewood birdcage. Archives, Department of Furniture and Woodwork, Victoria and Albert Museum.
74 Clayton 1997, pp.99, 114, 182; *HSQS*, LX, p.54.
75 *HSQS*, LX, p.34.
76 Gribelin's 1704 *A New Book of Cyphers* and *A New Book of Ornaments*, Christ Church Picture Gallery, inv.3.12
77 Plates 10 and 12 of Vauquer's book are extremely close to plates 2 and 5 of Gribelin's 1697 pattern book. See Vauquer 1680 (1888), vols VI and VII.
78 The illustrated clock was sold at Bonhams, London, 29 June 2017, lot 103. In his will (Prob 11/578/449), Constantin left a bequest to the French church Threadneedle Street. He lived in the parish of Christ Church; after his death his wife Susanna lived in the parish of St Margaret's, Westminster. www.englishtableclocks.org/index.php/supplement/174-huguenot-engravers-come-to-england, accessed 29 March 2021.
79 Symonds 1951, p.134. François Asselin entered the Clockmakers' Company on 7 November 1687.

Another table clock by Asselin is in the Rothschild Collections at Ascott, Buckinghamshire.
80 Barker 2003, no.29, pp.104–6.
81 Ibid., no.28, p.104.
82 George Vertue noted that Gentot became insolvent so had to leave London. Ibid., p.105.
83 Grimwade 1988.
84 Murdoch 1980; www.collections.vam.ac.uk/item/O114105/portrait-of-the-goldsmith-louis-print-cossin-louis (accessed 20 March 2020). There are impressions at Waddesdon and in the Bibliothèque nationale, Paris, engraved by Louis Cossin (1627–1704) after Pierre Rabon (1619–1684). The portrait served as the title page to a suite of seven ornament prints engraved by Cossin after Rouppert. For a full set, see the auction of the Library of the Birmingham Assay Office, 20 March 2020, lot 116.
85 Murdoch 2018.
86 Oman 1978, p.63, pl.69.
87 *HSQS*, XXIX, p.32.
88 *HSQS*, XXVI, p.22.
89 The inscription inside the front cover of the volume reads: 'Gribelin's works compleat – made up by himself, very curious.'
90 Barker 2003, no.86, p.185. For Samuel Gribelin, see www.collections.vam.ac.uk/item/O674203/engraving-gribelin-samuel (accessed 20 March 2020).
91 Oman 1978, pp.76–7, 82.
92 Murdoch 2015.
93 Murdoch 2014.
94 Calloway, Snodin and Wainwright 1980, no.97.

13 Huguenots and Portraiture: Allegiance, Identity, Loyalty and Memory *pages 247–67*

1 Williams 2015, pp.8–9, 25.
2 *HSQS*, LX, pp.273–4. In 1776 Matthew Maty instructed his executrix, his wife, Mary, 'to employ Bartolozzi or other eminent engraver, to make print from the best drawing or picture done for 100 copies & no more'.
3 An impression is in the British Museum, see Griffiths 1998, no.148, pp.220–1.
4 *The Observator*, 12 January 1685: 'The exact draught of the marble statue of his Majesty in the Royall Exchange so long expected is now (by permission of authority) finished. Curiously engraven by Mr Vandrebanc, and printed on a large sheet of imperiall paper … Price 2s 6d.' The plate passed into the hands of David Mortier, Huguenot bookseller at Erasmus Head in The Strand. Swift 1983.
5 In 1685 Vandrebanc was in Princes Street, near Leicester Fields. By 1692 he had moved to the west side of Greek Street, Soho, and moved again to Dean Street in 1693–4. The engraving is inscribed: 'Ludovicus Magnus / ad vivum depictus a Gothefredo Knellero cum in finem a Divo Carolo II ex Anglia in Galliam Miss A. 1685 dein vero ob summam picturam excellentam Sculptus a P. Vandrebanc. Sold by P. Vandrebanc in Princes Street near Lister Fields.' Clayton 1997, p.28, fig.34.
6 Stewart 1971, pp.38–9; Stainton and White 1987, cat.143; Vertue V (*The Walpole Society*, vol.26 [1937–8]), p.19.
7 The portrait of Monnoyer was in the Earl of Oxford's collection by 1741 as no.36, 'Old Baptist, an excellent head … Sir G Kneller'. It is recorded in a mezzotint by George White (*c.*1684–1732) and a preparatory drawing is in the Witt Collection, Courtauld Institute of Art.
8 Jean 'Vansommer', who designed patterns for silk weaving, was living in the 'old Artillery Jamaicas Planter' in 1704, when he married Madeleine Obrisset. In 1733 he witnessed the marriage of his daughter Magdaleine to Louis Ferdinand Vigne. *HSQS*, XXXVII, nos 474, 561.
9 British Museum, inv.1902,1011.7819; Paul van Somer also produced portraits of André Lortie from La Rochelle, minister at the Savoy church, in 1681 (British Museum, inv.1902,1011.6045). For Jan van Somer's portrait of Prince George of Hanover, see Stewart 1971, no.61.
10 Wessely 1870. A set of eight portraits of Huguenot ministers are in the Pepys Collection, Magdalen College, Cambridge, invs 2980.129a, b, c, d, 2980.130a, b, c, d; Griffiths 1998, p.231; Charrington 1936, pp.7, 8, 50, 60, 71, 151.
11 *The London Gazette*, 1 October 1694; Griffiths 1998, p.273, no.190.
12 Bourseau received a grant of 10d from the Royal Bounty for lessons with van Somer at the Newport Street address; Phillips 1933. Paul van Somer also engraved ornament prints and published a drawing book, *Figurae variae*, for which the British Museum has 11 plates (inv.1937,0802.1.48–59; the title page is inv.1937,0802.1.48.
13 British Museum, inv.1868,0808.3309; Griffiths 1998, no.207, pp.297–8.
14 Vautier's wife, Marguerite Gribelin, was Simon Gribelin's aunt. She made her reconnaisance at the Savoy church on 24 August 1687; *HSQS*, XXII, p.26. For Vautier's will, see *HSQS*, LX, pp.31, 361.
15 The print is signed 'D. Vautier pinx. S.Gribelin Sculpt.1689'; *HSQS*, XI, p.169.
16 The Cole family of Florence Court, County Fermanagh, Northern Ireland collected memorabilia associated with William of Orange and framed and displayed their copy. See www.nationaltrustcollections.org.uk/object/631233 (accessed 1 April 2020).
17 Godfrey 1978, p.29.
18 Murdoch and Vigne 2009, fig.7, p.15.
19 Spannheim died in London in October 1710 and was buried in Westminster Abbey; see *ODNB* under 'Ezekiel Spannheim'.
20 Examples are included in Gribelin's presentation volume, Department of Prints and Drawings, British Museum, inv.1859-6-25-121.
21 In *Omnium Caesarum verissimae imagines ex antiquisnumismatis desumptis*, 1554.
22 Phillips 1935, pl.LXXXIII.
23 *The Daily Advertiser*, 24 January 1743, issue 3749.
24 Norman 1976, no.C165, p.320.
25 Murdoch 1985a, no.354, p.244. Lestourgeon's silver pair-case watch in the Museum of London (inv. A22344) is engraved with a skull, crossbones and the initial 'W', and inscribed 'Died March 8 1702'. The pierced outer case, engraved with a floral pattern and an armorial shield surmounted by a helmet, is attached to its original silver chain and winding key, a rare survival. The British Museum has another example by Lestourgeon, which celebrates the accession of Queen Anne in 1702. Further examples are in the Clockmakers' Company Collection (Science Museum) and the Metropolitan Museum of Art, New York.
26 *HSQS*, XVI, pp.3, 9.
27 Murdoch 1985a, no.359, p.248. The pair-case watch dated 1708 with portrait miniature has a gold case marked by Adam Roumieu, who joined the Clockmakers' Company in 1695 (see p.208; Morgan 1883); Thompson 1996, pp.421–2, pl.XXXVIIa. He may have been related to Simon Beauvais, who joined the Clockmakers' Company in 1690; see Hill 1948.
28 Sarrazin et al. 2016; Gribelin 1941; British Museum, inv.P,8.199.
29 Develle 1913; Vincent 2002.
30 See www.collections.vam.ac.uk/item/O111334/watch-goullons-jacques (accessed 1 April 2020).
31 Enamel on gold, 6.5 x 5.5 cm in original frame. The miniature is in the Rijksmuseum and illustrated in www.theframeblog.com/tag/gilles-legare (accessed 1 April 2020).
32 Peter Oliver's watercolour is in the Victoria and Albert Museum (inv.P.3&A-1950); for the joint miniature of husband and wife in Sherborne Castle see Sumner 1995, no.33, illustrated p.76.
33 Scarisbrick 2011, p.106.
34 Also recorded as James Harding, court flautist and composer (*GMO*).
35 Isaac Oliver's 1598 portrait is in the Burghley House collection. The engraving, of *c.*1579 by an unknown artist, depicts the *Collignei Fratres*: Rijksmuseum, inv.RP-P-1948-66. MacLeod et al. 2019, no.55 pp.150–1.
36 Foskett 1987, p.79, pl.13c.
37 Walpole 1849, vol.1, p.178.
38 For the latest account of Isaac Oliver's noble patrons, see www.britishartstudies.ac.uk/issues/issue-index/issue-17/isaac-oliver-and-the-essex-circle (accessed 6 October 2020).
39 Knowles 2017.
40 A profile self-portrait of Peter Oliver and full face of his wife, Anne, dating from the 1620s, are in the National Portrait Gallery (invs 4853, 4853a).
41 *Mercurius Politicus*, 22–29 January 1658; Whitley Papers, Department of Prints and Drawings, British Museum, vol.IV, p.441.
42 In 1628 Des Granges copied Lucas Vorsterman's 1627 print of Raphael's celebrated painting of St George and the Dragon.
43 The Waddesdon Bequest, British Museum, inv.168.
44 Apted and Hannabuss 1978, p.43.
45 Bimbenet-Privat and Farges 2015.
46 Truman 2013, no.98, pp.127–9.
47 Lightbown 1968.
48 Scouloudi 1940.

49 National Trust at Seaton Delaval. See www.fairfaxhouse.co.uk/articles/the-fairfax-jewel (accessed 1 April 2020). Fairfax holds a banner inscribed 'Sic radiant fideles'('Thus the faithful shine'). The Fairfax Jewel was later owned by Horace Walpole.
50 Reynolds 1999, p.350.
51 Fatio 2018, p.201, entry for 12 March 1687 ('reçu à la paix de l'église'): 'Monsieur Petitot de Paris et sa femme'.
52 Foskett 1972, vol.1, p.44.
53 Stroehlin 1905.
54 *HSQS*, LX, p.306.
55 Ibid., p.192; Scouloudi 1987, p.xiv.
56 Heinz Archive, National Portrait Gallery, Artists' Files.
57 Foskett 1972, p.369.
58 Ibid., p.375.
59 Ibid., p.170.
60 George Vertue noted 'a Mans head a limning Benjamin Arlaud pinxit 1715 curiously neat well colourd and well drawn this Mr Arlaud was limner to the King or Queen till he died whether he had a salary or not I can't tell by this picture he shows to be a Master of his Art'. Vertue II (*The Walpole Society*, vol.20 [1931–2]), p.90. Benjamin's brother Jacques Antoine Arlaud, based at the exiled Stuart court at St Germain *c.*1703–10, acted as a dealer in Paris, supplying the Duke of Chandos with Oliver Cromwell's portrait and *Jupiter and Leda* by Annibale Caracci. Collins-Baker 1949, p.77.
61 Ibid., p.139.
62 François Picot was nephew of the jeweller Isaac Picot; he studied under enamel painter Jean Cuchet (1674–1739) in Geneva in 1707 and in Paris, Italy and Germany.
63 Foskett 1972, pp.138, 448–9.
64 *London Evening Post*, 13–15 September 1753.
65 *Public Advertiser*, 31 March 1764.
66 Bibliothèque de l'Institut National d'Histoire de l'Art, Paris, collections Jacques Doucet, inv.NUM 8 RES 14.
67 Foskett 1972, p.417. Daniel Mussard from Geneva, who joined the London Clockmakers' Company in 1686, was probably a member of the same family. Morgan 1883.
68 In September 1751 *The General Advertiser* announced that Mussard lodged 'at Mr Trinketts, Stationers, in Black Fryars, Broad Way'.
69 Foskett 1972, p.217; L. Cust and A. Peach, 'Gresse, John Alexander (1741–1794), painter and drawing master', *ODNB* (accessed 29 March 2020).
70 *ODNB*; *Gentlemans Magazine* 1st series, 31 (1761), pp.171–8; Foskett 1972, p.284. Dr Matthew Maty presented Gardelle's portrait of Voltaire to the British Museum (inv.Painting.26).
71 Humbert 1897.
72 See www.apollo-magazine.com/how-liotards-chocolate-girl-charmed-the-city-of-dresden/20 November 2018 (accessed 1 April 2020).
73 Garrick was in Paris in 1751, recorded sitting to Liotard on 14 and 15 June and dined with him, 'a very sensible unaffected man, a little vain as they all are' (Alexander 1928, pp.28, 30).
74 By 1731 there were still 12 master carvers and 250 workers in ivory active in Dieppe.
75 In 1753 Milbanke wrote to Pelham, afterwards first Lord Chichester: 'I dined with him at Lord Rockingham's (where he was doing an excellent picture of Lord Rockingham, a half-length); he is in his Greek dress with beard down to his waist'. Liotard shaved off his beard upon his marriage to Marie Gargues in 1756, apparently at her insistence. The miniature is inscribed on the backing in ink: 'Liotard / by / Himself / 1753'.
76 *The Public Advertiser*, 28 February 1754 and 15 March 1755.
77 H. Wine, 'Liotard, Jean-Étienne (1702–1789), painter', *ODNB* (accessed 29 March 2020).
78 Heinz Archive, National Portrait Gallery, Artists' Files; *The Daily Advertiser*, 13 February 1745.
79 In 1753 William De La Cour was established as a 'portrait painter in oil and pastel at Mr Read's Grocers the sign of the Ship, Great Russell Street, Covent Garden' (Fleming 1962, p.1224).
80 The auction of 'Household Furniture, Pictures, Plate, China and Linen of Mr De la Cour at his dwelling the Green Door, in Winchester Street, New Broad Street' was announced in *The Public Advertiser* on 23 February 1753. Croft Murray 1970, nos 199b, 200b, 250a, 325a.
81 Fleming 1962.
82 De La Cour's oil portrait of Sir Stuart Threipland (1716–1805) and the posthumous portrait of his first wife, Lady Janet Sinclair (d. *c.*1756), signed and dated 1765, are still in family ownership. Paintings of Diana and Flora were in the collection of the Dukes of Hamilton. Heinz Archive, National Portrait Gallery.
83 *HSQS*, XVIII, p.162.
84 Cavalier's relief is inscribed 'D. GRAFTON I.CAVALIER 1684'. Another 1684 portrait signed 'I. Cavalier F. 1684' and inscribed 'IOHEN SEIGNETTE MED DOCT RUPEL' probably represents Jehan Seignette (1654–1701), son of Jehan Seignette (1623–1663) and nephew of Elie Seignette(1632–1698). The family is credited with the development of Rochelle salt for medicinal purposes.
85 Vertue I (*The Walpole Society*, vol.18 [1929–30]), p.129; Friedman (1981) suggested that this may be linked with the profile of the Duchess of Grafton, as the Duke was the favourite illegitimate son of Charles II. Grafton's Paris education influenced his patronage of French artists. His wife, Isabella, was the daughter of Henry Bennet, Earl of Arlington. See J. Davies, 'FitzRoy (formerly Palmer), Henry, first Duke of Grafton (1663–1690), naval officer', *ODNB* (accessed 13 October 2020).
86 Gunnis, 1951 under 'Iback'. The inscription 'Josias Iback Stadti Blarensis 1679 Fudit' is cut into one of the horses' hoofs.
87 Colvin et al. 1976, p.325.
88 The medal, signed 'Cavalier F.1686' and inscribed on the reverse 'J. CAVALIER FECIT A.D. 1688' and on the obverse 'SAM.PEPYS CAR. ET. IAC.ANGLREGIB A SECRETIS ADMIRALIA', was acquired by the Clothworkers' Company in 1931. I am grateful to the former archivist, Mr D.E. Wickham, for this information.
89 A receipt in the Sackville family archives dated July 1690 for £21 for 'two medals one of my Lord & ye other My Lady' is signed by the artist. The medals represented Charles, 6th Earl of Dorset, and his second wife, Mary, daughter of James Compton, 3rd Earl of Northampton, who died the following year. I am indebted to Gervase Jackson-Stops for this information.
90 Stewart 1971, no.4, p.16.
91 The legend reads 'GOTHOFRIDVS KNELLER. PRIM. PICT. REGIUS. MAG. BRITANIAE'. Another ivory, of Mary II, in Berlin is inscribed 'CAVALIER F. LONDINI 1690'. I am most grateful to Christian Theuerkauff, formerly of the Staatliche Museen Preussischer Kulturbesitz, Berlin, for providing a photograph of the original.
92 Julius 1926, p.145.
93 Prince George is wearing his Garter George (he became a knight on 1 January 1684).
94 One of the medallions is signed 'I.C.'.
95 Verbeck 1973; Hein 2018, nos 103–17, pp.201–6. I am grateful to Dr Charles Avery for this reference. Arne 1952, p.62 (trans. Lars Olof Larsson): 'This time Fabritius travelled with a company of 22 persons, one of them was the French sculptor Jean Cavalier ... As usual they travelled via Moscow and Astrachan, and from there by ship to Nizova, the first Persian town south of the border.... They continued the journey with a caravan consisting of 80 camels and 40 horses to Schemacha, arriving there in the middle of June. Because of the strong heat they had to stay there until August 8th. Cavalier seems to have died there, leaving a debt to Fabritius of 3.547,21 riksdaler copper.'
96 *A Catalogue of the Genuine & Entire Collection of Valuable Gems, Bronzes, Marbles, & other Busts and Antiquities of the late Dr. Mead*, 11–15 March 1755, first day's sale, lots 32 and 40.
97 Friedman and Clifford 1974, appendix B.
98 Hodgkinson 1965, pp.29–32, fig.2.
99 Murdoch 1985a, no.320, p.222.
100 Avery 1996, p.76. The wax of Guy is in the Gordon Museum, Guy's Hospital, London.
101 Kerslake 1972.
102 I am most grateful to Pierre Bazin, former Curator of Dieppe Castle Museum, for this information.
103 For the Huguenot church in Edinburgh, see Easson 1949–50.
104 Avery 1996, p.13. Charles Avery generously shared his files on Le Marchand with me. Le Marchand's earliest recorded portrait, an ivory medallion of John Locke, is inscribed 'Effi. IOHAS LOCKE/ Aetat:65/DLMSC.' It is also inscribed in ink inside right shoulder 'Raper'.
105 The former was in the collection of S.R. Houfe; the latter is at Anglesey Abbey, Cambridgeshire, and may represent the Grand Dauphin, not Louis XIV. Houfe 1971.
106 Christie's, 13 December 1976.
107 *HSQS*, LX, 2007, p.178.

108 Collection of the French Hospital, Rochester, Kent.
109 Walpole 1849, vol.2, p.625.
110 Stukeley 1882, p.48.
111 *HSQS*, LII, 1971, under 'Constantin': 'qui par Grand Maux Dyseux dont il a Esté afflige depuis bien des annees Ayant Empesché de Gagner sa vie ce qui le reduit dans une Extreme Pauvrete Estant malade & tres Infirme'.
112 See www.collections.vam.ac.uk/item/077787/king-james-ii-crowned-by-relief-constantin-jacobus (accessed 1 April 2020).
113 See www.collections.vam.ac.uk/item/0125405/frederick-louis-prince-of-wales-oil-painting-constantyn-rene-auguste (accessed 1 April 2020).
114 See, for example, Rysbrack's double wax relief of Sir Mark Pleydell Bouverie and his wife, Harriet. Smith 2017, p.96.
115 Foskett 1972, vol.1, p.162; S. Hoog, 'Benoist, Antoine', *GAO* (accessed 29 March 2020).
116 According to Buckeridge (1706, p.456), Le Pipre 'applied himself to the Study and Practice of Modelling in wax, in *basso-rilievo*, and wished he had thought of it sooner, for that sort of work suited better with his genius than any. Had he lived longer he would have arrived to great Perfection in it'.
117 These are now displayed in the Jubilee Gallery at Westminster Abbey.
118 'Diary of Sir J. Perceval', British Library, Add. MS 47061, 13 March 1730.
119 Pyke 1973, pl.53, pp.56–7. Museum of Art, Pittsburgh, Gift of Herbert DuPuy, invs 27.10.355 and 27.10.356.
120 Gosset 1892. I am most grateful to William Vaughan for an introduction to his cousin Mrs Eve Walsh, and to Mrs Walsh for allowing me to examine these waxes and the family papers in her possession. M. and L. Craske, 'Gosset, Isaac (1713–1799), frame maker and wax modeller', *ODNB* (accessed 2 April 2020).
121 Hollis 1808, vol.1, pp.490–1, quoted by Pyke 1973, under 'Gosset'.
122 Vertue continues that Gosset 'had the Honour of his Majestyes … sitting to him having done the King's portrait in wax him and the late Prince of Wales – the princess of Wales – the Duke of Cumberland – and the Present young Prince of Wales', Vertue III (*The Walpole Society*, vol.22 [1933–4]), pp.160–1.
123 Murdoch 1985a, no.316, pp.216–17.
124 At a cost of £2 12s 6d: an initial payment of 1 guinea and the balance of £1 11s 6d payable within two months (Whitley Papers, Department of Prints and Drawings, British Museum, vol.IV).
125 The archives of Petworth House record a payment to Isaac Gosset of £4 4s 0d in 1762–3 (P 377/CII). I am indebted to Gervase Jackson-Stops for this reference.
126 Calloway, Snodin and Wainwright 1980, no.117.
127 Phillips 1931, pp.19, 35.
128 Obrisset's portraits of Charles I and Queen Henrietta Maria are taken from memorial medals: Charles I from the 1649 medal by Heinrich Reitz the younger, his queen from the medal of 1670 by John Roettiers (1631–1703). Obrisset's Oliver Cromwell is taken from the 1650 Battle of Dunbar medal by Thomas Simon (1618–1665); Charles II from Roettiers's medal of the Battle of Lowestoft; and William and Mary from the 1689 Coronation medal by George Bower (fl.1664–89). Obrisset's lead medallions of Queen Anne and George I are after medals by John Croker (1670–1741). Phillips 1931, pp.59, 61, 62, 65.
129 Fedden 1972. I am indebted to Gervase Jackson-Stops for this information.
130 Woodwiss 1965, pp.18, 47–8;
131 See www.nationaltrustcollections.org.uk/object/1312028.1 (accessed 1 April 2020).
132 Ingamells and Raines 1976–8, p.1.
133 The National Portrait Gallery portrait of Frederick, Prince of Wales (NPG 2501, now on display at Beningborough Hall outside York), which was not engraved, is thought to have been painted towards the end of Mercier's period as principal painter, probably in 1736. See Offices of the Duchy of Cornwall, Frederick, Prince of Wales, Household Accounts, vol.5, fol.232, entry for 18 July 1735.
134 Vertue III (*The Walpole Society*, vol.22 [1933–4]), p.37.
135 Murdoch 1985a, pp.106–7, no.141.
136 Beard 1958.
137 British Museum, invs K,67.221 and 1902,111.1809.
138 Ingamells and Raines 1976–8, p.3.
139 Crookshank and FitzGerald 1969, p.16; Ingamells and Raines 1976–8, no.63, p.26.
140 I am indebted to Dr Robert Raines for this suggestion.
141 The Parmentier portrait is in York Minster Library.
142 Sarrazin et al. 2016, pp.32–3. Vertue III (*The Walpole Society*, vol.22 [1933–4]), p.46.
143 National Portrait Gallery (NPG 137), www.npg.org.uk/collections/search/portrait/mw01240 (accessed 1 April 2020).
144 *HSQS*, LX, p.117; Hayward 1930; Raines n.d., p.5. The original 1701 portrait is at Knole, Kent; the National Portrait Gallery copy is on loan to the National Trust at Lyme Park, Cheshire. Saint Evremond received a pension from Ralph Montagu.
145 The original is at Sledmere House, East Yorkshire; a version is in the Society of Antiquaries of London.
146 Raines n.d., p.5.
147 British Museum, Heal Collection, 100/51.
148 Heinz Archive, National Portrait Gallery. Kerslake 1977, vol.1, p.135; O'Connell 2003, pp.171–2.
149 Offices of the Duchy of Cornwall, Frederick, Prince of Wales, Household Accounts, 1728–51, vol.14, entry for October 1745.
150 Janssens 1975, p.41; *HSQS*, LX, pp.273–4.
151 *St James's Chronicle*, 19 May 1764, quoted in Whitley Papers, Department of Prints and Drawings, British Museum, vol.VIII.
152 Archives, Drummonds Bank (Royal Bank of Scotland). Payments to 'Mr Rhinold' of, £25 on 20 July 1757, £18 on 12 August 1757 and £17 on 10 December 1757 in Roubiliac's account with Drummond's Bank may be for Reynolds's copy of the Chandos portrait of Shakespeare.
153 This copy was presented to the British Museum in 1760 by Roubiliac's friend Dr Matthew Maty, with that sculptor's terracotta bust of Shakespeare. Dawson 1999, pp.200–1.
154 Esdaile 1928, p.124; Bindman and Baker 1995, p.79; Dawson 1999, pp.193–204.
155 Dawson 1999, pp.10, 11, 63, 65, 73, 74, 77, 140, 165, 201.
156 The busts included the 12 Roman Emperors, Cleopatra and Faustina, and surmounted the 14 presses to which they gave their names. See www.bl.uk/collection-guides/cotton-manuscripts# (accessed 29 March 2020).
157 Esdaile 1924, pp.9, 19, 23; Baker 1995b.
158 Janssens 1975, p.31; de Lisle and Myers 2019.
159 The bust of Dr Mead in the British Museum is of a classical format, whereas the version in the Royal College of Physicians is informal.
160 My thanks to Malcolm Baker and David Bindman for this information. Although there is a plaster bust of Plato in the library of Trinity College, Cambridge, it is based on an early seventeenth-century model.
161 Webb 1956, pp.804–5.
162 Esdaile 1928, pp.110–11, 182.
163 Farrer 1902, vol.1, pp.336–8.
164 Vertue III (*The Walpole Society*, vol.22 [1933–4]), p.101.
165 Baker 2014b, pp.26–7.
166 Baker 2014a, pp.285–6.
167 Mallet 1962.
168 *The Monthly Magazine*, 1 October 1804. The Aufrères' daughter Sophia married 1st Lord Yarborough in 1774. 'The late Sir Joshua Reynolds frequently said that Aufrère's collection contained a greater variety of pieces by the first masters of the Italian, Dutch and French and Flemish Schools than any other private collection in England; he estimated its value at £200,000.' Whitley Papers, Department of Prints and Drawings, British Museum, vol.1, under 'Aufrère'.
169 See *ODNB*, under 'Ligonier'.
170 In the nineteenth century, earlier miniatures were often set in gold boxes.
171 Watney 1974.
172 Honey 1937.
173 Kerslake 1977, vol.1, p.168. The bust of George II was presented to the National Portrait Gallery with that of Lord Ligonier, on 27 June 1817, by Thomas Lloyd of 112 Gloucester Place, London.
174 Friedman and Clifford 1974, nos 71, 74.
175 Victoria and Albert Museum, Wedgwood Collection, MS E35–18679 (presented by the Art Fund with major support from the Heritage Lottery Fund, private donations and a public appeal).
176 Avery 1996, p.77 no.46, p.87 nos 62b and 63; Christie's, London, 5 April 1864, lot 2035.
177 Reilly and Savage 1973, p.247.

Bibliography

Abbreviations

BHO
British History Online
(www.british-history.ac.uk)

BSHAF
Bulletin de la Société de l'histoire de l'art français

BSHPF
Bulletin de la Société de l'histoire du Protestantisme français (1903–2015)

GAO
Grove Art Online
(www.oxfordartonline.com/groveart)

GMO
Grove Music Online
(www.oxfordmusiconline.com/grovemusic)

HSQS
Huguenot Society Quarto Series

NAAF
Nouvelles archives de l'art français

ODNB
Oxford Dictionary of National Biography
(www.oxforddnb.com)

PHSL
Proceedings of the Huguenot Society of London

Adams, E., and Redstone, D., *Bow Porcelain* (London 1981)

Agnew, D.C., *Protestant Exiles from France in the Reign of Louis XIV: Or, the Huguenot Refugees and Their Descendants in Great Britain and Ireland*, 2 vols and index (London 1871–4, 3rd edn 1886)

Airs, M., 'David Papillon: architect, military engineer, developer, author and jeweller', *The Georgian Group Journal*, XXV (2017) pp.1–14

Alcorn, E.M., *English Silver in the Museum of Fine Arts, Boston*, vol.2: *Silver from 1697* (Boston 2000)

Alcorn, E. (ed.), *Beyond the Maker's Mark: Paul de Lamerie Silver in the Cahn Collection*, exh. cat., Victoria and Albert Museum, London; Brooks Museum, Memphis; St Louis Art Museum, Missouri; Powerhouse, Sydney (Cambridge 2006)

Alcouffe, D., *Les Artisans décorateurs du bois au Faubourg Saint-Antoine sous le règne de Louis XIV d'apres les minutes des notaires Parisiens* (Paris 2008)

Alexander, E.P. *The Journal of John Fontaine: An Irish Huguenot Son in Spain and Virginia 1710–1719* (Charlottesville, VA, 1972)

Alexander, R.C., *The Diary of David Garrick being a record of his memorable trip to Paris in 1751* (New York 1928)

Allen, B., 'Jonathan Tyers' Other Garden', *Journal of Garden History*, 1, no.3 (1981), pp.215–38

Allen, B., *Francis Hayman* (New Haven and London 1987)

An Accurate Description of the United Netherlands and of the most Considerable Parts of Germany, Sweden & Denmark Containing a Succinct Account of what is most remarkable in these Countries. And Necessary Instructions for Travellers Together with an exact Relation of the Entertainment of His Most Sacred Majesty King William At the Hague. Written by an English Gentleman (London 1691)

Andrews, H.C., 'Garrick's Statue of Shakespeare', *Architectural Review*, 39 (1916), pp.93–4

Ansell, R., 'Foubert's academy: British and Irish elite formation in seventeenth – and eighteenth-century Paris and London', in *Beyond the Grand Tour: Northern Metropolises and Early Modern Travel Behaviour*, eds R. Sweet, G. Verhoeven and S. Goldsmith (London 2017), pp.46–64

Apted, M., and S. Hannabuss, *Painters in Scotland 1301–1700: A Biographical Dictionary* (Edinburgh 1978)

Archer, C., 'Festoons of Flowers for fitting up print rooms', *Apollo*, 130 (December 1989), pp.386–91

Archer, M., 'Delft at Dyrham', *The National Trust Year Book 1975–1976* (London 1975), pp.12–18

Arne, T.J., *Svenskarna och Österlandet* (Stockholm 1952)

Atkins, S.A., and N.H. Overall, *Some Account of the Worshipful Company of Clockmakers of the City of London* (London 1881)

Auzas, P., 'Les Grands Mays de Notre Dame a Paris', *BSHAF*, II (Paris 1949b), pp.85–8

Avery, C., 'Hubert Le Sueur, The "Unworthy Praxiteles" of King Charles I', *The Walpole Society*, vol.48 (1980), pp.135–209

Avery, C., *David Le Marchand 1674–1726: 'An Ingenious Man for Carving in Ivory'* (London 1996)

Baarsen, R. (ed.), *Rococo in Nederland*, exh.cat., Rijksmuseum, Amsterdam (Zwolle 2001)

Baarsen, R., et al., *Courts and Colonies: The William and Mary Style in Holland, England and America*, exh. cat., Cooper Hewitt Museum, New York (New York 1988)

Baillie, H.M., 'Etiquette and the Planning of State Apartments in Baroque Palaces', *Archaeologia*, 101 (January 1967), pp.169–99

Baker, M., 'English responses to continental sculpture in the 18th century', *Handbook to the Grosvenor House Antiques Fair* (London 1993), pp.12–17

Baker, M., '"Squabby Cupids and Clumsy Graces": Garden Sculpture and Luxury in Eighteenth-Century England', *Oxford Art Journal*, 18 (1995a), pp.1–18

Baker, M., 'The Portrait Sculpture', in *The Making of the Wren Library, Trinity College, Cambridge*, ed. D. McKitterick (Cambridge 1995b) pp.110–37

Baker, M., *Figured in Marble: The Making and Viewing of Eighteenth-Century Sculpture* (London 2000)

Baker, M., *The Marble Index: Roubiliac and Sculptural Portraiture in Eighteenth-Century Britain* (New Haven and London 2014a)

Baker, M., *Fame and Friendship: Pope, Roubiliac and the Portrait Bust*, exh. cat., Waddesdon Manor, Buckinghamshire (New Haven and London 2014b)

Barker, N. (ed.), *The Devonshire Inheritance: Five Centuries of Collecting at Chatsworth*, exh. cat., Bard Gallery, New York (Alexandria, VA, 2003)

Barkla, R., and R. Barkla, 'Andrew Planché – life after Derby', *Derby Porcelain International Society Journal*, 3 (1995), pp.26–43 (summarized in R. and R. Barkla, 'Andrew Planché's life after Derby', *Transactions of the English Ceramic Circle*, vol.15, part 3 [1995], p.367)

Barr, E., *George Wickes, Royal Goldsmith 1698–1761* (London 1980)

Barrell, R.A., *The Correspondence of Abel Boyer Huguenot Refugee 1667–1729* (New York and Queenstown, Ontario, 1992)

Barrett, F.A., and A.L. Thorpe, *Derby Porcelain 1750–1848* (Cirencester 1971)

Barrington Haynes, E., *Glass through the Ages* (London 1948)

Battison, E.A., 'Stone-Cutting and Polishing Lathe, by Jacques Besson', *Technology and Culture*, 7, no.2 (spring 1966), pp.202–5

Bazin, P., *Les Ivoiriers Dieppois au Musée de Dieppe* (Dieppe 1972)

Beard, G., 'A Royal Painter in Yorkshire, *Country Life*, 124 (7 August 1958), pp.274–5

Beard, G., 'William Kent and the Royal Barge', *Burlington Magazine*, 112 (July 1970), pp.488–95

Beard, G., *Decorative Plasterwork in Great Britain* (London 1975)

Beard, G., 'Robert Adam and his Craftsmen', *Connoisseur*, 198 (July 1978), p.193

Beard, G., 'English Woodcarvers', *Connoisseur*, 207 (June 1981) p.143

Beard, G., *The Work of Grinling Gibbons* (London 1989)

Beard, G., *Upholsterers and interior furnishing in England, 1530–1840* (New Haven and London 1997)

Beard, G., and C. Gilbert, *Dictionary of English Furniture Makers, 1660–1840* (Leeds 1986)

Beard, G., and A. Westman, 'A French Upholsterer in England: Francis Lapiere 1653–1714', *Burlington Magazine*, 135, no.1085 (August 1993), pp.515–24

Bellamy Gardner, H.,'The Earliest References to Chelsea Porcelain', *Transactions of the English Porcelain Circle*, 1 (1928), pp.16–22

Belsey, H., 'The Gainsborough's House Collection: A Progress Report', *Apollo*, 146 (1 August 1997), pp.55–9

Belsey, H., *Gainsborough at Gainsborough's House* (Sudbury 2002)

Benedict, P., 'The Huguenot Population of France, 1600–1685: The Demographic Fate and Customs of a Religious Minority', *Transactions of the American Philosophical Society*, 81, no.5 (1991), pp.i–ix, 1–164

Bennet, Ann, 'The Goldsmiths of Hull 1400-1800' Ph.D. University of Hull, 2 vols (Hull 1991)

Benthall, G., 'Early art schools in London, 1635–1770' [a bibliography], typescript, *c.*1955 (V&A Library, inv.msl/1961/2252)

Benton, E., 'The London Enamellers', *Transactions of the English Ceramic Circle*, 8, no.2 (1972), pp.137–63

Berg, W.E.J., *De réfugiés in de Nederlanden, na de herroeping van het Edict van Nantes eene proeve van onderzoek naar den invloed, welken hunne overkomst gehad heeft op handel en nijverheid, letteren, beschaving en zeden* (Amsterdam 1845)

Best, E.J., *The Huguenots of Lisburn: The Story of the Lost Colony* (Lisburn 1997)

Betts, J., and R. Smith, 'Hubert Martinet's Elephant: an eighteenth-century automaton at Waddesdon Manor' (forthcoming)

Bignamini, I., 'George Vertue, Art Historian, and Art Institutions in London, 1689–1768', *The Walpole Society*, vol.54 (1988), pp.2–148

Bignamini, I., and M. Postle, *The Artist's Model: Its Role in British Art from Lely to Etty* (Nottingham 1991)

Bilbey, D., and M. Trusted, *British Sculpture 1470 to 2000* (London 2002)

Bimbenet-Privat, M., and F. Farges, *La boîte à portrait de Louis xiv* (Paris 2015)

Bindman, D., and M. Baker, *Roubiliac and the Eighteenth-Century Monument: Sculpture as Theatre* (New Haven and London 1995)

Binney, M., 'Worksop Manor, Nottinghamshire', I, *Country Life*, 151 (15 March 1973), pp.678–82

Blair, C., *Three Presentation Swords* (London 1972)

Bleuzen, A., 'Les Familles Harache, Margas et Pantin, Etude de cas d'orfèvres Huguenots, De leurs origins rouennaises au Refuge lodonien (1650–1750)', 2nd Masters thesis (Paris 2008–9)

Blunt, A., 'A group of late 17th-century drawings of the outskirts of Paris', in *Etudes d'Art français offertes à Charles Sterling* (Paris 1975), pp.257–64

Bourdieu, C., *Ligier Richier, sculpteur lorrain* (Paris 1998)

Bourriau, R.P., *Notes pour server à l'histoire des horlogers à La Rochelle de xvie siècle au debut de xviiie siècle* (Besançon 1934)

Bowett, A., *English Furniture 1660–1714 From* Charles *ii to Queen Anne* (Woodbridge, 2002)

Bowett, A., 'The Engravings of Daniel Marot', *Furniture History*, 43 (2007) pp.85–100

Bowett, A., and I. Fraser, 'An Imposter Unmasked: The "Duke of Leeds" suite at Temple Newsam. House', *Furniture History*, 51 (2015), pp.77–86

Boyer, A., *History of the Life and Reign of Queen Anne* (London 1722)

Bradshaw, P., *Derby Porcelain Figures, 1750–1848* (London 1990)

Bresc-Bautier, G., and G. Scherf, *Cast in Bronze: French Sculpture from Renaissance to Revolution*, exh. cat., Louvre, Paris; Metropolitan Museum of Art, New York; J. Paul Getty Museum, Los Angeles (Paris 2009)

Brett, V., 'The great (and lesser) toyshops', *The Silver Society Journal*, 16 (2004), pp.117–23

Brett, V., 'The paper trail of eighteenth-century retailers', *Silver Studies*, 26 (2010), pp.17–31

Brett, V., 'Nicholas Le Normand's Featherwork', *The Furniture History Society Newsletter*, 193 (February 2014a), pp.1–10

Brett, V., *Bertrand's Toyshop in Bath: Luxury Retailing 1685–1765* (Wetherby 2014b)

Bristow, I., 'The Balcony Room at Dyrham', *National Trust Studies* (1980), pp.141–6

Bromley, J., *Catalogue of the Clockmakers' Library* (London 1977)

Bryant, J., *Chevening* (London 2018)

Buccleuch, R., *Boughton: The House, Its People and Its Collections* (Edinburgh 2016)

Bucholz, R.O., *Office-Holders in Modern Britain, vol.11, Court Officers, 1660–1837* (revised), 2006, 'Joiner of the Privy Chamber 1660–1782', at www.british-history.ac.uk/office-holders/vol11/pp377-383 (accessed 28 April 2021)

Buckeridge, B., *An Essay Towards an English School* (London 1706)

Buckley, F., *Old London Glasshouses* (London 1915)

Buckley, V., *Madame de Maintenon: The Secret Wife of Louis xiv* (London 2008)

Burrell, F.E., 'Some Advertisements of Ceramic Interest', *Transactions of the English Ceramic Circle*, v, part 3 (1962), pp.176–9

Butler, J., *The Huguenots in America: A Refugee People in New World Society* (Cambridge, ma, and London 1983)

Calloway, S., M. Snodin and C. Wainwright, *Horace Walpole and Strawberry Hill*, exh. cat., Orleans House Gallery, Twickenham (London 1980)

Campbell, C., *Vitruvius Britannicus* (London 1715)

Campbell, R., *The London Tradesman* (London 1747; fascimile edn Newton Abbott 1969)

Carpenter, A.F., *J.T. Desaguliers: A Natural Philosopher, Engineer and Freemason in Newtonian England* (London 2011)

Cartier, N., and I. Cartier, 'The Elie Pacot surtout', *The Silver Society Journal*, 6 (1994), pp.296–302

Cartwright, J.J., *The Wentworth Papers* (London 1883)

Cassidy Geiger, M., 'The Federzimmer from the Japanisches palais in Dresden', *Furniture History*, 35 (1999) pp.87–111

Cerny, G., *Theology, Politics, and Letters at the Crossroads of European Civilization: Jacques Basnage and the Baylean Huguenot Refugees in the Dutch Republic* (Dordrecht 1987)

Chardin, J., *The travels of Sir John Chardin into Persia and the East Indies. The first volume, containing the author's voyage from Paris to Ispahan. To which is added, The coronation of this present king of Persia, Solyman the Third* (London 1686)

Charleston, R., 'John Voyez', *Transactions of the English Ceramic Circle*, 5, part 1 (1960), pp.8–41

Charleston, R., 'New Attributions', *Antiques*, 41 (October 1963), pp.429–33

Charleston, R.J., and J.V.G. Mallet, 'A Problematical Group of Eighteenth-Century Porcelain', *Transactions of the English Ceramic Circle*, 8, no.1 (1971), pp.80–117

Charrington, J., *A Catalogue of the Engraved Portraits in the Library of Samuel Pepys Esq now belonging to the Library of Magdalen College, Cambridge* (Cambridge 1936)

Chassin du Gerny, Y., *Généologie des potiers d'etain en Guyenne* (Bordeaux 2007)

Citroen, K.A., *Amsterdamse zilversmeden en hun merken / Amsterdam Silversmiths and their Marks* (Amsterdam 1975)

Clark, P., *British Clubs and Societies 1580–1800: The Origins of an Associational World* (Oxford 2000)

Clarke, T.H., 'French Influences at Chelsea', *Transactions of the English Ceramic Circle*, 4, no.5 (1959), pp.45–57

Clarke, T.H., 'Sir Charles Hanbury Williams and the Chelsea Factory', *Transactions of the English Ceramic Circle*, 13, no.2 (1988), pp.110–20

Clayton, T., *The English Print 1688–1802* (New Haven and London 1997)

Clutton, G., and C. Mackay, *Old Thorndon Hall, Essex: A History and Reconstruction of Its Park and Garden*, Garden History Society Occasional Paper, 2 (1970), pp.27–39

Coertzen, P., *The Huguenots of South Africa 1688–1988* (Cape Town 1988)

Cohen, H., *The South Carolina Gazette 1732–1775* (Columbia 1953)

Collins, F. (ed.), *Register of the Freemen of the City of York*, vol.2: *1559–1759* (Durham 1900)

Collins-Baker, C.H. and M.I., *The Life and Circumstances of James Brydges, First Duke of Chandos, Patron of the Liberal Arts* (Oxford 1949)
Colvin, H.M., *Calke Abbey: A Hidden House Revealed* (London 1985)
Colvin, H.M., *A Biographical Dictionary of British Architects 1660–1840* (New Haven and London 1995)
Colvin, H.M., et al., *History of the King's Works*, vol.5: *1660–1782* (Cambridge 1976)
Cordellier, D., 'Sur quelques dessins de Hugues Sambin ou qui lui sont traditionnellement attribués', in *Peindre à Dijon au XVIe siècle*, ed. F. Elsig (Milan 2016), pp.223–37
Cornforth, J., 'Boughton House', I, *Country Life*, 148 (3 September 1970), pp.564–8; II (10 September 1970), pp.624–8; III (17 September 1970), pp.684–7; 149, IV (25 February 1971), pp.420–3; V (11 March 1971), pp.536–9
Cornforth, J., 'Looking Glass Mysteries', *Country Life*, 187 (21 October 1993), pp.72–5
Cornforth, J., 'A Splendid Unity of Arts: The silver at Kedleston Hall, Derbyshire)', *Country Life*, 190 (13 June 1996), pp.128–31
Cornforth, J., 'How the Boughton Bed was remade', *Country Life*, 197 (6 February 2006), pp.56–9
Cornforth, J., and L. Schmidt, 'Holkham Hall, Norfolk', *Country Life*, part I (24 January 1980), pp.214–17; part II (31 January 1980), pp.298–301; part III (7 February 1980), pp.359–62; part IV (14 February 1980), pp.427–31
Cousins, J., 'Pierre Harache I and II: A challenge to current attributions', *Silver Studies*, 19 (2005), pp.71–7
Cox, R., 'Castle (Cassels), Richard', in *A Biographical Dictionary of Civil Engineers in Great Britain and Ireland*, vol.I: *1500–1830* (London 2002), pp.121–2
Coyne, P., *Dictionnaire des Familles protestantes de Bordeaux au 17ieme siècle* (Bordeaux 1994)
Craske, M., 'Contacts and Contracts: Sir Henry Cheere and the Formation of a New Commercial World of Sculpture in Mid-Eighteenth-Century London', in *The Lustrous Trade: Material Culture and the History of Sculpture in England and Italy c.1700–c.1860*, eds A. Yarrington and C. Sicca (London 2000), pp.94–110
Craske, M., *The Silent Rhetoric of the Body: A History of Monumental Sculpture and Commemorative Art in England, 1720–1770* (New Haven and London 2007)
Craven, M., 'Nadauld the Sculptor', *Country Life*, 182, no.45 (10 November 1988), p.157
Croft-Murray, E., *Decorative Painting in England, 1537–1837*, vol.I: *Early Tudor to Sir James Thornhill* (London 1962); vol.2: *The Eighteenth and Early Nineteenth Centuries* (London 1970)
Croft-Murray, E., and P. Hulton, *Catalogue of British Drawings in the British Museum*, 2 vols (London 1960–3)
Crookshank, A., and D. FitzGerald, *Irish Portraits 1660–1860* exh. cat., National Gallery of Ireland, Dublin; National Portrait Gallery, London; Ulster Museum, Belfast (London 1969)
Cross, A., *By the Banks of the Neva: Chapters from the Lives and Careers of the British in Eighteenth-Century Russia* (Cambridge 1997)
Crouch, J., 'York House, Battersea: Finds from the Excavation of the Enamel Manufactory Site', *English Ceramic Circle Transactions*, 19, part I (2005), pp.29–46
Cruikshank, D., *Spitalfields: The History of a Nation in a Handful of Streets* (London 2016)
Cunningham, J., 'Craft and Culture: The Design, Production and Consumption of Silver in Ireland in the Seventeenth Century', PhD thesis, University of Ireland at Maynooth, 2016
Cunningham, P., *Handbook of London Past and Present* (London 1850)
Curran, C.P., *Dublin Decorative Plasterwork*, (London 1967)
Darcel, M.A., 'Une manufacture de tapisseries des Gobelins à Fulham et à Exeter, 1748–1766', *NAAF*, 6 (1878), pp.286–314
D'Argenville, D., *Abrège de la Vie des plus fameux Peintres*, 4 vols (Paris 1762)
Davis, J.M., 'An introduction to the panel paintings, oil sketches, drawings and prints of Louis Laguerre', PhD thesis, University of Georgia, 1982
Dawson, A., *Portrait Sculpture: A Catalogue of the British Museum Collection, c.1675–1975* (London 1999)
Debauve, F., 'Nicholas Sprimont (1716–1771): Un Liégeois orfèvre et porcelainier à Londres', *Art and Fact*, 1 (1982), pp. 60–71
De Jonge, C.H., *Dutch Tiles* (New York 1971)
Delaforce, A., 'Paul Crespin's Silver-Gilt Bath for the King of Portugal', *Burlington Magazine*, 139, no.1126 (January 1997), pp.38–40
De Lisle, G., and R. Myers, *Two Huguenot Brothers: Letters of Andrew and Jame Coltée Ducarel, 1732–1773* (Leicester 2019)
Denis, P., *Ligier Richier, l'artiste et son œuvre* (Paris and Nancy 1911)
Develle, E., *Les horlogers blésois aux XVIe et XVIIe siècles* (Blois 1913; 3rd edn Chartres 1978)
Dingwall, C., 'The Hercules Garden at Blair Castle, Perthshire', *Garden History*, 20, no.2 (autumn 1992), pp.153–72
Dmitrieva, O., and T. Murdoch, *Treasures of the Royal Courts: Tudors, Stuarts and the Russian Tsars* (London 2013)
Dobson, H.A., *William Hogarth* (London 1891)
Dodd, D., '"Mr Studio's" Hand-Coloured Prints at Stourhead', *Print Quarterly*, 33 (2016), pp.263–77
Dragesco, B., *English Ceramics in French Archives* (London 1993)
Driancourt-Girod, J., *L'insolite histoire des luthériens de Paris de Louis XIII à Napoléon* (Paris 1992)
Drury, M., 'Diplomat's Prize' *Country Life*, 185 (3 October 1991), pp.54–5
du Boulay, A., 'Recent discoveries on Charles Gouyn, Nicholas Sprimont and other 18th-century workers of Huguenot origin in the English Porcelain industry', *PHSL*, XXVI, no.4 (1996), pp.443–52
Dussieux, L.E., *Les Artistes Françaises à l'Etranger* (Paris 1856)
Easson, D.E., 'French Protestants in Edinburgh', *PHSL*, XVIII, no.4 (1949–50) pp.325–44
Eastman, M.M.R., R. Donohoe and M.E.H. Thompson, *The Huguenot Church in Charleston* (Charleston 2018)
Edgcumbe, R., *The Art of the Gold Chaser in Eighteenth-Century* (Oxford 2000)
Edmunds, R., *The Huguenot Clockmakers of Spitalfields* (London 2013)
Edwards, I., 'A Midland family of Gatesmiths', *Country Life*, 131 (26 April 1962), pp.975–6
Edwards, I., 'Ironwork at Cholmondeley: New Light on George London, Henry Wise and Jean Tijou', *Apollo*, 101 (January 1975), pp.22–5
Edwards, I., *Davies Brothers, Gatesmiths* (Cardiff 1977)
Edwards, R., 'A Mirror with painted decoration', *Country Life*, 78 (26 October 1935), p.433
Einberg, E., *William Hogarth: A Complete Catalogue of the Paintings* (New Haven and London 2016)
Elliot, J., *The City in Maps: Urban Mapping to 1900* (London 1987)
300 Jahre Hugenottenstadt Erlangen Vom Nutzen der Toleranz, exh. cat., Erlangen Stadtmuseum (Erlangen 1986)
Esdaile, K.A., *Roubiliac's Work at Trinity College Cambridge* (Cambridge 1924)
Esdaile, K.A., *The Life and Works of Louis François Roubiliac* (London 1928)
Esdaile, K.A., 'Roubiliac: some unrecorded details connected with his life and work', *The Archaeological Journal*, 86 (1929), pp.178–87
Esdaile, K.A., 'A signed drawing by Sprimont', *Apollo*, 39 (May–June 1944a), p.134
Esterly, D., *Grinling Gibbons and the Art of Carving*, exh. cat, Victoria and Albert Museum, London (London 1998)
Evans, E.A., 'Jacques Rousseau: A Huguenot Decorative Artist at the Courts of Louis XIV and William III', *PHSL*, XXII, no.2 (1972), pp.142–61
Evans, J., 'Huguenot Goldsmiths in England and Ireland', *PHSL*, XIV, 3 (1930–3), pp.496–594
Evelyn, P., 'Hubert Le Sueur's Equestrian Bronzes at the Victoria and Albert Museum', *Burlington Magazine*, 137, no.1103 (February 1995), pp.85–92
Eyres, P., and J. Lomax (eds), *Diplomats, Goldsmiths and Baroque Court Culture: Lord Raby in Berlin, The Hague and Wentworth Castle* (Barnsley 2014)
Fairbanks, J., *Paul Revere's Boston, 1735–1818*, exh. cat., Museum of Fine Arts, Boston (Boston 1975)
Fairclough, O., 'Mrs Strangways' Silver', *Journal of the Silver Society*, 8 (1996), pp.469–74
Farrer, L., *Biographical Dictionary of Medallists*, 5 vols (London 1902)
Fatio, O. (ed.), *Mémoires du pasteur et professeur Michel Turrettini: seigneur de Turretin 1644–1720* (Neuchâtel 2018)
Fedden, R., 'John Obrisset: A Notable Huguenot Craftsman', *Connoisseur*, 180 (January 1972), pp.13–17
Finch, P., *Burley-on-the-Hill, from Saxon Times to the Present Day*, 2 vols (London 1901)

Finney, P.C., *Seeing Beyond the Word: Visual Arts and the Calvinist Tradition* (Grand Rapids 1999)
Fischer, D.H., *Paul Revere's Ride* (New York 1994)
Fitzpatrick, M., et al., *The Enlightenment World* (London and New York 2004)
Fleming, J., 'Enigma of a Rococo Artist', *Country Life*, 131 (24 May 1962), pp.1224–6
Ford, B., 'The Blathwayt Brothers of Dyrham in Italy on the Grand Tour', *The National Trust Year Book 1975–6* (London 1976), pp.19–31
Francis, P., *Irish Delftware: An Illustrated History* (London 2000)
Friedman, T., 'Cavalier's Charles II on Horseback', *Leeds Art Calendar*, no.88 (1981), pp.4–13
Friedman, T., *The Georgian Parish Church: Monuments to Posterity* (Reading 2004)
Friedman, T., and T. Clifford, *The Man at Hyde Park Corner, 'Sculpture by John Cheere, 1709–1787'*, exh. cat., Temple Newsam House, Leeds, and Marble Hill, Twickenham (Leeds 1974)
Friedman, T., and J. Linstrum, 'Country Houses through Georgian Eyes', *Country Life*, 153 (1 February 1973), pp.268–70
Foskett, D., *A Dictionary of British Miniature Painters*, 2 vols (London 1972)
Foskett, D., *Miniatures: Dictionary and Guide* (Woodbridge 1987)
Fowler, J., and J. Cornforth, *English Decoration in the 18th Century* (London 1974)
Fuhring, P., and M. Bimbenet-Privat, 'Le style Cosse de Pois: L'Orfèvrerie et La Gravure à Paris sous Louis XIII', *Gazette des Beaux Arts*, 139, no.540 (January 2002), pp.1–224
Funck-Brentano, F., *La Bastille des Comédiens: le For l'Evêque* (Paris 1903)
Gardener, B., 'An Early Allusion to English Porcelain, Gouyn's will and some Chelsea Models', *Transactions of the English Porcelain Circle* II (1930), pp.23–7
Gardener, B., 'Further History of the Chelsea Porcelain Manufactory', *Transactions of the English Ceramic Circle*, 2, no.8 (1942), pp.136–41
Garnier, R., 'Thomas Tompion: The Huguenot Connection', *PHSL*, XXVI, no.1 (summer 1994), pp.1–13
Garrioch, D., *The Huguenots of Paris and the Coming of Religious Freedom* (Cambridge 2014)
Gerstein, A., 'Silver, Silk and Industry: The Courtauld Businesses 1708 to 1946', in *The Courtauld Collection: A Vision for Impressionism*, eds K. Serres and E. Vegelin, exh. cat., Fondation Louis Vuitton, Paris (London 2019), pp.43–54
Gibbs, G.C., 'Some Intellectual and Political Influences of the Huguenot Emigrés in the United Provinces, *c*.1680–1730', *Bijdragen en Mededelingen betreffende de Geschiedenis der Nederlanden*, 90 (1975), pp.255–87
Gilbert, C., *Catalogue of the Furniture at Temple Newsam House*, 2 vols (Leeds 1978–98)
Gilbert, C., *Pictorial Dictionary of Marked London Furniture 1700–1840* (Leeds 1996)
Gill, C., *The Rise of the Irish Linen Industry* (Oxford 1925)
Girouard, M., 'The Smythson Collection of the Royal Institute of British Architects', *Architectural History*, v (1962a), pp. 21–184
Girouard, M., 'Dyrham Park, Avon', *Country Life*, 131 (February 1962b), pp.335–9, 396–9
Glin, The Knight of, and J. and Peill, *Irish Furniture: Woodwork and Carving in Ireland from the earliest times to the Act of Union* (New Haven and London 2007)
Glozier, M., *Marshal Schomberg 1615–1690, 'the ablest soldier of his age': international soldiering and the formation of state armies in seventeenth-century Europe* (Brighton 2005)
Godber, J., *Wrest Park and the Duke of Kent, Henry Grey (1671–1740)* (Bedford 1963)
Godfrey, R.T., *Printmaking in Britain* (Oxford 1978)
Goodison, N., 'Langlois and Dominique', *Furniture History*, 4 (1968), pp.105–6
Goodison, N., *Ormolu: The Work of Matthew Boulton* (London 1974)
Goodway, E., 'The Rapilliart Family: David Willaume, his son, their apprentices, part I', *Silver Society Journal*, 10 (1998), pp.56–9
Goodway, E., 'David Willaume and his apprentices, part II: further research', *Silver Society Journal*, 11 (1999), pp.140–2
Goodway, E., 'Gleanings on Daniel Garnier', *Journal of the Silver Society*, 12 (2000), pp.125ff.
Gosset, M.H., 'A Family of Modellers in Wax', *PHSL*, III no.4 (1892), pp.540–68
Goulding, R., *Dyrham Park and William Blathwayt: A Souvenir Guide* (Swindon 2017)
Gowing, L., 'Hogarth, Hayman, and the Vauxhall Decorations', *Burlington Magazine*, 95, no.598 (January 1953), pp.4–17, 19
Grant, A.J., *The Huguenots* (London 1934)
Gray, J.G., 'The Origin of the Word Huguenot', *Sixteenth Century Journal*, 14, no.3 (autumn 1983, pp.349–59
Grazebrook, H.S., *Collections for a genealogy of the noble families of Henzey, Tyttery, and Tyzack (de Hennezel, de Thiétry, and du Thisac), 'gentilshommes verriers', from Lorraine: with a narrative pedigree of the Stourbridge branch of the first-named family and its descendants, including the several families of Brettell, Bate, Dixon, Hill, Jeston, Jervis, Pidcock, and others* (Stourbridge 1877)
Greder, L., *Elizabeth Sophie Chèron de l'Academie Royal de Peinture et Sculpture* (Paris 1909)
Green, D., *Blenheim Palace* (London 1951)
Gribelin, S., *A New Book of ornaments Useful to all Artists*, 1704, facsimile of original owned by Philip Hofer (Connecticut 1941)
Griffiths, A., *The Print in Stuart Britain* (London 1998)
Griffiths, A., *The Print before Photography: An Introduction to European Printmaking, 1550–1820* (London 2016)
Grimwade, A., *London Goldsmiths 1697–1837* (1976; 3rd edn London 1990)
Grimwade, A., 'The Master of George Vertue: His Identity and Oeuvres', *Apollo*, 127 (February 1988), pp.83–9
Guiffrey, M.J.J., 'Listes des peintres, sculpteurs, architectes, graveurs et autres artistes de la maison du Roi de la Reine ou de Princes de Sang, XVIe, XVIIe, XVIIIe siècles', *NAAF*, 1 (1872) pp.55–108
Guiffrey, M.J.J., 'Logement d'Artistes au Louvre. Liste générale des brevets de logement…', *NAAF*, 2 (1873) pp.1–221
Guiffrey, M.J.J., 'Congés accordés à des artistes français pour aller travailler à l'étranger (1693–1792)', *NAAF*, 6 (1878) pp.1–68
Guiffrey, M.J.J., *Comptes des bâtiments du roi sous le règne de Louis XIV* (Paris 1887), vol.2
Guiffrey, M.J.J., and Barthélemy, *Liste des Pensionnaires de L'Academie de France à Rome* (Paris 1908)
Gunnis, R., *Dictionary of British Sculptors 1660–1851* (London 1951)
Guttery, D.R., *From Broad-Glass to Cut Crystal: A History of the Stourbridge Glass Industry* (London 1956)
Gwynn, R., 'The Distribution of Huguenot Refugees in England, II: London and its Environs', *PHSL*, XXII (1976), no.6, pp.509–68
Gwynn, R., 'James II: His Treatment of Huguenot Refugees 1685–1686', *PHSL*, XXIII, no.14 (1980), pp.212–24
Gwynn, R., *Huguenot Heritage: The History and Contribution of the Huguenots in Britain* (London 1985)
Gwynn, R., *The Huguenots in Later Stuart Britain*, vol.II: *Settlement, Churches and the Role of London* (Eastbourne 2018)
Hall, I., *Georgian Hull* (Hull 1979)
Halsband, R., *The Life of Lady Mary Wortley Montagu* (Oxford1960)
Hamlett, L., 'Painted Interiors', in T. Barber ed., *British Baroque: Power and Illusion*, exh. cat., Tate Britain, London (London 2020), pp.103–14
Hammelman, H., *Book Illustrators in Eighteenth Century England*, ed. T.S.R. Boase (London 1975)
Hans, N.A., *New Trends in Education in the Eighteenth Century* (London 1951)
Harcourt-Smith, S., *A Catalogue of various clocks, watches, automata & other miscellaneous objects of European workmanship dating from the XVIIIth and early XIXth Centuries in the Palace Museum* (Peiping 1930)
Hardwick, N. (ed.), *A Diary of the Journey through the North of England made by William and John Blathwayt of Dyrham Park in 1703* (Bristol 1977)
Hardy, J., and G. Jackson-Stops, 'The Second Earl of Warrington and the Age of Walnut', *Apollo*, 108 (July 1978), pp.32–9
Hardy, J., and A. Turpin, 'Cornelius Gole's Book of Ornament', *Apollo*, 137 (January 1993), pp.18–21
Hare, S. (ed.), *Paul de Lamerie: At the Sign of the Golden Ball. The Work of England's Master Silversmith*, exh. cat., Goldsmiths' Hall, London (London 1990)
Harkness, G., *John Calvin, The Man and His Ethics* (New York 1931)

HARRIS, J., 'Bodt and Stainborough', *Architectural Review*, CXXX (January 1961), pp.34–5

HARTOP, C., *The Huguenot Legacy: English Silver 1680–1760 from the Alan and Simone Hartmann Collection* (London 1996)

HARVEY, M., *Painter in a Savage Land: The Strange Saga of the First European Artist in North America* (New York 2008)

HARVEY, S., and E. Grist, 'The Rainbow Coffee House and the Exchange of Ideas in Early Eighteenth-Century England', in *The Religious Culture of the Huguenots, 1660–1750*, ed. A. Dunan Page (Aldershot 2006), pp.163–72

HATCHER, J., and T.C. Barker, *A Short History of the Worshipful Company of Pewterers of London and a Catalogue of Pewterware in its Possession* (London 1968)

HATCHER, J., and T.C. Barker, *A History of British Pewter* (London 1974)

HAYWARD, J. (ed.), *The letters of Saint-Evremond: Charles Marguetel de Saint-Denis Seigneur de Saint-Evremond* (London 1930)

HAYWARD, J., *Huguenot Silver in England, 1688–1727* (London 1959)

HAYWARD, J., 'The Huguenot Gunmakers of London', *PHSL*, XXI, no.6 (1963–4), pp.649–64

HEAL, A., *The Signboards of Old London Shops: A Review of the Shop Signs Employed by the London Tradesmen During the XVIIth and XVIIIth Centuries; Compiled from the Author's Collection of Contemporary Trade-Cards and Billheads* (London 1947)

HEAL, A., *The London Furniture Makers from the Restoration to the Victorian Era, 1660–1840* (London 1953)

HECKSCHER, M.H., 'Gideon Saint, An Eighteenth-Century Carver and his Scrapbook', *Bulletin of the Metropolitan Museum of Art*, 27 (February 1969), pp.299–311

HEFFORD, W., 'Soho and Spitalfields, Little-Known Tapestry Weavers in and around London 1680–1760', *PHSL*, XXIV (1983–4), pp.103–12

HEIN, J., *Ivories and Narwhal Tusks at Rosenborg Castle: Catalogue of Carved and Turned Ivories and Narwhal Tusks in the Royal Danish Collection 1600–1875* (Copenhagen 2018)

HELD, J., 'Rubens's Glynde Sketch and the Installation of the Whitehall Ceiling', *Burlington Magazine*, 112, no.806 (May 1970), pp.274–81

HETHERINGTON, K.M., 'Education and the shaping of Huguenot identity in England *c.*1685–*c.*1725', MPhil thesis, University of Cambridge, 2019

HILL, C., 'Protestantism and the Rise of Capitalism', in *Essays in the Economic and Social History of Tudor and Stuart England in Honour of R.H. Tawney* (Cambridge 1961), pp.15–39

HILL, D., 'James Pascall and the Long Gallery Suite at Temple Newsam', *Furniture History*, 17 (1981), pp.70–4

HILL, N., 'Huguenot Clock and Watchmakers, Additions and Amendments to Britten', *Connoisseur*, 121 (March 1948), pp.26–30, 62

HINTON, M., and O. Impey (eds), *Kensington Palace and the Porcelain of Queen Mary II* (London 1998)

HOBBS, C., and D. Oakey, 'Two Fredericks and a Frame: A Rediscovered Giltwood Masterpiece by Paul Petit', *Furniture History*, 51 (2015), pp.87–104

HODGKINSON, T., 'Handel at Vauxhall', *Bulletin of the Victoria and Albert Museum*, 1, no.4 (October 1965), pp.1–13

HOLLIS, T.B., *Memoirs*, ed. F. Blackburne, 2 vols (London 1808)

HOMER, R.F., 'The Story of James Taudin', *The Journal of the Pewter Society*, 4, no.4 (1984), pp.118–22

HONEY, W.B., 'Royal Portraits in Pottery and Porcelain', *Burlington Magazine*, 70 (1937), pp.218–29

HOOD, G., 'The Career of Andrew Duche', *Art Quarterly*, XXXI, no.2 (1968), pp.168–84

HOUFE, S.R., 'A Whig Artist in Ivory', *Antique Collector*, 42 (April–May 1971), pp.66–70

HOWATT, A.P., and H.G. Widdowson, *A History of English Language Teaching*, 2nd edn (Oxford 2004)

HSIEH, C., 'Publishing the Raphael Cartoons and the Rise of Art-Historical Consciousness in England, 1707–1764', *The Historical Journal*, 52 (1974), pp.899–920

HSQS, II: *Les Actes des Colloques des Eglises françaises et des Synodes des Eglises Etrangères réfugiées en Angleterre, 1581–1654* (Lymington 1890)

HSQS, IV: *Registre de l'Eglise Wallonne de Southampton* (Lymington 1890)

HSQS, V: *Registers of the Walloon Church in Canterbury* (Lymington 1898)

HSQS, VII: *Registers of the French Conformed Churches of St Patrick and St Mary, Dublin* (Dublin 1893)

HSQS, X: *List of Aliens Resident in London, Henry VIII to* James I, part I (Aberdeen 1900)

HSQS, XI: *Register of the French Church of La Patente, Spitalfields, London, 1689–1785* (London 1898)

HSQS, XIII: *Register of the French Church of Threadneedle Street, London*, part II (Lymington 1899)

HSQS, XVI: *Registers of the French Church of Threadneedle Street, London*, part III (Aberdeen 1906)

HSQS, XVIII: *Letters of Denization and Acts of Naturalization of Aliens in England and Ireland 1603–1700* (Lymington 1911)

HSQS, XX: *Registers of the French Churches, Bristol, Plymouth, Stonehouse and Thorpe-le-Soken* (London 1912)

HSQS, XXI: *Le Livre des Temoinages de l'Eglise de Threadneedle Street, 1669–1789* (Frome 1909)

HSQS, XXII: *Le Livre des Conversions et des Reconaissances faites à L'Eglise française de la Savoye, 1684–1702* (Frome 1914)

HSQS, XXV: *Registers of the French Church of Le Carre and Berwick Street, London* (Frome 1922)

HSQS, XXVI: *Registers of the French Churches of the Savoy, Spring Gardens and Les Grecs, London* (Frome 1922)

HSQS, XXVII: *Registers of the Church of St Martin Orgars with its history and that of the Swallow Street Church* (Frome 1935)

HSQS, XXVIII: *Registers of the French Churches of the Chapel Royal, St James, and Swallow Street, London* (Manchester 1924)

HSQS, XXIX: *Registers of the French Churches of the Tabernacle, Glasshouse Street, and Leicester Fields, London* (Frome 1926)

HSQS, XXX: *Registers of the French Church of Rider Court, London* (Frome 1927)

HSQS, XXXI: *Register of the French Church of Hungerford Market, later Castle Street, London* (Frome 1928)

HSQS, XXXV: *A Supplement to Dr W.A. Shaw's Letters of Denization and Acts of Naturalization* (Frome 1932)

HSQS, XXXVII: *Register of the Church of St Martin Orgars with its history and that of the Swallow Street Church* (Frome 1935)

HSQS, XLII: *Register of the Artillery Church, London* (Frome 1948)

HSQS, XLV: *Registers of Wheeler Street, Swanfields, Hoxton, La Patente de Soho, Répertoire Générale* (Frome 1956)

HSQS, XLIX *Relief of French Protestant Refugees, 1681–1687* (London 1971)

HSQS, LII, LIII: *French Protestant Hospital: inmates of, and applicants to, 1718–1957 and applicants for the Coqueau Charity 1745–1901* (London 1971)

HSQS, LVI: *Catalogue of the Remaining Manuscripts in the Huguenot Library* (London 1983)

HSQS, LX: *Huguenot Wills and Administrations in England and Ireland 1617–1849* (London 2007)

HUGHES, G.B., '600 years of Corporation Plate', *Country Life*, 111 (13 June 1952), pp.1825–6

HUGHES, T. and B., *English Painted Enamels Illustrated from the Collections of Her Majesty Queen Mary and Mrs Ionides* (London 1967)

HULTON, P. (ed.), *The Work of Jacques Le Moyne de Morgues: A Huguenot Artist in France, Florida and England* (London 1977)

HUMBERT, A., *La vie et les œuvres de Jean Étienne Liotard (1702–1789:) étude biographique et iconographique* (Amsterdam 1897)

HUNT, L., M.C. Jacob and W. Mijnhardt, *The Book That Changed Europe: Picard and Bernard's Religious Ceremonies of the World* (Cambridge 2010)

HUYGENS, C., 'Journal', *Werken van het Historisch Genootschap Nieuwe Serie*, 23 (Utrecht 1876) (see also *Le séjour de Christian Huygens à Paris et ses relations avec les milieux scientifiques français; suivi de son Journal de voyage à Paris et à Londres*, ed. H.L.Brugmans [Paris 1935])

HYLTON, R.P., 'The Huguenot Settlement at Portarlington, 1692–1771', *Irish Economic and Social History*, 11 (January 1984), pp.126–8

INGAMELLS, J., and R. Raines, 'A Catalogue of the Paintings, Drawings and Etchings of Philip Mercier', *The Walpole Society*, vol.26 (1976–8), pp.1–70

IRELAND, S., *Graphic Illustrations of Hogarth*, 2 vols (London 1799)

IVANOFF, N., 'La Piscina Probatica di Louis Cheron Nella Chiesa di San PANTALEONE a Venezia', *Arte Veneta*, XVI (1962), pp.174–6

Jackson-Stops, G., 'English Baroque Ironwork', I: 'The Sources of Tijou's Designs', *Country Life*, 149 (28 January 1971a), pp.182–3; II: 'The Influence of Tijou', 150 (4 February 1971a), pp.262–6
Jackson-Stops, G., 'William III and French Furniture', *Furniture History*, 7 (1971b), pp.121–6
Jackson-Stops, G., 'Petworth and the Proud Duke', *Country Life*, 153 (28 June 1973a), pp.180–7
Jackson-Stops, G., 'Ribston Hall, Yorkshire', *Country Life*, 154 (11 October 1973b), pp.1050–3
Jackson-Stops, G., 'The Rebirth of a Dutch Versailles: The Restoration of Het Loo', *Country Life*, 158 (21 August 1975), pp.458–9
Jackson-Stops, G., 'Bordering on Works of Art, Picture Frames at Petworth, I', *Country Life*, 168 (4 September 1980), pp.798–800; II, 'Great Carvings for a Connoisseur', 170 (25 September 1980) pp.1030–2
Jackson-Stops, G., 'Daniel Marot and the 1st Duke of Montagu', *Nederland Kunsthistorisch Jaarboek*, 31 (1981), pp.244–62
Jacobsen, H., *Luxury and Power: The Material World of the Stuart Diplomat* (Oxford 2012)
Janssens, U., *Mathieu Maty and the Journal Britannique, 1750–1755* (Amsterdam 1975)
Jenkins, S., *Portrait of a Patron: The Patronage and Collecting of James Brydges, 1st Duke of Chandos (1674–1744)* (Oxford, 2007)
Jones, E.A., *The Old Silver Sacramental Vessels of Foreign Protestant Churches in England* (London 1908)
Jones, K., and C. Garibaldi, 'Crespin or Sprimont? A question revisited', *Silver Studies*, 21 (2006), pp.25–42
Julius, A., *Jean Cavalier Och Nagen Andra Elfenbeissnidare* (Stockholm, 1926)
Kaellgren, P., 'French influence in a toilet service by David Willaume I', *Journal of the Silver Society*, 4 (1994), pp.162–72
Kemp, M., *The Chapel of Trinity College* (Oxford 2013)
Kemp, M., *A Guide to the Restored Chapel Trinity College Oxford* (Oxford 2019)
Kent, T., *West Country Silver Spoons and their Makers 1550–1750* (London 1992)
Kenworthy-Browne, J., *Dyrham House, Avon*, 5th edn (London 1978)
Kerslake, J., 'Sculptor and Patron: Two portraits by Highmore', *Apollo*, 95 (January 1972), pp.25–9
Kerslake, J., *Early Georgian Portraits*, 2 vols (London 1977)
Kingdon, R.M., *Geneva and the Coming of the Wars of Religion in France* (Geneva 1956)
Kirby, E.E., 'Roubiliac's Receipt (Bill for the Monument to George Lynn)', *Country Life*, 131 (28 June 1962), p.1589
Knecht, R., *The French Renaissance Court 1483–1589* (New Haven and London 2008)
Knowles, M.T., 'Ornament in the Kitchen Garden: The Pea as Motif for Goldsmith in the France of Louis XIII', *Association of Art Historians*, 40, no.5 (2017), pp.965–93
Kroll, M. (trans. and ed.), *Letters from Liselotte: Elizabeth Charlotte, Princess Palatine and Duchess of Orléans* (London 1970)
Kuke, H.-J., *Jean de Bodt 1670–1745. Architekt and Inenieur im Zeitalter des Barock* (Worms 2002)
Labib-Rahman, L., 'Sir Jean Chardin, the Great Traveller (1643–1712/13), *PHSL*, XXIII, no.5 (1981), pp.309–18
La Chapelle, V. *The Modern Cook* (London 1733; facsimile edn Farmington Hills, MI, 2010)
Lachenicht, S., 'Huguenot Immigrants and the Formation of National Identities', *The Historical Journal*, 50, no.2 (2007), pp.309–31
Laffan, W., and C. Monkhouse (eds), *Ireland: Crossroads of Art and Design, 1690–1840*, exh. cat., Art Institute of Chicago (New Haven and London 2015)
Laharie, P., 'La confrérie Sainte-Anne des orfèvres parisiens, 1449–1712', in *Les Mays de Notre-Dame de Paris*, ed. A. Notter, exh. cat., Musée des Beaux-Arts, Arras (Arras 1999), pp.3–21
Lami, S., *Dictionnaire de sculpteurs français sous Louis XIV* (Paris 1906)
Landes, D.S., *Revolution in Time: Clocks and the Making of the Modern World* (Cambridge, MA, 1983)
Lane, A., 'Daniel Marot, Designer of Delft Vases and of Gardens at Hampton Court', *Connoisseur*, 123 (March 1949), pp.19–24
Lane, A., *English Porcelain Figures of the Eighteenth Century* (London 1961)
Lane, A., and R. Charleston, 'Girl-in-a-Swing Porcelain and Chelsea', *Transactions of the English Ceramic Circle*, 5, no.3 (1962), pp.111–36
Lane Poole, R., *A History of the Huguenots of the Dispersion at the Recall of the Edict of Nantes* (London 1880)
Latham, R., and W. Matthews (eds), *The Diary of Samuel Pepys*, 11 vols (London 1971–83)
Lee, G.L., *The Huguenot Settlements in Ireland* (1936, reprint London 2008)
Lee-Wolfe, T., 'James Thornhill's Travel Diary to Paris', *The Walpole Society*, vol.80 (2018), pp.202–61
Lees-Milne, J., *Earls of Creation: Five Great Patrons of Eighteenth-Century Art* (London 1962)
Le May, K., 'The London Engravers Liart and Audinet', *PHSL*, XXVIII, no.1 (2003), pp.67–82
Le May, K., 'A Fresh Look at the Harache Family of Goldsmiths, *PHSL*, XXVIII, no.3 (2005), pp.364–76
Lemonnier, H., 'Les Dessins originaux de Desgodetz pour "Les Edifices Antiques de Rome" (1676–1677)', *Revue Archéologique*, 5 series, 6 (July–Dec. 1917), pp.213–30
Lestringant, F., *Bernard Palissy 1510–1590: L'Écrivain, Le Réformé, Le Céramiste* (Niort 2010)
Lewis, W.S. (ed.), *The Yale Edition of Horace Walpole's Correspondence*, 48 vols (New Haven 1937–83)
Libson, L., and J. Yarker, *The Spirit and Force of Art: Drawing in Britain 1600–1750* (London 2018)
Lightbown, R., 'Jean Petitot and Jacques Bordier at the English court', *Connoisseur*, 168 no.676 (June 1968), pp.82–91
Lightbown, R., 'Isaac Besnier, Sculptor to Charles I and his work for Court Patrons, *c.*1624–1634', in D. Howarth (ed.), *Art and Patronage in the Caroline Courts* (Cambridge 1993), pp.132–67
Ligier Richier et la sculpture en Lorraine au XVIe siècle, exh. cat., Musée de Bar-le-Duc (Bar-le-Duc 1985)
Lippincott, L., 'Arthur Pond's Journal of Receipts and Expenses, 1734–1750', *The Walpole Society*, 54 (1991), p.323
Llanover, Lady (ed.), *The Autobiography and Correspondence of Mary Granville, Mrs Delany*, 3 vols (London 1861)
Lomax, J., and J. Rothwell, *Country House Silver from Dunham Massey* (London 2006)
Louw, H.J., 'The Origin of the Sash Window', *Architectural History*, 26 (1983), pp.49–72, 144–50
Lunsingh Scheurleer, T., 'Pierre Gole, ébéniste du roi Louis XIV', *Burlington Magazine*, 122 (June 1980), pp.378, 380–94
Lunsingh Scheurleer, T., *Pierre Gole, ébéniste de Louis XIV* (Dijon 2005)
Luria, K.P., 'Rituals of Conversion: Catholics and Protestants in Seventeenth-Century Poitou', in *Culture and Identity in Early Modern Europe (1500–1800): Essays in Honor of Natalie Zemon Davis* (Chicago 1993), pp.65–81
McDonnell, J., 'The Cramillion Lectern', *Irish Arts Review*, 24, no.4 (winter 2007), pp. 122–5
McEvansoneya, P., 'A Note on Hubert Le Sueur and Isaac Besnier', *Burlington Magazine*, 135, no.1085 (August 1993), pp.532–4
McInnes, M.D., and A. Mack, *In Pursuit of Refinement: Charlestonians Abroad 1740–1860* (Columbia 1999)
McKinley, D., 'Huguenot Silversmiths in London', *Huguenot Society Journal*, 30, no.1 (2013), pp.94–100
McKinley, D., 'The Foundation of Huguenot Silversmithing in London', *Huguenot Society Journal*, 30, no.5 (2017), pp.648–9, 652–5
MacLeod, C. (ed.), *The Lost Prince: The Life and Death of Henry Stuart*, exh. cat., National Portrait Gallery, London (London 2012)
MacLeod, C., et al. (eds), *Elizabethan Treasures: Miniatures by Hilliard and Oliver* exh. cat., National Portrait Gallery, London (London 2019)
McNeill, J.T., *The History and Character of Calvinism* (Oxford 1954)
Malcolm, J.P., *Londinium Redevivium*, vol.4 (London 1807)
Mallet, J.V.G., 'Some Portrait Medallions by Roubiliac', *Burlington Magazine*, 104 (1962), pp.153–8
Mallet, J.V.G., 'Hogarth's pug in porcelain', *Bulletin of the Victoria and Albert Museum*, III, no.2 (April 1967), pp.45–54
Manchee, W.H., 'The Fouberts and their Royal Academy', *PHSL*, XVI, no.1 (1937), pp.77–97
Mansel, P., *King of the World: The Life of Louis XIV* (London 2019)
Marandet, F., 'Louis Chéron (1660–1725) à Boughton House: Nouvelles Réflexions Sur La

Genèse Et La Signification Du Décor Peint De "Mister Charron"', *The British Art Journal*, XVIII, no.1 (2017), pp. 48–56

MARANDET, F. (ed.), *Louis Chéron (Paris, 1655– Londres, 1725): l'ambition du dessin parfait*, exh. cat., Musée des Beaux-arts de Caen (Paris 2021)

MATY, M., *The Miscellaneous Works of the late Philip Dormer Stanhope Earl of Chesterfield, consisting of Letters to his friends never before printed and various other articles to which are prefixed Memoirs of his Life tending to illustrate the Civil, Literary and Political History of his time*, 2 vols (London 1777)

MAURY, A., *Memoirs of a Huguenot family from the original autobiography of the Rev. James Fontaine, and other family manuscripts; comprising an original journal of travels in Virginia, New-York, etc., in 1715 and 1716* (New York 1853)

MELCHIOR-BONNET, S., *The Mirror: A History* (London 2002)

MENTZER, R., and B. van Ruymbeke, *A Companion to the Huguenots* (Boston 2016)

METEYARD, E., *The Life of Josiah Wedgwood*, 2 vols (London 1865)

MEW, E., 'Battersea Enamels and the Antigallican Society', *Apollo*, 7 (May 1928), pp.216–21

MICIO, P., 'Early French surtouts, unpublished drawings and documents', *The Journal of the Silver Society*, 19 (2005), pp.79–97

MILLAR, O., *Tudor Stuart and Early Georgian Pictures in the Royal Collection* (London 1963)

MITCHELL, D.M., 'Transfer of Jewellery Designs and Manufacturing Techniques between Northern European Cities', in *Netherlandish Fashion in the Seventeenth Century*, eds J. Pietsch and A. Jolly, Riggesberger Berichte no.19 (2012), pp.139–51

MITCHELL, D.M, *Elizabethan and Stuart Silversmiths in London: Their Lives and Their Marks* (London 2017)

MONTFAUCON, B. de, *Les Edifices Antiques de Rome dessiné et mesurés tres exactement* (Paris 1682)

MONSON, E., 'The three Esthers: noblewomen of the Huguenot refuge', *PHSL*, XXVII, no.1 (1998), pp.1–19

MORGAN, L., *Nature as Model: Salomon de Caus and Early Seventeenth-Century Landscape Design* (Philadelphia 2007)

MORGAN, O.S., 'List of Members of the Clockmakers' Company of London from the year of Incorporation in 1631 to the year 1732', *Archaeological Journal*, 40, no.1 (January 1883), pp.193–214

MORRIS, C. (ed.), *The Illustrated Journeys of Celia Fiennes 1685–c.1712* (London 1982)

MORRIS, N. (ed.), *Stowe House: Saving an Architectural Masterpiece* (London 2018)

MORTLOCK, D.P., 'Thomas Coke and the Family Silver', *Journal of the Silver Society*, 9 (1997), pp.552–8

MOUNTFORT, A., 'Thomas Briand a Stranger', *Transactions of the English Ceramic Circle*, 7, no.2 (1969), pp.87–95

MUNRO, J. (ed.), *Silent Partners: Artist and Mannequin from Function to Fetish*, exh. cat., Fitzwilliam Museum, Cambridge (New Haven and London 2014)

MURDOCH, T., 'A French Silversmith', *Country Life*, 168 (13 November 1980), p.1764

MURDOCH, T., 'Huguenot Artists, Designers and Craftsmen in Great Britain and Ireland', PhD thesis, University of London, 2 vols, 1982

MURDOCH, T., 'Louis François Roubiliac and his Huguenot connections', *PHSL*, XXIV, no.1 (1983), pp.26–45

MURDOCH, T., 'Some Huguenot Craftsmen from Dieppe in London', *Seventeenth-Century French Studies*, no.6 (1984), pp.60–74

MURDOCH, T. (ed.), *The Quiet Conquest: The Huguenots 1685–1985*, exh. cat., Museum of London (London 1985a)

MURDOCH, T., 'Courtiers and Classics, The Gosset Family', *Country Life* (9 May 1985b), pp.1282–3

MURDOCH, T., 'Harpies and Hunting Scenes, Paul Crespin (1694–1770) Huguenot Goldsmith', *Country Life* (29 August 1985c), pp.556–8

MURDOCH, T., 'The Huguenots and the English Rococo', in *The Rococo in England: A Symposium*, ed. C. Hind (London 1986), pp.60–81

MURDOCH, T., 'Carving a Brighter Niche: Nadauld the Sculptor', *Country Life*, 182 (13 October 1988), pp.240–1

MURDOCH, T. (ed.), *Treasures and Trinkets: Jewellery in London from Pre-Roman to Victorian Times*, exh. cat., Museum of London (London 1991)

MURDOCH, T. (ed.), *Boughton House: The English Versailles* (London 1992)

MURDOCH, T., 'The Dukes of Montagu as Patrons of the Huguenots', *PHSL*, XXV (1992b), pp.340–55

MURDOCH, T., 'The Furniture for the King's Apartments (Hampton Court Palace), "Walnuttree", gilding, japanning and marble', *Apollo*, 140 (August 1994) pp.55–9

MURDOCH, T., 'Jean, René and Thomas Pelletier: A Huguenot Family of Carvers and Gilders in England 1682–1726', part I, *Burlington Magazine*, 139 (November 1997), pp.732–42

MURDOCH, T., 'Jean, René and Thomas Pelletier: A Huguenot Family of Carvers and Gilders in England 1682–1726', part II, *Burlington Magazine*, 140 (June 1998), pp.363–74

MURDOCH, T., 'Worthy of the monarch: immigrant craftsmen and the production of state beds 1660–1714', in *From Strangers to Citizens: The Integration of Immigrant Communities in Britain, Ireland and Colonial America, 1550–1750* (Eastbourne 2001a), pp.151–9

MURDOCH, T., 'Pierre Langlois: cabinet-maker to the world of fashion', *PHSL*, XXVII, no.4 (2001b), pp.497–508

MURDOCH, T., 'Fit for a King: The State Bed from Melville House, Fife', *Apollo*, 155 (January 2002), pp.3–9

MURDOCH, T., 'Hugenottische Goldschmiede aus Metz in London und Kassel', in *Die Hugenotten – Flucht und Vertreibung*, exh. cat., Deutsches Historisches Museum, Berlin (Berlin 2005a), pp.101–12

MURDOCH, T., 'Edward Feline, Goldsmith', *PHSL*, XXVIII, 3 (2005b), pp.316–24

MURDOCH, T., 'A French Carver at Norfolk House: The Mysterious Mr Cuenot', *Apollo*, 159 (June 2006a), pp.54–63

MURDOCH, T., 'Autour de Willaume. Orfèvres messins établis à Londres et Cassel', in *Huguenots de la Moselle à Berlin, Les Chemins de L'éxil*, exh. cat., Temple-Neuf, Metz (Metz 2006b), pp.127–44

MURDOCH, T. (ed.), *Noble Households. Eighteenth-Century Inventories of Great English Houses: A Tribute to John Cornforth* (Cambridge 2006c)

MURDOCH, T., 'Ducal splendour: Silver for a Military Hero. The Elie Pacot Ewer and Basin made for John Churchill, 1st Duke of Marlbrough', *Journal of the Silver Society*, 22 (2007), pp.4–14

MURDOCH, T. (ed.), *Beyond the Border: Huguenot Goldsmiths in Northern Europe and North America* (Brighton 2008)

MURDOCH, T., 'Some Directors of the French Hospital: A Time of Gifts', *PHSL*, XXIX, no.2 (2009a), pp.188–201

MURDOCH, T., 'Time's Melody: Charles Clay's Musical Clocks', *Apollo*, 178, no.614 (November 2013), pp.78–85

MURDOCH, T., 'A Glimpse of the Apprentice William Hogarth Engraving his Master's Shop-Bill: The Sign of the Angel', *Silver Studies*, 31 (2014), pp.63–5

MURDOCH, T., 'Power and Plate: Sir Robert Walpole's Silver', *Burlington Magazine*, 157, no.1346 (May 2015), pp.318–24

MURDOCH, T., 'A Royal Acquisition for the Victoria and Albert Museum', *Antiquarian Horology*, 38, no.1 (March 2017), pp.51–60

MURDOCH, T., 'A set of silver-gilt waiters by Benjamin Pyne for the Courtenay Family of Powderham Castle, Devon', *Burlington Magazine*, 160 (June 2018), pp.478–85

MURDOCH, T., 'Measuring Time at the Hanoverian Court: Caroline, Augusta and Charlotte as Promoters of Clock and Watchmaking in London, *Furniture History*, 56 (2020a), pp.49–68

MURDOCH, T., 'Ivory Piqué: The Huguenot Tradition 1680–1760', *Huguenot Journal*, 33 (2020b), pp.1–26

MURDOCH, T., 'Verre églomisé at Masterpiece 2020', *Furniture History Society Newsletter*, 220 (November 2020c), p.18

MURDOCH, T., 'The Business Practice of Louis François Roubiliac 1752–1762', *Sculpture Journal*, 30, no.3 (forthcoming, 2021a)

MURDOCH, T. 'A Performance for the Service of the Table': New Light on Eighteenth Century Dining, *Getty Research Journal*, 14 (forthcoming, 2021b), pp.181–90

MURDOCH, T., book review, 'Hopetoun Scotland's Finest Stately Home', *Furniture History Society Newsletter*, 222 (May 2021)

MURDOCH, T., and P. Boucher, 'Montagu House, Bloomsbury: A French household in London, 1673–1733', in *A History of the French in London: Liberty,*

Equality, Opportunity, eds D. Kelly and M. Cornyck (London 2013), pp.43–67
Murdoch, T., and S. Robinson, 'Roubiliac and Sprimont: A Friendship Revisited', *Burlington Magazine* (forthcoming, 2021/2)
Murdoch, T., and M. Snodin, 'Admiral Keppel's Freedom Box', *Burlington Magazine*, 135, no.1083 (June 1993), pp.403–10
Murdoch, T., and R. Vigne, *The French Hospital in England: Its Huguenot History and Collections* (Cambridge 2009)
Murdoch, T., and H. Zech, *Going for Gold: The Craftsmanship and Collecting of Gold Boxes* (Brighton 2014)
Nathan, M., *The Huguenots in South Africa* (Pretoria 1939)
Nichols, R.H., and Wray, F.A., *The History of the Foundling Hospital* (London 1935)
Nito, M.J., and F. Rilo, 'John Cheere's Lead Garden Statues Workshop and the Important Commission of Prince Pedro of Portugal in 1755–6', *Sculpture Journal*, 15, no.1 (2006), pp.5–18
Norman, A.V.B., *Wallace Collection, Catalogue of Ceramics*, vol.1: *Pottery, Maiolica, Faience, Stoneware* (London 1976)
Oakley, A., *Eglise Protestante Française de Cantorbéry* (Canterbury 2015)
O'Connell, S., 'Simon Gribelin (1661–1733): Printmaker and Metal-Engraver', *Print Quarterly*, 2 (March 1985), pp.27–38
O'Connell, S., 'The Nosts: A Revision of the Family History', *Burlington Magazine*, 129, no.1017 (December 1987), pp.802–6
O'Connell, S., 'Shaftesbury in Naples, 1711–13', *The Walpole Society*, 54 (1988), pp.149–219
O'Connell, S., *London 1753*, exh. cat., British Museum, London (London 2003)
O'Mullane, B., 'The Huguenots in Dublin', part 1, *Dublin Historical Record*, 8, no.4 (September–November 1946), pp.121–34
Oman, C., *The English Silver in the Kremlin 1557–1663* (London 1961)
Oman, C., *English Engraved Silver 1150–1900* (London 1978)
Oswald, A., 'Stanmer, Sussex, the Seat of the Earl of Chichester', *Country Life*, 71 (2 January 1932), pp.14–20
Ozinga, D.M., *Daniel Marot, de schepper van den Hollandschen Lodewijk XIV-stijl* (Amsterdam 1938)
Paknadel, F., 'Shaftesbury's Illustrations of Characteristics', *Journal of the Warburg and Courtauld Institutes*, 37 (1974), pp.290–312
Pannier, J., and J. Vergnet-Ruiz, 'Une prétendue allégorie de la Révocation peinte par Louis Chéron, *BSHPF*, 85 (January–March 1936), pp.62–6
Pavord, A., *The Tulip* (London 1999)
Pears, I., *The Discovery of Painting: The Growth of Interest in the Arts in England, 1680–1768* (New Haven and London 1991)
Penny, N., 'The Macabre Garden at Denbies and its Monument', *Garden History*, 3, no.3 (summer 1975) pp.58–61
Perigal, F., 'Story of John Perigal of Dieppe', *PHSL*, 11 (1886), pp.14–42
Pevsner, N., and B. Cherry, *The Buildings of England*, vol.1: *London: The City and Westminster* (London 1978)
Phillips, H., 'John Rocque's Career', *London Topographical Record*, 20 (1952), pp.9–25
Phillips, P.A.S., *John Obrisset, Huguenot: Carver, Medallist, Horn and Tortoiseshell Worker and Snuffbox Maker: with Examples of his Works Dated 1705 to 1728* (London 1931)
Phillips, P.A.S., 'Huguenot Goldsmiths in England, 1687–1737', typescript, copies in Goldsmiths' Company Library; Library of the Huguenot Society of London; Metalwork Collection Library, Victoria and Albert Museum (London 1933)
Phillips, P.A.S., *Paul de Lamerie, his Life and Work* (London 1935)
Physick, J., *Designs for English Sculpture, 1680–1860* (London 1969)
Pomet, P., N. Lémery and J. Pitton de Tournefort, *A Complete History of Drugs* (London 1748)
Portal, C., *Abraham Portal 1726–1809* (Castle Cary c.1993)
Portalis, R., *Henri Pierre Danloux et son journal durant l'emigration* (Paris 1910)
Pyke, E.J., *A Biographical Dictionary of Wax Modellers* (Oxford 1973; supplement 1981)
Raines, R., 'James Parmentier, the celebrated painter from France', n.d.
Raines, R., and K. Sharpe, 'The Story of Charles I', *Connoisseur*, 184 (September 1973), pp.35–46, and 185 (July 1974), pp.192–5
Ramsay, W.H., A. Gabszewicz and E.G. Ramsay, 'Unaker or Cherokee Clay and its Relationship to the "Bow" porcelain manufactory, *Transactions of the English Ceramic Circle*, 17, no.3 (2001), pp.474–99
Reff, T., 'Puget's Fortunes in France', *Essays in History of Art presented to Rudolf Wittkower* (London 1967), pp.274–84
Reilly, R.L., and G. Savage, *Wedgwood: The Portrait Medallions* (London 1973)
Report on the Manuscripts of the late Allan George Finch, Esq., of Burley-on-the-Hill, Rutland, vols III (London 1957), IV (London 1965)
Ressinger, D.W. (ed. and trans.), *Memoirs of Isaac Dumont de Bostaquet, a Gentleman of Normandy: Before and After the Revocation of the Edict of Nantes*, Huguenot Society, n.s., 4 (London 2005)
Reynolds, G., *The Sixteenth and Seventeenth-Century Miniatures in the Collection of Her Majesty the Queen* (London 1999)
Ricketts, C., *Pewterers of London 1600–1900* (London 2001)
Robinson, S., 'Simon Pantin and His Children: Seven Goldsmiths in Two Generations, 1666 – 1771', *Silver Studies*, 37 (2021 forthcoming)
Romadzka, J., 'Guide to Luxury: Firm that Laid the Golden Eggs', *Country Life*, 199 (17 November 2005), pp.78–9
Root, R.K. (ed.), *Lord Chesterfield's Letters to His Son and Others* (London 1929)
Roscoe, I., et al., *Biographical Dictionary of Sculptors in Britain 1660–1851* (New Haven and London 2009)
Rose, R., *English Dial Clocks* (Woodbridge 1978)
Rosenberg, J., S. Slive, and E.H.ter Kuile, *Dutch Art and Architecture, 1600–1800* (London 1972)
Rosenfeld, M.N., 'From Drawn to Printed Model Book: Jacques Androuet Du Cerceau and the Transmission of Ideas from Designer to Patron, Master Mason and Architect in the Renaissance', *Canadian Art Review*, 16, no.2: *Études sur l'architecture et son environnement / Studies on Architecture and its Environment* (1989), pp.131–45, 219–50
Rothstein, N., *Silk Designs of the Eighteenth Century: In the Collection of the Victoria and Albert Museum, London, with a Complete Catalogue* (London 1990)
Rothwell, J., *Silver for Entertaining: The Ickworth Collection* (London, 2017)
Rowell, C. (ed.), *Ham House: 400 Years of Collecting and Patronage* (New Haven and London 2013)
Rouquet, A., *The Present State of the Arts in England* (Paris 1755, facsimile edn London 1970)
Royal Institute of British Architects, *Catalogue of the Drawings Collection, 1969–1976* (Farnborough 1972)
Russell, F., 'Louis Chéron: A Sale Catalogue', *Burlington Magazine*, 130 (June 1988), pp.464–7
Sackville West, R., *Knole*, National Trust Guidebook (London 1998)
Salmon, J.H.M., *Society in Crisis, France in the Sixteenth Century* (London 1975)
Salvi, C., 'Jean-Baptiste Monnoyer et Antoine Monnoyer. Problèmes d'attributions', *Revue du Louvre*, 2 (April 2002), pp.55–63
Samuel, E., 'Gems from the Orient: The Activities of Sir Jean Chardin (1643–1713) as a Diamond Importer and East India Merchant', *PHSL*, XXVII (2000), pp.351–68
Sanxay, T., *The Sanxay Family and descendants of Rev. Jacques Sanxay Huguenot Refugee to London in Sixteen Hundred and Eighty-Five* (New York 1907)
Sarrazin, B., et al. (eds), *Charles de la Fosse (1636–1716): Le triomphe de la couleur*, exh. cat., Palais de Versailles and Musee des Beaux-Arts, Nantes (Paris 2016)
Saumarez Smith, C., *The Building of Castle Howard* (London 1990)
Saunders, E., 'Tijou the Smith', *Country Life*, 168 (14 August 1980), p.569
Saunders, E., 'Biographical Dictionary of English Wrought Iron Smiths of the Seventeenth and Eighteenth Centuries', *The Walpole Society*, 67 (2005), pp.237–384
Scarisbrick, D., *Portrait Jewels: Opulence and Intimacy from the Medici to the Romanovs*, (London 2011)

Scott-Thomson, G., *Life in a Noble Household, 1641–1700* (London 1937)
Scott-Thomson, G., *The Russells in Bloomsbury, 1669–1771* (London 1940)
Scouloudi, I., 'Sir Theodore Turquet de Mayerne, *PHSL*, XVI (1940), pp.301–37
Scouloudi, I., 'The French Protestant Church, Southampton 1703–1936', *PHSL*, XX (1958–64), pp.679–80
Scouloudi, I., 'Louis Crommelin: Director of the Linen Manufactury', *PHSL*, XX, no.6 (1964), p.681
Scouloudi, I. (ed.), *Huguenots in Britain and their French Background, 1550–1800* (Basingstoke 1987)
Scoville, W.C., 'The Huguenots and the Diffusion of Technology', I, *Journal of Political Economy*, 60, no.4 (August 1952), pp.294–311; no.5 (October 1952), pp.392–411
Scoville, W.C., *The Persecution of the Huguenots and French Economic Development, 1680–1720* (Berkeley 1960)
Seelig, L., *Golddosen des 18. Jahrhunderts aus dem Besitz der Fürsten von Thurn und Taxis* (Munich 2007)
Seelig, L., 'Eighteenth-century Hanau gold boxes', *Silver Society of Canada Journal*, vol.18 (2015), pp.32–55 (www.silversocietyofcanada.ca/sites/default/files/Seelig.pdf, accessed 30 January 2020)
Seelig, L., 'Ignaz Peter Krafft und die Hanauer Luxuswarenproduktion des 18. Jahrhunderts', *Neues Magazin für Hanauische Geschichte* (2018), pp.62–103
Seelig-Teuwen, R., 'Barthélmy Prieur (1536–1611)', PhD thesis, University of Munich, 1973
Shears, P.J., 'Huguenot Connections with the Clockmaking Trade in England,' *PHSL*, XX, no.2 (1959–60), pp.158–76
Sheppard, F.H.W. (ed.), *Survey of London*, vol.XXVII: *Spitalfields and Mile End New Town* (London 1957) (BHO/survey-london/vol27)
Sheppard, F.H.W. (ed.), *Survey of London*, vols XXXI and XXXII: *St James Westminster*, parts 1 and 2 (London 1963) (BHO/survey-london/vols31–2/pt2)
Sheppard, F.H.W. (ed.), *Survey of London* vols XXXIII and XXXIV: *St Anne Soho*, parts 1 and 2 (London 1966) (BHO/survey-london/vols 33–4)
Sherlock, R., 'West Country Chandeliers and their Makers', *The Journal of the Antique Metalware Society*, 10 (June 2002), pp.1–12
Simon, J., *English Baroque Sketches*, exh. cat., Marble Hill House, Twickenham (London 1974)
Simon, J. (ed.), *Handel: A Celebration of his Life and Times, 1685–1759*, exh. cat., National Portrait Gallery, London (London 1985)
Simon, J., 'New Light on Joseph Goupy (1689–1769)', *Apollo*, 139 (February 1994), pp.15–18
Simon, J., *The Art of Picture Frame: Artists, Patrons and the Framing of Portraits in Britain*, exh. cat., National Portrait Gallery, London (London 1996)
Simon, R., *Hogarth, France and British Art: The rise of the arts in eighteenth-century Britain* (London 2007)
Simpson, P., *The Forgotten Fourdrinier: The Life, Times and Work of Paul Fourdrinier, Huguenot Master Printmaker in London (1720–1758)* (Authorhouse 2017)
Simpson, P., 'Peter Fourdrinier: A re-assessment', *Huguenot Journal*, 33 (2020), pp.42–60
Sitwell, H.D.W., 'The Jewel House and the Royal Goldsmiths', *Archaeological Journal*, 117, no.1 (1960), pp.131–55
Skerry, J., 'Beyond the Working Dates: Reconstructing the Life and Career of Elizabeth Pantin Buteux Godfrey', *Silver Sudies*, 34 (2018), pp.75–88
Sloan, K. (ed.), *A Noble Art: Amateur Artists and Drawing Masters*, exh. cat., British Museum, London (London 2000)
Sloman, S., *Gainsborough in Bath* (New Haven and London 2002)
Smith, A., *Longford Castle: The Treasures and the Collectors* (London 2017)
Smith, J.T., *Nollekens and his Times: Memoirs of Contemporary Artists from the Time of Roubiliac, Hogarth and Reynolds to that of Fuseli, Flaxman and Blake*, ed. W. Whitten, 2 vols (London 1920)
Smith, R., 'James Cox (*c.*1723–1800): A Revised Biography', *Burlington Magazine*, 142 (June 2000), pp.353–61
Smith, R., 'Justin Vulliamy (1712–1797) and the Protestant Swiss Community', *Huguenot Journal*, 30, no.3 (autumn 2015), pp.327–45
Smith, R., 'Les artisans étrangers au service de James Cox. Entrepreneurs et transfert international de savoir-faire techniques au XVIIIe siècle', in *La Suisse manufacturière au XVIIIe siècle, Lectures Croisées: Journal Societe Suisse pour l'etude du XVIIIe siècle* (2018), pp.73–100
Smith, S., 'Norwich China Dealers of the Mid-eighteenth Century', *Transactions of the English Ceramic Circle*, 9, no.2 (1974), pp.193–211
Snodin, M. (ed.), *Rococo: Art and Design in Hogarth's England*, exh. cat., Victoria and Albert Museum, London (London 1984)
Snodin, M., *Horace Walpole's Strawberry Hill*, exh. cat., Victoria and Albert Museum, London (New Haven and London 2009)
Snowman, A.K., *Eighteenth-Century Gold Boxes of Europe* (Woodbridge 1990)
Somers Cocks, A., 'The non-functional use of ceramics in the English Country House during the eighteenth century', *Studies in the History of Art*, 25 (1989), pp.195–216
Somerville, P., *The Savoy: Manor, Hospital, Chapel* (London 1960)
Stainton, L., and C. White, *Drawing in England from Hilliard to Hogarth* (London 1987)
Stewart, J.D. (ed.), *Sir Godfrey Kneller*, exh.cat., National Portrait Gallery, London (London 1971)
Strickland, W., *Dictionary of Irish Artists* (Dublin 1913)
Stroehlin, E., *Jean Petitot et Jaques Bordier, deux artistes huguenots du XVIIme siècle* (Geneva 1905)
Strong, R., *The Renaissance Garden in England* (London 1979)
Stuart Mason, A., and J. Bensusan-Butt, 'P.B. Scalé: Surveyor in Ireland, Gentleman of Essex', *PHSL*, XXIV, no.6 (1987–8), pp.508–18
Stukeley, Revd W., 'The family memoirs of the Rev. William Stukeley, ed. W.C.Lukis, *The Surtees Society*, 3 vols. 73 (1882), 76, 80 (1885–7)
Sumner, A. (ed.), *Death, Passion and Politics: Van Dyck's Portraits of Venetia Stanley and George Digby*, exh. cat., Dulwich Picture Gallery (London 1995)
Swift, K., 'Huguenot Booksellers in The Strand', *PHSL*, XXV, no.2 (1983), pp.123–40
Symonds, R.W., 'A Royal Scrutoire: English Furniture in Portugal', *Connoisseur* (June 1940), pp.233–6
Symonds, R.W., *Thomas Tompion: His Life and Work* (London 1951)
Symonds, R.W., *Furniture Making in Seventeenth and Eighteenth Century England: An Outline for Collectors* (London 1955)
Tait, H., 'Huguenot Silver made in London, 1690–1723: The Peter Wilding Bequest to the British Museum', *Connoisseur*, 180 (August 1972), pp.267–77; 181 (September 1972), pp.25–36
Tait, H., 'Nicholas Sprimont at Chelsea, his apprentice William Brown and the "anchor and dagger mark"', *Ars Ceramica*, 15 (1998–9), pp.24–33
Tapp, M., 'Lecture on Derby China', *Journal of the Derbyshire Archaeological Society*, 10 (1936–7), pp.157–61
Thalmann, J., *40 years of Christ Church Picture Gallery: Still One of Oxford's Best Kept Secrets* (Oxford 2008)
Thomassin, S., *Recueil des Figures, Statues de Versailles* (Paris 1694)
Thompson, D., 'Huguenot Watchmakers in England: With Examples from the British Museum Horological Collections', *PHSL*, XXVI, no.4 (1996), pp.417–30
Thompson, D., *Clocks* (London 2004)
Thompson, D., *Watches in the Ashmolean* (Oxford 2007)
Thompson, D., *Watches* (London 2008)
Thompson, F., *A History of Chatsworth* (London 1949)
Thomson, W.G., *A History of Tapestry* (London 1930)
Thornton, P., *Seventeenth-Century Interior Decoration in England, France and Holland* (New Haven and London 1978)
Thornton, P., and W. Rieder, 'Pierre Langlois, Ebeniste', part I, *Connoisseur*, 178 (December 1971), pp.283–8; part II, *Connoisseur*, 179 (February 1972), pp.105–12; part III, *Connoisseur*, 179 (March 1972), pp.176–87; part IV, *Connoisseur*, 179 (April 1972), pp.257–65; part V, *Connoisseur*, 180 (May 1972), pp.30–5
Thorpe, A.L., 'An Early Reference to China Making', *Journal of the Derbyshire Archaeological Society*, LXXV (1955), p.151
Thurley, S., *Somerset House: The Palace of England's Queens, 1551–1692* (London 2009)
Tillyard, S., *Aristocrats: Caroline, Emily, Louisa and Sarah Lennox 1740–1832* (London 1994)

Tipping, H.A., *English Homes*, period v, vol.i (London 1921)

Toesca, I., 'Alessandro Galilei in Inghilterra', *English Miscellany: A Symposium of History, Literature and the Arts*, ed. M. Praz, vol.3 (Rome 1952), pp.189–220

Toppin, A.J., 'Early Bow Muses', *Burlington Magazine*, 51 (1929), pp.188–92

Toynbee, P.J. (ed.), *The Letters of Horace Walpole*, vol.3 (Oxford 1903–5)

Treasure, G., *The Huguenots* (New Haven and London 2013)

Treasures from Chatsworth: The Devonshire Inheritance, exh. cat., The Dixon Gallery and Gardens, Memphis, TN; The Bard Graduate Center, New York; Peabody Essex Museum, Salem, MA; The Society of the Four Arts, Palm Beach, FL; Mobile Museum of Art, Mobile, AL; Tyler Museum of Art, Tyler, TX (Washington 1979)

Trench, L., *Materials and Techniques in the Decorative Arts: An Illustrated Dictionary* (London 2000)

Troeltsch, E., 'The Economic Ethic of Calvinism,' in *Protestantism and Capitalism: The Weber Thesis and its Critics*, ed. R. Green (Boston 1959), pp.21–8

Truman, C., *The Gilbert Collection of Gold Boxes* (New York 1991)

Truman, C., *The Wallace Collection: Catalogue of Gold Boxes* (London 2013)

Tunnicliffe, W.R., 'Anne Ribouleau: Augustin Courtauld's wife', *Huguenot Journal*, 32 (2019), pp.104–5

Turner, A., 'The Tribulations of Jean Helot', *Antiquarian Horology*, 32 (June 2011), pp.779–804

Turpin, A., 'A Table for Queen Mary's Water Gallery at Hampton Court', *Apollo*, 149, no.443 (January 1999), pp.3–14

Turpin, A., 'The Career of Cornelius Gole: An unrecognized cabinetmaker in late seventeenth-century England', *Furniture History*, 50 (2014), pp.75–87

Valpy, N., 'Charles Gouyn and the Girl-in-a-swing Factory', *Transactions of the English Ceramic Circle*, 15, no.2 (1994), pp.318–26

Van der Linden, D., *Experiencing Exile: Huguenot Refugees and the Dutch Republic 1680–1700* (Farnham 2015)

van Gelder, J.G. (ed.), 'The Stadholder King William III as Collector and Man of Taste', in *William and Mary and their House*, exh. cat., The Pierpont Morgan Library (New York and Oxford 1979)

Van Ruymbeke, B., 'Lieux de mémoire et musées huguenots aux États-Unis et en Afrique du Sud', *BSHPF*, 157 (October 2011), pp.597–618

van Wely, B., et al., *SingSong: Schatten uit de Verboden Stad / Treasures from the Forbidden City*, exh. cat., Museum Speelklok, Utrecht 2010

Vauquer, J., *Livres de Fleurs Propres pour orfevres et graveurs* (Blois 1680, repr. London 1888), vols VI, VII

Verbeck, J., 'A Dutchman portrayed in Sweden by a French ivory carver', *Antiek*, 8 (June–July 1973), pp.35–42

Vertue, G., 'Notebooks', *The Walpole Society*, I, vol.18 (1929–30); II, vol.20 (1931–2); III, vol.22 (1933–4); IV, vol.24 (1935–6); V, vol.26 (1937–8); VI, vol. 29 (1940–2); VII, vol.30 (1948–50)

Vial, E., *Gens et Choses de Lyon, Notes sur le Corporation des Peintres, Sculpteurs et Verriers de Lyon* (Lyon 1945), pp.151–68

Vincent, C., 'Some Seventeenth-Century French Painted Enamel Watch Cases', *Metropolitan Museum Journal* (New York 2002), pp.89–103

Wagner, H., 'Pedigree of the Huguenot Refugee Families of Berchere and Baril', *The Genealogist*, n.s., 23 (April 1907), pp.248–51

Walford, T., and H. Young (eds), *British Ceramic Design, 1600–2002* (London 2003)

Walker, R.J.B., *Old Westminster Bridge: The Bridge of Fools* (Newton Abbot 1979)

Wallace, R.S., *Calvin, Geneva and the Reformation: A Study of Calvin as Social Reformer, Churchman, Pastor and Theologian* (Edinburgh 1988)

Walpole, H., *Anecdotes of Painting*, 3 vols (London 1769), ed. H.G. Bohn (London 1849)

Walton, K. (ed.), *The Golden Age of English Furniture Upholstery, 1660–1840*, exh. cat., Temple Newsam House, Leeds (Leeds 1973)

Wardropper, I., 'The Flowering of the French Renaissance', *The Metropolitan Museum of Art Bulletin*, 62, no.1 (summer 2004), pp.3–48

Ward-Jackson, P., *English Furniture Designs* (London 1958)

Watney, B., 'The Origin of Some Ceramic Designs', *Transactions of the English Ceramic Circle*, 9, no.3 (1974), pp.267–75

Watney, B., 'Some Parallels and Prototypes in Ceramics', *Transactions of the English Ceramic Circle*, 10, nos 4, 5 (1975), pp.350–69

Watney, B., 'Pre-1756 Derby Domestic Wares contemporary with "Dry-Edge Figures"', *Burlington Magazine*, 109, no.766 (January 1976), pp.16–20

Webb, M.I., 'Roubiliac Busts at Wilton', *Country Life*, 119 (19 April 1956), pp.804–5; 'Portraits of Bolingbroke', op. cit., pp.1131–2

Welch, C., *History of the Worshipful Company of Pewterers of the City of London*, 2 vols (London 1902)

Wells-Cole, A., 'Two Rococo Masterpieces', *Leeds Art Calendar*, 79 (1976), pp.13–24

Wendel, F., *Calvin: The Origins and Development of his Religious Thought*, trans. P. Mairet (London 1963; rev. edn London 1980)

Wengraf, P., *Renaissance and Baroque Bronzes from the Hill Collection* (London 2014)

Wessely, J.E., 'Paul van Somer, Verzeichniss seiner Kupferstiche', *Archiv für die zeichnenden Künste*, 16 (1870), pp.39–87

Westman, A., *Fringe, Frog and Tassel, The Art of the Trimmings-Maker in Interior Decoration* (London 2019)

Westropp, M.S.D., *General Guide to the Art Collections, Pottery and Porcelain, National Museum of Ireland* (Dublin 1935)

Wheeler, R., 'Prince Frederick and Liberty: The Gardens of Hartwell House, Buckinghamshire, in the Mid-Eighteenth Century', *Garden History*, 34, no.1 (summer 2006), pp.80–91

Whinney, M., *Sculpture in Britain 1530 to 1830* (1963), rev. J. Physick (London 1988)

White, A., 'Church Monuments in Britain, circa 1560–1660', PhD thesis, University of London, 1992

Whitelock, W., *The Life and Times of John Jay, Statesman* (New York 1887)

Wilkinson, J.J., *Worthies, families, and celebrities of Barnsley and the district* (Derby 1883)

Williams, H., *Académie Royale: A History in Portraits* (Farnham 2015)

Wills, G., *English Furniture 1650–1750* (New York 1971)

Wittkower, R., 'Chance, Time and Vertue', *Journal of the Warburg and Courtauld Institutes*, 1 (1937–8), pp.313–21

Wood, L., *The Upholstered Furniture in the Lady Lever Art Gallery* (New Haven and London 2008)

Wood, L., 'A Royal Relic: The State Bedroom Suite at Warwick Castle', *Furniture History*, 48 (2012), pp.45–104

Wood, L., 'New Light on Pierre Langlois', *Newsletter of the Furniture History Society*, 196 (November 2014), pp.1–7

Woodwiss, J., *British Silhouettes* (London 1965)

Wren, C., *Parentalia* (Farnborough 1750)

Wren Society, eds A.T. Bolton and H.D. Hendry, vol.VII: *The Royal Palaces of Winchester, Whitehall, Kensington and St James's* (Oxford 1930); vol.VIII: *Thirty-two large drawings for Whitehall, Windsor and Greenwich 1694–1698* (Oxford 1931); vol.XV: *Photographic Supplement of St Paul's Cathedral and Part III of the Building Accounts from October 1st, 1695 to June 24th, 1713, Also the Chapter House Accounts 1712–14, and Outline of Cathedral Accounts* (1938); vol.XVI: *St Paul's Cathedral, Minutes Contracts and frauds and Abuses Controversy Construction Drawings* (1939); vol.XVIII: *The Wren MS 'Court orders' with a supplement of official papers from the Public Record Office, Welbeck Abbey, &c.: A biographical note on Sir Chr. Wren's visit to Paris 1665 and his death and funeral in 1723* (1941); vol.XIX: *The City Churches, Vestry Minutes and Churchwarden's Accounts* (1942)

Wright, G., 'Limestone Heritage, the English Dolomite', *Country Life*, 172 (19 August 1982), pp.502–4

Young, H., 'A Drawing from the Circle of James Cox', *Burlington Magazine*, 138, no.1119 (June 1996), pp.402–4

Young, H., 'Anti-Gallicanism at Chelsea: Protestantism, Protectionism and Porcelain', *Apollo*, 147, no.436 (June 1998), pp.35–41

Young, H., *English Porcelain 1745–95* (London 1999)

Zech, H.J. *Gold Boxes: Masterpieces from the Rosalinde and Arthur Gilbert Collection* (London 2015)

Photographic Credits

References are to plate numbers

The Art Institute of Chicago 216

Alamy Stock Photo:
Artokoloro / Alamy Stock Photo 3, 5. Ian Bottle / Alamy Stock Photo 78. Steve Fisher / Alamy Stock Photo 71. Heiner Heine / Alamy Stock Photo 117. Historic Images / Alamy Stock Photo 4, 53. ICP / Alamy Stock Photo Endpapers, 60. Infrequent_ Flyer / Alamy Stock Photo 125. Albert Knapp / Alamy Stock Photo 65. Chris Lacey / Alamy Stock Photo 67. NTPL/Jerry Harpur / Alamy Stock Photo 126. PURPLE MARBLES YORKSHIRE / Alamy Stock Photo 127. Marco Secchi / Alamy Stock Photo 197. Robert Thrift / Alamy Stock Photo 193

© Ashmolean Museum, University of Oxford 37, 213

Bibliothèque de Genève 10

Bibliothèque Nationale de France 30

Bridgeman images:
Conway Library, The Courtauld, London © The Courtauld / Bridgeman Images 265. © Gerard Degeorge / Bridgeman Images 110. © French Hospital / Bridgeman Images 11, 15, 16, 21, 199, 221. © Huntington Art Collections /Bridgeman Images 17. Huntington Library, Art Museum, and Botanical Gardens, San Marino, CA, USA © Huntington Art Collections / Bridgeman images 171. © Leeds Museums and Art Galleries (Temple Newsam House) UK / Bridgeman Images 183. Bridgeman images / Lindley Library, RHS, London, UK 18. © Museum of the Home (previously Geffrye Museum) / Bridgeman Images 101. Private Collection / Bridgeman images 20. © Peter Willi / Bridgeman Images 111

©Trustees of the British Museum, London. All rights reserved. 2, 12, 25, 26, 27, 29, 34, 35, 39, 41, 45, 76, 102, 109, 115, 169, 134, 138, 159, 161, 169, 172, 198, 200, 222, 228, 229, 230, 234, 236, 237, 241, 245, 261

© The Buccleuch Collections 38, 42, 43, 44, 46, 48, 50, 63, 64, 85, 92, 94, 95, 96, 97, 98

Canadian Centre for Architecture 75

Photograph © 2021 Carnegie Museum of Art, Pittsburgh 255

The Clothworkers' Company 239, 253

The Colonial Williamsburg Foundation 177

DeAgostini Picture Library/Scala, Florence 112

© Drayton Archive / photo: John Roan 104

© Fitzwilliam Museum, University of Cambridge 244

Fondation Custodia, Collection Frits Lugt, Paris 246

© Photo courtesy of the Fowler Museum at UCLA 175

Digital image courtesy of the Getty's Open Content Program 7

Getty Research Institute, Los Angeles 188 (2019-B592 vol.3), 189 (2019-B592 vol.2)

© Gloucestershire Archives (D1799/E236) 68

Colin Hepburn 69, 106

© 2021 Hopetoun 105

Photography Nick Howard. The Castle Howard Collection. 123, 124

Huguenot Museum, Rochester 167, 195, 211 (Photos: Rikard Österlund)

© London Metropolitan Archives (City of London) 1, 73, 74

Longford Castle Collection 6

E & H Manners 155

The Metropolitan Museum of Art 174

William Murphy 93

Museum of Fine Arts, Boston:
Gift of Edward Jackson Holmes 30.871, photograph © 2021 Museum of Fine Arts, Boston 13. Theodora Wilbour Fund in memory of Charlotte Beebe Wilbour 1973.482, photograph © 2021 Museum of Fine Arts, Boston 231

Museum of London 36, 206

© Museums at the Royal College of Surgeons 33

The National Archives 19

National Galleries of Scotland 252

© National Portrait Gallery, London Frontispiece, 28, 118, 240, 242

© National Trust 52, 180 (images/Brenda Norrish), 192 (Andrew Patterson), 219 (Robert Thrift)

© Courtesy of The Parish & Priory Church of St George, Dunster 81

By the kind permission of the Prince's Foundation. Image: Christie's 24

Private collection 194, 225, 259

Photo: Will Pryce © Country Life picture library. Future Publishing Ltd 70

Photo courtesy of Raffety Clocks 238

© Ravage Productions 14

RIBA Collections 62

Rijksmuseum, Amsterdam 59, 209, 210

Ronald Phillips Ltd 87

Royal Armouries 82, 83, 84

Royal Collection Trust / © Her Majesty Queen Elizabeth II 2021 58, 99, 100, 103, 107, 214, 224, 247, 248, 251, 266

Image courtesy of Saint Louis Art Museum / Private collection 182

© SCORPIAUX 80

Cooper Hewitt, Smithsonian Design Museum. Purchased for the Museum by the Advisory Council. 108

Photograph courtesy of Sotheby's 119

Photo: Bob Speel 263

Staatliche Schlösser, Burgen und Gärten Sachsen gGmbH, Schloss Moritzburg und Fasanenschlösschen, Fotograf: Jürgen Karpinski, Dresden 91

Photo © Tate 72, 220

© The Time Museum 23

Toledo Museum of Art, Purchased with Funds from the Florence Scott Libbey Bequest in Memory of Her Father, Maurice A. Scott (1964.51) 190

The President and Fellows of Trinity College, Oxford 40

© Victoria and Albert Museum, London 8, 9, 17, 22, 31, 47, 49, 51, 55, 56, 57, 61, 66, 77, 79, 88, 89, 90, 113, 114, 116, 120, 121, 132, 133, 136, 137, 139, 140, 141, 142, 143, 144, 145, 146, 147, 148, 149, 150, 151, 152, 153, 154, 156, 157, 158, 160, 164, 165, 166, 168, 178, 179, 181, 184, 185, 186, 187, 191, 196, 201, 202, 203, 204, 205, 207, 208, 212, 215, 217, 223, 226, 227, 232, 233, 235, 249, 250, 254, 256, 257, 258, 260, 264

Waddesdon Image Library 129 (Hugh Palmer), 218 (Andrew Peppard)

The Walters Art Museum 243

© 2021 Dean and Chapter of Westminster 122, 128, 131, 135

The Worshipful Company of Goldsmiths 130, 162, 163, 170, 173

© permission granted by the Worshipful Company of Pewterers 86

By the permission of Antony Usher and the Worshipful Company of Upholders 176

The Yale Center for British Art 32, 262

© ZAC and ZAC 54

Index

Illustrations and captions are indicated by the use of italics. All works are entered under the relevant surname.

D

E

F

G

H

W

Y

Z

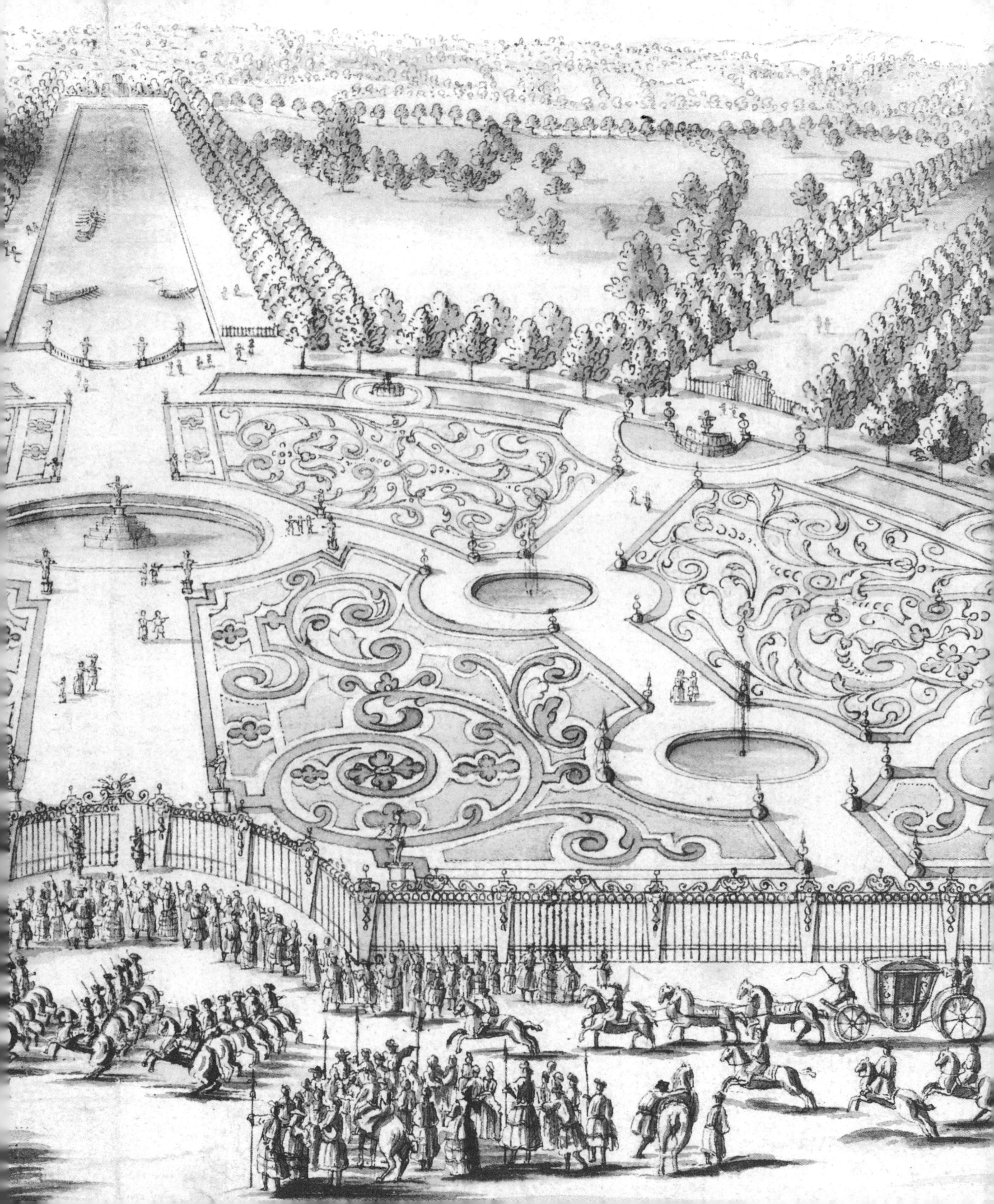